Managerial Accounting

An Introduction to Concepts, Methods, and Uses

Second Edition

Sidney Davidson, Ph.D., CPA
University of Chicago

Michael W. Maher, Ph.D., CPA
University of Michigan

Clyde P. Stickney, D.B.A., CPA
Dartmouth College

Roman L. Weil, Ph.D., CPA, CMA
University of Chicago

The Dryden Press
Chicago New York Philadelphia San Francisco Montreal Toronto
London Sydney Tokyo Mexico City Rio de Janeiro Madrid

Acquisitions Editor:	Larry Armstrong
Project Editors:	Russell Hahn, Anne Knowles
Managing Editor:	Jane Perkins
Design Director:	Alan Wendt
Production Manager:	Mary Jarvis
Copy Editor:	Lynne Lackenbach
Permissions Editor:	Doris Milligan
Indexer:	Cherie Worman
Compositor:	Waldman Graphics
Text Type:	10/12 Times Roman

Library of Congress Cataloging in Publication Data

Managerial accounting.

Includes bibliographical references and index.
1. Managerial accounting.   I. Davidson, Sidney,
1919–
HF5635.M2358   1985   658.1′511   84-8119
ISBN 0-03-059726-9

Printed in the United States of America
567-039-987654321

Materials from Uniform CPA Examination Questions and Unofficial Answers copyright © 1974, 1975, 1976, 1977, 1978, 1979, 1981 by the American Institute of Certified Public Accountants, Inc., are adapted with permission.

Materials from the Certificate in Management Accounting Examinations, Copyright © 1972–1977, 1978, 1979, 1980, 1981 by the National Association of Accountants are adapted with permission.

Address orders:
383 Madison Avenue
New York, NY 10017

Address editorial correspondence:
One Salt Creek Lane
Hinsdale, IL 60521
(800) 323-7437

CBS College Publishing
The Dryden Press
Holt, Rinehart and Winston
Saunders College Publishing

Thank you, thank you, thank you.

Whatever be the detail with which you cram
your students, the chance of their meeting in
after-life exactly that detail is almost
infinitesimal; and if they do meet it, they
will probably have forgotten what you taught
them about it. The really useful training yields
a comprehension of a few general principles
with a thorough grounding in the way they
apply to a variety of concrete details. In
subsequent practice the students will have
forgotten your particular details; but they will
remember by an unconscious common sense
how to apply principles to immediate
circumstances.

Alfred North Whitehead
The Aims of Education and Other Essays

The Dryden Press Series in Accounting

Preface

The purpose of this book is to provide an introduction to managerial accounting that (1) is logically organized around the major uses of managerial accounting; (2) is comprehensive in its coverage of managerial accounting topics; and (3) treats managerial accounting as a subject in its own right, not as a subset of financial accounting, economics, or operations research. The book can be used in introductory undergraduate, graduate, or executive programs. We have included a variety of end-of-chapter materials, including straightforward exercises, thought-provoking problems, and decision-making cases.

We assume that the majority of readers are present or future users, not providers, of accounting information. Hence, the examples and end-of-chapter materials focus on the uses of accounting for managerial purposes. We do not deal with accounting superficially, however. We believe that it is important for users of accounting information to understand enough about accounting to communicate effectively with accountants and to provide input to accounting system design.

Students who intend to be providers of accounting data will find the book particularly useful in two ways. First, the book provides a comprehensive introduction to managerial accounting that will be good background for subsequent courses in cost accounting, management control, and advanced management accounting. Second, the user perspective will help students ascertain decision makers' needs for accounting information.

Organization

Managerial accounting topics are often distributed throughout textbooks, thus giving the appearance that the subject is made up of many diverse and unrelated topics. In our experience, student response to this apparent lack of structure has been negative. We have organized this book into parts that provide a logical connection among chapters. For example, Part Three contains five chapters all dealing with the use of accounting information for managerial decision making.

Whereas all chapters in a part are logically connected, any chapter can be covered out of sequence or omitted. Chapter 6 in Part Three, for example, discusses estimating cost behavior. Chapter 6 could be covered *after* Chapter 7 or omitted without creating difficulties in covering other chapters in Part Three.

The book is divided into five major parts, as follows:

Part One. Fundamental Concepts, Chapters 1–2.
Part Two. Cost Methods and Systems, Chapters 3–5.
Part Three. Managerial Decision Making, Chapters 6–10.
Part Four. Managerial Planning and Performance Evaluation, Chapters 11–14.
Part Five. Special Topics, Chapters 15–18.

Part One covers fundamental concepts and provides an overview of managerial accounting. The other parts could be covered in any sequence, or omitted, after Part One, as shown in the diagram below:

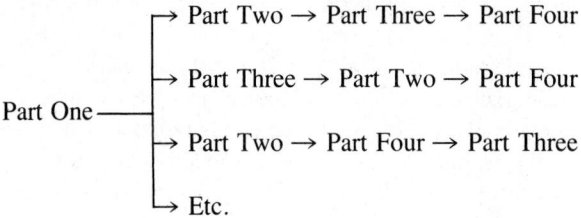

Part Two, Chapters 3–5, describes costing methods and systems used by companies. Chapter 3 discusses alternative methods of measuring product costs. Chapters 4 and 5 show how cost flows appear in the accounting systems commonly used by companies.

Part Three, Chapters 6–10, discusses concepts and methods useful for managerial decision making. Chapter 6 discusses methods of estimating cost behavior. Chapters 7 and 8 discuss the use of accounting data in short-run decision making, where capacity is held constant. Chapters 9 and 10 discuss the use of accounting in long-run decision making involving capital budgeting.

Part Four, Chapters 11–14, discusses managerial planning, control, and internal performance evaluation. Chapter 11 provides an overview of the planning and control process and discusses economic and behavioral issues in performance evaluation. Chapter 12 considers the development of budgets as tools for planning. Chapter 13 deals with the use of budgets, or standards, for controlling operations of a firm. Chapter 14 focuses on the control of decentralized operations.

Part Five, Chapters 15–18, deals with special topics. Chapter 15 discusses cost allocation. Chapter 16 both synthesizes materials in previous chapters and compares managerial decision making with the way managerial actions are reported. This chapter describes situations where managers may have incentives to take actions that are not in the best interests of the firm, but that make them look good to readers of accounting reports. Chapters 17 and 18 present an overview of financial accounting. If readers have had an introduction to financial accounting, these chapters will serve as a review. Readers who have not had financial accounting can use these chapters as an introduction to financial accounting concepts, methods, and uses. These chapters are independent of the rest of the book and can be read at any time.

The Appendix to the book discusses compound interest calculations used in discounted cash flow analysis. This Appendix is also independent of the rest of the book. The Glossary is a comprehensive set of definitions of more than 1,000 concepts and terms used in accounting.

Changes in This Edition

This edition contains substantially more material than the first edition. The relation between major chapters in the first edition and this edition are shown below.

Chapters in First Edition	→	Chapters in Second Edition
1		1, 2
—		3
12		4, 5
4, 5, 6, 7, 16		6, 7, 8, 9, 10
8, 9, 10, 11		11, 12, 13, 14
13		15
14		16
2, 3		17, 18
Compound Interest Appendix		Compound Interest Appendix
Glossary		Glossary

Major Features of the Book

This book contains the following characteristics that help differentiate it from other textbooks in the field.

Organization

Chapters are logically organized to provide a cohesive theme for each of the major parts of the book.

Extensive Assignment Materials

Extensive assignment materials cover a wide range of questions, exercises, problems, and cases. The assignment material is divided into three groups:

1. *Questions* that review important concepts and terms in the chapter;
2. *Exercises* dealing with single concepts or techniques in the chapter; and
3. *Problems and cases* with thought-provoking requirements, usually asking students to make decisions using accounting information.

Self-Study Materials

Self-study problems are a vital part of this text. Many chapters have three or four self-study problems. In addition to self-study problems, we have included *suggested solutions to even-numbered exercises* at the end of every chapter with exercises. This gives students ample opportunity for feedback on their understanding of the text material.

Cases

We have included numerous cases in this text. These range from short cases/long problems to lengthy "MBA-style" cases. We have included enough cases to provide ample material for instructors who use 10 to 15 cases each term.

Synthesis Chapter

Chapter 16 is a unique chapter that synthesizes materials from previous chapters. This chapter also discusses situations where data designed for one purpose are inappropriately used for a different purpose. The discussion incorporates many examples and cases that present complex issues and require students to draw upon previous chapters to address the issues. This chapter is particularly useful in graduate and executive classes.

Variance Analysis

Variance analysis is often presented as a series of formulas for students to memorize (which they usually forget shortly after the final examination). Our presentation of variances in Chapters 12 and 13 starts with a "big picture" comparison of budgeted and actual results, then presents variance calculations as a finer division of the budget versus actual comparison. There are two advantages to this approach. First, it keeps the "big picture" and the purpose of variance calculations in students' minds; they do not lose sight of their overall objectives as they analyze detailed variances. Second, the approach is one that students find intuitive. They may forget how to compute particular variances, but they will remember the overall model, which will enable them to "reinvent" variance analysis at a later date.

Related Materials Accompanying the Text

Instructor's Manual

The manual includes sample course outlines, lecture notes and outlines, examination questions and solutions, and additional problems.

Solutions Manual

This manual contains responses to questions and solutions to all exercises, problems, and cases. These solutions have been thoroughly checked by students to eliminate errors. The Solutions Manual is perforated, three-hole punched, and includes transparency masters.

Study Guide to Accompany Text

Professor Anne J. Rich has prepared a student study guide to accompany this text. For each chapter and the Appendix, it includes:

1. An outline of the chapter with emphasis on the key points;
2. A set of matching (term and definition) questions and answers for students' self-help;
3. Several exercises and problems for students' self-help with answers or suggested solutions;
4. A study plan which is designed to help the students solve the problems in the text.

Acknowledgments

We gratefully acknowledge the helpful criticisms and suggestions from the following people who reviewed the manuscript at various stages: John F. Bowen, Ripon College; Penelope Sue Campbell, University of Iowa; George J. Chorba, Villanova University; Robert Colson, University of Michigan; Dennis C. Daly, University of Minnesota; Leon J. Hanouille, Syracuse University; W. Thomas Lin, University of Southern California; Anne J. Rich, University of Hartford; Blaine A. Ritts, Bowling Green State University; Frank Sbrocchi, Concordia University – Canada; Kenneth P. Sinclair, Lehigh University; Gary W. Studnicka, Illinois Benedictine College.

Thomas Horton and Daughters, Inc., has given us permission to reproduce material from *Accounting: The Language of Business*. The following have consented to let us use problems or cases prepared by them: Case Clearing House, David O. Green, David Solomons, George Sorter, James Reece, James Patell, Gordon Shillinglaw, Jean Lim, Robert Colson, and Edward Deakin. Material from the Uniform CPA Examinations and Unofficial Answers, copyright by the American Institute of Certified Public Accountants, Inc., is adapted with permission. Permission has been granted by the Institute of Management Accounting of the National Association of Accountants to adapt problem materials from past Certified Management Accounting Examinations.

We thank the following people for their help in preparing this book: Jean Lim, Anne Greene, Christine Handt, Jongwook Cheh, Katherine Xenophon-Rybowiak, Raymonde Rousselot, Sandra Myers, Cherie Worman, and several hundred University of Michigan students who class-tested this material. Rick Antle, Robert Colson, and Anne Greene have provided particularly thought-provoking comments.

Finally, we would like to thank Susan Layton, John Bragg, Larry Armstrong, Anne Knowles, and Russell Hahn of the Dryden Press for their assistance in the development of this book.

S.D.
M.W.M.
C.P.S.
R.L.W.

Contents

Part One   **Fundamental Concepts**

This part contains two chapters that lay the foundation for subsequent chapters. Chapter 1 provides an overview of managerial accounting, shows ways in which it is useful to decision makers, and contrasts it with financial accounting. Chapter 2 discusses the major cost concepts that are used in this book.

Chapter 1   The Management Process and Accounting Information

Accounting affects virtually everyone working in business, not-for-profit organizations, governmental units, and other organized activities. Accounting is used to make such decisions as: Should we expand or contract our business? Should we close a particular store? Should we expand a governmental program? Accounting is also used in numerous planning and performance evaluation contexts, including forecasting, budgeting, and employee performance evaluation.

Even employees who do not use accounting directly are affected by it. Workers in fast food outlets may not use accounting themselves, for example, but their superiors use accounting information to ascertain whether a particular outlet should remain open, whether employees' hours should be increased or decreased, and in other decisions that affect these employees.

About 80 percent of small businesses do not survive for more than 5 years. One of the main reasons for this failure rate is that they have inadequate accounting information to help control costs, to forecast cash needs, and to plan for growth. Organizations with poor accounting systems have considerable difficulty obtaining financing from banks and shareholders. Also, cost overruns on electrical utility construction projects, cost overruns by defense contractors, small business failures, and rising health care costs are only a few examples of problems resulting from inadequate cost control.

In short, accounting touches our lives more than we might think. If you have observed store or mill openings or closings, airline fare discounting, clothing store merchandise sales, or employee hirings to help with seasonal increases in activity at ski resorts or department stores, then you have seen the results of decisions that use accounting information.

As shown in Exhibit 1.1, accounting is part of an organization's information system, which includes both financial and nonfinancial data. Accounting is commonly divided into (1) financial accounting and (2) managerial accounting. *Financial accounting* refers to the preparation of general-purpose reports for use by persons outside an organization. Such users include shareholders (owners) of a corporation, creditors (those who lend money to a business), financial analysts, labor unions, government regulators, and the like. External users are interested primarily in reviewing and evaluating the operations and financial status of the business as a whole.

Managerial accounting, on the other hand, refers to the providing of information to managers inside the organization. For example, a production manager may want a report on the number of units of product manufactured by various workers in order to evaluate their performance. A sales manager might want a report showing the relative profitability of two products in order to pinpoint selling efforts. Whereas the financial accounting reports prepared by publicly held companies are readily available in libraries or from the companies themselves, managerial accounting reports are not widely distributed outside of companies because they often contain confidential information. Consequently, we have relied on research and consulting experience to develop actual managerial accounting examples for this book.

Exhibit 1.1
Accounting as Part of the Information System

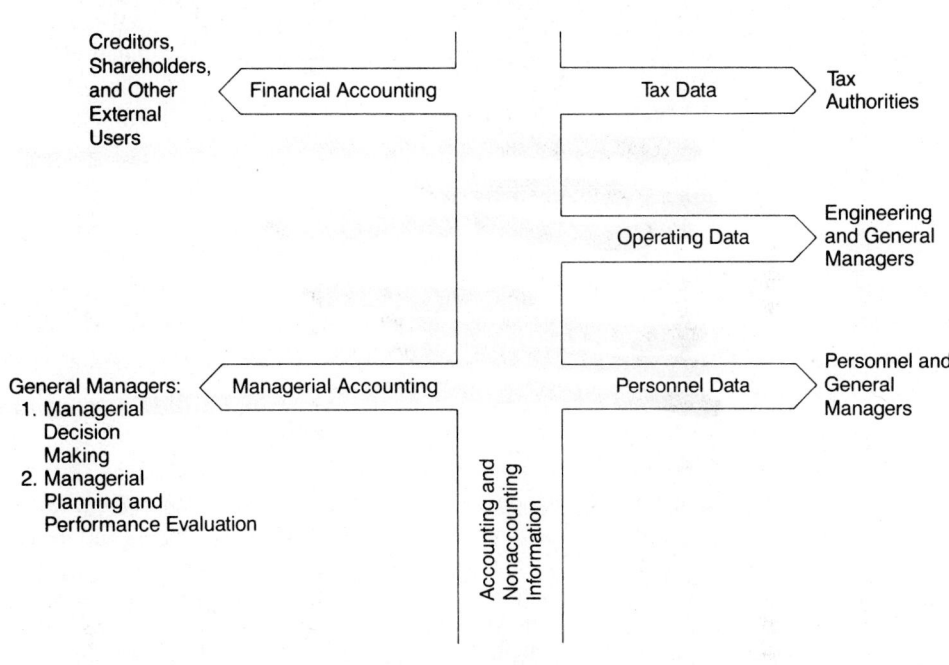

This book focuses primarily on managerial accounting. We consider how accounting aids management in making decisions and in planning and controlling operations. We assume that all of the readers of this book will be users of accounting data in their careers, though some readers will also be accounting professionals. Consequently, we take a user's perspective of accounting—we are concerned with understanding accounting systems so that the data generated by those systems can be used effectively by managers.

Uses of Accounting Information

Accounting provides information for three general uses: (1) managerial decision making; (2) managerial planning, control, and internal performance evaluation; and (3) financial reporting and external performance evaluation by shareholders and creditors. Whereas financial accounting books and courses focus on the third use, this book focuses primarily on the first two uses.

Managerial Decision Making

Management is continually confronted with the need to make decisions. Some of these decisions affect operations for only a few weeks or months, whereas others may have consequences for many years in the future. For example, what prices should be set for a firm's product during the next year? Should an important component of a firm's product be manufactured by the firm or purchased from outsiders? Should existing equipment be replaced with newer, more efficient equipment? Should a more sophisticated computer be purchased that will save clerical labor costs? These are just some of the decisions that face management.

The decision-making process includes the following steps:

1. Identifying a problem requiring managerial action.
2. Specifying the objective or goal to be achieved (for example, maximizing returns on investment).
3. Listing the possible alternative courses of action.
4. Gathering information about the consequences of each alternative.
5. Making a decision by selecting one of the alternatives.

Managerial accounting plays a critical role in step **4** of the decision-making process.

Example A manufacturer of electronic equipment is considering the introduction of portable computers into its product line. Management wishes to predict the expected costs of manufacturing the portable computers and the revenues that might be generated. The managerial accountant has a record of the costs incurred in the past to manufacture similar electronic equipment. These past costs might be classified into various groups (for example, materials, labor, and overhead). An attempt can then be made to project the future costs of manufacturing the portable computers. It is probable that data would also be available concerning the amount of advertising costs required to market similar products and the amount of sales revenue generated. Projections from these data could provide management with the information necessary to decide whether to add portable computers to the product line.

Managerial Planning, Control, and Internal Performance Evaluation

The planning and control process might be described as including the following steps or components:

1. Specifying a criterion (standard or budget) as to what actual performance should be.
2. Measuring the results of actual performance.
3. Evaluating performance by comparing actual performance with the criterion. This evaluation aids management in assessing actions already taken and in deciding which courses of action should be taken in the future.

Managerial accounting plays an important role in the planning and control process. By assisting management in the decision-making process, as discussed earlier, information is provided for establishing the expectation or standard as to what performance should be. In addition, the accounting system processes actual transactions, so it provides actual results to compare with projections.

Example The electronics manufacturer in the previous example decided to add portable computers to the firm's product line based, in part, on expectations about sales for several years. In the first year that portable computers would be sold, management projected sales revenue of $5 million. This amount might serve as the budget or standard for evaluating the performance of the marketing manager responsible for the portable computers product line.

If annual sales vary significantly from $5 million, an effort would be made to ascertain the cause of the difference, or *variance* as it is called in accounting, between anticipated and actual sales. If factors or conditions that are not under the control of the marketing manager caused the variance, then the marketing manager would not be held responsible for it. For example, a strike by production workers might cause a shortage of products and, thereby, a loss in sales that could not be controlled by the sales manager.

If the marketing manager can control the causes of the variance, then the variance would be attributable to the marketing manager in evaluating that manager's performance. For example, good design and implementation of an effective sales incentive program by the sales manager might lead to higher than expected sales. On the other hand, poor coordination of the sales force might lead to lower than expected sales. In both cases, the marketing manager would be held accountable.

Financial Accounting: External Financial Reporting and Performance Evaluation

In contrast to managerial accounting reports prepared for internal use, the financial reports prepared for users external to publicly held firms must follow certain standard formats and measurement rules. For example, a publicly held firm is required to present its statement of financial position (or balance sheet), statement of net income, and statement of changes in financial position each year in accordance with *generally accepted accounting principles.*

Relation Among Three Uses of Accounting

Exhibit 1.2 illustrates the relation among the three principal uses of accounting information discussed in this section. You will note that the managerial decision-making process and the managerial planning and control process are closely related. In making a decision, management forms an expectation as to what the results of actual performance should be if everything goes according to plan. The results of the internal performance evaluation in one period become an input into the planning and decision-making process of the next period.

Exhibit 1.2
Managerial Processes and Accounting Information

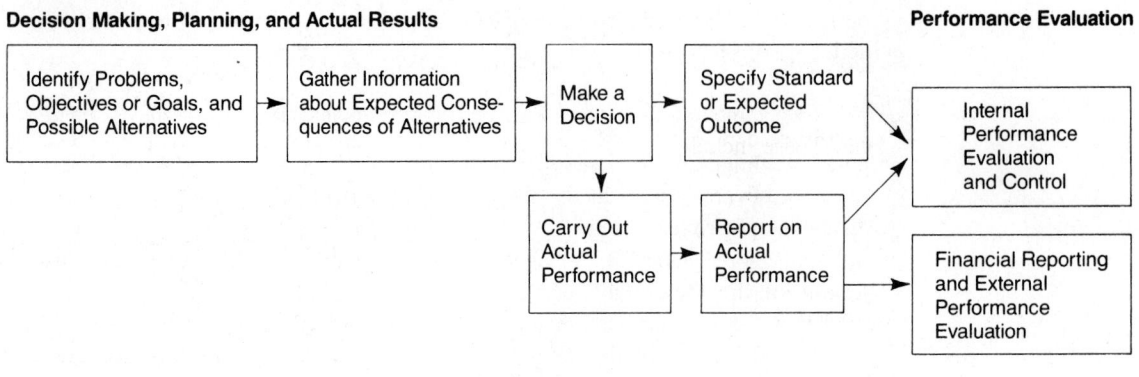

Decision Making, Planning, and Actual Results   **Performance Evaluation**

Misuse of Accounting Information

When accounting data are used for many purposes, including external reporting, tax return preparation, report preparation for regulatory authorities, and for managerial purposes, it is easy to mistakenly use data for one purpose that were intended for another. For example, many companies use the LIFO (last-in, first-out) inventory method and accelerated depreciation for tax purposes; however, these may not be appropriate for internal, managerial uses. An underlying theme in this book is that managerial accounting should be user-driven. Managers should identify the problems, goals, and alternatives first; then obtain the appropriate information for decision making.

Managers sometimes assume that the accounting data provided for financial reporting to shareholders and tax return preparation are the accounting data they must use for decision making, planning, and other managerial activities. That is simply not true. If basic transaction recording and processing is computerized, then the data can be easily adapted to meet multiple needs. One of the challenges currently facing accountants is to design systems with sufficient flexibility to provide data for many different purposes. And one of the challenges facing managers is to understand accounting well enough to know what to request and what may be expected from accountants.

The ideal situation is

1. For the decision-making process to be based on sound logic and economic reasoning, and
2. For the control process and financial reporting process to be based on measures of performance that realistically reflect the economic consequences of decisions made and actions taken.

In this way,

1. Managers will be encouraged to take actions that are in the best interests of shareholders, employees, and other constituents of the firm, and

2. The accounting reports—both internal and external—will not mislead readers about the results of managers' actions.

Differences between Financial and Managerial Accounting

There are some fundamental differences between managerial and financial accounting. These include:

Financial Accounting	Managerial Accounting
Users	
External users of information—usually shareholders, financial analysts, and creditors.	Internal users of information—usually managers.
GAAP	
Compliance with generally accepted accounting principles.	Need not comply with generally accepted accounting principles.
Future Versus Past	
Uses historical data in evaluating performance of the firm and its managers by outsiders.	Uses estimates of the future for decision making and historical data for internal performance evaluation.
Reporting Requirements	
Regulations often determine how much information is enough.	Internal cost/benefit evaluation determines how much information is enough.

Organizational Environment

Who manages the accounting function in organizations? In most corporate organizations, the *controller* is the chief accounting official. Recognizing the importance of this function, many organizations place the controller in the same organization rank as the other corporate vice-presidents. In other organizations, the controller and the treasurer may both report to a financial vice-president who is responsible for both the accounting and financial affairs of the corporation. (The activity that we call "managerial accounting" is known as "finance" in many organizations.)

An example of an organization structure appears in Exhibit 1.3. This is an abbreviated version of du Pont's organization chart. Although each organization develops its organization chart to fit its needs, the general structure of the du Pont organization chart is typical.

Controller

As the chief accounting officer, the controller usually exercises authority both for accounting within the organization and for external reporting. Internally, the controller oversees the supplying of accounting data to operating management. The controller also usually oversees the company's internal control system.

Exhibit 1.3
Organization Chart
E. I. du Pont de Nemours & Company

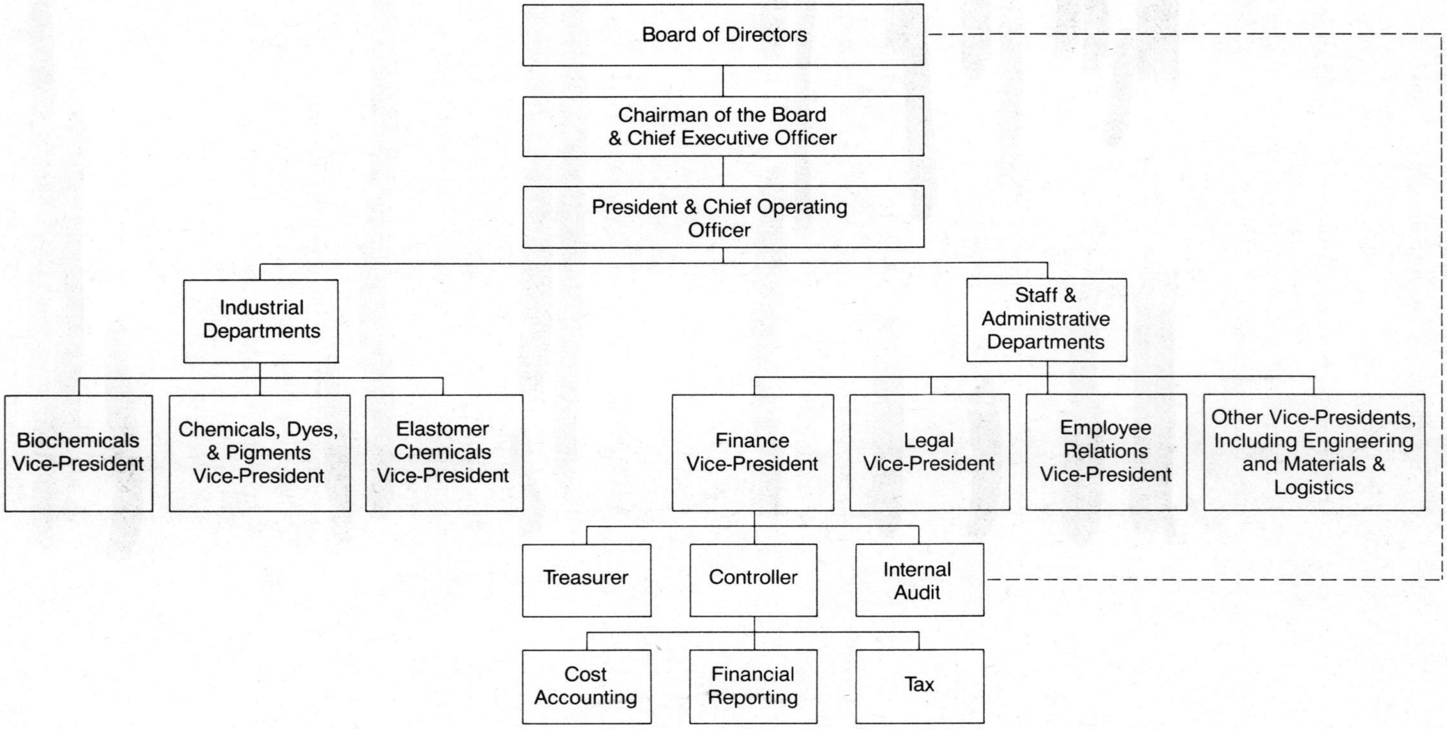

External reports include reports to taxing authorities and regulatory bodies such as the Securities and Exchange Commission, as well as the financial statements for shareholders. The controller generally is in charge of all accounting records, including those for inventories; receivables and payables; and property, plant, and equipment. The controller sometimes supervises data processing operations, but frequently data processing is an independent department.

Internal Audit

The *internal audit* department provides a variety of auditing and consulting services in many organizations, including auditing internal controls, auditing data reported inside the company, and assisting external auditors in their audit of an organization's external financial reports. In some organizations, internal auditors are internal consultants who provide an independent perspective on problems faced by operating managers. Such auditors are usually called *operational auditors*. Many auditors in the federal government are operational auditors.

The internal audit manager sometimes reports directly to the controller. Some companies recognize the possibility for conflicts between the controller's record-keeping role and the audit function, however, so they have the internal audit supervisor report directly to the controller's superior. The internal audit director is usually given authority to communicate directly to the audit committee of the board of directors.

Treasurer

The corporate *treasurer* is the manager in charge of obtaining capital for operations and for managing cash and near-cash assets. The treasurer handles credit reviews and sets policy for collecting receivables. The treasurer normally handles relationships with banks and other lending or financing sources, including public issues of shares or debt.

Professional Environment

Accountants are not only part of the management team, they are also part of a profession. Their professional environment influences the types of reports and data bases developed in companies.

Accounting Authorities

Frequent references are made throughout this book to the ''generally accepted accounting principles'' that govern financial accounting. These ''principles'' are the accounting methods used by firms in preparing their external financial statements. While managerial accounting is not constrained by ''generally accepted accounting principles'' or other rules such as the income tax laws, the fact that the accounting system must produce reports conforming with those regulations has implications for managerial accounting. The accounting system in some companies is designed primarily to comply with such rules and only secondarily to meet managerial needs.

Generally accepted accounting principles are not all codified, nor are they all promulgated by a single governmental, private, or professional authority. Rather, they are found in the literature of the field, including pronouncements of interested professional organizations and security exchanges, governmental regulations, articles, and textbooks. Thus management, the accounting profession, the users of financial statements, and governmental agencies contribute to the continuing development of generally accepted principles of accounting. The following organizations are important regulatory agencies.

Securities and Exchange Commission By Congressional act, the *Securities and Exchange Commission* (SEC) has been granted the legal authority to prescribe accounting principles to be followed by most corporations. The SEC has used its power sparingly, however.

Financial Accounting Standards Board Since 1973, the *Financial Accounting Standards Board* (FASB) has been the highest nongovernmental authority on generally accepted accounting principles. The FASB issues *Statements of Financial Accounting Standards* (and *Interpretations* of these statements) from time to time, establishing or clarifying generally accepted accounting principles.

American Institute of Certified Public Accountants The *American Institute of Certified Public Accountants* (AICPA) is the national organization of certified public accountants. Its publications and committees are influential in the development of accounting principles and auditing practices. It actively promulgates standards of ethics and reviews conduct within the profession.

Internal Revenue Service Income tax legislation and administration have influenced the practice of accounting, although income tax requirements in themselves do not establish principles and practices for external or internal reporting. The *Internal Revenue Code* (passed by the Congress), the *Regulations* and *Rulings* (of the Internal Revenue Service), and the opinions of the U.S. Tax Court form the basis for income tax reporting rules.

Cost Accounting Standards Board The *Cost Accounting Standards Board* (CASB) was established by the U.S. Congress in 1970 to set accounting standards for computing costs in cost-based contracts (for example, cost plus a profit) by defense contractors. The diversity in cost accounting systems used by defense contractors made it difficult for the U.S. government to evaluate proposals and to determine the payments due contractors. The CASB attempted to set standards to achieve uniformity and consistency in contract proposals and cost reporting. Most of the work of the CASB does not directly affect the form of financial statements, but its requirements have considerable weight in many areas of practice, especially those dealing with the allocation of costs. The CASB was terminated in 1980, but its standards are still applied to many transactions between defense contractors and the U.S. government.

Certifications

Certified Public Accountant The *Certified Public Accountant* (CPA) is a designation indicating that an individual is registered or licensed as a Certified Public Accountant. To qualify as a CPA, an individual must pass a written examination and satisfy audit experience requirements. The CPA examination includes questions on managerial accounting. We have included several questions from prior CPA examinations in this book.

Certificate in Management Accounting In 1972, a Certificate in Management Accounting (CMA) program was established to recognize educational achievement and professional competence in management accounting. The examination, educational requirements, and experience requirements are similar to those for the CPA examinations, but they are aimed at the professional in management and cost accounting. We have included many problems from prior CMA examinations in this book.

Canadian Certifications Examinations and certifications are given in Canada by the *Society of Management Accountants* and the *Certified General Accountants Association*.

Costs and Benefits of Accounting

A division of National Steel Company recently installed a particular managerial accounting system that cost several million dollars. How did management justify such an expenditure? They believed that the benefits from cost control and increased efficiency would save the company more than the cost of the system.

The question "How much accounting for managerial purposes is enough?" is resolved on a cost/benefit basis like similar managerial questions, such as "How much advertising is enough?" or "Should a computerized inventory system be installed?" More accounting information for managerial purposes is justified only if the benefits of the information exceed its costs.

In practice, it is difficult to measure the costs and benefits of accounting. In deciding to install the accounting system, the management of National Steel Company could be certain of only some of the costs and few of the benefits of the system. Despite these difficulties in measuring costs and benefits, accounting for managerial uses must meet cost/benefit requirements, in principle.

The analysis of costs and benefits requires considerable communication and cooperation between users and accountants. Users are more familiar with the benefits of information, whereas accountants are more familiar with its costs. As shown in Exhibit 1.4, users identify their needs based on the decisions they make and request data from accountants who develop information systems to supply information when it is cost/benefit-justified. In practice, the process sometimes works in reverse. But if accountants and users interact, they eventually settle on a cost/benefit-justified supply of accounting data that meets users' needs.

Exhibit 1.4
Supply and Demand for Accounting Information

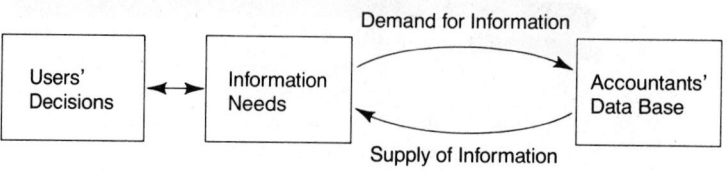

The Value of Information for Particular Decisions

Determining the value of information for particular decisions is important in many managerial settings besides accounting. For example, should an additional marketing study involving expanded sampling of a new product by consumers be undertaken? Should the company discontinue its marketing tests and proceed directly to full-scale production? Should a doctor order laboratory tests before taking action in an emergency situation? Should a production manager stop production to test a sample of products for defects, or allow production to continue?

The problem is solved conceptually by comparing the improvement in the value of actions because of information with the cost of information.

Scholars in economics, accounting, and decision theory are working on ways to deal with the difficult problem of measuring the value of information. The appendix to this chapter presents a formal analytical model for evaluating the "economics of information."

The main point is that both users and accountants recognize that information is not free. The costs and benefits of information should be taken into account in deciding how much accounting is enough.

Organization of the Book

Part One of this book (Chapters 1 and 2) provides background concepts for later use. Part Two (Chapters 3–5) provides an overview of cost systems to help users of accounting understand how accounting systems are designed. This understanding of accounting systems will help users communicate their information needs to accountants. Parts Three and Four discuss the two major uses of managerial accounting information. Part Three (Chapters 6–10) discusses the use of accounting for managerial decision making, and Part Four (Chapters 11–14) discusses the use of accounting for managerial planning and performance evaluation. Part V (Chapters 15–18) discusses special topics.

Summary

Accounting is often divided into financial accounting and managerial accounting. *Financial accounting* refers to the preparation of general-purpose reports for external users; *managerial accounting* refers to providing information to managers inside the organization. This book focuses primarily on the use of accounting for managerial decision making and for managerial planning and performance evaluation.

Whereas financial accounting is subject to externally imposed restrictions and rules, managerial accounting is not. The focus of managerial accounting is on providing the information needed for managerial decision making and other managerial activities, rather than on satisfying rules. Hence, managerial accounting reports can differ considerably from organization to organization. Further, managerial accounting comprises many special-purpose reports.

Although managerial accounting is not directly subject to external regulations, it is affected by them. Generally accepted accounting principles, tax laws, and other regulations affect the design of accounting systems; hence, they affect the kind of data that are routinely produced by accounting systems. Information that is required by regulations can also be used for managerial purposes at very low cost—perhaps only for the cost of an additional computer printout. This information need not, however, be prepared in a form that is relevant or useful for managerial purposes. Care must be continually expended to ensure that information designed for one purpose is not improperly used for another purpose.

Managerial accounting is user-oriented. In the ideal setting, users know what type of accounting data can be feasibly provided and whether it is worthwhile to obtain the data. Hence, it is important for users to understand accounting well enough to communicate effectively with accountants. Thus, they can obtain the data they want for decision making, and they can influence the design of accounting systems to meet their needs.

Appendix:
The Value of Information

(*Note*: This appendix assumes that students have some background in elementary probability theory.)

The decision about "how much information is enough" is usually made judgmentally. In this appendix, we show how formal decision theory models can be applied to the issue. These models require data that may not be readily available in many organizations; hence, this approach should be viewed more as a systematic method of thinking about the problem than as a tool that can be easily implemented and routinely applied. The methods described in this appendix have been applied to numerous practical problems, however, including obtaining information for drilling oil wells.

To make the analysis concrete, we consider the case of an owner-manager of a small company who is trying to decide whether to accept a special order from a customer. This is a one-time order. Rejection of the order results in no present or future impact on profits. If the order is accepted, the increased revenue to the company will be $1 million. The costs of making the products for the special order are not known with certainty, but they are estimated to be either $800,000 or $1,200,000, depending on how much time is needed for its manufacture. Hence, acceptance of the order would result in a net gain of $200,000 *or* a net loss of $200,000, whereas rejection will produce neither gain nor loss.

The proprietor regards the two production cost events as having the following probabilities: (1) there is a .6 probability that production costs will be $800,000, hence, a $200,000 profit would be made on the order; (2) there is a .4 probability that production costs will be $1,200,000, hence, a $200,000 *loss* would be incurred if the order is accepted. Consequently, the expected value of accepting the order is computed as follows:[1]

$$EV = \sum_i Pr_i \, V_i$$

$$= (.6 \times \$200,000) + (.4 \times -\$200,000)$$

$$= +\underline{\$40,000}$$

where EV = the expected value of the outcomes,

Pr_i = the probability of each outcome occurring,

V_i = the value of each outcome.

Value of Information

Note that the owner-manager has enough information to estimate a revenue outcome and two cost outcomes. Suppose that *before* deciding whether to accept or reject the order, the owner-manager has the option of obtaining more information, namely, the cost of a set of special orders already in production. The cost of setting up the necessary accounting records and analyzing these data are estimated to be $50,000. Note that (1) the decision whether to obtain this information is made before (2) the decision whether to accept the special order is made. The information would not be obtained, obviously, unless its benefits were greater than $50,000.

Suppose that the information would tell the owner-manager for certain whether production costs would be $800,000 or $1,200,000; that is, the information is perfect. What is the value of that information to the owner-manager? Exhibit 1.5 diagrams the analysis in a decision tree.

The sequence of events is as follows if the owner-manager obtains information:

1. Obtain information.

2a. Either information accurately predicts low production costs of $800,000, so accept the order to make a profit of $200,000; or

2b. Information accurately predicts high production costs of $1,200,000, so reject the order to avoid losing $200,000.

Note that the owner-manager's probability estimates of the information signal are the same as the estimates of the event—that is, .6 for low costs and .4 for high

---

[1]We assume that the owner-manager is risk-neutral to avoid complicating the issue. For applications to the risk-averse case, see Joel S. Demski, *Information Analysis* (Reading, Mass.: Addison-Wesley, 1980).

Exhibit 1.5
Decision Tree for Computing the Value of Perfect Information

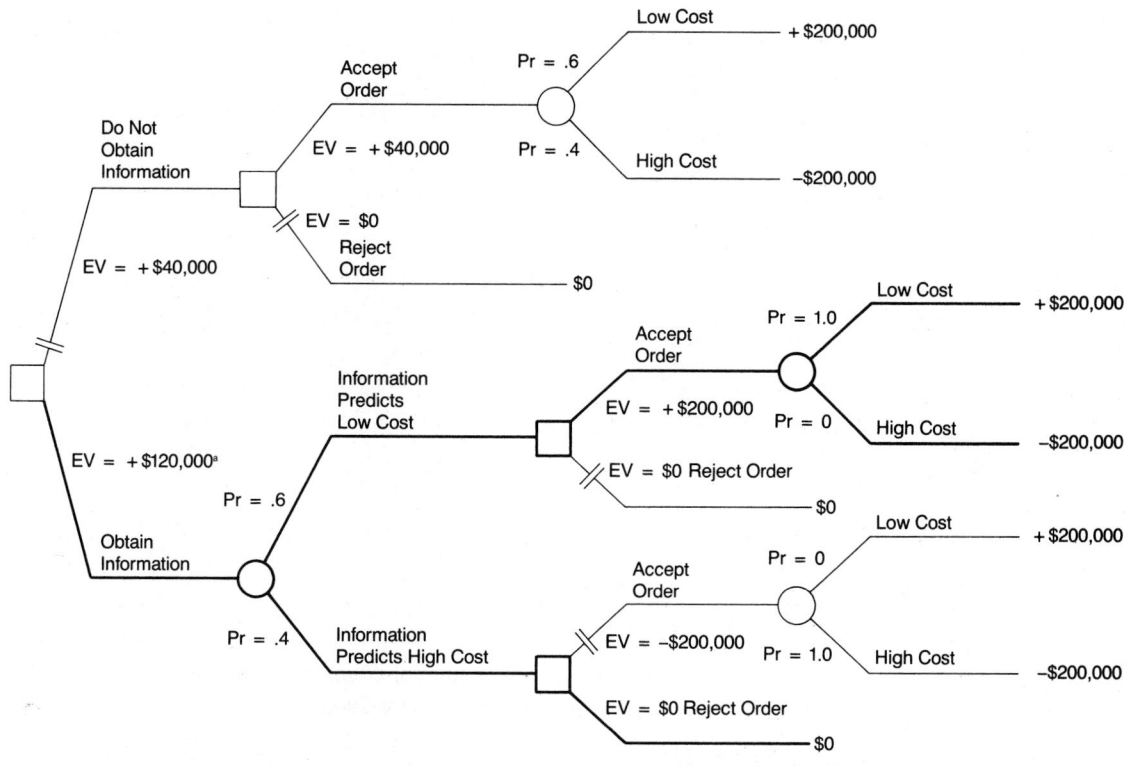

EV = expected value of the alternative.
Pr = owner-manager's subjective probability.
☐ = decision point.
◯ = event.
Note: The cost of information is excluded. The increase in expected value by using information of $80,000 is the expected value of perfect information, which is greater than the information cost of $50,000.
[a]$120,000 = (.6 × $200,000) + (.4 × $0). Expected value of perfect information is

$120,000 − $40,000 = \underline{\underline{$80,000}}$.

costs. If information is perfect, the probability estimates of what information will predict about events is the same as the probability estimates about the events themselves.

What does the owner-manager gain by obtaining information? If the information accurately predicts that production costs will be $800,000, the owner-manager gains nothing from the information. (We assume that the $50,000 cost of information has been incurred—and there are no refunds.) The value of the information is that it tells the owner-manager when to avoid the loss from accepting an order and *then* learning that production costs are high. This could save the owner-manager

$200,000. There is a .4 probability that this savings would occur, hence, the *expected value of perfect information* is $80,000 (= .4 × $200,000). The expected value of perfect information can also be seen by taking the difference in the expected values of the "obtain information" and "do not obtain information" alternatives in Exhibit 1.5:

Expected Value of Perfect Information	=	Expected Value of Alternative with Information	−	Expected Value of Alternative without Information
	=	$120,000	−	$40,000
	=	$ 80,000.		

The rational owner-manager would acquire the information because its expected benefits of $80,000 exceed its cost of $50,000.

Most information is not perfect, of course. The expected value of *perfect* information is a ceiling on the amount that should be paid for information. The *imperfect information* case is discussed in cost and advanced managerial accounting textbooks and textbooks on decision making under uncertainty.[2]

Problem 1 for Self-Study

Overview of the Use of Information for Decision Making, Performance Evaluation, and External Reporting

Cheers Warbuck, Incorporated, is a large publicly held corporation that operates a chain of retail department stores throughout the United States. It is currently faced with a decision whether or not to build a new "super store" in a rapidly growing regional shopping center in Phoenix.

a. What type of financial information would top management need in making this decision?

b. Assume that a decision has been made to open the new store. Identify the types of information that top management would be likely to need in order to evaluate the performance of the Phoenix store each year.

c. Identify the types of information that shareholders and potential investors would need for evaluating Cheers Warbuck's decision to open the store. How, if at all, would the information needed by shareholders and potential investors differ from that needed by top management for internal performance evaluation?

d. Discuss similarities and differences in the uses of accounting data identified in parts **a, b,** and **c.**

---

[2]For example, see N. Dopuch, J. G. Birnberg, and J. S. Demski, *Cost Accounting*, 3rd ed. (New York: Harcourt Brace Jovanovich, 1982), chap. 1; E. B. Deakin and M. W. Maher, *Cost Accounting* (Homewood, Ill., R. D. Irwin, 1984); or R. S. Kaplan, *Advanced Management Accounting* (Englewood Cliffs, N.J.: Prentice-Hall, 1982).

Suggested Solution

a. The appropriate basis for decisions is an analysis of the cash inflows and outflows that would result from the decision to open the store in Phoenix.[3] Part Three of this book discusses methods of estimating these cash flows and making decisions such as this.

b. Top management would need some basis for evaluating the performance of the Phoenix store. Return on investment, profits, and net cash flows are commonly used for this purpose. The use of financial performance measures is discussed at length in Part Four of this book.

c. First, the reports to shareholders must be prepared in accordance with generally accepted accounting principles, whereas the measures used by top management evaluation can follow whatever method management feels will provide the most useful information. Second, financial reports to shareholders are highly aggregated. Management usually wants much more detailed information than do shareholders.

d. The following chart summarizes similarities and differences among different uses of accounting data:

Item	Managerial Decision Making	Internal Performance Evaluation	External Performance Evaluation
Time Dimension	Future	Past	Past
Frequency	As Needed	More Frequent, Usually Monthly	Less Frequent
Degree of Aggregation	Detailed	Detailed	More Aggregated
Flexibility in Content	Flexible	Flexible	Relatively Inflexible; Must Follow GAAP
Range of Focus	Cash Flows	Division Profits, Revenues, Costs, and Return on Investment	Net Income, Cash Flows, Return on Shareholders' Equity

Problem 2 for Self-Study (Appendix)

Soong's Soybean Products After several years of supplying tofu to several supermarket chains, the Soong family decided that it was time to diversify their operations in the light of increasing competition from other tofu manufacturers.

At a recent family conference, several members came up with new product ideas as possible alternatives to tofu. A dehydrated soybean protein was considered too low-margin. Soybean jello, despite popularity with some communities, was rejected on the grounds that it was highly perishable and appealed to a small market segment.

[3]Readers familiar with discounted cash flow methods will recognize that these cash flows should be discounted to their present value using a risk-adjusted discount rate. We discuss discounted cash flow methods in Chapter 9.

Laura Soong, a recent biochemistry graduate, then suggested that they exploit the growing diet and health food market by introducing a soybean ice cream. "I've perfected it in the lab," she said. "It is low in cholesterol and has only one-quarter the calories of regular ice cream. But more important, it tastes almost like the real thing!" She then provided her estimates of costs for the project.

Based on Laura's figures, David Soong, the family accountant, estimates that if sales are high, the product will increase the company's profits by $150,000 per year. If sales are low, the product will reduce company profits by $100,000 per year. David assigns a prior probability of .5 for high sales and .5 for low sales.

The company can conduct a survey of various health food outlets to obtain information about the true demand for the new product. The costs of such a survey are $20,000.

a. Construct a decision tree like the one in Exhibit 1.5 to show the action they will take without the survey. What is the expected value of one year's increase or decrease in profits without information?

b. How much would the Soong family be willing to pay for perfect information?

Suggested Solution

a.

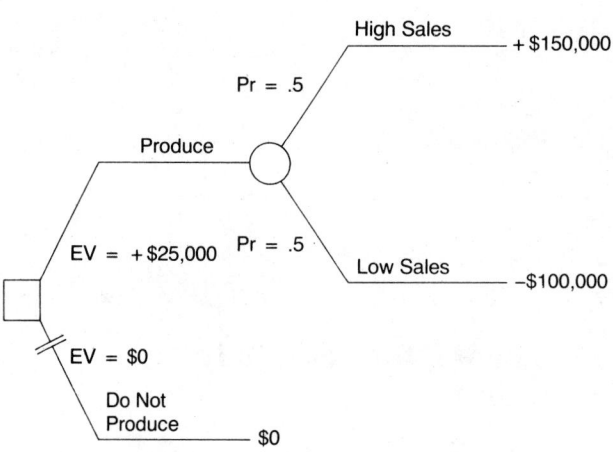

The expected value of profit without information is

$$.5(\$150,000) + .5(-\$100,000) = +\$25,000.$$

Decision: Produce.

b. See the following diagram.

The expected value of perfect information = $75,000 − $25,000 = $50,000. The expected value of perfect information, $50,000, exceeds the cost of the information, $20,000; hence, the information should be acquired.

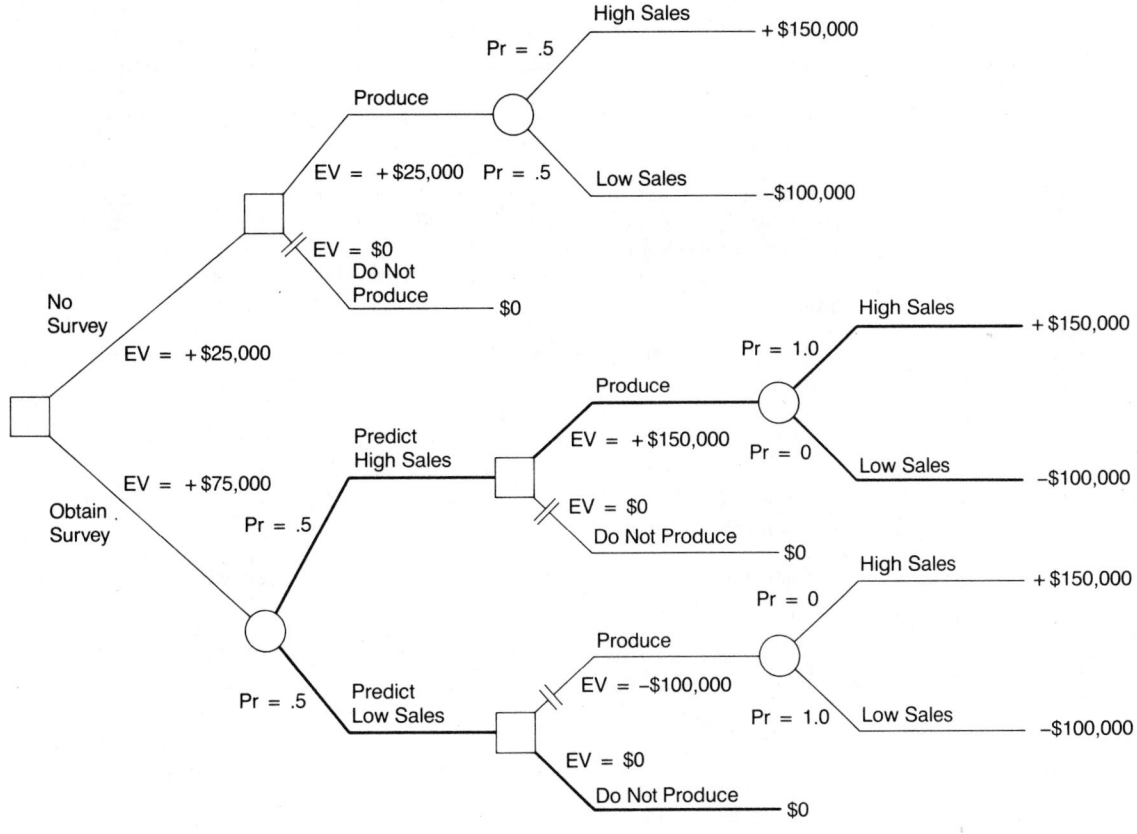

Questions

1. Review the meaning of the following concepts or terms introduced in this chapter.

a.	Managerial accounting.	**i.**	Internal audit.
b.	Financial accounting.	**j.**	Certificate in Management
c.	SEC.		Accounting.
d.	FASB.	**k.**	Certified Public Accountant.
e.	GAAP.	**l.**	Cost/benefit criterion.
f.	CASB.	**m.**	Expected value of perfect
g.	Controller.		information (appendix).
h.	Treasurer.		

2. Distinguish between financial accounting and managerial accounting.

3. Generally accepted accounting principles are the methods of accounting used by publicly held firms in preparing their financial statements. A principle in physics, such as the law of gravity, serves as a basis for developing theories and explaining the relationships among physical objects. In what ways are generally accepted accounting principles similar to and different from principles in physics?

4. "Managerial accounting is not important in nonprofit organizations, such as agencies of the federal government and nonprofit hospitals, because they do not have to earn a profit." Do you agree with this statement? Why or why not?

5. What are the steps involved in the managerial decision-making process? What role does accounting play in that process?

6. What are the steps involved in the managerial planning, control, and internal performance evaluation process? What role does accounting play in that process?

7. Distinguish between internal performance evaluation and external performance evaluation.

8. Why is it important that financial reports to shareholders not misrepresent the actions taken by managers?

9. "It is important for managerial accountants to understand the uses of accounting data and for users of data to understand accounting. Only in this way can the appropriate accounting data be provided for the correct uses." Do you agree with this statement? Why or why not?

10. A student planning a career in management wondered why it was important to learn about accounting. How would you respond?

11. "The best management accounting system is one that provides managers with all of the information they would like to have." Do you agree with this statement? Why or why not?

12. What are the two major uses of managerial accounting information?

13. (Appendix) What is the expected value of information?

Problems and Cases

14. *Value of Information—Nonbusiness Setting.* Consider the following value of information in a medical context.

Suppose that a patient visits a doctor's office and that the doctor decides on the basis of the signs that the patient's appendix should be removed immediately. Meanwhile the doctor orders a white cell blood count. The doctor decides that the appendix must be removed no matter what the blood count happens to be.

a.   What is the value of the information (in the cost/benefit sense discussed in this chapter) about the blood count to the doctor?

b.   Why might the doctor order the test anyway?

15. *Objectives and Uses of Financial Statements (CMA adapted).* Financial statements are an important means by which entities communicate economic information to interested parties. The objectives of financial reporting have received the attention of the accounting profession, the business community, the government, and the general public at various times and in various degrees for many years.

In the past 5 years there has been increased concern and intensive study of financial reporting objectives. The objectives recommended range from "the statements are the management's report on its stewardship of the investors' capital'' to ''the statements provide information to investors for predicting, comparing, and evaluating the economic activities of an enterprise.''

The objectives established for financial reporting will depend on whether the reports are prepared by management or some other party, what the reports are to represent (results of past activities or predictions of future actions), for whom the statements are intended, and how the statements will be used.

a. Discuss the responsibilities of management for the entity's financial reporting.

b. Does management prepare financial reports in order to reflect past performance of the business entity or to help predict the future performance of the entity? Discuss briefly.

c. Discuss briefly how financial reports can be used by investors in making investment decisions.

16. *Decision Making and Financial Reporting.* Harry Morris, a taxi driver in Washington, D.C., recently considered whether to sell his old Dodge and purchase a new one. The old car is completely depreciated for accounting (book) purposes and has zero net book value. However, Harry has a buyer who would pay him $300 cash for it. The new car would cost $7,000 to acquire, and Harry believes that he could keep it for 5 years, after which it would be worth $500. If Harry keeps the old car for the next 5 years, instead of buying the new one, he expects to incur large maintenance costs. In fact, keeping the old Dodge would cost $1,200 more per year for operating costs than would the new model. There would be no differences in revenues or in costs other than those noted above. Depreciation is on a straight-line basis.

Show the impact on operating profit (which equals revenues minus cash operating costs minus depreciation for this problem) and cash flows for each of the 5 years, assuming that (a) the old Dodge is kept for 5 years; and (b) the old Dodge is sold and the new Dodge is purchased. What would you recommend to Harry? Ignore income taxes and the time value of money. Compared to keeping the old car, would buying the new car make Harry's reported operating profit better or worse each year? The following format may help you address the problem:

	Year 1	Year 2	Year 3	Year 4	Year 5
Operating Profit:					
Keep Old Car:					
Buy New Car:					
Cash Flow:					
Keep Old Car:					
Buy New Car:					

17. *Decision Making Under Uncertainty and the Value of Information (Appendix) (CMA adapted).* Vendo Company operates the concession stands at the University football stadium. Records of past sales indicate that there are basically four kinds of football weather, that sales of hot dogs depend on the weather, and that the percentage of football games played in each kind of weather is as follows:

Weather	Percentage of Game Days	Hot Dogs Sold
Snow	10%	10,000
Rain.	20	20,000
Clear/Warm	40	30,000
Clear/Cold	30	40,000

Hot dogs cost Vendo Company $.30 each and are sold for $.50. Hot dogs unsold at the end of each game are worthless. Ignore income taxes.

a. Prepare a table with four rows and four columns showing the contribution margin from each of the four purchasing strategies of buying 10,000, 20,000, 30,000, or 40,000 hot dogs and the four weather conditions, snow, rain, clear/warm, and clear/cold.

b. Assuming that the chances of snow, rain, clear/warm, and clear/cold are 10, 20, 40, and 30 percent, respectively, compute the expected contribution margin from each of the following purchasing strategies:

(**i**) Buy 10,000 hot dogs.
(**ii**) Buy 20,000 hot dogs.
(**iii**) Buy 30,000 hot dogs.
(**iv**) Buy 40,000 hot dogs.

c. What is the optimal purchasing strategy in the absence of a weather forecast, and what is the expected contribution margin from following this strategy? (This answer will be the largest of the four expected payoffs computed in part **b.**).

d. If Vendo had a perfect weather forecast for each game, it would buy 10,000 hot dogs when snow is predicted, 20,000 when rain is predicted, 30,000 when clear/warm is predicted, and 40,000 when clear/ cold is predicted. What is the expected average contribution margin per football game assuming the availability of a perfect weather forecast and that the four kinds of weather will occur in the frequencies 10, 20, 40, and 30 percent?

e. What is the expected dollar value to Vendo Company of a perfect weather forecast per football game? That is, what is the expected dollar value of the information from a perfect weather forecast?

18. *Decision Making Under Uncertainty and the Value of Information (Appendix).* If a mother with Rh negative blood bears a child whose father is Rh positive, there may be complications (the medical name is *erythroblastosis foetalis*) in subsequent pregnancies unless a shot of Rhogam is given to the mother soon after the first child is born. Assume that 87 percent of all people have Rh positive blood, that 13 percent have Rh negative blood, and that matings occur randomly among blood types. Assume that the complications occur in 5 percent of the matings where the mother is negative and the father is positive and that the cost of the complications is $12,000.

a. In what percentage of matings will the complication arise?

b. What is the expected cost per mating from the complication if the Rhogam shot is not given to any mothers?

c. What is the cost per mating if every mother is given the shot, which costs $50?

d. Comparing your answers to parts **b** and **c**, what is the optimal action in the absence of information about blood types, and what is the expected cost per mating from following that action?

e. Suppose that information on blood types is known. What is the expected cost per mating if the Rhogam shot is given only in matings with Rh negative mothers and Rh positive fathers?

19. *Value of Information: CVC Hi-Tech (J. Lim) (Appendix).* Carl Valentine, chief executive of CVC Hi-Tech, a high-technology company, is thinking of signing a contract to provide personal computer software. The contract lasts for only 1 year, and Carl does not believe that it would be renewed. CVC Hi-Tech's sales of the software would be a function of the demand for the personal computer using the software.

Carl estimates that a high volume of sales would earn CVC Hi-Tech $500,000 in profits. A medium volume would give CVC Hi-Tech zero profits, and a low volume of sales would cause CVC Hi-Tech to incur a loss of $300,000. Valentine considers all three events to be equally likely.

a. What should Carl Valentine's decision be at this point? Assume that he is risk-neutral and a wealth maximizer.

b. Suppose that Carl Valentine can hire the services of a market research company for a fee of $30,000. Should he use their services if they can give him perfect information?

Chapter 2   Cost Concepts

As we noted in Chapter 1, managerial accounting deals with the information needs of managers for making decisions and for planning and performance evaluation. The primary information needs are generally the *costs* of carrying out the organization's activities. Questions that managers ask include: "What does product #101X cost?" "What is the cost of the assembly department in our Des Moines plant?" "What are the costs of caring for a patient for 1 day in the hospital?" Cost information is also important to value inventory and measure expenses in external financial reports. In this chapter, we introduce important cost concepts that are used throughout this book and in practice.[1]

Fundamental Cost Concepts

In principle, a *cost* is a *sacrifice* of resources. For example, if you were to purchase an automobile for a cash payment of $6,000, the cost to purchase the automobile would be $6,000. A promise to pay $6,000 would be treated the same as a cash payment for purposes of measuring costs.

Although this is a simple concept, it can be difficult to apply. For example, what is sacrificed to obtain a college education? Cash is sacrificed to pay for tuition and books. What about cash paid for living costs? If these costs would be incurred whether or not the student attends college, they should not be considered "costs" of getting a college education.

Cash is not all that students sacrifice. They also sacrifice their time. Placing a value on that time is difficult; it depends on the best foregone alternative use of the time. For students who sacrifice high-paying jobs to attend college, the total cost of college may be much larger than the cash sacrificed. Other students may not sacrifice as much in terms of foregone alternatives, so their college costs would be lower. In each case, costs are a sacrifice of resources. The most important resources sacrificed to attend college are time and money.

The term "cost" is meaningful only if it is used in some particular context. To say "the cost of this building is $1 million" is ambiguous unless the context of the cost is identified. Does "cost" mean the original price paid by the current owner, the price that would be paid to replace it new, or the price to replace it today in its current condition? Is it the annual rental fee paid to occupy the building? Is it the cash foregone from not selling it? Is it the original price paid minus

---

[1] A *Glossary* of accounting terms and concepts appears at the back of this book to facilitate finding definitions. See especially the compendium of cost definitions at "cost terminology."

accumulated depreciation? The context in which the term "cost" is used is needed to reduce its ambiguity. Much of this chapter is devoted to describing how different contexts affect the meaning of costs.

Opportunity Costs

The definition of cost as a "sacrifice" leads directly to the *opportunity cost* concept. If an asset is used for one purpose, the opportunity cost of using it for that purpose is the return foregone from the best alternative use of it.

The opportunity cost of a college education includes foregone earnings. Here are some other illustrations of the meaning of opportunity cost:

1. The opportunity cost of funds invested in a government bond is the interest that could be earned on a bank certificate of deposit (adjusted for differences in risk).[2]

2. The opportunity cost of using a plant to produce a particular product is the sacrifice of profits that would be made by producing other products (adjusted for differences in risk).

3. Proprietors of small businesses often take a nominal salary. But the opportunity cost of their time may be much higher than the nominal salary recorded on the books. The opportunity cost to the proprietor is the salary that could be earned in other jobs (adjusting for differences in risk and nonpecuniary costs and benefits of being a proprietor).

Costs and Expenses

It is important to distinguish *cost*, as used in managerial accounting, from *expense*, as used in financial accounting. Whereas a cost is a sacrifice of resources, an expense is a cost that is used up to produce revenues in a particular accounting period.

In managerial accounting, we are concerned primarily with *costs*, not expenses. Generally accepted accounting principles and regulations such as the income tax laws specify when costs are treated as expenses to be deducted from revenues. We shall reserve the term "expense" to refer to expenses for external reporting as defined by generally accepted accounting principles.

General Cost Structure

Direct and Indirect Costs

A distinction is made between direct and indirect costs. Costs that can be related directly to a cost object are called *direct costs*. Those that cannot are *indirect costs*.

---

[2]A principle in finance is that investors and creditors are compensated for taking risk. For example, U.S. Treasury notes are usually considered to be less risky than commercial notes; hence, commercial notes pay interest at a higher rate.

A *cost object* is any item for which a measure of cost is needed or desired. Departments, stores, divisions, product lines, or units produced are typical cost objects. The cost object establishes the context for labeling a cost as direct or indirect.

Example Umbrella Makers produces umbrellas. They buy the frame, handle, and nylon covering material; cut the nylon to the proper size; then assemble the pieces to make the umbrella. The company rents its factory facilities. If the cost object is an umbrella, the materials and labor that can be traced directly to the production of each umbrella are direct. Umbrella Makers considers the frame, handle, and nylon material to be direct material, and workers' time to cut nylon and assemble the umbrella to be direct labor. The factory rent, however, is an indirect cost of each umbrella.

In this example, when the cost object is an umbrella, the factory rent is *indirect*. Now suppose that the purpose of calculating costs is to evaluate the performance of the factory manager. In this case, the cost object is the entire factory, not a unit produced, so factory rent would be a direct cost. Factory rent is direct to the factory, but indirect to an umbrella produced. The distinction between direct and indirect is meaningful only in some contexts; that is, a cost is direct or indirect only with respect to a particular cost object.

Common Costs When indirect costs are common to, or shared by, two or more cost objects, they are called *common costs*. A common cost results from the common use of facilities (for example, building or equipment) or services (for example, data processing or the legal staff) by several products, departments, or processes.

Examples of common costs include:

1. The factory rent paid by Umbrella Makers is common to departments within the factory.
2. The cost of buildings that house a business school are usually common to each of the departments (accounting, finance, marketing, and so forth) within the school.
3. The cost of a computer is common to its uses.

The allocation of common costs involves assigning these costs to cost objects. Cost allocation pervades both internal and external accounting reports. Cost allocation will come up in numerous places in this text, where we discuss it in the context of managerial decision making and performance evaluation. Also, it is discussed at length in Chapter 15.

Manufacturing Costs

Costs are affected by the type of organization and the nature of its activities. The most complex organization, in terms of costs, is the manufacturing firm. It includes production, marketing, administration, and service activities. An understanding of the cost structure of a manufacturing organization can be useful for understanding the cost structure of all types of organizations.

Manufacturing involves the transformation of materials into a finished good using labor and capital invested in machines and production facilities. Manufacturing costs comprise three elements: direct materials, direct labor, and manufacturing overhead.

As previously indicated, *direct materials* (also called ''raw materials'') are those that can be traced directly to a unit of output. They can range from natural materials, such as iron ore to make steel and logs to make lumber, to more synthetic materials such as electronic chips used in making calculators and plastics used in making toys.

The adjective ''direct'' is important for classifying materials in this category. Many materials that are used in manufacturing are difficult to trace to particular units of output. Examples of these *indirect materials* include lubricants for machines, lightbulbs, welding rods, cleaning materials, and the like. Indirect materials are classified as part of overhead, which is described below.

Direct labor represents the wages of workers who transform raw materials into a finished product. Examples of direct labor costs are the costs of assembly-line workers who make automobiles, construction workers who build houses, and others whose labor can be traced directly to particular units of a product.

Labor costs that cannot be traced directly to the creation of products, yet are required as part of the production process, are known as *indirect labor*. Examples include wages of maintenance personnel, supervisors, materials handlers, and inventory storekeepers. Like indirect materials, indirect labor costs are classified as overhead. The sum of direct material and direct labor is sometimes called *prime cost*.

The third major category of manufacturing costs is *manufacturing overhead*. Included in manufacturing overhead are all *manufacturing* costs that are not traceable to particular units of product as either direct material or direct labor. These are costs that give the firm the capacity to produce, such as indirect materials and indirect labor, as previously noted, and the cost of utilities, property taxes, depreciation, insurance, rent, and other costs of operating the manufacturing facilities. Manufacturing overhead and direct labor are the costs of converting raw materials into final products. Thus, they are often known as *conversion costs*. The relation between the full cost of manufacturing a good, and the materials, labor, and manufacturing overhead required to produce it is diagrammed in Exhibit 2.1.

How indirect can a cost be to the manufacturing activity and still be considered part of manufacturing overhead? For example, are the costs of operating a factory employee cafeteria, or the plant manager's salary, or the cost of employing the plant's accounting staff part of manufacturing costs? In practice it is difficult to distinguish between such manufacturing and nonmanufacturing costs, so firms typically set their own guidelines and follow them consistently from period to period.

Although we use the term ''manufacturing overhead,'' many synonyms are found in practice, including *overhead, burden, factory burden, factory overhead*, and *factory expense*. The term ''overhead,'' as we use it, refers only to manufacturing costs, not to nonmanufacturing marketing and administrative costs.

Nonmanufacturing Costs

Nonmanufacturing costs comprise two elements: marketing costs and administrative costs. *Marketing costs* are those required to obtain customer orders and to provide the customer with the finished product. These include advertising, sales commissions, shipping, and building occupancy costs, among others. (These are also known as marketing and *distribution* costs. We refer to these costs as simply

Exhibit 2.1
Components of Manufactured Product Costs

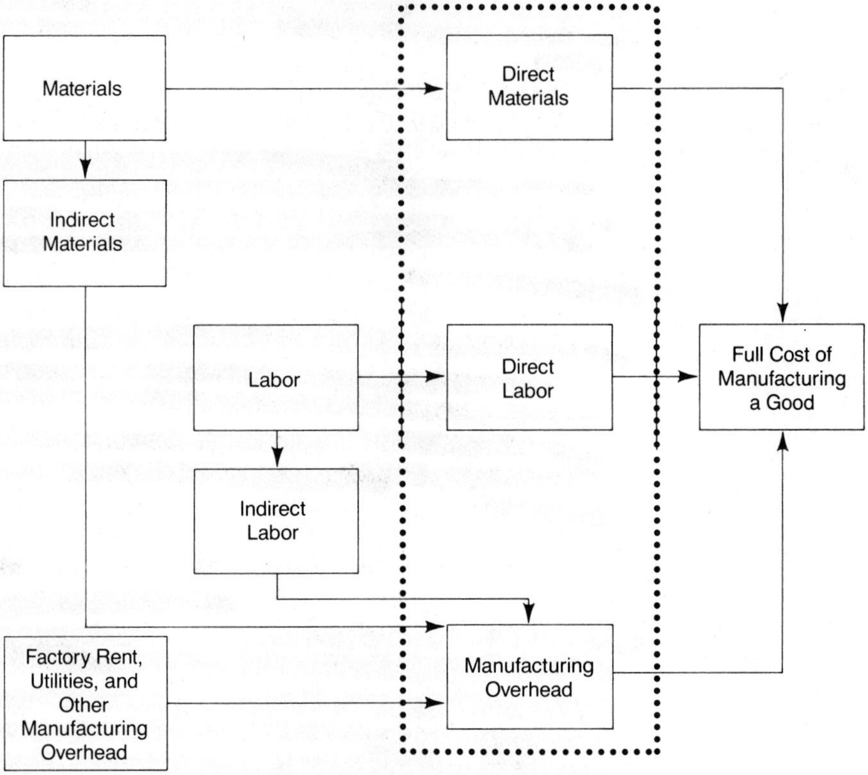

Prime Costs = Direct Materials + Direct Labor
Conversion Costs = Direct Labor + Manufacturing Overhead

marketing costs.) *Administrative costs* are those required to manage the organization, including executive and clerical salaries, and to provide staff support, such as legal, data processing, and accounting.

Period and Product Costs

Costs that can be more easily attributed to time intervals are known as *period costs*, whereas those more easily attributed to products are called *product costs*. An example of a period cost is the annual lease on an office building, or the salary of an organization's top executive. An example of a product cost is the cost of materials used to make a good, or the cost of merchandise purchased for resale.

Generally accepted accounting principles and income tax regulations require that manufacturing companies treat all *manufacturing costs* as product costs, to be held in inventory as an asset until the accounting period in which the product is sold.[3]

---

[3]These principles and regulations are not precise in stating which costs are manufacturing costs and which costs are nonmanufacturing costs.

Then they are expensed for financial accounting and tax purposes. All nonmanufacturing costs are treated as period expenses. In merchandising companies, only merchandise purchased for resale is treated as a product cost for financial accounting and tax purposes. There are no product costs for financial accounting or tax purposes in service organizations, because there is no tangible inventory. In short, product costs are inventoried for financial accounting and tax purposes.

Many managerial accountants argue that fixed manufacturing costs are really period costs and should be treated as such for managerial accounting purposes, regardless of when the product is sold. For example, they argue that the rent on a factory is better thought of as a period cost for managerial purposes because it does not vary with production activity. This difference between financial and managerial accounting appears in several places in this book, particularly when we reconcile the use of accounting for managerial purposes with its use for financial reporting.

Cost Concepts for Managerial Decision Making

In this section, we discuss concepts important for managerial decision making.

Cost Behavior: Fixed and Variable Costs

Perhaps the most useful classification of costs for managerial decision making is by cost behavior. That is, do total costs vary with activity (for example, production volume)? If so, they are *variable* costs. If not, they are *fixed*.

Example Umbrella Makers has received a special order for 10,000 umbrellas. The company must decide whether to accept or reject the order. Past experience enables management to predict that each umbrella made to fill the special order will require $1.00 of direct materials, $2.00 of direct labor, and $1.00 of variable manufacturing overhead. (Variable manufacturing overhead includes indirect materials, power to run machines, and indirect labor required to handle materials.) These are the only variable costs in manufacturing each umbrella. In addition, each umbrella requires $.50 variable marketing cost. Hence, the total variable cost per unit to make and sell each umbrella is $4.50. Knowing which costs are variable permits Umbrella Makers to estimate the amount of costs to be incurred if the special order is accepted, which is 10,000 units times $4.50 per unit or $45,000.

Umbrella Makers rents its factory facilities for $4,000 per month. The rental fee is the same regardless of the level of activity—it is a *fixed cost*. Knowing that the rent behaves in a fixed cost pattern for any level of activity permits Umbrella Makers to exclude rent from the analysis of which costs will be affected if the special order is accepted. Whether or not the special order is accepted, the rent will be $4,000 per month. Other examples of fixed costs at Umbrella Makers are property taxes, utilities to heat and light buildings, and marketing and administrative personnel costs. In total, fixed costs are $37,000 per month, comprised of $12,000 manufacturing and $25,000 marketing and administrative.

The breakdown of these costs for Umbrella Makers into fixed and variable com-

Exhibit 2.2
UMBRELLA MAKERS
Fixed and Variable Costs

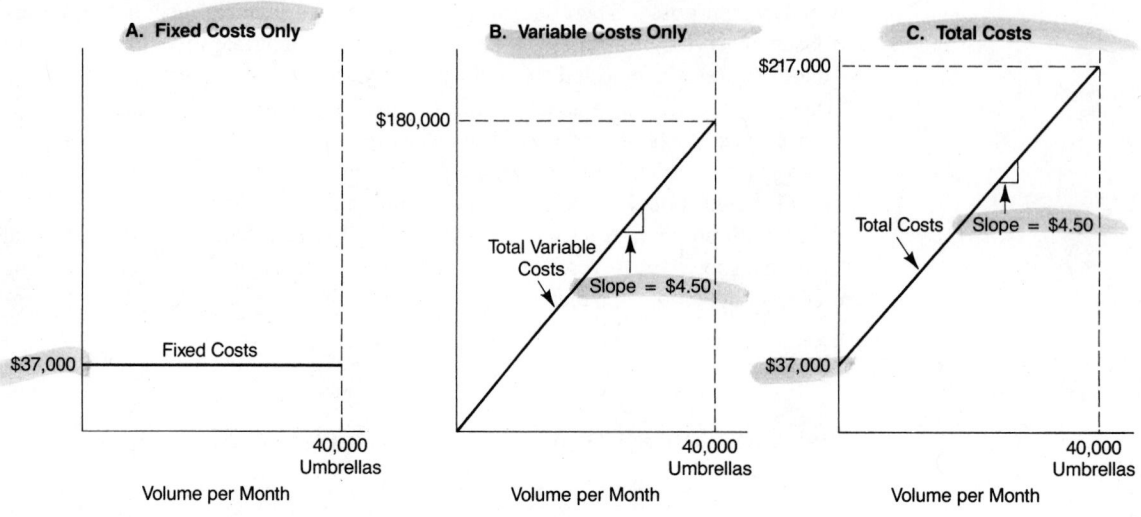

ponents appears in Exhibit 2.2. For a volume up to 40,000 umbrellas per month, fixed costs are assumed to remain constant. Total variable costs are assumed to increase at the constant rate of $4.50 per umbrella made and sold, which is the slope of the total variable cost line. Note that the slope of the total cost line is $4.50—the variable cost per unit—whereas the intercept of the total cost line (that is, where it intersects the vertical axis) is $37,000—the fixed cost per month.

It is important to note that fixed costs will not necessarily remain at the same level, even if there is no inflation. For example, suppose that Umbrella Makers can produce a maximum of 40,000 umbrellas per month with their present facilities. Assume that if management wants to increase production and sales volume beyond 40,000 units per month, additional facilities will have to be acquired, additional utilities costs will be incurred, and more administrative and marketing personnel will have to be hired. Assume that if additional facilities are added to expand capacity by 35,000 umbrellas per month, then $43,000 per month would be added to Umbrella Makers' fixed costs. Thus, for an additional capacity of 35,000 umbrellas, fixed costs would increase from $37,000 per month to $80,000 per month. Exhibit 2.3 illustrates this cost behavior. (This could be a long-term commitment.)

In a sense, the marginal cost of the 40,001st umbrella is $43,004.50 (that is, $43,000 additional fixed cost for the additional capacity plus $4.50 variable cost for the umbrella). Of course, such a cost would not be charged to that particular umbrella. Instead, the $43,000 is considered to be a *capacity cost*, that is, a cost of providing the additional capacity to produce and sell up to 75,000 umbrellas. If capacity is less than 40,000 umbrellas per month, fixed costs are $37,000 per month. If capacity is increased to a maximum of 75,000 umbrellas per month, fixed costs are $80,000 per month.

Exhibit 2.3
UMBRELLA MAKERS
Fixed and Variable Costs
Additional Capacity

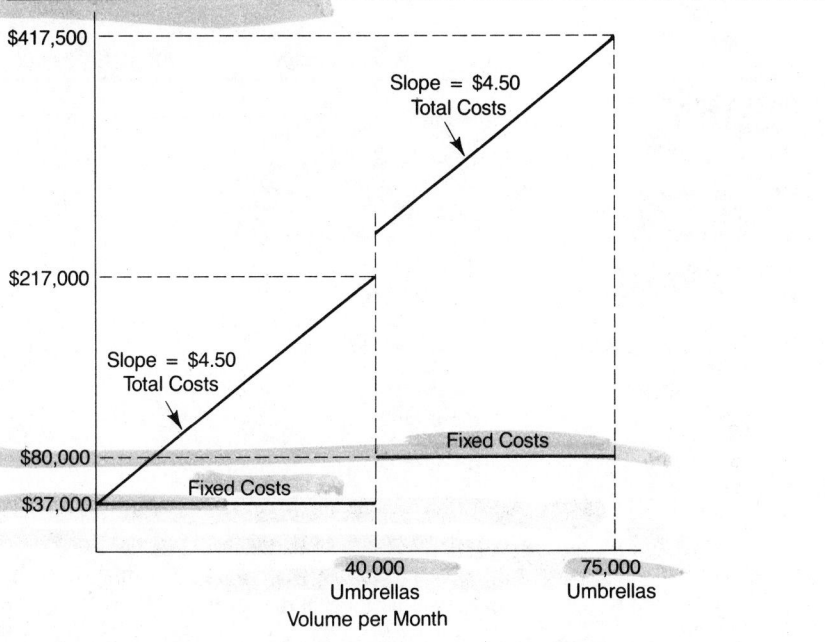

Long-Run Nature of Fixed Costs Decisions to increase or reduce capacity are usually long-term decisions. The decision to increase capacity is usually made under the assumption that the additional capacity will be needed for a long time, say, several years. The length of the commitment to a particular level of capacity varies. For an airplane manufacturer, the commitment could be decades. For a consulting firm, the commitment could be as short as the shortest lease obtainable for office space.

In short, fixed costs are not fixed forever; they can be changed when capacity is changed. In fact, we define fixed costs as those that remain the same for a given level of capacity. This definition is consistent with that of economists, who say that fixed costs do not vary in the short run, and that the short run is the period over which capacity remains unchanged. For practical purposes, the short run is usually defined to be about 1 year.

Comparison of Direct Costs with Variable Costs The terms "direct" and "variable" are often used interchangeably in the business world, because many costs that can be directly traced to a unit are variable. Direct materials and direct labor are often variable costs, for example. Variable manufacturing overhead costs, however, are *variable but not direct* if the implied cost object is a unit produced. A comparison of variable/fixed and direct/indirect costs for Umbrella Makers' manufacturing costs appears in Exhibit 2.4. (This example assumes that the company has not added additional capacity.)

Exhibit 2.4
UMBRELLA MAKERS
Comparison of Direct Costs with Variable Costs

	Amount	Direct Versus Indirect Cost		Assumed Cost Behavior	
		Direct[a]	Indirect	Variable	Fixed
Manufacturing Costs:					
Direct Materials	$1.00 per unit	X		X	
Direct Labor	$2.00 per unit	X		X	
Variable Manufacturing Overhead (e.g., indirect materials, power to operate machines)	**$1.00 per unit**		**X**	**X**	
Fixed Manufacturing Overhead (e.g., factory rent, property taxes) . . .	$12,000 per month		X		X

[a]By "direct" we mean traceable directly to the production of a unit, in this case.

Differential Costs

In making decisions, managers often want to know which costs would be affected if a contemplated action were taken. These costs are *differential costs*, that is, the costs that *differ* because of an action. You may have heard of incremental costs. Differential costs include both incremental costs (cost increases) and decremental costs (cost decreases).

If the contemplated action is an increase or decrease in volume with no change in capacity, differential costs will be variable costs. In the Umbrella Makers example, recall that management was considering filling a special order of 10,000 umbrellas. Only variable costs were assumed to be affected; to be specific, an increase in costs of $45,000 (that is, 10,000 umbrellas times $4.50 per unit variable cost) was expected. These are the differential costs of the special order.

Differential costs are not limited to variable costs, however. If an action affects fixed costs, then those costs are differential. Virtually any long-run action involving changes in capacity affects fixed costs. Consider the case in which Umbrella Makers increased capacity. The additional fixed costs (of $43,000) would be differential costs of the additional capacity.

The differential concept is important in using accounting information for managerial decision making. A question uppermost in the minds of decision makers is "How are costs affected by the actions we are contemplating?" An understanding of how to use accounting data to estimate these differential costs is such an important part of decision making that we devote a good share of Chapters 6–9 to it.

When we refer to differential cost analysis, we implicitly refer to all costs and revenues affected by decisions. As a practical matter, we hold constant other variables that decision makers may also consider important (for example, the impact of an action on employee morale or public relations). This is because managerial accountants have a comparative advantage in estimating differential costs, but not the other variables. Differential revenues are usually included in our analysis for completeness, but they are most often taken from estimates by marketing personnel.

Sunk Costs

Sunk costs result from past expenditures. Sunk costs are not affected by a decision, because sunk costs were incurred in the past, whereas decisions made now affect the future. This is a difficult concept for many decision makers to understand. Some managers, in an effort to overcome the results of unwise decisions in the past, will attempt to ''recover their investment'' and include sunk costs in their analyses. Such behavior often leads to incorrect decisions, as demonstrated by the following example.

Example The buyer for a sporting goods store purchased 200 pairs, at $20 per pair, of a new type of sandal, called jog-sandals (sandals that could be used for jogging). ''These are the coming thing!'' claimed the buyer. Unfortunately, in a year, the store sold only 2 pairs at the retail price of $40 per pair, and 3 pairs more at a reduced price of $25 per pair.

When the store manager suggested selling all the jog-sandals at $10 per pair at a local running club, ''just to get rid of the things,'' the store's merchandise buyer questioned: ''How can we make a profit when we buy at $20 and sell at $10?'' The store manager believed the buyer's argument and held the price at $25 per pair. After another year without a single sale, the manager threw away the shoes, stating, ''It's unfortunate that these jog-sandals didn't sell better, but at least we didn't sell them at a loss.'' Thus, the manager missed an opportunity to recover $1,950 (= 195 pairs at $10 each).

The relevant factors in the preceding example include the range of prices and the volume of jog-sandals that could be sold at those prices, inventory carrying costs, and so forth. But the original cost of the jog-sandals was a sunk cost, and should not have been considered in deciding how and whether to dispose of the goods.

In general, past expenditures are sunk costs (unless you can get your money back if the product is returned), and irrelevant for decisions. (This ignores income tax considerations.) Common examples of sunk costs include the past cost of inventory, whether bought or produced, the past cost of long-term assets (including residential homes), nonrefundable tuition paid for college, and the cost of a large dinner. (Moral: Don't feel obligated to eat all of your dinner just because it has been purchased.)

The fact that past expenditures are sunk costs does not mean that information about past amounts spent is totally irrelevant. Information about the past can be used to help predict differential costs of future actions. Further, past expenditures are used in performance evaluation.

Cost Concepts for Planning and Performance Evaluation

Many of the concepts already discussed are important for planning and performance evaluation. For example, knowing which costs are expected to change with changes in activity levels (variable costs) is important for planning. One concept that has not been discussed, *controllability*, is particularly important for performance evaluation.

Controllable and Noncontrollable Costs

The notion of *controllability* is important when accounting data are used for performance evaluation. If employees are risk-averse, they will prefer to have the rewards for their work based on factors they can control, all other things being equal. For example, the St. Louis plant manager would be held responsible for costs in the St. Louis plant, but not for costs in other plants.

Further, knowing which costs are controllable allows managers to set priorities in performing one of their most important missions—cost control. Knowing that, in the short run, factory rent is a *noncontrollable* cost,[4] whereas direct labor hours worked are *controllable*, enables managers to focus their attention on costs which can be more easily managed.

It is important to recognize the relative nature of controllable and noncontrollable. First, costs that are not controllable in the short run are likely to become controllable in the long run at some level in the organization. For example, a district manager of a merchandise company with outlets in shopping centers was taken to task because the costs of store leases in the territory were never reevaluated. "But these rental costs were labeled noncontrollable in the accounting reports," was the response of the district manager. Because of its failure to act on these "noncontrollable" costs, the company lost opportunities for better locations at cheaper prices within the shopping centers.

Second, as one moves up the organization to higher levels of management, more and more costs become controllable (see Exhibit 2.5). A cost is considered to be controllable at some level in the organization if the management at that level has the power to authorize the cost. If the advertising budget can be authorized by top management, but not by district sales managers, advertising costs are controllable by top management, but not by the district sales managers.

The controllable cost concept is applied in a variety of ways. In some companies, the fuel price increases of the 1970s were considered outside the control of *anyone* in the company. In other companies, however, the argument was made that top management had the authority to change (or close) operations and thus affect fuel usage, so even this cost was controllable by them. In short, the classification of costs as controllable or noncontrollable is sometimes a discretionary matter that must be decided by management.

---

[4]The term "noncontrollable" does not mean that costs are out of control. Instead it means that once a commitment has been made (for example, signing a lease), the level of spending cannot be changed.

Exhibit 2.5
Relation of Cost Control to Organization Level

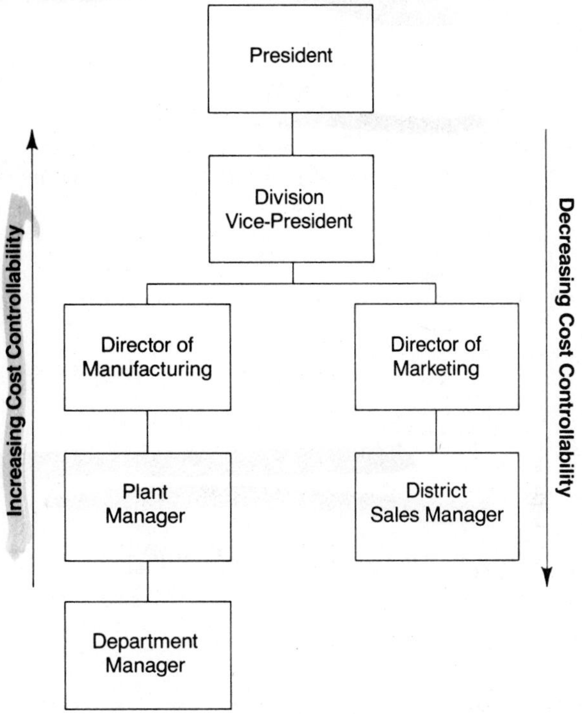

Costs Reported on Income Statements

This section compares the way costs would be presented on three types of income statements: (1) external financial reports, (2) managerial decision making, and (3) managerial performance evaluation.

Assume the following facts for Umbrella Makers for the month of February:

Units Produced and Sold in February	16,000 Units
Sales Price per Unit	$8.00 per Unit
Variable Manufacturing Cost per Unit:	
Direct Materials	$1.00 per Unit
Direct Labor	$2.00 per Unit
Variable Manufacturing Overhead	$1.00 per Unit
Fixed Manufacturing Costs:	
Fixed Manufacturing Overhead:	
Rent	$4,000 per Month
Other Manufacturing Overhead	$8,000 per Month
Marketing and Administrative:	
Fixed Costs	$25,000 per Month
Variable Costs	$.50 per Unit

Exhibit 2.6
UMBRELLA MAKERS
Income Statement for External Financial Reporting
For the Month Ending February 28

Sales Revenue.	$128,000[a]
Less Cost of Goods Sold	(76,000)[b]
Gross Margin	$ 52,000
Less Marketing and Administrative Expenses	(33,000)[c]
Net Income Before Taxes	$ 19,000

[a]$128,000 = 16,000 units sold × $8 selling price per unit.
[b]$76,000 = ($4.00 variable cost per unit + $.75 per unit share of fixed manufacturing costs) × 16,000 units.
[c]$33,000 = $25,000 fixed cost + ($.50 × 16,000 units sold).

Income Statement for External Reporting

The income statement for external reporting is shown in Exhibit 2.6. To comply with generally accepted accounting principles, fixed manufacturing overhead is allocated to each unit produced:

$$\text{Fixed Cost per Unit} = \frac{\text{Fixed Manufacturing Costs}}{\text{Units Produced}}$$

$$= \frac{\$12,000}{16,000 \text{ Units}}$$

$$= \$.75 \text{ per Unit.}$$

Adding this $.75 per unit to the $4.00 variable manufacturing cost per unit makes the "full cost" of manufacturing a unit $4.75. Hence, *cost of goods sold* is $76,000 (= $4.75 × 16,000 units).

Income statements for external reporting use a method of product costing known as *full absorption costing* (sometimes called "absorption costing"). Under full absorption costing, each unit of a good produced is assigned the unit's variable manufacturing cost plus a share of fixed manufacturing costs for inventory valuation. Full absorption costing is generally required for inventory valuation in external financial reports under generally accepted accounting principles and for income tax purposes.

Income Statement for Managerial Decision Making

The income statement for external reporting does not show actual manufacturing cost behavior because it "unitizes" fixed manufacturing costs to assign a share of these costs to each unit produced. The income statement in Exhibit 2.7 is prepared for managerial use—it presents cost behavior.

Note the difference between the *gross margin* in Exhibit 2.6 and the *contribution margin* in Exhibit 2.7. The gross margin is the difference between revenue and cost of goods sold, whereas the contribution margin is the difference between revenue and variable costs, including variable marketing and administrative costs.

Exhibit 2.7
Income Statement for Managerial Decision Making

Sales Revenue.		$128,000
Less Variable Costs:		
Variable Cost of Goods Sold	$(64,000)[a]	
Variable Marketing and Administrative Costs	(8,000)[b]	
Total Variable Costs		(72,000)
Contribution Margin		$ 56,000
Less Fixed Costs:		
Fixed Manufacturing Costs.	$(12,000)	
Fixed Marketing and Administrative Costs	(25,000)	
Total Fixed Costs		(37,000)
Operating Profit		$ 19,000

[a]$64,000 = 16,000 units $\times$ $4.00 variable manufacturing cost per unit.
[b]$8,000 = 16,000 units $\times$ $.50 variable marketing and administrative costs per unit.

The contribution margin is so called because it shows the contribution of units sold toward covering fixed costs and providing a profit. The *unit contribution margin,* which is the difference between selling price and variable cost per unit, is used in many managerial decision models. (For example, it is used in linear programming models to determine optimal product mix.) The contribution margin is such an important concept that it appears throughout this book in many contexts.

We use the term *operating profit* at the bottom of income statements prepared for managerial use to distinguish it from net income used in external reporting.

Income statements like that shown in Exhibit 2.7 use a method of product costing known as *variable costing* (also called "direct costing"). Under variable costing, each unit of a good produced is assigned the unit's variable manufacturing cost for inventory valuation. Fixed manufacturing costs are treated as period costs; they are not assigned to units for inventory valuation. (Nonmanufacturing costs are not assigned to units for inventory valuation under either variable or full absorption costing.) Variable costing is often used for internal reporting because it reflects cost behavior better than does full absorption costing.

Income Statement for Performance Evaluation

Income statements prepared for performance evaluation by managers inside the organization usually have two characteristics that distinguish them from the previous income statements. First, they partition costs (and perhaps revenues) into amounts that are controllable by the managers being evaluated and those that are noncontrollable. Second, they assign costs and revenues to responsibility centers. A *responsibility center* is any part of the organization for which a manager has responsibility. Department managers, for example, have responsibility for the revenues and costs in their departments.

Assume the following facts for the Wizard Bank, which has two branches: Anacortes and Bellingham. Each branch had the following costs and revenues for August:

	Anacortes Branch	Bellingham Branch
Revenues	$100,000	$150,000
Variable Costs (mostly interest costs). . . .	70,000	115,000

In addition, the bank had $60,000 in fixed costs, of which $20,000 was controllable by the Anacortes branch and $30,000 was controllable by the Bellingham branch.

Exhibit 2.8 presents an income statement showing costs and revenues controllable by branches. For performance evaluation, the actual amounts shown for each branch would be compared with predetermined budgeted controllable costs and revenues.

Exhibit 2.8
Income Statement for Performance Evaluation

	Controllable by Branches		Noncontrollable by Branches	Total for Bank
	Anacortes Branch	Bellingham Branch		
Revenues	$100,000	$150,000		$250,000
Variable Costs	70,000	115,000		185,000
Contribution Margin	$ 30,000	$ 35,000		$ 65,000
Fixed Costs Assigned to Branches.	20,000	30,000		50,000
Other Fixed Costs			$ 10,000	10,000
Operating Profit	$ 10,000	$ 5,000	$(10,000)	$ 5,000

Summary

Knowledge of cost concepts is important for external reporting, managerial decision making, and planning and performance evaluation. In concept, a cost is a sacrifice of resources. An opportunity cost is the best alternative use of resources foregone because of some action.

Distinguishing between costs and expenses is important. Whereas costs are a sacrifice of resources, expenses are costs that are used up (and matched against revenue) in a particular accounting period for external reporting.

Manufacturing costs are made up of direct materials, direct labor, and manufacturing overhead. Direct materials and direct labor (which are sometimes called "prime costs") can be attributed directly to each unit produced, whereas manufacturing overhead cannot. Nonmanufacturing costs are usually classified as either administrative or marketing.

A number of cost classifications have been found to be useful in practice. The most common are product versus period; direct versus indirect; controllable versus noncontrollable; and fixed versus variable. Manufacturing costs that can be inventoried are product costs, whereas those that cannot are classified as period expenses for external reporting purposes.

Direct costs are those that can be attributed directly to a particular cost object; indirect costs cannot. This classification is meaningful only within some context; that is, the cost object must be specified before it is meaningful to refer to a cost as being related directly to the cost object. The same holds for costs that can be classified as controllable and noncontrollable. Virtually all costs are controllable by top management, but at lower levels of the organization, managers do not have the authority to control as many costs. The time interval is also important for classifying costs as controllable or noncontrollable, because costs become more controllable for longer time intervals.

An important classification for decision making is by cost behavior: Variable costs are affected by activity levels, whereas fixed costs are not. This classification is meaningful only over some specified range of activity levels. Other important cost concepts for decision making are differential costs and sunk costs. Differential costs are those that differ because of an action. Sunk costs are past expenditures irrelevant for future decisions.

We have introduced many concepts and terms in this chapter that will be used throughout the book. To ensure that you understand them, refer to this chapter from time to time as you proceed through the book.

Problem 1 for Self-Study

A product manager uses the following "cost and price" cube to help relate prices to costs and contribution margins.

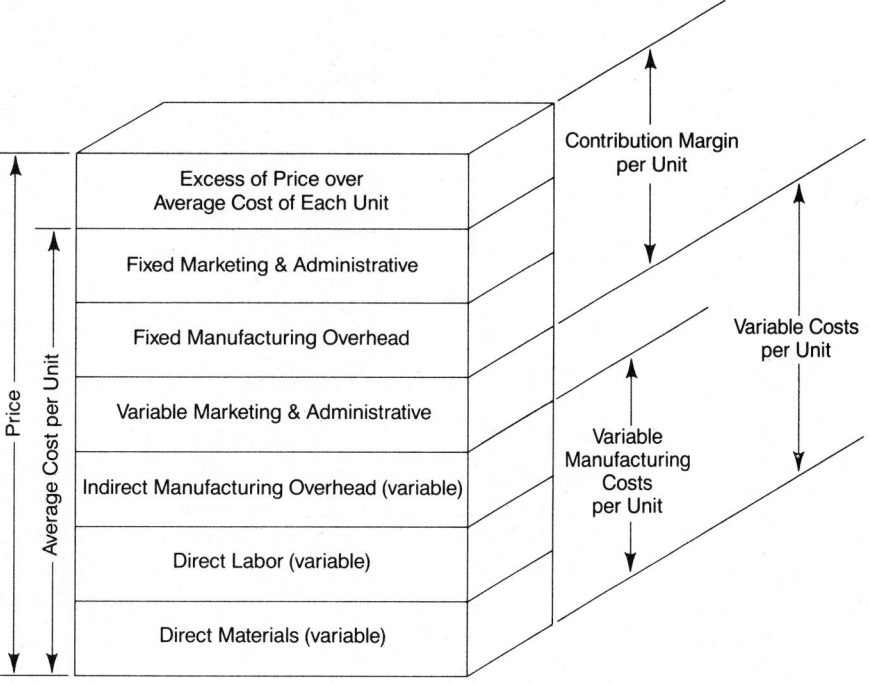

The manager has asked you to complete the cube, given the following data:

Price per Unit	$ 100
Contribution Margin per Unit	18
Gross Margin for 1,000 Units	21,000
Variable Manufacturing Costs per Unit	70
Direct Materials per Unit	40
Direct Labor per Unit	20
Fixed Marketing and Administrative Cost per Unit	6

You are also asked to indicate the inventory value of each unit under variable costing and full absorption costing.

Suggested Solution

Inventory Values:

Variable Costing . . . . $70 per Unit Variable Manufacturing Cost

Full Absorption Costing = $100 $- \dfrac{\$21,000}{1,000 \text{ Units}}$ . . . . $79 per Unit

Direct Materials . . . . $40 per Unit

Direct Labor . . . . $20 per Unit

Variable Manufacturing Overhead = $70 − ($40 + $20) = ... $10 per Unit

Variable Costs per Unit = Price − Unit Contribution Margin
= $100 − $18 = ... $82 per Unit

Variable Marketing and Administrative = $82 − $40 − $20 − $10 = . . $12 per Unit

Fixed Manufacturing Costs per Unit = Manufacturing Costs
per Unit − Variable Manufacturing Costs per Unit
= (Price − Gross Margin per Unit) − Variable Manufacturing

Costs per Unit = $\left(\$100 - \dfrac{\$21,000}{1,000 \text{ Units}} \right)$ − $70 = ... $9 per Unit

Fixed Marketing and Administrative Cost per Unit = ... $6 per Unit

Excess of Price over Average Cost of Each Unit
= $100 − ($40 + $20 + $10 + $12 + $9 + $6) = ... $3 per Unit

Problem 2 for Self-Study

Klogs, Inc.

After the death of his uncle Sven early this year, Peter Sorensen left his $40,000 a year job at an electronics company to assume control of Klogs, Inc., a manufacturer of quality clogs. His $28,000 salary at Klogs was substantially less than what he had earned in his previous job as a sales manager, but a sense of family duty persuaded him to head the ailing company. Besides, this was a chance for him to test his managerial skills.

Klogs, Inc., a Sorensen family concern for three generations, had been under the conservative leadership of Sven Sorensen for almost half a century. While maintaining a reputation for high-quality craftmanship, Klogs was never particularly innovative in the styles they put out. In fact, in the last 5 years, Klogs experienced a steady decline in sales due to a shrinking consumer demand for Klogs' clogs.

Reduced to only one product line, Klogs produced 70,000 pairs of clogs last year. At capacity, Klogs could put out 100,000 pairs of clogs. Klogs also has an old inventory of 3,000 pairs of clogs from a discontinued line. The inventory was still valued at $30,000—the inventory cost from 3 years ago.

On Peter Sorensen's first visit to the Klogs factory, Hansen, the young manager, gave him a tour of the place. Peter made extensive notes on the tour and obtained the following breakdown of last year's costs.

Item		
(a)	Sandpaper	$ 200
(b)	Nails	500
(c)	Leather	140,000
(d)	Factory Rent—10 Years Remaining on Lease	12,000
(e)	Labor—Cutting	210,000
(f)	Supervisor's Salary	15,000
(g)	Maintenance—Equipment	1,000
(h)	Utilities—Factory (fixed)	6,000
(i)	Varnish	7,700
(j)	Sven's Salary	28,000
(k)	Labor—Assembling	175,000
(l)	Sales Commission to Dealers ($.15 per Unit)	9,750
(m)	Shipping Costs ($.10 per Unit)	6,500
(n)	Administrative Manager's Salary	20,000
(o)	Office Supplies	100
(p)	Secretary's Salary	10,000
(q)	Depreciation—Equipment	1,000
(r)	Wood	70,000
(s)	Advertising	1,000

Klogs sold 65,000 pairs of clogs last year.

In his conversation with Hansen, Peter discovered that Klogs had conducted very favorable marketing tests on a new clog. But plans for the introduction of this new product line in the fall of last year were shelved because Sven had insisted that the old inventory be disposed of at no less than its book value before any new ventures be taken. Hansen felt that this new product line could be introduced this fall, and predicted that Klogs could expect to sell 40,000 pairs of this new product line. Peter recognized the sales potential in this new clog, which was radically different from the traditional Klogs' clog. It was trendy but did not sacrifice the quality and comfort of a Klogs clog. Hansen had done his homework and supplied Peter with the following facts and figures:

Cost of Producing 40,000 New Klogs

Leather	$100,000
Wood.	48,000
Nails, Varnish, and Sandpaper	1,000
Labor—Cutting	140,000
Labor—Assembling	120,000
Shipping Costs	4,000
Sales Commission to Dealers	6,000

Assuming that Klogs continues to produce 70,000 pairs of traditional Klogs, the Klogs factory will have to operate on Saturdays to meet the additional capacity requirements. The additional costs of operating on Saturday would be:

Supervisor's Overtime Salary	$4,000
Utilities	1,200

So far, Klogs has spent $3,000 in the development of New-Klogs, and $2,000 in a survey of retail outlets.

Armed with these figures, Peter realized that he needed to analyze current operations and come up with a strategy to reverse the Sorensen fortunes.

a. Ignoring any noneconomic value of self-employment, what is Peter Sorensen's opportunity cost of working for Klogs?

b. Identify the following costs using last year's figures.
  (1) Unit direct materials cost.
  (2) Unit direct labor costs.
  (3) Unit variable manufacturing overhead, comprised of indirect materials.
  (4) Fixed manufacturing overhead.
  (5) Unit variable marketing costs.
  (6) Fixed marketing costs.
  (7) Administrative costs.

c. What was the average unit value of last year's inventory under full absorption costing?

d. Identify the costs that Peter would consider uncontrollable.

e. How should the cost of the unsalable old inventory be treated in any Klogs decision? In analyzing the New-Klogs project, identify the costs that require similar treatment.

f. If Klogs wishes to produce an additional 40,000 new clogs, list the differential costs.

g. In Peter's list of last year's costs, what costs are treated as product costs and what costs are period costs for full absorption costing?

h. With two product lines, some costs will be common to both lines. Identify them.

Suggested Solution

a. Opportunity cost = $40,000.

b. (1) Items **(c)** and **(r)**:

$$\frac{\$140,000 + \$70,000}{70,000 \text{ Units}} = \$3.00.$$

(2) Items **(e)** and **(k)**:

$$\frac{\$210,000 + \$175,000}{70,000 \text{ Units}} = \$5.50.$$

(3) Items **(a)**, **(b)**, and **(i)**:

$$\frac{\$200 + \$500 + \$7,700}{70,000 \text{ Units}} = \$.12.$$

(4) Items **(d)**, **(f)**, **(g)**, **(h)**, and **(q)**:

$$\$12,000 + \$15,000 + \$1,000 + \$6,000 + \$1,000 = \$35,000.$$

(5) Items **(l)** and **(m)**:

$$\frac{\$9,750 + \$6,500}{65,000 \text{ Units}} = \$.25.$$

(6) Item **(s)**: $1,000.

(7) Items **(j)**, **(n)**, **(o)**, and **(p)**: $28,000 + $20,000 + $100 + $10,000 = $58,100.

c. $3.00 + $5.50 + $0.12 + $\dfrac{\$35,000}{70,000 \text{ Units}}$ = $9.12.

d. Factory rent would be considered uncontrollable in the next few years. In addition, some depreciation and utilities may not be controllable.

e. The unsalable old inventory should be treated as a sunk cost. Other sunk costs (*re* New-Klogs project) would be the development costs (= $3,000) and marketing survey costs (= $2,000).

f. Differential costs:

Direct Materials ($100,000 + $48,000)	$148,000
Direct Labor ($140,000 + $120,000).	260,000
Variable Manufacturing Overhead	1,000
Variable Marketing ($4,000 + $6,000)	10,000
Supervisor's Overtime	4,000
Utilities	1,200
Total	$424,200

g. All manufacturing costs are treated as product costs, whereas all nonmanufacturing costs are treated as period costs.

h. Common costs would include fixed manufacturing overhead, fixed marketing, and administrative costs.

Questions

1. Review the meaning of the following concepts or terms discussed in this chapter.

a. Opportunity cost.	**k.** Common costs.
b. Manufacturing costs.	**l.** Controllable versus
c. Prime costs.	noncontrollable costs.
d. Conversion costs.	**m.** Contribution margin.
e. Nonmanufacturing costs.	**n.** Gross margin.
f. Period versus product costs.	**o.** Full absorption costing.
g. Fixed versus variable costs.	**p.** Variable costing.
h. Differential costs.	**q.** Direct costing.
i. Sunk costs.	**r.** Responsibility centers.
j. Direct versus indirect costs.	

2. "The cost of my trip to Hawaii was $3,000." Using the concept of cost developed in this chapter, explain why this statement is ambiguous.

3. Zappa, a mechanic, left his $25,000 a year job at Joe's Garage to start his own body shop. Zappa drew an annual salary of $15,000. Identify his *opportunity costs*.

4. Expenses and costs are often used interchangeably, yet they do not always mean the same thing. Distinguish between the two terms.

5. Identify and describe the three elements that make up *manufacturing costs*.

6. Compare and contrast prime costs and conversion costs.

7. Nonmanufacturing costs are usually classified as either marketing costs or administrative costs. What are the differences between these two types of costs?

8. "Since fixed manufacturing overhead costs such as factory rent or property taxes are independent of the number of units produced, they should be treated as period costs rather than product costs." Comment.

9. In financial accounting, manufacturing costs are always treated as product costs, and nonmanufacturing costs as period costs. Is this a hard-and-fast rule in accounting in general? Explain.

10. Can costs that are normally considered fixed be variable? Conversely, can normally variable costs be fixed?

11. "All differential costs are variable costs." Comment.

12. Mark Burchinshaw, a member of the Shaughnessy Heights Country Club, paid $400 for unlimited tennis court time for the entire summer, because he anticipated spending many hours improving his game. In early June, Mark slipped on a wet floor at work, severely wrenching his ankle. Mark's ankle was put in a cast for 8 weeks, and despite some insurance coverage his medical bills totaled $300. With 3 weeks left on his summer tennis deal, Mark was back on the courts the moment his cast came off, despite his doctor's advice to avoid strenuous exercise for a month. "This summer's tennis court time cost me $400," Mark said. "I have to get my money's worth." Given your understanding of cost concepts, comment.

13. "An excellent feasibility study of our new product, Hughes. But why have you not included the cost of the test marketing we carried out last month in the analysis?" How should Hughes reply?

14. What do managerial accountants mean when they speak of cost behavior? Why is it important in managerial decision making?

15. What is a cost object? How are the concepts of direct and indirect costs related to it? Can direct costs be indirect, or vice versa?

16. Why is the idea of "controllability" important when accounting data are used for performance evaluation and decision making?

17. "Fixed costs are really variable. The more you produce, the smaller the unit cost of production." Is that statement correct? Why or why not?

18. *(CPA adapted).* You are to match each of the numbered "items" that follow with one of the "terms" listed below that *most specifically* identifies the cost concept indicated parenthetically. The same term may be used more than once.

Terms
- **a.** Common cost.
- **b.** Controllable cost.
- **c.** Direct cost.
- **d.** Estimated cost.
- **e.** Fixed cost.
- **f.** Historical cost.
- **g.** Differential cost.
- **h.** Indirect cost.
- **i.** Opportunity cost.
- **j.** Original cost.
- **k.** Prime cost.
- **l.** Replacement cost.
- **m.** Sunk cost.
- **n.** Full absorption costing.
- **o.** Variable costing.

Items

1. The management of a corporation is considering replacing a machine that is operating satisfactorily with a more efficient new model. Depreciation on the cost of the existing machine is omitted from the data used in judging the proposal, because it has little or no significance with respect to such a decision. (*The omitted cost.*)

2. One of the problems encountered by a bank in attempting to establish the cost of a commercial deposit account is the fact that many facilities and services are shared by many revenue-producing activities. (*Costs of the shared facilities and services.*)

3. A company declined an offer received to rent one of its warehouses and elected to use the warehouse for storage of extra raw materials to ensure uninterrupted production. Storage cost has been charged with *the monthly amount of the rental offered.* (*This cost is known as?*)

4. A manufacturing company excludes all "fixed" costs from its valuation of inventories, assigning to inventory only *applicable portions of costs that vary with changes in volume of product.* (*The term accounting employs for this costing procedure.*)

5. The sales department urges an increase in production of a product and, as part of the data presented in support of its proposal, indicates the total additional cost involved for the volume level it proposes. (*The increase in total cost.*)

6. The "direct" production cost of a unit includes those portions of *labor* and *materials* that are obviously traceable directly to the unit. (*The term used to specify the sum of the two named components.*)

19. Assuming that there are no income taxes, how should each of the following costs be used in a decision to replace old equipment?
   a. Book value of old equipment.
   b. Disposal value of old equipment.
   c. Cost of new equipment.

20. Below is a list of costs. Classify each of them as variable or fixed or a combination of the two. For each fixed cost, attempt to judge the time period over which the cost is fixed.

a. Depreciation of an office building.

b. Costs of raw materials used in producing a firm's products.

c. Leasing costs of a delivery truck, which is $250 per month and $.18 per mile.

d. Costs of internal programs for teaching recent business school graduates about the operating procedures and policies of the firm.

e. Local property taxes on land and buildings.

f. Compensation of sales staff on straight commission.

g. Compensation of sales staff on salary plus commission.

h. Fees paid to an independent firm of CPAs for auditing and attesting to financial statements.

21. The pathology laboratory at Presbyterian University Hospital is staffed by a medical doctor (pathologist) and several laboratory technicians. The lab contains equipment of two basic kinds: microscopes and the like for doing individual tests, and sophisticated testing equipment for doing 12 tests simultaneously on batches of specimens from several patients. Below is a list of costs.

(1) In your judgment, are these variable, fixed, or a combination of these?

(2) For each cost with a fixed component—all but strictly variable—attempt to judge the time period over which the cost is fixed.

a. Salary of the pathologist.

b. Hourly wages of the lab technicians.

c. Depreciation of a microscope.

d. Leasing costs of sophisticated testing equipment. The equipment is leased for $2,000 per month plus a charge of $1 per batch of specimens run plus a charge of $.10 per specimen in each batch.

e. Supplies for tests.

f. Fees paid to a local university professor of accounting who has been helping the hospital director to understand the causes of total costs shown for each month.

Exercises

22. *Opportunity Cost Analysis.* Geoff Parkhurst operates a covered parking structure that can accommodate up to 300 cars. Geoff charges $1 per hour for parking, and on average days the structure is 80 percent full. Parking attendants are paid $4.00 an hour to staff the cashier's booth at Parkhurst Parking. Utilities and other fixed costs average $500 per month. Recently, the manager of a nearby hotel approached Geoff concerning the reservation of 50 spots for a lump sum of $300 over an upcoming weekend for a small convention party. Normally, Geoff welcomed such opportunities to make a little extra, but this particular weekend was a football weekend. Because of the structure's proximity to the football stadium, all spots would be taken 2 hours before game time on football Sundays, and the structure would stay full until the end of the game—6 hours later. What is the opportunity cost of accepting the offer?

23. *Manufacturing Cost Concepts.* Bubba Brothers, a toy manufacturer, produces a variety of inflatable plastic toys. One day, the owner (Bubbles, as he is affectionately known to his employees) decided to take a look at the manufacturing costs of Squeaky Duck, a product the company introduced 2 years ago. Squeaky Duck is an inflatable plastic duck with a whistle attached to its beak. In the last 6 months, Bubba Brothers produced 10,000 Squeaky Ducks; the costs incurred were as follows:

Plastic Material	$2,000
Labor—Cutting	1,000
Labor—Assembling.	5,000
Whistle	3,000
Paint (nontoxic)	500
Machine Time[a]	2,000
Fixed Manufacturing Overhead[b]	2,500

[a]Allocated factory machine cost (for example, depreciation and maintenance) based on machine-hours used by product.
[b]Allocated on the basis of machine-hours.

    a.   Calculate **(1)** unit prime costs, and **(2)** total conversion costs.
    b.   Identify probable common costs.

24. *Manufacturing Costs.* Whizz Incorporated produced 3,000 Kiddy Kars in May. The costs incurred by their plant for that month were as follows:

Cutting			Fabrication			Assembly		
Wood	. . . .	$3,000	Labor	. . . .	$6,000	Paint.	. . . .	$ 1,000
Labor	. . . .	4,500	Nails.	. . . .	500	Labor	. . . .	7,500
			Sandpaper	. .	100	Wheels.	. . . .	12,000
						Axles	. . . .	6,000

Plant Supervisor's Salary.	$1,200
Utilities (independent of units)	200
Depreciation—Machinery.	300
Plant Rent	500

For each Kiddy Kar, calculate:
    a.   Direct materials cost.
    b.   Direct labor cost.
    c.   Variable manufacturing overhead.
    d.   Fixed manufacturing overhead.

25. *Nonmanufacturing Costs.* Trailblaster, a sleeping bag manufacturer, sold 10,000 sleeping bags in 1986 and filed the following year-end income statement:

Sales Revenue.	$500,000
Less Cost of Goods Sold	(300,000)
Gross Margin	$200,000
Less:	

Advertising	$(1,000)	
Sales Commissions to Dealers	(5,000)	
Office Rent	(4,800)	
Office Supplies	(200)	
Depreciation—Office Equipment	(100)	
Sales Promotion	(2,000)	(13,100)
Operating Profit		$186,900

    a.   Calculate variable marketing costs.
    b.   Calculate fixed marketing costs.
    c.   Calculate administrative costs.

26. *Product and Period Costs.* Refer to Trailblaster in Exercise **25.** Suppose that the cost of goods sold could be broken down into the following costs:

Direct Materials	$ 50,000
Direct Labor	100,000
Variable Overhead	80,000
Fixed Overhead	70,000

Assuming that production equals sales,
    a.   What would the product costs and period costs be according to generally accepted accounting principles?
    b.   If management wants to make an internal decision that only variable costs be treated as product costs, what would the product costs and period costs be?

27. *Differential Cost Analysis.* The Exten Company is considering a bid on a contract to supply the Defense Department with 500,000 gallons of chemicals. The capacity of the plant is 10,000,000 gallons a year, and Exten is currently producing and selling at the rate of 8,500,000 gallons a year. The fixed manufacturing costs of the plant total $5,400,000 per year regardless of the level of operations. The variable costs of chemicals of this type are approximately $2 per gallon. The sales manager says that a bid of no more than $1,200,000 would probably enable the company to get the contract.
    a.   Calculate the current unit manufacturing cost per gallon of chemical.
    b.   What is the differential cost if Exten bids for the government contract? Should a bid of $1,200,000 be made? Explain.

28. *Differential Costs.* Vito Enterprises, Inc., has a plant capacity that can produce 2,500 units annually. Its predicted operations for the year are as follows:

Sales (2,000 units at $40 each)	$80,000
Manufacturing Costs:	
Variable	$24 per Unit
Fixed	$17,000
Marketing and Administrative Costs:	
Variable	$2.50 per Unit
Fixed	$2,500

Should the company accept a special order for 400 units at a selling price of $32 each? Assume these units are subject to half the usual sales commission rate per unit, and assume no effect on regular sales at regular prices. What is the effect of the decision on the company's operating profit?

Problems and Cases

29. *Alternative Concepts of Cost: George Jackson (CMA adapted).* George Jackson operates a small machine shop. He manufactures one standard product available from many other similar businesses and he also manufactures products to customer order. His accountant prepared the annual income statement shown below.

	Custom Sales	Standard Sales	Total
Sales	$50,000	$25,000	$75,000
Material.	$10,000	$ 8,000	$18,000
Labor	20,000	9,000	29,000
Depreciation	6,300	3,600	9,900
Power	700	400	1,100
Rent	6,000	1,000	7,000
Heat and Light	600	100	700
Other	400	900	1,300
Total Costs	$44,000	$23,000	$67,000
Operating Profit	$ 6,000	$ 2,000	$ 8,000

The depreciation charges are for machines used in the respective product lines. The power charge is apportioned on the estimate of power consumed. The rent is for the building space, which has been leased for 10 years at $7,000 per year. The rent and the heat and light are apportioned to the product lines based on amount of floor space occupied. All other costs are variable expenses identified with the product line causing them.

A valued custom parts customer has asked Mr. Jackson if he would manufacture 5,000 special units for him. Mr. Jackson is working at capacity and would have to give up some other business in order to take this business. He can't renege on custom orders already agreed to, but he could reduce the output of his standard product by about one-half for 1 year and use the free standard product machine time to produce the specially requested custom part. The customer is willing to pay $7.00 for each part. The material cost will be about $2.00 per unit and the labor will be $3.60 per unit. Mr. Jackson will have to spend $2,000 for a special device that will be discarded when the job is done.

    a. Calculate and present the following costs related to the 5,000-unit custom order:

        (1) The differential cash cost of filling the order.
        (2) The opportunity cost of taking the order.
        (3) The sunk costs related to the order.

    b. Should Mr. Jackson take the order? Explain your answer.

30. *Differential Analysis: Justa Corporation (CMA adapted).* The Justa Corporation produces and sells three products. The three products, A, B, and C, are sold in a local market and in a regional market. At the end of the first quarter of the current year, the following income statement has been prepared:

	Total	Local	Regional
Sales	$1,300,000	$1,000,000	$300,000
Cost of Goods Sold	1,010,000	775,000	235,000
Gross Margin	$ 290,000	$ 225,000	$ 65,000
Marketing Costs	$ 105,000	$ 60,000	$ 45,000
Administrative Costs.	52,000	40,000	12,000
Total Marketing and Admin. Costs	$ 157,000	$ 100,000	$ 57,000
Operating Profit	$ 133,000	$ 125,000	$ 8,000

Management has expressed special concern with the regional market because of the extremely poor return on sales. This market was entered a year ago because of excess capacity. It was originally believed that the return on sales would improve with time, but after a year no noticeable improvement can be seen from the results as reported in the above quarterly statement.

In attempting to decide whether to eliminate the regional market, the following information has been gathered:

	Products		
	A	B	C
Sales	$500,000	$400,000	$400,000
Variable Manufacturing Costs as a Percentage of Sales	60%	70%	60%
Variable Marketing Costs as a Percentage of Sales	3%	2%	2%

Sales by Markets		
Product	Local	Regional
A	$400,000	$100,000
B	300,000	100,000
C	300,000	100,000

All administrative costs and fixed manufacturing costs are common to the three products and the two markets and are fixed for the period. Remaining marketing costs are fixed for the period and separable by market. All fixed costs are based on a pro-rated yearly amount.

a. Prepare the quarterly income statement showing contribution margins by markets.

b. Assuming that there are no alternative uses for the Justa Corporation's present capacity, would you recommend dropping the regional market? Why or why not?

c. Prepare the quarterly income statement showing contribution margins by products.

d. It is believed that a new product can be ready for sale next year if the Justa Corporation decides to go ahead with continued research. The new product can be produced by simply converting equipment presently used in producing product C. This conversion will increase fixed costs by $10,000 per quarter. What must be the minimum contribution margin per quarter for the new product to make the changeover financially feasible?

31. *Fixed and Variable Cost Analysis (Adapted from a problem by David Green.)* The sales representatives of the Piney Paper Company have secured two special orders, *either* of which, in addition to regular orders, will keep the plant operating at capacity through the slack season. Hence, the company can accept one order, or the other, or neither. One order is for 20 million printed placemats and the other is for 30 million sheets of engraved office stationery. The proposed prices are $.0070 per mat for the placemats and $.0062 per sheet for the stationery. Cost estimates are as follows:

	Mats (Cost per 100 mats)	Stationery (Cost per 100 sheets)
Direct Materials	$0.3550	$0.2775
Labor costs:		
Variable	0.1100	0.0993
Fixed	0.0300	0.0089
Manufacturing Overhead Costs:		
Variable	0.0430	0.0330
Fixed	0.0370	0.0523
Variable Marketing and Administrative Cost (already incurred to procure order)	0.0900	0.0912
Fixed Marketing and Administrative Cost (already incurred to procure order)	0.0950	0.0878
Total Cost per 100 Items	$0.7600	$0.6500
Selling Price per 100 Items	$0.7000	$0.6200

After reviewing these figures, management decides to reject the orders on the basis that "we cannot make much money if it costs more than we can sell it for."

Is management correct? Based on the above data, prepare a schedule to show which alternative should be accepted, if either.

32. *Estimating Cash Flows for Decision Making—Sensitivity Analysis.* An automobile manufacturer offers its Excalibre model in two versions—one with a gasoline engine and one with a diesel engine. The gasoline version has a list price of $12,500, and the diesel version a list price of $13,900. Assume for the purposes of this problem that the list prices are actually charged in purchase transactions. According to federal EPA mileage tests, the gasoline version gets, on average, 23 miles per gallon of gasoline, which costs $1.50 per gallon. The diesel version gets, on average, 30 miles per gallon of diesel fuel, which costs $1.40 per gallon. Assume that a purchaser had decided to acquire one of these two cars and that other operating costs of the two models of cars are identical. The purchaser expects to drive 12,000 miles a year for 5 years before disposing of the car. The gasoline version is expected to have a resale value 5 years hence of $2,500, and the diesel a resale value of $2,600.

Assume that costs per gallon of gasoline and diesel fuel are expected to remain constant over the 5 years.

    a.   What are the cash flows for each year relevant to the purchaser who wants to decide which of the two models of Excalibre to buy?

    b.   Assume that each of the cars can be purchased for a 10 percent discount from list price. Repeat the instructions in part **a**.

    c.   Assume that fuel costs increase at the rate of 10 percent per year and that the full list price is paid. Repeat part **a**.

33. *Cost Data for Multiple Purposes: Omega Auto Supplies (J. Lim)*. Omega Auto Supplies manufactures an automobile safety seat for children that it sells through several retail chains. Omega's sales are made exclusively within its five-state region in the Midwest. The cost of manufacturing and marketing children's automobile safety seats at the company's normal volume of 15,000 units per month is shown below:

Variable Materials	$300,000	
Variable Labor	150,000	
Variable Overhead	30,000	
Fixed Overhead	180,200	
Total Manufacturing Costs		$660,200
Variable Nonmanufacturing Costs	$ 75,000	
Fixed Nonmanufacturing Costs	105,000	
Total Nonmanufacturing Costs		180,000
Total Costs		$840,200

The following questions refer only to the data given above. Unless otherwise stated, assume that there is no connection between the situations described in the questions; each is to be treated independently. Unless otherwise stated, a regular selling price of $70 per unit should be assumed. Ignore income taxes and other costs that are not mentioned in the data above or in a question itself.

    a.   In any normal month, what would be the inventory value per completed unit according to generally accepted accounting principles?

    b.   On April 1, a special-order contract is offered to Omega Auto Supplies by a nonprofit charitable organization to supply 2,000 units to several orphanages for delivery by April 30. Production for April was initially planned for 15,000 units, and this special order can be easily accommodated without any additional capacity costs. (Thus, a total of 17,000 units would be produced.) The special-order contract will reimburse Omega for all production costs plus a fixed fee of $25,000. (There would be no variable marketing costs incurred on the special order.) Should Omega accept the special order?

    c.   Early in July, the senior management of Omega Auto Supplies met to evaluate the firm on performance for the first half of the year. The following exchange ensued.

    Bob Wilson (President): "Our performance for the first half of this year leaves much to be desired. Despite higher unit sales than forecast, our actual profits are $200,000 lower than what we expected."

Sam Brown (Sales Manager): "I suspect production needs to shape up" (he says smugly). "We in sales have pursued an aggressive marketing strategy and the three-quarters of a million increase in sales revenue is proof enough of our improved performance."

Linda Lampman (Production Manager): "Wait a minute, now! We managed to bring down unit costs from $44.00 to $43.00—with no help from sales, I must add! What's the use of production plans when Sales can change them any time they like? In February, Sam wanted a rush order for 4,000. In March, it was 8,000 units. Then in April he said to hold off on production; then in June he wanted 6,000. You know what I think. . . ."

Bob Wilson (President): "Hold on now! I refuse to let this degenerate into a witch-hunt. We have to examine this problem with more objectivity." (He turns to his assistant, who has been quietly taking notes.) "Do you have any ideas, Smith?"

Suppose that you are in Smith's position: What would you tell the president? You know that planned production and sales for each month of the year is 15,000 units per month. You also know that 108,000 units were produced and sold in the first 6 months of this year, and the income statement was as follows:

Sales Revenue		$7,020,000
Manufacturing Costs:		
Variable Materials	$2,160,000	
Variable Labor.	1,134,000	
Variable Overhead	324,000	
Fixed Overhead	1,026,000	(4,644,000)
Gross Margin		$2,376,000
Marketing Costs:		
Variable Marketing	$ 648,000	
Fixed Marketing	650,000	(1,298,000)
Operating Profit		$1,078,000

Suggested Solutions to Even-Numbered Exercises

22. *Opportunity Cost Analysis.* On normal days,

$$\text{Excess Capacity} = 20\% \times 300 \text{ Spots for Cars}$$

$$= 60 \text{ Spots for Cars.}$$

Therefore, Parkhurst's structure can accept the offer on normal business days at an opportunity cost of zero.

On football Sundays, however, the opportunity cost is

$$50 \text{ Spots for Cars} \times 6 \text{ Hours} \times \$1 = \underline{\$300}$$

24. *Manufacturing Costs*

  a. Direct materials cost:

Wood	$ 3,000
Wheels	12,000
Axles	6,000
	$21,000

Unit direct materials cost = $7.00.

b. Direct labor cost:

Labor—Cutting	$ 4,500
Labor—Fabrication	6,000
Labor—Assembly	7,500
	$18,000

Unit direct labor cost = $6.00.

c. Variable manufacturing overhead:

Nails	$ 500
Sandpaper	100
Paint	1,000
	$ 1,600

Unit variable overhead = $0.53.

d. Fixed manufacturing overhead:

Plant Supervisor's Salary	$ 1,200
Utilities	200
Depreciation	300
Plant Rent	500
	$ 2,200

26. *Product and Period Costs*

    a. Product costs are all manufacturing costs. Therefore,

$$\text{Product Costs} = \$300,000.$$

Period costs are all nonmanufacturing costs. Therefore,

$$\text{Period Costs} = \$13,100.$$

    b. All variable costs are treated as product costs. Therefore,

$$\text{Product Costs} = \$50,000 + \$100,000 + \$80,000 + \$5,000$$

$$= \$235,000.$$

All fixed costs are treated as period costs. Therefore,

$$\text{Fixed Costs} = \$70,000 + \$3,000^{a} + \$5,100^{b}$$

$$= \$78,100.$$

[a]Fixed marketing costs ($1,000 + $2,000).
[b]Administrative costs (fixed) ($4,800 + $200 + $100).

28. *Differential Costs.* Yes.

Special-Order Sales (400 × $32)		$12,800
Less Variable Costs:		
Manufacturing (400 × $24)	$(9,600)	
Sales Commissions (400 × $1.25)	(500)	(10,100)
Addition to Company Profit		$ 2,700

Part Two   Cost Methods and Systems

Each organization has unique features that make its accounting system unique. Users of accounting information need to know differences in accounting systems for two reasons. First, different accounting systems measure costs differently; without knowing the type of system that generated the cost, decision makers do not know whether they have the appropriate cost for their purpose. Second, a knowledge of alternative accounting systems is necessary if decision makers are to have an input into the design of accounting systems.

Chapter 3 presents the six alternative methods of computing the cost of an inventory item for manufacturing companies. Chapter 4 presents a model for describing cost and revenue flows. This model will help you to visualize the flow of costs and revenues in any organization and to see how they are assigned to departments, products, and the people responsible for them. Chapter 5 describes different accounting systems in different types of organizations: service, manufacturing, and merchandising. We also show how cost systems in organizations that focus on jobs, such as construction and consulting, differ from those with a process orientation such as steel, cereals, and most consumer products.

Chapter 3   Product Costing Methods

Chapter 2 emphasizes that there is no single measure of cost correct for all contexts or relevant for all decisions. Different types of costs are relevant for different purposes. For example, if we are making decisions about increasing the volume of activity, we need to know which costs are fixed and which are variable. If we are preparing financial statements for reporting to shareholders, then we need inventory values and cost of goods sold. This theme of "different costs for different purposes" appears throughout this book.

This chapter expands the concepts of costs discussed in Chapter 2 to consider alternative ways of measuring *unit manufacturing costs*. This chapter shows how these different methods of measuring unit manufacturing costs can have a substantial impact on inventory values and computations of operating profit. If users of accounting data understand these differences, then they can be more certain that they are obtaining the data appropriate for their purposes.

Product Costing for Managerial Purposes Versus Product Costing for External Financial Reporting

There are many different ways to measure the costs of producing a good. The value of a unit in inventory includes, under generally accepted accounting principles, unit variable manufacturing costs and a share of fixed manufacturing costs. When the product's cost is used for managerial decision making, it might include only the unit's variable manufacturing costs. When used for performance evaluation, unit costs are often measured using both standard variable costs and actual variable costs. In short, unit costs can be measured in different ways for different purposes.

Users of accounting information should know the alternative ways of measuring unit costs to avoid inappropriately using unit costs for one purpose that were intended for another purpose. Users of accounting can also put their knowledge of alternative product costing methods to good use by providing meaningful input to designing accounting systems.

The importance of understanding product costing methods was emphasized by a former student in an MBA class. The student, who was employed as an industrial engineer by a large manufacturing company, told of an assignment to operate a computerized model to ascertain the optimal product mix for the company.[1] This

---

[1] Readers familiar with production and management science techniques will recognize this as a "linear programming" problem.

model required as input, among other things, the *variable cost* of each product produced. When the model was first implemented, the former student asked plant managers and their accountants for the *unit cost* of each product produced in each plant.

The plant managers and accountants did not realize that the model specifically required *variable* unit costs. They provided data on the unit costs used for finished goods inventory valuation, which were *full absorption* costs. (Recall from Chapter 2 that full absorption unit costs include unit variable manufacturing costs *plus* a share of fixed manufacturing costs.) In addition, the costs provided were the actual (historical) costs incurred, not the future costs estimated for the period in which the product mix was to be computed.

Without realizing that the unit costs provided were inappropriate for the model, the company's industrial engineers computed the product mix. That the results were suboptimal should come as no surprise. The problem was eventually tracked down and corrected, but not without some lost profits and embarrassment to those involved.

Cases like this are common in industry. They lead us to emphasize, as we did in Chapter 1, the importance of better communication between the users and suppliers of accounting information.

Overview of the Alternatives

This chapter discusses the following six alternative ways of measuring unit manufacturing costs:

	Cost Measure		
Cost Inclusion	**Actual Costing**	**Normal Costing**	**Standard Costing**
Variable Costing	X	X	X
Full Absorption Costing	X	X	X

A manufacturing company's inventory costing system results essentially from answers to the following questions:

1. *Cost inclusion.* What costs are to be included in per-unit manufacturing costs? The choices are *variable costing* and *full absorption costing*.
2. *Cost measure.* How are costs to be measured? The choices are *actual costing*, *normal costing*, and *standard costing*.

Note that we are dealing with manufacturing costs only in this chapter. Nonmanufacturing costs, such as marketing and administrative costs, are not part of inventory, even in manufacturing companies.

Exhibit 3.1 shows these major different methods of computing unit manufacturing costs in more detail. (Exhibit 3.1 contains some new terminology to be made clear later.) Virtually all companies use one or more of these unit manufacturing cost methods. Some companies use a slight variation of these alternatives, but if you understand each of these six alternatives, you will be able to understand any variation encountered. Exhibits 3.1 (here) and 3.9 (later in this chapter) summarize the comparison of the six product costing methods.

Exhibit 3.1
Comparison of Unit Product Costs Under Alternative Costing Methods

| | Cost Measure | | |
Cost Inclusion	Actual Costing	Normal Costing	Standard Costing
Variable Costing			
Direct Materials	Actual	Actual	Standard
Direct Labor	Actual	Actual	Standard
Variable Manufacturing Overhead.	Actual	Normal	Standard
Fixed Manufacturing Overhead.	—	—	—
Full Absorption Costing			
Direct Materials	Actual	Actual	Standard
Direct Labor	Actual	Actual	Standard
Variable Manufacturing Overhead.	Actual	Normal	Standard
Fixed Manufacturing Overhead.	Actual	Normal	Standard

---

We next describe each of these alternatives using a comprehensive example that shows how unit costs differ under each of these costing methods. As we proceed, we shall add more detailed explanation and numbers to Exhibit 3.1, so the meaning of the terms contained in the exhibit will be made clear.

Cost Inclusion: Variable Versus Full Absorption Costing

Variable Costing[2]

Under a variable costing system, unit manufacturing costs for inventory valuation are the variable manufacturing costs. These variable manufacturing costs are a subset of total unit variable costs, which could include nonmanufacturing costs as well as manufacturing costs. In Exhibit 3.1, and throughout this book, we assume that direct materials, direct labor, and variable manufacturing overhead are variable costs. It is possible, of course, for some or all direct labor and manufacturing

---

[2]This method is also known as "direct costing."

overhead to be fixed in the short run. If so, these fixed costs are treated just as fixed manufacturing overhead is treated in our examples. Although variable costing measures unit costs in a way that is useful for managerial purposes, variable costing is not permitted for external reporting under generally accepted accounting principles.

Example During June, Umbrella Makers produced 10,000 umbrellas. The total and unit variable manufacturing costs were as follows:

	Total Cost	÷ 10,000 Units =	Cost per Unit
Direct Materials	$11,000		$1.10
Direct Labor (1,100 hours @ $21)	23,100		2.31
Variable Overhead	9,600		.96
Total	$43,700		$4.37

Exhibit 3.2 shows these unit costs.

Exhibit 3.2
Product Costs Under Variable Costing

	Cost Measure: Actual Costing
Variable Costing:	**Per Unit:**
Direct Materials.	Actual = $1.10
Direct Labor	Actual = 2.31
Variable Manufacturing Overhead	Actual = .96
Fixed Manufacturing Overhead ─DO NOT INCLUDE IN VARIABLE	—
Total Unit Cost	$4.37

Full Absorption Costing

Under *full absorption costing*, all manufacturing costs are charged to the product, including both variable and fixed manufacturing costs. That is, all fixed and variable manufacturing costs are "fully absorbed" in the product. In financial reporting these costs are held in inventory until the units are sold, then matched against revenue as an expense.

Exhibit 3.1 lists the difference between variable and full absorption costing. Under full absorption costing, a share of fixed manufacturing costs is allocated to each unit and included in the measure of unit costs. Fixed manufacturing costs are *not* unit costs. They are *total costs*. They are *converted* to unit costs by the following formula:

$$\text{Unit Fixed Manufacturing Cost} = \frac{\text{Total Fixed Manufacturing Costs for the Period}}{\text{Activity for the Period}}.$$

Example Umbrella Makers' fixed manufacturing costs for June were $12,300. The company made 10,000 umbrellas, so the "fixed unit cost" per umbrella is

$$\frac{\$12,300}{10,000 \text{ umbrellas}} = \$1.23.$$

Exhibit 3.3 compares full absorption and variable costing. Note that the $1.23 computed above is added to the variable costing unit cost to derive the full absorption unit cost of $5.60. (Recall that these are manufacturing costs only. Nonmanufacturing costs are not part of inventory under either full absorption or variable costing.)

Note how full absorption costing "unitizes" fixed costs. A total cost that was fixed over a range of activity levels is converted to a "unit" cost by allocating the total cost equally to the units produced. A naive user of the full absorption unit cost might believe that $5.60 is the product cost, and that if production were to increase by 100 umbrellas, manufacturing costs would increase by $560 (= 100 × $5.60). Of course this is not true. We would expect *only* variable costs to increase if production increased by 100 umbrellas [that is, a cost increase of $437 (= 100 × $4.37)].

When accountants measure and report full absorption unit costs, decision makers sometimes mistake them for variable costs. This problem, which occurs repeatedly in companies, is discussed in numerous contexts throughout this book. A good rule of thumb for decision-making purposes is "Never unitize fixed costs."

Exhibit 3.3
Comparison of Product Costs Under Variable and Full Absorption Costing

Cost Inclusion	Cost Measure: Actual Costing
Variable Costing:	**Per Unit:**
Direct Materials.	Actual = $1.10
Direct Labor	Actual = 2.31
Variable Manufacturing Overhead	Actual = .96
Fixed Manufacturing Overhead	—
Total Unit Cost	$4.37
Full Absorption Costing:	**Per Unit:**
Direct Materials.	Actual = $1.10
Direct Labor	Actual = 2.31
Variable Manufacturing Overhead	Actual = .96
Fixed Manufacturing Overhead	Actual = 1.23
Total Unit Cost	$5.60

Full absorption unit costing information is readily available in companies because these data are required for external financial reporting under generally accepted accounting principles and income tax regulations. This information is easily misused for managerial decisions. Variable costs per unit may not be as readily available, however, because costs often are not broken down into fixed and variable components.

Comparative Income Statements for Variable and Full Absorption Costing

In this section we compare income statements for variable and full absorption costing. Assume the following facts for Umbrella Makers for a month:

1. 10,000 units produced and sold.

2. Manufacturing costs according to the previous example: Variable costs:

    Direct material is $1.10 per unit produced.
    Direct labor is $2.31 per unit produced.
    Variable manufacturing overhead is $.96 per unit produced.
    Total unit variable manufacturing cost is $4.37 per unit.
    Fixed manufacturing overhead is $12,300 for the month.
    Total unit full absorption cost for 10,000 units produced is $5.60 [= $4.37 + ($12,300/10,000 units) = $4.37 + $1.23].

3. Sales price is $9 per unit sold.

4. Variable marketing costs are $.50 per unit sold.

5. Fixed marketing and administrative costs are $25,000 for the month.

Income statements for variable and full absorption costing appear in Exhibit 3.4. The variable costing statement presents more detail about cost behavior because it divides costs into fixed and variable components.

Exhibit 3.4
Comparative Income Statements:
Variable and Full Absorption Costing
Production Volume Equals Sales Volume

Variable Costing

Sales Revenue	$90,000
Variable Cost of Goods Sold (10,000 units @ $4.37)	(43,700)
Variable Marketing Costs	(5,000)
Contribution Margin	$41,300
Fixed Manufacturing Costs	(12,300)
Fixed Marketing and Administrative Costs	(25,000)
Operating Profit	$ 4,000

Full Absorption Costing

Sales Revenue	$90,000
Cost of Goods Sold (10,000 units @ $5.60)	(56,000)
Gross Margin	$34,000
Marketing and Administrative Costs	(30,000)
Operating Profit	$ 4,000

The operating profit under both methods is the same in Exhibit 3.4 because the number of units produced equals the number sold. Exhibit 3.5, which is discussed next, shows the results when units produced and sold are not the same.

Comparison of Variable and Full Absorption Costing: Production Is Greater Than Sales. Assume the following change in facts from the previous example:

1. Umbrella Makers had 1,000 umbrellas in beginning inventory. These umbrellas were valued under each method as follows:

	Total (1,000 units)	Per Unit
Variable Costing	$4,370	$4.37
Full Absorption Costing	5,600	5.60

2. During the month, Umbrella Makers produced 10,000 units, incurring the manufacturing costs noted in the previous example, and sold 9,000 units. Ending inventory comprised 2,000 units (= 1,000 units + 10,000 units produced − 9,000 units sold) valued as follows:

	Total (2,000 units)	Per Unit
Variable Costing	$ 8,740	$4.37
Full Absorption Costing	11,200	5.60

3. Sales revenue was $81,000 (= 9,000 units sold × $9), and variable marketing costs were $4,500 (= 9,000 units sold × $.50).

Exhibit 3.5 shows the comparative income statements with an increase in inventory. Variable and full absorption costing showed the same profit in Exhibit 3.4 when units produced and units sold were the same; however, Exhibit 3.5 shows a different profit for each method. Profits are different under each method because of the different treatment of fixed manufacturing overhead. Under variable costing, all of the fixed manufacturing overhead, $12,300, is expensed (that is, written off) for the month. Under full absorption costing, some of the period's fixed manufacturing overhead remains in ending inventory. To be precise, only $11,070 of fixed manufacturing overhead is expensed, computed as follows:[3]

1. The first 1,000 units sold were from beginning inventory. Fixed manufacturing overhead in first 1,000 units (1,000 × $1.23 fixed overhead per unit). . . . . $ 1,230
2. The next 8,000 units sold were produced this period. Fixed manufacturing overhead in next 8,000 units (8,000 × $1.23 fixed overhead per unit) 9,840

Total fixed manufacturing overhead costs expensed under full absorption costing $11,070

---

[3]This example assumes first-in, first-out inventory flows for convenience in presentation. The results in this example are not affected by the assumed inventory flows.

Exhibit 3.5
Variable and Full Absorption Costing:
Comparative Income Statements with Production (10,000 units) Greater Than Sales
(9,000 units)

Variable Costing

Sales Revenue (9,000 units sold @ $9)		$81,000
Variable Cost of Goods Sold:		
Beginning Inventory (1,000 units @ $4.37)	$ 4,370	
Add Current Month's Production (10,000 units @ $4.37) . . .	43,700	
	$48,070	
Subtract Ending Inventory (2,000 units @ $4.37)	(8,740)	
Variable Cost of Goods Sold.		(39,330)
Variable Marketing Costs		(4,500)
Contribution Margin		$37,170
Fixed Manufacturing Costs		(12,300)
Fixed Marketing and Administrative Costs		(25,000)
Operating Profit (Loss)		$ (130)

Full Absorption Costing

Sales Revenue (9,000 units sold @ $9)		$81,000
Cost of Goods Sold:		
Beginning Inventory (1,000 units @ $5.60)	$ 5,600	
Add Current Month's Production (10,000 units @ $5.60) . . .	56,000	
	$61,600	
Subtract Ending Inventory (2,000 units @ $5.60)	(11,200)	
Cost of Goods Sold		(50,400)
Gross Margin		$30,600
Marketing and Administrative Costs		(29,500)[a]
Operating Profit		$ 1,100

[a]$29,500 = $25,000 + $4,500.

Under full absorption costing, fixed manufacturing overhead costs expensed are $1,230 lower and therefore profits are $1,230 higher, as shown by the following computations:

Difference in fixed manufacturing overhead expensed = $12,300 (variable costing) − $11,070 (full absorption costing)	$1,230
Difference in profits = $1,100 profit under full absorption costing + $130 loss under variable costing	$1,230

Comparison of Variable and Full Absorption Costing: Production Is Less Than Sales In the previous example, the company had a beginning inventory of 1,000 units, produced 10,000 units, and sold 9,000 units, leaving an ending inventory of 2,000 units. Now assume that it is the next month, with the following change in facts:

1. Umbrella Makers had 2,000 units in beginning inventory, valued as follows (this is the previous month's ending inventory):

	Total (2,000 units)	Per Unit
Variable Costing	$ 8,740	$4.37
Full Absorption Costing	11,200	5.60

2. During the month, Umbrella Makers produced 10,000 units, incurring the production costs noted in the previous examples, and sold 11,000 units. Ending inventory comprised 1,000 units (= 2,000 units + 10,000 produced − 11,000 units sold), valued as follows:

	Total (1,000 units)	Per Unit
Variable Costing	$4,370	$4.37
Full Absorption Costing	5,600	5.60

3. Sales revenue was $99,000 (= 11,000 units sold × $9), and variable marketing costs were $5,500 (= 11,000 units sold × $.50).

Exhibit 3.6 shows comparative income statements with a decrease in inventory. Full absorption costing shows a lower profit than variable costing. Under variable costing, only the $12,300 fixed manufacturing overhead cost incurred during the period is expensed. Under full absorption costing, more than $12,300 fixed manufacturing overhead is expensed, as shown below:

1. The first 2,000 units sold were from beginning inventory. Fixed manufacturing overhead in the first 2,000 units (2,000 × $1.23 fixed overhead per unit) . . $ 2,460
2. The next 9,000 units sold were produced this period. Fixed manufacturing overhead in the next 9,000 units (9,000 × $1.23 fixed overhead per unit) . . 11,070
Total fixed manufacturing overhead expensed under full absorption costing . . $13,530

The amount of fixed manufacturing overhead expensed under variable costing is $12,300. The difference in the amount of costs expensed, $1,230 (= $13,530 − $12,300), is the difference in profits ($1,230 = $8,130 − $6,900) between variable and full absorption costing shown in Exhibit 3.6.

Exhibit 3.7 compares full absorption and variable costing for the 2 months presented in Exhibit 3.5 (first month) and Exhibit 3.6 (second month). It presents some important comparisons. First, the operating profit for the *2-month period* is the same under either method—$8,000. That is because the fixed manufacturing costs expensed, $24,600, are the same under both methods.

Second, operating profits are higher under full absorption costing in the first month because units produced exceed units sold (so some fixed costs that were expensed under variable costing are not under full absorption costing). The reverse is true in the second month.

Third, the difference in monthly operating profits between the two costing methods equals the *difference in inventory change* between the two methods.

Exhibit 3.6
Variable and Full Absorption Costing:
Comparative Income Statements with Sales Greater Than Production

Variable Costing

Sales Revenue (11,000 units sold @ $9)		$99,000
Variable Cost of Goods Sold:		
Beginning Inventory (2,000 units @ $4.37)	$ 8,740	
Add Current Month's Production (10,000 units @ $4.37) . . .	43,700	
	$52,440	
Subtract Ending Inventory (1,000 units @ $4.37)	(4,370)	
Variable Cost of Goods Sold.		(48,070)
Variable Marketing Costs		(5,500)
Contribution Margin		$45,430
Fixed Manufacturing Costs		(12,300)
Fixed Marketing and Administrative Costs		(25,000)
Operating Profit		$ 8,130

Full Absorption Costing

Sales Revenue (11,000 units sold @ $9)		$99,000
Cost of Goods Sold:		
Beginning Inventory (2,000 units @ $5.60)	$11,200	
Add Current Month's Production (10,000 units @ $5.60) . . .	56,000	
	$67,200	
Subtract Ending Inventory (1,000 units @ $5.60)	(5,600)	
Cost of Goods Sold		(61,600)
Gross Margin		$37,400
Marketing and Administrative Costs		(30,500)[a]
Operating Profit		$ 6,900

[a]$30,500 = $25,000 + $5,500.

Fourth, the difference in monthly operating profits equals the difference in fixed manufacturing costs expensed under the two systems. When the amount of fixed manufacturing costs in the beginning inventory under full absorption costing is the same as the amount in ending inventory for a period, then the fixed manufacturing costs expensed and operating profits are equal under both methods. A good rule of thumb is that *when the inventory of manufactured goods does not change from the beginning of the period to the end of the period*, operating profits are *identical* under both methods.

Our example assumes that the only fixed manufacturing cost is a portion of manufacturing overhead. If other manufacturing costs, such as direct labor, are fixed, they are treated as a *product* cost under full absorption and a *period* cost under variable costing, just like manufacturing overhead is in our example.

The difference between full absorption and variable costing is due only to *fixed manufacturing costs*, which are the only costs inventoried. It is *not* due to any portion of marketing and administrative costs; these costs are period costs, and are therefore not an inventoriable product cost, under either variable or full absorption costing.

Exhibit 3.7
Variable and Full Absorption Costing Comparison:
Comparative Income Statements for 2 Months

	First Month	Second Month	Total
Units			
Beginning Inventory	1,000	2,000	—
Units Produced	10,000	10,000	20,000
Units Sold	9,000	11,000	20,000
Ending Inventory	2,000	1,000	—
Dollars: Variable Costing			
Sales Revenue	$81,000	$99,000	$180,000
Variable Cost of Goods Sold.	(39,330)	(48,070)	(87,400)
Variable Marketing and Administrative Costs . .	(4,500)	(5,500)	(10,000)
Contribution Margin	$37,170	$45,430	$ 82,600
Fixed Manufacturing Costs	(12,300)	(12,300)	(24,600)
Fixed Marketing and Administrative Costs . . .	(25,000)	(25,000)	(50,000)
Operating Profit (Loss)	$ (130)	$ 8,130	$ 8,000
Change in Inventory.	$ 4,370[a]	$ 4,370	$ –0–
	Increase	Decrease	
Fixed Manufacturing Costs Incurred	$12,300	$12,300	$ 24,600
Fixed Manufacturing Costs Expensed	$12,300	$12,300	$ 24,600
Dollars: Full Absorption Costing			
Sales Revenue	$81,000	$99,000	$180,000
Cost of Goods Sold	(50,400)	(61,600)	(112,000)
Gross Margin	$30,600	$37,400	$ 68,000
Marketing and Administrative Costs	(29,500)	(30,500)	(60,000)
Operating Profit	$ 1,100	$ 6,900	$ 8,000
Inventory Change.	$ 5,600[b]	$ 5,600	$ –0–
	Increase	Decrease	
Fixed Manufacturing Costs Incurred	$12,300	$12,300	$ 24,600
Fixed Manufacturing Costs Expensed	$11,070	$13,530	$ 24,600

[a]$4,370 increase = 1,000 unit increase × $4.37 variable manufacturing cost per unit.
[b]$5,600 increase = 1,000 unit increase × $5.60 full absorption cost per unit.

Summary: Variable Versus Full Absorption Costing

The variable costing method measures unit costs with only variable manufacturing costs. The variable costing method treats variable costs as *unit* costs and fixed costs as *total* costs. Managers usually find the variable costing method more useful than the full absorption costing method for managerial decision making, planning, and performance evaluation.

Full absorption costing adds fixed manufacturing costs to variable manufacturing costs to arrive at a unit product cost. Thus, units "fully absorb" all manufacturing costs. The full absorption method is required for external financial reporting. Virtually all manufacturing companies use full absorption costing for external reporting; but many also use variable costing for management purposes. This is a classic case where the type of accounting information that is used for one purpose may not be useful for another.

Cost Measure: Actual, Normal, or Standard Cost

Normal Costing

Our previous comparison of variable and full absorption costing methods assumed that costs are measured as *actual costs* incurred. This section describes commonly used alternatives to actual costs, known as *normal costing* and *standard costing*. Normal costing uses *actual* direct material and direct labor costs, plus an amount representing "normal" manufacturing overhead. Under normal costing, a rate for applying overhead to units produced is determined before the production period. This rate is used in applying overhead to each unit as it is produced. We first discuss the rationale for using normal manufacturing overhead costs; then we show how normal costing works.

Normal overhead costs have advantages over actual costs. First, actual total manufacturing overhead costs may fluctuate because of seasonality (the cost of utilities, for example), recording adjustments (compare actual with accrued property taxes, for example), or other reasons that are not related directly to activity levels. Also, if production is seasonal and overhead costs remain unchanged, the per-unit costs in low-volume months will be higher than the per-unit costs in high-volume months, as shown in the following example:

	Production	Total Monthly Variable and Fixed Manufacturing Overhead	Per-Unit Overhead Cost
January.	1,000 Units	$20,000	$20
July	6,000 Units	30,000	5

Normal costs enable companies to smooth, or "normalize," these fluctuations. The *per-unit* overhead cost would be the same throughout the year, regardless of month-to-month fluctuations in actual costs and activity levels.

Actual direct material and direct labor costs can be known within a day after the costs are incurred in companies that use perpetual inventory systems and a computerized payroll system in which labor time is entered daily. In contrast, it may take a month or more to learn about the actual overhead costs for the same units. For example, often 2 weeks to a month (or longer) will lapse after the end of an accounting period before invoices for utilities are received. The cost of supplies used will not be known until the end of a quarter or year when an inventory of supplies is taken. Thus, a *predetermined overhead rate* is frequently used to estimate the actual cost in advance of recording the actual cost. (We use the terms *predetermined* rate and *normal* rate interchangeably.)

Computing the Overhead Rate How are manufacturing overhead rates computed? The procedure may be as simple as estimating the activity level, or normal volume, for the year, estimating the amount of manufacturing overhead for the year, and dividing the latter by the former. Or it may be more complex, involving the use of statistical models. The basic idea is to estimate the rate from the following formula:

$$\text{Predetermined Manufacturing Overhead Rate} = \frac{\text{Estimated Manufacturing Overhead}}{\text{Normal Activity Level}} \; .$$

Example Umbrella Makers used the general formula presented above. In a previous year, the company's total variable manufacturing overhead cost was $96,000 and the activity level was 12,000 direct labor hours. The company expected the same level of activity for the coming year and costs were expected to increase to $108,000 because of inflation. So:

$$\text{Predetermined Variable Manufacturing Overhead Rate} = \frac{\$108,000}{12,000 \text{ hours}} = \$9.00 \text{ per hour.}$$

The fixed manufacturing predetermined overhead rate may be computed in a similar fashion. Umbrella Makers estimated fixed manufacturing overhead to be $120,000 and the activity level to be 12,000 direct labor hours, giving:

$$\text{Predetermined Fixed Manufacturing Overhead Rate} = \frac{\$120,000}{12,000 \text{ hours}} = \$10.00 \text{ per hour.}$$

If the actual overhead costs and activity levels coincide with the estimates, normal costs and actual costs will be the same. If the estimates turn out to be incorrect, normal unit costs and actual unit costs will be different.

The predetermined overhead rates mean that for each direct labor hour worked, the product is charged with $9.00 for variable manufacturing overhead and $10.00 for fixed manufacturing overhead at Umbrella Makers.

To summarize, the conceptual formulas for applying overhead to products are as follows:

$$\text{Normal Unit Overhead Cost} = \frac{\left(\text{Predetermined Overhead Rate} \times \text{Actual Basis} \right)}{\text{Actual Number of Units Produced}} \; .$$

ACTIVITY LEVEL
OR
DIRECT LABOR
HOURS

The computations require the following steps:

1. *Compute the predetermined (that is, normal) overhead rates.* These rates usually cover 1 year. For Umbrella Makers, these rates were:

Variable Manufacturing Overhead Rate . . . . $ 9.00 per Direct Labor Hour
Fixed Manufacturing Overhead Rate . . . . $10.00 per Direct Labor Hour

2. *Multiply these rates by a measure of the actual level of activity for the period* (in this example, direct labor hours is the measure of activity). This gives the *total* fixed and *total* variable overhead charged to production for that period. For Umbrella Makers there were 1,100 labor hours for the month:

Variable Manufacturing Overhead: 1,100 Direct Labor Hours at $9.00 . . . . . $ 9,900
Fixed Manufacturing Overhead: 1,100 Direct Labor Hours at $10.00. . . . . . $11,000

3. *Divide the total cost by the actual number of units produced to derive a unit cost.*

Variable Manufacturing Overhead:

$$\frac{\$9 \times 1{,}100 \text{ Hours}}{10{,}000 \text{ Units}} = \frac{\$9{,}900}{10{,}000 \text{ Units}} = \$.99.$$

Fixed Manufacturing Overhead:

$$\frac{\$10 \times 1{,}100 \text{ Hours}}{10{,}000 \text{ Units}} = \frac{\$11{,}000}{10{,}000 \text{ Units}} = \$1.10.$$

Note: The predetermined rates are usually set for a year; these annual rates are applied to each month's production to derive a product cost.

Exhibit 3.8 compares unit costs under actual and normal costing. It also compares full absorption and variable costing. In comparing the methods, note that only the overhead costs are different.

Exhibit 3.8
Comparison of Product Costs Under Actual and Normal Costing

	Cost Measure	
Cost Inclusion	**Actual Costing**	**Normal Costing**
Variable Costing:		
Direct Materials.	Actual = $1.10	Actual = $1.10
Direct Labor	Actual = 2.31	Actual = 2.31
Variable Manufacturing Overhead	**Actual** = .96	**Normal**[a] = .99
Fixed Manufacturing Overhead	—	—
Total Unit Cost	$4.37	$4.40
Full Absorption Costing:		
Direct Materials.	Actual = $1.10	Actual = $1.10
Direct Labor	Actual = 2.31	Actual = 2.31
Variable Manufacturing Overhead	**Actual** = .96	**Normal**[a] = .99
Fixed Manufacturing Overhead	**Actual** = 1.23	**Normal**[b] = 1.10
Total Unit Cost	$5.60	$5.50

[a]$.99 = $\dfrac{\$9 \text{ Predetermined Variable Overhead Rate} \times 1{,}100 \text{ Hours Worked}}{10{,}000 \text{ Units Produced}}$

[b]$1.10 = $\dfrac{\$10 \text{ Predetermined Fixed Overhead Rate} \times 1{,}100 \text{ Hours Worked}}{10{,}000 \text{ Units Produced}}$

Alternative Activity Bases for Applying Overhead Like many companies, Umbrella Makers uses direct labor hours as the activity base for applying overhead. Other companies use different bases for applying overhead. These include the following examples:

Actual Base	Predetermined Rate
Direct Labor Hours	Dollars per Direct Labor Hour
Machine Hours	Dollars per Machine Hour
Pounds of Raw Materials Used	Dollars per Pound
Direct Labor Dollars	Percentage of Direct Labor Dollars
Units of Output	Dollars per Unit of Output

(Self-Study Problem No. 2 at the end of this chapter shows how to apply overhead using various bases.)

The base that is easiest to use is units of output produced. Companies with only one product generally apply overhead on that basis. Output is difficult to measure, however, in companies with multiple products. Consider a company such as Hewlett-Packard, which makes several types of calculators, electronic parts, medical equipment, and numerous other products. With multiple products, companies look for a common denominator for their measure of activity. A typical common denominator is some input measure such as direct labor hours or direct labor dollars. Unless otherwise specified, in this book we use actual direct labor hours as the measure of activity to apply overhead to products under the normal costing method.

Standard Costing

Under standard costing, a standard or predetermined manufacturing cost is developed for each unit. In most cases, these are the costs that management establishes as a norm. In that sense, they are the costs that "should" be incurred to produce each unit. Standards are developed for each input—direct materials, direct labor, and manufacturing overhead.

Why Do Companies Use Standard Costs?

Standards are "norms": They are benchmarks for performance. By comparing the actual costs against the standards, companies can measure how well they are controlling costs.

Planning and decision making require estimates of what costs would be if a proposed action were taken. Standard costs can be used as those estimates.

Standard costs are also used in inventory valuation for financial reporting. Much of the clerical work needed to accumulate costs and allocate them to each unit produced is reduced if standard costing systems are used.

In short, standard costs can be used for all three purposes of accounting information: managerial decision making, planning and performance evaluation, and external reporting. In the following example, we describe how standard costs were developed at Umbrella Makers. The approach described is similar to that followed in many companies.

Example The standard cost of each umbrella at Umbrella Makers was computed as follows. (Like many companies, Umbrella Makers revises its standards yearly.)

Direct Materials Based on engineering studies of the amount of direct materials required to make an umbrella, and the estimated costs of those materials, the standard was set at

Direct Materials . . . . $1.00 per Umbrella

Direct Labor Based on studies of the time required to make an umbrella and inevitable idle time, the standard direct labor time was set at .1 hour per umbrella. Labor costs, including fringe benefits and employer-paid payroll taxes, were estimated to be $20.00 per hour. This gave the direct labor cost:

Direct Labor (.1 hour at $20). $2.00 per Umbrella

Variable Manufacturing Overhead The standard variable overhead *rate* is the same as the predetermined rate determined under normal costing. That rate ($9.00 per direct labor hour) was multiplied by the standard direct labor hours per unit to give the standard variable manufacturing overhead cost per unit:

Variable Manufacturing Overhead Cost (.1 hour at $9.00) . . . . . $ .90 per Umbrella

Fixed Manufacturing Overhead The standard fixed overhead *rate* is also the same as the predetermined rate for normal costing. That rate ($10.00 per direct labor hour) was multiplied by the standard direct labor hours per unit to give the standard fixed manufacturing overhead cost per unit:

Fixed Manufacturing Overhead Cost (.1 hour at $10.00) . . . . . . $1.00 per Umbrella

Note that whereas the overhead *rates* are the same under both normal and standard costing, the unit *costs* are not. That is because standard costing multiplies the rate by the *standard* direct labor hours (that is, a standard input activity base), whereas normal costing multiplies the rate by the *actual* direct labor hours (that is, an *actual* input activity base).

Summary of Standard Costs Umbrella Makers' unit standard cost is

Direct Materials	$1.00
Direct Labor (.1 hour at $20)	2.00
Variable Manufacturing Overhead (.1 hour at $9).	.90
Total Standard Variable Unit Cost	$3.90
Fixed Manufacturing Overhead (.1 hour at $10)	1.00
Total Standard Full Absorption Unit Cost	$4.90

Comparison of Costing Methods

Exhibit 3.9 summarizes the six combinations of major product costing methods and warrants special study. Note that full absorption unit costs are systematically higher than variable costing unit costs because variable costing excludes fixed manufacturing overhead from product costs. This relation holds as long as fixed manufacturing overhead costs are greater than zero.

This relation is important for decision making. Recall that full absorption unit costs are used in inventory valuation for external financial reporting, whereas variable costs are used for many internal decisions. If decision makers mistakenly use full absorption costs when they think they are using variable costs, their unit cost estimates will be systematically overstated.

Exhibit 3.9
Comparison of Unit Product Costs Under Alternative Costing Methods

	Cost Measure		
Cost Inclusion	Actual Costing	Normal Costing[a]	Standard Costing
Variable Costing:			
Direct Materials	Actual = $1.10	Actual = $1.10	Standard = $1.00
Direct Labor	Actual = 2.31	Actual = 2.31	Standard = 2.00
Variable Manufacturing Overhead.	Actual = .96	Normal = .99	Standard = .90
Fixed Manufacturing Overhead.	—	—	—
Total Unit Cost.	$4.37	$4.40	$3.90
Full Absorption Costing:			
Direct Materials	Actual = $1.10	Actual = $1.10	Standard = $1.00
Direct Labor	Actual = 2.31	Actual = 2.31	Standard = 2.00
Variable Manufacturing Overhead.	Actual = .96	Normal = .99	Standard = .90
Fixed Manufacturing Overhead.	Actual = 1.23	Normal = 1.10	Standard = 1.00
Total Unit Cost.	$5.60	$5.50	$4.90

[a]Overhead is applied on the basis of direct labor hours.

Example A special order for 100 umbrellas is received at Umbrella Makers. Only variable manufacturing costs will be affected if this order is filled. Revenue from the order would be $480, that is, $4.80 per umbrella. The company's best estimate of the unit cost for this order is the *standard* cost.

A manager at Umbrella Makers argues: "We cannot accept this order. Each unit costs $4.90 (standard full absorption cost), and the per-unit price is only $4.80."

The manager's error, of course, is that the appropriate per-unit cost is only $3.90 (standard variable cost), not $4.90. The full absorption unit cost includes some fixed costs that have been allocated to units based on an expected activity level. But fixed costs would not be affected by this order. In short, the confusion between full absorption and variable unit costs can lead to systematic errors in cost estimation and wrong decisions.

There is no similar systematic relationship among *actual, normal,* and *standard* costing unit costs. If standard cost estimates are set at the best estimate of the expected value, then actual unit costs will be distributed around the standard unit cost—sometimes actual unit costs will be greater than standard, sometimes less. An exception can be found in companies that set standards very "tight"; that is, standard costs are set below the expected value. In these cases, actual unit costs will usually exceed standard unit costs.

Are Some Accounting Methods Systematically "Better" Than Others?

Managers frequently ask: "What is the best accounting system?" The answer is usually "It depends"—it depends on the use of the accounting system.

There are rare cases, however, where a ranking of accounting systems can be made for managerial purposes. For example, if two accounting systems are equally costly, the system that is "finer" (more detailed) is more desirable than the "coarser" system.[4] Suppose that data from System 1 contain all of the data that are in System 2, and more. System 1 would be considered "finer." For example, suppose that we compare cost data about a product from two accounting methods: one in which fixed and variable manufacturing costs are separated (System 1 below), and one in which they are not (System 2 below):

	System 1	System 2
Direct Materials.	$ 4.00	$ 4.00
Direct Labor.	3.00	3.00
Variable Manufacturing Overhead	1.00	
Unit Variable Cost.	$ 8.00	
Sum of Variable and Fixed Manufacturing Overhead.		3.00
Fixed Manufacturing Overhead Allocated to Each Unit . . .	2.00	
Total Unit Cost.	$10.00	$10.00

System 1 would be considered "finer" in this case, because it divides manufacturing overhead into variable and fixed elements, whereas System 2 shows only the sum. In a sense, the data are broken down more "finely" under System 1; thus, System 1 contains at least as much information as System 2, and possibly more. System 1 would be preferred to System 2 if they were equally expensive systems to develop and operate.

This is one more example of an economic analysis of accounting information. Accounting, like any other factor of producing and marketing products, is subject to cost/benefit tests.

---

[4]Readers interested in a more technical, comprehensive discussion should consult J. Demski and G. Feltham, *Cost Determination* (Ames, Iowa: Iowa State University Press, 1976), p. 26; J. Demski, "Basic Ideas in the Economic Analysis of Information," in G. Lobo and M. Maher (Eds.), *Information Economics and Accounting Research* (Ann Arbor, Mich.: School of Business, University of Michigan, 1980), pp. 11–13; or D. Blackwell and M. Girschick, *Theory of Games and Statistical Decisions* (New York: Wiley, 1954).

Summary

This chapter analyzes alternative product costing methods typically used by manufacturing companies. Understanding these costing methods is important if we are to know which cost we should use in decision making. This is particularly an issue in choosing between unit costs under full absorption and variable costing. Decision makers frequently use full absorption unit costs when they intended to use variable costing unit costs.

The key difference between full absorption and variable costing is the treatment of fixed manufacturing costs—full absorption costing "unitizes" them and treats them as product costs; variable costing treats them as period costs. This implies that operating profits will differ under each method if units produced and sold are not the same, as shown in Exhibit 3.10.

Under *normal* costing, direct materials and direct labor are charged to products at actual costs, but overhead is not. A *predetermined* rate is used for variable and fixed manufacturing overhead. The *total* variable and *total* fixed overhead charged to products for the period is the predetermined rate times a measure of *actual* activity (for example, direct labor hours). The *unit* variable and *unit* fixed overhead is the total normal cost divided by the actual number of units produced. Under *standard* costing, *all* unit costs are predetermined.

Exhibit 3.10
Summary Comparison of Full Absorption and Variable Costing

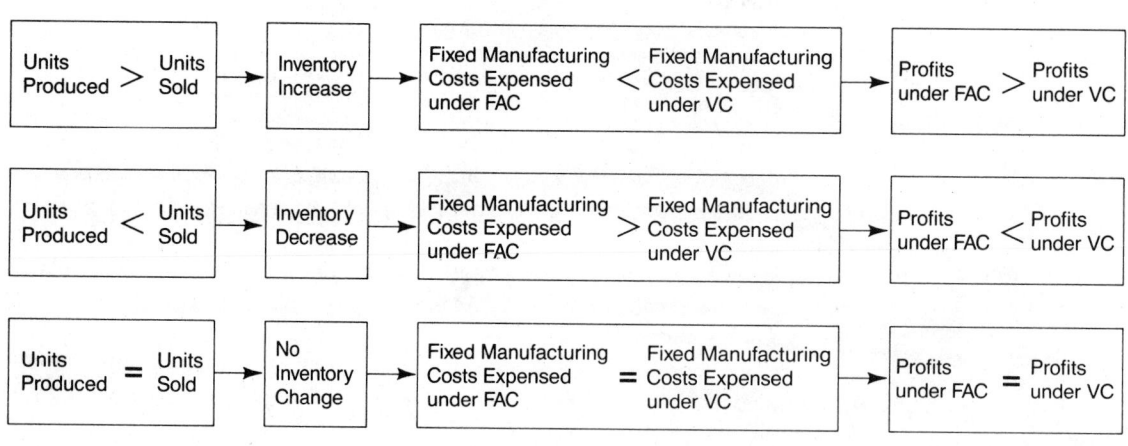

Note: These relations assume that unit costs of inventory do not change from period to period.
FAC = full absorption costing.
VC = variable costing.
> = "are greater than."
< = "are less than."

Comparisons of the six product costing methods are summarized in Exhibit 3.1 (in words) and in Exhibit 3.9 (in numbers).

Problem 1 for Self-Study

Comparison of Variable to Full Absorption Costing: Chelwood, Inc.

Chelwood Corporation manufactures a single product with the following costs:

Selling Price . . . . $8.00 per Unit
Variable Manufacturing Costs (direct materials and direct labor) . . . $4.80 per Unit
Fixed Manufacturing Overhead (all manufacturing overhead is fixed) . $160,000 per Month
Marketing and Administrative Costs (all fixed) . . . . $80,000 per Month
Beginning Inventory:
   Variable Manufacturing Costs . . . . $4.80 per Unit
   Fixed Manufacturing Costs . . . . 1.60 per Unit
     Total . . . . $6.40 per Unit

There are no work-in-process inventories, and FIFO inventory flow assumption is used.

The president of Chelwood wants an analysis on the effects of variations in sales and production units. To help you, the following charts have been included for you to complete. Complete the charts using actual costing, and comment on the reasons for differences in operating profits.

Units[a]

	Sales = Production			Sales > Production			Sales < Production		
Sales	100	80	110	115	90	125	90	75	100
Production	100	80	110	100	80	110	100	80	110
Beginning Inventory	0	0	0	15	10	15	0	0	0
Ending Inventory	0	0	0	0	0	0	10	5	10

[a]All numbers in thousands.

Full Absorption Costing

Revenue									
Cost of Goods Sold									
Gross Margin									
Marketing and Administrative									
Operating Profit									
Beginning Inventory									
Ending Inventory									

Variable Costing

	Sales = Production			Sales > Production			Sales < Production		
Revenue									
Variable Cost of Goods Sold									
Contribution Margin									
Fixed Manufacturing Costs									
Fixed Marketing and Administrative									
Operating Profit									
Beginning Inventory									
Ending Inventory									

Suggested Solution

Full Absorption Unit Manufacturing Cost[a]	$6.40	$6.80	$6.2545	$6.40	$6.80	$6.2545	$6.40	$6.80	$6.2545
Variable Costing Unit Manufacturing Cost	4.80	4.80	4.80	4.80	4.80	4.80	4.80	4.80	4.80

Full Absorption Costing[b]

Revenue (at $8 per unit)	$800	$640	$880	$920	$720	$1000	$720	$600	$800
Cost of Goods Sold[c]	640	544	688	736	608	784	576	510	625
Gross Margin	160	96	192	184	112	216	144	90	175
Marketing and Administrative	80	80	80	80	80	80	80	80	80
Operating Profit	80	16	112	104	32	136	64	10	95
Beginning Inventory	0	0	0	96	64	96	0	0	0
Ending Inventory	0	0	0	0	0	0	64	34	63

[a]Full absorption unit cost is:

$$\$4.80 + \frac{\$160,000}{100,000} = \$6.40,$$

$$\$4.80 + \frac{\$160,000}{\text{Units Produced}} = \$4.80 + \frac{\$160,000}{80,000} = \$6.80,$$

$$\$4.80 + \frac{\$160,000}{110,000} = \$6.2545.$$

[b]All amounts in thousands.
[c]Cost of goods sold = Full absorption cost of beginning inventory
+ Full absorption cost of current month's production
− Full absorption cost of ending inventory

Examples:	Sales = 100 Production = 100	Sales = 90 Production = 80	Sales = 100 Production = 110
Beginning Inventory	$ 0	10 units @ 6.40 = $ 64	$ 0
+ Current Production	100 units @ $6.40 = $640	80 units @ 6.80 = $544	110 units @ 6.2545 = $688
− Ending Inventory	$ 0	$ 0	10 units @ 6.2545 = $ 63
= Total Cost of Goods Sold	$640	$608	$625

Variable Costing[a]

Revenue	$800	$640	$880	$920	$720	$1000	$720	$600	$800
Variable Cost of Goods Sold[b]	480	384	528	552	432	600	432	360	480
Contribution Margin	320	256	352	368	288	400	288	240	320
Fixed Manufacturing Costs	160	160	160	160	160	160	160	160	160
Fixed Marketing and Administrative	80	80	80	80	80	80	80	80	80
Operating Profit	80	16	112	128	48	160	48	0	80
Beginning Inventory	0	0	0	72	48	72	0	0	0
Ending Inventory	0	0	0	0	0	0	48	24	48

[a]All amounts in thousands.
[b]Variable cost of goods sold equals variable costing unit cost times number of units sold: $4.80 × 100,000 = $48,000; $4.80 × 80,000 = $384,000; and so forth.

When units produced equal units sold, operating profits are the same under both variable costing and full absorption costing. When units sold exceed units produced, operating profits reported are higher under variable costing. Conversely, when units produced exceed units sold, operating profits are higher under full absorption costing. This difference in operating profits reported under the two product costing methods when units sold do not equal units produced is due to the fact that fixed manufacturing costs are carried in inventory under full absorption costing, whereas fixed manufacturing costs are expensed as period costs under variable costing.

Problem 2 for Self-Study

Use of Alternative Overhead Bases in Normal Costing: Umbrella Makers

Compute predetermined overhead rates, overhead costs per unit, and unit product costs for Umbrella Makers for each of the following:

a. Direct labor hours (as used in the example in this chapter).

b. Percentage of direct labor dollars.

c. Dollars per unit of output.

Assume that Umbrella Makers made the following estimates before the accounting period in which the predetermined rates were to be used:

(1) Estimated variable manufacturing overhead $108,000
(2) Estimated fixed manufacturing overhead $120,000
(3) Estimated labor hours . . . . 12,000 Hours
(4) Estimated labor dollars per hour $20
(5) Estimated rate of output . . . . 10 Units per Direct
                                                            Labor Hour

Actual values for the month were as follows:
(1) Actual direct labor hours . . . . 1,100 Hours
(2) Actual number of units produced . . . . 10,000 Units
(3) Actual labor dollars per hour $21
(4) Actual direct labor cost per unit $2.31
(5) Actual direct materials cost per unit $1.10

Suggested Solution

The rates would be computed as shown below.

Base		Variable Manufacturing Overhead	Fixed Manufacturing Overhead
a.	Direct Labor Hours	Rate $= \dfrac{\$108,000}{12,000 \text{ Hours}}$	Rate $= \dfrac{\$120,000}{12,000 \text{ Hours}}$
		$= \$9$ per Hour	$= \$10$ per Hour
b.	Direct Labor Dollars	Rate $= \dfrac{\$108,000}{\$20 \times 12,000 \text{ Hours}}$	Rate $= \dfrac{\$120,000}{\$20 \times 12,000 \text{ Hours}}$
		$= \dfrac{\$108,000}{\$240,000}$	$= \dfrac{\$120,000}{\$240,000}$
		$= 45$ percent per Labor Dollar	$= 50$ percent per Labor Dollar
c.	Units of Output	Rate $= \dfrac{\$108,000}{10 \times 12,000 \text{ Hours}}$	Rate $= \dfrac{\$120,000}{10 \times 12,000 \text{ Hours}}$
		$= \dfrac{\$108,000}{120,000 \text{ Units}}$	$= \dfrac{\$120,000}{120,000 \text{ Units}}$
		$= \$.90$ per Umbrella	$= \$1.00$ per Umbrella

The overhead costs per umbrella would be computed as shown below.

Base		Variable Manufacturing Overhead	Fixed Manufacturing Overhead
a.	Direct Labor Hours	$\dfrac{\$9 \times 1,100 \text{ Hours}}{10,000 \text{ Umbrellas}}$	$\dfrac{\$10 \times 1,100 \text{ Hours}}{10,000 \text{ Umbrellas}}$
		$= \$.99$ per Umbrella	$= \$1.10$ per Umbrella
b.	Direct Labor Dollars	$\dfrac{45 \text{ percent of Actual Direct Labor Costs}}{10,000 \text{ Umbrellas}}$	$\dfrac{50 \text{ percent of Actual Direct Labor Costs}}{10,000 \text{ Umbrellas}}$
		$= \dfrac{.45 \times \$23,100}{10,000 \text{ Umbrellas}}$	$= \dfrac{.50 \times \$23,100}{10,000 \text{ Umbrellas}}$
		$= \$1.0395$ per Umbrella	$= \$1.155$ per Umbrella
c.	Units of Output (computed above when predetermined rates were computed) . . .	$\$.90$ per Umbrella	$\$1.00$ per Umbrella

Note that the overhead cost per umbrella is different for each base because the expected relationships among labor hours, labor dollars, and units of output did not hold. For example, the hourly labor rate was expected to be $20, but the actual rate was $21. Hence, the *direct labor dollar* base gives a higher cost per umbrella than does the *direct labor hour* base. A comparison of units costs for each of the three bases is shown below. Note that the normal overhead cost is different for each base.

Actual Costs			Normal Overhead Costs Using Alternative Bases			Normal Costing: Total Unit Cost per Umbrella
Direct Materials	+ Direct Labor	+	Variable Manufacturing Overhead	+ Fixed Manufacturing Overhead	=	
			Base			
			Direct Labor Hours $ .99	+ $1.10	=	$5.50
$1.10	+ $2.31	+	Direct Labor Dollars $1.0395	+ $1.155	=	$5.6045
			Units of Output $ .90	+ $1.00	=	$5.31

Problem 3 for Self-Study

Comparing Alternative Product Costing Methods:
Gourmet's Choice (Part I)[5]

In January 1986 an East Coast tuna fish canner named Sam Peabody, the owner of Gourmet's Choice, was feeling increasingly dissatisfied with the company's current product costing methods. The company had until now used an actual full absorption costing method for costing its output for both external reporting and internal managerial decision making. However, fluctuations in the price of tuna had resulted in sizable changes in unit cost. In addition, delays in the recording of all overhead costs resulted in inefficiencies.

Early one Thursday morning that month, Sam summoned his managerial accountant, John Phillips, a recent business school graduate, and told him to prepare a report on alternative product costing methods that Gourmet's Choice could use.

Because Phillips was in the midst of preparing last year's books for closing, he decided to compare various product costing methods. Leafing through the minutes of previous production meetings, he discovered the following facts from the annual production meeting in the beginning of 1985.

(1) Production planned for 1985 was 1 million 3-ounce cans of raw tuna.
(2) Only 75 percent of raw tuna fish would end up in the finished product; that is, 4 ounces of raw tuna fish would yield 3 ounces of finished product.
(3) Average raw tuna fish price for 1985 was expected to be $1.20 per pound.
(4) Cans were projected to cost $.05 per can.
(5) Direct labor would cost $12 per hour.
(6) Each can of finished product requires .01 direct labor hour (including idle time).
(7) Variable manufacturing overhead was estimated to be $200,000.
(8) Fixed manufacturing overhead was estimated to be $100,000.

[5]Prepared by J. Lim.

At the end of 1985, actual production was 1,100,000 cans of tuna. The costs incurred were as follows:

```
Tuna Fish (275,000 pounds @ $1.30 per pound)  . . . . . . . . . . $357,500
Tin Cans (1,105,000 cans @ $.05 per can)  . . . . . . . . . .       55,250
Direct Labor (11,500 hours @ $12.00 per hour). . . . . . . . .     138,000
Variable Manufacturing Overhead. . . . . . . . . . . . . . .       225,000
Fixed Manufacturing Overhead. . . . . . . . . . . . . . . . .      100,000
```

Phillips decided that direct labor hours would be the most appropriate measure of activity for applying overhead.

a. Using a 2 × 3 matrix corresponding to Exhibit 3.9, calculate the six alternative product costing values Gourmet's Choice could come up with, using 1985 manufacturing costs.

b. Would actual costs go up by the full absorption amount if production increases to 1,200,000 cans? (Assume that Gourmet's Choice has the capacity to produce 1,200,000 cans.) If not, by how much would costs increase?

c. Is the manufacturing overhead applied the same under normal as under standard costing? Why or why not?

Suggested Solution

		Actual	Normal	Standard
a.	**Variable Costing**			
	Direct Materials:			
	Tuna Fish	0.3250	0.3250	0.3000[c]
	Tin Cans	0.0502	0.0502	0.0500
	Direct Labor	0.1255	0.1255	0.1200[d]
	Variable Manufacturing Overhead	0.2045	0.2091[a]	0.2000[e]
	Fixed Manufacturing Overhead	—	—	—
	Unit Inventory Cost	0.7052	0.7098	0.6700
	Full Absorption Costing			
	Direct Materials:			
	Tuna Fish	0.3250	0.3250	0.3000[c]
	Tin Cans	0.0502	0.0502	0.0500
	Direct Labor	0.1255	0.1255	0.1200[d]
	Variable Manufacturing Overhead	0.2045	0.2091[a]	0.2000[e]
	Fixed Manufacturing Overhead	0.0909	0.1045[b]	0.1000[f]
	Unit Inventory Cost	0.7961	0.8143	0.7700

[a] $\dfrac{\$200,000}{0.01 \times 1,000,000} \times \dfrac{11,500}{1,100,000}$.

[b] $\dfrac{\$100,000}{0.01 \times 1,000,000} \times \dfrac{11,500}{1,100,000}$.

[c] $\dfrac{3}{0.75} \times \dfrac{\$1.20}{16}$.

[d] $0.01 \times \$12$.

[e] $\left[\dfrac{\$200,000}{0.01 \times 1,000,000} \right] \times \left[\dfrac{0.01 \times 1,100,000}{1,100,000} \right] = \$.20$.

[f] $\left[\dfrac{\$100,000}{0.01 \times 1,000,000} \right] \times \left[\dfrac{0.01 \times 1,100,000}{1,100,000} \right] = \$.10$.

b. No. Costs would go up by variable unit cost × 100,000 cans. For example, actual costs would be estimated to increase by $.7052 × 100,000 cans = $70,520.

c. No. Under normal costing,

$$\begin{matrix} \text{Overhead} \\ \text{Applied} \end{matrix} = \begin{matrix} \text{Predetermined} \\ \text{Rate} \end{matrix} \times \begin{matrix} \text{Actual Activity} \\ \text{Level} \end{matrix}.$$

whereas under standard costing,

$$\begin{matrix} \text{Overhead} \\ \text{Applied} \end{matrix} = \begin{matrix} \text{Predetermined} \\ \text{Rate} \end{matrix} \times \begin{matrix} \text{Standard Activity} \\ \text{Level} \end{matrix}.$$

Problem 4 for Self-Study

Evaluation of Cost Behavior: Gourmet's Choice (Part II)[6]

Sam Peabody decided that for 1986 his company would start applying overhead at a predetermined rate to cost the company's product. He figured that this would speed up Gourmet's Choice's accounting process.

Gourmet's Choice produced 950,000 cans of finished product for the year 1986. Manufacturing costs were as follows:

	Total	**Unit**
Direct Materials:		
Tuna Fish (237,500 pounds @ $1.18 per pound	$280,250	$.295
Tin Cans	47,525	.050
Direct Labor (10,500 hours @ $12.00 per hour)	126,000	.133
Variable Manufacturing Overhead (10,500 hours @ $20 per hour)[a] . .	210,000	.221
Fixed Manufacturing Overhead (10,500 hours @ $10 per hour)[a] . . .	105,000	.110
	$768,775	$.809

[a]Uses predetermined rate.

Making a quick division, Sam found to his dismay that the unit product cost of $.809 was substantially more than the standard unit cost that Phillips had derived last year. Immediately, Sam sent a memo to Phillips saying "Raw tuna fish prices are lower, so why have our costs gone up?"

How should Phillips comment on Sam Peabody's evaluation?

Suggested Solution

Sam Peabody should be careful about comparing *normal costing* unit costs of $.809 with his expectations, because normal costs are not actual costs. In fact, the actual overhead costs of producing 950,000 cans of tuna are not known from the information given above.

[6]Prepared by J. Lim.

The primary reason for the difference is the average in direct labor hour usage, which showed up not only in direct labor costs but also in overhead because direct labor hours are used as the activity base.

Sam might find *variable* unit costs more useful than *full absorption* unit costs in making unit cost comparisons, because full absorption costs include "unitized" fixed costs, which change as volume changes even when the total fixed costs themselves do not change.

Questions

1. Review the meaning of the following concepts or terms discussed in this chapter.

a.	Variable costing.	**e.**	Predetermined overhead rate.
b.	Full absorption costing.	**f.**	Standard costing.
c.	Actual costing.	**g.**	Standard manufacturing
d.	Normal costing.		overhead.

2. Distinguish between full absorption costing and variable costing. Which method of costing would a firm use to evaluate the effects of decreasing production by 5 percent if it is currently producing at close to capacity?

3. How are marketing and administrative costs treated under variable costing? Under full absorption costing?

4. Under what circumstances do you find operating profit under variable costing equal to full absorption costing profits? When are variable costing profits smaller? When are they greater?

5. How can a company using full absorption costing manipulate profits without changing sales?

6. Describe comparative inventory changes under both variable costing and full absorption costing when
   a. Sales volume exceeds production volume.
   b. Production volume exceeds sales volume.

7. What is the variable costing method also known as? Does variable costing imply that every variable cost associated with a product is reflected in its inventory cost?

8. "A 15 percent price increase to cover rising costs!" fumed an angry customer. "I know for a fact that there has been no increase in materials cost, and the company has not given their workers any pay increases. I bet the owner is lining his pockets!" Suppose that the company uses actual costs to value their products. Give possible explanations for the increase in costs.

9. Give reasons why the use of normal overhead costs is often preferred to actual overhead costs in product costing.

10. Is the applied overhead in normal costing the same as the applied overhead in standard costing? Explain.

11. ''I think the use of a predetermined rate to apply overhead to my products will make product costing easier. But I fill orders according to customer specifications, hence one product is very different from another. How, then, can I allocate overhead fairly among these very different products?'' Explain to the shopowner how best to allocate/apply overhead to the products.

12. Estimated costs differ from actual costs most of the time, so why do companies bother with standard costs?

Exercises

13. *Computing Unit Costs for Variable and Full Absorption Costing.* Star Corporation manufactured 300,000 units of a component for video game machines. The manufacturing costs incurred were as follows:

Direct Materials	$ 750,000
Direct Labor	900,000
Variable Manufacturing Overhead	150,000
Fixed Manufacturing Overhead	450,000
Total	$2,250,000

    a. Calculate the unit manufacturing variable cost.
    b. Calculate the unit manufacturing full absorption cost.

14. *Computing Inventory Value Using Variable Costing and Full Absorption Costing.* The following data pertain to operations of the Sikes Company in Year 1 and Year 5.

	Year 1	Year 5
Opening Inventory in Units	0	6,000
Units Produced	50,000	48,000
Units Sold	48,000	50,000
Fixed Overhead Production Costs	$12,000	$12,000
Variable Overhead Production Costs	12,000	14,000
Fixed Marketing Costs	10,000	10,000
Direct Labor	36,000	40,000
Direct Materials	48,000	50,000

There are no work-in-process inventories, and a FIFO inventory flow assumption is used.

    a. Compute the dollar value of ending finished goods inventory in Year 1 under actual full absorption costing.

b. Compute the dollar value of ending finished goods inventory in Year 1 under actual variable costing, assuming that all fixed overhead production costs would be incurred even if there were no production.

c. Which method, full absorption or variable costing, implies larger reported operating profit for Year 1?

15. *Computing Inventory Value Using Variable Costing and Full Absorption Costing.* Refer to the data in the preceding problem for Sikes Company.

a. Compute the dollar value of ending finished goods inventory in Year 5 under actual full absorption costing.

b. Compute the dollar value of ending finished goods inventory in Year 5 under actual variable costing, assuming that all fixed overhead production costs would be incurred even if there were no production.

c. Which method, full absorption or variable costing, implies larger reported operating profit for Year 5?

16. *Computing Allocated Overhead and Finished Goods Value.* The Speedway Boat Company allocates factory overhead to jobs on a direct labor hour basis at the rate of $3 per hour.

a. Job 745 for four sailboats required $8,400 of direct materials and $10,000 of direct labor at an average rate of $4 per hour. What was the total cost shown for job 745?

b. Job 305 for a small trawler required $6,300 of direct materials and $20,000 of direct labor at an average rate of $5 per hour. Job 305 sold for $40,000. What was the "gross margin" on this sale? (Gross margin is revenue less total manufacturing costs for the goods sold.)

17. *Comparative Impact of Full Absorption and Variable Costing on Unit Costs and Profits.* Mortlake, Inc., produces a single product that sells for $20.50. In Year 2, Mortlake produced 100,000 units and sold 85,000 units. There was no beginning nor ending work-in-process inventory that year.

Manufacturing costs and marketing and administrative costs for Year 2 were as follows:

	Variable	Fixed
Direct Materials	$400,000	–0–
Direct Labor	280,000	–0–
Manufacturing Overhead	115,000	$220,000
Marketing and Administrative Costs	97,750	180,000

a. Compute the unit product cost for Year 2 under variable costing.

b. Compute the unit product cost for Year 2 under full absorption costing.

c. What would Mortlake's operating profit be for Year 2 using the variable costing method? Using the full absorption costing method?

18. *Comparison of Full Absorption and Variable Costing in Income Statement Formats.* Consider the following facts:

	Year 1	Year 2
Sales Volume	70,000 Units	130,000 Units
Production Volume	100,000 Units	100,000 Units
Selling Price	$20 per Unit	$20 per Unit
Variable Manufacturing.	$13 per Unit	$13 per Unit
Fixed Manufacturing.	$340,000	$340,000
Nonmanufacturing costs (all fixed)	$150,000	$150,000

Prepare comparative income statements under variable costing and full absorption costing.

19. *Computing Applied Overhead Under Normal and Standard Costing.* Matthew Products Company uses machine time as the basis for allocating overhead to its products. On January 1, it was estimated that production for the coming year would be 800,000 units. It was also estimated that total overhead for the same year would be $2,000,000 and that estimated machine time would be 40,000 hours. The actual overhead, units produced, and machine time for the four quarters were as follows:

Quarter	Actual Overhead Costs	Actual Units Production	Actual Machine Time
1st	$600,000	300,000 Units	16,000 Hours
2nd	$700,000	300,000 Units	15,000 Hours
3rd	$500,000	200,000 Units	9,000 Hours
4th	$400,000	100,000 Units	6,000 Hours

  a. Compute the standard machine time per unit produced.
  b. Compute the predetermined overhead rate for applying overhead on the basis of machine hours.
  c. Compute the amount of overhead applied under both normal costing and standard costing for each quarter.

20. *Computing Actual Unit Costs and Normal Unit Costs Under Both Variable and Full Absorption Costing.* Wyman Company uses a predetermined rate for applying overhead to production. The rates for Year 1 were as follows: variable, $2 per labor dollar; fixed, $3 per labor dollar. Actual overhead costs incurred were as follows: variable, $40,000; fixed, $50,000. Actual direct materials costs were $10,000, and actual direct labor costs were $18,000. Wyman produced 20,000 units that year.

  a. Calculate unit actual costs using variable costing and full absorption costing.
  b. Calculate unit normal costs using variable costing and full absorption costing.

21. *Computing Applied Manufacturing Overhead from Two Different Activity Bases.* The Tall Texas Company makes a single product: Lone Star belt buckles. The following information is available about this product for January of Year 2:

Belt Buckles

Actual Volume:	Units	4,200 Buckles
	Direct Labor Hours	3,300 Hours
Normal (Estimated) Volume: Units	4,000 Buckles
	Direct Labor Hours	3,000 Hours
Predetermined Average Wage Rate	$20 per Hour
Actual Average Wage Rate	$19 per Hour
Actual Manufacturing Overhead	$92,000
Actual Direct Materials Cost per Unit	$5 per Buckle
Normal (Estimated) Manufacturing Overhead:		
Fixed Portion.	$66,000
Variable Portion.	$8 per Labor Hour

(Round all calculations to the nearest cent.)

   a. Derive *unit manufacturing costs* under **(1)** *variable, normal* and **(2)** *full absorption, normal* costing for belt buckles. Assume that fixed and variable manufacturing overhead is applied using actual direct labor hours as the basis and the predetermined manufacturing overhead rates are per direct labor hour.

   b. Repeat part **a**, except assume that manufacturing overhead is applied as a predetermined percentage of direct labor cost. You will need to derive the predetermined percentage.

22. *Computing Standard Unit Cost Using Two Possible Activity Bases for Manufacturing Overhead Application.* The Kool Kentuckian Company makes a single product: leather cowboy hats. The following information is available about these products for January of Year 3:

Cowboy Hats

Actual Volume:	Units	2,100 Hats
	Direct Labor Hours	1,100 Hours
Standard Volume: Units	2,000 Hats
	Direct Labor Hours	1,000 Hours
Predetermined Average Wage Rate	$20 per Hour
Actual Average Wage Rate	$19 per Hour
Actual Manufacturing Overhead	$33,000
Actual Direct Materials Cost per Unit	$15 per Hat
Standard Direct Materials Cost per Unit	$14 per Hat
Standard Manufacturing Overhead:		
Fixed Portion.	$25,000
Variable Portion.	$8 per Labor Hour

(Round all calculations to the nearest cent.)

   a. Derive *unit manufacturing costs* under **(1)** *variable, standard* and **(2)** *full absorption, standard* costing for cowboy hats. Assume that fixed and variable manufacturing overhead is applied using standard direct labor hours as the basis and the predetermined manufacturing overhead rates are per direct labor hour.

   b. Repeat part **a**, except assume that manufacturing overhead is applied as a predetermined percentage of direct labor cost. You will need to derive the predetermined percentage.

23. *Computing Overhead Using Normal and Standard Costing (R. Colson).* Mayhew Production Corporation uses machine time as the basis for allocating manufacturing overhead to products. On January 1, Year 2, Mayhew's production superintendent estimated that 900,000 units would be produced in Year 2, requiring 45,000 hours of machine time. The controller estimated that total manufacturing overhead cost for Year 2 would be $2,500,000.

Records of the actual overhead costs, units produced, and machine time were collected on a quarterly basis in Year 2 as follows:

Quarter	Actual Overhead Costs	Actual Units Produced	Actual Machine Time
1st	$800,000	333,333	17,000 Hours
2nd	900,000	333,333	18,000 Hours
3rd	500,000	222,223	11,000 Hours
4th	500,000	111,111	5,000 Hours

Compute the amount of overhead under normal costing and standard costing for each quarter (round to two decimal places).

Quarter	Normal Overhead	Standard Overhead
1st		
2nd		
3rd		
4th		

Problems and Cases

24. *Computing Actual and Standard Costs.* In January of Year 4, Sweet Tooth Products, a New England sugar refinery, was forced to review its method of product costing upon receiving a persistent stream of complaints from regular customers concerning the wide fluctuations in sugar prices. Sweet Tooth had used quarterly actual costs as a basis of pricing their product. Raw sugar prices had always followed a distinct seasonal pattern, and utilities costs were always higher in winter than in summer.

Year 3's actual quarterly costs were as follows:

Quarter	1st	2nd	3rd	4th
Tons Processed	1,000	1,000	1,000	1,000
Direct Materials Cost (raw sugar)	$300,000	$150,000	$100,000	$250,000
Variable Manufacturing Overhead	$ 20,000	$ 20,000	$ 20,000	$ 20,000
Fixed Manufacturing Overhead	$120,000	$ 80,000	$ 60,000	$100,000

Direct material prices in Year 4 were expected to duplicate Year 3's seasonal pattern with a general increase of 5 percent. Fixed manufacturing overhead was also expected to follow the present seasonal pattern with a 10 percent increase in cost.

Production volume would be 1,000 tons per quarter as before, and variable manufacturing overhead would remain unchanged.

Year 4's actual first quarter costs were as follows:

Tons Processed	1,100
Direct Materials	$349,800
Variable Manufacturing Overhead.	$ 20,900
Fixed Manufacturing Overhead.	$130,900

Calculate an actual cost and standard cost per ton for the first quarter. Given the considerable difference between actual and standard costs, should Sweet Tooth adopt standard costing for their product? Explain why or why not.

25. *Preparing Income Statements Using Variable and Full Absorption Costing. (This problem and the next are adapted from an article by Raymond P. Marple in* The Accounting Review, *July 1956.)*

The All Fixed Costs Company is so named because it has no variable costs—all of its costs are fixed and vary with time rather than output. The All Fixed Costs Company is located on the bank of a river and has its own hydroelectric plant to supply power, light, and heat. The company manufactures a synthetic material from air and river water, and sells its product on a long-term, fixed-price contract. It has a small staff of employees, all hired on an annual salary basis. These employees are kept on the payroll at full salary even if the company produces no output for a month. The output of the plant can be increased or decreased by adjusting a few dials on the control panel. The following data show production, sales, and cost information for the first two months of operations.

All Fixed Costs Company

	Month 1	Month 2
Production.	20,000 tons	0 tons
Sales	10,000 tons	10,000 tons
Selling Price per Ton	$ 30	$ 30
Costs (all fixed):		
Production.	$280,000	$280,000
General and Administrative	$ 40,000	$ 40,000

a. Prepare income statements for each of the two months, using full absorption costing.

b. Prepare income statements for each of the two months, using variable costing.

c. Which costing method is management likely to prefer? Why?

26. *Preparing Income Statements Using Variable and Full Absorption Costing.* The Semi-Fixed Costs Company is just like the All Fixed Costs Company (see the preceding problem) except that its fixed production costs are $210,000 per month and variable production costs are $7 per ton. The production units, sales units, selling price, and general and administrative cost data for months 1 and 2 for the All Fixed Costs Company apply to the Semi-Fixed Costs Company as well.

a. Prepare income statements for each of the two months, using full absorption costing.

b. Prepare income statements for each of the two months, using variable costing.

c. Which costing method is management likely to prefer? Why?

27. *Computing Unit Costs Using Normal Costing.* Baehr Company, a manufacturing company, uses a predetermined overhead rate based on direct labor hours to apply overhead to products. An estimate of overhead costs was prepared for Year 7 as shown below.

Direct Labor Hours	100,000	120,000	140,000
Variable Overhead Costs	$325,000	$390,000	$455,000
Fixed Overhead Costs	216,000	216,000	216,000
Total Overhead	$541,000	$606,000	$671,000

Although the annual ideal capacity is 150,000 direct labor hours, company officials have determined 120,000 direct labor hours as normal capacity for the year.

The information presented below is for November of Year 7. Jobs 77-50 and 77-51 were completed during November.

Inventories November 1, Year 7

Direct Materials and Supplies	$ 10,500
Work in Process (job 77-50)	54,000
Finished Goods	112,500

Purchases of Direct Materials and Supplies

Direct Materials	$135,000
Supplies	15,000

Materials and Supplies Requisitioned for Production

Job 77-50	$ 45,000
Job 77-51	37,500
Job 77-52	25,500
Supplies	12,000
	$120,000

Factory Direct Labor Hours (DLH)

Job 77-50	3,500 DLH
Job 77-51	3,000 DLH
Job 77-52	2,000 DLH

Labor Costs

Direct Labor Wages	$ 51,000
Indirect Labor Wages (4,000 hours)	15,000
Supervisory Salaries	6,000
	$ 72,000

Building Occupancy Costs (heat, light, depreciation, etc.)

Factory Facilities	6,500
Sales Offices	1,500
Administrative Offices	1,000
	$ 9,000

Administrative Costs

Depreciation on Office Equipment	$ 1,500
Other	6,500
	$ 8,000

a. Calculate the predetermined overhead rates to be used to apply variable and fixed manufacturing overhead to individual jobs during Year 7.

b. Compute the total cost of job 77-50.

c. Compute the total manufacturing overhead costs applied to job 77-52 during November.

d. Compute the total amount of overhead (fixed and variable) applied to jobs during November.

e. Compute actual manufacturing overhead incurred during November.

f. Compare the amounts computed in parts **d** and **e** above. Which is greater?

28. *Applying Overhead Under Normal Costing Using Multiple Bases (CMA adapted).* The Herbert Manufacturing Company is a manufacturer of custom-designed restaurant and kitchen furniture. Actual overhead costs incurred during the month are applied to the products on the basis of actual direct labor hours required to produce the products. The overhead consists primarily of supervision, employee benefits, maintenance costs, property taxes, and depreciation.

Herbert Manufacturing recently won a contract to manufacture the furniture for a new fast food chain that is expanding rapidly in the area. In general, this furniture is durable but of a lower quality than Herbert Manufacturing normally manufactures. To produce this new line, Herbert Manufacturing must purchase more molded plastic parts for the furniture than for its current line. Through innovative industrial engineering, an efficient manufacturing process for this new furniture has been developed that requires only a minimum capital investment. Management is optimistic about the profit improvement the new product line will bring.

At the end of October, the start-up month for the new line, the controller has prepared a separate income statement for the new product line. On a consolidated basis the gross profit percentage was normal; however, the profitability for the new line was less than expected.

At the end of November, the results improved somewhat. Consolidated profits were good, but the reported profitability for the new product line was less than expected. John Herbert, president of the corporation, is concerned that knowledgeable shareholders will criticize his decision to add this lower-quality product line at a time when profitability appeared to be increasing with their standard product line.

The results as published for the first 9 months, for October, and for November are presented in Exhibit 3.11 on page 92.

Mr. Jameson, Cost Accounting Manager, has stated that the overhead allocation based only on direct labor hours is no longer appropriate. On the basis of a recently completed study of the overhead accounts, Mr. Jameson feels that only the supervision and the employee benefits should be allocated on the basis of direct labor hours and the balance of the overhead should be allocated on a machine hour basis. In his judgment, the increase in the profitability of the custom-design furniture is due to a misallocation of overhead in the present system.

The actual direct labor hours and machine hours for the past two months are shown on the following page.

	Fast Food Furniture	Custom Furniture
Machine Hours		
October:		
Forming	660	10,700
Finishing	660	7,780
Assembly	—	—
	1,320	18,480
November:		
Forming	1,280	9,640
Finishing	1,280	7,400
Assembly	—	—
	2,560	17,040
Direct Labor Hours		
October:		
Forming	1,900	9,300
Finishing	3,350	12,000
Assembly	4,750	8,700
	10,000	30,000
November:		
Forming	3,400	8,250
Finishing	5,800	10,400
Assembly	8,300	7,600
	17,500	26,250

The actual overhead costs for the past 2 months were as follows:

	October	November
Supervision	$ 13,000	$ 13,000
Employee Benefits	95,000	109,500
Maintenance	50,000	48,000
Depreciation	42,000	42,000
Property Taxes.	8,000	8,000
All Other	32,000	24,500
Total	$240,000	$245,000

a. Based on Mr. Jameson's recommendation, reallocate the overhead for October and November using direct labor hours as the allocation base for supervision and employee benefits. Use machine hours as the base for the remaining overhead costs.

b. Support or criticize Mr. Jameson's conclusion that the increase in custom-design profitability is due to a misallocation of overhead. Use the data developed in part **a** to support your analysis.

c. Mr. Jameson has also recommended that consideration be given to using predetermined overhead absorption rates calculated on an annual basis rather than allocating actual cost over actual volume each month. He stated that this

Exhibit 3.11
HERBERT MANUFACTURING COMPANY
(000 omitted)

	Fast Food Furniture	Custom Furniture	Consolidated
Nine Months Year-to-Date, Year 8			
Sales	—	$8,100	$8,100
Direct Material	—	$2,025	$2,025
Direct Labor:			
Forming	—	758	758
Finishing	—	1,314	1,314
Assembly	—	558	558
Manufacturing Overhead	—	1,779	1,779
Cost of Sales	—	$6,434	$6,434
Operating Profit.	—	$1,666	$1,666
Operating Profit Percentage	—	20.6%	20.6%
October, Year 8			
Sales	$400	$ 900	$1,300
Direct Material	$200	$ 225	$ 425
Direct Labor:			
Forming	17	82	99
Finishing	40	142	182
Assembly	33	60	93
Manufacturing Overhead	60	180	240
Cost of Sales	$350	$ 689	$1,039
Operating Profit.	$ 50	$ 211	$ 261
Operating Profit Percentage	12.5%	23.4%	20.1%
November, Year 8			
Sales	$800	$ 800	$1,600
Direct Material	$400	$ 200	$ 600
Direct Labor:			
Forming	31	72	103
Finishing	70	125	195
Assembly	58	53	111
Manufacturing Overhead	98	147	245
Cost of Sales	$657	$ 597	$1,254
Operating Profit.	$143	$ 203	$ 346
Operating Profit Percentage	17.9%	25.4%	21.6%

is particularly applicable now that the company has two distinct product lines. Discuss the advantages of using annual predetermined overhead rates.

29. *Effect of Changes in Production and Costing Method on Operating Profit: "I Enjoy Challenges."* Kelly Company uses an actual cost system to apply all production costs to the units produced. Although production has a maximum production capacity of 40 million units, only 10 million units were produced and sold during Year 5. There were no beginning or ending inventories.

KELLY COMPANY
Income Statement
for the Year Ending December 31, Year 5

Sales (10,000,000 units @ $3.00)		$30,000,000
Less Cost of Goods Sold:		
Variable (10,000,000 @ $1)	$(10,000,000)	
Fixed	(24,000,000)	(34,000,000)
Gross Margin		$ (4,000,000)
Less Marketing and Administrative		
Costs (all fixed)		(5,000,000)
Operating Profit (Loss)		$ (9,000,000)

The board of directors is concerned about this loss. A consultant approached the board with the following offer: "I agree to become president for no fixed salary. But I insist on a year-end bonus of 10 percent of operating profit (before considering the bonus)." The board of directors agreed to these terms, and the consultant was hired.

The new president promptly stepped up production to an annual rate of 30,000,000 units. Sales for Year 6 remained at 10,000,000 units.

The resulting Kelly Company income statement for Year 6 is presented below:

KELLY COMPANY
Income Statement
for the Year Ending December 31, Year 6

Sales (10,000,000 units @ $3.00)		$30,000,000
Less Cost of Goods Sold:		
Cost of Goods Manufactured:		
Variable (30,000,000 @ $1)	$(30,000,000)	
Fixed	(24,000,000)	
Total Cost of Goods Manufactured	$(54,000,000)	
Ending Inventory:		
Variable (20,000,000 @ $1)	$ 20,000,000	
Fixed ($20/30 \times 24,000,000$)	16,000,000	
Total Inventory	$ 36,000,000	
Cost of Goods Sold		(18,000,000)
Gross Margin		$12,000,000
Less Marketing and Administrative		
Costs (all fixed)		(5,000,000)
Operating Profit Before Bonus		$ 7,000,000
Less Bonus		(700,000)
Operating Profit After Bonus		$ 6,300,000

The day after the statement was verified, the president took his check for $700,000 and resigned to take a job with another corporation. He remarked, "I enjoy challenges. Now that Kelly Company is in the black, I'd prefer tackling another challenging situation.'' (His contract with his new employer is similar to the one he had with Kelly Company.)

a. As a member of the board of directors, comment on the Year 6 income statement.

b. Using variable costing, what would operating profit be for Year 5? For Year 6? What are the inventory values at the end of Year 6?

c. At what sales level would the president be indifferent to the product costing approach used to determine his bonus? Why?

d. At what sales level would the outside executive prefer variable costing to full absorption costing?

30. *Deriving Normal and Standard Unit Costs for Multiple Products.* The Fleetwood Mac Manufacturing Company makes three products: X1, X2, and X3. The standard manufacturing costs for each product for Year 3 have been computed as follows:

	X1	X2	X3
Direct Materials	$20	$25	$30
Direct Labor	20 (= 1 hour @ $20)	30 (= 1.5 hours @ $20)	$40 (= 2 hours @ $20)
Manufacturing Overhead (fixed and variable combined). . . .	36 (= 1 hour @ $36)	54 (= 1.5 hours @ $36)	72 (= 2 hours @ $36)

Activity measures for January, Year 3:

Normal (estimated) volume per month, in units	1,000 Units	1,000 Units	2,000 Units
Normal (estimated) volume per month, in direct labor hours	1,000 Hours	1,500 Hours	4,000 Hours
Actual volume for January, Year 3, in units. .	800 Units	1,200 Units	1,500 Units
Actual volume for January, Year 3, in direct labor hours	900 Hours	1,700 Hours	3,200 Hours

The company has not kept past records of manufacturing overhead for each product, nor has a breakdown of manufacturing overhead into fixed and variable components been made. The available data about actual costs in January, Year 3, are as follows:

Actual Direct Materials Costs:

X1	$17,600
X2	28,800
X3	46,500
Actual Manufacturing Overhead	$232,000
All Other Costs (marketing and administrative)	$100,000
Actual Labor Rates Averaged $21 per Hour	

The company is experimenting with normal costing, using the following two methods of applying manufacturing overhead:

(1) Predetermined rate times actual direct labor hours.

(2) Predetermined percentage times actual direct labor costs.

a. Derive predetermined rates for each of these two methods for each of the three products.

b. Calculate the *normal unit cost* for each of the three products for January, Year 3, using both methods of applying manufacturing overhead.

c. Given the data provided, can you compare the January, Year 3, *actual unit* cost for X3 with the *standard unit* cost for X3? If so, make the comparison. If not, state why you cannot make the comparison.

d. *Additional information.* Suppose that you analyze manufacturing overhead costs and derive the following *estimates* for Year 3:

Fixed Manufacturing Overhead. . . . . $156,000 per Month
Variable Manufacturing Overhead. . . . . $12 per Direct Labor Hour

(1) What is the *full absorption, normal* cost per unit for X1, X2, and X3 and (2) the *variable normal* cost per unit for X1, X2, and X3 based on this new information? (Note: Full absorption normal unit cost *may* now differ from previous calculations.) Assume that overhead is applied based on rates per labor hour.

Suggested Solutions to Even-Numbered Exercises

14. *Computing Inventory Value Using Variable Costing and Full Absorption Costing.*
a and **b**.

	a Full Absorption Costing	b Variable Costing
Direct Materials	$ 48,000	$48,000
Direct Labor	36,000	36,000
Variable Overhead	12,000	12,000
Fixed Overhead	12,000	—
Total Production Costs.	$108,000	$96,000

$$\text{Ending Inventory Costs} = \frac{2,000}{50,000} \text{ of Costs of Units Produced.}$$

$$\frac{2,000}{50,000} \times \$108,000 = \$4,320 \text{ Full Absorption Costing Ending Inventory.}$$

$$\frac{2,000}{50,000} \times \$96,000 = \$3,840 \text{ Variable Costing Ending Inventory.}$$

c. There is an increase in inventory, so a portion of the fixed costs, under full absorption costing, is included in ending inventory. Total expenses, therefore, will be less under full absorption costing and income will be larger.

16. *Computing Allocated Overhead and Finished Goods Value.*

   a. Job 745:

Raw Materials	$ 8,400
Direct Labor	10,000
Overhead (10,000/4 × $3)	7,500
Total Manufacturing Costs	$25,900

   b. Job 305:

Revenue		$40,000
Less: Raw Materials	$ (6,300)	
Direct Labor	(20,000)	
Overhead (20,000/5 × $3)	(12,000)	(38,300)
Gross Margin		$ 1,700

18. *Comparison of Full Absorption and Variable Costing in Income Statement Formats.*

Variable Costing:
Contribution Margin Format
(000 omitted)

	Year 1	Year 2	Total
Sales	$ 1,400	$ 2,600	$ 4,000
Variable Cost of Goods Sold:			
Beginning Inventory	$ –0–	$ (390)	$ –0–
Current Period Manufacturing Costs . . .	(1,300)	(1,300)	(2,600)
Less Ending Inventory	390	(–0–)	(–0–)
Variable Cost of Goods Sold	$ (910)	$(1,690)	$(2,600)
Total Contribution Margin	$ 490	$ 910	$ 1,400
Fixed Manufacturing Costs	(340)	(340)	(680)
Nonmanufacturing Costs	(150)	(150)	(300)
Operating Profits	$ –0–	$ 420	$ 420

Full Absorption Costing:
Traditional Income Statement Format
(000 omitted)

	Year 1	Year 2	Total
Sales	$ 1,400	$ 2,600	$ 4,000
Full Cost of Goods Sold:			
Beginning Inventory	$ –0–	$ (492)	$ –0–
Current Period Manufacturing Costs . . .	(1,640)	(1,640)	(3,280)
Less Ending Inventory	492	–0–	–0–
Full Absorption Cost of Goods Sold	$(1,148)	$(2,132)	$(3,280)
Gross Margin	$ 252	$ 468	$ 720
Nonmanufacturing Costs	(150)	(150)	(300)
Operating Profits	$ 102	$ 318	$ 420

20. *Computing Actual Unit Costs and Normal Unit Costs Under Both Variable and Full Absorption Costing.*

		Variable	Full Absorption
a.	**Actual Costing**		
	Direct Materials	$0.50	$0.50
	Direct Labor	0.90	0.90
	Variable Manufacturing Overhead	2.00	2.00
	Fixed Manufacturing Overhead	—	2.50
	Total Unit Cost	$3.40	$5.90
b.	**Normal Costing**		
	Direct Materials	$0.50	$0.50
	Direct Labor	0.90	0.90
	Variable Manufacturing Overhead	1.80	1.80
	Fixed Manufacturing Overhead	—	2.70
	Total Unit Cost	$3.20	$5.90

22. *Computing Standard Unit Cost Using Two Possible Activity Bases for Manufacturing Overhead Application.*

a.	**Unit Standard Costs**	**Cowboy Hats**
	Direct Materials	$14.00 per Hat
	Direct Labor ($20 × 1,000 hours) ÷ 2,000 Hats	= $10.00
	Variable Manufacturing Overhead ($8 × 1,000 hours) ÷ 2,000 Hats	= $ 4.00
	Variable, Standard Unit Cost.	= $28.00 per Hat
	Fixed Manufacturing Overhead[a] ($25 × 1,000 hours) ÷ 2,000 Hats	= $12.50
	Full Absorption, Standard Unit Cost	= $40.50 per Hat

[a]Fixed manufacturing overhead rate: $25 = $25,000 ÷ 1,000 hours.

b.	**Unit Standard Costs**	**Cowboy Hats**
	Direct Materials (see above)	$14.00 per Hat
	Direct Labor (see above)	$10.00
	Variable Manufacturing Overhead[a] (0.4 × $20 × 1,000 hours) ÷ 2,000 Hats	= $4.00
	Variable, Standard Unit Cost.	$28.00 per Hat
	Fixed Manufacturing Overhead[b] (1.25 × $20 × 1,000 hours) ÷ 2,000 Hats	= $12.50
	Full Absorption, Standard Unit Cost	$40.50 per Hat

[a]Variable Overhead: 40 percent = $8 ÷ $20.
[b]Fixed Overhead: 125 percent = $25,000 ÷ ($20 × 1,000 hours).

Chapter 4   Accounting for Resource Flows: Cost Accumulation

This chapter shows how the accounting system records and reports the flow of resources in organizations. The accounting system accumulates costs to help answer questions such as these:

What is the cost of a job in a print shop or a CPA firm?

How do the costs of Department A compare with the department's budget?

What is the manufacturing cost of a unit? How does that cost compare to standards?

These and other questions asked by managers require an understanding of how the accounting system works. An understanding of how the accounting system works equips managers to have better input into designing and redesigning the system to provide the needed data.

Chapter 3 shows six different methods of measuring unit manufacturing costs. This chapter describes the accounting procedures used to obtain and report the data to measure these costs for each product costing method.

The focus is on manufacturing organizations because they are the most complex and comprehensive types of organizations. A thorough understanding of accounting in manufacturing will equip you to deal with accounting in all types of organizations. (Chapter 5 applies the analysis to merchandising and service organizations.)

Although the level of technical accounting detail in this chapter is less than that of a text on cost accounting, it does provide a broad overview of the way accounting systems record and report the flow of resources.

Cost Accumulation and Cost Allocation

As discussed in earlier chapters, a managerial accounting system must be designed to serve several purposes. For planning and performance evaluation, costs are accumulated by department or other *responsibility centers*. (A *responsibility center* is simply an *organizational unit*. One or more managers are responsible for the activities in each responsibility center in a company. Examples of responsibility centers are divisions, territories, plants, product lines, and departments.) Costs are then allocated to products to derive inventory costs for external reporting and other purposes.

Exhibit 4.1 shows the relation between cost accumulation and cost allocation for a typical manufacturing firm. A separate purchasing department is responsible for acquiring materials. There are two manufacturing departments, Assembling and

Exhibit 4.1
Relation Between Cost Accumulation and Cost Allocation

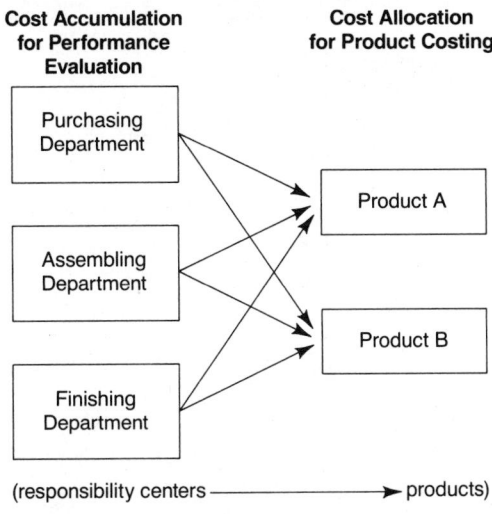

Finishing. The accounting system is designed so that, for control purposes, costs are initially accumulated for the three responsibility centers. The actual cost of materials purchased is accumulated in an account for the Purchasing Department. The costs of direct materials, direct labor, and manufacturing overhead incurred in production are accumulated in separate accounts for the manufacturing departments: Assembling and Finishing. The actual costs incurred are then compared with the standard or budgeted amounts and significant variances are investigated, as discussed later in Chapters 12 and 13. Then the accounting system has served its function of providing data for performance evaluation and control.

For the accounting system to provide product cost information, the data must be allocated along product lines rather than by responsibility centers. This process allocates costs from responsibility centers to products. This allocation process is the primary focus of this chapter.

Fundamental Accounting Model of Resource Flows

Exhibit 4.2 shows how materials are transformed into finished goods. Note that Work-in-Process is the account that both *describes* the transformation of inputs into outputs in a company and *accounts* for the costs incurred in the process. (Later in this chapter we add the accounts that show the sources of inputs.)

In most companies, costs are controlled by department (for example, the Assembly Department or the Finishing Department). Thus, each department has a separate Work-in-Process account, as shown in Exhibit 4.3, which accumulates the costs

Exhibit 4.2
Flow of Costs Through the Accounts

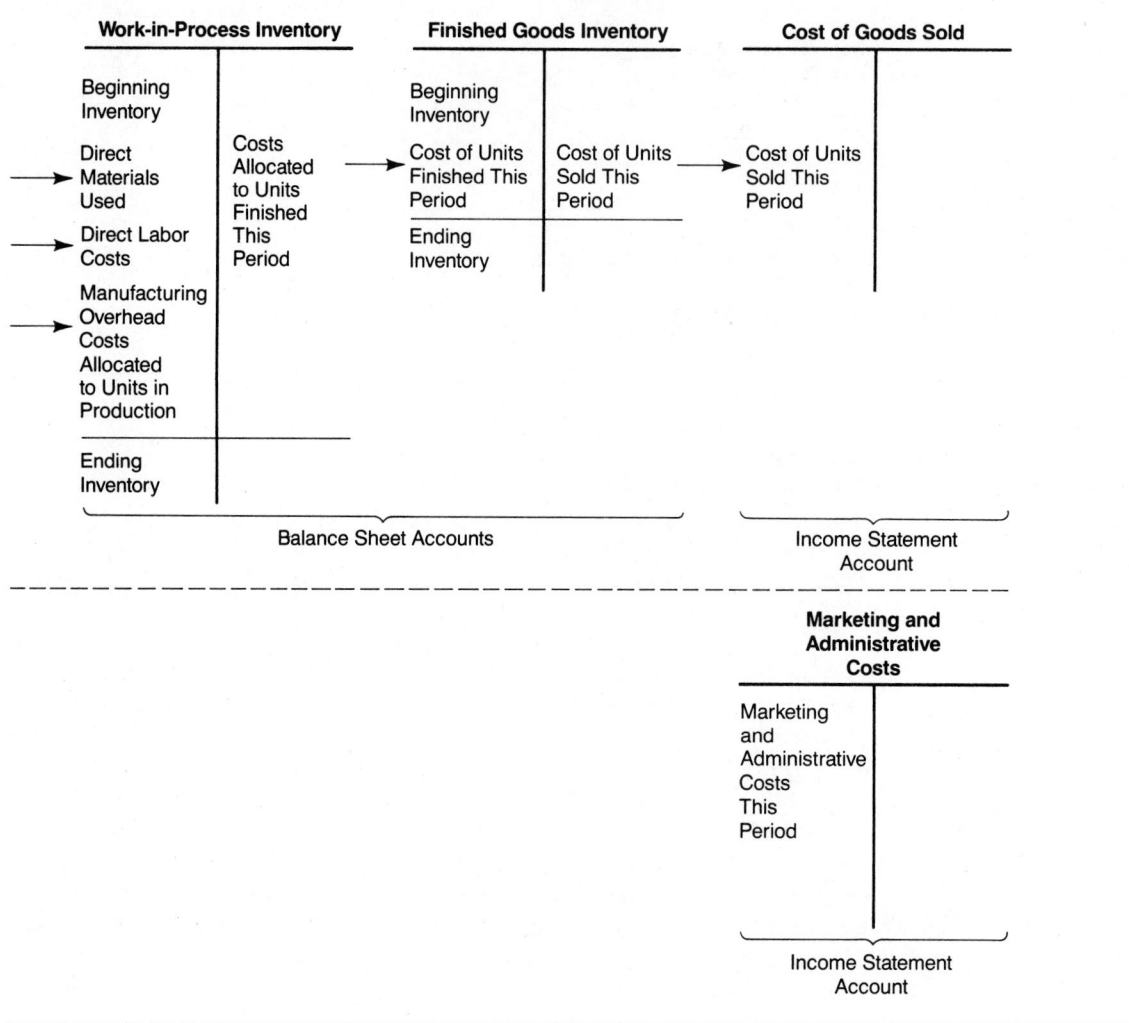

of the department. Department managers are held accountable for the costs accumulated in their departments.

Companies that operate in competitive markets have little direct control over prices paid for materials or prices received for finished goods. Thus, a key factor for the success of a company is how well it can control the conversion costs (conversion costs are direct labor and manufacturing overhead). Companies closely monitor those costs in the Work-in-Process Inventory account.

In short, the accounting system has two purposes in manufacturing: (1) to accumulate costs by responsibility center (department) for performance evaluation and cost control; and (2) to allocate manufacturing costs to units produced for product costing. The next section illustrates the process, using the data from Chapter 3 for Umbrella Makers.

Accounting for the Flow of Resources in a Manufacturing Firm: An Example

Recall from Chapter 3 that there are six major methods for costing products:

| | Cost Measure | | |
Cost Inclusion	Actual Costing	Normal Costing	Standard Costing
Variable Costing	1	3	5
Full Absorption Costing	2	4	6

The following pages describe the flow of costs for each method. Because full absorption costing is required for financial reporting under generally accepted accounting principles, it is more commonly used for product costing than is variable costing. Although we show the flow of costs for variable costing as well, keep in mind that you are most likely to find the full absorption system in practice.

Facts The following information will be used to demonstrate how the accounting system works for each product costing method. Umbrella Makers produced and sold 10,000 umbrellas in June. For now, assume that there were no beginning or ending inventories in June. Actual costs for June were as follows:

Manufacturing Costs:
Direct Materials $11,000
Direct Labor (1,100 hours @ $21) 23,100
Variable Manufacturing Overhead (including $2,000 indirect materials and
    $2,400 indirect labor) 9,600
Fixed Manufacturing Overhead (including $2,100 indirect labor) 12,300
    Total Manufacturing Costs $56,000

Marketing and Administrative Costs
  (all expensed for financial reporting):
Variable (with units sold). . . . . $ 5,000
Fixed 25,000
    Total $30,000
Sales (10,000 umbrellas @ $9) $90,000

Assume for this example that all acquisitions and sales are on account (accounts or wages payable and accounts receivable).

To illustrate the flow of costs through departments, assume that Umbrella Makers has two manufacturing departments:

Department	Responsibility
Work-in-Process: Assembly	Assembles Umbrellas from Direct Materials
Work-in-Process: Finishing	Paints, Inspects, and Packages Umbrellas

In addition, there are a number of support departments such as purchasing, warehousing, and maintenance. The costs of operating these support departments are included in manufacturing overhead.

Exhibit 4.3
Flow of Resources Through Work-in-Process Departments

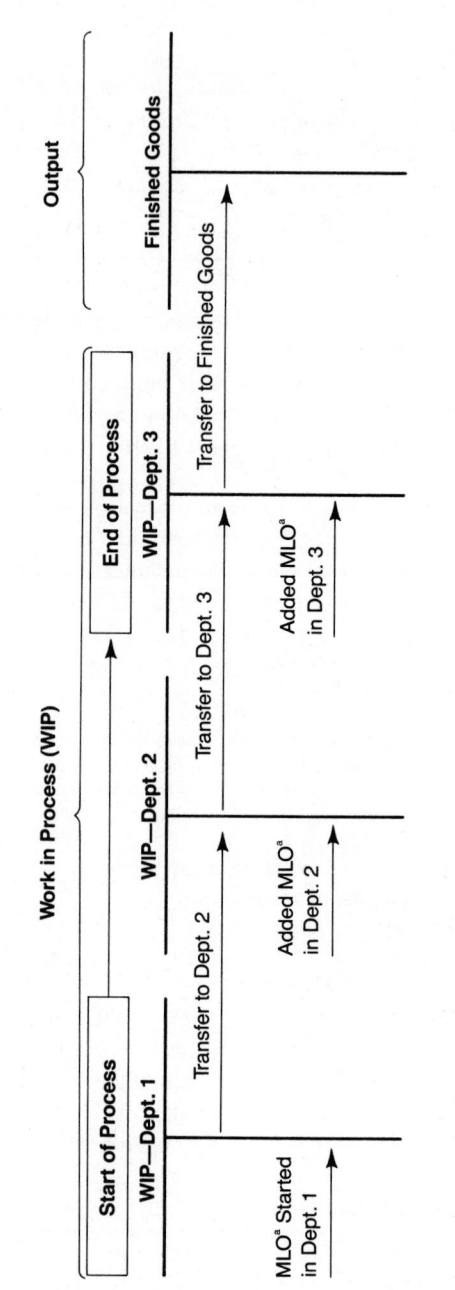

aMLO = Direct Materials, Direct Labor and Manufacturing Overhead.

The manufacturing costs were initially charged to the two production departments as follows:

	Assembly	Finishing	Source of Information
Direct and Indirect Materials Purchased:			Invoices indicating the quantity and price of materials purchased
Direct Materials	$11,000	$ –0–	
Indirect Materials	$ 2,000	$ –0–	
Direct Materials Used	$11,000	$ –0–	Materials requisition requests prepared by the production manager indicating the quantity of materials needed for production
Direct Labor Costs	$16,800 800 Hours	$6,300 300 Hours	Allocation of time between departments based on time cards filled out by workers
Variable Manufacturing Overhead . . .	$ 7,300	$2,300	Many sources
Fixed Manufacturing Overhead	$ 9,100	$3,200	Many sources

Allocating Manufacturing Overhead Costs to Production Departments Overhead costs are indirect costs and often difficult to assign to production departments. At Umbrella Makers, for example, assume that Assembly and Finishing occupy the same building. Assume also that all occupancy costs (for example, rent, building utilities, and building maintenance) are allocated to each department on the basis of square footage.

This is a reasonable, but arbitrary, basis because occupancy costs are not *necessarily incurred* on the basis of square feet. For example, if Finishing were moved to another building, would all of the costs allocated to it be saved? Surely not. The costs allocated to the Assembly Department would go up simply because Finishing no longer occupied the square footage in the building and absorbed a portion of the occupancy costs.

In general, manufacturing overhead costs are allocated among production departments in a reasonable and systematic fashion. There is an inherent arbitrariness in cost allocation, however, when costs that are common to two or more departments are divided among those departments.

Cost Flows: Actual Costing/Full Absorption Costing

Cost Inclusion	Cost Measure		
	Actual Costing	**Normal Costing**	**Standard Costing**
Variable Costing			
Full Absorption Costing			

The following journal entries describe the flow of resources for June based on the above information. These entries are numbered and keyed to the T-accounts in Exhibit 4.4. Tracing the entries through the T-accounts will help you visualize the flow of resources through the company. To save space, each entry summarizes transactions for the month. In fact, many of these revenues and costs would be recorded weekly or even daily. (All transactions are assumed to be on account.)

(1) Materials were purchased.

Materials Inventory	13,000	
Accounts Payable		13,000

(2) Direct materials amounting to $11,000 were requisitioned for production of 10,000 umbrellas, and indirect materials of $2,000 were used in June:

Work-in-Process Inventory: Assembly	11,000	
Variable Manufacturing Overhead.	2,000	
Materials Inventory		13,000

(3) Employees earned wages of $27,600. Direct labor costs were charged to production departments and indirect labor of $4,500 was charged to manufacturing overhead. $2,400 of the indirect labor represented materials handling and other labor assumed to be variable manufacturing overhead; $2,100 of indirect labor represented supervisory salaries that were considered to be a fixed manufacturing cost.

Work-in-Process Inventory: Assembly	16,800	
Work-in-Process Inventory: Finishing.	6,300	
Variable Manufacturing Overhead.	2,400	
Fixed Manufacturing Overhead.	2,100	
Wages Payable		27,600

(4) Manufacturing overhead costs were recorded for rent, power, costs of running the purchasing, factory maintenance and warehousing departments, and all other manufacturing overhead except indirect materials and labor. Other than indirect materials and indirect labor, variable overhead was $5,200; fixed overhead was $10,200.

Variable Manufacturing Overhead.	5,200	
Fixed Manufacturing Overhead.	10,200	
Accounts Payable		15,400

(5) After the variable manufacturing overhead costs for June were recorded, they were allocated to production departments. This entry was made in July for the month of June.

Work-in-Process Inventory: Assembly	7,300	
Work-in-Process Inventory: Finishing.	2,300	
Variable Manufacturing Overhead		9,600

(6) After all of the fixed manufacturing overhead costs for June had been recorded, they were charged to production departments. This entry was made in July for the month of June.

Work-in-Process Inventory: Assembly	9,100	
Work-in-Process Inventory: Finishing.	3,200	
Fixed Manufacturing Overhead		12,300

(7) Assembled units were transferred to Finishing. Goods were transferred from Assembly to Finishing during the month as they were completed, so this entry summarizes those made daily. The total cost of units was $44,200.

Work-in-Process Inventory: Finishing.	44,200	
Work-in-Process Inventory: Assembly		44,200

(8) 10,000 finished umbrellas were transferred to the finished goods warehouse. The total manufacturing cost of these umbrellas was $56,000 ($44,200 from Assembly; $11,800 was additional cost from Finishing).

Finished Goods Inventory	56,000	
Work-in-Process Inventory: Finishing		56,000

(9) Sales of 10,000 umbrellas for the month were made on account for $90,000:

Cost of Goods Sold	56,000	
Finished Goods Inventory		56,000
Accounts Receivable	90,000	
Sales Revenue		90,000

(10) Marketing and administrative costs were incurred and treated as period costs:

Variable Marketing and Administrative Costs	5,000	
Fixed Marketing and Administrative Costs	25,000	
Wages and Accounts Payable		30,000

Exhibit 4.4
Flow of Resources for Umbrella Makers, Full Absorption Costing

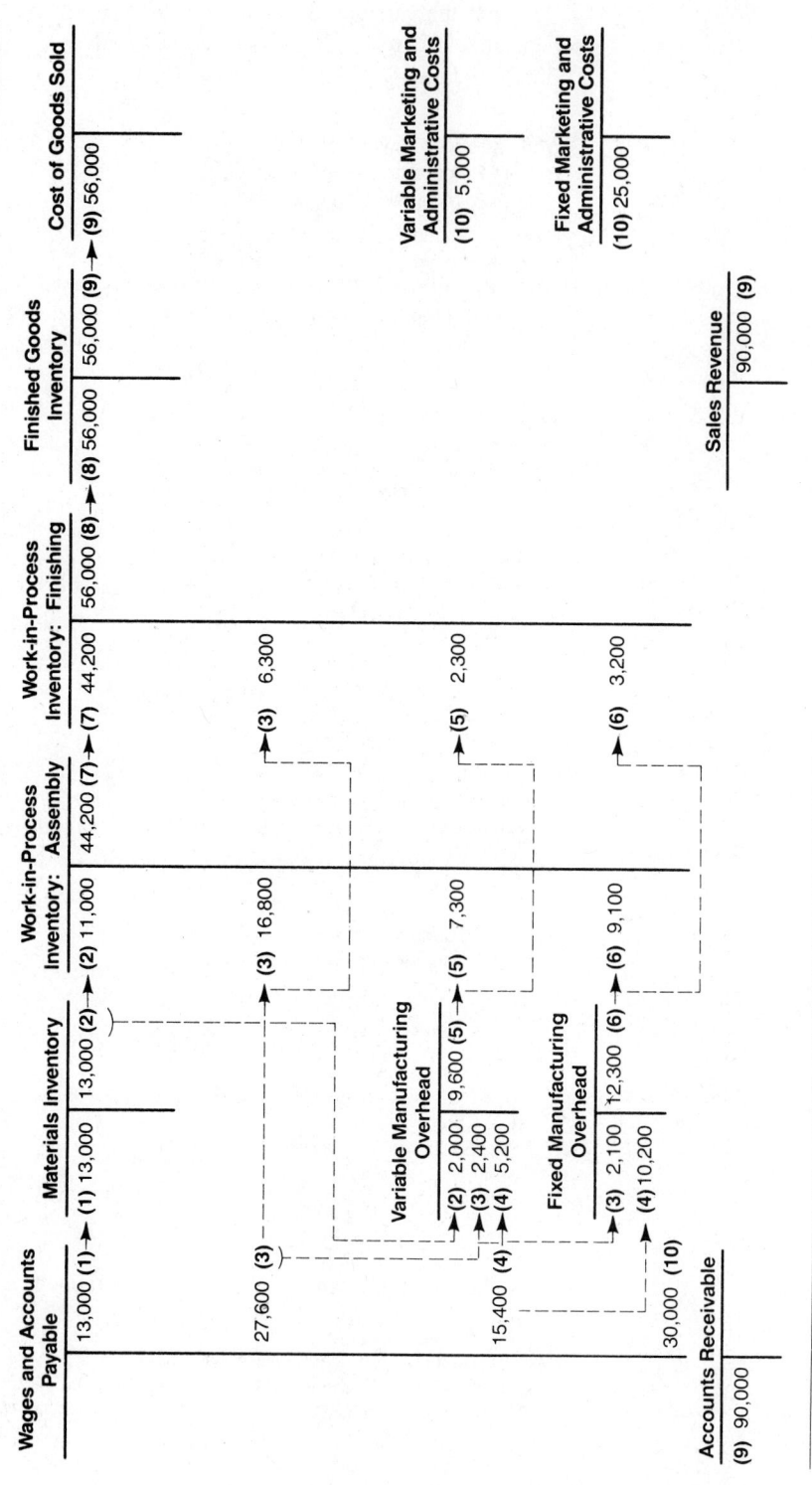

These 10 entries describe the flow of resources from the production and sale of umbrellas for the month of June. To complete the operating cycle, we show the closing entry below and the income statement in Exhibit 4.5.[1]

(11) Close temporary accounts for June:

Sales Revenue	90,000	
Cost of Goods Sold		56,000
Variable Marketing and Administrative Costs		5,000
Fixed Marketing and Administrative Costs		25,000
Retained Earnings		4,000

Exhibit 4.5
UMBRELLA MAKERS
Full Absorption Income Statement
For the Month Ending June 30

Sales Revenue	$90,000
Less Cost of Goods Sold	(56,000)
Gross Margin	$34,000
Less Marketing and Administrative Costs	(30,000)
Operating Profit	$ 4,000

Statement of Cost of Goods Sold

Manufacturing Costs:

Direct Materials	$11,000
Direct Labor	23,100
Variable Manufacturing Overhead	9,600
Fixed Manufacturing Overhead	12,300
Total Manufacturing Costs	$56,000[a]

[a]These are the total costs charged (debited) to Work-in-Process Inventory. Because there is no beginning or ending Work-in-Process or Finished Goods Inventory, total cost of manufacturing the product in June is also the cost of the goods sold.

Comparison of Full Absorption/Actual Costing with Variable and Normal Costing

The previous pages described full absorption/actual costing. The following pages show how variable costing and normal costing differ from full absorption/actual. Recall that these methods differ only in the way manufacturing overhead is treated. These differences are summarized on the next page.

---

[1]We use the term "operating profits" to describe the bottom line of the "income" statement. We use that term whenever the income statement is prepared for internal use rather than for financial reporting in compliance with generally accepted accounting principles (GAAP). We also distinguish "operating profits" from an economic notion of "profits." Economic profits are sales revenue minus the sum of operating costs recorded in the accounting records *and* implicit opportunity costs, which are not recorded in the accounting records. Operating profits are sales revenue minus only the operating costs recorded in the accounting records.

	Actual Costing	Normal Costing
Variable Costing: Variable Manufacturing Overhead	Actual Costs Assigned to Products	Costs Assigned to Products Using Predetermined Rates
Fixed Manufacturing Overhead	Actual Costs Treated as Period Costs	Actual Costs Treated as Period Costs
Full Absorption Costing: Variable Manufacturing Overhead	Actual Costs Assigned to Products	Costs Assigned to Products Using Predetermined Rates
Fixed Manufacturing Overhead	Actual Costs Assigned to Products	Costs Assigned to Products Using Predetermined Rates

A comprehensive comparison of these four methods appears in Exhibit 4.6. Part A shows overhead cost flows under full absorption/actual costing, which were previously described in Exhibit 4.4. You may find it helpful to refer to Exhibit 4.6 as we compare and contrast the other methods.

Note that the *actual costs incurred* for materials, labor, and overhead are identical, regardless of method. Direct materials and direct labor charged to production departments are identical for each method. Revenues, marketing costs, and administrative costs are unaffected by the choice of product costing method. The treatment of manufacturing overhead explains the entire difference in product costs among the four methods.

Cost Flows: Actual Costing/Variable Costing

	Cost Measure		
Cost Inclusion	Actual Costing	Normal Costing	Standard Costing
Variable Costing			
Full Absorption Costing			

When *variable* costing is used, fixed manufacturing costs are *not* charged to Work-in-Process Inventory and subsequently carried to Finished Goods Inventory and to Cost of Goods Sold. Instead, these costs are written off as a period cost. Parts A and B of Exhibit 4.6 highlight these differences. Self-Study Problem No. 1 at the end of the chapter presents cost flows through T-accounts under variable costing.

Exhibit 4.6
Comparison of Overhead Treatment Under Four Different Product Costing Methods

	Actual Overhead Cost	Applied to Work-in-Process		Under - or Overapplied Overhead	Period Cost
		Assembly	Finishing		

A. Full Absorption, Actual Costing

Variable	$ 9,600	$7,300	$2,300	
Fixed	$12,300	$9,100	$3,200	

B. Variable Costing, Actual Costing

Variable	$ 9,600	$7,300	$2,300		
Fixed	$12,300				$12,300

C. Full Absorption, Normal Costing

Variable	$ 9,600	$7,200 [a]	$2,700 [b]	$300 Overapplied	
Fixed	$12,300	$8,000 [c]	$3,000 [d]	$1,300 Underapplied	

D. Variable Costing, Normal Costing

Variable	$ 9,600	$7,200 [a]	$2,700 [b]	$300 Overapplied	
Fixed	$12,300				$12,300

[a] $9 per direct labor hour × 800 direct labor hours worked in the Assembly Department.
[b] $9 per direct labor hour × 300 direct labor hours worked in the Finishing Department.
[c] $10 per direct labor hour × 800 direct labor hours worked in the Assembly Department.
[d] $10 per direct labor hour × 300 direct labor hours worked in the Finishing Department.

Cost Flows: Normal Costing/Full Absorption Costing

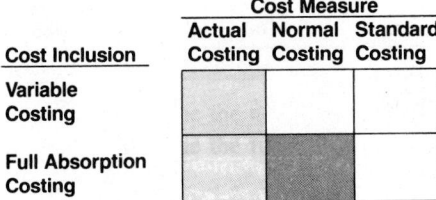

	Cost Measure		
Cost Inclusion	Actual Costing	Normal Costing	Standard Costing
Variable Costing			
Full Absorption Costing			

Normal costing differs from actual costing in the treatment of manufacturing overhead. As discussed in Chapter 3, manufacturing overhead is charged to production using a predetermined rate. This "normalizes" product costs and allows companies to estimate product costs before the actual overhead costs are known.

The accounting difference between actual and normal costing can be seen by comparing the following manufacturing overhead accounts:

Actual Costing Manufacturing Overhead		**Normal Costing Manufacturing Overhead**	
Accumulation of actual costs.	Application of actual costs to units produced.	(Actual) Accumulation of actual costs.	(Applied) Application of normal costs to units produced.

Actual and applied costs are generally not equal in normal costing, so the manufacturing overhead account is closed to an overhead adjustment account at the end of the period, as shown in the following example.

Example. For Umbrella Makers, assume that the predetermined rates are as follows:

$$\text{Variable Manufacturing Overhead Rate} = \frac{\text{Estimated Variable Manufacturing Overhead for the Year}}{\text{Estimated Direct Labor Hours for the Year}}$$

$$= \frac{\$108,000}{12,000 \text{ Hours}}$$

$$= \$9.00 \text{ per Direct Labor Hour.}$$

$$\text{Fixed Manufacturing Overhead Rate} = \frac{\text{Estimated Fixed Manufacturing Overhead for the Year}}{\text{Estimated Direct Labor Hours for the Year}}$$

$$= \frac{\$120,000}{12,000 \text{ Hours}}$$

$$= \$10.00 \text{ per Direct Labor Hour.}$$

The amounts charged to production under full absorption normal costing are as follows:

		Rate		Actual Direct Labor Hours		Total Charged to Work-in-Process
Variable Manufacturing Overhead	Assembly . . .	$9	×	800	=	$7,200
	Finishing . . .	$9	×	300	=	$2,700
Fixed Manufacturing Overhead	Assembly . . .	$10	×	800	=	$8,000
	Finishing . . .	$10	×	300	=	$3,000

Part C of Exhibit 4.6 shows the debit to Work-in-Process for manufacturing overhead under *full absorption/normal* costing for Umbrella Makers. This can be compared with part A to see the difference between full absorption *actual* and full absorption *normal* costing.

The actual overhead does not equal the amount applied or charged to Work-in-Process; hence, there is under- or overapplied overhead computed as follows:

	(1) **Actual Cost**	(2) **Amount Applied**	**Underapplied** (1) − (2)	**Overapplied** (2) − (1)
Variable Overhead	$ 9,600	$7,200 + $2,700 = $ 9,900	—	$300
Fixed Overhead	$12,300	$8,000 + $3,000 = $11,000	$1,300	—

These under- or overapplied overhead accounts are entered in a temporary account, as shown in the T-accounts below, which is closed at the end of each accounting period. The amount of under- or overapplied overhead is usually treated as a period cost expensed for managerial purposes.[2]

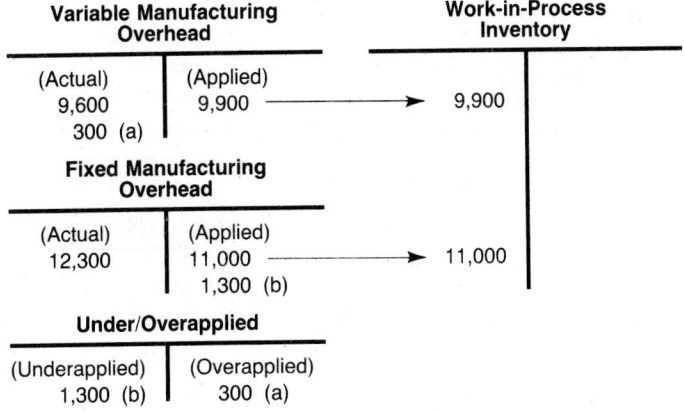

We caution decision makers and managers who use this information for performance evaluation to note that the amount charged or applied to Work-in-Process under normal costing is *not actual* manufacturing overhead. For example, assume that the manufacturing vice-president at Umbrella Makers wants to know what the actual variable overhead costs for each of the two production departments were for June. The vice-president's assistant reports: "Assembly's costs were $7,200 and Finishing's costs were $2,700." Is this statement correct? No. Those amounts are *normal* costs, not actual costs.

---

[2]The under- or overapplied overhead is sometimes "pro-rated" or allocated between units sold and those not sold, particularly if the under- or overapplied amount is material to the amounts shown on financial statements. For example, if 80 percent of current period's production is sold, many companies will allocate 80 percent of the under- or overapplied overhead to cost of goods sold on the income statement, and 20 percent to the increase in inventory on the balance sheet. Other companies would not "pro-rate" under- or overapplied overhead, but would allocate all of it to cost of goods sold or show all of it as a period cost or expense on the income statement. More detailed explanations of this procedure appear in cost accounting books.

In short, users of accounting information should know whether the data are from an actual or normal costing system. Actual and normal costing not only report different unit costs, as we saw in Chapter 3, but also the amounts charged to Work-in-Process accounts differ under these two systems. Users who want actual cost data, when their companies use a normal costing system, will usually have to make special efforts to get them. On the other hand, some users prefer the normal cost data because normalizing the data smoothes periodic fluctuations in actual costs. There are no clear-cut theoretical advantages of one system over the other. Like many managerial accounting alternatives, situation-specific advantages and disadvantages dictate whether a company uses normal costing, actual costing, or both.

Cost Flows: Normal Costing/Variable Costing

Cost Inclusion	Actual Costing	Normal Costing	Standard Costing
Variable Costing			
Full Absorption Costing			

Only a slight modification from normal/full absorption is needed for normal/variable costing. Actual fixed manufacturing overhead costs are treated as period costs; only *variable* manufacturing overhead is applied to Work-in-Process accounts.

Self-Study Problem 1 presents comparative cost flows through T-accounts and comparative income statements for each method. We encourage you to work through Self-Study Problem 1 to see how the accounting is different for each of these four product cost methods.

Cost Flows: Standard Costing

Cost Inclusion	Actual Costing	Normal Costing	Standard Costing
Variable Costing			
Full Absorption Costing			

Many organizations use standard costs for planning and performance evaluation. In addition, standard costs may be used to value inventory and measure the amount of cost of goods sold for external financial reporting. The use of standards can save considerable clerical costs. When standard costs are used for this purpose, the standard costs replace actual production costs in the accounting records.

Standard Costs Versus Standard Cost Systems We distinguish between standard costs and standard cost *systems*. Many organizations, including banks, hospitals, fast food franchises, and governmental units to name a few, use standard costs for planning and performance evaluation, without incorporating standard costs in the accounting record-keeping system. That is, comparisons of actual costs and standard costs are made "off the books." With a standard cost *system,* standard costs are part of the accounting record-keeping system. Standard cost *systems* are frequently found in manufacturing operations making a relatively homogeneous product (for example, particular product lines of steel, automobiles, electronic calculators). Standard cost *systems* are found less frequently in operations that make customized, heterogeneous units (for example, construction contractors making large construction projects, or defense contractors making prototype military hardware).

When a standard costing *system* is used in manufacturing, the *standard cost* of each unit (for example, each umbrella) is charged to Work-in-Process. Differences between the actual costs incurred to produce some quantity of output and the standard costs allowed for that quantity of output are called "variances." These variance accounts reconcile actual and standard costs. (See Exhibit 4.7.)

Exhibit 4.7
Flow of Manufacturing Costs:
Standard Cost System

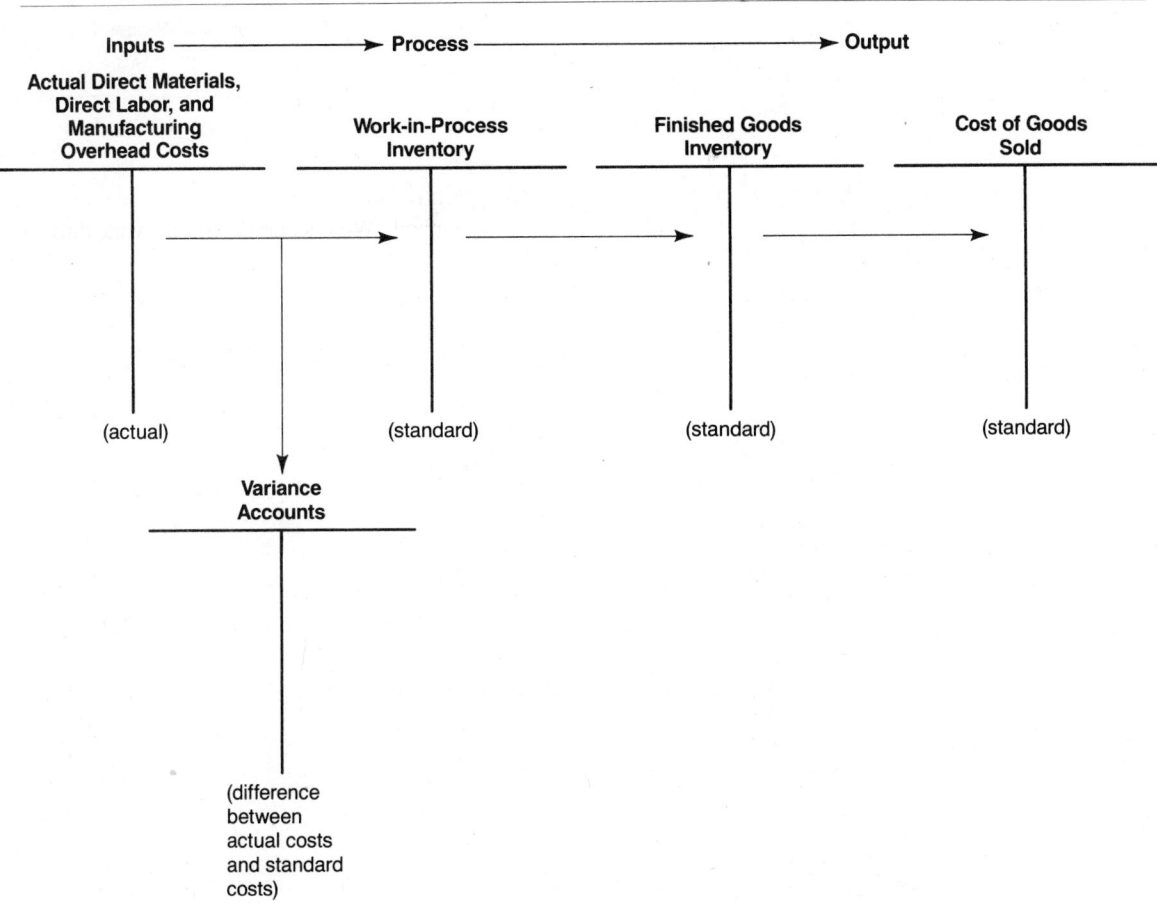

Example Based on the facts for Umbrella Makers given in Chapter 3, the standard direct materials cost per umbrella is $1.00. Umbrella Makers produced 10,000 umbrellas in June, so the total standard direct materials costs for June were $10,000 (= $1.00 × 10,000 umbrellas). However, Umbrella Makers actually spent $11,000 on direct materials for the 10,000 umbrellas produced in June, so there is a variance of $1,000.

The flow of costs for this transaction is shown in Exhibit 4.8. The journal entry is

Work-in-Process Inventory: Assembly (Standard)	10,000	
Direct Materials Variance (Unfavorable).	1,000	
Accounts Payable: Materials (Actual)		11,000

Exhibit 4.8
UMBRELLA MAKERS
Flow of Standard Direct Materials Costs

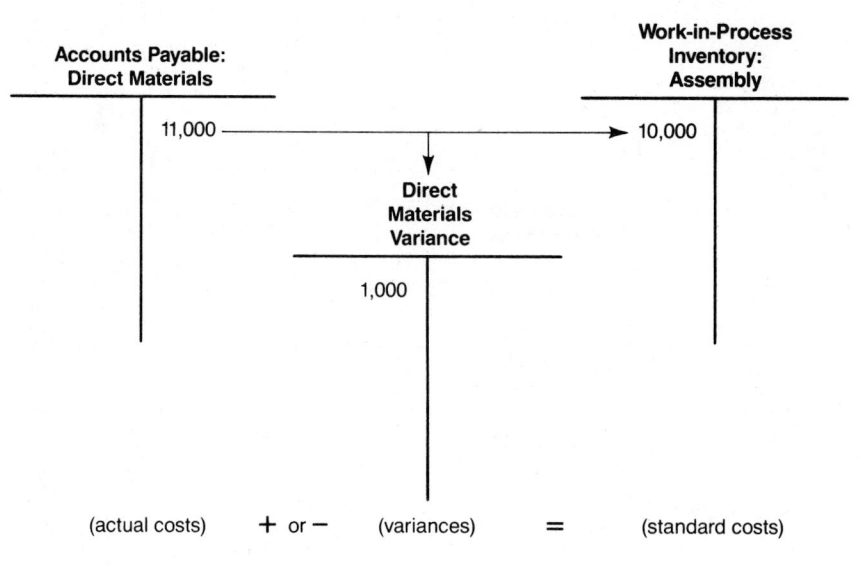

The following labels are used to describe cost variances:

		Label
When	Actual Cost > Standard Cost:	"Unfavorable" Variance
	Actual Cost < Standard Cost:	"Favorable" Variance.

The direct materials variance in the preceding example is "unfavorable" because actual costs exceed standard cost.

The complete model of standard cost accounting systems, including resource flows through T-accounts and journal entries, appears in the appendix to Chapter 13.

In summary, using a standard cost system means that the costs charged to units produced will be at standard cost, not actual costs. All of the costs of production in Work-in-Process appear at standard cost. The units in Finished Goods Inventory and in Cost of Goods Sold on the income statement appear at standard cost. The differences between actual and standard costs (the variances) are carried to the income statement. For Umbrella Makers, the total actual costs incurred and the standard costs allowed for the production of 10,000 umbrellas in June are shown in Exhibit 4.9 and the income statement is presented in Exhibit 4.10.

Exhibit 4.9
UMBRELLA MAKERS
Standard Costs and Variances

	Total Actual Costs Incurred	Standard Costs Allowed		Variances
		Per Unit	Total (for 10,000 units)	
Direct Materials . . .	$11,000	$1.00	$10,000	$1,000 Unfavorable
Direct Labor	23,100	2.00	20,000	3,100 Unfavorable
Variable Manufacturing Overhead.	9,600	.90	9,000	600 Unfavorable
Fixed Manufacturing Overhead.	12,300	1.00	10,000	2,300 Unfavorable
Total	$56,000	$4.90	$49,000	$7,000 Unfavorable

Standard Costing/Variable Costing

Cost Inclusion	Cost Measure		
	Actual Costing	Normal Costing	Standard Costing
Variable Costing			
Full Absorption Costing			

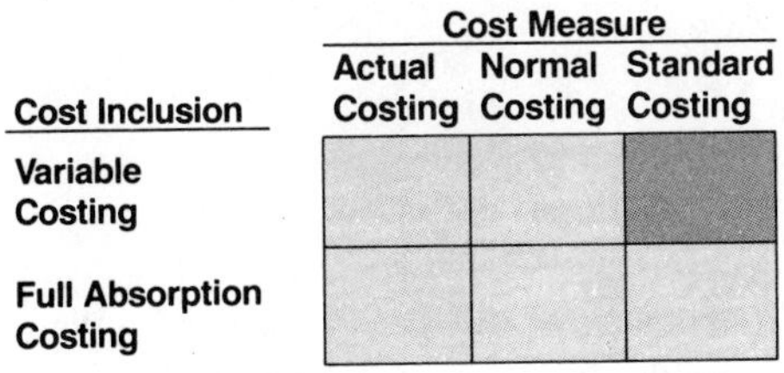

Under variable costing, only variable manufacturing costs are treated as product costs (that is, unit costs). Hence, standard costs would include only variable manufacturing costs.

Exhibit 4.10
UMBRELLA MAKERS
Standard Cost Income Statement
for the Month Ending June 30

Sales Revenue		$90,000
Cost of Goods Sold, at Standard Cost		(49,000)
Gross Margin Before Variances		$41,000
Manufacturing Variances:		
Direct Materials	$(1,000)	
Direct Labor	(3,100)	
Variable Manufacturing Overhead	(600)	
Fixed Manufacturing Overhead	(2,300)	
Total Variances (unfavorable)[a]		(7,000)
Gross Margin		$34,000
Marketing and Administrative Costs		(30,000)
Operating Profits		$ 4,000

[a]These variances are "unfavorable," so they are subtracted from sales revenue to arrive at gross margin. Variances that are "favorable" (that is, actual cost is less than standard cost) would be added in deriving gross margin. For example, suppose that all facts are the same as above, except that the manufacturing variances are favorable. Then the format would be

Sales Revenue		$90,000
Cost of Goods Sold, at Standard Cost		(49,000)
Gross Margin Before Variances		$41,000
Manufacturing Variances:		
Direct Materials	$1,000	
Direct Labor	3,100	
Variable Manufacturing Overhead	600	
Fixed Manufacturing Overhead	2,300	
Total Variances (favorable)		$ 7,000
Gross Margin		$48,000
Marketing and Administrative Costs		(30,000)
Operating Profits		$18,000

Flow of Costs When There Are Inventory Balances

Accounting systems are based on the following *basic accounting equation:*

$$\text{Beginning Balance} + \text{Transfers In} = \text{Transfers Out} + \text{Ending Balance}.$$

In symbols:

$$BB \quad + \quad TI \quad = \quad TO \quad + \quad EB.$$

This equation applies to all accounts. Our examples of cost flows so far have shown TI and TO, but not BB and EB.

We present this equation for two reasons: (1) it is a fundamental equality in accounting; and (2) knowing this equation can help you to solve for unknown data, as demonstrated by the following example.

Example Lay-Z Manufacturing Company keeps only partial records of cost flows. (The company president claims: "We spend our money on production and marketing; we don't waste it on accounting systems.") You are able to piece together the following data for last year:

Account	Beginning Balance, Dec. 1	Ending Balance, Dec. 31	Other Information
Accounts Payable (for direct and indirect production materials only) . .	$10,000	$15,000	$245,000 Paid on Account During the Month
Materials Inventory	$18,000	$21,000	None
Indirect Materials Used			$31,000 Used During the Month; All Charged to Manufacturing Overhead
Wages Payable.	$7,000	$4,000	$140,000 Used During the Month (10,000 hours at $14 per hour); $14,000 Indirect labor, $126,000 Direct Labor
Manufacturing Overhead (variable and fixed are combined)	–0–	$2,000 Underapplied	Applied at a Predetermined Rate of $12 per Hour Times Actual Direct Labor Hours
Work-in-Process Inventory	?	$36,000	—
Finished Goods Inventory	$18,000	$22,000	—
Cost of Goods Sold	—	—	$510,000 for the Month

Exhibit 4.11 shows the above information in T-accounts. The unknown amounts can be found as follows, using the basic accounting equation and the above information (it may be helpful to put the amounts in Exhibit 4.11 as they are derived below):

	Beginning Balance	+	Transfers in	=	Transfers out	+	Ending Balance
(1) Accounts payable	BB	+	TI	=	TO	+	EB
	$10,000	+	TI	=	$245,000	+	$15,000
			TI	=	$245,000	+	$15,000 − $10,000
			TI	=	$250,000, Total Materials Purchased		
(2) Total Materials Used . . .	BB	+	TI	=	TO	+	EB
	$18,000	+	$250,000 [from **(1)** above]	=	TO	+	$21,000
			TO	=	$18,000 + $250,000 − $21,000		
			TO	=	$247,000, Total Direct and Indirect Materials Used		
(3) Direct Materials Used . . .	Total Materials Used [from **(2)** above]	−	Indirect Materials Used	=	Direct Materials Used		
	$247,000	−	$31,000	=	$216,000, Direct Materials Used		
(4) Wages Payable	BB	+	TI	=	TO	+	EB
	$7,000	+	$140,000	=	TO	+	$4,000
			TO	=	$7,000 + $140,000 − $4,000		
			TO	=	$143,000, Wage Payments		

Exhibit 4.11
Lay-Z Manufacturing Company
Incomplete Description of Manufacturing Cost Flows for the Month of December[a]

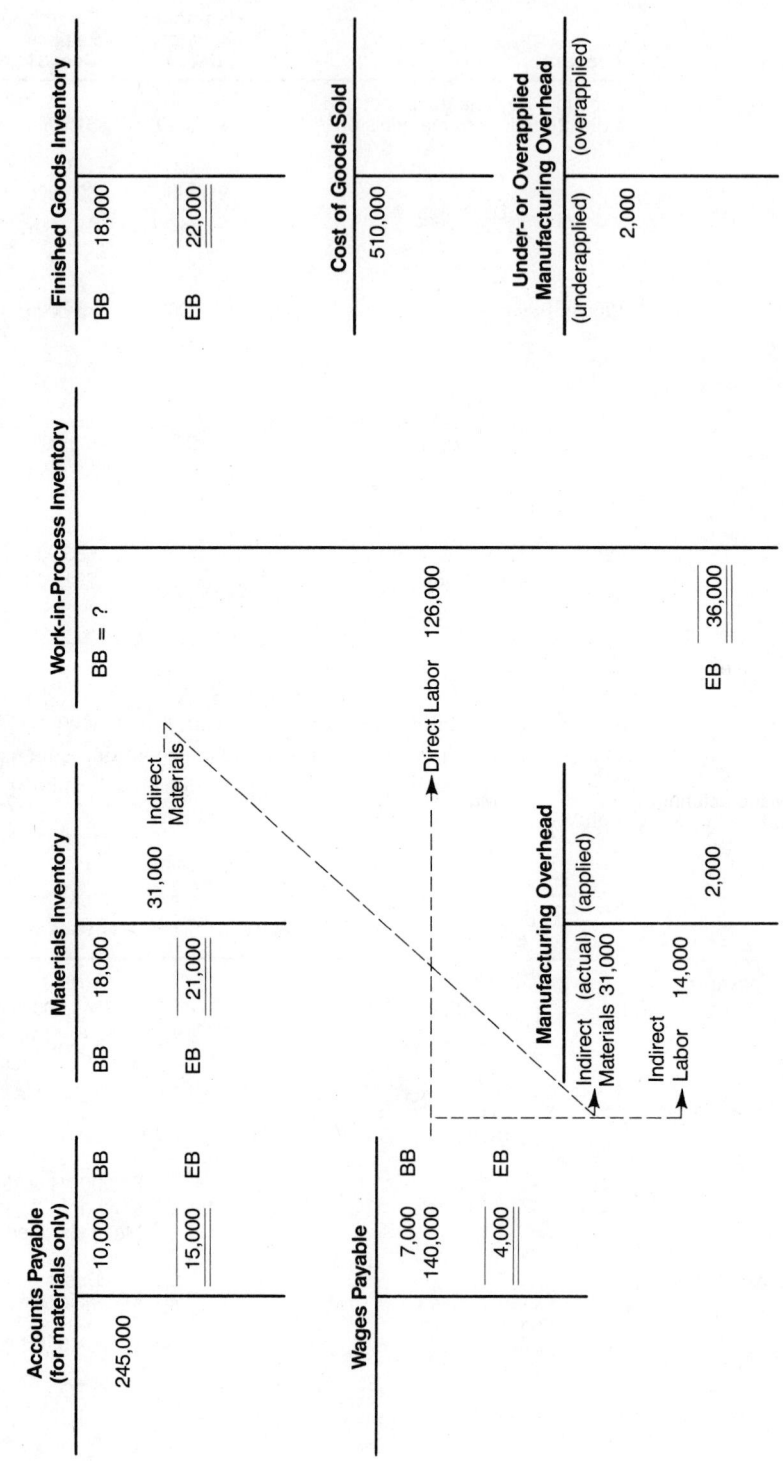

[a]BB = beginning balance.
 EB = ending balance.

	Beginning Balance	+	Transfers in	=	Transfers out	+	Ending Balance

(5) Manufacturing Overhead Applied to Production (MOH) . . . . .

$$MOH = \$12 \text{ per Hour} \times \frac{\text{Direct Labor}}{\text{Hours Worked (DLH)}}$$

$$DLH = \frac{\$126,000 \text{ Charged to Production}}{\$14 \text{ per Hour Labor Wage Rate}}$$

DLH = 9,000

MOH = $12 × 9,000 DLH

= $108,000

At this point, we are unable to solve for Work-in-Process Inventory unknowns because there are two—BB and TO; hence, we proceed with Finished Goods Inventory.

(6) Finished Goods Inventory

BB + TI = TO + EB

$18,000 + TI = TO + $22,000

TO = $510,000, Cost of Goods Sold, so

TI = $510,000 + $22,000 − $18,000

TI = $514,000, which is also the Work-in-Process Inventory Transfer out (TO)

(7) Work-in-Process Inventory

BB + TI = TO + EB

BB + ($216,000 + $126,000 + $108,000) = $514,000 + $36,000

BB = $514,000 + $36,000 − ($216,000 + $126,000 + $108,000)

BB = $550,000 − $450,000 = $100,000

(8) Actual Manufacturing Overhead . . . .

= Manufacturing Overhead Applied to Production + Underapplied Overhead

= $108,000 + $2,000

= $110,000

An amount of $31,000 has already been recorded for indirect materials and $14,000 for indirect labor, so the balance of actual manufacturing overhead to be charged is $65,000 (= $110,000 − $31,000 − $14,000).

Exhibit 4.12 shows the flow of manufacturing costs using the amounts just derived.

Relation of the Flow of Costs to the Cost of Goods Manufactured and Sold Statement

The presence of inventories complicates the statements of cost of goods manufactured and sold. In general, these statements summarize the flow of costs in T-accounts as shown in Exhibit 4.13. On the left of the exhibit is the basic accounting equation restated from BB + TI = TO + EB to TI + BB − EB = TO; the middle presents the descriptions used in the statements; the right shows the activity in the manufacturing cost accounts. You may not remember the format of these statements, but if you remember the basic accounting equation, you will know all of the elements of these statements.

Exhibit 4.12
LAY-Z MANUFACTURING COMPANY
Complete Description of Manufacturing Cost Flows for the Month of December[a]

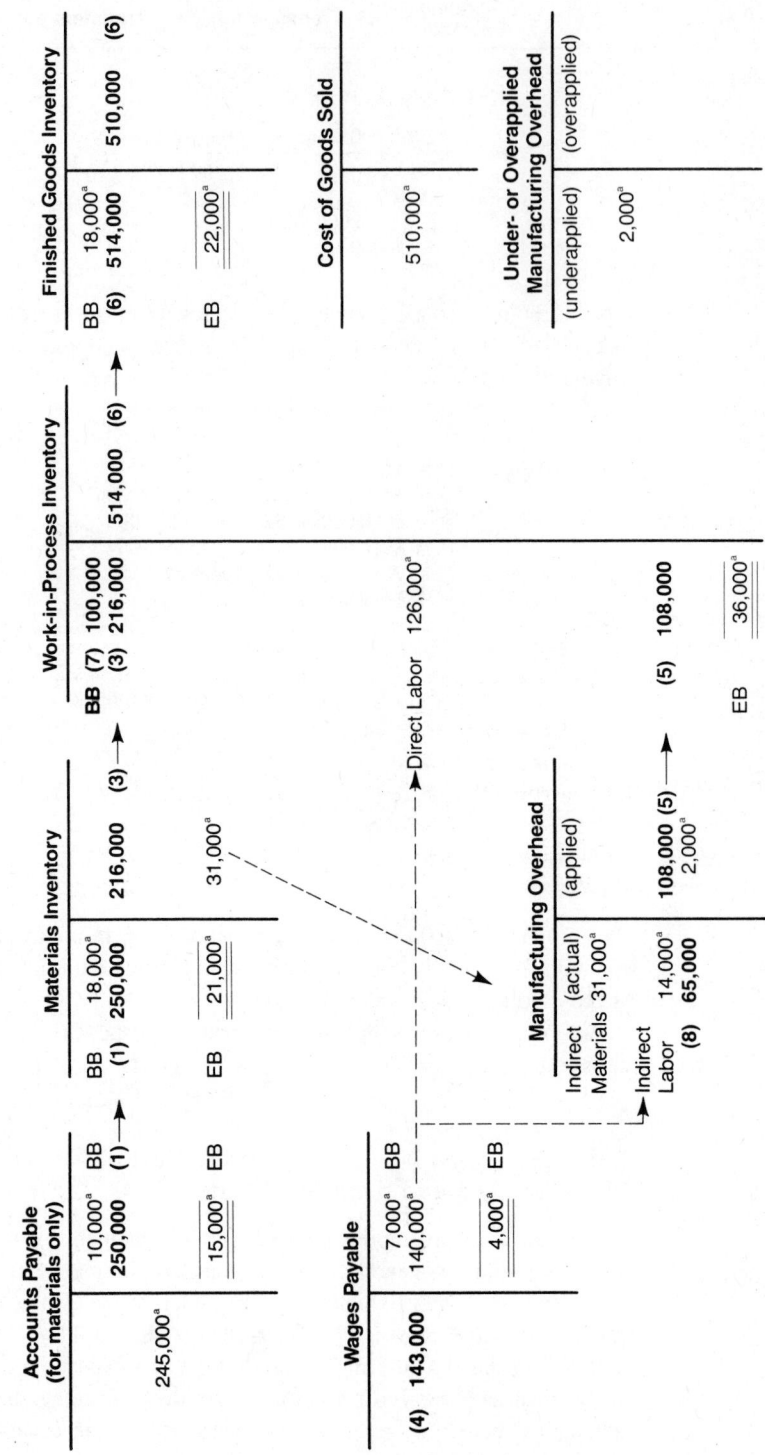

[a]These amounts were given in the text.
[b]Numbers in parentheses correspond to solution steps in text.

Exhibit 4.13
Relation Between the Flow of Costs and Cost of Goods Manufactured and Sold

Accounting Equation	Statement Description	Activity in Account
Work-in-Process Inventory		
TI	Manufacturing Costs Incurred During the Period	Materials, Labor, and Overhead Debited to Work-in-Process During the Period
+ BB	+ Beginning Work-in-Process Inventory	Beginning Balance
− EB	− Ending Work-in-Process Inventory	Ending Balance
= TO	= Cost of Goods Manufactured During the Period[a]	Amount Credited to Work-in-Process and Debited to Finished Goods During the Period
Finished Goods Inventory		
TI	Cost of Goods Manufactured During the Period	Same as Work-in-Process Transfer Out
+ BB	+ Beginning Finished Goods Inventory	Beginning Balance
− EB	− Ending Finished Goods Inventory	Ending Balance
= TO	= Cost of Goods Sold During the Period	Amount Credited to Finished Goods and Debited to Cost of Goods Sold

[a]Cost of goods manufactured could also be called "cost of goods *finished* during the period."

Exhibit 4.14 shows how the activity for Lay-Z Manufacturing Company would be presented in a statement format. To complete the income statement in Exhibit 4.14, assume that sales revenue was $900,000, and marketing and administrative costs were $250,000 for December. Note how the statement of cost of goods manufactured and sold describes the flow of costs starting with material, labor, and overhead inputs at the top, and ending with the sale of the finished product at the bottom. The format of this statement varies from company to company, but it always includes the amounts in the basic accounting equation.

Summary

This chapter discusses accounting methods of recording and reporting cost flows for transforming inputs into output. Part of the accounting function for both external reporting and managerial purposes is to trace the flow of resources and account for them through this process.

In manufacturing, costs of inputs are accumulated in work-in-process departments as production occurs. As these work-in-process departments are the basic responsibility centers in manufacturing, the costs collected in those departments provide important information for performance evaluation and cost control. The information is also needed for product costing for external financial reporting and managerial decision making. Thus, Work-in-Process Inventory accounts are the focal point of accounting in manufacturing organizations.

Exhibit 4.14
LAY-Z MANUFACTURING COMPANY
for the Month Ending December 31

Income Statement

Sales Revenue	$900,000
Less:	
Cost of Goods Sold	(510,000)
Underapplied Overhead	(2,000)[a]
Gross Margin	$388,000
Less Marketing and	
Administrative Costs	(250,000)
Operating Profit	$138,000

Statement of Cost of Goods Manufactured and Sold

Manufacturing Costs:		
Direct Materials:		
Beginning Inventory	$ 18,000	
Add Purchases	250,000	
Materials Available	$268,000	
Less: Indirect Materials Used	(31,000)	
Ending Inventory	(21,000)	
Direct Materials Used		$216,000
Direct Labor		126,000
Manufacturing Overhead		
Applied		108,000
Total Manufacturing Costs		$450,000
Add Beginning Work-in-Process		
Inventory		100,000
Less Ending Work-in-Process		
Inventory		(36,000)
Cost of Goods Manufactured		$514,000
Add Beginning Finished Goods		
Inventory		18,000
Less Ending Finished Goods		
Inventory		(22,000)
Cost of Goods Sold		$510,000

[a]Under- or overapplied overhead is treated as a period cost in this example; it is not pro-rated to inventories and cost of goods sold.

Product costs in manufacturing comprise direct materials, direct labor, and manufacturing overhead. Direct materials and direct labor can be traced directly to products, but manufacturing overhead usually must be allocated or applied to products using an overhead rate times some "basis," such as direct labor hours. Under variable costing, only *variable* manufacturing overhead need be allocated to units using this rate times basis. Under full absorption costing, both variable and fixed overhead are allocated to units.

The Manufacturing Overhead accounts accumulate actual costs on the left/debit side and allocate those costs to Work-in-Process Inventory on the right/credit side. The costs that are allocated depend on the costing method used:

Costing Method	Costs Allocated to Work-in-Process Inventory
Actual	Actual Costs
Normal	*Predetermined Rate* Times *Actual Basis* (for example, predetermined rate times actual direct labor hours worked)
Standard	*Predetermined Rate* Times *Standard Basis* (for example, predetermined rate times standard direct labor hours allowed for the actual output produced)

When standard costing is used, Work-in-Process is charged with the standard cost of each unit produced. This standard is a predetermined cost allowance or norm. The difference between the actual costs incurred and the standard costs allowed for the actual output produced is a "variance." Variances are usually computed for each input (that is, each category of direct materials, direct labor, and manufacturing overhead) and for each responsibility center (for example, the Assembly Department and the Finishing Department).

The basic accounting equation,

$$\frac{\text{Beginning}}{\text{Balance}} + \frac{\text{Transfers}}{\text{In}} = \frac{\text{Transfers}}{\text{Out}} + \frac{\text{Ending}}{\text{Balance}}$$

$$\text{BB} + \text{TI} = \text{TO} + \text{EB}.$$

relates the flow of costs through the accounts to beginning and ending inventory balances. This equation can be helpful for finding unknown balances and cost flows.

Problem 1 for Self-Study

Comprehensive Review Problem

Show the flow of manufacturing costs through accounts for the information in the text example, Umbrella Makers, for each of the following four product costing methods:

a. Full absorption/actual costing.

b. Variable costing/actual costing.

c. Full absorption/normal costing.

d. Variable costing/normal costing.

Present income statements for each of these four methods.

124

Suggested Solution

a. Full-Absorption Costing/Actual Costing

Accounts and Wages Payable

13,000 (1)	
27,600 (3)	
15,400 (4)	

Materials Inventory

(1) 13,000	13,000 (2)

Variable Manufacturing Overhead

(2) 2,000	9,600 (5A)
(3) 2,400	
(4) 5,200	

Fixed Manufacturing Overhead

(3) 2,100	12,300 (6A)
(4) 10,200	

Work-in-Process: Assembly

(2) 11,000	44,200 (7A)
(3) 16,800	
(5A) 7,300	
(6A) 9,100	

Work-in-Process: Finishing

(7A) 44,200	56,000 (8A)
(3) 6,300	
(5A) 2,300	
(6A) 3,200	

Finished Goods

(8A) 56,000	56,000 (9A)

Cost of Goods Sold

(9A) 56,000	

b. Variable Costing/Actual Costing

Accounts and Wages Payable

13,000 (1)	
27,600 (3)	
15,400 (4)	

Materials Inventory

(1) 13,000	13,000 (2)

Variable Manufacturing Overhead

(2) 2,000	9,600 (5B)
(3) 2,400	
(4) 5,200	

Fixed Manufacturing Overhead

(3) 2,100	
(4) 10,200	

Work-in-Process Assembly

(2) 11,000	35,100 (7B)
(3) 16,800	
(5B) 7,300	

Work-in-Process: Finishing

(7B) 35,100	43,700 (8B)
(3) 6,300	
(5B) 2,300	

Finished Goods

(8B) 43,700	43,700 (9B)

Cost of Goods Sold

(9B) 43,700	

c. Full-Absorption Costing/Normal Costing

Accounts and Wages Payable
	13,000 (1)
	27,600 (3)

15,400 (4)

Materials Inventory
(1) 13,000	13,000 (2)

Variable Manufacturing Overhead
(Actual)	(Applied)
(2) 2,000	
(3) 2,400	
(4) 5,200	9,900 (5C)
(12) 300	

Fixed Manufacturing Overhead
(Actual)	(Applied)
(3) 2,100	
(4) 10,200	11,000 (6C)
	1,300 (12)

Work-in-Process: Assembly
(2) 11,000	43,000 (7C)
(3) 16,800	
(5C) 7,200^a	
(6C) 8,000	

Work-in-Process: Finishing
(7C) 43,000	55,000 (8C)
(3) 6,300	
(5C) 2,700^b	
(6C) 3,000	

Finished Goods
(8C) 55,000	55,000 (9C)

Cost of Goods Sold
(9C) 55,000	

Under/Over Applied Overhead (Fixed and Variable)
(12) 1,300	300 (12)

d. Variable Costing/Normal Costing

Accounts and Wages Payable
	13,000 (1)
	27,600 (3)

15,400 (4)

Materials Inventory
(1) 13,000	13,000 (2)

Variable Manufacturing Overhead
(Actual)	(Applied)
(2) 2,000	
(3) 2,400	
(4) 5,000	9,900 (5D)
(12) 300	

Fixed Manufacturing Overhead
(3) 2,100	
(4) 10,200	

Work-in-Process: Assembly
(2) 11,000	35,000 (7D)
(3) 16,800	
(5D) 7,200^a	

Work-in-Process: Finishing
(7D) 35,000	44,000 (8D)
(3) 6,300	
(5D) 2,700^b	

Finished Goods
(8D) 44,000	44,000 (9D)

Cost of Goods Sold
(9D) 44,000	

Under/Over Applied Overhead (Variable, Only)
	300 (12)

^{a}$9 per Direct Labor Hour × 800 Direct Labor Hours worked in the Assembly Department = $7,200.
^{b}$9 per Direct Labor Hour × 300 Direct Labor Hours worked in the Finishing Department = $2,700.

UMBRELLA MAKERS
Comparative Income Statements
for the Month Ending June 30

A. Actual/Full Absorption Costing[a]		C. Normal/Full Absorption Costing	
Sales Revenue	$90,000	Sales Revenue	$90,000
Less Cost of Goods Sold . . .	(56,000)	Less: Cost of Goods Sold	
Gross Margin	$34,000	(normal)	(55,000)
Less Marketing and		Underapplied Overhead. .	(1,000)
Administrative Costs	(30,000)	Gross Margin	$34,000
Operating Profits	$ 4,000	Less Marketing and	
		Administrative costs	(30,000)
		Operating Profits	$ 4,000
B. Actual/Variable Costing		**D. Normal/Variable Costing**	
Sales Revenue	$90,000	Sales Revenue	$90,000
Less:		Less:	
Variable Cost of Goods		Variable Cost of Goods Sold	
Sold	(43,700)	(normal)	(44,000)
Variable Marketing and		Marketing and Administrative	
Administrative Costs . . .	(5,000)	Costs.	(5,000)
Contribution Margin	$41,300	Add Overapplied Variable	
Less:		Overhead	300
Fixed Manufacturing		Contribution Margin	$41,300
Overhead	(12,300)	Less:	
Fixed Marketing and		Fixed Manufacturing	
Administrative Costs . . .	(25,000)	Overhead	(12,300)
Operating Profits	$ 4,000	Fixed Marketing and	
		Administrative Costs . . .	(25,000)
		Operating Profits	$ 4,000

[a]See also Exhibit 4.5.

Comparative Income Statements For managerial purposes, the variable costing reports shown in parts B and D are potentially more useful than the corresponding full absorption statements in parts A and C, because the variable costing statements present more information about cost behavior. One of the full absorption statements, A or C, would be used for external reporting, however. In this example, the bottom line—operating profits—is the same for each of the four methods. This is a special case that occurs when inventories in Work-in-Process and Finished Goods at the beginning of the period equal those at the end of the period (as in this case where there are no inventories).

Problem 2 for Self-Study[3]

Standard Costs

One morning, as Sam Peabody sat in his office flipping through *The Wall Street Journal,* he came across an article about standard costing systems. "Well," thought Sam to himself, "we are already using standard costs for performance evaluation. Why not try incorporating them into the system and using them for planning, inventory valuation, and valuing cost of goods sold for financial reporting? After

[3]From J. Lim.

all, one can of tuna fish is pretty much the same as another. How much more homogeneous can a product get?''

Increasingly intrigued as to how well the standard cost system would fit Gourmet's Choice, Sam summoned his accountant, John Phillips, to his office. ''I want a report on how 1986 would have looked if we had used a standard cost system. Use the standard costs you developed the beginning of last year. Our costs may have fluctuated, but they have not deviated that much from the standard figures.''

Looking through his notes, Phillips noted that at standard, each can required:

(1) 4 ounces of raw tuna at $1.20 per pound to fill a 3-ounce can.

(2) One can at $0.05 each.

(3) .01 direct labor hour at $12 per hour.

(4) Variable manufacturing overhead at $20 per direct labor hour.

(5) Fixed manufacturing overhead at $10 per direct labor hour.

Actual production in 1986 was 950,000 cans of tuna, and total actual costs were as follows:

Tuna Fish (237,500 pounds @ $1.18)	$280,250
Tin Cans (950,500 cans @ $0.05)	47,525
Direct Labor (10,500 hours @ $12.00)	126,000
Variable Manufacturing Overhead.	192,000
Fixed Manufacturing Overhead.	100,000

900,000 cans were sold in 1986 at $.85 a can. Marketing and administrative costs were $20,000.

Assuming that there were no beginning and ending work-in-process inventories, and no beginning finished goods inventory:

a. Calculate standard costs and variances for the manufacturing costs.

b. Prepare an income statement for 1986. Assume that all variances are expensed in the year incurred. Use full absorption costing.

Suggested Solution

a.

	Actual Costs	Standard Costs	Variances
Tuna Fish	$280,250	$1.20 × $\frac{4 \text{ oz.}}{16 \text{ oz.}}$ × 950,000 cans = $285,000	$ 4,750 F
Cans	$ 47,525	$0.05 × 950,000 cans = $ 47,500	$ 25 U
Direct Labor	$126,000	$12 × .01 hr. × 950,000 cans = $114,000	$12,000 U
Variable Overhead . .	$192,000	$20 × .01 hr. × 950,000 cans = $190,000	$ 2,000 U
Fixed Overhead . . .	$100,000	$10 × .01 hr. × 950,000 cans = $ 95,000	$ 5,000 U

F = favorable variance
U = unfavorable variance

b. Income statement for the year ending December 31, 1986:

Sales Revenue	$765,000
Less Cost of Goods Sold, at Standard Cost	(693,000)
Gross Margin Before Variances.	$ 72,000

Manufacturing Variances:

Tuna Fish (favorable).	$ 4,750	
Tin Cans (unfavorable)	(25)	
Direct Labor (unfavorable)	(12,000)	
Variable Manufacturing Overhead (unfavorable)	(2,000)	
Fixed Manufacturing Overhead (unfavorable)	(5,000)	
Total Variances (unfavorable)		(14,275)
Gross Margin		$57,725
Less Marketing and Administrative Costs		(20,000)
Operating Profits		$ 37,725

Problem 3 for Self-Study

Finding Unknown Flows and Balances

The management of Wheeler Industrial Equipment Company wishes to compute various unknown balances and has asked you for assistance. The following data are available:

Account Balances	January 1, Year 1	December 31, Year 1
Materials Inventory	$205,000	$?
Work-in-Process Inventory	68,550	?
Finished Goods Inventory.	31,000	65,000
Accounts Payable (all for direct and indirect materials)	16,000	24,000
Cost of Goods Sold	–0–	769,650

The work-in-process balances are for jobs in process at the balance sheet dates. On January 1, Year 1, there were two jobs in process, as follows:

Date Started	Job Number	Direct Materials	Direct Labor
10/15/Year 0	101	$14,200	$ 8,400
12/17/Year 0	103	6,500	9,000
		$20,700	$17,400

On December 31, Year 1, there was only one job in process, number 204. However, the only available information on the job was the accumulated direct labor costs of $12,000 and direct materials of $21,900. The company uses full absorption, normal costing. Overhead is applied to jobs as a percentage of direct labor costs.

The following additional information is available to you for Year 1:

Payments Made to Suppliers of Materials in Year 1	$342,000
Indirect Materials Issued from Inventory.	14,000
Direct Labor Costs Incurred	140,000
Direct Materials Costs Transferred to Finished Goods Inventory	403,800
Current Period Applied Overhead in Finished Goods Inventory on December 31, Year 1	30,000
Actual Manufacturing Overhead Costs Incurred . . . . (fixed and variable are combined)	247,000

(*Hint:* It may be helpful to set up T-accounts with the amounts given in the problem entered.)

Find the following unknown balances and transaction cost flows.

a. Materials purchased in Year 1.

b. Direct materials issued to production (Work-in-Process Inventory) in Year 1.

c. Materials Inventory, December 31, Year 1.

d. Rate at which overhead is applied to Work in Process.

e. Overhead applied to work in process.

f. Under- or overapplied overhead.

g. Cost of goods manufactured (that is, transferred to Finished Goods Inventory).

h. Work-in-Process Inventory, December 31, Year 1.

i. Applied overhead in ending Work-in-Process Inventory, December 31, Year 1.

Suggested Solution

The basic accounting equation, BB + TI = TO + EB, can be used to solve for the unknowns. (Cost flows through T-accounts are shown at the end of this solution.)

a. *Accounts Payable Account*

TI	=	TO	+	EB	−	BB
Materials Purchased	=	Payments to Suppliers	+	Accounts Payable Balance—12/31/01	−	Accounts Payable Balance—1/1/01
	=	$342,000	+	$24,000	−	$16,000
	=	$350,000.				

b. *Work-in-Process Account*

$$TI \quad = \quad TO \quad + \quad EB \quad - \quad BB$$

Direct Materials = Issued	Direct Materials Costs Transferred to Finished Goods (given)	+	Direct Materials in Ending Work-in-Process Inventory— 12/31/01 (given)	−	Direct Materials in Beginning Work-in-Process Inventory— 1/1/01 (given)
=	$403,800	+	$21,900	−	$20,700

$$= \quad \underline{\underline{\$405,000.}}$$

c. *Materials Inventory Account*

$$EB \quad = \quad BB \quad + \quad TI \quad - \quad TO$$

Ending Materials Inventory— 12/31/01	=	Beginning Materials Inventory— 1/1/01	+ Purchases −	$\left(\begin{array}{ccc} \text{Direct} & & \text{Indirect} \\ \text{Materials} & + & \text{Materials} \\ \text{Issued} & & \text{Issued} \end{array} \right)$
	=	$205,000	+ $350,000 −	($405,000 + $14,000)

$$= \quad \underline{\underline{\$136,000.}}$$

d. *Overhead Application Rate*

(i) The easiest way to proceed is to find:

$$\frac{\text{Overhead}}{\text{Application}} = \frac{\text{Overhead Applied to Jobs in Beginning Inventory}}{\text{Direct Labor Costs of Jobs in Beginning Inventory}}$$
(Rate)

$$= \frac{\text{Overhead Applied to Jobs—1/1/01}}{\$17,400}.$$

(ii) Next, find the overhead applied to the jobs in beginning Work-in-Process inventory:

$$\begin{array}{l} \text{Overhead} \\ \text{Applied to} \\ \text{Jobs—1/1/01} \end{array} = \$68,550 - \$20,700 - \$17,400$$

$$= \underline{\underline{\$30,450.}}$$

(iii) So the rate is

$$\begin{array}{c} \text{Overhead} \\ \text{Application} \\ \text{Rate} \end{array} = \frac{\$30,450}{\$17,400}$$

$$= \underline{\underline{175\%.}}$$

e. *Overhead Applied to Work-in-Process*

$$\frac{\text{Amount}}{\text{Applied}} = \text{Rate} \times \text{Base (direct labor costs)}$$

$$= 175\% \times \$140,000$$

$$= \underline{\$245,000}.$$

f. *Under- or Overapplied Overhead*

$$\frac{\text{Underapplied}}{\text{Overhead}} = \frac{\text{Actual}}{\text{Overhead}} - \frac{\text{Overhead}}{\text{Applied}}$$

$$= \$247,000 - \$245,000$$

$$= \underline{\$2,000} \quad \text{(underapplied)}.$$

g. *Finished Goods Inventory Account*

	TI	=	TO	+	EB	−	BB

$$\frac{\text{Cost of Goods}}{\text{Manufactured}} = \frac{\text{Cost of}}{\text{Goods Sold}} + \frac{\text{Ending finished}}{\text{Goods—12/31/01}} - \frac{\text{Beginning Inventory}}{\text{Goods—1/1/01}}$$

$$= \$769,650 + \$65,000 \qquad \$31,000$$

$$= \underline{\$803,650}.$$

h. *Work-in-Process Inventory Account*

	EB	=	BB	+	TI	−	TO

| Ending Work-in-Process Inventory—12/31/01 | = | Beginning Work-in-Process Inventory—1/1/01 | + | Direct Materials, Direct Labor and Manufacturing Overhead Charged to the Account During Year 1 | − | Cost of Goods Manufactured |

$$= \$68,550 + (\$405,000 + \$140,000 + \$245,000) - \$803,650$$

$$= \underline{\$54,900}.$$

i. *Applied Overhead in Ending Work-in-Process Inventory*

$$\frac{\text{Applied}}{\text{Overhead}} = \frac{\text{Overhead}}{\text{Rate}} \times \text{Base (that is, direct labor costs)}$$

$$= 175\% \times \$12,000 \text{ (given)}$$

$$= \underline{\$21,000}.$$

WHEELER INDUSTRIAL EQUIPMENT COMPANY
Manufacturing Cost Flows

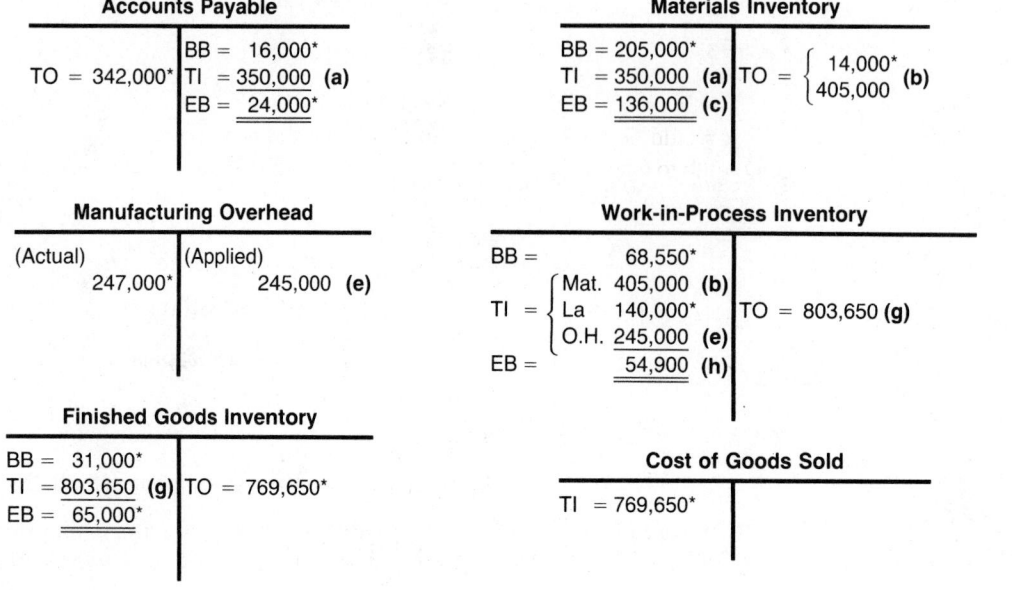

BB refers to Beginning Balance.
EB refers to Ending Balance.
TI refers to Transfers In.
TO refers to Transfers Out.
* indicates that the amount was given in the problem.
( ) letter in parentheses indicates the part of the solution in which the amount was derived.

Questions

1. Review the meaning of the following concepts or terms discussed in this chapter.

a. Accounting system.
b. Work-in-Process Inventory account.
c. Finished Goods Inventory account.
d. Cost accumulation.
e. Cost allocation.
f. Variable costing.
g. Full absorption costing.
h. Gross margin.

i. Net operating profit.
j. Contribution margin.
k. Actual costing system.
l. Normal costing system.
m. Standard costing.
n. Standard cost system.
o. Variances.
p. Pro-rating variances.
q. Basic accounting equation.

2. What purpose(s) does the accounting system serve in a manufacturing organization?

3. What are the basic problems encountered in trying to allocate overhead costs to various departments within an organization?

4. How is a normal costing system different from an actual costing system? Explain how accounting data obtained from one system may differ from the other.

5. Distinguish between standard costs and a standard cost system. To what kind of organization is a standard cost system more suited?

6. How are variances treated in a standard cost system?

7. "It would be a whole lot easier to allocate the actual overhead costs incurred each month to the actual units produced each month than to fool with predetermined overhead rates." Comment.

8. A firm incurred manufacturing overhead costs of $500,000 for the year. Overhead applied to units produced during the year totaled $600,000. What are some of the reasons for this difference?

9. Assuming that other factors work out as planned, what is the effect on the application of overhead of:

a. An excess of actual direct labor cost over estimated direct labor cost, when overhead is allocated as a percentage of direct labor cost.

b. A decrease in the pace of operations so that estimated machine hours exceed actual machine hours, when a machine hour rate of allocating overhead is used.

c. An excess of the actual amount of overhead incurred over the estimated overhead for the period.

Exercises

10. *Variable and Full Absorption Income Statements.* The actual cost flows for Martinez Tortilla Factory in Year 5 were as follows:

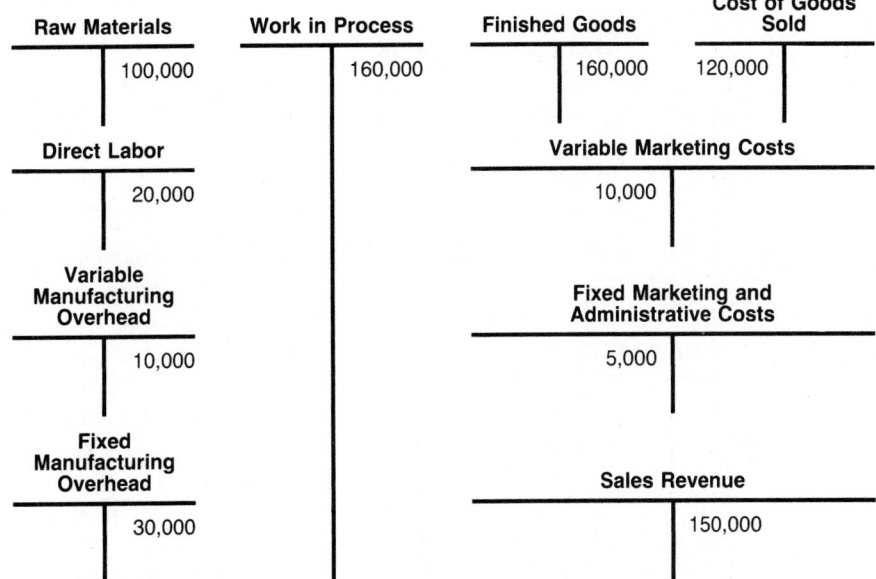

   a. Prepare a full absorption costing income statement.
   b. Prepare a variable costing income statement.

11. *Computing Overhead Rate*. Trapp Electronics Corporation estimated its overhead costs for 19X0 to be as follows: fixed, $400,000; variable, $6 per unit. Trapp expected to produce 100,000 units during the year.
   a. Determine the rate to be used to apply overhead costs to products.
   b. During 19X0, Trapp incurred overhead costs of $950,000 and produced 90,000 units. Determine the amount of overhead costs applied to units produced.
   c. Refer to part **b.** Determine the amount of under- or overapplied overhead for the year.

12. *Computing Overhead Costs*. Pender Company uses a predetermined rate for applying overhead costs to production. The rates for 19X0 were as follows: variable, $2 per unit; fixed, $1 per unit. Actual overhead costs incurred were as follows: variable, $95,000; fixed $45,000. Pender expected to produce 45,000 units during the year, but produced only 40,000 units.
   a. What was the amount of budgeted fixed costs for the year?
   b. What is the amount of under- or overapplied overhead for the year?

13. *Computing Overhead Costs*. Hoffman Corporation began business on January 1, 19X0. It expected to incur manufacturing overhead costs during 19X0 as follows: fixed, $300,000; variable, $4 per unit. Hoffman planned to produce 100,000 units during the year. Only 90,000 were actually produced at the following total manufacturing costs:

	Number of Units	Total Manufacturing Costs
Units Finished and Sold	70,000	$1,050,000
Units Finished But Not Sold	20,000	270,000
	90,000	$1,320,000

Hoffman incurred overhead costs of $657,000 during the year. Determine the amount of under- or overapplied overhead for the year.

14. *Tracing Manufacturing Cost Flows Using T-Accounts*. Set up T-accounts for Materials Inventory, Work-in-Process Inventory, Finished Goods Inventory, Cost of Goods Sold, and Manufacturing Overhead. Enter the following items in the T-accounts as appropriate for the month of June:
   (1) Beginning inventory accounts were as follows: Materials Inventory, $40,000; Work-in-Process Inventory, $150,000; Finished Goods Inventory, $120,000.
   (2) Materials purchased during June were $300,000.
   (3) Materials used during June totaled $270,000.
   (4) Direct labor costs incurred during the month were $400,000.
   (5) Manufacturing overhead costs incurred during June totaled $130,000.
   (6) Manufacturing overhead costs applied to units produced totaled $120,000.

(7) The cost of units completed during June was $910,000.

(8) The cost of goods sold during June was $850,000.

15. *Computing Manufacturing Costs Under Normal Costing.* Haskell Company applies overhead costs to products at a rate of 40 percent of direct labor cost. The company uses a separate overhead account. The following data relate to the manufacturing activities of Haskell Company during March:

	March 1	March 31
Direct Materials Inventory	$32,400	$32,900
Work-in-Process Inventory.	55,800	43,200
Finished Goods Inventory	44,200	46,300

Factory costs incurred during the month were as follows:

Direct Materials Purchased	$ 65,700
Direct Labor Cost Incurred	125,000
Factory Heat, Light, and Power	5,000
Factory Rent	10,000
Depreciation on Factory Equipment	25,000

a. Determine the cost of direct materials used during March.

b. Determine the cost of the units completed during March and transferred to the finished goods storeroom.

c. Determine the cost of goods sold during March.

16. *Computing Manufacturing Costs Under Normal Costing.* Cornell Company applies overhead to products at a rate of 10 percent of direct labor cost. It maintains a separate manufacturing overhead account during the year. The following data relate to the manufacturing activities of Cornell Company during June:

	June 1	June 30
Direct Materials Inventory	$22,600	$18,900
Work-in-Process Inventory	68,600	76,500
Finished Goods Inventory	54,300	51,900

Factory costs incurred during the month were as follows:

Direct Materials Purchased	$344,000
Labor Services Received	280,300
Factory Heat, Light, and Power	3,300
Factory Insurance	1,800
Depreciation on Factory Equipment	20,800
Factory Rent	2,400

a. Determine the cost of direct materials used during June.

b. Determine the cost of units completed during June and transferred to the finished goods storeroom.

c. Determine the cost of goods sold during June.

d. Determine the amount of under- or overapplied overhead for the month of June.

17. *Computing Manufacturing Overhead.* The Matron Products Company uses the direct labor hours basis of allocating overhead to jobs. On January 1, it was estimated that total overhead for the coming year would be $400,000 and that 100,000 direct labor hours would be worked.

The actual overhead and direct labor hours for the first 5 months of the year were as follows:

	Actual Overhead	Actual Direct Labor Hours
January	$ 51,000	12,500
February	40,000	9,600
March	61,000	15,500
April	58,500	14,200
May	50,000	13,000
	$260,500	64,800 hrs.

Determine the amount of under- or overpaid overhead for each month.

18. *Computing Variances and Preparing Income Statements Under Full Absorption/Standard Costing.* Last year Bonanza Incorporated manufactured 900,000 lightbulbs. The standard costs per unit were as follows:

Raw Materials	$0.10
Direct Labor	0.05
Manufacturing Overhead	0.20

Actual costs were

Raw Materials	$ 89,000
Direct Labor	45,500
Manufacturing Overhead	185,000
Marketing and Administrative Costs	10,000

a. Calculate the various manufacturing variances.

b. Given that Bonanza Incorporated sold 890,000 of the 900,000 lightbulbs at $.40 each, prepare an income statement as one would under a full absorption standard costing system.

19. *Manufacturing Cost Variances Under a Full Absorption/Standard Costing System.* Mickey's Munch, a breakfast cereal company, had revenue of $820,000 and total marketing and administrative costs of $120,000 in Year 6. Mickey's Munch uses a standard costing system. Standard cost of raw materials was estimated to be $.30 per pound. Variable and fixed manufacturing overhead were estimated to be $2 and $5 per machine hour, respectively. Standard machine hours per pound was .08 hour. Actual production and sales for Mickey's Munch was 410,000 pounds, and actual costs incurred were as follows:

Raw Materials.	$125,000
Variable Manufacturing Overhead.	64,900
Fixed Manufacturing Overhead.	161,500

    a. Calculate the manufacturing cost variances.
    b. Prepare an income statement using full absorption/standard costing.

20. *Comparison of Cost Flows Under Full Absorption and Variable Costing.* Gibsons Products manufactures the Shuswap Monster, a stuffed toy. Variable manufacturing overhead is applied at the rate of $1.50 per labor hour and fixed manufacturing overhead at a rate of $2.25 per labor hour. Actual costs incurred in Year 3 were as follows:

Direct Materials	$ 62,500
Direct Labor ($8.50 per hour)	255,000
Actual Variable Overhead	50,000
Variable Marketing and Administrative Costs.	56,250
Actual Fixed Overhead	65,000
Fixed Marketing and Administrative Costs.	35,000

    In Year 3, 25,000 units were produced and 24,200 units were sold. There were no beginning inventories in Year 3, and ending Work-in-Process inventory for Year 3 was zero.
    a. Using T-accounts, show the cost flows through Cost of Goods Sold under the variable/normal costing approach.
    b. Using T-accounts, show the cost flows through Cost of Goods Sold under the full absorption/normal costing approach.

21. *Preparing Income Statements.* Refer to Exercise **20.** Assume that the selling price of each Shuswap Monster is $25.
    a. Prepare an income statement for Year 3 using the variable costing approach.
    b. Prepare an income statement for Year 3 using the full absorption costing approach.

22. *Comparison of Cost Flows Under Full Absorption and Variable Costing.* In Year 4, Brixton Products incurred the following costs for its line of drainpipes:

	Variable	Fixed
Direct Materials	$625,000	—
Labor	593,750	$125,000
Supplies	100,000	—
Depreciation	—	87,500
Repairs and Maintenance	50,000	150,000
Other Manufacturing Costs	37,500	50,000
Marketing and Administrative Costs	50,000	137,500

100,000 units were produced and 80,000 units were sold that year. There were no beginning inventories in Year 4, and ending Work-in-Process inventory was zero.

    a. Using T-accounts, show the manufacturing cost flows under the variable/actual costing approach.

    b. Using T-accounts, show the manufacturing cost flows under the full absorption/actual costing approach.

23. *Preparing Income Statements*. Refer to Exercise **22.** Assume the selling price of drain pipes to be $25 per unit.

    a. Present the income statement based on variable costing for Year 4.

    b. Present the income statement based on full absorption costing for Year 4.

    c. Explain the difference in the operating profits.

Problems and Cases

24. *Tracing Cost Flows Under Normal and Actual Costing*. Kowalski Company applies overhead costs to products at a rate of 40 percent of direct labor costs. The company uses a separate overhead account. The following data relate to the manufacturing activities of Kowalski Company during March:

(1) Beginning and ending raw materials inventory were $32,400 and $32,900, respectively. $65,700 of raw materials were purchased that month.

(2) Direct labor costs incurred were $125,000.

(3) Beginning and ending work-in-process inventories were $55,800 and $0, respectively.

(4) Beginning finished goods inventory was $44,200. Kowalski Company used the FIFO method for its inventories. Of the total amount transferred into finished goods inventory that month, 85 percent of the units were sold.

(5) Actual overhead costs were $40,000.

    a. Using T-accounts, trace the cost flows through Cost of Goods Sold for March.

    b. Suppose that Kowalski Company had used an actual costing system for March. Again using T-accounts, trace the cost flows through Cost of Goods Sold.

25. *Deriving Income Statement Amounts*. Hastings Products uses the following unit costs for one of the products it manufactures:

Direct Materials	$70.20
Direct Labor	44.46
Manufacturing Overhead:	
Variable	14.04
Fixed (based on 8,000 units per month) YEAR	11.70
Marketing and Administrative Costs:	
Variable	9.36
Fixed (based on 8,000 units per month) YEAR	6.55

In Year 4, there were 1,600 units in beginning Finished Goods Inventory; 8,800 units were produced; and 10,400 units were sold at $180 per unit. There was no beginning nor ending Work-in-Process Inventory. Actual costs for Year 4 were as estimated. Over- or underapplied overhead is expensed to Cost of Goods Sold.

   a. Prepare an income statement for Year 4 using variable costing.

   b. Would reported operating profits be more, less, or equal if full absorption costing had been used? Prove it with an income statement using full absorption costing.

26. *Tracing Cost Flows Under Full Absorption/Normal Costing.* Cambie Company uses a full absorption/normal costing system. Cambie incurred the following costs during the month of June:

	Balance, June 1	Balance, June 30
Direct Materials Inventory	?	$ 52,000
Work-in-Process Inventory	?	364,000
Finished Goods Inventory	$130,000	104,000

Other Information:

Direct Labor Costs	$312,000
Manufacturing Overhead (actual)	145,600
Overapplied Manufacturing Overhead	41,600
Direct Materials Purchases	234,000
Cost of Goods Sold (before correction for overapplied manufacturing overhead)	468,000
Direct Materials Requisitioned for Production	260,000

Show the flow of costs for June for Cambie Company. Be as thorough as possible.

27. *Evaluating Full Absorption and Variable Costing Using Normal Costs (CMA adapted).* The vice-president for sales of Huber Corporation has received the income statement for November. The statement has been prepared on the variable costing basis and is reproduced below. The firm has just adopted a variable costing system for internal reporting purposes.

HUBER CORPORATION
Income Statement
for the Month of November
(in thousands)

Sales Revenue	$2,400
Less Variable Cost of Goods Sold	(1,200)
Manufacturing Contribution Margin	$1,200
Less Fixed Manufacturing Costs	(600)
Gross Margin	$ 600
Less Nonmanufacturing Costs (all fixed)	(400)
Operating Profit	$ 200

The controller attached the following notes to the statements:

1. The unit sales price for November averaged $24.
2. Actual fixed manufacturing costs equaled the amount budgeted.
3. The normal unit manufacturing costs for the month were

Variable Cost	$12
Fixed Cost	4
Total Cost	$16

4. The unit rate for fixed manufacturing costs is a predetermined rate based on a normal monthly production of 150,000 units.
5. Production for November was 45,000 units in excess of sales.
6. The inventory on November 30 consisted of 80,000 units.

a. The vice-president for sales is not comfortable with the variable cost basis and wonders what the operating profit would have been under the prior full absorption cost basis.

(1) Present the November income statement on a full absorption cost basis.
(2) Reconcile and explain the difference between the variable costing and the full absorption costing operating profit figures.

b. Explain the features associated with variable cost income measurement that should be attractive to the vice-president for sales.

28. *Reconciling Variable Costing Operating Profit with Full Absorption Costing Operating Profit.* Point Grey Corporation employs a full absorption costing system for its external reporting as well as for internal management purposes. The latest annual income statement appears as follows:

Sales Revenue		$581,000
Cost of Goods Sold:		
Beginning Inventory.	$ 30,800	
Cost of Current Production	441,000	
Less Ending Inventory	(120,400)	
Less Total Cost of Goods Sold		(351,400)
Gross Margin.		$229,600
Less:		
Marketing Costs		(116,200)
Administrative Costs		(69,720)
Operating Profit Before Taxes		$ 43,680
Less Income Taxes		(20,300)
Operating Profit After Taxes		$ 23,380

Company management is somewhat concerned that although they are showing adequate profits, there has been a shortage of cash to meet operating costs. The following information has been provided to you to assist management with its evaluation of the situation:

Statement of Cost of Goods Manufactured

Direct Materials:		
Beginning Inventory	$ 22,400	
Purchases	86,800	
Less Ending Inventory	(30,800)	$ 78,400
Direct Labor		175,140
Manufacturing Overhead:		
Variable	$ 55,160	
Fixed (including depreciation of $42,000)	132,300	187,460
Cost of Goods Manufactured		$441,000

There are no work-in-process inventories. Management reports that it is pleased that this year manufacturing costs are 70 percent variable compared to last year, when these costs were only 45 percent variable. This, management notes, provides more insurance against volume declines. Although 80 percent of the marketing costs are variable, only 40 percent of the administrative costs are considered variable. Assume FIFO inventory flow.

   a.   Prepare a variable costing income statement for the year.

   b.   Reconcile the difference between the full absorption costing statement given in the problem to the variable costing statement in part **a.** Use net operating profit before taxes.

29. *Incomplete Records.* On December 31, Year 3, a fire destroyed the bulk of the accounting records of Houdini Company, a small, one-product manufacturing firm. In addition, the chief accountant mysteriously disappeared. You have the task of reconstructing the records for Year 3. The general manager has said that the accountant had been experimenting with both full absorption costing and variable costing on an actual costing basis.

The records are a mess, but you have gathered the following data for Year 3:

(1) Sales Revenue	$585,000
(2) Actual Fixed Manufacturing Costs Incurred	$85,800
(3) Actual Variable Manufacturing Costs per Unit for Year 3 and for Units in	
Inventory on January 1, Year 3	$3.90
(4) Operating Profit, Full Absorption Costing Basis.	$78,000
(5) Notes Receivable from Chief Accountant	$18,200
(6) Contribution Margin	$234,000
(7) Direct Material Purchases	$227,500
(8) Actual Marketing and Administrative Costs (all fixed).	$27,300
(9) Gross Margin	$105,300

You also learn that full absorption costs per unit in beginning Finished Goods Inventory equals the Year 3 full absorption production cost per unit.

   a.   Prepare a comparative income statement on a full absorption and variable costing basis.

   b.   Determine the number of units sold.

   c.   Determine the full absorption cost per unit.

d. Determine the number of units produced.

e. Reconcile the operating profit under variable costing with that under full costing, showing the exact source of the difference.

30. *Completing Missing Data.* After a dispute concerning wages, Ernest Arson tossed an incendiary device into the Flash Company's record vault. Within moments, only a few charred fragments were readable from the company's factory ledger, as shown below:

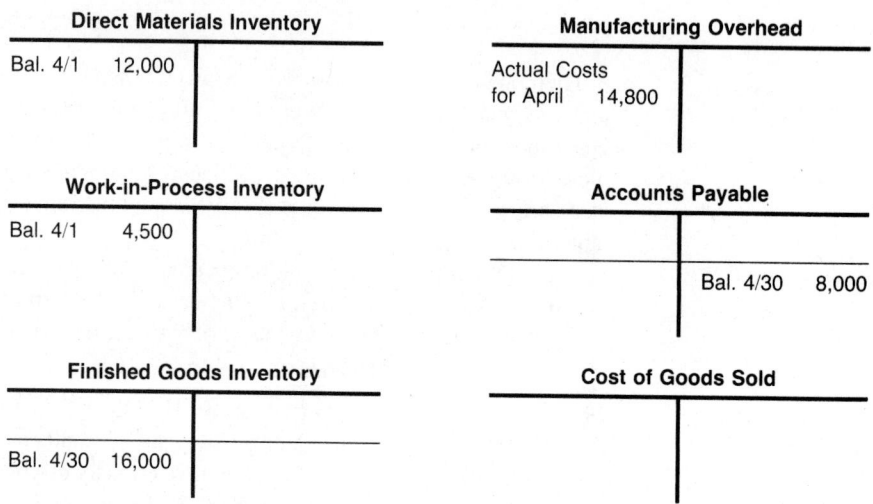

Sifting through the ashes and interviewing selected employees have turned up the following additional information:

(1) The controller remembers clearly that the predetermined overhead rate was based on an estimated 60,000 direct labor hours to be worked over the year, and an estimated $180,000 in manufacturing overhead costs.

(2) The production superintendent's cost sheets showed only one job in process on April 30. Materials of $2,600 had been added to the job, and 300 direct labor hours had been expended at $6 per hour.

(3) The accounts payable are for direct materials purchases only, according to the accounts payable clerk. He clearly remembers that the balance in the account was $6,000 on April 1. An analysis of canceled checks (kept in the treasurer's office) shows that payments of $40,000 were made to suppliers during the month.

(4) A charred piece of the payroll ledger shows that 5,200 direct labor hours were recorded for the month. The employment department has verified that there are no variations in pay rates among employees (this infuriated Ernest, who felt that he was underpaid).

(5) Records maintained in the finished goods warehouse indicate that the finished goods inventory totaled $11,000 on April 1.

(6) From another charred piece in the vault you are able to discern that the cost of goods manufactured for April was $89,000.

Determine the following amounts:
- **a.** Work-in-process inventory, April 30.
- **b.** Direct materials purchased during April.
- **c.** Overhead applied to work in process.
- **d.** Cost of goods sold for April.
- **e.** Over- or underapplied overhead for April.
- **f.** Direct materials usage during April.
- **g.** Direct materials inventory, April 30.

31. *Comparative Income Statements and Solving for Unknowns.* A client has requested your help in analyzing the operations of one of her divisions, the Robson Division. "I don't understand this! I received this income statement yesterday for the Robson Division managers (see Exhibit 4.15), but one of our internal auditors came across this other one (see Exhibit 4.16). The second statement shows a lower net income! I think something strange is going on here. It looks like the division managers are sending me this first statement (in Exhibit 4.15) that makes them look good, while they're hiding the second statement (in Exhibit 4.16), which shows what's really going on. I want you to look into this for me."

Exhibit 4.15
ROBSON DIVISION
Income Statement
April

Sales Revenue	$1,080,000
Less Cost of Goods Sold	(720,000)
Overapplied Overhead	45,000
Gross Margin	$ 405,000
Less Selling and Administrative Costs	(180,000)
Operating Profit	$ 225,000

Notes:
1. Fixed manufacturing costs applied at predetermined rate of $1.80 per unit.
2. No under- or overapplied overhead is prorated to inventories.
3. Ending Inventory is $576,000.

Exhibit 4.16
ROBSON DIVISION
Income Statement
April

Sales Revenue	$1,080,000
Less Variable Cost of Goods Sold	(540,000)
Contribution Margin	540,000
Less Fixed Costs	(270,000)
Less Selling and Administrative Costs	(180,000)
Operating Profit	$ 90,000

a.   Determine the number of units sold in April.
b.   Determine *expected* and *actual* production in April.
c.   Determine *beginning* and *ending* inventory in April.
d.   Reconcile (assume FIFO flow of units):

(1) Actual Fixed Costs Incurred in April. . . . . $
   Add:
   Deduct:
   Fixed Costs Expensed Under Full Absorption Costing . . . . . $
(2) Components of Fixed Costs Expensed Under Full Absorption
   Costing:
   Through Cost of Goods Sold . . . . $
   Other (identify) . . . .
   Total . . . . $

e.   Summarize the transactions for the month in journal entry or T-account form. Show the difference between full absorption and variable costing in your summary. Use one summary account, Other Assets and Liabilities, for transactions that are not specifically identified with an account. Use one inventory account for both work in process and finished goods.

32. *Computing Income Statement Values Under Both Variable and Full Absorption Costing Using Actual and Normal Costing Methods.* Fred Byacarco, president of a (formerly) large automobile manufacturing company, is surprised to see the company's second quarter financial statements for the car division. Due to a decrease in quantity demanded, sales were cut 20 percent from the first quarter. Perhaps of greater significance was the 50 percent decrease in production to reduce inventory levels. "I expected about a 20 percent decrease in profits because of the sales decline," said Fred, "but nothing like this. I'm going to see what went wrong in the accounting department. You can bet some heads will roll!" (Fred's other comments are not repeatable.)

Here are the data Fred saw (000 omitted):

	First Quarter	Second Quarter
Sales Revenue.	$2,500,000	$2,000,000
Less:		
Cost of Goods sold	(2,000,000)	(1,600,000)
(Over-) Underapplied Fixed Manufacturing Costs	–0–	(300,000)
Gross Margin	$ 500,000	$ 100,000
Less Marketing and Administrative costs (all fixed)	(300,000)	(300,000)
Operating Profit Before Taxes	$ 200,000	$ (200,000)
Sales Units	500	400
Production Units	600	300

Note: The company uses a full absorption "normal" costing system, which it defines as "actual variable costs plus a predetermined rate for fixed costs." Fixed costs per quarter were unchanged and variable costs per unit remained constant for both quarters. There was no beginning inventory at the start of the first quarter. There was no work-in-process inventory; all inventories are in finished goods. The same estimate of units for the predetermined fixed cost rate is used in both quarters.

    a. Show the operating profit before taxes for each quarter using:
        (1) Full absorption/actual costing.
        (2) Variable/actual costing.
    For each costing method, what were
        (1) Unit variable manufacturing costs?
        (2) Total fixed manufacturing costs expensed?
    b. Indicate the value of the beginning inventory of finished goods (there are no work-in-process inventories) at the beginning of the second quarter under:
        (1) Full absorption/normal costing, using the company's definition of "normal" costing.
        (2) Full absorption/actual costing.
        (3) Variable/actual costing.
    c. Explain what happened to Mr. Byacarco. Remember, he is a layperson and impatient with long, technical explanations. However, be precise.

33. *Job Costing for Pricing and Performance Evaluation.*[4] Deborah Carr, founder and president of E-Z Printing Company, was worried. The company was doing more business than ever before—sales were at an annual rate of about $625,000 a year—but operating profits had declined slightly during recent months, and the ratio of income to sales had dropped sharply. Ms. Carr wondered what had gone wrong and what she could do about it. She called in her chief (and only) accountant, Gene Hockman, and asked him to find out what was happening.

    E-Z Printing did a general printing business on a customer-order basis. Ms. Carr set the price to be charged for each job. When possible, she waited until the work was done and then quoted a price equal to 140 percent of the cost of the paper stock used, plus $25 for each labor hour. Straight-time wage rates in the past, adjusted for recent wage rate increases, had averaged about $8 per hour, and this formula seemed to provide an adequate margin to cover overhead costs and provide a good profit. No attempt was made to modify these prices for seasonality, even though business was usually slow in the winter months and heavy in the spring and fall.

    Most of E-Z Printing's work was done on the basis of predetermined contract prices. In bidding on these jobs, Ms. Carr applied her standard pricing formula to her own estimates of the amount of labor and paper stock the job would require. She prided herself on her ability to make these estimates, but she sometimes quoted a price that was higher or lower than the formula price, depending on her judgment of the market situation.

    The company's production procedures were fairly simple. When a customer's order was received, it was assigned a production order number and a production order was issued. The material to be printed, known as the customer's copy, was

---

[4]© 1968 by l'Institut pour l'Étude des Méthodes de Direction de l'Entreprise (IMEDE), Lausanne, Switzerland, under the title Tipografia Stanca S.P.A. This case was revised and updated in 1984.

given to a copy editor, who indicated on the copy the sizes and styles of type that should be used. The editor sometimes made changes in the copy, usually after telephoning the customer to discuss the changes.

Once the customer's material had been copy-edited, it was sent to the composing room, where it was set in type. A proof copy was printed by hand and returned to the copy editor, who checked the printed copy against the original. Any errors in the proof were indicated in the margin, and the marked proof was sent to the customer for approval. At this point, the customer might decide to make changes in the copy, and these changes, as well as corrections of typesetting errors, were made as soon as the corrected proof was returned to the composing room.

In some cases a second proof was sent to the customer for his or her approval, but at E-Z Printing most orders were sent to the pressroom as soon as the customer's corrections had been made and the second proof had been approved by the copy editor.

At this point, the order was ready for production on one of the presses in the pressroom. Printing instructions were contained in the production order, which specified the particular press to be used; the number of copies to be printed; the color, size, style, weight, and finish of the stock or paper to be used; and similar details. Copies were then printed, bound, and packaged for delivery to the customer.

An order could take as little as 1 day in the copy editing and composing room stages or as long as several weeks. Printing, binding, and packaging seldom took more than 2 days except on very large production runs of multipage booklets.

E-Z Printing's before-tax profit had fluctuated between 13 and 15 percent of net sales. The interim profit report for the first half of Year 4 came as a shock to Ms. Carr. Although volume was slightly greater than in the first half of Year 3, profit was down to 8.8 percent of sales, an all-time low. The comparison, with all figures expressed as percentages of net sales, was as follows:

	June 30, Year 4	June 30, Year 3
Net Sales .	100.0%	100.0%
Production Costs .	77.6	72.3
Selling and Administrative Costs.	13.6	13.9
Profit	8.8	13.8

Mr. Hockman knew that the company's problem must be either low prices or excessive costs. Unfortunately, the cost data already available told him little about the cost/price relation for individual jobs. E-Z's operating costs were classified routinely into 20 categories, such as salaries, pressroom wages, production materials, depreciation, and so forth. Individual job cost sheets were not used, and the cost of goods in process was estimated only once a year, at the end of the fiscal year.

Detailed data were available on only two kinds of items: paper stock issued and labor time. When stock was issued, a requisition form was filled out, showing the kind of stock issued, the quantity, the unit cost, and the production order number. Similar details were reported when unused stock was returned to the stockroom.

As for labor, each employee engaged directly in working on production orders filled in a time sheet each day, on which the time spent on a specific production order and the order number were recorded. The employee's department number and pay grade were recorded on the time sheet by the payroll clerk.

Mr. Hockman's first step was to establish some overall cost relations. Employees, for example, fell into three different pay grades, with the following regular hourly wage rates:

Grade	Rate
1	$12
2	8
3	6

These rates applied to a regular work week of 40 hours a week. For work in excess of this number of hours, employees were paid an overtime premium of 50 percent of their hourly wage. Overtime premiums were negligible when the workload was light, but in a normal year they averaged about 5 percent of the total amount of hourly wages computed at the regular hourly wage rate. In a normal year, this was approximately $.40 per direct labor hour.

In addition to their wages, the employees also received various kinds of benefits, including vacation pay, health insurance, and old-age pensions. The cost of these benefits to E-Z Printing amounted to about 70 percent of direct labor cost, measured at regular straight-time hourly rates. The overtime premiums did not affect the amount of fringe benefits paid or accrued.

Mr. Hockman estimated that all other shop overhead costs, that is, all copy department, composing room, and pressroom costs other than direct materials, direct labor, overtime premiums, and employee benefits on direct labor payrolls, would average $4 a direct labor hour in a normal year.

Armed with these estimates of general relationships, Mr. Hockman proceeded to determine the costs of several recent production orders. One of these was Job No. A-467. This was received for copy editing on Monday, April 3, and delivered to the customer on Friday, April 7. Ms. Carr had quoted a price of $1,800 on this job in advance, on the basis of an estimate of $480 for paper stock costs and 45 direct labor hours. All actual requisitions and time records relating to Job No. A-467 are included in the lists in Exhibits 4.17 and 4.18. (To save space, some of the details shown on the requisitions and time tickets have been omitted from these exhibits.)

a. Diagram or explain to your own satisfaction the flow of actual material, labor, and overhead costs to Job No. A-467.

b. Develop a costing rate or rates for labor costs, to be used to charge a job cost sheet or Factory Overhead account for an hour of labor time. You must decide whether to use a single rate for all pay grades or a separate rate for each. You must also decide whether to include various kinds of fringe benefit costs in the labor costing rates or to regard these as overhead.

Exhibit 4.17
Partial List of Material Requisitions for the Week of April 3–7

Requisition Number	Job No.	Amount[a]
4058	A-467	$300
R162	A-469	(20)
4059	A-467	60
4060	A-442	6
R163	A-455	(10)
R164	A-472	(8)
4060	A-467	36
R165	A-465	(12)
4062	A-467	96
4063	A-471	320
4064	A-473	264
4065	A-458	22
R166	A-467	(32)
4066	A-481	176

[a]Amounts in parentheses are returned materials.

Exhibit 4.18
Partial Summary of Labor Time Sheets
for the Week of April 3–7

Employee Number	Pay Grade	Department	Job No.[a]	Hours
14	2	Copy	A-463	6.6
14	2	Copy	A-467	1.4
15	1	Copy	A-467	3.3
15	1	Copy	—	2.7
15	1	Copy	A-467	8.8
18	3	Press	A-467	4.0
18	3	Press	A-472	4.6
22	1	Composing	A-455	3.8
22	1	Composing	A-467	8.4[b]
22	1	Composing	—	1.5
23	2	Press	A-458	3.4
23	2	Press	A-467	4.7[b]
23	2	Press	—	1.1
23	2	Press	A-459	2.5
24	2	Copy	A-470	7.4
28	1	Press	A-467	7.0
28	1	Press	A-458	1.0
31	3	Press	—	8.0
33	1	Composing	A-471	7.6
33	1	Composing	A-472	4.2
40	2	Press	A-469	3.6
40	2	Press	A-467	4.9
40	2	Press	—	0.2
43	1	Press	A-467	3.5
43	1	Press	A-481	5.8

[a]A dash indicates time spent on general work in the department and not on any one job.
[b]Employee No. 22 worked 6 hours of overtime during the week, none of them on Job No. A-467, while Employee No. 23 worked 8 hours of overtime, including 4 hours on Job No. A-467.

c. Prepare a price quota sheet for Job No. A-467 and enter the costs that would be assigned to this job, using the costing rates you developed in the answer to part **b.** Use estimated labor hours: Grade 1—30 hrs.; Grade 2—11 hrs.; Grade 3—4 hrs.

d. What could be the advantages of developing costs for each job? Do you think these advantages would be great enough to persuade Ms. Carr to hire an additional clerk for this purpose at an annual cost of about $20,000?

Suggested Solutions to Even-Numbered Exercises

10. *Variable and Full Absorption Income Statements.*

a.

Sales Revenue	$150,000
Less Cost of Goods Sold	(120,000)
Gross Margin.	$ 30,000
Less Marketing and Administrative Costs	(15,000)
Net Operating Profit	$ 15,000

b.

Sales Revenue	$150,000
Less:	
Variable Cost of Goods Sold	(97,500)*
Variable Marketing Costs.	(10,000)
Contribution Margin	$ 42,500
Less:	
Fixed Manufacturing Overhead.	(30,000)
Fixed Marketing and Administrative Costs	(5,000)
Net Operating Profit	$ 7,500

$$*(\$100,000 + 20,000 + 10,000) \times \frac{120,000}{160,000} = \$97,500$$

12. *Computing Overhead Costs.*

  a. Budgeted Fixed Costs = $1.00 per Unit × 45,000 Units
$$= \$45,000.$$

  b. Applied Overhead = ($1.00 × 40,000) + ($2.00 × 40,000)
$$= \$120,000.$$

$$\$140,000 - \$120,000 = \$20,000 \text{ Underapplied.}$$

14. *Tracing Manufacturing Cost Flows Using T-Accounts.*

Materials Inventory		Work-in-Process Inventory		Finished Goods Inventory	
(1) 40,000		**(1)** 150,000		**(1)** 120,000	
(2) 300,000	270,000 **(3)**	**(3)** 270,000	910,000 **(7)**	**(7)** 910,000	850,000 **(8)**
		(4) 400,000			
		(6) 120,000			

Manufacturing Overhead Control		Cost of Goods Sold	
(5) 130,000	120,000 **(6)**	**(8)** 850,000	

16. *Computing Manufacturing Costs Under Normal Costing.*

Direct Materials		
BI 22,600		
344,000	347,700	**(2)**
———		
EI 18,900		

Work-in-Process		
BI 68,600		
280,300	648,130	**(3)**
(1) 28,030		
(2) 347,700		
EI 76,500		

Finished Goods		
BI 54,300		
(1) 648,130	650,530	**(4)**
———		
EI 51,900		

Factory Overhead		
3,300		
1,800	28,030	**(1)**
20,800		
2,400		

Cost of Goods Sold		
(4) 650,530		

(1) Factory overhead applied = .10 × $280,300 (direct labor) = $28,030.
(2) $22,600 + $344,000 − $18,900 = $347,700.
(3) $68,600 + $280,300 + $28,030 + $347,700 − $76,500 = $648,130.
(4) $54,300 + $648,130 − $51,900 = $650,530. Overhead underapplied =
$28,300 − $28,030 = $270.
   a. Cost of direct materials used = $347,700.
   b. Cost of units transferred to finished goods = $648,130.
   c. Cost of goods sold = $650,530.
   d. Underapplied overhead = $28,300 (actual) − $28,030 (applied) = $270.

18. *Computing Variances and Preparing Income Statements Under Full Absorption/Standard Costing.*
   a.

	Standard	Actual	Variance
Direct Materials.	$ 90,000	$ 89,000	$1,000F
Direct Labor	45,000	45,500	500U
Manufacturing Overhead	180,000	185,000	5,000U

   b.

Income Statement

Sales Revenue	$356,000
Cost of Goods Sold, at Standard Cost	$311,500
Gross Margin Before Variances.	$ 44,500
Manufacturing Variances:	
Direct Materials 1,000	
Direct Labor. . . . . (500)	
Manufacturing Overhead . . . . (5,000)	
Total Variances	(4,500)
Gross Margin	$ 40,000
Less Marketing and Administrative Costs	(10,000)
Operating Profit	$ 30,000

20. *Comparison of Cost Flows Under Full Absorption and Variable Costing.*
     a. *Variable Costing*

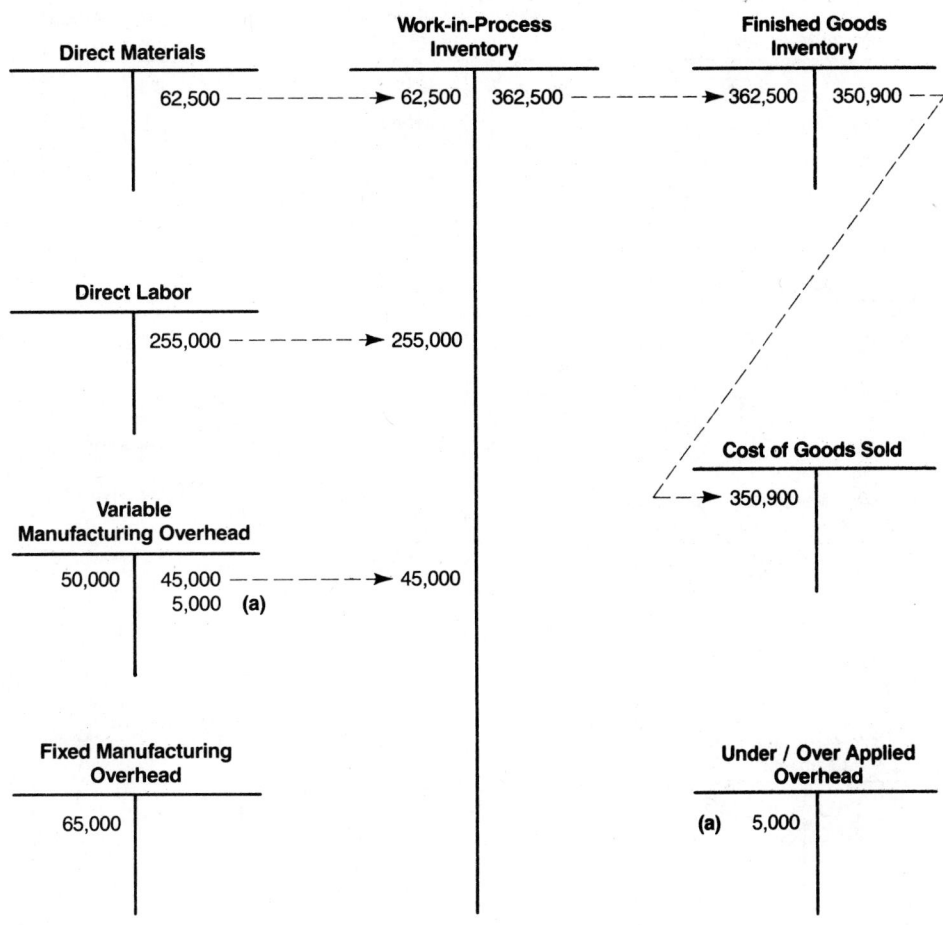

b. *Full Absorption Costing*

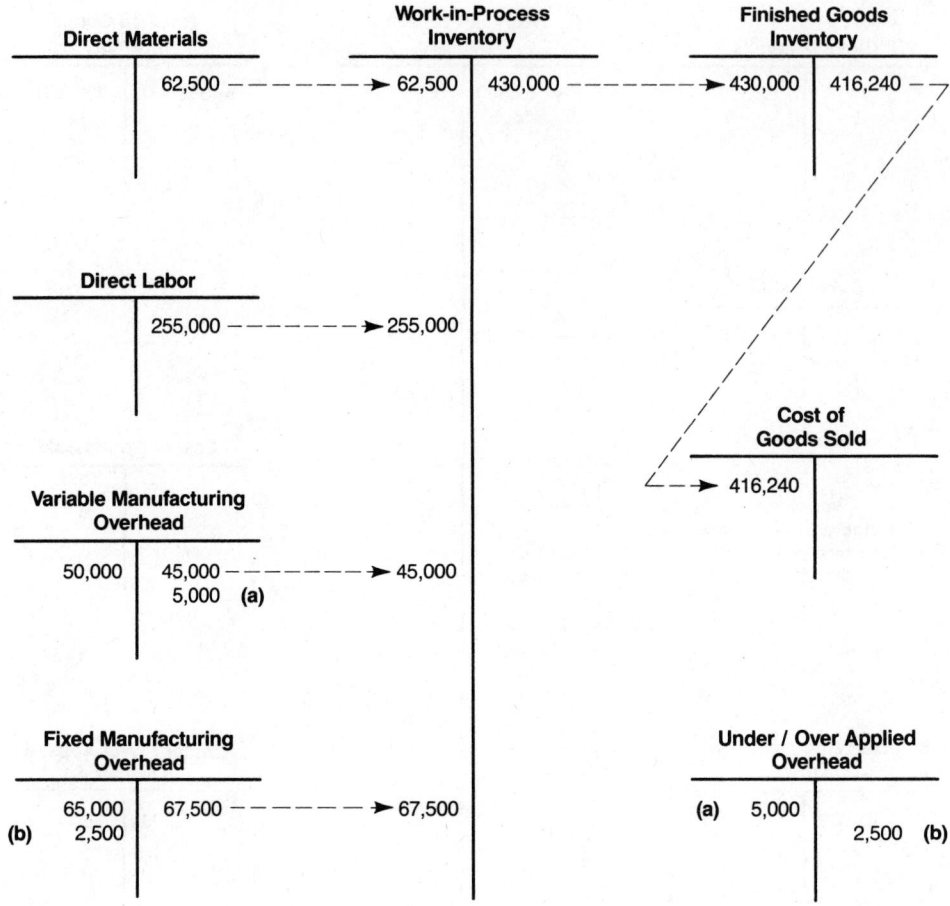

22. *Comparison of Cost Flows Under Full Absorption and Variable Costing.*
   a. *Variable/Actual Costing*

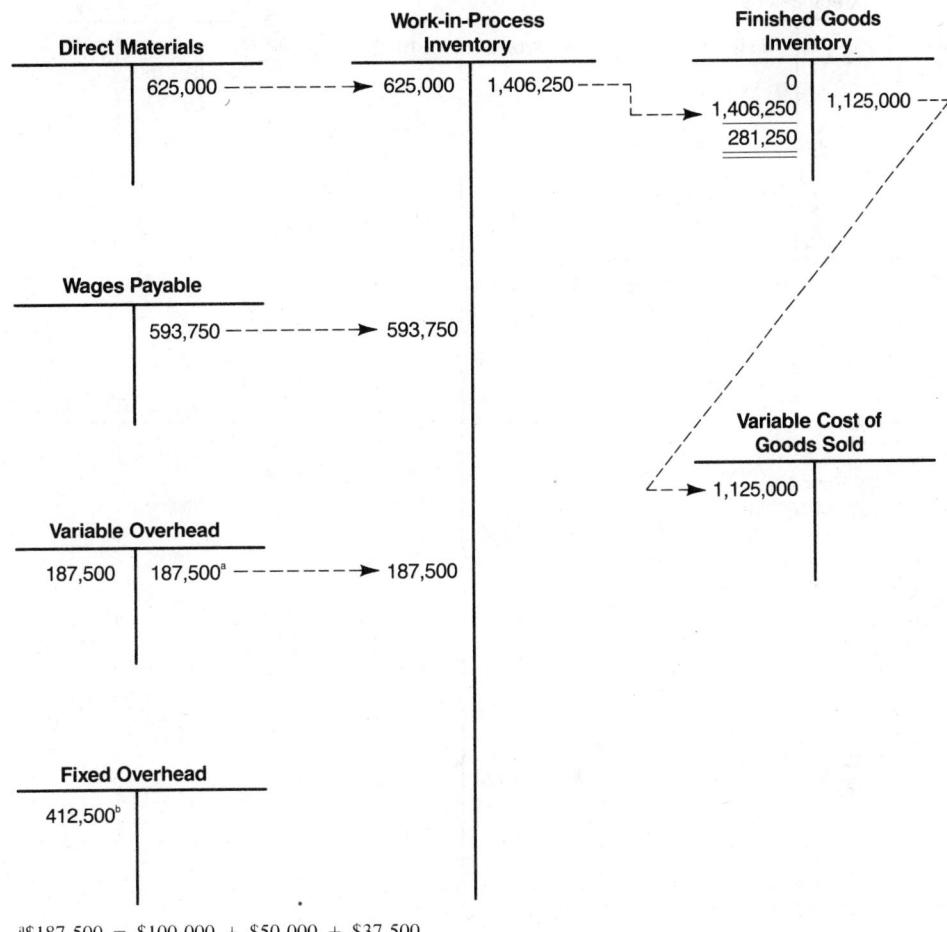

^{a}\$187,500 = \$100,000 + \$50,000 + \$37,500.
^{b}\$412,500 = \$87,500 + \$150,000 + \$50,000 + \$125,000.

b. *Full Absorption/Actual Costing*

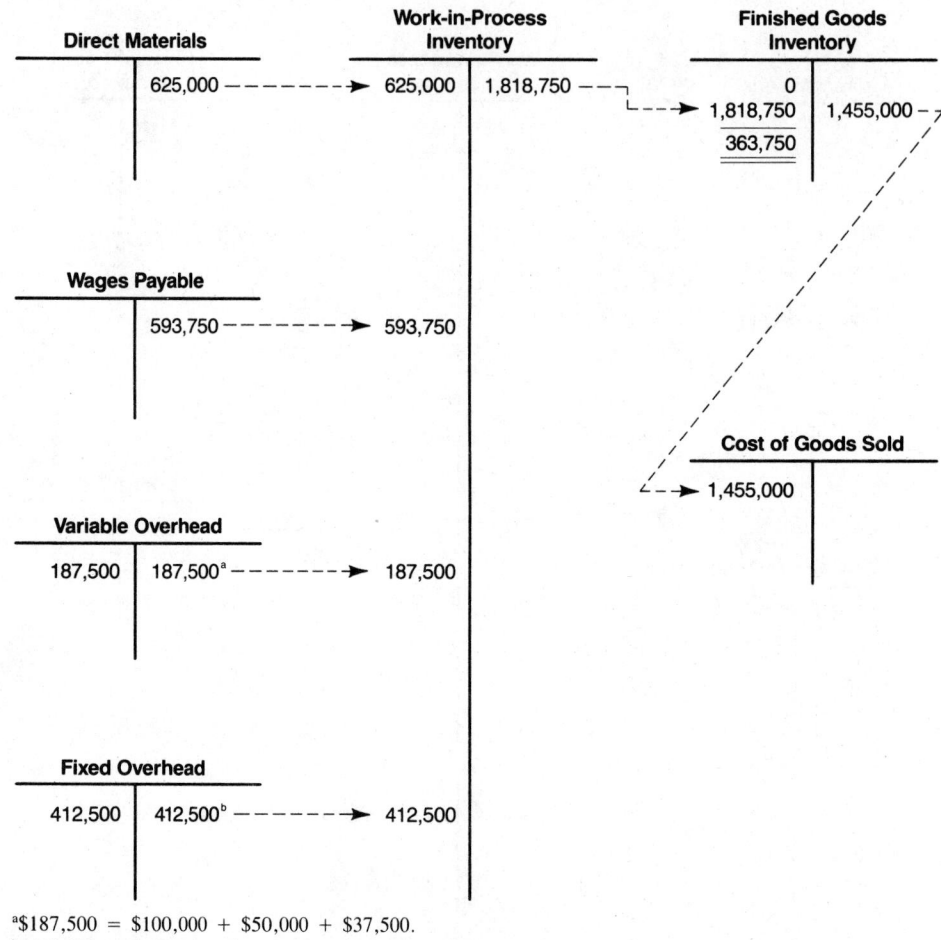

a$187,500 = $100,000 + $50,000 + $37,500.
b$412,500 = $87,500 + $150,000 + $50,000 + $125,000.

Chapter 5   Accounting for Resource Flows in Different Types of Organizations

Different types of organizations require different types of accounting systems. Generally, cost accounting systems differ depending on whether the organization is

1. A *job-order manufacturing company*, such as a custom construction company or a print shop;
2. A *manufacturing company using process production methods*, such as an oil refining company;
3. A *merchandising company;* or
4. A *service organization*.

This chapter provides an overview of how the accounting system differs for each type of organization. We show that accounting systems differ for each of these four major types of companies because of the unique characteristics of each type of organization.

To integrate this chapter with Chapters 3 and 4, recall that Chapter 3 presented the following six product costing methods:

	Cost Measure		
Cost Inclusion	Actual Costing	Normal Costing	Standard Costing
Variable Costing	1	3	5
Full Absorption Costing	2	4	6

Chapter 4 showed how these costs are accounted for in manufacturing organizations. Any of these six product costing methods could be used in either of the two types of manufacturing companies, job and process, that we discuss in this chapter. Hence, the accounting system design question is resolved in manufacturing organizations by first asking: "What type of production operation is this—job or process?", then by choosing one or more of the six methods for product costing.

The General Model

The essential business of any organization is the transformation of inputs into outputs. Exhibit 5.1 shows this process for each of three major types of organi-

Exhibit 5.1
Transformation of Inputs to Outputs

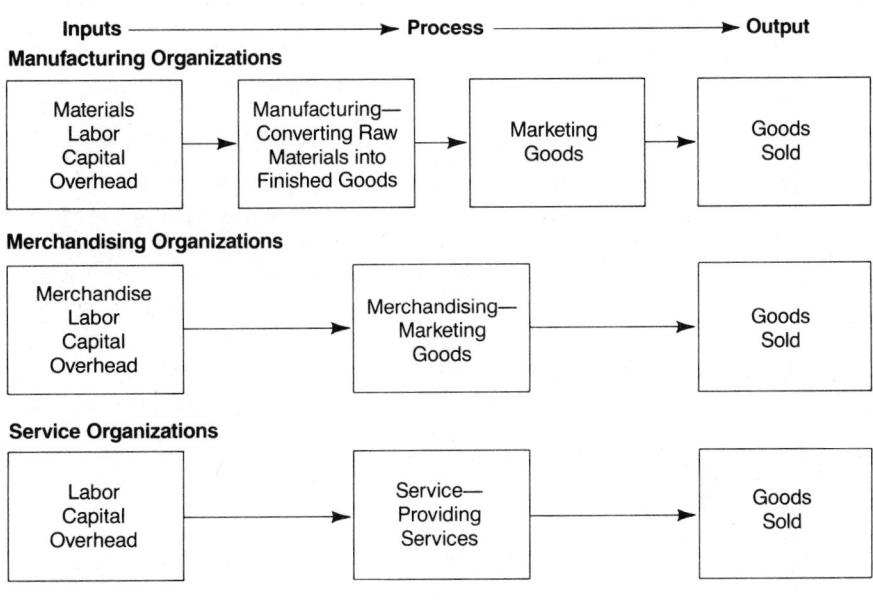

zations: manufacturing, merchandising, and service. Note the many similarities among the three types of organizations. All require inputs, and all transform those into a product for the market.

There are, however, some essential differences in the accounting system found in these different organizations. Much of the *manufacturing* activity is the conversion of raw materials into a final product, so the focus of the accounting system is on "work in process," that is, on the transformation process. Manufacturing can be thought of as creating inventory. Of course, manufacturing companies not only manufacture goods, they also market them.

Merchandising is similar to manufacturing in that both deal with inventory. However, merchandising starts where manufacturing stops—that is, with the manufactured product. Accounting for manufacturing operations requires a great deal of effort to compute the cost of the product. This product cost computation is not as difficult in merchandising because inventories are acquired in finished form and their "cost" is simply the purchase price (plus transportation costs of bringing in the merchandise). Although a major task of accounting systems in manufacturing is to assign costs to units produced for inventory valuation, this is a relatively small job in merchandising. The major task of the accounting system in merchandising is to accumulate costs by responsibility center.

Unlike manufacturing and merchandising, *service* has no inventory (other than supplies). Costs are accumulated by responsibility centers for performance evaluation. In public accounting firms, for example, costs are accumulated in the auditing department, the tax department, and so forth. As discussed later in this chapter, costs also may be broken down by job, as shown on the next page:

| | Department | |
Job	Audit	Tax
Z-Mart, Inc.	$XX	$XX
Joanna Smith		$XX

This breakdown facilitates performance evaluation—say, comparison with a budget—for both department managers and job managers.

The remainder of this chapter details these general concepts and provides some concrete examples. Of the three types of organizations, manufacturing is the most comprehensive and complex. For example, most manufacturing companies include elements of merchandising and service in their operations. Because accounting in manufacturing organizations is complex and comprehensive, we devote considerable space to it in this text. Keep in mind, however, that although many of managerial accounting's concepts and methods have been developed in a manufacturing context, they are increasingly being applied to merchandising and service organizations.

Job-Order and Process Costing Systems

This section provides an overview of product cost accounting in the two major types of production operations: job operations and process operations.

In *job-order costing,* costs are collected for each "unit" produced. Job-order systems are useful for companies whose manufacturing operations are designed for specific jobs or orders, such as print shops, custom furniture manufacturing, and construction. Companies that produce on contract, such as defense contractors, use job-order costing. Costs are often collected by department, too, for evaluating the performance of departmental personnel. For example, in a print shop, costs are collected for each order. For a defense contractor, costs are collected for each contract. For a custom home builder, costs are collected for each house.

Example Unique Buildings makes a customized product. In April, three jobs were started and completed (no beginning inventories). The manufacturing cost of each job was

Job No. 1001 . . . . $8,000
Job No. 1002 6,000
Job No. 1003 7,000

Job No. 1001 was sold. The flow of costs for this company that manufactures jobs is shown in the top panel of Exhibit 5.2.

In *process costing,* costs are accumulated in a department or production process during an accounting period (for example, a month), then spread evenly, or "averaged," over the units produced that month. The basic formula is

$$\text{Unit Cost} = \frac{\text{Total Manufacturing Costs}}{\text{Total Units Produced}}$$

Exhibit 5.2
Flow of Costs
Job-Order and Process Costing

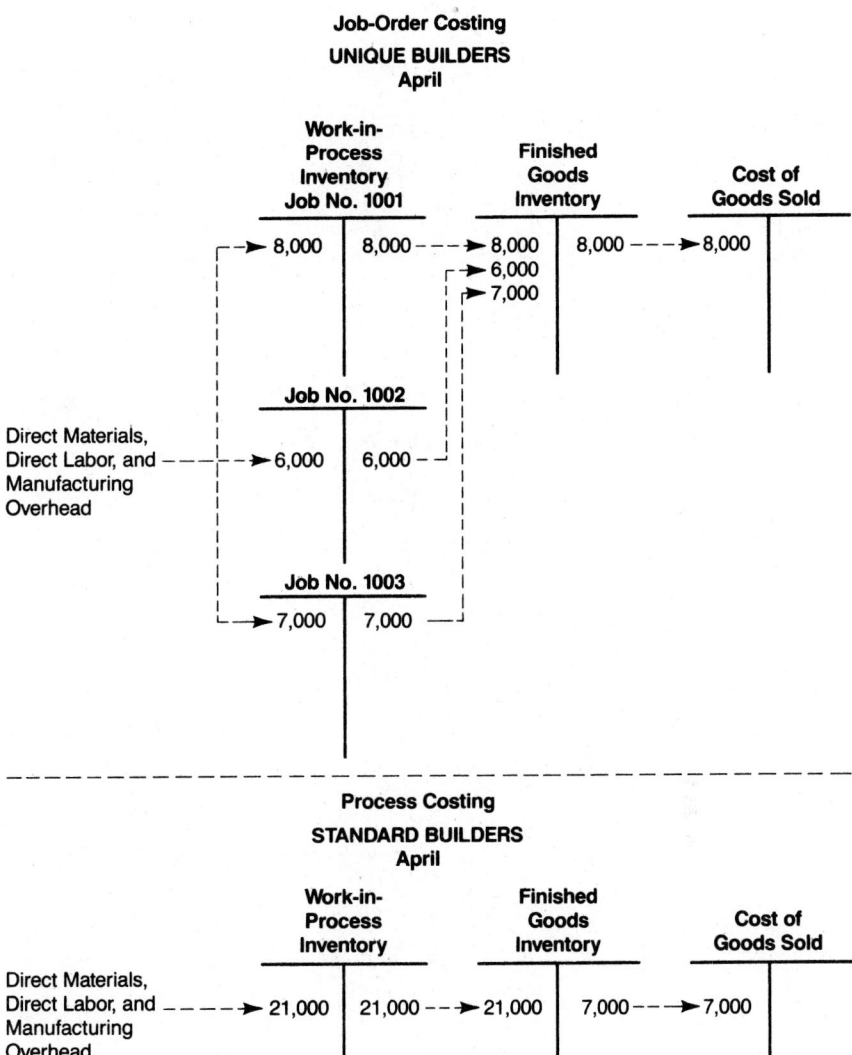

Process costing is used when units being produced are relatively uniform. Industries using process costing include chemicals, automobile manufacturing, steel, and oil refining.

Example Standard Builders started and completed three homogeneous units in April (no beginning or ending inventories). Total manufacturing costs were $21,000,

Exhibit 5.3
CUSTOM MANUFACTURING CORPORATION
Accounting for Manufacturing Costs in a Job-Order System

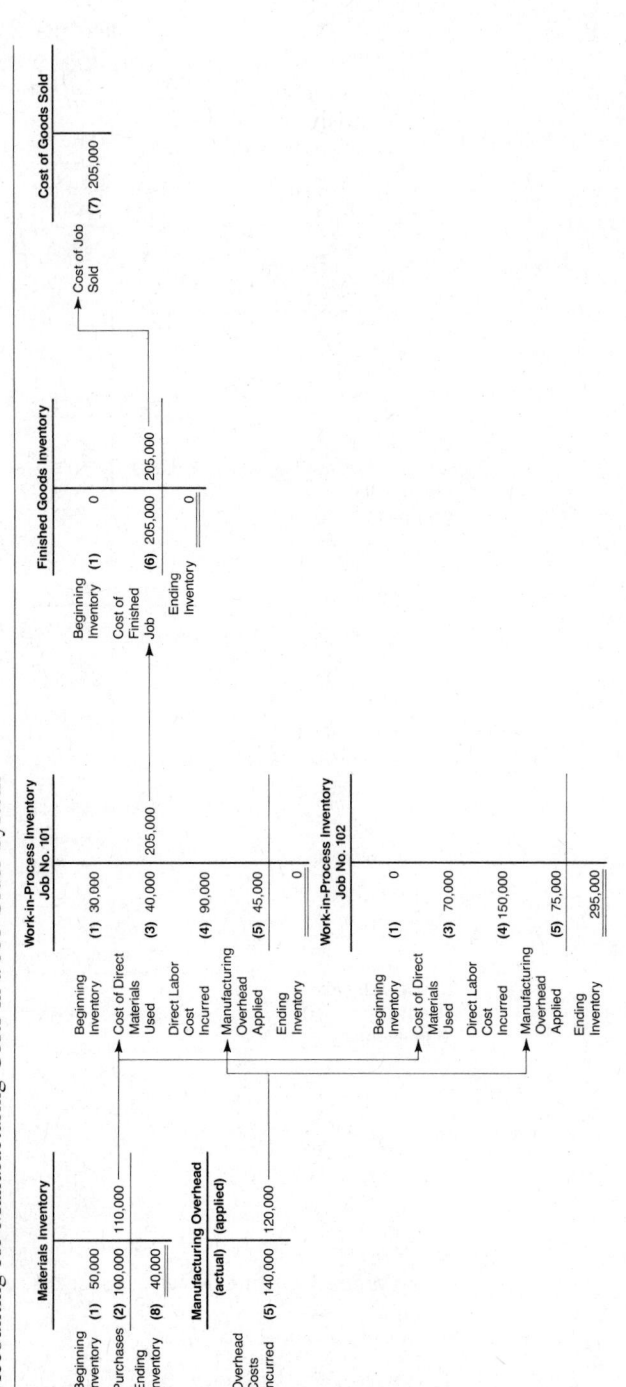

so each unit was assigned a cost of $7,000. One unit was sold. This flow of costs is shown in the bottom panel of Exhibit 5.2. Note how much more detail would be required under job-order costing for a large number (say, 10,000) of jobs or units.

We have just presented an overview of costing in companies with job or process operations. Next, we examine these two production systems in more detail, using comprehensive examples.

Job-Order System Example

The illustration of a job-order system is based on the transactions of Custom Manufacturing Corporation for January. This company manufactures custom-order heavy equipment. Costs are accumulated in separate accounts for each job or order. Exhibit 5.3 presents the flow of costs for January using full absorption, normal costing. Custom Manufacturing Corporation worked on two jobs during January: Job 101 and Job 102. Note that there is a separate Work-in-Process Inventory account for each job. (The numbers in parentheses in Exhibit 5.3 correspond to the transactions or events described below.)

1. At the beginning of January, direct materials costing $50,000 were in the materials storeroom. There was one job in the factory, Job 101, that was partially complete. Manufacturing costs accumulated on Job 101, as of the beginning of January, were $30,000. Another job, Job 102, was started during the month.

2. Direct materials costing $100,000 were purchased during January. These purchases are shown on the left side of the Materials Inventory account. (Indirect materials are not carried in the Materials Inventory account at Custom Manufacturing. Costs of indirect materials are debited to manufacturing overhead when they are purchased and used.)

3. Direct materials costing $110,000 were issued to the factory. Direct materials costing $40,000 were used on Job 101 and direct materials costing $70,000 were used on Job 102.

4. Direct labor costs incurred in the factory during January totaled $240,000, of which $90,000 was attributable to Job 101 and $150,000 was attributable to Job 102.

5. At the beginning of January, manufacturing overhead costs were estimated for the year. Fixed costs were estimated to be $750,000. Variable overhead costs were estimated to vary with direct labor costs at the rate of $.25 per dollar of direct labor cost. Custom Manufacturing Corporation expected to incur $3,000,000 of direct labor cost for the year. Thus, the total overhead cost expected for the year was $1,500,000 [= $750,000 + (.25 × $3,000,000)]. The predetermined rate for applying manufacturing overhead costs to jobs is 50 percent of direct labor costs (= $1,500,000 ÷ $3,000,000).

Actual manufacturing overhead costs, including indirect materials and indirect labor, of $140,000 are shown on the debit (left) side of Manufacturing Overhead. Overhead costs were allocated to Job 101 and Job 102 at the rate of 50 percent of

Exhibit 5.4
WALSH PROCESSING CORPORATION
Accounting for Manufacturing Costs in a Process System

Materials Inventory

Beginning Inventory (1)	200,000		
Purchases (2)	600,000	550,000	
Ending Inventory (8)	250,000		

Manufacturing Overhead

Overhead Costs Incurred (5)	180,000	205,000	

Work-in-Process Inventory

Beginning Inventory (1)	140,600	1,130,000	
Cost of Direct Materials Used (3)	550,000		
Direct Labor Costs Incurred (4)	410,000		
Manufacturing Overhead Costs Applied (5)	205,000		
Ending Inventory (6)	175,600		

Finished Goods Inventory

Beginning Inventory (1)	300,000		
Cost of Units Completed (6)	1,130,000	1,030,000	Cost of Units Sold (7)
Ending Inventory (8)	400,000		

Cost of Goods Sold

Cost of Units Sold (7)	1,030,000

Calculation of Equivalent Units and Allocation of Manufacturing Costs

	Equivalent Units					Costs Allocated to:	
	Units Completed (1)	Units Incomplete (2)	Total Equivalent Units (3)	Total Costs (4)	Cost per Equivalent Unit (5)[d]	Units Completed (6)[e]	Units Incomplete (7)[f]
Direct Materials	100,000	20,000	120,000	$ 600,000 [a]	$ 5.00	$ 500,000	$100,000
Direct Labor	100,000	12,000	112,000	470,400 [b]	4.20	420,000	50,400
Manufacturing Overhead	100,000	12,000	112,000	235,200 [c]	2.10	210,000	25,200
Total				$1,305,600	$11.30	$1,130,000	$175,600

[a] Beginning inventory costs + costs incurred = $50,000 + $550,000; see text.
[b] $60,400 + $410,000; see text.
[c] $30,200 + $205,000; see text.
[d] Column (4) ÷ column (3).
[e] Column (1) × column (5).
[f] Column (2) × column (5).

the direct labor cost incurred on each job. [These amounts are shown on the credit (right) side of the Manufacturing Overhead account and on the debit (left) side of the Work-in-Process Inventory accounts.]

6. During January, Job 101 was completed and transferred to the finished goods storeroom. The accumulated costs on Job 101 were $205,000. This amount flows, or is transferred, from the Work-in-Process Inventory to the Finished Goods Inventory account.

7. Job 101 is shipped to the customer. The cost of Job 101 is transferred from Finished Goods Inventory to Cost of Goods Sold.

8. The Direct Materials Inventory account shows that direct materials costing $40,000 should be in the materials storeroom at the end of January. (A physical count might be taken to ensure that inventory of this amount is actually on hand.)

9. Job 102 is incomplete as of the end of January. Costs accumulated on this job during the month total $295,000. This amount becomes the beginning inventory for Work-in-Process Inventory, Job 102, for February.

The distinctive feature of a job-order system is that costs are accumulated by job. The allocation or assignment of these costs to "output" is relatively simple, because the product is a well-defined, specific customer's order.

Process System Example

A process cost system is used when many units of a uniform product are processed continually during the period. That is, at any time there are units at all stages of completion. The illustration that follows is for Walsh Processing Corporation for January. Walsh's only product passes through a single manufacturing process. Direct labor and manufacturing overhead costs are incurred uniformly over the production process. Exhibit 5.4 presents the flow of costs for January.

Note that there is just one Work-in-Process Inventory account for the manufacturing process, in contrast to a job-order system in which there is a Work-in-Process account for each job. The numbers in parentheses correspond to the transactions and events described below.

1. At the beginning of January, balances in inventory accounts were Materials Inventory, $200,000; Work-in-Process Inventory, $140,600 (composed of $50,000 direct materials, $60,400 direct labor, and $30,200 manufacturing overhead); Finished Goods Inventory, $300,000.

2. Direct materials purchased during January totaled $600,000.

3. Direct materials costing $550,000 were issued to the factory. Materials are added to the product at the beginning of the production process.

4. Direct labor costs incurred during January totaled $410,000.

5. Annual budgeted manufacturing overhead costs were as follows: fixed, $400,000; variable, 40 percent of direct labor costs. Direct labor costs were estimated to be

$4,000,000 for the year. Thus, the total overhead cost expected to be incurred during the year was $2,000,000 [= $400,000 + (.40 × $4,000,000)]. The predetermined rate for applying overhead costs to production each month is thus 50 percent of direct labor cost (= $2,000,000 ÷ $4,000,000). Actual manufacturing overhead costs, including indirect materials and indirect labor, were $180,000 in January. During January, direct labor costs were $410,000. Manufacturing overhead cost assigned to January's production was therefore $205,000.

6. We now come to the step in a process costing system that distinguishes it from job-order costing: the assignment or allocation of costs to units completed and to units in ending Work-in-Process Inventory. During January, 100,000 units were completed and transferred to the finished goods storeroom. At the end of January, 20,000 units were still in the factory at various stages of completion. It was determined that these unfinished units were, on average, 60 percent complete.

It would be inappropriate to take the total manufacturing costs (including the cost of beginning inventory) incurred of $1,305,600 (= $140,600 beginning Work-in-Process Inventory + $550,000 direct materials + $410,000 direct labor + $205,000 manufacturing overhead) and allocate it 2/12 (= 20,000 units ÷ 120,000 units) to units in ending inventory, because units in ending inventory have not received the full production effort that a completed unit has received. Instead, the allocation of costs is made by expressing units in ending inventory in terms of *equivalent whole* or *completed units*.

For example, the units in ending inventory are 60 percent complete, on average, as of the end of January. The 20,000 partially completed units in ending inventory therefore have received direct labor and overhead effort equal to that of 12,000 (= 60 percent × 20,000) complete units. The total equivalent units for direct labor and manufacturing overhead is therefore 112,000 units (= 100,000 complete + 12,000 partially completed). The direct labor and overhead costs are allocated 100/112 to the units completed and 12/112 to the units in ending inventory.

The calculation of equivalent units for direct material is somewhat different because direct materials are added at the beginning of processing at Walsh Processing Corporation. Therefore, the 20,000 units in ending inventory have received all of the direct material they will receive. That is, the 20,000 partially completed units have received the same amount of direct materials as 20,000 completed units.

With respect to direct materials, there are 120,000 equivalent whole units (= 100,000 units + 20,000 units). The direct materials costs therefore are allocated 100/120 to units completed and 20/120 to units in ending inventory.

The lower panel of Exhibit 5.4 shows the calculation of equivalent units for each of the three elements of manufacturing cost. The total cost in column (4) is the cost in beginning inventory plus the cost incurred during the period.

For example, the total direct materials cost of $600,000 is composed of $50,000 from beginning inventory [see item (1)] and $550,000 of costs incurred during January. The total cost is expressed in terms of cost per equivalent unit in column (5) by dividing the total cost in column (4) by the equivalent units in column (3). The total costs are then assigned to units completed in column (6) and units in ending inventory in column (7). The basis for the cost allocations in columns (6) and (7) is the equivalent units in columns (1) and (2) and the cost per equivalent unit in column (5).

7. The cost of units sold during January is determined to be $1,030,000.

8. Records show that an ending inventory of direct materials costing $250,000 and an ending inventory of finished goods costing $400,000 should be on hand at the end of January.

The distinctive feature of process costing systems is that costs are accumulated for *all* units in a production process, not for *each* unit as in job costing. Because there are a relatively large number of identical units being produced, all in various stages of completion, it is necessary to assign or allocate costs according to equivalent whole units rather than simply to the total number of units being processed.

The process costing procedure illustrated here follows a *weighted-average cost flow assumption*. That is, costs from beginning inventory are added to costs incurred during the current period and a weighted-average cost per equivalent unit is computed for each element of cost. (A FIFO or LIFO cost flow assumption could also be used. These methods are discussed in cost accounting texts.)

Job Versus Process Costing: Cost Benefit Considerations

Why is one accounting system preferred to another? The answer lies in cost/benefit analysis. In general, the costs of record keeping under job-order systems are greater than under process costing. Consider a house builder. Under job-order costing, the costs must be accumulated for each house. If lumber is sent on a truck for delivery to several houses, it is not sufficient to record the total issued. Records must be kept of the amount delivered to, and subsequently returned from, each house. If laborers work on several houses, they must keep track of the time spent on *each* house. Process costing, however, simply requires recording the total cost. For the house builder, process costing would report the average cost of all houses built. (In practice, house builders generally use job-order for custom-built houses, and process costing for houses within a particular model type or floor plan.)

Under process costing, the direct cost incurred for a particular unit is not reported. If all units are homogeneous, this loss of information is probably minimal. Is it important for Kellogg's to know whether the cost of the 1,001st box of Raisin Bran differs from the 1,002nd's cost? Not likely! Cost control and performance evaluation will take place by department or activity, not by unit produced. Thus, the additional benefits of job-order costing would not justify the additional record-keeping costs.

In Chapter 3, we indicate that a "finer" information system is superior to a "coarser" one if the cost of the two is the same. A job-order costing system is usually "finer" than a process costing system, because the former contains all of the information that is in the latter (that is, total manufacturing costs and total units), and more. The additional information in job-order costing is the cost of *each* unit. In process costing, that information is not available—only the *aggregate* of costs is available, which is then spread over units to give an *average* unit cost.

Although job-order costing is "finer" than process costing, it is usually a more costly system. Thus, management and accountants must examine the costs and benefits of information and pick the method that best fits the organization's production operations.

Example In this example, a custom house builder explains benefits of job-order costing for companies that make heterogeneous products.

> "We estimate the costs of each house for pricing purposes. Unless we know the actual costs of each house, we cannot evaluate our estimation methods. We use the information for performance evaluation and cost control, too. We assign a manager to each house who is responsible to see that actual costs don't exceed the estimate. If we come in less than 10 percent over estimate, the manager gets a bonus.
>
> "We need a job-order system to help us charge customers for any cost overruns, too. Usually, customers make changes as we build. If the changes have a small impact on costs, we absorb them. But if the costs added by these changes mount up, we like to go to the customer with our tally of estimated and actual costs, and get an adjustment in the price of the house. Sometimes, we build on a cost-plus basis, in which case we *must* know and be able to document costs for each house so we can collect from the customer."

In summary, the comparative costs and benefits of job and process costing are usually evaluated as follows:

Nature of Production Operations	Costing System Used
Heterogeneous Units, Each Unit Large	Job Costing
Homogeneous Units, Continuous Process, Many Small Units . .	Process Costing

Merchandising

The merchandising activity can be thought of as starting where manufacturing left off, that is, at Finished Goods Inventory. Merchandising companies purchase goods already manufactured. There are no Direct Material, Direct Labor, Manufacturing Overhead, or Work-in-Process accounts in merchandising firms. Finished Goods Inventory is simply called "Merchandise Inventory."

Exhibit 5.5 shows the flow of costs through the accounts. Note that the top accounts in Exhibit 5.5 deal with the purchase and sale of inventory. The purchase operation in merchandising parallels that in manufacturing. The inventory account displays the costs for which buyers are responsible. One measure of buyers' performance is a comparison of the actual costs charged or debited to inventory and the budget costs allowed for the goods purchased.

The cost of the units sold during the period is transferred to Cost of Goods Sold, just as in manufacturing.

Exhibit 5.5
Flow of Costs: Merchandising

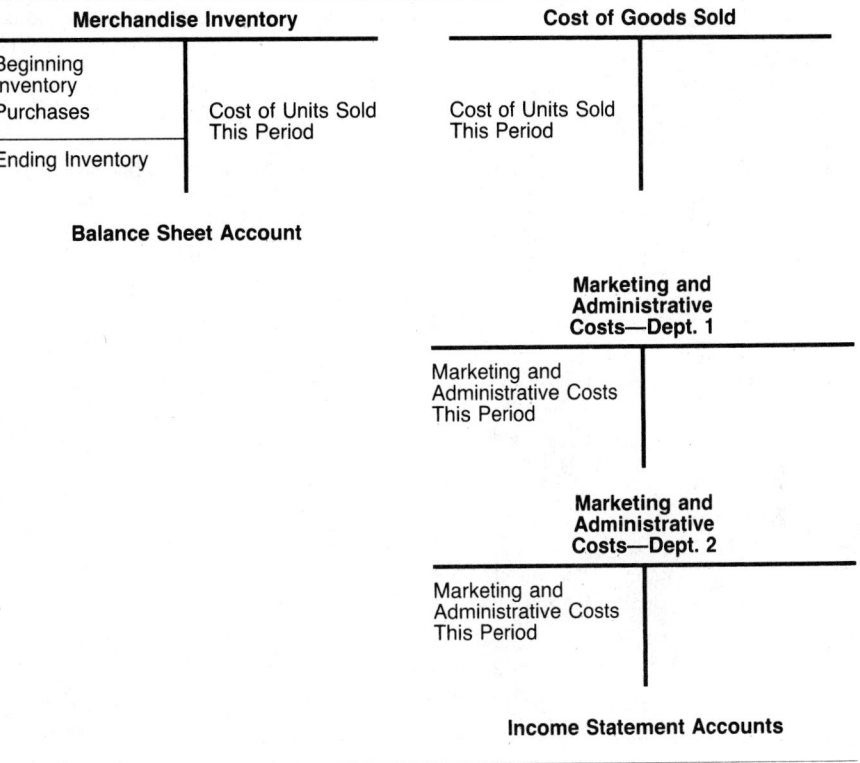

Merchandise Inventory		**Cost of Goods Sold**	
Beginning Inventory Purchases	Cost of Units Sold This Period	Cost of Units Sold This Period	
Ending Inventory			

Balance Sheet Account

Marketing and Administrative Costs—Dept. 1	
Marketing and Administrative Costs This Period	

Marketing and Administrative Costs—Dept. 2	
Marketing and Administrative Costs This Period	

Income Statement Accounts

The two lower accounts in Exhibit 5.5 show the costs required to run the company and market the product. These costs can be thought of as the ''value added'' in merchandising. Unlike the value added in manufacturing, however, these costs are not added to the value of inventory.

Product costing is easier in merchandising than in manufacturing. The choice of product costing method—for example, full absorption versus variable costing, actual versus normal costing—does not arise in merchandising. In merchandising, a product's cost is generally its purchase price plus costs of transporting the merchandise.[1]

Example Weather Beaters buys umbrellas from Umbrella Makers and sells them in its retail store. In June, Weather Beaters purchased 1,100 umbrellas at $9.00 each plus $.50 each for freight-in, and sold 600 of them for $15.00 each. Weather Beaters had 50 umbrellas on hand on June 1 at an inventory cost of $9.50 each.

---

[1]This is not to minimize important financial reporting issues involving inventory such as flow assumptions (for example, first-in, first-out or last-in, first-out) or cost basis (current value versus historical cost) assumptions. These issues come up in both merchandising and manufacturing.

Direct marketing and administrative costs of the umbrella operation were $3,000 for June. All transactions were on account.

The following entries would record these transactions:

(1) Merchandise Inventory. 10,450
  Accounts Payable to Umbrella Makers 9,900
  Accounts Payable: Freight-in. 550
  To record the purchase of 1,100 umbrellas at $9.00 each plus freight-in of $.50 per umbrella.

(2) Accounts Receivable 9,000
  Sales 9,000
  Cost of Goods Sold. 5,700
  Merchandise Inventory 5,700
  To record the sale of 600 umbrellas at $15.00. (Each umbrella is assigned a cost of $9.50. If the units have different values, it is important to specify cost flow assumptions—for example, FIFO, LIFO.)

(3) Marketing and Administrative Costs 3,000
  Accounts Payable 3,000
  To record marketing and administrative costs for June.

Exhibit 5.6 shows the flow of costs, and Exhibit 5.7 shows the income statement for this example. Note how much simpler the merchandising inventory accounting system is than the manufacturing accounting system. Merchandising does not require the extensive product costing apparatus that manufacturing does. Performance evaluation and cost control in merchandising focus on marketing and administrative costs, which are usually accounted for by product line and department. For example, in a retail department store, costs are collected and reported for each major product line and department—sportswear, housewares, furniture, and so on.

Service

The flow of costs in service organizations is similar to manufacturing. Input costs include labor and overhead that are part of the service provided. Costs are often collected by departments in multidepartment organizations for performance evaluation. In consulting, public accounting, and similar service organizations, costs are also collected by job or "client." The accounting method is analogous to that used in manufacturing job shops. As in manufacturing, costs are collected by job for performance evaluation, to provide information for cost control, and to compare actual with estimated costs for pricing of future jobs.

A key difference between service organizations and manufacturing or merchandising organizations is that service organizations do not show inventories (other than supplies) on the financial statements for external reporting. Service organizations sometimes maintain "Work-in-Process Inventory" in their internal records. This is the cost of service performed for a client but not yet billed, which is like the accumulation of unbilled costs for a special contract or job in a manufacturing job shop.

Exhibit 5.6
WEATHER BEATERS
Merchandise Cost Flows
June

Accounts Payable		Merchandise Inventory		Cost of Goods Sold	
	9,900 (1)	Beg. Bal. 475	5,700 (2)	(2) 5,700	
	550 (1)	(1) 10,450			
		End. Bal. 5,225			

				Marketing and Administrative Costs	
	3,000 (3)			(3) 3,000	

Accounts Receivable				Sales	
(2) 9,000					9,000 (2)

Note: Numbers in parentheses correspond to journal entries in text.

Exhibit 5.7
WEATHER BEATERS
Income Statement
for the Month Ending June 30

Sales Revenue.	$9,000
Less Cost of Goods Sold[a].	(5,700)
Gross Margin	$3,300
Less Marketing and Administrative Costs	(3,000)
Operating Profit	$ 300

[a]Statement of cost of goods sold:

Beginning Merchandise Inventory	$ 475
Add: Purchases	9,900
Freight-in	550
Goods Available for Sale.	$10,925
Less Ending Inventory	(5,225)
Cost of Goods Sold	$ 5,700

Example For the month of July, Conehead Consulting Group (CCG) has the following activity:

Client A: 400 hours.

Client B: 600 hours.

Billing rate to client: $100 per hour.

Labor costs (all consulting staff): $40 per hour.

Total consulting hours worked in July: 1,200 hours. (200 hours could not be charged to a client and are called "direct labor–unbillable.")

Actual overhead costs for July: $24,000. (Overhead includes travel, secretarial work, telephone, copying, supplies, and postage.)

Overhead charged to jobs based on hours worked:

$$\text{Rate per Hour} = \frac{\text{Actual Overhead Costs}}{\text{Actual Labor Hours}}$$

$$= \frac{\$24,000}{1,200 \text{ Hours}}$$

$$= \$20 \text{ per Hour.}$$

Marketing and administrative costs: $12,000.

All transactions are on account.

Entries to record these transactions are as follows:

(1) Direct Labor—Client A   16,000
Direct Labor—Client B   24,000
Direct Labor–Unbillable   8,000
   Wages Payable.   48,000
To record labor costs for July and to assign direct labor costs to Client A (400 hours @ $40 = $16,000) and Client B (600 hours @ $40 = $24,000).

(2) Overhead—Client A   8,000
Overhead—Client B   12,000
Unassigned Overhead   4,000
   Various Payables   24,000
To record overhead costs for July and to assign overhead costs to Client A (400 hours @ $20 = $8,000), to Client B (600 hours @ $20 = $12,000), and Unassigned (200 hours @ $20 = $4,000).

(3) Marketing and Administrative Costs   12,000
   Payables   12,000
To record marketing and administrative expense for July.

(4) Accounts Receivable.   100,000
   Revenue—Client A   40,000
   Revenue—Client B   60,000
To record billing for services in July to Client A (400 hours @ $100 = $40,000) and to Client B (600 hours @ $100 = $60,000).

Exhibits 5.8 and 5.9 show the flow of costs and the income statement.

Exhibit 5.8
CONEHEAD CONSULTING GROUP
Flow of Costs in a Service Organization, July

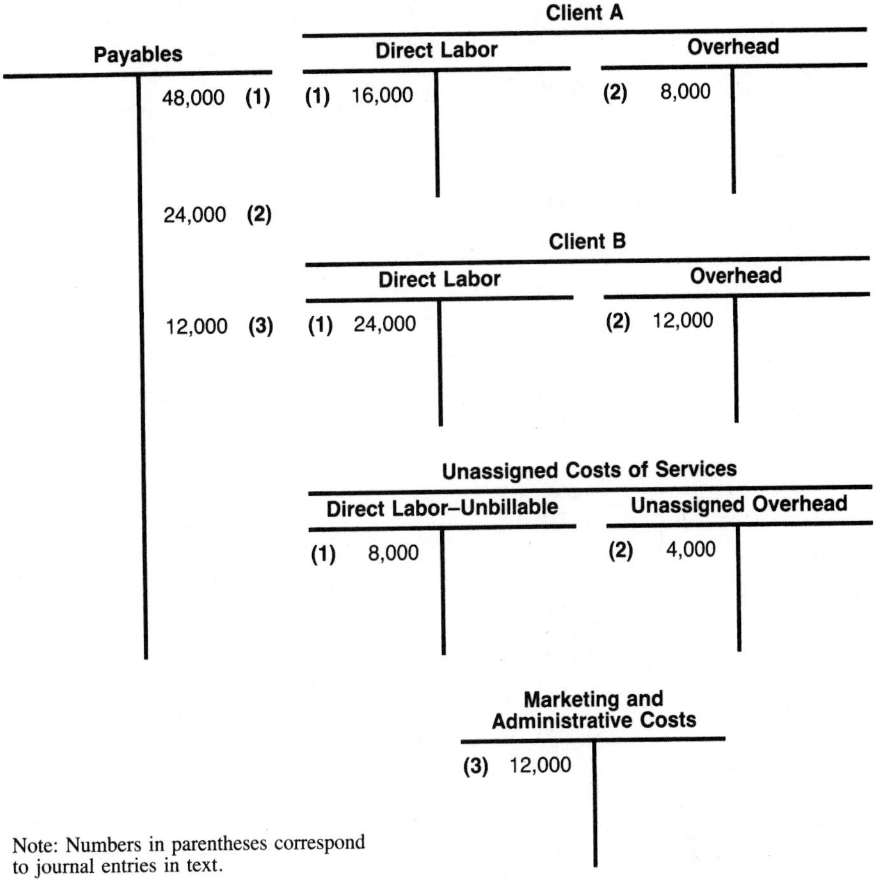

Client A

Payables		Direct Labor		Overhead	
	48,000 (1)	(1) 16,000		(2) 8,000	
	24,000 (2)				

Client B

	Direct Labor		Overhead	
12,000 (3)	(1) 24,000		(2) 12,000	

Unassigned Costs of Services

Direct Labor–Unbillable		Unassigned Overhead	
(1) 8,000		(2) 4,000	

Marketing and Administrative Costs

(3) 12,000	

Note: Numbers in parentheses correspond
to journal entries in text.

Exhibit 5.9
CONEHEAD CONSULTING GROUP
Income Statement
for the Month Ending July 31

Revenue from Services for Clients	$100,000
Less Direct Costs of Services to Clients:	
Labor	(40,000)
Overhead	(20,000)
Gross Margin	$ 40,000
Less Other Costs:	
Labor	(8,000)
Overhead	(4,000)
Marketing and Administrative	(12,000)
Operating Profit	$ 16,000

Summary

Job-order accounting systems are used when manufacturing operations are designed for special jobs or customer orders. Process accounting systems are used when manufacturing operations are designed for production of standardized products that pass through several production processes. In job-order costing, costs are accumulated for each unit or job produced; in process costing, costs are accumulated for an entire operation or department and averaged over the units produced.

Chapters 3 and 4 presented a 2 × 3 matrix of alternative costing methods. This chapter adds a comparison of two manufacturing systems, job-order and process costing, as shown below:

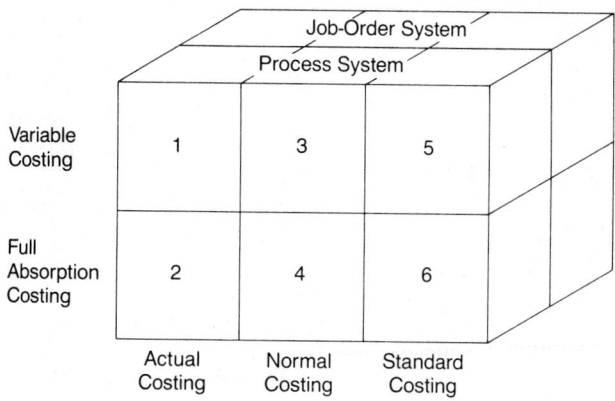

Any of the six product cost methods could be used in process systems; *any* could be used in job-order systems. Process systems tend to use standard costing, however. This is because standard costs are more easily assigned to the homogeneous units of a process manufacturing system than to the heterogeneous units of a job-order system. Job-order systems tend to use actual (or normal) costing. Actual costs are often used for pricing and performance evaluation of jobs.

Merchandising starts where manufacturing ends. Product costing is easier in merchandising than in manufacturing. Product costs are simply the purchase price plus direct costs of obtaining the product (for example, freight-in). Thus, product costing for external financial reporting is not as complicated in merchandising as in manufacturing. For managerial purposes, the accounting system should be designed to assign costs to merchandising responsibility centers—primarily product lines and departments.

Service organizations have costing systems similar to manufacturing, with one important difference—there are usually no inventories (except for supplies) for external reporting. Job-order costing is found in many service organizations, such as consulting firms. Some service organizations, notably banks, use standard costing. In short, knowledge of costing in manufacturing companies can, with a few modifications, be applied to service organizations.

Problem 1 for Self-Study

Comprehensive Cost Flow Problem in a Job-Order Company[2]

One clear April morning, Patrick O'Leary and James Hughes sat morosely in the office adjacent to their jointly owned factory. They had spent an entire day trying to devise a better way of pricing their job orders. Last year was a very busy year, but Donegal Woolens posted a loss. "Jim, we ought to go to a management consulting firm before things get worse," O'Leary said. "I guess you're right," Hughes agreed with resignation, "but we can hardly afford to spend any more money."

Both Pat and Jim were recent graduates of a well-known fashion design school. Extremely talented, the pair had attracted the attention of several well-known fashion designers. Their company, Donegal Woolens, supplied custom-ordered, hand-knit woolens for a few exclusive stores. Their specialty was classic Irish knits, but they were occasionally willing to create *avante garde* designs. Donegal Woolens employed 20 full-time knitters at $5 per hour. Pat and Jim assembled and packed the knitted pieces themselves, and each took a salary of $1,500 per month. Since beginning operations last year, they had priced the various jobs by applying a markup of 20 percent on direct labor and direct material costs. However, despite operating at capacity, last year's performance was a great disappointment to them. In total, 10 jobs were taken and completed, incurring the following costs:

Jobs	Raw Materials	Direct Labor Costs
101	$ 7,650	$ 30,740
102	3,230	14,050
103	6,840	23,190
104	4,100	15,260
105	5,900	21,560
106	4,580	18,810
107	7,240	25,950
108	2,060	10,650
109	2,870	12,440
110	7,300	27,350
	$51,770	$200,000
Manufacturing Overhead Costs		$52,000

[2]From J. Lim.

Thirty percent of the $52,000 manufacturing overhead was considered variable overhead; 70 percent was considered fixed.

Donegal Woolens expected to operate at the same activity level as last year, and overhead costs and the wage rate were not expected to change.

For the first quarter of this year, Donegal Woolens had just completed two jobs and was beginning on the third. The costs incurred were as follows:

Jobs	Raw Materials	Direct Labor Costs
111	$6,860	$24,500
112	4,650	15,620
113	4,700	9,880
Total Factory Overhead		$13,560
Total Marketing and Administrative Costs		5,600

You are an associated consultant with Vesting Concerns Management Consultants, the firm Donegal Woolens has approached. The senior partner of your firm has examined Donegal Woolens' books and has decided to divide actual factory overhead by job into fixed and variable portions as follows:[3]

	Actual Factory Overhead	
Jobs	Variable	Fixed
111	$1,495	$ 5,200
112	1,375	4,410
113	230	850
	$3,100	$10,460

In the first quarter of this year, 40 percent of marketing and administrative costs were variable, 60 percent were fixed.

You have been asked by the senior partner to do the following for Donegal Woolens:

a.   Present in T-accounts the full absorption/actual manufacturing cost flows for the three jobs in the first quarter of this year.

b.   Using last year's overhead costs and direct labor hours, calculate a predetermined overhead rate per direct labor hour for variable and fixed overhead.

c.   Present in T-accounts the full absorption/normal manufacturing cost flows for the three jobs in the first quarter of this year. Use the overhead rates derived in part **b.**

---

[3] Actual manufacturing costs that are not traceable directly to specific jobs have to be allocated. For example, depreciation may be allocated on the basis of machine hours, and factory rent on the basis of area used. Allocation can be arbitrary.

d. Prepare income statements for the first quarter of this year under:
   (1) Full absorption/actual.
   (2) Full absorption/normal.
   (3) Variable costing/actual.
   (4) Variable costing/normal.

You are told that Jobs 111 and 112 are priced at $42,500 and $27,500, respectively. All over- or underapplied overhead for the quarter is expensed on the income statement.

Suggested Solution

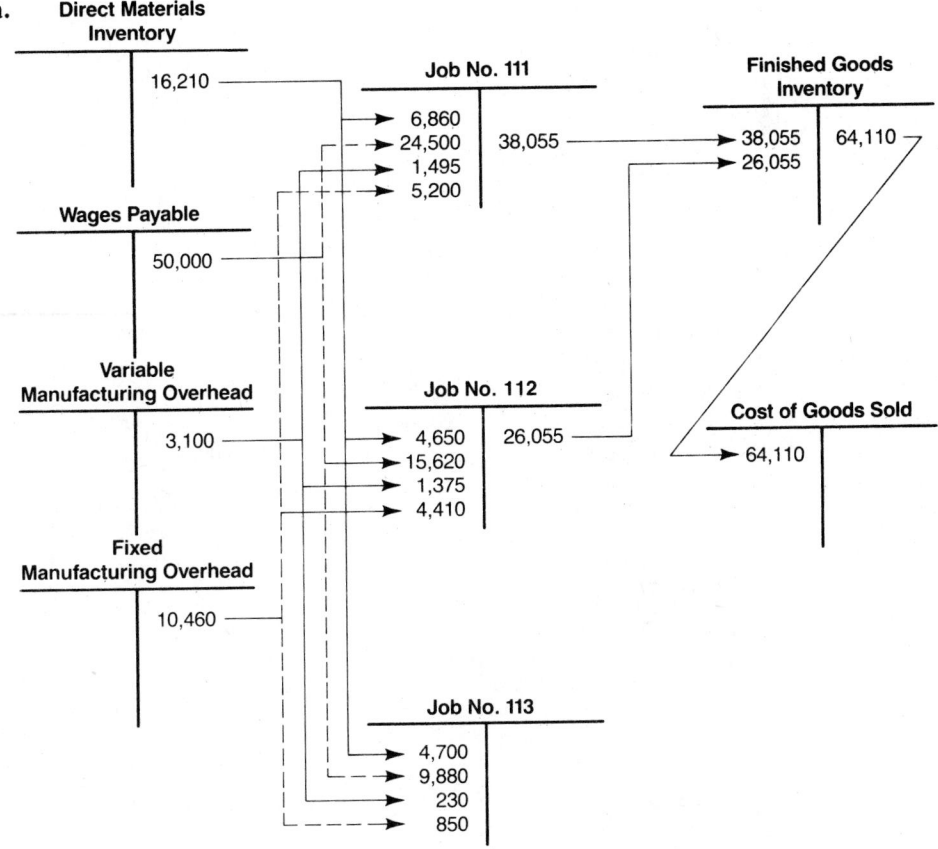

b. Total Direct Labor Costs = $200,000.

$$\text{Total Direct Labor Hours} = \frac{\$200,000}{\$5/\text{hr.}} = 40,000.$$

Variable Manufacturing Overhead $= 0.30 \times \$52,000$
$= \$15,600.$

Predetermined Variable Overhead Rate $= \dfrac{\$15,600}{40,000}$

$= \$0.39$ per Direct Labor Hour.

Fixed Manufacturing Overhead $= 0.70 \times \$52,000$
$= \$36,400.$

Predetermined Fixed Overhead Rate $= \dfrac{\$36,400}{40,000}$

$= \$0.91$ per Direct Labor Hour.

c.

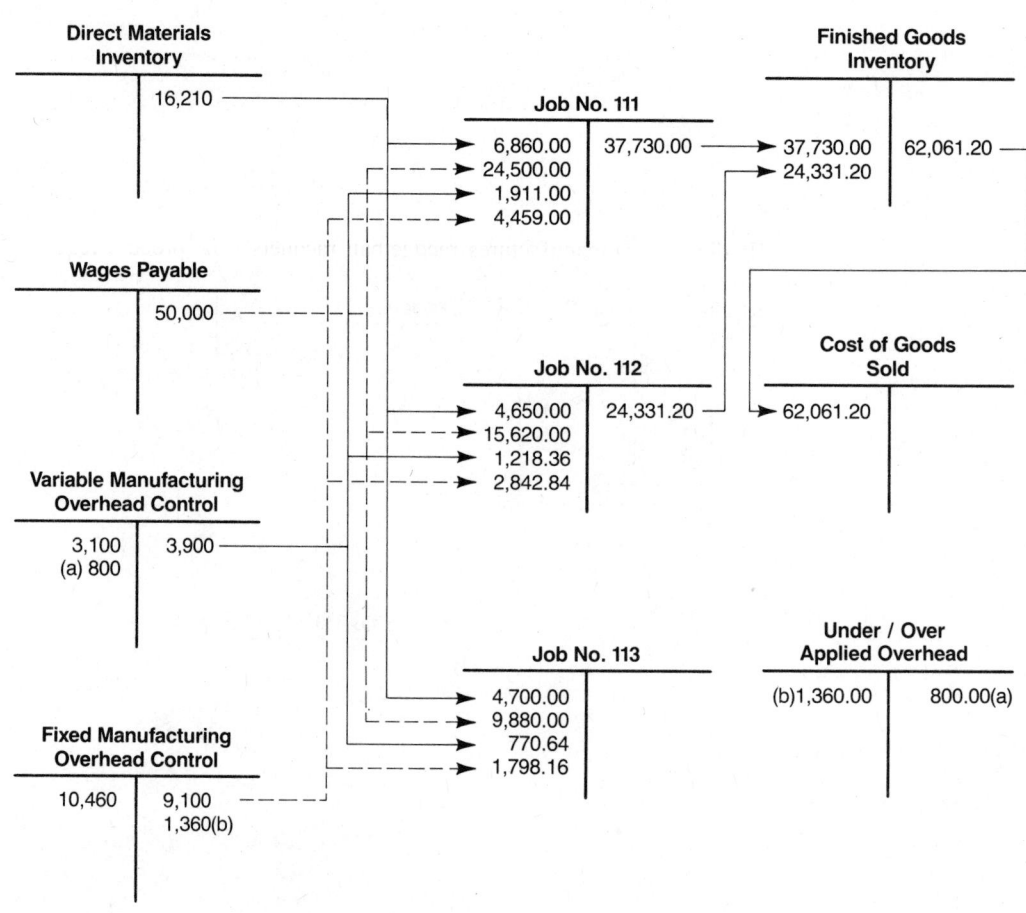

d.

	Actual	Normal
Full Absorption Costing		
Sales Revenue	$70,000	$70,000.00
Less Cost of Goods Sold	(64,110)	(62,061.20)
Gross Margin.	$ 5,890	$ 7,938.80
Less:		
(Under-) Overapplied Overhead	—	(560.00)
Marketing and Administrative Costs	(5,600)	(5,600.00)
Operating Profit (Loss)	$ 290	$ 1,778.80
Variable Costing		
Sales Revenue	$70,000	$70,000.00
Less:		
Variable Manufacturing Costs	(54,500)	(54,759.36)
Variable Marketing and Administrative Costs	(2,240)	(2,240.00)
Contribution Margin	$13,260	$13,000.64
Less:		
Fixed Manufacturing Costs	(10,460)	(10,460.00)
(Under-) Overapplied Overhead	—	800.00
Fixed Marketing and Administrative Costs	(3,360)	(3,360.00)
Operating Profit (Loss)	$ (560)	$ (19.36)

Problem 2 for Self-Study

Tracing Manufacturing Cost Flows in a Process Costing Company

Hardball, Inc. manufactures racquetball racquets. The process requires two manufacturing departments: assembling and finishing. Racquets are formed in the assembling department using aluminum tubing, handle materials, and frame accessories. The completed frames are sent to the finishing department, where the racquets are stringed and packaged for shipment to sporting goods stores. Six thousand frames were transferred to the finishing department this month.

Because the racquets are manufactured in such large numbers, the company uses a process cost accounting system to assign costs to racquets. The following information is available for Hardball manufacturing activities of the finishing department during the past month:

	Units	Prior Department Costs[a]	Direct Materials	Conversion Costs
Physical Flow				
Beginning Inventory	1,000	100 Percent Complete	60 Percent Complete	75 Percent Complete
Ending Inventory	2,700	100 Percent Complete	80 Percent Complete	45 Percent Complete
Costs Incurred:				
Beginning Inventory	—	$ 7,100	$ 600	$ 420
Current Costs		43,200	2,500	6,475

[a]Prior department costs are costs passed on from the assembling department to the finishing department.

Assume that no units were lost or spoiled.

a. Prepare a schedule showing equivalent units produced in the finishing department using weighted-average process costing.

b. Use a T-account to show cost flows in the finishing department using weighted-average costing.

Suggested Solution

a. Equivalent units—weighted average, finishing department:

	Prior Department Costs	Direct Materials	Conversion Costs
Units Transferred Out	4,300[a]	4,300	4,300
Ending Inventory	2,700	2,160[b]	1,215[c]
	7,000	6,460	5,515

[a] $BB + TI = TO + EB$
$1,000 + 6,000 = TO + 2,700$
$TO = 1,000 + 6,000 - 2,700$
$= 4,300.$
[b] $2,160 = 80\% \times 2,700.$
[c] $1,215 = 45\% \times 2,700.$

b.

Work in Process Inventory—Finishing Department

Prior Department Costs	To Finished Goods Inventory:
Beginning Inventory . . . . . $ 7,100	Prior Department Costs
Current 43,200	(50,300 ÷ 7,000) × 4,300 . . . $30,899
Total $50,300	Materials: (3,100 ÷ 6,460) ×
	4,300 2,063
Materials:	Conversion Costs: (6,895 ÷
Beginning Inventory 600	5,515) × 4,300 5,376
Current 2,500	Total Transferred to Finished
Total 3,100	Goods Inventory . . . . . $38,338[a]
Conversion Costs:	
Beginning Inventory 420	
Current 6,475	
Total 6,895	
Total Costs to Be Accounted for . . $60,295[a]	
Ending Inventory:	
Prior Department Costs (50,300	
− 30,899) $19,401	
Materials (3,100 − 2,063) . . . 1,037	
Conversion Costs (6,895 −	
5,376) 1,519	
Total ending inventory . . . . $21,957[a]	

[a]Of the $60,295 total costs to be accounted for, $38,338 were transferred to Finished Goods Inventory and $21,957 remained in ending Work-in-Process Inventory.

Problem 3 for Self-Study

Cost Flows in a Service Organization

For the month of September, Touche Andersen & Company worked 200 hours for Client A and 700 hours for Client B. Touche Andersen bills clients at the rate of $80 per hour, whereas the labor cost for its audit staff is $30 per hour. The total number of hours worked in September was 1,000 (100 hours were not billable to clients), and overhead costs were $10,000. (Examples of unbillable hours are hours spent in professional training and meetings unrelated to particular clients.) Overhead is assigned to clients based proportionally on direct labor hours, so Client A is assigned $2,000, Client B is assigned $7,000, and $1,000 remains unassigned. In addition, Touche Andersen & Company had $5,000 in marketing and administrative costs. All transactions are on account.

a. Using T-accounts, trace manufacturing costs and revenue flows.

b. Prepare a full absorption income statement for the company for the month of September.

Suggested Solution

a. TOUCHE ANDERSEN & COMPANY
September

Accounts Receivable	Revenue—Client A	Revenue—Client B	Unassigned Costs
(4) 72,000	16,000 **(4)**	56,000 **(4)**	

Wages and Accounts Payable	Direct Labor— Client A	Direct Labor— Client B	Direct Labor— Unbillable
30,000 **(1)**	**(1)** 6,000	**(1)** 21,000	**(1)** 3,000

	Overhead— Client A	Overhead— Client B	Unassigned Overhead
10,000 **(2)**	**(2)** 2,000	**(2)** 7,000	**(2)** 1,000

			Marketing and Administrative Costs
5,000 **(3)**			**(3)** 5,000

b. TOUCHE ANDERSEN & COMPANY
Income Statement
For the Month Ended September 30

Revenue from Service for Clients		$72,000
Less Costs of Services to Clients:		
Labor	$(27,000)	
Overhead	(9,000)	
Total Costs of Services to Clients.		(36,000)
Gross Margin		36,000
Less Other Costs:		
Labor	(3,000)	
Overhead	(1,000)	
Marketing and Administrative Costs.	(5,000)	
Total Other Costs		(9,000)
Operating Profit.		$27,000

Questions

1. Compare and contrast job-order systems and process costing systems.

2. Manufacturing overhead is sometimes assigned to job orders in proportion to material cost. Do you think this is likely to be a satisfactory procedure? Explain.

3. Management of a company that manufactures small appliances is trying to decide whether to install a job-order or process costing system. The manufacturing vice-president has stated that job-order costing gives them the best control because it is possible to assign costs to specific lots of goods. The controller, however, has stated that job-order costing would require too much record keeping. Is there another costing system that might meet the manufacturing vice-president's control objectives? Explain.

4. Describe the activities of each of the following types of organizations: manufacturing, merchandising, and service.

5. Why are there no inventories in a service organization?

6. A merchandiser comments: "I perform services that add to the value of the products that I sell. My marketing staff facilitates economic efficiency by purchasing the right product, informing the consuming public of its availability, and distributing it in an efficient manner. Why shouldn't I be allowed to include my marketing and administrative costs as a part of the value of my inventory?" Reply to this comment.

Exercises

7. *Tracing Cost Flows in a Job-Order Costing System.* The Kelly-Kar Products Company uses a job-order costing system. For Year 6, total overhead was estimated to be $80,000 and the number of direct labor hours is estimated to be 20,000. In the last quarter, the following jobs were completed:

Job	No. 242	No. 301
Direct Materials Cost	$ 3,200	$ 4,600
Direct Labor Costs.	$11,000	$14,000
Direct Labor Hours	2,200 Hours	2,800 Hours

    a. Based on the above information, what overhead rate might be used?

    b. Using T-accounts, trace the cost flows for the two jobs.

8. *Computing Manufacturing Costs of a Job Order.* The Johnson Products Company uses a job-order cost accounting system. For Year 4, total overhead is estimated to be $40,000 and the number of direct labor hours is estimated to be 10,000.

    a. Based on the above information, what overhead rate might be used?

    b. Job 247 is a special order for 100 special-design tables. The Work-in-Process Inventory account for this job shows raw material costs of $4,600 and direct labor costs of $7,600. It is determined that 1,200 direct labor hours have been charged to the job. What is the total cost of Job 247? What is the unit cost of each table on that job?

9. *Computing Over- or Underapplied Overhead.* The Falcon Manufacturing Company distributes its factory overhead over its job orders as a percentage of direct labor cost. The rate set for the third quarter of the year was 150 percent, based on an estimated total overhead of $75,000 and an estimated total direct labor cost of $50,000.

Indicate the amount of *overapplied* or *underapplied* overhead for the quarter under each of the following assumptions:

    a. Actual overhead, $70,000; actual direct labor, $48,000.

    b. Actual overhead, $79,000; actual direct labor, $52,000.

    c. Actual overhead, $80,000; actual direct labor, $50,000.

    d. Actual overhead, $84,000; actual direct labor, $56,000.

    e. Actual overhead, $68,000; actual direct labor, $44,000.

    f. Actual overhead, $76,000; actual direct labor, $49,000.

10. *Cost Flows in a Merchandising Organization.* Howard's Pharmacy carries three product lines: drugs, cosmetics, and toiletries. Two days after the store's month-end inventory taking, Howard Rose, the owner, was given the following figures:

Product Line	Beginning Inventory	Ending Inventory	Purchases
Drugs.	$30,500	$31,600	$40,200
Cosmetics	20,150	21,900	28,400
Toiletries	24,360	23,240	30,600
Marketing Costs			10,000
General and Administrative Costs			8,000

Use T-accounts to describe the above cost flows. Assume all costs are on account.

11. *Cost Flows in a Service Company.* Quick Sell, an advertising consulting firm, charges clients $80 per hour for their services. Direct labor costs are $30 per hour and the predetermined overhead rate is $10 per labor hour. In August, Quick Sell began and completed the following jobs:

Job A: 150 hours.

Job B: 200 hours.

Job C: 400 hours.

Actual overhead costs were $8,000, and marketing and administrative costs (all fixed) were $5,000.

    a. Using T-accounts, trace the cost flows for the month of August.

    b. Assuming that 40 percent of the overhead is variable, prepare a variable-cost income statement for August.

    c. How would Quick Sell deal with the discrepancy between actual and applied overhead?

12. *Computing Equivalent Units Using the Weighted-Average Method.* A company's records show the following information concerning the work in process in a manufacturing plant:

(1) Beginning inventory, 6,000 units (30 percent complete—materials; 40 percent complete—conversion costs).
(2) Transferred out, 17,000 units.
(3) Ending inventory (10 percent complete—materials; 5 percent complete—conversion costs).
(4) Started this month, 21,000 units.

  Compute the equivalent units produced with respect to materials and conversion costs using the weighted-average method.

13. *Computing the Cost of Job Orders.* Records of the McKinley Machine Company on May 31, before recording the application of factory overhead to products and before recording the transfer of completed units to Finished Goods Inventory, are as follows:

Work-in-Process Inventory $16,842
Factory Overhead   3,100

Job-order cost records show the following data:

	Job 576	Job 577	Job 578	Job 579	Job 580
Work in Process, May 1					
Material.	$ 953	$ 824			
Direct Labor	1,250	1,507			
Factory Overhead	1,075	945			
Direct Costs Incurred in May					
Material.	$ 170	$ 520	$1,240	$ 950	$1,312
Direct Labor	1,260	842	2,500	1,302	192

Manufacturing overhead is applied at the rate of 50 percent of direct labor cost. Jobs 576, 577, and 578 were completed during May. Jobs 579 and 580 are still in process at the end of May.

    a. Compute the total costs allocated to Job 576, to Job 577, and to Job 578.

    b. Compute the total costs allocated to Job 579 and to Job 580.

14. *Preparing Income Statement for a Merchandiser.* Sellout Corporation experienced the following events during a current year:

(1) Incurred marketing costs of $197,000 on account.

(2) Purchased $971,000 of merchandise.

(3) Paid $26,000 in transportation-in costs.

(4) Incurred $400,000 of administrative costs.

(5) Took a periodic inventory on December 31 and learned that goods with a cost of $297,000 were on hand. This compared with a beginning inventory of $314,000 on January 1.

(6) Sales revenue during the year was $1,850,000.

    Prepare an income statement based on these data.

15. *Computing Equivalent Units.* In the Assembling Department, material A is added at the beginning of processing, material B is added when units reach the 50 percent stage of completion, and direct labor and manufacturing overhead costs are incurred evenly throughout processing. There were no units in Work-in-Process Inventory at the beginning of May. During May, 80,000 units were started and completed. Another 20,000 units were started and are 30 percent complete as of the end of May. Compute the equivalent whole units of work performed during May for material A, material B, direct labor, and manufacturing overhead.

16. *Computing Equivalent Units.* Refer to the data in Exercise **15.** The Finishing Department receives semifinished products from the Assembly Department. Material C is added at the beginning of processing and material D is added at the end of processing. Direct labor and manufacturing overhead costs are incurred evenly throughout processing. During May, 80,000 units are received from the Assembly Department. Fifty thousand units are completed and transferred to the finished goods storeroom. The remaining 30,000 units are 60 percent of the way through the process as of the end of May.

    Compute the equivalent whole units for transferred-in costs, material C, material D, direct labor, and manufacturing overhead.

17. *Tracing Cost Flows Under Job-Order Costing.* The Robinson Machine Company uses a job-order cost accounting system. Manufacturing overhead is applied to jobs on a direct labor cost basis at a rate of 50 percent of direct labor cost. A Manufacturing Overhead account is used to accumulate actual overhead costs.

    At August 1, the balance in the Work-in-Process Inventory account was $34,524. The following jobs were in process at August 1:

Job No.	Materials	Direct Labor	Overhead	Total
478.	$ 5,100	$ 9,620	$4,810	$19,530
479.	3,470	3,960	1,980	9,410
480.	4,120	976	488	5,584
Total	$12,690	$14,556	$7,278	$34,524

Selected transactions for the month of August are as follows:

(1) Materials issued: Job 480, $449; Job 481, $3,570; Job 482, $2,100; general factory use, $390; total, $6,509.
(2) Labor costs are assigned as follows: Job 478, $334; Job 479; $2,650; Job 480, $7,800; Job 481, $5,890; Job 482, $1,726; general factory, $853; total, $19,253.
(3) The employer's share of payroll taxes is 8 percent of wages earned. All factory payroll taxes are treated as manufacturing overhead costs.
(4) Depreciation of factory equipment for the month is $3,200.
(5) Building depreciation for the month is $1,200.
(6) Other manufacturing costs for the month include: power, $730; repairs, $520; utility services, $450; fire insurance, $183; property taxes, $317.   TOTAL = 2200
(7) Manufacturing overhead for the month is applied to jobs.
(8) Jobs 478 and 479 are completed and transferred to the finished goods warehouse for delivery in September.

Set up T-accounts for Direct Materials Inventory, Work-in-Process Inventory, Finished Goods Inventory, and Manufacturing Overhead. The T-account for Work-in-Process Inventory should be set up so as to accumulate the costs of each of the jobs separately. Enter the August 1 amounts plus each of the eight transactions in the T-accounts.

Problems and Cases

18. *Computing Equivalent Units and Costs Under Process Costing.* The Homes Metals Company uses a process cost accounting system. Process E is the fifth in their series of seven processes. Material is added proportionately throughout processing. The following data relate to the operations of that process during March:

Work in Process, March 1, None.
Costs Incurred During the Month:

Direct Materials	$139,000
Direct Labor	157,000
Factory Overhead Applied	82,000

Units Transferred from Process D, 75,000 at a Cost of $12 per Unit.
Work in Process, March 31, 20,000 Units, 40 Percent Completed.

    a. Compute the equivalent whole units for transferred-in costs, direct material, direct labor, and factory overhead.
    b. Compute the cost per equivalent unit for each of the costs in part **a.**
    c. Compute the amount of costs allocated to units completed in process E during March and the costs allocated to units incomplete in process E at the end of March.

19. *Computing Equivalent Units and Costs Under Process Costing.* The General Manufacturing Company uses a process cost accounting system. Process C is the third in their series of five processes. The following data relate to the operations of that process during August. There were no goods in process at August 1.

Costs Incurred During August:
Direct Materials.	$67,500
Direct Labor	91,000
Manufacturing Overhead Applied	41,500

Units transferred from process B: 65,000, at cost of $9 per unit. Work in process at August 31: 25,000 units, which are on the average 40 percent complete as to the work of process C. Materials, labor, and overhead are added continuously throughout the process.

    a. Compute the equivalent whole units for transferred costs, direct material, direct labor, and manufacturing overhead.

    b. Compute the cost per equivalent unit for each of the costs in part **a.**

    c. Compute the amount of costs allocated to units completed in process C during August and the costs allocated to units incomplete as of the end of August.

20. *Computing Equivalent Units and Cost Flows Under Process Costing.* Wilson Manufacturing Corporation maintains a process cost accounting system. Materials are added at the start of processing, and direct labor and manufacturing overhead costs are incurred evenly over processing. On January 1, there were 5,000 units in process with the following accumulated costs:

Direct Material	$50,000
Direct Labor	40,000
Manufacturing Overhead	10,000

During January, 45,000 units were started in process. The following costs were incurred during January:

Direct Material	$450,000
Direct Labor	420,000
Manufacturing Overhead	105,000

During January, 40,000 units were completed. The units in ending inventory are, on average, 60 percent complete.

    a. Prepare an analysis showing the calculation of equivalent whole units for direct material, direct labor, and manufacturing overhead.

    b. Compute the amount of costs allocated to units completed during January and to units incomplete as of January 31.

21. *Computing Equivalent Units and Cost Flows Under Process Costing.* Denver Products Company maintains a process cost accounting system. Material A is added at the start of processing, and material B is added at the end of processing. Direct labor and manufacturing overhead costs are incurred evenly during processing. On September 1, there were 20,000 units in process with the following accumulated costs:

Material A.	$78,000
Material B.	0
Direct Labor	40,000
Manufacturing Overhead	30,000

During September, 110,000 units were started in process. The following costs were incurred during September:

Material A $442,000
Material B 180,000
Direct Labor 490,000
Manufacturing Overhead 367,500

During September, 90,000 units were completed. The units in ending inventory were, on average, 40 percent complete.

    a. Prepare an analysis showing the calculation of equivalent whole units for material A, material B, direct labor, and manufacturing overhead.

    b. Compute the amount of cost allocated to units completed during September and to units incomplete as of September 30.

22. *Tracing Cost Flows in a Service Organization* (*K. McGarvey*). White and Brite Dry Cleaners operates with five employees and the president, Hexter Strength. Hexter and one of the five employees attend to all the marketing and administrative duties. The remaining four employees work throughout the operation. White and Brite has four service departments: dry cleaning, coin washing and drying, special cleaning, and sewing repairs and altering. Timecards are marked, and records are kept to monitor the time each employee spends working in each department. When business is slow or when all is under control, there is idle time, and this is also marked on the timecard. (Note: It is necessary to have some idle time because White and Brite promises 60-minute service, and it is necessary to have available direct labor hours to accommodate fluctuating peak demand periods throughout the day and the week.)

    A summary of November operating data is as follows:

	Idle Time	Dry Cleaning	Coin Washing and Drying	Special Cleaning	Sewing Repairs and Altering
Sales Revenue		$2,625	$5,260	$2,000	$625
Direct Labor (in hours)	25	320	80	125	90
Direct Overhead:					
Cleaning Compounds . . .		500	250	400	–0–
Supplies		325	700	265	150
Electricity Usage		250	625	100	25

    Other data are as follows:

(1) The four employees working in the service departments all make $4 per hour.

(2) The person in charge of marketing earns $1,000 per month, and Hexter earns $1,500 per month.

(3) Indirect overhead amounted to $512 and is assigned to departments based on direct labor hours used. Because there are idle hours, some overhead will not be assigned to a department.

(4) In addition to salaries paid, marketing costs for such items as Yellow Pages advertising, radio advertising, and special promotions totaled $400.

(5) In addition to Hexter's salary, administrative costs amount to $150.

(6) All revenue transactions are cash, and all others are on account.

   a. Using T-accounts, show the flow of costs.

   b. Prepare an income statement for White and Brite for the month of November. No inventories were kept.

23. *Tracing Costs in a Job-Order Company.* On January 1, two jobs were in process at the Bondview Printing Company. Details of the jobs are as follows:

Job No.	Direct Materials	Direct Labor
A-15	$87	$32
A-38	16	42

Materials inventory at January 1 totaled $460, and $58 in materials were purchased during the month. A requisition for $8 in supplies was filled. On January 1, finished goods inventory consisted of two jobs: Job No. A-07 costing $196 and Job No. A-21 with a cost of $79. Both of these jobs were sold during the month.

Also during January, Jobs No. A-15 and A-38 were completed. To complete Job No. A-15 required an additional $34 in direct labor. The completion costs for Job No. A-38 included $54 in direct materials and $100 in direct labor.

Job No. A-40 was started during the period but was not finished. A total of $157 of direct materials was brought from the storeroom during the period, and total direct labor costs during the month amounted to $204. Overhead has been estimated at 150 percent of direct labor costs, and this relationship has remained fairly stable throughout the past few years.

Compute costs of Jobs No. A-15 and A-38 and balances in the January 31 inventory accounts.

24. *Tracing Costs in a Job-Order Company.* The following transactions occurred at the March Production Company, a job-order custom manufacturer:

(1) Purchased $40,000 in materials.

(2) Issued $2,000 in supplies from the materials inventory.

(3) Received materials with a cost of $31,600 at the storeroom.

(4) Paid for the materials purchased in **(1)**.

(5) Issued $34,000 in materials to the production department.

(6) Incurred wage costs of $56,000, which were debited to a temporary account called Payroll. Of this amount, $18,000 was withheld for payroll taxes and other similar liabilities. The remainder was paid in cash to the employees. [See transactions **(7)** and **(8)** for additional information about Payroll.]

(7) Recognized $28,000 in fringe benefit costs, which were incurred as a result of the wages paid in **(6)**. This $28,000 was debited to the temporary account called Payroll.

(8) Analyzed the payroll account and determined that 60 percent was direct labor, 30 percent indirect manufacturing labor, and 10 percent administrative and marketing costs.

(9) Paid for utilities, power, equipment maintenance, and other miscellaneous items for the manufacturing plant. The total amount was $43,200.

(10) Paid $53,500 for new equipment.

(11) Applied overhead on the basis of 175 percent of direct labor costs.

(12) Recognized depreciation on manufacturing property, plant, and equipment of $21,000.

    a.   Prepare journal entries to record the above transactions.

    b.   The following balances appeared in the accounts of March Manufacturing Company:

	Beginning	Ending
Materials Inventory	$74,100	—
Work-in-Process Inventory	16,500	—
Finished Goods inventory.	83,000	$ 66,400
Cost of Goods Sold.	—	131,700

Prepare T-accounts to show the flow of costs during the period.

25. *Reconstructing Missing Data.* Disaster struck the only manufacturing plant of the Complete Transaction Equipment Corporation on December 1. All of the work-in-process inventory was destroyed. A few records were salvaged from the wreckage and from a set of records located at the company's headquarters office. The loss is fully insured if adequate documentation can be supplied to the insurance company. The insurance company has also stated that it will pay the "normal" cost of the lost inventory, because company policy is that seasonal and other nondirect costs should be apportioned to inventories on an annualized basis. Hence, the value of work-in-process inventory is made up of direct materials, direct labor, and applied overhead.

The following information about the plant appears on the October 31 financial statements at the company's headquarters:

Materials Inventory, October 31	$ 49,000
Work-in-Process Inventory, October 31	86,200
Finished Goods Inventory, October 31	32,000
Cost of Goods Sold through October 31	348,000
Accounts Payable, Materials Suppliers on October 31	21,600
Manufacturing Overhead through October 31.	184,900
Payroll Payable on October	–0–
Withholding and Other Payroll Liabilities on October 31	9,700
Overhead Applied through October 31	179,600

A quick count of the inventories on hand on December 1 shows:

Materials Inventory	$43,000
Work-in-Process Inventory	–0–
Finished Goods Inventory	37,500

The accounts payable clerk tells you that there are outstanding bills to suppliers of $50,100 and that cash payments of $37,900 have been made during the month to these suppliers.

The payroll clerk informs you that the payroll costs last month included $82,400 for the manufacturing section and that $14,700 of this was indirect.

At the end of November, the following balances were available from the main office:

Manufacturing Overhead Applied through November 30	$217,000
Cost of Goods Sold through November 30.	396,600

You recall that each month there is only one requisition for indirect materials. Among the ashes you find the requisition for $2,086.

You also learn that during the month the overhead was overapplied by $1,200.

Compute the "normal" cost of the work-in-process inventory lost in the disaster.

26. *Job-Order Costs for Contracting.* Empire Industries, Inc., had a contract to produce a machine for the R2D2 Company. The machine would be produced in departments A, B, and C. The costs incurred in the three departments are as follows:

	Dept. A	Dept. B	Dept. C
Materials Used.	$6,200	$7,000	–0–
Direct Labor Cost.	3,500	6,000	$8,000
Direct Labor Hours	1,000	1,500	2,000
Machine Hours	100	50	500
Overhead Allocation Basis	$3 per Direct Labor Hour	150 Percent of Direct Labor Cost	$14 per Machine Hour

Management was concerned about the complexities of this allocation method and about the impact of different cost allocations on the computed job costs. The estimated total overhead in each department and the estimated total overhead bases for this year are as follows:

	Dept. A	Dept. B	Dept. C
Estimated Overhead	$240,000	$330,000	$140,000
Direct Labor Cost	280,000	220,000	120,000
Direct Labor Hours	80,000	55,000	30,000
Machine Hours	10,000	1,500	10,000

One member of management suggested that a plant-wide overhead rate be established based on direct labor cost. Another stated that plant-wide rates are not very useful.

    a. Compute plant-wide rates and rates by department based on:
        (1) Direct labor cost.
        (2) Direct labor hours.
        (3) Machine hours.
    b. Calculate the costs of the R2D2 job using:
        (1) Overhead as initially allocated.
        (2) Overhead based on plant-wide direct labor costs.
        (3) Overhead based on plant-wide direct labor hours.
        (4) Overhead based on plant-wide machine hours.
        (5) Overhead based on department direct labor costs.
        (6) Overhead based on department direct labor hours.
        (7) Overhead based on department machine hours.

27. *Comprehensive Job Costing Problem with Equivalent Units* (*CPA adapted*). The Custer Manufacturing Corporation, which uses a job-order cost system, produces various plastic parts for the aircraft industry. On October 9, Year 4, production was started on Job No. 487 for 100 front bubbles (windshields) for commercial helicopters.

Production of the bubbles begins in the fabricating department, where sheets of plastic (purchased as raw material) are melted down and poured into molds. The molds are then placed in a special temperature and humidity room to harden the plastic. The hardened plastic bubbles are then removed from the molds and hand-worked to remove imperfections.

After fabrication the bubbles are transferred to the testing department, where each bubble must meet rigid specifications. Bubbles that fail the tests are scrapped, and there is no salvage value.

Bubbles that pass the tests are transferred to the assembly department, where they are inserted into metal frames. The frames, purchased from vendors, require no work prior to installing the bubbles.

The assembled unit is then transferred to the shipping department for crating and shipment. Crating material is relatively expensive, and most of the work is done by hand.

The following information concerning Job No. 487 is available as of December 31, Year 4 (the information is correct as stated):

(1) Direct materials charged to the job:
    (a) One thousand square feet of plastic at $12.75 per square foot was charged to the fabricating department. This amount was to meet all plastic material requirements of the job, assuming no spoilage.
    (b) Seventy-four metal frames at $408.52 each were charged to the assembly department.
    (c) Packing material for 40 units at $75 per unit was charged to the shipping department.

(2) Direct labor charges through December 31 were as follows:

	Total	Per Unit
Fabricating Department	$1,424	$16
Testing Department	444	6
Assembly Department	612	12
Shipping Department	256	8
	$2,736	

(3) Differences between actual and applied manufacturing overhead for the year ended December 31, Year 4, were immaterial. Manufacturing overhead is charged to the four production departments by various allocation methods, all of which you approve.

Manufacturing overhead charged to the fabricating department is allocated to jobs based on heat-room hours; the other production departments allocate manufacturing overhead to jobs on the basis of direct labor dollars charged to each job within the department. The following reflects the manufacturing overhead rates for the year ended December 31, Year 4.

	Rate per Unit
Fabricating Department	$.45 per Hour
Testing Department	.68 per Direct Labor Dollar
Assembly Department	.38 per Direct Labor Dollar
Shipping Department	.25 per Direct Labor Dollar

(4) Job No. 487 used 855 heat-room hours during the year ended December 31.

(5) Following is the physical inventory for Job No. 487 as of December 31:

Fabricating department:

(a) Fifty square feet of plastic sheet.

(b) Eight hardened bubbles, one-fourth complete as to direct labor.

(c) Four complete bubbles.

Testing Department:

(a) Fifteen bubbles that failed testing when two-fifths of testing was complete. No others failed.

(b) Seven bubbles complete as to testing.

Assembly department:

(a) Thirteen frames with no direct labor.

(b) Fifteen bubbles and frames, one-third complete as to direct labor.

(c) Three complete bubbles and frames.

Shipping department:

(a) Nine complete units; two-thirds complete as to packing material; one-third complete as to direct labor.

(b) Ten complete units; 100 percent complete as to packing material; 50 percent complete as to direct labor.

(c) One unit complete for shipping was dropped off the loading docks. There is no salvage.

(d) Twenty-three units have been shipped prior to December 31.

(e) There was no inventory of packing materials in the shipping department at December 31.

(6) Following is a schedule of equivalent units in production by department for Job No. 487 as of December 31.

CUSTER MANUFACTURING CORPORATION
Schedule of Equivalent Units in Production for Job No. 487
December 31

		Fabricating Department		
		Bubbles (units)		
	Plastic (sq. ft.)	Materials	Labor	Overhead
Transferred in from Direct Materials . .	1,000	—	—	—
Production to Date	(950)	95	89	95
Transferred out to other Departments . .	—	(83)	(83)	(83)
Spoilage	—	—	—	—
Balance at December 31	50	12	6	12

	Testing Department (units)		
	Bubbles		
	Transferred In	Labor	Overhead
Transferred in from Other Departments	83	—	—
Production to Date	—	74	74
Transferred out to Other Departments	(61)	(61)	(61)
Spoilage	(15)	(6)	(6)
Balance at December 31	7	7	7

	Assembly Department (units)			
	Transferred In	Frames	Labor	Overhead
Transferred in from Direct Materials	—	74	—	—
Transferred in from Other Departments.	61	—	—	—
Production to Date	—	—	51	51
Transferred out to Other Departments.	(43)	(43)	(43)	(43)
Balance at December 31	18	31	8	8

	Shipping Department (units)			
	Transferred In	Packing Material	Labor	Overhead
Transferred in from Direct Materials	—	40	—	—
Transferred in from Other Departments.	43	—	—	—
Production to Date	—	—	32	32
Shipped	(23)	(23)	(23)	(23)
Spoilage	(1)	(1)	(1)	(1)
Balance at December 31	19	16	8	8

Prepare a schedule for Job No. 487 of ending inventory costs for **(a)** direct materials by department, **(b)** work in process by department, and **(c)** cost of goods shipped. All spoilage costs are charged to cost of goods shipped.

28. *Solving for Missing Data.* After a dispute with the company president, the controller of Vancouver Company resigned in January, Year 5. At that time, his office was converting the internal reporting system from full absorption to variable costing. You have been called in to prepare financial reports for the previous year. Your investigation reveals that much data are missing, but you piece together the following information.

(1) From the production department, you learn that the company manufactures fishing rods that pass through one department. All materials are added at the beginning of production, and processing is applied evenly throughout the department. There is no spoilage.

(2) From the sales department you learn that 95,000 units were sold at a price of $35 each during Year 4.

(3) From various sources you determine that variable manufacturing overhead was $396,000 and fixed manufacturing overhead was $252,000 for Year 4. Nonmanufacturing costs (all fixed) were $336,000.

(4) In one of the desk drawers of the former controller, you discover the draft of a report with the following information:

(a) "To improve our present accounting system we will be adopting the normal costing approach for both internal and external reporting in Year 4. We will write off over- or underabsorbed overhead as part of cost of goods sold in Year 4 rather than allocate it to inventories."

(b) "Direct unit costs remained the same in Year 4 as in previous years: $4.80 per unit for materials cost and $2.40 per unit for direct labor. Variable overhead will be applied at a rate of $1.80 per direct labor dollar, and fixed overhead at $1.20 per direct labor dollar."

(c) "132,000 units were transferred from work-in-process inventory to finished goods inventory. 144,000 units of materials were purchased and 138,000 units requisitioned to work in process."

Inventory Summary (in units)

	January 1, Year 4	December 31, Year 4
Work-in-Process Inventory	12,000 (40 percent complete)	18,000 (20 percent complete)
Finished Goods Inventory	No records	38,000
Direct Materials Inventory	No records	12,000

a. Show the flow of whole units, including units started, in Work-in-Process Inventory, transferred to finished goods, and sold. Be sure to include both beginning and ending inventories.

b. Show the flow of manufacturing costs during the year, including beginning and ending inventories, using full absorption normal costing. Prepare the income statements using:

(1) Full absorption/actual costing.

(2) Full absorption/normal costing.

(3) Variable/actual costing.

(4) Variable/normal costing.

Vancouver Company uses the weighted-average method of inventory valuation.

29. *Evaluate Cost Systems Used in Insurance Companies.* John Frank, controller of Midwest Insurance Company, recently returned from a management education program where he had spent considerable time talking to Peter Montgomery, his counterpart at Northern Insurance Company. Both companies had mortgage departments, but whereas Midwest gave loans only to businesses, Northern gave only home mortgage loans.

Peter Montgomery had described the use of standard costs at Northern as follows: "We have collected data over several years that give us a pretty good idea how much it costs to process each batch of loans. There are three main categories of loans that we receive: (1) FHA and VA mortgages, (2) conventional home mortgages, and (3) development loans. Banks and other financial institutions make these loans initially; the loans are packaged and offered to us as a package. The Mortgage Division is responsible for establishing terms for determining whether the property being mortgaged and the mortgagor are acceptable to us, and for legal work on the loan. We assume that each loan in a category costs about the same. To determine how much it costs to process loans, we periodically have people in the Mortgage Division keep track of their time on each package of loans. Our overhead is about 130 percent of direct labor costs, so we assign overhead accordingly to each package of loans. We don't keep track of the actual costs of processing each package of loans. What we lose in knowing the actual cost of processing each loan, we make up by saving clerical costs that would be incurred to keep track of the time spent on each package of loans." A cost statement for a recent month is shown in Exhibit 5.10.

Montgomery's comment about saving clerical costs struck a respondent chord with John Frank. Midwest's accounting costs had reached alarming levels, according to the company president, and Frank was looking for ways to reduce costs. Midwest kept track of the following costs for each loan: labor; telephone costs; travel; and outside services, such as appraisals, legal fees, and the cost of consultants. The costs of processing these loans were often several thousand dollars. A sample of these loans and their processing costs are shown in Exhibit 5.11.

When Frank told the Mortgage Division manager about the methods used by Northern, the manager responded: "That sounds fine for them because each package of loans in a category has about the same processing costs. The processing costs of each loan in our company vary considerably. I believe it would be invalid to establish standards for our loans."

Frank thought the Mortgage Division manager's comments were reasonable, but he thought there must be some way to save clerical costs by not recording the costs of processing each loan. At the same time, he knew there were potential benefits of having a standard against which to compare actual costs.

    a.   What would you advise Mr. Frank to do? Compare the advantages and disadvantages of the system used by each company.

    b.   Diagram the flow of costs for each company using the data available in Exhibits 5.10 and 5.11. Treat each loan or category of loans as a separate product in your diagram.

Exhibit 5.10
NORTHERN INSURANCE COMPANY
Mortgage Division
Loan Processing Costs
Month of October

Category of Loans	Labor	Overhead	Number of Loans Processed
Standard Costs			
FHA and VA	$ 4,200	$ 5,460	14
Conventional	31,160	40,508	82
Development	20,440	26,572	73
Total	$55,800	$72,540	
Actual Costs	$58,172	$74,626	
Variance	$ 2,372 Unfavorable	2,086 Unfavorable	

Exhibit 5.11
MIDWEST INSURANCE COMPANY
Mortgage Division
Loan Processing Costs
Month of July

Loan No.	Labor	Telephone	Travel	Outside Services Appraisal	Legal	Other
A48-10136	$ 1,184	$ 113	$ 415	$ 1,500	—	—
A48-11237	3,631	42	—	2,300	—	—
B42-19361	814	78	—	—	1,500	150
C39-21341	4,191	240	$ 110	—	2,200	—
.	.	.	.	.	.	.
.	.	.	.	.	.	.
.	.	.	.	.	.	.
Total	$47,291	$4,843	$2,739	$11,800	$9,950	$1,470

Suggested Solutions to Even-Numbered Exercises

8. *Computing Manufacturing Costs of a Job Order.*

    a. $4 per direct labor hour. $40,000/10,000 hours.

b.

Raw Material	$ 4,600
Direct Labor	7,600
Overhead (1,200 × $4)	4,800
Total Cost	$17,000
Cost per Unit	$ 170

10. *Cost Flows in a Merchandising Organization.*

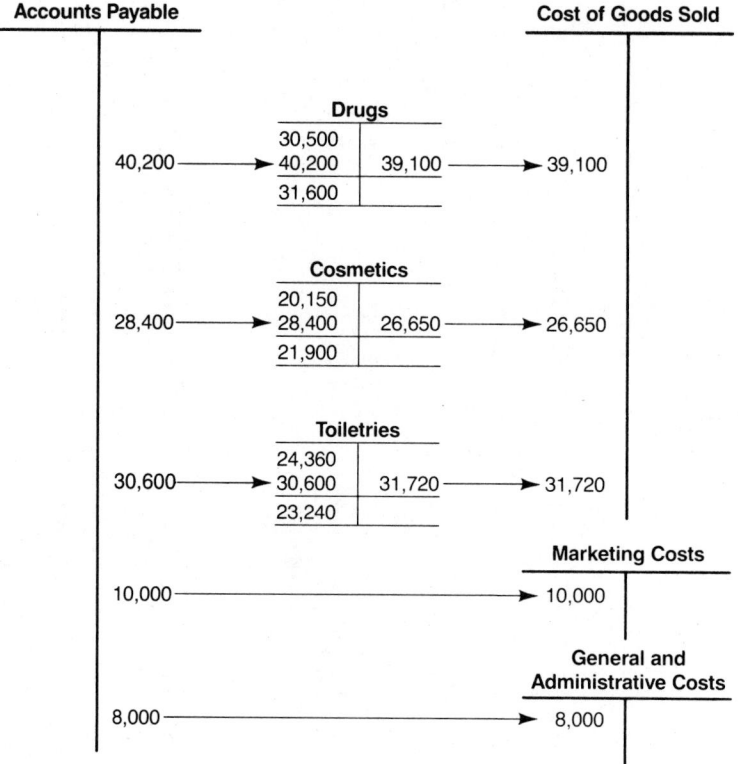

12. *Computing Equivalent Units Using the Weighted-Average Method.* For each method, it is necessary to determine the physical count in the ending inventory. This can be done by taking the inventory relationship:

$$BI + TI = TO + EI,$$

and substituting the information from the problem:

$$6,000 + 21,000 = 17,000 + EI$$

$$EI = 10,000.$$

Equivalent units—weighted-average method:

		Equivalent Units	
Item	Physical Count	Direct Materials	Conversion Costs
Transferred out.	17,000	17,000	17,000
Ending Inventory	10,000	1,000[a]	500[b]
Total	27,000	18,000	17,500

[a]1,000 = 10 percent × 10,000.
[b]500 = 5 percent × 10,000.

14. *Preparing Income Statement for a Merchandiser.*

Revenues		$1,850,000
Cost of Goods Sold:		
Beginning Inventory	$ 314,000	
Purchases	971,000	
Freight-in	26,000	
Goods Available for Sale.	$1,311,000	
Less Ending Inventory	(297,000)	
Less Total Cost of Goods Sold		(1,014,000)
Gross Margin		$ 836,000
Less: Marketing costs	$ (197,000)	
Administrative Costs	(400,000)	
Less Total Costs		(597,000)
Operating Profit.		$ 239,000

16. *Computing Equivalent Units.*

	Units Completed in Assembly	Equivalent Units Complete in Finishing	Total
Transferred-in Costs	50,000	30,000	80,000
Material C	50,000	30,000	80,000
Material D	50,000	—	50,000
Direct Labor	50,000	18,000	68,000
Overhead	50,000	18,000	68,000

Part Three   **Managerial Decision Making**

At the beginning of this book, we stated that there are two major uses of managerial accounting information: (1) managerial decision making, and (2) managerial planning, control, and internal performance evaluation. This part of the book, Chapters 6 through 10, deals with the first use, *managerial decision making*. This use of accounting information emphasizes performing financial analyses of alternative courses of action to answer such questions as:

What costs will be saved if production volume is reduced?

What is the minimum price at which a good or service will be profitable?

At what volume will a product line's revenues cover its costs?

Should a proposed hospital be built?

Is it cheaper to perform services internally or to acquire them from external sources?

These are a few examples of many economic decisions made by managers that require accounting information. Note that all of these decisions have one thing in common—they are future-oriented. This means that managers are attempting to estimate the future costs and benefits of alternative operations. The data in the accounting records are, of course, data about the past. These data are, nevertheless, a potentially good source of information about the future if they are used wisely. Chapter 6 presents methods of estimating cost behavior. We focus on *costs* because cost differences among options are particularly important and difficult to estimate.

Chapter 7 shows the interrelations among selling prices, volume, costs, and profits. Chapters 8 through 10 present applications of "differential analysis" to many important business decisions. Chapter 8 deals with short-term decisions, whereas Chapters 9 and 10 focus on long-term capacity decisions and on capital budgeting.

Chapter 6   Estimating Cost Behavior

The fundamental distinction between fixed and variable costs was discussed in Chapter 2. This chapter discusses methods of *estimating* or deriving the breakdown of costs into fixed and variable components, as follows:

$$TC = F + VX$$

where TC refers to the *total cost* for a time period, F refers to the *total fixed cost* for the time period, V refers to the *variable cost per unit*, and X refers to the *number of units of activity* for the time period. Nearly all managerial decisions deal with alternative activity levels; hence, it is important to estimate which costs will vary with activity and how much they will vary.

The process of cost estimation works as follows. Suppose management is considering the temporary reduction in production at a particular plant. What costs will be saved? Some costs will not be reduced, while others will. Management would estimate the relation between costs and units produced to ascertain which costs would vary. The unit variable cost, V, would be multiplied by the number of units to be reduced, X, to derive the cost savings, VX. These would be estimates of future costs because the decision involves reducing production in the future.

Many costs cannot be neatly identified as "fixed" or "variable." This is one reason for using statistical and other techniques for estimating cost behavior. In effect, these techniques explore costs to identify an underlying cost behavior pattern that may not be apparent on the surface.

The Nature of Fixed and Variable Costs

Short Run Versus Long Run

Variable costs are those costs that change as the level of activity is changed, whereas fixed costs are those costs that do not change as the activity level changes. If the time period is long enough—many years would be required—there will be no fixed costs. But during short time periods, say, 1 year, the firm must operate with a relatively fixed set of productive facilities, sales force, and managerial staff.

This fact provides the basis for the distinction drawn in economics between the short run and the long run and in accounting between variable costs and fixed costs. To the economist, the *short run* is a time period long enough to allow management to change the level of production or other activity within the constraints of current total productive capacity. Total productive capacity can be changed only in the *long run*.

Exhibit 6.1
Long-Run Versus Short-Run Nature of Costs

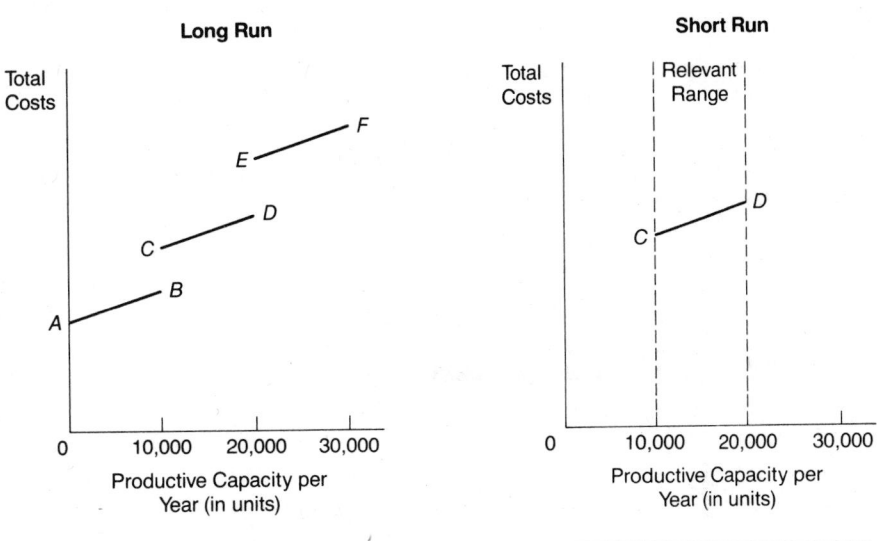

To the manager, costs that vary with activity levels in the short run are variable costs; costs that will not vary in the short run no matter what the level of activity are fixed costs. The accounting concepts of variable and fixed costs are, then, short-run concepts. They must be defined in terms of a particular period of time and related to a particular level of productive capacity.

Consider, for example, the total costs (both variable and fixed) for a firm as shown in Exhibit 6.1. The graph on the left shows the total costs in the long run. If the productive capacity of the firm is 10,000 units per year, total costs will be measured by line *AB*. If new production facilities are acquired in order to increase capacity to 20,000 units, then total costs will be measured by line *CD*. An increase in capacity to 30,000 units will increase the total costs to that shown by line *EF*. These shifts in capacity represent long-run commitments. Of course, there will be some overlap; production of 10,000 units per year could be at the high volume end of the *AB* line or at the low volume end of the *CD* line.

In the short run, there is only one capacity level, that of the existing plant. The total costs in the short run are shown in the graph at the right on the assumption that the capacity of the existing plant is 20,000 units per year. Note that line *CD* represents costs for the production level of approximately 10,000 units to 20,000 units only. For production levels outside of this range, a different plant capacity is needed and the total costs line will shift up or down. The level of activity likely to be undertaken with existing plant is referred to as the *relevant range* of activity. Estimates of variable and fixed costs are applicable only if the contemplated level of activity is within the relevant range. If an alternative under consideration requires a level outside the relevant range, then new plant facilities must be acquired and the total cost line will be different than that for current production facilities.

Example Exotic Eats is a profitable restaurant featuring a menu of Far Eastern dishes. Because it is located in the financial district of a city, it was open only from 11:00 A.M. until 2:00 P.M., Monday through Friday, for lunch business. Although the restaurant can serve a maximum of 210 customers per day, it has been serving a daily average of 200 customers. The daily costs and revenues of operations are as follows:

Revenues	$1,000
Less Variable Costs	(400)
Less Fixed Costs	(350)
Operating Profits	$ 250

Based on this information, the restaurant's management is considering doubling capacity. Initial calculations indicate that the number of customers would double. Management wants to know: "Would operating profits double?" A simple extrapolation indicates that operating profits would *more* than double, as shown in Exhibit 6.2, because total revenues would double while total costs would not.

This simple extrapolation assumes that total revenues and total variable costs double to $2,000 and $800, respectively, while fixed costs remain constant at $350. For a decision such as this, which involves a change in capacity, fixed costs are not likely to remain constant. The management of Exotic Eats realizes that with additional capacity and increased customers, additional cooks would have to be hired, occupancy costs (for example, space rental) would increase, and other fixed

Exhibit 6.2
EXOTIC EATS
Simple Extrapolation of Variable Costs
Accompanying Expansion

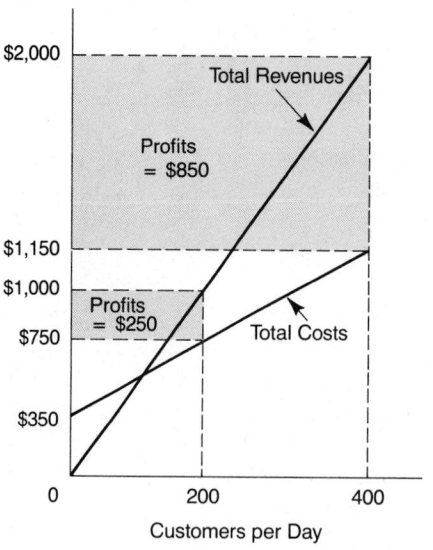

Exhibit 6.3
EXOTIC EATS
Increase in Fixed Costs
Accompanying Expansion

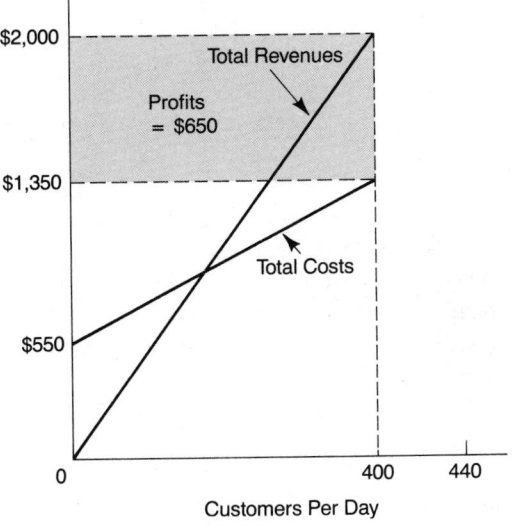

costs would increase. The projected new volume is outside the "relevant range" of volume over which the original assumed cost behavior pattern would hold, so the original cost behavior pattern was invalid.

A revised, more realistic analysis of the cost behavior pattern estimates the unit variable cost of $2 per customer to be the same as before, but fixed costs are estimated to increase from $350 to $550 per day. The revised cost behavior pattern appears in Exhibit 6.3. Exhibit 6.4 compares profits at the original activity level, 200 customers per day, with the projected increase to 400 per day. These estimates

Exhibit 6.4
EXOTIC EATS
Comparison of Profits at Original and Projected Activity Levels

		Alternative: 400 Customers per Day	
	Status Quo: 200 Customers per Day	Incorrect Assumption of Constant Fixed Costs	Correct Assumption of Change in Fixed Costs
Revenues	$1,000	$2,000	$2,000
Less Variable Costs	(400)	(800)	(800)
Total Contribution Margin. . . .	$ 600	$1,200	$1,200
Less Fixed Costs	(350)	(350)	(550)
Operating Profits.	$ 250	$ 850	$ 650

of costs would be input to the decision about increasing capacity. Of course, decisions involving long-run changes in capacity usually require discounted cash flow analysis, which is discussed in Chapter 9.

Types of Fixed Costs

Where the short run stops and the long run starts is a fuzzy distinction in practice. Thus, the accounting concept of fixed costs contains several subclassifications that are helpful in understanding the relationship between particular types of fixed costs and current capacity.

Capacity Costs Many resources used during a period provide a firm with the capacity to produce or to sell or both. These fixed costs are called *capacity costs*.

Some capacity costs will be incurred even if operations are temporarily shut down completely. Examples include property taxes and some executive salaries.

Other capacity costs will cease if operations are shut down completely, but must be incurred in fixed amounts if operations are carried out at any level. A security force can be laid off if production ceases, but once the force is employed, it guards the plant no matter how little or how much activity is going on inside.

Discretionary Costs In contrast to fixed capacity costs, other fixed costs are not necessary to give productive or selling capacity to the firm. These costs are usually called *discretionary* costs, *programmed* costs, or *managed* costs. Activities such as research, development, and advertising to generate new business are examples.

These costs are sometimes considered "discretionary" in the sense that they are not necessary in the short run to operate the business. They are, however, usually essential for achieving long-run goals. Imagine the short-run and long-run effects to Proctor & Gamble of eliminating media advertising. Or consider the effects of dropping research and development at Hewlett-Packard. Although these companies would survive for a period of time, after a bit they would become quite different, and probably smaller, companies. In short, programmed costs reflect top management's policies and commitments to activities. Once such commitments are made, these programmed costs are considered to be fixed in the short run.

Other Cost Behavior Patterns

We have made a simple distinction between fixed and variable costs: Total fixed costs remain constant for a period of time (the "short run") over a range of activity levels (the "relevant range"), whereas total variable costs change as the volume of activity changes.

Curvilinear Variable Costs The straightforward linear fixed and variable cost behavior patterns, as shown in Exhibits 6.2 and 6.3, are not always found in practice. Total variable cost behavior may be curvilinear, as shown by the three different examples of variable cost behavior in Exhibit 6.5. Curvilinear costs indicate that the costs vary with the volume of activity, but not proportionately. For example, as volume increases, the unit prices of some inputs such as materials and

Exhibit 6.5
Examples of Curvilinear
Total Variable Cost Behavior

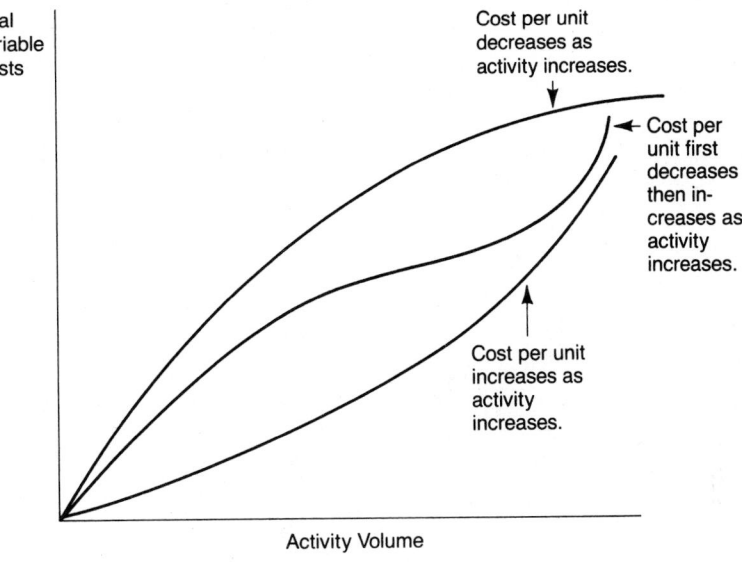

power may decrease. Another example of curvilinear cost behavior can occur when employees become more efficient with experience, as discussed next.

Learning Curves There is often a systematic learning from experience. As employees' experience increases, productivity improves and costs per unit decrease. This phenomenon is frequently found whenever new products or processes are initiated, or when a group of new employees is hired.

The nature of the learning phenomenon is typically described as a constant percentage reduction in the *average* direct labor input time required per unit as the *cumulative output* doubles. For example, assume a time reduction rate of 20 percent (that is, an 80 percent cumulative learning curve), and that the first unit takes 125 hours. Then the *average* for two units should be 100 hours per unit (.80 × 125 hours), a total of 200 hours for both units. Four units would take an average of 80 hours each (= .80 × 100 hours), or a total of 320 hours. The mathematical formula for the learning curve is discussed in the appendix to this chapter.

These results are summarized below:

Quantity		Time in Hours	
Unit	**Cumulative Units**	**Cumulative**	**Cumulative Average per Unit**
First	1	125	125
Second	2	200	100 (= .80 × 125)
Third and Fourth	4	320	80 (= .80 × 100)
Fifth through Eighth	8	512	64 (= .80 × 80)

Exhibit 6.6
Impact of Learning Curves on Time and Cost Behavior

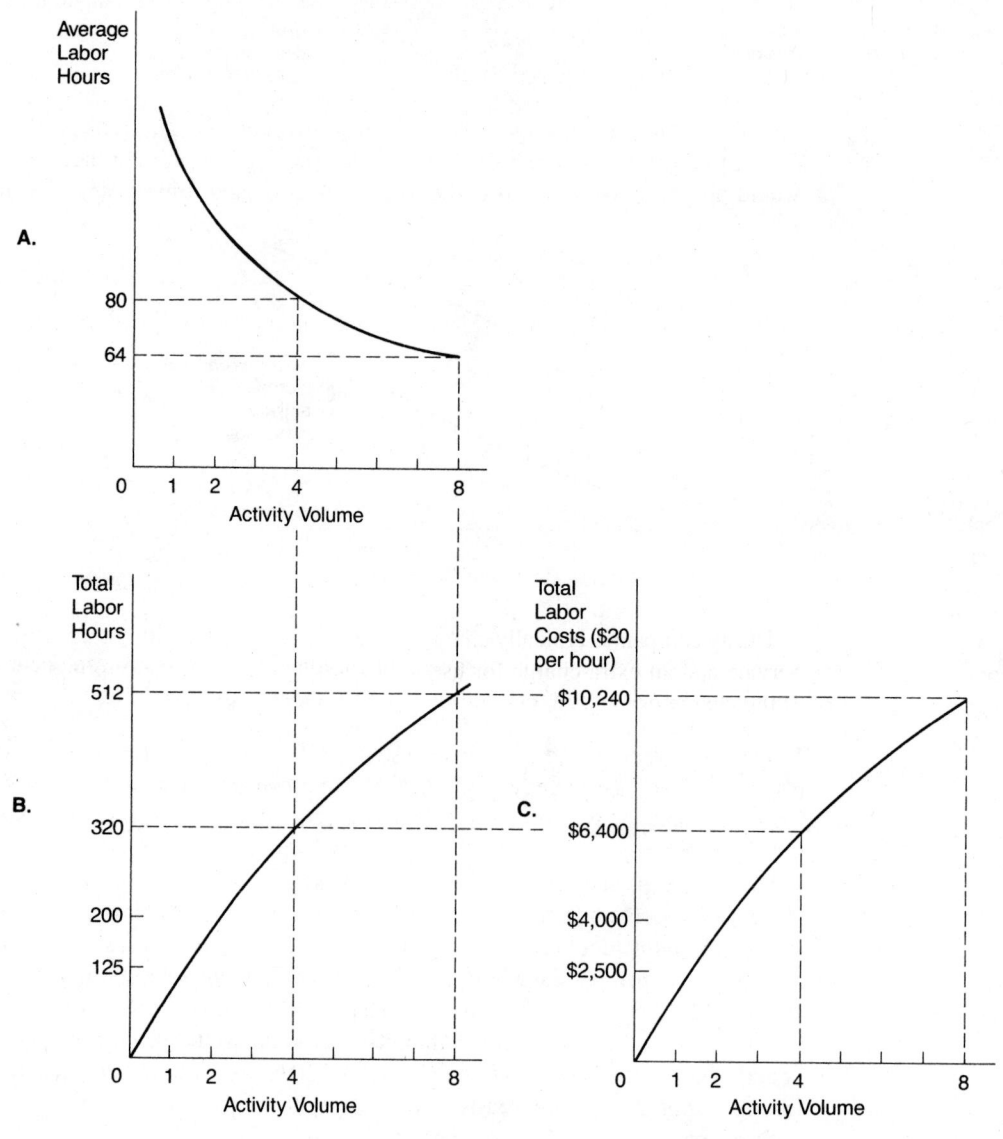

Exhibit 6.6 shows the relations between volume and *average* labor hours in part A, between volume and *total* labor hours in part B, and the relation between volume and total labor costs in part C, assuming a labor cost of $20 per hour.

The possible effects of learning on costs can be important for decision making and performance evaluation. Suppose that you are trying to decide whether to make a new product that would be subject to the 80 percent cumulative learning curve.

Using the data in Exhibit 6.6, if you assumed that the product would require labor costs of $2,500 per unit for the first 8 units made, you would be seriously over-stating labor costs for the 8 units. If you used $2,500 per unit as a standard against which you would compare actual cost performance, you would be setting a very loose standard for all but the first unit.

To what costs do learning curves apply? The "learning" phenomenon results in savings of time; thus, any costs that are a function of time could be affected. Therefore, hourly labor costs would be affected, whereas straight piece-work pay would not. Any overhead costs that are affected by labor time would be affected. For example, if power to run machinery is a variable cost that is related to the amount of time that laborers run machines to perform a task, then reduction in labor time could reduce machine time and machine power costs. Costs of direct materials and fixed overhead are usually assumed to be unaffected by the learning phenomenon.

Semivariable Costs Semivariable costs, by convention, refer to costs that have fixed and variable components such as represented by lines *CD*, *CE*, and *CF* in Exhibit 6.7A. Repair and maintenance costs or utility costs exemplify semivariable cost behavior. There is a fixed cost (0C) to provide a minimum repair service capability within a plant (for example, the cost of regular salaries of repair personnel). When repairs are actually performed, costs increase as materials are used and overtime wages are paid.

Utility companies typically charge a fixed minimum per month (0C) for providing service and an extra charge for uses of the service above some minimum amount. If the charge per unit of, say, electricity decreases at certain stages as consumption

Exhibit 6.7
Patterns of Cost Behavior: Semivariable and Semifixed Costs

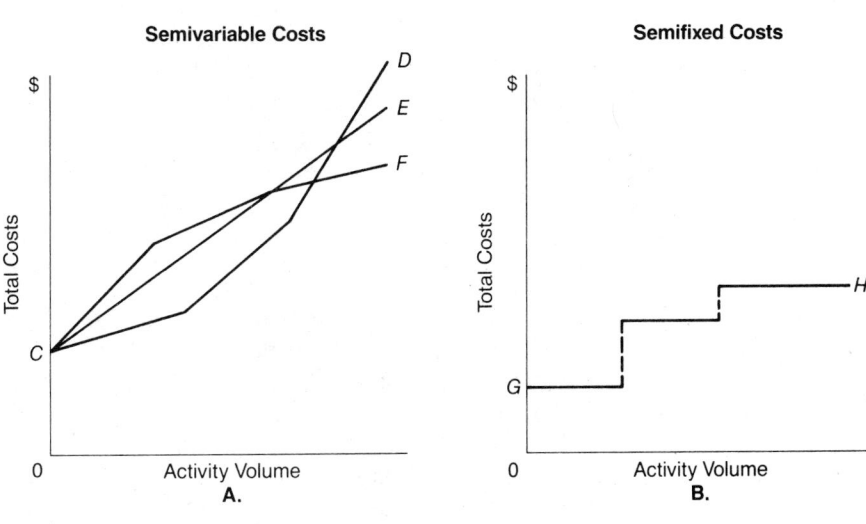

increases, then the cost curve would look like line *CF*. If the per unit charge increases at certain stages as usage increases, then the costs would look like *CD*. Semivariable costs are often called *mixed costs*.

Example Miller Corporation has a highly automated plant. There is a direct relationship between the hours of electricity used and the number of units produced. Past experience suggests that electricity costs behave in a semivariable pattern as follows:

Up to 50,000 Units	$300
Next 20,000 Units	.006/Unit
Next 20,000 Units	.005/Unit

Miller Corporation expects to produce 65,000 units if a special order is not accepted. The expected cash outflow for electricity is $390 [= $300 + (15,000 × $.006)]. If the special order is accepted, production will be increased to 75,000 units (= 65,000 + 10,000). Electricity costs will therefore be $445 [= $300 + (20,000 × $0.006) + (5,000 × $.005)]. The incremental cash outflow for electricity from accepting the special order is $55 (= $445 − $390).

Semifixed Costs The term *semifixed costs,* by convention, refers to costs that increase in steps, such as shown by the broken line *GH* in Exhibit 6.7B. Semifixed costs are sometimes described as *step costs*. If a quality control inspector can examine 1,000 units per day, then inspection costs will be semifixed, with a break for every 1,000 units per day examined.

Example Johnson Corporation hires one quality control inspector for each 25,000 units produced. The annual salary is $12,000 per inspector. Before a special order is accepted, production is 65,000 units; so the company has three inspectors. If a special order would increase volume from 65,000 to 75,000 units, no additional inspectors would be hired. If the special order would increase production to a level greater than 75,000 units (say, to 85,000 units), a fourth inspector would be hired.

The distinction between fixed and semifixed costs is subtle. A change in fixed costs (other than for price changes) usually involves a change in long-term assets, whereas a change in semifixed costs usually does not.

Summary

There are a variety of relations between costs and the volume of activity. Some costs do not vary in the short run over a relevant range—that is, they are *fixed*. Others vary with volume—that is, they are *variable*. Some costs are neither strictly fixed nor strictly variable, but contain components of both.

In considering the behavior of costs for decision making, managers usually simplify the complexities of cost behavior and assume that costs are either strictly fixed or linearly variable. The reason is that the incremental cost of analyzing the more complex data is often greater than the incremental benefits of doing so.[1] Although the assumed simple linear variable/fixed cost behavior does not fully describe reality, it is usually sufficiently close for many decision-making purposes. Of course, there may be cases where estimating and analyzing more complex cost behavior is worthwhile.

Cost Estimation

A major purpose of cost estimation is to break down total costs into fixed and variable cost components. As previously indicated, some costs, such as rent and insurance, will have only a fixed portion, whereas others, such as direct materials and direct labor, will have only a variable portion. Many costs, however, are mixed, having both fixed and variable components.

The total cost of an item can be expressed as

$$\begin{matrix} \text{Total} \\ \text{Cost} \\ \text{During} \\ \text{Period} \end{matrix} = \begin{matrix} \text{Fixed} \\ \text{Cost} \\ \text{During} \\ \text{Period} \end{matrix} + \left(\begin{matrix} \text{Variable} \\ \text{Cost per} \\ \text{Unit of} \\ \text{Activity} \end{matrix} \times \begin{matrix} \text{Units of} \\ \text{Activity} \\ \text{During} \\ \text{Period} \end{matrix} \right),$$

or, using briefer but fairly standard notation,[2]

$$TC = F + VX.$$

where F is total fixed costs during the period, V is variable cost per unit of activity, and X is the number of units of activity. For example, assume that the total cost of utilities per month is found to be $400 plus $.05 per kilowatt-hour used. If the use of 100,000 kilowatt-hours is anticipated next month, utilities cost is estimated to be $5,400 (= $400 + $.05 per kilowatt-hour × 100,000 kilowatt-hours).

The activity represented by X is often called the *independent variable* and the amount of total costs is the *dependent variable*. In some sophisticated analyses, more than one activity or independent variable is presumed to influence total cost.

---

[1]Simplification of complex cost behavior patterns into strictly fixed and variable costs is analogous to our discussion of the costs and benefits of information in Chapter 1. The basic concept of "simplification" is that by simplifying we lose some information, but we reduce the costs of information and analysis. Any time we sacrifice understanding the full complexities of cost causation, depreciation measurement, revenue recognition, and so forth, we are simplifying, presumably because the costs of more complex analysis exceed the benefits.

For an expanded discussion of "simplification," see Joel S. Demski, *Information Analysis* (Reading, Mass.: Addison-Wesley, 1980), pp. 44–61.

[2]This is a specific form of the general functional relationship

$$Y = a + bX,$$

where Y is the dependent variable, a is the intercept, b is the slope, and X is the independent variable. This is the equation for a straight line.

The symbolic representation of such a relation might be

$$TC = F + V_1X_1 + V_2X_2 + \cdots + V_nX_n,$$

where F is total fixed cost per period, V_1 is the variable cost per unit of activity X_1 carried out, V_2 is the variable cost per unit of activity X_2 carried out, and so on. The activities might be direct labor hours worked and number of units produced. In this discussion of cost estimation, we assume only one activity, or independent variable.

What follows is an explanation of the major methods of estimating cost behavior. In each method, the goal is to estimate the equation $TC = F + VX$ for the particular cost item under study.

Engineering Method of Estimating Costs

Engineering estimates indicate what costs *should be*. The engineering method is probably so named because it was first used in estimating manufacturing costs from engineers' specifications of the required inputs to the manufacturing process for a unit of manufactured output. The method is not, however, confined to manufacturing. Time-and-motion studies have been used in banks, fast food companies, governmental units, hospitals, and many other nonmanufacturing operations.

Virtually all business activities are designed to produce a defined output from a variety of labor, material, and capital equipment inputs. The engineers' cost estimates are based on a study of the physical relation between the quantities of these inputs and each unit of output (what economists call the ''production function''). It is then a relatively simple matter to assign costs to each of the physical inputs (wages, material prices, insurance charges, etc.) in order to estimate the cost of the outputs.

There are several difficulties in using the engineering method to estimate costs. The cost estimate will be of low quality to the extent that the actual amounts of inputs used, such as materials and labor, vary during the production process because of waste, spoilage, and varying labor efficiency. Another difficulty of this method is that workers have varying degrees of skill and correspondingly varying wage rates. The engineering estimate of the appropriate skill level and wage rate may be subject to large errors.

It is difficult to estimate the indirect costs of production—the cost of utilities, supervision, maintenance, security—with the engineering method. So the method is most reliable when costs are related directly to output (for example, direct labor and direct materials). Finally, the engineering method is surprisingly costly to use. Analysis of time, motion, materials, operating characteristics of equipment, and the ability of labor with varying skills requires an expert. Expert engineers are costly.

In short, the engineering method of estimating costs is most useful when input/output relationships are well defined and fairly stable over time. For a company that does not change its production function over time, the engineering method is usually quite good for estimating the amount of direct materials, direct labor, and some overhead required to make the product.

Account Analysis

In contrast to the engineering method, other methods of estimating cost behavior use actual accounting data. The account analysis calls for a review of each cost account and a classification of the account according to cost behavior. This classification is done by people who are thoroughly familiar with the activities of the firm and have developed an understanding of the way its costs behave. Most building occupancy costs might be classified as fixed, for example, whereas direct materials and direct labor would probably be classified as variable.

This analysis can be built into the chart of accounts, which is the system of assigning numerical codes to accounts to indicate cost behavior. For example, as shown in Exhibit 6.8, variable costs are coded "01," whereas fixed costs are coded "02." If a more complex cost behavior classification is desired (for example, classification into "discretionary fixed costs," "semivariable costs," and so forth), appropriate digits may be added to the coding system.

Account analysis also may be done after the fact. That is, costs recorded in an account are analyzed at the end of a time period and classified according to cost behavior.

Example The management of Chicago Manufacturing Company wants a breakdown of manufacturing overhead costs into fixed and variable components. The information will be used for the following purposes: (1) to develop predetermined variable and fixed manufacturing overhead rates for product costing; (2) to estimate basic cost behavior patterns for a variety of decisions about cost-volume-profit relationships and the impact of various economic decisions on costs; and (3) to estimate cost behavior for profit planning, budgeting, and determining standard costs.

Exhibit 6.8
CHICAGO MANUFACTURING COMPANY
Cost Behavior
Account Analysis

Account	Account Codes	
	Item[a]	Behavior[b]
Direct Material	101	01
Direct Labor	102	01
Manufacturing Overhead:		
Indirect Materials	103	01
Indirect Labor	104	01
Lease	105	02
Utilities (heat, lights)	106	02
Power	107	01
Insurance	108	02

[a]Each account is assigned a different number.
[b]01 = variable cost; 02 = fixed cost.
Note: Additional codes can be used to assign costs to departments or other responsibility centers.

Manufacturing overhead costs include all manufacturing costs except those for raw materials and direct labor. The overhead costs include utility costs, property taxes on the factory building, supervisors' wages, wages for security and maintenance staff, insurance on the factory building and depreciation on factory buildings, machinery, and equipment.

Each manufacturing overhead account for Chicago Manufacturing Company was assigned a code to indicate whether it was fixed or variable. At the end of the year, the total amounts in the respective fixed and variable cost categories were summed, as shown below. 57,000 direct labor hours were worked during the year.

Code	Cost Behavior	Amount
01	Variable.	$39,900
02	Fixed.	14,910
		$54,810

Dividing the fixed costs by 12 to give a monthly average of $1,242.50, and the variable costs by the 57,000 direct labor hours worked to give a variable cost rate per hour of $.70, results in the following monthly estimated cost equation:

$$TC = \$1,242.50 + \left(\$.70 \times \begin{array}{c} \text{Direct Labor} \\ \text{Hours Worked} \\ \text{During Month} \end{array} \right).$$

An advantage of account analysis is that it involves a detailed examination of the data base, presumably by accountants and managers who are familiar with it. This expert judgment can uncover cost behavior patterns that might be overlooked using the other methods. Account analysis is a subjective, judgmental approach, however, so different analysts are likely to provide different estimates of cost behavior.

Estimation of Costs Using Historical Data

When a firm has been carrying out activities for some time and future activities are expected to be similar to those of the past, then the firm can analyze the historical data to estimate the variable and fixed components of total cost and to determine likely future costs. The procedure for analyzing historical cost data requires two steps:

1. An estimate is made of the relationship $TC = F + VX$. This is an estimated relation for the *past*.
2. This estimate is updated so it is appropriate for the present or future period for which the estimate is desired. This requires adjusting costs for inflation and for changes in the relationship between costs and activity that have oc-

curred. For example, if a production process is expected to be more capital intensive in the future, variable costs may be reduced and fixed costs increased.

These are several methods used to estimate costs from historical data; these range from simple "eyeball estimates" to sophisticated statistical methods. Whatever method is used, the manager should take some preliminary steps before relying on cost estimates based on historical data.

Preliminary Steps in Analyzing Historical Cost Data

In the several decades since computers have become a cost-effective tool for analysis, the expression GIGO, "garbage-in, garbage-out," has become well known to data analysts. GIGO means that the results of an analysis cannot be better than the input data. Before using cost estimates, the analyst should be confident that the estimates make sense and are based on valid assumptions.

Keep in mind that we are trying to find fixed costs per period, F, and variable cost per unit, V, of some activity variable, X, in the relation

$$TC = F + VX.$$

The historical data will consist of several observations. An observation is the amount of total costs for a period and the level of activity carried out during that period. Thus, we might have total labor costs by months (the dependent variable) and the number of units produced during each of the months or the number of direct labor hours worked during each of the months (the independent variable). (For an example, see Exhibit 6.9, which shows 12 observations, one for each month, for the Chicago Manufacturing Company.)

We do not provide here an exhaustive list of all the steps to take in analyzing historical data, but the following are some of the more important.

1. Review Alternative Activity Bases (Independent Variables) In deciding which measure of activity to use, there are often several alternatives. The activity base chosen should have some logical relation to the cost item. The total cost for an item might be a function of number of units produced, labor hours used, labor costs incurred, machine hours used, quantities of materials used, cost of materials used, and so on. The objective in selecting an activity base is to find one whose variation is closely associated with the cost item being estimated. In principle, there is no reason not to use more than one activity base or independent variable, but a given cost estimation usually focuses on just one. (In order to have more than one independent variable, the number of observations must be large if the statistical relations are to be robust and reliable.)

2. Plot the Data One of the simplest procedures, but one often omitted by careless analysts, is to plot each of the observations of total costs against activity levels. Such plots can indicate an "outlier" observation—one that is unlike the others. Such outliers may indicate faulty data collection, incorrect arithmetic, or merely a time period when production was so far out of control that it would make sense to ignore the observation in determining the average relationships among total, fixed, and variable costs. Moreover, plotting the data may make it clear that no relation or only a nonlinear relation exists between the activity base and actual costs.[3]

3. Examine the Data and Method of Accumulation Do the time periods for the cost data and the activity correspond? Occasionally, accounting systems will record costs actually incurred late on a given day as occurring on the following day. It is difficult to deduce valid relations when the data for the dependent variable (total costs, in our case) are not compiled for the same period as the data for the independent variable (activity base, in our case).

Are the time periods covered by each observation of total costs and the activity base long enough to be meaningful, but short enough to allow for variations in activity levels? If, for example, observations are collected by the hour, variations in the relationship between the dependent and independent variables might be highlighted. Workers may be more efficient in the morning and less so in the late afternoon. On the other hand, observations collected by month may smooth over meaningful variations of activity level and cost that could be observed if the data were based on weekly observations.

Be aware that a number of common recording procedures can make data appear to exhibit incorrect cost behavior patterns. As discussed in Chapters 3 and 4, fixed manufacturing overhead is often applied or charged to production on the basis of some activity measure such as direct labor hours. This unitizing of fixed manufacturing costs makes them appear to be variable. So the manufacturing overhead cost observations should be *actual total costs, not* the *applied unit cost.*

Sometimes there appears to be an inverse relation between activity and particular costs—when activity is high, these costs are low; when activity is low, these costs are high. An excellent example is maintenance, which is sometimes purposely done when activity is slow. High levels of maintenance are often incurred during plant shutdowns for automobile model changes, for example. The analyst would be naive to infer that high maintenance costs are caused by low activity levels.

These are a few examples of data-recording methods that could lead the analyst astray. In general, cost allocations, accruals, correcting and reversing entries, and relationships between costs and activity levels should be investigated to ensure that costs and activities have been matched in the appropriate time period for cost estimation purposes.[4] Invalid relationships between activity and costs should be restated on a valid basis or the cost should be omitted from the analysis.

Methods of Cost Estimation Using Historical Data

Once the preliminary steps have been taken to analyze the historical data, any one of several methods may be used to estimate the historical relationship between total costs and activity levels; that is, to estimate $TC = F + VX$.

---

[3]The cost estimation methods discussed in this chapter assume that a linear relationship exists between the dependent and independent variables. If a nonlinear relationship is found to exist, more sophisticated estimation methods are required.

[4]For an extension of these remarks, see G. Benston, ''Multiple Regression Analysis of Cost Behavior,'' *The Accounting Review* (October 1966), pp. 657–672.

We discuss the estimation of variable and fixed manufacturing overhead for Chicago Manufacturing Company in this section. After this estimate is computed from past data, analysts can adjust the estimate for known changes in costs (for example, inflation) and the relationship between costs and the activity base (for example, a change in the production process). Keep in mind that although this is a manufacturing example, the concepts can be (and are) also applied to nonmanufacturing costs.

Exhibit 6.9
CHICAGO MANUFACTURING COMPANY
Overhead Cost Data by Month

Month	Total Overhead Costs Incurred During Month	Direct Labor Hours Worked During Month
January	$ 5,580	$ 6,000
February	4,330	5,500
March	4,080	3,500
April	2,830	3,000
May	2,455	2,500
June	3,080	2,000
July	3,580	4,000
August	4,455	4,500
September	5,330	5,000
October	6,580	6,500
November	5,580	7,000
December	6,930	7,500
	$54,810	$57,000

Total manufacturing overhead costs of the Chicago Manufacturing Company for each month during the previous year are shown in Exhibit 6.9 and plotted in Exhibit 6.10. The problem is to estimate the relationship between total overhead costs and activity.[5] The activity base that is suspected to correlate best with total overhead costs per month is the number of direct hours worked during the month. Exhibit 6.9 shows total overhead costs and direct labor hours worked each month.

The cost relationship to be estimated is

$$\begin{pmatrix} \text{Total Overhead} \\ \text{Costs per} \\ \text{Month} \end{pmatrix} = \begin{pmatrix} \text{Fixed} \\ \text{Costs} \\ \text{per Month} \end{pmatrix} + \begin{pmatrix} \text{Variable Overhead} \\ \text{Cost per Direct} \\ \text{Labor Hour} \end{pmatrix} \times \begin{pmatrix} \text{Direct Labor} \\ \text{Hours} \\ \text{Worked During} \\ \text{Month} \end{pmatrix}$$

$$TC = F + VX.$$

Before estimating the cost relationship, we plot the data, as in Exhibit 6.10. There are no apparent outliers for the 12 observation pairs in Exhibit 6.9. Two outliers

---

[5]Alternatively, we could study the behavior of each of these overhead costs individually and aggregate the fixed and variable cost components to obtain an estimate of total overhead costs. These alternative approaches normally yield approximately the same results.

Exhibit 6.10
CHICAGO MANUFACTURING COMPANY
Scatter Plot of Total Monthly Overhead Costs
and Direct Labor Hours Used During Month

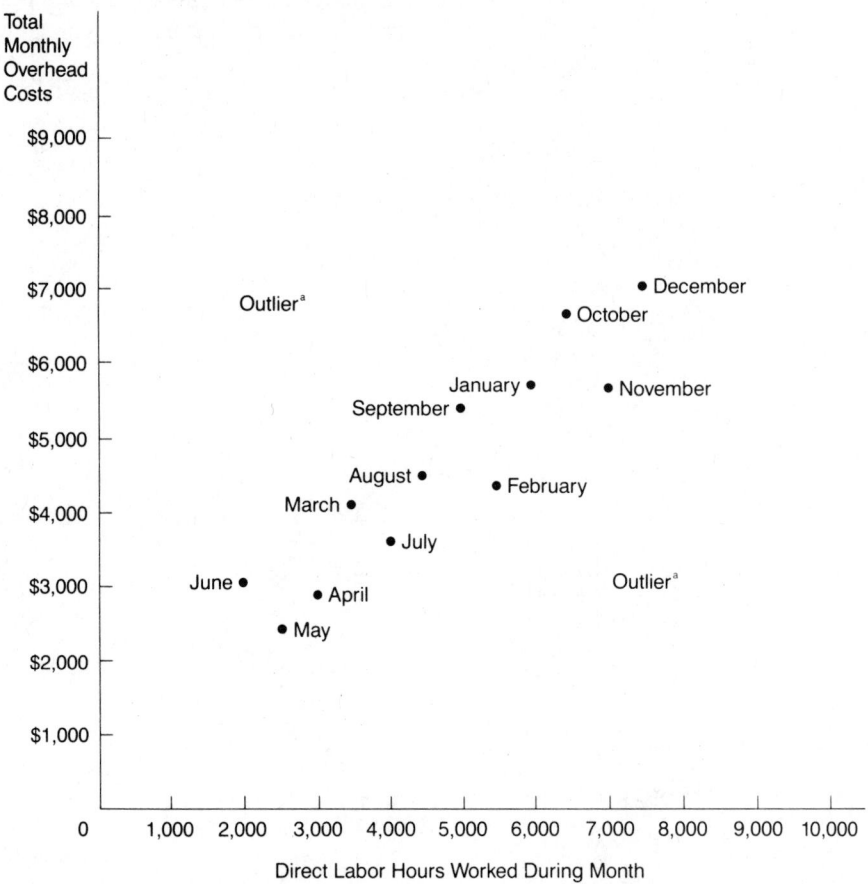

[a]Outliers assumed and plotted for purposes of illustration. They are not drawn from data in Exhibit 6.9.

are drawn on the plot so that you can see what we mean by an outlier.[6] If there were one or two months with outliers such as those shown, we should investigate what happened during those months and possibly discard the observations once we understood their cause.

Two common methods of estimating the cost relationship, that is, identifying F and V in the above equation, are illustrated next.

[6]One of the outliers, the one corresponding roughly to 7,000 hours and $3,000 of total costs, has total costs much less than they apparently should be. We suspect that the cause here is faulty recording of data, but if not, then we would want to know what happened that month. Investigation of outliers illustrates the concept called "management by exception." Understanding the cause of outlier observations is particularly important for managerial control, as we discuss in the topic of "variance analysis" in Chapters 12 and 13.

Visual Curve-Fitting Method One method of estimating costs from data such as those in Exhibit 6.10 is visual curve fitting. In visual curve fitting, a straight line is drawn through the data points that seems to "fit" well. By "fit," we mean a straight line that goes through the middle of data points as closely as possible. (A curved, kinked, or step function could also be drawn if more complex cost estimates are desired.) To demonstrate the procedure to yourself, try drawing such a line to fit the observations in Exhibit 6.10. The line that we visually fit to these data intercepts the vertical axis of $1,000 and has a slope of $.75 per hour as shown in Exhibit 6.11. The chances are that the line you drew is not exactly the same as ours. Yours and ours might each give roughly the same estimate of total costs for activity ranging from 3,000 to 6,000 direct labor hours per month, but would probably give significantly different estimates of total costs for 1,000 or 8,000 direct labor hours per month. The shortcoming of this method has, we hope, been demonstrated by the difference between your visually fit line and ours. The visually fit line is subjective, and different analysts may reach different conclusions from examining the same data.

Exhibit 6.11
CHICAGO MANUFACTURING COMPANY
Visual Curve-Fitting Method of Estimating Fixed Overhead Costs per Month
and Variable Overhead Costs per Direct Labor Hour Worked

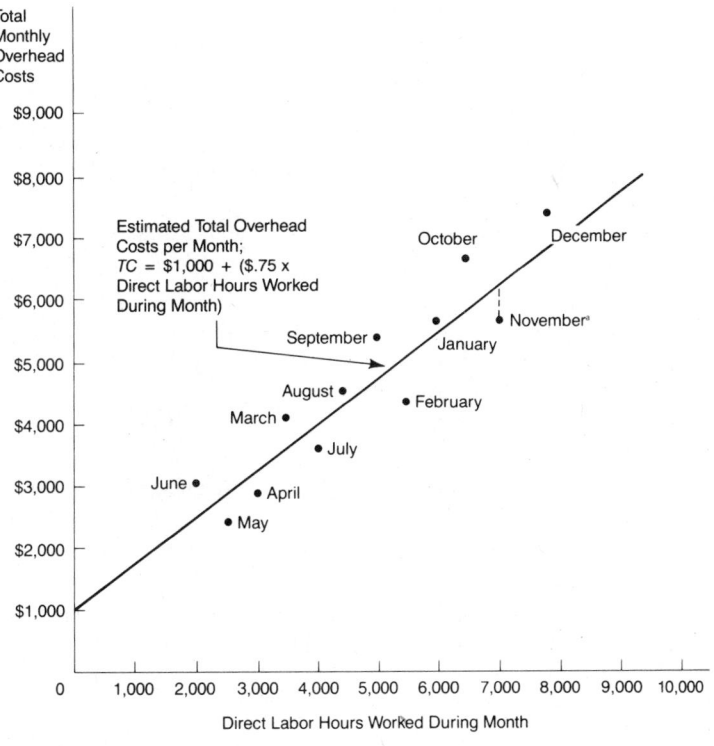

Note: This illustration is based on data in Exhibit 6.9.
[a]The vertical distance between the line and the observation, called *deviation,* is shown for November.

Once you have drawn a line to fit the data, the estimate of the fixed cost component, F, is the total cost for a zero level of activity—the amount at the point where the line crosses the vertical axis.[7] The estimate of the variable cost per unit of activity can be found by reading the numbers for any two points *on the line*. The relation is as follows, where subscripts 1 and 2 refer to the two points:

$$\begin{matrix} \text{Variable Cost} \\ \text{per Unit of} \\ \text{Base Activity} \end{matrix} = V = \frac{TC_1 - TC_2}{X_1 - X_2} =$$

$$\frac{\text{Change in Costs Between Two Points}}{\text{Change in Activity Between the Two Points}} = \frac{\text{Slope of}}{\text{Total Cost Line.}}$$

In our case, we use the points

Point 1: 8,000 hours; $7,000 total costs.

Point 2: 0 hours; $1,000 total costs.

Using the formula above, we find that

$$V = \frac{\$7,000 - \$1,000}{8,000 \text{ Hours} - 0 \text{ Hours}} = \frac{\$6,000}{8,000 \text{ Hours}} = \$.75 \text{ per Hour.}$$

Thus, total overhead cost is estimated as

$$\begin{matrix} \text{Total Overhead} \\ \text{Costs per Month} \end{matrix} = \$1,000 + \$.75 \text{ per Direct Labor Hour.}$$

Your estimate of the fixed and variable overhead costs will be different if the line you drew differs from ours.

A variation of the visual curve fitting approach is the *high-low* method in which a curve is fitted to the highest and lowest total cost observations.

Regression Analysis When computing facilities are available, by far the most cost-effective and accurate method for estimating cost relations is the statistical method known as *regression analysis*. Rather than estimating the cost relationship by the high–low or visual curve-fitting methods, the regression analysis "fits" a line to the data by the method of least squares. That is, a line is fit to the observations in such a way that the sum of the squares of the vertical distance of the observation points from the point on the regression line is minimized. (See November in Exhibit 6.11 for an illustration of the "vertical distance.") The statistical regression locates the line that best goes through the data points using the least-squares criterion. (The sum of the absolute deviations might just as well be minimized, but the computational problems are somewhat more difficult. Nearly all "canned" computer library programs use the least-squares criterion.)

In our example, an observed actual value of total overhead cost is TC, and the line we fit by the least-squares regression will be of the form

$$\hat{TC} = \hat{F} + \hat{V}X$$

---

[7]This estimate of F is outside of the range of observations, so it should be viewed with some skepticism.

where the $\wedge$ on $\hat{TC}$ indicates that the value of TC is estimated. The right-hand side of the equation should already be familiar to you. The vertical distance between the actual and the fitted values, $TC - \hat{TC}$ is called the *residual*. The method of least squares therefore fits a line to the data so as to minimize the sum of all the squared residuals.

It is beyond the scope of this text to do more than introduce the methods of regression analysis, but virtually every computer system has a program in its library that will perform the calculations. Furthermore, pocket calculators available for less than $50 will perform many calculations. Our purpose here is to show the results of using the statistical methods and to give a brief introduction to interpreting the results. You should be aware, however, that entire books have been devoted to these methods and their use.

Running the data in Exhibit 6.9 through a computer "least-squares regression" program gives the following results, which will be explained below.

Estimated
Total
Overhead $=$ $1,002 + $.751 × Direct Labor Hours Worked During Month
Costs   ($470)   ($.093)
per Month

$$R^2 = 0.85.$$

The line implied by this equation is presented in Exhibit 6.12.

By now, you should be able to interpret the $1,002 and $.751 amounts. The first is the estimate of the fixed overhead cost per month, and the second is the estimate of the variable overhead cost per unit of base activity, direct labor hours worked during the month. The two numbers, $1,002 (for fixed costs) and $.751 (for variable costs), are called *coefficients* of the regression equation.

The previous discussion dealt only with one independent variable. *Multiple regression* has more than one independent variable.

Standard Errors of the Coefficients The numbers shown in parentheses below these coefficients are called "standard errors of the coefficients." These standard errors are measures of variation and give a rough idea of the confidence we can have in the above fixed and variable cost coefficients. The smaller the standard error relative to its coefficient, the more precise the estimate. (Such computational precision does not necessarily indicate that the estimating procedure is *theoretically correct*, however.)

For example, the standard error of the fixed overhead cost per month is $470; the estimate of fixed costs of $1,002 is 2.13 times (= $1,002 ÷ $470) as large as the standard error. The ratio between an estimated regression coefficient and its standard error is called the "*t*-value" or "*t*-statistic." If the *t*-value is approximately 2 or larger, then a commonly used rule of thumb is that we can be relatively confident that the actual coefficient is different from zero.[8] The estimated variable

---

[8]Statistics books provide "*t*-tables" that make the analysis of *t*-statistics more precise.

Exhibit 6.12
CHICAGO MANUFACTURING COMPANY:
Statistical (Least-Squares Regression) Method of Estimating Fixed Overhead Costs
per Month and Variable Overhead Costs per Direct Labor Hour Worked

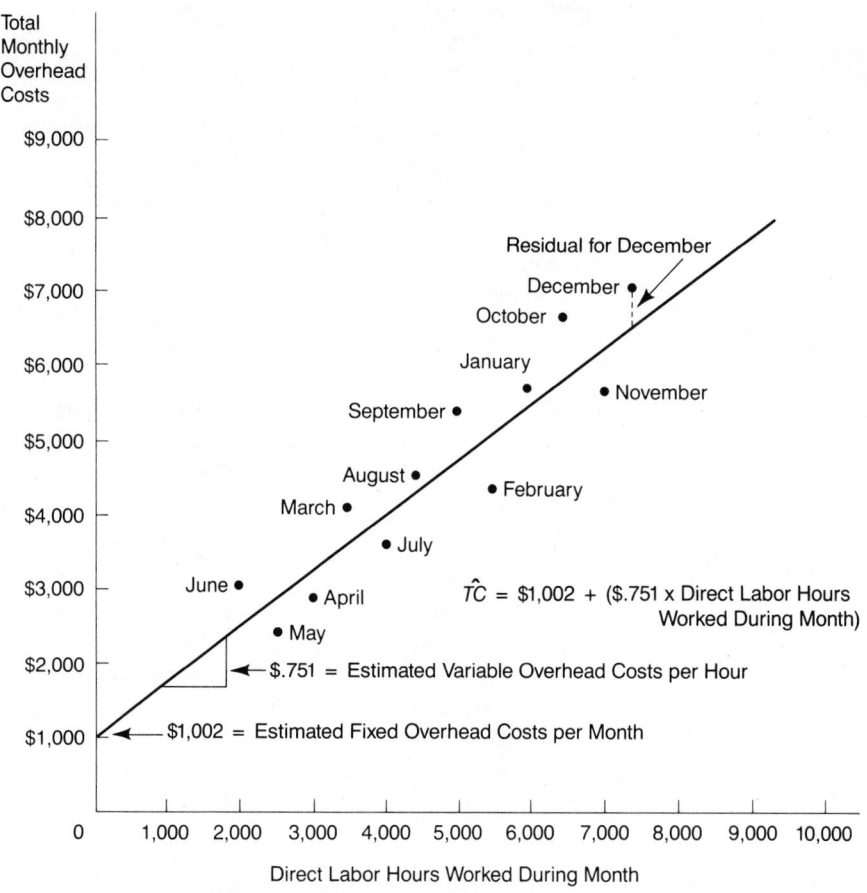

Note: This illustration is based on data in Exhibit 6.9.

cost coefficient is relatively large compared to the standard error of the variable cost coefficient in this example; the *t*-value is relatively large: $0.751 \div \$.093 = 8.08$. We conclude, therefore, that there is a statistically significant relationship between changes in total overhead costs and changes in direct labor hours: Larger amounts of direct labor hours worked per month are correlated with larger amounts of total overhead costs.

In cases where the standard error of the cost coefficient is large relative to the coefficient (small *t*-value), the cost coefficient is not significantly different from zero. If a variable cost coefficient has a small *t*-value, we would conclude that there is little, if any, relationship between this particular activity (or independent variable) and changes in costs. If a fixed cost coefficient has a low *t*-value, we might conclude that these costs have little, if any, fixed cost component (which we would expect for direct materials, for example).

R^2 The "R^2" attempts to measure how well the line fits the data (that is, how closely the data points cluster about the fitted line). If all the data points were on the same straight line, then the R^2 would be 1.00—a perfect fit. If the data points formed a circle or disk, then the adjusted R^2 would be zero, indicating that no line passing through the center of the circle or disk fits the data better than any other.[9] Technically, R^2 is a measure of the fraction of the total variance of the dependent variable about its mean that is explained by the fitted line.[10] An R^2 of one means that all of the variance is explained; an R^2 of zero means that none of the variance is explained.

Many users of statistical regression analysis believe that low R^2's indicate a weak relation between the total costs (dependent variable) and the activity base (independent variable). Whether or not the activity base is a good explanatory variable for total costs is signalled by a low standard error (or high t-value) for the estimated variable cost coefficient. If there are sufficiently many data observations, there can be both low R^2 and significant regression coefficients. This possibility is shown graphically in Exhibit 6.13.

Exhibit 6.13
Relation Between Statistical Significance of Variable Cost Coefficient and R^2

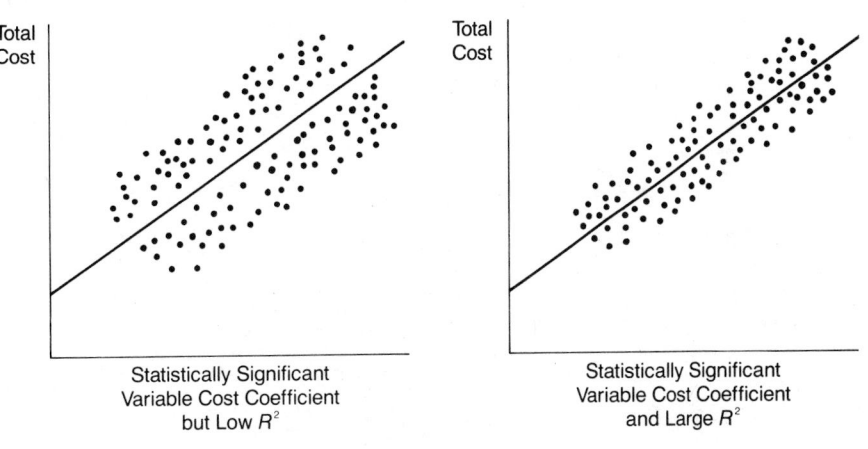

Statistically Significant
Variable Cost Coefficient
but Low R^2

Statistically Significant
Variable Cost Coefficient
and Large R^2

[9]Other situations can also lead to an R^2 of zero.
[10]Many books and computer outputs report both an "adjusted" and an "unadjusted" R^2. The adjustment takes into account the number of coefficients that have been fit to the data—two in a linear regression of the kind illustrated here: one for the constant (fixed costs in our applications) and one for the coefficient of the activity variable. An adjusted R^2 is a better measure than an unadjusted R^2 because the R^2 is appropriately penalized for the use of more independent variables. (If you used as many independent variables as you have observations, you would always get an unadjusted R^2 of 1.00.) The unadjusted R^2 for a simple linear regression is merely the square of the correlation coefficient between the independent and dependent variables.

Using the Regression to Estimate Costs The least-squares regression equation

$$TC = \$1,002 + \$.751 \times \text{Direct Labor Hours Worked}$$

is graphed as a heavy straight line in Exhibit 6.14 with the observations shown and identified by month. The dashed line graphed on Exhibit 6.14 shows that these same data observations may have been generated by a nonlinear relation between costs and activity that appears to be linear in the range of observations.

We should be wary of predicting total costs for direct labor hours worked less than about 2,000 per month or more than about 8,000 per month. This means that we should be wary of our estimate of fixed costs, because it is outside the "relevant

Exhibit 6.14
CHICAGO MANUFACTURING COMPANY:
Comparison of Regression Estimate to Possible Nonlinear Relation

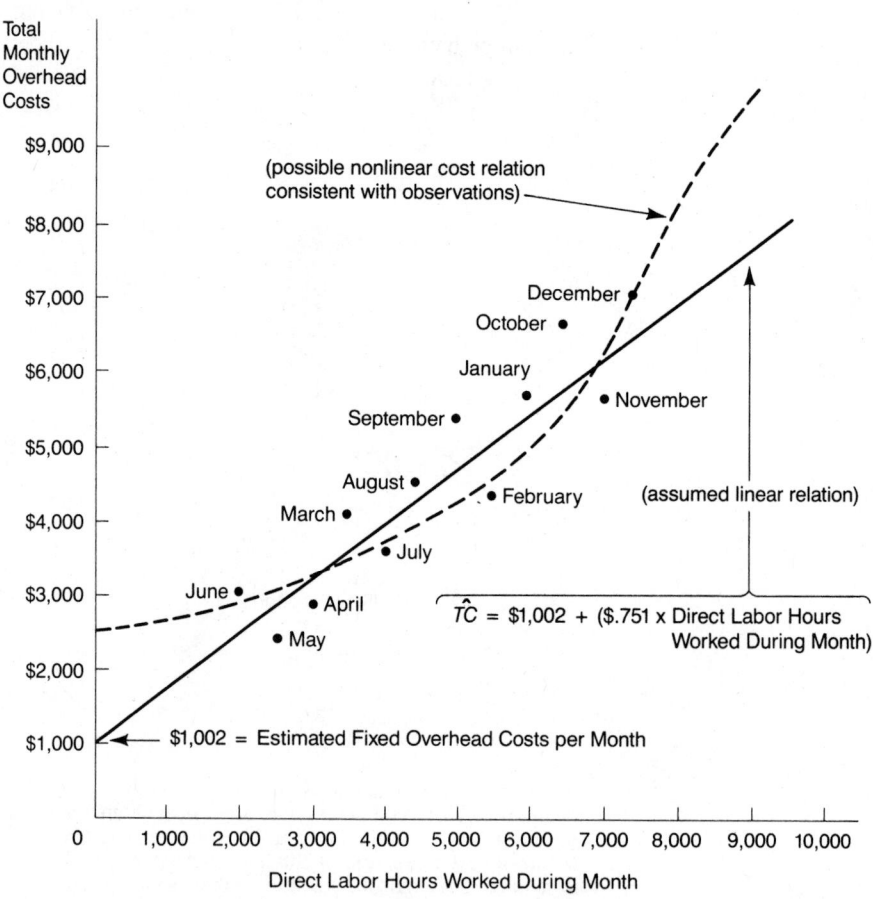

Note: This illustration is based on data in Exhibit 6.9.

range.'' This regression estimate of fixed costs can be checked with the account analysis or other methods to be sure that it makes sense. Were this done here, we might find that the true relation between costs and activity is that shown by the dashed line in Exhibit 6.14, not the assumed straight line.

Warning Probably the major difficulty of using statistical estimating techniques is that they are so easy to do in this day of inexpensive computing devices, but the necessary warnings are not printed on the computer packages. We conclude this section by providing three warnings. First, a relation achieved in a regression analysis does not imply a causal relation. That is, a correlation between two variables does not imply that changes in one will cause changes in the other. An assertion of causality must be based on either *a priori* knowledge or some analysis other than a regression analysis.

Second, users of regression analysis should be wary of drawing too many inferences from the results unless they are familiar with such statistical estimation problems as *multicollinearity, autocorrelation,* and *heteroscedasticity* and how to deal with them.[11] Statistical estimation problems are beyond the scope of this book; they are dealt with at length in statistics books.

Third, users of regression analysis should be aware of problems inherent in the data base, as discussed earlier in this chapter.

Strengths and Weaknesses of Cost Estimation Methods

Each of the methods discussed has advantages and disadvantages. Probably the most informative estimate of cost behavior is one that would use all of the methods discussed because each method has the potential to provide information not provided by the others. In practice, the cost of each method must be compared with the benefits to decide which to use. Exhibit 6.15 summarizes the strengths and weaknesses of these methods.

---

[11]Briefly, *multicollinearity* refers to the problem caused in multiple linear regression (more than one independent variable) when the independent variables are not independent of each other but are correlated. When there is severe multicollinearity, the regression coefficients are unreliable. For example, direct labor hours worked during a month are likely to be strongly correlated with direct labor costs during the month, even when wage rates change over time. If both direct labor hours and direct labor costs are used in a multiple linear regression, we would expect to have a problem of multicollinearity. *Autocorrelation* refers to the phenomenon that occurs when, for example, a linear regression is fit to data where there is actually a nonlinear relation between the dependent and independent variables. In that case, the deviation of one observation from the fitted line can be predicted, to one degree or another, from the deviation of the prior observation(s). For example, if there is seasonal demand for a product and production is also seasonal, then a month of large total costs is more likely to be followed by another month of large total costs than by a month of small total costs. In such a case, we would have autocorrelation in the deviations of the data points from a fitted straight line. *Heteroscedasticity* refers to the phenomenon that occurs when the average deviation of the dependent variable from the best-fitting linear relationship is systematically larger on one part of the range of independent variable(s) than in others. For example, if less reliable equipment and less skilled labor are brought into use in months of large total production, then there is likely to be more variation in total costs during months of large total production than in months of small total production.

Exhibit 6.15
Strengths and Weaknesses of Cost Estimation Methods

Method	Strengths	Weaknesses
Engineering Method	Based on studies of what future costs should be rather than what past costs have been.	Not particularly useful when the physical relationship between inputs and outputs is indirect. Can be costly to use.
Account Analysis	Provides a detailed expert analysis of the cost behavior in each account.	Subjective.
Visual Curve-Fitting Method	Uses all the observations of cost data. Relatively easy to understand and apply.	The fitting of the line to the observations is subjective. Difficult to do where several independent variables are to be used.
Regression Method	Uses all of the observations of cost data. The line is statistically fit to the observations. A measure of the goodness of fit of the line to the observations is provided. Relatively easy to use with computers and sophisticated calculators.	The regression model requires that several relatively strict assumptions be satisfied in order for the results to be valid.

Summary

Estimates of cost behavior are needed to apply manufacturing overhead to products, to estimate how costs will be affected by managerial decisions, and for planning and budgeting.

For these purposes, categorizing costs into fixed and variable components is useful. Variable costs change with the level of activity, whereas fixed costs remain constant. This categorization is valid within some assumed time period (usually called the *short run*) and range of activity (the *relevant* range).

Many fixed costs are called *capacity costs;* they will remain constant (in the absence of inflation) as long as capacity is not changed. Other fixed costs are called *discretionary costs.* These costs include such things as advertising and research and development, which may not be absolutely essential to operate the business but are essential for achieving long-run goals.

Many costs are not simply fixed or variable. Variable costs may be *curvilinear* as well as linear. An example of curvilinear variable costs is the impact of learning which reduces labor and labor-related costs per unit as workers gain experience with a new product or process.

Costs also may be *semivariable,* having both fixed and variable components. *Semifixed* costs are those that increase in steps.

There are numerous methods for estimating cost behavior. Each attempts to estimate *TC, F,* and *V* in the equation

$$TC = F + VX,$$

where *TC* is the total cost during the period, *F* is the fixed cost during the period, *V* is the variable cost per unit of activity, and *X* is the number of units of activity during the period.

The *engineering* method involves a study of the physical inputs required to produce each unit of output. This is the basis for estimating the costs of each unit of output. The *account analysis* method calls for an analysis of each cost account and a classification of the account according to cost behavior—usually either fixed or variable.

Two methods, *visual curve fitting* and *regression,* rely on historical data in the accounting records. Keeping in mind the adage, "garbage-in, garbage-out," we recommend the following steps in analyzing these data:

1. Select an activity base (that is, the independent variable) whose variation is closely associated with the cost item being estimated.
2. Plot the data.
3. Examine the data and cost accumulation methods. Be sure that the costs (dependent variable) are matched with the activity expected to cause the costs (independent variable) in the same time period.
4. Examine the constancy of the production process to ensure that data are collected over a period when there were no major changes in the production process.

The *visual curve-fitting* method estimates the relationship between costs and activity from a line drawn to provide the best visual "fit" of the data. *Regression* analysis also provides the best "fit" of a line to the data such that the sum of the squares of the vertical distance of each observation point from the regression line is minimized.

The results of computerized regression analyses provide more than fixed and variable cost estimates. *Standard errors of the coefficients* of the regression equation give a rough idea of the confidence we have in the coefficients—the smaller the standard error is relative to its coefficient, the better. The R^2 attempts to measure how well the data fit the regression line.

Users of regression for cost estimation should be sure that (1) a logical relation exists between the underlying activity base and the costs being estimated, (2) statistical estimation problems have been considered and dealt with, and (3) the data base has been examined.

Appendix: Derivation of Learning Curves

Mathematically, the learning curve effect can be expressed in exponential form as

$$Y = aX^b,$$

where

Y = *average* number of labor hours required per unit for *X* units,
a = number of labor hours required for the first unit,
X = cumulative number of units produced,
b = *index* of learning equal to the log of the learning rate divided by the log of 2.

For the learning curve example in the text, $b = -0.322$, which can be shown as follows:

If the first unit takes a hours, then the average for 2 units is $0.8a$ hours according to the model. Because $X = 2$, the equation gives $0.8a = a2^b$. Taking logs, log $0.8 + \log a = \log a + b \log 2$. Simplifying, $b = \log 0.8/\log 2 = -.322$.

Thus, the average number of labor hours from the example in the text could be derived as follows:

X	Y	
1	125	
2	100	$Y = 125 \times (2^{-.322}) = 100$
3	88	$Y = 125 \times (3^{-.322}) = 88$
4	80	$Y = 125 \times (4^{-.322}) = 80$
.	.	
.	.	
.	.	
8	64	$Y = 125 \times (8^{-.322}) = 64$

The function

$$Y = aX^b$$

is curvilinear, as shown in the text. The function is linear when expressed in logs, because

$$\log Y = \log a + b \log X,$$

so the function is linear when plotted on log-log paper as shown below.

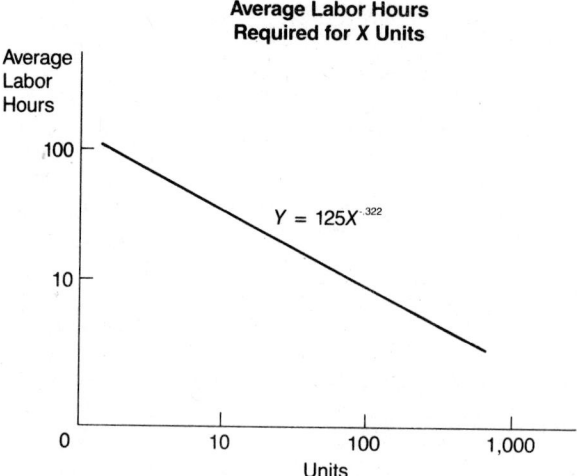

Average Labor Hours Required for X Units

For an expanded discussion, consult an operations management textbook. For accounting applications of learning curves, see F. P. Kollaritsch and R. B. Jordan,

"The Learning Curve: Concepts and Application," in *The Managerial and Cost Accountant's Handbook,* H. A. Black and J. D. Edwards, Eds. (Homewood, Ill.: Dow Jones–Irwin, 1979), pp. 971–1017; W. J. Morse, "Reporting Production Costs That Follow the Learning Curve Phenomenon," *The Accounting Review* (October 1972), pp. 761–773; and N. Baloff and J. W. Kennelly, "Accounting Implications of Product and Process Startups," *Journal of Accounting Research* (Autumn 1967), pp. 131–143.

Problem 1 for Self-Study

Sketch appropriate cost graphs for each of the following situations.

a. Costs of raw materials used in producing a firm's products.

b. Wages of delivery truck drivers. One driver is required, on average, for each $1 million of sales.

c. Leasing costs of a delivery truck, which is $250 per month and $.18 per mile.

d. Fixed fee paid to an independent firm of CPAs for auditing and attesting to financial statements.

e. Compensation of sales staff with salary of $10,000 plus commission rates that increase as sales increase: 4 percent of the first $100,000 of annual sales, 6 percent of all sales from $100,000 to $200,000, and 8 percent for sales in excess of $200,000.

f. Cost of electricity, where a flat rate of $50 is charged for the first 5,000 units, $.005 per unit for the next 45,000 units, and $.004 per unit for all units in excess of the first 50,000 units.

Suggested Solution

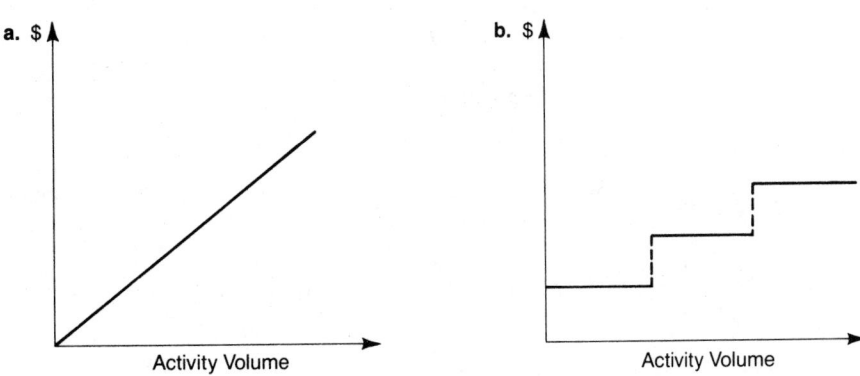

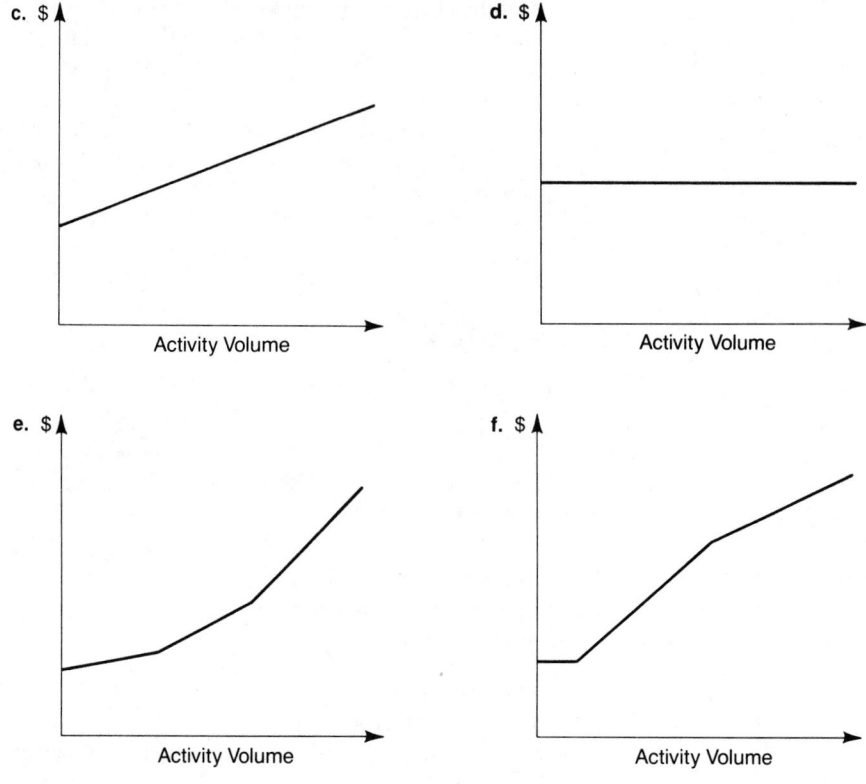

Problem 2 for Self-Study

Propylon Textiles[13]

Propylon, the wonder fabric of the 1980s, was the brainchild of Henry Carr, scion of an old banking family. Pursuing his special interest in polymers as a chemistry graduate student, Carr created a synthetic compound whose polymer threads were far superior to any of the synthetics used by the textile industry. The fabric was crease-resistant, wrinkle-free, and simulated the appearance and feel of natural-fiber fabrics. Propylon took the world by storm when production began 3 years ago. In addition to its versatility, propylon is extremely strong and durable, heat-resistant, and "breathes" like natural fibers.

By the second year, Propylon Textiles had reached its current production level with 10 product lines. Now, after the third year of production, Natalie Martin, the controller, has decided that the company has enough data to merit a detailed analysis of its overhead cost behavior.

The following monthly overhead costs were recorded for the previous 2 years.

---

[13]This case was written by Jean Lin under the supervision of Michael Maher.

Cost Data for Propylon Textiles (in thousands)

Month, First Year

	J	F	M	A	M	J	J	A	S	O	N	D	2-Year Totals
Indirect Materials	$22	$20	$23	$24	$22	$21	$20	$19	$19	$18	$18	$20	$ 503
Indirect Labor	40	30	40	40	40	30	20	10	10	10	10	20	630
Lease	12	12	12	12	12	12	12	12	12	12	12	12	288
Utilities	9	9	8	8	8	7	8	7	8	8	9	9	206
Power	5	4	5	6	6	5	3	3	3	2	2	4	104
Insurance	1	1	1	1	1	1	1	1	1	1	1	1	24
Maintenance	20	6	6	6	6	6	20	6	6	6	6	6	200
Depreciation	2	2	2	2	2	2	2	2	2	2	2	2	72
Research and Development	7	8	10	9	8	10	6	6	7	4	5	8	171
Total Overhead	$118	$92	$107	$108	$105	$94	$92	$66	$68	$63	$65	$82	$2,198
Direct Labor Hours	36.0	34.2	37.4	37.8	36.4	35.0	33.2	30.8	30.9	29.4	30.0	33.4	815.8 hours
Direct Labor Costs ($)	216.0	205.2	224.4	226.8	218.4	210.0	199.2	184.8	185.4	176.4	180.0	200.4	$4,997.4
Machine Hours	45.0	42.6	45.0	47.0	45.2	43.6	41.2	40.0	39.4	37.2	36.5	42.0	1,022.7 hours
Units Produced	8.9	8.6	9.2	9.5	8.9	8.6	8.0	7.8	7.6	7.4	7.2	8.1	202.5 units

Month, Second Year

	J	F	M	A	M	J	J	A	S	O	N	D
Indirect Materials	$21	$21	$23	$24	$24	$21	$22	$20	$19	$19	$21	$22
Indirect Labor	20	30	40	50	30	30	30	20	10	10	30	30
Lease	12	12	12	12	12	12	12	12	12	12	12	12
Utilities	10	10	9	9	8	8	8	8	9	9	10	10
Power	5	5	6	7	6	4	5	4	2	2	5	5
Insurance	1	1	1	1	1	1	1	1	1	1	1	1
Maintenance	20	6	6	6	6	6	20	6	6	6	6	6
Depreciation	4	4	4	4	4	4	4	4	4	4	4	4
Research and Development	6	8	1	9	8	8	7	7	7	5	8	9
Total Overhead	$99	$97	$102	$122	$99	$94	$109	$82	$70	$68	$97	$99
Direct Labor Hours	33.2	34.2	36.9	39.6	35.2	34.0	35.2	32.4	30.2	30.4	34.2	35.8
Direct Labor Costs ($)	207.5	213.7	230.6	247.5	220.0	212.5	220.0	202.5	188.7	190.0	213.7	223.7
Machine Hours	43.4	43.2	46.4	50.0	44.2	42.6	43.2	41.2	38.2	37.6	43.8	44.2
Units Produced	8.4	8.6	9.1	9.8	8.9	8.4	8.7	8.1	7.7	7.5	8.6	8.9

You are a financial analyst at Propylon Textiles and have been asked by the controller to prepare a report on the firm's overhead cost behavior, using the data for the two-year period. Computer output to help you with the analysis is presented below.

Subproblem No. 1:

Dependent Variable = Overhead
Independent Variable: DL Hours
R-Square = .8848

Variable Name	No.	Estimated Coefficient	Standard Error	T-Value 22 DF
DL Hours	1	5.9676	.45910	12.999
Intercept		−1112.7	156.54	−7.1079
24 Observations				

Subproblem No. 2:

Dependent Variable = Overhead
Independent Variable: DL Cost
R-Square = .8712

Variable Name	No.	Estimated Coefficient	Standard Error	T-Value 22 DF
DL Cost	2	.91426	.07493	12.201
Intercept		−987.9	156.57	−6.3096
24 Observations				

Subproblem No. 3:

Dependent Variable = Overhead
Independent Variable: M Hours
R-Square = .8630

Variable Name	No.	Estimated Coefficient	Standard Error	T-Value 22 DF
M Hours	3	4.9015	.41645	11.770
Intercept		−1,172.8	117.96	−6.5902
24 Observations				

Subproblem No. 4:

Dependent Variable = Overhead
Independent Variable: Units Produced
R-Square = .8700

Variable Name	No.	Estimated Coefficient	Standard Error	T-Value 22 DF
Units Produced	4	23.799	1.9610	12.136
Intercept		−1,092.2	165.97	−6.5805
24 Observations				

a. Using the account analysis method, calculate the monthly average for fixed costs and the variable cost rate per:

(**1**) Direct labor hour.

(**2**) Machine hour.

(**3**) Unit of output.

Write the cost equation for each of the three activity bases.

To help you, the controller has classified the various accounts as follows:

Account	Cost Behavior
Indirect Materials	Variable
Indirect Labor	Variable
Lease	Fixed
Utilities	Fixed
Power	Variable
Insurance	Fixed
Maintenance	Fixed
Depreciation	Fixed
Research and Development	Fixed

b. Plot direct labor costs against total overhead. Are there any outliers? If so, determine possible causes.

c. Subproblems 1 through 4 in the computer output above are simple linear regressions with overhead as the dependent variable and direct labor hours, direct labor costs, machine hours, and units of output, respectively, as the independent variables. Select the most appropriate activity base for overhead cost and explain your choice.

d. Plot indirect labor costs against direct labor hours. What kind of cost balance pattern do you observe?

e. Using the activity base selected in part (**c**), label and sketch the overhead cost function. What does this overhead cost function tell you about the relation between current production levels and capacity?

Suggested Solution

a.

Indirect Materials	$ 503,000
Indirect Labor	630,000
Power	104,000
Total Variable Costs	$1,237,000
Lease	$ 288,000
Utilities	206,000
Insurance	24,000
Maintenance	200,000
Depreciation	72,000
Research and Development	171,000
Total Fixed Costs	$ 961,000

$$\text{Monthly Fixed Costs} = \frac{\$961,000}{24} = \$40,042.$$

$$\text{Variable Cost per Direct Labor Hour} = \frac{\$1,237,000}{815,800} = \$1.516.$$

$$\text{TC} = \$40,042 + (\$1.516 \times \text{Direct Labor Hours})$$

$$\text{Variable Cost per Machine Hour} = \frac{\$1,237,000}{1,022,700} = \$1.210.$$

$$\text{TC} = \$40,042 + (\$1.210 \times \text{Machine Hours})$$

$$\text{Variable Cost per Unit Produced} = \frac{\$1,237,000}{202,500} = \$6.109.$$

$$\text{TC} = \$40,042 + (\$6.109 \times \text{Units Produced})$$

b.

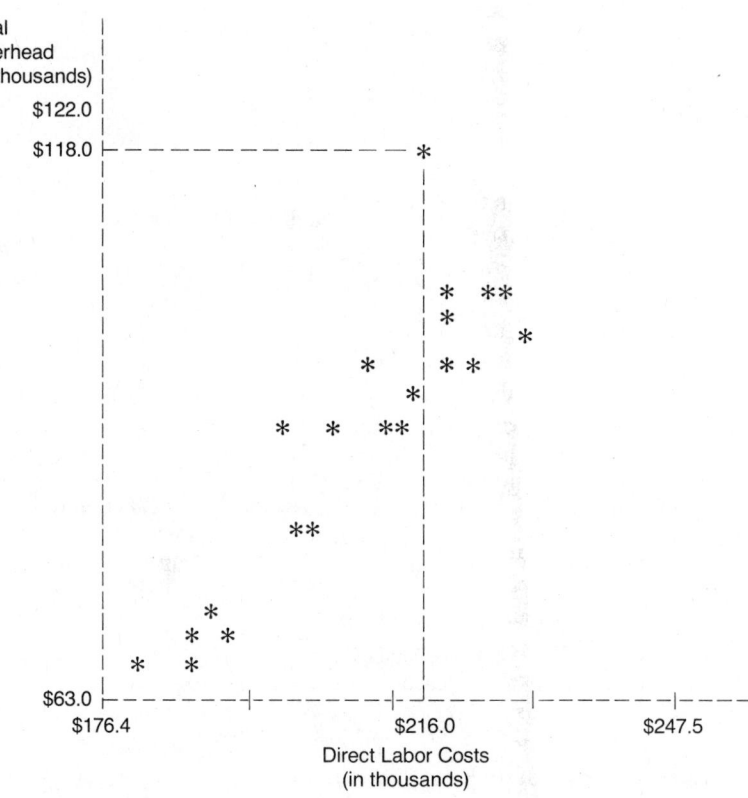

The first observation ($216,000, $118,000) appears to be an outlier. The most probable cause for the higher overhead cost is the relatively higher amount spent on maintenance that month.

c. Based on the R_2 and t-values, the four regressions are about the same. They should search for a logical relation between overhead and the most appropriate activity base. Machine hours may not be appropriate if machine processes for the various product lines are radically different. Direct labor cost is not a good measure if wage rates are varied and unrelated to overhead. Units of output may not be a good activity base because there are 10 different product lines.

d.

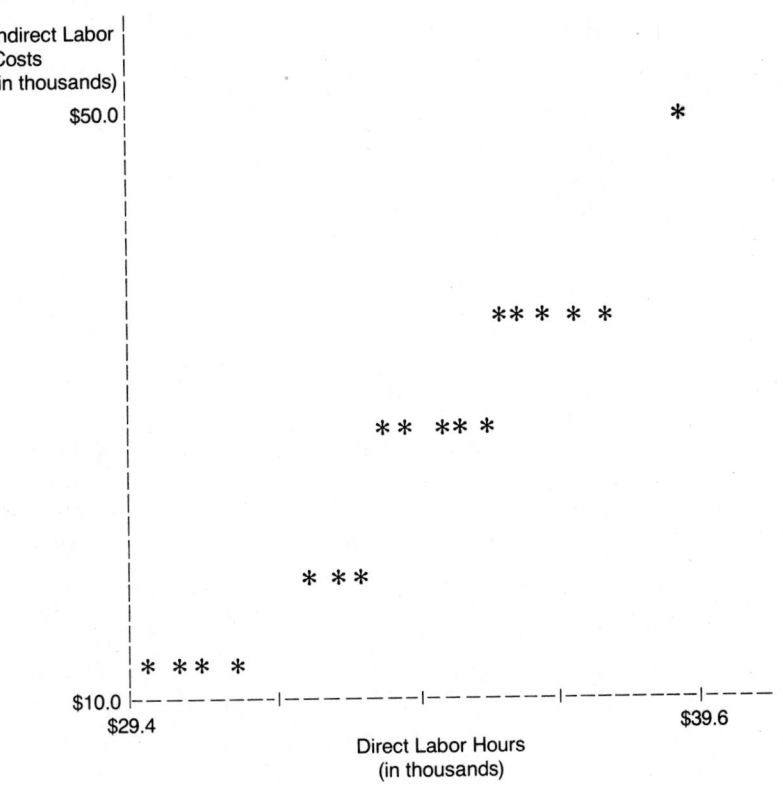

e. The costs are semifixed or step costs.

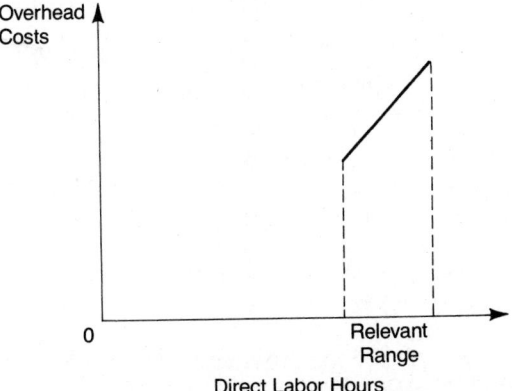

f. The steepness of the overhead function within the relevant range seems to imply that the firm is currently operating at capacity and is facing increasing marginal costs. In the long run, the company should seriously consider capacity expansion.

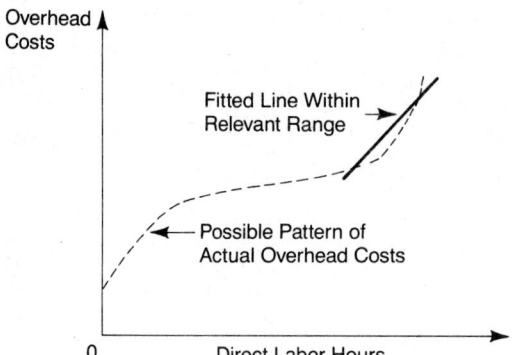

Questions

1. Review the meaning of the following concepts or terms discussed in this chapter.

a. Cost behavior.
b. Fixed costs.
c. Variable costs.
d. Short run versus long run.
e. Relevant range.
f. Capacity costs.
g. Discretionary (programmed, managed) costs.
h. Curvilinear variable costs.
i. Learning curves.
j. Semivariable costs.
k. Semifixed costs.
l. Cost estimation.

m. Independent variable versus dependent variable.
n. Engineering method of cost estimation.
o. Account analysis method.
p. Activity bases.
q. Outlier.
r. Visual curve-fitting method.
s. Regression analysis.
t. t-Value.
u. R^2.
v. Standard error of the coefficients.

2. "The concepts of short-run costs and long-run costs are so relative: Short run could mean a day, a month, a year or even 10 years, depending on what you are looking at." Comment.

3. "My variable costs are $2 per unit. If I want to increase production from 100,000 units to 150,000 units, my costs should only go up by $100,000." Comment.

4. Describe the phenomenon that gives rise to learning curves. To what type of costs do learning curves apply?

5. "Simplification of all costs into just fixed and variable costs distorts the actual cost behavior pattern of a firm. Yet businesses rely on this method of cost classification." Comment.

6. Which method of cost estimation does not rely primarily on historical cost data? What are the drawbacks of this method?

7. "The account analysis method is based on subjective judgment. So we cannot really consider it a valid method of cost estimation." Comment.

8. What methods of cost estimation rely primarily on historical data? Discuss the problems an unwary user may encounter with the use of historical cost data.

9. Why is knowledge of the range of observations included in a data set for cost estimation purposes?

10. If an analyst simply enters data into a program to compute regression estimates, what major problems might he or she encounter?

11. When estimating fixed and variable costs, it is possible to have an equation with a negative intercept. Does this mean that at zero production level the company has negative fixed costs?

12. Suggest ways that one can compensate for the effects of price instability when preparing cost estimates.

Exercises

13. *Graphical Representation of Cost Relationships.*
Sketch cost graphs for the following situations:
    a. A 20 percent increase in fixed costs will enable Twickenham Products to produce up to 50 percent more. Variable costs will remain unchanged.
    b. Refer to part **a.** What if Twickenham Products' variable costs double for the additional units they intend to produce?
    c. Aerodyne's variable production costs per unit decline as more units are produced.
    d. Richmond Paper pays a flat fixed charge per month for electricity plus an additional rate of $.10 per unit for all consumption over the first thousand units.
    e. Surrey Steel's indirect labor costs are composed entirely of supervisors' salaries. Surrey Steel requires one supervisor for every 40 workers.
    f. Petersham Plastics is currently operating at close to capacity. A short-run increase in production would result in increasing unit costs for every additional unit produced.

14. *Cost Behavior in Event of Capacity Change.* Muller's Gasthaus, a lodge located in a fast-growing ski resort, is planning on opening their new wing this coming winter, increasing the number of beds by 40 percent. Although variable costs per guest-day will remain unchanged, fixed costs will increase by 25 percent. Last year's costs were

Variable Costs	$50,000
Fixed Costs	$30,000

The occupancy rate percentage is expected to stay the same as last year.
    a. Sketch the cost function.

b. Calculate the additional operating costs that Muller's Gasthaus will incur next year.

15. *Cost Behavior When Costs Are Semivariable.* Data from the shipping department of Weston Company for the last 2 months are as follows:

	Number of Packages Shipped	Shipping Department Costs
November	3,000	$4,500
December	4,500	6,000

a. Sketch a line describing these costs as a function of the number of packages shipped.

b. The line should indicate that these shipping costs are semivariable. What is the apparent fixed cost per month of running the shipping department during November and December?

c. What is the apparent variable cost per package shipped?

16. *Cost Behavior When Costs Are Semivariable.* Data from the shipping department of Kennelly Company for the last 3 months are as follows:

	Number of Packages Shipped	Shipping Department Costs
June	2,000	$3,500
July	2,500	4,500
August	1,500	3,000

What is the apparent relation between shipping department costs and the number of packages shipped?

17. *Cost Estimation Using Visual Curve Fitting.* Data on total manufacturing costs and production output of the Anwell Company for the past 6 months are shown below.

a. Estimate fixed costs per month and variable cost per unit produced from the above data using a straight line visually fit to a plot of the above data.

b. Estimate total monthly costs for a month when 250 units are produced using the estimates of fixed and variable costs from **a**.

ANWELL COMPANY

Month	Units Produced	Total Costs
March	200	$16,000
April	280	19,200
May	300	19,800
June	260	19,000
July	260	18,600
August	240	16,400

18. *Effect of Learning on Cost Behavior (Appendix).* Zipper Incorporated manufactures aircraft parts for various commercial airlines. On one particular contract, including the design and manufacture of special containers, the following costs were recorded.

Cumulative Number of Units Produced, X	Average Manufacturing Costs (in real dollars), Y
1	$1,333
2	1,000
3	845
4	750
5	684
6	634
7	594
8	562

a. Sketch the relationship between X and Y.

b. If there is a "learning" phenomenon, determine the constant percentage reduction in manufacturing costs.

19. *Average Cost Calculations.* Soma Beds has the following cost equation:

$$\text{Total Costs} = \$13{,}266 + \$150n,$$

where n = units of output.

a. Calculate Soma's average fixed cost per unit when output is 500 units.

b. Calculate the average variable cost per unit when output is 500 units.

c. Calculate the average cost per unit when output is 500 units.

20. *Repair Cost Behavior.* An analysis of repair costs by month in the Baiman Company was made using linear regression analysis. The equation fit was of the form

$$\begin{matrix} \text{Total} \\ \text{Repair} \\ \text{Costs} \end{matrix} = \begin{matrix} \text{Fixed} \\ \text{Costs} \end{matrix} + \left(\begin{matrix} \text{Variable Repair Costs} \\ \text{per Machine Hour Used} \\ \text{During Month} \end{matrix} \times \begin{matrix} \text{Machine Hours} \\ \text{Actually Used} \\ \text{During Month} \end{matrix} \right)$$

$$TRC = a + bx.$$

The results were as follows (standard error of coefficients shown in parentheses):

$$TRC = \$20{,}000 - \$.75x$$
$$\quad\quad\quad (\$7{,}000) \quad (\$.25)$$

The R^2 was 0.90.

Average monthly repair costs have been $18,800 and machine hours used have averaged 1,600 hours per month. Management is concerned about the ability of the analyst who carried out this work because of the *negative* coefficient for variable cost. What is your evaluation of these results?

21. *Interpreting Regression Results.* The output of overhead on direct labor costs is shown on the top of the next page.

Regression Results:

Equation:

Intercept.	$16,400
Slope	2.150

Statistical Data:

Correlation Coefficient	.92
R-Square	.85

The company is planning on operating at a level that would call for direct labor costs of $14,000 per month for the coming year.

    a. Use the regression output to write the overhead cost equation.

    b. Based on the cost equation, compute the estimated overhead cost per month for the coming year.

    c. Comment on the regression.

22. *Interpreting Regression Data.* A marketing manager of a company used a pocket calculator to estimate the relation between advertising expenditures (the independent variable) and sales dollars. Monthly data for the past 3 years were entered into the calculator. The regression results indicated the following equation:

$$\text{Sales Dollars} = \$97,000 - 145 \times \text{Advertising Dollars}$$
$$\text{Correlation Coefficient} = -.814$$

Do these results imply that advertising hurts sales? Why would there appear to be a negative relation between advertising expenditures and sales?

23. *Cost Estimation Using Visual Curve Fitting.* Okanagan Beer has observed the following overhead costs for the past 12 months:

Month	Overhead Costs	Gallons of Output
Jan..	$45,600	18,000
Feb.	$62,400	44,000
Mar.	$67,200	48,000
Apr..	$48,000	22,000
May.	$56,400	36,000
June	$62,400	42,000
July	$52,800	30,000
Aug.	$49,200	20,000
Sep.	$62,400	46,000
Oct..	$51,600	24,000
Nov.	$57,600	34,000
Dec.	$60,000	40,000

    a. Prepare a scatter plot of the data.

    b. By visual inspection, fit a line through the plotted points and calculate the approximate monthly fixed cost and unit variable cost.

Problems and Cases

24. *Interpreting Multiple Regression Results.* In order to select the most appropriate activity base for allocating overhead, Mercury Gas, an oil refinery, ran a multiple linear regression of several independent variables against their nonmaintenance overhead cost. The results were as follows for 24 observations:

Variable Name	Coefficient	Standard Error	t-Value
Direct Labor Hours	.876	2.686	.326
Units of Output.	10.218	5.378	1.900
Maintenance Costs	− 12.786	1.113	− 11.488
Cost of Utilities.	.766	.079	9.696
Intercept	12.768	6.359	2.008
$R^2 = 0.90$			

Discuss the appropriateness of each of the variables and select the most appropriate.

25. *Interpreting Regression Results (adapted from an example by George Benston, The Accounting Review, October 1966, pp. 657–672).* The Benston Company manufactures widgets and digits. The widgets are assembled in batches, whereas digits are made one at a time. The cost of producing widgets is believed to be independent of the number of digits produced in a week. Cost data were gathered for 156 weeks. The following notation is used:

C = Total Manufacturing Costs per Week,
N = Number of Widgets Produced During a Week
B = Average Number of Widgets in a Batch During the Week, and
D = Number of Digits Produced During the Week.

A multiple linear regression was fit to the observations, with the following results (standard errors of estimated coefficients are shown in parentheses under the coefficients):

$$C = \$265.80 + \$8.21N - \$7.83B + \$12.32D$$
$$(\$110.80) \quad (\$.53) \quad (\$1.69) \quad (\$2.10)$$

The adjusted R^2 was .89.

a. According to the regression results, by how much are weekly costs expected to increase if the number of widgets is increased by one?

b. What are the expected costs for the week if 500 widgets are produced in batches of 20 each and the number of digits produced during the week is 300?

c. Interpret the negative coefficient ($-\$7.83$) estimated for the variable B.

26. *Comprehensive Problem in Estimating Costs for Historical Data.* The internal accounting department at Ling Company has available the data shown in the accompanying table: observations by month for the last 3 years on total overhead costs for the month on direct labor hours worked for the month, and on direct labor costs for the month in dollars. The problem is to estimate the fixed overhead costs per month and the variable overhead costs per unit of base activity. Analysis of the overhead costs indicates that direct labor hours required and direct labor costs are both closely related to variable overhead costs. The procedures and questions below mirror the steps taken by the accountants at Ling Company in determining estimates of fixed and variable overhead costs.

    a. Before the data are used in establishing estimated costs, what questions should be raised and answered about how data shown in the accompanying table were processed through the accounting system? Assume that these questions have been satisfactorily answered before the following steps are taken.

    b. Prepare a graph with total overhead costs on the vertical axis and direct labor *hours* on the horizontal axis. Plot the 36 monthly observations.

    c. Prepare a graph with total overhead costs on the vertical axis and direct labor *costs* in dollars on the horizontal axis. Plot the 36 monthly observations.

    d. Visually fit a linear cost relation to the graphs drawn in parts **b** and **c**, and determine the fixed cost and variable cost coefficients from your visually fit lines.

    e. The data were run through a computer linear regression program. The first regression used total overhead costs as the dependent variable and direct labor hours as the independent variable. The results were as follows:

	Coefficient	Standard Error	t-Value
Fixed Costs	$9,553	$558.08	17.1
Direct Labor Hours	$.03527	$.00226	15.6
$R^2 = 0.88$			

Second, a regression was run using total overhead costs as the dependent variable and direct labor costs in dollars as the independent variable. The results were as follows:

	Coefficient	Standard Error	t-Value
Fixed Costs	$5,707	$542.47	10.5
Direct Labor Costs	$0.00723	$0.00031	23.0
$R^2 = 0.94$			

Interpret the results of these regressions. Which appears to be the most useful? What cost estimates result?

LING COMPANY
Observations by Month of Total Overhead Costs, Direct Labor Hours, and Direct Labor Costs

	Direct Labor Hours Worked During Month	Direct Labor Costs Incurred During Month	Total Overhead Costs for Month
Year 1			
January	300,000	$1,920,000	$19,200
February	300,000	1,920,000	20,000
March	315,000	2,016,000	20,000
April	285,000	1,824,000	19,200
May	315,000	2,016,000	19,600
June	330,000	2,112,000	20,000
July	330,000	2,112,000	20,800
August	345,000	2,208,000	22,000
September	360,000	2,304,000	22,000
October	345,000	2,208,000	21,600
November	300,000	1,920,000	22,000
December	315,000	2,268,000	22,400
Year 2			
January	285,000	2,052,000	20,000
February	225,000	1,620,000	18,000
March	240,000	1,728,000	18,400
April	210,000	1,512,000	16,800
May	225,000	1,620,000	17,200
June	210,000	1,512,000	16,400
July	225,000	1,620,000	17,600
August	225,000	1,620,000	16,800
September	150,000	1,080,000	12,800
October	195,000	1,404,000	15,200
November	180,000	1,296,000	15,200
December	180,000	1,440,000	15,600
Year 3			
January	165,000	1,320,000	15,200
February	150,000	1,200,000	14,800
March	180,000	1,440,000	16,400
April	180,000	1,440,000	16,000
May	195,000	1,572,000	16,800
June	195,000	1,572,000	17,200
July	210,000	1,692,000	18,000
August	210,000	1,692,000	18,400
September	150,000	1,200,000	14,400
October	180,000	1,452,000	16,800
November	195,000	1,572,000	17,600
December	210,000	1,704,000	17,200

27. *Overhead Cost Estimation Using Scattergraph and Regression Methods* (*CMA adapted*). The Franklin Plant of the Ramon Company manufactures electrical components. Plant management has been experiencing some difficulties with fluctuating monthly overhead costs. Management wants to be able to estimate overhead costs accurately to plan its operations and its financial needs. A trade association publication reports that for companies manufacturing electrical components, overhead tends to vary with direct labor hours.

A member of the controller's staff proposed that the cost behavior pattern of these overhead costs be determined. It would then be possible to estimate overhead costs using direct labor hours.

Another member of the accounting staff suggested that a good starting place for determining cost behavior or patterns would be to analyze historical data.

Following this suggestion, monthly data were gathered on direct labor hours and overhead costs for the past 2 years. It should be noted that there were no major changes in operations over this period of time.

The raw data are as follows:

Month Number	Direct Labor Hours	Overhead Costs
1	20,000	$84,000
2	25,000	99,000
3	22,000	89,500
4	23,000	90,000
5	20,000	81,500
6	19,000	75,500
7	14,000	70,500
8	10,000	64,500
9	12,000	69,000
10	17,000	75,000
11	16,000	71,500
12	19,000	78,000
13	21,000	86,000
14	24,000	93,000
15	23,000	93,000
16	22,000	87,000
17	20,000	80,000
18	18,000	76,500
19	12,000	67,500
20	13,000	71,000
21	15,000	73,500
22	17,000	72,500
23	15,000	71,000
24	18,000	75,000

These data were entered into a computer regression program. The following output was obtained:

Regression Output:

R-Square 9109
Coefficients of the Equation:
  Intercept $39,859
  Independent Variable (slope) 2.1549

a. Prepare a scattergraph showing the overhead costs plotted against direct labor hours.

b. Use the results of the regression analysis to prepare the cost estimation equation and to prepare a cost estimate for 22,500 direct labor hours.

c. Evaluate how well the regression equation estimates overhead cost behavior at the Franklin Plant.

28. *Regression Analysis in Process and Loss Prediction (CMA adapted).* The Johnstar Company makes an expensive chemical product. The costs average about $1,000 per unit of weight, and the material sells for $2,500 per unit of weight. Materials storage is extremely hazardous; therefore, a batch is made each day to fill customer orders for the day. Failure to deliver the required quantity results in a shutdown for the customers with a corresponding cost penalty assessed against Johnstar. However, excess chemical on hand at the end of the day must be disposed of in costly, secure facilities.

The chemical increases in weight during processing, but the exact increase varies depending on temperature and pressure conditions as well as on the impurities present in the input materials. It is important for the company to know the final weight from any batch as soon as possible so that a new batch can be started should the expected final weight be smaller than required for customer needs.

A consultant was hired to advise the company on how to estimate the final weight of the product. The consultant recommended that the product be weighed after 3 hours and that the weight after 3 hours be used to predict the weight at the end of processing. Based on 20 processed batches, the following observations were made:

Batch No.	Weight at 3 Hours	Final Weight	Batch No.	Weight at 3 Hours	Final Weight
1	55	90	11	60	80
2	45	75	12	35	60
3	40	80	13	35	80
4	60	80	14	55	60
5	40	45	15	35	75
6	60	80	16	50	90
7	50	80	17	30	60
8	55	95	18	60	105
9	50	100	19	50	60
10	35	75	20	20	30

Data obtained from the regression analysis included the following:

R^2	.4126
Coefficients of the Regression:	
Constant	28.6
Slope	1.008
Standard Error of Slope Coefficient.	0.2834
t-Value for Slope	3.5559

a. Use the results of the regression to calculate the estimate of the final weight of today's batch, which at the end of 3 hours weighs 42 units.

b. Customer orders for today total 68 units. The smallest batch that can be started must weigh at least 20 units at the end of 3 hours. What factors should be considered in deciding whether to start a new batch?

29. *Learning Curves* (*CMA adapted*). The Kelly Company plans to manufacture a product called Electrocal, which requires a substantial amount of direct labor on each unit. Based on the company's experience with other products that required similar amounts of direct labor, management believes that there is a learning factor in the production process used to manufacture Electrocal.

Each unit of Electrocal requires 50 square feet of direct material at a cost of $30 per square foot for a total material cost of $1,500. The standard direct labor rate is $25 per direct labor hour. Variable manufacturing overhead is assigned to products at a rate of $40 per direct labor hour. The company adds a markup of 30 percent on variable manufacturing cost in determining an initial bid price for all products.

Data on the production of the first two lots (16 units) of Electrocal is as follows:

1. The first of 8 units required a total of 3,200 direct labor hours.
2. The second lot of 8 units required a total of 2,240 direct labor hours.

Based on prior production experience, Kelly anticipates that there will be no significant improvement in production time after the first 32 units. Therefore, a standard for direct labor hours will be established based on the average hours per unit for units 17–32.

    a. What is the basic premise of the learning curve?

    b. Based on the data presented for the first 16 units, what learning rate appears to be applicable to the direct labor required to produce Electrocal? Support your answer with appropriate calculations.

    c. Calculate the standard for direct labor hours that Kelly Company should establish for each unit of Electrocal.

    d. After the first 32 units have been manufactured, Kelly Company was asked to submit a bid on an additional 96 units. What price should Kelly bid on this order of 96 units? Explain your answer.

    e. Knowledge of the learning curve phenomenon can be a valuable management tool. Explain how management can apply the learning curve in the planning and controlling of business operations.

30. *Learning Curves, Differential Analysis* (*CMA adapted*). The Xyon Company has purchased 80,000 pumps annually from Kobec, Inc. The price has increased each year and reached $68 per unit last year. Because the purchase price has increased significantly, Xyon management has asked that an estimate be made of the cost to manufacture it in its own facilities. Xyon's products consist of stamping and castings. The company has little experience with products requiring assembly.

The engineering, manufacturing, and accounting departments have prepared a report for management that included the estimate shown below for an assembly run of 10,000 units. Additional production employees would be hired to manufacture the subassembly. However, no additional equipment, space, or supervision would be needed.

The report states that total costs for 10,000 units are estimated at $957,000 or $95.70 a unit. The current purchase price is $68 a unit, so the report recommends a continued purchase of the product.

Components (outside purchases).	$120,000
Assembly Labor[a]	300,000
Factory Overhead[b].	450,000
General and Administrative Overhead[c].	87,000
Total Costs	$957,000
Fixed Overhead.	50 percent of Direct Labor Dollars
Variable Overhead.	100 percent of Direct Labor Dollars
Factory Overhead Rate	150 percent of Direct Labor Dollars

[a]Assembly labor consists of hourly production workers.

[b]Factory overhead is applied to products on a direct labor dollar basis. Variable overhead costs vary closely with direct labor dollars.

[c]General and administrative overhead is applied at 10 percent of the total cost of material (or components), assembly labor, and factory overhead.

a. Was the analysis prepared by the engineering, manufacturing, and accounting departments of Xyon Company and the recommendation to continue purchasing the pumps that followed from the analysis correct? Explain your answer and include any supportive calculations you consider necessary.

b. Assume Xyon Company could experience labor cost improvements on the pump assembly consistent with an 80 percent learning curve. An assembly run of 10,000 units represents the initial lot or batch for measurement purposes. Should Xyon produce the 80,000 pumps in this situation? Explain your answer.

Suggested Solutions to Even-Numbered Exercises

14. *Cost Behavior in Event of Capacity Change.*

a.

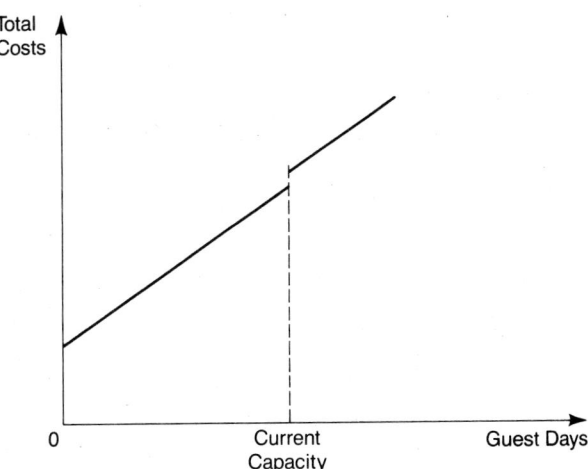

    b. Additional Operating Costs = 0.40(50,000) + 0.25(30,000)

$$= \underline{\underline{\$27,500}}.$$

16. *Cost Behavior When Costs Are Semivariable.*

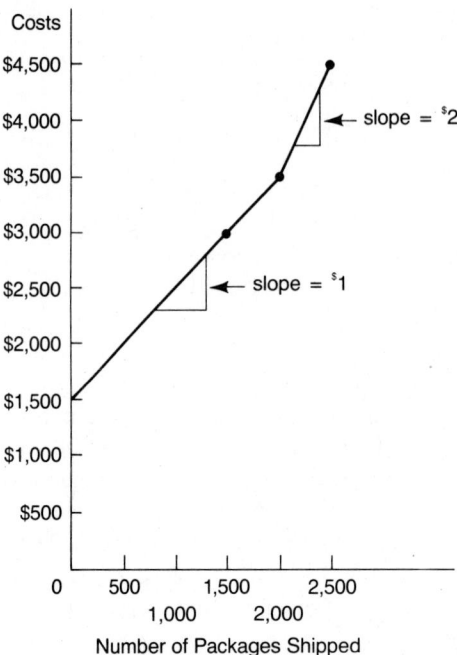

Costs are semivariable. The fixed-cost component is estimated to be $1,500 and the variable cost component is $1 per package up to 2,000 packages. With only three data points, these estimates should be viewed skeptically.

18. *Effect of Learning on Cost Behavior (Appendix).*
   a.

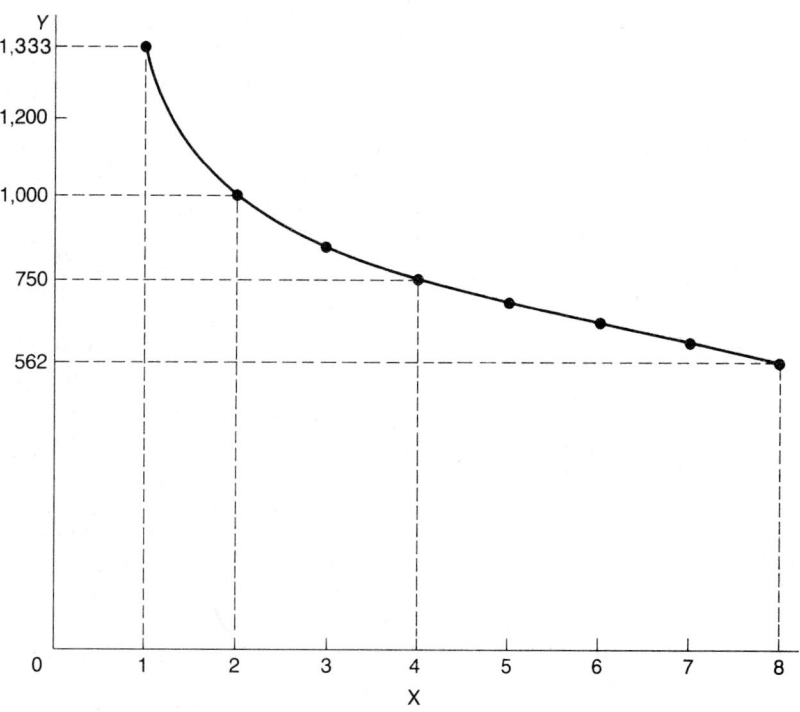

   b. $\dfrac{Y_2}{Y_1} = \dfrac{Y_4}{Y_2} = \dfrac{Y_8}{Y_4} = \underline{\underline{0.75}}$ cumulative learning curve = 25% time reduction
   rate.

20. *Repair Cost Behavior.* The *t*-value of the variable cost coefficient is -3 ($= -.75 \div .25$), which should help convince management that the variable cost coefficient is significantly different from zero. The most likely explanation for the inverse relation between production and repair costs is that repair work is scheduled during slow rather than busy times.

22. *Interpreting Regression Data.* This problem is frequently encountered when applying analytical techniques to certain costs. Quite often the advertising expenditures result in sales being generated in the following month or so. In addition, many companies increase their advertising when sales are declining and cut back on advertising when there is capacity business. A better model might be developed by relating this month's sales to last month's advertising.

Similar problems exist for repair and maintenance costs, because machines are usually given routine repairs and maintenance during slow periods. An inverse relationship often exists between salespersons' travel expenses and sales, if the salesperson spends more time traveling when the sales are more difficult to make.

Chapter 7   Cost-Volume-Profit Analysis

An understanding of the relations among revenues, costs, the volume of activity, and profits is essential for successful management. In a sense, the cost-volume-profit model is *the* underlying model of the firm; virtually all financial decisions affect costs, volume, or profits. Thus, it can be used as a macro model to describe a firm's financial activities. For example, an automotive company executive recently stated that the company did not show a quarterly profit because, "Given the prices we can charge and the costs we incur, we simply did not have enough volume to break even last quarter."

In addition, cost-volume-profit analysis can be used as a micro tool to answer questions such as "What level of activity is required for Product T-21 to break even?" "What is the expected profit from Product S-29 if advertising is increased by $20,000?"

The analysis relies on concepts of fixed and variable cost behavior that were discussed in Chapters 2 and 6. This chapter presents the cost-volume-profit model and demonstrates how it can be used (or misused) in a number of managerial decision-making situations. This chapter focuses on short-run operating decisions, which are those that do not involve a change in capacity.

After reading this chapter, you should understand the nature of the cost-volume-profit model, applications of the model, and the model's limitations and assumptions.

The Cost-Volume-Profit Model

The cost-volume-profit model adds revenues to the cost equation discussed in Chapter 6 to give the following comprehensive cost-volume-profit equation:

$$\pi = TR - TC,$$

where π = operating profit for the period, TR = total revenues for the period, and TC = total costs for the period.

The cost-volume-profit equation can be described in more detail as

$$\pi = TR - TC$$

$$= PX - (F + VX),$$

where P = unit selling price, X = number of units sold in the period, F = fixed operating costs for the period, and V = unit variable costs.

"Profits" derived in managerial models or shown on internal reports may differ from "net income" for external financial reporting under generally accepted accounting principles (GAAP). For example, costs in the managerial model might include as "depreciation" an estimate of the decline in economic value of an asset because of its use over a period of time. This is in contrast to depreciation for external reporting, which is an allocation over time of the price paid for the asset. Also, the cost-volume-profit model treats fixed manufacturing overhead as a cost of the period (that is, the *variable costing method*), not as a unit cost as required for external reporting under GAAP (the *full absorption method*).

Example Our discussion for the rest of this chapter is based on the illustrative data for Baltimore Manufacturing Company shown in the top panel of Exhibit 7.1.

Exhibit 7.1
BALTIMORE MANUFACTURING COMPANY
Cost-Volume-Profit Data

Selling Price per Unit $30		

Cost Classification	Variable Cost (per unit)	Fixed Cost (per month)
Manufacturing Costs:		
Direct Materials	$ 4	—
Direct Labor	9	—
Manufacturing Overhead	4	$3,060
Total Manufacturing Costs	$17	$3,060
Marketing and Administrative Costs	5	1,740
Total Costs	$22	$4,800

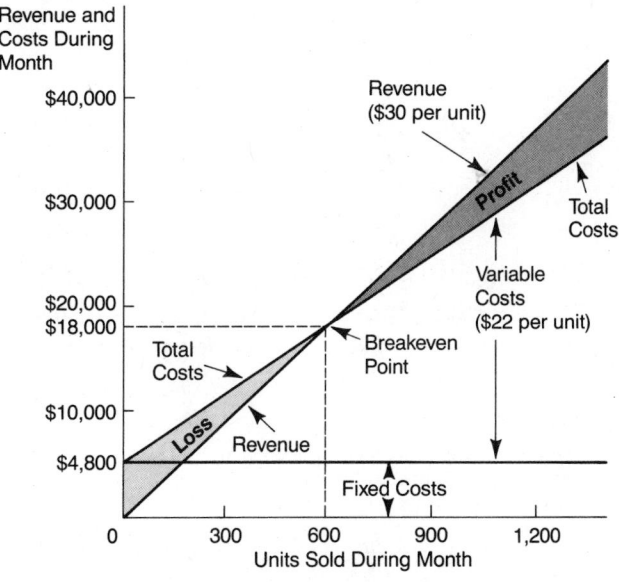

The cost-volume-profit equation for Baltimore Manufacturing is

$$\pi = PX - (F + VX)$$

$$= \$30X - (\$4{,}800 + \$22X).$$

The bottom panel of Exhibit 7.1 presents two linear relations. First, total revenue, $TR = PX = \$30X$, is plotted. Because revenue is zero when the sales volume, X, is zero, the revenue line goes through the origin (the zero point) of the graph. It has a slope of $30; for each unit increase in sales, the revenues go up by $30, so that, for example, at 600 units sold, total revenues are $18,000. The second linear relation graphed in Exhibit 7.1 is total cost as a function of activity (units sold[1]): $TC = \$4{,}800 + \$22X$. Because the fixed costs are $4,800 per month, the total cost line goes through the vertical axis at $4,800. Because variable costs are $22 per unit, the total cost line increases $22 for each increase in units produced and sold during the month. At 600 units, for example, total costs are $18,000: $4,800 of fixed costs plus $13,200 (= $22 per unit × 600 units) of variable costs.

The Contribution Concept Many of the questions that can be answered with the cost-volume-profit model are easier to answer by use of the contribution concept. Each unit sold makes a contribution to fixed costs and the earning of profit. The *contribution margin* per unit is the excess of unit selling price over unit variable cost.[2] In terms of our symbols, the contribution margin is defined by

$$\text{Contribution Margin per Unit} = P - V.$$

For the Baltimore Manufacturing Company, the contribution margin is

$$\$8 = \$30 \text{ Selling Price per Unit} - \$22 \text{ Variable Cost per Unit.}$$

The contribution margin has some particularly important applications in product choice decisions. Suppose that you have the opportunity to produce and sell *one* of the following products to a customer (not both):

	Price
Product A	$12
Product B	$15

Which would you sell? Product B? Is it more profitable? We cannot tell which product is more profitable until we consider respective variable costs. Suppose that we find the information shown on the top of the next page.

---

[1] We assume the units were produced and sold in the same time period to keep the analysis from becoming unnecessarily complex.

[2] The concepts of "sales revenue less total variable cost" and "sales revenue per unit less variable cost per unit" are both often called *contribution margin*. The former is actually *total contribution margin*, whereas the latter is *contribution margin per unit*. We, and others, often use the term *contribution margin* to mean one or the other, depending on the context.

	Price	Variable Cost	Contribution Margin
Product A	$12	$ 7	$5
Product B	$15	$11	$4

Although B's price is higher and it would provide more revenues, A's contribution to fixed costs and profits is higher.[3]

Breakeven Point The point where total costs and total revenues are equal, which is 600 units as shown in Exhibit 7.1, is called the *breakeven point*.[4] At sales volumes less than 600 units per month, the firm incurs a loss equal to the vertical distance between the total cost line and the revenue line. [For example, verify that at a sales volume of 300 units, there would be a loss of $2,400 ($TR = \$30 \times 300$ units $= \$9,000$); ($TC = \$4,800 + (\$22 \times 300) = \$11,400$).]

Without resorting to a graph such as the one in Exhibit 7.1, you can derive the breakeven point by using the equation

$$\pi = PX - (F + VX).$$

At the breakeven point, profit, π, must be zero. In our example, we know that $P = \$30$, $F = \$4,800$, and $V = \$22$. Thus, the breakeven sales volume is represented by X_b in the equation

$$0 = \$30X_b - (\$4,800 + \$22\,X_b),$$

or

$$0 = \$8X_b - \$4,800$$

$$\$8X_b = \$4,800$$

$$X_b = \frac{\$4,800}{\$8}$$

$$= 600 \text{ Units.}$$

In general, the breakeven equation is

$$\text{Breakeven Point in Units} = \frac{\text{Fixed Costs per Period}}{\text{Contribution Margin per Unit}},$$

or, in symbols,

$$X_b = \frac{F}{P - V}.$$

---

[3]This raises an interesting incentive problem if sales personnel are paid a commission that is a percent of revenue. They would have an incentive to sell the higher-priced, but less profitable, product.
[4]Cost-volume-profit analysis is sometimes called "breakeven analysis." Finding the breakeven point, however, is only one application of cost-volume-profit analysis.

Target Profits The above equations can easily be applied to finding the volume required for a target profit. For example, if Baltimore Manufacturing Company wants to know the sales required in a month to achieve a profit of $5,000, it can solve the following:

$$\$5,000 = \$30X - (\$4,800 + \$22X)$$

$$\$5,000 = \$8X - \$4,800$$

$$\$8X = \$9,800$$

$$X = 1,225 \text{ Units per Month.}$$

The Profit-Volume Model

The cost-volume-profit graph shown in Exhibit 7.1 is convenient enough for finding the breakeven point or getting a rough idea of profit or loss at various sales levels. However, because the profit or loss is measured as the vertical distance between two lines, neither of which is horizontal, it is not convenient for precisely observing the profit or loss as a function of sales volume. Consequently, the relation between profit and volume is often graphed as in Exhibit 7.2, the *profit-volume graph*.

Exhibit 7.2
BALTIMORE MANUFACTURING COMPANY
Profit-Volume Graph

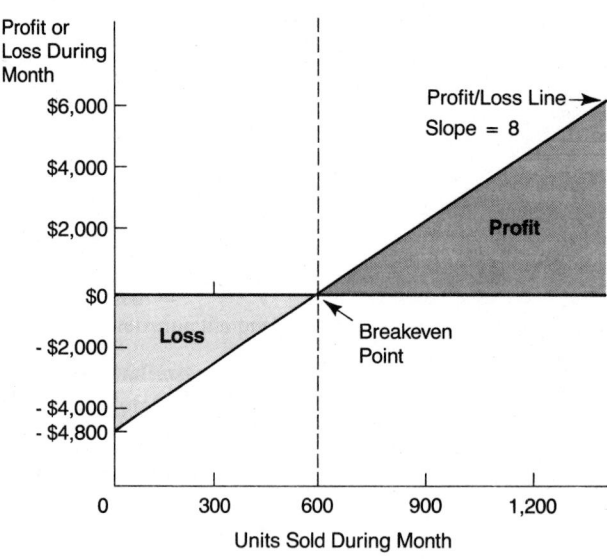

The relation between the profit-volume and the cost-volume-profit graphs can be seen by rearranging the cost-volume-profit equation. The cost-volume-profit equation is

$$\pi = PX - (F + VX).$$

Rearranging terms gives

$$\pi = PX - F - VX,$$

and

$$\pi = -F + (P - V)\,X$$

which is the *profit-volume* equation.

The vertical axis of the profit-volume graph shows the amount of profit or loss for the period—1 month in our example. At zero sales, the loss is equal to the fixed costs, F, of \$4,800. At the breakeven point, 600 units in our example, the profit is zero. The slope of the profit line is equal to $P - V$ ($= \$30 - \$22 = \$8$), which is the *contribution margin* per unit sold.

Applications of the Cost-Volume-Profit Model

In this section, we illustrate several uses of the cost-volume-profit model.

Example 1: Required Selling Price The manager of Baltimore Manufacturing Company wants to know what price must be charged if sales are 800 units per month and the target profit is \$4,000 per month. Fixed costs per month are \$4,800 and unit variable costs are \$22. We can solve for the required selling price as follows:

$$\text{Profit} = \text{Revenues} - \text{Costs}$$
$$\$4,000 = 800P - [\$4,800 + (800 \times \$22)]$$
$$800P = \$17,600 + \$4,800 + \$4,000$$
$$800P = \$26,400$$
$$P = \$33 \text{ Required Selling Price per Unit.}$$

Example 2: New Breakeven with an Increase in Fixed Costs The manager of Baltimore Manufacturing Company wants to know how many units must be sold per month to break even under the following conditions: Fixed costs increase to \$5,600 per month, but variable costs remain at \$22 per unit and selling price remains at \$30 per unit. Solving for X, which represents the number of units produced and sold, we have

$$\text{Profit} = \text{Revenues} - \text{Costs}$$
$$\$0 = \$30X - (\$5,600 + \$22X)$$
$$\$8X = \$5,600$$
$$X = 700 \text{ Units Required to Break Even.}$$

Example 3: Sensitivity Analysis One of the most useful applications of cost-volume-profit analysis, particularly for planning, is sensitivity analysis.[5] In sensi-

---

[5] For example, see "What-If Help for Management," *Business Week*, January 21, 1980, p. 73.

tivity analysis, "what-if" questions are asked, and "if-then" statements follow. For example, the manager of Baltimore Manufacturing Company wants to know the impact of changing costs, prices, and volume on profits. Specifically, consider the following alternative cases ("what-if's"):

Costs: (1) No change

(2) 10 percent increase.

Price and volume:

(1) No change

(2) 10 percent price increase and 5 percent volume decrease.

The matrix below shows the results (that is, the "if-thens") from applying the following cost-volume-profit equation:

$$\text{Profit} = \text{Revenues} - \text{Costs}$$

$$\pi = PX - (F + VX).$$

The status quo is assumed to be

$$\$1{,}600 = (\$30 \times 800) - [\$4{,}800 + (\$22 \times 800)].$$

		Costs	
		No Change	10 Percent Increase
Price and Volume	No Change	(\$30 × 800) − [\$4,800 + (\$22 × 800)] = **\$1,600**	(\$30 × 800) − [\$5,280 + (\$24.20 × 800)] = **−\$640**
	10 Percent Price Increase, 5 Percent Volume Decrease	(\$33 × 760) − [\$4,800 + (\$22 x 760)] = **\$3,560**	(\$33 × 760) − [\$5,280 + (\$24.20 × 760)] = **\$1,408**

These results show the manager that a 10 percent cost increase, with no change in selling price or volume, would result in a loss for the company. On the other hand, if there are no cost increases, but prices could be increased by 10 percent with a 5 percent drop in volume, profits would more than double. If the cost-volume-profit equation is in a computer, it is very easy to perform extensive sensitivity analysis.

Example 4: Comparison of Alternatives The manager of Baltimore Manufacturing Company is considering a proposed alternative production method. Under the current method, variable costs are $22 per unit and fixed costs are $4,800. The proposed alternative would substitute machines for labor; variable costs would drop to $18 per unit, but the annual lease of the machines and machine maintenance would increase fixed costs to $6,000 per month. (No initial investment in the machines is required.) Under both alternatives, the selling price will be $30 per unit and 800 units will be sold each month. The expected profit under the status quo is

$$\text{Profit} = \text{Revenues} - \text{Costs}$$
$$= (\$30 \times 800) - [\$4,800 + (\$22 \times 800)]$$
$$= \$24,000 - \$22,400$$
$$= \$1,600.$$

The expected profit under the proposed alternative is

$$\text{Profit} = \text{Revenues} - \text{Costs}$$
$$= (\$30 \times 800) - [\$6,000 + (\$18 \times 800)]$$
$$= \$24,000 - \$20,400$$
$$= \$3,600.$$

The analysis indicates that expected profits would increase under the proposed alternative.

Margin of Safety

Another calculation made from cost-volume-profit analysis is the *margin of safety*. The margin of safety is the excess of projected (or actual) sales over the breakeven sales level. The formula for margin of safety is

$$\text{Sales} - \frac{\text{Breakeven}}{\text{Sales}} = \frac{\text{Margin of}}{\text{Safety}}.$$

In our example, the level of activity is 800 units, whereas the breakeven point is at 600 units. Therefore, the *margin of safety* is 200 units. Sales volume can drop 25 percent before a loss is incurred, other things held constant.

Companies that become more capital-intensive, and substitute fixed costs for variable costs, often find that their margin of safety goes down. Consider two companies that are alike in every respect, except that 75 percent of Variable Company's total costs are variable, whereas 75 percent of Fixed Company's total costs are fixed at current volume levels. (See Exhibit 7.3.)

Fixed Company has a lower margin of safety, hence it will incur losses more quickly than Variable Company if sales volume decreases. Companies in industries such as automobiles and steel that have shifted costs from the variable category to the fixed category have found that relatively small decreases in sales volume can result in losses.

Exhibit 7.3
Comparison of Variable Company and Fixed Company

	Variable Company (1,000,000 units)	Fixed Company (1,000,000 units)
Sales	$1,200,000	$1,200,000
Variable Costs	750,000	250,000
Contribution Margin	$ 450,000	$ 950,000
Fixed Costs	250,000	750,000
Operating Profit	$ 200,000	$ 200,000

(Variable Costs + Fixed Costs) Total Costs = $1,000,000 — for each company

Breakeven Point

Variable Company:
$$X_b = \frac{F}{P - V}$$
$$= \frac{\$250,000}{\$1.20 - .75}$$
$$= 555,556 \text{ Units}$$

Fixed Company:
$$X_b = \frac{F}{P - V}$$
$$= \frac{\$750,000}{\$1.20 - .25}$$
$$= 789,474 \text{ Units}$$

Margin of Safety (units)

Variable Company:
= Sales Volume − Breakeven Volume
= 1,000,000 − 555,556
= 444,444 Units

Fixed Company:
= Sales Volume − Breakeven Volume
= 1,000,000 − 789,474
= 210,526 Units

Margin of Safety as a Percentage of Sales Volume

Variable Company:
$$\frac{444,444}{1,000,000} = 44 \text{ Percent}$$

Fixed Company:
$$\frac{210,526}{1,000,000} = 21 \text{ Percent}$$

Using Sales Dollars as a Measure of Volume

Most companies have multiple products, or products that are not easily defined as units. For example, in the manufacture of computers, one company is likely to have many product lines. When products are not uniform or are difficult to measure, sales dollars are often used to measure the volume of activity.

When sales dollars are used to measure volume, the cost-volume-profit equation remains the same as before, except that PX is total revenue, not "price times quantity," and VX is total variable costs, not "unit variable cost times quantity." We substitute PX for X when solving for volume of activity. For example, the breakeven volume in units for Baltimore Manufacturing Company is

$$X_b = \frac{F}{P - V}$$

$$= \frac{\$4,800}{(\$30 - \$22)}$$

$$= 600 \text{ Units.}$$

When volume is defined as PX, we multiply both sides of the breakeven formula by P to express volume in sales dollars:

$$PX_b = \left(\frac{F}{P - V}\right)P$$

$$= \frac{F}{(P - V)/P}$$

$$= \frac{\$4,800}{(\$30 - \$22)/\$30}$$

$$= \frac{\$4,800}{.26667}$$

$$= \$18,000.$$

Thus, the breakeven volume expressed in sales *dollars* is $18,000. (You can verify that this is the same as 600 units.)

The term $(P - V)/P$ in the denominator of the breakeven equation is called the *contribution margin ratio,* that is, the ratio of the unit contribution margin to unit price. Hence, the formula is stated (in words):

$$\text{Breakeven Sales Dollars} = \frac{\text{Fixed Costs}}{\text{Contribution Margin Ratio}}.$$

In the example, this ratio states that each dollar of sales generates $.26667 of contribution.

Also, the profit equation can be expressed as profit equals revenue times contribution margin ratio minus fixed costs, derived as follows:

$$\text{Profit} = \text{Total Revenue} - \text{Total Variable Costs} - \text{Fixed Costs}$$

$$\pi = PX$$

$$= X(P - V) - F$$

$$= PX\left[\frac{(P - V)}{P}\right] - F$$

If revenue = \$18,000, then

$$\pi = (\$18,000 \times .26667) - \$4,800$$

$$= 0.$$

Income Taxes

Income taxes are incorporated into the cost-volume-profit model as follows:

$$\text{Aftertax Profit} = \text{Before-tax Profit} \times (1 - \text{Tax Rate}).$$

This means that the aftertax profit equals the before-tax profit minus taxes, where taxes equal the tax rate times the before-tax profit. If we let π_{at} designate "aftertax profits," π_{bt} designate "before-tax profits," and t designate the tax rate, we have

$$\pi_{at} = \pi_{bt}(1 - t)$$

$$= [(P - V)X - F](1 - t).$$

Example The management of Baltimore Manufacturing Company wants to know what volume of sales is required to provide \$1,920 profit *after taxes* in April. $P = \$30$, $V = \$22$, $F = \$4,800$, and let $t = .4$ (that is, an average tax rate for April of 40 percent). To find the volume that provides an aftertax profit of \$1,920:

$$\pi_{at} = \pi_{bt}(1 - t)$$

$$\$1,920 = [(P - V)(X) - F](1 - t)$$

$$= [(\$30 - \$22)(X) - \$4,800](1 - .4)$$

$$= [(\$8X - \$4,800)(.6)]$$

$$= \$4.8X - \$2,880$$

$$\$4,800 = \$4.8X$$

$$\frac{\$4,800}{\$4.8} = X$$

$$X = 1,000 \text{ Units.}$$

Using the Contribution Format
for Income Statements[6]

Traditional income statement formats do not lend themselves to cost-volume-profit analysis because fixed and variable costs are not identified and separated on the income statement. The contribution format for a manufacturing company looks like:

Revenue		xxxx
Less Variable Costs:		
Variable Cost of Goods Sold	xx	
Variable Marketing and Administrative Costs	xx	xxx
Total Contribution Margin		xxx
Less Fixed Costs:		
Fixed Manufacturing Costs	xx	
Fixed Marketing and Administrative Costs	xx	xxx
Operating Profit		xx

Note: The contribution format is based on the *variable costing* product costing method.

This format helps in a number of ways. Managers can estimate the impact of increases or decreases in volume on profits. It helps managers to focus on variable costs on a unit basis and fixed costs on a lump-sum basis. And it helps managers see relations among costs, volume, and prices.

To compare the contribution format with the traditional one, we refer to the Baltimore Manufacturing Company example.

Example Recall the following facts for Baltimore Manufacturing Company:

Selling Price	$30 per Unit
Variable Costs	$22 per Unit
Fixed Costs	$4,800 per Month
Volume	800 Units per Month

Costs were partitioned into manufacturing and nonmanufacturing costs as follows:

	Manufacturing	**Marketing and Administrative**
Variable	$ 17	$ 5
Fixed	3,060	1,740

Inventory values under full absorption costing, which is used in the traditional income statement format, are measured as shown on the top of the next page.

---

[6]Chapter 2 introduced this idea, which is expanded here.

Variable Manufacturing Costs (e.g., direct materials, direct labor, variable manufacturing overhead)	$17 per Unit
Fixed Manufacturing Costs ($3,060 ÷ 800 units)	$3.825 per Unit
Total Full Absorption Product Cost.	$20.825 per Unit

A comparison of the contribution and traditional formats appears in Exhibit 7.4.

Although the "bottom line" is the same for both formats in this example, it is important to note some significant differences.[7] One is the difference between *total contribution margin* and *gross margin*. Another is the different costs matched with revenue. The traditional format treats both fixed and variable manufacturing costs as unit (that is, product) costs, and treats both variable and fixed nonmanufacturing costs as period costs. Note that *both* manufacturing and nonmanufacturing variable costs are included in unit cost calculations for the contribution format.

The contribution format displays all of the information that the traditional format does and more by presenting costs in fixed and variable components. Of course, this assumes that costs have been partitioned into fixed and variable components. This breakdown of costs is, itself, costly, so managers and accountants must ascertain whether the benefits of estimating cost behavior, including benefits from cost-volume-profit analyses and contribution format income statements, justify the costs of estimating cost behavior. We use the contribution format for internal

Exhibit 7.4
BALTIMORE MANUFACTURING COMPANY
Comparative Income Statements

Contribution Format[a]				Traditional Format[b]	
Revenue		$24,000[c]	Revenue		$24,000[c]
Less Variable Costs:			Less Cost of Goods Sold		(16,660)[f]
Variable Manufacturing Costs . .	($13,600)[d]		Gross Margin.		$ 7,340
Variable Marketing and Administrative Costs.	(4,000)[e]	(17,600)	Less Marketing and Administrative Costs.		(5,740)[g]
Total Contribution Margin		$ 6,400	Operating Profit		$ 1,600
Less Fixed Costs:					
Fixed Manufacturing Costs . . .	$ (3,060)				
Fixed Marketing and Administrative Costs.	(1,740)	4,800			
Operating Profit		$ 1,600			

[a]The contribution format uses the *variable costing* method of product costing.
[b]The traditional format uses the *full absorption* product costing method.
[c]$30 × 800 units = $24,000.
[d]$17 × 800 units = $13,600.
[e]$5 × 800 units = $4,000.
[f]$20.825 × 800 units = $16,660.
[g]$4,000 = $5 × 800 units + $1,740 = $5,740.

[7]Under certain conditions, the "bottom line" may differ, too. Variable costing and full absorption costing give different profit figures if the fixed manufacturing costs, which are expensed (that is, treated as a period cost) in the period incurred under variable costing, are not expensed in that same period under full absorption costing. This difference occurs when the company produces more than it sells or less than it sells. When it produces more than it sells, some fixed manufacturing costs, which are expensed under variable costing, are inventoried under full absorption costing. Hence, variable costing profits would be lower in this case.

Exhibit 7.5
Comparative Income Statement Formats

Contribution Format			Traditional Format	
Merchandising			**Merchandising**	
Revenue		xxxx	Revenue	xxxx
Less Variable Costs:			Less Cost of Goods Sold	xxx
Cost of Goods (merchandise) Sold . . .	xxx		Gross Margin	xxx
Marketing and Administrative Costs . .	xx	xxx	Less Marketing and Administrative Costs . .	xx
Total Contribution Margin		xxx	Operating Profit	xx
Less Fixed Marketing and Administrative				
Costs		xx		
Operating Profit		xx		
Service			**Service**	
Revenue		xxxx	Revenue	xxxx
Less Variable Costs:			Less: Cost of Providing Services	xxx
Costs of Providing Services	xx		Marketing and Administrative Costs . .	xxx
Marketing and Administration Costs . .	xx	xxx	Operating Profit	xx
Total Contribution Margin		xxx		
Less Fixed Costs:				
Cost of Providing Services	xx			
Marketing and Administration Costs . .	xx	xx		
Operating Profit		xx		

reporting and the traditional format for external reporting in this book. This is one of many aspects of accounting where the method used for one purpose may not be well suited for another.

The difference in formats discussed for Baltimore Manufacturing Company also applies to merchandising and service organizations. Comparisons are shown in Exhibit 7.5. The cost of goods sold in merchandising are assumed to be variable costs only.

Multiproduct Cost-Volume-Profit

Most companies produce and/or sell many products. This poses problems for some uses of cost-volume-profit analysis, as shown by the following example.

Example Sport Autos is a sports car dealership selling two models: Sleek and Powerful. The relevant prices and costs of each are as follows:

		Sleek		Powerful	
Average Selling Price per Car . . .		$20,000		$30,000	
Less Average Variable Costs:					
Cost of Car	$(11,000)		$(15,000)		
Cost of Preparing Car for Sale . .	(3,000)		(3,000)		
Sales Commissions	(1,000)	(15,000)	(2,000)	(20,000)	
Average Contribution Margin per					
Car		$ 5,000		$10,000	

Average monthly fixed costs of the new car department are $100,000.

The cost-volume-profit equation presented earlier now must be expanded to consider the contribution of each product:

$$\pi = (P_s - V_s)X_s + (P_p - V_p)X_p - F,$$

where the subscript s designates the Sleek model, and the subscript p designates the Powerful model. Based on the information for Sport Autos, the company's profit equation is

$$\pi = (\$20{,}000 - \$15{,}000)X_s + (\$30{,}000 - \$20{,}000)X_p - \$100{,}000$$

$$= \quad \$5{,}000X_s \quad + \quad \$10{,}000X_p \quad - \$100{,}000.$$

The fact that there are multiple products poses no particular problem if the multiproduct cost-volume-profit model is used to describe the firm's operations or to do sensitivity analyses. If the managers of Sport Autos want to know the impact of cost, or price, or volume changes on profits, holding all other things constant, the multiproduct model is useful. But other applications, such as deriving the breakeven point or target level of profits, are more difficult.

For example, the chief executive of Sports Autos has been listening to a debate between two of the sales personnel about the breakeven point for the company. According to one, "We have to sell 20 cars a month to break even." But the other one claims that 10 cars a month would be sufficient. The chief executive wonders how these two sales personnel could hold such different views.

The breakeven volume is the volume that provides a contribution that just covers all fixed costs. That is, for Sport Autos:

$$\$5{,}000X_s + \$10{,}000X_p = \$100{,}000.$$

The claim that 20 cars must be sold to break even is correct if *only* the *Sleek* model is sold, whereas the claim that only 10 cars need be sold is correct if *only* the *Powerful* model is sold. In fact, there are many possible product mix combinations at which the company would break even.

All of the possible breakeven points for Sport Autos are listed in Exhibit 7.6.

Exhibit 7.6
SPORT AUTOS
Combinations of Breakeven Quantities

Sleek Model		Powerful Model		Total Contribution	Fixed Costs	Profit
Quantity	Contribution	Quantity	Contribution			
20	$100,000	0	$ 0	$100,000	$100,000	$–0–
18	90,000	1	10,000	100,000	100,000	–0–
16	80,000	2	20,000	100,000	100,000	–0–
14	70,000	3	30,000	100,000	100,000	–0–
12	60,000	4	40,000	100,000	100,000	–0–
10	50,000	5	50,000	100,000	100,000	–0–
8	40,000	6	60,000	100,000	100,000	–0–
6	30,000	7	70,000	100,000	100,000	–0–
4	20,000	8	80,000	100,000	100,000	–0–
2	10,000	9	90,000	100,000	100,000	–0–
0	–0–	10	100,000	100,000	100,000	–0–

Exhibit 7.7
Possible Breakeven Volumes for Sport Autos

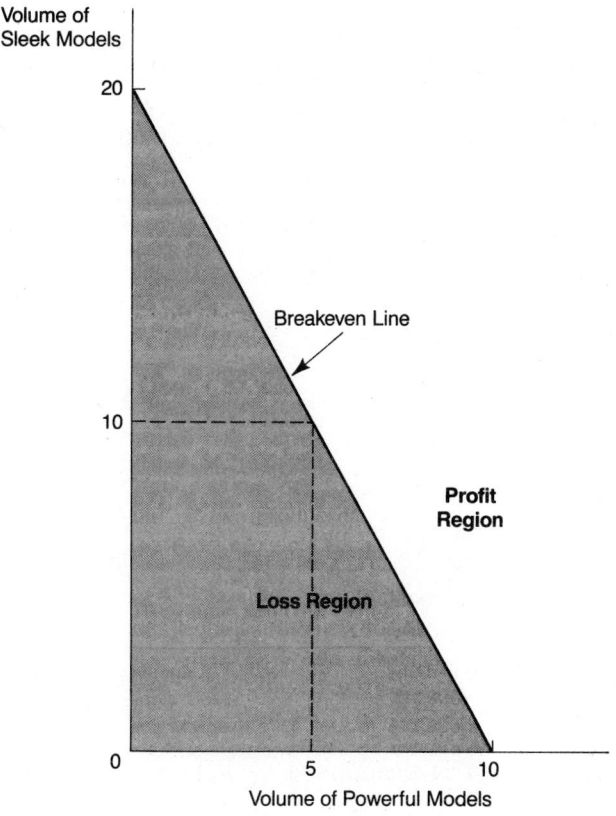

Exhibit 7.7 is a graphical presentation of the possible breakeven volumes for Sport Autos. The breakeven line in Exhibit 7.7 is one of a family of lines known as "isoprofit" lines ("iso" means "equal"). Profits are the same for any combination of product volumes on that line. (To see this, find a couple of breakeven points from Exhibit 7.6 on the breakeven line in Exhibit 7.7.) Any combination of product volumes to the right of the line provides a profit; any to the left results in a loss.

This simple example should demonstrate how complex multiproduct cost-volume-profit analysis can become. In a company with many products, the combinations of product volumes that will provide a specific target profit can easily be so large that not even a computer can store them all. To deal with this problem, managers and accountants can: (1) assume that all products have the same contribution margin; (2) assume that a particular product mix does not change; (3) assume a weighted-average contribution margin; (4) treat each product line as a separate entity. In addition to these simplifications, multiproduct analyses can be made using a mathematical method known as *linear programming,* as discussed in Chapter 8.

1. Assume the Same Contribution Margin Products can often be grouped so that they have equal or nearly equal contribution margins. It does not matter whether a unit of Product A is sold or a unit of Product B, if both have the same contribution margin. (This approach would not be valid for Sport Autos.)

2. Assume a Fixed Product Mix Suppose the experience at Sport Autos is that Sleeks outsell Powerfuls at a rate of 2-to-1. Define a "package sale," X^*, to be the sale of two Sleeks and one Powerful. The contribution from this "package" is

$$
\begin{array}{lr}
\text{Sleek:} & 2 \times \$5,000 = \$10,000 \\
\text{Powerful:} & \underline{10,000} \\
\text{Total:} & \underline{\underline{\$20,000}}
\end{array}
$$

The breakeven point is

$$
X_b^* = \frac{\$100,000}{\$20,000}
$$

$$
= 5.
$$

This means that the sale of five "packages," each made up of two Sleeks and a Powerful, would contribute enough to break even. In other words, the breakeven volume for the month is 15 units—10 Sleeks and 5 Powerfuls.

3. Assume a Weighted-Average Contribution Margin Another way of applying the assumed product mix is to use a weighted-average contribution margin. If the product mix is assumed to be two Sleeks for every Powerful, the per-unit weighted-average contribution margin is

$$
\begin{array}{cc}
\textit{Sleeks} & \textit{Powerful} \\
(\tfrac{2}{3} \times \$5,000) + (\tfrac{1}{3} \times \$10,000) = \$6,667.
\end{array}
$$

The breakeven point is

$$
X_b = \frac{\$100,000}{\$6,667}
$$

$$
= 15 \text{ Cars,}
$$

of which 10 are Sleeks and 5 are Powerfuls, according to the product mix assumption required to derive the weighted-average unit contribution margin.

What is the effect of incorrect assumptions in the above analysis about product mix? If the actual mix is richer than assumed (more Powerfuls, in our example), fewer units are required to break even than predicted. More units are required to break even than predicted if the mix is poorer than assumed. (For example, see the data in Exhibits 7.6 and 7.7.)

4. Treat Each Product Line as a Separate Entity This method requires allocating fixed costs to product lines. For example, part of the Sport Autos' $100,000 monthly fixed costs would be allocated to Sleek automobiles and the rest to Powerfuls. The problem is to find a reasonable method of allocating costs. Often these costs are common to the product lines, so any allocation method would be arbitrary. In situations like this, companies often resort to allocation methods such as "allocate on the basis of relative sales dollars" or "allocate on the basis of quantities of the product lines." Other allocation bases used include relative total contributions, relative direct costs, relative number of employees per product line (particularly to allocate labor-related costs), or relative square feet of space used by each product line (particularly to allocate space-related costs).

Suppose that Sport Autos arbitrarily allocates the $100,000 fixed costs, which are common costs, 40 percent to Sleeks and 60 percent to Powerfuls. Now break-even analysis and other cost-volume-profit analyses can be done by product line:

For Sleeks:

$$\pi = (P - V)X - F$$

$$= (\$20,000 - \$15,000)X - \$40,000$$

$$X_b = \frac{\$40,000}{\$5,000}$$

$$= 8 \text{ Units.}$$

For Powerfuls:

$$\pi = (P - V)X - F$$

$$= (\$30,000 - \$20,000)X - \$60,000$$

$$X_b = \frac{\$60,000}{\$10,000}$$

$$= 6 \text{ Units.}$$

Allocating fixed costs to product lines facilitates product line cost-volume-profit analysis. But decision makers should be wary of any analysis that relies on arbitrary cost allocations. It would be a mistake to believe that each product line at Sport Autos causes fixed costs of $40,000 (Sleeks) and $60,000 (Powerfuls), respectively. The two product lines *combined* cause fixed costs of $100,000; the breakdown of those costs is arbitrary. Further note that a change in the arbitrary allocation method would change the breakeven volumes. (For example, if the $100,000 were allocated $20,000 to Sleeks and $80,000 to Powerfuls, four Sleeks (= $20,000 ÷ $5,000 per unit) and eight Powerfuls (= $80,000 ÷ $10,000 per unit) would now be required for each product line to break even.)

Simplifications and Assumptions

The cost-volume-profit model is often a simplified description of cost, revenues, and volume to make the analysis easier. Although it is possible to provide a more complete description of reality, it is also costly. The careful user of cost-volume-profit analysis should be aware of the following common assumptions, and be prepared to perform sensitivity analysis to see how the assumptions affect the model's results.

Comparison with Economists' Profit Maximization Model

Textbooks in economics usually present nonlinear cost and revenue curves, as in Exhibit 7.8. Total revenue is assumed to increase at a decreasing rate *if* the firm faces a downward-sloping demand curve. Total costs are assumed to increase at an increasing rate as volume approaches capacity. In Exhibit 7.8, the economists' cost curve includes the opportunity cost of owners' invested capital, whereas the linear approximation from the accounting records typically does not. Neither the "economists" nor the "accountants" cost and revenue curves should be considered correct in an absolute sense. Both are approximations of actual cost and revenue behavior.

Exhibit 7.8
Comparison of Economics and Accounting Assumed Cost and Revenue Behavior

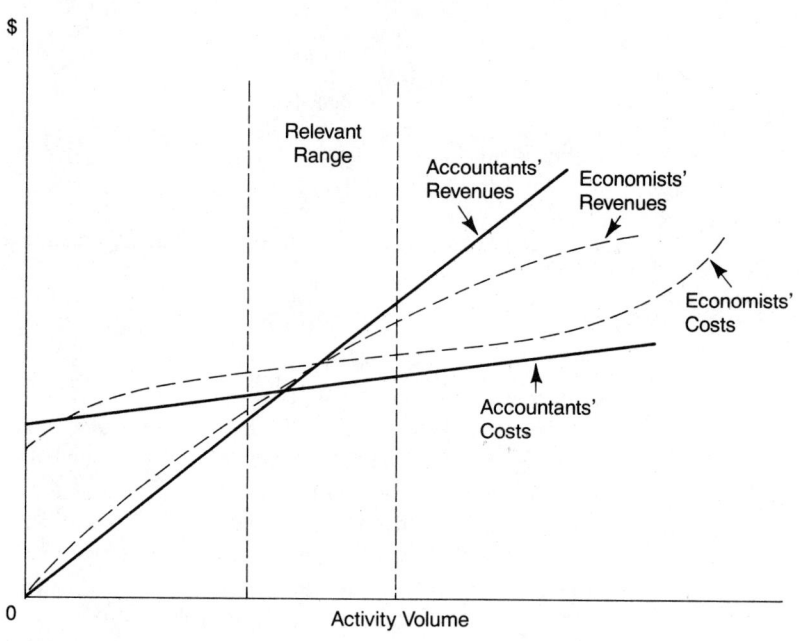

Basic Assumption Required to Make the Model Work: Total Cost Breakdown into Fixed and Variable Components

The cost-volume-profit model is most powerful when used as a tool for analyzing the effects of various alternatives on operations. This is because the model captures most of the important operating relationships of the firm in a single equation. We can analyze the effects of changes in any of the following variables on the remaining variables: selling price, number of units sold, variable cost, fixed cost, sales mix, and production mix. The major assumption required by the model is that *total costs can be broken down into fixed and variable components.*

Our illustrations in this chapter assumed that there was a linear relation between revenues and volume, and between costs and volume. It is possible, however, to apply the model with nonlinear revenue and cost functions. In practice, cost and revenue curves are usually assumed to be linear over some *relevant range* of activity, as discussed in Chapter 6. Exhibit 7.8 presents an example where cost and revenue curves may be reasonably linear within the relevant range limits, even though the curves are nonlinear outside the relevant range.

We also implicitly assumed that the variables in the model could be predicted with certainty. This assumption is likewise not required. Techniques have been developed for applying the cost-volume-profit model under conditions of uncertainty.[8]

Assumptions Required to Derive Breakeven Point

If the cost-volume-profit (CVP) model is used to derive a unique breakeven point, two more assumptions are required:

1. Selling price per unit, total fixed costs, and variable costs per unit will not change as the level of activity is changed. This implies that prices paid and charged are constant, and there is no change in workers' productivity during the period.
2. The production mix and sales mix will not change as the level of activity is changed.

Assumption Required to Reconcile CVP Profits with External Financial Statement Net Income

If the cost-volume-profit model is used to predict the effect of changes in prices, costs, or volumes on the net income that is reported to readers of external financial statements, then revenues and costs computed for the cost-volume-profit model must be the same as the revenues and expenses computed for external reporting. One difference is that the cost-volume-profit model assumes that fixed manufacturing costs are expensed in the period incurred (in accordance with *variable costing*), whereas external reporting (in accordance with *full absorption costing*) allocates fixed manufacturing costs to units produced and does not expense these costs until the period when the units are sold.

If all units are produced and sold in the same period, as we assume in our example, then the fixed manufacturing costs will be expensed in the period in

---

[8]These techniques are discussed in advanced cost accounting textbooks, and in Robert K. Jaedicke and Alexander A. Robichek, "Cost-Volume-Profit Analysis Under Conditions of Uncertainty," *The Accounting Review,* XXXIX (October 1964), pp. 917–926; Rene Manes, "A New Dimension to Breakeven Analysis," *Journal of Accounting Research* (Spring 1966), pp. 87–100; and Glenn L. Johnson and S. Stephen Simik II, "Multiproduct C-V-P Analysis Under Uncertainty," *Journal of Accounting Research* (Autumn 1971), pp. 278–286.

which they were incurred.[9] Suppose, however, that fixed manufacturing costs were $10,000 in March, and that 1,000 units were produced, but only 500 of them were sold (assume no beginning inventory). External reporting, using full absorption/ actual costing, would expense only 50 percent, or $5,000 of the fixed manufacturing cost. The other $5,000 would remain in inventory until the units were sold.

Summary of Assumptions

The following list summarizes the above assumptions:

1. Total costs are partitioned into fixed and variable components.

2. Cost and revenue behavior is linear throughout the relevant range of activity. This assumption implies:
   a. Total fixed costs do not change throughout the relevant range of activity.
   b. Variable costs *per unit* remain constant throughout the relevant range of activity.
   c. Selling price per unit remains constant throughout the relevant range of activity.

3. Product mix remains constant throughout the relevant range of activity.

4. No change in inventory. Otherwise, it is necessary to reconcile the treatment of fixed manufacturing costs under CVP (that is, period costs), with their treatment for external financial reporting purposes (that is, product costs which are expensed when the units are sold).

Assumptions of the cost-volume-profit model make it easy to use, but they also make it "unrealistic." Before criticizing the model for being "unrealistic," however, one needs to consider the costs and benefits of relaxing those assumptions to create more realism. Often the cost of more realism exceeds the benefits from improved decision making.

One method of dealing with the assumption is to perform some sensitivity or "what-if" analyses. For example, whereas the mean or expected value of Baltimore Manufacturing Company's variable costs per unit is $22, suppose that a reasonable range of values is from $15 to $29; that is, management estimates that there is a nonzero, but very small, probability that variable costs are less than $15 or greater than $29. Managers would probably want a sensitivity, or "what-if," analysis performed to ascertain whether decisions would change if variable costs were (say) $15 or $29 instead of $22 per unit.

Summary

The cost-volume-profit model shows relations among revenues, costs, volume, and profits. It can be used as an economic model to describe a firm's activities, or it can be used as an analytical model to derive, for example, a product line breakeven point, target profits for a store, or the impact of a change in volume on profits.

---

[9]This is also known as the "no change in inventory" assumption.

In equation form, the model is

$$\pi = TR - TC$$
$$= PX - (VX + F)$$
$$= (P - V)X - F,$$

where

$$\pi = \text{Operating Profit}$$
$$TR = \text{Total Revenues}$$
$$TC = \text{Total Costs}$$
$$P = \text{Selling Price per Unit}$$
$$V = \text{Variable Cost per Unit}$$
$$F = \text{Fixed Costs per Period}$$
$$X = \text{Volume per Period}$$
$$(P - V) = \text{Contribution Margin per Unit.}$$

Sensitivity analysis is one of the most useful applications of the cost-volume-profit model, particularly for planning. It enables managers to respond to "what-if" questions such as "If costs are 10 percent higher than expected, or if volume is 5 percent higher than expected, what will be the impact on profits?"

The contribution format for income statements uses cost behavior as the primary classification method. Thus, the contribution format is based on the cost-volume-profit model.

The simple cost-volume-profit model assumes a single product. Most organizations, however, have multiple products. This does not affect the usefulness of the model as a tool for descriptive work or sensitivity analysis, but it makes it more difficult to derive breakeven points. Some ways of dealing with this are to (1) assume that all products have the same contribution margin so the breakeven point is not affected by product mix; (2) assume a particular product mix; (3) assume a weighted-average contribution margin based on an assumed product mix; or (4) treat each product as a product line, which usually requires an arbitrary allocation of common costs.

The careful user of the cost-volume-profit model will recognize that it is just a model, not a complete description of reality. The simpler the model, the greater its potential applications, but the less realistic it is. Although it is possible to make the model more realistic, there is a cost of doing so. For example, a more realistic nonlinear model of cost behavior can be used if the benefits of better decisions exceed the additional costs of building nonlinear relationships into the model.

Problem 1 for Self-Study

Refer to the profit graph shown in Exhibit 7.9. Use the following list of concepts in answering each of the questions.

Exhibit 7.9

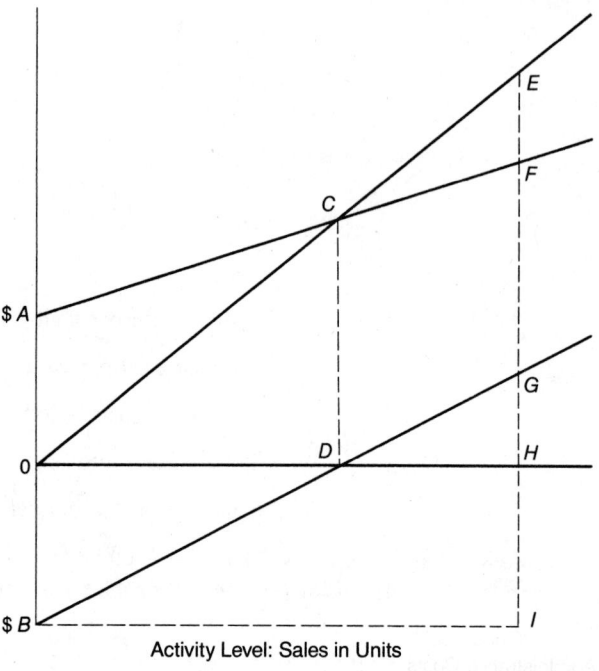

(1) Variable cost per unit.
(2) Fixed cost per period.
(3) Revenue.
(4) Contribution margin per unit.
(5) Margin of safety in units.
(6) Breakeven sales in units.
(7) None of the above.

For each of the following segments on the graph, identify the concept from the list above that corresponds to the line segment.

a.	0A	**c.**	0D	**e.**	0H—0D	**g.**	HF + HG
b.	IG	**d.**	B0	**f.**	B0/0D		

Refer to the graph in Exhibit 7.9. Answer each of the following as "true" or "false."

    h. If revenue is CD, then the margin of safety is zero.
    i. If revenue is HE, then the margin of safety is D0.
    j. Total profit could never be larger than total expense.
    k. If selling price is increased, breakeven sales in units would decrease.
    l. If selling price is increased, HF would increase.
    m. FE = HG.

Suggested Solution

a. 0A   (2) Fixed Cost per Period
b. IG   (7) Total Contribution Margin
c. 0D   (6) Breakeven Sales in Units
d. B0   (2) Fixed Cost per Period; Also, Operating Loss When Sales Are Zero.
e. 0H—0D   (5) Margin of Safety in units.
f. B0/0D   (4) Contribution Margin per Unit
g. HF + HG   (3) Revenue
h. True.
i. False.
j. False.
k. True.
l. False.
m. True.

Problem 2 for Self-Study

The operating data of the Snavely Company for April are as follows:

	Fixed	Variable	Total
Sales			$2,200,000
Operating Costs:			
Cost of Goods Sold	$550,000	$610,000	$1,160,000
Administrative Costs	110,000	30,000	140,000
Selling Costs	185,000	42,000	227,000
Total Costs.	$845,000	$682,000	$1,527,000
Profit.			$ 673,000

There were 110,000 units sold during April.

a. What is the breakeven point in terms of units of product?

b. If sales can be increased to 200,000 units, determine the amount of profits.

c. For a revenue of $1,800,000, estimate the amount of profits.

Suggested Solution

a.
$$\text{Selling Price} = \frac{\$2,200,000}{110,000} = \$20 \text{ per Unit}$$

$$\text{Variable Cost} = \frac{\$682,000}{110,000} = \$6.20 \text{ per Unit}$$

$$\text{Contribution Margin} = \$20 - \$6.20 = \$13.80 \text{ per Unit}$$

$$\text{Contribution Margin Percentage} = \frac{\$13.80}{\$20} = 69 \text{ Percent}$$

$$0 = (\$13.80 \times \text{Units}) - \$845,000$$

$$\text{Units} = 61,232.$$

b.   Profit = ($13.80 × 200,000) − $845,000 = $1,915,000.

c.   Profit = (.69 × $1,800,000) − $845,000 = $397,000.

Problem 3 for Self-Study

Surfer Company

Given the following information for Surfer Company for July:

Sales.	$180,000
Fixed Manufacturing Costs	22,000
Fixed Marketing and Administrative Costs.	14,000
Unit Price	9
Unit Variable Manufacturing Cost.	5
Unit Variable Marketing Costs.	1

Find:

a.   Breakeven quantity.

b.   Quantity that would produce an operating profit of $30,000.

c.   Quantity that would produce an operating profit of 20 percent of sales dollars.

d.   Breakeven sales quantity if unit variable costs are reduced by 10 percent per product unit, assuming no changes in total fixed costs.

e.   Sales dollars required to generate an operating profit of $20,000.

f.   Number of units sold in July.

Suggested Solution

a.   Breakeven $X = \dfrac{F}{P - V}$

$$= \frac{\$36,000}{\$9 - 6}$$

$$= 12,000 \text{ Units.}$$

b. $X = \dfrac{F + \text{Target } \pi}{P - V}$

$$= \frac{\$36,000 + 30,000}{\$9 - 6}$$

$$= 22,000 \text{ Units.}$$

c.   Target $\pi = .2PX = .2(\$9X)$

$$.2(\$9X) = (P - V)X - F$$

$$\$1.8X = \$3X - \$36,000$$

$$\$1.2X = \$36,000$$

$$X = \frac{\$36,000}{\$1.20}$$

$$X = 30,000 \text{ Units.}$$

d. $X = \dfrac{F}{P - V}$

$$= \frac{\$36,000}{\$9 - (.9)(\$6)}$$

$$= \frac{\$36,000}{\$3.60}$$

$$= 10,000 \text{ Units.}$$

e. $PX = \dfrac{F + \text{Target } \pi}{(P - V)/P}$

$$= \frac{\$36,000 + 20,000}{(\$9 - \$6)/\$9}$$

$$= \frac{\$56,000}{3/9}$$

$$= \$168,000.$$

f. Units sold in July:

$$X = \frac{\$180,000}{\$9}$$

$$= 20,000 \text{ Units.}$$

Problem 4 for Self-Study

Triple X Company

Triple X Company produces these products with the following characteristics:

	Product I	Product II	Product III
Price per Unit	$5	$6	$7
Variable Cost per Unit	$3	$2	$4
Expected Sales (units)	100,000	150,000	250,000

Total fixed costs for the company are $1,240,000.

Assuming that the product mix would be the same at the breakeven point, compute the breakeven point in:

a. Units (total and by product line).

b. Sales dollars (total and by product line).

Suggested Solution

a. Compute weighted-average contribution margin:

	Product I	Product II	Product III
Product Mix:	$\dfrac{100,000 \text{ Units}}{500,000 \text{ Units}}$	$\dfrac{150,000}{500,000}$	$\dfrac{250,000}{500,000}$
	= .20	= .30	= .50
Weighted-Average Contribution Margin $(P^* - V^*)$	.20($2) + .30($4) + .50($3)		
	= $3.10		

Or

$$\frac{(100,000 \text{ Units})(\$2) + (150,000)(\$4) + (250,000)(\$3)}{500,000} = \$3.10$$

$$X = \frac{\$1,240,000}{\$3.10}$$

$$X = 400,000 \text{ Units.}$$

b. To compute breakeven sales dollars, find the weighted-average price and variable costs:

$$P^* = (.20)(\$5) + (.30)(\$6) + (.50)(\$7)$$

$$P^* = \$6.30$$

$$V^* = (.20)(\$3) + (.30)(\$2) + (.50)(\$4)$$

$$V^* = \$3.20$$

$$\text{Breakeven } PX = \frac{F}{\dfrac{P - V}{P}} = \frac{\$1,240,000}{\$3.10/\$6.30}$$

$$= \frac{\$1,240,000}{.492 \text{ (rounded)}}$$

$$= \$2,520,000 \text{ (rounded to nearest } \$1,000).$$

(Check: 400,000 units × $6.30 = 2,520,000.)

Product line amounts:

	Total (100%)	Product I (20%)	Product II (30%)	Product III (40%)
Units	400,000	80,000	120,000	200,000
Unit Price.	$6.30	$5	$6	$7
Sales Dollars	$2,520,000	$400,000	$720,000	$1,400,000

Questions

1. Review the meaning of the following terms or concepts discussed in this chapter.

   a. Cost-volume-profit model.

   b. Breakeven point.

   c. Cost-volume-profit graph.

   d. Profit-volume equation.

   e. Contribution margin per unit.

   f. Sensitivity analysis.

   g. Margin of safety.

   h. Gross margin (compared to contribution margin).

   i. Isoprofit lines.

   j. Contribution margin ratio.

   k. Relevant range.

   l. Variable costing (compared to full absorption costing).

2. Define the profit equation.

3. Define the term "contribution margin."

4. How does the total "contribution margin" differ from the "gross margin" that is often shown on companies' financial statements?

5. Compare cost-volume-profit analysis with profit-volume analysis. How do they differ?

6. Is a company really breaking even if it produces and sells at the "breakeven" point? What costs might not be covered?

7. What is usually the difference between cost-volume-profit analysis on a cash basis and that on an accrual accounting basis? For a company having depreciable assets, would you expect the accrual breakeven point to be higher, lower, or the same as the cash breakeven point?

8. How is the profit equation expanded when multiproduct cost-volume-profit analysis is used?

9. Why is a constant product mix often assumed in multiproduct cost-volume-profit analysis?

10. When would the sum of the breakeven quantities for each of a company's products not be the breakeven point for the company as a whole?

11. What is the difference between economic "profits" and accounting "net income" or "operating profit"?

12. Name three common assumptions of a linear cost-volume-profit analysis.

13. Why might there be a difference between the operating profit calculated by cost-volume-profit analysis and the net income reported in financial statements for external reporting?

14. Fixed costs are often defined as "fixed over the short run." Does this mean that they are not fixed over the long run? Why or why not?

15. Why do accountants use a linear representation of cost and revenue behavior in cost-volume-profit analysis? How can this use be justified?

16. What effect could the following changes, occurring independently, have on **(1)** the breakeven point, **(2)** the contribution margin, and **(3)** the expected profit?
- **a.** An increase in fixed costs.
- **b.** A decrease in wage rates applicable to direct, strictly variable labor.
- **c.** An increase in the selling price of the product.
- **d.** An increase in production volume.
- **e.** An increase in insurance rates.

17. Assume the linear cost relation of the cost-volume-profit model for a single-product firm and use the following answer key:

(1) More than double.
(2) Double.
(3) Increase, but less than double.
(4) Remain the same.
(5) Decrease.

Complete each of the following statements, assuming that all other quantities remain constant.
- **a.** If price is doubled, revenue will _____.
- **b.** If price is doubled, the total contribution margin (contribution margin per unit times number of units) will _____.
- **c.** If price is doubled, profit will _____.
- **d.** If contribution margin per unit is doubled, profit will _____.
- **e.** If fixed costs are doubled, the total contribution margin will _____.
- **f.** If fixed costs are doubled, profit will _____.
- **g.** If fixed costs are doubled, the breakeven point of units sold will _____.
- **h.** If total sales of units are doubled, profit will _____.
- **i.** If total sales dollars are doubled, the breakeven point will _____.
- **j.** If the contribution margin per unit is doubled, the breakeven point will _____.
- **k.** If both variable costs per unit and selling price per unit are doubled, profit will _____.

Exercises

18. *Breakeven and Target Profits.* Analysis of the operations of the Homes Company shows the fixed costs to be $100,000 and the variable costs to be $4 per unit.

Selling price is $8 per unit.
- **a.** Derive the breakeven point expressed in units.
- **b.** How many units would have to be sold to earn a profit of $140,000?
- **c.** What would profits be if revenue from sales were $1,000,000?

19. *Cost-Volume-Profit; Volume Defined in Sales Dollars.* An excerpt from the income statement of the Wooster and Valley Company is shown below.

WOOSTER AND VALLEY COMPANY
Income Statement
Year Ended December 31, Year 1

Sales		$2,000,000
Operating Expenses:		
Cost of Goods Sold	$950,000	
Selling Costs.	300,000	
Administrative Costs	150,000	
Total Operating Costs.		1,400,000
Profit		$ 600,000

It was estimated that fixed costs in Year 1 were $440,000.
- **a.** What percentage of sales revenue is variable cost?
- **b.** What is the breakeven point in sales dollars for Wooster and Valley Company?
- **c.** Prepare a cost-profit-volume graph for Wooster and Valley Company.
- **d.** If sales revenue falls to $1,800,000, what will be the estimated amount of profit?
- **e.** What volume of sales would be required to produce a profit of $1,120,000?

20. *Cost-Volume-Profit Graph.* Identify each of the following on the graph below:
- **a.** The total cost line.
- **b.** The total revenue line.
- **c.** The total variable costs.
- **d.** Variable cost per unit.
- **e.** The total fixed costs.
- **f.** The breakeven point.
- **g.** The profit area (or volume).
- **h.** The loss area (or volume).

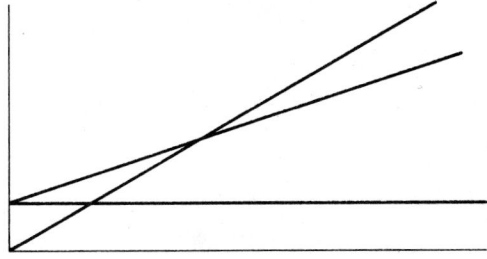

21. *Profit-Volume Graph.* Identify the places on the profit-volume graph indicated by the letters below:

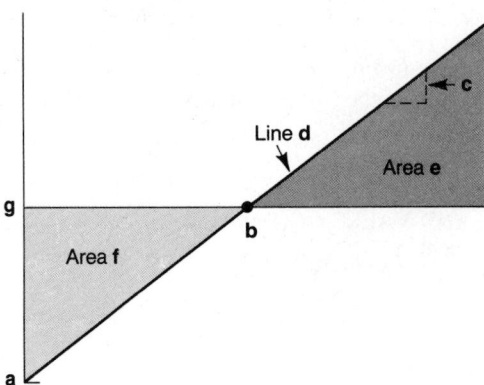

22. *Cost-Volume-Profit Analysis.* Surf's Up Company produces one type of sunglasses with the following costs and revenues for the year:

Total Revenues	$5,000,000
Total Fixed Costs.	$1,000,000
Total Variable Costs.	$3,000,000
Total Quantity Produced and Sold	1,000,000 Units

    a.   What is the selling price per unit?
    b.   What is the variable cost per unit?
    c.   What is the contribution margin per unit?
    d.   What is the breakeven point?
    e.   What quantity of units is required for Surf's Up Company to make an operating profit of $2,000,000 for the year?

23. *Breakeven and Target Profits; Volume Defined in Sales Dollars.* The estimate of operating costs of the Tarmin Company for the year is that fixed costs will total $300,000 and that variable costs will be $2 per unit.
    a.   Determine the breakeven point in sales dollars at a selling price of $3 per unit (*Hint:* Find the contribution margin ratio first.)
    b.   Determine the breakeven point in sales dollars at a selling price of $4 per unit.
    c.   How many units must be sold at a price of $5 per unit in order to generate a profit of $150,000?

24. *CVP—Sensitivity Analysis.* Giovanni, Inc., is considering introduction of a new product with the following price and cost characteristics:

Sales Price	$100 Each
Variable Cost	$60 Each
Fixed Costs	$200,000 per Year

a. What quantity is required for Giovanni, Inc., to break even?

b. What quantity is required for Giovanni, Inc., to make an operating profit of $100,000 for the year?

c. Assume that the projected quantity for the year is 8,000 units for each of the following situations:

(1) What will be the operating profit for 8,000 units?

(2) What would be the impact on operating profit if the sales price decreases by 10 percent? Increases by 20 percent?

(3) What would be the impact on operating profit if variable costs per unit decrease by 10 percent? Increase by 20 percent?

(4) Suppose that fixed costs for the year are 10 percent lower than projected, whereas variable costs per unit are 10 percent higher than projected. What would be the impact on operating profit for the year?

25. *Multiple Product Profit Analysis.* Company BE produces two products, B and E, with the following characteristics:

	Product B	Product E
Selling Price per Unit	$5	$6
Variable Cost per Unit.	$3	$2
Expected Sales (Units)	100,000	150,000

The total fixed costs for the company are $700,000.

a. What is the anticipated level of profits for the expected sales volumes?

b. Assuming that the product mix would be the same at the breakeven point, compute the breakeven point in terms of each of the products.

c. If the product sales mix were to change to 4 B:1 E, what would the new breakeven volume equal in terms of each of the products?

26. *Multiple Product Profit Analysis.* The Multiproduct Company produces and sells three different products. Operating data for the three products are shown below.

	Selling Price per Unit	Variable Cost per Unit	Fixed Cost per Month
Product P	$3	$2	—
Product Q	5	3	—
Product R	8	5	—
Entire Company.	—	—	$48,000

Define a unit as the sum of one unit of product R sold, two units of product Q sold, and three units of product P sold.

a. Draw a cost-volume-profit graph for the Multiproduct Company.

b. At what sales revenue does the Multiproduct Company break even?

    c. If the Company sells two units of product P for every two units of product Q and one unit of product R, at what sales revenue does it break even?

Problems and Cases

27. *Explaining Sales and Cost Changes (CPA adapted).* You have acquired the following data for the calendar years 1984 and 1985 for Celebration, Inc.:

	1984		1985		Dollar Increase
Sales	$750,000	100%	$840,000	100%	$90,000
Variable Cost of Goods Sold . . .	495,000	66	560,000	66⅔	65,000
Contribution Margin	$255,000	34%	$280,000	33⅓%	$25,000
Unit Selling Price	$10		$12		

Explain the increase in sales and cost of goods sold between 1984 and 1985.

28. *CVP—Missing Data (CPA adapted).* Freedom, Inc., management has performed cost studies and projected the following annual costs based on 40,000 units of production and sales:

	Total Annual Costs	Percent of Total Annual Cost That Is Variable
Direct Material	$400,000	100%
Direct Labor	360,000	75
Manufacturing Overhead.	300,000	40
Selling, General, and Administrative.	200,000	25

    a. Compute Freedom's unit selling price that will yield a projected profit of 10 percent of sales dollars, given sales of 40,000 units.
    b. Assume that management selects a selling price of $30 per unit (40,000 units). Compute Freedom's dollar sales that will yield a projected 10 percent profit on sales assuming that the above variable-fixed costs relationships are valid.

29. *CVP—Sensitivity Analysis.* In the last year, the sales of the Woodward Company were $1,200,000, fixed costs were $400,000, and variable costs were $600,000.
    a. At what sales volume would the company break even?
    b. If sales volume increased by 15 percent but prices are unchanged, by how much will profit increase?
    c. If fixed costs were reduced by 10 percent, by how much would profit increase?
    d. If variable costs were reduced by 10 percent, by how much would profit increase?

30. *Solving for Unknowns.* (*This problem and the next three are adapted from problems by David O. Green.*) When Britain's auto business slumped in 1921, William R. Morris (the "Henry Ford of Britain") gambled on cost saving from his new assembly lines and cut prices to a point where his expected loss per car in 1922 would be $240 if sales were the same as in 1921, or 1,500 cars. However, sales in 1922 rose to 60,000 cars, and profits for the year were $810,000. For 1922, calculate:

    a. The contribution margin per car.
    b. Total fixed costs.
    c. Breakeven point in cars.

31. *Solving for Unknowns.* During 1983, a division of an automobile company sold 90,000 cars for $250 million and realized a loss for the year of $24 million. The breakeven point was 120,000 cars. For 1983, calculate:

    a. The contribution margin per car.
    b. Total fixed costs.
    c. Profits for 1983 had sales been twice as large.

32. *Solving for Unknowns.* In 1967, reported *Time* magazine, the future of the American Motor Company seemed so shaky that its creditors, a consortium of banks headed by Chase Manhattan, examined the books every 10 days. The new management trimmed fixed costs by $20 million to cut the breakeven point from 350,000 cars in 1967 to 250,000 cars in 1968. From this information, calculate:

    a. The contribution margin per car (assumed constant for 1967 and 1968).
    b. Fixed costs for 1967 and 1968.
    c. 1967 losses, assuming sales of 300,000 cars.
    d. 1968 profits, assuming sales of 400,000 cars.

33. *Solving for Unknowns.* Reporting on Chrysler Corporation's performance for 1969, *The Wall Street Journal* pointed out that Chrysler had boosted its market share from 10 percent in 1962 to 18 percent in 1968. In 1969, however, countermeasures by Ford and General Motors, coupled with a 10 percent decline, or 1 million cars, in industry sales, created problems for Chrysler. Chrysler cut prices and increased advertising so that the contribution margin per car was $100 less in 1969 than in 1968. Fixed costs were reduced 20 percent in 1969 from what they had been in 1968. Nevertheless, Chrysler's 1969 profits were only $80 million on sales of 1.4 million autos, whereas 1968 profits had been $300 million. From this information, calculate:

    a. Industry sales (in autos) for 1968 and 1969.
    b. Chrysler's total fixed costs for 1968 and 1969.
    c. Chrysler's contribution margin per car in 1968 and 1969.

34. *Solving for Unknowns.* The Unitec Corporation had Year 0 revenues of $400,000 and profit equal to $4 per unit sold. Early in Year 1, the president of Unitec learned that a rival firm had contracted for a nationwide advertising program of extraordinary proportions to launch a competing product. Thereupon, the president of Unitec Corporation ordered a price cut for Unitec's single product. At the start of Year 1, the president ordered an increase of $48,000 in advertising expenditures to publicize the price cut. The price cut and increased advertising produced Year l sales in units double the Year 0 sales in units, but left profit unchanged in Year 1 compared to Year 0.

Had the new, Year 1 price been in effect during Year 0, revenues on its actual Year 0 sales volume would have been $96,000 less than actual Year 0 revenues, and the loss would have been equal to $2 per unit sold.

Compute each of the following quantities for Year 1:

    a. Sales volume in units.

    b. Revenues.

    c. Profit.

    d. Contribution margin per unit.

    e. Fixed costs.

35. *Solving for Unknowns.* Lecarla Company increased its market share from 12 percent in 19X0 to 36 percent in 19X5. By 19X6, however, actions by competitors and a 10 percent decline of 1,000 units in total industry sales from their 19X5 level created severe problems for Lecarla Company. In an unsuccessful effort to maintain its market share, the company reduced selling prices during 19X6, resulting in a decrease in contribution margin of $10 per unit compared to 19X5. Cutbacks in administrative activities reduced total fixed costs by 20 percent in 19X6. Operating profit in 19X6 was only $12,000 on sales of 2,800 units, whereas 19X5 operating profit was $54,000.

Compute each of the following:

    a. Fixed costs during 19X5.

    b. Fixed costs during 19X6.

    c. Contribution margin per unit during 19X5.

    d. Contribution margin per unit during 19X6.

    e. Breakeven sales in units during 19X5.

    f. Breakeven sales in units during 19X6.

36. *CVP—Missing Data; Assumptions.* Despite an increase in sales revenue from $4,704,000 in 19X8 to $4,725,000 in 19X9, the American Steel Corporation recently reported a decline in net income of $129,500 from 19X8 to an amount equal to 2 percent of sales revenue in 19X9. Among other factors, an increase in average total cost per unit of $2.05 from the average total cost per unit of $20 in 19X8 was provided as an explanation.

    a. Determine the changes, if any, in average selling price and sales in units from 19X8 to 19X9.

    b. Determine the total fixed costs and variable cost per unit during 19X9. Assuming that such a calculation is improper given the above information, illustrate why with a graph and discuss any important assumptions of the cost-volume-profit model that have apparently been violated.

37. *Alternatives to Reduce Breakeven Sales.* The Ronald Tool Corporation operated near the breakeven point of $1,125,000 during 19X1, while incurring fixed costs of $450,000. Management is considering two alternatives to reduce the breakeven level. Alternative A trims fixed costs by $100,000 annually; doing so will, however, reduce the quality of the product and result in a 10 percent decrease in selling price, though no change in the number of units sold. Alternative B substitutes automatized processing equipment for certain operations now performed manually. Alternative B will result in an annual increase in $150,000 in fixed costs, but will lead to a 5 percent decrease in variable costs per unit produced.

    a. What was the total contribution margin (contribution margin per unit times number of units sold) during 19X1?

    b. What is the breakeven sales in dollars under alternative A?

    c. What is the breakeven sales in dollars under alternative B?

    d. What should the company do?

38. *CVP—Partial Data; Special Order.* Partial income statements of the Ford Corporation for the first two quarters of 19X2 appear below.

FORD CORPORATION
Partial Income Statements
For First and Second Quarters of 19X2

	First Quarter	Second Quarter
Sales at $.90 per Unit	$36,000	$63,000
Total Costs	49,000	67,000
(Loss)	($13,000)	($ 4,000)

Each dollar of variable cost per unit is made up of 50 percent direct labor, 25 percent direct materials, and 25 percent variable overhead costs. Sales during the third quarter are expected to remain at the same level as during the second quarter, 70,000 units.

    a. What is the breakeven point in units?

    b. The company has just received a special order from the government for 30,000 units at a price of $.80 per unit. The company's regular market for 70,000 units in the third quarter would be unaffected if the order is accepted. The additional units can be produced with existing capacity, but if they are, direct labor costs will increase by 10 percent for *all* units produced because of the need to hire and use new labor. Additional insurance and administrative costs will result in an increase in fixed costs of $3,000 if the new order is accepted. Should the government order be accepted?

    c. Assume that the order in part **b** is accepted. What level of sales to non-government customers would be required for third-quarter profit to be $6,800?

39. *Solving for Cost-Based Selling Price.* United Instruments Corporation follows a cost-based approach to pricing. Prices are set equal to 120 percent of cost. The annual cost of producing one of its products is as follows:

Variable Manufacturing Costs.	$40 per Unit
Fixed Manufacturing Costs.	$100,000 per Year
Variable Selling and Administrative Costs	$10 per Unit
Fixed Selling and Administrative Costs	$60,000 per Year

    a. Assuming that 10,000 units are produced and sold, calculate the selling price per unit.

    b. Assuming that 20,000 units are produced and sold, calculate the selling price per unit.

40. *Solving for Cost-Based Selling Price.* Western Electronics Company follows a cost-based approach to pricing. Prices are set equal to 110 percent of cost. The company has annual fixed costs of $600,000. The variable costs of the company's products are as follows:

Product	Variable Cost per Unit
A	$10
B	20
C	30

The company expects to produce and sell 10,000 units of product A, 40,000 units of product B, and 10,000 units of product C.

    a. Compute the selling price of each product if fixed costs are allocated to products on the basis of the number of units produced.

    b. Compute the selling price of each product if fixed costs are allocated to products on the basis of total variable costs.

41. *CVP Under Uncertainty.* (This problem should be assigned only to students who have had some introduction to statistics and who have access to tables for the normal distribution.) The Brown Corporation provides the following estimates of quantities relating to its business operations:

Selling Price	$2.00 per Unit
Variable Costs	$1.50 per Unit
Fixed Costs	$5,000 per Month
Expected (Mean) Level of Sales, Which Are Normally Distributed	16,000 Units per Month
Standard Deviation of Monthly Sales	4,000 Units

    a. What is the breakeven level of sales units?

    b. What is the profit at the expected level of sales?

    c. Determine the probability of the company's at least breaking even in a given month.

    d. Determine the probability of profit being at least $5,000 for a given month.

42. *CVP Analysis with Semifixed (Step) Costs.* Level Co. has one product. The sales price of $10 remains constant per unit regardless of volume, as does the variable cost of $6 per unit. The company is considering operating at one of the following three monthly levels of operations:

	Volume Range (production and sales)	Total Fixed Costs	Increase in Fixed Costs from Previous Level
Level 1	0–16,000	$40,000	—
Level 2	16,001–28,000	72,000	$32,000
Level 3	28,001–38,000	94,000	22,000

a. Calculate the breakeven point(s).

b. If the company can sell everything it makes, should it operate at level 1, level 2, or level 3? Support your answer.

43. *CVP Analysis with Semifixed Costs and Changing Unit Variable Costs.* The Eades Company manufactures and sells one product. The sales price, $50 per unit, remains constant regardless of volume. Last year's sales were 15,000 units and operating profits were $200,000. "Fixed" costs depended on production levels, as shown below. Variable costs per unit are 40 percent *higher* for level 2 (two shifts) than for level 1 (day shift only), because of additional labor costs due primarily to higher wages required to employ workers for the night shift.

	Annual Production Range (in units)	Annual Total Fixed Costs
Level 1 (day shift)	0–20,000	$100,000
Level 2 (day and night shifts)	20,001–36,000	164,000

Last year's cost structure and selling price are not expected to change this year. Maximum plant capacity is 36,000. The company sells everything it produces.

a. Compute the contribution margin per unit for last year for each of the two production levels.

b. Compute the breakeven points for last year for each of the two production levels.

c. Compute the volume in units that will maximize operating profits. Defend your choice.

44. *CVP Analysis with Semifixed Costs.* Beverly Miller, director and owner of the Discovery Day Care Center, has a master's degree in elementary education. In the 7 years she has been running the Discovery Center, her salary has ranged from nothing to $10,000 per year. "The second year," she says, "I made 62 cents an hour."

Her salary is what's left over after all other expenses are met.

Could she run a more profitable center? She thinks perhaps she could if she increased the student-teacher ratio, which is currently five students to one teacher. (Government standards for a center like this set a maximum of 10 students per teacher.) However, she refuses to increase the ratio to more than six-to-one. "If you increase the ratio to more than 6:1, the children don't get enough attention. In addition, the demands on the teacher are far too great." She does not hire part-time teachers.

Beverly rents the space for her center in the basement of a church for $450 per month, including utilities. She estimates that supplies, snacks, and other nonpersonnel costs are $40 per student per month. She charges $190 per month per student. Teachers are paid $600 per month, including fringe benefits. There are no other operating costs. At present, there are 30 students and six teachers.

a. What is the present operating profit per month of the Discovery Day Care Center before Ms. Miller's salary?

b. What is (are) the breakeven point(s), assuming a student-teacher ratio of 6:1?

c. What would be the breakeven point(s) if the student-teacher ratio were allowed to increase to 10:1?

d. Ms. Miller has an opportunity to increase the student body by six students. She must take all six or none. Should she accept the six students, if she wants to maintain a maximum student-teacher ratio of 6:1?

e. (Continuation of part **d**.) Suppose that Ms. Miller accepts the 6 children. Now she has the opportunity to accept one more. What would happen to profit if she did?

45. *CVP with Taxes (CMA adapted).* R. A. Ro and Company, maker of quality, hand-made pipes, has experienced a steady growth in sales for the past 5 years. However, increased competition has led Mr. Ro, the president, to believe that an aggressive advertising campaign will be necessary next year to maintain the company's present growth. To prepare for next year's advertising campaign, the company's accountant has prepared and presented Mr. Ro with the following data for the current year, 1983.

Cost Schedule

Variable Costs:

Direct Labor	$ 8.00/pipe
Direct Materials	3.25/pipe
Variable Overhead	2.50/pipe
Total Variable Costs	$13.75/pipe

Fixed Costs:

Manufacturing	$ 25,000
Selling	40,000
Administrative	70,000
Total Fixed Costs	$135,000
Selling Price, per Pipe	$25.00
Expected Sales, 1983 (20,000 units)	$500,000

Tax Rate: 40 Percent

Mr. Ro has set the sales target for 1984 at a level of $550,000 (or 22,000 pipes).

a. What is the projected aftertax operating profit for 1983?

b. What is the breakeven point in units for 1983?

c. Mr. Ro believes that an additional selling expense of $11,250 for advertising in 1984, with all other costs remaining constant, will be necessary to attain the sales target. What will be the aftertax operating profit for 1984 if the additional $11,250 is spent?

d. What will be the breakeven point in dollar sales for 1984 if the additional $11,250 is spent for advertising?

e. If the additional $11,250 is spent for advertising in 1984, what is the required sales level in dollar sales to equal 1983 aftertax operating profit?

f. At a sales level of 22,000 units, what is the maximum amount that can be spent on advertising if an aftertax operating profit of $60,000 is desired?

46. *Comprehensive CVP Case.*[10] Bill French picked up the phone and called his boss, Wes Davidson, controller of Duo-Products Corporation. "Say, Wes, I'm all set for the meeting this afternoon. I've put together a set of breakeven statements that should really make the boys sit up and take notice—and I think they'll be able to understand them, too." After a brief conversation about other matters, the call was concluded and French turned to his charts for one last check-out before the meeting.

French had been hired 6 months earlier as a staff accountant. He was directly responsible to Davidson and, up to the time of this case, had been doing routine types of analysis work. French was an alumnus of a liberal arts undergraduate school and graduate business school, and was considered by his associates to be quite capable and unusually conscientious. It was this latter characteristic that had apparently caused him to "rub some of the working guys the wrong way," as one of his co-workers put it. French was well aware of his capabilities and took advantage of every opportunity that arose to try to educate those around him. Wes Davidson's invitation for French to attend an informal manager's meeting had come as some surprise to others in the accounting group. However, when French requested permission to make a presentation of some breakeven data, Davidson acquiesced. The Duo-Products Corporation had not been making use of this type of analysis in its review or planning programs.

Basically, what French had done was to determine the level at which the company must operate in order to break even. As he phrased it:

> The company must be able to at least sell a sufficient volume of goods so that it will cover all the variable costs of producing and selling the goods; further, it will not make a profit unless it covers the fixed, or nonvariable, costs as well. The level of operation at which total costs (that is, variable plus nonvariable) are just covered is the breakeven volume. This should be the lower limit in all our planning.

The accounting records had provided the following information that French used in constructing his chart:

Plant capacity—2 million units.

Past year's level of operations—1.5 million units.

Average unit selling price—$1.20.

Total fixed costs—$520,000.

Average variable unit cost—$.75.

From this information, French observed that each unit contributed $.45 to fixed overhead after covering the variable costs. Given total fixed costs of $520,000, he

---

[10]Copyright (1959) by the President and Fellows of Harvard College. This case was prepared by R. C. Hill under the direction of Neil E. Harlan as a basis for class rather than to illustrate either effective or ineffective handling of an administrative situation. Reprinted by permission of the Harvard Business School.

calculated that 1,155,556 units must be sold in order to break even. He verified this conclusion by calculating the dollar sales volume that was required to break even. Because the variable costs per unit were 62.5 percent of the selling price, French reasoned that 37.5 percent of every sales dollar was left available to cover fixed costs. Thus, fixed costs of $520,000 require sales of $1,386,667 in order to break even.

When he constructed a breakeven chart to present the information graphically, his conclusions were further verified. The chart also made it clear that the firm was operating at a fair margin over the breakeven requirements, and that the profits accruing (at the rate of 37.5 percent of every sales dollar over breakeven) increased rapidly as volume increased (see Exhibit 7.10).

Exhibit 7.10

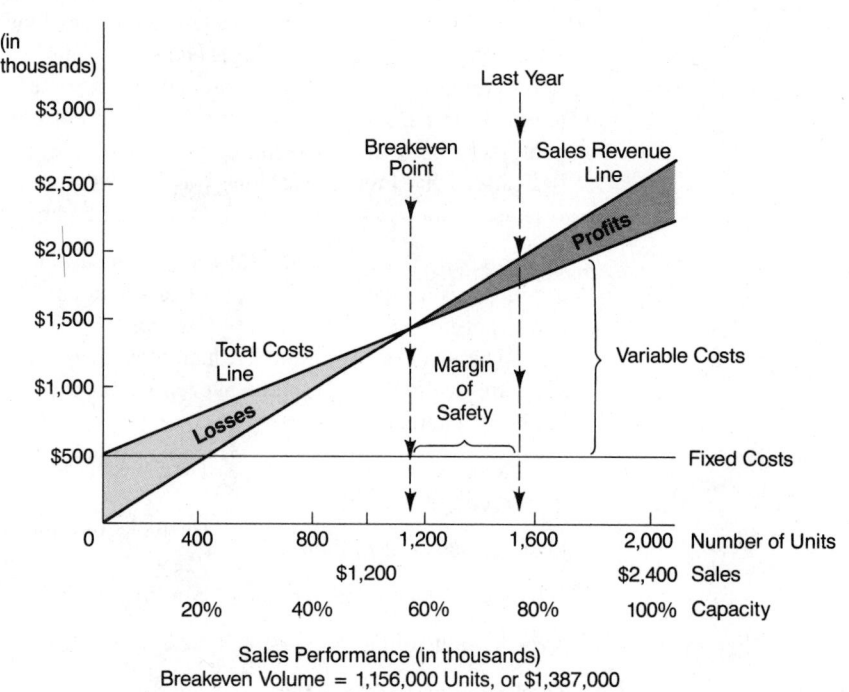

Sales Performance (in thousands)
Breakeven Volume = 1,156,000 Units, or $1,387,000

Shortly after lunch, French and Davidson left for the meeting. Several representatives of the manufacturing departments were present, as well as the general sales manager, two assistant sales managers, the purchasing officer, and two people from the product engineering office. Davidson introduced French to the few people he had not already met, and then the meeting got under way. French's presentation was the last item on Davidson's agenda, and in due time the controller introduced French, explaining his interest in cost control and analysis.

French had prepared enough copies of his chart and supporting calculations for everyone at the meeting. He described carefully what he had done and explained how the chart pointed to a profitable year, dependent on meeting the volume of sales activity that had been maintained in the past. It soon became apparent that some of the participants had known in advance what French planned to discuss; they had come prepared to challenge him and soon had taken control of the meeting. The following exchange ensued (see Exhibit 7.11 for a checklist of participants with their titles):

Exhibit 7.11
List of Participants in the Meeting

Bill French.	Staff Accountant
Wes Davidson	Controller
John Cooper	Production Control
Fred Williams	Manufacturing
Ray Bradshaw	Assistant Sales Manager
Arnie Winetki.	General Sales Manager
Anne Fraser	Administrative Assistant to the President

COOPER (production control): You know, Bill, I'm really concerned that you haven't allowed for our planned changes in volume next year. It seems to me that you should have allowed for the sales department's guess that we'll boost sales by 20 percent, unit-wise. We'll be pushing 90 percent of what we call capacity then. It sure seems that this would make quite a difference in your figuring.

FRENCH: That might be true, but as you can see, all you have to do is read the cost and profit relationship right off the chart for the new volume. Let's see—at a million-eight units we'd. . . .

WILLIAMS (manufacturing): Wait a minute, now!!! If you're going to talk in terms of 90 percent of capacity, and it looks like that's what it will be, you had better note that we'll be shelling out some more for the plant. We've already got okays on investment money that will boost your fixed costs by $10,000 a month, easy. And that may not be all. We may call it 90 percent of plant capacity, but there are a lot of places where we're just full up and we can't put things up any tighter.

COOPER: See, Bill? Fred Williams is right, but I'm not finished on this bit about volume changes. According to the information that I've got here—and it came from your office—I'm not sure that your breakeven chart can really be used even if there were to be no changes next year. Looks to me like you've got average figures that don't allow for the fact that we're dealing with three basic products. Your report here (see Exhibit 7.12) on costs, according to product lines, for last year makes it pretty clear that the "average" is way out of line. How would the breakeven point look if we took this on an individual product basis?

FRENCH: Well, I'm not sure. Seems to me that there is only one breakeven point for the firm. Whether we take it product by product or in total, we've got to hit that point. I'll be glad to check for you if you want, but. . . .

Exhibit 7.12
Product Class Cost Analysis
(Normal Year)

	Aggregate	"A"	"B"	"C"
Sales at Full Capacity (units) . . .	2,000,000			
Actual Sales Volume (units). . . .	1,500,000	600,000	400,000	500,000
Unit Sales Price	$ 1.20	$ 1.67	$ 1.50	$ .40
Total Sales Revenue	$1,800,000	$1,000,000	$600,000	$200,000
Variable Cost per Unit	$ .75	$ 1.25	$ .625	$ .25
Total Variable Cost	$1,125,000	$ 750,000	$250,000	$125,000
Fixed Costs	$ 520,000	$ 170,000	$275,000	$ 75,000
Net Profit	$ 155,000	$ 80,000	$ 75,000	—
Ratios:				
Variable Costs to Sales	.63	.75	.42	.63
Variable Income to Sales	.37	.25	.58	.37
Utilization of Capacity	75.0%	30.0%	20.0%	25.0%

BRADSHAW (assistant sales manager): Guess I may as well get in on this one, Bill. If you're going to do anything with individual products, you ought to know that we're looking for a big swing in our product mix. Might even start before we get into the new season. The "A" line is really losing out and I imagine that we'll be lucky to hold two-thirds of the volume there next year. Wouldn't you buy that, Arnie? [Agreement from the general sales manager.] That's not too bad, though, because we expect that we should pick up the 200,000 that we lose, and about a quarter million units more, over in "C" production. We don't see anything that shows much of a change in "B." That's been solid for years and shouldn't change much now.

WINETKI (general sales manager): Bradshaw's called it about as we figure it, but there's something else here too. We've talked about our pricing on "C" enough, and now I'm really going to push our side of it. Ray's estimate of maybe half a million—450,000 I guess it was—up on "C" for next year is on the basis of doubling the price with no change in cost. We've been priced so low on this item that it's been a crime—we've got to raise, but good, for two reasons. First, for our reputation; the price is out of line class-wise and is completely inconsistent with our quality reputation. Second, if we don't raise the price, we'll be swamped and we can't handle it. You heard what Williams said about capacity. The way the whole "C" field is exploding, we'll have to answer to another half-million units in unsatisfied orders if we don't jack the price up. We can't afford to expand that much for this product.

At this point, Anne Fraser (administrative assistant to the president) walked up toward the front of the room from where she had been standing near the rear door. The discussion broke for a minute, and she took advantage of the lull to interject a few comments.

FRASER: This has certainly been enlightening. Looks like you fellows are pretty well up on this whole operation. As long as you're going to try to get all the things together that you ought to pin down for next year, let's see what I can add to help you:

Number One: Let's remember that everything that shows in the profit area here on Bill's chart is divided just about evenly between the government and us. Now, for last year we can read a profit of about $150,000. Well, that's right. But we were left with half of that, and then paid our dividends of $50,000 to the stockholders. Since we've got an anniversary year coming up, we'd like to put out a special dividend of about 50 percent extra. We ought to hold $25,000 in for the business, too. This means that we'd like to hit $100,000 *after* the costs of being governed.

Number Two: From where I sit, it looks like we're going to have a talk with the union again, and this time it's liable to cost us. All the indications are—and this isn't public—that we may have to meet demands that will boost our production costs—what do you call them here, Bill—variable costs—by 10 percent across the board. This may kill the bonus-dividend plans, but we've got to hold the line on past profits. This means that we can give that much to the union only if we can make it in added revenues. I guess you'd say that that raises your breakeven point, Bill—and for that one I'd consider the company's profit to be a fixed cost.

Number Three: Maybe this is the time to think about switching our product emphasis. Arnie Winetki may know better than I which of the products is more profitable. You check me out on this Arnie—and it might be a good idea for you and Bill French to get together on this one, too. These figures that I have (Exhibit 7.12) make it look like the percentage contribution on line ''A'' is the lowest of the bunch. If we're losing volume there as rapidly as you sales folks say, and if we're as hard-pressed for space as Fred Williams has indicated, maybe we'd be better off grabbing some of that big demand for ''C'' by shifting some of the facilities over there from ''A.''

That's all I've got to say. Looks to me like you've all got plenty to think about.

DAVIDSON: Thanks, Anne. I sort of figured that we'd get wound up here as soon as Bill brought out his charts. This is an approach that we've barely touched, but, as you can see, you've all got ideas that have got to be made to fit here somewhere. I'll tell you what let's do. Bill, suppose you rework your chart and try to bring into it some of the points that were made here today. I'll see if I can summarize what everyone seems to be looking for.

First of all, I have the idea buzzing around in the back of my mind that your presentation is based on a rather important series of assumptions. Most of the questions that were raised were really about those assumptions; it might help us all if you try to set the assumptions down in black and white so that we can see just how they influence the analysis.

Then, I think that Cooper would like to see the unit sales increase taken up, and he'd also like to see whether there's any difference if you base the calculations on an analysis of individual product lines. Also, as Bradshaw suggested, since the product mix is bound to change, why not see how things look if the shift materializes as sales has forecast?

Arnie Winetki would like to see the influence of a price increase in the ''C'' line; Fred Williams looks toward an increase in fixed manufacturing costs of $10,000 a month, and Anne Fraser has suggested that we should consider taxes, dividends, expected union demands, and the question of product emphasis.

I think that ties it all together. Let's hold off on our next meeting, fellows, until Bill has time to work this all into shape.

With that, the participants broke off into small groups and the meeting disbanded. French and Wes Davidson headed back to their offices and French, in a tone of concern, asked Davidson, "Why didn't you warn me about the hornet's nest I was walking into?"

"Bill, you didn't ask!"

a. What are the assumptions implicit in Bill French's determination of his company's breakeven point?

b. On the basis of French's revised information, what does next year look like:

(1) What is the breakeven point?

(2) What level of operations must be achieved to pay the extra dividend, ignoring union demands?

(3) What level of operations must be achieved to meet the union demands, ignoring bonus dividends?

(4) What level of operations must be achieved to meet both dividends and expected union requirements?

c. Can the breakeven analysis help the company decide whether to alter the existing product emphasis? What can the company afford to invest for additional "C" capacity?

d. Is this type of analysis of any value? For what can it be used?

Suggested Solutions to Even-Numbered Exercises

18. *Breakeven and Target Profits.*

a. Contribution Margin (per unit) = Unit Selling Price − Unit Variable Cost

$$= \$8 - \$4$$

$$= \$4$$

Profit = (Contribution Margin per Unit × Units) − Fixed Costs

$$0 = (\$4 \times \text{Units}) - \$100,000$$

Units = 25,000.

b. $\$140,000 = (\$4 \times \text{Units}) - \$100,000$

$\$240,000 = \$4 \times \text{Units}$

$60,000 = \text{Units}.$

c. Profit = (.5 × \$1,000,000) − \$100,000

$$= \$400,000$$

$$\text{Contribution Margin Percentage} = \frac{\text{Unit Selling Price} - \text{Unit Variable Cost}}{\text{Unit Selling Price}}$$

$$= \frac{\$8 - \$4}{\$8} = \frac{\$4}{\$8} = 50\%.$$

20. *Cost-Volume-Profit Graph.*

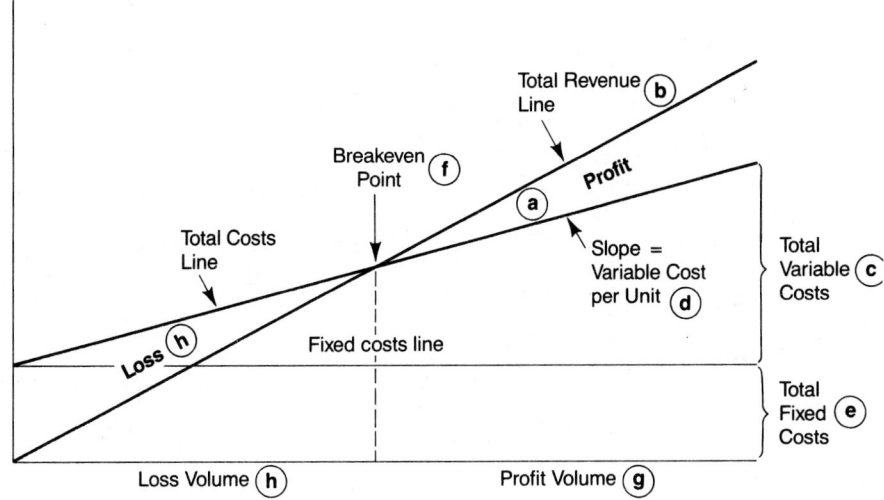

22. *Cost-Volume-Profit Analysis.*
   a. $\$5,000,000 \div 1,000,000$ Units $= \$5$ per Unit.
   b. $\$3,000,000 \div 1,000,000$ Units $= \$3$ per Unit.
   c. $\$5 - \$3 = \$2$ per unit.
   d. $\pi = (\$5 - \$3)X - \$1,000,000.$

   Let $\pi = 0.$

   $0 = (\$5 - \$3)X - \$1,000,000.$

   $X = \dfrac{1,000,000}{(\$5 - \$3)} = 500,000$ Units.

   e. Let $\pi = \$2,000,000.$

   $\$2,000,000 = (\$5 - \$3)X - \$1,000,000.$

   $X = \dfrac{\$3,000,000}{(\$5 - \$3)} = 1,500,000$ Units.

24. *CVP—Sensitivity Analysis.*
   a. $\pi = (P - V)X - F$

   $0 = (\$100 - \$60)X - \$200,000$

   $X = \dfrac{\$200,000}{(\$100 - \$60)} = 5,000$ Units.

b. $100,000 = (\$100 - \$60)X - \$200,000$

$$X = \frac{\$300,000}{(\$100 - \$60)} = 7,500 \text{ Units.}$$

c. **(1)** $\pi = (\$100 - \$60)8,000 - \$200,000$

$= \$120,000.$

(2) *10 percent price decrease. Now P* $= \$90$.

$\pi = (\$90 - \$60)8,000 - \$200,000$

$= \$40,000.$

π decreases by \$80,000 (67 percent).

20 percent price increase. Now P $= \$120$.

$\pi = (\$120 - \$60)8,000 - \$200,000$

$= \$280,000.$

π increases by \$160,000 (133 percent).

(3) *10 percent variable cost decrease. Now V* $= \$54$.

$\pi = (\$100 - \$54)8,000 - \$200,000$

$= \$168,000$

π increases by \$48,000 (40 percent).

20 percent variable cost increase. Now V $= \$72$.

$\pi = (\$100 - \$72)8,000 - \$200,000$

$= \$24,000.$

π decreases by \$96,000 (80 percent).

(4) $\pi = (\$100 - \$66)8,000 - \$180,000$

$= \$92,000.$

π decreases by \$28,000 (23 percent).

26. *Multiple Product Profit Analysis.*

a.

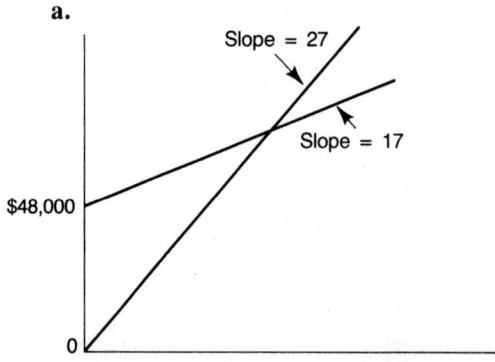

A unit = production of one product R, two product Q's, and three product P's.

Variable Cost per Unit = $(3 \times \$2) + (2 \times \$3) + (1 \times \$5) = \$17$

Revenue per Unit = $(3 \times \$3) + (2 \times \$5) + (1 \times \$8) = \$27$.

b. $0 = $ Total Revenue $-$ Total Cost

$0 = \$27X - (\$17X + \$48,000)$

$\$10X = \$48,000$

$X = 4,800$ Units.

Production at breakeven point is

Product P $= 3 \times 4,800 = 14,400$

Product Q $= 2 \times 4,800 = 9,600$

Product R $= 1 \times 4,800 = 4,800$.

Total Revenue at breakeven level $= 4,800$ units $\times \$27 = \$129,600$.

c. A unit $=$ two product P's, two product Q's, and one product R.

Variable Cost per Unit = $(2 \times \$2) + (2 \times \$3) + (1 \times \$5) = \$15$

Revenue per Unit = $(2 \times \$3) + (2 \times \$5) + (1 \times \$8) = \$24$

$0 = $ Total Revenue $-$ Total Cost

$0 = \$24X - (\$15X + \$48,000)$

$\$9X = \$48,000$

$X = 5,333$ Units.

Production at breakeven point is

Product P $= 2 \times 5,333.3 = 10,667$

Product Q $= 2 \times 5,333.3 = 10,667$

Product R $= 1 \times 5,333.3 = 5,333$.

Total Revenue at breakeven $= 5,333$ units $\times \$24 = \$127,992$.

Chapter 8   Short-Run Decisions and Differential Analysis

This chapter continues our discussion of the use of accounting information for managerial decision making. This chapter deals with the use of accounting information in making such managerial decisions as pricing, accepting special orders, making versus buying products, and choosing the optimal mix of products.

These are "short-run" decisions, which means that capacity is assumed to be fixed. Chapter 9 deals with long-run decisions involving changes in capacity.

This chapter deals with several applications of one principle: *differential analysis*.[1] Management's performance is usually judged on the basis of a firm's profitability. Thus, managers are interested in ascertaining the differential effect of various alternative actions on profits. After reading this chapter, you should understand how to apply differential analysis. As you go through each application of differential analysis, we encourage you to keep the following questions in mind: What differs among the alternatives? By how much?

The Differential Principle

Managerial decision making is the process of making choices. If a choice is to be made among alternatives, then there must be differences among the alternatives. The analysis of the differences among alternatives is called *differential analysis*.

The differential analysis model, shown in Exhibit 8.1, extends the cost-volume-profit model discussed in Chapter 7. The first two columns represent the cost-volume-profit equation for the status quo, or current situation, and for the alternative being considered. The third column shows the difference between the

Exhibit 8.1
Differential Analysis Model[a]

	Alternative	− Status Quo	= Difference
Revenue	$P_1 X_1$	$P_0 X_0$	ΔPX
Less Variable Costs	$V_1 X_1$	$V_0 X_0$	ΔVX
Total Contribution Margin	$(P_1 - V_1)X_1$	$(P_0 - V_0)X_0$	$\Delta(P - V)X$
Less Fixed Costs	F_1	F_0	ΔF
Operating Profit	π_1	π_0	$\Delta \pi$

[a]P = price per unit; X = volume per period; V = variable cost per unit; $P - V$ = contribution margin per unit; F = fixed costs per period; π = operating profit per period; Δ = amount of difference.

---

[1]"Differential" analysis is also known as "incremental" analysis or "marginal" analysis.

status quo and the alternative. If the difference is such that $\pi_1 > \pi_0$, then the alternative is more profitable than the status quo. If $\pi_0 > \pi_1$, the the status quo is more profitable.

The following example illustrates the important dimensions of differential analysis. To provide continuity, we use the facts from this example throughout the chapter. We illustrate using a manufacturing firm because it is the most comprehensive and complex of any type of organization. The concepts apply as well to service, financial, merchandising, and other types of organization.

Example Assume the following status quo data for Baltimore Manufacturing Company:

Units Manufactured and Sold . . . . 800 Units per Month
Maximum Production and Sales Capacity . . . . 1,200 Units per Month
Selling Price $30

Cost Classification	Variable Cost (per unit)	Fixed Cost (per month)
Manufacturing:		
Direct Materials	$ 4	
Direct Labor	9	
Manufacturing Overhead	4	$3,060
Total Manufacturing Costs.	$17	$3,060
Marketing and Administrative Costs	5	1,740
Total Costs	$22	$4,800

The management of the Baltimore Manufacturing Company believes that it can increase volume from 800 units to 900 units per month by decreasing the selling price from $30 to $28 per unit. Would the price reduction be profitable? The result of differential analysis for this problem, as shown in Exhibit 8.2, indicates that the alternative would not increase profits.

Exhibit 8.2
BALTIMORE MANUFACTURING COMPANY
Differential Analysis of a Price Reduction[a]

	Alternative P = $28 X = 900	−	Status Quo P = $30 X = 800	=	Difference
Revenue	$25,200[b]	−	$24,000[d]	=	$ 1,200
Less Variable Costs	(19,800)[c]	−	(17,600)[e]	=	(2,200)
Total Contribution Margin.	$ 5,400	−	$ 6,400	=	$−1,000
Less Fixed Costs	(4,800)	−	(4,800)	=	—
Operating Profit	$ 600	−	$ 1,600	=	$−1,000

[a]Numbers with parentheses are costs; numbers with minus signs are the result of row operations in which the *status quo* amount is greater than the *alternative* amount.
[b]$25,200 = $28 × 900 units.
[c]$19,800 = $22 × 900 units.
[d]$24,000 = $30 × 800 units.
[e]$17,600 = $22 × 800 units.

Relevant Costs

Note in Exhibit 8.2 that not all costs were differential for *this* decision; specifically, fixed costs in this example were assumed to be unchanged. Thus, only revenues and *total* variable costs were *relevant* to the analysis; fixed costs were not. Differential analysis is sometimes called "relevant cost" analysis because of the importance of identifying which costs (or revenues) are relevant to the decision. A cost or revenue is "relevant" if an amount appears in the "Difference" column; all others are irrelevant. Thus, fixed costs could have been ignored in this example. (This is not true in general. Fixed costs are nearly always differential in long-run decisions involving changes in capacity, and they are sometimes differential in short-run operating decisions, as we shall see later in this chapter.)

As you become familiar with differential analysis, you will find shortcuts by ignoring irrelevant costs (and revenues) from the outset of your work. For example, you needed to work only with revenues and total variable costs in the previous example to get the answer.

Problems in Identifying Costs

Focus on Cash Flows

The most difficult part of decision making is estimating the benefits and costs of each alternative. Although benefits and costs have several dimensions, the most important dimensions for business decisions are the amounts and timing of cash flows. (Chapter 9 provides analytical methods of dealing with the *timing* of cash flows; this chapter deals only with the *amount* of cash flows.) The emphasis on cash flow is fundamental for two reasons:

1. Cash is the medium of exchange. It can be used immediately to pay debts or dividends or to purchase equipment. Noncash assets can eventually be converted into cash, but this takes time and perhaps some additional costs.
2. Cash serves as a common, highly objective, measure of the benefits and costs of alternatives. If one alternative is stated in terms of units of inventory to be produced and another in terms of the number of machines to be acquired, then the alternatives are not expressed in a common measuring unit. Before these alternatives can be compared, their benefits and costs must be reexpressed in a common measuring unit. Cash flows are used as the common measuring unit because they represent the most objective and quantifiable measure of benefits and costs.

Consequently, differential analysis focuses mostly on differential cash flows. In the previous example, differential revenues and costs were both assumed to be cash flows or near-cash flows (for example, revenues and costs on account are assumed to be cash flows). Focusing on cash flows is not enough, however, because two additional costs may be overlooked: opportunity costs and economic depreciation.

Opportunity Costs

As discussed in Chapter 2, the benefits from alternative uses of assets are opportunity costs. Suppose that the increase in volume from 800 units to 900 units in the previous example means using additional building space that could have been rented to a tenant, generating $200 cash inflow per month. The differential opportunity cost of the increase in volume would have been $200, making the alternative to increase volume even less attractive. (Specifically, the differential net operating profits would have been $-$1,200 in Exhibit 8.2.)

It is easy to overlook opportunity costs because they are not recorded as transactions in the accounting records. It is important, however, to consider them in comparing alternative actions.

Economic Depreciation

Depreciation creates a special problem because there is an amount in the records labeled "depreciation" that is an allocation of a past cost. In differential analysis we are concerned with economic depreciation, which is the change in the economic value of an asset because of its use. Focusing on cash flows usually means that the cash outflow to acquire an asset and the cash inflow when it is sold are taken into account. If so, economic depreciation, which is the decline in value of an asset, would be considered automatically.

Example Management of a rental car company is trying to decide between the purchase of a fleet of Oldsmobile or Buick automobiles. All costs of operating both models are assumed to be equal. However, economic depreciation differs. The Buicks would cost $11,600 and have a salvage value of $8,800 when the cars are sold after 6 months. The Oldsmobiles would cost $11,000 each and have a salvage value of $8,400 when the cars are sold after 6 months. As shown below, the Oldsmobiles have a lower economic depreciation in this case. (We have excluded the time value of money for ease of illustration. Such lease decisions are typically made over longer time periods and include consideration of the time value of money.)

	Alternative 1: Buick	Alternative 2: Oldsmobile	Difference (1 − 2)
Cost of Car	$(11,600)	$(11,000)	$(600)
Salvage Value After 6 Months . . .	8,800	8,400	400
Economic Depreciation (decline in value)	$ (2,800)	$ (2,600)	$(200)

In short, the use of an asset has both costs: *economic depreciation* because of the decline in its value, and the *opportunity cost* of investing funds in the asset instead of elsewhere.

The practical difficulties of considering *all* costs in differential analysis should be apparent. It is important to keep in mind that although opportunity costs and economic depreciation may be relevant to a decision, it may not be worthwhile to try to measure them. This is one of many situations in management where the benefits of obtaining all relevant information for a decision may not justify the cost of doing so.

We recommend identifying the relevant cash flows first. If the decision would not be affected if any reasonable estimate of opportunity costs and economic depreciation were added to the differential costs already estimated, then there is no reason to obtain an estimate of those costs. If the decision is close, however, it may be worthwhile to obtain estimates of opportunity costs and economic depreciation.

Uncertainty and Differential Analysis

Cost and revenue estimates for the status quo are usually more certain than estimates for alternatives. The status quo represents something known, whereas alternatives are often little more than educated guesses. There is a high probability that some critical aspect of the alternative may be omitted.

If managers are averse to risk and uncertainty, then they prefer the known to the unknown, all other things being equal. Consequently, we sometimes find managers rejecting an alternative that is expected to be more profitable than the status quo because of uncertainty. Managers often deal with uncertainty and differential analysis by setting high standards for the alternative (for example, ''The alternative must increase profits by 25 percent before it will be accepted.'').

Pricing Decisions

Decisions regarding the prices to be charged for a firm's products are complex, involving such factors as competitors' actions and market conditions. In many cases a firm will not be in a competitive position to set prices. The more highly competitive the market, the more likely that the market price will have to be accepted as given. In some situations, however, firms do have at least some control over the prices charged. For example, many firms sell to government agencies or other buyers with cost-plus-fixed-fee contracts. In this section, we consider pricing decisions to show that correct pricing decisions involve the principles of differential analysis.

Cost-Based Approach to Pricing

One approach to setting prices is to add a markup to the firm's costs. Suppose that the management of the Baltimore Manufacturing Company has set a goal of reporting profits of $2,000 per month. If the volume were estimated to be 800 units per month, the per-unit price would be calculated as follows:

$$\pi = PX - (VX + F)$$

$$\$2{,}000 = (P \times 800) - [(\$22 \times 800) + \$4{,}800]$$

$$= (P \times 800) - \$22{,}400$$

$$\$24{,}400 = P \times 800$$

$$P = \frac{\$24{,}400}{800}$$

$$= \$30.50.$$

So the unit price would be set at $30.50.

If a firm is to remain in business in the long run, it must recover all of its costs plus provide an adequate return to its owners. It is desirable, then, that long-run *average* prices approximate the amount derived from a cost-based approach to pricing. There are some shortcomings, however, to using this approach in making pricing decisions.

First, the relation between P and X in the market is being ignored. If the Baltimore Manufacturing Company faces a downward-sloping demand curve, it may not be feasible to sell 800 units at a price of $30.50.

Second, cost-plus pricing is often done in a simplistic manner, such as: "Add $2.50 to the total cost of producing and selling each unit to get the price." There is a circularity in pricing decisions when this type of cost-based approach is used. The per-unit cost of a product is critically affected by the number of units produced. As the number of units is increased, the amount of fixed cost allocated to each unit decreases. Thus, the per-unit cost of a product if 800 units are produced at the Baltimore Manufacturing Company is

$$\$22 + \frac{\$4{,}800}{800} = \$28,$$

whereas the per-unit cost if 1,000 units are produced is

$$\$22 + \frac{\$4{,}800}{1{,}000} = \$26.80.$$

In the former case,

$$P = \$2.50 + \$28$$

$$= \$30.50,$$

whereas in the latter case,

$$P = \$2.50 + \$26.80$$

$$= \$29.30.$$

If management were to price in this manner, it could be dropping prices when demand was stronger and raising them when it was weaker.

Moral: If prices are based on per-unit costs, and per-unit costs are related to

Exhibit 8.3
BALTIMORE MANUFACTURING COMPANY
Differential Analysis of a Special Order

	Alternative	−	Status Quo	=	Difference
Revenue	$26,500[a]	−	$24,000	=	$2,500
Less Variable Costs	(19,800)[b]	−	(17,600)	=	(2,200)
Total Contribution	$ 6,700	−	$ 6,400	=	$ 300
Less Fixed Costs	(4,800)	−	(4,800)	=	—
Operating Profit	$ 1,900	−	$ 1,600	=	$ 300

[a]$26,500 = $24,000 + ($25 × 100 units).
[b]$19,800 = $17,600 + ($22 × 100 units).

volume, and volume is related to prices, then prices are highest when volume is lowest and vice versa.

Third, the "costs" attributable to a particular product may be affected by several questionable accounting practices and conventions. For example, the cost of using plant and machinery is usually based on the acquisition cost of these assets. No recognition is given to the opportunity cost of using the plant and machinery in manufacturing the product. Also, the portion of the acquisition cost of these assets attributable, or allocated, to each period is affected by the depreciable life and depreciation method used. The allocation of various costs to specific products becomes particularly questionable as the cost items become more and more indirect with respect to the product. Consider, for example, the allocation of the president's salary to each of a firm's products. Accounting practices such as these raise questions about the validity of product "cost" amounts.

Fourth, cost-based pricing can lead to incorrect decisions, particularly in the short run. For example, assume that the Baltimore Manufacturing Company has received a special order for 100 units for $25 per unit. This order will have no effect on the firm's regular market, and the order can be filled with existing capacity. If a cost-based approach to pricing were used, this special order would probably be rejected because the $25 price is less than the $28 per-unit full cost ($28 = $22 + $4,800/800). An argument could be made that the fixed costs should be spread over 900 units. That would give a per-unit full cost of $22 + $4,800/900 = $27.33, which is still higher than the special-order offer price. As Exhibit 8.3 demonstrates, rejection of this order is incorrect. Applying the differential approach to pricing results in the correct decision.

Differential Approach to Pricing

The differential approach to pricing presumes that the price must at least be equal to the *differential* cost of producing and selling the product. In the short run, this will result in a positive contribution to the coverage of fixed costs, and generation of profit. In the long run, this will require the coverage of all costs, because both fixed and variable costs become differential costs in the long run.

The differential approach is particularly useful in special-order decisions. Consider the special order discussed above. Exhibit 8.3 presents an analysis of the effects of not accepting and of accepting the special order, assuming that the regular market consists of 800 units sold at a price of $30 a unit. Exhibit 8.3 demonstrates that the special order at $25 per unit should be accepted, because that price permits the firm to cover the differential costs of $22 per unit and provide a contribution of $3 per unit toward coverage of fixed costs and profit. (A shortcut is to compute the per-unit contribution margin on the special order, $3, and multiply it by the number of units, 100. This gives the additional total contribution from the special order, $300.)

The differential approach to pricing works well for special orders but has been criticized for pricing a firm's regular products. It is suggested that following the differential approach in the short run (that is, setting prices equal to variable cost) will lead to underpricing in the long run, because there will be inadequate contribution to covering fixed costs or generating profits.

There are two responses to this criticism. First, the differential approach does lead to correct short-run pricing decisions. Once plant capacity has been set and fixed costs have been incurred, the fixed costs become irrelevant to the short-run pricing decision. The firm must attempt to set a price at least equal to the differential, or variable, costs. Second, in both the short and long run, the differential approach provides only an indicator of the *minimum* acceptable price. The actual price charged will be some higher amount, taking market demand, competitor's actions, and similar factors into consideration.

Consider the data for the Baltimore Manufacturing Company in Exhibit 8.4. The minimum acceptable price in the short run is the differential cost of $22 per unit. In the long run, the minimum acceptable price is $28 per unit, because both variable and fixed costs must be covered. A more desirable long-run price is $30, which includes a profit. Between the $22 short-run minimum price and the (say) $30 long-run desired price lies the range of price flexibility for the firm. A price slightly higher than the variable cost might be set for a special order as long as there is excess capacity and the firm's regular market will not be affected.

If extensive market competition exists for the firm's regular product, a price slightly higher than the $22 minimum might be set. The firm hopes to underprice competitors and to capture a larger share of the market. The increase in quantity sold may more than offset the reduction in the contribution margin per unit from a lower selling price, resulting in a larger *total* contribution margin.[2]

Exhibit 8.4
BALTIMORE MANUFACTURING COMPANY
Data for Pricing

Short-Run Differential Costs (variable costs)	$22	= Short-Run Minimum Price
Fixed.	6[a]	
Long-Run Incremental Costs	$28	= Long-Run Minimum Price
Expected Profits.	2	
Target Selling Price	$30	= Long-Run Desired Price

[a]$6 = $4,800/800. This assumes a long-run volume of 800 units.

[2]This assumes an elastic demand curve such that the negative effects on total contribution margin of percentage decreases in the contribution margin per unit are more than offset by the positive effects of percentage increases in quantity.

If a firm is the only supplier of this product, it will be in a position to charge a price much higher than $28. In this case, however, the earning of high profits may induce other firms to manufacture the product, thereby reducing the initial firm's market share. Thus, the pricing decision should include an analysis of short-run and long-run differential costs, market conditions, and competitors' actions.

Make-or-Buy Decisions

Any decision in which a firm decides whether to meet its needs internally or to acquire goods or services from external sources is a "make-or-buy" decision. A restaurant that serves its meals from frozen entrees "buys," whereas one that uses fresh ingredients "makes." A steel company that mines its own iron ore and coal and processes it through to final product "makes" the pig iron, whereas one that purchases these raw materials "buys." Housing contractors who do their own site preparation and foundation work "make," whereas those who hire subcontractors "buy."

The advantages and disadvantages of relying on outsiders include both cost comparisons and factors not easily quantified, such as dependability of suppliers and quality control of purchased materials. These decisions sometimes appear to be simple one-time choices between making or buying, but usually they are part of a firm's strategy to become more or less self-reliant.

Example The Baltimore Manufacturing Company has an opportunity to buy part of its product for $12 per unit. This would have the following effect on prices, volume, and costs:

	Alternative: Buy	Status Quo: Make
Unit Selling Price	$30	$30
Volume	800 per Month	800 per Month
Unit Variable Manufacturing Costs	$6	$17
Purchased Parts, per Unit	$12	$0
Unit Variable Marketing and Administrative Costs . .	$5	$5
Fixed Manufacturing Costs	$2,100	$3,060
Fixed Marketing and Administrative Costs	$1,740	$1,740

As shown in Exhibit 8.5, the alternative to buy is more profitable.

Adding and Dropping Parts of Operations

Managers must decide when to add or drop products from the product line and when to open or abandon sales territories. These can be either long-run decisions involving a change in capacity or short-run decisions in which capacity does not change. This chapter deals with these as short-run decisions.

Exhibit 8.5
BALTIMORE MANUFACTURING COMPANY
Differential Analysis of Make-or-Buy Decision

	Alternative: Buy	_	Status Quo: Make	=	Difference
Revenue	$24,000	–	$24,000	=	—
Less:					
Variable Costs to Produce and Sell	(8,800)ᵃ	–	(17,600)	=	$ – (8,800)
Variable Costs of Goods Bought	(9,600)ᵇ	–	—	=	(9,600)
Total Contribution Margin	$ 5,600	–	$ 6,400	=	$ – 800
Less Fixed Costs	(3,840)ᶜ	–	(4,800)	=	– (960)
Operating Profit	$ 1,760	–	$ 1,600	=	$ + 160

ᵃ$8,800 = ($6 + $5) × 800 units.
ᵇ$9,600 = $12 × 800 units.
ᶜ$3,840 = $2,100 + $1,740.

The differential principle implies the following analysis. If the differential revenue from the sale of a product is greater than the differential costs required to provide the sales, then the product generates profits and should be continued. This is the correct decision even though the product may show a loss in financial statements because of the allocation of overhead costs to it. If the product more than covers its differential costs, and if no other alternative use of the production and sales facilities exists, then the product should be retained.

Example Suppose that the Baltimore Manufacturing Company had three products, instead of only one as in the previous examples, and used common facilities to produce and sell all three products. Each product is independent of, and has no effect on sales of, the others. The relevant data for these three products are as follows:

	Product			
	A	B	C	Total
Sales Volume per Month	800	1,000	600	—
Unit Sale Price	$30	$20	$40	—
Sales Revenue	$24,000	$20,000	$24,000	$68,000
Unit Variable Cost	$22	$14	$35	—
Fixed Cost per Month	—	—	—	$13,600

Management has asked the accounting department to allocate fixed costs to each product so "We can evaluate how well each product is doing." Total fixed costs were 20 percent of total dollar sales, so fixed costs were charged to each product at 20 percent of the product's sales. For example, Product C was charged for $4,800 (= .20 × $24,000 sales) of fixed costs.

The product-line income statements are shown in the top panel of Exhibit 8.6. As shown, a "loss" of $1,800 was reported for Product C. One of Baltimore's managers argued: "We should drop Product C. It is losing $1,800 per month." A

Exhibit 8.6
BALTIMORE MANUFACTURING COMPANY
Differential Analysis of Dropping a Product

Income Statement Analysis

	Product			
	A	B	C	Total
Sales	$24,000	$20,000	$24,000	$68,000
Less Variable Costs	(17,600)	(14,000)	(21,000)	(52,600)
Total Contribution Margin	$ 6,400	$ 6,000	$ 3,000	$15,400
Less Fixed Costs Allocated to Each Product	(4,800)[a]	(4,000)[a]	(4,800)[a]	(13,600)
Operating Profit (Loss)	$ 1,600	$ 2,000	$ (1,800)	$ 1,800

[a]Allocations of the $13,600 of fixed costs made in proportion to sales: 20 percent of sales dollars charged to each product as fixed costs.

Differential Analysis

	Alternative: Drop Product C	−	Status Quo	=	Difference
Sales	$44,000	−	$68,000	=	$−24,000
Less Variable Costs	(31,600)	−	(52,600)	=	−(21,000)
Total Contribution Margin	$12,400	−	$15,400	=	$ −3,000
Less Fixed Costs	(13,600)	−	(13,600)	=	—
Operating Profit (Loss)	$ (1,200)	−	$ 1,800	=	$ −3,000

second manager suggested they perform a differential analysis to see which costs would be saved and which revenues would be lost if the Product C were dropped. As shown in the bottom panel of Exhibit 8.6, differential analysis indicated that the company would be less profitable if it dropped Product C.

The first manager was incorrect in assuming that fixed costs would be saved by dropping the product, because all products use common facilities. The firm might want to investigate more profitable uses of the facilities used in producing and selling Product C, because its contribution margin appears to be the weakest of the three products. Until such alternatives emerge, it pays to continue producing and selling Product C.

Product Choice Decisions

"Which products should we sell?" is a question frequently faced by managers. Most firms have a number of options about the goods and services they can supply to the market, but there are also limitations on what can be done. A small CPA firm may have to choose between performing work for Client A or for Client B because of a shortage of personnel. Students have to choose how to allocate their study time between accounting and finance, or their time between Question 1 and Question 2 on a final exam. An automobile manufacturer with limited production facilities must decide whether to produce subcompacts, compacts, or some other model.

We normally think of these product-choice problems as short-run decisions. The automobile manufacturer may be able to produce both subcompacts and compacts in the *long-run* by increasing capacity. The CPA firm could serve both Client A and Client B in the *long run* by hiring more professional staff. With enough time, students can study for *both* accounting and finance. In the short-run, however, capacity limitations require choices among such options.

Example The Baltimore Manufacturing Company has just purchased one machine that can make Products L, M, and N. The market for these products is such that all of them, or any combination, can be sold in the market. Management wants to pick the most profitable product, or combination of products, to produce. Only 400 hours of time is available on the machine each month.

The time requirements for each of the three products, their selling prices, and their variable costs appear in Exhibit 8.7. For this example, assume that all marketing and administrative costs are fixed. Also assume that fixed manufacturing, marketing, and administrative costs are the same (that is, not differential) whichever product or combination of products is produced.

Even though Product N has a per-unit contribution of $10.00, whereas Product L has a per-unit contribution of only $2.00, Product L is still the best product to produce given the capacity constraint on the machine. Product L contributes $4.00 per hour (= $2.00 per unit ÷ .5 hour per unit) of time on the machine, whereas Product N contributes only $2.50 per hour ($10.00 per unit ÷ 4 hours per unit) of time on the machine. Differential analysis indicates that the total contribution

Exhibit 8.7
Rationing Scarce Capacity
(Machine Is Available only 400 Hours per Month)

	Product		
	L	**M**	**N**
Time Required on the Machine per Unit Produced	0.5 Hour	2.0 Hours	4.0 Hours
Selling Price per Unit	$5.00	$12.00	$16.00
Less Variable Costs to Produce One Unit	(3.00)	(5.00)	(6.00)
Contribution Margin per Unit . .	$2.00	$ 7.00	$10.00
Contribution Margin per Hour on the Machine (contribution margin per unit ÷ time requirement in hours)	$4.00 per Hour[a]	$3.50 per Hour[b]	$2.50 per Hour[c]
Total Contribution from Using 400 Hours on the Machine . .	$1,600	$1,400	$1,000

[a]$4.00 per hour = $2.00 ÷ 0.5 hour.
[b]$3.50 per hour = $7.00 ÷ 2.0 hours.
[c]$2.50 per hour = $10.00 ÷ 4.0 hours.

margin from using the machine to produce Product L is $1,600, whereas the contribution from producing Product M is $1,400, and that from producing Product N is $1,000.

If there were no limitations on the amount of machine time available, the Baltimore Manufacturing Company should produce and sell all three products in the short run because all have a positive contribution margin. But with time limits, the most profitable product is *the one that contributes the most per unit of time.* As a general rule, the optimal use of a scarce resource is the use that contributes the most per unit of resource consumed. (If you face time constraints on an examination and must choose between Question 1 and Question 2, and if working on Question 1 provides 1 point per minute and Question 2 provides 2 points per minute, then you should work on Question 2.)

When there is only one scarce resource, as in this example where the scarce resource is time on the machine, the decision is easy to make: Choose the product that gives the largest contribution per unit of the scarce resource used. When there are several scarce resources and each product uses different proportions of each of them, the computational problem becomes more difficult. Appendix A to this chapter describes *linear programming,* which is a mathematical tool for solving such constrained decision problems. Textbooks on operations research and quantitative methods describe these techniques in more detail.

Incorrect Use of Accounting Data Many accounting systems routinely provide unit cost information that includes an *allocation* of fixed costs to each unit. This is the *full absorption* method of product costing, whereas we have assumed the variable costing method so far in this chapter. Use of the full absorption unit costs for short-run decision making is not correct, as demonstrated by the following example.

Example We have seen that production of Product L is optimal because its total monthly contribution is the highest of the three products. (Refer to Exhibit 8.7.) Suppose that fixed manufacturing costs were charged to each product at a rate of 100 percent of direct labor costs, using the *full absorption, normal costing* method described in Chapter 3.[3] The unit cost for each product under full absorption,

---

[3]The full absorption costing system derives unit costs by adding an allocation of fixed manufacturing costs to variable costs. Thus, the two methods calculate different unit margins as shown below:

Variable Costing:

$$\text{Selling Price per Unit} - \text{Variable Manufacturing Cost per Unit} = \text{Contribution Margin per Unit}.$$

Full Absorption Costing

$$\text{Selling Price per Unit} - \left(\text{Variable Manufacturing Cost per Unit} + \text{Allocation of Fixed Manufacturing Cost to Each Unit} \right) = \text{Gross Margin per Unit}.$$

Under *normal* costing, the allocation of fixed manufacturing cost is made with a predetermined "normal" rate. Any differences between actual fixed manufacturing costs and the amount charged to units produced is assumed to be written off as a period cost.

Exhibit 8.8
Rationing Scarce Capacity by Incorrectly Using Full Absorption Unit Costs

		Product	
	L	**M**	**N**
(1) Time Required on the Machine per Unit Produced . .	0.5 Hour	2.0 Hours	4.0 Hours
(2) Selling Price per Unit.	$5.00	$12.00	$16.00
Variable Costs to Produce One Unit:			
(3) Direct Materials	$1.00	$2.00	$2.50
(4) Direct Labor	1.50	2.00	2.50
(5) Variable Manufacturing Overhead	.50	1.00	1.00
(6) Total Variable Costs per Unit .	$3.00	$5.00	$6.00
(7) Allocation of Fixed Costs at 100 Percent of Direct Labor . .	1.50	2.00	2.50
(8) Full Absorption Cost per Unit .	$4.50	$7.00	$8.50
(9) Gross Margin per Unit [line **(2)** minus line **(8)**].	$ .50	$5.00	$7.50
(10) Gross Margin per Hour . . .	$1.00 per Hour	$2.50 per Hour	$1.875 per Hour

normal costing is shown on line **(8)** of Exhibit 8.8. Users of the accounting data would typically see only the unit costs shown on line **(8)** of Exhibit 8.8, so the margin-per-hour calculation would use the *gross* margin (that is, selling price minus full absorption unit cost) instead of contribution margin. As shown on line **(10)** of Exhibit 8.8, use of full absorption cost may lead to an incorrect assessment that Product M is most profitable and Product L is least profitable per machine hour.

The above is one example of how use of accounting data intended for one purpose may not be as useful for other purposes. Full absorption unit cost data are intended primarily for external reporting. Most managerial decision models assume that *variable* unit costs are used. Unsophisticated users of accounting data often incorrectly assume that any calculated unit cost is a variable cost.

We have used a manufacturing example to demonstrate this point about incorrectly assuming unit costs calculated by accounting systems to be variable costs. The problem is much more general than this setting, however. You should not *assume* that the unit cost reported by an accounting system in any organization is a variable cost.

Inventory Management Decisions

Inventory management is important in merchandising, manufacturing, and other organizations that have inventories. One of the reasons claimed for the success of Japanese business in recent years has been their ability to manage inventory such that inventory levels are very low.[4] American manufacturers have also made dramatic reductions in inventory levels. Firestone Tire and Rubber Company, finding

---

[4]See Robert H. Hayes, "Why Japanese Factories Work," *Harvard Business Review* (July–August 1981).

that it had $300,000,000 in excess inventory, overhauled its inventory system.[5] If inventory carrying costs were 20 percent of the inventory value, then Firestone could save $60 million per year by reducing excess inventory. A Buick plant was able to reduce its inventory of a part by 80 percent by changing delivery times from alternate-day rail deliveries to three times-daily truck deliveries.[6]

Key inventory management questions include:

1. How many units of inventory should be on hand and available for use or sale?
2. What is the optimal number of times a particular item should be ordered during a period of time? What is the optimal size of the order?

The Inventory Management Problem

Inventory management decisions involve two types of opposing costs. There are differential costs incurred each time an order is placed or a production run is made (for example, the cost of processing each purchase order or the cost of preparing machinery for each production run). These "setup" or "order" costs could be minimized by minimizing the number of orders or production runs.

By ordering or producing less frequently, however, each order or production run must be for a larger number of units. The firm must carry a larger inventory so that sufficient inventory will be on hand between orders or production runs. Larger inventories imply larger costs of carrying these inventories, or "carrying" costs (for example, the cost of maintaining warehouse facilities).

The inventory management problem is to find the optimal trade-off between these two types of opposing costs, carrying costs and setup costs, as shown in Exhibit 8.9. (We refer to both order costs and setup costs as "order costs" for the rest of our discussion.) The problem translates into a question of calculating the optimal number of orders or production runs each year and the optimal number of units to be ordered or produced. The optimal number of units ordered or produced is known as the *economic order* quantity.

Example California Merchandising sells 6,000 units of a product per year, spread evenly throughout the year. Each unit costs $1 to purchase. The differential cost of preparing and following up on an order is $100 per order. The cost of carrying a unit in inventory is 30 percent of the unit's cost. Thus, if one order is placed for the year, 6,000 units would be purchased, and the company would have, *on average,* 3,000 units ($3,000) in inventory during the year. The carrying cost would be $900 (= $3,000 × .30) for the year. Exhibit 8.10 presents the inventory carrying costs, order costs, and total costs of the inventory. Note the trade-off between carrying costs and order costs: As one decreases, the other increases. The optimal number of orders per year is three, which has the lowest total costs [see column (6) in Exhibit 8.10].

[5]*The Wall Street Journal,* August 15, 1980, p. 15.
[6]Reported in Robert S. Kaplan, "Measuring Manufacturing Performance: A New Challenge for Management Accounting Research," *The Accounting Review* (October 1983).

Exhibit 8.9
Inventory Costs

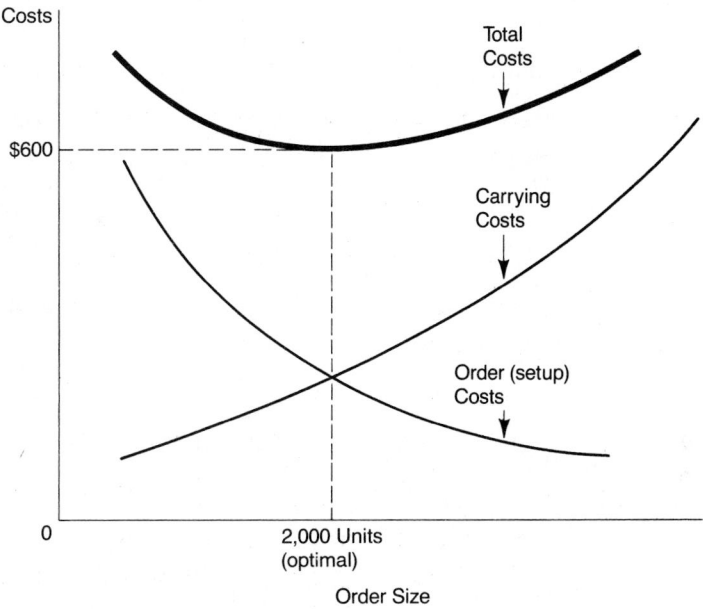

Exhibit 8.10
CALIFORNIA MERCHANDISING
Economic Order Quantity Calculation

Differential Costs per Order Are $100.
Annual Requirement Is 6,000 Units.
Inventory Carrying Costs Are at 30 Percent per Year.
Purchase Cost per Unit Is $1.00.

Orders (1)	Order Size[a] (2)	Average Number of Units in Inventory[b] (3)	Inventory Carrying Costs[c] (4)	Order Costs[d] (5)	Total Costs[e] (6)
1	6,000	3,000	$900	$ 100	$1,000
2	3,000	1,500	450	200	650
3	2,000	1,000	300	300	600[f]
4	1,500	750	225	400	625
5	1,200	600	180	500	680
6	1,000	500	150	600	750
12	500	250	75	1,200	1,275

[a]6,000 units ÷ number of orders from column (1).
[b]Number of units in an order from column (2) ÷ 2.
[c]Amount in column (3) × $1 cost per unit × .30.
[d]$100 × number of orders from column (1).
[e]Amount in column (4) + amount in column (5).
[f]Lowest total cost.

A formal model for deriving the optimal number of orders (or setups of production runs) and the optimal number of items in an order (or production run) appears in Appendix B to this chapter.

Estimating Inventory Costs

Managers, industrial engineers, analysts, and others who attempt to derive optimal solutions to inventory management problems typically use costs provided by the accounting system. An important but difficult task for management accountants is to estimate inventory order (or setup) costs and carrying costs. Keep in mind that only *differential* costs are relevant. For example, suppose that one purchasing agent is used whether there is one order or 12 orders per year, and the agent's salary is not affected by the number of orders made. Assume that there is no opportunity cost of the agent's time. Then the agent's salary would not be differential, and it would not be part of the order costs.

Order (Setup) Costs To estimate differential order (setup) costs, consider whether any salaries or wages differ because of the number of orders (or setups) and whether there are opportunity costs of lost time. Production setups, in particular, usually result in lost time for production employees. Order costs should include differential costs of receiving and inspecting orders, of processing invoices from suppliers, and freight costs. It is important to ascertain the amount by which costs will differ if the number of orders per period differs. If freight costs are a constant amount (say, $.10) per unit, they would not be differential to the number of orders placed. If freight is charged per *shipment*, however (say, $50 per shipment), they would be differential.

Carrying Costs Differential carrying costs include insurance, inventory taxes, the opportunity cost of funds invested in inventory, and other costs that differ with the number of units held in inventory. If additional wages are paid or additional warehouse space is leased because of an increase in inventory quantity, then these costs would be differential carrying costs. Carrying costs should not include an allocated portion of warehouse depreciation or rent if these costs are fixed regardless of the number of units in inventory. In this case, the depreciation and rent do not represent *differential* carrying costs.

Example Consider the following data obtained from the records of EOQ Incorporated:

Orders Handled per Year on Average	40 Orders
Average Order Size	1,000 Units
Total Units Purchased per Year	40,000 Units
Purchase Price of Merchandise	$12.00 per Unit
Freight-in	$.50 per Unit
Costs to Place an Order:	
Fixed Cost (per year)	$2,000
Variable Cost (per order)	$11.00

Cost to Unload a Shipment (fixed labor costs of $4,000 per
  year ÷ 40 shipments per year + variable costs of $30
  per shipment) . . . . $130 per Shipment
Inventory Taxes . . . . 10 Percent of Inventory Value
Salary of Supervisor . . . . $18,000 per Year
Insurance on Inventory . . . . 4 Percent of Inventory Value
Warehouse Rental (fixed rental of $2,000 per year; average
  inventory level is 500 units) . . . . $4.00 per Unit
Costs to Inspect and Count Inventory . . . . $1.10 per Unit
Cost of Capital . . . . 20 Percent

    In the past, the company had an average of 40 orders per year and an average inventory level of 500 units. Management is not convinced that those figures are optimal. Which costs should be included in computing the optimal order size computation?

    Differential carrying costs per unit include the following:

(1) Inventory Taxes: 10 percent × $12.50 (Inventory value is
  assumed to include freight-in) . . . . $ 1.25 per Unit
(2) Inventory Insurance: 4 Percent × $12.50 . . . . .50 per Unit
(3) Costs to Inspect and Count Inventory . . . . 1.10 per Unit
(4) Cost of Capital: 20 Percent × $12.50 . . . . 2.50 per Unit
    Total per Unit . . . . $ 5.35

    Percentage Carrying Cost . . . . $\dfrac{\$\,5.35}{\$12.50}$ = 42.8 Percent

    Note that the purchase price and freight-in are not differential, because the total number of units purchased for a year is not affected by the number of orders placed or the average level of inventory. Warehouse rental is a fixed cost, even though it is expressed as a unit cost. EOQ Incorporated's carrying cost per year would be $2,675 (= 500 × $5.35), excluding fixed costs.

    Differential order costs include the following:

(1) Cost of Placing an Order (variable portion only) $11.00
(2) Cost of Unloading (variable portion only) 30.00
    Total per Order $41.00

    The salary of the supervisor is fixed, and the fixed portions of ordering costs and unloading costs are excluded. EOQ Incorporated's order cost per year would be $1,640 (= 40 × $41).

    The optimal order size turns out to be 784 (rounded) units per order, giving an average inventory level of 392 units. The optimal number of orders per year is 51 (= 40,000 units per year ÷ 784 units per order). (All numbers rounded to nearest whole number.) We derived these amounts using an economic order quantity model as described in Appendix B to this chapter. Problem 3 for Self-Study at the end of this chapter computes the minimum total cost using the format shown in Exhibit 8.10. As shown in Exhibit 8.11, the company could save $127 per year with the proposed order size and inventory level.

Exhibit 8.11
Differential Cost Analysis for Inventory Management

	Alternative	−	Status Quo	= Difference
Differential Carrying Costs	$2,097 (= $5.35 × 392 units)		$2,675 (= $5.35 × 500 units)	$ − 578
Differential Order Costs	2,091 (= $41 × 51 orders)		1,640 (= $41 × 40 orders)	451
Total Differential Costs. . . .	$4,188		$4,315	$ − 127
Nondifferential Costs:				
Fixed Cost of Placing an Order .	2,000		2,000	−0−
Fixed Cost to Unload a Shipment	4,000		4,000	−0−
Fixed Salary of Supervisor	18,000		18,000	−0−
Fixed Warehouse Rental. . . .	2,000		2,000	−0−
Total Costs.	$30,188		$30,315	$ − 127

Costs of Not Carrying Sufficient Inventory

In addition to the two types of costs just discussed—order costs and carrying costs—there is a third category of costs: costs of not carrying sufficient inventory. These costs include production shutdowns or customer ill will if inventory is not available for production or sale, and added freight and handling charges to expedite special handling. In a conceptual sense, managing inventory levels takes this third category of cost into account.

Safety stocks are buffers against running out of inventory. Our EOQ Incorporated example assumed that the optimal pattern of ordering and inventory depletion was as follows:

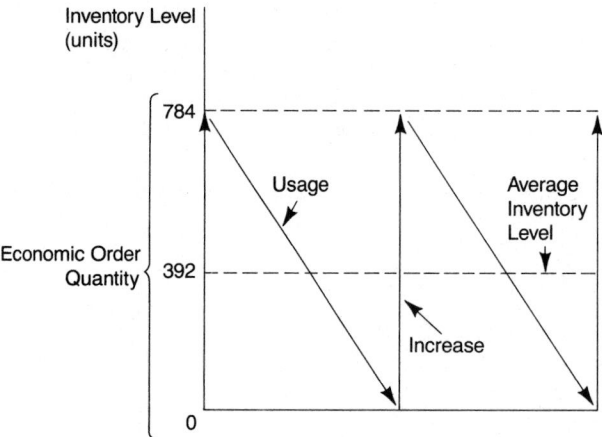

The inventory is assumed to be replenished just as inventory levels reach zero. Many events could result in a stock-out—a delivery truck could be delayed, for example. Hence, production or sales might have to be halted to await the delivery of inventory. To prevent this stock-out, management will provide a *safety stock,* as shown on top of the next page for EOQ Incorporated:

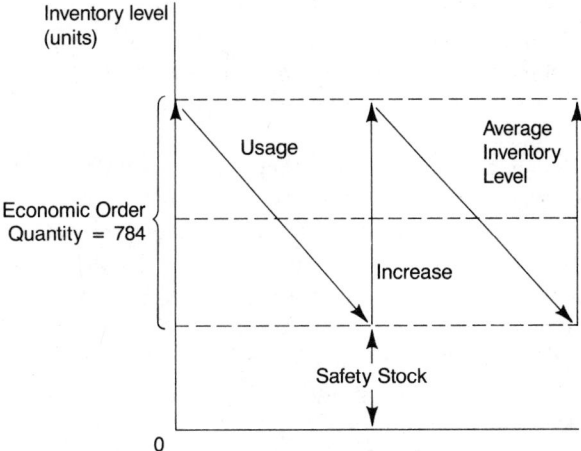

What is the optimal level of safety stock? This depends on the trade-off between stock-out costs and holding costs. The higher the stock-out costs, the higher the safety stock, whereas the higher the holding costs, the lower the safety stock.

Summary

The most important concept in this chapter is *differential analysis;* that is, ascertaining *what* would differ and by *how much* if an alternative action is taken instead of the status quo. Differential analysis is performed by comparing alternatives to the status quo, or present situation, as follows:

	Alternative	−	Status Quo	=	Difference
Revenue	$P_1 X_1$	−	$P_0 X_0$	=	ΔPX
Less Variable Costs	$V_1 X_1$	−	$V_0 X_0$	=	ΔVX
Total Contribution Margin	$(P_1 - V_1)X_1$	−	$(P_0 - V_0)X_0$	=	$\Delta(P - V)X$
Less Fixed Costs	F_1	−	F_0	=	ΔF
Operating Profit	π_1	−	π_0	=	$\Delta \pi$

where the terms are the same as defined earlier in the chapter.

We have applied differential analysis to several short-run operating decisions, and we have focused on identifying and measuring *differential costs*.

Identifying relevant costs is an important part of decision making. These are costs that will be different because of an action. Costs that do not differ are not relevant for ascertaining the financial consequences of a contemplated action.

Differential costs are usually made up of differential cash flows. Two noncash differential costs that, though difficult to measure, should not be ignored are *opportunity costs* and *economic depreciation* that differ because of an action.

Opportunity costs, that is, the benefits from foregone alternatives, are not recorded in the accounting records. Thus, they are easily overlooked in differential analysis. Economic depreciation is the change in economic value of an asset because of its use. Economic depreciation usually differs from the depreciation recorded in the accounting records.

Pricing decisions are sometimes based on costs as well as market factors. There are special cost-based contracts, such as those between government agencies and defense contractors. And for any organization, prices must at least cover differential costs if the organization is to maximize its profit position. In the short run, this practice will result in a positive contribution toward covering fixed costs and generating a profit. In the long run, this practice will cover all costs, because both fixed and variable costs become differential in the long run.

In addition to pricing, differential analysis is commonly applied to decisions to accept special orders, make-or-buy decisions, and decisions to add products or close parts of operations. The relevant costs for these decisions are rarely provided in routine accounting reports; special analysis of cost behavior is nearly always necessary. Choice of the optimal product mix when there are capacity limitations requires not only estimating differential cost (that is, variable cost) per unit, but also differential cost per unit of scarce resource consumed by each product. Inventory management decisions require an estimate of differential order or production setup costs and differential inventory carrying costs. In general, these are opposing costs, as shown below. Assume a constant demand for the products.

Number of Orders (Setups)	Order (Setup) Costs	Level of Inventory and Inventory Carrying Costs
Increases ⟶	Increase ⟶	Decrease
Decreases ⟶	Decrease ⟶	Increase

Part of the inventory management problem is to find the optimal trade-off between number of orders (production runs) and the level of inventory so that total costs are minimized.

Appendix A: Linear Programming

Most decisions made by managers are subject to such constraints as factory capacity, personnel time, floor space, and so forth. If there is enough time before a decision has to be implemented, constraints can be avoided by increasing capacity. In the *short run*, however, decision makers are faced with a constrained amount of resources available to them. *Linear programming* solves problems of this type. We refer to it as a *constrained optimization* technique because it solves for the optimal use of scarce (that is, constrained) resources.

Two simple examples demonstrate how linear programming works. We solve these using graphs and simple algebra. More complex problems can be solved using a systematic procedure called the *simplex method,* described in textbooks on operations research and quantitative methods. Most linear programming problems are solved with computer programs that use the simplex method, or variations of it.

Profit Maximization

Example Moline Company produces two products, Product 1 and Product 2. The contribution margins per unit of the two products are as follows:

Product	Contribution Margin Per Unit
1	$3
2	$4

Fixed costs are the same regardless of the combination of 1 and 2 produced; therefore, the objective is to maximize the total contribution per period of these two products.

Both products have a positive contribution. If there were no constraints, Moline Company should make (and sell) both products and our problem would be solved. When there are constrained resources (for example, machine time), but Product 1 and Product 2 each consume the same amount of the scarce resource (say, 1 hour of machine time) per unit of each product, the solution is to produce and sell only the highest-contribution item, Product 2, all else being equal. Products usually do not consume equal amounts of scarce resources, however. So the problem is to find the optimal mix of products considering how much scarce resource each product consumes.

Moline Company uses two scarce resources to make the two products: labor time and machine time. There are 24 hours of labor time and 20 hours of machine time available each day. The amount of time required to make each product is as follows:

	Product	
	1	2
Labor Time	1 Hour per Unit	2 Hours per Unit
Machine Time . . . . :	1 Hour per Unit	1 Hour per Unit

This problem is formulated as follows (X_1 and X_2 refer to the quantity of Products 1 and 2 produced and sold):

(1) Maximize: $\$3X_1 + \$4X_2$

(2) Subject to: $X_1 + 2X_2 \leq 24$ Labor Hours

(3) $X_1 + X_2 \leq 20$ Machine Hours.

The first line, the *objective function,* states that the objective is to maximize total contribution where each unit of Product 1 contributes $3 and each unit of Product 2 contributes $4. Line **(2)** is the labor time constraint, which states that each unit of Product 1 requires 1 labor hour and each unit of Product 2 requires 2 labor hours. Total labor hours cannot exceed 24 per period (that is, one day). Line **(3)** is the machine time constraint, which states that Product 1 and Product 2 each use 1 machine hour per unit, and total machine hours cannot exceed 20.

Exhibit 8.12 graphs the constraints. The shaded area is the feasible production; production does not use up more scarce resources than are available. The lowercase letters show the "corner points." We find the optimal solution by deriving the total contribution margin at each point, using the following steps.

Exhibit 8.12
Linear Programming, Graphic Solution
Comparison of Corner and Noncorner Points

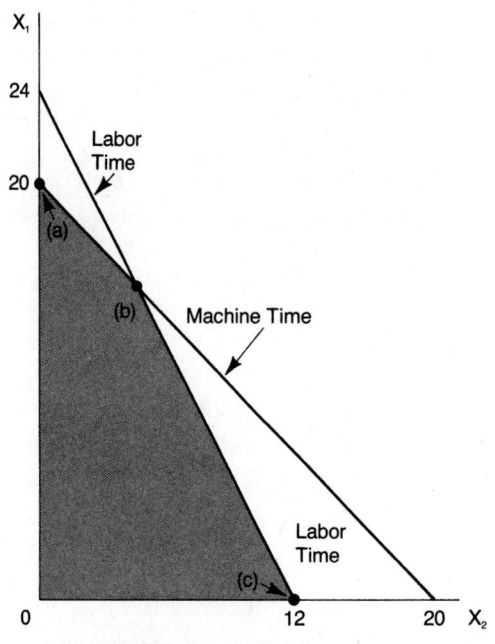

Step 1. Find the production of Product 1 and Product 2 at each point. Points (a) and (c) are straightforward. At (a), $X_1 = 20$ and $X_2 = 0$; at (c), $X_2 = 12$ and $X_1 = 0$. Point (b) requires solving for two unknowns using the two constraint formulas:

$$\text{Labor Time:} \qquad X_1 = 24 - 2X_2$$

$$\text{Machine Time:} \qquad X_1 = 20 - X_2.$$

Setting these two equations equal, we have

$$X_1 = 24 - 2X_2$$

$$X_1 = 20 - X_2,$$

so

$$24 - 2X_2 = 20 - X_2$$

$$4 = X_2.$$

If $X_2 = 4$, then

$$X_1 = 20 - X_2$$

$$= 20 - 4$$

$$= 16.$$

At point (b), therefore, 16 units of Product 1 and 4 units of Product 2 are produced.

Step 2. Find the total contribution margin at each point. (Recall that the unit contribution margins of Products 1 and 2 are $3 and $4.) The solution is shown in Exhibit 8.13.

Exhibit 8.13
Optimal Product Mix

	Production		Contribution		
Point	X_1	X_2	1	2	Total
(a)	20	0	$60	$ 0	$60
(b)	16	4	$48	$16	$64
(c)	0	12	$ 0	$48	$48

It is optimal to produce at point (b), where $X_1 = 16$ and $X_2 = 4$.

Why must the optimal solution be at a corner? If production moves away from the corner at point (b) in any feasible direction, total contribution will be lower. Exhibit 8.14 shows a movement away from (b) in four feasible directions. Exhibit 8.15 compares contributions at those noncorner points with the contribution at corner point (b). These examples are intended to show intuitively that the contribution margin is lower away from the corner point, but our assertion that the optimal solution always lies on a corner point can be proved mathematically.[7]

Cost Minimization

Example In our last example, we found the product mix that maximized total contribution, and therefore maximized profits. In this example, the objective is to

---

[7]Sometimes multiple corners have equal total contributions. Any point on a straight line joining these corners has a total contribution equal to the total contribution at the adjoining corners.

Exhibit 8.14
Linear Programming, Graphic Solution
Comparison of Corner and Noncorner Points

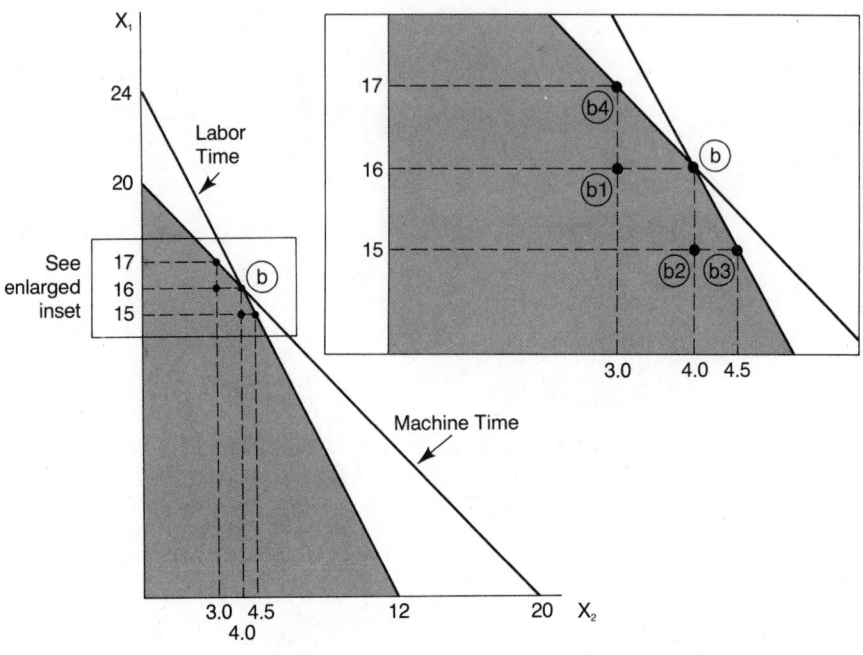

Exhibit 8.15
Comparison of Corner Point with Noncorner Points

| Point | Production | | Contribution | | |
	X_1	X_2	1	2	Total
(b)	16	4	$48	$16	$64
(b1)	16	3	$48	$12	$60
(b2)	15	4	$45	$16	$61
(b3)[a]	15	4.5	$45	$18	$63
(b4)[b]	17	3	$51	$12	$63

[a]Let $X_1 = 15$ and find X_2 as follows:

$$X_1 = 24 - 2X_2$$
$$15 = 24 - 2X_2$$
$$2X_2 = 9$$
$$X_2 = 4.5.$$

[b]Let $X_2 = 3$ and find X_1 as follows:

$$X_1 = 20 - X_2$$
$$= 20 - 3$$
$$= 17.$$

minimize costs. Two raw materials, A and B, are used to make one product. The cost of each raw material is

A . . . . $4 per Pound
B . . . . $3 per Pound

The constraints are that at least 5 pounds of A must be used, and at least 10 pounds of A plus B must be used. The problem would be formulated as follows:

$$\text{Minimize:} \quad \$4X_A + \$3X_B$$

$$\text{Subject to:} \quad X_A \quad\quad \geq 5$$

$$X_A + X_B \geq 10.$$

The objective is to find the combination of X_A and X_B that minimizes the cost of producing a unit of output. As shown in Exhibit 8.16, the optimal (that is, least costly) use of raw materials is 5 units of A and 5 units of B.

Exhibit 8.16
Minimization Problem

Point	Raw Material		Cost		
	X_A	X_B	A	B	Total
(a)	10	0	$40	$ 0	$40
(b)[a]	5	5	$20	$15	$35

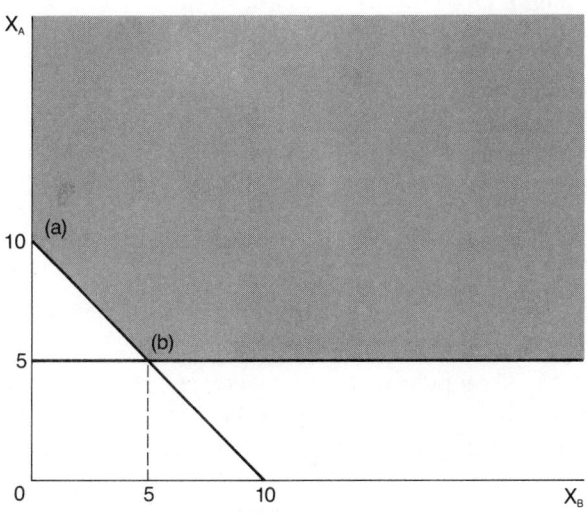

Note: Shaded area is the feasible region.
[a]To find the amount of A used when $X_A = 5$, let
$X_A = 10 - X_B$
$5 = 10 - X_B$
$X_A = 5$.

Sensitivity Analysis

The contribution margins and costs that are used in the objective functions are estimates and subject to error. Decision makers frequently need to know how much error can be tolerated to make a difference in the decision. This helps ascertain how much effort should be put into making the cost and revenue estimates.

To demonstrate our point, we use our earlier profit-maximization problem for Moline Company, which was formulated as follows:

$$\text{Maximize:} \quad \$3X_1 + \$4X_2$$

$$\text{Subject to:} \quad X_1 + 2X_2 \leq 24 \text{ Labor Hours}$$

$$X_1 + X_2 \leq 20 \text{ Machine Hours.}$$

Suppose that the variable cost estimate for Product 2 was $.50 per unit too low, so Product 2's unit contribution margin should have been $3.50 instead of $4.00. What effect would this have? We have calculated the new contributions in Exhibit 8.17. If you compare Exhibit 8.17 with 8.13, you will see that the contribution for Product 2 changes, thus the total contribution changes. The optimal decision to produce 16 units of Product 1 and 4 units of Product 2 does not change, however. In spite of the change in costs and thus in contributions, the *decision* does not change. In this example, the unit contribution margin of Product 2 would have to drop to less than $3 per unit before there would be a change in the optimal decision, assuming that all other things remained constant.

Exhibit 8.17
Optimal Product Mix: Revised Cost Estimates

	Production		Contribution		
Point[a]	X_1	X_2	1	2	Total
(a)	20	0	$60	$ 0	$60
(b)	16	4	$48	$14[b]	$62
(c)	0	12	$ 0	$42	$42

[a]These are points on the graph presented in Exhibit 8.12.
[b]Four units × $3.50 per unit.

Most linear programming computer programs can provide this type of sensitivity analysis so that managers and accountants can ascertain how much a cost or contribution margin can change before the optimal decision would change.

Opportunity Costs

Any constrained resource has an opportunity cost, which is the foregone profits of not having an additional unit of the resource. For example, suppose that Moline Company in our previous example could obtain one additional hour of machine time. With one more hour of machine time, the machine constraint would have

Exhibit 8.18
Linear Programming, Graphic Solution
Increase in Machine Time from 20 to 21 Hours

Point	Production		Contribution		
	X_1	X_2	1	2	Total
(a1)	21	0	$63	$ 0	$63
(b1)[a]	18	3	$54	$12	$66
(c1)	0	12	$ 0	$48	$48

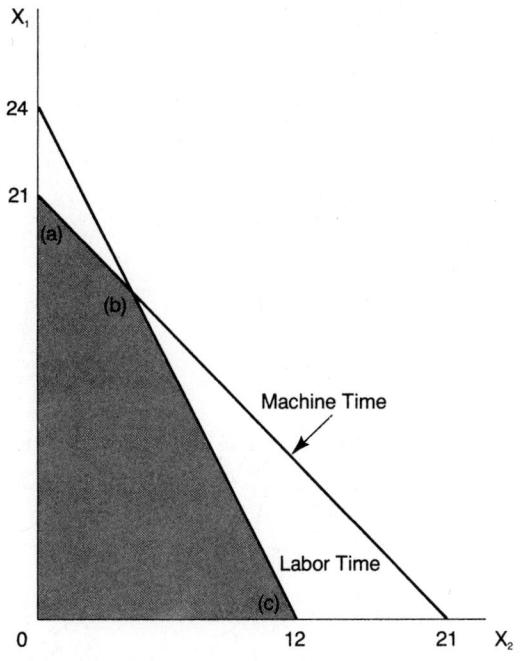

[a]$X_1 = 24 - 2X_2$ and $X_1 = 21 - X_2$, so
$$24 - 2X_2 = 21 - X_2$$
$$X_2 = 3$$
$$X_1 = 21 - X_2$$
$$= 21 - 3$$
$$= 18.$$

moved out, as shown in Exhibit 8.18. The new production at point (b) would be computed as follows:

$$X_1 = 24 - 2X_2$$

$$X_1 = 21 - X_2$$

$$24 - 2X_2 = 21 - X_2$$

$$X_2 = 3$$

$$X_1 = 18.$$

The new total contribution at point (b) would be $3(18) + $4(3) = $66, compared to $64 when machine time was constrained to 20 hours per day, as shown for point (b) in Exhibit 8.13. Thus, the opportunity cost of not having an extra hour of machine time is $2 (= $66 − $64).

Linear programming computer programs regularly provide opportunity costs. (Sometimes they are called "shadow prices" or values of the "dual variables.") Opportunity cost data can be used to ascertain whether it is worthwhile to acquire more units of a scarce resource. For example, if Moline Company were offered one more machine hour for a rental fee of less than $2 per hour, it would be profitable for the company to acquire the hour, all other things being equal.

Appendix B: Economic Order Quantity Model

The optimal number of orders or production runs per period can be derived from the following formula:

$$N = \frac{D}{Q},$$

where

$$Q = \sqrt{\frac{2K_0D}{K_c}};$$

N = The optimal number of orders or production runs for the period;

Q = the *economic order quantity,* or the optimal number of items in an order or production run;

D = the period demand in units;

K_0 = the order or setup cost;

K_c = the cost of carrying one unit in inventory for the period.

The formula $Q = \sqrt{2K_0D/K_c}$ is derived by using calculus to minimize total cost with respect to Q. The total cost (TC) formula is

$$\frac{\text{Total Cost}}{\text{per Period}} = \frac{\text{Carrying Costs}}{\text{per Period}} + \frac{\text{Order (Setup) Costs}}{\text{per Period}}$$

$$TC = K_c\frac{Q}{2} + K_0\frac{D}{Q}.$$

Take the first derivative of TC with respect to Q, set it equal to zero, and solve for Q:

$$\frac{dTC}{dQ} = \frac{d}{dQ}\left(K_c\frac{Q}{2} + K_0\frac{D}{Q}\right)$$

$$= K_c\left(\frac{1}{2} - \frac{K_0D}{Q^2}\right) = 0.$$

$$Q = \sqrt{\frac{2K_0D}{K_c}}.$$

Example The following facts were presented in the California Merchandising example in the text:

D = period demand = 6,000 units per year.

K_0 = order cost = $100 per order.

K_c = carrying cost = 30 percent of the cost of inventory or $.30 per unit ($.30 = 30 percent $\times$ $1.00 per unit).

Solving for Q (the optimal number of items in an order), we have

$$Q = \sqrt{\frac{K_0 D}{K_c}}$$

$$= \sqrt{\frac{2 \times \$100 \times 6{,}000 \text{ Units}}{\$.30}}$$

$$= \sqrt{4{,}000{,}000 \text{ Units}}$$

$$= 2{,}000 \text{ Units per Order.}$$

$$N = \frac{D}{Q}$$

$$= \frac{6{,}000 \text{ Units}}{2{,}000 \text{ Units}}$$

$$= 3 \text{ Orders per Year.}$$

From these equations, we derived the optimal order size, 2,000 units, and the optimal number of orders per year, 3. This is the same result that we derived in the text when we sought the least costly order. The economic order quantity model is usually more efficient, however, than using trial and error to find the least costly size and number of orders (or productions).

We have presented the basic *economic order quantity* model. There are many variations and modifications of this model in textbooks on operations research and quantitative methods.

Problem 1 for Self-Study

Skedaddle Snowblasters[8]

Memories of dogsled travel during his childhood in Alaska had prompted Scott Cameron to start Skedaddle Snowblasters 5 years ago. An experienced engineer with an entrepreneurial streak, Cameron had left his research and development job with a major auto company to exploit what he perceived to be a growing market in snowmobiles.

Currently, Skedaddle Snowblasters produces two lines of snowmobiles: the Standard Snowblaster and the Deluxe Snowblaster. Operating at capacity, the company ran into bottlenecks in both its body fabrication department and engine production

---

[8]by J. Lim.

department. Last month, Skedaddle Snowblasters put out 15,000 Standard Snowblasters and 6,250 Deluxe Snowblasters, and the unit costs incurred were as follows:

	Standard	Deluxe
Body Fabrication		
Materials	$210	$290
Direct Labor	75	120
Variable Overhead	20	25
Fixed Overhead[a]	85	115
Total Costs	$390	$550
Engine Production		
Materials	$450	$ 520
Direct Labor	150	280
Variable Overhead	30	20
Fixed Overhead[a]	260	490
Total	$890	$1,310
Assembly		
Materials	$ 40	$ 35
Direct Labor	60	95
Variable Overhead	30	15
Fixed Overhead[a]	80	120
Total	$210	$ 265
Marketing and Administrative Costs (all fixed[a])	$10	$15
Selling Price	$1,800	$2,500

[a]All fixed costs are allocated.

Beginning and ending inventories in all departments were zero.

Cameron has several decisions facing him this coming month, and he feels that each alternative should be considered in isolation. Analyze each of the following alternatives independently, using last month's data as the status quo.

a. An outside supplier has offered to supply Deluxe bodies for $600 each. This would allow production of 15,000 Standard Snowblasters and 10,000 Deluxe Snowblasters. Should Cameron accept the offer to buy 3,750 Deluxe bodies?

b. The Canadian government has offered to buy 1,000 modified Deluxe Snowblasters for $2,600 each. These modifications will require extra time in the fabrication department, incurring additional labor costs of $20 per unit and reducing standard production by 100 units. Should Skedaddle Snowblasters accept the contract?

c. (Appendix A) At capacity, the engine production department can produce either 30,000 Standards or 20,000 Deluxes. The body fabrication department can produce 20,000 Standards or 25,000 Deluxes. Given these constraints, what is Skedaddle Snowblasters' optimal product mix?

d. Assume the status quo to be the optimal calculated in part **c**. Increasing fixed costs in body fabrication and engine production by 20 percent can expand capacity to allow either:

(1) Production of 10,000 Standards and 15,000 Deluxes, or

(2) Production of 5,000 units of an Economy model with total variable costs of $1,250 and priced at $1,400, in addition to 15,000 Standards and 6,250 Deluxes.

Which is the better alternative?

Suggested Solution

a.

	Alternative	Status Quo	Difference
Sales Revenue	$52,000,000ᶜ	$42,625,000ᵃ	$9,375,000
Less Variable Costs	(30,593,750)ᵈ	(24,725,000)ᵇ	(5,868,750)
Contribution Margin. . . .	$21,406,250	$17,900,000	$3,506,250
Less Fixed Costs	(11,150,000)ᵉ	(11,150,000)	—
Operating Profit	$10,256,250	$ 6,750,000	$3,506,250

ᵃ$1,800(15,000) + $2,500(6,250).
ᵇ$1,065(15,000) + $1,400(6,250).
ᶜ$1,800(15,000) + $2,500(10,000).
ᵈ$24,725,000 + $1,565(3,750).
ᵉ$435(15,000) + $740(6,250).

Skedaddle Snowblasters should *accept* the supplier's offer.

b.

	Alternative	Status Quo	Difference
Sales Revenue	$42,545,000ᵃ	$42,625,000	$ (80,000)
Less Variable Costs	(24,638,500)ᵇ	(24,725,000)	86,500
Contribution Margin	$17,906,500	$17,900,000	$ 6,500
Less Fixed Costs	(11,150,000)	(11,150,000)	—
Net Operating Profit	$ 6,756,500	$ 6,750,000	$ 6,500

ᵃ$1,800(14,900) + $2,500(5,250) + $2,600(1,000).
ᵇ$1,065(14,900) + $1,400(5,250) + $1,420(1,000).

Skedaddle Snowblasters should *accept* the contract offer.

c. Let X_S and X_D refer to the volume of Standard and Deluxe.

$$\text{Maximize: } 735\, X_S + 1{,}100\, X_D$$

Subject to:

$$5X_S + 4X_D \leq 100{,}000 \quad (\text{Body}),$$

$$2X_S + 3X_D \leq 60{,}000 \quad (\text{Engine}).$$

Points (X_S, X_D)	Total Contribution
(a) 20,000; 0	$735(20,000) = $14,700,000
(b) 8,570; 14,290	$735(8,570) + $1,100(14,290) = $22,017,950ᵃ
(c) 0; 20,000	$1,100(20,000) = $22,000,000

ᵃOptimal mix. See top of next page for additional computations.

Additional computations for point (b):

$$5\left(\frac{60,000 - 3X_D}{2}\right) + 4X_D = 100,000;$$

$X_S = 8,570$ and $X_D = 14,290$, rounded to the next 10.

d.

	Status Quo	Alternative (1)	Alternative (2)
Sales Revenue	$51,151,000[a]	$55,500,000[c]	$58,151,000[f]
Less Variable Costs . . .	(29,133,050)[b]	(31,650,000)[d]	(35,383,050)[g]
Contribution Margin . . .	$22,017,950	$23,850,000	$22,767,950
Less Fixed Costs	(11,150,000)	(12,941,250)[e]	(12,941,250)
Operating Profit	$10,867,950	$10,908,750	$ 9,826,700

[a]$1,800(8,570) + $2,500(14,290).
[b]$1,065(8,570) + $1,400(14,290).
[c]$1,800(10,000) + $2,500(15,000).
[d]$1,065(10,000) + $1,400(15,000).
[e]$11,150,000 + 0.20($8,956,250).
[f]$51,151,000 + $1,400(5,000).
[g]$29,133,050 + $1,250(5,000).

Skedaddle Snowblasters should accept alternative (1).

Problem 2 for Self-Study

Regulator Valve[9]

Regulator Valve produces a regulator valve that is used in electric turbine systems. Major customers include electric utility companies. Regulator valve has several competitors.

The costs of the regulator valve at the company's normal volume of 5,000 units per month are shown in Exhibit 8.19.

Exhibit 8.19

Unit Manufacturing Costs:		
Variable Materials	$250	
Variable Labor	175	
Variable Overhead	75	
Fixed Overhead	150	
Total Unit		
Manufacturing Costs		$ 650
Unit Nonmanufacturing Costs:		
Variable	200	
Fixed	175	
Total Units Nonmanufacturing Costs		375
Total Unit Costs		$1,025

---

[9]By R. Colson.

The following questions refer only to the data in Exhibit 8.19. Unless stated otherwise, each question should be treated independently. Unless given otherwise, the regular selling price per unit is $1,750. Ignore income taxes and other costs not shown in Exhibit 8.19 unless specifically given in a question.

a. Market research estimates that a price increase to $1,900 per unit would decrease monthly volume to 4,500 units. The accounting department estimates that the only cost affected by such a price change would be to increase fixed manufacturing costs to $165 per unit. Would you recommend that this action be taken? What would be the impact on monthly revenues, costs, and profits?

b. Refer to part a. Given the information available, what is the opportunity cost of keeping the price of regulator valves at $1,750?

c. A proposal is received from an outside contractor who will make and ship 1,000 regulator valves per month directly to Regulator Supply's customers as orders are received from Regulator Supply's sales force. Regulator Supply's fixed nonmanufacturing costs would be unaffected, but its variable nonmanufacturing costs would be cut by 25 percent for the 1,000 units produced by the contractor. Regulator Supply's plant would operate at 80 percent of its normal level, and total fixed manufacturing costs would be cut by 15 percent. What in-house unit cost should be used to compare with the price quotation received from the contractor?

d. Assume the same facts as in part c, except that the idle facilities would be used to produce 600 modified regulator valves for use in nuclear reactors. These modified valves could be sold for $2,500 each. The variable costs of manufacturing these units would be $700, and variable nonmanufacturing costs would be $225 per unit. In addition, Regulator Supply would have to pay a $25,000 inspection fee to satisfy a government regulation that all nuclear reactor valve manufacturers meet certain minimum safety standards. To satisfy these safety standards, Regulator Supply would have to incur a 20 percent increase in normal fixed manufacturing costs. What is the maximum purchase price per unit that Regulator Supply should be willing to pay the outside contractor in this case?

Suggested Solution

a.

	Alternative	−	Status Quo	Difference
Price	$1,900		$1,750	
Volume	4,500		5,000	
Revenue	$8,550,000	−	$8,750,000	$ − 200,000
Variable Costs	(3,150,000)	−	(3,500,000)	− (350,000)
Contribution Margin	5,400,000	−	5,250,000	$ 150,000
Fixed Costs	(1,617,500)[a]	−	(1,625,000)	− (7,500)
Operating Profit	$3,782,500	−	$3,625,000	$ 157,500

[a](4,500 × $165) + ($175 × 5,000) = $1,617,500.

If monthly profits are the principal concern, they should raise their prices to $1,900.

b. $3,782,500 - 3,625,000 = \$157,500.$

c.

	Alternative: Contract for 1,000 Units	−	Status Quo: All Production In-House	Difference
Revenue	$8,750,000	−	$8,750,000	$ −0−
Variable Manufacturing Costs.	(2,000,000)	−	(2,500,000)	−(500,000)
Variable Nonmanufacturing Costs	(950,000)	−	(1,000,000)	− (50,000)
Contribution Margin	$5,800,000	−	$5,250,000	$ 550,000
Fixed Manufacturing Costs	(637,500)	−	(750,000)	−(112,500)
Fixed Nonmanufacturing Costs	(875,000)	−	(875,000)	−0−
Payment to Contractor	(X)	−	−	(X)
Operating Profit	$4,287,500 − X	−	$3,625,000	$662,500 − X

$$X = \$4,287,500 - 3,625,000$$

$$= 662,500 \text{ for } 1,000 \text{ Units}$$

Or

$$\frac{\$662,500}{1,000} = \$662.50 \text{ per Unit.}$$

d. *Differential analysis table (dollars in thousands):*

	Alternative					Status Quo	
	Contract 1,000 Regular Valves, Produce 4,000 Regular and 600 Modified					5,000 Regular Valves In-House	
	Regular (in)	Regular (out)	Modified	Total			Difference
Revenue	$7,000	$1,750	$1,500	$10,250	−	$8,750	$1,500
Variable Manufacturing Costs	(2,000)	—	(420)	(2,420)	−	(2,500)	−(80)
Variable Nonmanufacturing Costs	(800)	(150)	(135)	(1,085)	−	(1,000)	(85)
Contribution Margin . . .	$4,200	$1,600	$ 945	$ 6,745	−	$5,250	$1,495
Fixed Manufacturing Costs				(900)	−	(750)	(150)
Fixed Nonmanufacturing Costs				(900)	−	(875)	(25)
Contractor Payment . . .				(X)	−	—	(X)
Operating Profit.				$4,945 − X		$3,625	$1,320 − X

X = $4,945 Thousand − 3,625 Thousand = $1,320 Thousand for the Order or $1,320 per unit

Alternative method of analysis:

$$X = \text{Increase in Revenue} - \text{Increase in Costs}$$

$$= \$1,500 + 80 - 85 - 150 - 25 = \underline{\$1,320} \text{ (in thousands).}$$

Problem 3 for Self-Study

EOQ Incorporated

Compute the minimum total costs for EOQ Incorporated, given the following summary facts, which are presented in more detail in the text:

Differential Costs per Order $41
Total Units Purchased per Year . . . . 40,000 Units
Differential Carrying Costs per Unit of Inventory . . . . $5.35 per Unit

Find the minimum total costs of ordering and holding the inventory. [*Hint:* The optimal number of orders per year is 51 (rounded).]

Suggested Solution

a. Compute total costs using trial and error:

Annual Orders	Order Size[a]	Average Number of Units in Inventory	Inventory Carrying Costs[b]	Order Costs[c]	Total Costs
40	1,000	500	$2,675	$1,640	$4,315
•					
•					
•					
50	800	400	2,140	2,050	4,190
51	784	392	2,097	2,091	4,188
52	769	384.5	2,057	2,132	4,189
53	755	377.5	2,020	2,173	4,193
•					
•					
•					
60	667	333.5	1,784	2,460	4,244

[a]40,000 units ÷ number of orders.
[b]Average units in inventory × $5.35.
[c]Number of orders × $41.

Minimum total costs are $4,188 at 51 orders per year.

b. (Appendix B). The optimal number of orders can also be derived from the formula presented in Appendix B.

$$N = \frac{D}{Q}$$

where

$$Q = \sqrt{\frac{2K_0D}{K_c}};$$

N = optimal number of orders or production runs for the period;

Q = *economic order quantity,* or optimal number of items in an order or production run;

D = period demand in units = 40,000 units per year;

K_0 = order or setup cost = $41 per order;

K_c = cost of carrying one unit in inventory for the period = $5.35 per unit.

Thus,

$$Q = \sqrt{\frac{2 \times \$41 \times 40,000 \text{ Units}}{\$5.35}}$$

$$= \sqrt{613,084}$$

$$= 783$$

$$N = \frac{D}{Q} = \frac{40,000}{783} = 51.086 \text{ Orders.}$$

We have rounded to whole numbers so that there are 51 orders per year, 784 units per order, and 392 average inventory balance.

Questions

1. Review the meaning of the following terms and concepts.

a. Differential analysis.

b. Status quo.

c. Relevant costs.

d. Cash flows.

e. Opportunity costs.

f. Economic depreciation.

g. Differential costs.

h. "Make-or-buy" decision.

i. Gross margin versus contribution margin.

j. "Setup" or "order" costs.

k. Carrying costs.

l. Objective function.

m. Sensitivity analysis.

n. Shadow price.

o. Linear programming.

p. EOQ model.

2. "Users of differential analysis should use revenues and expenses of a particular period rather than cash flows, because they are more representative of a firm's performance during a given period." Comment.

3. "A proper evaluation of any project using differential analysis would require the consideration of all relevant costs—past, present, and future." Comment.

4. Assuming that there are no income taxes, how should each of the following costs enter into a decision to replace old equipment?

a. Book value of old equipment.

b. Disposal value of old equipment.

c. Cost of new equipment.

5. How significant are opportunity costs and economic depreciation in differential analysis? When will you use/not use these costs?

6. State and explain the shortcomings of using a cost-based approach to product pricing.

7. What is a common criticism made against the differential approach to product pricing? How can you refute this criticism?

8. When a firm is faced with one or several scarce resources, how does it make optimal use of the resources it has? Describe one technique a firm could use to solve such a constrained decision problem.

9. If you were asked to supply profit figures for a linear program your firm wishes to run, would you give the gross margin per unit or contribution margin per unit? Why?

10. Inventory management problems usually involve two types of opposing costs. Describe them and sketch a graph depicting their behavior with order size.

Exercises

11. *Special Order.* Fraser Enterprises has the capacity to produce 4,000 units per year. Its predicted operations for the year are:

Sales (3,000 units @ $60)	$180,000
Manufacturing Costs:	
Variable	$38 per Unit
Fixed	$22,000
Marketing and Administrative Costs:	
Variable	$3 per Unit
Fixed	$6,000

Should the company accept a special order for 500 units at a selling price of $50? Variable marketing and administrative costs for this order will be zero, and regular sales will not be affected. What is the effect of the decision on the company's operating profit?

12. *Product Choice.* Maximillian Steel Refinery can sell the iron it refines as ingots, semifinished steel, or as finished steel. Additional refining requires no special facilities, and all additional refining costs are variable. Estimated costs for producing 10,000 ingot tons are $40,000. Additional refining would yield 9,360 tons of semifinished steel at an additional cost of $30,000. An additional $25,000 is required to transform the product to 8,470 tons of finished steel. The market price for ingots is $96 per ton, $105 for semifinished steel, and $130 for finished steel. Fixed costs are $600,000.

What should Maximillian Steel produce?

13. *Special Order.* Anticipating unusually high sales for May, Mr. Twinkles, a breakfast cereal company, has plans to produce 40,000 pounds of cereal, using up all available capacity. Production and marketing costs for May are anticipated to be as follows:

Unit Manufacturing Costs per Pound:

Variable Direct Materials Cost	$0.15
Variable Labor	0.02
Variable Overhead	0.03
Fixed Overhead	0.10
Total Manufacturing Costs	$0.30

Unit Marketing Costs per Pound:

Variable	$0.03	
Fixed	0.20	
Total Marketing Costs		0.23
Total Unit Costs		$0.53
Selling Price per Pound		$0.80

On April 30, Mr. Twinkles received a contract offer from Feed the Hungry (FTH), a government agency, to supply 5,000 pounds of cereal for delivery by May 31. The FTH offer would reimburse the government's share of manufacturing costs plus a fixed fee of $2,000. Variable marketing costs will be zero for this order; fixed costs will not be affected. Should Mr. Twinkles accept the offer?

14. *Make or Buy*. Reliant Enterprises, a sailboat manufacturer, is currently operating at 70 percent capacity and producing about 10,000 units a year. In order to use more capacity, the manager has been considering the research and development department's suggestion that Reliant Enterprises manufacture its own sails. Currently Reliant purchases sails from a supplier at a unit price of $28. Estimates show that Reliant Enterprises can manufacture its own sails at $10 per unit direct materials cost and $8 direct labor cost. The factory overhead is $2 per direct labor dollar, of which 20 percent is variable.

    a.   Should Reliant Enterprises make or buy the sails?

    b.   Suppose that Reliant Enterprises could rent out the currently unused part of the factory for $1,000 a month. How would this affect the decision in part **a**?

15. *Dropping a Product Line*. British Columbia Wood Products is currently operating at 75 percent capacity. Worried about the company's performance, Blondell, the general manager, segmented the company's income statement product by product and obtained the following picture:

	Product		
	A	**B**	**C**
Sales	$32,600	$42,800	$51,200
Less Variable Costs	(22,000)	(38,000)	(40,100)
Total Contribution Margin	$10,600	$ 4,800	$11,100
Less Allocated Fixed Costs	(4,700)	(5,600)	(7,100)
Net Operating Profit (Loss)	$ 5,900	$ (800)	$ 4,000

Should British Columbia Wood Products drop Product B, if that would reduce total fixed costs by 20 percent?

16. *Product Mix Decisions.* Timeless Products, a clock manufacturer, is operating at capacity. Constrained by machine time, the company has decided to drop the most unprofitable of its three product lines. The accounting department came up with the following data from last year's operations.

	Manual	Electric	Quartz
Machine Time per Unit.	0.4 Hour	2.5 Hours	5.0 Hours
Selling Price per Unit	$20	$30	$50
Less Variable Costs per Unit	(10)	(14)	(28)
Contribution Margin	$10	$16	$22

Which line should Timeless Products drop?

17. *Product Choice Using Linear Programming (Appendix A).* Fortuna Corporation manufactures two products whose contribution margins are as follows:

Product	Contribution Margin
A	$ 9
B	$15

Each month, Fortuna Corporation has only 6,000 hours of machine time and 7,200 hours of available labor time. The amount of time required to make Products A and B is as follows:

	Product A	Product B
Labor Time	2 Hours per Unit	4 Hours per Unit
Machine Time	3 Hours per Unit	2 Hours per Unit

All units produced are sold.

Set the problem up in the linear programming format and solve for the optimal production mix.

18. *Economic Order Quantity.* (This exercise can be worked using either trial and error or the model in Appendix B.) The Magee Foundry regularly uses 1,000 bolts per day, 250 days per year. Bolts can be purchased in lots of 1,000 for $10 per lot or in lots of 10,000 for $96.10 per lot. Ordering costs are $10 per order, and the holding costs of items in inventory are estimated to be 20 percent of cost per year.

   a. What is the economic order quantity and associated annual costs, assuming that only lots of 1,000 items are available?

   b. What is the economic order quantity and associated annual costs, assuming that only lots of 10,000 items are available?

   c. Compare the costs of the two answers above and state the optimal ordering policy for these bolts, assuming that lots of 1,000 or 10,000 can be ordered.

19. *Economic Order Quantity.* (This exercise can be worked using either trial and error or the model in Appendix B.) The purchasing agent responsible for ordering cotton underwear for Soares Retail Stores estimates that 10,000 packages of cotton underwear are sold evenly throughout each year, that each order costs $24 to place, and that it costs $.12 to hold a package of underwear in inventory for a year.

    a.   How many packages of underwear should be ordered in each order?

    b.   How many times per year should underwear be ordered?

20. *Product Mix Decisions (Appendix A) (CPA adapted).* The Random Company manufactures two products, Zeta and Beta. Each product must pass through two processing operations. All materials are introduced at the start of Process No. 1. There are no work-in-process inventories. Random may produce either one product exclusively or various combinations of both products, subject to the following constraints:

	Process No. 1	Process No. 2	Contribution Margin per Unit
Hours Required to Produce One Unit of:			
Zeta	1 Hour	1 Hour	$4.00
Beta	2 Hours	3 Hours	5.25
Total Capacity in Hours per Day	1,000 Hours	1,275 Hours	

A shortage of technical labor has limited Beta production to 400 units per day. There are *no* constraints on the production of Zeta other than the hour constraints in the above schedule. Assume that all relationships between capacity and production are linear.

What is the total contribution that would be obtained at the optimal product mix?

21. *Product Mix Decisions (Appendix A).* Using the information for the Random Company in Exercise **20** and assuming that the present Process No. 1 cost for each unit of Zeta is $2.35, what is the maximum price that Random would be willing to pay for an additional hour of Process No. 1 time?

22. *Finding Most Profitable Price-Quantity Combination.* The Culler Company is introducing a new product and must decide what price should be set. An estimated demand schedule for the product is as follows:

Price	Quantity Demanded (in units)
$10	40,000
12	36,000
14	28,000
16	24,000
18	18,000
20	15,000

Estimated costs are as follows:

Variable Manufacturing Costs	$4 per Unit
Fixed Manufacturing Costs	$40,000 per Year
Variable Selling and Administrative Costs	$2 per Unit
Fixed Selling and Administrative Costs	$10,000 per Year

    a. Prepare a schedule showing the total revenue, total cost, and total profit or loss for each selling price.

    b. Which price should be selected? Explain.

Problems and Cases

23. *Special Order.* Eastern Furniture Company has a capacity of 100,000 tables per year. The company is currently producing and selling 80,000 tables per year at a selling price of $200 per table. The cost of producing and selling one table at the 80,000-unit level of activity is as follows:

Variable Manufacturing Costs	$ 80
Fixed Manufacturing Costs	20
Variable Selling and Administrative Costs	40
Fixed Selling and Administrative Costs	10
Total Costs	$150

The company has received a special order for 10,000 tables at a price of $130. Because no sales commission would be paid on the special order, the variable selling and administrative costs would be only $25 per table. The company has rejected the offer based on the following computations:

Selling Price per Table	$130
Variable Manufacturing Costs	(80)
Fixed Manufacturing Costs	(20)
Variable Selling and Administrative Costs	(25)
Fixed Selling and Administrative Costs	(10)
Net Loss per Table	$ (5)

Should Eastern Furniture Company have accepted the special order? Show your computations.

24. *Using Fixed Costs in Analyzing Alternatives.* MacInnes Electronics Corporation manufactures citizens' band (CB) radios. Early in 1976 it invested $20 million in manufacturing facilities that could produce 23-channel CB radios. Data for 1976 are as follows:

Number of Radios Produced and Sold	40,000
Variable Cost per Radio	$30
Fixed Cost per Radio	25
Selling Price per Radio	80

Early in 1977, the federal government increased the number of channels permitted from 23 to 40. The result was that market demand for 23-channel radios decreased significantly and market price dropped to $50 a radio. Management has decided to close down its production facilities. The president stated: "We are hurt no matter what we do. We cannot adapt our current production facilities to manufacture 40-channel radios. However, if we continue manufacturing 23-channel radios, we will lose $5 on each unit produced and sold. We are, therefore, better off just to close down."

    a. Show how the president calculated the $5 loss on each 23-channel radio.

    b. Do you agree with the president's decision? If not, explain why and show your computations.

25. *Special Order.* Whitley Electronics Company produces precision instruments for airplanes. It is currently operating at capacity. It has received an invitation to bid on a government contract for 1,000 specially designed precision instruments. The company has estimated its costs for the contract to be as follows:

Variable Manufacturing Costs.	$20,000
Allocated Fixed Manufacturing Costs	15,000
Special Design and Production Setup Costs	10,000
Shipping Costs	5,000
Special Administrative Costs	5,000
Total Costs	$55,000
Cost per Precision Instrument ($55,000/1,000).	$ 55

If Whitley accepts the government contract, it will have to forgo regular sales of 1,000 units. These 1,000 units would have a selling price of $80 each, variable costs of $40 each, and fixed costs of $20 each.

    a. What is the lowest per-unit price that Whitley can bid on this contract without sacrificing profits?

    b. Whitley has learned that it will receive the contract if it bids $78 or less per unit. What action should Whitley take?

26. *Economic Order Quantity.* (This problem can be worked using trial and error or the model in Appendix B.) The Lewis Company sells 3,000 medium-priced stereo sets per year in addition to many other items. The medium-priced stereo sets cost Lewis Company $100 each. Total costs of holding inventory for a year are 16 percent of an item's cost. A single purchasing department processes all purchase orders. Data on purchasing department costs for each of the last several years is shown below.

LEWIS COMPANY
Total Orders Placed and Costs Incurred in Purchasing Department

Year	Orders Placed	Total Ordering Costs
1	5	$3,997
2	75	4,000
3	98	4,002
4	130	4,595
5	200	6,010
6	250	6,995

The purchasing department will be placing about 130 orders during the next year for items other than medium-priced stereo sets.

    a. What is the apparent relation between orders placed and total order costs? What is the incremental cost of placing an order for medium-priced stereo sets?

    b. What is the optimal number of medium-priced stereo sets to order at a time?

    c. What is the optimal number of orders to place each year for medium-priced stereo sets?

27. *Dropping a Machine from Service.* The Brunson Grain Company has four large milling machines of approximately equal capacity. Each was run at close to its full capacity during 19X5. Each machine is depreciated separately using an accelerated method. Data for each machine are as follows:

	No. 1	No. 2	No. 3	No. 4
Date Acquired	1/1/X0	1/1/X1	1/1/X3	1/1/X4
Cost.	$50,000	$60,000	$75,000	$80,000
Operating Costs: 19X5				
Labor	$20,000	$18,000	$22,000	$21,500
Materials	5,000	6,000	4,500	3,000
Maintenance.	1,000	1,000	700	550
Depreciation	3,363	5,454	10,910	13,091
Total	$29,363	$30,454	$38,110	$38,141

Activity in 19X6 is expected to be less than in 19X5, so that one machine is to be dropped from service. It has been proposed that No. 4 should be that machine on the grounds that it has the highest operating costs. Do you agree or disagree with this proposal? Why or why not?

28. *Make or Buy.* The Dodd Manufacturing Company produces machinery of which part No. 301 is a subassembly. Part No. 301 is presently being produced by the Dodd Manufacturing Company in its own shops, but the West Products Company offers to supply it at a cost of $200 per 500 units. An analysis of the costs of producing part No. 301 by the Dodd Manufacturing Company reveals the following information:

	Cost per 500 Units
Direct (Variable) Material	$ 65
Direct (Variable) Labor	90
Other Variable Costs	22
Fixed Costs[a]	110
Total	$287

[a]Fixed overhead consists largely of depreciation on general-purpose equipment and factory buildings.

    a. Should the offer by the West Products Company be accepted if the plant is operating well below capacity?

b.   Should the offer be accepted if the price is reduced to $165 per 500 units?

c.   If other profitable uses can be found for the facilities now used in turning out part No. 301, what maximum purchase price should be accepted?

29. *Bidding on a Contract.* The Exton Company is considering making a bid on a contract to supply the Defense Department with 500,000 gallons of chemicals. The capacity of the plant is 10,000,000 gallons a year, and Exton is currently producing and selling at the rate of 8,500,000 gallons a year. The fixed costs of the plant total $5,400,000 per year regardless of the level of operations. The variable costs of chemicals of this type is approximately $2 per gallon. The sales manager says that a bid of no more than $1,200,000 would probably enable the company to get the contract.

a.   Should a bid of $1,200,000 be made? Explain.

b.   Assume that the present production is being sold at an average price of $3 per gallon and average variable costs equal $2 per gallon. Compute the operating profit (1) if the government contract were not obtained and (2) if the government contract were obtained at a bid of $1,200,000.

30. *Accepting or Rejecting an Order.* The Milky Way Company produces a precision part for use in rockets, missiles, and a variety of other products. In the first half of 19X0, it operated at 80 percent of capacity and produced 160,000 units. Manufacturing costs in that period were as follows:

Direct Material	$430,000
Direct Labor	770,000
Other Variable Costs	150,000
Fixed Costs	450,000

The parts were all sold at a price of $14 per unit.

The AMF Aircraft Company offers to buy as many units of the part as the Milky Way Company can supply at a price of $10 per unit. It is estimated that to increase operations to a 100 percent capacity level would increase office and administrative costs by $50,000 for a 6-month period. Management feels that sales to AMF at this price will not affect their ability to reach the previous level of sales at the regular price and that there are no legal restrictions on selling at the lower price.

Present a schedule indicating if it would be worthwhile to accept the AMF offer. (Show your calculations.)

31. *Machine Replacement.* On the last day of last year Oliver bought a new, special-purpose machine for $150,000 for use during a project that will last for 3 years. One week after purchase of the machine a salesperson from another company showed Oliver a different machine that costs $180,000. The latter machine is technically superior. Neither machine will have any salvage or disposal value in 3 years. As compared to the "old machine," the new machine will save $55,000 per year in operating costs—raw materials and labor. The "old" machine can be sold now for only $50,000.

Oliver is confident that the new machine would save $55,000 each year for 3 years, but hesitates to recognize a loss on the old machine by selling it now. "I will use the old machine for 3 years and I will have no loss; by using the machine for 3 years, I'll get my money out of it."

Annual cash operating costs for the old machine are $80,000; this amount does not include any charge for depreciation. Sales, all for cash, will be $1 million each year. All other expenses will amount to $700,000 each year and will be paid for in cash. The amount of all other cash expenses is independent of the machine used. The machine in question is the only long-term asset that Oliver uses. Ignore income taxes and compound interest considerations.

    a. Prepare a statement of cash receipts and disbursements for each of 3 years assuming that the old machine is kept.

    b. Repeat part **a** assuming that the new machine is acquired.

    c. What is the total net difference between cash flows over the 3 years of the alternatives? Which one has the higher cash flows?

    d. Calculate the operating profit for each of the 3 years assuming that the old machine is kept and straight-line depreciation is used.

    e. Repeat part **d** assuming that the new machine is acquired and straight-line depreciation is used.

    f. What is the total net difference between operating profits over the 3 years of the two alternatives, and which one has the larger total operating profit?

    g. How would the answers to parts **c** and **f** differ if the old machine had cost $200,000 instead of $150,000? $300,000 instead of $150,000?

    h. What is the name for the kind of cost represented by the $150,000 cost of the old machine just after its purchase?

32. *Cost Estimate for Bidding.* The Norwood Printing Company operates a medium-sized printing shop. In May, it received an inquiry from a prospective customer about its prices for furnishing an advertising booklet in quantities of 2,000 copies, 8,000 copies, and 15,000 copies. After analyzing the job, the estimating staff furnished the following estimates of cost:

Setup Costs for Job	$500
Material Cost per 100 Booklets	50
Direct Labor Cost per 100 Booklets	45

In the company's cost accounting records, fixed costs are allocated to jobs on a direct-labor-cost basis, at a rate of 80 percent of direct labor costs. Thus, for example, if direct labor costs for a job are $100, the job would also be charged with $80 of fixed costs. The company seeks to make a profit of 10 percent of the bid price on each order. (For this purpose, profit is defined as revenue minus costs, including allocated fixed costs.) The printing shop was operating with sufficient excess capacity to fill the orders up to 15,000 copies.

    a. Assuming that the bid was to be based on average *total* cost (including fixed costs charged to products at the rate of 80 percent of direct labor costs) and a 10 percent profit margin, what price would be quoted for each quantity? (Show computations for this and all other parts of the question.)

    b. By how much would operating profit of the firm increase if the price quoted in part **a** for 8,000 copies were accepted?

    c. Repeat part **b** for 15,000 copies.

    d. What is the minimum bid that should be accepted for 2,000 copies? For 8,000 copies?

33. *Alternative Machines.* The Able Bakery now purchases frozen precut cookie dough at a cost of $.03 per cookie. Management is considering purchasing either an automatic or semiautomatic cookie cutter. If the automatic machine is purchased, the annual fixed costs will be $8,000. In addition, there will be a $.010 variable cost per cookie. Use of a semiautomatic machine will lead to $4,500 in fixed costs per year, plus $.015 of variable cost per cookie.

   a.   At what volume of operations will the total annual costs incurred by using the semiautomatic machine equal outside purchase costs?

   b.   At what volume of operations will the total annual costs incurred by using the automatic machine equal outside purchase costs?

   c.   Which of the three alternatives is least costly if annual production volume is 600,000 cookies?

   d.   Which of the three alternatives is least costly if annual production volume is 800,000 cookies?

   e.   At which level of production volume are the costs incurred by using the two machines equal?

34. *Product Mix Decision.* The Vancil Company has one machine on which it can produce either of two products, Y or Z. Sales demand for both products is such that the machine could operate at full capacity on either of the products and all output could be sold at current prices. Product Y requires 2 hours of machine time per unit of output and Product Z requires 4 hours of machine time per unit of output. Machine time (depreciation) is charged to products at the rate of $8 per hour.

The following information summarizes the per-unit cash inflows and costs of Products Y and Z.

	Per Unit	
	Product Y	**Product Z**
Selling Price	$60	$110
Materials.	$ 9	$ 11
Labor	3	5
Machine Depreciation[a]	16	32
Allocated Portion of Fixed Factory Costs[b]	12	20
Total Cost of Unit sold	$40	$ 68
Gross Margin per Unit	$20	$ 42

[a]This item under these circumstances could be referred to as "variable factory costs."
[b]Allocated in proportion to (direct) labor costs.

Selling costs are the same whether product Y or Z, or both, are produced, and can be ignored. Should Vancil Company plan to produce product Y, product Z, or some mixture of both? Why?

35. *Department Closing.* Prior to 19X0, Kahn Wholesalers Company had not kept departmental income statements. In order to achieve better management control, the Company decided to install department-by-department accounts. At the end of 19X0, the new accounts showed that although the business as a whole was profitable, the Dry Goods Department had shown a substantial loss. The income statement for the Dry Goods Department, shown here, reports on operations for 19X0.

KAHN WHOLESALERS COMPANY
Dry Goods Department
Partial Income Statement for 19X0

Sales	$500,000	
Cost of Goods Sold	(375,000)	
Gross Margin.		$125,000
Costs:		
Payroll, Direct Labor, and Supervision.	$(33,000)	
Commissions of Sales Staff[a]	(30,000)	
Rent[b]	(26,000)	
State Taxes[c].	(3,000)	
Insurance on Inventory	(4,000)	
Depreciation[d]	(7,000)	
Administration and General Office[e]	(22,000)	
Interest for Inventory Carrying Costs[f]	(5,000)	
Total Costs		(130,000)
Loss Before Allocation of Income Taxes		$ (5,000)

Additional computations:

(a) All sales staff are compensated on straight commission, at a uniform 6 percent of all sales.

(b) Rent is charged to departments on a square-foot basis. The company rents an entire building, and the Dry Goods Department occupies 15 percent of the building.

(c) Assessed annually on the basis of average inventory on hand each month.

(d) Eight and one-half percent of cost of departmental equipment.

(e) Allocated on basis of departmental sales as a fraction of total company sales.

(f) Based on average inventory quantity multiplied by the company's borrowing rate for 3-month loans.

Analysis of these results has led to a suggestion that the Dry Goods Department be closed down. Members of the management team agree that keeping the Dry Goods Department is not essential to maintaining good customer relations and supporting the rest of the company's business. That is, eliminating the Dry Goods Department is expected to have no effect on the amount of business done by the other departments.

What action do you recommend to management of Kahn Wholesalers Company? Why?

36. *CVP and Differential Costs (CPA adapted).* You have been asked to assist the management of the Arcadia Corporation in arriving at certain decisions. Arcadia has its home office in Ohio and leases factory buildings in Texas, Montana, and Maine, all of which produce the same product. The management of Arcadia has provided you with a projection of operations for 1987, the forthcoming year, as follows:

	Total	Texas	Montana	Maine
Sales Revenue.	$4,400,000	$2,200,000	$1,400,000	$800,000
Fixed Costs:				
Factory.	$1,100,000	$ 560,000	$ 280,000	$260,000
Administration	350,000	210,000	110,000	30,000
Variable Costs	1,450,000	665,000	425,000	360,000
Allocated Home Office Costs	500,000	225,000	175,000	100,000
Total	$3,400,000	$1,660,000	$ 990,000	$750,000
Profit from Operations	$1,000,000	$ 540,000	$ 410,000	$ 50,000

The sales price per unit is $25.

Due to the marginal results of operations of the factory in Maine, Arcadia has decided to cease operations and sell that factory's machinery and equipment by the end of 1986. Arcadia expects that the proceeds from the sale of these assets would be greater than their book value and would cover all termination costs.

Arcadia, however, would like to continue serving its customers in that area if it is economically feasible and is considering one of the following three alternatives:

(1) Expand the operations of the Montana factory by using space presently idle. This move would result in the following changes in that factory's operations:

	Increase Over Factory's Current Operations
Sales Revenue	50%
Fixed Costs:	
Factory	20
Administration	10

Under this proposal, variable costs would be $8 per unit sold.

(2) Enter into a long-term contract with a competitor who will serve that area's customers. This competitor would pay Arcadia a royalty of $4 per unit based on an estimate of 30,000 units being sold.

(3) Close the Maine factory and not expand the operations of the Montana factory.

In order to assist the management of Arcadia Corporation in determining which alternative is more economically feasible, prepare a schedule computing Arcadia's estimated profit from total operations that would result from each of the following methods:

    a.   Expansion of the Montana factory.
    b.   Negotiation of long-term contract on a royalty basis.
    c.   Shutdown of Maine operations with no expansion at other locations.

Note: Total home office costs of $500,000 will remain the same under each situation.

37. *Product Choice Decisions (CPA adapted).* Ocean Company manufactures three different products: Ex, Why, and Zee. Projected income statements by product line for the year are presented below:

	Ex	Why	Zee	Total
Unit Sales	10,000	500,000	125,000	635,000
Revenue	$925,000	$1,000,000	$575,000	$2,500,000
Variable Cost of Units Sold	(285,000)	(350,000)	(150,000)	(785,000)
Fixed Cost of Units Sold	(304,200)	(289,000)	(166,800)	(760,000)
Gross Margin	$335,800	$ 361,000	$258,200	$ 955,000
Variable Nonmanufacturing Costs . .	(270,000)	(200,000)	(80,000)	(550,000)
Fixed Nonmanufacturing Costs . . .	(125,800)	(136,000)	(78,200)	(340,000)
Operating Profit	$ (60,000)	$ 25,000	$100,000	$ 65,000

Production costs are similar for all three products. Fixed nonmanufacturing costs are allocated to products in proportion to revenues. The fixed cost of units sold is allocated to products by various allocation bases, such as square feet for factory rent and machine hours for repairs, and so forth.

Ocean management is concerned about the loss for product Ex and is considering two alternative courses of corrective action.

Alternative A. Ocean would purchase some new machinery for the production of product Ex. This new machinery would involve an immediate cash outlay of $650,000. Management expects that the new machinery would reduce variable production costs so that total variable costs (cost of units sold and nonmanufacturing costs) for product Ex would be 52 percent of product Ex revenues. The new machinery would increase total fixed costs allocated to product Ex to $480,000 per year. No additional fixed costs would be allocated to products Why or Zee.

Alternative B. Ocean would discontinue the manufacture of product Ex. Selling prices of products Why and Zee would remain constant. Management expects that product Zee production and revenues would increase by 50 percent. Some of the present machinery devoted to product Ex could be sold at scrap value that equals its removal costs. The removal of this machinery would reduce fixed costs allocated to product Ex by $30,000 per year. The remaining fixed costs allocated to product Ex include $155,000 of rent expense per year. The space previously used for product Ex can be rented to an outside organization for $157,500 per year.

Prepare a schedule analyzing the effect of Alternative A and Alternative B on projected total company operating profit.

38. *Analyzing the Differential Costs of a New Market (CMA adapted).* The Calco Corporation has been a major producer and distributor of molded and assembled plastic products for industrial use in its region for the past 20 years. Annual sales have averaged $60,000,000 for the past 4 years. Several times during this 20-year period the company has considered entering the consumer products market with items that could be manufactured in its facilities. Each time the product idea was sold to another company because Calco had no experience in the consumer markets, and its facilities were at or near full capacity.

Late last year the product engineering department presented a proposal to produce a plastic storage unit designed especially for the consumer market. The product was very well suited for the company's manufacturing process. No costly modification of machinery or molds would be required, nor would operations in the assembly department have to be changed in any way. In addition, there was an adequate amount of manufacturing capacity available due to the recent expansion of facilities and a leveling of the sales growth in its industrial product lines.

The Calco management was receptive to this proposal. Although they had rejected consumer products in prior years, the arguments for the product were more persuasive this year—there was excess capacity, the products fit very well into the manufacturing process, and Calco's industrial markets appeared to be maturing. Therefore, entering the consumer market would give the company added opportunity to expand its sales.

The management is considering two alternatives for marketing the product. The first is to add this responsibility to Calco's current marketing department. The other alternative is to acquire a small, new company named Jasco, Inc. Jasco was started by some former employees of a firm that specialized in marketing plastic products for the consumer market when they lost their jobs as a result of a merger. Jasco has not yet started operations.

Calco has never used independent distributors. Consequently, the management would prefer to acquire a distributor rather than merely enter into a contract for distribution of the product. The founders of Jasco are receptive to such an approach. In fact, Calco could acquire Jasco complete with personnel for a very nominal sum.

The manufacturing costs will be the same for either marketing alternative. The product engineering department has prepared the following estimates of the unit manufacturing costs for the new storage unit.

Direct Materials	$14.00
Direct Labor	3.50
Fixed Manufacturing Overhead	10.00
Total	$27.50

The total overhead rate for all of Calco's manufacturing activities is $20 per hour. The rate is composed of $5 per hour for supplies, employee benefits, power, and so on; and $15 per hour for supervision, depreciation, insurance, taxes, and so on.

Calco's marketing department has used their experience in the sale of industrial products to develop a proposal for the distribution of the new consumer product. The marketing department would be reorganized so that several positions that were scheduled for elimination now would be assigned to the new product. The marketing department's forecast of the annual financial results for its proposal to market the new storage units appears below.

Sales Revenue (100,000 units @ $45)		$4,500,000
Costs:		
Cost of Units Sold (100,000 units @ $27.50)		$2,750,000
Marketing Costs:		
Positions That Were to Be Eliminated		600,000
Sales Commissions (5 percent of sales)		225,000
Advertising Program		400,000
Promotion Program		200,000
Share of Current Marketing Department's Management Costs		100,000
Total Costs		$4,275,000
Net Income Before Taxes		$ 225,000

The Jasco founders also prepared a forecast of the annual financial results based on their experience in marketing consumer products. The forecast presented below was based on the assumption that Jasco would become part of Calco and would be responsible for marketing the new storage unit in the consumer market.

Sales Revenue (120,000 units @ $50)	$6,000,000
Costs:	
Cost of Units sold (120,000 units @ $27.50)	3,300,000
Marketing Costs:	
Personnel—Sales	660,000
Personnel—Sales Management	200,000
Commissions (10 percent)	600,000
Advertising Program	800,000
Promotion Program.	200,000
Office Rental (the annual rental of a long-term lease already signed by Jasco)	50,000
Total Costs	$5,810,000
Net Income Before Taxes	$ 190,000

Prepare a schedule of differential costs and revenues to assist management in deciding whether to enter the consumer market.

39. *Product Choice with Constraints (Appendix A) (CMA adapted).* Leastan Company manufactures a line of carpeting that includes a commercial carpet and a residential carpet. Two grades of fiber—heavy-duty and regular—are used in manufacturing both types of carpeting. The mix of the two grades of fiber differs in each type of carpeting, with the commercial grade using a greater amount of heavy-duty fiber.

Leastan will introduce a new line of carpeting in 2 months to replace the current line. The present fiber in stock will not be used in the new line. Management wants to exhaust the present stock of regular and heavy-duty fiber during the last month of production.

Data regarding the current line of commercial and residential carpeting are as follows:

	Commercial	**Residential**
Selling Price per Roll	$1,000	$800
Production Specifications per Roll of Carpet:		
Heavy-Duty Fiber.	80 Pounds	40 Pounds
Regular Fiber	20 Pounds	40 Pounds
Direct Labor Hours	15 Hours	15 Hours
Standard Cost per Roll of Carpet:		
Heavy-Duty Fiber ($3 per pound)	$240	$120
Regular Fiber ($2 per pound)	40	80
Direct Labor ($10 per direct labor hour)	150	150
Variable Manufacturing Overhead (60 percent of direct labor cost)	90	90
Fixed Manufacturing Overhead (120 percent of direct labor cost)	180	180
Total Standard Cost per Roll	$700	$620

Leastan has 42,000 pounds of heavy-duty fiber and 24,000 pounds of regular fiber in stock. All fiber not used in the manufacture of the present types of carpeting during the last month of production can be sold as scrap at $.25 a pound.

There are a maximum of 10,500 direct labor hours available during the month. The labor force can work on either type of carpeting.

Sufficient demand exists for the present line of carpeting so that all quantities produced can be sold.

a. Calculate the number of rolls of commercial carpet and residential carpet Leastan Company must manufacture during the last month of production to exhaust completely the heavy-duty and regular fiber still in stock.

b. Can Leastan Company manufacture these quantities of commercial and residential carpeting during the last month of production? Explain your answer.

40. *Product Choice with Constraints (Appendix A) (CMA adapted).* Excelsion Corporation manufactures and sells two kinds of containers—paperboard and plastic. The company produced and sold 100,000 paperboard containers and 75,000 plastic containers during the month of April. A total of 4,000 and 6,000 direct labor hours were used in producing the paperboard and plastic containers, respectively.

The company has not been able to maintain an inventory of either product, due to the high demand; this situation is expected to continue in the future. Workers can be shifted from the production of paperboard to plastic containers and vice versa, but additional labor is not available in the community. In addition, there will be a shortage of plastic material used in the manufacture of the plastic container in the coming months due to a labor strike at the facilities of a key supplier. Management has estimated there will be only enough direct material to produce 60,000 plastic containers during June.

The income statement for Excelsion Corporation for the month of April is shown below. The costs presented in the statement are representative of prior periods and are expected to continue at the same rates or levels in the future.

EXCELSION CORPORATION
Income Statement
For the Month Ended April 30

	Paperboard Containers	Plastic Containers
Sales Revenue	$220,800	$222,900
Less:		
Returns and Allowances	$ 6,360	$ 7,200
Discounts.	2,440	3,450
	$ 8,800	$ 10,650
Net Sales	$212,000	$212,250
Cost of Sales:		
Direct Material Cost	$123,000	$120,750
Direct Labor.	26,000	28,500
Indirect Labor (variable with direct labor hours)	4,000	4,500
Depreciation—Machinery	14,000	12,250
Depreciation—Building	10,000	10,000
Cost of Sales	$177,000	$176,000
Gross Profit.	$ 35,000	$ 36,250
Nonmanufacturing Expenses:		
Variable	$ 8,000	$ 7,500
Fixed	1,000	1,000
Commissions—Variable.	11,000	15,750
Total Operating Expenses	$ 20,000	$ 24,250
Income Before Tax	$ 15,000	$ 12,000
Income Taxes (40 percent)	6,000	4,800
Net Income.	$ 9,000	$ 7,200

a. What is the contribution per unit of scarce resource?

b. What is the optimal product mix given the constraints in the problem?

41. *Multiple Products—Continuing Operations (CMA adapted).* Stac Industries is a multiproduct company with several manufacturing plants. The Clinton Plant manufactures and distributes two household cleaning and polishing compounds—regular and heavy-duty—under the Cleen-Brite label. The forecasted operating results for the first 6 months of 1985, when 100,000 cases of each compound are expected to be manufactured and sold, are presented in the following statement.

CLEEN-BRITE COMPOUNDS
Clinton Plant
Forecasted Results of Operations
For the 6-Month Period Ending June 30, 1985
(in thousands)

	Regular	Heavy Duty	Total
Sales Revenue	$2,000	$3,000	$5,000
Cost of Sales	(1,600)	(1,900)	(3,500)
Gross Profit	$ 400	$1,100	$1,500
Nonmanufacturing Costs:			
Variable	$ (400)	$ (700)	$(1,100)
Fixed[a]	(240)	(360)	(600)
Total Nonmanufacturing costs	$ (640)	$(1,060)	$(1,700)
Income (Loss) Before Taxes	$ (240)	$ 40	$ (200)

[a]The fixed nonmanufacturing costs are allocated between the two products on the basis of dollar sales volume on the internal reports.

The regular compound sold for $20 a case and the heavy-duty sold for $30 a case during the first 6 months of 1985. The manufacturing costs by case of product are presented in the schedule at the top of the next column. Each product is manufactured on a separate production line. Annual normal manufacturing capacity is 200,000 cases of each product. However, the plant is capable of producing 250,000 cases of regular compound and 350,000 cases of heavy-duty compound annually.

	Cost per Case	
	Regular	Heavy-Duty
Direct Materials	$ 7.00	$ 8.00
Direct Labor	4.00	4.00
Variable Manufacturing Overhead	1.00	2.00
Fixed Manufacturing Overhead[a]	4.00	5.00
Total Manufacturing Cost	$16.00	$19.00
Variable Nonmanufacturing Costs	$ 4.00	$ 7.00

[a]Depreciation charges are 50 percent of the fixed manufacturing overhead of each line.

The schedule below reflects the consensus of top management regarding the price-volume alternatives for the Cleen-Brite products of the last 6 months of 1985.

These are essentially the same alternatives management had during the first 6 months of 1985.

Regular Compound		Heavy-Duty Compound	
Alternative Prices (per case)	**Sales Volume (in cases)**	**Alternative Prices (per case)**	**Sales Volume (in cases)**
$18	120,000	$25	175,000
20	100,000	27	140,000
21	90,000	30	100,000
22	80,000	32	55,000
23	50,000	35	35,000

Top management believes the loss for the first 6 months reflects a tight profit margin caused by intense competition. Management also believes that many companies will be forced out of this market by next year and profits should improve.

a. What unit selling price should Stac Industries select for each of the Cleen-Brite compounds (regular and heavy-duty) for the remaining 6 months of 1985? Support your selection with appropriate calculations.

b. Without prejudice to your answer to part **a**, assume that the optimum price-volume alternatives for the last 6 months were a selling price of $23 and a volume level of 50,000 cases for the regular compound and a selling price of $35 and a volume of 35,000 cases for the heavy-duty compound.

(1) Should Stac Industries consider closing down its operations until 1986 in order to minimize its losses? Support your answer with appropriate calculations. (Stac could save none of its fixed costs by temporarily closing.)

(2) Identify and discuss the qualitative factors that should be considered in deciding whether the Clinton Plant should be closed down during the last 6 months of 1985.

42. *Formulating a Linear Programming Problem (Appendix A) (CMA adapted).* The Witchell Corporation manufactures and sells three grades, A, B, and C, of a single wood product. Each grade must be processed through three phases—cutting, fitting, and finishing—before it is sold.

The following unit information is provided:

	A	B	C
Selling Price	$10.00	$15.00	$20.00
Direct Labor	5.00	6.00	9.00
Direct Materials	.70	.70	1.00
Variable Overhead	1.00	1.20	1.80
Fixed Overhead	.60	.72	1.08
Materials Requirements in Board Feet	7	7	10
Labor Requirements in Hours:			
Cutting	$3/6$	$3/6$	$4/6$
Fitting	$1/6$	$1/6$	$2/6$
Finishing	$1/6$	$2/6$	$3/6$

Only 5,000 board feet of direct materials per week can be obtained. The cutting department has 180 hours of labor available each week. The fitting and finishing departments each have 120 hours of labor available each week. No overtime is allowed.

Contract commitments require the company to make 50 units of A per week. In addition, company policy is to produce at least 50 additional units of A, 50 units of B, and 50 units of C each week to actively remain in each of the three markets. Because of competition, only 130 units of C can be sold each week.

Formulate and label the objective function and the constraint functions necessary to maximize the contribution margin.

43. *Inventory Usage Analysis* (knowledge of probabilities needed for part **c**) *(CMA adapted)*. Thoran Electronics Company began producing pacemakers last year. At that time, the company forecasted the need for 10,000 integrated circuits annually. During the first year, the company placed orders when the inventory dropped to 600 units so that it would have enough to produce pacemakers continuously during a 3-week lead time. Unfortunately, the company ran out of this component on several occasions, causing costly production delays. Careful study of last year's experience resulted in the following expectations for the coming year:

Weekly Usage	Related Probability of Usage	Lead Time	Related Probability of Lead Time
280 Units	.2	3 Weeks.	.1
180 Units	.8	2 Weeks.	.9
	1.0		1.0

The study also suggested that usage during a given week was statistically independent of usage during any other week and usage was also statistically independent of lead time.

    a. The expected average usage during a regular production week is
      (1) 180 units.
      (2) 200 units.
      (3) 280 units.
      (4) 460 units.
      (5) Some usage other than those given above.
    b. The expected usage during lead time is
      (1) 840 units.
      (2) 400 units.
      (3) 360 units.
      (4) 420 units.
      (5) Some usage other than those given above.
    c. If the company reorders circuits when the inventory has dropped to a level of 700 units, the probability that it will run out of this component before the order is received is
      (1) .0008.
      (2) .0040.

(3) .0104.

(4) .0400.

(5) Some amount other than those given above.

44. *Computing Optimal Safety-Stock Levels (CMA adapted).* The Starr Company manufactures several products. One of its main products requires an electric motor. The management of Starr Company used the EOQ model to determine that the optimum number of motors to order is 3,000 per order. Management now wants to determine how much safety stock to keep on hand.

The company uses 30,000 motors annually at the rate of 100 per working day. The motors regularly cost $60 each. The lead time for an order is 5 days. The cost to carry a motor in stock is $10. If a stock-out occurs, management must purchase motors at retail from an alternate supplier. The alternate supplier charges $80 per motor.

Starr Company has analyzed the usage during the past reorder periods by examining inventory records. The records indicate the following usage patterns during past reorder periods:

Usage During Lead Time	Number of Times Quantity Was Used
440	6
460	12
480	16
500	130
520	20
540	10
560	6
	200

Compute the least-cost safety stock level and the total differential costs at that level.

45. *Inventory Costs Versus Costs for Inventory Management (CMA adapted).* Pointer Furniture Company manufactures and sells office furniture. To compete effectively in different markets, it produces several brands of office furniture. The manufacturing operation is organized by the item produced rather than by the furniture line. Thus, the desks for all brands are manufactured on the same production line. The desks are manufactured in batches. For example, 10 high-quality desks might be manufactured during the first 2 weeks in October and 50 units of a lower-quality desk during the last 2 weeks. Because each model has its own unique manufacturing requirement, the change from one model to another requires the factory's equipment to be adjusted.

Management of Pointer wants to compute the most economical production run for each of the items in its product lines. One of the cost parameters that must be determined before the model can be employed is the setup cost incurred when there is a change to a different furniture model. The accounting department has been asked to determine the setup cost for the desk (Model JE 40) in its junior executive line as an example.

The equipment maintenance department is responsible for all of the changeover adjustments on production lines in addition to the preventive and regular maintenance of all the production equipment. The equipment maintenance staff has a 40-hour work week; the size of the staff is changed only if there is a change in the work load that is expected to persist for an extended period of time. The equipment maintenance department had 10 employees last year, and they each averaged 2,000 hours for the year. They are paid $9 an hour, and employee benefits average 20 percent of wage costs. The other departmental costs, which include such items as supervision, depreciation, insurance, and so on, total $50,000 per year.

Two workers from the equipment maintenance department are required to make the change on the desk line for Model JE 40. They spend an estimated 5 hours setting up the equipment. The desk production line on which Model JE 40 is manufactured is operated by five workers. During the changeover, these workers assist the maintenance workers when needed and operate the line during the test run. (The test run takes one machine hour.) However, they are idle for approximately 40 percent of the time required for the changeover.

The production workers are paid a basic wage rate of $7.50 an hour. Two overhead bases are used to apply the overhead costs of this production line because some of the costs vary in proportion to direct labor hours whereas others vary with machine hours. The overhead rates applicable for the current year are as follows:

	Based on Direct Labor Hours	Based on Machine Hours
Variable	$2.75	$ 5.00
Fixed	2.25	15.00
	$5.00	$20.00

These department overhead rates are based on an expected activity of 10,000 direct labor hours and 1,500 machine hours for the current year. This department is not scheduled to operate at full capacity because production capability currently exceeds sales potential.

The estimated cost of the direct materials used in the test run totals $200. Salvage material from the test run should total $50. Pointer's cost of capital is 20 percent.

    a. Prepare an estimate of Pointer Furniture Company's setup cost for desk Model JE 40 for use in the economic production run model. For each cost item identified in the problem, justify the amount and the reason for including the cost item in your estimate. Explain the reason for excluding any cost item from your estimate.

    b. Identify the cost items that would be included in an estimate of Pointer Furniture Company's cost of carrying the desks in inventory.

46. *Comprehensive Differential Costing Case.* Hospital Supply, Inc., produced hydraulic hoists that were used by hospitals to move bed-ridden patients. The costs of manufacturing and marketing hydraulic hoists at the company's normal volume of 3,000 units per month are shown in Exhibit 8.20.

Exhibit 8.20
Costs per Unit for Hydraulic Hoists

Unit Manufacturing Costs:		
Variable Materials	$100	
Variable Labor	150	
Variable Overhead	50	
Fixed Overhead	120	
Total Unit Manufacturing Costs		$420
Unit Marketing Costs:		
Variable	$ 50	
Fixed	140	
Total Unit Marketing Costs		190
Total Unit Costs.		$610

The following questions refer only to the data given above. Unless otherwise stated, assume that there is no connection between the situations described in the questions; each is to be treated independently. Unless otherwise stated, a regular selling price of $740 per unit should be assumed. Ignore income taxes and other costs that are not mentioned in Exhibit 8.20 or in a question itself.

a. What is the breakeven volume in units? In sales dollars?

b. Market research estimates that volume could be increased to 3,500 units, which is well within hoist production capacity limitations, if the price were cut from $740 to $650 per unit. Assuming that the cost behavior patterns implied by the data in Exhibit 8.20 are correct, would you recommend that this action be taken? What would be the impact on monthly sales, costs, and income?

c. On March 1, a contract offer is made to Hospital Supply by the federal government to Supply 500 units to Veterans Administration hospitals for delivery by March 31. Because of an unusually large number of rush orders from their regular customers, Hospital Supply plans to produce 4,000 units during March, which will use all available capacity. If the government order is accepted, 500 units normally sold to regular customers will be lost to a competitor. The contract given by the government would reimburse the government's share of March manufacturing costs, plus pay a fixed fee (profit) of $50,000. (There would be no variable marketing costs incurred on the government's units.) What impact would accepting the government contract have on March income?

d. Hospital Supply has an opportunity to enter a foreign market in which price competition is keen. An attraction of the foreign market is that demand there is greatest when demand in the domestic market is quite low; thus idle production facilities could be used without affecting domestic business.

An order for 1,000 units is being sought at a below-normal price in order to enter this market. Shipping costs for this order will amount to $75 per unit, while total costs of obtaining the contract (marketing costs) will be $4,000. Domestic business would be unaffected by this order. What is the minimum unit price Hospital Supply should consider for this order of 1,000 units?

e. An inventory of 230 units of an obsolete model of the hoist remains in the stockroom. These must be sold through regular channels at reduced prices, or the inventory will soon be valueless. What is the minimum price that would be acceptable in selling these units?

f. A proposal is received from an outside contractor who will make and ship 1,000 hydraulic hoist units per month directly to Hospital Supply's customers as orders are received from Hospital Supply's sales force. Hospital Supply's fixed marketing costs would be unaffected, but its variable marketing costs would be cut by 20 percent for these 1,000 units produced by the contractor. Hospital Supply's plant would operate at two-thirds of its normal level and total fixed manufacturing costs would be cut by 30 percent. What in-house unit cost should be used to compare with the quotation received from the supplier? Should the proposal be accepted for a price (that is, payment to the contractor) of $425 per unit?

g. Assume the same facts as above in part **f**, except that the idle facilities would be used to produce 800 modified hydraulic hoists per month for use in hospital operating rooms. These modified hoists could be sold for $900 each, while the costs of production would be $550 per unit variable manufacturing expense. Variable marketing costs would be $100 per unit. Fixed marketing and manufacturing costs would be unchanged whether the original 3,000 regular hoists were manufactured or the mix of 2,000 regular hoists plus 800 modified hoists were produced. What is the maximum purchase price per unit that Hospital Supply should be willing to pay the outside contractor? Should the proposal be accepted for a price of $425 per unit to the contractor?

47. *Make Versus Buy—Liquid Chemical Case.* See Problem 35 at the end of Chapter 9. Identify four alternative actions and the differential costs (that is, cash flows) for each alternative.

Suggested Solutions to Even-Numbered Exercises

12. *Product choice.*
Alternative 1: Sell ingots only
Alternative 2: Sell semi-finished steel only
Alternative 3: Sell finished steel only

	Alternative		
	1	**2**	**3**
Revenue	$960,000	$982,800	$1,101,100
Less Variable Costs	(40,000)	(70,000)	(95,000)
Total Contribution Margin	$920,000	$912,800	$1,006,100
Less Fixed Costs	(600,000)	(600,000)	(600,000)
Net Operating Profit	$320,000	$312,800	$ 406,100

Maximillian Steel should produce finished steel.

14. *Make-or-Buy.*

a.

	Buy	Make	Difference
Raw Materials	—	$ 80,000	—
Direct Labor	—	100,000	—
Variable Overhead	—	32,000	—
Total Variable Costs	$280,000	$212,000	$68,000

Reliant Enterprises can save $68,000 by making its own sails.

b. The opportunity cost of utilizing the factory space will be $12,000 per year. This will not alter the decision in **a** above but the net benefits will be reduced to $56,000.

16. *Product mix decisions.*

	Manual	Electric	Quartz
Machine Time per Unit	0.4 hr.	2.5 hr.	5.0 hr.
Contribution Margin	$10.00	$16.00	$22.00
Contribution Margin per Machine Hour	$25.00	$ 6.40	$ 4.40

Timeless Products should drop the quartz line.

18. *Economic order quantity.*

a. $D = 250$ batches of 1,000 bolts

$K_0 = \$10$

$K_c = 0.20 \times \$10 = \$2$

$$Q = \sqrt{\frac{2 \times \$10 \times 250}{\$2}} = 50$$

$$N = \frac{D}{Q} = \frac{250}{50} = 5$$

Annual ordering costs $= \$50$.

b. $D = 25$ batches of 10,000 bolts

$K_0 = \$10$

$K_c = 0.20 \times \$96.10 = \$19.22$

$$Q = \sqrt{\frac{2 \times \$10 \times 25}{\$19.22}} = 5.1$$

$$N = \frac{D}{Q} = \frac{25}{5.1} = 4.9.$$

Annual ordering costs $=$ \$49. But it would not be possible to order 51,000 bolts at a time, because bolts are only available in 10,000 bolt batches.

c. If both size batches can be ordered, the optimum solution is to make 4.9 orders per year of 51,000 bolt batches (5 lots of 10,000 and one lot of 1,000).

20. *Product mix decisions.*

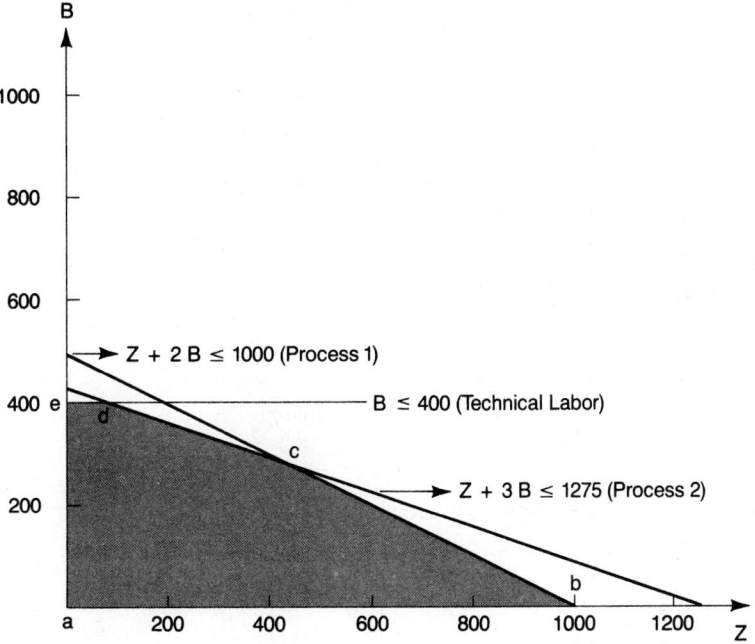

Problem Formulation:

Maximize Total Contribution Margin $= 4.00\,Z + 5.25\,B$.

Subject to:

Process 1 Constraint: $Z + 2B \leq 1000$

Process 2 Constraint: $Z + 3B \leq 1275$

Technical Labor Constraint: $B \leq 400$.

| Critical Points | Produce and Sell | | Total Contribution |
	Z	B	Margin[c]
a	–0–	–0–	–0–
b	1000	–0–	$4000.00*
c	450[a]	275[a]	$3243.75
d	75[b]	400[b]	$2400.00
e	–0–	400	$2100.00

*Optimal Solution

[a]$Z + 2 B = 1000$ (Process 1 Constraint)

$Z + 3 B = 1275$ (Process 2 Constraint)

Solving simultaneously:

$(1000 - 2 B) + 3 B = 1275$

$$B = \underline{275}$$

$$Z + 2(275) = 1000$$

$$\therefore Z = \underline{450}$$

[b]$Z + 3 B = 1275$

$B = 400.$

Solving Simultaneously:

$Z + 3(400) = 1275$

$Z = \underline{75}.$

[c]Total Contribution Margin $= \$4.00\ Z + \$5.25\ B.$

22. *Finding most profitable price-quantity combination*

a.

(1) Price	(2) Quantity Demanded	(3) Revenues	(4) Total[a] Variable Manufacturing Costs	(5) Total[b] Variable Selling and Administrative Costs	(6) Total Costs[c]	(7) Total Profit[d]
$10	40,000	$400,000	$160,000	$80,000	$290,000	$110,000
$12	36,000	$432,000	$144,000	$72,000	$266,000	$166,000
$14	28,000	$392,000	$112,000	$56,000	$218,000	$174,000
$16	24,000	$384,000	$ 96,000	$48,000	$194,000	$190,000
$18	18,000	$324,000	$ 72,000	$36,000	$158,000	$166,000
$20	15,000	$300,000	$ 60,000	$30,000	$140,000	$160,000

[a]Quantity demanded $\times$ \$4.

[b]Quantity demanded $\times$ \$2.

[c]Columns (4) + (5) + $50,000 [fixed manufacturing + administrative costs].

[d]Column (3) − (6).

b. A price of $16 should be selected because it results in the most profit.

Chapter 9 · Long-Run Decisions and Capital Budgeting

Earlier chapters considered the application of the differential principle to several kinds of short-run operating decisions. In each of the cases discussed, the firm's capacity was fixed. The objective was to decide how best to use that fixed capacity in the short run—for example, how many units should be produced? This chapter shifts attention to the long run. We focus on decisions to change operating capacity. Should a larger plant be built? Should a new branch bank be opened? Should a retail store be enlarged? Should new machinery be acquired to replace older, less efficient machinery? Should machinery be acquired that will perform services currently performed by workers? No decision is more important to the long-run success of a firm than deciding which investment projects to undertake.

Short-run operating decisions and long-run capacity decisions are similar in that both rely on an incremental analysis of cash inflows and cash outflows. There is one important difference, however. Long-run capacity decisions involve cash flows over several future periods, whereas typical operating decisions involve only short-range cash flows. When the cash flows extend over several future periods in different patterns for various alternatives, some technique must be employed for making the cash flows comparable. This technique is *present value analysis,* sometimes called *discounted cash flow* or *DCF* analysis. The Appendix at the back of this book discusses present value analysis. You should be familiar with its contents before studying this chapter.

Capital Budgeting: Investment and Financing Decisions

Capital budgeting involves making decisions about which long-term investments to undertake and how to finance them. A firm faced with a decision to acquire a new plant or equipment must decide:

1. Whether to acquire the new asset (the investment decision); and
2. How to raise the funds required to obtain the new asset (the financing decision).

The funds might be raised through borrowing, by retaining earnings (curtailing dividends), or by issuing additional capital stock.

One of the most significant contributions to the theory of finance in recent years is the principle that the investment decision should generally be made independently of the financing decision. That is, the investment decision should be made first, and only after a project gets the go-ahead should management begin to consider how to finance it.

The rationale for separating investment and financing decisions is the premise that all of a firm's assets are financed by all of a firm's equities (that is, liabilities plus owners' equity). A new asset will involve investing funds, but once the asset is added to the firm's portfolio of assets, it is financed by all of the firm's equities. This chapter focuses on the investment decision. Specific equities generally do not finance specific assets. Chapter 10 discusses this issue.

Discounted Cash Flow Methods

If you have an opportunity to invest $1 today in return for $2 in the future, your evaluation of the attractiveness of the opportunity depends, in part, on how long you have to wait for the $2. If you must wait only 1 week after making the initial investment, you are much more inclined to accept the offer than if you have to wait 10 years to receive the $2. Discounted cash flow (DCF) methods are designed to aid the evaluation of investments involving cash flows over time where the time between cash payment and receipt is significant. The two discounted cash flow methods most often discussed and used are the *net present value (NPV) method* and the *internal rate of return (IRR) method*. This chapter discusses the net present value method. Chapter 10 discusses the internal rate of return method.

The Net Present Value Method

The net present value method involves the following steps:

1. Estimating the amounts of future cash inflows and future cash outflows for each alternative under consideration.
2. Discounting the future cash flows to the present using the firm's cost of capital.
3. Accepting or rejecting the proposed project or selecting from a set of mutually exclusive projects.

If the net present value of the future cash inflows and outflows for an alternative is positive, then the alternative should be accepted. If the net present value of the future cash flows is negative, then the alternative should be rejected. If one from a set of mutually exclusive alternatives must be chosen, select the one with the largest net present value of cash flows.

This three-step procedure summarizes a complex process involving many esti-mates and predictions. These complexities are considered later in this chapter. For now, however, we examine two illustrations of the net present value method, the first ignoring income taxes and the second considering income taxes.

Illustration Ignoring Income Taxes

The example in this section illustrates the steps of the net present value method. After we introduce the basics here, the example is complicated somewhat in a later section. Finally, the Problems for Self-Study at the end of the chapter also show more complicated examples.

Garden Winery Company is contemplating the acquisition of equipment that will allow it to bring a new variety of wine to the market. The equipment costs $100,000 and is expected to last 4 years. Exhibit 9.1 shows the cash inflows and cash outflows expected from this equipment during each of the 4 years of its useful life. At the end of Year 0, that is, at the start of the project, the equipment is purchased for $100,000. The decreasing pattern of cash inflows over the 4 years results in part from the equipment becoming less productive over time and in part from the expected reaction of other wine sellers, who will copy the new wine variety and force down the selling price.

The cash outflows for each of the 4 years are for labor, grapes, bottles, and similar costs. We have assumed that the equipment has a zero salvage value at the end of 4 years. Column (4) shows the net cash flow for each year.

Exhibit 9.1
GARDEN WINERY COMPANY
Cash Flows Associated with a New Wine Project
(ignoring income taxes)[a]

Cash Flow Analysis

End of Year (1)	Cash Inflows (2)	Cash Outflows (3)	Net Cash Inflow (Outflows) (4)	Present Value Factor at 25 Percent (5)	Present Value of Cash Flows (6)
0	—	$100,000	$(100,000)	1.00000	$(100,000)
1	$ 60,000	10,000	50,000	.80000	40,000
2	55,000	10,000	45,000	.64000	28,800
3	50,000	10,000	40,000	.51200	20,480
4	40,000	10,000	30,000	.40960	12,288
Total	$205,000	$140,000	$ 65,000		$ 1,568

Accounting Income Data

Year (7)	Revenues (8)	–	Other Expenses (9)	–	Depreciation (10)	=	Net Income (11)
0	—		—		—		—
1	$60,000	–	$10,000	–	$25,000	=	$25,000
2	55,000	–	10,000	–	25,000	=	20,000
3	50,000	–	10,000	–	25,000	=	15,000
4	40,000	–	10,000	–	25,000	=	5,000
Total							$65,000

[a]Amounts in columns are derived as follows:
(2), (3), (8), (9): given.
(4) = (2) − (3).
(5) is based on the factors in Table 2 at the back of the book.
(6) = (4) × (5).
(10) = $100,000 ÷ 4.
(11) = (8) − (9) − (10).

The cash flow related to equipment represents the initial outlay for its acquisition, not its depreciation, which appears in the financial statements, as in the bottom panel of Exhibit 9.1. Depreciation is an accounting *allocation* of cost to periods of benefit. Although the acquisition has no immediate impact on income, it does affect cash flow at the time of acquisition. (In practice, there can be a cash inflow upon disposal of the asset at the end of the project's life.) The cash flow data show the correct timing of cash flows, whereas accrual accounting data do not. Hence, cash flows enable decision makers to compute the time value of money as needed for investment decisions, thus making cash flow data the correct input for investment decision making.

Because cash can be invested over time to earn interest, cash received or paid today has a higher present value than cash to be received or paid at some time in the future. To put the cash flows in column **(4)** on an equivalent basis, they are discounted to their present value. The discount rate used in this illustration is 25 percent. (We discuss the selection of an appropriate discount rate later.) If cash can be invested to earn 25 percent, the right to receive $50,000 at the end of Year 1 is equivalent to receiving $40,000 today. Column **(5)** shows the discount factors for the present value of $1 for various periods at 25 percent. Column **(6)** shows the present value of each cash flow.

This project results in a positive net present value of $1,568. That is, the present value of the net future cash inflows exceeds the initial investment by $1,568. This project should therefore be accepted because its net present value is greater than zero. Accepting positive net present value projects increases the value of the firm, assuming that the discount rate is the firm's opportunity cost of capital, as discussed later.

Identifying Cash Flows

In practice, analysts consider a variety of cash flows. The following checklist of cash flows is reasonably detailed. Later sections explain and illustrate some of the more difficult steps. The cash flows associated with an investment project can be classified as those at the inception of the project (the initial cash flows), those occurring during the life of the project (the periodic cash flows), and those occurring at the conclusion of the project (the terminal cash flows). This three-way classification of cash flows includes the following.

Initial Cash Flows

1. Asset cost—outflow.

2. Freight and installation costs—outflow.

3. Salvage or other disposal value of existing asset—inflow.

4. Income tax effect, gain or loss, on disposal of existing asset—outflow (if gain) or inflow (if loss).

5. Investment tax credit on new asset—inflow.

Periodic Cash Flows

1. Receipts (*not* revenues, which generally precede receipt) from sales—inflow.

2. Lost "other" revenues caused by undertaking this particular project, if any—outflow. (For example, the new equipment for Garden Winery allows the company to market a new wine. If this results in a decrease in the sales of other wine, then there would be lost "other" revenues.)

3. Expenditures for fixed and variable production costs—outflow (at time of incurrence, which generally precedes date of sale).

4. Savings for fixed and variable production costs, if any—inflow.

5. Selling, general, and administrative expenditures—outflows.

6. Savings in selling, general, and administrative expenditures, if any—inflows.

7. Income tax effects of flows **1–6**—inflow if item is an outflow and outflow if item is an inflow. The tax effect may occur in a different period from the above items. For example, the tax effect of cost of goods manufactured and sold occurs for the period of sale, which generally follows the period of cash outflow to purchase raw materials and manufacture the goods.

8. Savings in taxes caused by deductibility of depreciation on tax return (sometimes called "depreciation tax shield")—inflow.

9. Loss in tax savings from lost depreciation, if any—outflow.

10. Do *not* count noncash items such as depreciation expense or allocated items of overhead not requiring incremental cash expenditures.

Terminal Cash Flows

1. Proceeds of salvage of equipment—inflow.

2. Tax on gain (or loss) on salvage, if any—outflow (or inflow).

The example in the next section illustrates some of the complexities introduced by income taxes.

Illustration Considering Income Taxes

Income taxes affect both the *amounts* of cash flows and the *timing* of cash flows, and, consequently, must be considered in making investment decisions.

Reconsider the proposed equipment acquisition for Garden Winery Company. In this case, assume an income tax rate of 40 percent and a discount rate for aftertax cash flows of 15 percent [= .25 × (1 − .40)]. Also assume that straight-line depreciation is used. The top panel of Exhibit 9.2 shows the calculation of the net present value of the proposed project, assuming that the equipment is depreciated using the straight-line method for income tax purposes. Although depreciation is not a cash flow, it does represent a deductible expense. Hence, depreciation affects cash flows by way of its effect on taxable income and the income taxes paid. Using

Exhibit 9.2
GARDEN WINERY COMPANY[a]
Cash Flows Associated with a
New Wine Project
(considering income taxes)

End of Year (1)	Cash Inflows (2)	Cash Outflows (3)	Pretax Net Cash Flow (4)	Depreciation Expense (5)	Taxable Income (6)	Income Tax Payable[b] (7)	Net Cash Inflow (Outflow) (8)	Present Value Factor at 15 Percent (9)	Present Value of Cash Flows (10)
A. Straight-Line Depreciation Method									
0 . .	—	$100,000	$(100,000)	—	—	—	$(100,000)	1.00000	$(100,000)
1 . .	$ 60,000	10,000	50,000	$ 25,000	$25,000	$10,000	40,000	.86957	34,783
2 . .	55,000	10,000	45,000	25,000	20,000	8,000	37,000	.75614	27,977
3 . .	50,000	10,000	40,000	25,000	15,000	6,000	34,000	.65752	22,356
4 . .	40,000	10,000	30,000	25,000	5,000	2,000	28,000	.57175	16,009
Total	$205,000	$140,000	$ 65,000	$100,000	$65,000	$26,000	$ 39,000		$ 1,125
B. Accelerated Cost Recovery Method									
0 . .	—	$100,000	$(100,000)	—	—	—	$(100,000)	1.00000	$(100,000)
1 . .	$ 60,000	10,000	50,000	$ 25,000	$25,000	$10,000	40,000	.86957	34,783
2 . .	55,000	10,000	45,000	38,000	7,000	2,800	42,200	.75614	31,909
3 . .	50,000	10,000	40,000	37,000	3,000	1,200	38,800	.65752	25,512
4 . .	40,000	10,000	30,000	–0–	30,000	12,000	18,000	.57175	10,292
Total	$205,000	$140,000	$ 65,000	$100,000	$65,000	$26,000	$ 39,000		$ 2,496

[a]Amounts in columns are derived as follows:

(2), (3): given.   (5) Panel B: $100,000 × .25 = $25,000.   (6) = (4) − (5).   (9) Based on the factors
(4) = (2) − (3). $100,000 × .38 = $38,000.   (7) = .40 × (6).   from Table 2 at the
(5) Panel A = $100,000 ÷ 4. $100,000 × .37 = $37,000.   (8) = (4) − (7).   back of the book.
                                                                                                        (10) = (8) × (9).

[b]Excludes effect of investment tax credit.

a 15 percent discount rate, the project has a positive net present value of $1,125 and should be accepted.

Accelerated Cost Recovery One of the most important effects of income tax laws on investment decisions arises from the firm's ability to use accelerated depreciation methods, called the "accelerated cost recovery system" or ACRS, in the income tax laws. ACRS shifts depreciation charges from later to earlier years as compared to the straight-line method. This has the effect of shifting taxable income and tax payments from earlier to later years. Although accelerated cost recovery does not change the total tax liability generated by a project over its life, it does influence the desirability of the project by affecting the timing of cash flows.

The lower panel of Exhibit 9.2 shows the calculation of the net present value of the project assuming that ACRS is used. (The investment tax credit is discussed later.) Assume that equipment with a 4-year life such as that acquired by Garden Winery can be depreciated over *3* years for tax purposes under ACRS: 25 percent in the first year, 38 percent in the second, and 37 percent in the third, according to the tax law in effect when this book was published. Note that the total depreciation expense in column **(5)** is $100,000 under both straight-line and ACRS. In the latter case, however, the deductions are more accelerated. The net cash flows in column **(8)** total $39,000 in both cases, but they occur in a different pattern. The net present value of the project is $1,371 (= $2,496 − $1,125) greater if accelerated cost recovery, rather than straight-line, is used for tax purposes.

The Cost of Capital—An Opportunity Cost

Economic theory suggests that the appropriate discount rate to use in evaluating investment projects is the firm's *cost of capital*. The cost of capital (or the "normal rate of return" or the "hurdle rate") is the *opportunity cost* of funds. The opportunity cost of funds used for an investment is the income the owner could have earned if the funds were invested elsewhere. The term *cost of capital* means the minimum rate of return required by the owner of an asset to justify using it. The term is short for "opportunity cost of capital."

Measuring the Cost of Capital

Often, firms *measure* the cost of capital by computing the cost of all of the liabilities and owners' equity on the balance sheet. All of the assets of a corporation are financed with funds raised from various sources. When financial markets are in equilibrium, the required rates of return on the assets can be deduced from the cost of raising the funds used to acquire assets. Measuring the cost of capital as the weighted average of the sources of funds is often useful, but it confuses some people into thinking that the average cost of liabilities and owners' equity *is* the cost of capital. It is not; the cost of capital is the required rate of return on the assets themselves.

Cost of capital is a notion about *assets;* the measurement just described concerns liabilities and other equities. As an extreme example,[1] suppose that we have $10,000 cash to invest. Assume that the required rate of return on that asset is determined by the highest risk-free interest that can be earned from using that cash. If this is 12 percent per year, then the cost of capital is 12 percent per year. Notice that the derivation of the required rate of return, the cost of capital, does not require knowing how the asset, $10,000 cash, was raised. If the $10,000 was earned by hard physical labor harvesting crops, its cost of capital is 12 percent. If the $10,000 was found in the street or won in a lottery, its cost of capital is 12 percent. No matter the origin of the funds, the cost of capital—the required rate of return on the asset cash—is 12 percent. The important point is that the cost of capital does *not* depend on the source of funds used to acquire those assets. It does depend on the risk characteristics of the alternative investments: the riskier the project, the higher the cost of capital.

---

[1]This example was first suggested, to our knowledge, by Professor Ezra Solomon of Stanford University.

One may choose *to measure* the cost of capital by looking at the cost of liabilities and owners' equity, but one should not confuse that *measure* of the cost of capital with the actual cost of capital, which is the required rate of return on assets of comparable risk.

Using the Cost of Capital in Making Investment Decisions

Because we separate the investment and financing decisions, we expect each investment project (with risk equal to the average for the firm) to earn a rate of return equal to at least the *average* cost of capital for the firm. If the project earns just the cost of capital (that is, the project has a zero net present value), then the market value of the firm's shares will remain unchanged as a result of the new investment project. If a project has a positive net present value, then the market value of the firm's shares should increase when that project is undertaken. This occurs because the firm is able to generate a higher rate of return than the average rate required by the suppliers of capital. Because the returns to creditors and preferred shareholders are fixed, this excess return accrues to the benefit of the common shareholders.

The subtleties of computing the cost of capital rate are properly the subject of finance books.[2] Here, the emphasis is on using that rate. The decision rule is: *A firm should undertake an investment project if the net present value of the cash flows is positive when the cash flows are discounted at the cost of capital rate.*

Sensitivity of Net Present Value to Estimates

The calculation of the net present value of a proposed project requires three types of predictions or estimates:

1. The amount of future cash flows.
2. The timing of future cash flows.
3. The cost of capital rate.

There is likely to be some error in the amount predicted or estimated for each of these three items. The net present value model exhibits different degrees of sensitivity to such errors.

Amounts of Future Cash Flows

Errors in predicting the amounts of future cash flows are likely to have the largest impact of the three items. Exhibit 9.2 indicated that the proposed project for Garden Winery Company had a net present value (using the straight-line depreciation method)

---

[2]See, for example, J. Fred Weston and Eugene F. Brigham, *Managerial Finance*, 7th ed. (Hinsdale, Ill.: Dryden Press, 1981); or Thomas E. Copeland and J. Fred Weston, *Financial Theory and Corporate Policy* (Reading, Mass.: Addison-Wesley, 1979).

of $1,125 based on the cash flows initially predicted. Suppose that there is a 10 percent error in these predictions and that the estimate of future cash flows (excluding the initial $100,000 outlay and the investment tax credit) each year should have been 10 percent less than the amounts shown in column **(8)** of Exhibit 9.2. The net present value of the proposed project using the same 15 percent discount rate is *minus* $8,988.[3] The total error in present value dollars is $10,113 (= $1,125 + $8,988), which is about 10 percent of the initial investment, $100,000. Given the sensitivity of the net present value to errors in the predictions of cash flows, accurate predictions are desirable. Statistical techniques have recently been developed for dealing with the uncertainty inherent in predictions of cash flows. These techniques, which build on the net present value model, are beyond the scope of this book.[4]

Timing of Future Cash Flows

The degree of sensitivity of the net present value model to shifts in the pattern, but not in the total amount, of cash flows depends on the extent of the shifting. Column **(8)** of Exhibit 9.2 shows net cash flows for Years 1 through 4 of $40,000, $37,000, $34,000, and $28,000, or $139,000 in total when the straight-line depreciation method is used. Suppose that the pattern of cash flows should have been estimated to be relatively stable as follows: $35,000, $35,000, $35,000, $34,000, again a total of $139,000. The net present value in the latter case would be *minus* $647, as compared to $1,125 in Exhibit 9.2.[5] The error is $1,772 (= $1,125 + $647) in present value terms, or about 2 percent of the initial investment. Other examples could be constructed that would result in a different percentage effect. It seems clear, however, that errors in predicting the amount of cash flows tend to be more serious than in predicting their pattern.

Calculation of Cost of Capital

A third uncertain factor in the net present value calculation is the cost of capital. The difficulty here lies not in predicting a future cash flow but in estimating returns to alternative uses of capital. No satisfactory techniques have yet been developed for empirically verifying a firm's estimate of its cost of capital rate.

What loss does a firm suffer if it incorrectly calculates its cost of capital? Using the 15 percent aftertax cost of capital for Garden Winery Company in Exhibit 9.2 results in a net present value of $2,496 for the proposed project using ACRS depreciation (ignoring the investment tax credit). If the aftertax cost of capital

---

[3]Note that $-\$100,000 + .90 \times (\$34,783 + \$27,977 + \$22,356 + \$16,009) = -\$8,988$.

[4]Interested readers might consult the following books for additional discussion of capital budgeting under uncertainty: Harold Bierman, Jr., and Seymour Smidt, *The Capital Budgeting Decision*, 5th ed. (New York: Macmillan, 1980); J. Fred Weston and Eugene F. Brigham, *Managerial Finance*, 7th ed. (Hinsdale, Ill.: Dryden Press, 1981), chap. 14.

[5]$-\$100,000 + (\$35,000 \times .86957) + (\$35,000 \times .75614) + (\$35,000 \times .65752) + (\$34,000 \times .57175) = -\$647$.

should have been estimated to be 20 percent, the net present value for this project would have been about minus $6,227. Management miscalculated the cost of capital by one-third $[= (.20 - .15) \div .15]$. That large error resulted in a misestimate of the net present value by about $8,723 $(= \$2,496 + \$6,227)$, or less than 10 percent of the initial investment. In general, if a project is marginally desirable for a given cost of capital, it will ordinarily not be grossly undesirable for slightly higher rates. If a project is clearly worthwhile when the cost of capital is 15 percent, for example, it is likely to be worthwhile even when the cost of capital is 18 or 20 percent.

Complications in Computing Periodic Cash Flows

The steps for using the net present value method have been described and illustrated. In practice, decision makers sometimes have difficulty in computing the periodic aftertax cash flows whose present values are to be summed. Some of the difficulty results from confusion between accounting data and cash flow data. Other difficulty stems from an inability to state clearly which cash flows are differential and which are not. This section describes and illustrates a number of such potential difficulties. Problem 2 for Self-Study at the end of the chapter contains a comprehensive example.

New Asset Acquisition: Deriving the Net Proceeds When Assets Are Retired

Often, when a new investment is to be undertaken, an already-owned product line must be, or can be, discontinued, and already-owned assets sold or otherwise retired. Clear thinking is required in treating the proceeds from selling off such assets. Generally, it is best to construct a series of mutually exclusive investment alternatives, evaluate each, and choose the best.

Example A kitchen appliance manufacturer currently makes food blenders. It is considering manufacturing a more versatile and complex food processor. The existing product line of blenders will generate net cash flows of $200,000 at the end of each of the next 10 years if the manufacturer continues to make and sell blenders. The currently owned equipment to manufacture blenders could be sold today for $1,000,000. This equipment will last 10 years; by then it will have no salvage value. New equipment for manufacturing food processors will cost $5,000,000 but will generate net cash flows of $900,000 at the end of each of the next 15 years. After 15 years, it will have no salvage value. Ignore tax considerations. The two cases below illustrate the construction of the mutually exclusive alternatives.

Case A If food processors are made, there will be no further market for blenders. Although there are several ways to get to the right answer, one can easily err if one tries to combine the cash flow implications of the various strategies. The three mutually exclusive alternatives and their cash flows are as follows:

1. Sell the existing blender equipment and get out of the business. This implies cash flow $+\$1,000,000$ today, a net present value of $+\$1,000,000$ at any discount rate.
2. Stay in the blender business. This implies net cash flows of $+\$200,000$ at the end of each of the next 10 years.
3. Sell the blender equipment and purchase the processor equipment. This implies cash flow of $-\$4,000,000$ ($= -\$5,000,000$ for new $+ \$1,000,000$ from selling old) today and $\$900,000$ at the end of each of the next 15 years.

Using the cost of capital, one computes three net present values and chooses the alternative with the largest one. If alternative 1 is not a realistic alternative, ignore it.

Case B The manufacturer has the alternative of keeping the blender business while adding the processor business. For simplicity, however, we assume that the net cash flow for the first 10 years is $\$1,050,000$ if both blenders and processors are sold. In this case, a fourth mutually exclusive project can be added to the list of three above:

4. Stay in the blender business and add the processor business. This implies cash flow of $-\$5,000,000$ today, $+\$1,050,000$ per year at the end of the next 10 years, and $+\$900,000$ per year at the end of the following 5 years.

Disposal of Currently Owned Assets: Sale or Trade-in

Much of the impact on aftertax cash flows results from the effect of income taxes. If one sells an asset below its taxable "basis" (book value for tax purposes), then the loss can be used to offset otherwise taxable income and reduce income taxes otherwise payable. Special income tax rules apply, however, to trade-in transactions. If the equipment is traded in on the new asset, the amount that would have been a loss had the equipment been sold is not currently deductible, but is added to the tax basis of the new asset. The increase in tax basis results in higher depreciation charges over the life of the new asset, which reduces taxes payable in those years. A loss that is deductible today is more valuable than deductions over the next several years because of the time value of money.

Example The currently owned blender equipment in the preceding example that can be sold for $\$1,000,000$ has a taxable basis of $\$3,000,000$. The income tax rate is 40 percent of pretax income and the manufacturer has sufficient other taxable income to offset losses or depreciation or both on equipment transactions. The owner has been offered $\$1,000,000$ cash for the old equipment or a trade-in of $\$1,200,000$ toward the new processor-making equipment, which would otherwise cost $\$5,000,000$. If the manufacturer sells the equipment for $\$1,000,000$ cash, there will be a tax loss of $\$2,000,000$ ($= \$3,000,000$ basis $- \$1,000,000$ proceeds of sale) to be deducted on the tax return. This loss results in cash savings of $\$800,000$ ($= .40 \times \$2,000,000$) from reduced income taxes otherwise payable. Then the manufacturer will have to pay $\$5,000,000$ cash for the equipment and the depreciable basis for taxes will be $5,000,000. The total cash outflow is $3,200,000 (= $1,000,000 + $800,000 − $5,000,000).

If, on the other hand, the manufacturer trades in the old equipment on the new, then the initial cash outflow will be $3,800,000 (= $5,000,000 − $1,200,000). The journal entry to record the new equipment for tax purposes will be

Equipment—New	6,800,000	
Equipment—Old (Net)		3,000,000
Cash		3,800,000

No gain or loss recognized on trade-in; the tax basis of the new asset is equal to the cash paid for it plus the tax basis of the old asset traded in. (The journal entry for financial reporting may differ from this.)

The depreciable basis of the new asset is larger than the $5,000,000 cost by the $1,800,000 implied loss from trading in an asset for a $1,200,000 allowance when the asset has a book value of $3,000,000. In this case, the analyst must consider two mutually exclusive projects:

1. Initial cash outlay of $3,200,000 (= $5,000,000 for equipment reduced by $1,000,000 proceeds of sale and $800,000 in tax savings) followed by depreciation charges (reducing income taxes in later years) based on asset cost of $5,000,000.
2. Initial cash outlay of $3,800,000 followed by depreciation charges (reducing income taxes in later years) based on asset cost of $6,800,000.

Another way to view this choice is to ask if one should pay $600,000 (= $3,800,000 − $3,200,000) today in return for an extra $1,800,000 (= $6,800,000 − $5,000,000) in depreciation deductions over the life of the asset. The depreciation deductions of $1,800,000 will total $720,000 (= .40 × $1,800,000) in cash savings for income taxes otherwise payable over the depreciable life of the equipment. The net present value analysis will show whether paying $600,000 now for $720,000 over time is a worthwhile investment. Shortcuts such as this are often available, but making mistakes in constructing them is common.

Acquisition of New Assets: Investment Credit

To provide a stimulus for the acquisition of new capital equipment, the federal government reduces income taxes otherwise payable in years when a firm purchases qualifying equipment. Even though some companies account for this cash savings in income taxes over the life of the equipment, the cash flow all occurs in the year the qualifying equipment is put into operation. There is, however, a trade-off between the amount of the investment credit taken and the amount of depreciation that can be deducted for tax purposes, and there can be a trade-off between the amount of the investment credit and the depreciable life of the assets.

Example A corporation plans to acquire a new automobile. It will pay $15,000 cash for this automobile. The firm may depreciate the automobile over either 3 years or 5 years. If it depreciates the automobile over *3* years for tax purposes, it can take an investment credit of 4 percent of the asset's cost, $600 (= .04 × $15,000), and depreciate the asset's entire cost; or it can take an initial investment credit of 6 percent of the asset's cost, $900 (= .06 × $15,000), but then the depreciable basis for tax purposes will be reduced by one-half of the investment credit taken, to $14,550 [= $15,000 × (1.00 − .50 × .06)]. If it depreciates the automobile over *5* years for tax purposes, it can take an investment credit of 8 percent of the asset's cost, $1,200 (= .08 × $15,000), and depreciate the asset's entire cost; or it can take an initial investment credit of 10 percent of the asset's cost, $1,500 (= .10 × $15,000), but then the depreciable basis for tax purposes will be reduced by one-half of the investment credit taken, to $14,250 [= $15,000 × (1.00 − .50 × .10)].[6] In this example, the analyst must choose the best of four mutually exclusive projects:

1. Cash outlay of $14,400 (= $15,000 cost − $600 investment credit) followed by depreciation of $15,000 over 3 years.
2. Cash outlay of $14,100 (= $15,000 cost − $900 investment credit) followed by depreciation of $14,550 over 3 years.
3. Cash outlay of $13,800 (= $15,000 cost − $1,200 investment credit) followed by depreciation of $15,000 over 5 years.
4. Cash outlay of $13,500 (= $15,000 cost − $1,500 investment credit) followed by depreciation of $14,250 over 5 years.

Depreciation and Cash Flow

Depreciation is an expense reducing income, but it does not use cash. The cash effects occur in the year the asset is acquired. Depreciation itself is ignored in deriving cash flows for net present value analysis. Insofar as depreciation is deductible on the tax return, however, it shields otherwise taxable income from taxation. The analyst must be careful to focus on the tax shield provided by depreciation while recognizing that depreciation itself does not affect cash.

Example An automobile costing $15,000 will be depreciated over 5 years using the straight-line method for financial reporting. On the tax return the automobile will be depreciated over 3 years using ACRS: 25 percent in the first year, 38 percent in the second, and 37 percent in the third. The income tax rate is, and is expected to remain, 40 percent of taxable income. The company has sufficient other taxable income that the depreciation deductions can reduce taxable income dollar for dollar. Ignoring investment credits, the cash flows relevant for a net present value analysis are −$15,000 today followed by +$1,500 (= $15,000 × .25 × .40) at the end of the first year, $2,280 (= $15,000 × .38 × .40) at the

---

[6]Three different sets of rules for depreciation and the investment credit have been in force within the 2 years preceding the writing of this chapter. The numbers in this example, and throughout the chapter and its end-of-chapter materials, reflect the rules for 1985, but the rules may have changed by the time you read this.

end of the second year, and $2,220 (= $15,000 × .37 × .40) at the end of the third year. (Of course, the automobile must produce some other positive cash inflows or savings in outflows to be worthwhile.)

Salvage Value of Equipment

When an asset is acquired specifically for a project, the asset's cost (reduced by appropriate investment credits) will be a cash outflow at the start of the project. At the end of the project, the asset will be scrapped or sold or may have some other use. The cash flow impact of the disposal and any tax implications thereof should be included in the analysis as a cash flow of the last period.

Example The food processing equipment described earlier is expected to have a fair market value of $400,000 at the end of the 15-year period of production of food processors. At that time, the manufacturer plans to sell the equipment to a manufacturer of spare parts. The cash flows for the fifteenth year should be increased by $400,000. (There may be tax consequences to consider as well.)

Impact on Working Capital

Ordinarily, when one starts a new business, one expects to tie up cash in inventories, accounts receivable, and bank accounts. Eventually these inventories will be sold for cash, the accounts receivable will be collected, and the cash can be withdrawn from the bank accounts. No special treatment is needed for the cash spent to acquire inventories, for the cash not immediately received from customers who purchase on account, and for the cash in bank accounts. The analyst needs merely to show all cash outlays in the period when they occur and all cash inflows in the period collected, which may differ from the period of sale.[7]

Effect of Inflation on Cash Flows

The cost of capital or discount rate used in computing net present values reflects, at least in part, current market interest rates. Recall that the cost of capital is an opportunity cost, and one alternative opportunity available to all investors is the purchase of relatively risk-free bonds issued by the federal government and of some low-risk corporate bonds. Market interest rates, a factor determining the cost of capital, reflect three separate phenomena:

---

[7]Some textbooks on managerial finance, in treating the subject of working capital requirements for investments projects, show explicit investments in working capital at the start of the project and a specific recovery of it sometime later. This special treatment of the investment in working capital is more likely to confuse than to help. Why should this particular investment be treated differently from any other? We prefer to show all cash inflows and outflows in parallel, not treating any of them differently from the others. The important point is to make sure that, in constructing a dated schedule of cash flows, for example for sales, the time of collection of cash from a sale, not the time of the sale, is used.

1. A "pure" rate of interest reflecting the productive capability of capital assets. (Economists debate the results of empirical research, but most would agree that the pure rate of interest generally lies between 0 and 5 percent per year.)

2. A risk factor reflecting the likelihood of default of the particular borrower. (The federal government has the lowest probability of default, so government bonds usually have the lowest risk premiums.)

3. A premium reflecting inflation expected to occur over the life of the loan. (A lender lends out dollars with a particular purchasing power and receives at maturity dollars with a smaller purchasing power if there has been inflation during the loan term. As the expected rate of inflation increases, the lender will charge a higher interest rate to compensate for the correspondingly larger expected decline in the purchasing power of the dollars loaned out.)

If the pure rate of interest is p, the risk premium is r, and the expected inflation is e, then the market rate of interest i satisfies the following equations:

$$(1 + i) = (1 + p)(1 + r)(1 + e),$$

or

$$i = (1 + p)(1 + r)(1 + e) - 1.$$

Example Assume a pure rate of interest of 3 percent, a risk premium for the Fisher Corporation of 2 percent, and an expected rate of inflation for the next year of 9 percent. The market rate of interest i for Fisher Corporation is

$$i = (1.03)(1.02)(1.09) - 1$$

$$= .145 \quad \text{or} \quad 14.5 \text{ percent.}$$

Thus, in times of expected general inflation, interest rates are higher than in times of lower expected general inflation. High costs of capital, other things being equal, reflect high expected inflation.[8] Decision makers using the net present value method with market interest rates influencing the cost of capital therefore are reflecting anticipated inflation in the discounting process. Such decision makers would be inconsistent if they did not also reflect the effects of anticipated future inflation on cash flows.

Example An owner of a plot of land zoned for commercial use is considering renting the land to the operator of a supermarket. Rental payments to the owner will be based on a percentage of retail sales. Analysis shows that, given the traffic patterns in the area, 4,000 families per week can be expected to do their shopping in this store. Because of competing stores in nearby neighborhoods and the fact that there is little room for further real estate development in the market area of

---

[8]Compare, for example, the rate of interest and rates of inflation in the early 1960s to those of the late 1970s.

the proposed supermarket, the owner is fairly sure that the number of families using the store will not change substantially over time. The owner's aftertax cost of capital is 15 percent per year. The owner can easily estimate the rental payments for the first year.

Given an estimate that the number of families shopping will not increase over time, it would be easy for the analyst to project level cash flows for the 10-year proposed lease term. Assume, for example, that the proposed rental terms are projected to result in a payment by the supermarket to the lessor of $100,000 at the end of the first year. If the owner projects rental payments of $100,000 each year for 10 years and discounts them at 15 percent per year, the present value of the cash flows is computed to be $501,877 (= $100,000 × 5.01877; see Table 4, 10-period row, 15 percent column). An aftertax cost of capital of 15 percent per year is so high for projects of this risk that it seems likely that the cost of capital anticipates substantial general inflation over the life of the lease. It would be inconsistent not to anticipate that such inflation will increase disposable incomes of shoppers and prices of the merchandise they purchase in the store. Thus, careful analysis will probably project price increases for the items sold in the stores, in the net sales of the store, and in the rental revenues to the owner. If, for example, sales prices increase at the rate of 6 percent per year, then the stream of rental payments will be $106,000 (= $100,000 × 1.06) at the end of the first year, $112,360 (= $100,000 × 1.06^2) at the end of the second year, . . . , $179,085 (= $100,000 × 1.06^{10}) at the end of the tenth year. The net present value of that stream of payments discounted at 15 percent per year is $656,411.[9] This is almost one-third larger than the net present value assuming no increase in selling price and rentals.

Summary

In deciding whether to invest cash today in return for cash payoffs in the future, the decision maker should take into account the time value of money using a discounted cash flow method.

The net present value method involves making forecasts of future cash inflows and outflows for the proposed project. Making effective investment decisions requires careful analysis of accounting data to derive cash flows, which are not identical with revenues and expenses. The estimated cash flows are discounted to present value with a rate equal to the required rate of return on assets. This required rate of return is called the "cost of capital" or the "hurdle rate." The cost of capital is often measured by taking a weighted average of the equities that provide

---

[9]Note that

$$\sum_{i=1}^{10} \frac{\$100,000 \times (1.06)^i}{(1.15)^i} = \sum_{i=1}^{10} \frac{\$100,000}{(1.15/1.06)^i}.$$

Because $1.15 \div 1.06 - 1 = 8.49$ percent, the computation is equivalent to computing the present value of a level annuity of $100,000 per year discounted at 8.49 percent per year.

a firm's financing, even though the cost of capital reflects the opportunity cost of the assets to be committed to the proposed project.

Problem 1 for Self-Study

Kary Kinnard has an opportunity to open a franchised pizza outlet. The building can be leased, so Mr. Kinnard need only invest in equipment, which he estimates will cost $60,000. He will take an investment tax credit of $6,000 (= 10 percent times $60,000) at the end of Year 1. The equipment will be depreciated over 5 years using ACRS percentages of 15, 22, 21, 21, and 21 percent. The depreciable base of the equipment will be reduced to 95 percent of cost because the 10 percent tax credit will be taken. For financial reporting, the equipment will be depreciated over 6 years using the straight-line method. For purposes of this analysis, assume the equipment will last for 6 years, after which it will be sold for $6,000. Any tax gain on the disposal will be taxed at 40 percent at the end of Year 6.

Mr. Kinnard estimates the following revenues, variable costs, and fixed costs from operations for the 6-year period. Expected inflation is reflected in these estimates. Assume end-of-year cash flows.

	1	2	3	4	5	6
Revenues	$30,000	$36,000	$41,000	$45,000	$48,000	$50,000
Variable Costs	12,000	14,400	16,400	18,000	19,200	20,000
Fixed Costs (includes depreciation of $9,000 per year)	14,000	14,200	14,500	14,900	15,400	16,000

Use an aftertax cost of capital of 12 percent per year, and an income tax rate of 40 percent for this analysis. The $60,000 outlay for the equipment will be made at the beginning of Year 1.

Should Mr. Kinnard make the investment?

Suggested Solution

Depreciation Schedule

Year	ACRS Depreciation base = $57,000
1	$ 8,550
2	12,540
3	11,970
4	11,970
5	11,970
	$57,000

Operating Cash Flow Analysis

	1	2	3	4	5	6
Revenues	$30,000	$36,000	$41,000	$45,000	$48,000	$50,000
Less variable costs	12,000	14,400	16,400	18,000	19,200	20,000
Less cash fixed costs.	5,000	5,200	5,500	5,900	6,400	7,000
(1) Income before taxes and depreciation . . .	$13,000	$16,400	$19,100	$21,100	$22,400	$23,000
Depreciation (ACRS)	8,550	12,540	11,970	11,970	11,970	—
Taxable income	$ 4,450	$ 3,860	$ 7,130	$ 9,130	$10,430	$23,000
(2) Tax (40% rate)	1,780	1,544	2,852	3,652	4,172	9,200
Cash flows from operations (1)-(2)	$11,220	$14,856	$16,248	$17,448	$18,228	$13,800
Present value factors (12%)	.89286	.79719	.71178	.63552	.56743	.50663
Present Value . . . . . . $61,849 =	$10,018 +	$11,843 +	$11,565 +	$11,089 +	$10,343 +	$ 6,991

Analysis of All Cash Flows

Operating Cash Flows	$ 61,849
Cash Outlay for Machinery—Year 0	(60,000)
Investment Tax Credit—Year 1 $6,000 (.89286)	5,357
Salvage Proceeds from Selling Machinery—Year 6, $6,000 (.50663)	3,040
Taxes on Salvage Proceeds—Year 6 $6,000 (.40)(.50663)	(1,216)
Net Present Value	$ 9,030

The company should take the project, as it has a positive net present value.

Problem 2 for Self-Study

This comprehensive problem illustrates the analysis of accounting data to derive cash flows for an investment decision and the choice among mutually exclusive alternatives.

Problem Data

Magee Company is contemplating undertaking a new product line. If it does so, it must acquire new equipment with a purchase price of $150,000 at the beginning of Year 1. The equipment will last for 5 years and is expected to have a salvage value of $2,500 in terms of today's purchasing power. Equipment prices, including prices of used equipment of this sort, are forecast to rise at an annual rate of 12 percent, so that the actual salvage expected to be realized at the end of the fifth year is $4,406 (= $2,500 \times 1.12^5$). Any gain on disposal will be taxed at 40 percent, and the taxes on the gain will be payable at the end of Year 6.

Magee Company owns old manufacturing equipment with a book value of $18,000 that must be disposed of, independent of whether the new machine is acquired. The old equipment can be sold for $25,000 cash or traded in on the new equipment for a reduction of $28,000 in cash purchase price. If the old equipment is sold, the gain of $7,000 (= $25,000 − $18,000) will be taxed at the rate of 40 percent, but the taxes will not be payable until the end of Year 1. If the old equipment is traded in, the "gain" on disposal will not be taxed, but will reduce the depreciable basis of the new asset (and future depreciation charges) both for financial accounting and for tax purposes. If there is a trade-in with cash payment of $122,000 (= $150,000 − $28,000), the journal entry will be

New Equipment	140,000	
Old Equipment (Net)		18,000
Cash		122,000

Book value of new equipment is $140,000 for both tax and financial reporting.

New equipment, if acquired, will be depreciated over 5 years for tax purposes using the following ACRS cost percentages: 15, 22, 21, 21, and 21. The equipment is eligible for an investment tax credit that will decrease tax payments at the end of Year 1. The amount of the investment credit is determined jointly by:

1. Whether the equipment is purchased outright for $150,000 or acquired via trade-in for $140,000; and
2. Whether the asset's depreciable basis is reduced by one-half of the investment credit taken, in which case the investment credit is 10 percent of the asset's cost and the depreciable tax basis is 95 percent (= 100 percent − one-half of 10 percent), or the asset's depreciable basis for tax purposes is unreduced by the investment credit taken, in which case the investment credit is 8 percent of the asset's cost.

If the asset is purchased, Magee Company will earn an investment credit of either 8 percent or 10 percent of $150,000. If the asset is acquired with a trade-in, the investment credit will be either 8 percent or 10 percent of $140,000. If the 10 percent credit is taken, the depreciable basis will be reduced by 5 percent, either to $142,500 (= .95 × $150,000) or to $133,000 (= .95 × $140,000). If the 8 percent credit is taken, there will be no reduction in the depreciable basis for tax purposes.

Salvage value need not be considered in computing ACRS deductions for tax purposes, but must be for financial reporting purposes. The equipment will be depreciated for financial reporting over 5 years using the straight-line method. (These combinations result from the rules of generally accepted accounting principles and the income tax law, not from our wish to make the example complicated.) Magee Company spreads the benefit of the investment credit over 5 years in its financial statements. (This is called the "deferral method" and contrasts with the "flow-through method," which reports all the benefits in the year of acquisition.)

Sales volume is forecast to be 15,000 units each year. Sales price is $7.00 per unit for Year 1, but is forecast to increase by 10 percent per year to $7.70 in Year 2, $8.47 in Year 3, and so on. Variable costs of production are $3.00 per unit in Year 1, but are forecast to increase by 8 percent per year to $3.24 in year 2, and so on. Selling costs are $5,000 per year plus $.50 per unit in Year 1; in subsequent years the variable portion of selling costs is forecast to increase at the rate of 10 percent per year to $.55 in Year 2, $.61 in Year 3, and so on. All variable manufacturing costs are assumed to be paid in cash at the beginning of each year. All selling costs are assumed to be paid in cash at the end of each year. All sales and receipts are assumed to occur at the end of each year.

Income taxes on a given year's operations are paid at the end of the year. Although selling costs become deductions on the tax return in the year incurred, manufacturing costs become deductible for taxes only when the goods are sold. Income taxes are paid at the rate of 40 percent of pretax income. Magee Company has sufficient other taxable income that losses on this project can be used to offset other income, saving $.40 in taxes for every $1.00 of operating loss.

Production in each year must be sufficient to meet each year's sales, except that 20,000 units must be produced in the first year to provide a continuing inventory of 5,000 units. Hence, production in Year 5 need be only 10,000 units so that at the end of Year 5, ending inventory will be zero. Inventory will be accounted for with LIFO cost flow. All depreciation charges for a year are product costs to be allocated to units produced in that year.

The Magee Company has an aftertax cost of capital of 15 percent per year.

a. List the mutually exclusive alternatives that Magee Company faces.

b. Magee Company must choose a combination of investment credit and depreciable tax basis. If the investment credit is 8 percent, then the full cost is depreciable for tax purposes. If the investment credit is 10 percent, then the depreciable basis for tax purposes is only 95 percent of the asset's cost. Consider an asset costing $1,000 that can be fully depreciated under ACRS for tax purposes with a 5-year life (cost percentages of 15, 22, 21, 21, and 21) and earns an investment credit of $80 or can have its depreciable tax basis reduced to $950 but earns an investment credit of $100.

Assume an income tax rate of 40 percent and an aftertax cost of capital of 15 percent. Assume that the investment credit can be used to reduce income tax payments at the end of Year 1 and there is sufficient taxable income that the depreciation each year can be used to reduce otherwise taxable income, providing $.40 of cash flow for each $1.00 of depreciation deduction.

Construct a schedule deriving the net present values of the acquisition cost of the equipment, the investment credit, and the depreciation tax shield. Explain why this analysis enables Magee Company to choose a combination of investment credit and depreciable basis that minimizes the present value of the cost of equipment, even though Magee Company uses full absorption costing so depreciation charges are a product cost, not immediately deductible.

c. Construct a schedule of cash flows for the alternative of trading in the old equipment on the new. Assume for the remainder of the problem that an 8 percent investment credit is taken and the depreciable basis is the full $140,000 of cost.

d. Explain why the trade-in alternative in part **c** must dominate the alternative of selling outright the old equipment and purchasing the new.

e. Analyze the alternatives and suggest a decision to management of Magee Company.

f. Prepare income statements for Years 1–5, assuming the treatment in part **c**. Explain the causes of the differences between net income and net cash flow for each year.

g. Consider the alternative of trading in the old asset on the new. Compare the sum of the net incomes over the 5 years of the project to the sum of the cash flows over the same 5 years. Note that the sum of the incomes is less than the sum of the cash flows by $18,000, exactly equal to the book value of the old asset traded in on the new. Is this relation coincidence? Comment.

Suggested Solution

a. *The Alternatives:*

    (1) Sell the old equipment and do not acquire the new.
    (2) Trade in the old equipment on the new equipment.
    (3) Sell the old equipment and purchase the new.

Note that this problem does not have an alternative to retain the old equipment and continue using it, which would be possible in many situations.

b. *Choosing Combination of Investment Credit and Depreciable Basis.* Exhibit 9.3 derives the cash flows. Note that the cost of using a 10 percent investment credit with a 5 percent reduction in depreciable basis is slightly smaller than from using an 8 percent investment credit: the larger investment credit outweighs the disadvantages of smaller depreciation charges over 5 years. As the discount rate increases, the larger investment credit becomes even more preferred. (In spite of the slight advantage to the 10 percent credit combined with the 5 percent basis reduction, the rest of the problem uses the 8 percent credit and no basis reduction because the *financial* accounting statements required in part **f** are simpler that way. If the basis is reduced for tax purposes, then income tax permanent differences are created that require special financial accounting treatments.)

    Because Magee Company is required to use full absorption costing for inventories, some of the depreciation charges for the first year are carried in inventory until the fifth year. Thus, some of the tax shield from the first year's depreciation charge will not be realized until the fifth year.[10]

c. *Trade in Old Asset on New Asset.* Exhibits 9.4 and 9.5 consider the case of trading in the old equipment on the new. Exhibit 9.4 derives the operating cash flows, including income tax effects. Exhibit 9.5, discussed later, combines operating and nonoperating cash flows. The various lines of Exhibit 9.4 are derived on the next page.

---

[10]This reduces the benefits of the larger depreciation from choosing an 8 percent investment credit. If a 10 percent credit is preferred to an 8 percent credit when all first-year depreciation charges can be deducted in the first year, then it will be even more preferred when some of the first-year charges must be deducted on the fifth-year tax return. If the analysis in Exhibit 9.3 had indicated that an 8 percent investment credit with no basis reduction has a lower cost than 10 percent credit with basis reduction, then some further computations would be required to decide whether the 8 percent credit is preferred to the 10 percent credit under absorption costing.

Exhibit 9.3
Analysis of Trade-off Between Benefits of Investment Credit
and Depreciation Basis for 5-Year Economic Lives
Discount Rate of 15 Percent per Year
(Part **b** of Problem for Self-Study)
Amounts rounded to the nearest whole dollar.

	10 Percent Investment Credit Basis Reduction of 5 Percent to $950			8 Percent Investment Credit. No Reduction: Basis Is $1,000		
	Amount	Cash Inflow (Outflow)	Present Value of Flow at 15 Percent	Amount	Cash Inflow (Outflow)	Present Value of Flow at 15 Percent
Start of Year 1						
Cash Outflow for Purchase	$1,000	$(1,000)	$(1,000)	$1,000	$(1,000)	$(1,000)
End of Year 1						
Investment Credit	100	100	87	80	80	70
Depreciation Charge (15 percent). . .	143			150		
Tax Shield at .40.	57	57	50	60	60	52
End of Year 2						
Depreciation Charge (22 percent) . . .	209			220		
Tax Shield at .40.	84	84	64	88	88	67
End of Year 3						
Depreciation Charge (21 percent) . . .	200			210		
Tax Shield at .40.	80	80	53	84	84	55
End of Year 4						
Depreciation Charge (21 percent) . . .	200			210		
Tax Shield at .40.	80	80	46	84	84	48
End of Year 5						
Depreciation Charge (21 percent) . . .	198[a]			210		
Tax Shield at .40.	79	79	39	84	84	42
Net Present Value at Start of Year 1 of Acquisition and Depreciation Tax Shield Cash Flows			$(661)			$(666)

[a]$(.95 \times \$1,000) - \$143 - \$209 - \$200 - \$200.$

Line (1). 15,000 units are sold each year and the amounts to be produced.equal the number sold, except in Year 1 when production is 20,000, or 5,000 units more than sales, and in Year 5, when production is 10,000, or 5,000 units fewer.

Line (2). Variable cost per unit is given as $3.00 for Year 1, $3.24 for Year 2, and increases at the rate of 8 percent per year thereafter to $3.50 in Year 3, $3.78 in Year 4, and $4.08 in Year 5.

Line (3). Total variable costs result from multiplying lines **(1)** by line **(2)**. This amount is paid in cash at the beginning of the year, so is transferred to line **(17)** as a cash outflow at the beginning of each year.

Line (4). Depreciation charge for the year results from multiplying the taxable depreciable basis, $140,000, by the ACRS percentages: 15, 22, 21, 21, and 21.

Exhibit 9.4
Analysis of Cash Flow Data by Year for Magee Company[a]
(Part **c** of Problem 2 for Self-Study)

	1	2	3	4	5	
Production and Selling Costs During Year						
(1)[a] Number of Units Produced.	20,000	15,000	15,000	15,000	10,000	
(2) Variable Manufacturing Cost per Unit . . .	$ 3.00	$ 3.24	$ 3.50	$ 3.78	$ 4.08	
(3) Total Variable Costs (at beginning of year) = (1) × (2)	$ 60,000	$ 48,600	$ 52,500	$ 56,700	$ 40,800	
(4) Depreciation Charge for Year for Taxes . .	$ 21,000	$ 30,800	$ 29,400	$ 29,400	$ 29,400	
(5) Total Manufacturing Costs for Taxes = (3) + (4)	$ 81,000	$ 79,400	$ 81,900	$ 86,100	$ 70,200	
(6) Manufacturing Costs per Unit for Taxes = (5) ÷ (1)	$ 4.05	$ 5.29	$ 5.46	$ 5.74	$ 7.02	
(7) Variable Selling Cost per Unit.	$ .50	$ .55	$ .61	$ .67	$ .73	
Revenues, End of Year						
(8) Number of Units Sold	15,000	15,000	15,000	15,000	15,000	
(9) Selling Price per Unit.	$ 7.00	$ 7.70	$ 8.47	$ 9.32	$ 10.25	
(10) Total Revenues = (8) × (9)	$105,000	$115,500	$127,050	$139,800	$153,750	
Tax Return for Year						
(11) Revenues = (10)	$105,000	$115,500	$127,050	$139,800	$153,750	
(12) Less Manufacturing Costs of Sales. . . .	60,750	79,400	81,900	86,100	90,450	
(13) Less Selling Expenses	12,500	13,250	14,150	15,050	15,950	
(14) Taxable Income = (11) − (12) − (13) . .	$ 31,750	$ 22,850	$ 31,000	$ 38,650	$ 47,350	
(15) Income Taxes Payable = .40 × (14). . .	$ 12,700	$ 9,140	$ 12,400	$ 15,460	$ 18,940	
Cash Flow at:						
End of Year	0	1	2	3	4	5
Beginning of Year	1	2	3	4	5	6
(16) Revenues = (10)	—	$105,000	$115,500	$127,050	$139,800	$153,750
(17) Less Variable Cost = (3)	$ 60,000	48,600	52,500	56,700	40,800	—
(18) Less Selling Expenses = (13), Lagged . .	—	12,500	13,250	14,150	15,050	15,950
(19) Less Income Taxes for Year = (15), Lagged	—	12,700	9,140	12,400	15,460	18,940
(20) Net Cash Flow (Outflow) = (16) − (17) − (18) − (19).	($ 60,000)	$ 31,200	$ 40,610	$ 43,800	$ 68,490	$118,860
(21) Present Value at 15 Percent = $124,890 .	($ 60,000)	$ 27,131	$ 30,707	$ 28,799	$ 39,159	$ 59,094

[a]See text for discussion of line-by-line derivation.

The financial statement depreciation will be $27,119 [= ($140,000 − $4,406) ÷ 5)] per year, but this fact is irrelevant for the analysis of cash flows. Tax depreciation is relevant only because of its impact on tax deductible cost of goods sold, which is deducted in computing taxable income and therefore affects income tax payments.

Line (5). Total manufacturing costs is the sum of the preceding two lines.

Line (6). Manufacturing cost per unit is generally irrelevant for decision making in the absence of taxes. Because, however, there is a buildup of inventory in

Year 1 not sold until Year 5 and because full absorption costing is required for tax purposes, the full cost of the units put into inventory in Year 1 must be computed. Such unit costs must be computed to derive tax effects whenever production volume differs from sales volume.

Line (7). Variable selling costs of $.50 per unit per year increase at the rate of 10 percent per year. The figure is used to compute total selling costs later on line (13) and cash outflow for selling costs on line (18).

Line (8). The number of units sold is given.

Line (9). Selling price per unit increases at the rate of 10 percent per year. (The numbers shown here result from using this formula: Selling price at the end of Year $t = \$7.00 \times 1.10^{t-1}$. One might multiply each year's price by 1.10 to derive the next year's price. There is no material difference between these two procedures, but because of differing rounding conventions, analysts may reach differing numbers by the fifth year.)

Line (10). Total revenue results from multiplying the preceding two lines. The product is carried to line (11) for tax purposes and to line (16) for cash flow calculations.

Line (11). See discussion of line (10).

Line (12). Manufacturing cost is taken from line (5) except for Years 1 and 5. In Year 1, manufacturing cost is the product of manufacturing cost per unit, line (6), times number of units sold, line (8): $\$4.05 \times 15,000 = \$60,750$. Recall that a LIFO cost flow assumption is used. In Year 5, 10,000 units carry Year 5 manufacturing costs and 5,000 units carry Year 1 manufacturing costs: $\$70,200 + (\$4.05 \times 5,000) = \$90,450$.

Line (13). Selling expenses are variable costs per unit on line (7) multiplied by the number of units sold from line (8) plus $5,000.

Line (14). Taxable income is revenues, line (11), less expenses on lines (12) and (13).

Line (15). Income taxes are 40 percent of the amount on line (14). The amounts are to be paid at the end of the year of sale.

Lines (16)–(20). These lines show all cash flows. Generally, careful thought is required to align the timing of the cash flows. Note that the preceding lines show operations for a period. Here each cash flow is assumed to occur at a specific moment. Because the end of one year is also the beginning of the next, we find it convenient to label these moments with both their end-of-year and beginning-of-year designations to aid analysis. Note, for example, how the cash flows for variable manufacturing costs appear in one column, but the revenues from sale of the items produced appear in the next column.

Line (21). The present values at the beginning of Year 1 result from multiplying the numbers on line (20) by the appropriate factor from the 15 percent column in Table 2 at the back of the book. The sum of the numbers on line (21) is $124,890.

Exhibit 9.5
Analysis of All Cash Flows from Trading in Old Equipment
on New Equipment for Project of Magee Company
(Parts **c** and **g** of Problem 2 for Self-Study)

	Present Value at Beginning of Year 1	Undiscounted Cash Flows
Operating Cash Flows (Exhibit 9.4).	$124,890	$242,960
Cash Outlay for Equipment at Beginning of Year 1 ($150,000 cost − $28,000 trade-in).	(122,000)	(122,000)
Investment Credit of $11,200 Received at End of Year 1 ($11,200 × .86957)	9,739	11,200
Salvage Proceeds from Selling Equipment at End of Year 5 ($4,406 × .49718)	2,191	4,406
Taxes at 40 Percent on Salvage Proceeds of $4,406 Paid at the End of Year 6 ($4,406 × .40 × .43233). . . .	(762)	(1,762)
Total.	$ 14,058	$134,804

Analysis of All Cash Flows Exhibit 9.5 shows all the cash flows, operating and nonoperating, for the trade-in decision with present values at the beginning of Year 1. Note that the benefit of the investment credit occurs 1 year after the purchase of the equipment. The salvage proceeds at the end of Year 5 are taxed at the end of Year 6. Because salvage value is ignored for tax purposes in computing depreciation, the entire depreciable basis of $140,000 is written off through ACRS. Thus, the gain on sale is equal to all the salvage proceeds, $4,406 (= $4,406 − $0).

The net present value of this project is positive, $14,058. It would be wrong to undertake it, however, without considering the net present value of its mutually exclusive alternatives.

d. *Sell Old Equipment and Acquire New for Cash.* The alternative of selling the old equipment and acquiring the new equipment for cash is clearly dominated by the trade-in alternative analyzed in Exhibits 9.4 and 9.5. The skeptic would have to construct an analysis such as that in Exhibits 9.4 and 9.5 with depreciation charges based on $150,000, rather than $140,000 on line **(4)**, plus cash proceeds from selling the equipment outright, offset with taxes, as analyzed in the preceding paragraph, and a slightly larger investment credit. Trade-in is clearly superior, because:

1. It leads to immediately reduced cash outflow of $2,200: $28,000 lower cost for the equipment reduced by the $25,000 cash proceeds from selling and the $800 loss of investment credit; and

2. The taxes on the gain on sale are payable immediately, but the same taxes are in effect paid over the depreciable life of the new equipment.

e. *Selling the Old Equipment.* If the old equipment is sold outright, there will be cash proceeds of $25,000 received immediately and a taxable gain upon sale of $7,000 (= $25,000 proceeds − $18,000 net book value). The taxes of $2,800 (= .40 × $7,000) will not be paid until the end of Year 1, so have a net present value of $2,435 ($= \$2,800 \times .86957$). Thus, the present value of selling the old equipment outright is $22,565 ($= \$25,000$ cash proceeds $- \$2,435$ present value of tax on gain).

The Decision Selling the old equipment has a net present value of $22,565, whereas trading it in on the new has a net present value of only $14,058. The analysis suggests that the old equipment be sold and the new equipment not be acquired, but the decision is close. Other factors would probably influence a decision as close as this. Note, for example, that the aftertax cost of capital used in the analysis is 15 percent and that the income tax rate is 40 percent. Thus, the pretax cost of capital is 25 [$= .15 \div (1.00 - .40)$] percent. A pretax cost of capital as large as 25 percent incorporates substantial inflation or risk premium, or both, into the analysis.[11] If the undertaking is not particularly risky, the analyst might wonder why inflation on the order of 15 percent is being implicitly assumed for the cost of capital, but sales revenues and costs for the project are being forecast to increase at rates less than the inflation rate.

If the aftertax cost of capital were sufficiently lower than 15 percent, then acquiring the new equipment via trade-in would have an edge over not acquiring it. (Exercise **22** at the end of this chapter requires working through this analysis using an aftertax cost of capital of 14 percent per year to show that the net present value of selling remains about $22,500; whereas that of trading in on the new increases to more than $19,000.)

Because the new equipment does not generate substantial amounts of positive cash flows in the last few years and because the result is not substantially better than selling the old equipment outright, we prefer the outright sale, assuming that is a realistic business alternative. We would not conclude, however, that these data indicate a clearcut decision either way. Whatever Magee Company does is not likely to be too costly, as compared to the rejected alternative.

f. *Income Statements.* Exhibit 9.6 shows the income statements for each of the 5 years. Lines **(22)**–**(24)** derive total manufacturing costs for use in computing cost

---

[11]If the pretax cost of capital (interest rate) is 25 percent, the real rate of interest is 3 percent, and the risk premium for a firm is 6 percent, then the implied expected rate of inflation can be found using a transposition of the interest formula discussed in the chapter.

From

$$1 + i = (1 + p)(1 + r)(1 + e),$$

we derive

$$1 + e = \frac{1 + i}{(1 + p)(1 + r)}$$

or

$$e = \frac{1 + i}{(1 + p)(1 + r)} - 1$$

$$= \frac{1.25}{1.03 \times 1.06} - 1$$

$$= 14.5 \text{ percent.}$$

Exhibit 9.6
Financial Statements for Magee Company[a]
(Part **f** of Problem 2 for Self-Study)

	1	2	3	4	5
Schedule of Manufacturing Costs for Year					
(22)[a] Variable Costs of Production	$ 60,000	$ 48,600	$ 52,500	$ 56,700	$ 40,800
(23) Depreciation	27,119	27,119	27,119	27,119	27,118
(24) Total Manufacturing Costs = (22) + (23) . . .	$ 87,119	$ 75,719	$ 79,619	$ 83,819	$ 67,918
Income Statement for Year					
(25) Revenues	$105,000	$115,500	$127,050	$139,800	$153,750
(26) Less Cost of Goods Sold	65,339	75,719	79,619	83,819	89,698
(27) Less Selling Costs	12,500	13,250	14,150	15,050	15,950
(28) Pretax Income = (25) − (26) − (27)	$ 27,161	$ 26,531	$ 33,281	$ 40,931	$ 48,102
(29) Income Taxes = .40 × (28)	(10,864)	(10,612)	(13,312)	(16,372)	(19,241)
(30) Investment Credit	2,240	2,240	2,240	2,240	2,240
(31) Net Income = (28) − (29) + (30)	$ 18,537	$ 18,159	$ 22,209	$ 26,799	$ 31,101

[a]See text for discussion of derivation, line by line. Lines (1)–(21) are in Exhibit 9.4.

of goods sold. [Line numbers start with **(22)** because lines **(1)**–**(21)** appear in Exhibit 9.4.]

Line (22). Variable costs of production appear on line **(3)** of Exhibit 9.4.

Line (23). Financial statement depreciation per year, based on the straight-line method, is $140,000 book value less $4,406 estimate of salvage value, divided by 5 years. In the last year the amount is $1 smaller to correct for cumulative rounding error.

Line (24). Total manufacturing costs are the sum of the preceding two lines.

Line (25). Revenues appear on line **(10)** of Exhibit 9.4.

Line (26). Cost of goods sold is taken from line **(24)** except in Years 1 and 5, when the number of units sold differs from the number produced. In Year 1, cost of goods sold is $87,119 × 15,000 ÷ 20,000 = $65,339 because only 15,000 of the 20,000 units produced are sold. The remainder of the costs of $21,780 (= $87,119 − $65,339) are carried in inventory (assuming LIFO cost flow) until Year 5, when they are added to the manufacturing costs of that year's production to derive cost of goods sold for Year 5: $21,780 + $67,918 = $89,698.

Line (27). Selling expenses appear on line **(13)** of Exhibit 9.4.

Line (28). Pretax income is revenues less cost of goods sold and selling expenses.

Line (29). Income tax expense before the investment credit is 40 percent of pretax income. This amount differs from income taxes payable because of the financial accounting treatment of timing differences, discussed briefly below and in more detail in financial accounting textbooks.

Line (30). Magee Company uses the deferral method of accounting for the investment credit. Even though all of the cash benefits of the investment credit occur in the year the new equipment is put into operation, the financial accounting benefits of it are spread, under this method, over the life of the equipment. The amount for each year is $2,240 (= $11,200 ÷ 5).

Line (31). Net income is pretax income less income taxes plus the recognized portion of the investment credit.

The amounts of income in each year differ from the amounts of cash flow for each year for five reasons:

1. Expenditure for asset acquisition affects cash flows, whereas depreciation affects financial statement amounts.
2. Revenues and cost of goods sold are matched on the financial statements although the cash expenditures to produce inventory occur in periods different from the collection from its sale.
3. Income tax expense differs from income taxes payable. Financial statement income tax expense is based on pretax financial statement income, not on taxable income as reported on the tax return. (Whenever the financial statements and the tax return differ in amounts that will eventually reverse, the differences are called "timing differences" and income tax expense is based on financial statement pretax income.)
4. While the investment credit increases cash flows in the year earned, under the deferral method its benefits are spread over the life of the equipment whose acquisition provided the investment credit. Under the flow-through method, not used by Magee Company, the benefits of the investment credit would be used to increase income only in the year the credit is earned.
5. Cash flow from disposal of the asset at the end of its life appears in Exhibit 9.5, but so long as actual salvage value equals estimated salvage value, there is no effect on reported income. If actual salvage value differs from book value at the time of disposal, there will be a gain or loss at that time.

g. *Net Income.* Net income over the life of the project is computed by adding the numbers on line **(31)** of Exhibit 9.6: $18,537 + $18,159 + $22,209 + $26,799 + $31,101 = $116,805. The sum of the cash flows over the life of the project is $134,804, as computed in the second column of Exhibit 9.5. The difference between these two numbers of $17,999 (= $134,804 − $116,805) differs from the $18,000 book value of the old asset traded in on the new by only $1, a rounding error. This is not coincidence. Over long enough time periods in accounting, income equals cash inflows less cash outflows. $18,000 of cost of the old equipment (its net book value) had not yet been charged to income in any period. That cost increased the cost of the new asset, so the sum of depreciation charges for the new asset is $18,000 larger than the cash expenditure for the new asset at the time of its acquisition. The $18,000 cash was spent at the time the old asset was acquired. Without the trade-in transaction (and rounding error), the sum of the cash flows would equal the sum of the net incomes.

Questions

1. Review the meaning of the following concepts or terms discussed in this chapter:

a.	Investment decision versus financing decision.	**e.**	Effect of depreciation expense on cash flows.
b.	Net present value of cash flows.	**f.**	Mutually exclusive projects.
c.	Opportunity cost of capital.	**g.**	Investment credit.
d.	Required rate of return.	**h.**	ACRS.

2. The capital budgeting decision consists of two distinct problems. Describe these.

3. Assume a margin of error of plus or minus 10 percent in estimating any number required as an input for a capital budgeting decision. Under ordinary conditions, the net present value of a project is most sensitive to the estimate of which of the following:

(1) Amounts of future cash flows,

(2) Timing of future cash flows,

(3) Cost of capital?

4. Financial accounting writers emphasize that "Depreciation is not a source of funds." This chapter states that accelerated cost recovery methods result in larger cash flows than does the straight-line depreciation method. Reconcile these two statements.

5. How, if at all, should the amount of inflation incorporated in the cost of capital influence projected future cash flows for a project?

6. In *measuring* the cost of capital, one often measures the cost of the individual equities. There is no contractual obligation to pay anything to common shareholders. How can the capital they provide be said to have a cost other than zero?

7. A firm has a choice of three alternative investments:

(1) Short-term government note promising a return of 14 percent.

(2) Short-term commercial paper (issued by a blue-chip corporation) promising a return of 18 percent.

(3) Short-term, lower-grade commercial paper (issued by a less well-established corporation) promising a return of 20 percent.

How can the opportunity cost of capital be defined by the marginal investments available to the firm when there are at least three such alternatives, each with a different promised rate?

8. Assume no change in marginal income tax rates over the life of new equipment about to be acquired. "So long as the trade-in allowance for an already-owned asset is at least as large as its book value for tax purposes, it will never pay to sell the asset, rather than trading in."

Comment.

9. Assume no change in marginal income tax rates over the life of new equipment about to be acquired. "Whenever the trade-in allowance for an already-owned asset is smaller than its book value for tax purposes, it will always pay to sell the asset, rather than trading in."
Comment.

10. "Cash received sooner is more valuable than cash received later. Therefore, the flow-through method of treating the investment credit (taking all the benefits of the investment credit in the year qualifying assets are acquired) is preferred to the deferral method (spreading the benefits over the depreciable lives of the qualifying assets)."
Comment.

11. "Because salvage value is ignored for tax purposes in computing depreciation charges under the Accelerated Cost Recovery System and the only cash flow effect of depreciation is on cash flows for income taxes, salvage value can safely be ignored in capital budgeting analysis."
Comment.

12. Describe the factors that influence the market rate of interest a company must pay to borrow.

13. Describe the chain of influence, if any, between the rate of anticipated inflation in an economy and the opportunity cost of capital to a firm in that economy.

14. "But Mr. Miller, you have said that the opportunity cost of capital is the rate of return on alternative investment projects available to the firm. So long as the firm has debt outstanding, one opportunity for idle funds will be to retire debt. Therefore, the cost of capital cannot be higher than the current cost of debt for any firm with debt outstanding."
How should Mr. Miller reply?

Exercises

15. *Computing Net Present Value.* A firm has an aftertax cost of capital of 10 percent. Compute the net present value of each of the five projects listed below.

Project	Aftertax Cash Flow End of Year			
	0	1	2	3
A	$(10,000)	$4,000	$4,000	$4,000
B	(10,000)	6,000	4,000	2,000
C	(10,000)	2,000	4,000	6,000
D	(10,000)	4,400	4,400	4,400
E	(10,000)	3,600	3,600	3,600

16. *Computing Net Present Value.* Compute the net present value of:
   a.   An investment of $15,000 that will yield $1,000 for 28 periods at 4 percent per period.

      b.   An investment of $100,000 that will yield $250,000 eight years from now at 10 percent compounded semiannually.

17. *Computing Net Present Value.* Westminster Products is considering a project that requires an initial investment of $800,000 and will generate the following cash inflows for the next 6 years:

Year	Cash Inflow at End of Year
1	$100,000
2	200,000
3	300,000
4	400,000
5	300,000
6	200,000

Ignoring tax effects, calculate the net present value of this project if Westminster's cost of capital is

      a.   12 percent.

      b.   20 percent.

18. *Computing Net Present Value.* Hammersmith Homes is considering four possible housing development projects, each requiring an initial investment of $5,000,000. The cash inflows from each of the projects are as follows:

Year	Project A	Project B	Project C	Project D
1	$2,000,000	$4,000,000	–0–	$1,000,000
2	2,000,000	2,000,000	–0–	2,500,000
3	2,000,000	2,000,000	–0–	3,000,000
4	2,000,000	1,000,000	–0–	2,500,000
5	2,000,000	1,000,000	$10,000,000	1,000,000

      a.   Ignoring tax effects, compute the net present value of each of the projects. Hammersmith's cost of capital is 15 percent.

      b.   Hammersmith can take on only one project; which should it choose? Explain why this project is superior to the others.

19. *Computing Net Present Value.* Megatech, a computer software manufacturer, is considering a software development project that requires an initial investment of $200,000 and subsequent investments of $150,000 and $100,000 at the end of the first and second years. This project is expected to yield annual aftertax cash inflows for 6 more years: $90,000 for the third through eighth years.

    If Megatech's aftertax cost of capital is 10 percent, calculate the net present value of this project.

20. *Interaction of Investment Credit and ACRS Asset Lives.* The Dopuch Company purchases a machine for $10,000 that has no salvage value at the end of its useful life. The machine is to be depreciated under accelerated cost recovery for tax purposes. If the depreciable life is chosen to be 3 years, Dopuch Company will receive an investment tax credit of $400; but if a 5-year depreciable life is chosen, $800 will be granted as a credit toward Dopuch Company's income tax bill at the time of purchase. Accelerated cost recovery percentages for a 3-year life are 25, 38, and 37; for a 5-year life they are 15, 22, 21, 21, and 21.

Calculate the present value of the difference in tax savings for 3- and 5-year depreciable lives of the machine. Round calculations to the nearest dollar. Assume a 40 percent marginal tax rate.

a. Which depreciable life should be chosen if the aftertax cost of capital is 15 percent compounded annually?

b. Which depreciable life should be chosen if the aftertax cost of capital is 25 percent compounded annually?

c. Estimate the aftertax cost of capital at which the Dopuch Company will be indifferent as to which life is used.

21. *Deriving Cash Flows and Computing Net Present Value.* The Eastern States Railroad (ESRR) is considering replacing its power jack tamper, used to maintain track and roadbed, with a new automatic-raising power tamper. The present power jack tamper cost $36,000 five years ago and was estimated to have a total life of 12 years. If it is kept, it will require an overhaul 2 years from now that is estimated to cost $10,000. It can be sold for $5,000 now; it will be worthless 7 years from now.

A new automatic-raising tamper costs $46,000 delivered and has an estimated physical life of 12 years. ESRR anticipates, however, that because of developments in maintenance machines, the new machine should be disposed of at the end of the seventh year for $10,000. Furthermore, the new machine will require an overhaul costing $14,000 at the end of the fourth year. The new equipment will reduce wages and fringe benefits by $8,000 per year.

Track maintenance work is seasonal, so the equipment is normally used only from May 1 through October 31 of each year. Track maintenance employees are transferred to other work and receive the same rate of pay for the rest of the year.

The new machine will require $2,000 per year of maintenance, whereas the old machine requires $2,400 per year. Fuel consumption for the two machines is identical. ESRR's cost of capital is 12 percent per year and, because of operating losses, ESRR pays no income tax.

Should the new machine be purchased?

22. *Observing the Effects of Using Different Discount Rates.* Refer to the data and analysis developed for the Magee Company in Exhibits 9.4 and 9.5. Evaluate the alternatives using an aftertax cost of capital of 14 percent. Use the following five-place discount factors for 14 percent:

Number of Periods	Factor	Number of Periods	Factor
0	1.00000	4	.59208
1	.87719	5	.51937
2	.76947	6	.45559
3	.67497		

23. *Deriving Cash Flows and Computing Net Present Value.* The Largay Corporation is contemplating selling a new product. The equipment necessary to distribute and sell the product can be acquired for $100,000. It has an estimated life of 10 years and no salvage value. In addition, it will be eligible for an immediate 8 percent investment tax credit. That is, if the asset is acquired, the income taxes otherwise payable in the year of acquisition will be reduced by $8,000 (= .08 × $100,000). The following schedule shows the expected sales volume, selling price, and variable cost per unit of production:

Year		Sales Volume	Selling Price	Variable Cost of Production
1	. . . . .	10,000 Units	$5.00	$3.00
2	. . . . .	12,000	5.00	3.10
3	. . . . .	13,000	5.50	3.25
4	. . . . .	15,000	5.75	3.25
5	. . . . .	20,000	6.00	3.30
6	. . . . .	25,000	6.00	3.40
7	. . . . .	20,000	6.10	3.50
8	. . . . .	18,000	6.10	3.50
9	. . . . .	15,000	6.25	3.50
10	. . . . .	15,000	6.30	3.75

Production in each year must be sufficient to meet each year's sales. In addition, 5,000 extra units will be produced in Year 1 to provide a continuing inventory of 5,000 units. Thus, production in Year 1 will be 15,000 units, but in Year 10 will be only 10,000 units, so that at the end of Year 10, ending inventory will be zero. Inventory will be accounted for using the LIFO (last-in, first-out) cost flow assumption. The corporation's income tax rate is 40 percent, and its aftertax cost of capital is 10 percent per year. Cash is received at the end of the year when sales are made and expended at the end of the year when costs are incurred. Variable selling expenses are estimated at $1 per unit sold. Depreciation on the new distribution equipment is not a product cost but is an expense each period. Depreciation deductions are based on the following accelerated cost recovery percentages for each year: 15 in the first, 22 in the second, 21 in the third, 21 in the fourth, 21 in the fifth, and zero thereafter. The Largay Corporation generates sufficient cash flows from other operations so that the investment tax credit and depreciation deductions can all be used to reduce current tax payments.

    a.   Prepare a schedule of cash flows for this project.
    b.   Verify that the net present value of the project is approximately $14,450.

Problems and Cases

24. *Net Present Value Graph and Indifference Cost of Capital.* The aftertax net cash flows associated with two mutually exclusive projects, G and H, are as follows:

Project	Cash Flow End of Year		
	0	1	2
G	$(100)	$125	—
H	(100)	50	$84

a. Calculate the net present value for each project using discount rates of 0, .04, .08, .12, .15, .20, and .25.

b. Prepare a graph as follows. The vertical axis should be labeled "Net Present Value in Dollars" and the horizontal axis should be labeled "Discount Rate in Percent per Year." Plot the net present value amounts calculated in part **a** for project G and project H.

c. State the decision rule for choosing between projects G and H as a function of the firm's cost of capital.

d. What generalizations can be drawn from this exercise?

25. *Deriving Cash Flows for Asset Disposition.* The Wisher Washer Company purchased a made-to-order machine tool for grinding washing machine parts. The machine cost $100,000 and was installed yesterday. Today, a machine tool is offered that will do exactly the same work but costs only $50,000. Assume that the cost of capital is 12 percent, that both machines will last for 5 years, that both machines will be depreciated on a straight-line basis for tax purposes with no salvage value, that the income tax rate is and will continue to be 40 percent, and that Wisher Washer Company earns sufficient income that any loss from disposing of or depreciating the "old" machine can be used to offset other taxable income. Ignore the investment credit.

How much, at a minimum, must the "old" machine fetch upon resale at this time to make purchasing the new machine worthwhile?

26. *Deriving Cash Flows for Abandonment Decision.* The Ingram Company must decide whether to continue selling a line of children's shoes manufactured on a machine that can be used for no other purpose by the company. The machine has a current book value of $12,000 and can be sold today for $7,000. The machine is being depreciated on a straight-line basis for tax purposes assuming no salvage value and could continue in use for 4 more years. If the machine is kept in use, it can be disposed of at the end of 4 years for $600, although this will not affect the depreciation charge for the next 4 years. The variable cost of producing a pair of shoes on the machine is less than the cash received from customers by $13,000 per year. To produce and sell the children's shoes requires cash outlays of $10,000 per year for administrative and overhead expenditures as well. The tax rate paid by Ingram Company is 40 percent. The rate applies to any gain or loss on disposal of the machine as well as to other income. From its other activities, Ingram Company earns more income than any losses from the line of children's shoes or from disposal of the machine.

a. Prepare a schedule showing all the cash and cost flows that Ingram Company needs to consider in order to decide whether to keep the machine.

b. Should Ingram Company keep the machine if its aftertax cost of capital is 12 percent?

c. Repeat part **b** assuming an aftertax cost of capital of 15 percent.

27. *Deriving Cash Flows and Performing Breakeven Analysis.* In the mid-1970s, Peugeot offered its automobile Model 504 in two versions—one with a gasoline engine and one with a diesel engine. The gasoline version had a list price of $6,270, and the diesel version a list price of $6,986. Assume for the purpose of this problem that the list prices were actually charged in purchase transactions. According to federal EPA mileage tests and using then-current fuel prices, the operating cost savings for the diesel over the gasoline model amounted to $.01108 cent per mile or $133 per year assuming that 12,000 miles are driven each year. Assume that a purchaser decided to acquire one of these two cars and that the purchaser expected to drive 12,000 miles a year for 5 years before disposing of the car. The gasoline version is expected to have a resale value 5 years hence of $1,500, and the diesel a resale value of $1,675.

Assume that the operating cost differential was expected to remain constant over the 5 years. Assume that the automobile is purchased and the first year's fuel payments are made on January 1 of Year 1. Subsequent cash payments are made on January 1 of each year, and the automobile is sold on January 1 of Year 6.

a. If the purchaser uses a discount rate of 12 percent per year, which version should the purchaser acquire, and what is the net present value of the savings from buying this version rather than the other?

b. At what mileage driven each year, assuming equal annual mileage per year for 5 years, constant resale values, and a discount rate of 12 percent, is the purchaser indifferent between the two versions?

c. Assuming that 12,000 miles are driven each year, at what discount rate is the purchaser indifferent between the two versions? (Find the approximate answer, using the tables at the back of the book.)

28. *Net Present Value Analysis of Tax Advantages of ACRS.* Assume an aftertax cost of capital of 15 percent per year, an income tax rate of 40 percent, and that all cash flows for taxes occur at year-end.

a. Compute the present value of the tax shield provided by straight-line depreciation over 10 years of an asset costing $10,000.

b. Compute the present value of the tax shield provided by accelerated cost recovery over 5 years using the following percentages: 15, 22, 21, 21, and 21.

c. Assuming that firms are allowed to use straight-line depreciation, which gives a larger incentive to the investment in depreciable assets, the switch to accelerated cost recovery for tax purposes or an 8 percent investment credit?

29. *Outright Sale Versus Trade-in of Existing Asset* (*adapted from problems by David O. Green*). Brogan Company must buy a crane. It can buy a new one from the factory for $150,000. Cromwell Company, a competitor, bought an identical model last week for $150,000, finds that it needs a larger crane, and offers to sell its crane to Brogan. The new factory crane and the Cromwell crane have economic lives of 5 years with no salvage value. Ignore the investment credit.

Cromwell Company can sell its crane to Brogan or can trade in the crane on the larger model, which also has a 5-year life with no salvage value. The cash price of the larger model is $300,000, and the factory will give Cromwell an allowance of $135,000 if the "old" crane is traded in. If an asset is traded in, there is no tax loss recognizable at the time of trade-in, and the depreciable cost of the new asset is the book value of the old plus any cash paid at the time the new asset is purchased. Cromwell uses accelerated cost recovery for tax purposes with the following percentages of cost claimed in the 5 years: 25, 38, 37, 0, and 0. It has a cost of capital of 12 percent and is taxed at a marginal rate of 40 percent. If Cromwell sells to Brogan, any loss is fully deductible from taxable income at the time of sale, that is, immediately. Round dollar calculations to the nearest hundred dollars.

a. What is the lowest price Cromwell can get from Brogan and be as well off as by trading in?

b. At what price will the two parties agree for Cromwell to sell to Brogan?

30. *Deriving Cash Flows for Two Mutually Exclusive Alternatives; No Income Taxes.* The director of Reinhardt Hospital needs a new automobile. The alternatives have been narrowed to buying an Oldsmobile with either a gasoline or a diesel engine. The gasoline model costs $15,000, whereas the diesel model costs $19,000. The gasoline model gets 20 miles per gallon of gasoline, whereas the diesel model gets 30 miles per gallon of diesel fuel. Gasoline currently costs $1.40 per gallon and is expected to increase in price at the rate of 12 percent per year. Diesel fuel costs $1.20 per gallon and is expected to increase in price at the rate of 8 percent per year. The car will be driven for 4 years: 36,000 miles in the first year, 30,000 miles each in the second and third years, and 24,000 miles in the fourth year. The salvage value of the diesel is expected to be $7,000 at the end of the fourth year. The salvage value of the gasoline model is expected to be $6,000 at the end of the fourth year. Assume that all other operating costs (oil, insurance, and so on) will be the same for the two different kinds of cars.

Assume that all cash flows occur at the start of the year but that salvage proceeds are received at the end of the fourth year. Because Reinhardt Hospital is a tax-exempt, not-for-profit institution, income taxes need not be considered. The cost of capital to the hospital is 15 percent per year.

Observe that there are two mutually exclusive alternatives for which separate cash flow streams can be derived. But observe also that one can subtract the cash flows from acquiring the diesel from those of acquiring the gasoline model to derive the cash flows of an investment project called "acquisition of diesel rather than gasoline model." Using this shortcut, derive the cash flows of acquiring the diesel rather than the gasoline model, compute the net present value of those cash flows, and decide which model car the hospital should acquire.

31. *Deriving Cash Flows for Two Mutually Exclusive Alternatives, Including Income Taxes.* Refer to the data in the preceding problem for Reinhardt Hospital. Assume now that the hospital is a private, profit-seeking hospital that must pay taxes at the rate of 40 percent of its pretax income. Assume that the hospital has sufficient income otherwise taxable that all depreciation and operating costs for the automobile can be used to reduce the income tax payments by $.40 for each $1.00 of deduction. Whichever car is acquired will be depreciated under accelerated cost recovery over 3 years using the following depreciation percentages in each year: 25 percent in the first year, 38 percent in the second, and 37 percent in the third. Assume that although operating costs save taxes at the beginning of the year (as the costs are incurred), depreciation deductions save taxes at the end of the year. Ignore the investment credit and assume an aftertax cost of capital of 15 percent.

  a. Compute the aftertax cash flows from acquiring the diesel rather than the gasoline model and their net present value. Which model should the taxable hospital acquire?

  b. How large an investment credit (as a percentage of original cost), if any, would change the decision reached above?

32. *Bond Refunding Decision.* The Hornbeer Company issued $1 million of callable 10-year, 16 percent, annual coupon bonds on January 1, Year 1, to mature on December 31, Year 10. The bonds were issued at par, so proceeds to the company were exactly $1 million. Late in Year 5, when interest rates had dropped so that Hornbeer Company could borrow for 12 percent, it decided to call the outstanding bonds at 106 percent of par, the price required by the bond indenture. That is, the company was required to pay $1.06 million (plus any interest accrued at that time) to the holders of the bonds. On December 31, Year 5, the company borrowed $1 million from an insurance company at 12 percent interest, payable annually through December 31, Year 10. The proceeds of the loan and $60,000 additional cash were used to retire the bond issue after the interest payment for Year 5 was made.

Compute the net present value of the costs of new borrowing, using the proceeds to retire the old bond issue. Decide whether such action should be taken. Assume a discount rate of 12 percent per year. (Ignore income tax considerations.)

33. *Income Tax Impact on Bond Refunding Decision.* Refer to the data in the preceding problem for the Hornbeer Company. Assume that the original 16 percent bond issue had been issued at 96 percent of par and that discount is being amortized on a straight-line basis. At the time the 16 percent issue is called at the end of Year 5, the book value of the bonds is 98 percent of par. The loss on bond retirement is deductible for tax purposes in Year 5, and is shown as an extraordinary item on the financial statements for Year 5.

Compute the net present value of these bond refunding transactions assuming a discount rate of 12 percent per year, a marginal income tax rate of 40 percent per year, and that a loss on bond retirement can be used to reduce otherwise taxable income.

34. *Computing Present Value of Operating Cost Savings and Replacement Cost of Used Asset.* The Pepper River Electric Company (PREC) produces electricity. Its current oil-burning plant is several years old and is capable of producing electricity for 20 more years. It can produce 15 million kilowatt-hours of electricity per year by burning oil costing $500,000 per year. If PREC were to rebuild a 20-year oil-burning plant today, the cost would be $10 million. Because of drastic increases in oil prices since the current plant was built, PREC would not build an oil-burning plant today. Instead, it would build a coal-burning plant. The coal-burning plant would cost $11 million to build, have a 20-year useful life, and produce 15 million kilowatt-hours of electricity per year by burning coal costing $100,000 per year.

Assume a cost of capital of 12 percent per year, that the fuel cost differential stays constant for 20 years, and that all fuel costs are incurred at the beginning of each year. Ignore income tax considerations.

    a. What is the present value of the cash savings from lower fuel costs resulting from operating a coal-burning plant rather than an oil-burning plant?

    b. What is the current replacement cost of the productive capacity owned by PREC? (The chapter does not give guidance on this question, which is designed to cause consideration of issues beyond those discussed.)

35. *Deriving Cash Flows for Mutually Exclusive Alternatives.*[12] The Liquid Chemical Company manufactured and sold a range of high-grade products throughout Great Britain. Many of these products required careful packing, and the company had always made a feature of the special properties of the containers used. They had a special patented lining, made from a material known as GHL, and the firm operated a department especially to maintain its containers in good condition and to make new ones to replace those that were past repair.

Mr. Walsh, the general manager, had for some time suspected that the firm might save money, and get equally good service, by buying its containers from an outside source. After careful inquiries, he approached a firm specializing in container production, Packages, Ltd., and asked for a quotation from it. At the same time he asked Mr. Dyer, his chief accountant, to let him have an up-to-date statement of the cost of operating the container department.

Within a few days, the quotation from Packages, Ltd., came in. The firm was prepared to supply all the new containers required—at that time running at the rate of 3,000 a year—for £125,000[13] a year, the contract to run for a guaranteed term of 5 years and thereafter to be renewable from year to year. If the required number of containers increased, the contract price would be increased proportionally. Additionally, and irrespective of whether the above contract was concluded or not, Packages, Ltd., undertook to carry out purely maintenance work on containers, short of replacement, for a sum of £37,500 a year, on the same contract terms.

Mr. Walsh compared these figures with the cost figures prepared by Mr. Dyer, covering a year's operations of the container department of the Liquid Chemical Company, which were as follows:

Materials		£ 70,000
Labour:		
Foreman		5,000
Workers		45,000
Department Overheads:		
Manager's Salary	£ 8,000	
Rent on Container Department	4,500	
Depreciation of Machinery	15,000	
Maintenance of Machinery	3,600	
Other Expenses.	15,750	
		46,850
		£166,850
Proportion of General Administrative Overheads		22,500
Total Cost of Department for Year		£189,350

---

[12]Copyright by Professor David Solomons, Wharton School, University of Pennsylvania, and reproduced by permission.
[13]At the time of this case, one British pound (£) was worth about $2.35.

Walsh's conclusion was that no time should be lost in closing the department and in entering into the contracts offered by Packages, Ltd. However, he felt bound to give the manager of the department, Mr. Duffy, an opportunity to question this conclusion before he acted on it. He therefore called him in and put the facts before him, at the same time making it clear that Duffy's own position was not in jeopardy; even if his department were closed, there was another managerial position shortly becoming vacant to which he could be moved without loss of pay or prospects. The manager Duffy would replace also earns £8,000 per year, so there are no net cash consequences for the firm of transferring Duffy to the other position.

Mr. Duffy looked thoughtful and asked for time to think the matter over. The next morning he asked to speak to Mr. Walsh again, and said he thought there were a number of considerations that ought to be borne in mind before his department was closed. "For instance," he said, "what will you do with the machinery? It cost £120,000 four years ago, but you'd be lucky if you got £20,000 for it now, even though it's good for another 4 years at least. And then there's the stock of GHL (a special chemical) we bought a year ago. That cost us £100,000, and at the rate we're using it now, it'll last us another 4 years or so. We used up about one-fifth of it last year. Dyer's figure of £70,000 for materials probably includes about £20,000 for GHL. But it'll be tricky stuff to handle if we don't use it up. We bought it for £500 a ton, and you couldn't buy it today for less than £600. But you wouldn't have more than £400 a ton left if you sold it, after you'd covered all the handling expenses."

Walsh thought that Dyer ought to be present during this discussion. He called him in and put Duffy's points to him. "I don't much like all this conjecture," Dyer said. "I think my figures are pretty conclusive. Besides, if we are going to have all this talk about 'what will happen if,' don't forget the problem of space we're faced with. We're paying £8,500 a year in rent for a warehouse a couple of miles away for other corporate purposes. If we closed Duffy's department, we'd have all the warehouse space we need without renting."

"That's a good point," said Walsh. "Though I must say, I'm a bit worried about the workers if we close the department. I don't think we can find room for any of them elsewhere in the firm. I could see whether Packages can take any of them. But some of them are getting on. There's Walters and Hines, for example. They've been with us since they left school 40 years ago. I'd feel bound to give them a small pension—£1,500 a year each, say."

Duffy showed some relief at this. "But I still don't like Dyer's figures," he said. "What about this £22,500 for general administrative overheads? You surely don't expect to sack anyone in the general office if I'm closed, do you?" "Probably not," said Dyer, "but someone has to pay for these costs. We can't ignore them when we look at an individual department, because if we do that with each department in turn, we shall finish up by convincing ourselves that directors, accountants, typists, stationery, and the like don't have to be paid for. And they do, believe me."

"Well, I think we've thrashed this out pretty fully," said Walsh, "but I've been turning over in my mind the possibility of perhaps keeping on the maintenance work ourselves. What are your views on that, Duffy?"

"I don't know," said Duffy, "but it's worth looking into. We shouldn't need any machinery for that, and I could hand the supervision over to a foreman. You'd save £3,000 a year there, say. You'd only need about one-fifth of the workers, but you could keep on the oldest. You wouldn't save any space, so I suppose the rent would be the same. I shouldn't think the other expenses would be more than £6,500 a year." "What about materials?" asked Walsh. "We use about 10 percent of the total on maintenance," Duffy replied.

"Well, I've told Packages, Ltd., that I'd let them know my decision within a week," said Walsh. "I'll let you know what I decide to do before I write to them."

a. Assume no income tax effects, a cost of capital of 10 percent per year, and that no additional information can be readily obtained. What action should be taken? Support your conclusion with a net present value analysis of all the mutually exclusive alternatives.

b. What, if any, additional information do you think is necessary for a sound decision? Why?

36. *Comprehensive Review.* Demski Company is contemplating undertaking a new product line. If it does so, it must acquire new equipment at the beginning of Year 1 for $135,000. The equipment requires installation expenditures of $15,000. The equipment, if purchased, qualifies for an investment credit of $12,000, which results in decreased tax payments at the end of Year 1. The equipment will last for 10 years and is expected to have a salvage value of $2,000 in terms of today's purchasing power. Equipment prices, including prices of used equipment of this sort, are forecast to rise at an annual rate of 6 percent, so the actual salvage expected to be realized at the end of the tenth year is $3,582 (= $2,000 × 1.06^{10}). Any gain on disposal will be taxed at 40 percent and the taxes on the gain will be payable at the end of Year 10.

Demski Company owns old manufacturing equipment with a book value of $18,000 that must be disposed of. The old equipment can be sold for $27,000 cash or traded in on the new equipment for a reduction of $28,000 in cash purchase price. If the old equipment is sold, the gain will be taxed at the rate of 40 percent, but the taxes will not be payable until the end of Year 1. If the old equipment is traded in, the "gain" on disposal will not be taxed, but will reduce the depreciable basis of the new asset (and future depreciation charges) both for financial accounting and for tax purposes. If there is a trade-in with cash payment of $122,000 (= $150,000 − $28,000), the journal entry will be

New Equipment	140,000	
Old Equipment (Net)		18,000
Cash		122,000

The investment credit will be only $11,200 if the old asset is traded in.

New equipment, if acquired, will be depreciated for financial reporting over 10 years using the straight-line method but will be depreciated over 5 years using

ACRS for tax purposes. Depreciation deductions on the tax return will equal the following percentages of depreciable basis: 15 percent in the first year, 22 percent in the second, 21 percent in the third, 21 percent in the fourth, 21 percent in the fifth, and zero thereafter. Recall that salvage value need not be considered in computing ACRS deductions for tax purposes.

Sales volume, by year, is forecast as follows:

Year 1	10,000 Units
Year 2	12,000
Year 3	15,000
Year 4	18,000
Year 5	20,000
Year 6	25,000
Year 7	28,000
Year 8	23,000
Year 9	19,000
Year 10	15,000

Sales price is $5.50 per unit for Year 1, but is forecast to increase by 10 percent per year to $6.05 in Year 2, $6.66 in Year 3, and so on. Variable costs of production are $3.00 per unit in Year 1, but are forecast to increase by 8 percent per year to $3.24 in Year 2, and so on. Selling costs are $5,000 per year plus $.50 per unit in Year 1; in subsequent years the variable portion of selling costs is forecast to increase at the rate of 10 percent per year to $.55 in Year 2, $.61 in Year 3, and so on. All variable manufacturing costs are assumed to be paid in cash at the *beginning* of each year. All selling costs are assumed to be paid in cash at the *end* of each year. All sales and receipts therefrom are assumed to occur at the end of each year.

Income taxes on a given year's operations are paid at the end of the year. Although selling costs become deductions on the tax return in the year incurred, manufacturing costs become deductible for taxes only when the goods are sold. Income taxes are paid at the rate of 40 percent of pretax income. Demski Company has sufficient other taxable income that losses on this project can be used to offset other income, saving $.40 in taxes for every $1.00 of operating loss.

Production in each year must be sufficient to meet each year's sales, except that 15,000 units must be produced in the first year to provide a continuing inventory of 5,000 units. Hence, production in Year 10 need be only 10,000 units so that at the end of Year 10 ending inventory will be zero. Inventory will be accounted for with LIFO cost flow. All depreciation charges for a year are product costs to be allocated to units produced in that year.

The Demski Company has an aftertax cost of capital of 15 percent per year.

a. List the mutually exclusive alternatives facing Demski Company.

b. Construct a schedule of cash flows for the alternative of trading in the old equipment on the new and using the new equipment.

c. Explain why the alternative in part **b** dominates the alternative of selling outright the old equipment and purchasing the new, rather than trading in.

d. Analyze the alternatives and suggest a decision to management of Demski Company.

Suggested Solutions to Even-Numbered Exercises

16. *Computing Net Present Value.*

   a. Net Present Value = $-\$15{,}000 + \$1{,}000\ (16.66306)$

$$= \underline{\$1{,}663}.$$

   b. Net Present Value = $-\$100{,}000 + \$250{,}000(0.45811)$

$$= \underline{\$14{,}528}.$$

18. *Computing Net Present Value.*

a.

Year	Present Value Factor	Discounted Cash Flows			
		Project A	Project B	Project C	Project D
0	1.00000	$(5,000,000)	$(5,000,000)	$(5,000,000)	$(5,000,000)
1	.86957	1,739,140	3,478,280	–0–	869,570
2	.75614	1,512,280	1,512,280	–0–	1,890,350
3	.65752	1,315,040	1,315,040	–0–	1,972,560
4	.57175	1,143,500	571,750	–0–	1,429,375
5	.49718	994,360	497,180	4,971,800	497,180
		$1,704,320	$2,374,530	$(28,200)	$1,659,035

b. Hammersmith should take Project B, which has the largest net present value. Even though all four projects have similar undiscounted total cash flow streams, that is, $10,000,000, Project B is superior in that the bulk of the cash returns come in the earlier years.

20. *Interaction of Investment Credit and ACRS Asset Lives.*

Effects of Depreciation of $10,000 Asset

	3-Year Life		40 Percent Tax Shield	5-Year Life		40 Percent Tax Shield
Year	Depreciation (percent)	Charge (dollars)		Depreciation (percent)	Charge (dollars)	
1	25%	$2,500	$1,000	15%	$1,500	$600
2	38	3,800	1,520	22	2,200	880
3	37	3,700	1,480	21	2,100	840
4	–0–	–0–	–0–	21	2,100	840
5	–0–	–0–	–0–	21	2,100	840

Cash Flow Differences of 3-Year Versus 5-Year Life

End of Year		Life 3-Year	5-Year		Difference
0	Investment Credit	$ 400 −	$800	=	$ − 400
1	Depreciation	1,000 −	600	=	400
2	Depreciation	1,520 −	880	=	640
3	Depreciation	1,480 −	840	=	640
4	Depreciation	−0− −	840	=	− 840
5	Depreciation	−0− −	840	=	− 840

a. The answer to **a** is 5 years. At 15 percent, the present value of the difference in tax savings between a 3-year and a 5-year life is $(45). See below.

b. The answer to **b** is 3 years. At 25 percent, the present value of the difference is $39. See below.

End of Year	Cash Inflow (Outflow)	**a.** 15 Percent Present Value Factor	Value	**b.** 25 Percent Present Value Factor	Value
0	$(400)	1.00000	$(400)	1.00000	$(400)
1	400	.86957	348	.80000	320
2	640	.75614	484	.64000	410
3	640	.65752	421	.51200	328
4	(840)	.57175	(480)	.40960	(344)
5	(840)	.49718	(418)	.32768	(275)
			$(45)		$ 39

c. At an aftertax cost of capital of about 20 percent, the net present value will be about zero, indicating indifference. Linear interpolation indicates a rate of

$$15\% + \left(\frac{45}{45 + 39}\right)(25\% - 15\%)$$

$$= 15\% + \left(\frac{45}{84}\right)(10\%)$$

$$= 20.4\%.$$

At 20 percent, the net present value is $ + 5.

22. *Observing the Effects of Using Different Discount Rates.*

MAGEE COMPANY
Operating Cash Flows
End of Year
(Cost of Capital 14 Percent)

(1) End of Year	(2) Cash Flow	(3) Present Value Factor at 14 Percent	(4) Present Value at 14 Percent = (2) × (3)
0	$ (60,000)	1.00000	$ (60,000)
1	31,200	.87719	27,368
2	40,610	.76947	31,248
3	43,800	.67497	29,564
4	68,490	.59208	40,552
5	118,860	.51937	61,732
Total			$130,464

Present Value of All Cash Flows from Trading-in Old Equipment on New Equipment

Operating Cash Flow	$130,464
Cash Outlay for Equipment	(122,000)
Investment Credit: $11,200 × .87719	9,825
Salvage Proceeds End of Year 5: $4,406 × .51937	2,288
Taxes on Salvage End of Year 6: $4,406 × .40 × .45559	(803)
Net Present Value	$ 19,774

Present Value of Outright Sale

Sale Proceeds	$ 25,000
Taxes Paid on Gain 1 Year Later: $7,000 × 0.40 × .87719	(2,456)
Net Present Value.	$ 22,544

Chapter 10   Capital Budgeting: A Closer Look

The preceding chapter introduced the fundamentals of capital budgeting: separating the investment decision from the financing decision, analyzing cash flows, and summing the cash flows after discounting them at the firm's opportunity cost of capital. This chapter:

1. Describes other methods for making capital budgeting decisions, evaluating their strengths and weaknesses;

2. Introduces the problem of capital rationing;

3. Explores in greater depth the requirement that, for sound analysis, the investment decision be separated from the financing decision; and

4. Illustrates the need to separate the investment and financing decisions in the context of evaluating leases.

Alternative Methods for Evaluating Projects

Many methods are used for evaluating projects, but most are conceptually inferior to using the net present value (or discounted cash flow) method with a discount rate equal to the cost of capital. Some methods that take the time value of money into account often give the same decision results as the net present value rule and, in practice, prove to be satisfactory. Alternative methods that do not take the time value of money into account are easy to use because they do not involve present value computations, but this simplicity is their chief virtue.

The strength of the net present value method for making capital budgeting investment decisions rests on its focus on discounted cash flows. The net present value itself, a dollar number with a sign—positive or negative—is sometimes hard to compare across alternatives. Some decision makers believe that comparing a project with a net present value of $10,000 to one with a net present value of $100,000 may not be meaningful if the first project requires an initial investment much different from that of the second. Decision makers are sometimes uncomfortable with the net present value method because it seems to be independent of the size of the underlying investment. The net present value rule states merely that a positive net present value is good and a negative one is bad.

In order to take into account the *size* of the projects being considered, variants of the discounted cash flow method, called the *internal rate of return analysis* and the *excess present value index,* have been proposed. We discuss these and other alternative methods next. We show that these variants can cause other problems and that the net present value is the superior aid to decision making.

Internal Rate of Return

The *internal rate of return*, sometimes called the *time-adjusted rate of return*, of a stream of cash flows is defined as the discount rate that equates the net present value of that stream to zero. Stated another way, it is the rate that discounts the future cash flows to the present so that the present value of the future cash flows is equal to the initial investment.

Calculating the Internal Rate of Return To illustrate the calculation of the internal rate of return, assume that a proposed project requires an initial investment of $11,059 and is expected to yield net cash inflows for the next 4 years as follows: Year 1, $5,000; Year 2, $4,000; Year 3, $3,000; Year 4, $2,000. To calculate the internal rate of return, we compute the rate that will discount the net cash *inflows* during Years 1 to 4 so that they have a present value of $11,059; that is, the net present value of the inflows and outflows is zero. Mathematically, this involves solving the following equation for *r*, the discount rate:

$$\$11,059 = \frac{\$5,000}{(1 + r)^1} + \frac{\$4,000}{(1 + r)^2} + \frac{\$3,000}{(1 + r)^3} + \frac{\$2,000}{(1 + r)^4}.$$

Computers and some pocket calculators can compute this discount rate quickly. Whatever device is used, it is necessary to try various discount rates until the proper one is found. We begin by trying a discount rate of 10 percent. Columns (3) and (4) of Exhibit 10.1 show that at this discount rate the net present value is positive. This suggests that the internal rate of return must be larger than 10 percent. So we try 12 percent. We can see from column (6) of Exhibit 10.1 that 12 percent is the discount rate that equates the net present value to zero. Twelve percent therefore is the internal rate of return for this project. (If the net present value for a given trial rate were *negative*, then we should try a *smaller* rate at the next trial.) One can devise efficient, systematic trial-and-error procedures to minimize the tedium of the calculation. The compound interest appendix at the back of this book provides further illustrations of finding the internal rate of return.

Exhibit 10.1
Calculation of Internal Rate of Return

End of Year (1)	Cash Inflow (Outflow) (2)	Present Value Factor at 10 Percent (3)	Present Value of Cash Flows at 10 Percent (4)	Present Value Factor at 12 Percent (5)	Present Value of Cash Flows at 12 Percent (6)
0	$(11,059)	1.00000	$(11,059)	1.00000	$(11,059)
1	5,000	.90909	4,545	.89286	4,464
2	4,000	.82645	3,306	.79719	3,189
3	3,000	.75131	2,254	.71178	2,135
4	2,000	.68301	1,366	.63552	1,271
Net Present Value . .			$ 412		$ –0–

Using the Internal Rate of Return When using the internal rate of return to evaluate investment alternatives, one specifies a *cutoff rate*, such as 15 percent for the Garden Winery Company example in the previous chapter. Projects are accepted if their internal rates of return exceed the cutoff rate and rejected if their internal rates of return are less than the cutoff rate. The cutoff rate is sometimes called the *"hurdle rate."*

Advocates of the internal rate of return argue that the method does not require knowing the firm's cost of capital, and is therefore easier to use in practice than the net present value rule. For the internal rate of return rule to give the correct answers, however, the cutoff rate must be the cost of capital. Otherwise, some projects that will increase the value of the firm to its owners will either be rejected when they should be accepted or vice versa. The net present value method does not require more data than the internal rate of return method.

The net value method is superior to the internal rate of return method for several reasons, explained next.

Simplicity The net present value method is easier to calculate. Both methods require estimates of future cash flows and the cost of capital rate. The internal rate of return requires, however, a "search" for the proper discount rate on each project. This is, however, a minor disadvantage, given the power of modern computing devices.

Single Ranking Measure The net present value method provides a single net present value amount for each project that can be used for making the accept/reject decision. The internal rate of return method, however, may give more than one internal rate of return for a particular project. This mathematical phenomenon can occur when the pattern of yearly net cash flows contains an intermixing of net cash inflows and outflows. For example, if at the end of a project's life, cash expenditures will be made to return the plant site to its original condition, then individual cash flows can be negative both at the beginning and at the end of a project's life, but positive in between. Projects with intermixing of cash inflows and outflows are likely to have multiple internal rates of return.[1] Examples of multiple internal rates of return have been discovered in practice for coal mining companies that use strip mining to generate cash inflows from coal but that are required to spend large amounts of cash at the completion of the mining phase to reclaim the stripped land.

Better Ranking of Alternatives Under the net present value rule, projects are either acceptable or unacceptable. When projects are mutually exclusive, only one of a set of projects can be chosen. Under these conditions the rule tells us to choose the project with the largest net present value. The internal rate of return rule ranks projects in the same way as the net present value rule only when each of the following four conditions is met:

1. If the cutoff rate used for the internal rate of return is equal to the cost of capital.

---

[1]Solving for the internal rate of return involves finding the roots of a polynomial. Descartes' rule of signs tells how to determine the limit to the number of roots of such a polynomial. See the Glossary for an explanation of this rule.

2. If projects are not mutually exclusive.

3. If projects have the same life.

4. If there is only one internal rate of return.

Otherwise, the internal rate of return leads to incorrect decisions about projects, as demonstrated next.

Mutually Exclusive Projects *Mutually exclusive projects* are projects where acceptance of one alternative eliminates the need to consider further the rejected alternatives. For example, a firm needing a new truck might prepare a net present value analysis for trucks meeting the firm's specifications from each of four different suppliers. After one of the trucks is selected, there is no need to consider the other three trucks as viable investment alternatives. Only one truck is needed. The net present value decision rule for choosing among mutually exclusive projects is to accept the project with the largest net present value and reject the others. The internal rate of return analysis can give wrong answers when projects are mutually exclusive. Assume that the aftertax cost of capital is 10 percent per year and that only one of the projects, A or B, as shown in Exhibit 10.2, can be chosen. Project A provides a simple illustration for calculating the internal rate of return. The internal rate of return on project A is the rate r such that

$$\$100 = \frac{\$120}{1 + r}.$$

Solving for r gives $r = .20$. The internal rate of return in project B is similarly easy to calculate. The internal rate of return rule would rank project A as better than project B, whereas the net present value rule prefers project B. To see that project B is better for the firm, consider what the firm must do with the "idle" $200 it will have to invest if project A is chosen. That $200 must be invested, by definition, at the aftertax cost of capital of 10 percent and will provide $220, after taxes, at the end of the first year. So the total flows available at the end of the first year from project A and from the investment of the idle funds at 10 percent will be $120 + $220 = $340, which is less than the $345 available after taxes from project B. The firm will prefer the results from choosing project B as the net present value rule signals.

Exhibit 10.2
Data for Projects A and B

Project Name	Aftertax Cash Flows by Year		Internal Rate of Return	Net Present Value at 10 Percent
	End of Year			
	0	1		
A	$(100)	$120	20%	$ 9.09
B	(300)	345	15	13.64

To understand better why the net present value ranking is superior, decide whether you would rather invest $.10 today to get $2 a year from now ($r = 1,900$ percent) or invest $1,000 today to get $2,500 a year from now ($r = 150$ percent). *You may not do both.* We presume that you would prefer the second alternative even though the internal rate of return on the first is more than 12 times larger than for the second. The internal rate of return rule, applied to mutually exclusive projects, ignores the *amount* of funds that can be invested at that rate. This shortcoming is sometimes called the "scale effect."[2]

Projects with Different Lifetimes Consider projects C and D shown in Exhibit 10.3. The internal rate of return on project D is the rate r that satisfies the equation

$$\$100 = \frac{\$50}{(1 + r)} + \frac{\$84}{(1 + r)^2}.$$

You can verify that the internal rate of return is 20 percent by using the 20 percent column of Table 2 at the back of the book. The internal rate of return rule ranks project C as better than project D, whereas the net present value rule ranks project D better than project C.

To see why project D is better for the firm, consider what the firm must do during Year 2. If project C is accepted, $125 must be invested in the average investment project available to the firm. The return from such an average project is, by definition, the cost of capital, 10 percent. At the end of Year 2, the firm will have $125 \times 1.10 = \$137.50$. If project D is accepted, the $50 cash inflow at the end of the first year will also be invested at 10 percent and will grow to $50 \times 1.10 = \$55$ by the end of Year 2. Thus, the total funds available at the end of the second year are $55 + \$84 = \$139$, which is larger than the $137.50 if project C were accepted. The internal rate of return rule ignores the fact that the idle funds must be invested at the cost of capital.

Exhibit 10.3
Data for Projects C and D

Project Name	Cash Flows by Year End of Year			Internal Rate of Return	Net Present Value at 10 Percent
	0	1	2		
C	$(100)	$125	—	25%	$13.64
D	(100)	50	$84	20	14.88

---

[2]The scale effect problem often arises in using the internal rate of return method in evaluating alternatives to existing projects. Refer to Case A (food blenders and processors) on pages 369–70 of Chapter 9. What is the internal rate of return on alternative (2) described there? It is infinite because there is no initial cash outflow. Whenever there is a "status quo" to be compared to alternatives requiring initial cash outflows, the internal rate of return analysis is likely to be difficult.

Excess Present Value Index

The excess present value index is computed as follows:

$$\text{Excess Present Value Index} = \frac{\text{Present Value of Future Cash Flows}}{\text{Initial Investment}}.$$

This index indicates the number of present value dollars generated per dollar of investment. For example, if the present value of the *future* cash flows is $17,000 and the initial investment is $12,000, then the excess present value index is 1.42 (= $17,000 ÷ $12,000).

In the absence of mutually exclusive projects, the net present value and the excess present value methods result in the same accept/reject decisions. Projects with an excess present value index greater than 1.0 (positive net present value) are accepted. Projects with an excess present value index less than 1.0 (negative net present value) are rejected.

When projects are mutually exclusive, the net present value and excess present value index methods might give conflicting results. Consider the data in Exhibit 10.4. The rankings of the four projects differ depending on whether the rankings are based on net present values or excess present value indexes. The difference in the rankings is caused by the fact that in the excess present value index method, the excess present value is related to the dollars of investment required, rather than to the absolute size of the net present value. Using the net present value rule will maximize the wealth of the firm because that rule focuses on total dollar return, not the rate of return per dollar. The point of this example is valid only if the four projects are mutually exclusive *and* all funds not invested in one of these projects must be invested elsewhere at a rate no greater than the cost of capital.

Payback Period

Another method often used in evaluating investment projects involves the payback period. The *payback period* is the length of time that elapses before total cumulative

Exhibit 10.4
Ranking of Projects According to Net Present Value and Excess Present Value Index Methods

Project (1)	Initial Cash Outlay Required (2)	Present Value of Future Cash Flows (3)	Net Present Value (4)	Ranking by Net Present Value (5)	Excess Present Value Index (6)	Ranking by Excess Present Value Index (7)
E	$120,000	$170,000	$50,000	1	1.42	3
F	110,000	150,000	40,000	2	1.36	4
G	70,000	100,000	30,000	3	1.43	2
H	30,000	55,000	25,000	4	1.83	1

Column **(4)** = column **(3)** − column **(2)**.
Column **(6)** = column **(3)** ÷ column **(2)**.

aftertax cash inflows from the project equal the initial cash outlay for the project. Refer to Exhibit 10.1. The proposed project has a payback period of about 2.7 years. By the end of the first year, $5,000 of the initial investment has been "recovered." By the end of the second year, the cumulative cash inflows total $9,000 (= $5,000 + $4,000). The remaining $2,059 (= $11,059 − $9,000) is received approximately two-thirds of the way through the third year. Hence the payback is 2.7 years. The payback period decision rule states that projects be accepted when the payback period is as short as some designated cutoff time period, such as 2 years, and rejected otherwise.

The weakness in the payback period rule is that both the time value of money and all cash flows subsequent to the payback date are ignored. One project could have a shorter payback period than another but much smaller net present value. The payback period rule is designed to emphasize concern with the firm's liquidity and to facilitate calculations when many small, similar projects are considered. The net present value rule, however, also takes liquidity into account because the cost of capital is the rate of return required to justify employing additional assets in the business should a possibility arise.

A mathematical artifact of the payback method is that when many not-mutually exclusive projects are being considered, each of which has the same life and uniform cash inflows over its life, then the results of using the payback method will be the same as using the net present value method.[3] This fact, plus the fact that in earlier times computing devices were not as accessible and inexpensive as they are today, led to the education of a generation of managers with the techniques of payback analysis. Be aware that some in the business world still use payback methods; they will not necessarily get wrong answers.

Advocates of the payback period argue that the net present value rule, even with its discounting of future cash flows, gives too much weight to cash flows to be received more than 3 or 4 years into the future. They point out that many managers have favorite "pet" projects in which they would like to see the company invest. Managers have learned that marginal projects can be made to look acceptable under the net present value method if some of the distant cash inflows are made unrealistically large. (This might be achieved by making very optimistic projections of future increases in sales revenues or by making optimistic estimates of the rate at which production costs will decline as workers learn new skills.) Such managers might figure that they will not be on the same job by the time top management learns that the cash inflows projected for, say, 5 years hence were too optimistic. Such managers might reasonably expect to have been promoted or fired by the time 5 years elapse. Thus, they expect not to be held accountable for their distant projections. Analysts who fear being misled by overly optimistic managers insist on using a payback rule to find out the near-term profitability of a project. Advo-

[3]If the net cash inflows per year from a project are constant and occur for a number of years at least twice as long as the payback period and when the discount rate is reasonably large— say, 10 percent per year or more—then the reciprocal of the payback period is approximately equal to the internal rate of return on the project. Thus, the payback period will rank projects in the same way as the internal rate of return and, hence, the net present value method, if the stated conditions are met.

cates of the net present value method caution about accepting cash flow projections without careful study, but maintain that the net present value method is still conceptually superior.

Discounted Payback Period

Given the widespread use[4] of the payback period rule and its inability to yield good decisions for the most general case, some accountants have suggested that firms that want a payback rule should use the discounted payback period. The *discounted payback period* is similar to the ordinary payback period, but it is defined as the length of time that elapses before the *present value* of the cumulative cash inflows is at least as large as the initial cash outlay. The discount rate used in this calculation is most often the cost of capital. The discounted payback period gives some recognition to the time value of funds that flow before payback is accomplished. The ordinary payback periods of projects J and K in Exhibit 10.5 are the same, 3 years, but the discounted payback criteria will properly rank K as better than J.

Either payback rule would improperly prefer both J and K to project L. Yet analysts sometimes recommend the discounted payback rule to firms that are wary of applying the net present value rule to projects like project L. As we pointed out above, the manager who made the original forecast for $50,000 cash inflow for Year 5 may not be around to be held accountable by the time it is learned that the forecast was too optimistic.

Exhibit 10.5
Illustrative Data for Payback Rules, Projects J, K, and L

Project Name	Cash Flow at End of Year					
	0	1	2	3	4	5
J	$(10,000)	$2,000	$3,000	$5,000	$2,000	—
K	(10,000)	5,000	3,000	2,000	2,000	—
L	(10,000)	—	—	—	—	$50,000

Bailout and Discounted Bailout Periods

The payback period criteria ignore the cash flows after payback has been achieved and the possible residual value of equipment of a project that for whatever reason does not last its estimated life. The *bailout period* is the shortest elapsed time from the start of the project until the cumulative cash inflows from a project plus the residual value of the equipment at the end of the period equal the cash outflows

---

[4]See the results of the following surveys: T. Klammer, "Empirical Evidence of the Adoption of Sophisticated Capital Budgeting Techniques," *Journal of Business,* 45 (July 1972), p. 393; L. Schall, G. Sundem, and W. Geijsbeck, "Survey and Analysis of Capital Budgeting Methods," *Journal of Finance,* 33 (March 1978), pp. 281–287; S. H. Kim and E. J. Farragher, "Current Capital Budgeting Practices," *Management Accounting* 62, 12 (June 1981), pp. 26–32.

for the project. Assume, for example, that a project with an initial cash outflow of $100 has cash inflows of $20 at the end of each year. Also assume that the equipment could be sold for $60 at the end of the first year, $50 at the end of the second year, $40 at the end of the third year, $30 at the end of the fourth year, and so on until salvage is zero at the end of the seventh year. The payback period is 5 years (5 years = $100 ÷ $20 per year). Note, however, that by the end of the third year cumulative cash inflows have been $60 and the equipment can be salvaged for $40. Thus, bailout occurs after three periods.

The *discounted bailout period* is calculated from present values of estimated cash flows and residual values. The bailout period (or the discounted bailout period) will always be shorter than the payback period (or the discounted payback period) if the equipment has any residual value at the end of the payback period. The bailout criteria are superior to payback criteria because bailout takes into account the residual value subsequent to the termination date being considered. Because the estimated residual value at any date incorporates an estimate of the present value of the cash flows from the equipment after that date, the bailout criteria use more of the relevant information available than do the payback criteria.

As far as we know, the bailout methods are seldom seen in practice.

Accounting Rate of Return

The *accounting rate of return*, sometimes called the *rate of return on investment* or *ROI*, is defined for a project as

$$\frac{\text{Average Yearly Income from the Project}}{\text{Average Investment in the Project}}.$$

Assume that a project requiring an investment of $10,000 is expected to yield total income of $3,300 over 4 years. The average yearly income is $825. The average investment in the project, assuming straight-line depreciation and no salvage value, is $5,000 [= ($10,000 − $0)/2]. Hence, the accounting rate of return is $825 ÷ $5,000 = 16.5 percent. The accounting rate of return pays no attention to the time value of money and it uses accounting income, rather than cash flow, data.

Assume that the project results in equal annual aftertax cash flows of $3,325 at the end of each of the 4 years. Net income over the life of the project is, then, $3,300 (= 4 × $3,325 − $10,000). Because the internal rate of return on an investment of $10,000 to yield $3,325 in arrears for 4 years is about 12.5 percent, the net present value of this project will be positive only for discount rates less than 12.5 percent. If the firm has an aftertax cost of capital of 15 percent, this project is not a worthwhile undertaking because it has a negative net present value of about −$500 at that rate. The ROI is 16.5 percent, which might induce the manager making decisions with ROI to think the project is worthwhile.[5]

---

[5]Furthermore, the ROI will be the same, 16.5 percent, even if all the cash flow from the project occurs at the end of the fourth year, whereas the internal rate of return drops to 7.4 percent in this case. To take another extreme case, assume that $12,300 of cash flows occurred at the end of the first year and $1,000 occurred at the end of the fourth. The ROI would remain 16.5 percent, but the internal rate of return would increase dramatically, to more than 26 percent.

Because the accounting rate of return ignores the time value of money and uses accounting data, rather than cash flow data, it is generally an inferior decision-making tool. To see why ROI is often used in spite of this, consider three points. First, ROI is easy to compute. Second, the ROI and the internal rate of return for some projects are not drastically different, so using ROI for decision making will not always lead to wrong decisions. Third, as discussed in later chapters, ROI is often used in performance measurement. Managers who know they will be evaluated by ROI after decisions have been implemented will not always ignore ROI in considering which decisions to make.

Thus, we can understand why some companies, particularly those that use ROI for performance measurement after decisions are implemented, will use ROI as a decision-making technique. Chapter 14 shows that a refinement of ROI, residual income, is preferred for purposes of performance evaluation, so that ROI need not be used for either decision making, before plans are undertaken, or for performance evaluations, after the fact.

Evaluation of Capital Budgeting Decision-Making Tools

The manager must make a decision: whether to undertake some investment project. Analytically, we have seen that the net present value method applied to cash flow data will lead to maximizing the wealth of owners and that the internal rate of return is almost as good. Sometimes, however, other methods such as payback and ROI are used because the computational work is so much less burdensome for these methods. When computations must be done by hand, there is an important trade-off to be considered between the costs of applying the more complex discounted cash flow methods and their benefits. When thousands of dollars are at stake, however, the costs of using computers should be considered as well. When managers have computer terminals available to them as readily as they do pencil sharpeners, there is little reason not to use the computationally more complex discounted cash flow methods.

Capital Rationing

Another capital budgeting problem arises in connection with "capital rationing." Suppose that a manager is faced with a set of investment alternatives, each of which requires current cash outlays and has a positive net present value. Altogether they require more funds this year than have been made available by higher management. For example, assume that a manager has $200,000 to invest in projects, is told to use a 15 percent aftertax cost of capital, and may choose from the set of four projects shown in Exhibit 10.4. Aside from the capital constraint, each of the four projects is independent of the others; that is, they are not mutually exclusive projects.

All four projects represent worthwhile investments, but the manager, given a $200,000 constraint on the first-year cash outlays, may not undertake all of them. Juggling the possibilities, we can see from Exhibit 10.6 that the manager must choose one from several combinations of projects.

What is the manager to do? To maximize the net present values of the cash flows

Exhibit 10.6
Dilemma Caused by Capital Rationing

Project Combinations (1)	For Each Project Combination, the Sum of		
	Initial Cash Outlays (2)	Present Value of Cash Inflows (3)	Net Present Values (4) = (3) − (2)
E, G	$190,000	$270,000	$80,000
E, H	150,000	225,000	75,000
F, G	180,000	250,000	70,000
F, H	140,000	205,000	65,000
G, H	100,000	155,000	55,000

to the firm, the manager must choose the combination of projects E and G and reject the others. (Any funds not invested in these five projects must be used elsewhere in the firm and will, presumably, earn the 15 percent aftertax cost of capital.)

The problem of capital rationing arises from the inherent contradiction in telling a manager to use a cost of capital of, say, 15 percent while simultaneously limiting the capital budget. A limited capital budget implies a high, if not infinite, cost of securing additional funds. With a budget constraint, the firm is implicitly telling the manager that the cost of funds in excess of $200,000 per year is so large that capital expenditures in excess of $200,000 per year should not be considered at *any* cost. Using the cost of capital to calculate net present values of cash flows contains the only needed budgeting device: Managers will not invest funds in projects returning less than the cost of capital because the net present values of such projects will be negative. Capital rationing has no place in a profit-seeking firm that chooses between investment alternatives by taking the time value of money into account.

If management perceives a constraint on funds available for investment, then all managers should be told to use a higher cost of capital than had been used before. If, when the higher discount rate is used by managers in evaluating projects, the total funds required still exceed the perceived constraints, then the discount rate should be increased to still a higher level. If at the higher discount rate not all of the "available funds" would be used, the rate should be reduced. By a series of successive approximations, the discount rate to allocate available funds will be optimally determined.

Although capital rationing logically should not occur for long-run decisions in the absence of uncertainty, it is nonetheless a problem encountered in business practice when managers face uncertainty. Techniques similar to those shown in Exhibit 10.6 are generally used for allocating the capital budget each period.

Separating Investment and Financing Decisions

Investment decisions should be made independently of financing decisions. If a project can earn a return at least as large as the firm's cost of capital, then it should be undertaken. The manner in which the specific funds needed for the project will be obtained is a separate question.

Apparent Net Present Value Benefits to Borrowing

Combining the investment and financing decisions can mislead decision makers into believing that a project financed with debt is more worthwhile than the same project financed with cash on hand. The examples in Exhibit 10.7 are constructed to show how the confusion can result. Assume that a firm borrows money at the market rate of interest and makes the required debt service payments, both principal and interest, on schedule. Such an undertaking, by itself, can never be "worthwhile" in the same sense that an investment project with a positive net present value is worthwhile. Such borrowing increases the leverage of the firm, increasing the risk of the owners' equity. Such increased leverage is a "gamble," but in a

Exhibit 10.7
Net Present Values from Borrowing
at Various Interest Rates,
Discounted at 15 Percent Cost of Capital

			Cash Flows		
End of Year (1)	Event (2)	Pretax (3)	From Reduced Income Taxes Caused by Deducting Interest Expense (4)	Aftertax (5)	Present Value at 15 Percent (6)
12 Percent Loan					
0	Borrow	$ + 1,000	—	$ + 1,000	$ + 1,000
1	Interest	− 120	$ + 48	− 72	− 63
2	Interest	− 120	+ 48	− 72	− 54
2	Repayment	− 1,000	—	− 1,000	− 756
	Net Present Value				$ + 127
18 Percent Loan					
0	Borrow	$ + 1,000	—	$ + 1,000	$ + 1,000
1	Interest	− 180	$ + 72	− 108	− 94
2	Interest	− 180	+ 72	− 108	− 82
2	Repayment	− 1,000	—	− 1,000	− 756
	Net Present Value				$ + 68
25 Percent Loan					
0	Borrow	$ + 1,000	—	$ + 1,000	$ + 1,000
1	Interest	− 250	$ + 100	− 150	− 130
2	Interest	− 250	+ 100	− 150	− 114
2	Repayment	− 1,000	—	− 1,000	− 756
	Net Present Value				$ −0−

Column (3): Interest expense determined by terms of loan: 12, 18, or 25 percent.
Column (4): .40 × (3) when column (3) is deductible on tax return.
Column (5): (3) + (4).
Column (6): Amount in column (5) discounted at 15 percent using factors from Table 2.

End of Year 0	1.00000
End of Year 1	.86957
End of Year 2	.75614

technical sense it is a fair gamble. In this framework, a positive net present value project would be called a "favorable gamble" because it promises a rate of return higher than those otherwise available to the firm.

Exhibit 10.7 illustrates the net present values that result from analyzing borrowing activity as though it were an investment project. It assumes a firm with a pretax cost of capital of 25 percent, an income tax rate of 40 percent, and thus an aftertax cost of capital of 15 percent. The firm has sufficient other income that interest expense deducted on the tax return reduces cash outflows for taxes by $.40 for each $1.00 of interest expense.

In Exhibit 10.7, column (3) shows the pretax cash flows from borrowing and column (5) shows the cash flows after tax effects for the deductibility of interest expense. Column (6) shows the net present values of the cash flows, positive in the top two panels and zero in the third.

The top two panels of Exhibit 10.7 show apparently positive net present value from an outright borrowing. In the top panel, the market interest rate—12 percent—is lower than the aftertax cost of capital of 15 percent. The other two panels show interest rates—18 percent and 25 percent—higher than the aftertax cost of capital. Twenty-five percent is the breakeven rate—the borrowing rate at which the net present value of the borrowing goes to zero. One would not expect ever to see a case where the borrowing rate was as high as the pretax cost of capital. This case is illustrated to show the breakeven point.

In analyzing the cash flows from a loan, in a net present value analysis, one will find a positive net present value whenever the pretax borrowing rate is less than the pretax cost of capital. In this example, the pretax cost of capital is 25 percent $[= .15/(1.00 - .40)]$. Put differently, a loan will show positive net present value whenever the aftertax cost of borrowing is less than the cost of capital. In this case, the aftertax cost of borrowing is the interest rate multiplied by .60 $(= 1.00 - .40$ income tax rate).

When a loan is analyzed independent of the uses to which the funds will be put, as in Exhibit 10.7, it shows a positive net present value; this will occur whenever the aftertax cost of capital exceeds the aftertax borrowing rate. This positive net present value appears even though the loan does not improve the borrower's risk-adjusted expected returns. That the present value is positive and the firm is not better off shows the weakness of embedding the financing arrangement in the net present value analysis. Next, we illustrate such an embedding and the misleading signal it causes. The general result is that when interest on a loan is paid at an aftertax rate less than the discount rate used in present value calculations, the loan will always appear to have a positive net present value.

Managerial Evaluation of Leases

Types of Leases

Leases are of two broad types. Cancelable leases, such as for the use of telephones by the month or of cars rented by the day or week, are generally short-term and can be canceled by either party in the rental transaction. These leases do not present any problems because they are not a form of borrowing and, in any case, would not normally be analyzed as part of a firm's capital budgeting system.

Noncancelable leases, on the other hand, run for much longer periods of time. Under these leases, a firm commits itself to payments over the term of the lease whether or not the leased asset is continued in use. The obligation under a non-cancelable lease is, in an economic sense, not significantly different from a loan from a bank or other creditor. These leasing arrangements are in effect installment purchases of the property. The noncancelable lease is a means of financing the acquisition of an asset's service for a specified period of time.

Procedure for Evaluating Leases

To evaluate a leasing proposal properly, the investment and financing decisions must be separated. The procedure we illustrate in this section for evaluating leases is summarized as follows:

1. Decide if acquisition of the asset's services is a desirable investment alternative (the investment decision). To do this, calculate the net present value of the cash flows expected to be generated by the asset, *assuming that the asset is purchased immediately for cash*. The discount rate used should be the cost of capital. If the net present value is positive, then go to step 2. If the net present value is negative, do not consider the proposal further.

2. Decide the best means of financing the acquisition of the asset's services. The financing decision requires several steps.
   a. Compute the net present value of leasing. To do this, substitute the periodic rental payments for the outright cash payment at the time of the acquisition. Then calculate the net present value of leasing using the firm's cost of capital.
   b. Compute the net present value assuming that the acquisition of the asset is financed by borrowing the necessary funds. It is important that the pattern of amounts to be repaid under the assumed borrowing be roughly the same as the pattern of the assumed lease payments. If they are not, then the method illustrated here may not give the right answer. For example, if the proposed lease requires equal annual payments at the end of the year, then the assumed borrowing should be like a mortgage (with equal annual payments) rather than like a bond (with small interest payments until maturity, when the entire principal is repaid).
   c. Substitute the periodic interest and principal payments for the single outright cash payment at the time of acquisition.
   d. Compute the net present value of the purchase-borrowing alternative; use the firm's cost of capital in computing discount factors.

The financing alternative with the largest net present value should be used.

Illustration of the Lease Evaluation Procedure

Return to the example of the Garden Winery Company discussed in Chapter 9. The company is contemplating the acquisition of equipment that will permit it to produce a new type of wine. The manufacturer of the equipment is asking an

Exhibit 10.8

Annual Net Cash Flows and Net Present Values of Alternatives Available to Garden Winery Company for Acquiring Use of Asset

(discount rate is 15 percent per year; income taxes are 40 percent of pretax income)

End of Year (1)	Pretax Cash Inflows Less Cash Outflow Expenses (2)	Depreciation (3)	Lease Payments (4)	Payments to Service Debt — Total (5) =	Interest Expense (6) +	Principal Repayment (7)	Pretax Income (8)	Income Tax Expense (9)	Net Cash Inflows (Outflows) (10)	Present Value of Net Cash Flows at (11)
Purchase Asset Outright; No Borrowing (See Exhibits 9.1 and 9.2)										
0	—	—	—	—	—	—	—	—	$(100,000)	$(100,000)
1	$ 50,000	$ 25,000	—	—	—	—	$25,000	$10,000	40,000	34,783
2	45,000	25,000	—	—	—	—	20,000	8,000	37,000	27,977
3	40,000	25,000	—	—	—	—	15,000	6,000	34,000	22,356
4	30,000	25,000	—	—	—	—	5,000	2,000	28,000	16,009
	$165,000	$100,000					$65,000	$26,000	$ 39,000	$ 1,125
Lease Asset; Lease Payment Made at the End of Each Period										
0	—	—	—	—	—	—	—	—	—	—
1	$ 50,000	—	$ 38,629	—	—	—	$11,371	$ 4,548	$ 6,823	$ 5,933
2	45,000	—	38,629	—	—	—	6,371	2,548	3,823	2,891
3	40,000	—	38,629	—	—	—	1,371	549[b]	822	541
4	30,000	—	38,628[a]	—	—	—	(8,628)	(3,451)	(5,177)	(2,960)
	$165,000		$154,515				$10,485	$ 4,194	$ 6,291	$ 6,405
Purchase Asset; Borrow $100,000 at 20 Percent to Be Repaid in Four Annual Installments										
0	—	—	—	—	—	—	—	—	$ –0–[c]	$ –0–
1	$ 50,000	$ 25,000	—	$ 38,629 =	$20,000 +	$ 18,629	$ 5,000	$ 2,000	9,371	8,149
2	45,000	25,000	—	38,629 =	16,274 +	22,355	3,726	1,490	4,881	3,691
3	40,000	25,000	—	38,629 =	11,803 +	26,826	3,197	1,279	92	60
4	30,000	25,000	—	38,628[a] =	6,438 +	32,190	(1,438)	(575)	(8,053)	(4,604)
	$165,000	$100,000		$154,515 =	$54,515 +	$100,000	$10,485	$ 4,194	$ 6,291	$ 7,296

Column (2) Refer to Exhibit 9.2; the amounts shown here are the amounts shown in column (3) of Exhibit 9.2. The initial outlay is not an expense; it appears first in column (10).

Column (3) Straight-line method; $100,000 cost/4-year life.

Column (6) Twenty percent of outstanding loan. Outstanding loan is $100,000 less cumulative principal repayments shown in column (7); see Exhibit 10.9.

Column (7) Lease payment less portion allocated to interest expense from column (6); see Exhibit 10.9.

Column (8) Amount in column (2) less amounts in columns (3), (4), and (6).

Column (9) Forty percent of amount in column (8).

Column (10) Amount in column (2) less amounts in columns (4), (5), and (9).

Column (11) Amount in column (11) multiplied by present value factor for 15 percent discount rate: 1.00000 for cash flow at end of Year 0; .86957 for cash flows at end of Year 1, .75614 for cash flows at end of Year 2; .65752 for cash flows at end of Year 3; .57175 for cash flows at end of Year 4.

[a]See Exhibit 10.9 for derivation of payment for Year 4.

[b]By actual multiplication, .40 × $1,371, this number is $548; rounding to the nearest dollar has caused the sum of numbers in this column to be in error by $1. Note that .40 × $10,485 = $4,194. This number has been changed to $549 to undo the rounding effects.

[c]At the end of Year 0, $100,000 is borrowed and used immediately to acquire asset; this number is + $100,000 − $100,000 = $0.

immediate cash price of $100,000 for the equipment. Alternatively, the manufacturer will lease the asset to Garden Winery Company for a rental fee of $38,629 a year for 4 years, after which the asset will be scrapped.

Investment Decision The first step is to decide if acquisition of the asset's services is a desirable investment alternative, as in Exhibit 9.2. The analysis is repeated in the top panel of Exhibit 10.8. The analysis assumes that the asset is purchased outright and that annual cash flows are discounted at the firm's cost of capital of 15 percent per year. If the asset is purchased, then the net present value of the investment project is $1,125. Acquiring the asset is, therefore, a worthwhile undertaking.

Financing Decision Next we must consider how the investment should be financed. It is necessary that we consider this second question because leasing is a form of financing.

The middle panel of Exhibit 10.8 shows the calculation of the net present value assuming that the asset is acquired through leasing. Instead of a cash outflow of $100,000 at time zero, there is a cash outflow of $38,629 per year for lease payments except in the last year, when the payment is $38,628; see Exhibit 10.9. To simplify the illustration, we assume that lease payments are made at the end of each year. Because Garden Winery Company is only leasing the asset, it will not deduct depreciation expense in calculating taxable income. It does, however, deduct rent expense in calculating taxable income. The net aftertax cash flows are again discounted using the firm's cost of capital of 15 percent. The net present value of acquiring the asset's services through leasing is $6,405. Notice that the net present value of leasing is almost six times as large as the net present value of outright purchase.

Some managers would note the much larger net present value for the leasing plan and conclude that leasing is surely better for the firm than buying outright. *Comparing the net present values of buying outright versus leasing is invalid.* The investment decision has been confounded with the financing decision. A noncancelable lease is a form of borrowing. In the first case, the firm is not borrowing; in the second case, it is borrowing. To evaluate the leasing plan, the manager should construct a series of cash flows in which the firm borrows equivalent amounts of funds for equivalent interest rates and then compare a borrow-purchase alternative with the leasing alternative. Correct managerial decisions require comparable financing plans. Because the leasing contract effectively combines the financing and investment decisions, the valid alternative to leasing is a borrow-purchase alternative.

The lower panel of Exhibit 10.8 analyzes the borrow-purchase alternative. We begin by computing the rate at which Garden Winery Company could borrow $100,000 today, with repayments being made over the next 4 years. In the illustration we have used a 20 percent rate. This is the rate that the manufacturer/lessor is *implicitly* charging Garden Winery Company in the leasing arrangement. It is the discount rate that discounts the annual rental payments of $38,629 back to the present so that they have a present value equal to the cost of the asset of $100,000. If the leasing company is willing to lend to Garden Winery Company at 20 percent, then the Company can presumably borrow from a bank at 20 percent per year. If

Exhibit 10.9
Separation of Loan Payments into Interest and Principal for a $100,000, Four-Year, 20 Percent Loan; Annual Payment $38,629[a]

End of Year (1)	Unpaid Liability at Beginning of Period (2)	Interest Expense (3)	Principal Payment (4)	Unpaid Liability at End of Period (5)
0	—	—	—	$100,000
1	$100,000	$20,000	$ 18,629	81,371
2	81,371	16,274	22,355	59,016
3	59,016	11,803	26,826	32,190
4	32,190	6,438	32,190	–0–
Total		$54,515	$100,000	

[a]Except in last year, when only $38,628 (= $6,438 + $32,190) is required.
Column (3) = .20 × column (2).
Column (4) = $38,629 − column (3), except in Year 4.
Column (5) = column (2) − column (4).

payments on the loan are made in annual installments at the end of the year, then the payments will be $38,629 for each of the 4 years, just as for the lease. After all, the same amount is being borrowed and at the same interest rate as in the lease. Part of each payment to the bank is for interest and part is for principal repayment. The separation of the annual payment into interest and principal follows the effective interest method as described in financial accounting texts. Exhibit 10.9 illustrates this separation. These amounts appear in columns (6) and (7) of Exhibit 10.8. Separating the annual payment into interest and principal repayment is required for the computation of income taxes, because the interest expense is a deduction in computing taxable income whereas repayment of the loan principal is not.

If the company borrows and purchases the asset, it will report depreciation each year identical with that if it purchases without borrowing. Column (3) shows the depreciation charges. In the case of borrow-purchase, pretax income is cash inflows less cash outflows, column (2), less depreciation, column (3), and interest expense, column (5). Column (9) shows income taxes, which are 40 percent of pretax income. Net cash flow for the period shown in column (10) is cash inflows less cash outflows, column (2); less payments to the bank to service the debt, column (5); less income taxes, column (9). Column (11) shows the present values of each of the net cash flows discounted at 15 percent per year.

The net present value of the borrow-purchase alternative is $7,296, which is somewhat larger than the net present value of the lease alternative ($6,405) because of the timing of income tax payments. In this illustration, borrowing turns out to be slightly superior to leasing as a form of financing.

Why Do Leasing and Borrow-Purchase Appear More Attractive Than Outright Purchase?

Both leasing and borrow-purchase have net present values more than six times as large as the net present value of the outright purchase. Why? We can rephrase this question to make the managerial implications clearer. Suppose that the cash flow in Year 1 were only $45,000, and not $50,000. Then the analysis of the outright purchase shows a negative net present value, indicating that the project is not worthwhile for the company; but the analyses of leasing and borrow-purchase both show positive net present values, indicating that the project is worthwhile when financed with debt. What should the manager conclude?

The answers to both questions involve the difference between the aftertax interest cost of debt and the cost of capital used in making investment decisions. In the illustration for Garden Winery Company, the aftertax cost of capital is 15 percent, whereas the borrowing rate is 20 percent. In the net present value of the leasing and borrow-purchase alternatives, the company is charged with interest on borrowings at 20 percent with an aftertax cost of 12 percent [$= (1.00 - .40) \times 20$ percent], but the cash flows are discounted at 15 percent. Any time a series of interest payments is discounted with a higher rate than the aftertax rate implied by the loan contract, the present value of the payments to service the loan will have a lower present value than the face amount of the borrowing. Recall the discussion of financing methods illustrated with Exhibit 10.7.

The phenomenon of *leverage* occurs when the rate of return on total capital can be increased because the rate paid to borrow is less than the rate typically earned by the company on its projects. The difference between the net present values of borrowing and outright purchase results from showing the expected returns to leverage as a part of the return to the *specific* project. But, of course, the firm always has the option to borrow at the current market rate of interest. The returns and risks of leverage accrue to the firm's financing policy *as a whole*, and should not be attributed to any one investment project.

Thus, if the net present value for outright purchase is negative even though the net present value for one of the borrowing alternatives is positive, then the firm should not undertake the project. Lease contracts by their very nature involve a simultaneous consideration of investment and financing. Because the two aspects cannot easily be separated in general, the manager should first evaluate the project assuming outright purchase. Only after outright purchase appears worthwhile, because the project has a positive net present value, should the form of financing be considered. Once the lease terms are specified, the manager should ascertain the payment schedule for a straight loan that is as similar as possible in terms of amounts borrowed and timing of repayments as are implicit in the lease. Then the borrowing and leasing alternatives can be compared.[6]

---

[6]The nature of leasing contracts can be somewhat more complicated than indicated here. For example, lease payments can be made in advance, with the initial lease payment being immediately deductible for tax purposes. It is not usually possible to arrange a straight loan with interest payable in advance that is deductible for tax purposes. (In theory, there is no such thing as interest paid in advance. If payments are made before interest has accrued, then theory says that those payments must be a reduction in the principal amount of the loan, not interest.) Another complication arises when the manufacturer offers a "package deal," where the combined interest payments and asset cost are together smaller than they would be separately. (Automobile dealers often are willing to sell at a lower price when the buyer borrows from the dealer than when the buyer makes an outright purchase.) The advanced questions raised by some leasing contracts are beyond the scope of this introductory, but already sophisticated, discussion. The reader interested in a more advanced discussion is referred to Chapter 8 of the *Handbook of Modern Accounting,* 2nd ed., edited by Sidney Davidson and Roman L. Weil (New York: McGraw-Hill, 1977); and S. Basu, *Leasing Arrangements: Managerial Decision Making and Financial Reporting Issues* (Hamilton, Ont.: Society of Management Accountants of Canada, 1980).

Considering Investment and Financing Decisions Simultaneously Can Be Acceptable

Are there conditions under which the analysis in the second panel of Exhibit 10.8 is correct for making an investment decision? That is, can it ever be correct to consider the net present value of the combined operating and financing cash flows? Yes.

If the lessor allows the lessee to make debt service (lease) payments from the cash flows produced by the leased asset only, then the financing plan and the operating cash flows can be combined for analysis. This is *not* the same thing as saying that the leased asset is "collateral" for the loan.

Example The Western Railroad leases for 12 years from the General Products Credit Company a new heavy-duty locomotive for hauling coal from the Powder River Basin in Wyoming to Chicago. It promises to pay $200,000 per year for 12 years. The payments must be made whatever use, if any, is made of the locomotive. If the railroad fails to make payments, then the Credit Company is allowed to take back the locomotive, which it owns.

Case A The Credit Company expects to be paid from whatever cash the railroad has on hand, independent of the business that generated the cash. If the railroad should go bankrupt, the Credit Company is entitled to payment of amounts due to it, just the same as any other creditor. In this case, the decision to acquire the locomotive is independent of the particular financing arrangements offered by the lessor. The railroad ought to make the investment decision on the basis of the cash flows from using the locomotive, assuming that it is purchased for cash.

Case B The Credit Company is willing to have debt service (lease) payments made solely from the revenues of hauling coal with this particular locomotive. If the locomotive is unused for any reason for a given year, then the railroad is not required to make the $200,000 payment for that year. In this case the financing decision can be considered along with the investment decision, because the railroad's acquisition of the debt in becoming the lessee of the locomotive will not affect its ability to borrow funds (or issue new equity shares) to finance other parts of its business. This situation would be unusual, but is occasionally seen, particularly in some leveraged leases.

Summary

The optimal method for evaluating investment projects should take the time value of money into account. All the methods that do take the time value of money into account require a cutoff rate or discount rate, sometimes called a "hurdle rate." If optimal economic decisions are to result, the cutoff or discount rate must be set equal to the cost of capital. If the cost of capital rate is to be used at all, the net present value rule is no more complex than the others. Using the net present value rule will lead to decisions that will make present value of the firm's wealth equal to or larger than that from using any of the other rules.

Under many circumstances, the net present value method and the internal rate of return method give identical answers. In some circumstances, particularly those involving mutually exclusive projects, the internal rate of return method can give a misleading message. Thus, the net present value method should be used in making the investment decision.

The investment decision and the financing decision for investment projects should be kept separate. The use of the present value rule and the differential principle for making decisions will enable the manager to choose between various methods of financing only if the contending financing plans involve equal amounts of borrowing for equal amounts of time. Otherwise, the benefits of financial leverage will be confused with the benefits from a particular investment project.

Problem 1 for Self-Study

Management of the Antle Company is considering an investment project that requires an initial investment of $10,000 and that promises to return $17,490, after taxes, at the end of 4 years. Because the aftertax cost of capital of the firm is 15 percent per year, the net present value of the investment is zero. An investment banker points out, however, that if the firm borrows the $10,000 via a 4-year annual coupon bond issue, the annual interest expense (based on 20 percent coupons) will be $2,000, but will be only $1,200 after taxes at a 40 percent rate. The net present value of the project will increase from zero to $857, and the project will be worthwhile. The banker offers to arrange a $10,000 loan at a 20 percent rate.

a.   Verify that the net present value of the project is zero.

b.   Reproduce the investment banker's analysis; use five-place present value factors.

c.   Comment on the investment banker's proposal and advise the Antle Company as to how it should evaluate the project.

Suggested Solution

a.   Table 2, 4-period row, 15 percent column is .57175; $17,490 × .57175 = $10,000.
b.   See Exhibit 10.10.
c.   The analysis in Exhibit 10.10 confounds the investment and financing decision. The investment banker's advice should be ignored unless the loan can be arranged so that the only collateral for the loan is the investment project itself *and* the only source of debt service payments for the bond issue is cash flows from the project. (Because the project has cash flows only in the last year, it is unlikely that such a loan can be arranged.) Otherwise, this analysis indicates that Antle Company should be indifferent to this project.

Exhibit 10.10
ANTLE COMPANY
(Problem 1 for Self-Study)

End of Year (1)	Cash Flow If Borrow $10,000 (2)			Present Value	
				Factor at 15 Percent (3)	Amount = (2) × (3) (4)
0	$+10,000 − $10,000	=	$ −0−	1.00000	$ −0−
1	−2,000 × (1 − .40)	=	−1,200	.86957	(1,043)
2	−2,000 × (1 − .40)	=	−1,200	.75614	(907)
3	−2,000 × (1 − .40)	=	−1,200	.65752	(789)
4	−2,000 × (1 − .40)	=	−1,200	.57175	(686)
4	+17,490 − 10,000	=	+7,490	.57175	4,282
					$ 857

Problem 2 for Self-Study

Fabco Manufacturing Company was considering the purchase of two different types of machines to manufacture rubber gaskets, one of the many products it produced for industrial markets. The two machines were alike in the following ways: Each required an initial investment of $750,000; lasted five years, after which the salvage value was 0; and had sufficient capacity to meet the projected steady demand. The main difference between the two machines was the timing and amount of operating cash flows. Machine A's operating cash costs would start out high and then decrease in subsequent years. For machine B, constant operating cash costs were predicted. The incremental net cash flows (revenues minus operating cash costs) for the two machines were expected to be as follows:

	Aftertax Cash Flow per Year					
	0	1	2	3	4	5
Machine A . . .	$(750,000)	$100,000	$200,000	$200,000	$300,000	$550,000
Machine B . . .	(750,000)	250,000	250,000	250,000	250,000	250,000

Fabco needed to determine which, if either, of the two machines to buy to manufacture rubber gaskets. Unsure of which method of evaluation to use, the vice-president asked that calculations be made for the following methods:

(1) Payback period (assume, for this calculation only, that cash flows are spread evenly throughout the year).
(2) Accounting rate of return.
(3) Internal rate of return.
(4) Net present value (cost of capital = 10 percent).
(5) Net present value (cost of capital = 12 percent).

a. Perform the above calculations for each machine. (Use discount factors rounded to five decimal places.) For each method state which machine looks like the better investment.

b. Why does the net present value method yield different decisions at the two different discount rates? Does the internal rate of return method exhibit the same phenomenon?

c. Comment on the usefulness of each of the above methods for choosing between the two machines.

Suggested Solution

The following table provides data used in various parts of the solution.

	Cash Flow	Discount Factor at 10 Percent	Present Value at 10 Percent	Discount Factor at 12 Percent	Present Value at 12 Percent
Machine A					
Year 0	$(750,000)	1.00000	$(750,000)	1.00000	$(750,000)
Year 1	100,000	.90909	90,909	.89286	89,286
Year 2	200,000	.82645	165,290	.79719	159,438
Year 3	200,000	.75131	150,262	.71178	142,356
Year 4	300,000	.68301	204,903	.63552	190,656
Year 5	550,000	.62092	341,506	.56743	312,087
Net present value . . .			$ 202,870		$ 143,823
Machine B					
Year 0	$(750,000)	1.00000	$(750,000)	1.00000	$(750,000)
Year 1	250,000	.90909	227,273	.89286	223,215
Year 2	250,000	.82645	206,613	.79719	199,298
Year 3	250,000	.75131	187,828	.71178	177,945
Year 4	250,000	.68301	170,753	.63552	158,880
Year 5	250,000	.62092	155,230	.56743	141,858
Net present value . . .			$ 197,697		$ 151,196

a. **(1)** Payback period:

Machine A: Cumulative cash inflow at the end of Year 3 = $500,000. Total investment of $750,000 − $500,000 = $250,000 remaining to be recouped in Year 4.

$$\frac{\$250,000}{300,000} = .83.$$

Thus, payback period = 3.83 years.

Machine B:

$$\text{Payback Period} = \frac{\$750,000}{250,000 \text{ per Year}} = 3.0 \text{ Years.}$$

Purchase decision: Purchase machine B if a payback period of 3 years is acceptable.

(2) Accounting rate of return (or return on investment):

Machine A:

$$\text{Average Net Income} = \frac{\text{Total Cash Flow} - \text{Total Depreciation}}{5}$$

$$= \frac{\$1,350,000 - \$750,000}{5}$$

$$= \$120,000.$$

$$\text{Average Investment} = \frac{\$750,000}{2}$$

$$= \$375,000.$$

$$\text{ROI} = \frac{\$120,000}{\$375,000} = 32\%.$$

Machine B:

$$\text{Average Net Income} = \frac{\$1,250,000 - \$750,000}{5} = \$100,000.$$

$$\text{Average Investment} = \frac{\$750,000}{2} = \$375,000.$$

$$\text{ROI} = \frac{\$100,000}{\$375,000} = 26.7\%$$

Decision: Purchase machine A if 32 percent is an acceptable ROI.

(3) Internal rate of return:

Machine A:

$$\text{At } 12\%, \quad \text{NPV} = \$143,823,$$

$$\text{At } 20\%, \quad \text{NPV} = \$(46,330),$$

calculated using five-decimal-place discount factors.
By interpolation, IRR is approximated as follows:

$$\frac{\$(46,330)}{\$143,823 + \$46,330} \times (20\% - 12\%) = -1.95\%$$

$$20\% - 1.95\% = 18.05\% \text{ IRR}.$$

Or, using a pocket calculator, IRR = 17.78 percent.

Machine B:

$$\text{At } 12\%, \quad \text{NPV} = \$151,195,$$

$$\text{At } 20\%, \quad \text{NPV} = \$(2,350),$$

calculated using five-decimal-place discount factors.

Interpolating:

$$\frac{\$(2,350)}{\$151,195 + \$2,350} \times (20\% - 12\%) = -.12\%$$

$$20\% - .12\% = 19.88\% \text{ IRR.}$$

Or, using a pocket calculator, IRR = 19.86 percent.

Decision: Purchase machine B if 19.86 percent is considered a sufficiently high IRR.

(4) Net present value at 10 percent (see table above):

Machine A: NPV = $202,870,

Machine B: NPV = $197,697.

Decision: Purchase machine A. Both have a positive NPV, and the NPV for machine A is higher.

(5) Net present value at 12 percent (see table above)

Machine A: NPV = $143,823,

Machine B: NPV = $151,196.

Decision: Purchase machine B. Both have a positive NPV, and machine B's is higher.

b. Machine A's cash inflows occur later than those of machine B. Therefore, at higher discount rates, machine A looks less attractive than machine B. But because machine A's total cash inflows are greater, at a low enough discount rate its NPV is greater than that of machine B. The crossover point occurs somewhere between the discount rates of 10 percent and 12 percent. The internal rate of return is higher than the discount rate at which machine B becomes more attractive than machine A; hence, machine B dominates machine A using IRR.

c. The payback period and ROI methods both ignore the time value of money. As these two machines differ mainly in the timing of their cash inflows, failure to consider the time value of money results in an incomplete comparison of cash flows.

The internal rate of return method considers all the cash flows and the time value of money, but still does not always lead to the same decision as the net present value method. As discussed in part **b.**, the IRR for each machine is constant, whereas the relative NPV's for the two machines depends on the firm's cost of capital. The most useful method for making the purchase decision is the net present value method, with careful thought about the firm's measure of its cost of capital.

Problem 3 for Self-Study

The purpose of this problem is to expand on the text's discussion of the impact of financing on capital budgeting decisions.

Only in exceptional cases will a specific financing instrument be tied so closely to a specific investment project that the capital cost of the investment is the cost of the specific financing instrument.

Consider two firms, Company A and Company B. Both companies operate two lines of business of the same size. The first line of business is owning and leasing to others railroad oil tank cars. The second line of business is owning and leasing vacation homes near recreational lakes. In financing the two businesses, Company A and Company B borrow funds from local banks to supplement the funds invested by the owners. For purchases of oil tank cars to be put on lease, First National Bank is willing to supply 80 percent of the purchase price through long-term, fixed-interest-rate loans. For purchases of vacation homes, Second National Bank is willing to lend only 40 percent of the purchase price through long-term, fixed-interest-rate loans. First National Bank finances only tank car loans and Second National Bank finances only vacation home loans.

Company A First National Bank has agreed that interest payments on the tank car debt and all tank car debt principal repayments will be paid only out of tank car rentals. The only collateral for the loans is the tank cars. The rentals from vacation homes are not to be used in any way to service the tank car debt to First National Bank. The vacation homes are similarly financed: Debt service payments to Second National Bank are to come only from rentals of vacation homes, and the only collateral for the loan is the home being financed with a given loan.[7]

Company B Company B, while identical in its assets and operations to Company A, has conventional installment note financing for both its tank car and vacation home purchases. That is, both banks look to all income of the firm—from whatever source—for payment of interest and principal on debt. The banks are entitled to receive payments as they come due from whatever assets Company B has on hand. Thus, Company B will be required to pay interest due First National Bank, for example, with earnings from vacation homes if tank car rentals are insufficient. Moreover, if Company B defaults on its loans to the First National Bank, the bank can expect to receive some of the proceeds of disposing of the vacation homes.

Analyze the differences between Company A's and Company B's financings. What are the implications of these differences for making capital budgeting decisions?

Suggested Solution

The risks assumed by the banks in lending to Company A are clearly different from risks assumed in lending to Company B. Management of Company A would be

---

[7]These simplified facts are chosen to highlight the issue. Only in the cases of some leveraged leases and certain loans from the federal Small Business Administration to new businesses have we actually seen financing of this sort.

correct to consider simultaneously the investment and financing decision for a new tank car debt. The interest rate on the loan is the appropriate cost of funds for management of Company A to consider in making decisions about new tank cars. At Company B, however, a new loan for a new tank car deal affects the likelihood of repayment of *all* old loans. Thus, the impact of new loans on the Company's entire business must be considered. Management of Company B must consider more than mere cost of the new debt used to acquire new assets. Situations like Company A, where specific financings are tied only to specific assets, are unusual enough that any decision maker encountering one ought to be careful to make sure all aspects of the financing are, in fact, understood.

Questions

1. Review the meaning of the following concepts or terms discussed in this chapter.

a.	Internal rate of return.	**h.**	Discounted payback period.
b.	Mutually exclusive projects.	**i.**	Bailout period.
c.	Scale effect.	**j.**	Discounted bailout period.
d.	Excess present value index.	**k.**	Accounting rate of return.
e.	Cutoff rate.	**l.**	Capital rationing.
f.	Payback period.	**m.**	Cancelable lease.
g.	Reciprocal of payback period.	**n.**	Noncancelable lease.

2. a. The internal rate of return rule and the net present value rule both take the time value of money into account and usually give the same decision. When may they give different decisions?

b. "The internal rate of return is more difficult to compute than the net present value of a project. The internal rate of return method can never give a better answer than the net present value method." Why, then, do you suppose that so many people use the internal rate of return method?

3. What are the weaknesses of using the payback period as a device for capital budgeting decisions?

4. For mutually exclusive projects, the project with the lowest net present value of cash inflow per dollar of initial cash outlay can be the best alternative for the firm. How can this be?

5. "Under no conditions should the investment decision be made simultaneously with the financing decision."

Comment.

6. Assume that a firm borrows cash at a fair market interest rate less than its opportunity cost of capital. The net present value of the cash flows from this loan is positive when the cash flows are discounted at the firm's cost of capital.

Why will this loan *not* necessarily increase the wealth of the firm or its owners?

7. Assume that a firm borrows at a fair market interest rate and computes the net present value of the cash flows—proceeds of borrowings and aftertax debt-service payments—using the aftertax cost of capital. Generally, the result will be a positive number, indicating that the borrowing "project" is a worthwhile undertaking according to the net present value rule.

Comment on this phenomenon.

Exercises

8. *Net Present Value and Mutually Exclusive Projects.* The Larson Company must choose between two mutually exclusive projects. The cost of capital is 12 percent. Given the data below, which project should Larson choose, and why?

		Aftertax Cash Flows End of Year			
Project Label		0	1	2	3
M		$(500,000)	$175,000	$287,500	$400,000
N		(450,000)	477,000	195,000	60,000

9. *Computing Internal Rate of Return.* What is the internal rate of return on the following projects, each of which requires a $10,000 cash outlay now and returns the cash flows indicated?

a. $5,530.67 at the end of Years 1 and 2.
b. $1,627.45 at the end of Years 1 through 10.
c. $1,556.66 at the end of Years 1 through 13.
d. $2,053.39 at the end of Years 1 through 20.
e. $2,921.46 at the end of Years 3 through 7.
f. $2,101.77 at the end of Years 2 through 10.
g. $24,883.20 at the end of Year 5 only.

10. *Computing Payback.* What is the payback period of the projects in Exercise **9, a** through **g**?

11. *Relation between internal rate of return and payback period.* Compare the internal rate of return on the projects in Exercise **9, a** through **d**, with the *reciprocal* of the payback period for those projects computed in Exercise **10**. Notice that the internal rate of return on **d** is exactly equal to the reciprocal of its payback period, but this relation does not hold for the other projects. Explain.

12. *Computing payback.* What is the payback period of the projects in Exercise **9, a** through **g**, assuming that cash flows occur uniformly throughout the year?

13. *Working backwards with net present value method.* A manager's favorite project requires an aftertax cash outflow on January 1 of $4,000 and promises to return $1,000 of aftertax cash inflows at the end of each of the next 5 years. The aftertax cost of capital is 10 percent per year.

a. Use the net present value method to decide whether this favorite project is a good investment.

b. How much would the projected cash inflow for the end of Year 5 have to be increased for the project to be acceptable?

c. How much would the projected cash inflow for the end of Year 5 have to be increased for the project to have a net present value of +$100?

14. *Computing internal rate of return.* Carlo Company is considering the acquisition of a machine that costs $40,000 and that is expected to save $8,000 in cash outlays per year, after taxes, at the end of each of the next 12 years. The new machine is estimated to have no salvage value at the end of its useful life. (You may compute the actual return on your calculator or use Table 4 and interpolate.)

a. Compute the internal rate of return for this project.

b. Compute the internal rate of return, assuming that the cash savings were to last only 6, instead of 12, years.

c. Compute the internal rate of return, assuming that the cash savings were to last 20, rather than 12, years.

d. Compute the internal rate of return, assuming that the cash savings will be $6,000 rather than $8,000 per year for 12 years.

15. *Computing Net Present Value of Leverage.* Compute the apparent benefits of financial leverage for each of the following annual coupon bond issues. Assume an income tax rate of 40 percent and an aftertax cost of capital of 12 percent.

a. $100,000 borrowed for 5 years at 12 percent.

b. $100,000 borrowed for 10 years at 12 percent.

c. $100,000 borrowed for 5 years at 15 percent.

d. $100,000 borrowed for 5 years at 20 percent.

Problems and Cases

16. *Managerial Incentives of Performance Evaluation Based on Accounting Data.* A firm with an opportunity cost of capital of 20 percent faces two mutually exclusive investment projects:

(1) Acquiring certain goods at the start of the year, shipping them to Japan, and selling them at the end of the year. The internal rate of return on this project is 25 percent, and it has positive net present value.

(2) Making certain expenditures today that will cause reported earnings for the year to decline. This will result, however, in large cash flows at the ends of the second and third years. The internal rate of return on this project is 35 percent, and it has even larger net present value than the first project.

Management observes that the second project will result in smaller earnings for the current year reported to its shareholders than the first.

How might management's observation influence its choice between the two investment projects?

17. *Multiple IRRs.* Consider an investment in a strip-mining operation where the cash flows are negative at the outset, positive during the intermediate years, and negative at the end because of expenditures to restore the mine site to its premining environment. For simplicity, assume that there are only three periodic cash flows: $100,000 initial investment, $225,000 cash inflow from ore at the end of the first period, and a $126,500 cash outflow for restoration at the end of the second period.

    a.   Demonstrate that this project has two internal rates of return: 10 percent per period and 15 percent per period. Observe that the internal rate of return methodology for capital budgeting as usually stated ("compute the internal rate of return and accept the project if the rate exceeds the hurdle rate") fails to give clear guidance in this case.

    b.   Compute the net present value of this project at discount rates of 5 percent, 12 percent, and 20 percent.

    c.   Using the net present value methodology, state a decision rule for accepting or rejecting this project as a function of the cost of capital.

18. *Leverage and Decision Making.* Management of the Xenophon Company is considering an investment project that requires an initial investment of $100,000 and promises to return $176,234, after taxes, at the end of 5 years. Because the after tax cost of capital of the firm is 12 percent per year, the net present value of this investment is zero. Management finds itself indifferent to the project. A financial analyst points out, however, that if the firm will borrow the $100,000 via a 5-year annual coupon bond issue, the annual interest expense will be $15,000, or $9,000 after taxes, the net present value of the project will increase from zero to $10,814, and it will become worthwhile.

    a.   Verify that the net present value of the project is zero.

    b.   Reproduce the analysis that the financial analyst has in mind.

    c.   Comment on the suggestion of the financial analyst.

19. *Definition of Alternatives to Be Considered.* Consider two mutually exclusive alternatives facing a manufacturer of food blenders:

(1) Sell the existing blender equipment and get out of the business, netting $+$1,000 cash proceeds from sale.

(2) Stay in the blender business, generating $+$200 of net cash inflows per year at the end of each of the next 10 years.

    a.   Why is there no well-defined internal rate of return on alternative **(1)**?

    b.   Why is there no well-defined internal rate of return on alternative **(2)**?

    c.   Some who favor the internal rate of return methodology would "rescue" that methodology from the difficulty in situations such as the above by defining the "incremental" investment project, which is the algebraic difference between the cash flows of the two alternatives. Consider the incremental project defined as cash flows from alternative **(2)** minus cash flows from alternative **(1)**, as described above. Such a project shows an outflow of $1,000 now in return for inflows of $200 at the end of each of the next 10 years. (One might be tempted to say that this incremental project represents the opportunity cost—an investment of $1,000—of staying in business, followed by the actual cash inflows of staying in business—$200 per year. Such intermixing of opportunity costs and actual cash flows can confuse even the experienced analyst.) Demonstrate that such a project has an internal rate of return of about 15 percent and that staying in the blender business is superior to getting out so long as the cost of capital is less than or equal to 15 percent.

d. Consider the third alternative facing the manufacturer of food blenders:

(3) Sell the blender equipment and purchase equipment for manufacturing food processors. This implies cash expenditures of $4,000 currently and cash flows of $900 per year in arrears for 15 years.

How can such an alternative be compared to alternatives **(1)** and **(2)**, with the internal rate of return methodology?

e. Consider the fourth alternative facing the manufacturer:

(4) Stay in the blender business and add the processor business. This implies cash outflow of $5,000 currently, followed by cash inflows of $1,050 at the end of each of the next 10 years and cash inflows of $900 at the end of each of the 5 years thereafter.

How can such an alternative be compared to **(1)**, **(2)**, and **(3)**, with the internal rate of return methodology?

f. What do you conclude about "rescuing" the internal rate of return methodology via the technique of constructing incremental investment projects?

20. *Analyzing a Lease.* The Myers company wonders whether to acquire a computer that has a 3-year life, costs $30,000, and will save $25,000 per year before taxes in cash operating costs as compared to the present data processing system. Myers Company can borrow for 3 years at 12 percent per year. The computer manufacturer is willing to sell the computer for $30,000 or to lease it for three years on a noncancelable basis—that is, on the basis that Myers Company must make payments for the three years no matter what happens. The annual lease payment will be $12,490, except in the third year when it is $12,491. The income tax rate is 40 percent. If purchased, the computer will be depreciated using accelerated cost recovery over three years, using accelerated cost recovery percentages of 25 percent in the first year, 38 percent in the second, and 37 percent in the third.

Prepare an analysis that will help Myers Company decide what it should do. Round discount factor to two places. The aftertax cost of capital is 10 percent.

21. *Compare lease with borrow/buy.* The Carom Company plans to acquire, as of January 1, 19X0, a computerized cash register system that costs $100,000 and that has a 5-year life and no salvage value. The new computerized system will save $35,000 in cash operating costs per year. The company is considering two plans for acquiring the system:

(1) Outright purchase. To finance the purchase, $100,000 of par value 5-year, 15-percent annual coupon bonds will be issued January 1, 19X0, at par.

(2) Lease. The lease required five annual payments to be made on December 31, 19X0, 19X1, 19X2, 19X3, and 19X4. The lease payments are to be $29,832 and they have a present value of $100,000 on January 1, 19X0, when discounted at 15 percent per year.

The firm's aftertax cost of capital is 12 percent. Accelerated cost recovery will be used for tax purposes with the following percentages in each of the 5 years, respectively: 25, 38, 37, 0, and 0. The income tax rate is 40 percent.

a. Construct an exhibit similar to Exhibit 10.8. Round discount factors to two decimal places. Use three panels, one for each of the following alternatives:

(1) Outright purchase for cash.

(2) Outright purchase with borrowing as explained in **(1)**.

(3) Lease under terms as explained in **(2)**.

b. Should the services of the asset be acquired? How do you reach this conclusion?

c. Which of the financing plans, borrowing via a bond issue or leasing, appears preferable? How can one financing plan with an interest cost of 15 percent per year (bond issue) appear preferable to another financing plan with an interest cost of 15 percent per year (lease)? What can you conclude from the answers to these two questions?

d. Now assume that the lease contract calls for payments of $28,500 per year (an implicit interest rate of only 13.1 percent). Construct a fourth panel in the exhibit called for in part **a**. Which financing plan, leasing at 13.1 percent or borrowing at 15 percent, appears preferable? How can one plan of financing with an interest cost of 15 percent per year (bond issue) appear preferable to another plan of financing with an interest cost of 13.1 percent per year (lease)? What can you conclude from the answers to these two questions?

e. Should Carom Company lease the asset or purchase it? How can you tell? If you judge that purchase is preferable, what is the minimum aftertax payment that the lessor could offer to make Carom Company indifferent to leasing?

22. *Merits of Internal Rate of Return.* A well-known university sponsors a continuing education program for engineers. One of its programs is called "Evaluating Project Alternatives by Rate of Return." The advertising copy for this program says, in part:

Why You Should Attend Traditionally, a large percentage of business decisions have been based solely on payback. Although the payback method has the advantage of computational simplicity, it is not a true measure of life-cycle cost effectiveness and can lead to erroneous accept-reject decisions.

Why Use Rate of Return

(1) Takes into account:

Cash flows beyond the payback period;

Timing of cash flows within the payback period.

(2) Does not discriminate against long-lived projects.

(3) Does not ignore the time value of money.

(4) Differentiates between debt and equity capital.

(5) Does not require stipulation of an interest rate.

(6) Provides for:

Return of and on debt and equity capital;

Income taxes, income tax write-offs;

Inflation;

Costs that escalate at a rate greater than the rate of inflation.

(7) Permits an accurate ranking of alternatives.

(8) Gives correct choice among independent alternatives.

(9) Maximizes return on investment.

Assume that by "rate of return," this advertising means the "internal rate of return."

Comment on the nine numbered points from the copy. Consider these points as they apply both to the internal rate of return method and the net present value method.

23. *Merits of Lessee's Benefits of Leasing.* A well-known company with a financing subsidiary promotes its leasing activities (as lessor) with material containing the following statements. Evaluate these statements.

Retain Favorable Tax Advantages Many companies in capital-intensive industries are not in a position to use investment tax credits to full advantage. Neither can they benefit from accelerated depreciation. Yet these companies often need new equipment. Leasing offers a solution to the problem: The lessee can assign tax benefits—benefits it cannot use—to the lessor in exchange for reduced lease payments. No other form of equipment financing provides this important advantage.

Conserve Cash Normally, leasing affords 100 percent financing. There are no down payments or compensating balances. If a company ties up its cash to purchase equipment, the earning power of the cash itself is lost. But if the same company were to lease equipment, it could still put the cash into other, profitable investments. It is for this reason that, in the long run, leasing can help maximize the use of a company's resources. Leasing gives a company the opportunity to use more equipment or to spend less for equipment. Leasing, in fact, can often do both.

Match Income and Expense, and Stay Within Capital Budgets If a company purchases equipment, it immediately pays for the last day of production as well as the first. But leasing allows the payment for equipment to be made from the income generated by its use. Furthermore, lease payments can be tailored to fit even the tightest capital equipment budgets. Combined, these attributes make leasing an effective way for companies to sustain rapid growth.

Reduce the Impact of Inflation If inflation continues, a company that purchases capital equipment will find in the future that the true value of its depreciation allowance has been reduced. But companies that lease equipment will benefit from a reduction in the true value of future lease payments. It is for this reason that leasing can provide an effective hedge against inflation; and to maximize the advantage, many companies choose to lease depreciating assets such as equipment, while purchasing appreciating assets such as property.

Preserve Other Sources of Financing Growing companies need many sources of financial assistance. When they lease equipment, companies preserve the flexibility to use alternative credit sources in other ways. If a company leases its income-producing equipment, it can still use its bank lines of credit for short-term needs, or it can hold them open in anticipation of future capital requirements.

Control the Use of Equipment It is the use—not the ownership—of equipment that generates income. A unit of equipment has the same productive capacity regardless of whether it is leased or owned. When equipment is leased, however, its disposition is much easier. At the end of the lease period, the equipment can be leased again, can be purchased, or can be returned to the lessor. The decision is made on the basis of whether the equipment is still profitable, not whether it is owned.

Obtain Favorable Balance Sheet Treatment When correctly structured, some leases can qualify as operating leases for the purpose of the lessee's accounting treatment. Operating lease payment obligations are not capitalized on the lessee's balance sheet as a liability.

Suggested Solutions to Even-Numbered Exercises

8. *Net Present Value and Mutually Exclusive Projects.*
   Choose Project N. See below.

End of Year	Discount Factors at 12 Percent	Cash Flows in $000's		Present Value of Cash Flows in $000's	
		M	N	M	N
0	1.00000	−$500	−$450	−$500.0	−$450.0
1	.89286	175	477	156.3	425.9
2	.79719	287.5	195	229.2	155.5
3	.71178	400	60	284.7	42.7
				$170.2	$174.1

Net present value of cash flows discounted at 12 percent is larger for N.

10. *Computing Payback.*
   In years: **a.** 2   **e.** 6
            b. 7   **f.** 6
            c. 7   **g.** 5
            d. 5

12. *Computing payback.*
In years: **a.** 1.81 **e.** 5.42
b. 6.14 **f.** 5.76
c. 6.42 **g.** 4.40
d. 4.87

14. *Computing internal rate of return.*
Actual internal rate of return:
a) 16.94% **c)** 19.43%
b) 5.47% **d)** 10.45%
Using Table 4 and interpolating:
a. $40,000 ÷ $8,000 = 5.0
Present Value of Annuity, 12 periods, 12% = 6.19437
Present Value of Annuity, 12 periods, 20% = 4.43922
                                                          1.75515

6.19437 − 5.0 = 1.19347
1.19437 ÷ 1.75515 = .68049
.68049 × (20% − 12%) = 5.44392%
12% + 5.44392% = 17.44392%

b. $40,000 ÷ $8,000 = 5.0
Present Value of Annuity, 6 periods, 5% = 5.07569
Present Value of Annuity, 6 periods, 6% = 4.91732
                                                      0.15837

5.07569 − 5.0 = .07569
.07569 ÷ .15837 = .47793
.47793 × (6.0% − 5.0%) = .47793%
5% + .47793% = 5.47793%

c. $40,000 ÷ $8,000 = 5.0
Present Value of Annuity, 20 periods, 12% = 7.46944
Present Value of Annuity, 20 periods, 20% = 4.86958
                                                        2.59986

7.46944 − 5.0 = 2.46944
2.46944 ÷ 2.59986 = .94983
.94983 × (20% − 12%) = 7.59864%
12% + 7.59472% = 19.59864%

d. $40,000 ÷ $6,000 = 6.66667
Present Value of Annuity, 12 periods, 10% = 6.81369
Present Value of Annuity, 12 periods, 12% = 6.19437
                                                        .61932

6.81369 − 6.66667 = .14702
.14702 ÷ .61932 = .23739
.23739 × (12% − 10%) = .47478%
10% + .47478% = 10.47478%

After taking out the loan...

Part Four   **Managerial Planning
and Performance Evaluation**

At the beginning of this book, we stated that there are two major uses of managerial accounting information: (1) managerial decision making, and (2) managerial planning, control, and internal performance evaluation. This part of the book deals with the second use: *managerial planning, control, and internal performance evaluation*. (We refer to this as *planning and performance evaluation* for short.)

Part Three of this book, Chapters 6 through 10, focused on managerial decision making. If management applies the principles of differential analysis, it should make economically sound decisions. Once management has made a decision, its job is only partially complete. The alternatives selected must be translated into action. Then the actions, once taken, must be evaluated to ensure that performance coincides as closely as possible with expectations. These latter tasks make up the planning and performance evaluation process. We discuss the use of accounting in planning and performance evaluation in this part of the book.

Managers use accounting information to address such planning and performance evaluation questions as these:

After taking our decisions into account, what is our projected level of profits for the year?

If volume drops 10 percent, how much should budgeted costs go down?

How is the efficiency of production activities measured?

How can the performance of decentralized parts of the organization be measured?

How can we design performance measurement systems to encourage employees to act in the best interests of the organization?

These are a few examples of the numerous planning and performance evaluation issues faced by managers. Managerial accounting plays an important role in dealing with these issues. Managers use accounting to assign responsibility for actions, primarily through the use of budgets and standards. The accounting system provides information about actual performance to compare with expectations, such as budgets and standards.

Chapter 11 is an overview of the planning and performance evaluation process. We think it is important to see the ''big picture'' before going into detailed methods and concepts. It is particularly important to see how the planning and performance evaluation process ties together goals for the organization, plans for achieving these goals, decisions and activities, and evaluation of performance. All of this becomes an ongoing cycle in the organization.

Chapter 12 goes into more detail about developing budgets and comparing actual results of actions with those expected. Chapter 13 extends Chapter 12 by going into more detail about ways to measure and interpret variances from the budget.

Chapter 14 considers performance evaluation in decentralized operations that have both investment and profit responsibilities.

Chapter 11   The Planning and Control Process

This chapter provides an overview of the planning and control process that takes place in organizations. It shows how the planning and control process fits the ongoing cycle of setting goals, making plans, making decisions and taking actions, measuring the results of those actions, and comparing results with goals. This chapter is more qualitative than quantitative; Chapters 12 through 14 go into more extensive quantitative analysis.

The Planning and Control Process

The purpose of planning and control processes is to plan how to use resources, including people, to achieve particular goals, and to control the use of resources to achieve those goals. The planning and control process comprises the following phases (see Exhibit 11.1):

Setting organizational goals.

Strategic planning.

Capital budgeting.

Operating budgeting.

Comparison with actual results.

Performance evaluation and corrective action.

Revisions of goals, plans, and budgets.

Organizational Goals

Management establishes organizational goals, the set of broad objectives toward which employees work. For example, a manufacturing firm's management recently stated the firm's goals as follows:

> Our long range objective is to increase earnings consistently while maintaining our current share of market sales, and maintain an ROI which is within the top one-third of our industry. We plan to achieve these goals while providing our customers with high quality products, and meeting our social responsibilities to our employees and the communities in which they live.[1]

---

[1]Taken from an internal company document. Management of the company prefers that the company remain anonymous.

Exhibit 11.1
Overview of the Planning and Control Process

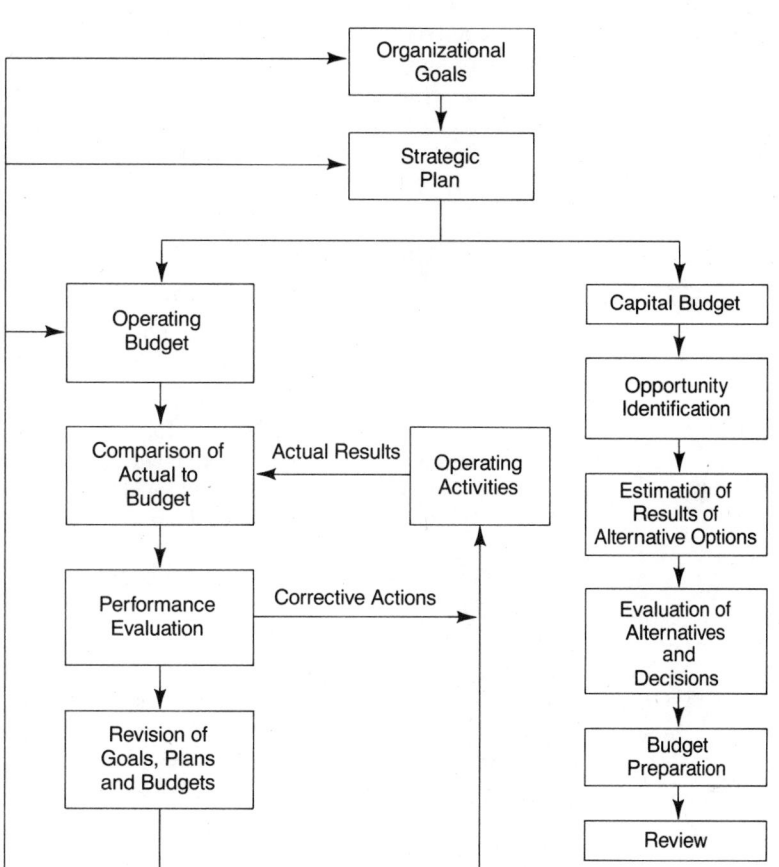

Strategic Plan

The strategic plan states the method or strategy for achieving organizational goals. For example, the previously mentioned manufacturing firm's strategies include:

1. *Cost control.* Optimize contribution from existing product lines by holding product cost increases to less than the rate of inflation. This will involve implementing new machinery proposed in the capital budget as well as replacing our five least efficient plants over the next 5 years.

2. *Market share.* Maintain market share by providing a level of service and quality comparable to our top competitors. This requires improving our quality control so that customer complaints are reduced from a current level of 4 percent to 1 percent within 2 years.

Strategic plans include long-range (typically 5 years or more) forecasts of sales, including new products, production and capacity requirements, aggregate levels of costs, and financing requirements. The plans also address the major capital investments required to maintain present facilities, increase capacity, or diversify to other products. In short, the strategic plan states the long-run strategy for achieving organizational goals. Capital and operating budgets, discussed later, are more specific, more detailed, and (particularly the operating budget) focus on near-term time periods.

Planning and Control of Capital Expenditures

Capital investment decisions are important because they involve large dollar amounts and commit organizations to long-term plans that are not easily changed. For example, National Steel, Inc.'s decision to install a continuous slab caster committed the company to a particular production process for a long time.

Chapters 9 and 10 discuss techniques for making capital investment decisions. Capital budgeting decision making is, however, only one step in planning and controlling capital expenditures. The entire process comprises the following five steps.

1. *Identify Opportunities for Capital Expenditures.* Opportunities for capital expenditures can be classified as (a) those dealing with ongoing operations, including replacement, cost-saving methods, and quality improvement methods; and (b) those dealing with major changes in operations, including adding or dropping product lines, and opportunities for vertical or horizontal integration. Ideas about new opportunities for ongoing operations often come from operating personnel—those closest to day-to-day activities. Ideas about major changes in operations usually come from top management and high-level staff positions.

2. *Identify Alternative Options and Estimate Results of Each.* Many opportunities will be dropped early because they are totally infeasible or inappropriate. For the remaining opportunities being considered, alternatives are identified, and estimates are made of the results that would occur if the alternatives were implemented. Because of the uncertainty inherent in this process, an "optimistic," "pessimistic," "most likely," and perhaps other estimates are made. If simulation capabilities are available on a computer, it is possible to assign probabilities to events and simulate a large number of possibilities.[2]

3. *Evaluate Alternatives and Make Decisions.* This step selects the most appropriate alternative. As discussed in Chapters 9 and 10, choices are usually based on a combination of financial factors. These include the amount and timing of estimated cash flows, the risk of the project, and nonfinancial factors, such as regulatory requirements, employee safety, corporate image, and community responsibility. Although the decisions require judgment, techniques such as discounted cash flow analysis help quantify the financial analysis.

---

[2]For example, see the classic paper by David B. Hertz, "Risk Analysis in Capital Investment," *Harvard Business Review* (January–February 1964).

4. *Prepare the Capital Budget.* After projects are accepted, their cash flows are combined in the capital budget. Approvals are obtained from management and the board of directors (or legislators in governmental units). Then the budget becomes the expenditure authorization. Most organizations have controls that preclude expenditures above a predetermined amount unless approved by top management or the board.

5. *Follow-up and Performance Review.* An important but sometimes omitted step is the follow-up and performance review. This step has three purposes: (a) to ascertain if expenditures were in accordance with intentions and authorizations; (b) to evaluate the success of the capital project (for example, ''Were expected cost savings realized?''); and (c) to evaluate the capital budgeting process (for example, ''Were cash flow estimates biased?'').

This completes the capital budgeting cycle, from identifying opportunities through follow-up and performance review.

Operating Budgets

After management selects the best products, makes capital investment decisions, selects production techniques, and makes other decisions, management can develop a formal short-run plan of action. This short-run plan is known as the operating budget. The operating, or period, budget is usually prepared for 1 year at a time. Many firms prepare detailed budgets for the coming year, but less detailed budgets for the following years. Some firms prepare these for as many as 10 years into the future.

One way to visualize period budgets is to imagine preparing a set of estimated financial statements for each month of the forthcoming year. (Of course, these estimates would not necessarily be prepared in accordance with generally accepted accounting principles, because they would be used for managerial purposes only.) For managerial purposes, some financial statements are more useful than others. Budgets of changes in financial position and of cash flows are useful for financing decisions, particularly for helping the treasurer's department. The income statement, or *profit plan* as it is often called, forecasts the results of operations, so it is generally the most useful to managers. We focus on it in later chapters.

Feedback Phase

The remaining parts of the planning and control process depicted in Exhibit 11.1—comparison of actual to budget, performance evaluation, and revision of goals, plans, and budgets—are the *feedback phase*. The feedback phase serves three purposes: (1) to motivate employees, (2) to guide corrective actions, and (3) to help revise goals and plans. By comparing actual performance with the budget and investigating the reasons for any variances, management has a basis for evaluating past performance of employees. For example, a production supervisor might compare the actual number of units produced by various workers with the standard for a period to decide which workers should receive bonuses or be promoted. A company president might compare the rate of return on assets of an operating division with a standard to assess the division manager's performance.

A second use of the information from the feedback phase is to alert management to particular activities that need attention. Managers generally cannot keep a close watch on all the activities for which they are responsible. Managers rely heavily on planning and control systems to do a large part of the surveillance. In this way managers can focus on the large variances between actual performance and the budget or standard.[3] Then they can take corrective actions where necessary. Basing action on exceptional variances is often referred to as *management by exception.*

Finally, information about actual performance provides feedback for revising goals and plans.

Variance between actual results and budgets need not result from good or bad performance, but can result from unrealistic goals and plans. Sometimes budgets are not carefully prepared. Also, events can occur that were not foreseen and built into the plan. For example, a severe winter storm in the Midwest made the activities of one of National Steel's plants so inefficient that virtually all unit variable costs were higher than standard.

Motivating Agents

When planning and control systems are used to evaluate performance, they are expected to motivate in a particular way. In simplest terms, evaluating employees' effort, and rewarding (penalizing) them for high (low) effort is expected to motivate them to work harder.

The motivation problem occurs because *principals* (for example, supervisors) have delegated duties or entrusted responsibilities to their *agents* (for example, subordinates).[4] We find these principal-agent relationships in many settings, including the following:

Principals	Agents
Shareholders	Board of Directors
Board of Directors	Corporate (Top) Management
Corporate (Top) Management	Divisional Managers
Divisional Managers	Plant Managers
Owner of a Taxi Company	Drivers of the Taxicabs
Retail Store Managers	Department Managers
Nursing Supervisor	Staff Nurses

[3]The terms "budget" and "standard" are often used interchangeably.

[4]For comprehensive reviews of analytical research in this area, see L. Peter Jennergen, "On the Design of Incentives in Business Firms—A Survey of Some Research," *Management Science,* XXV (February 1980); Joel Demski, *Information Analysis,* 2nd ed. (Reading, Mass.: Addison-Wesley, 1980); and Stanley Baiman, "Agency Research in Managerial Accounting: A Survey," *Journal of Accounting Literature,* 1 (Spring 1982).

Much of both financial and managerial accounting has been developed to monitor agency relationships. Corporate management, for example, provides financial statements to shareholders. Division managers report on their activities to their superiors at corporate headquarters. In general, accounting provides information about subordinates (agents) to superiors (principals) for performance evaluation. This allows superiors to make decisions about future employment prospects of the subordinates. (For example, should they be promoted? Fired?) In addition, accounting information is used in employment contracts. Often an employee is given a bonus based on accounting performance measures.

Thus, accounting affects motivation. Subordinates who know they are being evaluated on the basis of accounting information have incentives to make themselves ''look good'' on that basis. (Analogously, consider how students wishing to enter graduate school have incentives to manipulate grade-point averages, if admissions offices use grade-point averages without regard to difficulty of courses taken.)

How Much Information Is Enough? Like other accounting systems, planning and control systems should be cost-effective. If information were costless to generate and to process, superiors would always prefer more information to less. But information is not costless, so the cost of obtaining more information about subordinates must be compared to the benefits of (1) evaluating their future employment prospects, and (2) motivating them to take desired actions.

Goal Congruence

When all members of an organization have incentives to perform in the common interest, *goal congruence* occurs.

Although complete goal congruence is unlikely to exist, there are many cases where we do observe team efforts. Examples include some military units and athletic teams. Many companies attempt to achieve this *esprit de corps* by, for example, carefully selecting employees whom management believes will be loyal. Observers of the Japanese management style report that Japanese managers and owners have created team orientations with considerable goal congruence.

Complete goal congruence, however, is unlikely to be found in most business settings.[5] For example, employees generally prefer to work less hard than the firm would like. Consequently, performance evaluation and incentive systems are set

---

[5]There is some evidence that risk-averse employees may be induced by control systems to take actions that are suboptimal for the organization. See R. O. Swalm, ''Utility Theory— Insight into Risk Taking,'' *Harvard Business Review* (November–December 1966); and J. L. Zimmerman, ''Budget Uncertainty and the Allocation Decision in a Nonprofit Organization,'' *Journal of Accounting Research,* 14 (Autumn 1976). Also, there is some evidence that employee performance is directly related to goal congruence. See M. W. Maher, K. V. Ramanathan, and R. B. Peterson, ''Preference Congruence, Information Accuracy and Employee Performance: A Field Study,'' *Journal of Accounting Research,* 17 (Autumn 1979); and A. Harrell, ''The Decision-Making Behavior of Air Force Officers and the Management Control Process,'' *The Accounting Review,* 52 (October 1977).

up to increase goal congruence by encouraging employees to behave more in the firm's interest.

The classroom setting is a good example. Examinations, written assignments, indeed, the entire grading process is part of a performance evaluation and incentive system to encourage students to behave in a certain manner. Sometimes the system appears to encourage the wrong type of behavior, however. For example, if the goal is to encourage students to learn, then students might be better off electing difficult courses. But their grades may suffer, so students who believe that later payoffs depend on grade-point averages may elect easier courses.

Problems of this type occur in all organizations where it may not be in the employees' best interest to take actions that are in the best interest of the organization. Consider the case of a plant manager who wants to look good on the basis of plant operating profits for this year. The manager believes that a promotion and bonus will follow from high plant operating profits. Profits will be lowered in the short run if a needed maintenance program is undertaken, but the company will be better off in the long run. The manager faces a classic trade-off between doing what looks good and doing what is in the best interest of the company. (This is analogous to the problem faced by a student in deciding between an easy course that will bolster the grade-point average or a hard course that will have more long-term benefits.)

It can be costly to design planning and control systems that induce employees to act in the best interest of the organization. Management must trade off the costs and benefits of planning and control systems. The optimal expenditure on planning and control might still allow employees considerable opportunity for behavior contrary to the best interest of top management.

Criteria for Evaluating Planning and Control Systems

Goal conflicts cannot be entirely removed, but if recognized, they can be dealt with to minimize the conflict. We discuss some criteria for evaluating planning and control systems in this section. Planning and control systems that meet these criteria will tend to encourage employees to act in the firm's best interest.

A planning and control system is established for an activity (for example, production, selling, research and development) to increase the probability that the original objective or goal for that activity will be achieved. The objectives and preferences of the individuals performing various tasks also need to be considered. Management involves "getting things done through people." To design a good planning and control system, the behavioral reactions of employees to levels of standards, measures of actual performance, and form and frequency of feedback must be taken into account.

When evaluating a planning and control system, the following two questions should be asked:

1. What types of behavior does the system motivate?
2. Is this behavior in the best interests of the organization?

Responsibility Is Based on Controllability

A desirable attribute of planning and control systems is that employees are given responsibility for and evaluated in the performance of activities they can control. If responsibility for performing an activity is fixed, then (1) managers and other employees will know what is expected of them, and (2) they can be held accountable for variances in their performance from the standards and budgets. Planning and control systems are therefore developed around responsibility centers within a firm. A *responsibility center* is a unit of activity within a firm that has control over, and responsibility for, an activity during a particular time period. Responsibility centers are classified according to the activities controlled, as follows:

1. *Cost center,* where the center controls only costs incurred;
2. *Revenue center,* which controls only revenues;
3. *Profit center,* where the center has control over both revenues and costs; and
4. *Investment center,* in which the responsibility center has control over revenues, costs, and assets.

In a responsibility center, a particular manager or group of employees *controls* specific activities. The basic principle is that employees are assigned responsibility for what they can control, and their performance is measured in terms of things they can control. The following examples illustrate that this principle is not easy to apply.

Example 1 Horton Corporation has a purchasing department that is responsible for the acquisition of materials for the production departments. Production supervisors inform the purchasing department of the quantities and qualities of materials that will be needed at various times. The purchasing department then searches for suppliers that will provide the needed materials at the best price. The purchasing department is held accountable if the actual prices paid vary from the standard prices allowed.

The purchasing department is a responsibility center with respect to the price paid for raw materials. Suppose, however, that, as a result of poor production planning, a production foreman places a rush order for raw materials that must be received within 3 days. In order to obtain the raw materials on time, the purchasing department agrees to pay a higher price to expedite the order. As a consequence, the actual price paid is significantly higher than the standard price. Should the purchasing department be held accountable for this unfavorable price variance? This is a difficult question to answer. The response depends on the behavioral reactions of employees in the purchasing and producing departments of having the variance assigned to them.

The main point of this example is that control is not always easily assigned. Control runs along a continuum from absolute control to no control. Most cases fall between these extremes. The guideline generally followed is that the unit in the firm with the most influence over the item is held accountable for it. In the rush-order example, the production department would probably be held responsible for the unfavorable price variance, even though the excess price paid would normally be the responsibility of the purchasing department.

To define control requires specifying a particular time period. Most variable costs tend to be controllable by some unit within the firm each time period. Some fixed costs are also controllable in the short run. Most fixed costs, however, are controllable only in the long run. Once capacity level decisions have been made, managers are generally locked into a particular level of fixed costs. For purposes of evaluating performance in the short run, the question arises as to whether or not managers should be held accountable for fixed cost variances.

Example 2 The producing departments of Horton Corporation submit capital budgeting proposals to central corporate headquarters. Given various constraints on growth (for example, market demand and availability of managerial talent), personnel in central corporate headquarters decide which capital investment proposals will be accepted and which will be rejected. In the long run, then, the producing departments, which generate capital investment proposals, and central corporate headquarters, which selects particular proposals, share the responsibility for fixed capacity costs (for example, depreciation on building and equipment, property taxes and insurance on the manufacturing facilities). In the short run, however, neither of these two units controls fixed capacity costs.

Suppose that property tax rates or insurance premiums are increased so that during a particular time period there is an unfavorable fixed cost variance with respect to these costs. Who should be held accountable for the variance? A response is again difficult, because it depends on who can control the costs. The main point is that control must be defined in terms of a particular time period. In this case, the producing departments have little control over property taxes and insurance in the short run and probably should not be held accountable for any cost variances.

Showing the variances on the cost report for the producing departments, however, makes the producing departments' employees more aware of these costs, which they can partially and indirectly control in the long run. Evaluating the responsibility center as an economic unit need not use the same data as evaluating the people within that unit. To evaluate the center, we might assign costs, revenues, and assets even though they are not controlled by the people in the center.

The identification of responsibility centers within a firm is an important first step in designing planning and control systems. Setting the boundaries of control for a particular responsibility center is far from precise. Nonetheless, an attempt must be made if the planning and control system is to be effective.

Controllability and Risk Aversion ''You should hold employees responsible only for those things they can control'' is sometimes claimed to be an important behavioral factor in designing planning and control systems. Moreover, holding employees responsible only for the things they can control reduces their risk. To induce an employee to bear more risk generally requires that the employee be paid higher returns. Risk-averse employees will demand a higher wage to assume greater risk, all other things being equal.[6]

---

[6]An extensive literature has emerged in recent years dealing with risk sharing and incentives in organizations. The work so far has been done in simplified analytical settings, and the results are difficult to generalize to organizations. Some fundamental principles about incentives, risk sharing, and the role of information in employment contracts have nevertheless been developed. For discussion, see Joel Demski, *Information Analysis*.

Performance Measure Is Relevant to Objectives

A second desirable attribute of planning and control systems is the following: The measures used for evaluating performance should be relevant to the objectives or purposes of the responsibility centers. If the purpose of a producing department is to manufacture products of a particular quality at the lowest cost, then manufacturing cost per unit passing quality inspection might be used as the performance measure. If the objective of a secretarial typing pool is to type quality copy at the lowest cost, then the evaluation measure might be correct lines typed per dollar of cost in the pool.

An improperly designed performance measure will provide data of questionable usefulness to the firm. It may also misdirect the efforts of employees who attempt to perform so that they succeed relative to the measure. For example, a performance measure for the traveling sales staff that relates revenue generated to the number of calls made to customers (that is, sales divided by calls made) may lead salespersons to *reduce* the number of calls made in order to improve their performance report. If the development of a good relationship between the salespeople and the customers is critical and depends on frequent calls by the sales staff, then this performance measure could lead to action (reduced numbers of sales calls) that is clearly not in the best interest of a firm.

Use of Nonquantitative Performance Measures One problem in designing planning and control systems for some activities is that it is often difficult to design a quantitative measure for evaluating performance. In most cases this occurs because there is no clear-cut relationship between inputs and outputs. For example, consider the order-procuring activities of the sales staff. The amount of revenue generated by a particular salesperson cannot be related directly to the hours of time worked or the cost of promotional materials developed. There are too many intervening variables, such as general economic conditions, the behavior of competitors, and geographical diversity.

As another example, consider the research and development activity. The desired output is a set of new inventions and developments that will permit a firm to maintain or improve its market position. There is no precise relationship, however, between the salaries of research scientists or the cost of supplies used (inputs) and the value of new discoveries and developments. It is difficult, therefore, to design a quantitative measure that captures the relevant aspects of performance for this activity.

When a quantitative performance measure is not possible, the planning and control systems tend to be less formalized and more intuitive. As a manager of a research and development department put it:

> We hire people we can trust to work hard even though their output is not easily measured. We encourage peer group pressure and a sense of loyalty to the company. And we have them submit a written annual report of their activities. If we tried to impose quantitative performance measures on our research and development people, we would not only incur system costs, but also we would damage morale such that our people's performance would probably go down, not up.

The Planning and Control System Is Matched to the Nature of the Organization

Planning and control systems should "fit" the organization, not vice versa. A steel company may find a formal, quantitative system designed to regulate output and control costs the most desirable. A company that does research and development for a governmental agency under cost-plus-fixed-fee contracts would not be as concerned about regulating output and controlling costs. They would desire a system that encouraged quality and meeting contract deadlines, while accounting for costs by job or contract so the company can be paid.

The following examples describe three different kinds of control mechanisms— markets, bureaucracies, and clans—for different types of activities. These examples are based on an article describing planning and control systems for a specific company.[7]

Example 1:
Controlling the Purchasing Agent Using a Market Mechanism The work of the purchasing agent is largely subject to market mechanisms.

> [The agent] simply puts each part out for competitive bids and permits the competitive process to define a fair price. . . . The work of the manager who supervises these agents is also greatly simplified, because he needs only to check their decisions against the simple criterion of the cost minimization rather than observing the steps through which they work. . . .[8]

Example 2:
Controlling the Warehousing Function Using a Bureaucratic Mechanism

> In marked contrast to purchasing, warehousing . . . is subject to a variety of explicit routines of monitoring and directing. . . . The fundamental mechanism of control involves close personal surveillance and direction of subordinates by supervisors.[9]

This "bureaucratic mechanism" conforms to the idea of formal planning and control systems in companies. Unlike the market mechanism in which the market coordinates and controls activities of participants, in a "bureaucracy" a superior coordinates and controls the activities of "subordinates." Superiors control subordinates by setting standards and budgets, or other rules, against which the subordinate's performance is compared.

Example 3:
Informal Controls
Ouchi also found evidence of informal controls that could be used to control activities. These informal controls were particularly useful when precise evaluation

---

[7]Examples are taken from an article by William Ouchi, "A Conceptual Framework for the Design of Organizational Control Mechanisms," *Management Science* (September 1979), pp. 833–848. For a discussion of the use of informal controls in U.S. companies, see R. K. Mautz et al., *Internal Control in U.S. Companies* (New York: Financial Executives Research Foundation, 1980), particularly pp. 174–176 and 338ff.

[8]Ouchi, "A Conceptual Framework," pp. 834–835.

[9]Ouchi, "A Conceptual Framework," p. 835.

of an individual's work is sometimes difficult (as described earlier for research and development). Other examples include many governmental and health care employees, auditors in public accounting firms, financial analysts, and data processing systems designers. A key informal control in these cases is the process of socialization, during which would-be employees are indoctrinated with a set of values. (When large groups are socialized, they are often called "professions.")

When the outputs of an individual are difficult to measure, it is sometimes less costly for organizations to hire people with a particular set of values or to instill a set of values than to use formal control methods. For example, one of the largest retailers in the United States has would-be store managers go through a several-year program of on-the-job training before promotion to store manager. These employees are observed by superiors during this period, and as a company executive told us, "those who do not have the appropriate degree of team spirit and loyalty are weeded out before we trust them with a store of their own."

In short, different activities and organizations call for different types of planning and control systems. Market mechanisms may work best when there are market exchanges and little teamwork is required—which is the case, for example, for some sales personnel, buyers, and piece-work employees. Formal planning and control systems are most commonly used when market exchanges are infeasible, yet employees' performance is measurable. Informal controls (for example, socialization) are commonly used when employees' outputs are difficult to measure.

Performance Standards Are Effective

A good control system incorporates performance standards that serve to motivate employees. In setting performance standards, two principal behavioral concerns must be addressed: (1) the extent of employee participation in setting standards, and (2) the tightness of the standards.

Employee Participation Employee participation is costly to the organization because it consumes employee time, but it provides data to management that might not be available otherwise. Whether employee participation has a positive motivational effect remains an open question. An appreciation of the issues can be obtained by considering some of the questions that have been addressed in the research on this issue.

1. Does participation lead employees to feel that they are a more integral part of an organization and, because of this ego involvement, result in improved performance?

2. Does participation merely lead to greater group cohesiveness among employees, which can then work either to the advantage or disadvantage of the firm, depending on the group's feeling about the benefits of the participation?

3. Are the results of participation different in the following two situations?
   a. Employees merely provide inputs to the standard-setting process but have no voice in the actual standard-setting.
   b. Employees both supply inputs and participate in setting specific standards.

4. Are the results of participation different depending on the managerial style of supervisors (authoritarian, democratic) and the personality characteristics of employees?

5. Are the results of participation different depending on the educational backgrounds and technical skills of employees and the nature of the tasks (production versus research and development or legal services)?

6. How is participation related to the creation of slack in organizations (a term referring to the difference between the resources available to a firm and the amount necessary to maintain the organization coalition of individuals and groups)?

Interested readers might consult the references listed below to explore these questions more fully.[10]

Tightness of Standards Standards for performance may be set very loose and be met a large percentage of the time or set very tight and be met only a small percentage of the time. Empirical research tends to suggest that employees underperform when standards are set too loose. Introducing a moderate level of tension by way of tighter standards leads to higher employee motivation and, therefore, better performance. The principal question, then, is just how tight the standards should be. Two types of standards have been described in the literature: (1) ideal standards, and (2) normal or currently attainable standards.

Ideal standards are those that can be met under the most efficient operating conditions for existing resources (plant, equipment, employees). Ideal standards are used when management feels that such standards provide the best incentive to good performance. Generally, however, empirical research tends to show that standards do not provide an incentive to perform well unless the employee, whose performance is measured against the standard, perceives the standard to be reasonable and attainable.[11] Ideal standards can be criticized, then, because employees may lose initiative for seeking more efficient performance and become discouraged because the standards are seldom achievable.

Normal or *currently attainable standards* are those that can be met under reasonably efficient operating conditions with provision for normal spoilage, rest periods, and other time that is lost because of, for example, normal machine breakdowns. Normal standards are, by definition, those that management can reasonably expect, but stringent enough so that workers who achieve them have reason to be satisfied with their performance.

---

[10]Andrew C. Stedry, *Budget Control and Cost Behavior* (Englewood Cliffs, N.J.: Prentice-Hall, 1960); Chris Argyris, "Organizational Leadership and Participative Management," *Journal of Business*, 27 (January 1955), pp. 1–7; Selwyn Becker and David Green, Jr., "Budgeting and Employee Behavior," *Journal of Business*, 35 (October 1962), pp. 392–402; Michael Schiff and Arie Y. Lewin, "The Impact of Budgets on People," *The Accounting Review*, 45 (April 1970), pp. 259–268; Ken Milani, "The Relationship of Participation in Budget-Setting to Industrial Supervisor Performance and Attitudes: A Field Study," *The Accounting Review*, 50 (April 1975), pp. 274–284.

[11]Stedry, *Budget Control and Cost Behavior;* also see Gary L. Holstrum, "The Effect of Budget Adaptiveness and Tightness on Managerial Decision Behavior," *Journal of Accounting Research*, 9 (Autumn 1971), pp. 268–277.

It is difficult to generalize as to how tight standards should be. All that can be said is that there are dangers in setting the standards too loose or too tight. Standards that are currently attainable but sufficiently tight to motivate employees are probably best.

Feedback Is Timely

A control system requires timely feedback if it is to be effective. Management needs to be aware of significant variances of actual performance from the standards in time to take corrective action. Employees need to know whether their performance is judged to be satisfactory or unsatisfactory. Satisfactory performance tends to reinforce employee behavior and leads to greater employee motivation. Unsatisfactory performance may lead to greater employee motivation (if standards are still considered to be attainable) or to withdrawal (when the standards are not considered attainable or the employee no longer feels a part of the management-employee coalition in the firm).[12]

The frequency of feedback differs depending on the nature of the activity. For an automated production line, feedback may be required within seconds or minutes so that corrective action can be taken quickly. For purposes of evaluating the overall performance of a division of a firm, monthly or quarterly feedback is probably sufficient.

Benefits Exceed Costs

As we have emphasized repeatedly, accounting should be subject to cost/benefit analysis like other activities. One of the most important criteria for evaluating a planning and control system is that the benefits of the system exceed the costs of designing and implementing it. For example, the benefits of a sophisticated system for the acquisition and use of paperclips is not likely to justify the costs to be incurred.

The costs and benefits of planning and control systems are difficult to measure because they tend to be indirect or not easily quantified. So managers *judgmentally* assess costs and benefits of planning and control systems.[13]

Types of Planning and Control Systems

There are three broad types of planning and control systems: operational, divisional, and organization-wide. To understand the distinction better, refer to the organization chart in Exhibit 11.2.

---

[12]Doris M. Cook, "The Effect of Frequency of Feedback on Attitudes and Performance," *Empirical Research in Accounting: Selected Studies (Journal of Accounting Research, Supplement* 1967), pp. 213–224; James E. Sorensen and David D. Franks, "The Relative Contribution of Ability, Self-Esteem and Evaluative Feedback to Performance: Implications for Accounting Systems," *The Accounting Review*, 47 (October 1972), pp. 735–746.

[13]The method we used to assess the value of information in the appendix to Chapter 1 could, in theory, be applied to cost/benefit decisions about planning and control systems.

Exhibit 11.2
Types of Planning and Control Systems
at Different Organizational Levels

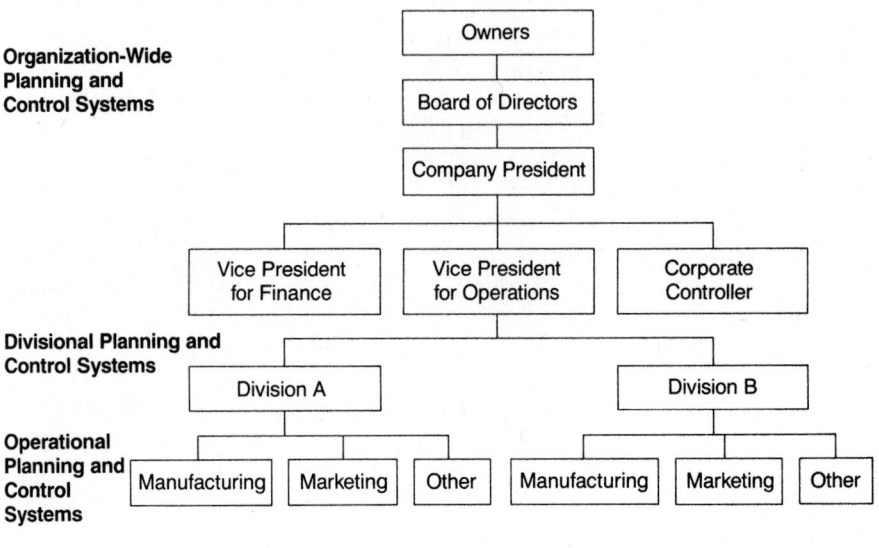

**Organization-Wide
Planning and
Control Systems**

**Divisional Planning and
Control Systems**

**Operational
Planning and
Control
Systems**

Operational Planning and Control Systems

As shown in the organization chart in Exhibit 11.2, operational planning and control systems are designed for activities closest to day-to-day manufacturing, marketing, and other activities of the organization. For example, operational control systems would be designed for such activities as raw materials acquisition and storage, office typing and record keeping, and order-getting activities of the sales personnel.

The agency relationships are usually as follows (from lower to upper levels):

$$\text{Workers} \rightarrow \text{Supervisors} \rightarrow \begin{array}{c}\text{Department} \\ \text{Heads}\end{array} \rightarrow \begin{array}{c}\text{Plant Managers,} \\ \text{Store Managers,} \\ \text{District Managers,} \\ \text{etc.}\end{array} \rightarrow \begin{array}{c}\text{Division} \\ \text{Managers.}\end{array}$$

For planning and control purposes, an organization is divided into *responsibility centers*. A particular individual or group is assigned responsibility for the activities in that unit. A plant's manager is assigned responsibility for the activities in the plant, a department head has responsibility for the activities in the department, and so forth. Responsibility centers carry names associated with the activities for which the manager is responsible. Manufacturing departments are usually called *cost centers*, because the managers are responsible for costs.

Marketing departments are often called *revenue centers* (or *contribution margin centers*) if the manager is responsible for revenue (or contribution margins). If marketing managers have responsibility for marketing costs—for example, sales commissions and advertising—these are sometimes called *marketing centers*. Accounting for performance measurement in manufacturing and marketing responsibility centers is discussed in Chapters 12 and 13.

There are two categories of cost centers, based on the type of costs incurred in the center. Most manufacturing costs are assumed to be *engineered;* that is, input/output relationships are sufficiently well established that a particular set of inputs will provide a predictable and measurable output. Input/output relations are not as well specified for many activities, however. Output is relatively unpredictable and difficult to measure for most staff functions of all organizations (research, administration, legal, and advertising) and for most activities in governmental units. Responsibility centers in which input/output relationships are not well specified are called *discretionary cost* (or *expense*) *centers*. Managers of such centers receive from their superiors a cost budget that provides a ceiling on the center's costs. It is nearly impossible to ascertain effectiveness of such centers from the accounting numbers; managerial judgment is required.

Management by Objectives Many organizations attempt to plan and control discretionary costs using *management by objectives* (MBO).[14] In principle, responsibility center managers state their objectives, the things they will do to attain those objectives, uncertainties and known impediments, resources required, and costs of achieving the objectives. Actual performance in terms of objectives achieved, costs incurred, and so forth, is compared with the plan for performance evaluation.

Zero-Base Budgeting[15] There have been many attempts to tie MBO to the accounting system. Many organizations, including Texas Instruments, Xerox, Control Data, many state and local governmental units, and many parts of the federal government have used variations of *zero-base budgeting*. In principle, zero-base budgeting requires responsibility center managers to justify every dollar of costs from a zero base, in contrast to *incremental budgeting*, which justifies only additions to previous cost levels. In practice, budgeting from an absolute zero base has proved too costly for the benefits obtained in many cases. Nevertheless, many aspects of zero-base budgeting are currently in use, particularly for discretionary cost centers.

Divisional Planning and Control Systems

Divisional planning and control systems are designed for the next major level above operational control in the organization chart where the agency relationships are usually between top management (the principal) and division managers (the agents). Divisions combine and coordinate the activities of operating units and, in effect,

---

[14]Management by objectives can be used anywhere in an organization for any activity.

[15]Similar methods have gone by different names over the years. It is often politically useful to develop a new title for an old idea. (For an excellent discussion, see Robert N. Anthony, "Zero-Base Budgeting: Useful Fraud?", *Government Accountants Journal,* Summer 1977.) Although the methods described here are often called *zero-base budgeting,* other names are given to the same idea.

are "organizations within an organization." A company that produces and markets a single product may have no divisions or only one division. Companies with multiple products or with geographically dispersed facilities often have many divisions. Divisional planning and control systems typically focus on the profit performance of the divisions, which may be either a measure of the divisional operating profits or return or the company's investment in the division. Hence, divisions are *profit centers* or *investment centers*. Chapter 14 discusses divisional performance measurement and control.

Organization-Wide Planning and Control Systems

Organization-wide planning and control systems tend to be less formal than for divisions or operational activities. These planning and control systems essentially involve a periodic review of the organization's activities by the board of directors, by trustees, or, in the case of governmental units, by legislative bodies. The comparison of actual with the expected level of performance may occur quarterly or perhaps only once a year.

In recent years, various regulatory and other trends have increased top management's accountability for their organization's actions. For example, the New York Stock Exchange requires audit committees of all companies whose stock is traded on the exchange. To ensure that there is some outside monitoring of top management's activities, the audit committee must comprise people who are not employees of the company.

One of the audit committee's functions has been to oversee the activities of the firm's external auditors. The audit committee sometimes requests the external auditors to extend the usual audit of the financial statements to search for management fraud or illegal payoffs. As these audit committees have become established, they have increased the scope of their activities. Greater attention is given to other aspects of the firm's activities, such as community relations, employee morale, and environmental protection. Management consulting firms have been hired to study various aspects of a company's operations and make recommendations for changes. The scope of activities of corporate audit committees is expected to continue to broaden in the future.

Government regulation of top management's activities is a form of *top* management control. Many of the securities laws, antitrust regulations, affirmative action, and environmental protection laws attempt to "control" top management. A recent example of such regulation was the Foreign Corrupt Practices Act of 1977, which regulated not only kickbacks and bribes to foreign government officials, but also the adequacy of internal accounting control systems.[16]

Managerial accounting focuses on operating and divisional planning and control, not on organization-wide planning and control. Organization-wide planning and control methods involve external financial reporting, external auditing, executive incentive systems, and various government regulations, all designed to make top management accountable to its constituents.

---

[16]For a discussion of this regulation and managers' responses to it, see M. Maher, "The Impact of Regulation on Controls: Firms' Response to the Foreign Corrupt Practices Act," *The Accounting Review,* 56 (October 1981).

Summary

This chapter introduces the planning and control process and shows the role of accounting in this process. Strategic plans for achieving an organization's goals are formulated. These plans include long-range forecasts of sales, capacity requirements, aggregate levels of costs, and financing arrangements. Capital budgets authorize the expenditure of funds to satisfy the capacity requirements for the strategic plan. Operating budgets are annual short-run plans that provide much more detail about how the coming year's operations will carry out the organization's strategic plans.

The capital budgeting cycle comprises five steps:

1. Identify opportunities for capital expenditures.
2. Identify alternatives and estimate results.
3. Evaluate alternatives and make decisions.
4. Prepare the capital budget.
5. Follow-up and performance review.

Operating budgets include pro forma financial statements prepared before the period. Their chief uses are for planning, for coordinating activities among various people in the organization, and for authorizing expenditures. They become benchmarks for performance evaluation.

The feedback phase of budgeting involves comparing actual results to the budget. The purposes of feedback are:

1. To evaluate performance of people and responsibility centers.
2. To guide management in making changes in the organization's activities.
3. To revise goals, plans, and budgets.

Accounting systems exist in large part to report on activities of agents (for example, subordinates) to their principals (for example, superiors). These systems both motivate agents and inform principals about their agents' performance.

Goal congruence occurs when all members of an organization have incentives to perform in the common interest. Planning and control systems that enhance goal congruence encourage employees to work in their own best interest while, at the same time, working in the organization's best interest.

A good planning and control system will:

1. Tie an employee's performance evaluation to the activities the employee can control.
2. Evaluate performance using measures that are relevant for achieving desired objectives.
3. Match the planning and control system to the nature of the organization.
4. Provide timely feedback.
5. Provide benefits that exceed the costs of the system.

Two behavioral issues affect the setting of performance standards:

1. Should there be employee participation in budgeting?
2. Should standards for performance norms be set loose or tight?

Participation is costly, but it may have a positive motivational impact on employees, and it may provide a source of data not otherwise available to management.

The conventional wisdom (based at least partially on research) is to set standards that are tight, but attainable.

Operational planning and control deals with day-to-day operations, usually at departmental levels. Divisional systems are designed for the next level up in the organization. Operating systems usually deal with one aspect of an organization's activities—for example, purchasing or selling or production. Divisional systems, on the other hand, take into account multiple activities (for example, purchasing *and* production *and* selling) of a responsibility center. Organization-wide systems deal with broader questions of top management's accountability and the organization's responsibility to various constituents, including shareholders, employees, customers, and government regulators. Except for formal constraints imposed on top management by regulation and boards of directors, organization-wide planning and control systems tend to be informal.

Problem for Self-Study
(CMA adapted)

Springfield Corporation operates on a calendar-year basis. It begins the annual budgeting process in late August, when the president establishes targets for the total dollar sales and net income before taxes for the next year.

The sales target is given to the marketing department, where the marketing manager formulates a sales budget by product line in both units and dollars. From this budget, sales quotas by product line in units and dollars are established for each of the corporation's sales districts.

The marketing manager also estimates the cost of the marketing activities required to support the target sales volume, and prepares a tentative marketing expense budget.

The executive vice-president uses the sales and profit targets, the sales budget by product line, and the tentative marketing expense budget to determine the dollar amounts that can be devoted to manufacturing and corporate office expense. The executive vice-president prepares the budget for corporate expenses and then forwards to the production department the product-line sales budget in units and the total dollar amount that can be devoted to manufacturing.

The production manager meets with the factory managers to develop a manufacturing plan that will produce the required units when needed within the cost constraints set by the executive vice-president. The budgeting process usually comes to a halt at this point because the production department does not consider the financial resources allocated to be adequate.

When this standstill occurs, the vice-president of finance, the executive vice-president, the marketing manager, and the production manager meet together to determine the final budgets for each of the areas. This normally results in a modest increase in the total amount available for manufacturing costs, while the marketing expense and corporate office expense budgets are cut. The total sales and net income figures proposed by the president are seldom changed. Although the participants are seldom pleased with the compromise, these budgets are final. Each executive then develops a new detailed budget for the operations in his or her area.

None of the areas has achieved its budget in recent years. Sales often run below the target. When budgeted sales are not achieved, each area is expected to cut costs so that the president's profit target can still be met. However, the profit target is seldom met because costs are not cut enough. In fact, costs often run above the original budget in all functional areas. The president is disturbed that Springfield has not been able to meet the sales and profit targets. He hires a consultant with considerable experience with companies in Springfield's industry. The consultant reviews the budgets for the past 4 years and concludes that the product-line sales budgets were reasonable, and that the cost and expense budgets were adequate for the budgeted sales and production levels.

a. Discuss how the budgeting process as employed by Springfield Corporation contributed to the failure to achieve the president's sales and profit targets.

b. Suggest how Springfield Corporation's budgeting process could be revised to correct the problems.

c. Should the functional areas be expected to cut their costs when sales volume falls below budget? Explain your answer.

Suggested Solution

a. The budget at Springfield is an imposed "top down" budget which fails to consider both the need for realistic data and the human interaction essential to an effective budgeting/control process. The president has not given any basis for his goals, so one cannot know whether they are realistic for the company. True participation of company employees in preparation of the budget is minimal and limited to mechanical gathering and manipulation of data. This suggests there will be little enthusiasm for implementing the budget.

The budget process is the merging of the requirements of all facets of the company on a basis of sound judgment and equity. Specific instances of poor procedures include the following:

The sales by product line should be based upon an accurate sales forecast of the potential market. Therefore, the sales by product line should have been developed first to derive the sales target rather than the reverse.

Production costs probably would be the easiest and most certain costs to estimate. Given variable and fixed production costs, one could estimate the sales volume needed to cover manufacturing costs plus the costs of other aspects of the operation. This would be helpful before budgets for marketing costs and corporate office expenses are set.

The initial meeting between the vice president of finance, executive vice president, marketing manager, and production manager should be held earlier. This meeting is held too late in the budget process.

b. Springfield should consider the adoption of a "bottom-up" budget process. This means that the people responsible for performance under the budget would participate in the decisions by which the budget is established. This approach provides information from sales, financial, and production personnel. Although time consuming, the approach should produce a more acceptable, informative and workable goal/control mechanism.

The sales forecast should be developed considering internal sales forecasts as well as external factors. Costs within departments should be divided into fixed and variable, controllable and noncontrollable, discretionary and nondiscretionary categories.

c. The functional areas should not necessarily be expected to cut costs when sales volume falls below budget. The time frame of the budget (1 year) is short enough so that many costs are relatively fixed in amount. For those costs which are fixed, there is little hope for a reduction as a consequence of short-run changes in volume. However, the functional areas should be expected to cut costs should sales volume fall below target when:

Control is exercised over the costs within their function.

Budgeted costs were more than adequate for the originally targeted sales, i.e., slack was present.

Budgeted costs vary to some extent with changes in sales.

There are discretionary costs which can be delayed or omitted with no serious effect on the department.

Questions

1. Review the meaning of the following concepts or terms discussed in this chapter.

a.	Planning and control process.	**l.**	Quantitative performance measure.
b.	Strategic plan.		
c.	Operating budget.	**m.**	Ideal standards.
d.	Feedback phase.	**n.**	Normal or currently attainable standards.
e.	Capital budget.		
f.	Management by exception.	**o.**	Operational control.
g.	Goal congruence.	**p.**	Divisional control.
h.	Responsibility center.	**q.**	Company-wide control.
i.	Cost center.	**r.**	Management audit.
j.	Revenue center.	**s.**	Audit committee.
k.	Investment center.		

2. Explain the difference between strategic plans and the budget plan.

3. Why would more detail be included in a budget for the coming period than appears in a longer-range forecast?

4. The chief executive officer of a large company remarked, ''I don't understand why other companies waste so much time in the budgeting process. I set our company goals, and everyone strives to meet them.'' Comment on the executive's budgeting method.

5. What is the danger in relying entirely on lower management estimates of sales, costs, and other data used in budget planning?

6. A company recently established a bonus plan for its employees. An employee receives a bonus if the employee's subunit meets the cost levels specified in the annual budget plan. If the subunit's costs exceed the budget, no bonus is earned by employees of that subunit. What problems might arise with this bonus plan?

7. How does budgeting help coordinate a company's activities?

8. You are the manager of the assembling division of a manufacturing firm. A report on the division's performance for February shows the following:

Cost Item	Standard	Actual	Variance
Raw Materials	$ 3,500	$4,000	$500 Unfavorable
Direct Labor	3,500	3,000	500 Favorable
Supplies	400	300	100 Favorable
Insurance	600	500	100 Favorable
Depreciation	2,000	2,000	—
Total	$10,000	$9,800	$200 Favorable

What action would you take next? Explain.

9. Who, among management personnel, is most likely to be able to control each of the following?
   a. Raw materials used (quantity).
   b. Electricity for machinery.
   c. Charge for floor space.
   d. Machinery depreciation.
   e. Unit price of materials.
   f. Insurance on machinery.
   g. Direct labor (quantity).

10. Accounting is supposed to be a neutral, relevant, and objective measure of performance. Why would problems arise when applying accounting measures to performance evaluation contexts?

11. A company prepares the master budget by taking each division manager's estimate of revenues and costs for the coming period and entering the data into the budget without adjustment. At the end of the year, division managers are given a bonus if their division "profit" is greater than the budget. Do you see any problems with this system?

12. When is top management an agent in a principal-agent relationship as discussed in the chapter?

13. When is top management a principal in a principal-agent relationship as discussed in the chapter?

14. Sales personnel in a company are paid a bonus based on the number of units sold, regardless of the number of defective units returned. How might that incentive system lead to dysfunctional consequences?

Problems and Cases

15. *Assigning Responsibility for Variances.* The Dominick Manufacturing Company is organized into two divisions, Assembling and Finishing. The Assembling Division combines raw materials into a semifinished product. The product is then sent to the Finishing Division for painting, polishing, and packing.

During May, the Assembling Division incurred significantly higher raw materials costs than expected because poor-quality raw materials required extensive rework. Because of the rework, fewer units than expected were transferred to the Finishing Division. The Finishing Division incurred higher labor costs per unit of finished product because workers had substantial idle time.

    a. Who should be held responsible for the raw materials variance in the Assembling Department? Explain.

    b. Who should be held responsible for the labor (idle time) variance in the Finishing Department? Explain.

16. *Performance Evaluation in a CPA Firm.* Cameron and MacInnes, Certified Public Accountants, employ 30 staff accountants. The accountants are involved primarily in auditing the financial statements of the firm's clients. At the completion of each audit assignment, the supervisor evaluates the performance of each staff accountant using a numerical scoring system. The quantitative measures are then used for promotion and compensation decisions. The scoring system involves assignment of a 0, 1, or 2 for each of the following factors scored:

(1) General physical appearance.
(2) Impression made on client.
(3) Ability to work with other staff accountants.
(4) Meeting, surpassing, or falling short of last year's audit time on each assigned task.
(5) Potential for advancement to partnership.

Evaluate the strengths and weaknesses of this numerical scoring system as a tool for evaluating and controlling performance.

17. *Internal Control of Petty Cash.* The Langston Advertising Agency maintains a petty cash fund of $500 in its office. The fund is used to make cash payments for postage, freight, business luncheons, and other costs that do not exceed $25 per expenditure. Before cash can be distributed, an invoice or other evidence must be submitted to the petty cash custodian. The initials of two people other than the custodian are required to authorize the payment. At the end of each day, the petty cash fund is counted to ensure that the custodian has cash and authorized receipts totaling $500. The fund is then replenished with cash equal in amount to the authorized receipts. As a further check on the custodian, surprise counts are made of the fund during the day approximately twice each week.

Evaluate the strengths and weaknesses of these control procedures for the petty cash fund.

18. *Performance Evaluation of Airline Reservations.* Trans Union Airlines is a large domestic airline servicing all major cities throughout the United States. It employs rather sophisticated control systems for many of its activities, including airplane maintenance, baggage handling, customer check-in, and others. One such control system, for telephone reservation services, is described below.

The objective of the control system is to increase the likelihood that customers will receive prompt, courteous, and efficient service when they phone in for reservations. The standards for performance are stated in terms of a list of quantitative and qualitative attributes regarding the telephone conversation.

(1) The telephone call should be answered no later than the third ring.
(2) If a customer is placed "on hold" because of a backlog of calls, the hold period should be no longer than 1 minute.
(3) The reservation clerk should present a pleasant and helpful disposition to the customer.
(4) In cases where a requested flight is full, the reservation clerk should make an effort to place the customer on other Trans Union flights before offering information on flights of other airlines.
(5) After the flight reservations have been made, the reservation clerk should read the flight numbers and times back to the customer.

The company uses two methods of monitoring the telephone reservation service. First, personnel in the controller's department listen to the telephone conversations by way of telephone taps located in central corporate headquarters. They then prepare a written evaluation of the reservation clerk's performance using the above standards. Because the clerks are unaware that their conversations are being heard, they do not act unnaturally. The second monitoring method involves a periodic call to customers to have them evaluate the conversation.

Evaluate the strengths and weaknesses of this control system as a basis for evaluating the performance of the reservation clerks.

19. *Control System to Screen Employees.* An Atlanta-based textile firm employs 30,000 workers in its local plant. A personnel department has been set up to handle hiring and some aspects of training. Before a worker is hired, the personnel department checks his or her credit standing, previous job experience references, and any other factors felt to have a bearing on performance. If the "checker" is satisfied, the applicant is hired immediately or placed on a short waiting list.

Ten individuals are involved in this initial processing in the personnel department. The department supervisor allocates new employment applications to one of the 10 checkers and carries out other personnel department activities.

Outline what you feel would be an effective control system for this initial processing activity. Note important strengths and weaknesses as you proceed.

20. *Controls over Planning Function.* United Manufacturing Corporation has recently set up an independent planning department at the central corporate level.

This department is responsible for most aspects of budgeting (revenue forecasting, production scheduling, profit planning, capital investment). Planning department personnel are responsible to the vice-president for administration. The resulting budgets are incorporated into the control system designed and administered by the controller's department.

Outline what you feel would be an effective control system for the planning department's activities (that is, how the performance of the planning department is to be evaluated).

21. *Controls over Research and Development.* Consolidated Electronics Corporation conducts its research and development activities in a separate building near the central corporate headquarters. The research staff consists of 20 scientists and engineers and 30 research assistants. Approximately 60 percent of the staff's time is devoted to improvement of existing products and processes. Most of this work is performed at the request of personnel in the firm's operating divisions. The remaining 40 percent of the staff's time is devoted to projects of particular interest to the scientists and engineers. In some cases, these efforts result in patents for new products or processes that are either used by Consolidated or sold to other companies. In other cases, these research efforts lead to publishable papers in professional journals. In some instances, no usable results are obtained and the projects are discontinued.

Design what you feel would be an effective control system for this research and development activity.

22. *Effect of Participation and Standard Setting on Budgets.* Stedry (*Budget Control and Cost Behavior*) studied the relationships among **(1)** participation in standard setting, **(2)** tightness of standards, and **(3)** performance. The task performed by a group of students was the solving of a series of short numerical problems. Performance was measured in terms of the number of correct solutions in a 7-minute period.

Students operated under one of three types of budgeting arrangements:

(1) Imposed budgets—students were told how many correct solutions were expected of them in each 7-minute period with no participation on their part.
(2) Pseudoparticipation budgets—students were asked to write down the number of solutions they aspired to get correct in each 7-minute period. After doing this, the students were given a *preset* budgeted amount. The students were not aware that their input was not considered in setting the budget amounts.
(3) Imposed/aspiration-level budgets—students were told how many correct solutions were expected of them in each 7-minute period. They were then asked to write down the number of solutions they aspired to get correct.

Students operated under one of three types of standards with respect to tightness: **(1)** low, **(2)** medium, or **(3)** high. These amounts were set based on performance during the preceding 7-minute period but were adjusted to reflect the different degrees of tightness. Everyone started with a budget of five correct solutions.

Shown below are the average number of correct solutions for students in each of the nine combinations of budgeting arrangements and tightness of standards.

Tightness of Standard	Budgeting Arrangement		
	Imposed Budget	Pseudoparticipation Budget	Imposed/ Aspiration-Level Budget
Low	4.09	4.70	4.56
Medium	4.35	5.45	5.50
High	5.13	4.04	5.85

a. What observations can be made from these results regarding the relationship between participation in setting standards and performance?

b. What observations can be made from these results regarding the relationship between tightness of standards and performance?

23. *Budget Process: Behavioral Issues (CMA adapted).* RV Industries manufactures and sells recreation vehicles. The company has eight divisions strategically located to be near major markets. Each division has a sales force and two to four manufacturing plants. These divisions operate as autonomous profit centers responsible for purchasing, operations and sales.

John Collins, the corporate controller, described the divisional performance measurement system as follows:

We allow the divisions to control the entire operation from the purchase of direct materials to the sale of the product. We, at corporate headquarters, get involved only in strategic decisions, such as developing new product lines. Each division is responsible for meeting its market needs by providing the right products at a low cost on a timely basis. Frankly, the divisions need to focus on cost control, delivery, and services to customers in order to become more profitable.

While we give the divisions considerable autonomy, we watch their monthly income statements very closely. Each month's actual performance is compared with the budget in considerable detail. If the actual sales or contribution margin is more than 4 or 5 percent below the budget, we jump on the division people immediately. I might add that we don't have much trouble getting their attention. All of the management people at the plant and division level can add appreciably to their annual salaries with bonuses if actual net income is considerably greater than budget.

The budgeting process begins in August when division sales managers, after consulting with their sales personnel, estimate sales for the next calendar year. These estimates are sent to plant managers, who use the sales forecasts to prepare production estimates. At the plants, production statistics including direct material quantities, labor hours, production schedules, and output quantities, are developed by operating personnel. Using the statistics prepared by the operating personnel, the plant accounting staff determines costs and prepares the plant's budgeted variable cost of goods sold and other plant expenses for each month of the coming calendar year.

In October, each division's accounting staff combines plant budgets with sales estimates and adds additional division expenses. Collins says:

> After the divisional management is satisfied with the budget, I visit each division to go over their budget and make sure it is in line with corporate strategy and projections. I really emphasize the sales forecasts because of the volatility in the demand for our product. For many years, we lost sales to our competitors because we didn't project high enough production and sales, and we couldn't meet the market demand. More recently, we were caught with large excess inventory when the bottom dropped out of the market for recreational vehicles.
>
> I generally visit all eight divisions during the first two weeks in November. After that the division budgets are combined and reconciled by my staff, and they are ready for approval by the board of directors in early December. The board seldom questions the budget.
>
> One complaint we've had from plant and division management is that they are penalized for circumstances beyond their control. For example, they failed to predict the recent sales decline. As a result, they didn't make their budget and, of course, they received no bonuses. However, I point out that they are well rewarded when they exceed their budget. Furthermore, they provide most of the information for the budget, so it's their own fault if the budget is too optimistic.

    a.   Identify and explain the biases the corporate management of RV Industries should expect in the communication of budget estimates by its division and plant personnel.

    b.   What sources of information can the top management of RV Industries use to monitor the budget estimates prepared by its divisions and plants?

    c.   What services could top management of RV Industries offer the divisions to help them in their budget development, without appearing to interfere with the division budget decisions?

    d.   The top management of RV Industries is attempting to decide whether it should get more involved in the budget process. Identify and explain the variables management needs to consider in reaching its decision.

24. *Budgeting Research Expenditures.*[17] According to an article by Peter F. Drucker, innovative companies have two separate budgets, an operating budget and an innovative budget. "The operating budget contains everything that is already being done. The innovation budget contains the things that are to be done differently and the different things to be worked on."

In reviewing the different budgets, top management asks different questions. For the operating budget, management asks: What is the optimization point? "But for innovations, top management asks: Is this the right opportunity? And if the answer is yes; top management asks: What is the *most* this opportunity can absorb by way of resources at this stage?"

---

[17]Based on Peter F. Drucker, "The Innovative Company," *The Wall Street Journal*, February 26, 1982, p. 22.

Suppose that the top management of your company wants the budget to encourage innovation. How would the budgeting and performance evaluation methods differ for ''innovative'' activities compared to routine operating activities?

25. *Divisional Performance Measurement: Behavioral Issues (CMA adapted).* Divisional managers of SIU Incorporated have been expressing growing dissatisfaction with the methods currently being used to measure divisional performance. Divisional operations are evaluated every quarter by comparison with the budget prepared during the prior year. Divisional managers claim that many factors are completely out of their control but are included in this comparison. This results in an unfair and misleading performance evaluation.

The managers have been particularly critical of the process used to establish standards and budgets. The annual budget, stated by quarters, is prepared 6 months prior to the beginning of the operating year. Pressure by top management to reflect increased earnings has often caused divisional managers to overstate revenues and/ or understate expenses. In addition, once the budget has been established, divisions were required to ''live with the budget.'' Frequently, external factors such as the state of the economy, changes in consumer preferences, and actions of competitors have not been adequately recognized in the budget parameters that top management supplied to the divisions. The credibility of the performance review is curtailed when the budget cannot be adjusted to incorporate these changes.

Top management, recognizing the current problems, has agreed to establish a committee to review the situation and to make recommendations for a new performance evaluation system. The committee consists of each division manager, the corporate controller, and the executive vice-president, who serves as the chairman. At the first meeting, one division manager outlined an Achievement of Objectives System (AOS). In this performance evaluation system, divisional managers would be evaluated according to three criteria:

(1) Doing better than last year. Various measures would be compared to the same measures of the prior year.
(2) Planning realistically. Actual performance for the current year would be compared to realistic plans and/or goals.
(3) Managing current assets. Various measures would be used to evaluate the divisional management's achievements and reactions to changing business and economic conditions.

A division manager believed this system would overcome many of the inconsistencies of the current system because divisions could be evaluated from three different viewpoints. In addition, managers would have the opportunity to show how they would react and account for changes in uncontrollable external factors.

A second division manager was also in favor of the proposed AOS. However, the manager cautioned that the success of a new performance evaluation system would be limited unless it had the complete support of top management. Further, this support should be visible within all divisions. The manager believed that the committee should recommend some procedures that would enhance the motivational and competitive spirit of the divisions.

    a. Explain whether or not the proposed AOS would be an improvement over the measure of divisional performance now used by SIU Incorporated.

b. Develop specific performance measures for each of the three criteria in the proposed AOS that could be used to evaluate divisional managers.

c. Discuss the motivational and behavioral aspects of the proposed performance system. Also, recommend specific programs that could be instituted to promote morale and give incentives to divisional management.

26. *Change to More Centralized Organization Structure: Behavioral Issues (CMA adapted).* Greengrass Company is an established manufacturer and wholesaler of a broad line of lawn fertilizer and yard maintenance products. Greengrass Company has annual sales of approximately $100 million and has been a wholly owned subsidiary of a large conglomerate, KSU Corporation, for the past 5 years. Prior to that, it was an independent corporation with the stock controlled by the founding and managing family.

Al B. Cardwell, son of the founder, is currently the president of the company, but he is scheduled to retire in May of next year. His nephew, B. C. Cardwell, is currently executive vice-president and has been heir apparent to the presidency ever since Al B. Cardwell became president.

Greengrass Company had maintained a pattern of increasing profits for many years. During the past 3 years, however, profits have decreased significantly. Management has attributed this to reduced demand caused by cool, wet summers in the company's primary marketing area, coupled with intense competitive activity.

Following his return from a week-long corporate management planning meeting, Al B. Cardwell called a staff meeting to discuss plans for next year's marketing season. At the close of the meeting, he announced that the KSU Board had named William Thoma to become president of Greengrass Company in May of next year. Cardwell explained that KSU's management was concerned with the subsidiary's slumping profits and had decided to assume a greater degree of control over Greengrass operations. Thoma's appointment was the first step in this direction. In addition, a new system of financial reporting to KSU management is to be installed.

Mr. Thoma's reputation was well known to the entire staff. He had been executive vice-president of two other KSU-owned companies during the previous 3 years. In both cases, the companies had records of declining profits prior to his appointment. A significant management reorganization occurred in each of those companies within 12 months after his appointment. In each case, some members of senior management were given early retirement or released, depending on their ages. Their replacements usually came from other KSU companies with which Thoma had been associated. Although earnings did increase following the reorganizations, the entire ''personality'' of the companies was changed.

a. Discuss the ways the change to a more centralized organization and decision structure can be expected to influence the behavior of Greengrass managers.

b. Discuss the impact of William Thoma's selection as the new president on the behavior of Greengrass managers.

27. *Controlling Operations: Nonprofit Organization.*[18] On November 1, 1983, Captain William Shefford, USN, was assigned as the seventeenth commanding

---

[18]David Croll © 1983.

officer of the Admiral Mahon Weapons Station. Except during the war years, the billet of commanding officer for Mahon had been seen as a nice, restful final duty station after 30 years in the Navy. This time, however, the Bureau of Personnel told Captain William Shefford that this was not the case. The Mahon Weapons Station had some major problems that necessitated the attention of a bright, hard-charging, career-minded captain still in the running for promotion—or at least that's what the Bureau of Personnel told him.

He was briefed by the assigning officer that: "because the commanding officer's billet had been seen as the final step before full retirement, control had become very lax." Captain Jennings, the commanding officer he would replace, presented this picture of the CO's job: "It is mostly ceremonial. The work here is so technical that it is impossible to learn even a rudimentary level in the 3 years the tour lasts." Since there were Naval personnel assigned to the base in support positions, he, Jennings, limited his involvement with civilian personnel to official functions, and spent his time with the military problems of the Naval personnel. There was a high-level civilian technical director assigned to the base, who dealt with the technical problems. The actual day-to-day operations, however, were not handled by the technical director but by the 13 research directors who reported to him. The technical director's time was taken up with refereeing turf fights among the 13 research directors.

The research directors nominally covered 13 separate areas of research. In practice, the research directors made proposals and contracted for research jobs directly with "clients" (that is, other Naval commands). When they were awarded a contract, the research directors would assemble a team of researchers and other employees to complete the contract. The more contracts a research director brought in, the more resources he received. When interest in a specific area of research ended, the research director was faced with the choice of either seeing his allocation of resources and personnel greatly diminish or branching out into an associated, more currently popular area of research. It was no wonder that the technical director spent so much of his time arguing over who should do the research and how the personnel and resources should be allocated.

On his second day as commanding officer, Bill Shefford called a meeting with the technical director, the research directors, and the heads of all the support activities. He was greatly disappointed to find that even though only one of the research directors called to be excused, only the technical director arrived in person. The remaining 12 research directors sent their number-two people, and the support people sent secretaries. None of the important items on the agenda could be discussed, because none of the people at the meeting, with the exception of the technical director, felt competent to make a decision for his area.

Within the next 3 weeks, Captain Bill Shefford averaged two calls a day from other military commanders and technical directors of similar facilities complaining that work their operations had done in the past were being bid on by the Admiral Mahon Weapons Station. Although much less frequently, Bill also received calls from commanding officers of "client" commands demanding to know why Mahon had not bid on their project even though they had bid on similar projects in the past. Bill was further frustrated because without the help of the technical director he was unable to determine which research director was responsible for which projects. The base was at full employment, and everyone seemed overworked and happy but Bill.

To make matters worse for Bill, a congressman was publicly complaining about duplication of effort within the military and was being fed examples of military duplication by the staff of a competing Naval research station. Bill was sure he was going to be called on to justify certain proposals made by Mahon on projects previously done at other stations.

The final straw came when an old classmate from the Naval Academy asked Bill, "What exactly do you people do down there on the bay?", and Bill didn't have an answer.

> **a.** Outline chronologically what Bill Shefford must do to get control of his command.
>
> **b.** What problems will he face as he tries to implement the solution outlined above?
>
> **c.** Why was Bill's meeting so poorly attended?

28. *Project Performance Reporting (CMA adapted).* Walton Research does electronics research for business firms and the federal government. Most of the company's work is based on contracts calling for prototypes, or models, of new products. Each project has two phases: a "design phase" and a "build phase." The "design phase" involves designing the product in accordance with the customer's guidelines. Several designs are usually prepared before one is acceptable to the customer.

The "build phase" of the project involves building the prototype to meet the specifications. After the prototype is built, the specifications and the prototype are turned over to the customer. Walton Research never mass-produces the project; it only prepares specifications and builds prototypes.

Walton Research's reputation for building quality prototypes on time is extremely important for the company's long-term success. Most of Walton's contracts are "cost-plus" a fixed fee (that is, "profit"), with shared costs over a specific amount. For example, Walton currently has a contract to make a product called XT-214, which is a navigational device for use on spaceships. The specified cost limit has been negotiated with the customer to be $800,000. The fixed fee on the contract is $80,000. The customer has agreed to pay for 50 percent of the costs in excess of $800,000. If the project actually costs $760,000, for example, Walton Research will receive $840,000 (equals cost of $760,000 plus fixed fee of $80,000). If the project costs $860,000, Walton will receive $910,000 (equals cost limit of $800,000 plus 50 percent of the $60,000 cost overrun, or $30,000, plus the fixed fee of $80,000).

A recent project performance report provides the following data about the XT-214 project:

Project	Budget	Actual	Remaining	Status
XT-214	$800,000	$750,000	$50,000	95 Percent Complete

Top management of Walton Research meets in the second week of each month to review the performance of the preceding month. One of the managers at the meeting commented that the project manager for the XT-214 project was performing well. "The manager is doing well at holding the line on costs on the XT-214 project," the manager stated. "I hope that's taken into account at promotion time."

Another manager at the meeting stated, "I disagree. Project XT-214 is a disaster! The 95 percent completion figure is provided by the manager, and according to him, this project has been 95 percent complete for 2 months. The preliminary quality control tests have come across my desk, and they indicate that a complete teardown and rework will be necessary. Further, the customer is furious because the project is 2 months behind schedule. I realize the project looks good on the performance report, but I can assure you that the report does not present the full story about Project XT-214."

a. How is the present project performance report inadequate for projects like the XT-214?

b. What improvements would you recommend in the report? Give particular attention to the way that things important to Walton Research are reported. Consider the costs and benefits of your recommendations to the extent possible.

29. *Comprehensive Planning and Control Case.*[19] Empire Glass Company was a diversified company organized into several major product divisions. Each division was headed by a vice-president who reported to the company's executive vice-president, Landon McGregor. The Glass Products Division, the focus of this case, was responsible for manufacturing and selling glass food and beverage bottles.

McGregor's corporate staff included three financial people—the controller, chief accountant, and treasurer. The controller's department consisted of only two people—James Walker and his assistant, Ellen Newell. The market research and labor relations departments also reported in a staff capacity to McGregor.

All the product divisions were organized along similar lines. Reporting to each division vice-president were staff members in the customer service and product research areas. Reporting in a line capacity to each vice-president were also general managers of manufacturing and of marketing, who were respectively responsible for all the division's manufacturing and marketing activities. Both of these executives were assisted by a small staff of specialists. Exhibit 11.3 presents an organization chart of top management and of the Glass Product Division's management group. All corporate and divisional managers and staff were located in British City, Canada. Exhibit 11.4 shows the typical organization structure of a plant within the Glass Products division.

Products and Technology Glass Products operated seven plants in Canada. Of their products, food jars constituted the largest group, including jars for products such as catsup, mayonnaise, jams and jellies, honey, and instant coffee. Milk, beer,

[19]Copyright © 1964 by the President and Fellows of Harvard College. This case was prepared by David F. Hawkins as a basis for class discussion rather than to illustrate either effective or ineffective handling of an administrative situation. Reproduced by permission of the Harvard Business School.

Exhibit 11.3
Top Management and Glass Products Management

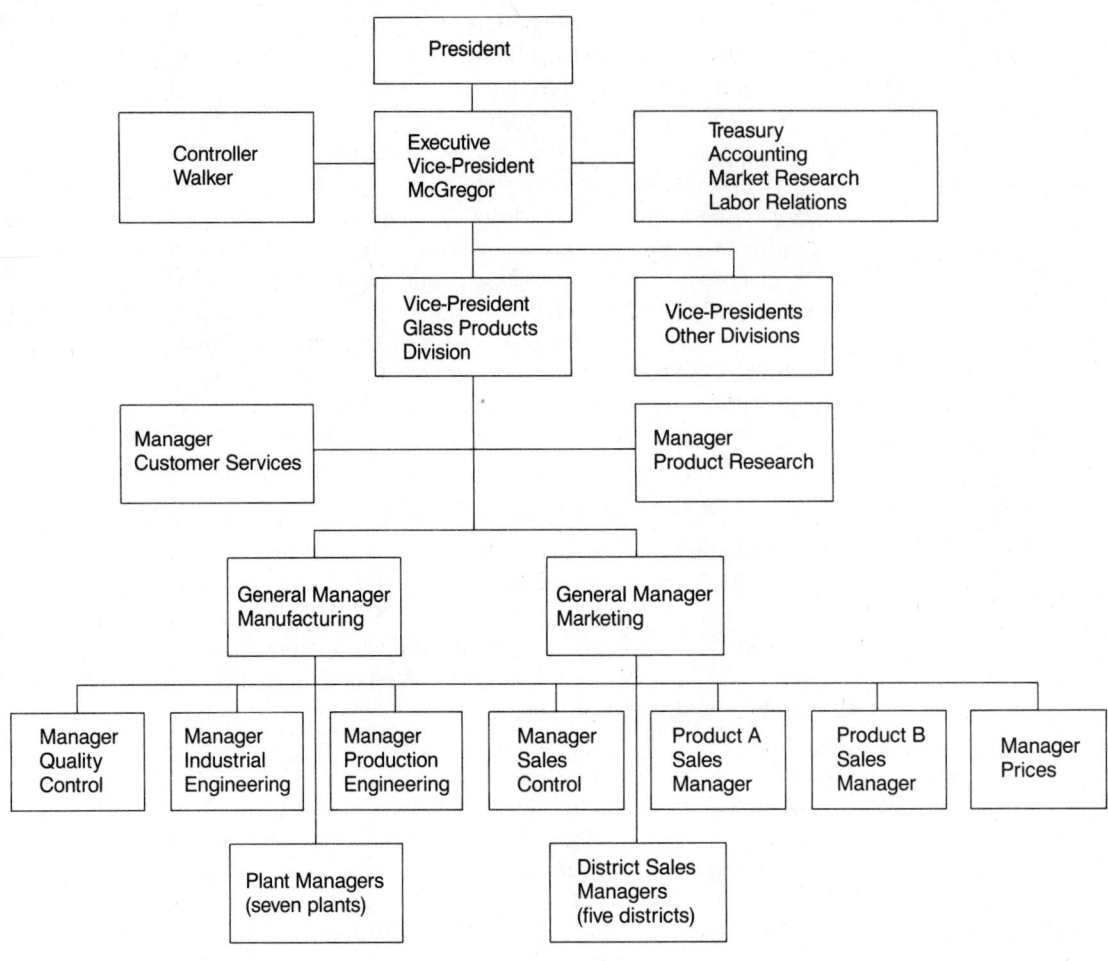

and soft-drink bottles were also produced in large quantities. A great variety of containers for wines, liquors, drugs, cosmetics, and chemicals were produced in smaller quantities.

Most of the thousands of different products, varying in size, shape, color, and decoration, were produced to order. According to Glass Products executives, the typical lead time between a customer's order and shipment from the plant was between 2 and 3 weeks.

The principal direct materials for container glass were sand, soda ash, and lime. The first step in the manufacturing process was to melt batches of these materials in furnaces or "tanks." The molten mass was then passed into automatic or semi-automatic machines, which filled molds with the molten glass and blew the glass into the desired shape. The ware then went through an automatic annealing oven

Exhibit 11.4
Typical Plant Organization: Glass Products Division

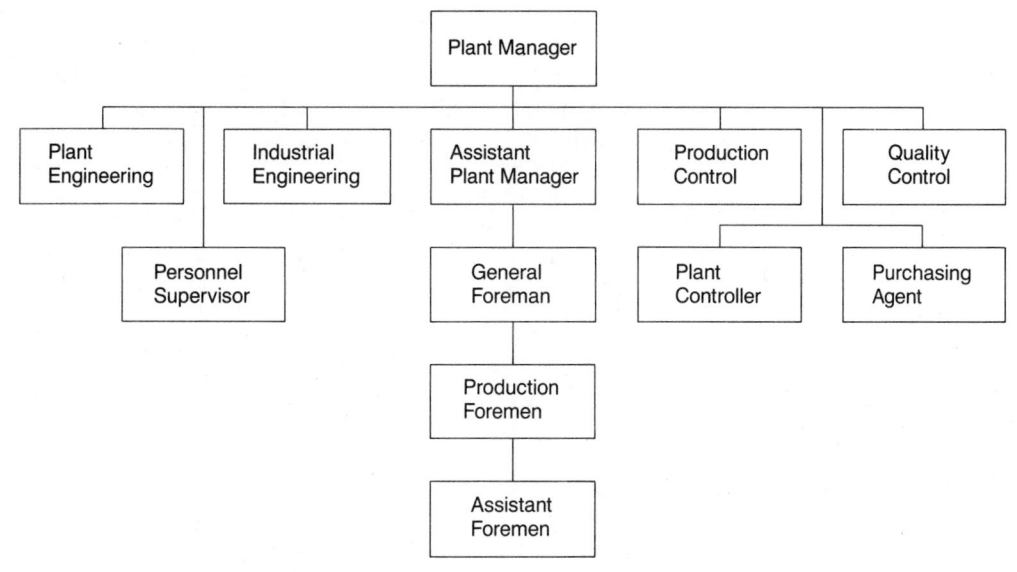

or lehr, where it was cooled slowly under carefully controlled conditions. If the glass was to be coated on the exterior to increase its resistance to abrasion and scratches, this coating—often a silicone film—was applied at the lehr. Any decorating (such as a trademark or other design) was then added, the product inspected again, and the finished goods packed in corrugated containers (or wooden cases for some bottles).

Quality inspection was critical in the manufacturing process. If the melt in the furnace was not completely free from bubbles and stones, or if the fabricating machinery was slightly out of adjustment or molds were worn, the rejection rate was very high. Although a number of machines were used in the inspection process, including electric eyes, much of the inspection was still visual.

Although glassmaking was one of the oldest arts, and bottles had been machine molded at relatively high speed for more than half a century, Glass Products had spent substantial sums each year to modernize its equipment. These improvements had greatly increased the speed of operations and had substantially reduced the visual inspection and manual handling of glassware.

Most of the jobs were relatively unskilled, highly repetitive, and gave the worker little control over work methods or pace. The moldmakers who made and repaired the molds, the machine repairpersons, and those who made the equipment setup changes between different products were considered to be the highest classes of skilled workers. Wages were relatively high in the industry, in part because the plants were noisy and hot. Production employees belonged to two national unions, and bargaining was conducted on a national basis. Output standards were established for all jobs, but no bonus was paid to hourly plant workers for exceeding standard.

Marketing Over the years, Glass Products' sales had grown at a slightly faster rate than had the total glass container market. Until the late 1950s, the division had charged a premium for most of its products, primarily because they were of better quality than competitive products. Subsequently, however, the quality of the competitive products had improved to the point where they now matched the division's quality level. In the meantime, the division's competitors had retained their former price structure. Consequently, Glass Products had been forced to lower its prices to meet its competitors' lower market prices. According to one division executive:

> Currently, price competition is not severe, particularly among the two or three larger companies that dominate the glass bottle industry. Most of our competition is with respect to product quality and customer service. . . . In fact, our biggest competitive threat is from containers other than glass. . . .''

Each of the division's various plants shipped some products throughout Canada to some extent, although transportation costs limited each plant's market primarily to its immediate vicinity. Although some of the customers were large and bought in huge quantities, many were relatively small.

Budgetary Control System James Walker, Empire Glass Company controller for more than 15 years, described the company's budgetary control system to a casewriter. Excerpts from that interview are reproduced below.

> To understand the role of the budgetary control system, you must first understand our management philosophy. Fundamentally, we have a divisional organization based on broad product categories. These divisional activities are coordinated by the company's executive vice-president, whereas the head office group provides a policy and review function for him. Within the broad policy limits, we operate on a decentralized basis; each of the decentralized divisions performs the full management job that normally would be inherent in any independent company. The only exceptions to this are the head office group's sole responsibilities for sources of funds and labor relations with those bargaining units that cross division lines.
>
>   Given this form of organization, the budget is the principal management tool used by the head office to coordinate the efforts of the various segments of the company toward a common goal. Certainly, in our case, the budget is much more than a narrow statistical accounting device.

Sales Budget As early as May 15 of the year preceding the budget year, top management of the company asks the various division vice-presidents to submit preliminary reports stating what they think their division's capital requirements and outlook in terms of sales and income will be during the next budget year. In addition, top management wants an expression of the division vice-president's general feelings toward the trends in these items over the 2 years following the upcoming budget year. At this stage, the head office is not interested in much detail. Since all divisions plan their capital requirements 5 years in advance and had made predictions of the forthcoming budget year's market when the budget estimates were prepared last year, these rough estimates of next year's conditions and requirements are far from wild guesses.

After the opinions of the division vice-presidents are in, the market research staff goes to work. They develop a formal statement of the marketing climate in detail for the forthcoming budget year and in general terms for the subsequent 2 years. Once these general factors have been assessed, a sales forecast is constructed for the company and for each division. Consideration is given to the relationship of the general economic climate to our customers' needs and Empire's share of each market. Explicitly stated are basic assumptions as to price, weather conditions, introduction of new products, gains or losses in particular accounts, forward buying, new manufacturing plants, industry growth trends, packaging trends, inventory carryovers, and the development of alternative packages to or from glass. This review of all the relevant factors is followed for each of our product lines, regardless of its size and importance. The completed forecasts of the market research group are then forwarded to the appropriate divisions for review, criticism, and adjustments.

The primary goal of the head office group in developing these sales forecasts is to assure uniformity among the divisions with respect to the basic assumptions on business conditions, pricing, and the treatment of possible emergencies. Also, we provide a yardstick so as to assure us that the company's overall sales forecast will be reasonable and obtainable.

The division top management then asks the district managers what they expect to do in the way of sales during the budget year. Head office and the divisional staffs will give the district managers as much guidance as they request, but it is the sole responsibility of each district manager to come up with the district's forecast.

After the district sales managers' forecasts are received by the divisional top management, the forecasts are consolidated and reviewed by the division's general manager of marketing, who may suggest revisions. The district managers know little of what's happening outside their territories; but at headquarters we can estimate the size of the whole market for, say, liquor, and each of our customer's market share. That's where the market research group's forecasts come in handy. Let me emphasize, however, that nothing is changed in the district manager's budget unless the district manager agrees. Then, once the budget is approved, nobody is relieved of responsibility without top management approval. Also, no arbitrary changes are made in the approved budgets without the concurrence of all the people responsible for the budget.

Next, we go through the same process at the division and headquarters levels. We continue to repeat the process until everyone agrees that the sales budgets are sound. Then, each level of management takes responsibility for its particular portion of the budget. These sales budgets then become fixed objectives.

I would say a division has four general objectives in mind in reviewing its sales budget:

(1) A review of the division's competitive position, including plans for improving that position.
(2) An evaluation of its efforts to gain either a larger share of the market or offset competitors' activities.

(3) A consideration of the need to expand facilities to improve the division's products or introduce new products.

(4) A review and development of plans to improve product quality, delivery methods and service.

Manufacturing Budgets Once the division vice-presidents, executive vice-president, and company president have given final approval to the sales budget, we make a sales budget for each plant by breaking down the division sales budget according to the plants from which the finished goods will be shipped. These plant sales budgets are then further broken down on a monthly basis by price, volume, and end use. With this information available, the plants then budget their contribution, fixed expenses, and income before taxes. Contribution is the difference between gross sales, less discounts, and variable manufacturing costs. Income is the difference between contribution and fixed costs. It is the plant manager's responsibility to meet this budgeted *profit* figure, even if actual dollar sales drop below the budgeted level.

Given the plant's sales budget, it is up to the plant manager to determine the fixed overhead and variable costs—at standard—that the plant will need to incur so as to meet the demands of the sales budget. In my opinion, requiring the plant managers to make their own plans is one of the most valuable things associated with the budget system. Each plant manager divides the preparation of the overall plant budget among the plant's various departments. First, the departments spell out the program in terms of the physical requirements, such as tons of direct material, and then the plans are priced at standard cost.

The plant industrial engineering department is assigned responsibility for developing engineered cost standards. This phase of the budget also includes budgeted cost reductions, budgeted unfavorable variances from standards, and certain budgeted programmed fixed costs in the manufacturing area, such as service labor. The industrial engineer prepares this phase of the budget in conjunction with departmental line supervision.

Before each plant sends its budget in to British City, a group of us from the head office goes out to visit each plant. For example, in the case of Glass Products, Ellen Newell, assistant controller, and I, along with representatives of the division's manufacturing staffs, visit each of the division's plants. Let me stress this point: We do not go on these trips to pass judgment on the plant's proposed budget. Rather, we go with two purposes in mind. First, we wish to acquaint ourselves with the thinking behind the figures that each plant manager will send in to British City. This is helpful, because when we come to review these budgets with the top management—that is, the president and executive vice-president—we will have to answer questions about the budgets, and we will know the answers. Second, the review is a way of giving guidance to the plant managers in determining whether or not they are in line with what the company needs to make in the way of profits.

Of course, when we make our field reviews, we do not know what each of the other plants is planning. Therefore, we explain to the plant managers that although their budget may look good now, when we put all the plants together in a consolidated budget the plant managers may have to make some changes because the projected profit is not high enough. When this happens, we tell the plant managers that it is not their programs that are unsound. The problem is that the company cannot afford the programs. I think it is very important that the plant managers have a chance to tell their story. Also, it gives them the feeling that we at headquarters are not living in an ivory tower.

These plant visits are spread over a 3-week period, and we spend an average of half a day at each plant. The plant managers are free to bring to these meetings any of their supervisors they wish. We ask them not to bring in anybody below the supervisory level—then, of course, you get into organized labor. During the half day we spend at each plant, we discuss the budget primarily. However, if I have time I like to wander through the plant and see how things are going. Also, I go over in great detail the property replacement and maintenance budget with the plant manager.

About September 1, the plant budgets come into British City, and the accounting department consolidates them. Then the division vice-presidents review their respective division budgets to see if they are reasonable in terms of what the vice-president thinks the corporate management wants. If the vice-president is not satisfied with the consolidated plant budgets, the various plants within the division will be asked to trim their budgeted costs.

When the division vice-presidents and the executive vice-president are satisfied, they will send their budgets to the company president. He may accept the division budgets at this point. If he doesn't, he will specify the areas to be reexamined by division and, if necessary, by plant. The final budget is approved at our December board of directors meeting.

Comparison of Actual and Standard Performance At the end of the sixth business day after the close of the month, each plant wires to the head office certain operating variances, which we put together on what we call the variance analysis sheet. Within a half-hour after the last plant report comes through, variance analysis sheets for the divisions and plants are compiled. On the morning of the seventh business day, these reports are on the desks of top management. The variance analysis sheet highlights the variances in what we consider to be critical areas. Receiving this report as soon as we do helps us at the head office to take timely action. Let us emphasize, however, we do not accept the excuse that plant managers have to go to the end of the month to know what happened during the month. They have to be on top of these particular items daily.

When the actual results come into the head office, we go over them on the basis of exception; that is, we only look at those figures that are in excess of the budgeted amounts. We believe this has a good effect on morale. The plant managers don't have to explain everything they do. They have to explain only where they go off base. In particular, we pay close attention to the net sales, gross margin, and the plant's ability to meet its standard manufacturing cost. When analyzing sales, we look closely at price and mix changes.

All this information is summarized on a form known as the Profit Planning and Control Report No. 1 (see Exhibit 11.5). This document is backed up by a number of supporting documents (see Exhibit 11.6). The plant PPCR No. 1

Exhibit 11.5
Profit Planning and Control Report No. 1

Prev. Year	Budget	Actual	Ref.		Actual	Budget	Prev. Year
MONTH — Income Gain (+) or Loss (−) From					YEAR TO DATE — Income Gain (+) or Loss (−) From		
			1	Gross Sales to Customers			
			2	Discounts & Allowances			
			3	Net Sales to Customers			
%	%		4	% Gain (+)/Loss (−)		%	%
				DOLLAR VOLUME GAIN (+)/ LOSS (−) DUE TO:			
			5	Sales Price			
			6	Sales Volume			
			6(a)	Trade Mix			
			7	Std. Variable Cost of Sales			
			8	Contribution Margin			
				CONTRIB. MARGIN GAIN (+)/ LOSS (−) DUE TO:			
			9	Profit Volume Ratio (P/V)*			
			10	Dollar Volume			
%	%	%	11	Profit Volume Ratio (P/V)*		%	%	%
			12	Budgeted Fixed Mfg. Cost			
			13	Fixed Manufacturing Cost-Transfers			
			14	Plant Income (standard)			
%	%	%	15	% of Net Sales		%	%	%
%	%	%	16	% Mfg. Efficiency		%	%	%
			17	Manufacturing Variances			
			18	Methods Improvements			
			19	Other Revisions of Standards			
			20	Material Price Changes			
			21	Division Special Projects			
			22	Company Special Projects			
			23	New Plant Expense			
			24	Other Plant Expenses			
			25	Income on Seconds			
			26				
			27				
			28	Plant Income (actual)			
%	%		29	% Gain (+)/Loss (−)		%	%
%	%	%	30	% of Net Sales		%	%	%
			36A				
				CAPITAL EMPLOYED			
			37	Total Capital Employed			
%	%	%	38	% Return		%	%	%
			39	Turnover Rate			

_____   _____   _____ 19 ____
Plant   Division   Month

*The *P/V* ratio was defined to be (price − variable cost) ÷ price.

Exhibit 11.6
Brief Description of PPCR No. 2–PPCR No. 11

Report	Individual Plant Reports, Description
PPCR No. 2 . . .	Manufacturing expense: plant materials, labor, and variable overhead consumed. Detail of actual figures compared with budget and previous year's figures for year to date and current month.
PPCR No. 3 . . .	Plant expense: plant fixed expenses incurred. Details of actual figures compared with budget and previous year's figures for year to date and current month.
PPCR No. 4 . . .	Analysis of sales and income: part operating gains and losses due to changes in sales revenue, profit margins, and other sources of income. Details of actual figures compared with budget and previous year's figures for year to date and current month.
PPCR No. 5 . . .	Plant control statement: analysis of plant direct material gains and losses, spoilage costs, and cost reduction programs. Actual figures compared with budget figures for current month and year to date.
PPCR No. 6 . . .	Comparison of sales by principal and product groups: plant sales dollars, profit margin, and P/V ratios broken down by end product use (that is, soft drinks, beer). Compares actual figures with budgeted figures for year to date and current month.

Report	Division Summary Reports, Description
PPCR No. 7 . . .	Comparative plant performance, sales, and income: gross sales and income figures by plants. Actual figures compared with budget figures for year to date and current month.
PPCR No. 8 . . .	Comparative plant performance, total plant expenses: profit margin, total fixed costs, manufacturing efficiency, other plant expenses, and P/V ratios by plants. Actual figures compared with budgeted and previous year's figures for current month and year to date.
PPCR No. 9 . . .	Manufacturing efficiency: analysis of gains and losses by plant in areas of materials, spoilage, supplies, and labor. Current month and year to date actuals reported in total dollars and as a percentage of budget.
PPCR No. 10. . .	Inventory: comparison of actual and budget inventory figures by major inventory accounts and plants.
PPCR No. 11. . .	Status of capital expenditures: analysis of the status of capital expenditures by plants, months, and relative to budget.

and the month-end trial balance showing both actual and budget figures are received in British City at the close of the eighth business day after the end of the month. These two very important reports, along with the supporting reports (PPCR No. 2–PPCR No. 11) are then consolidated by the accounting department to show the results of operations by division and company. The consolidated reports are distributed the next day.

In connection with the fixed cost items, we want to know whether the plants carried out the programs they said they would carry out. If they have not, we want to know why. Also, we want to know if they have carried out their projected programs at the cost they said they would.

In addition to these reports, at the beginning of each month the plant managers prepare current estimates for the upcoming month and quarter on forms similar to the variance analysis sheets. Since our budget is based on known programs, the value of this current estimate is that it gets the plant people to look at their programs. We hope that they will realize they cannot run their plants just on a day-to-day basis.

If we see a sore spot coming up, or if the plant manager draws our attention to a potential trouble area, we may ask that daily reports concerning this item be sent to division top management. In addition, the division top management may send a division staff specialist—say, a quality control expert if it is a quality problem—to the plant concerned. The division staff members can make recommendations, but it is up to the plant manager to accept or reject these recommendations. Of course, it is well known throughout the company that we expect the plant managers to accept gracefully the help of the head office and division staffs.

Sales-Manufacturing Relations If a sales decline occurs during the early part of the year, and if the plant managers can convince us that the change is permanent, we may revise the plant budgets to reflect these new circumstances. However, if toward the end of the year the actual sales volume suddenly drops below budget, we don't have much time to change the budget plans. What we do is ask the plant managers to go back over their budgets with their staffs and see where reduction of expense programs will do the least harm. Specifically, we ask them to consider what they may be able to eliminate this year or delay until next year.

"I believe it was Confucius who said: "We make plans so we have plans to discard." Nevertheless, I think it is wise to make plans, even if you have to discard them. Having plans makes it a lot easier to figure out what to do when sales fall off from the budgeted level. The understanding of operations that comes from preparing the budget removes a lot of potential chaos that might arise if we were under pressure to meet a stated profit goal and sales declined quickly and unexpectedly at year-end, just as they did last year. In these circumstances, we don't try to ram anything down the plant managers' throats. We ask them to tell us where they can reasonably expect to cut costs below the budgeted level.

Whenever a problem arises at a plant between sales and production, the local people are supposed to solve the problem themselves. For example, a customer's purchasing agent may insist he wants an immediate delivery, and this delivery will disrupt the production department's plans. The production group can make recommendations as to alternative ways to take care of the problem, but it's the sales manager's responsibility to get the product to the customer. The sales force are supposed to know their customers well enough to judge whether or not the customer really needs the product. If the sales manager says the customer needs the product, that ends the matter. As far as we are concerned, the customer's wants are primary; our company is a case where sales wags the rest of the dog. Of course, if the change in the sales program involves a major plant expense that is out of line with the budget, then the matter is passed up to division top management for a decision.

The sales department has the sole responsibility for product price, sales mix, and volume. They do not have direct responsibility for plant operations or profit. That's the plant management's responsibility. However, it is understood that the sales group will cooperate with the plant people whenever possible.

Motivation There are various ways in which we motivate the plant managers to meet their profit goals. First of all, we only promote capable people. Also, a monetary incentive program has been established that stimulates their efforts to achieve their profit goals. In addition, each month we put together a bar chart that shows, by division and plant, the ranking of the various manufacturing units with respect to manufacturing efficiency.[20] We feel the plant managers are fully responsible for variable manufacturing costs. I believe this is true, since all manufacturing standards have to be approved by plant managers. Most of the plant managers give wide publicity to these bar charts, The efficiency bar chart and efficiency measure itself is perhaps a little unfair in some respects when you are comparing one plant with another. Different kinds of products are run through different plants. These require different setups, and so forth, which have an important impact on the position of a plant. However, in general, the efficiency rating is a good indication of the quality of the plant managers and their supervisory staffs.

Also, a number of plants run competitions within plants that reward department heads based on their relative standing with respect to a certain cost item. The plant managers, their staffs, and employees have great pride in their plants.

The number one item now stressed at the plant level is *quality*. The market situation is such that in order to make sales you have to meet the market price and exceed the market quality. By quality I mean not only the physical characteristics of the product but also delivery schedules. The company employee publications' message is that if the company is to be profitable, it must produce high-quality items at a reasonable cost. This is necessary so that the plants can meet their obligation to produce the maximum profits for the company in the prevailing circumstances.

The Future An essential part of the budgetary control system is planning. We have developed a philosophy that we must begin our plans where the work is done—in the line organization and out in the field. Perhaps, in the future, we can avoid or cut back some of the budget preparation steps and start putting together our sales budget later than May 15. However, I doubt if we will change the basic philosophy. Frankly, I doubt if the line operators would want any major change in the system; they are very jealous of the management prerogatives the system gives them.

It is very important that we manage the budget. We have to be continually on guard against its managing us. Sometimes, the plants lose sight of this fact. We have to be made conscious daily of the necessity of having the sales volume to make a profit. And when sales fall off and their plant programs are reduced, they do not always appear to see the justification for budget cuts—although I do suspect that they see more of the justification for these cuts than they will admit. It is this human side of the budget to which we have to pay more attention in the future.

---

[20]Manufacturing Efficiency $= \dfrac{\text{Total Standard Variable Manufacturing Costs}}{\text{Total Actual Variable Manufacturing Costs}} \times 100\%.$

a.   Describe each step of Empire's budget process from its start on May 15 until its final approval. Relate each step to the organization charts in Exhibits 11.3 and 11.4.

b.   Evaluate Empire's budgeting process. Have they related the budget to organizational goals? What incentives do participants have for biasing information?

c.   Evaluate the strength and weaknesses of Empire's performance evaluation methods and organization structure. Should the plants continue to be profit/investment centers, or should they be cost centers? Why? (This question may be postponed until Chapter 14.)

Chapter 12   Operating Budgets

This chapter focuses on developing and using the short-term operating budget. As previously indicated, this budget states quantitatively management's plan of action for the coming year. This chapter considers the principal uses of such budgets, how they are developed, and how actual results of operations are compared with budgets to derive variances for performance evaluation.

Uses of Operating Budgets

Budgets are useful tools for (1) planning, (2) control, and (3) employee motivation.

Tool for Planning

After management selects the best alternatives with respect to products, prices, levels of output, production techniques, and so on, these choices are translated into a formal, integrated plan of action. This is one of the most important purposes of the budgeting process. It forces management to take each of the choices made and to make sure that it coordinates with other alternatives selected. It also presents management with a comprehensive picture of the expected effects of its decisions on the firm as a whole. Put another way, budgets are estimates of financial statements prepared before the actual transactions occur.

When used as a tool for planning, budgets are generally static. That is, the budgets are developed for a particular expected level of activity, usually sales or production in units. A single set of estimates is derived for sales, manufacturing costs, selling and administrative expenses, and profit. Such budgets are referred to as *static* budgets.

Tool for Control

Budgets provide estimates of what performance is expected to be. As such, they serve as criteria or standards for evaluating performance. A comparison of budgeted and actual amounts provides a basis for evaluating past performance and guiding future action. To be effective as tools for control, the budgets must be initially developed for individual responsibility centers. Budgets are developed for production, marketing, purchasing, administration, and so on. They are then integrated into a master budget for the firm as a whole. In this way, the performance of each responsibility center can be evaluated with respect to those activities over which it had control during a particular period.

Flexible Budgets When used as tools for control, budgets are generally *flexible*. That is, the budget for each responsibility center is expressed in the form of a particular level of fixed cost that is expected to be incurred regardless of the level of activity, and a variable cost per unit of activity that can change *in total* as the level of activity changes. The "flex" in a flexible budget is with respect to variable costs (that is, those costs that vary with changes in activity levels). The budget for fixed costs is static.

Example Studies of past cost behavior indicate that the Assembling Division of Standard Manufacturing Corporation should incur total fixed costs of $100,000 and variable costs of $10 per unit next period. For planning purposes, Standard estimates that 50,000 units will be produced by the Assembling Division. The static cost budget for the division used for planning purposes is therefore $600,000 [= $100,000 + ($10 × 50,000)]. Suppose, however, that due to unexpected demand during the period, the Assembling Division produced 70,000 units. It is not particularly useful *for control purposes* to compare the actual cost of producing 70,000 units with the expected cost of producing 50,000 units. The underlying levels of activity are different. To evaluate actual performance, the budget, or standard, must be expressed in terms of what costs should have been to produce 70,000 units. This is where the flexible budget comes in. It indicates that manufacturing costs should have been $800,000 [= $100,000 + ($10 × 70,000)] during the period. This is the most appropriate standard for control. Note that the estimates of fixed and variable costs form the inputs into both the static budget for planning and the flexible budget for control.

Tool for Employee Motivation

The importance of the human factor in the planning and control process is well known. Standards, or budgets, can serve as motivating devices for employees if the standards are set at levels that are tight but currently attainable with reasonably efficient performance. It is desirable that the budgets used for planning and control also serve as tools for employee motivation. In this way, a single budgeting and accounting system can be designed that will serve multiple purposes. In some instances, however, the budget of what costs are *expected to be* for planning purposes may be different from the level of costs that, when used as a standard for evaluating performance, will best motivate employees. In these cases, the budgeting and accounting system must be adaptable if it is to serve all purposes.

The Master Budget

The master budget, sometimes called the *comprehensive budget,* is a complete blueprint of the planned operations of the firm for a period. It emphasizes the relation of the various inputs in all areas of the company to final output and sales.

Its preparation requires a recognition of the interrelations among the various units of a firm. For example, to prepare a master budget requires knowing how a projected increase in sales of product A affects each of the following: the several producing departments; the selling, general, and administrative effort; and the financial position of the company.

Preparation of a master budget is a difficult, complex process that requires much time and effort by management at all levels. The difficulties of fitting all pieces together may be great, especially the first few times a master budget is prepared. Despite these difficulties, or perhaps because of them, the master budget is an effective instrument for planning and control. Its value has been proved so often that almost all organizations of any size recognize master budget preparation as a vital task of management.

No simple example can effectively convey the complexity of the process, but the illustration in the following pages is designed to indicate some of the problems and possible solutions.

Example The budget preparation process will be illustrated for Victoria Corporation for a single period of time. This example is continued in our discussion of performance evaluation in this chapter and in Chapter 13. An organization chart of Victoria Corporation appears in Exhibit 12.1. Each box in the organization chart is a responsibility center. The production, marketing, and corporate staff departments are not broken down further into additional responsibility centers to keep the illustrations simple.

Phase 1: Organizational Goals, Strategic Plans, and the Capital Budget

Operating budgets exist within a larger planning and control framework, as discussed in Chapter 11. Organizational goals and strategies for achieving them have a direct bearing on budgeted operations.

There is an ongoing interface between operating budgets and capital budgets as well. Capital investment decisions rely on cash flow forecasts that are presumably consistent with forecasts for operating budgets. Operations for a future period are constrained by the level of capacity, type of equipment, and so forth, provided by the capital budget.

Knowing where to start in forecasting activity levels may be a problem, but generally there is one critical or constraining factor that determines the level of activity. This is the factor that constrains the firm from doing everything management would like. For most firms the critical factor is the volume of anticipated sales. The critical factor could also be the availability of raw materials, or the supply of labor, or manufacturing capacity. We assume that budgeted sales is the critical factor for Victoria Corporation. We start with the sales budget; the other budgets build on the sales budget, as we shall soon see.

Phase 2: The Sales Forecast

The sales budget appears in Exhibit 12.2. Responsibility for preparing the budget usually belongs to the chief marketing executive of the firm. The marketing executive

Exhibit 12.1
VICTORIA CORPORATION
Organization Chart

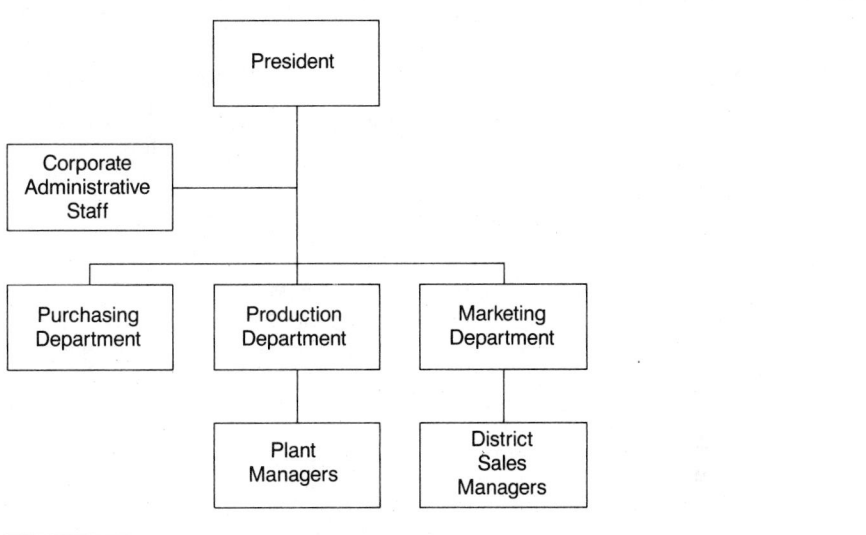

relies on inputs from the market research group as well as from salespersons or district managers in the field. The discussions among sales groups in budget preparation frequently serve to bring out problems in the firm's selling and advertising programs and to broaden the participants' thinking about the firm's place in the market.

Exhibit 12.2
VICTORIA CORPORATION
Sales Budget for Period 1

Optimistic	90,000 Units at $7	= $630,000
Median	70,000 Units at $6	= $420,000
Pessimistic	50,000 Units at $5	= $250,000

Previous sales experience is usually the starting point for sales budget estimates. These historical data are then modified to recognize market trends, anticipated changes in general economic conditions, altered advertising plans, and any other factors deemed relevant. In the end, the marketing executive usually makes the final decisions on the precise quantities and dollar amounts to be shown in the sales budget for each product.

Example Victoria Corporation produces one product that is expected to sell 70,000 units at $6 per unit. An initial sales forecast at Victoria Corporation was developed by the market research group, who estimated pessimistic, optimistic, and median forecasts of (1) total product sales in the market and (2) Victoria's market share.

The company defined "optimistic" as "probability of sales this high or higher is .2"; they defined "pessimistic" as "probability of sales this low or lower is .2"; and median sales were "50-50." The marketing vice-president also had district sales managers prepare optimistic, pessimistic, and median forecasts for their districts.

According to the marketing vice-president, who is the chief marketing executive at Victoria Corporation, the data bases used by the two groups differed:

> The market research group uses consumer studies, economic forecasts, and past data about the company. They provide a good macro-level forecast of economic conditions and consumer preferences for our products, but they know little about the day-to-day efforts of our sales personnel.
>
> This is where our sales managers' forecasts are most valuable. They know about potential customers, they know which of our present customers we are likely to lose, and they can forecast sales quite accurately for the first few months of the budget year. When I combine the forecasts of both the market research group and the sales managers, I have a good idea of both the market conditions affecting the demand for our product and the immediate needs of our customers.

The marketing vice-president combined the forecasts from the two groups with personal experience and knowledge of the company to prepare the forecasts shown in Exhibit 12.2. Although all three forecasts—optimistic, pessimistic, and median—are shown, only the median is used in our subsequent discussion to keep the example simple.

Production Budget

The sales budget, combined with knowledge of beginning inventory and estimates of desired ending inventories, form the basis of the production budget for the Victoria Corporation shown in the top panel of Exhibit 12.3. The number of units shown for ending inventory reflects management's desired inventory to service customers in the period following the one being budgeted.[1]

The quantity of each product to be produced is budgeted by using a variant of the basic accounting equation:

$$\text{Beginning Balance} + \text{Transfers in} = \text{Transfers out} + \text{Ending Balance},$$
$$BB + TI = TO + EB.$$

Expressing the equation in units, and relating it to the relationship between units produced and sold, the basic accounting equation is expressed as

$$\text{Units to Be Produced} = \text{Number of Units Sold} + \text{Units in Ending Inventory} - \text{Units in Beginning Inventory}.$$

The costs to be incurred in producing the desired number of units appear in the lower panel of Exhibit 12.3

---

[1]Chapter 8 discusses models for deriving optimal inventory levels.

Exhibit 12.3
VICTORIA CORPORATION
Production Budget
for the Budget Period

Units to Be Produced

Budgeted Sales, in Units (see sales budget)	70,000
Desired Ending Inventory (assumed)	8,000
Total Units Needed	78,000
Less Beginning Inventory (assumed)	(8,000)
Units to Be Produced	70,000

Cost Expected to Be Incurred

Direct Materials (1 pound per unit at $1.00 per pound)	$ 70,000
Direct Labor (⅛ hour per unit at $20 per hour)	175,000
Manufacturing Overhead:	
Indirect Labor ($.10 per unit)	7,000
Supplies ($.04 per unit)	2,800
Power ($1,000 per period plus $.03 per unit)	3,100
Maintenance ($13,840 per period)	13,840
Rent ($6,000 per period)	6,000
Insurance ($1,000 per period)	1,000
Depreciation ($10,360 per period)	10,360
Total Production Costs	$289,100

Direct Materials Direct materials are raw materials that are traceable to, or associated directly with, individual units produced. Direct materials are almost always a variable cost item. Each finished unit is estimated to require 1 pound of direct materials. The quantities of direct materials required per finished unit are based on engineering studies of material usage. The $1.00 cost per pound of the direct materials is based on studies of past cost behavior and projected prices of suppliers. Hence, the budgeted or standard direct materials cost per finished unit is $1.00 × 1 pound per finished unit = $1.00 per finished unit.[2]

Direct Labor Direct labor represents work traceable directly to particular units of product. Engineering time and motion studies and studies of past labor time usage behavior indicate that a unit requires about 7.5 minutes of labor time. This estimate allows for normal, periodic rest periods. The standard is sufficiently tight so that employees are motivated to perform efficiently. The standard wage rate, including fringe benefits and payroll taxes (for example, employer's share of Social Security and unemployment taxes) for production workers in Victoria Corporation's plant is $20.00 per hour and results from negotiations with the local labor union.

Manufacturing Overhead Whereas direct material and direct labor are traceable directly to particular units produced, manufacturing overhead costs are not. Manufacturing overhead costs either give a firm the capacity to produce (these are

---

[2]The terms "budgets" and "standards" are often used interchangeably when referring to estimated costs per finished unit.

usually fixed manufacturing overhead costs), or they are costs that vary with units produced but are not traceable directly to the units produced (that is, variable manufacturing overhead costs). As shown in Exhibit 12.3, indirect labor and supplies are variable manufacturing overhead costs. Power is a semivariable, or mixed, cost, having both variable and fixed components. Maintenance, rent, insurance, and depreciation are fixed manufacturing overhead costs.

These estimates are often based on past experience modified by projected changes in costs and production methods. Statistical regression methods can be applied to overhead to (1) separate fixed from variable overhead and (2) find the relationship between variable overhead and a measure of activity (for example, direct labor hours, output).[3] For Victoria Corporation, the measure of activity is output and variable manufacturing overhead is assumed to be $.17 per unit of output.

Summary of Production Budget The production budget in Exhibit 12.3 is a plan of production department activity for the period. The production manager must schedule production so that 70,000 units are manufactured. The production budget can help in evaluating the performance of the production department at the end of the period. If production in units and input costs are as projected, then the production department should incur costs of $289,100 during the period.

If the level of production differs from the projected amounts, then the flexible budget amounts must be applied to determine the amount of costs that should have been incurred. The flexible budget for the production department is

$$\begin{array}{l}\text{Total Budgeted}\\\text{Manufacturing}\\\text{Costs for}\\\text{Production}\\\text{Departments}\end{array} = \$32,200 + \left(\$3.67 \times \begin{array}{l}\text{Units}\\\text{Produced}\end{array}\right).$$

Fixed costs comprise the estimates for power, maintenance, rent, insurance, and depreciation: $32,200 = $1,000 + $13,840 + $6,000 + $1,000 + $10,360. Variable costs comprise the estimates for direct materials, direct labor, indirect labor, supplies, and power: $3.67 = $1.00 + $2.50 + $.10 + $.04 + $.03.

Marketing and Administrative Costs The budget for marketing costs for the Victoria Corporation's marketing department appears in Exhibit 12.4. All of the items except commissions and shipping costs are expected to be fixed. Commissions are 2 percent of sales dollars, or $.12 per unit if the selling price is $6 per unit as budgeted; $.12 = 2% × $6. Shipping costs are $.02 per unit shipped. Hence, the variable marketing cost per unit sold is $.14. Note that variable marketing costs vary with units *sold,* whereas variable manufacturing costs vary with units *produced.*

All of the central corporate administrative costs in Exhibit 12.5 are estimated to be fixed.

---

[3]Chapter 6 discusses methods of dividing manufacturing overhead costs into variable and fixed components.

Exhibit 12.4
VICTORIA CORPORATION
Marketing Cost Budget

Variable Cost

Commissions (2 percent of sales; see Exhibit 12.2, sales budget)	$ 8,400[a]	
Shipping Costs ($.02 per unit shipped; see Exhibit 12.2, sales budget)	1,400	
Total Variable Marketing Costs.		$ 9,800

Fixed Costs

Salaries ($25,000 per period)	$25,000	
Advertising ($30,000 per period)	30,000	
Sales Office ($8,400 per period)	8,400	
Travel ($2,000 per period)	2,000	
Total Fixed Marketing Costs		65,400
Total Marketing Cost Budget		$75,200

[a]Also, $.12 per unit sold × 70,000 units sold = $8,400.

Discretionary Fixed Costs Many of the so-called fixed costs in the production, marketing, and administration budgets are, in fact, discretionary costs. Maintenance, advertising, and donations are examples. Although they are budgeted as fixed costs, managers realize that these costs are not like committed costs (for example, factory rent), which are required to provide the firm's basic capacity to produce and market its product.

When economic conditions make it doubtful that the firm will achieve its budgeted profit goals, discretionary costs are often cut. When managers state that they have reduced their fixed costs, or reduced their breakeven points, often the cuts are discretionary costs, not committed costs. Discretionary costs are a tempting cost-cutting target because their reduction does not have serious short-term effects on production and marketing. The long-term consequences could be disastrous, however, if maintenance and advertising programs are discontinued.

Profit Plan (Budgeted Income Statement) The profit plan, or budgeted income statement, appears in Exhibit 12.6. The top part presents this statement on a var-

Exhibit 12.5
VICTORIA CORPORATION
Administrative Cost Budget

President's Salary	$10,000
Salaries of Other Staff Personnel	17,000
Supplies	2,000
Heat and Light	1,400
Rent	4,000
Donations and Contributions	1,000
General Corporate Taxes	8,000
Depreciation—Staff Office Equipment	1,400
Total Administrative Cost Budget.	$44,800

Exhibit 12.6
VICTORIA CORPORATION
Master Budget Profit Plan (income statement)

Variable Costing Basis

Sales (70,000 units at $6)	$420,000
Less: Variable Manufacturing Cost of Goods Sold (70,000 units at $3.67) . . .	(256,900)
Variable Marketing Costs (70,000 units at $.14)	(9,800)
Contribution Margin	$153,300
Less: Fixed Manufacturing Costs	(32,200)
Fixed Marketing and Administrative Costs	(110,200)
Operating Profits (variable costing)	$ 10,900

Full Absorption Costing Basis

Sales (70,000 units at $6)	$420,000
Less: Cost of Goods Sold (70,000 units at $4.13)[a].	(289,100)
Gross Margin.	$130,900
Less: Marketing and Administrative Costs.	(120,000)
Operating Profits (full absorption costing)	$ 10,900

[a]Full absorption manufacturing cost per unit
= Total Manufacturing Costs ÷ Total Units Produced
= $289,100 ÷ 70,000 Units
= $4.13 per Unit.

iable costing basis for internal, managerial use at Victoria Corporation; the bottom part shows the income statement prepared using full absorption costing, which is required for external financial reporting by generally accepted accounting principles and income tax regulations. Earlier chapters indicated that full absorption costing "unitizes" fixed manufacturing costs, which can be misleading for management decision making.

Note that although the format of the two statements differs, the operating profits are the same, because *units produced and sold are the same.* Later discussions examine the case when the two differ. For the rest of this chapter and the next, we rely on the variable costing profit plan, unless otherwise specified, in discussing the use of accounting for performance evaluation.

After compiling the budget, management finds that an operating profit of $10,900 has been projected. (Recall that this is *before taxes* and miscellaneous income and expenses.) If top management finds this budgeted result satisfactory, and adequate cash can be made available to carry out the operations, the master budget will be approved. If the budgeted results are considered unsatisfactory, additional thought and meetings will be devoted to considering ways in which the budgeted results might be improved through cost reductions or sales increases.

Summary of the Master Budget

The master budget comprehensively summarizes management's plans for the period covered. The master budget includes a budgeted balance sheet, a cash flow budget, and other budgets, as well as the profit plan developed in the preceding pages. Appendix A to this chapter presents the comprehensive master budget including the profit plan, budgeted balance sheets, and the cash flow budget.

Preparing the master budget usually requires the participation of all managerial groups from local plant and sales managers to the top executives of the company. Once the budget is prepared and adopted, it becomes a major planning and control instrument. Further, it becomes the authorization to produce units, to purchase materials, to hire employees, and to carry out other similar actions. In governmental units, the budget becomes the *legal* authorization for expenditure.

Master budgets are almost always static budgets; that is, they consider the likely results of operations at the one level of operations specified in the budget. This may facilitate the planning process, but it weakens the effectiveness of the budget as a control device if the scale of operations deviates from the planned level. Under those circumstances, flexible budgets are necessary. Flexible budgets consider the varying amounts of revenues and costs that are appropriate at various levels of operations. Flexible budgets are described in more detail below.

Using the Budget for Performance Evaluation and Control

This section shows how actual results are compared with budgets and how variances are derived for performance evaluation. The emphasis is on the use of the budget to control operations; hence, only the master budget profit plan is discussed.

Comparison of Actual Results with the Flexible and Master Budgets

The following presents a comparison of the master budget with the flexible budget and with actual results. This comparison ties the results of the planning process (which results in the master budget) with flexible budgeting, and forms the basis for analyzing differences between plans and actual results.

Flexible Versus Master Budget Exhibit 12.7 compares the flexible budget with the master budget profit plan for Victoria Corporation. The master budget is based on the profit plan in Exhibit 12.6. To review, some of the important amounts are as follows:

Sales Price per Unit	$6.00
Sales Volume per Period	70,000 Units
Variable Manufacturing Costs per Unit	$3.67
Variable Marketing Costs per Unit (2 percent sales commission plus $.02 per unit shipping costs)	$.14
Fixed Manufacturing Costs per Period	$32,200
Fixed Marketing Costs per Period	$65,400
Fixed Administrative Costs per Period	$44,800

Exhibit 12.7
VICTORIA CORPORATION
Flexible Budget and Profit Plan Volume Variance

	Flexible Budget (based on actual sales volume of 80,000)	Sales Volume Variance	Master Budget (based on a prediction of 70,000 units sold)
Sales	$480,000[a]	$60,000 F	$420,000[d]
Less:			
Variable Manufacturing Costs. . .	293,600[b]	36,700 U	256,900[e]
Variable Marketing Costs	11,200[c]	1,400 U	9,800[f]
Contribution Margin	$175,200	$21,900 F	$153,300
Less:			
Fixed Manufacturing Costs . . .	32,200	—	32,200
Fixed Marketing Costs	65,400	—	65,400
Fixed Administration Costs . . .	44,800	—	44,800
Operating Profit	$ 32,800	$21,900 F	$ 10,900

[a]80,000 units sold at $6.00.   [c]70,000 units sold at $3.67.
[b]80,000 units sold at $3.67.   [f]70,000 units sold at $.14.
[c]80,000 units sold at $.14.   U denotes "unfavorable" variance.
[d]70,000 units sold at $6.00.   F denotes "favorable" variance.

The flexible budget in this case is based on the actual sales volume.[4] Variable costs and revenues *should* change as volume changes. The flexible budget indicates what revenues and costs should be at various activity levels. The flexible budget can be thought of as the cost equation: $TC = F + VX$, where TC = total costs, F = budgeted fixed costs, V = budgeted variable cost per unit, and X = actual volume.

During the period, 80,000 units were sold. The difference of $21,900 between operating profits in the master budget and the flexible budget is due in part to this 10,000-unit difference in sales volume from the sales plan of 70,000 units. The $21,900 resulting from the 10,000-unit increase times the budgeted contribution margin per unit of $2.19 ($2.19 = $6.00 − $3.67 − $.14) is called a *sales volume variance* (also known as an *activity variance*).

What Is the Meaning of "Favorable" and "Unfavorable?" Note the use of "F" (favorable) and "U" (unfavorable) beside each of the variances in Exhibit 12.7. These terms describe the impact of the variance on the budgeted operating profits. A *favorable* variance means that the variance would *increase* operating profits, holding all other things constant. An *unfavorable* variance would *decrease* operating profits, holding all other things constant.

These terms are not used in a normative sense; thus, a "favorable" variance is

---

[4]The relevant activity variable is *sales* volume because this is a profit plan (that is, an income statement). If the objective were to compare the flexible *production* budget with the master production budget, then the relevant activity variable would be production volume. Sales and production volumes are assumed to be equal throughout this example, so we can avoid allocating fixed manufacturing costs to inventories. Later in this chapter, we relax this assumption.

not *necessarily* good, and an "unfavorable" variance is not *necessarily* bad. Further note the variable cost variances—they are labeled "unfavorable." Does this reflect unfavorable conditions in the company? Highly unlikely! These are variable costs that are *expected* to increase because the actual sales volume is higher than planned. In short, the labels "favorable" or "unfavorable" do not automatically connote "good" or "bad" conditions. Rather, a "favorable" variance implies that actual profits are higher than budgeted, all other things (for example, other variances) being ignored; conversely, an "unfavorable" variance implies that actual profits are lower than budgeted, all other things being ignored.

Information Use The information presented in Exhibit 12.7 has a number of uses. First, it shows that the increase in operating profits from the master budget is caused by the increase in sales volume over the level planned. Sales variances are usually the responsibility of the marketing department, so this information may be useful feedback to personnel in that department, and it may be informative for evaluating their performance. Second, the resulting flexible budget shows budgeted sales, costs, and operating profits *after* taking into account the volume increase, but *before* considering differences in *unit* selling prices, differences in *unit* variable costs, and differences in fixed costs from the master budgets.

Actual Results Versus Flexible Budget Assume that actual results for period 1 are as follows:

Sales Price per Unit	$6.10
Sales Volume for the Period	80,000 Units
Variable Manufacturing Costs per Unit	$3.82
Variable Marketing Costs per Unit	$.16
Fixed Manufacturing Costs for the Period	$34,000
Fixed Marketing Costs for the Period	$64,400
Fixed Administrative Costs for the Period	$44,600

Now the actual results can be compared with both the flexible budget and the master budget as shown in Exhibit 12.8. Columns (5), (6), and (7) are carried forward from Exhibit 12.7.

Column (1) in Exhibit 12.8 is calculated from the facts presented above. Column (2) summarizes purchasing and manufacturing variances, which are discussed in more detail later. Columns (3) and (4) show marketing and administrative variances. The favorable sales price variance of $8,000 is partly offset by increased commissions of $160 (= 2% × $8,000). The remaining $1,440 U marketing and administrative cost variance is just the residual: $12,800 actual − $11,200 flexible budget − $160 = $1,440. Variances would be presented in more detail to the managers of responsibility centers (for example, departments, plants, divisions) that have responsibility for them.

Overview of the Profit Variance

Exhibit 12.8 shows the source of the total variance from the profit plan—$15,700 favorable. First, a favorable variance of $21,900 is incurred because sales volume

Exhibit 12.8
VICTORIA CORPORATION
Comparison of Actual Results to Profit Plan Budget

	(1) Actual (based on actual sales volume of 80,000 units)	(2) Purchasing and Production Variances	(3) Marketing and Administrative Cost Variances	(4) Sales Price Variance	(5) Flexible Budget (based on actual sales volume of 80,000 units)	(6) Sales Volume Variance	(7) Master Budget (based on a plan of 70,000 units sold)
Sales	$488,000[a]	—	—	$8,000 F	$480,000[f]	$60,000 F	$420,000[i]
Less:							
Variable Manufacturing Costs	305,600[b]	$12,000 U	—	—	293,600[g]	36,700 U	256,900[j]
Variable Marketing Costs	12,800[c]	—	$1,440 U[d]	160 U[e]	11,200[h]	1,400 U	9,800[k]
Contribution Margin	$169,600	$12,000 U	$1,440 U	$7,840 F	$175,200	$21,900 F	$153,300
Less:							
Fixed Manufacturing Costs	34,000	1,800 U	—	—	32,200	—	32,200
Fixed Marketing Costs	64,400	—	1,000 F	—	65,400	—	65,400
Fixed Administrative Costs	44,600	—	200 F	—	44,800	—	44,800
Operating Profits	$ 26,600	$13,800 U	$ 240 U	$7,840 F	$ 32,800	$21,900 F	$ 10,900

Total Variance from Flexible Budget = $6,200 U

Total Variance from Master Budget = $15,700F

[a] 80,000 units sold at $6.10 per unit.
[b] 80,000 units sold at $3.82 per unit.
[c] 80,000 units sold at $.16 per unit.
[d] $1,440 U = $12,800 − $11,200 − $160.
[e] $160 U = .02 × $8,000 F sales price variance.
[f] 80,000 units sold at $6.00.
[g] 80,000 units sold at $3.67.
[h] 80,000 units sold at $.14.
[i] 70,000 units sold at $6.00.
[j] 70,000 units sold at $3.67.
[k] 70,000 units sold at $.14.
U denotes "unfavorable" variance.
F denotes "favorable" variance.

is 10,000 units higher than expected. If all else had gone according to plan, profits should have been $32,800—the flexible budget amount. However, profits are only $26,600 because of unfavorable cost variances, offset partly by a favorable selling price variance.

Think of Exhibit 12.8 as an *overview* of actual results, plans and variances. What is your overall assessment of Victoria Corporation's performance for the period? Clearly the company did better than expected, because sales prices and volume were both higher than expected. However, costs were also higher than expected, even after allowing for the increase in volume. The $12,000 unfavorable variable manufacturing cost variance could be particularly concerning. Note that the flexible budget has increased the allowance for variable manufacturing costs from $256,900 in the master budget to $293,600 in the flexible budget. However, the actual costs were even higher—$305,600. This implies either inefficiencies in manufacturing or that the company paid more than expected for variable manufacturing inputs, such as direct materials, direct labor, or variable manufacturing overhead items.

Reports like Exhibit 12.8 are important because they provide companies with an overview of variances from original plans. The master budget provides a financial expression of top management's plans for the company. It is a means of allocating resources to the organization's responsibility centers, and it helps coordinate purchasing, production, sales, financing, personnel hiring, and so forth. Variances from the master budget are followed closely to ascertain whether cutbacks or expansions of personnel are needed, whether additional or less financing is needed, whether material purchases should be curtailed or increased, and whether there are problems with operating efficiencies. These are only a few reasons why top management follows variances closely.

Key Variances Many top executives receive daily variance reports about a few key items. For example, airline officials receive variance reports on seats sold the previous day; officials in steel companies receive variance reports on the number of tons of steel produced; and officials of merchandising companies receive daily variance reports on sales. As these examples demonstrate, most of these key items deal with *output*. Input variances (that is, cost variances) usually require more detailed data collection and are reported weekly or monthly. Reports like Exhibit 12.8 that tie all the pieces together are less frequent; these reports are usually monthly, quarterly, or yearly.

Although reports like Exhibit 12.8 present the "big picture," they do not provide enough detail for analyzing variances. The next step in analyzing variances is to assign responsibility for them, to ascertain whether variances should be investigated further and corrective steps taken, and to reward or penalize employees where appropriate. Chapter 13 discusses these issues in more detail.

An Extension: Production Volume Does Not Equal Sales Volume

The previous example assumes that production volume equals sales volume. Although there are no new conceptual issues when production volume does not equal

Exhibit 12.9
VICTORIA CORPORATION
Comparison of Actual to Budget
When Production and Sales Volumes Are Not Equal
(incomplete report)

	(1) Actual (based on actual sales volume of 80,000 units)	(2) Purchasing and Production Variances	(3) Marketing and Administrative Cost Variances	(4) Sales Price Variance	(5) Flexible Budget (based on actual sales volume of 80,000 units)	(6) Sales Volume Variance	(7) Master Budget (based on a plan of 70,000 units sold)
Sales	$488,000	—	—	$8,000 F	$480,000	$60,000 F	$420,000
Less: Variable Manufacturing Costs	?	?			?	?	?
Variable Marketing and Administrative Costs	12,800	—	1,440 U	160 U	11,200	1,400 U	9,800
Contribution Margin	$?	$?	$1,440 U	$7,840 F	$?	$?	$?
Less: Fixed Manufacturing Costs	34,000	1,800 U	—	—	32,200	—	32,200
Fixed Marketing Costs	64,400	—	1,000 F	—	65,400	—	65,400
Fixed Administrative Costs	44,600	—	200 F	—	44,800	—	44,800
Operating Profits	$?	$?	$ 240 U	$7,840 F	$?	$?	$ 10,900

sales volume, managerial accounting students and managers who use accounting data sometimes find the effects of this inequality confusing. (Hence, we encourage you to be familiar with Exhibit 12.8 before continuing.)

Production Volume Greater Than Sales Volume

Assume the following *new* facts for Victoria Corporation:

Planned Production Volume . . . . 75,000 Units
Actual Production Volume . . . . 85,000 Units

Other facts are the same as in the previous example—they are repeated here for convenience:

	Actual	Budget/ Standard
Sales Price per Unit	$6.10	$6.00
Sales Volume for the Period	80,000 Units	70,000 Units
Variable Manufacturing Costs per Unit.	$3.82	$3.67
Variable Marketing Costs per Unit	$.16	$.14
Fixed Manufacturing Costs for the Period.	$34,000	$32,200
Fixed Marketing Costs for the Period	$64,400	$65,400
Fixed Administrative Costs for the Period.	$44,600	$44,800

Variable selling and administrative costs are affected by *sales* volume only. Assume that there was no beginning inventory.

Exhibit 12.9 presents the amounts that are not changed when we relax the assumption that sales and production volumes are equal. For example, all of the marketing and administrative costs are the same in Exhibit 12.9 as in Exhibit 12.8, because they do not vary with production volume. The amounts that may change because sales and production volumes are not equal are indicated by a ''?'' in Exhibit 12.9.

Manufacturing Costs Are the budgeted variable manufacturing costs in columns (5) and (7) based on budgeted *sales volume* or budgeted *production volume?* Are the actual costs in column (1) based on actual *sales* volume or actual *production* volume? The answer may be surprising. Both the flexible and master budgets are based on *sales* volume; hence, the variable manufacturing costs in columns (5) and (7) of Exhibit 12.9 are the same as in Exhibit 12.8: $293,600 and $256,900, respectively. As a result, the variable manufacturing cost amount in column (6) would be $36,700 U—the same as in Exhibit 12.8.

The total variable manufacturing cost variance based on units *manufactured* is calculated as follows:

$$\begin{array}{l} \text{Total} \\ \text{Variable} \\ \text{Manufacturing} \\ \text{Cost Variance} \end{array} = \begin{array}{c} \text{Actual Variable} \\ \text{Manufacturing Cost} \\ \text{per Unit Times} \\ \textit{Actual} \text{ Number} \\ \text{of Units } \textit{Produced} \end{array} - \begin{array}{c} \text{Budgeted (or } \textit{Standard}\text{)} \\ \text{Variable Manufacturing} \\ \text{Cost per Unit Times} \\ \textit{Actual} \text{ Number of} \\ \text{Units } \textit{Produced} \end{array}$$

$$= (\$3.82 \times 85{,}000 \text{ Units}) - (\$3.67 \times 85{,}000 \text{ Units})$$

$$= \$.15 \times 85{,}000 \text{ Units}$$

$$= \$12{,}750 \text{ Unfavorable.}$$

Although the variance *per unit* is the same here as in the previous example—$.15 per unit—the total variance is higher by $750 because 85,000 units were produced here, whereas only 80,000 units were produced in the previous example ($750 = $.15 per unit × 5,000 additional units produced).

Prorating Variances The amount of the $12,750 variance that is allocated to column (2) in Exhibit 12.9 depends on whether or not manufacturing variances are *prorated* (that is, allocated) between units sold and those in ending inventory. If variances are prorated, the calculation is as follows:

$12,750 × (80/85) = $12,000 Assigned to Units Sold

$12,750
Total Variable
Manufacturing $12,750 × (5/85) = $750 Assigned to Units Still in Inventory
Cost Variance

In this case, the amounts in columns (1) and (2) would be the same in Exhibit 12.9 as in Exhibit 12.8—$305,600 actual variable manufacturing cost and a $12,000 unfavorable variance. The $750 variance allocated to inventory would not be reported as a variance in the income statement until those units are sold.

Variances Not Prorated If variances are *not prorated* for Victoria Corporation, the amounts in Exhibit 12.9 would be as follows: column (2), $12,750; column (1), $306,350 (= $293,600 allowed in the flexible budget plus $12,750 unfavorable variance). Hence, the actual variable manufacturing costs in column (1) would be based on actual costs of the 80,000 units sold (that is, $305,600) plus the variance attached to the 5,000 units produced but not sold.

Common Practice Is Not to Prorate Variances Companies generally do *not* prorate variances for internal reporting purposes. If prorating has little effect on inventory values and measures of profit, managers may consider it a waste of time.

In addition, production variances are often not prorated because they are considered to be *period* costs by managers. If a variance results from production in a particular period, managers want it reported that period, not in some future period.

What if variances are sufficiently large that failure to prorate would materially misstate inventories or net income for financial reporting to shareholders? In such a case, variances would be prorated for external reporting. Even so, they need not be prorated for internal reporting if prorating them serves no useful purpose.

Exhibit 12.10 shows the completed statement, assuming that variable manufacturing cost variances are not prorated.

Incentives for Accurate Forecasts

You can see the importance of the sales forecast to the entire budget process from our Victoria Corporation example. If the sales forecast is too high, for example, and the company produces to meet the forecast, then the company will have excess inventory.

If the sales forecast is too low, sales opportunities are likely to be missed because purchasing and production were planning on lower operating levels. Or, to meet unexpected sales demand, employees will be worked overtime and paid a premium, emergency purchases of materials and supplies will be made at prices above normal, and other costs will be incurred because production, purchasing, personnel, and other departments were not prepared to meet the sales demand. Yet sales personnel might ''look good'' because there are favorable sales variances.

Rewarding managers only for accurate forecasting could create disincentives for better performance—managers would try just to meet the forecast, but not to beat it. Companies use many different methods of providing incentives for both accurate forecasting *and* performance. These methods include comparing sales forecasts from year to year, and obtaining forecasts from multiple sources. Probably the most common method of ascertaining the reasonableness of forecasts is for sales managers to know enough about their subordinates' products and territories that they have intuitive knowledge of what is reasonable. Formal incentive models have also been developed; these are discussed in Appendix B to this chapter.

Our emphasis has been on the sales forecast in this section. The discussion applies, however, to any type of forecast where the forecaster has incentives to bias the forecast.

Summary

This chapter discusses the 1-year operating budget, which is used for planning, control, and employee motivation. After management makes decisions about products to produce, pricing, levels of output, production techniques, and so forth, the choices are translated into a formal plan of action, known as the master budget profit plan. This plan starts with goals and objectives—a plan is not very helpful unless goals are specified.

The first item to be forecast is the critical factor that most constrains the firm. This is the marketplace for most firms; hence, the sales forecast is usually the place to start. Input for sales forecasts is usually provided by both sales personnel and market research staff. These groups are increasingly being asked to provide probabilistic estimates of sales. The budgeted volume is a function of the sales forecast and desired beginning and ending inventory levels. Budgeted material purchases and labor needs are a function of the production budget. The quantities of direct materials and direct labor required to make a product are estimated using

Exhibit 12.10
VICTORIA CORPORATION
Comparison of Actual to Budget
When Production and Sales Volumes Are Not Equal
(complete report)

	(1) Actual (based on actual sales volume of 80,000 units)	(2) Purchasing and Production Variances	(3) Marketing and Administrative Cost Variances	(4) Sales Price Variance	(5) Flexible Budget (based on actual sales volume of 80,000 units)	(6) Sales Volume Variance	(7) Master Budget (based on a plan of 70,000 units sold)
Sales	$488,000	—	—	$8,000 F	$480,000	$60,000 F	$420,000
Less:							
Variable Manufacturing Costs	306,350	$12,750 U	—	—	293,600	36,700 U	256,900
Variable Marketing Costs	12,800	—	$1,440 U	160 U	11,200	1,400 U	9,800
Contribution Margin	$168,850	$12,750 U	$1,440 U	$7,840 F	$175,200	$21,900 F	$153,300
Less:							
Fixed Manufacturing Costs	34,000	1,800 U	—	—	32,200	—	32,200
Fixed Marketing Costs	64,400	—	1,000 F	—	65,400	—	65,400
Fixed Administrative Costs	44,600	—	200 F	—	44,800	—	44,800
Operating Profits	$ 25,850	$14,550 U	$ 240 U	$7,840 F	$ 32,800	$21,900 F	$ 10,900

engineering studies, blueprints, and product specifications. The cost per unit of input is based on projected materials' prices and labor wage rates, fringe benefits, and payroll taxes. Whereas direct materials and direct labor costs are often "engineered"—that is, traceable directly to a unit of finished product—manufacturing overhead costs are not. Estimates of marketing and administrative costs complete the profit plan. (The profit plan is only one part of the master budget, which also includes the cash budget and budgeted balance sheet. Appendix A to this chapter presents the complete master budget.)

The master budget profit plan is fixed, that is, based on the *projected* sales volume. The flexible budget is based on the *actual* sales volume, however. Whereas the fixed budget shows budgeted costs at the projected sales volume, the flexible budget shows budgeted costs at the *actual* sales volume.

Exhibit 12.8 summarizes the following comparison:

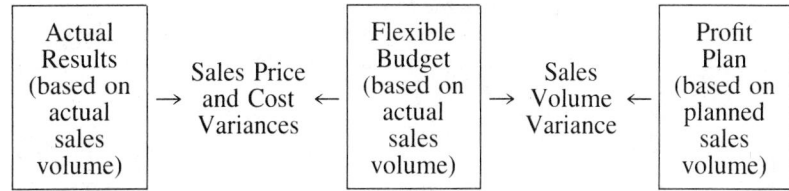

When production volume and sales volume are not equal, the purchasing and manufacturing variances will differ depending on whether or not variances are prorated to goods remaining in inventories and then sold. If variances are not prorated, then the purchasing and manufacturing variances shown in exhibits like Exhibit 12.10 are based on *production activity, not sales activity*. Hence, variances presented are a hybrid of variances based on sales activity and those based on production activity. The sales volume variance, sales price variance, and marketing cost variances are related to sales activity, whereas the manufacturing and purchasing cost variances are related to production activity. Administrative variances may be related to sales activity, to production activity, or to neither.

People who provide forecasts that will be used to establish budgets for performance evaluation are likely to have incentives to bias those forecasts. For example, sales personnel who know their performance will be evaluated based on whether or not they beat their forecasts have incentives to bias those forecasts down. If sales personnel are rewarded only for accurate sales forecasts, then they have incentives to bias their forecasts downward, thus making them easily achieved, and to keep actual performance results from bettering the forecast.

Appendix A: Comprehensive Master Budget—Victoria Corporation

This appendix presents the comprehensive master budget for Victoria Corporation. First, we summarize the profit plan developed in the chapter. Second, we tie the profit plan into the other budgets, such as the cash budget and the capital budget. Finally, we present the budgeted balance sheet. The master budget ties together the financial activities of the firm for the budget period. Hence, it can be very

Exhibit 12.11
VICTORIA CORPORATION
Summary of Sales, Production, and Cost Budgets

Sales Budget[a]

70,000 Units at $6 . . . . $420,000

Production Budget[b]

Units to Be Produced

Budgeted Sales, in Units (see sales budget).	70,000
Desired Ending Inventory (assumed)	8,000
Total Units Needed	78,000
Beginning Inventory (assumed)	8,000
Units to Be Produced	70,000

Cost Expected to Be Incurred

Direct Materials (1 pound per unit at $1.00 per pound)		$ 70,000
Direct labor (1/8 hour per unit at $20 per hour)		175,000
Manufacturing Overhead:		
Indirect Labor ($.10 per unit)	$ 7,000	
Supplies ($.04 per unit)	2,800	
Power ($1,000 per period plus $.03 per unit).	3,100	
Maintenance ($13,840 per period)	13,840	
Rent ($6,000 per period)	6,000	
Insurance ($1,000 per period)	1,000	
Depreciation ($10,360 per period)	10,360	44,100
Total Production Costs.		$289,100

Marketing Cost Budget[c]

Variable Costs

Commissions (2 percent of sales; see sales budget)	$ 8,400	
Shipping Costs ($.02 per unit shipped; see sales budget)	1,400	
Total Variable Marketing Costs.		$ 9,800

Fixed Costs

Salaries ($25,000 per period)	$25,000	
Advertising ($30,000 per period)	30,000	
Sales Office ($8,400 per period)	8,400	
Travel ($2,000 per period)	2,000	
Total Fixed Marketing Costs		65,400
Total Marketing Cost Budget		$ 75,200

Administrative Cost Budget[d]

President's Salary	$ 10,000
Salaries of Other Staff Personnel	17,000
Supplies.	2,000
Heat and Light	1,400
Rent	4,000
Donations and Contributions.	1,000
General Corporate Taxes.	8,000
Depreciation—Staff Office Equipment	1,400
Total Administrative Cost Budget	$ 44,800

[a]*Source:* Exhibit 12.2.   [c]*Source:* Exhibit 12.4.
[b]*Source:* Exhibit 12.3.   [d]*Source:* Exhibit 12.5.

useful for both planning and coordination. For example, planning for cash needs requires knowing cash flows from/to operating activities and knowing cash needs for the capital budget.

Exhibit 12.11 summarizes the information from the chapter about projected sales and production volumes, revenues, and costs. Exhibit 12.12 presents the master budget profit plan from the chapter.

Exhibit 12.12
VICTORIA CORPORATION
Master Budget Profit Plan

Variable Costing Basis

Sales (70,000 units at $6)	$420,000
Less:	
Variable Manufacturing Cost of Goods Sold (70,000 units at $3.67)	(256,900)
Variable Marketing Costs (70,000 units at $.14)	(9,800)
Contribution Margin	$153,300
Less:	
Fixed Manufacturing Costs	(32,200)
Fixed Marketing and Administrative Costs	(110,200)
Operating Profits (variable costing)	$ 10,900

Full Absorption Costing Basis

Sales (70,000 units at $6)	$420,000
Less:	
Cost of Goods Sold (70,000 units at $4.13)	(289,100)
Gross Margin	$130,900
Less:	
Marketing and Administrative Costs	(120,000)
Operating Profits (full absorption costing)	$ 10,900

Source: Exhibit 12.6.

Materials Purchases Budget

The purchasing department is responsible for purchasing materials in Victoria Corporation. Exhibit 12.13 presents the materials purchases budget. The production budget is the basis for the materials purchases budget. For simplicity in presentation, it is assumed that payments to suppliers equal purchases each period.

Exhibit 12.13
VICTORIA CORPORATION
Materials Purchases Budget

Quantities to Be Purchased (in pounds)	
Units to Be Used (see Exhibit 12.11)	70,000
Purchases Required at a Budgeted Cost of $1 per Pound	$70,000
There are no materials inventories.	

Capital Budget

The capital budget, Exhibit 12.14, shows the Victoria Corporation's plan for acquisition of depreciable, long-term assets during the next period. Management plans to purchase major items of equipment. Part of the cost will be financed by the issuance of notes payable in a later period to equipment suppliers. The note issuance is deducted from the cost of the acquisitions to determine current cash outlays for equipment. An alternative, accepted treatment would have viewed the note issuance as a cash inflow, with the entire cost of the equipment included in cash outflows.

Exhibit 12.14
VICTORIA CORPORATION
Capital Budget

	Period 1
Acquisition of New Factory Machinery	$12,000
Miscellaneous Capital Additions.	2,000
Total Capital Budget.	$14,000
Borrowings for New Machinery—Long-Term Notes Payable.	(6,000)
Current Cash Outlay.	$ 8,000

Cash Outlays Budget

A schedule of the planned cash outlays for the budget period is presented in Exhibit 12.15. The first six items are taken from the cash outlay lines of earlier exhibits. Each period, the Victoria Corporation pays the income taxes accrued in the previous period. Income taxes payable at the start of the budget period are shown to be $6,200 on the beginning balance sheet (column 1 of Exhibit 12.19). Dividends of $5,000 are expected to be declared and paid in the budget period.

Exhibit 12.15
VICTORIA CORPORATION
Cash Outflows Budget

	Period 1
Materials (Exhibit 12.13)	$ 70,000
Labor (Exhibit 12.11)	175,000
Manufacturing Overhead (Exhibit 12.11)[a]	33,740
Marketing Costs (Exhibit 12.11)	75,200
Administrative Costs (Exhibit 12.11)[b].	43,400
Capital Expenditures (Exhibit 12.14).	8,000
Payments on Short-Term Notes[c]	13,000
Interest[c].	3,000
Income Taxes[d]	6,200
Dividends[c].	5,000
Total Cash Outflows.	$432,540

[a]Manufacturing overhead costs − depreciation = $44,100 − $10,360 = $33,740.
[b]Administrative costs − depreciation = $44,800 − $1,400 = $43,400.
[c]Assumed for illustration.
[d]Income taxes on earnings of previous period are paid in current period. The amount is assumed in this case.

Receivables and Collections Budget

Most of the sales of each period are collected in the period of sale, but there is some lag in collections. The budget for cash collections from customers is shown in Exhibit 12.16. Collections for sales of a given period normally occur as follows: 85 percent in the period of sale and 15 percent in the next period. It would be possible to introduce sales discounts and estimates of uncollectible accounts into the illustration, but they are omitted for simplicity. The estimated accounts receivable at the start of the budget period of $71,400 are shown on the beginning balance sheet (column 1 of Exhibit 12.19). The amount represents 15 percent of the sales of $476,000 of the previous period ($71,400 = .15 × $476,000). In the budget period, 85 percent of sales is expected to be collected, leaving $63,000 in Accounts Receivable at the end of the budget period ($63,000 = 15 percent of budget period sales of $420,000).

Cash Budget

Cash flow is so important for any organization that no budget is more important for financial planning than the cash budget, illustrated in Exhibit 12.17. This budget is significant because it helps management in planning to avoid unnecessary idle cash balances on the one hand, or unneeded, expensive borrowing on the other. Most firms prepare a cash budget rather than a budgeted statement of changes in financial position.

The budgeted amounts for cash outflows and collections from customers are taken from Exhibits 12.15 and 12.16, respectively. The other income is made up of interest and miscellaneous revenues. It is estimated to be $2,000 for the period.

Budgeted (Pro Forma) Income and Retained Earnings Statement

All of the previous budget information is pulled together in the budgeted income and retained earnings statement and the budgeted balance sheet. The former is

Exhibit 12.16
VICTORIA CORPORATION
Receivables and Collections Budget

	Budget Period
Accounts Receivable, Start of Period:	
From the Period Immediately Preceding the Budget Period (15 percent of $476,000)	$ 71,400
Budget Period Sales	420,000
Total Receivables	$ 491,400
Less Collections:	
Current Period (85 percent of $420,000)	$(357,000)
Previous Period (15 percent of $476,000)	(71,400)
Total Collections	$(428,400)
Accounts Receivable, End of Period	$ 63,000

Exhibit 12.17
VICTORIA CORPORATION
Cash Budget

	Budget Period
Cash Receipts:	
Collections from Customers (Exhibit 12.16)	$428,400
Other Income[a]	2,000
Total Receipts	$430,400
Cash Outflows (Exhibit 12.15)	(432,540)
Increase (Decrease) in Cash During Period	$ (2,140)
Cash Balance at Start of Period[a]	79,800
Cash Balance at End of Period	$ 77,660

[a]Assumed for illustration.

illustrated in Exhibit 12.18. At this stage in the budgeting process, management's attention switches from decision making, planning, and control to external reporting to shareholders. That is, management becomes particularly interested in how the results of its decisions will be reflected in the income statement and balance sheet. Accordingly, the budgeted income statement and balance sheet are often prepared in accordance with generally accepted accounting principles. That is why we call the statement in Exhibit 12.18 an *income statement* rather than a profit plan, and we present it using full absorption costing as required for external reporting.

Compilation of all of the data for the period indicates a budgeted income of $6,039. If top management finds this budgeted result satisfactory, and adequate

Exhibit 12.18
VICTORIA CORPORATION
Budgeted (pro forma) Income and Retained Earnings Statement

Sales (70,000 units at $6)	$420,000
Less Cost of Goods Sold (70,000 units at $4.13)	(289,100)
Gross Margin.	$130,900
Less Marketing Expenses	(75,200)
Less Administrative Expenses.	(44,800)
Operating Income (Exhibit 12.12).	$ 10,900[a]
Other Income (Exhibit 12.17)	2,000
	$ 12,900
Less Interest Expense (Exhibit 12.15)	(3,000)
Pretax Income	$ 9,900
Less Income Taxes[b]	(3,861)
Net Income	$ 6,039
Less Dividends (Exhibit 12.15)	(5,000)
Increase in Retained Earnings.	$ 1,039
Retained Earnings at Start of Period (Exhibit 12.19)	56,500
Retained Earnings at End of Period (Exhibit 12.19)	$ 57,539

[a]This is the amount called operating profits on the master budget profit plan, Exhibit 12.12.

[b]Income taxes average approximately 39 percent of pretax income. The amount $3,861 is shown as the end of this period income taxes payable in Exhibit 12.19.

cash can be made available to carry out the operations as indicated by Exhibit 12.17, the master budget will be approved. If the budgeted results are not considered satisfactory, much additional thought and many additional meetings will be devoted to considering ways in which the budgeted results might be improved through cost reductions or altered sales plans.

Budgeted Balance Sheet

The final exhibit of this series, Exhibit 12.19, shows the budgeted balance sheets at the start and end of the period. (The budget is prepared before the beginning of the budget period; hence, the beginning balance sheet is unknown when the budget

Exhibit 12.19
VICTORIA CORPORATION
Budgeted Balance Sheet

	Start of Budget Period	End of Budget Period
Assets		
Current Assets		
Cash (Exhibit 12.17)	$ 79,800	$ 77,660
Accounts Receivable (Exhibit 12.16)	71,400	63,000
Finished Goods	33,040[a]	33,040[a]
Total Current Assets	$184,240	$173,700
Plant Assets		
Equipment (Exhibit 12.14)	460,000	474,000
Less Accumulated Depreciation	(162,000)[b]	(173,760)[b]
Total Assets	$482,240	$473,940
Equities		
Current Liabilities		
Accounts Payable	$ 96,540[b]	$ 96,540[b]
Short-term Notes and Other Payables	41,000[b]	28,000[b]
Income Taxes Payable (Exhibits 12.15 and 12.18)	6,200	3,861
Total Current Liabilities	$143,740	$128,401
Long-Term Liabilities		
Long-Term Equipment Notes (Exhibit 12.14)	82,000[b]	88,000[b]
Total Liabilities	$225,740	$216,401
Shareholders' Equity		
Capital Stock ($20 par value)	$200,000[b]	$200,000[b]
Retained Earnings (Exhibit 12.18)	56,500[b]	57,539[b]
Total Shareholders' Equity	$256,500	$257,539
Total Equities	$482,240	$473,940

[a]8,000 units in inventory according to Exhibit 12.11 at $4.13 per unit. $4.13 was given in the chapter as the full absorption manufacturing cost per unit.
[b]Assumed for purposes of illustration.

is prepared. For example, a budget prepared for the coming calendar year starting January 1 would usually be prepared the preceding September through November.)

Here, as in the budgeted income statement, management will have to decide if the budgeted overall results will be acceptable. Will cash balances be satisfactory? Is the receivables turnover up to plan? Will the final capital structure and debt-equity ratio conform to management's desires? If the budgeted balance sheet and income statement are satisfactory, they will become the initial benchmarks against which actual performance in the ensuing period is checked.

Summary of the Master Budget

The master budget is a summary of management's plans for the period covered. Preparing the master budget is usually a complex, dynamic process requiring the participation of all managerial groups from local plant and sales managers to the top executives of the firm and the board of directors. Once the budget is prepared and adopted, it becomes the major planning and control instrument.

Master budgets are almost always static budgets; that is, they consider the likely results of operations at the one level of operations specified in the budget. If preparing the master budget requires a lot of hand calculation, then it can be cumbersome and costly to prepare multiple master budgets. As the process is computerized, it becomes less costly to develop multiple master budgets that take into account the various uncertainties such as market conditions, material prices, labor difficulties, and government regulations facing the firm.

Appendix B: Incentive Model for Truthful Reporting

Methods of providing incentives for truthful reporting have been developed in the Soviet Union and independently reported in the literature.[5] The objective is to provide incentives *both* for truthful reporting *and* for high performance.

Example Assume that the Harrison Raviv Company solicits sales forecasts from each of its district sales managers. These forecasts become budgets against which actual sales are compared to evaluate performance.

The firm's general manager of marketing wants to provide each district sales manager with a salary and a bonus. Previously the bonus had been based on beating the budget. The managers, however, began to "low-ball" the forecasts. Management knew this was happening, but they did not know how high the forecasts *should* have been, because they did not have the information the managers had. The general manager of marketing explained:

---

[5]See M. Weitzman, "The New Soviet Incentive Model," *Bell Journal of Economics* (Spring 1976); J. Gonik, "Tie Salesmen's Bonuses to Their Forecasts," *Harvard Business Review* (May–June 1978); Y. Ijiri, J. Kinard, and F. Putney, "An Integrated Evaluation System for Budget Forecasting and Operating Performance with a Classified Bibliography," *Journal of Accounting Research* (Spring 1968); and Robert Kaplan, *Advanced Management Accounting* (Englewood Cliffs, N.J.: Prentice-Hall, 1982), chap. 17.

Managers could always counter our arguments with data that we could not audit. Their low estimates wreaked havoc with our production schedules, purchasing, and hiring decisions.

Next we tried to give them incentives for accurate forecasts. They were rewarded if the actual sales were close to the forecasts, and penalized if actual and forecast deviated a lot. With this system, the managers forecast sales at a level that was sufficiently low to be achievable, then they "managed" their sales such that actual was almost right at the forecast. The consequences were that they had disincentives to beat the budget. Also, our internal auditors found numerous cases where managers had delayed sales orders until the following year and even turned down some orders because they did not want the current year's sales to overshoot the forecast.

The incentive plan to deal with this problem has three components.

1. Rewards are positively related to forecasted sales to give managers incentives to forecast high rather than low. Thus, if b_1 is a bonus coefficient that is a percent of forecasted sales, and forecasted sales are $\hat{Y}$, then this component of the bonus is:

$$b_1\hat{Y}.$$

2. Incentives are given to increase sales even if the budget has been "beaten" by rewarding managers for the excess of actual sales, Y, over the forecast, $\hat{Y}$. If b_2 is the bonus coefficient that is a percent of the excess of Y over $\hat{Y}$, then this component of the bonus is:

$$b_2(Y - \hat{Y}), \qquad \text{for } Y \geq \hat{Y}.$$

3. When actual sales, Y, are less than the forecast, $\hat{Y}$, the manager is penalized. If b_3 is the bonus coefficient that is a percent of the shortfall, $\hat{Y} - Y$, then this component of the bonus is:

$$-b_3(\hat{Y} - Y), \qquad \text{for } \hat{Y} > Y.$$

If B is the dollar bonus paid to the manager, then the overall bonus plan is:

$$B = \begin{cases} b_1\hat{Y} + b_2(Y - \hat{Y}), & \text{for } Y \geq \hat{Y} \text{ (that is, when actual exceeds the forecast);} \\ b_1\hat{Y} - b_3(\hat{Y} - Y), & \text{for } \hat{Y} > Y \text{ (that is, when the forecast exceeds actual).} \end{cases}$$

The coefficients are set such that

$$b_3 > b_1 > b_2 > 0,$$

and a rule of thumb is that b_3 should be at least 30 percent greater than b_1, and b_1 should be at least 30 percent greater than b_2.[6] This incentive plan is intended to reward both accurate forecasts and outstanding performance.

---

[6]See Weitzman, "The New Soviet Incentive Model," pp. 253–254.

Example Harrison Raviv Company established an incentive system using the methods described above. Exhibit 12.20 shows the bonus that would be paid for various combinations of forecasted sales and actual sales. For example, if the forecast is $1,100,000 and the actual sales are $1,000,000, the district sales manager receives a bonus of $48,000; if both the forecast and actual sales are $1,100,000, the sales manager receives a bonus of $55,000; and so forth.

Implications

What are the implications of this incentive system? If you read down a column in Exhibit 12.20, you will see that after making the forecast, the manager is always rewarded for more sales even if an increase in sales makes the forecast inaccurate. Reading across the rows reveals that the highest bonus is paid when the forecast equals actual; hence, the manager is rewarded for accurate forecasts.

The major objective of this incentive system is to provide incentives for accurate forecasting and sales output simultaneously. Although our example has dealt with sales forecasts, the method described could be used for virtually any type of forecasting (for example, production levels, costs, productivity). At this point, there has been little practical experience with this incentive plan (outside the Soviet Union), so we have little evidence about implementation difficulties. Whereas the method appears to be a clever innovation, we shall have to see it in operation

Exhibit 12.20
HARRISON RAVIV COMPANY
Incentives for Accurate Forecasting
Bonus Paid to District Sales Managers
(000 omitted from sales and bonus amounts)

Let b_1 = 5 percent; b_2 = 3 percent, and b_3 = 7 percent

$$B = \begin{cases} .05\hat{Y} + .03(Y - \hat{Y}), & \text{for } Y \geq \hat{Y}; \\ .05\hat{Y} - .07(\hat{Y} - Y), & \text{for } \hat{Y} > Y. \end{cases}$$

		Forecasted Sales, $\hat{Y}$		
		$1,000	$1,100	$1,200
Actual Sales, Y	$1,000	50[a]	48[d]	46[g]
	$1,100	53[b]	55[e]	53[h]
	$1,200	56[c]	58[f]	60[i]

[a]$50 = .05($1,000).
[b]$53 = .05($1,000) + .03($1,100 − $1,000).
[c]$56 = .05($1,000) + .03($1,200 − $1,000).
[d]$48 = .05($1,100) − .07($1,100 − $1,000).
[e]$55 = .05($1,100).

[f]$58 = .05($1,100) + .03($1,200 − $1,100).
[g]$46 = .05($1,200) − .07($1,200 − $1,000).
[h]$53 = .05($1,200) − .07($1,200 − $1,100).
[i]$60 = .05($1,200).

before we pass judgment on it. (Note that the bonus coefficients, b_1, b_2, and b_3, can be adjusted to suit the needs of the particular situation. The examples shown here are reportedly similar to those used in the Soviet system.)

In summary, incentive methods have been developed that reward both for accurate forecasts and for good performance: (1) Rewards are positively related to forecasted sales to give incentives to forecast high rather than low; (2) additional rewards are given for beating the forecast; and (3) penalties are given for results worse than forecast.

Problem 1 for Self-Study[7]

In April, Computer Supply, Inc. produced and sold 50,000 minicomputer cases at a sales price of $10 each. (Budgeted sales were 45,000 units at $10.15.)

Budget

Standard Variable Costs per Unit This Month, as in Previous Months . .	$4.00
Fixed Manufacturing Overhead Cost: Monthly Budget	$ 80,000
Marketing and Administrative:	
Variable	$1.00 per Case
Fixed (monthly budget)	$100,000

Actual

Actual Manufacturing Costs:	
Variable Costs per Unit	$4.88
Fixed Overhead	$ 83,000
Actual Marketing and Administrative:	
Variable (50,000 at $1.04)	$ 52,000
Fixed	$ 96,000

Using variable costing, prepare a report comparing actual results with the flexible and master budgets for April. Include variances.

---

[7]This self-study problem continues in Chapter 13.

Suggested Solution

Comparison of Actual to Budget, April

	Actual (based on 50,000 units)	Purchasing and Production Variances	Marketing and Administrative Variances	Sales Price Variances	Flexible Budget (based on 50,000 units)	Sales Volume Variance	Master Budget (based on 45,000 units)
Sales Revenue	$500,000	—	—	$7,500 U	$507,500	$50,750 F	$456,750
Less:							
Variable Manufacturing Costs	244,000	$44,000 U	—	—	200,000	20,000 U	180,000
Variable Marketing and Administrative Costs .	52,000	—	$2,000[a] U	—	50,000	5,000 U	45,000
Contribution Margins . .	$204,000	$44,000 U	$2,000 U	$7,500 U	$257,500	$25,750 F	$231,750
Less:							
Fixed Manufacturing Costs	83,000	3,000 U	—	—	80,000	—	80,000
Fixed Marketing and Administrative Costs . .	96,000	—	4,000 F	—	100,000	—	100,000
Operating Profits	$ 25,000	$47,000 U	$2,000 F	$7,500 U	$ 77,500	$25,750 F	$ 51,750

Total Variance from
Flexible Budget = $52,500 U

Total Variance from
Master Budget = $26,750 U

[a]$2,000 = $.04 × 50,000 = ($1.04 − 1.00) 50,000 units.

Problem 2 for Self-Study (Appendix B)[8]

Starting with a pastry shop on the Upper West Side of New York more than 15 years ago, Peter Kirillov's current operation consists of a chain of 10 pastry shops scattered around the New York area. Capitalizing on recipes handed down from one of his ancestors, Kirillov's pastries were known for their excellence.

Recently, Kirillov became disturbed by the poor profit performance of some of the chain's branches, which he suspects is linked to poor production planning. Because of the high quality standards imposed on the pastry chain's products, branch managers are expected to match daily production as closely as possible to daily sales. Day-old pastries are marked down 50 percent. Should a particular type of pastry run out, a branch manager can schedule a rush order at his or her discretion. This, however, may increase production costs by as much as 40 percent above standard.

Kirillov is convinced that if branch managers forecasted sales more accurately, production planning would improve, resulting in greater profits. About a year ago, Kirillov's childhood friend, Raskolnikov, mentioned a new incentive plan in one of his letters. This plan, Raskolnikov said, was designed to provide an incentive for more accurate forecasting in the Soviet shoe factory he managed. Kirillov feels that such a bonus plan might provide the necessary incentive for his managers to forecast sales more accurately.

a. Suppose that daily sales for a typical pastry store range from $2,000 to $4,000. What bonus would a branch manager receive daily for forecasting daily sales of $2,000, $2,500, $3,000, $3,500, and $4,000 under the following incentive plan?

$$\text{Bonus} = \begin{cases} 0.03\hat{Y} + 0.01(Y - \hat{Y}) & \text{for } Y > \hat{Y}, \\ 0.03\hat{Y} - 0.05(\hat{Y} - Y) & \text{for } \hat{Y} > Y, \end{cases}$$

where

$$\hat{Y} = \text{Forecasted Sales in Dollars}$$

$$Y = \text{Actual Sales in Dollars}$$

b. Discuss the disincentives to overforecast or underforecast in the bonus plan developed in part **a**.

---

[8]J. Lim.

Suggested Solution

a.

Actual Sales, Y   **Forecasted Sales, Ŷ**

	$2,000	$2,500	$3,000	$3,500	$4,000
$2,000	$60[a]	$50[f]	$40[k]	$30[p]	$20[u]
$2,500	$65[b]	$75[g]	$65[l]	$55[q]	$45[v]
$3,000	$70[c]	$80[h]	$90[m]	$80[r]	$70[w]
$3,500	$75[d]	$85[i]	$95[n]	$105[s]	$95[x]
$4,000	$80[e]	$90[j]	$100[o]	$110[t]	$120[y]

[a]$60 $= 0.03(\$2,000)$.
[b]$65 $= 0.03(\$2,000) + 0.01(\$2,500 - \$2,000)$.
[c]$70 $= 0.03(\$2,000) + 0.01(\$3,000 - \$2,000)$.
[d]$75 $= 0.03(\$2,000) + 0.01(\$3,500 - \$2,000)$.
[e]$80 $= 0.03(\$2,000) + 0.01(\$4,000 - \$2,000)$.
[f]$50 $= 0.03(\$2,500) - 0.05(\$2,500 - \$2,000)$.
[g]$75 $= 0.03(\$2,500)$.
[h]$80 $= 0.03(\$2,500) + 0.01(\$3,000 - \$2,500)$.
[i]$85 $= 0.03(\$2,500) + 0.01(\$3,500 - \$2,500)$.
[j]$90 $= 0.03(\$2,500) + 0.01(\$4,000 - \$2,500)$.
[k]$40 $= 0.03(\$3,000) - 0.05(\$3,000 - \$2,000)$.
[l]$65 $= 0.03(\$3,000) - 0.05(\$3,000 - \$2,500)$.
[m]$90 $= 0.03(\$3,000)$.
[n]$95 $= 0.03(\$3,000) + 0.01(\$3,500 - \$3,000)$.
[o]$100 $= 0.03(\$3,000) + 0.01(\$4,000 - \$3,000)$.
[p]$30 $= 0.03(\$3,500) - 0.05(\$3,500 - \$2,000)$.
[q]$55 $= 0.03(\$3,500) - 0.05(\$3,500 - \$2,500)$.
[r]$80 $= 0.03(\$3,500) - 0.05(\$3,500 - \$3,000)$.
[s]$105 $= 0.03(\$3,500)$.
[t]$110 $= 0.03(\$3,500) + 0.01(\$4,000 - \$3,500)$.
[u]$20 $= 0.03(\$4,000) - 0.05(\$4,000 - \$2,000)$.
[v]$45 $= 0.03(\$4,000) - 0.05(\$4,000 - \$2,500)$.
[w]$70 $= 0.03(\$4,000) - 0.05(\$4,000 - \$3,000)$.
[x]$95 $= 0.03(\$4,000) - 0.05(\$4,000 - \$3,500)$.
[y]$120 $= 0.03(\$4,000)$.

b. From the bonus payoff matrix developed in part **a**, we see that overforecasting is penalized (5 percent of each forecasted sales dollar in excess of actual sales). On the other hand, underforecasting results in the excess of actual sales over forecasted sales being rewarded at a lower rate. For every level of actual sales, the highest bonus is paid when the forecast equals actual sales.

Questions

1. Review the meaning of the following concepts or terms discussed in this chapter.

   a. Budgets as planning tools.   **c.** Static budget.

   b. Budgets as control tools.   **d.** Flexible budget.

e. Master budget.

f. Variances.

g. Prorating variances.

h. Sales volume variance.

i. Favorable versus unfavorable variance.

2. "Last month we sold more units than planned, yet our performance report shows unfavorable sales volume variances for all variable manufacturing costs. I don't consider an increase in sales to be unfavorable." Please explain.

3. Why is a variable costing format more useful than a full absorption format for performance reporting?

4. A sales manager was criticized by a superior for selling high-revenue, low-profit items instead of lower-revenue but higher-profit items. The sales manager responded: "My income is based on commissions that are a percent of revenues. Why should I care about profits; I care about revenues!" Comment.

5. "The flexible budget is a poor benchmark. You should develop a budget and stay with it." Comment.

6. Why is the sales forecast so important in developing the master budget?

7. When would the master budget profit equal the flexible budget profit?

8. Managers in some companies claim that they do not use flexible budgeting, yet they compute a sales volume variance that takes into account total variable cost changes. How is that different from flexible budgeting?

9. The sales volume variance is sometimes computed using revenue only, and at other times is computed taking costs into account. What is the difference between these methods? What are the advantages and disadvantages of each?

Exercises

10. *Solving for Materials Requirements.* Bala Company expects to sell 84,000 units of finished goods over the next 3-month period. The company currently has 44,000 units of finished goods on hand and wishes to have an inventory of 48,000 units at the end of the 3-month period. To produce 1 unit of finished goods requires 4 units of raw materials. The company currently has 200,000 units of raw materials on hand and wishes to have an inventory of 220,000 units of raw materials on hand at the end of the 3-month period.

How many units of raw materials must the Bala Company purchase during the 3-month period?

11. *Solving for Budgeted Manufacturing Costs.* PQR Company expects to sell 100,000 units of product during the current year. Budgeted costs per unit are $120 for direct materials, $100 for direct labor, and $50 (all variable) for manufacturing overhead. PQR Company began the period with 30,000 units of finished goods on hand and wants to end the period with 10,000 units of finished goods on hand.

Compute the budgeted manufacturing costs of the PQR Company for the current period. Assume no beginning or ending inventory of work in process.

12. *Solving for Cash Collections (Appendix A).* Jones Corporation normally collects cash from credit customers as follows: 50 percent in the month of sale, 30 percent in the first month after sale, 18 percent in the second month after sale, and 2 percent are never collected. Sales, all on credit, of Jones Corporation are expected to be as follows:

January	$500,000
February	600,000
March	400,000
April	500,000

    a. Calculate the amount of cash expected to be received from customers during March.

    b. Calculate the amount of cash expected to be received from customers during April.

13. *Solving for Cash Payments (Appendix A).* Wallace Corporation purchases raw materials on account from various suppliers. It normally pays for 60 percent of these in the month purchased, 30 percent in the first month after purchase, and the remaining 10 percent in the second month after purchase. Raw materials purchases during the last 5 months of the year were as follows:

August.	$1,400,000
September	1,800,000
October	2,000,000
November	3,500,000
December	1,500,000

Determine the budgeted amount of cash payments to suppliers for the months of October, November, and December.

14. *Analyzing Contribution Margin Variances.* Austin Co. prepared a budget last period that called for sales of 7,000 units at a price of $12 each. The costs per unit were estimated to amount to $5 variable and $3 fixed. During the period, production was exactly equal to actual sales of 7,100 units. The selling price was $12.15 per unit. Variable costs were $5.90 per unit. Selling and administrative costs were all fixed at $15,000.

   Prepare a performance report to show the difference between the actual contribution margin and the master budget.

15. *Analyzing Gross Profit Changes (CPA adapted).* Garfield Company, which sells a single product, provided the following data for calendar years 1986 and 1987:

	1986	1987
Sales Volume.	180,000 Units	150,000 Units
Sales Revenue	$720,000	$750,000
Cost of Goods Sold	(575,000)	(525,000)
Gross Profit	$145,000	$225,000

What impact did the changes in sales volume and changes in sales price have on the gross profit?

16. *Preparing Budgets and Deriving Variances.* Alamo Products provided the following information about its 1985 results:

	Actual	Master Budget
Beginning Inventory:		
Fixed Costs.	$ 12,000	$ 12,000
Variable Costs.	6,000	6,000
Current Manufacturing Costs:		
Variable	280,000	300,000
Fixed	600,000	540,000
Ending Inventory:		
Variable	56,000	30,000
Fixed	120,000	108,000

There were 3,000 units in the beginning inventory. The master budget called for the production of 70,000 units; however, 65,000 were actually produced. Ending inventory contained 13,000 units. The company uses the FIFO inventory system.

Determine the budgeted and actual cost of goods sold.

17. *Preparing Flexible Budgets (CPA adapted).* The following information is provided concerning the operations of the Full Ton Company for the current period:

	Actual	Master Budget
Sales Volume	90 Units	100 Units
Sales Revenue	$9,200	$10,000
Manufacturing Cost of Goods Sold:		
Direct Labor.	$1,420	$ 1,500
Direct Materials	1,200	1,400
Variable Overhead	820	1,000
Fixed Overhead	485	500
Cost of Goods Sold	$3,925	$ 4,400
Gross Profit.	$5,275	$ 5,600
Operating Costs:		
Marketing Costs:		
Variable	$ 530	$ 600
Fixed	1,040	1,000
Administrative Costs:		
Variable	500	500
Fixed	995	1,000
Total Operating Costs.	$3,065	$ 3,100
Operating Profits	$2,210	$ 2,500

There are no inventories.

Prepare a flexible budget for the Full Ton Company.

18. *Comparing Master Budget to Actual Results.* Use the information for the Full Ton Company (Exercise **17**) to prepare a performance report that will enable management to isolate the variance between master budget and actual results.

19. *Prorating Variances.* Granada Company computed its total variable manufacturing cost variance for March to be $11,220 unfavorable. The company produced 224,400 units and sold 176,320 units. Assuming there was no beginning inventory, how much of the variance would be assigned to units sold and how much to ending inventory?

20. *Prorating Variances.* Fiero Company provides the following information for the month of August:

Beginning Inventory	10,000 units
Production.	90,000 units
Sales	92,000 units
Variable Manufacturing Cost Variances	$20,000 favorable

Fiero uses FIFO and prorates variances.
    a.   Prorate the $20,000 F variance to ending inventory and to units sold.
    b.   Compare the impact on operating profit of prorating versus not prorating variances.

21. *Incentives for Accurate Forecasting (Appendix B).* Compute the bonus, B, paid to a pizza company's franchise managers using the following formulas:

$$B = b_1\hat{Y} + b_2(Y - \hat{Y}), \text{ for } Y \geq \hat{Y}$$

$$B = b_1\hat{Y} - b_3(\hat{Y} - Y), \text{ for } \hat{Y} > Y$$

$$\text{where } b_1 = 4\%,$$

$$b_2 = 2\%,$$

$$b_3 = 6\%,$$

$$\hat{Y} = \text{forecasted sales revenue},$$

$$Y = \text{actual sales revenue}.$$

Let Y and $\hat{Y}$ each have values of $2,500, $3,000, and $3,500.

22. *Incentives for Accurate Forecasting (Appendix B).* Compute the monthly bonus, B, paid to an automobile dealership manager using the following formulas:

$$B = b_1\hat{Y} + b_2(Y - \hat{Y}), \text{ for } Y \geq \hat{Y}$$

$$B = b_1\hat{Y} - b_2(\hat{Y} - Y), \text{ for } \hat{Y} > Y$$

$$\text{where } b_1 = \$100 \text{ per car}$$

$$b_2 = \$70 \text{ per car}$$

$$b_3 = \$150 \text{ per car}$$

$$\hat{Y} = \text{forecasted sales of cars (in units)}$$

$$Y = \text{actual number of cars sold.}$$

Let Y and $\hat{Y}$ each have values of 20 cars, 21 cars, 22 cars, 23 cars, and 24 cars.

23. *Flexible Budgeting—Manufacturing Costs.* As a result of studying past cost behavior and adjusting for expected price increases in the future, Wilson Corporation estimates that its manufacturing costs will be as follows:

Direct Materials	$2.00 per Unit
Direct Labor.	$1.50 per Unit
Manufacturing Overhead:	
Variable	$ .50 per Unit
Fixed	$50,000 per Period

Wilson adopts these estimates for planning and control purposes.

    a. Wilson Corporation expects to produce 10,000 units during the next period. Prepare a schedule of the expected manufacturing costs.

    b. Suppose that Wilson Corporation produces only 8,000 units during the next period. Prepare a flexible budget of manufacturing costs for the 8,000-unit level of activity.

    c. Suppose that Wilson Corporation produces 13,000 units during the next period. Prepare a flexible budget of manufacturing costs for the 13,000-unit level of activity.

24. *Marketing Cost Budget.* Refer to the marketing cost budget of the Victoria Corporation shown in Exhibit 12.4. Prepare a flexible marketing cost budget for the period assuming the following levels of sales and shipments.

	Case 1	Case 2	Case 3
Units	60,000	75,000	64,000

25. *Administrative Cost Budget.* Refer to the central corporate administrative budget of the Victoria Corporation in Exhibit 12.5. Prepare a flexible central corporate administrative cost budget for the period, assuming that production and sales were 100,000 units. Is the term ''flexible budget'' a misnomer in this case? Explain.

26. *Computing Sales Price and Volume Variances.* Budgeted sales of Holt Electronics Corporation for 19X0 were as follows:

Product X (5,000 units)	$100,000
Product Y (200 units)	20,000
Product Z (50,000 units)	250,000
Total Budgeted Sales	$370,000

Actual sales for the period were as follows:

Product X (5,300 units)	$111,300
Product Y (240 units)	23,040
Product Z (48,000 units)	192,000
Total Actual Sales	$326,340

Calculate the sales price and volume variances for sales of each of the three products.

27. *Estimating Flexible Selling Expense Budget and Computing Variances.* Reynolds Products, Incorporated, estimates that the following selling expenses will be incurred next period:

Salaries (fixed)	$ 20,000
Commissions (.05 of sales revenue)	15,000
Travel (.03 of sales revenue)	9,000
Advertising (fixed)	50,000
Sales Office Costs ($4,000 plus $.05 per unit sold).	7,000
Shipping Cost ($.10 per unit sold).	6,000
Total Selling Expenses	$107,000

    a. Estimate the cost equation ($y = a + bx$) for selling expenses.

    b. Assume that 50,000 units are sold during the period at an average price of $6 per unit. Determine the sales price and volume variance.

    c. The actual selling expenses incurred during the period were $110,000. Assuming that sales were as given in part **b**, calculate the total selling expense variance.

Problems and Cases

28. *Comparing Actual to Budgeted Production Costs (CMA adapted).* The Melcher Co. produces farm equipment at several plants. The business is seasonal and cyclical in nature. The company has attempted to use budgeting for planning and controlling activities, but the fluctuating nature of the business has caused some company officials to be skeptical about the usefulness of budgeting to the company. The accountant for the Adrian plant has been using flexible budgeting to help the plant management control operations. The accountant presents the following data.

Planned Level of Production for January 19X0 (in units)	**4,000**

Budgeted Cost Data:	
Direct Materials ($9.00 per unit)	$36,000
Direct Labor ($6.00 per unit)	$24,000
Variable (with production):	
Indirect Labor	$ 6,650
Indirect Materials	600
Repairs.	750
Total Variable.	$ 8,000
Fixed:	
Depreciation	$ 3,250
Supervision	3,000
Total Fixed.	$ 6,250
Total Manufacturing Costs	$74,250

Actual Data for January 19X0	
Units Produced.	3,800
Costs Incurred:	
Material	$36,000
Direct Labor	25,200
Indirect Labor	6,000
Indirect Materials	600
Repairs	1,800
Depreciation	3,250
Supervision	3,000
Total.	$75,850

a. Prepare a flexible budget for January based on planned production levels of 3,800 units and of 4,000 units.

b. Prepare a report for January comparing actual and flexible budget costs based on the actual level of production for the month.

29. *Projected Income Statements.* The Norwood Corporation has patented a new household product and is now actively marketing it. Its income statement for the first quarter of 19X2 is shown below.

The $7 per unit manufacturing cost is presently made up of material cost, $2; direct labor cost, $4; and overhead costs, $1. The productive capacity of the present plant, working one 8-hour shift per day, is 50,000 units per quarter. The sales manager is certain that additional units could be sold if they were available. Top management is reluctant to increase the size of the plant and, instead, decides to consider the advisability of adding a second, and perhaps a third, shift.

The production manager estimates the following:

(1) Each additional shift would increase output by 50,000 units per quarter.

(2) If a second shift were added, labor costs per unit on the output of that shift would be 10 percent higher and total overhead cost would be increased 25 percent.

(3) If a third shift were added, labor costs per unit for the output of that shift would be 25 percent higher than for one-shift operations and total overhead would be 75 percent higher than for one-shift operations. With three-shift operations, it is estimated that material costs of all units could be reduced 4 percent due to larger quantity purchases.

The sales manager estimates the following:

(1) 100,000 units a quarter could be sold at the current price; but in order to sell 150,000 units each quarter, the unit price would have to be reduced by 5 percent.

(2) Selling expenses for 100,000 units per quarter will be 50 percent higher and for 150,000 units will be 90 percent higher than for 50,000 units.

Total administrative costs are expected to increase by 20 percent and by 40 percent from the 50,000 unit figure for sales of 100,000 units and 150,000 units, respectively.

Prepare projected second-quarter income statements assuming:
  a. Two-shift operations.
  b. Three-shift operations.

THE NORWOOD CORPORATION
Partial Income Statement
January 1 to March 31, 19X2

Sales (50,000 units at $10 per unit)		$500,000
Operating Costs:		
Cost of Goods Sold ($7 per unit)	$350,000	
Selling Costs	45,000	
Administrative Costs.	30,000	
Total Costs		425,000
Operating Profit		$ 75,000

30. *Solving for Unknowns in the Budgeted Income Statement (adapted from a problem by David O. Green).* A partial income statement for 19X0 of Baines Manufacturing Corporation appears below.

Inventories are usually kept at minimal levels, and production each year is equal to sales. Each dollar of finished product produced in 19X0 contained $.50 of direct materials. $.33⅓ of direct labor, and $.16⅔ of overhead costs. During 19X0, fixed overhead costs were $40,000. No changes in production methods or credit policies are anticipated for 19X1.

BAINES MANUFACTURING CORPORATION
Partial Income Statement for 19X0

Sales (100,000 units at $10)		$1,000,000
Cost of Goods Sold		600,000
Gross Margin		$ 400,000
Selling Costs.	$150,000	
Administrative Costs	100,000	
Operating Profit Before Taxes		250,000
		$ 150,000

Management has estimated the following changes for 19X1:

30 percent increase in number of units sold.

20 percent increase in unit cost of materials.

15 percent increase in direct labor cost per unit.

10 percent increase in variable overhead cost per unit.

5 percent increase in fixed overhead costs.

8 percent increase in selling costs because of increased volume.

6 percent increase in administrative costs arising solely because of increased wages.

There are no other changes.

a. What must the unit sales price be in 19X1 for Baines Manufacturing Corporation to earn $200,000 before taxes?

b. What will be the 19X1 profit before taxes if selling prices are increased, as above, but unit sales increase by 10 percent, rather than 30 percent? (Selling costs would go up by only one-third of the amount projected above.)

c. If selling price in 19X1 were to remain at $10 per unit, how many units must be sold in 19X1 for pretax profit to be $200,000?

31. *Differential Analysis and Budgeting.* The Monmouth Company is preparing its budget for the year 19X1. If the same selling policies that were in effect in 19X0 are continued in 19X1, the budget officer estimates that the profit plan will appear as shown below.

All variable costs vary with the number of units sold. The company could increase its output to 1 million units per year without increasing its fixed manufacturing and administrative costs. In order to increase its income, the company is seeking to utilize the presently unused capacity. Two plans have been suggested to improve the income picture.

Plan A. It is estimated that unit sales could be increased by 25 percent if **(1)** selling price per unit is reduced by 5 percent, and **(2)** an additional advertising campaign is instituted that would increase fixed selling costs by $15,000.

Plan B. The company has an opportunity to obtain a government contract for an additional 200,000 units if it quotes a low enough price. If the government contract were obtained, it would have no effect on the regular sales of 800,000 units.

a. Assuming that plan A were adopted and the results are as anticipated, present the profit plan for 19X1.

b. If it is anticipated that plan A would function as planned, what is the lowest price the company should bid on the government contract in Plan B? (Show your computations.)

c. If it is decided that plan A is not feasible, what is the lowest price the company should bid on the government contract? (Show your computations.)

THE MONMOUTH COMPANY
Projected Partial Profit Plan
Year 19X1

Sales (800,000 units at $2 per unit)			$1,600,000
Operating Costs:			
Cost of Goods Sold:			
Variable	$600,000		
Fixed	300,000		
Total Cost of Goods Sold		$900,000	
Administrative Costs:			
Variable	$ 20,000		
Fixed	100,000		
Total Administrative Costs.		120,000	
Selling Costs:			
Variable	$ 30,000		
Fixed	120,000		
Total Selling Costs		150,000	
Total Operating Costs			(1,170,000)
Operating Profit			$ 430,000

32. *Computing Master Budget Given Actual Data.* Enterprises lost the only copy of the master budget for this period. Management wants to evaluate this period's performance, but feels they need the master budget to do so. Actual results for the period were as follows:

Sales Volume.	120,000 Units
Sales Revenue	$672,000
Variable Costs:	
Manufacturing.	(147,200)
Marketing and Administrative	(61,400)
Contribution Margin	$463,400
Fixed Costs:	
Manufacturing.	(205,000)
Marketing and Administrative	(113,200)
Operating Profit	$145,200

The company planned to produce and sell 108,000 units at a price of $5 each. At that volume, the contribution margin would have been $380,000. Variable marketing and administrative costs are budgeted at 10 percent of sales revenue. Manufacturing fixed costs are estimated at $2 per unit at the normal production level. Management notes: "We budget an operating profit of $1 per unit."

    a. Construct the master budget for the period.

    b. Prepare a report comparing actual sales to the flexible budget and master budget.

33. *Adapting Budget Control Concepts to a Research Organization (CMA adapted).* The Argo Company has an extensive research program. The research activity is well organized. Each project is required to be broken down into phases, with the completion times and the cost of each phase estimated. The project descriptions and related estimates serve as the basis for development of the annual research department budget.

The schedule below presents the costs for the approved research activities for a recent year. The actual costs incurred by project or overhead category are compared to the approved activity and the variances noted on this same schedule.

The director of research prepared a narrative statement of research performance for the year to accompany the schedule. The director's statement follows the schedule.

ARGO COMPANY
Comparison of Actual with Budgeted Research Costs
(in thousands)

	Approved Activity for the Year	Actual Costs for the Year	(Over) Under Budget
Projects in Progress:			
4–1	$ 23.2	$ 46.8	$(23.6)
5–3	464.0[a]	514.8	(50.8)
New Projects:			
8–1	348.0	351.0	(3.0)
8–2	232.0	257.4	(25.4)
8–3	92.8	—	92.8
Total Research Costs	$1,160.0	$1,170.0	$(10.0)
General Research Overhead Costs			
(allocated to projects in proportion to their direct costs):			
Administration	$ 50.0	$ 52.0	$ (2.0)
Laboratory Facilities	110.0	118.0	(8.0)
Total	$ 160.0	$ (170.0)	$(10.0)
Allocated to Projects	(160.0)	(170.0)	(10.0)
Balance	–0–	–0–	–0–
Total Research Costs	$1,160.0	$1,170.0	$(10.0)

[a]Phases 3 and 4 only.

The year has been most successful. The two projects, 4–1 and 8–1, scheduled for completion in this year were finished. Project 8–2 is progressing satisfactorily and should be completed next year as scheduled. The fourth phase of project 5–3, with estimated direct research costs of $100,000 and the first phase of project 8–3, both included in the approved activity for the year, could not be started because the principal researcher left our employment. They were resubmitted for approval in next year's activity plan.

From the information given, prepare an alternative schedule that will provide the management of Argo Company with better information than the existing schedule by which to judge the research cost performance for the given year. (*Hint:* Separate direct from indirect costs.)

34. *Performance Evaluation Using Flexible Budgets (CMA adapted).* Persons Deli is planning to expand operations and, hence, is concerned that its performance reporting system may need improvement. The budgeted income statement for its Akron Persons Deli, which contains a delicatessen and restaurant operation, is (in thousands) as follows:

	Delicatessen	Restaurant	Total
Gross Sales	$1,000	$2,500	$3,500
Purchases.	$ 600	$1,000	$1,600
Hourly Wages	50	875	925
Franchise Fee	30	75	105
Advertising	100	200	300
Utilities	70	125	195
Depreciation	50	75	125
Lease Cost	30	50	80
Salaries	30	50	80
Total	$ 960	$2,450	$3,410
Operating Profit	$ 40	$ 50	$ 90

The performance report that the company uses for management evaluation is as follows:

PERSONS RESTAURANT-DELI
Akron, Ohio
Net Income for the Year
(in thousands)

	Actual Results				Over (Under) Budget
	Delicatessen	Restaurant	Total	Budget	
Gross Sales	$1,200	$2,000	$3,200	$3,500	$(300)[a]
Purchases[b]	780	800	1,580	1,600	(20)
Hourly Wages[b]	60	700	760	925	(165)
Franchise Fee[b]	36	60	96	105	(9)
Advertising.	100	200	300	300	—
Utilities[b]	76	100	176	195	(19)
Depreciation	50	75	125	125	—
Lease Cost	30	50	80	80	—
Salaries	30	50	80	80	—
Total	$1,162	$2,035	$3,197	$3,410	$(213)
Operating Profit	$ 38	$ (35)	$ 3	$ 90	$ (87)

[a]There is no sales price variance.
[b]Variable costs. All other costs are fixed.

Prepare a schedule to indicate the flexible budget and relevant variances for the delicatessen department.

35. *Comprehensive Problem.* The Krate Company, a small manufacturing firm, makes wooden crates. Its master budget income statement for the month of May is presented below.

	Master Budget (based on 8,000 units)
Sales Revenue (8,000 units at $20)	$160,000
Less:	
Variable Manufacturing Costs	80,000[a]
Variable Marketing and Administrative Costs	8,000[b]
Contribution Margin	$ 72,000
Less:	
Fixed Manufacturing Costs	20,000
Fixed Marketing and Administrative Costs	45,000
Operating Profit	$ 7,000

[a] 8,000 budgeted units at $10 unit.
[b] 8,000 budgeted units at $1 per unit.

The following estimates are used by the company to prepare the master budget:

Sales Price	$ 20 per Crate
Sales Volume.	8,000 Crates
Production Volume	8,000 Crates
Variable Manufacturing Costs	$ 10 per Crate
Variable Marketing and Administrative Costs.	$ 1 per Crate
Fixed Manufacturing Costs	$20,000
Fixed Marketing and Administrative Costs.	$45,000

Assume that the actual results for May were as follows:

	Actual
Sales Price	$ 19 per Crate
Sales Volume	10,000 Crates
Variable Manufacturing Costs	$105,440
Variable Marketing and Administrative Costs	$ 11,000
Fixed Manufacturing Costs	$ 21,000
Fixed Marketing and Administrative Costs	$ 44,000

Compare the master budget, flexible budget, and actual results for the month of May.

36. *Comprehensive Problem with Unequal Production and Sales Volumes.* Given the master budget in Problem **35,** assume that the actual results for May were as follows:

Sales Price	$ 19 per Crate
Sales Volume	10,000 Crates
Production Volume.	12,000 Crates
Variable Manufacturing Costs	$126,528 ($10.544 per crate)
Variable Marketing and Administrative Costs	$ 11,000
Fixed Manufacturing Costs	$ 21,000
Fixed Marketing and Administrative Costs	$ 44,000

Compare the master budget, flexible budget, and actual results for the months of May. Assume that variances are not prorated.

37. *Prorating Variances.* Using the results from Problem **36,** prorate variances to units sold and those in ending inventory, assuming no beginning inventory.

38. *Production Budget, Budgeted Income Statement, and Cash Forecast (Appendix A) (CPA adapted).* Modern Products Corporation, a manufacturer of molded plastic containers, determined in October 19X0 that it needed cash to continue operations. The corporation began negotiating for a 1-month bank loan of $100,000 starting November 1, 19X0. The loan would carry interest at the rate of 1 percent per month. Interest and principal would be repaid on November 30, 19X0. In considering the loan, the bank requested a projected income statement and cash budget for the month of November.

The following information is available:

(1) Sales were budgeted at 120,000 units per month in October 19X0, December 19X0, and January 19X1, and at 90,000 units in November 19X0.

The selling price is $2 per unit. Sales are billed on the 15th and last day of each month on terms of 2/10, net 30. (That is, a 2 percent discount is offered for payment within 10 days. Payment is due, in any case, within 30 days.) Experience indicates that sales occur evenly throughout the month and that 50 percent of the customers pay the billed amount within the discount period. The remainder pay at the end of 30 days, except for uncollectible amounts, which average ½ percent of gross sales. On its income statement the corporation deducts the estimated amounts for cash discounts on sales and expected uncollectibles from sales.

(2) The inventory of finished goods on October 1 was 24,000 units. The finished goods inventory at the end of each month is to be maintained at 20 percent of sales anticipated for the following month. There is no work in process.

(3) The inventory of raw materials on October 1 was 22,800 pounds. At the end of each month, the raw materials inventory is to be maintained at not less than 40 percent of production requirements for the following month. Materials are purchased as needed in minimum quantities of 25,000 pounds per shipment. Raw material purchases of each month are paid in the next succeeding month on terms of net 30 days.

(4) All salaries and wages are paid on the 15th and last day of each month for the period ending on the date of payment.

(5) All manufacturing overhead and selling and administrative expenses are paid on the 10th of the month following the month in which incurred. Selling expenses are 10 percent of gross sales. Administrative expenses, which include depreciation of $500 per month on office furniture and fixtures, total $33,000 per month.

(6) The manufacturing budget for molded plastic containers, based on expected production of 100,000 units per month, is as follows:

Materials (50,000 pounds, $1.00 each)	$ 50,000
Labor	40,000
Variable Overhead	20,000
Fixed Overhead (includes depreciation of $4,000)	10,000
Total	$120,000

(7) The cash balance on November 1 is expected to be $10,000.

Prepare the following for Modern Products Corporation, assuming that the bank loan is granted. Ignore income taxes.

    a. Schedules computing inventory budgets by months for

        (i) Finished goods production in units for October, November, and December.

        (ii) Raw material purchases in pounds for October and November.

    b. A projected income statement for the month of November. Cost of goods sold should be equal to the variable manufacturing cost per unit times the number of units sold plus the total fixed manufacturing cost budgeted for the period.

    c. A cash forecast for the month of November showing the opening balance, receipts (itemized by dates of collection), disbursements, and balance at the end of month.

39. *Incentives for Truthful Reporting (Appendix B).* Cellol, Inc., a wholesaler in the record industry, has approached All Purpose Consulting Agency to help them design an incentive system that will motivate their sales account managers to make accurate forecasts for monthly sales. Suppose that you are a consultant with Hoover All Purpose Intelligence (HAPI). Show the management of Cellol how the following bonus plan would work with forecasts of $8,000, $10,000, $12,000, $14,000, and $16,000.

$$\text{Bonus} = \begin{cases} 0.04\hat{Y} + 0.02(Y - \hat{Y}) & \text{for } Y > \hat{Y}, \\ 0.04\hat{Y} - 0.06(\hat{Y} - Y) & \text{for } \hat{Y} > Y, \end{cases}$$

$\hat{Y}$ − Forecasted Sales,

$Y =$ Actual Sales.

40. *Incentives for Accurate Forecasting (Appendix B) (J. Lim).* Kathy Kelly, the vice-president of production operations, was not at all pleased with the unfavorable sales volume variances that Kelowna's lawnmower line had been showing over the last four quarters. Kelly suspected that the source of her problem could be traced to the marketing department. The production department had a very good cost control system, but due to very long supplier lead times and a rigid production plan process, production scheduling had to be planned well in advance, based on quarterly sales forecasts. The current bonus system employed by the marketing department paid Kelowna's sales representatives a sales commission of 2 percent of actual dollar sales. Kelly felt that the present bonus system encouraged overly optimistic forecasting, since a large inventory reduced the risk of a stockout. Determined to motivate more accurate sales forecasting by the company's sales force, Kelly decided to present to top management an alternative bonus system based on the Soviet incentive system described at the All Purpose Consulting Agency seminar she attended a month ago. Briefly, Kelly hopes to propose a system whereby:

$$\text{Bonus} = \begin{cases} \$2\hat{Y} + \$1(Y - \hat{Y}) & \text{for } Y \geq \hat{Y}, \\ \$2\hat{Y} - \$3(\hat{Y} - Y) & \text{for } \hat{Y} \geq Y, \end{cases}$$

where

$$\hat{Y} = \text{Forecasted Sales in Units.}$$

$$Y = \text{Actual Sales in Units.}$$

    a. Suppose that you are Kathy Kelly's assistant. Prepare a bonus payoff matrix for actual and forecasted sales of 8,000 units, 10,000 units, 12,000 units, and 14,000 units to help her illustrate her bonus plan.

    b. Suppose that the average manufacturer's sales price per lawnmower is $90. How would the current bonus plan compare to Kelly's proposed alternative?

Suggested Solutions to Even-Numbered Exercises

10. *Solving for Materials Requirements.*

$$\begin{array}{c}\text{Finished Units} \\ \text{to Be Produced}\end{array} = \begin{array}{c}84,000 \text{ Units} \\ \text{to Be Sold}\end{array} + \begin{array}{c}48,000 \text{ Units in} \\ \text{Ending Inventory}\end{array} - \begin{array}{c}44,000 \text{ Units in} \\ \text{Beginning Inventory}\end{array}$$

$$\begin{array}{c}\text{Units to} \\ \text{Be Produced}\end{array} = \underline{\underline{88,000}}$$

$$\begin{array}{c}\text{Units of Raw} \\ \text{Materials to} \\ \text{Be Used}\end{array} = \begin{array}{c}4 \text{ Units of Raw} \\ \text{Materials per} \\ \text{Finished Unit}\end{array} \times 88,000 \text{ Finished Units} = 352,000$$

$$\begin{array}{c}\text{Units of Raw} \\ \text{Materials to} \\ \text{Be Purchased}\end{array} = \begin{array}{c}352,000 \text{ Units} \\ \text{to Be Used}\end{array} + \begin{array}{c}220,000 \text{ Units} \\ \text{Desired Ending} \\ \text{Inventory}\end{array} - \begin{array}{c}200,000 \text{ Units} \\ \text{in Beginning} \\ \text{Inventory}\end{array}$$

$$= \underline{\underline{372,000}}$$

12. *Solving for Cash Collections (Appendix A).*

   a. Budgeted cash collection in March:

From January Sales (.18 × $500,000) . . . . $ 90,000
From February Sales (.30 × $600,000) 180,000
From March Sales (.50 × $400,000) 200,000
    Total Budgeted Collections in March $470,000

   b. Budgeted cash collections in April:

From February Sales (.18 × $600,000) $108,000
From March Sales (.30 × $400,000) 120,000
From April Sales (.50 × $500,000). 250,000
    Total Budgeted Collections in April $478,000

14. *Analyzing Contribution Margin Variances.*

	Actual (7,100 units)	Manufacturing Variances	Sales Price Variance	Flexible Budget (7,100 units)	Sales Volume Variance	Master Budget (7,000 units)
Sales Revenue	$86,265[a]		$1,065 F	$85,200[c]	$1,200 F	$84,000[d]
Less: Variable Manufacturing Costs	41,890[b]	$6,390 U		35,500	500 U	35,000
Contribution Margin	$44,375	$6,390 U	$1,065 F	$49,700	$ 700 F	$49,000

[a]7,100 units × $12.15.
[b]7,100 units × $5.90.
[c]7,100 units × $12.
[d]7,000 units × $12.

16. *Preparing Budgets and Deriving Variances.*

	Actual	Master Budget
Beginning Inventory.	$ 18,000	$ 18,000
Add: Current Manufacturing Costs		
Variable	280,000	300,000
Fixed	600,000	540,000
	$898,000	$858,000
Less: Ending Inventory	(176,000)	(138,000)
Cost of Goods Sold.	$722,000	$720,000

18. *Comparing Master Budget to Actual Results.*

	Actual (90 units)	Manufacturing Variances	Marketing and Administrative Variances	Sales Price Variance	Flexible Budget (90 units)	Sales Volume Variance	Master Budget (100 units)
Sales Revenue . . .	$9,200			$200 F	$9,000	$1,000 U	$10,000
Variable Costs:							
Manufacturing							
Direct Labor . . .	1,420	$70 U			1,350	150 F	1,500
Materials	1,200	60 F			1,260	140 F	1,400
Overhead. . . .	820	80 F			900	100 F	1,000
Marketing	530		$10 F		540	60 F	600
Administrative . . .	500		50 U		450	50 F	500
Total Variable Costs .	$4,470				$4,500		$ 5,000
Contribution Margin . .	$4,730	$70 F	$40 U	$200 F	$4,500	500 U	$ 5,000
Fixed Costs:							
Manufacturing . . .	485	15 F			500	—	500
Marketing	1,040		40 U		1,000	—	1,000
Administrative . . .	995		5 F		1,000	—	1,000
Operating Profit . . .	$2,210	$85 F	$75 U	$200 F	$2,000	500 U	$ 2,500

20. *Prorating Variances.*

a. Variance assigned to ending inventory:

$$BB + TI = TO + EB$$

$$10,000 + 90,000 = 92,000 + EB$$

$$EB = 8,000 \text{ Units}$$

$$\frac{8,000 \text{ Units}}{90,000 \text{ Units}} \times \$20,000 = \begin{array}{l} \$1,778 \text{ (F) to} \\ \text{Ending Inventory;} \end{array}$$

$$\frac{92,000 \text{ Units} - 10,000 \text{ Units (from BB)}}{90,000 \text{ Units}} = \begin{array}{l} \$18,222 \text{ (F) to} \\ \text{Units Sold.} \end{array}$$

b. Without prorating variances: $20,000 (F) offset against expenses.
With prorating variances: $18,222 (F) offset against expenses.
Profits are $1,778 (= $20,000 − 18,222) higher in this case without prorating variances.

22. *Incentives for Accurate Forecasting (Appendix B).*

		Forecasted Sales, $\hat{Y}$				
		20	**21**	**22**	**23**	**24**
Actual Sales, Y	**20**	$2,000[a]	$1,950[f]	$1,900[i]	$1,850	$1,800
	21	2,070[b]	2,100[g]	2,050[j]	2,000	1,950
	22	2,140[c]	2,170[h]	2,200	2,150	2,100
	23	2,210[d]	2,240	2,270	2,300	2,250
	24	2,280[e]	2,310	2,340	2,370	2,400

[a]$2,000 = \$100\ (20)$.
[b]$2,070 = \$2,000 + \$70\ (21 - 20)$.
[c]$2,140 = \$2,000 + \$70\ (22 - 20)$.
[d]$2,210 = \$2,000 + \$70\ (23 - 20)$.
[e]$2,280 = \$2,000 + \$70\ (24 - 20)$.

[f]$1,950 = \$100\ (21) - \$150\ (21 - 20)$.
[g]$2,100 = \$100\ (21)$.
[h]$2,170 = \$2,100 + \$70\ (22 - 21)$, etc.
[i]$1,900 = \$100\ (22) - \$150\ (22 - 20)$.
[j]$2,050 = \$2,200 - \$150\ (22 - 21)$, etc.

24. *Marketing Cost Budget.*

Fixed Costs:

Salaries .	$25,000
Advertising .	30,000
Sales Office Costs .	8,400
Travel .	2,000
	$65,400

Variable Costs:

Shipping Costs $= \$.02$ per Unit Sold and Shipped.

Commissions $= 2$ Percent of Sales, or $.02 \times$ Units Sold $\times$ Selling Price per Unit.

$$\text{Variable Costs} = \left(\$.02 \times \frac{\text{Units}}{\text{Shipped}} \right) + \left(\$.02 \times \$6 \begin{array}{c} \text{Unit} \\ \text{Selling} \\ \text{Price} \end{array} \times \frac{\text{Units}}{\text{Sold}} \right).$$

Selling Expense Flexible Budget:

$$\$65,400 + \left(\$.02 \times \frac{\text{Units}}{\text{Shipped}} \right) + \left(\$.12 \times \frac{\text{Units}}{\text{Sold}} \right).$$

Case 1:

$$\$65,400 + (\$.02 \times 60,000) + (\$.12 \times 60,000)$$
$$= \$65,400 + \$1,200 + \$7,200$$
$$= \underline{\$73,800}.$$

Case 2:

$$\$65,400 + (\$.02 \times 75,000) + (\$.12 \times 75,000)$$
$$= \$65,400 + \$1,500 + \$9,000$$
$$= \underline{\$75,900}.$$

Case 3:

$$\$65,400 + (\$.02 \times 64,000) + (\$.12 \times 64,000)$$
$$= \$65,400 + \$1,280 + \$7,680$$
$$= \underline{\$74,360}.$$

26. *Computing Sales Price and Volume Variances.*

	Actual	Sales Price Variance	Flexible Budget	Sales Volume Variance	Master Budget
Product X Sales . . .	$111,300	$ 5,300 F	$106,000[a]	$ 6,000 F	$100,000
Product Y Sales . . .	23,040	960 U	24,000[b]	4,000 F	20,000
Product Z Sales . . .	192,000	48,000 U	240,000[c]	10,000 U	250,000
	$326,340	$43,660 U	$370,000	$ —0—	$370,000

[a]$5,300 \text{ Units } \times \dfrac{\$100,000}{5,000 \text{ Units}} = \$106,000.$

[b]$240 \text{ Units } \times \dfrac{\$20,000}{200 \text{ Units}} = \$24,000.$

[c]$48,000 \text{ Units } \times \dfrac{\$250,000}{50,000 \text{ Units}} = \$240,000.$

Chapter 13   Measuring and Interpreting Variances

In Chapter 11 we stated that an important part of the planning and control process is the *feedback phase*. As shown in Exhibit 13.1,[1] the feedback phase involves comparing actual results to budgets, evaluating performance, and revising goals, plans, and budgets. By comparing actual performance with the budget and investigating reasons for variances, management has a basis for evaluating past performance with an eye toward taking corrective actions where necessary, penalizing or rewarding employees, and revising goals, plans, and budgets. The use of variances is based on the philosophy of *management by exception,* which focuses managerial attention on exceptions, or variances, from the norm.

Chapter 12 provided an overview of the comparison of actual to budget; in this chapter we go into more detail. This chapter presents a variance analysis model that underlies the approach found in most organizations. An important point to remember as you encounter variance analysis in practice is that each organization is unique. That is, each organization calculates variances in a way that is unique, based on the nature of the organization, the tastes of the accounting and finance staff for particular types of variances, and the needs of decision makers.

Rather than attempt to describe the peculiarities of methods used in a large number of organizations, we have opted to set forth the fundamental variance analysis model that is the basis for methods commonly used. As you encounter variance analyses in practice, you may find that the concepts learned in this chapter are applied somewhat differently than in our examples. The basic concepts underlying the applications, however, are the same in virtually all organizations.

Variance Analysis

To keep the analysis from being purely an abstract exercise, we use the Victoria Corporation example discussed in Chapter 12. For convenience, we have reproduced Exhibit 12.8 as Exhibit 13.2. This exhibit presents an overall comparison of actual results with the budget.

As shown in Exhibit 13.2, the total variance in operating profits from the original plan was $15,700 favorable. The next step is to investigate and analyze the variance to find causes, to ascertain whether corrective steps need be taken, and to reward or penalize employees, where appropriate.

---

[1]Exhibit 13.1 is the same as Exhibit 11.1, and is reproduced here for the reader's convenience.

Exhibit 13.1
Overview of the Planning and Control Process

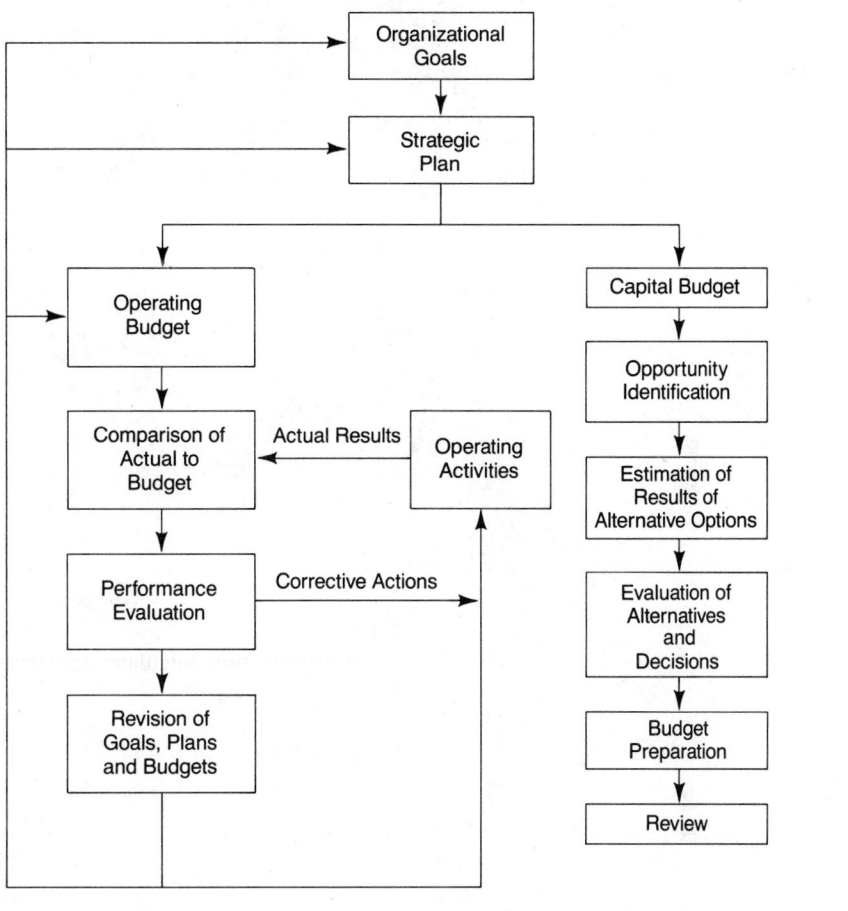

Responsibility for Variances

This section describes variance calculations for each of the major groups responsible for variances in organizations: marketing, administration, purchasing, and production. An important point in variance analysis is that each responsibility center's variances are calculated *holding all other things constant*. Hence, we try to separate marketing variances from production, production variances from purchasing, and so forth. After variances have been computed, managers can investigate the causes of variances and take corrective action if necessary.

Marketing

Marketing is usually assigned responsibility for the sales volume, sales price, and marketing cost variances. Thus, the marketing department at Victoria Corporation would be assigned the following variances (shown on page 541).

Exhibit 13.2
VICTORIA CORPORATION
Comparison of Actual Results to Profit Plan Budget

	(1) Actual (based on actual sales volume of 80,000 units)	(2) Purchasing and Production Variances	(3) Marketing and Administrative Cost Variances	(4) Sales Price Variance	(5) Flexible Budget (based on actual sales volume of 80,000 units)	(6) Sales Volume Variance	(7) Master Budget (based on a plan of 70,000 units sold)
Sales	$488,000[a]	—	—	$8,000 F	$480,000[f]	$60,000 F	$420,000[i]
Less:							
Variable Manufacturing Costs	305,600[b]	$12,000 U	—	—	293,600[g]	36,700 U	256,900[j]
Variable Marketing Costs	12,800[c]	—	$1,440 U[d]	160 U[e]	11,200[h]	1,400 U	9,800[k]
Contribution Margin	$169,600	$12,000 U	$1,440 U	$7,840 F	$175,200	$21,900 F	$153,300
Less:							
Fixed Manufacturing Costs	34,000	1,800 U	—	—	32,200	—	32,200
Fixed Marketing Costs	64,400	—	1,000 F	—	65,400	—	65,400
Fixed Administrative Costs	44,600	—	200 F	—	44,800	—	44,800
Operating Profits	$ 26,600	$13,800 U	$ 240 U	$7,840 F	$ 32,800	$21,900 F	$ 10,900

Total Variance from Flexible Budget = $6,200U

Total Variance from Budget Plan = $15,700F

[a] 80,000 units sold at $6.10 per unit.
[b] 80,000 units sold at $3.82 per unit.
[c] 80,000 units sold at $.16 per unit.
[d] $1,440 U = $12,800 − 11,200 − 160.
[e] $160 U = .02 × $8,000 favorable price variance.

[f] 80,000 units sold at $6.00.
[g] 80,000 units sold at $3.67.
[h] 80,000 units sold at $.14.
[i] 70,000 units sold at $6.00.

[j] 70,000 units sold at $3.67.
[k] 70,000 units sold at $.14.
U denotes "unfavorable" variance.
F denotes "favorable" variance.

Variable Marketing Cost	$ 1,440 U
Fixed Marketing Cost	1,000 F
Sales Volume	21,900 F
Sales Price (net of commissions)	7,840 F*

*($8,000 F price variance − $160 higher commissions associated with the higher than expected price = $7,840.)

Marketing may be given credit for the $21,900 favorable sales volume variance, which measures the favorable impact on profits of higher than expected sales volume. The sales volume variance also may be a function of other factors, such as unexpected changes in the market, unexpected changes in competitors' marketing or pricing strategies, or, of course, product price changes. The sales volume variance is a contribution margin variance, because it is the budgeted contribution margin times the difference between budgeted and actual sales volume. While each unit sold generates $6.00 of revenue, each unit has a budgeted, or standard, variable manufacturing cost of $3.67, a budgeted shipping cost of $0.02 per unit, and a budgeted sales commission of $0.12 (= 2 percent × $6.00). (These ''facts'' were presented in Chapter 12.) Thus, the contribution margin expected from each unit is $2.19 (= $6.00 − $3.67 − $0.02 − $0.12).

Why is the *standard* variable cost used instead of *actual?* Recall that we are calculating the sales *volume* variance alone. By using *standard* variable cost in computing contribution margins, we avoid mixing cost variances with the sales volume variance.

Marketing also may be given credit for the sales price variance. Note that the favorable sales price variance of $8,000 is partially offset by the increase in sales commission (2 percent of $8,000 = $160) as a result of the higher-than-budgeted selling price. Of the total marketing cost variance, $1,400 (unfavorable) is due to the sales volume variance and $160 (unfavorable) is due to the sales price variance. This leaves only $1,440 (unfavorable) variable marketing cost and $1,000 (favorable) fixed marketing cost variance to be explained by other factors.

An investigation of the variable marketing cost variance should start with the sales commissions. Were commissions inappropriately paid—for example, on sales that were returned? Was the percentage raised above the 2 percent that was budgeted? Were there commissions earned but unreported in previous periods that are recorded in the current period?

Similar questions would be asked about shipping costs. Did rates increase? Were discounts not taken? Were there recording errors? The accounting staff is usually responsible for ascertaining whether variances are due to bookkeeping adjustments or errors, whereas marketing managers who are familiar with marketing activities investigate marketing activities that may have caused the variances.

Fixed marketing costs are often somewhat discretionary. A favorable variance does not necessarily mean good performance. For example, the $1,000 favorable variance at Victoria Corporation could mean that the company did less advertising than intended, which could have negative consequences for future sales.

Administration

Administration is assigned a $200 favorable variance. Administrative variances are often the hardest to manage because they are not *engineered*. That is, there is no well-defined causal relation between administrative input and administrative output.

Administrative costs are usually budgeted with a discretionary cost budget. A discretionary cost budget places a ceiling on costs for a particular set of tasks. For example, suppose that an organization's corporate internal audit staff was given a budget of $2,000,000 for salaries for 40 people and an additional $400,000 for travel, supplies, and other costs. The internal audit department would not be allowed to spend more than those limits without obtaining approvals for a larger budget. Those approvals would normally come from top executives (for example, the president of the company) or the board of directors.

Although discretionary budgets can provide a ceiling for expenditure, they do not provide a norm in the manner of a flexible manufacturing cost budget. If there is no measure of output, then there is no measure of input-output relationships, and ascertaining the "proper" level of costs is quite difficult. These difficulties should be taken into account when evaluating an administrative cost variance, or any other discretionary cost variance.

Purchasing

A common method of evaluating the performance of the purchasing department is by using the materials price variance.[2] This measures the difference between actual and standard prices paid for materials. Materials often make up more than 50 percent of a product's manufacturing cost, so expected profits can quickly turn to losses when actual material prices exceed standard.

Assume that Victoria Corporation actually purchased 81,000 pounds of direct materials at $1.05 per pound. Recall that the standard cost was $1.00 per pound. Purchasing would be charged with an unfavorable price variance of $4,050 [= ($1.05 − $1.00) × 81,000 pounds].

Production

Production departments would usually be charged with the remaining variable manufacturing cost variance that was not assigned to purchasing and with the fixed manufacturing cost variance. For Victoria Corporation, the variances would be assigned as follows:

	Total	− Purchasing	= Production
Variable Manufacturing Cost Variance	$12,000 U −	$4,050 U	= $7,950 U
Fixed Manufacturing Cost Variance	$1,800 U −	−0−	= $1,800 U

[2]A study of internal control practices in U.S. companies found the purchase price variance to be the most common method of evaluating a purchasing department's performance. See R. K. Mautz, W. Kell, M. Maher, A. Merton, R. Reilly, D. Severance, and B. J. White, *Internal Control in U.S. Corporations* (New York: Financial Executives Research Foundation, 1980).

Separating Variances into Price and Efficiency Components

Variable manufacturing cost variances are often partitioned into *price* and *efficiency* components. The price component is the difference between the budgeted (or standard) prices and the actual price paid for each unit of input, whereas the efficiency variance is a measure of the efficiency with which inputs are used to produce output. To demonstrate this point, suppose that Victoria Corporation's $12,000 unfavorable variable manufacturing variance consists of the following manufacturing cost variances (for illustrative purposes, assume that 80,000 units were produced):

	Actual	Standard Allowed Based on Actual Production Output of 80,000 Units	Variance
Direct Materials . . .	81,000 Pounds at $1.05 = $85,050	80,000 Pounds at $1.00 = $80,000	$ 5,050 U
Direct Labor	10,955 Hours at $18.90 = $207,050 (rounded to the nearest dollar)	10,000 Hours (= 80,000 Units × ⅛ Hour) at $20 = $200,000	7,050 U
Variable Manufacturing Overhead.	$ 13,500	80,000 Units at $0.17 = $13,600	100 F
Total Variable Manufacturing Costs	$305,600	$293,600	$12,000 U
	Actual	**Fixed Budget**	**Variance**
Fixed Manufacturing Overhead.	$ 34,000	$ 32,200	$ 1,800 U

Note that these total manufacturing variances also appear in column (2) of Exhibit 13.2.

At this point, it would be useful for you to calculate price and efficiency variances without looking ahead. We recommend this exercise because variance calculations often result from memorization of formulas that are quickly forgotten. These formulas are incorporated into computer programs at most organizations, so it is more important that the variances you read in reports make sense, intuitively, than it is for you to memorize formulas.

A *price* variance is simply the difference between the price set as the norm—that is, the standard or budgeted price—and the actual price. For direct labor, this amount was −$1.10 (= $18.90 actual − $20.00 standard) per hour for Victoria Corporation. The company purchased 10,955 hours of labor, so the favorable labor price variance was $12,050 (= $1.10 × 10,955 hours), rounded down. The material purchase price variance could be calculated in a similar way, giving an unfavorable price variance of $4,050, as noted earlier.

An *efficiency* variance is simply the difference between the actual quantity of inputs used and those allowed at standard to make a unit of output. At Victoria Corporation, each unit produced is allowed 1 pound of direct material. If 81,000 pounds were actually used to produce 80,000 units, there is an unfavorable efficiency variance of 1,000 pounds in quantity, or $1,000 (= 1,000 pounds × $1 standard price per pound).

Variable Cost Variance Model

A general model for variance calculations appears in Exhibit 13.3. We apply that model to the calculation of direct materials, direct labor, and variable manufacturing overhead variances for Victoria Corporation in Exhibit 13.4. We have divided direct materials and direct labor variances into price and efficiency components. Additional analyses of variable and fixed manufacturing cost variances are made later in this chapter.

Note that Exhibit 13.4 breaks down the total variable manufacturing cost variance in column (2) of Exhibit 13.2 into more detail. Think of Exhibit 13.2 as the "big picture," with Exhibit 13.4 as a detailed supporting schedule.

The computations in column (3) of Exhibits 13.3 and 13.4 must be interpreted carefully. Note that the term SQ refers to the *standard quantity of input allowed to produce the actual output*. SQ is *not* the expected production volume. If each unit of output produced has a standard of ⅛ hour of direct labor time, and if 80,000 units of output are *actually produced*, then SQ = 10,000 hours (= ⅛ hour × 80,000 units).

Exhibit 13.3
General Model for Variance Analysis: Variable Manufacturing Costs

(1)	(2)	(3) FLEXIBLE PRODUCTION BUDGET
ACTUAL Actual input price (AP) times actual quantity (AQ) of input (AP × AQ)	**INPUTS AT STANDARD** Standard input price (SP) times actual quantity (AQ) of input (SP × AQ)	Standard input price (SP) times standard quantity (SQ) of input allowed for actual output (SP × SQ)

Price Variance[a]	Efficiency Variance[a]
(1) − (2)	(2) − (3)
(AP × AQ) − (SP × AQ)	(SP × AQ) − (SP × SQ)
= (AP − SP) × AQ	= SP × (AQ − SQ)

Total Variance
(1) − (3)
(AP × AQ) − (SP × SQ)

[a]The terms "price" and "efficiency" variances are general categories. Although terminology varies from company to company, the following specific variance titles are frequently used:

Input	Price Variance Category	Efficiency Variance Category
Direct Materials	Price (or purchase price) Variance	Usage or Quantity Variance
Direct Labor	Rate Variance	Efficiency Variance

We shall avoid unnecessary labeling by simply referring to these variances as either a "price" or "efficiency" variance.

Exhibit 13.4
VICTORIA CORPORATION
Calculation of Variable Manufacturing Cost Variance

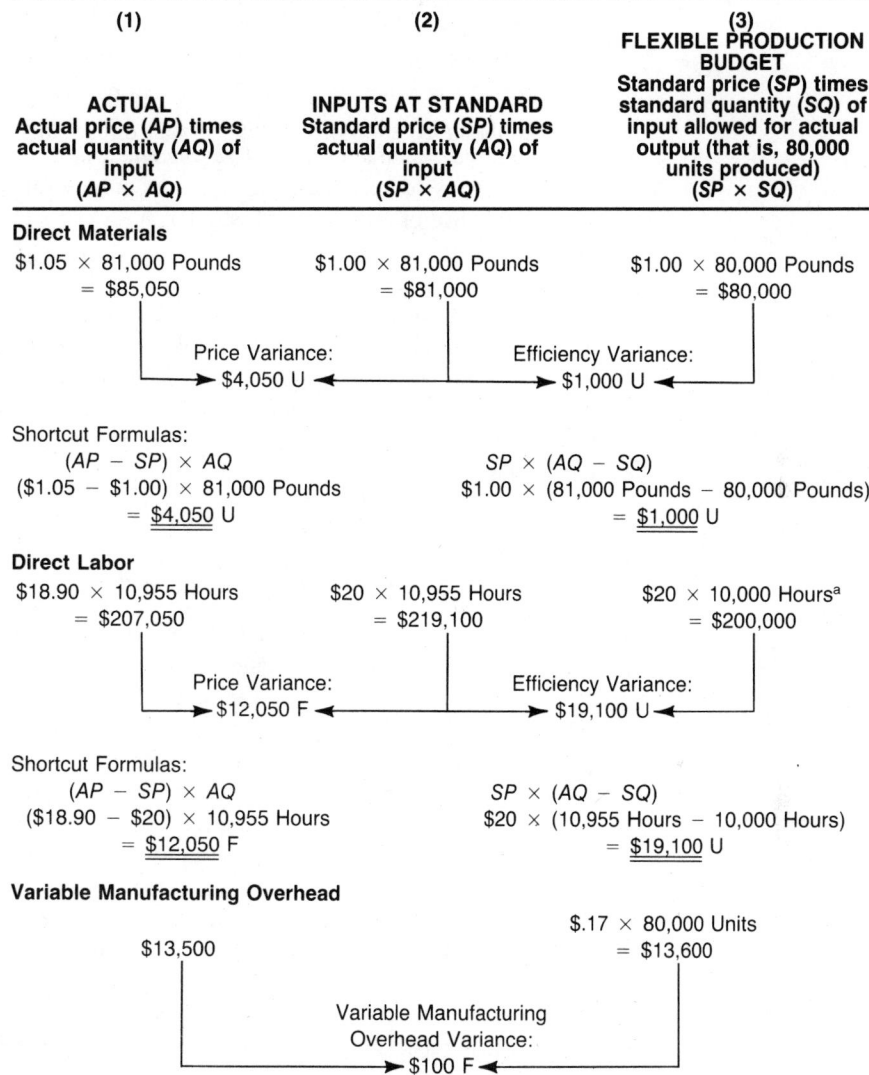

(1)	(2)	(3) FLEXIBLE PRODUCTION BUDGET Standard price (*SP*) times standard quantity (*SQ*) of input allowed for actual output (that is, 80,000 units produced) (*SP* × *SQ*)
ACTUAL Actual price (*AP*) times actual quantity (*AQ*) of input (*AP* × *AQ*)	**INPUTS AT STANDARD** Standard price (*SP*) times actual quantity (*AQ*) of input (*SP* × *AQ*)	

Direct Materials

$1.05 × 81,000 Pounds
= $85,050

$1.00 × 81,000 Pounds
= $81,000

$1.00 × 80,000 Pounds
= $80,000

Price Variance:
$4,050 U

Efficiency Variance:
$1,000 U

Shortcut Formulas:

$(AP − SP) × AQ$
($1.05 − $1.00) × 81,000 Pounds
= $\underline{4,050}$ U

$SP × (AQ − SQ)$
$1.00 × (81,000 Pounds − 80,000 Pounds)
= $\underline{1,000}$ U

Direct Labor

$18.90 × 10,955 Hours
= $207,050

$20 × 10,955 Hours
= $219,100

$20 × 10,000 Hours[a]
= $200,000

Price Variance:
$12,050 F

Efficiency Variance:
$19,100 U

Shortcut Formulas:

$(AP − SP) × AQ$
($18.90 − $20) × 10,955 Hours
= $\underline{12,050}$ F

$SP × (AQ − SQ)$
$20 × (10,955 Hours − 10,000 Hours)
= $\underline{19,100}$ U

Variable Manufacturing Overhead

$13,500

$.17 × 80,000 Units
= $13,600

Variable Manufacturing
Overhead Variance:
$100 F

---

[a]10,000 hours allowed = 80,000 units produced × ⅛ hours per unit allowed.

Note: It is sometimes difficult to see intuitively which variances are favorable (F) and which are unfavorable (U). Keep in mind that for cost variances you are comparing amounts on the left—actual—with those on the right—budget or standard. If the amount on the left—the actual—is more than the amount on the right—the budget or standard—then the variance is *unfavorable* because higher costs than budgeted mean lower profits than budgeted. The reverse is true for favorable variances—the amounts on the left—actuals—are lower than those on the right. *Caution:* We set up all of the cost variance calculations in this book consistently, with actual costs on the left, standard or budget on the right; so the above rule works in this book. Other books and company practices do not necessarily follow this practice consistently.

Note that column (3) is also called the flexible *production* budget. The flexible *sales* budget is used to analyze differences between actual and budgeted profits [see column (5) in Exhibit 13.2]. In Exhibits 13.3 and 13.4, the activity of interest is production, so the relevant budget is based on production volume. In short, column (3) of Exhibits 13.3 and 13.4 shows the *standard cost allowed to produce the actual output,* whereas column (1) of Exhibits 13.3 and 13.4 shows the *actual costs incurred to produce the actual output.* The differences between columns (1) and (3) are the manufacturing cost variances.

This overview of manufacturing variances provides the essential calculations for management use of variances. Most companies carry this analysis to much more detail.

Summary and Overview Exhibit 13.5 is a diagram of all the variances discussed. It breaks down the $15,700 total favorable variance from Exhibit 13.2 into components and shows their assignment to responsibility centers—marketing, administration, purchasing, and production. Generally, variances are reported in much more detail than shown here. They are divided into more detailed cost items—by type of direct material and labor, for example.

Reasons for Manufacturing Variances

Variance reports include explanations for the variances. This helps managers to ascertain whether variances should be investigated and corrective action taken, whether people responsible for variances should be rewarded, or whether other managerial action is warranted. Why do variances occur? First, a variance is simply the difference between a predetermined norm or standard and actual results. Some difference should be expected just because one measure is expected and the other is actual. For example, if you and several of your friends were each to flip a coin 10 times, not all of you would come up with five heads, even though five heads (= 50 percent of 10 coin flips) might be the expected value. In short, even when standards are unbiased expected values, and there are no *systematic* reasons that explain variances, some variances will occur anyway.

Second, the standards themselves may be biased. Sometimes standards are intentionally set "loose" or "tight." Sometimes they are unintentionally biased, such as when expected labor wage increases are omitted or an allowance for waste on direct material usage is omitted.

Reasons for Materials Variances There are numerous reasons for materials price variances. They could result from failure to take purchase discounts, from using a better (worse) grade of raw material than expected, so that the price paid was higher (lower) than expected, or from changes in the market supply or demand for the raw material that affected prices. Materials efficiency variances are caused by a number of factors. When management, industrial engineers, and others set standards for the amount of direct materials that should be used to make a unit of output, they usually allow for material defects, inexperienced workers who ruin materials, improperly used materials, and so forth. To the extent that material is used more

Exhibit 13.5
VICTORIA CORPORATION
Variance Diagram

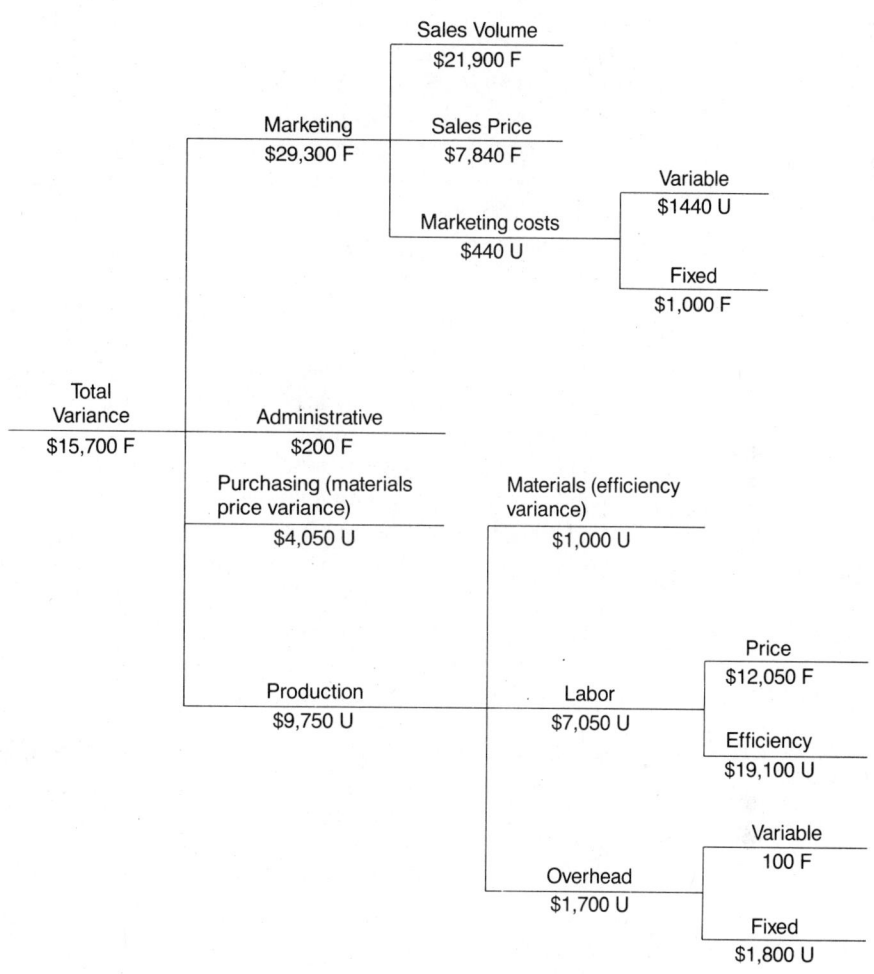

efficiently than these standards, there are favorable efficiency variances; usage worse than these standards results in unfavorable variances. Sometimes *purchasing*, not production, is responsible for a material efficiency variance. In an effort to reduce prices (and create a favorable price variance), purchasing departments have been known to buy a quality of materials inferior to standards. Purchasing may also be responsible for ordering the wrong materials.

Reasons for Labor Variances Labor price or wage variances can occur because changes in wage rates are not correctly anticipated. Wage rates established by union contract may be different from anticipated, for example. Also, a wage rate change may occur but standards are not adjusted to reflect it.

The labor efficiency variance is a measure of labor productivity. It is one of the most clearly watched variances because it is usually highly controllable. Many of the things that create variances affect all competitors about the same. If labor wage rates go up dramatically because of a union contract settlement, usually all companies in an industry are affected, so little competitive advantage or disadvantage results. Labor efficiency is unique to a firm, however. It can lead to competitive advantages or disadvantages.

A financial vice-president of a manufacturing company told us: "Raw materials are 57 percent of our product cost, direct labor is only 22 percent. Yet we carry out the labor efficiency variance to the penny, we break it down by product line, by department, and sometimes by specific operation, while we give the raw materials variances only a passing glance. Why? Because there's not much we can do about some of our other variances, like materials price variances, but there's a lot we can do to keep our labor efficiency in line."

Labor efficiency variances have many causes. The cause may be the workers themselves—poorly motivated or poorly trained workers will be less productive, whereas highly motivated and well-trained workers may generate favorable efficiency variances. Other causes include poor materials, faulty equipment, poor supervision, and scheduling problems.

Although managers are usually responsible for direct labor efficiency variances, responsibility is sometimes attributed to purchasing for buying faulty materials. Scheduling problems may be the fault of upstream production departments that have delayed production, the personnel department for providing the wrong type of worker, or numerous other sources.

Note that the labor price variance in the Victoria Corporation example was favorable, whereas the labor efficiency variance was unfavorable. The first question a manager would probably ask is: "Did we use workers who were lower paid and not as efficient as expected?" The point is that while firms go to great lengths to break variances down into small components that can be easily understood and traced to particular responsibility centers, managers should not overlook the fact that variances are usually interrelated.

Summary of the Fundamental Variance Analysis Model

We previously noted that variances can be divided into much more detail than presented here. Our objective is to present the conceptual model that underlies variance calculations. This model has the following characteristics:

1. A variance is simply the difference between a norm and the actual results. These norms may be called standards or budgets. By convention, the term *standard* is used to describe the norm for manufacturing costs.

2. Variances are often divided into a price component and an efficiency component.

    a. The price component refers to the difference between the actual price and the standard price allowed per unit. If the price variance is expressed as a total amount, that total is the price variance per unit times the actual units purchased.

b. The efficiency variance is a measure of productivity. It compares the actual input used to make the actual output with the standard allowed to make the actual output. Note that the efficiency variance is based on *actual* output, not budgeted output. If manufacturing cost efficiency is calculated (for example, efficiency in using labor to manufacture products), then the relevant measure of output is production volume.

Extensions of the Basic Variance Calculation Model

In this section, we extend the basic model to some variances not previously discussed.

Materials Purchased and Used Are Not Equal

In the Victoria Corporation example, the direct materials purchased and used were the same. What if they are not equal? Are direct materials variances based on *purchases* or *usage?* The answer is that the *price* variance is generally based on purchases, whereas the *efficiency* variance is based on materials used.

This enables managers to spot price variances at the time materials are purchased, rather than waiting until they are entered into production. In addition, it emphasizes that responsibility for purchase price variances is normally assigned to the purchasing department at the time of purchase, whereas responsibility for the efficiency variance is assigned to manufacturing departments.

For example, if Victoria Corporation had purchased 90,000 pounds of material at $1.05 per pound, used 81,000 pounds, and had a standard of 80,000 pounds, the purchase price variance would have been $4,500 U [= 90,000 × ($1.05 − $1.00)] instead of $4,050 U when only 81,000 pounds were purchased. The efficiency variance would still be $1,000 U [= (81,000 pounds − 80,000 pounds) × $1.00]. Materials inventory would increase by $9,000 [= (90,000 pounds − 81,000 pounds) × $1.00]. The variance model presented in Exhibits 13.3 and 13.4 would be modified as follows:

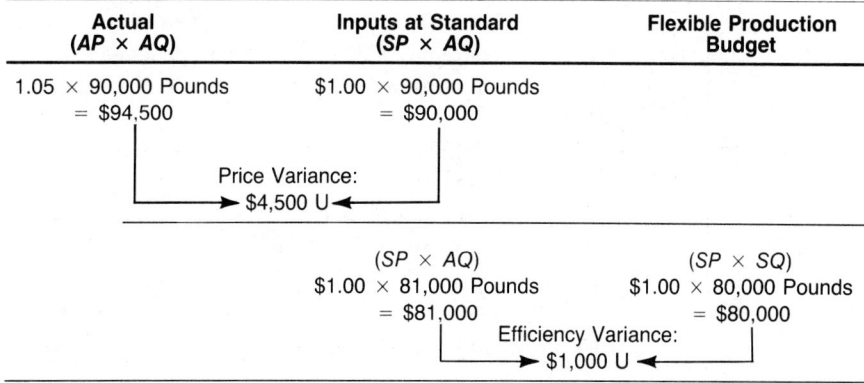

Actual (*AP* × *AQ*)	**Inputs at Standard** (*SP* × *AQ*)	**Flexible Production** **Budget**
1.05 × 90,000 Pounds = $94,500	$1.00 × 90,000 Pounds = $90,000	
	Price Variance: → $4,500 U ←	
	(*SP* × *AQ*) $1.00 × 81,000 Pounds = $81,000	(*SP* × *SQ*) $1.00 × 80,000 Pounds = $80,000
		Efficiency Variance: → $1,000 U ←

Variable Overhead Efficiency Variance

Variable overhead efficiency variances are sometimes calculated to help control particular overhead items. For example, energy costs in many firms are both sufficiently large and controllable to warrant special attention.

Example American Parcel Delivery is a parcel service that competes with the U.S. Postal Service and United Parcel Service. Each driver is responsible for picking up and delivering parcels in a particular geographic area. One of the company's major costs is fuel for the pick-up and delivery vans. One of the measures used to evaluate the performance of drivers is a fuel efficiency variance. A standard amount of fuel consumption per parcel, whether delivered or picked up, is calculated for each territory. These allowances take the population density of the territory into account—more fuel per parcel is allowed for sparsely populated territories, less for densely populated territories. Drivers control this variance primarily by scheduling trips to avoid unnecessary driving.

For a particular territory, the standard was .08 gallon of fuel per parcel. The driver assigned to this territory picked up or delivered 1,100 parcels during March; hence, 88 gallons were allowed ($= 1,100$ parcels $\times$ .08 gallon). In all, 93 gallons of fuel were actually used. Exhibit 13.6 shows the efficiency variance. Although the driver was not responsible for fuel price variances, Exhibit 13.6 presents it to complete the comparison of actual with standard. Note the similarity between these calculations and the direct materials and direct labor calculations presented earlier.

Although managers often calculate variances for particularly important, controllable overhead items, such as power or fuel costs, it is more difficult to compute price and efficiency variances for variable overhead as a total. Sometimes this is done when variable overhead is highly correlated with another production input. For example, suppose that variable overhead is highly correlated with direct labor hours. The manager responsible for direct labor efficiency variances could also be made responsible for variable overhead efficiency variances.

Mix Variances

Most organizations use multiple inputs for their output. A steel company uses a combination of iron ore, coke, and other raw materials to make its product. A hospital uses a combination of registered nurses, licensed practical nurses, and nurses' aides to provide nursing care to patients. A mix variance shows the impact on profits of using something other than the predetermined mix.

Example Engineering Associates is a consulting firm that bid on a particular consulting job, assuming 600 hours of partner time at a cost of $80 per hour and 1,400 hours of staff time at $30 per hour. Due to scheduling problems, the partner spends 1,000 hours and the staff member spends 1,000 hours. If the cost is actually $80 and $30 for partner and staff time, respectively, then there is no labor price variance. Further, the 2,000 hours required was exactly what was expected. Nevertheless, the job is $20,000 over budget, as shown on the next page:

Exhibit 13.6
AMERICAN PARCEL DELIVERY
Example Variable Overhead Efficiency Variance—Fuel Costs

Facts
Actual:

Output . . . . 1,100 Parcels Picked up or Delivered

Fuel Required. . . . . 93 Gallons

Cost per Gallon . . . . $1.58 per Gallon

Standard:

Fuel Allowed . . . . .08 Gallon per Parcel Picked up or Delivered

Cost per Gallon . . . . $1.60 per Gallon

Actual (AP × AQ)	Inputs at Standard (SP × AQ)	Flexible Production Budget (SP × SQ)
$1.58 per Gallon × 93 Gallons = $146.94	$1.60 per Gallon × 93 Gallons = $148.80	$1.60 per Gallon × (.08 Gallon × 1,100 Parcels) = $1.60 × 88 Gallons = $140.80

Price Variance: $1.86 F

Efficiency Variance: $8.00 U

Shortcut Formulas:

$(AP - SP) \times AQ$
$(\$1.58 - \$1.60) \times 93 \text{ Gallons}$
$= \underline{\$1.86} \text{ F}$

$SP \times (AQ - SQ)$
$\$1.60 \times [93 \text{ Gallons} - (.08 \text{ Gallon} \times 1,100 \text{ Parcels})]$
$= \$1.60 \times 5 \text{ Gallons}$
$= \underline{\$8} \text{ U}$

$$\text{Actual Cost} = (1,000 \text{ Hours} \times \$80) + (1,000 \text{ Hours} \times \$30)$$
$$= \$80,000 + \$30,000$$
$$= \underline{\$110,000}.$$

$$\text{Budgeted Cost} = (600 \text{ Hours} \times \$80) + (1,400 \text{ Hours} \times \$30)$$
$$= \$48,000 + \$42,000$$
$$= \underline{\$90,000}.$$

The $20,000 unfavorable variance is due neither to a price nor an efficiency variance. It results from the substitution of 400 hours (= 1,000 hours actual − 600 hours budgeted) of partner time at $80 for 400 hours of staff time at $30. The mix variance is the difference in labor costs per hour of $50 (= $80 − $30) times the 400 hours substituted.

If a mix variance had not been calculated for this job, then the variance would have been calculated as follows:

	AP × AQ	SP × AQ	SP × SQ
Partner	($80 × 1,000 Hours)	($80 × 1,000 Hours)	($80 × 600 Hours)
Staff	+ ($30 × 1,000 Hours)	+ ($30 × 1,000 Hours)	+ ($30 × 1,400 Hours)
	= $110,000	= $110,000	= $90,000

Price Variance:
→ $0 ←

Efficiency Variance:
→ $20,000 U ←

Note that the mix variance would have been called an efficiency variance if a separate mix variance had not been calculated.

This example demonstrates the general concept of a mix variance. Two factors are important for considering mix variances. First, there is an assumed *substitutability of inputs*. The presumption is that partner time was substitutable for staff time. Second, the prices must be different for a mix variance to be nonzero. If the cost per hour of both partners and staff were the same, the substitution of hours would have had no effect on the total cost of the job.

Fixed Manufacturing Overhead Variances

Price Variance Our Victoria Corporation example assumed that the firm uses variable costing for internal accounting purposes. Hence, variable manufacturing costs are assumed to be unit costs (that is, they are product costs), whereas fixed manufacturing costs are assumed to be lump-sum costs (that is, they are period costs). When variable costing is used, there is only one type of fixed manufacturing cost variance, the difference between the *actual* lump-sum costs and the *budgeted* lump-sum costs. This variance is known as the *price, spending,* or *budget* variance. (This variance is the $1,800 unfavorable fixed manufacturing overhead variance shown in Exhibits 13.2 and 13.5.)

Production Volume Variance The *production volume* variance is calculated when companies use full absorption costing. Under full absorption costing, fixed costs are added to the costs of units produced, using a predetermined fixed cost application rate as described in Chapter 3. The production volume variance occurs when the actual number of units produced differs from the number of units used to estimate the fixed cost per unit.

For example, assume that the estimated fixed manufacturing costs for Victoria Corporation were $32,200 and the estimated production volume for the period was 70,000 units. If this firm used full absorption costing, it would apply fixed manufacturing overhead to units as follows:

$$\text{Fixed Manufacturing Cost per Unit} = \frac{\text{Estimated Fixed Manufacturing Cost per Period}}{\text{Estimated Production Volume per Period}}$$

$$= \frac{\$32,200}{70,000 \text{ Units Planned}}$$

$$= \$.46 \text{ per Unit.}$$

During the period, 80,000 units were actually produced, so 80,000 units times $.46 per unit equals $36,800 "applied" to Work-in-Process Inventory.[3] The amount "applied" is the amount of fixed manufacturing overhead debited to Work-in-Process Inventory. This amount applied—$36,800—is greater than the amount budgeted—$32,200. Why? It is greater only because actual production volume was greater than estimated. If the production volume had been estimated to be 80,000 units, then the estimated unit cost would have been

$$\frac{\$32,200}{80,000 \text{ Units}} = \$.4025 \text{ per Unit.}$$

Applied fixed manufacturing overhead would have been $32,200 (= $.4025 × 80,000 units actually produced), which equals the budget amount. Thus, if the production volume were correctly estimated, there would be no production volume variance. In short, the production volume variance occurs because the estimate of production volume does not equal actual production volume.

The relationship among actual, budget, and applied fixed manufacturing overhead is shown in Exhibit 13.7.

The production volume variance applies only to fixed costs, and emerges because we are allocating a fixed period cost to products on a predetermined basis. It is a phenomenon unique to full absorption costing. The benefits of using this variance for control purposes are questionable. Some accountants argue that this variance signals a difference between expected and actual production levels; but then, so does a simple production report comparing actual and planned production volumes. Some argue that it measures the cost of the idle capacity when unfavorable, and the value of producing a greater level than expected when favorable.

Our approach in this book is to treat the production volume variance as an outcome of full absorption costing when predetermined rates are used, rather than as part of the planning and control framework we have developed. Note that the production volume variance does not appear in the budget versus actual framework for planning and performance evaluation presented in Chapter 12, Exhibit 12.8; nor does it appear in the analysis of manufacturing variances earlier in this chapter.

---

[3]Note that we use *production*, not *sales*, volumes. We have assumed that production and sales volumes are equal, for now, to keep the example simple. Later we assume that production and sales volumes are unequal. Then it will be important to remember that to unitize a fixed manufacturing cost you should divide the cost by *production* volume, not by sales volume. If you were to "unitize" fixed *marketing* costs, then you would divide the cost by *sales* volume.

Exhibit 13.7
VICTORIA CORPORATION
Fixed Manufacturing Overhead
Production Volume Variance

Actual	Budget[a]		Budget[a]		Applied
$34,000	$32,200		$32,200		$46 × 80,000 Units of Output = $36,800

Price Variance: $1,800 U

Efficiency Variance: Not Applicable

Production Volume Variance: $4,600 F

[a]Note that there is no difference between a master and flexible budget for fixed costs because fixed costs are assumed not to vary with volume. If fixed costs were different in the flexible budget than in the master budget, then the flexible budget fixed costs are used here because the flexible budget is the one used for performance evaluation and control purposes.

An Extension: Production Volume Does Not Equal Sales Volume

As noted in Chapter 12, there are no new concepts when we relax the assumption that production and sales volumes are equal. In the example so far in this chapter, we have assumed that planned production and sales volumes were 70,000 units, whereas actual production and sales volumes were 80,000 units for Victoria Corporation. Now let production and sales be unequal, as shown below:

	Actual	Planned
Production Volume	85,000	75,000
Sales Volume	80,000	70,000

Note that the facts for this modification of the Victoria Corporation example are the same here as the modification in Chapter 12; however, we go into more detail here. Total actual and standard variable costs are assumed to increase proportionately with volume (that is, actual and standard variable cost per unit remains constant). Fixed costs are assumed to remain fixed. Other facts for the modified example are shown in Exhibit 13.8. Exhibit 13.9 shows the variance calculations. This can be compared with Exhibit 13.4 to see the effects of producing 85,000 units instead of 80,000 units.

Exhibit 13.8
Modified Victoria Corporation Example When
Production Volume Does Not Equal Sales Volume

	Actual	Budget/Standard[a]
Variable Manufacturing Costs:		
Direct Materials	$1.05 per Pound × 81,000 Pounds × (85,000 ÷ 80,000)[b] = $1.05 × 86,063 = $90,366	$1.00 per Pound × 1 Pound per Unit × 85,000 Units Produced = $85,000
Direct Labor	$18.90 per Hour × 10,955 Hours × (85,000 ÷ 80,000)[b] = $18.90 × 11,640 Hours = $219,996	$20 per Hour × ⅛ Hour per Unit × 85,000 Units Produced = $20 × 10,625 Hours = $212,500
Variable Manufacturing Overhead	$13,500 × (85,000 ÷ 80,000)[b] = $ 14,344	$.17 per Unit × 85,000 Units Produced = $ 14,450
Total Variable Manufacturing Costs . .	$324,706	$311,950
Fixed Manufacturing Overhead . . .	$ 34,000	$ 32,200

[a]The terms "budget" and "standard" are often used interchangeably.

[b](85,000 ÷ 80,000) gives the ratio of the production volume in the current example to the production volume in the example earlier in this chapter. Multiplying input quantities by (85,000 ÷ 80,000) implies a proportional increase in total input quantities, total variable costs, and volume of units produced.

Note: Unit amounts are rounded to nearest whole cent; totals are rounded to the nearest whole dollar.

Exhibit 13.9
Calculation of Variable Manufacturing Cost Variances When Production Does Not
Equal Sales Volume
Modified Victoria Corporation Example

Variable Manufacturing Costs

ACTUAL Actual price (*AP*) times actual quantity (*AQ*) of input (*AP* × *AQ*)	INPUTS AT STANDARD Standard price (*SP*) times actual quantity (*AQ*) of input (*SP* × *AQ*)	FLEXIBLE PRODUCTION BUDGET Standard price (*SP*) times standard quantity (*SQ*) of input allowed for actual output (that is, 85,000 units produced) (*SP* × *SQ*)

Direct Materials

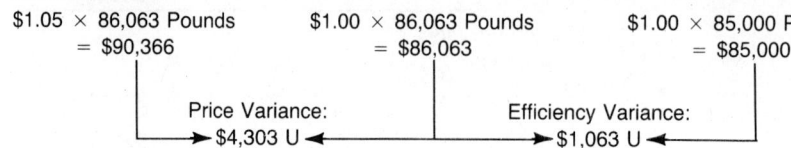

$1.05 × 86,063 Pounds = $90,366 $1.00 × 86,063 Pounds = $86,063 $1.00 × 85,000 Pounds = $85,000

Price Variance: → $4,303 U ←   Efficiency Variance: → $1,063 U ←

Shortcut Formulas:
   (*AP* − *SP*) × *AQ*   *SP* × (*AQ* − *SQ*)
($1.05 − $1.00) × 86,063 Pounds $1.00 × (86,063 Pounds − 85,000 Pounds)
      = $4,303 U   = $1,063 U

Direct Labor

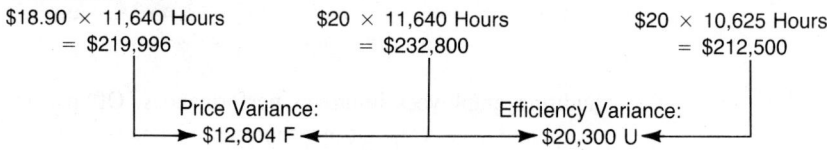

$18.90 × 11,640 Hours = $219,996 $20 × 11,640 Hours = $232,800 $20 × 10,625 Hours = $212,500

Price Variance: → $12,804 F ←   Efficiency Variance: → $20,300 U ←

Shortcut Formulas:
   (*AP* − *SP*) × *AQ*   *SP* × (*AQ* − *SQ*)
($18.90 − $20) × 11,640 Hours $20 × (11,640 Hours − 10,625 Hours)
      = $12,804 F   = $20,300 U

Variable Manufacturing Overhead

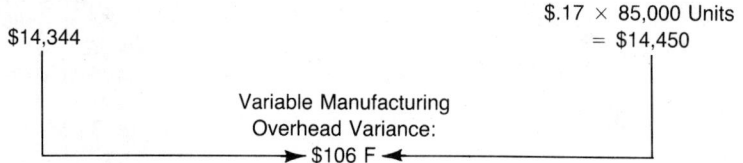

$14,344 $.17 × 85,000 Units = $14,450

Variable Manufacturing
Overhead Variance:
→ $106 F ←

Fixed Manufacturing Overhead

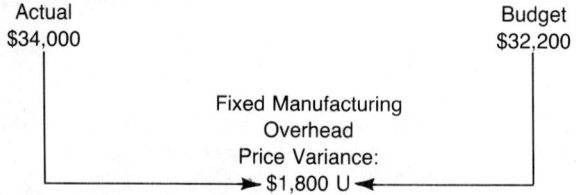

Actual
$34,000

Budget
$32,200

Fixed Manufacturing
Overhead
Price Variance:
→ $1,800 U ←

Note that the amount allowed—that is, the flexible budget amount—is based on 85,000 units of *actual production* output. It is *not* based on planned production nor on sales volume. A common source of error is to base variable manufacturing cost variances on something other than *actual production* volume. To remember this, recall that production managers are responsible for the cost variances that occur from their actual production; hence, variable manufacturing cost variances compare actual costs to costs allowed for the actual production volume.

Variance Investigation Models

Managers may receive reports that contain hundreds or even thousands of variances. Managerial time is a scarce resource—it is costly to follow up and investigate variances. When confronted with variance reports, managers ask: Which variances should be investigated?

The premise of variance analysis is that not all variances should be investigated. In fact, the decision whether to investigate a variance can be dealt with like other decisions—on a cost/benefit basis. Hence, variances should be investigated if the benefits from investigation are expected to exceed the costs of investigation. These benefits include improvements from taking corrective action, such as repairing defective machinery, instructing workers who were performing their tasks incorrectly, or changing a standard purchase order so that cheaper materials can be purchased. Further, managers generally believe that periodically investigating or auditing employees improves performances. Often it is quite difficult to measure the benefits and costs of investigation, so decisions about the value of investigating variances rely considerably on managerial judgments.

Periodic Variance

The major costs of variance investigation are the opportunity costs of employees' time. Investigators spend time, and usually those being investigated spend time, too. Although costs and benefits of variance investigation are difficult to measure, there are usually many cases where benefits are clearly too low or costs are clearly too high to make investigation worthwhile, or where variances are so large that something must be done about them.

Managers use a variety of methods to help them ascertain which variances to investigate, including "rules of thumb" (for example, any variance greater than 10 percent of standard cost, any variance that has been unfavorable for 3 months in a row) that have worked well in the past. Although we emphasize that managerial experience and good judgment are the most important ingredients for variance investigation decisions, some decision aids have been developed in recent years to assist managers.

Control Charts

Quality control techniques have long relied on the use of tolerance limits. Quality is allowed to fluctuate within predetermined tolerance limits. Applying this concept

Exhibit 13.10
Labor Efficiency Variance Report:
Friday Through Thursday
Control Chart[a]

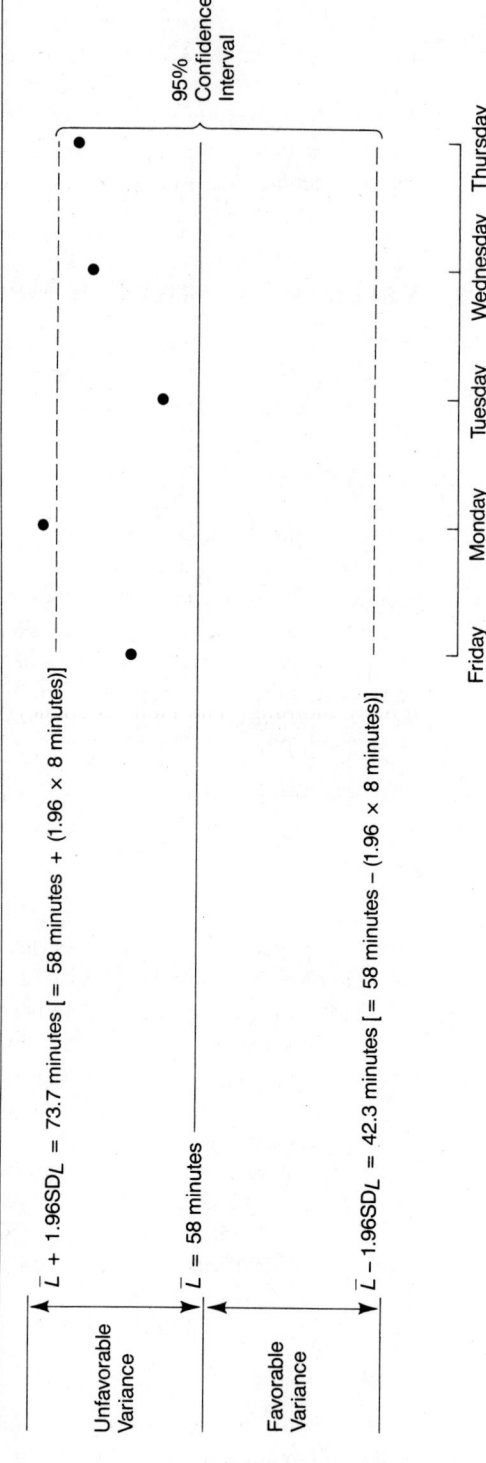

$\bar{L} + 1.96\mathrm{SD}_L = 73.7$ minutes [$= 58$ minutes $+ (1.96 \times 8$ minutes)]

Unfavorable Variance

$\bar{L} = 58$ minutes

Favorable Variance

$\bar{L} - 1.96\mathrm{SD}_L = 42.3$ minutes [$= 58$ minutes $- (1.96 \times 8$ minutes)]

95% Confidence Interval

Friday   Monday   Tuesday   Wednesday   Thursday

[a]$\bar{L}$ = expected labor time per unit of output; SD_L = standard deviation of labor time per unit of output.
95 percent of the area in a normal distribution lies between $\bar{L} - 1.96\mathrm{SD}_L$ and $\bar{L} + 1.96\mathrm{D}_L$, according to tables available in statistics texts.

to variances requires establishing some predetermined limits within which variances are allowed to fluctuate. Those limits may be different for different cost items. For example, greater tolerance is usually allowed for direct materials prices than for labor efficiency, because the former are less controllable when the variances are caused by market fluctuations. Some managers set differential tolerance limits depending on whether the variance is favorable or unfavorable, with unfavorable variances facing a tighter tolerance than favorable variances.

Statistical Significance Our knowledge about the properties of statistical distributions can help set tolerance limits. Managers can establish tolerance limits based on statistical confidence limits.

Example The manager of a plant that assembles calculators wants to set tolerance limits on labor efficiency variances such that variances fall outside the limits less than 5 percent of the time. Labor efficiency costs are assumed to be normally distributed; based on past experience, expected labor time is 58 minutes per unit of output, and estimated standard deviation is 8 minutes per unit of output.

Exhibit 13.10 presents a graphic display of actual observations reported to the plant manager for 5 days. A time series of these observations is presented so the manager can see trends and look for cumulative effects of variances. The manager gets this report at 8:00 a.m. each morning for the previous 5 working days. The report shown in Exhibit 13.10 was received by the plant manager at 8:00 a.m. Friday morning. The labor efficiency variance for Tuesday would have been investigated, presumably on Wednesday, because it was outside the tolerance limits. In addition, the manager would probably investigate this labor variance after receiving the report on Friday because of the trend indicating a shift away from standard.

Decision Models

Although control charts provide data about variances, they do not incorporate the costs and benefits of variance investigation. The simple decision model in the following example shows how this can be done.

Example Electromagnet, Inc., uses a stamping machine to make a product in 10,000 unit batches. The machine used for production of this product is adjusted at the beginning of a batch. During the production run, material usage variances are calculated and reported. If the machine is "out of adjustment," it will use considerably more materials than needed. Hence, adjusting the machine during a production run could save material costs. Sometimes the machine uses more materials than needed because of lower-quality materials, variance reporting errors, or other factors that would not be corrected by adjusting the machine. Experience has shown that materials usage variances are approximately normally distributed.

Midway through a particular production batch, the stamping department manager receives a report indicating a large negative materials usage variance. Based on past experience, the manager believes there is a 70 percent chance that the machine is out of adjustment.

The decision facing the manager is whether or not to investigate the machine. If the variance is investigated, the machine will be shut down temporarily and the adjustment will be checked. Once the machine is shut down, adjustments will be costless for practical purposes. Shutting down the machine, however, would result in idle worker time, loss of materials, and lost managerial time. After computing the opportunity cost of lost time and the cost of lost materials, the department manager estimates the cost of variance investigation, C, to be $1,000. There is some probability that after incurring the cost of investigation, the machine will not need adjustment after all. Hence, there would be no benefits from adjusting the machine. If the machine needs adjustment, however, the firm will save $2,000 in materials costs.

In this case, the manager estimates there is a 70 percent chance that the machine needs adjustment, hence, a 70 percent chance that the firm can save $2,000 in materials costs.[4]

Given the costs, C, and the benefits, B, from investigation, and the probability, Pr, that the benefits can be obtained, the decision rule is to investigate when expected benefits exceed expected costs.[5] In this case, investigating is worthwhile if

$$Pr\ B > C$$

$$.70 \times \$2,000 > \$1,000$$

$$\$1,400 > \$1,000.$$

This simple example shows how to model the variance investigation decision by applying statistical decision theory tools. In practice, the model is difficult to apply, because estimates of C, B, and Pr are difficult to make and subject to considerable error. At a minimum, managers should perform sensitivity analysis to see if the decision changes when their estimates of C, B, and Pr change.

The purpose of this discussion on variance investigation models is to indicate that statistical analysis can provide decision aids to managers. You should not infer from our discussion that these decision aids *must* be used in all situations. Like other decision aids—for example, regression for estimating cost behavior—managers find these more useful in some situations than in others, and some managers are more comfortable with them than are other managers. Also, keep in mind that we have barely explored the potential use of these models. Readers interested in pursuing these ideas further should consult advanced cost and managerial accounting textbooks.[6]

---

[4]Readers who have studied statistics will recognize this as the manager's posterior probability that the machine is out of adjustment, given a variance as high as the one reported. Calculation of posterior probabilities rely on Bayes' theorem, which is presented in statistics textbooks.

[5]We have assumed that decision makers are risk-neutral in this example.

[6]See R. Kaplan, *Advanced Management Accounting* (Englewood Cliffs, N.J.: Prentice-Hall, 1982), chap. 10; N. Dopuch, J. Birnberg, and J. Demski, *Cost Accounting* (New York: Harcourt Brace Jovanovich, 1982), chap. 8; R. Kaplan, "The Significance and Investigation of Cost Variances: Survey and Extensions," *Journal of Accounting Research* (Autumn 1975), pp. 311–337; R. Magee, "A Simulation Analysis of Alternative Cost Variance Investigation Models," *The Accounting Review* (July 1976), pp. 529–544, and Stanley Baiman and Joel Demski, "Variance Analysis Procedures as Motivational Devices," *Management Science* (August 1980).

Use of Variances in Nonmanufacturing Settings

Our variance analysis examples have mostly been in manufacturing settings. That is because manufacturing has the most comprehensive set of variances of any organization. You should not infer that manufacturing firms are the only ones to use variances. In fact, standard costs and variance analyses are used in retail stores, banks, fast food outlets, hospitals, and many other organizations.

Service organizations use the set of variances that we have calculated, with one exception—they do not have direct materials variances. Fast food outlets calculate limits for the actual versus standard amount of food served, and labor time incurred for food service, cooking, and other labor activities. Banks compute variances for labor time spent in processing transactions. Governmental units compute variances for labor costs required to make inspections, write parking tickets, and other labor activities.

Nondollar Variances

Many variances are not converted to dollars. That is, a variance is computed to measure performance, but no dollar value is placed on it. For example, variances from standard are sometimes computed for response time to emergency calls by fire, police, and medical personnel. Variances from standard in the length of time in grocery stores, banks, government offices, and other service organizations are computed to measure service performance and to decide if action should be taken to speed up service.

In short, variances are an integral part of performance evaluation and decision making. Any situation in which a standard, norm, or plan can be established lends itself to variance analysis. This chapter has presented a comprehensive model of variance analysis that can be generalized to many settings. A thorough understanding of that model will allow you to understand and use variances in virtually any setting you are likely to encounter.

Summary

Variances between actual results and a norm or standard provide a basis for management to take corrective actions where necessary, penalize and reward employees, and revise goals, plans, and budgets. This chapter presents fundamental variance analysis models that are the basis for variance calculations in organizations. Variance analysis is based on the philosophy of *management by exception*, which focuses managerial attention on exceptions, or variances, from the norm.

An important decision faced by managers is: Which variances should be investigated? The conceptual answer is to investigate only those variances for which the benefits of investigation exceed the cost.

Responsibility for variances is generally assigned as follows:

Departments	Responsible for
Marketing	Sales Price Variances, Sales Volume Variances, Sales Mix Variances, Marketing Cost Variances
Administration	Administrative Cost Variances
Purchasing	Materials Purchase Price Variances
Production	Direct Materials Usage Variances, Direct Materials Mix Variances, Direct Labor Variances, Manufacturing Overhead Variances

The general model for calculating variable cost variances is as follows:

Actual		Inputs at Standard		Flexible Production Budget
$AP \times AQ$		$SP \times AQ$		$SP \times SQ$
	Price Variance		Efficiency Variance	
	$(AP - SP) \times AQ$		$SP \times (AQ - SQ)$	

This model is commonly applied to direct materials and direct labor costs, but it also may be applied to variable marketing costs, variable overhead costs, or any other variable cost.

Why do variances occur? Most reasons for variances can be classified as one of the following:

1. Random variation of actual around standard. Some fluctuation is normal and not worth bothering about.

2. Bias in setting the standard (that is, standard is "tighter" or "looser" than the expected cost under normal operating conditions). If this bias is intended, the standard is left alone; if not, the standard is adjusted to remove the bias.

3. Systematic variance not due to bias in the standards.

Of these three reasons, only the third may require investigation and correction, assuming that the benefits of investigation and correction exceed the costs.

Mix variances are calculated when inputs or outputs are substitutes. They measure the cost of using more expensive material or labor in place of less expensive material or labor, for example.

The most common fixed manufacturing overhead variance for performance evaluation is the *price variance* (also called a *spending variance*), which measures the difference between budgeted and actual fixed costs. If rent costs are budgeted at $10,000 and actually are $12,000, the price variance is $2,000 unfavorable. This is a straightforward calculation with a clear meaning—the firm paid $2,000 more for rent than budgeted. The *production volume variance* occurs only if fixed costs are "unitized," such as when full absorption costing is used to value inventory and calculate the cost of goods sold. The production volume variance occurs when the estimate of activity in the denominator of the following equation does not equal actual activity.

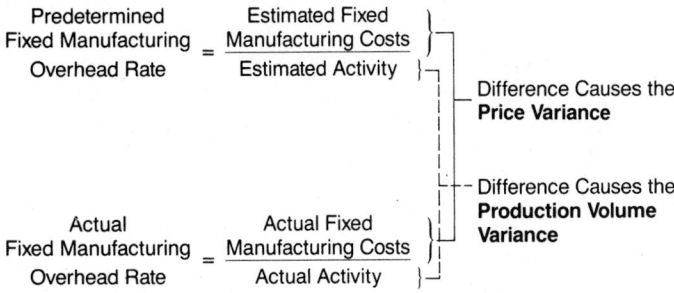

Managers usually investigate and correct only a small fraction of the variances computed, because investigation and correction is costly—it consumes both managerial and worker time. How do managers select the variances to be investigated? Often they use "rules of thumb," such as "investigate if the variance is greater than 10 percent of the standard." If the properties of frequency distributions can be estimated, managers can base variance tolerance limits on confidence intervals, as shown in Exhibit 13.10. It is also possible to model variance investigation using statistical decision theory and the following rule:

$$\text{Investigate if } Pr\, B > C,$$

where

B = benefits from investigation,

C = costs of investigation,

Pr = probability of achieving benefits if variance is investigated.

Whether a rule of thumb or a statistical model is used, the basic idea is to apply the simple cost/benefit criterion that is the foundation of all managerial activity: Take action only if its benefits exceed its costs.

Appendix: Standard Costs

We distinguish between *standard costs* and *standard cost systems*. Although many organizations use standard costs, only some use the standards to value inventory and product costs in the accounting records. Firms that most commonly use standard cost systems are manufacturing companies with process systems, for example, steel, chemical, or calculator manufacturers. (See Chapter 5 for a discussion of process costing systems.) The use of standard costs can provide significant savings in record-keeping costs, particularly in process manufacturing, where units are homogeneous and not easily identifiable. Although standard cost systems are found primarily in manufacturing, they could be adapted for product costing in any organization with goods or services.

Because we take a user perspective of accounting in this book, you may wonder why users of accounting information should study standard cost accounting systems. We believe that there are two reasons. First, study of this system will help solidify your understanding of variance measurement and analysis. As indicated in the text, our goal is to make your understanding of variances intuitive rather than mechanical. Looking at the way variances emerge from cost flows through the accounting system should help achieve that goal. Second, as indicated earlier in this book, the better users understand accounting systems, the more input they can have in designing and modifying them.

Standard Cost Flows

The general model for the flow of costs in standard cost accounting systems is shown in Exhibit 13.11. (This overview was also presented in Chapter 4.)

When a standard cost system is used, costs are transferred through the production process at standard. In process costing, units transferred between departments are valued at standard cost; whereas in job costing, standard costs are used to charge the job for its components. Actual costs are accumulated in the accounts where transactions are initially recorded on the books (for example, Accounts Payable, Wages Payable). The difference between the actual costs assigned to a department and the standard cost of the work done is the variance for the department.

In the following sections, we discuss the flow of costs and demonstrate how the variances are isolated in the accounting system. These variances will be the same as those calculated in the chapter for Victoria Corporation, when the actual production volume was 80,000 units. You may find it helpful to refer to Exhibit 13.4 as you work through the following entries. All the data necessary to make the direct materials, direct labor, and variable manufacturing overhead variances are presented in Exhibit 13.4. We caution you to recognize that standard cost systems vary from company to company. The model we present is typical, but it may be modified to meet the specific needs of a particular company.

Direct Materials

Materials are purchased for their actual cost, but usually carried in materials inventory at the standard price per unit of material. The entry for Victoria Corporation for materials purchased is as follows (numbers in parentheses are the journal entry numbers):

(1) Materials Inventory	81,000	
Materials Price Variance	4,050	
Accounts Payable		85,050

To record the purchase of 81,000 pounds of material at the actual cost of $1.05 per pound, and to record the purchase in Materials Inventory at the standard cost of $1.00 per pound.

(Note that unfavorable cost variances are always debits and favorable cost variances are always credits.) Exhibit 13.12 presents the flow of standard costs through T-accounts. Note that *actual costs* are generally shown in the accounts on the left

Exhibit 13.11
Standard Cost Flows

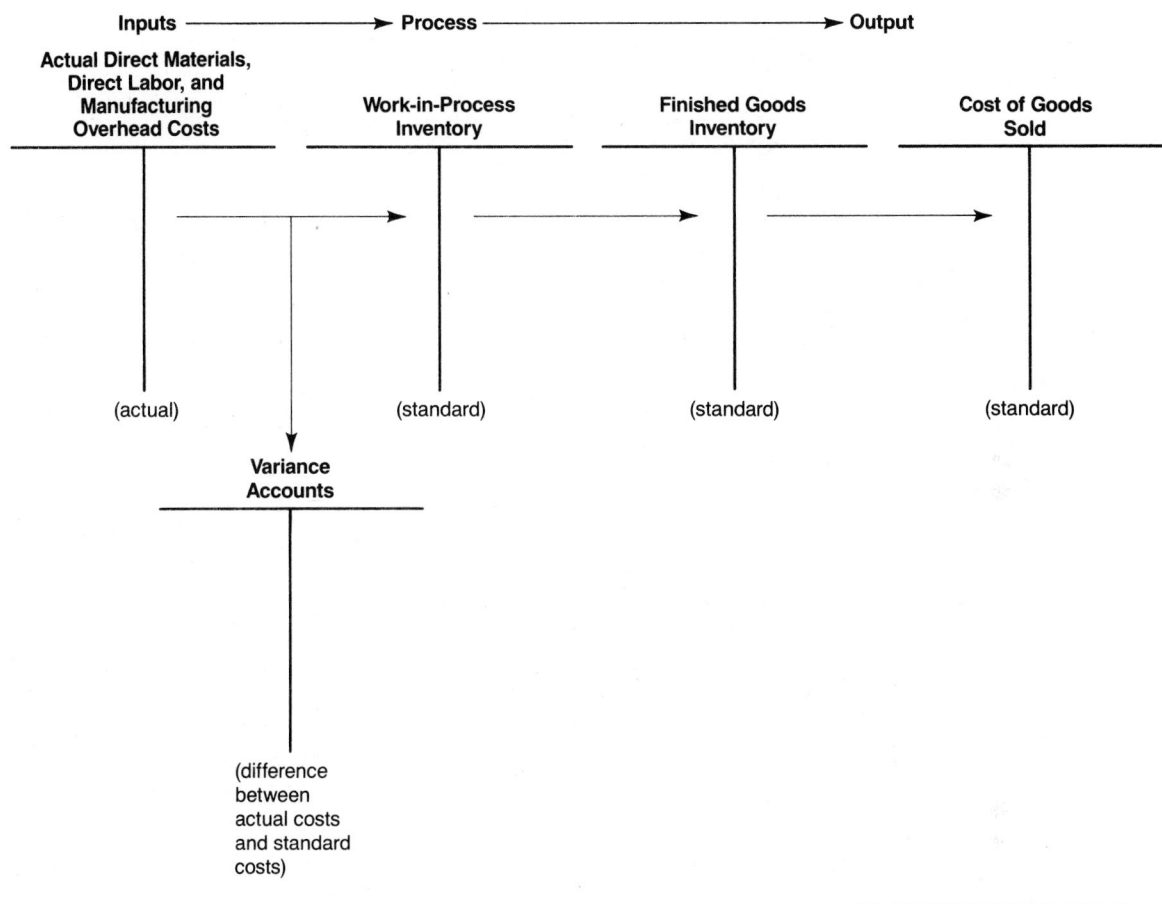

side of Exhibit 13.12 (for example, in Accounts Payable). The costs that are entered in Work-in-Process are *standard costs.*

The materials price variance appears in the accounting records at the time the materials are purchased. As noted in the text, it may be valuable for managers to know the materials price variances when materials are bought, so that corrective action can be taken if necessary.

We say that direct materials are being carried at standard cost because the $1.00 per pound is the standard allowed per unit of input. But a word of caution is in order. The standard cost referred to is the standard cost per unit of *input* (that is, pounds), *not* standard cost per unit of *output.*

When direct materials are placed into production, each operating department is assigned the *actual quantity* of input used at the *standard cost* per input unit. Thus, the production department at Victoria Corporation is assigned the actual quantity of 81,000 pounds of materials at the standard cost of $1.00 per pound. Production is not normally held responsible for the materials price variances, they are the

Exhibit 13.12
VICTORIA CORPORATION
Flow of Costs[a]
Full Absorption Costing with Standard Costs

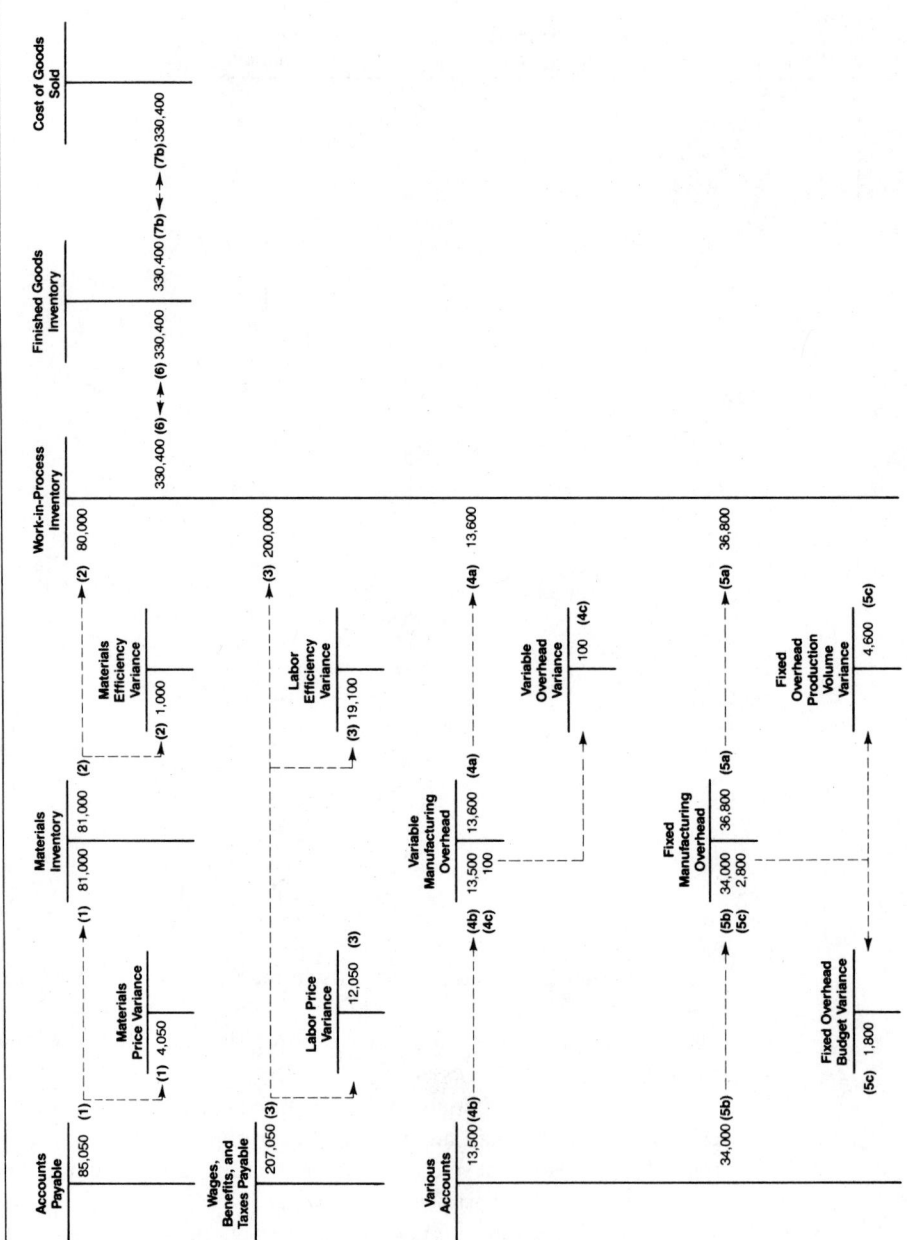

responsibility of the purchasing department. Production is held responsible for materials efficiency variances, however.

The entry charging production for the standard cost of materials used is

---

(2) Work-in-Process Inventory 80,000
    Materials Efficiency Variance 1,000
      Materials Inventory 81,000
To record the requisition of 81,000 pounds of material at the standard
cost of $1.00 per pound to make 80,000 units of output.

(Exhibit 13.12 presents this entry in T-accounts.)

Direct Labor

The actual direct labor, including fringe benefits and taxes, is credited to various payable accounts. To simplify the presentation, we assume that the credit is just to Wages, Benefits, and Taxes Payable. Direct labor is charged to Work-in-Process Inventory at the standard direct labor cost allowed for the output produced. This entry for Victoria Corporation is

---

(3) Work-in-Process Inventory 200,000
    Labor Efficiency Variance 19,100
      Labor Price Variance 12,050
      Wages Payable 207,050
To charge Production for the standard cost of direct labor at $20
per hour times 10,000 hours allowed (that is, ⅛ hour per unit of
output allowed), to record the actual direct labor cost, and to record
direct labor variances.

Variable Manufacturing Overhead

Standard overhead costs are charged to production based on output produced at the rate of $.17 per unit of output. Standard costs are often charged to production before the actual costs are known, as demonstrated by the following sequence of entries:

1. Standard overhead costs are charged to production during the period. The debit is to Work-in-Process Inventory, the credit is to Variable Manufacturing Overhead.

2. Actual costs are recorded in various accounts and transferred to Variable Manufacturing Overhead by crediting the various accounts and debiting Variable Manufacturing Overhead. Examples of the accounts credited include Accounts Payable for costs of utilities, and Wages, Benefits, and Taxes Payable for indirect labor costs. This is completed after actual costs are known, which will be after the end of the period.

3. Variances are computed as the difference between the standard costs charged to production and actual costs incurred.

This approach is essentially the same as that used in Chapter 4 for charging production with overhead costs using "normal" costing. However, variance accounts are used here in place of Under- or Overapplied Overhead accounts, as in Chapter 4.

The three entries for Victoria Corporation are as follows:

(4a)	Work-in-Process Inventory	13,600	
	Variable Manufacturing Overhead		13,600
	To charge Production for the standard variable overhead cost at $.17 per output unit times 80,000 units actually produced.		
(4b)	Variable Manufacturing Overhead	13,500	
	Various Accounts		13,500
	To record actual variable manufacturing overhead costs incurred.		
(4c)	Variable Manufacturing Overhead	100	
	Variable Overhead Variance		100
	To record the favorable variable overhead variance of $100, and to close the Variable Manufacturing Overhead account.		

The sequence of events makes it necessary to record the flow of variable manufacturing overhead costs in the three entries shown. However, if such sequencing is not important, only one entry would be necessary:

Work-in-Process Inventory at Standard	13,600	
Various Accounts at Actual		13,500
Variable Overhead Variance		100

Fixed Manufacturing Overhead

Fixed manufacturing overhead is treated as a product cost for full absorption costing, which is required for financial reporting under generally accepted accounting principles, but it is treated as a period cost under variable costing. In this book, we have treated fixed costs as period costs for managerial decision making, planning, and performance evaluation; that is, we have used variable costing. Standard cost systems may be designed for either full absorption or variable costing. If designed for variable costing, then the discussion ends with the preceding section on variable overhead. If designed for full absorption costing, then fixed manufacturing overhead costs are "unitized"; that is, each unit produced is allocated a share of fixed manufacturing overhead.

For Victoria Corporation, the fixed manufacturing overhead rate was computed as follows:

$$\begin{array}{c} \text{Fixed} \\ \text{Manufacturing} \\ \text{Rate} \end{array} = \frac{\text{Estimated Fixed Manufacturing Cost}}{\text{Estimated Production Volume}}$$

$$= \frac{\$32,200}{70,000 \text{ Units Planned}}$$

$$= \$.46 \text{ per Unit.}$$

The amount charged to production (that is, debited to Work-in-Process Inventory) was computed as follows:

$$\begin{array}{c}\text{Amount} \\ \text{Charged} \\ \text{to Production}\end{array} = \begin{array}{c}\text{Fixed} \\ \text{Manufacturing} \\ \text{Rate}\end{array} \times \begin{array}{c}\text{Actual Number} \\ \text{of Output} \\ \text{Units Produced}\end{array}$$

$$= \$.46 \times 80{,}000 \text{ Units Actually Produced}$$

$$= \$36{,}800.$$

Production Volume Variance In Chapters 12 and 13, we showed the fixed manufacturing price variance to be the difference between the actual and budgeted cost. However, the budgeted cost is not the amount charged to production, unless the actual and estimated production volumes are equal. In short, the amount applied, or charged, to production does not equal the budget if the estimated and actual activity levels used in the denominator of the calculation are different, which makes the rate incorrect.

The following diagram summarizes the relations among actual, budget, and applied fixed manufacturing cost for Victoria Corporation (taken from Exhibit 13.7):

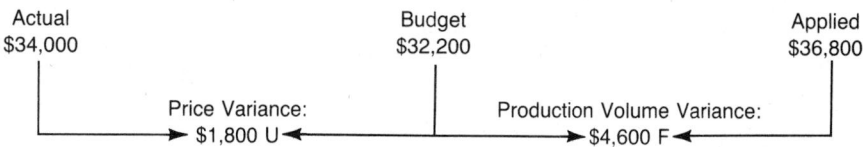

Journal Entries The method of charging fixed manufacturing standard overhead costs to production is similar to the one we used for variable manufacturing costs. For the aforementioned sequence of events, the three entries for Victoria Corporation are as follows:

(5a) Work-in-Process Inventory 36,800
    Fixed Manufacturing Overhead 36,800
    To charge production with standard fixed manufacturing overhead costs at $.46 per unit times 80,000 units produced.

(5b) Fixed Manufacturing Overhead. 34,000
    Various Accounts. 34,000
    To record actual fixed manufacturing overhead costs incurred.

(5c) Fixed Manufacturing Overhead. 2,800
    Fixed Overhead Budget Variance 1,800
      Fixed Overhead Volume Variance 4,600
    To record fixed manufacturing overhead variances and to close the Fixed Manufacturing Overhead account.

If this sequence is not followed, only one entry would be necessary:

Work-in-Process Inventory at Standard	36,800	
Fixed Overhead Budget Variance	1,800	
Various Accounts at Actual		34,000
Fixed Overhead Production Volume Variance		4,600

Note that both actual and applied fixed overhead show up in the accounts, but budgeted overhead does not.

Transfer out of Production

The total standard cost per unit is

Direct Materials	$1.00
Direct Labor	2.50
Variable Manufacturing Overhead	.17
Fixed Manufacturing Overhead	.46
	$4.13

When the units are completed, the transfer to Finished Goods Inventory is made at standard cost:

(6) Finished Goods Inventory	330,400	
Work-in-Process Inventory		330,400

To transfer 80,000 completed units from Work-in-Process to Finished Goods at a standard cost of $4.13 per unit.

The following entries record the sale of 80,000 cases (selling price = $6.10 per unit, per information in Chapter 12):

(7a) Accounts Receivable	488,000	
Sales		488,000

(7b) Cost of Goods Sold	330,400	
Finished Goods Inventory		330,400

To record the sale of 80,000 cases at an actual selling price of $6.10 per unit and a standard cost of $4.13 per unit.

Closing the Variance Accounts

To complete the accounting cycle, variance accounts would be closed to Income Summary or Retained Earnings, as follows:

Income Summary	9,200	
Labor Price Variance	12,050	
Fixed Overhead Production Volume Variance	4,600	
Variable Overhead Variance.	100	
Materials Price Variance		4,050
Materials Efficiency Variance.		1,000
Labor Efficiency Variance		19,100
Fixed Overhead Price Variance		1,800

Debiting the income summary means that the net variance was unfavorable.

Summary

Exhibit 13.12 shows the complete flow of standard costs through T-accounts. (You should find it helpful to trace each entry in this appendix to the flow of costs in Exhibit 13.12.)

Problem 1 for Self-Study[7]

During the past month, the following events took place at Computer Supply, Inc.:

(1) Produced 50,000 and sold 40,000 minicomputer cases at a sales price of $10 each. (Budgeted sales were 45,000 units at $10.15.)

(2) Standard variable costs per unit (that is, case):

Direct Materials: 2 Pounds at $1	$2.00
Direct Labor: .10 Hours at $15	1.50
Variable Manufacturing Overhead: .10 Hours at $5	.50
Total	$4.00 per Case

(3) Fixed manufacturing overhead cost:

Monthly Budget	$ 80,000

(4) Actual production costs:

Direct Materials Purchased: 200,000 Pounds at $1.20	$240,000
Direct Materials Used: 110,000 Pounds at $1.20	132,000
Direct Labor: 6,000 Hours at $14	84,000
Variable Overhead	28,000
Fixed Overhead	83,000

   a.   Compute variable manufacturing cost variances in as much detail as possible.

[7]This is a continuation of Problem 1 for Self-Study in Chapter 12.

b. Assume that the monthly fixed manufacturing overhead cost budget was $80,000 (given above) for a budgeted production volume of 4,000 direct labor hours (40,000 cases). Compute the fixed overhead price variance and production volume variance.

Suggested Solution

a. Variable manufacturing cost variances:

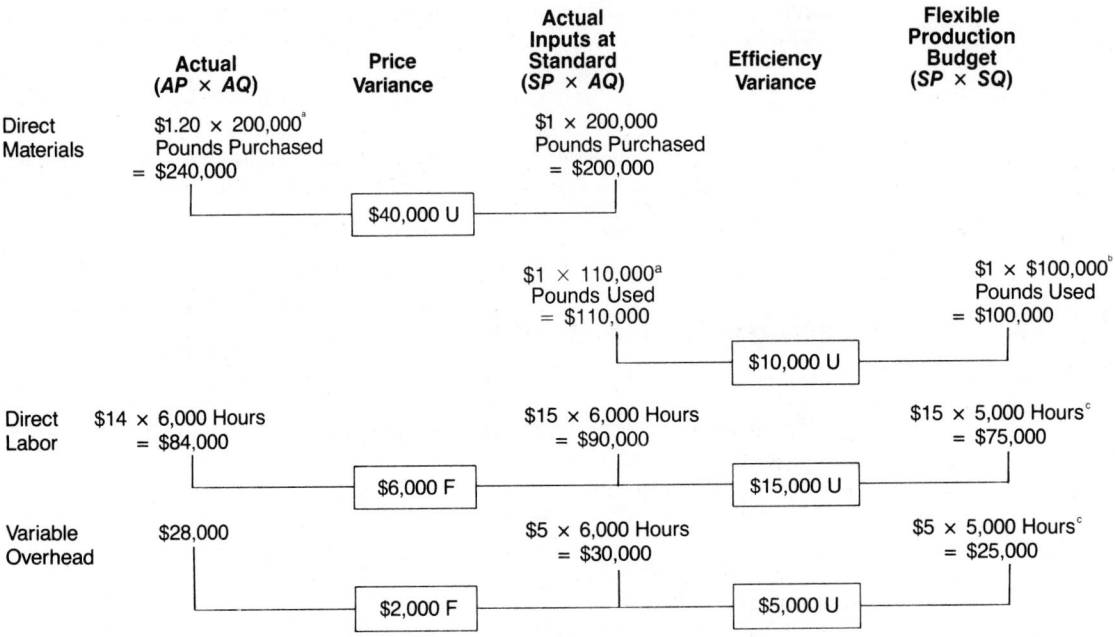

^aDirect materials—pounds purchased.
^bStandard direct materials pounds used in production per unit times units produced (2 pounds × 50,000 units).
^c10 × 50,000 units produced.

b. Fixed manufacturing cost variances:

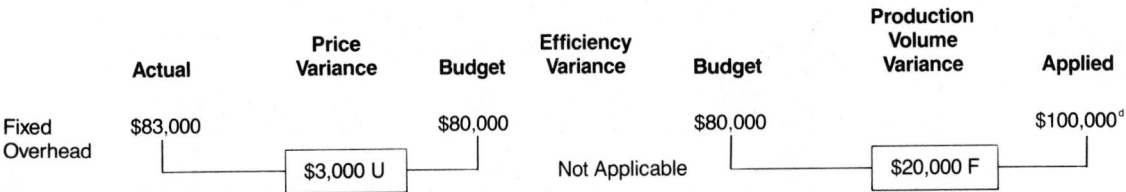

^dFixed overhead rate = $80,000 ÷ $40,000 = $2 per case, or $20 per standard labor hour.
50,000 cases actually produced × $2 = $100,000 fixed overhead applied (or 5,000 standard labor hours allowed × $20 = $100,000).

Problem 2 for Self-Study (Appendix)

Assume that the information in Self-Study Problem No. 1 is recorded using full absorption, standard costing. Assume that Work-in-Process Inventory has no beginning or ending inventories. Show how the information would be recorded using:

a. Journal entries.

b. T-accounts.

Suggested Solution

a. Journal entries:

(1)	Direct Materials Inventory	200,000	
	Materials Price Variance	40,000	
	Accounts Payable		240,000
	To record the purchase of 200,000 pounds of materials at an actual cost of $1.20 per pound and to record the transfer to Direct Materials Inventory at the standard cost of $1 per pound.		
(2)	Work-in-Process Inventory	100,000	
	Materials Efficiency Variance	10,000	
	Direct Materials Inventory		110,000
	To record the requisition of 110,000 pounds of materials at the standard cost of $1 per pound and to charge Work-in-Process Inventory with the standard usage of 100,000 pounds of materials at the standard price.		
(3)	Work-in-Process Inventory	75,000	
	Labor Efficiency Variance	15,000	
	Labor Price Variance		6,000
	Wages Payable		84,000
	To charge Work-in-Process Inventory for the standard cost of direct labor at $15 per hour times 5,000 standard hours allowed and to record the actual cost of $14 per hour times the 6,000 hours actually worked.		
(4)	Work-in-Process Inventory	25,000	
	Variable Overhead		25,000
	To apply overhead to production at $5 per standard direct labor hour times the 5,000 hours allowed.		
(5)	Variable Overhead (actual)	28,000	
	Various Accounts (Cash, Accounts Payable, etc.) . . .		28,000
	To record actual variable overhead.		
(6)	Variable Overhead Efficiency Variance	5,000	
	Variable Overhead Price Variance		2,000
	Variable Overhead		3,000
	To record variable overhead variances and to close the Variable Overhead account.		
(7)	Work-in-Process Inventory	100,000	
	Fixed Overhead (applied)		100,000
	To record fixed overhead at a standard cost of $20 per direct labor hour times 5,000 standard hours ($80,000 ÷ 4,000 hours = $20 per hour).		

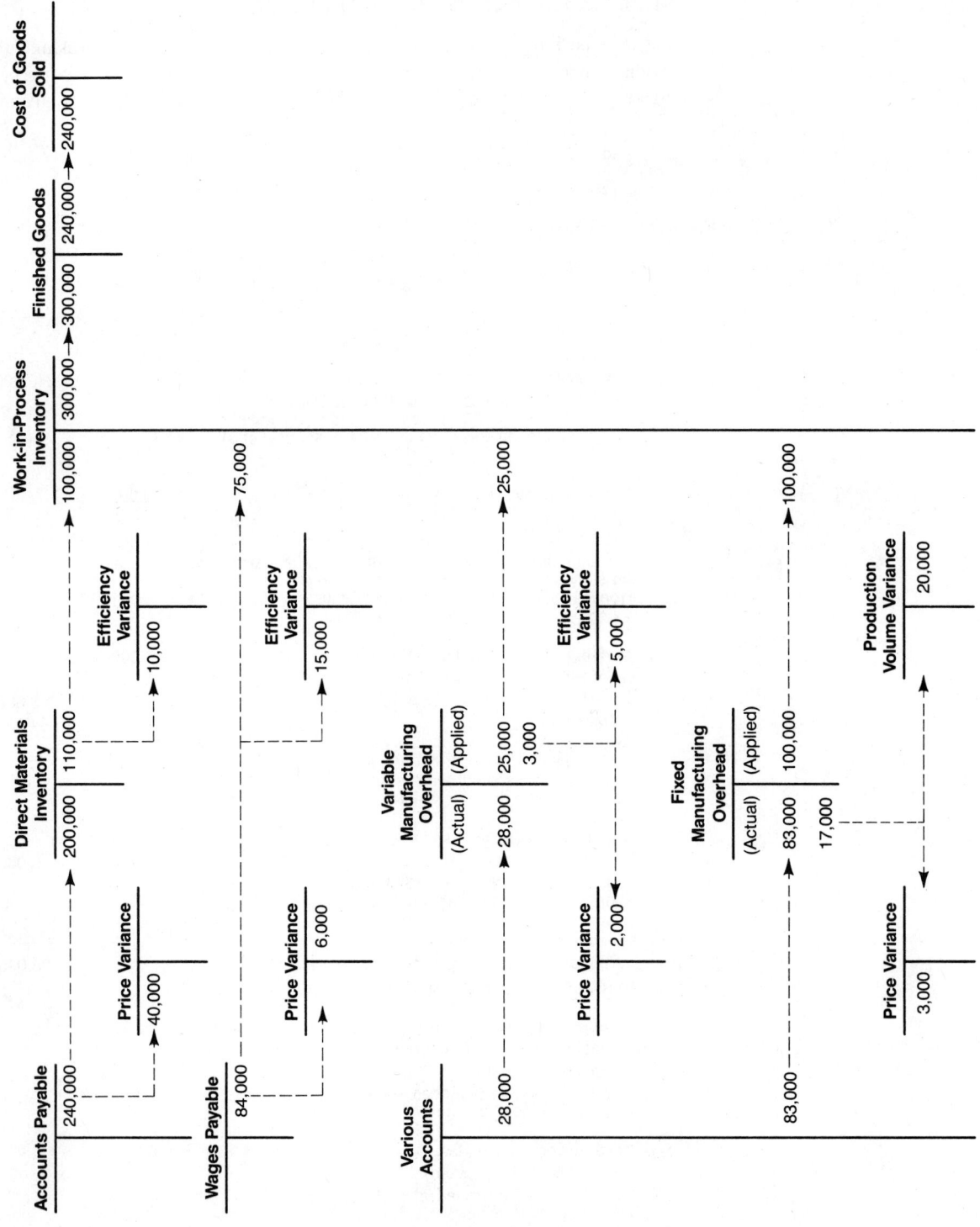

(8) Fixed Overhead (actual)   83,000
         Various accounts (Cash, Accounts Payable, etc.)   83,000
     To record actual fixed overhead.

(9) Fixed Overhead   17,000
     Fixed Overhead Price Variance   3,000
         Fixed Overhead Production Volume Variance   20,000
     To record fixed overhead variances and to close the Fixed
     Overhead account.

(10) Finished Goods Inventory   300,000
         Work-in-Process Inventory   300,000
     To record the transfer of 50,000 units of finished goods at
     the standard cost of $6 per unit.

(11) Cost of Goods Sold   240,000
         Finished Goods Inventory   240,000
     To record the sale of 40,000 units at a standard cost of $6
     per unit.

b. T-accounts: (See exhibit on the opposite page).

Questions

1. Review the meaning of the following concepts or terms discussed in this chapter.

a. Price variance.
b. Efficiency variance.
c. Standard cost allowed to make the actual output.
d. Materials price variance.
e. Materials efficiency (usage) variance.
f. Direct labor price (rate) variance.
g. Direct labor efficiency variance.
h. Variable overhead price (spending) variance.
i. Variable overhead efficiency variance.
j. Total fixed overhead variance.
k. Fixed overhead price (budget) variance.
l. Fixed overhead production volume variance.
m. Mix variance.
n. Management by exception.
o. Variance investigation.
p. Standard costs versus standard cost systems.

2. Why is a materials efficiency variance typically not calculated for the purchasing activity?

3. Why is a materials price variance typically not calculated for the production activity?

4. Comment on the following statement: "If both materials purchase and materials usage are the responsibility of the production department, it is just as well to calculate materials price variance at the time materials are used."

5. The total direct labor variance (price variance plus efficiency variance) is the difference between the actual cost of labor services acquired and the standard cost of labor services that should have been used to produce the actual level of output. The total materials variance, however, is not simply the difference between the actual cost of materials purchased and the standard cost of material that should have been used to produce the actual level of output. Why is there a difference?

6. Why might the total variable manufacturing overhead variance not be divided into price and efficiency components?

7. For control purposes, why is an efficiency variance not calculated for fixed manufacturing overhead?

8. "Timely feedback means different things for different types of costs." Explain.

9. "The control systems for manufacturing overhead and selling and administrative costs are not nearly as sophisticated as those for direct material and direct labor." Explain.

10. "It would be a lot easier to allocate the actual overhead costs incurred each month to the actual units produced each month than to fool with predetermined overhead rates." Comment.

11. A firm incurred fixed manufacturing overhead costs of $500,000 for the year. Fixed overhead applied to units produced during the year totaled $600,000. What are some of the reasons for this difference?

12. Why doesn't management investigate all unfavorable variances?

13. Describe the basic decision that management must make when considering whether to investigate a variance.

14. "The larger a variance, the more likely management is to investigate it." Comment on the rationale for this statement.

15. "Favorable variances should not be investigated." True? Comment.

16. Under what conditions would statistically based quality control charts be useful in responsibility reporting?

Exercises

17. *Materials and Labor Variances.* The Rubber Duckie Company produces toys. Recently established standard costs are as follows:

Materials: 5 pieces per unit at $.20 per piece.

Labor: .50 hour per unit at $4.50 per hour.

In November, 28,000 pieces of material were purchased for $5,040. Twenty-seven thousand pieces of material were used in producing 5,000 units of finished product. Labor costs were $12,015 for 2,700 hours worked.

    a. Compute the materials price variance.
    b. Compute the materials efficiency variance.
    c. Compute the labor price variance.
    d. Compute the labor efficiency variance.

18. *Materials and Labor Variances.* The Space Invader Company's budget contains these standards for materials and direct labor for a unit of 10 boxes:

Material—2 Pounds $.50 . . . . $1.00
Direct Labor—1 Hour $4.50 . . . .   4.50

Although 100,000 units were budgeted for September, only 97,810 were produced. Two hundred thousand pounds of materials were purchased for $105,500. Materials weighing 193,880 pounds were issued to production. Direct labor costs were $396,800 for 99,200 hours.

    a. Compute the materials price variance.
    b. Compute the materials efficiency variance.
    c. Compute the labor price variance.
    d. Compute the labor efficiency variance.

19. *Materials and Labor Variances.* Jonathan Company presents the following data for October:

	Standards per Batch	Actual
Materials	2 Pounds at $5 per Pound	195,000 Pounds
Labor	3 Hours at $6 per Hour	280,000 Hours
Units Produced		96,000 Batches

During the month, 100,000 pounds of materials were purchased for $505,500. Wages earned were $1,708,000. Compute all labor and material variances.

20. *Solving for Materials Quantities and Costs.* Weda Company presents the following variance data for the month: (F indicates favorable variance; U indicates unfavorable variance.)

	Material A	Material B	Material C
Material Price Variance	$ 42,000 F	$ 25,000 F	$ 21,000 U
Material Efficiency Variance	40,000 U	30,000 U	48,000 U
Net Material Variance	$ 2,000 F	$ 5,000 U	$ 69,000 U
Units Produced Requiring This Material . . .	100,000	110,000	125,000

Two pounds of each kind of material are allowed for each unit of output requiring that kind of material. For material A, the average price paid was $.20 per pound less than standard; for material B, $.10 less; for material C, $.07 greater. There are no opening or closing inventories of any kind of material (that is, materials are purchased and used in the same period).

    For each of the three materials, calculate the following:

    a. Number of pounds of material purchased.
    b. Standard cost per pound of material.
    c. Total standard material cost.

21. *Overhead Variances*. Castle Products Company uses a flexible budgeting system for controlling manufacturing overhead costs. As a result of studying past overhead cost data, it has established a flexible budget for overhead as follows:

Fixed Overhead: $500,000 per month.

Variable Overhead: $2 per unit.

Actual data for January, February, and March are as follows:

	Units Produced	Total Overhead Costs
January	50,000	$650,000
February	60,000	610,000
March	40,000	570,000

Determine the total overhead cost variance for each month.

22. *Labor and Overhead Variances (CPA adapted)*. The data below are related to the current month's activity of the Marilyn Corporation:

Actual Total Direct Labor	$43,400
Actual Hours Worked	14,000
Standard Hours Allowed for Actual Output (flexible budget)	15,000
Direct Labor Price Variance	1,400 U
Actual Total Overhead	32,000
Budgeted Fixed Costs	9,000
Master Budget (normal) Activity in Hours	12,000
Actual Fixed Costs	9,100
Total Overhead Application Rate per Direct Labor Hour	$2.25

Compute the labor and variable overhead price and efficiency variances, and the fixed overhead price variance.

23. *Materials Variances*. Information on Milwaukee Company's direct materials costs is as follows:

Actual Quantities of Direct Materials Used	20,000
Actual Costs of Direct Materials Used	$40,000
Standard Price per Unit of Direct Materials	$2.10
Flexible Budget for Direct Materials	$41,000

    a.   What was Milwaukee Company's direct material price variance?

    b.   What was the Company's direct materials efficiency variance?

24. *Overhead Variances*. Information on Omaha Company's combined fixed and variable overhead costs is as follows:

Overhead Applied	$80,000
Actual Overhead	86,000
Flexible Budget Overhead	83,000

    a. What is the amount of the over- or underapplied overhead, assuming that full absorption costing was used?

    b. What is the production volume variance?

25. *Solving for Labor Hours.* Labor Company reports the following direct labor information for product CER for the month of October:

Standard Rate	$6.00 per Hour
Actual Rate Paid	$6.10 per Hour
Standard Hours Allowed for Actual Production	1,500 Hours
Labor Efficiency Variance	$600 U

What are the actual hours worked?

26. *Overhead Variances.* Hyperspace, Inc., which uses standard costing, shows the following overhead information for the current period:

Actual Overhead Incurred	$12,600, of Which $3,500 Is Fixed
Budgeted Fixed Overhead	3,300
Variable Overhead Rate per Direct Labor Hour	$3
Standard Hours Allowed for Actual Production	3,500
Actual Labor Hours Used	3,200

What are the variable overhead price and efficiency variance, and the fixed overhead price variance?

27. *Production Volume Variance.* For the information given in Exercise **26**, what is the fixed overhead production volume variance, assuming that the budgeted fixed overhead is based on an estimated activity of 3,000 hours?

28. *Finding Purchase Price.* Information on Gretsky Company's direct materials cost is as follows:

Standard Price per Materials Unit	$3.60
Actual Quantity Used	1,600
Standard Quantity Allowed for Production	1,450
Materials Price Variance	$240 F

What was the actual purchase price per unit, rounded to the nearest cent?

29. *Overhead Variances.* Trapp Electronics Corporation estimated its overhead costs for 19X0 to be as follows: fixed, $400,000; variable, $6 per unit. Trapp expected to produce 100,000 units during the year.

    a. Determine the rate to be used to apply overhead costs to products.

    b. During 19X0, Trapp incurred overhead costs of $950,000 and produced 90,000 units. Determine the amount of overhead costs applied to units produced.

    c. Refer to part **b**. Determine the amount of under- or overapplied overhead for the year.

30. *Overhead Variances.* Wyman Company uses a predetermined rate for applying overhead costs to production. The rates for 19X0 were as follows: variable, $2 per unit; fixed, $1 per unit. Actual overhead costs incurred were as follows: variable, $95,000; fixed, $45,000. Wyman expected to produce 45,000 units during the year but produced only 40,000 units.

    a.   What was the amount of budgeted fixed costs for the year?
    b.   What is the amount of under- or overapplied overhead for the year?
    c.   Compute all possible overhead variances.

31. *Recording Overhead Costs (Appendix) (CMA adapted).* Standard Company has developed standard overhead costs based on a capacity of 180,000 direct labor hours as follows:

Standard Costs per Unit:	
Variable Portion: 2 Hours at $3	$ 6
Fixed Portion: 2 Hours at $5	10
	$16

During April, 90,000 units were scheduled for production; however, only 80,000 units were actually produced. The following data relate to April:

(1) Actual direct labor cost incurred was $644,000 for 165,000 actual hours of work.
(2) Actual overhead incurred totaled $1,378,000—$518,000 variable and $860,000 fixed.
(3) All inventories are carried at standard cost.

    Use T-accounts to show the recording of these overhead costs in Work-in-Process Inventory together with the related variances.

32. *Recording Overhead Costs (Appendix) (CPA adapted).* Union Company uses a standard cost accounting system. The following overhead costs and production data are available for August 1981:

Standard Fixed Overhead Rate per Direct Labor Hour	$1.00
Standard Variable Overhead Rate per Direct Labor Hour	$4.00
Budgeted Monthly Direct Labor Hours	40,000
Actual Direct Labor Hours Worked	39,500
Standard Direct Labor Hours Allowed for Actual Production.	39,000
Overall Overhead Variance—Favorable.	$ 2,000
Actual Variable Overhead	$159,500

Show the flow of these overhead costs in T-account form.

33. *Overhead Journal Entries (Appendix).* Using the data in Exercise **32**, prepare journal entries to reflect the events of the month as they would appear in a standard cost system.

Problems and Cases

34. *Overhead Variances.* The manufacturing overhead costs of Windum Industries, Incorporated, are separable into fixed and variable components. The flexible budget for overhead costs is

Fixed Costs: $100,000 per period.

Variable Costs: $10 per unit.

During the period, 20,000 units were produced. Actual manufacturing overhead costs were $350,000.

    a. Determine the total manufacturing overhead variance.

    b. Assume that, of the $350,000 total overhead costs incurred, $120,000 were fixed costs and $230,000 were variable costs. Determine the total fixed cost variance and the total variable cost variance.

    c. Assume that each unit of output requires 2 hours of labor and that variable overhead costs vary both with labor hours and units of output. Thus, variable overhead costs are expected to be $10 per unit or $5 per direct labor hour. During the period, 42,000 labor hours were worked in producing the 20,000 units of output. Disaggregate the total variable overhead variance determined in part **b** into a price variance and an efficiency variance.

35. *Labor and Overhead Variances.* Direct labor and variable overhead standards per finished unit for Columbia Metals Company are as follows:

Direct Labor: 10 hours at $5.00 per hour.

Variable Overhead: 10 hours at $2.00 per hour.

During July, 5,000 finished units were produced. Direct labor costs were $234,000 (52,000 hours). Actual variable overhead costs were $103,000.

    a. Determine the price and efficiency variances for direct labor.

    b. Determine the price and efficiency variances for variable overhead.

    c. What similarities are there likely to be between the factors that cause the direct labor price variance and the variable overhead price variance?

    d. What similarities are there likely to be between the factors that cause the direct labor efficiency variances and the variable overhead efficiency variance?

36. *Performance Evaluation in a Service Industry.* National Insurance Company estimates that its overhead costs for policy administration should cost $72 for each new policy obtained and $2 per year for each $1,000 face amount of insurance outstanding. The company set a budget of 5,000 new policies for the coming period. In addition, the company estimated that the total face amount of insurance outstanding for the period would equal $10,800,000.

During the period, actual costs related to new policies amounted to $358,400. A total of 4,800 new policies were obtained.

The cost of maintaining existing policies was $23,200. Had these costs been incurred at the same prices as were in effect when the budget was prepared, the costs would have amounted to $22,900. However, there was $12,100,000 in policies outstanding during the period.

Prepare a schedule to indicate the differences between a master production budget and actual costs for this operation.

37. *Manufacturing Variances.* The standard cost of product A of the Acme Company is composed of the following items:

Material: 6 pounds at $.75 per pound.

Labor: 1 hour at $5.00 per hour.

Overhead: $2,500 per month plus $2.50 per unit.

During January, 30,000 pounds of material were purchased at an average cost of $.76 a pound and 29,000 pounds were used; 5,000 direct labor hours were worked at an average rate of $5.05 per hour; and actual overhead costs were $15,500, of which $2,400 was fixed. There were 5,000 units started and completed during the month.

Compute the amount of each of the following variances:
  a. Materials price variance.
  b. Materials efficiency variance.
  c. Labor price variance.
  d. Labor efficiency variance.
  e. Total overhead variances in as much detail as possible.

38. *Manufacturing Variances.* Alger Company manufactures salad bowls. The company makes two types of bowls, A and B, from the same material. The company has no fixed overhead. The following are the standards and production data for November:

	Bowl A	Bowl B
Standard Costs		
Raw Materials	$ .25 (.05 lb at $5.00)	$ .50 (.10 lb at $5.00)
Labor	$ .40 (6 min at $4.00)	$ .45 (6 min at $4.50)
Overhead	$1.60 per direct labor hour	$1.50 per direct labor hour
Production Data for November		
Units	5,000	3,000
Pounds of Raw Materials Used	250	305
Direct Labor Hours Used . . .	500	299
Labor Costs Incurred	$2,060.00	$1,330.55

Total overhead was $1,236. This amount is to be allocated proportionately to the total costs of the two products on the basis of standard direct labor hours. One thousand pounds of raw materials were purchased for $5,020. The labor efficiency variance for bowl A was zero.

  a. Compute the raw material price variance.
  b. Compute the raw material efficiency variance for bowl A and for bowl B.
  c. Compute the direct labor price and efficiency variances for bowl A and for bowl B.

    d. Compute the variable overhead price and efficiency variances for bowl A and for bowl B.

39. *Solving for Materials and Labor.* Under the flexible budget of the Ceramic Tile Company, budgeted variable overhead is $60,000 when 60,000 direct labor hours are worked, whereas budgeted direct labor costs are $300,000. All data apply to the month of February.

    The following are some of the variances for February (F denotes Favorable; U denotes Unfavorable):

Variable Overhead Price Variance	$12,000 U
Variable Overhead Efficiency Variance	10,000 U
Materials Price Variance.	15,000 F
Materials Efficiency Variance	8,000 U

    $325,500 of direct labor costs were incurred in February. According to the standards, 1 pound of material should cost $2.00. One pound of material is the standard for each unit of product. One hundred thousand units were produced in February. The unit materials price variance was $.20 per pound, whereas the average wage rate exceeded the standard average rate by $.25.

    Compute the following for February, assuming that there are opening and closing inventories of materials:

    a. Pounds of materials purchased.
    b. Pounds of material usage over standard.
    c. Standard hourly wage rate.
    d. Standard direct labor hours for the total February production.

40. *Manufacturing Variances.* The Old Style Company mass produces pseudo-antique rolltop desks. The standard costs are

Wood	25 Pounds at $3.20 per Pound
Trim	8 Pounds at $5.00 per Pound
Direct Labor	5 Hours at $6.00 per Hour
Variable Overhead	$15 per Unit
Fixed Overhead	$62,000 per Period

Transactions during February were as follows:

(1) Eighty tons of wood were purchased at $3.25 per pound; 155,000 pounds were issued to production.
(2) Twenty-five tons (50,000 pounds) of trim were purchased at $4.80 per pound; 48,500 pounds were issued to production.
(3) The direct labor payroll was 31,000 hours at $5.75.
(4) Overhead costs were $151,000, of which $60,500 were fixed.
(5) Six thousand desks were produced during February.

Calculate all variances to the extent permitted by the data.

41. *Recording Standard Costs (Appendix).* Using the data in Problem **40**, present the flow of costs in T-accounts.

42. *Manufacturing Cost Variances.* The Seasonal Company manufactures Christmas cards and other greeting cards. Fixed overhead is budgeted at $6,000 per month. Variable overhead is budgeted at $9,500 when 10,000 direct labor hours are worked per month.

The following data are available for April (F denotes Favorable; U denotes Unfavorable):

Materials Purchased	20,000 Units
Direct Labor Costs Incurred	$36,000
Total Direct Labor Variance	$500 F
Average Actual Wage Rate ($.20 less than the standard wage rate)	$4.80
Variable Overhead Costs Incurred	$6,675
Materials Price Variance	$200 F
Materials Efficiency Variance	$610 F
Price of Purchased Materials	$.60 per Unit
Materials Used	15,000 Units
Actual Fixed Overhead	$7,200

Using the above data, identify and present computations for all variances.

43. *Manufacturing Cost Variances.* The standard materials and labor cost per unit for the manufacturing departments of the Davis Company are as follows:

Material, 2 Pounds of Material A at $3.00	$6.00
Labor, 4 Standard Hours at $2.00 per Hour.	8.00

The flexible budget shows the following monthly allowances for manufacturing overhead costs:

	8,000 Units	10,000 Units	12,000 Units
Units Produced			
Manufacturing Overhead Costs:			
Fixed	$30,000	$30,000	$30,000
Variable	32,000	40,000	48,000
Total Manufacturing Overhead Costs.	$62,000	$70,000	$78,000

During the month of December, 8,000 units were completed at the following costs:

Materials Purchased and Used, 16,200 Pounds at $3.20	$51,840
Direct Labor, 31,800 Hours at $2.10	66,780
Manufacturing Overhead Costs ($32,000 fixed, $31,000 variable)	63,000

Compute all variances possible.

44. *Investigating a Process.* A financial analyst is trying to determine if a particular production process is in control. The cost of investigation is $3,500; if the process is out of control, it will cost the company $7,500 to correct the error. By correcting the error, the present value of the cost savings until the next scheduled routine intervention will be $20,000. The probability of the process being in control is .80, and the probability of the process being out of control is .20.

Should the process be investigated? Why or why not?

45. *Controlling Labor Costs (CPA adapted).* The Clark Company has a contract with a labor union that guarantees a minimum wage of $500 per month to each direct labor employee with at least 12 years of service. One hundred employees currently qualify for coverage. All direct labor employees are paid $5 per hour.

The direct labor budget for 1985 was based on the annual usage of 400,000 hours of direct labor at $5, or a total of $2,000,000. Of this amount, $50,000 (100 employees × $500) per month (or $600,000 for the year) was regarded as fixed. Thus, the budget for any given month was determined by the formula $50,000 + $3.50 (direct labor hours worked).

Data on performance for the first 3 months of 1985 follows:

	January	February	March
Direct Labor Hours Worked.	22,000	32,000	42,000
Direct Labor Costs Budgeted	$127,000	$162,000	$197,000
Direct Labor Costs Incurred	110,000	160,000	210,000
Variance	17,000 F	2,000 F	13,000 U

The factory manager was perplexed by the results, which showed favorable variances when production was low and unfavorable variances when production was high, because the factory manager believed the control over labor costs was consistently good.

  a. Why did the variances arise? Explain and illustrate, using amounts and diagrams as necessary.

  b. Does this direct labor budget provide a basis for controlling direct labor cost? Explain, indicating changes that might be made to improve control over direct labor cost and to facilitate performance evaluation of direct labor employees.

46. *Variance Investigation (CMA adapted).* The Bilco Oil Company currently sells three grades of gasoline: regular, premium, and "regular plus," which is a mixture of regular and premium. Regular plus is advertised as being "at least 50 percent premium." Although any mixture containing 50 percent or more premium gas could be sold as "regular plus," it is less costly to use exactly 50 percent. The percent of premium gas in the mixture is determined by a valve in the blending machine. If the valve is properly adjusted, the machine provides a mixture that is 50 percent premium and 50 percent regular. If the valve is out of adjustment, the machine provides a mixture that is 60 percent premium and 40 percent regular.

Once the machine is started, it must continue until 100,000 gallons of "regular plus" have been mixed.

Cost data available:

Cost per Gallon—Premium	$.32
—Regular	$.30
Cost of Checking the Valve	$80
Cost of Adjusting the Valve	$40

The probabilities of the valve's condition are estimated to be

Event	Probability
In Adjustment	.7
Out of Adjustment	.3

    a. Should Bilco investigate the valve?

    b. At what probability would Bilco be indifferent about whether to investigate?

47. *Variance Investigation: Multiple Choice (CPA adapted).* The folding department foreman must decide each week whether the department will operate normally the following week. The foreman may order a corrective action if it is believed that the folding department will operate inefficiently; otherwise nothing is done. The foreman receives a weekly folding department efficiency variance report from the accounting department. A week in which the folding department operates inefficiently is usually preceded by a large efficiency variance. The graph gives the probability that the folding department will operate normally in the following week as a function of the magnitude of the current week's variance reported to the foreman.

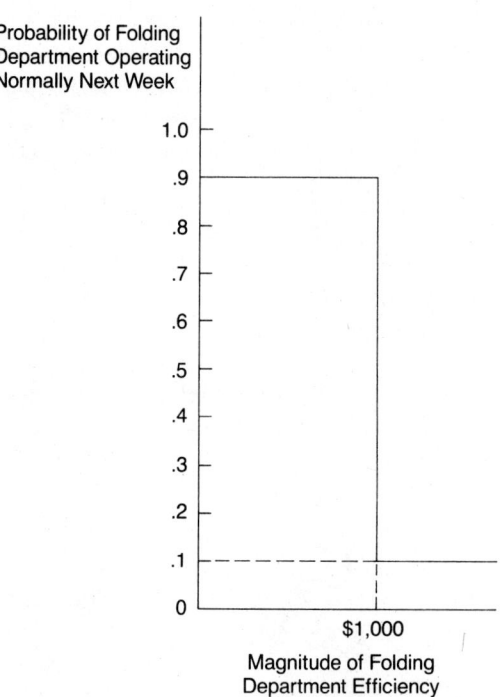

a. An efficiency variance of $1,500 this week means the probability of operating normally the following week is (choose one):

(1) 0.
(2) .1.
(3) .9.
(4) 1.

b. What are the possible relations between the current efficiency variance and next week's operations (choose one)?

(1) Large variance followed by normal operation, large variance followed by inefficient operation, small variance followed by normal operation, and small variance followed by inefficient operation.
(2) Large variance followed by normal operation, small variance followed by inefficient operation, and small variance followed by normal operation.
(3) Large variance followed by inefficient operation, small variance followed by normal operation, and small variance followed by inefficient operation.
(4) Large variance followed by 90 percent of normal operation, small variance followed by 10 percent of normal operation, large variance followed by inefficient operation, and small variance followed by inefficient operation.

c. If the foreman can determine for certain whether the folding department will operate normally next week and the cost of corrective action is less than the extra cost of operating the folding department inefficiently, then the best decision rule for the foreman to follow is (choose one):

(1) If normal operations are predicted, do not take corrective action; if inefficient operations are predicted, take corrective action.
(2) Regardless of the current variance, do not take corrective action.
(3) If normal operations are predicted, take corrective action; if inefficient operations are predicted, do not take corrective action.
(4) Regardless of the current variance, take corrective action.

d. The following cost information is relevant to the folding department foreman in deciding whether corrective action is warranted:

$500 = cost of corrective action that will assure normal operation of folding department for the following week.

$3,000 = excess cost of operating folding department inefficiently for one week.

The foreman receives a report that the folding department efficiency variance is $600. The expected benefit of taking corrective action is (choose one):

(1) $0.
(2) $300.
(3) $2,700.
(4) $3,000.

48. *Materials Variances.* Starship Steel Company had the following direct materials data for its product:

Standard costs for 1 unit of output:

   Material A, 10 units of input at $100.

   Material B, 20 units of input at $150.

During August the company had the following results:

Units of Output Produced	2,000 Units
Materials Purchased and Used:	
Material A	22,000 Units at $90
Material B	39,000 Units at $152

Compute materials price and efficiency variances.

49. *Labor Variances.* Quicki-Burger has two categories of direct labor: unskilled, which costs $8 per hour; and skilled, which costs $12 per hour. Management has established standards per "equivalent meal," which has been defined as a typical meal consisting of a sandwich, a drink, and a side order. Standards have been set as follows:

   Skilled labor: 4 minutes per equivalent meal.

   Unskilled labor: 10 minutes per equivalent meal.

During May, Quicki-Burger sold 30,000 equivalent meals and incurred the following labor costs:

Skilled Labor: 1,600 Hours	$19,000
Unskilled Labor: 4,200 Hours	37,000

Compute labor price and efficiency variances.

50. *Standard Cost Systems (Appendix) (CMA adapted).* Nanron Company has a process standard cost system for all its products. All inventories are carried at standard during the year. The inventories and cost of goods sold are adjusted for all variances considered material in amount at the end of the fiscal year for financial statement purposes. All products are considered to flow through the manufacturing process to finished goods and ultimate sale in a first-in, first-out (FIFO) pattern.

The standard cost of one of Nanron's products manufactured in the Dixon Plant, unchanged from the prior year, is shown below.

Direct Materials	$2
Direct Labor (.5 direct labor hour at $8)	4
Manufacturing Overhead	3
Total Standard Cost	$9

There is no work-in-process inventory of this product, because of the nature of the product and the manufacturing process.

The schedule below reports the manufacturing and sales activity measured at standard cost for the current fiscal year.

	Units	Dollars
Product Manufactured	95,000	$855,000
Beginning Finished Goods Inventory	15,000	135,000
Goods Available for Sale	110,000	$990,000
Ending Finished Goods Inventory	19,000	171,000
Cost of Goods Sold	91,000	$819,000

The manufacturing performance relative to standard costs both this year and last year was not good. The balance of the finished goods inventory, $140,800, reported on the balance sheet at the beginning of the year included a $5,800 adjustment for variances from standard cost. The unfavorable standard cost variances for labor for the current fiscal year consisted of a wage rate variance of $32,000 and a labor efficiency variance of $20,000 (2,500 hours at $8). There were no other variances from standard cost for this year.

Adjust the inventories and cost of goods sold to reflect the actual costs of this year's production.

51. *Standard Cost Systems and Revisions of Standards (Appendix) (CMA adapted).* The Lenco Company employs a standard cost system as part of its cost control program. The standard cost per unit is established at the beginning of each year. Standards are not revised during the year for any changes in material or labor inputs or in the manufacturing processes. Any revisions in standards are deferred until the beginning of the next fiscal year. However, in order to recognize such changes in the current year, the company includes planned variances in the monthly budgets prepared after such changes have been introduced.

The following labor standard was set for one of Lenco's products effective July 1, 1984, the beginning of the fiscal year.

Class I Labor: 4 Hours at $6	$24.00
Class II Labor: 3 Hours at $7.50	22.50
Class V Labor: 1 Hour at $11.50	11.50
Standard labor cost per 100 units	$58.00

The standard was based on the quality of material that had been used in prior years and what was expected to be available for the 1984–1985 fiscal year. The labor activity is performed by a team consisting of four persons with class I skills, three persons with class II skills, and one person with class V skills. This is the most economical combination for the company's processing system.

The manufacturing operations occurred as expected during the first 5 months of the year. The standard costs contributed to effective cost control during this period. However, there were indications that changes in the operations would be required in the last half of the year. The company had received a significant increase in orders for delivery in the spring. There were an inadequate number of skilled workers available to meet the increased production. As a result, the production teams, beginning in January, would be made up of more class I labor and less class II labor than the standard required. The teams would consist of six class I persons, two class II persons, and one class V person. This labor team would be less efficient than the normal team. The reorganized teams work more slowly, so that only 90 units are produced in the same time period that 100 units would normally be produced. No direct materials will be lost as a result of the change in the labor mix. Completed units have never been rejected in the final inspection process as a consequence of faulty work; this is expected to continue.

In addition, Lenco was notified by its material supplier that a lower-quality material would be supplied after January 1. One unit of direct material normally is required for each good unit produced. Lenco and its supplier estimated that 5 percent of the units manufactured would be rejected upon final inspection due to defective material. Normally, no units are lost due to defective material.

    a. How much of the lower-quality material must be entered into production in order to produce 42,750 units of good production in January with the new labor teams? Show your calculations.

    b. How many hours of each class of labor will be needed to produce 42,750 good units from the material input? Show your calculations.

    c. What amount should be included in the January budget for the planned labor variance due to the labor team and material changes? What amount of this planned labor variance can be associated with the **(1)** material change and **(2)** the team change? Show your calculations.

52. *Comprehensive Overview of Budgets, Variances, and Cost Systems.* "I just don't understand these financial statements at all!" exclaimed Mr. Elmo Knapp. Mr. Knapp explained that he had turned over management of Racketeer, Inc., division of American Recreation Equipment, Inc., to his son, Otto, the previous month. Racketeer, Inc., manufactures tennis rackets.

"I was really proud of Otto," he beamed. "He was showing us all the tricks he learned in business school and, if I say so myself, I think he was doing a rather good job for us. For example, he put together this budget for Racketeer, which makes it real easy to see how much profit we'll make at any sales volume (Exhibit 13.13). As best as I can figure it, in March we expected to have a volume of 8,000 units and a profit of $14,500 on our rackets. But we did much better than that! We sold 10,000 rackets, so we should have made almost $21,000 on them."

"Another one of Otto's innovations is this standard cost system," said Mr. Knapp proudly. "He sat down with our production people and came up with a standard production cost per unit (see Exhibit 13.14). He tells me this will tell us how well our production people are performing. Also, he claims it will cut down on our clerical work."

Mr. Knapp continued, "But one thing puzzles me. My calculations show that we should have shown a profit of nearly $21,000 in March. However, our accountants came up with less than $19,000 in the monthly income statement (Exhibit 13.15). This bothers me a great deal. Now I'm not sure our accountants are doing their job properly. It appears to be that they're about $2,200 short."

"As you can probably guess," Mr. Knapp concluded, "we are one big happy

Exhibit 13.13
RACKETEER, INC.
Profit Graph, Rackets

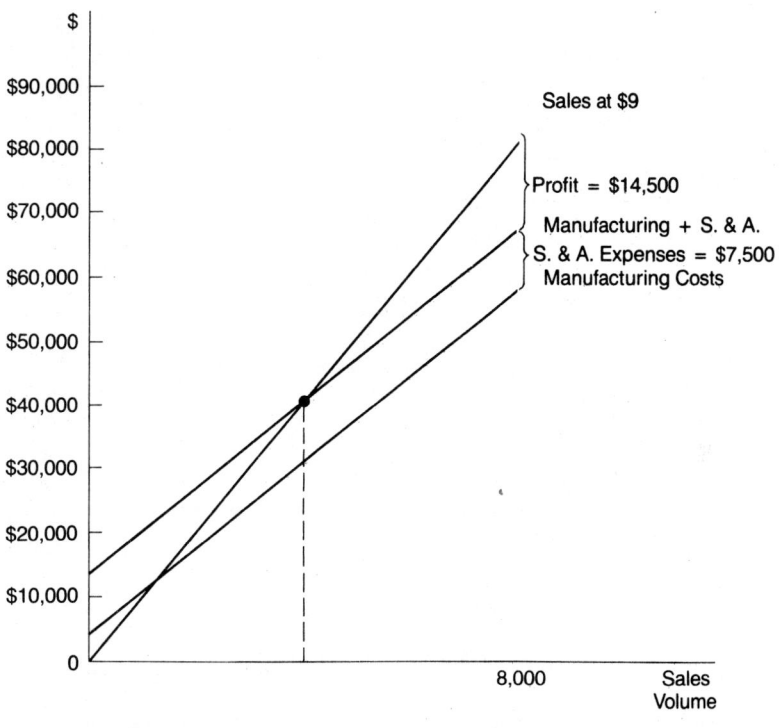

Exhibit 13.14
RACKETEER, INC.
Standard Costs,[a]

	Per Racket
Raw Material:	
Frame	$3.15
Stringing Materials: 20 Feet at $.03 per Foot	.60
Direct Labor:	
Skilled ⅛ Hour at $9.60 per Hour	1.20
Unskilled ⅛ Hour at $5.60 per Hour	.70
Plant Overhead:	
Indirect Labor	.10
Power	.03
Supervision	.12[b]
Depreciation	.20[b]
Other	.15[b]
Total Standard Cost per Frame	$6.25

[a]Standard costs are calculated for an estimated volume of 8,000 units each month.
[b]Fixed costs.

Exhibit 13.15
RACKETEER, INC.
Income Statement for March
Actual

Sales: 10,000 Rackets at $9	$90,000
Standard Cost of Goods Sold: 10,000 Rackets at $6.25	62,500
Gross Profit After Standard Costs	$27,500
Variances:	
Material Variance	(490)
Labor Variance	(392)
Overhead Variance	(660)
Gross Profit	$25,958
Selling and Administrative Expense	7,200
Operating Profit	$18,758

family around here. I just wish I knew what those accountants are up to—coming in with a low net income like that.''

Prepare a report for Mr. Elmo Knapp and Mr. Otto Knapp that reconciles the profit graph with the actual results for March. Show the source of each variance from the original plan (8,000 rackets) in as much detail as you can, and evaluate Racketeer's performance in March. (Actual production data for March appear in Exhibit 13.16.) Recommend improvements in Racketeer's profit planning and control methods.

53. *Standard Cost Flows* (Appendix). Refer to Problem **52.** Present the flow of costs in T-account form.

Exhibit 13.16
RACKETEER, INC.
Actual Production Data for March

Direct Materials Purchased and Used:	
Stringing Materials	175,000 Feet at $.025 per Foot
Frames	7,100 at $3.15 per Frame
Labor:	
Skilled ($9.80 per hour)	900 Hours
Unskilled ($5.80 per hour)	840 Hours
Overhead:	
Indirect Labor	$ 800
Power	250
Depreciation	1,600
Supervision	960
Other	1,250
Production	7,000 Rackets

Suggested Solutions to Even-Numbered Exercises

18. *Materials and Labor Variances.*

a. Materials Price Variance $= 200,000 \times \left(\dfrac{\$105,500}{200,000} - \$.50 \right) = \$5,500$ U.

b. Materials Efficiency Variance $= (193,880 - 195,620) \times \$.50$
$$= \$870 \text{ F.}$$

c. Labor Price Variance $= 99,200 \times \left(\dfrac{\$396,800}{99,200} - \$4.50 \right) = \$49,600$ F.

d. Labor Efficiency Variance $= (99,200 - 97,810) \times \$4.50 = \$6,255$ U.

20. *Solving for Materials Quantities and Costs.*
Material A:

a. Price Variance $= \$.20$ F per pound.
Total Price Variance $= \$42,000$ F.
Pounds Purchased and Used $= \dfrac{\$42,000}{\$.20} = 210,000.$

b. Standard Pounds Allowed for 100,000 Units $= 200,000.$
Used over Standard $= 210,000 - 200,000 = 10,000.$
Efficiency Variance $= \$40,000$ U.
Standard Unit Price $= \dfrac{\$40,000}{10,000} = \$4.00.$

c. 200,000 Pounds $\times \$4.00$ per Pound $= \$800,000.$

Material B:

a. Pounds Purchased and Used $= \dfrac{\$25,000}{\$.10} = 250,000.$

b. Standard Unit Price $= \dfrac{\$30,000}{(250,000 - 220,000)} = \dfrac{\$30,000}{30,000} = \$1.00.$

c. $220,000 \times \$1.00 = \$220,000.$

Material C:

a. Pounds Purchased and Used $= \dfrac{\$21,000}{\$.07} = 300,000.$

b. Standard Unit Price $= \dfrac{\$48,000}{(300,000 - 250,000)} = \$.96.$

c. $250,000 \times \$.96 = \$240,000.$

22. *Labor and Overhead Variances.*

	Actual Costs	Price Variance	Inputs at Standard Price	Efficiency Variance	Flexible Production Budget
Direct Labor			$43,400 - $1,400 = $42,000		15,000 × $3.00[b] = $45,000
	$43,400				
		⟶ $1,400 U ⟵		⟶ $3,000 F ⟵	
Variable Overhead	$32,000 - $9,100 = $22,900		14,000 × $1.50[a] = $21,000		15,000 × $1.50[a] = $22,500
		⟶ $1,900 U ⟵		⟶ $1,500 F ⟵	
Fixed Overhead	$9,100				$9,000
		⟶ $100 U ⟵			

[a]$1.50 per hour = $2.25 per hour total overhead minus $.75 per hour fixed overhead, where $.75 per hour = $9,000 budgeted fixed overhead ÷ 12,000 budgeted hours.

[b]$3.00 per hour = $\dfrac{\$42,000}{14,000\ \text{hours}}$.

24. *Overhead Variances.*

Actual Costs		Flexible Budget		Overhead Applied
$86,000		$83,000	Production Volume Variance:	$80,000
	Underapplied Overhead:		⟶ $3,000 U ⟵	
	⟶ $6,000 U ⟵			

26. *Overhead Variances.*

	Actual Costs	Price Variance	Inputs at Standard Prices	Efficiency Variance	Flexible Budget
Variable Overhead	$12,600 - $3,500 = $9,100		$3 × 3,200 Hours = $9,600		$3 × 3,500 Hours = $10,500
Fixed Overhead		⟶ $500 F ⟵		⟶ $900 F ⟵	
	$3,500				$3,300
		⟶ $200 U ⟵			

28. *Finding Purchase Price.*

Actual Costs	Price Variance	Inputs at Standard Prices
1,600 × AP		1,600 × $3.60 = $5,760

$\longrightarrow$ \$240 F $\longleftarrow$

1,600 × AP = $5,760 − $240
AP = $3.45

30. *Overhead Variances.*

a.   Budgeted Fixed Costs = $1.00 per Unit × 45,000 Units

= $45,000.

b.   Applied Overhead = ($1.00 × 40,000) + ($2.00 × 40,000)

= $120,000.

$140,000 − $120,000 = $20,000 Underapplied.

c. $\dfrac{\text{Total Variable}}{\text{Overhead Variance}}$ = $\dfrac{\text{Actual Costs} - \text{Flexible}}{\text{Production Budget Costs}}$

= $95,000 − (40,000 × $2.00)

= $15,000 U.

Fixed Overhead Variance Analysis:

Actual	Price Variance	Budget	Production Volume Variance	Applied
$45,000		$45,000		40,000

$\longrightarrow$ 0 $\longleftarrow$ $\longrightarrow$ \$5,000 U $\longleftarrow$

32. *Recording Overhead Costs.*

Variable Overhead		Variable Overhead Price Variance		Variable Overhead Efficiency Variance		Work-in-Process	
159,500	156,000[a]	1,500[d]		2,000[b]		156,000	
	3,500						

Fixed Overhead		Fixed Overhead Price Variance		Fixed Overhead Production Volume			
33,500[g]	39,000[f]		6,500[e]	1,000[c]		39,000	
5,500							

[a]39,000 direct labor hours at $4.00 = $156,000.

[b]$(39,500 \times \$4) - (39,000 \times \$4) = \$2,000$.

[c]$(40,000 \times \$1) - (39,000 \times \$1) = \$1,000$.

[d]$159,500 - (39,500 \times \$4) = \$1,500$.

[e]$2,000 F - \$1,500 U - \$2,000 U - \$1,000 U = \$6,500 F$.

[f]39,000 direct labor hours at $1.00 = $39,000.

[g]Actual − Applied = $−2,000.

$159,500 + X - (\$156,000 + \$39,000) = \$-2,000$.

$X = \$33,500$ Actual Fixed Overhead.

Chapter 14 Divisional Performance Measurement and Control

Companies like General Electric, Honeywell, and Du Pont have multiple products and divisions. Central corporate management determines broad corporate policies, establishes long-range plans, raises capital, and conducts other coordinating activities. But there are hundreds of corporate affiliates and divisions to oversee. How do companies like these measure and control the performance of their divisions in such widely diverse and geographically dispersed operating environments? Such companies rely heavily on their accounting systems to measure performance and to help control and coordinate their activities. This chapter discusses concepts and methods of measuring performance and controlling activities in multidivision companies.

Divisional Organization and Performance

The term "division" is used by different companies to mean different things. Some companies use the term to refer to segments organized according to product groupings, whereas other companies use it in reference to geographic areas served. We use the term "division" to refer to a segment that conducts both production and marketing activities.

As discussed in Chapter 11, a division may be either a *profit center,* having responsibility for both revenues and operating costs, or an *investment center,* having responsibility for assets in addition to revenues and operating costs. Many companies treat the division almost as an autonomous "company." Headquarters provides funds for its divisions, much as shareholders and bondholders provide funds for the company.

A partial organization chart for Honeywell, Incorporated, is presented in Exhibit 14.1 to show how divisions fit into the entire organization. The organization chart in Exhibit 14.1 presents only a small part of this complex organization. Honeywell has a layer of responsibility centers not previously discussed in this book, called "groups" of divisions. Groups, like divisions, are investment centers at Honeywell. Managers of groups and divisions are responsible for revenues, costs, and assets invested in the divisions and groups. Most operating units below the division level are responsible for either revenues or costs alone.

Exhibit 14.1
HONEYWELL, INCORPORATED
Partial Organization Chart

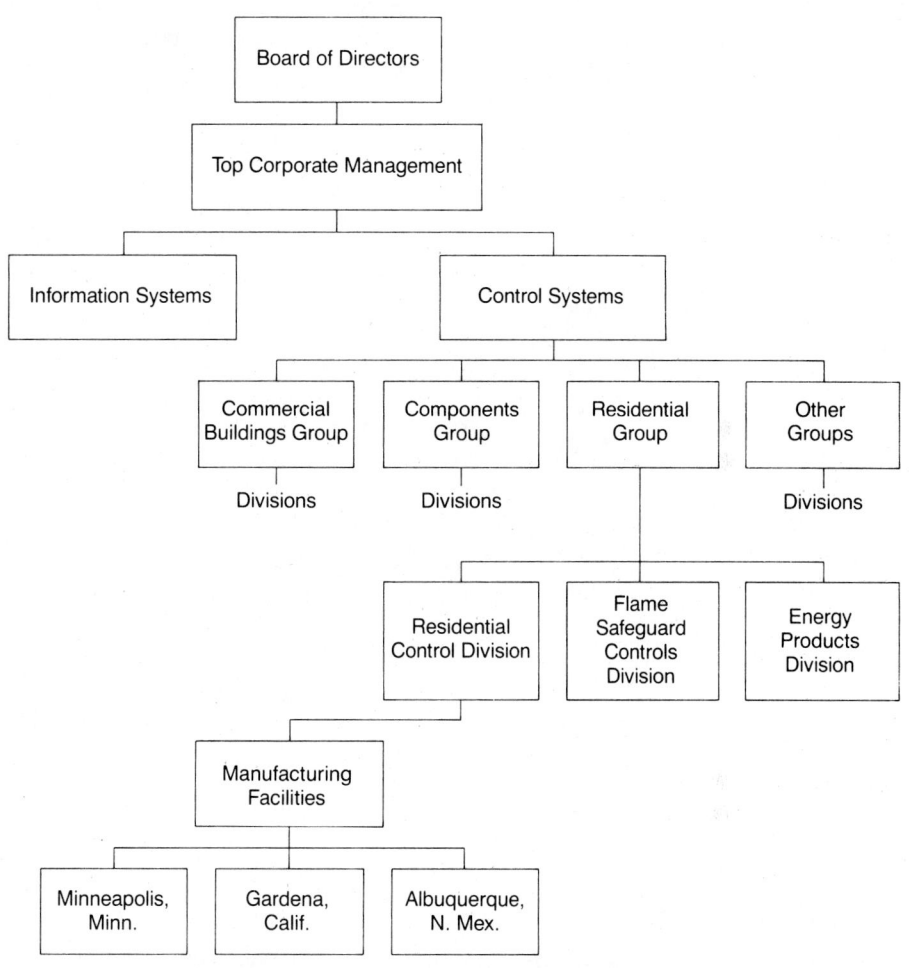

Source: Honeywell Annual Report, 1982.

The Nature of Divisionalized Organizations

The essence of divisionalization is the delegation, or decentralization, of decision-making authority and responsibility. Delegation of managerial duties is common in all but very small organizations. The major advantages of delegation are the following:

1. Delegation allows local personnel to respond quickly to a changing environment.

2. Delegation frees top management from detailed operating decisions.
3. Delegation divides large, complex problems into manageable pieces.
4. Delegation helps train managers and provides a basis for evaluating their decision-making performance.
5. Delegation motivates: Ambitious managers are likely to be frustrated if they implement only the decisions of others. Delegation allows managers to make their own decisions.

Delegation has disadvantages, however. Local managers may take actions that are not "congruent" with the overall goals of the organization. For example, a division manager might decide to purchase materials from an outside supplier even though another division of the firm could produce the materials at a lower incremental cost using currently idle facilities. Top management must be continually alert to situations where trade-offs are required between the benefits of decentralized decision-making authority in a divisionalized company and the possible conflicts between the goals of a division and those of the organization as a whole. Thus, divisional planning and control systems attempt to encourage division managers to take actions that are consistent with organizational goals.[1] This attempt is called seeking *behavioral congruence* or *goal congruence*.

Delegation is not unique to divisionalized organizations—it occurs in many employee-employer relationships. Divisionalized organizations carry delegation to an extreme, however, by giving divisional managers responsibility for nearly everything that occurs in their division.

Criteria for Divisional Performance Measurement

Control systems in general are more likely to be effective if there is a quantitative measure that captures the relevant aspects of performance of the unit being considered. This statement applies to divisional performance controls as well as other controls.

Desirable Dimensions of a Divisional Performance Measure

One desirable attribute is that the measure provides a *common basis* for comparing and evaluating the performance of divisions operating in widely different geographic and product markets. This is critical from the standpoint of top management. Because a principal goal of all divisions is to generate profits, the measure commonly used is based on divisional income or profits.

A second desirable attribute is that the divisional performance measure be *independent* from performance achieved in other parts of the company. This attribute is desirable so that responsibility can be pinpointed and divisional managers can

---

[1] For an expanded discussion, see David Solomons, *Divisional Performance Measurement and Control* (Homewood, Ill.: Richard D. Irwin, 1968).

be held accountable only for activities over which they have some degree of control. (Hence, this is also called the *controllability* attribute.) A divisional performance measure will not be independent if a portion of one division's costs or part of the central corporate headquarters' costs are allocated to another division. If the division had no control over these costs, they should not affect top management's evaluation of the division's performance.

A third desirable attribute is that the divisional performance measure indicate as closely as possible the *contribution* the division makes to company-wide results. This contribution may be somewhat different from the amount over which the division has control. One obvious example is the salary of the divisional manager. The amount of the salary is likely to be determined by top management and therefore not be controllable by the division manager. However, it is a necessary cost that must be covered before the division can contribute to the profits of the company and should, therefore, be included in any measure of the division's performance.

Separating a Manager's Performance from Divisional Performance In general, it is wise to discriminate between the measure of an organizational unit's performance and that of the unit's manager. Often we find managers performing well despite poor performance by the division due to factors outside of the manager's control.

Another example relates to interdivisional conflict. Assume a division purchased materials externally rather than buying from a division inside the company with idle capacity. By purchasing from a source outside of the company, the profits of the two divisions together are less than if the materials had been purchased from the division inside the company. Should the performance measure for each division reflect the results of its actual transactions? Or should the cost of idle capacity in the one division be charged against the profits of the other division? There are no easy answers to these questions. Top management needs to be informed of situations where actions of individual divisions are detrimental to overall company performance.

Return on Investment as the Performance Measure

Given that one of the principal goals of the divisions is to contribute to the profits of the company, it is not surprising that divisional operating profit is a commonly used measure of performance. Divisional operating profit by itself, however, does not provide a basis for measuring a division's performance in generating a return on the funds invested in the division. For example, the fact that Division A had an operating profit of $50,000 does not necessarily mean that it was more successful than Division B, which had an operating profit of $40,000. The difference between these profit levels could be attributable entirely to a difference in the size of the divisions. Some means must therefore be used to scale the division profit measure for the amount of capital invested in the division. One commonly used way to achieve the result is to measure the division return on investment, or ROI, calculated as follows:

$$\begin{array}{l} \text{Division} \\ \text{Return on} \\ \text{Investment} \\ \text{(ROI)} \end{array} = \frac{\text{Division Operating Profit}}{\text{Division Investment}}$$

$$= \frac{\text{Division Revenue} - \text{Division Operating Costs}}{\text{Division Investment}}.$$

If the investments of Division A and Division B in the preceding example were $500,000 and $250,000, respectively, then the ROIs would be 10 percent (= $50,000 ÷ $500,000) and 16 percent (= $40,000 ÷ $250,000). Thus, Division B was more profitable given its investment base than was Division A, even though Division A generated a larger absolute amount of profit.

There are several important questions that must be answered before ROI can be applied as a control measure:

1.   How are revenues measured, particularly when part of a division's output is transferred to another division rather than being sold externally?
2.   Which costs are deducted in determining divisional operating costs—only those that are controllable by the division, or also a portion of central corporate administration and staff costs?
3.   How is investment to be measured—total assets or net assets, at historical cost or some measure of current cost?

These questions are considered in the sections that follow.

Transfer Pricing: Measuring Divisional Revenue

In cases where, because of the nature of the product, none of a division's output can be sold to another division and all of the output is therefore sold externally, there are few unique revenue measurement problems beyond those encountered in financial accounting. That is, accounting policy questions must be made regarding whether revenue will be recognized as production takes place, at the point of sale, or as cash is collected. It may be of interest to top management to have all divisions follow the same accounting methods, thereby enhancing the comparability of the measures of ROI.

In cases where one division's output can be or is sold to another division, we are confronted with what is called the *transfer pricing problem*. The "price" assigned to the interdivisional transfer of goods or services represents a revenue of the selling division and a cost of the buying division.[2] Should the transfer price be

---

[2]Only rarely will cash equal to the transfer price actually change hands. Transfer prices are set at the time of the transfer so performance of the selling division can be assessed as of the time of the transfer rather than waiting several periods until all manufacturing is completed and the good is sold to someone outside the company.

set equal to the manufacturing cost of the selling division? Or should the transfer price be the amount at which the selling (buying) division could sell (purchase) the good or service externally? Or should the transfer price be a negotiated amount somewhere between the selling division's cost of manufacturing and the external market price?

A superficial consideration of the transfer pricing problem might suggest that the selection of a transfer price is of little consequence. After all, what comes out of one corporate pocket goes into another. This simplistic viewpoint ignores the fact that the amount of the transfer price may affect certain divisional decisions, which in turn may affect the overall profitability of the company. For example, suppose that a transfer price is set at $10 per unit and there is no external market in which to sell the product. If the buying division feels that this price is too high, it may take less than it would at a lower price. In this case the buying division may be doing what is best from the standpoint of its own profitability, but the actions of the two divisions together may not be best for the company as a whole.

The simplistic view of the transfer pricing problem also ignores the real possibility that a transfer price set arbitrarily by central corporate headquarters may undermine the entire divisional organizational structure. Division managers are supposed to be free, within limits, to make manufacturing and marketing decisions as if they were separate companies. If the return, or profit, from a significant portion of its operations is dictated by the transfer price imposed by top management, some motivational and other benefits of decentralized decision making will be lost. The selection of an appropriate transfer price can therefore have a significant impact on decision making.

We discuss several solutions to the "transfer pricing problem" under the following heads:

Direct intervention.

Top management-established transfer pricing policies:

Market prices,

Differential cost plus opportunity cost,

Use of full costs and standard costs,

Motivational problems when the supplier receives no "profit."

Negotiated transfer prices.

Direct Intervention

Top management could intervene directly and order a supplying division of the company to produce and transfer products to a buying division. Top management would specify a transfer price that would be incidental to the transaction. That is, the transfer price would have no bearing on the decision; rather, it would be set *after* the transaction. If this were an extraordinarily large order, or if these internal product transfers were rare, direct intervention could be the optimal solution because it would virtually ensure that division managers take the "right" actions.

But if the type of transaction is common, direct intervention reduces some of the value that comes from decentralization.[3] Further, direct intervention is a costly use of top management's time that might be better spent elsewhere. To avoid this, the company may set up a transfer pricing *policy* to encourage decentralized managers to make the "right" decisions without reducing their autonomy, as discussed in the next section.

Management-Established Transfer Pricing Policy

Rather than intervene directly and force a transaction, top management may establish rules for setting transfer prices that encourage division managers to optimize company goals. Whereas the transfer prices are secondary when top management intervenes on each transaction, here the transfer price is the basis for division managers' decisions. If the transfer price is incorrectly established, division managers will not make decisions that are in the best interests of the company. We discuss some bases for setting these transfer prices below. In each case, we assume that one division of the company—the selling division—produces a product that could be purchased by another division of the company—the buying division.

Market Prices as Transfer Prices *Market price* refers to a price in an intermediate market, not the price for the end product produced by the "buying division." When there is a competitive external market for the transferred product, market prices work well as transfer prices.[4] Both the selling and buying divisions can sell and buy as much as they want at the market price. Managers of both selling and buying divisions are indifferent between trading with each other or with outsiders. From a company-wide perspective, this is optimal as long as the selling division is operating at capacity. Use of a market price also helps assure profit independence of the divisions. Any gains or losses in efficiency of the selling division do not get passed on to the buying division. Use of competitive market prices is also relatively free from argument, thereby saving administrative costs.

A major problem with market prices can occur when a selling division operates below capacity, as demonstrated by the following example.

Example The Systems Division of Magna-Products, Incorporated, builds a navigational system that is standard equipment in many commercial and military airplanes. This division—which is the *selling* division—has the capacity to make 300 systems per year. Its variable cost per system is $1 million. (Differential costs are assumed to equal variable costs in this example.) The Aircraft Division of Magna-Products, Incorporated—the *buying* division—builds airplanes, and uses the selling

---

[3]For an expanded discussion, see Joshua Ronen and George McKinney, "Transfer Pricing for Divisional Autonomy," *Journal of Accounting Research* (Spring 1970).

[4]Classic work on the economic theory of transfer pricing can be found in Jack Hirschleifer, "On the Economics of Transfer Pricing," *Journal of Business* (July 1956), pp. 172–184. Also see Jack Hirschleifer, "Economics of the Divisionalized Firm," *Journal of Business* (April 1957), pp. 96–108; and David Solomons, *Divisional Performance: Measurement and Control* (Homewood, Ill.: Richard D. Irwin, 1965), app. A to chap. VI.

division's navigational system in those airplanes. The Systems (selling) Division can sell to outside airplane manufacturers, and the Aircraft (buying) Division can buy the system from outside suppliers.

The market for airplanes has temporarily worsened, such that the selling division can sell only 100 systems per year to outside buyers at a price of $2.5 million per system. The Aircraft (buying) division of Magna-Products could use 50 systems per year in the airplanes it builds. (The Aircraft Division also operates below capacity.)

If the market price of $2.5 million per system is the transfer price, the Aircraft (buying) Division treats the cost of the system as $2.5 million. Assume that the *other* variable costs of making an airplane are $16 million. From the Aircraft Division's perspective, its variable costs per airplane are $18.5 million (= $16 million + $2.5 million). Suppose that it has an offer to build and sell 6 airplanes for a price of $18 million each.

Given the soft market for airplanes, Magna-Products' company policy is to sell airplanes for any price greater than variable cost. Thus, it is in the company's best interest for the Aircraft Division to sell the airplanes, because the price of $18 million exceeds the variable cost to the company of $17 million (= $16 million + $1 million variable cost of making the part). The Aircraft Division turns down the order, however, because *its* variable costs are $18.5 million. Exhibit 14.2 summarizes this analysis.

Exhibit 14.2

Comparison of Total Company Perspective with Buying and Selling Divisions' Perspectives[a]

	Magna-Products: Company Perspective	Aircraft Division: Buying Division Perspective	Systems Division: Selling Division Perspective
Price per Airplane	$18,000,000	$18,000,000	—
Differential (Variable) Cost of Navigational System	$(1,000,000)	—	$(1,000,000)
Transfer Price	—	$(2,500,000)	$2,500,000
Differential (Variable) Cost of Remainder of Airplane	$(16,000,000)	$(16,000,000)	—
Profit (Loss)	$ 1,000,000	$(500,000)	$1,500,000
Decision	Although the company would make a profit of $1 million per airplane, the buying (Aircraft) division rejects the order because it incurs a loss.		

[a]Costs are in parentheses. The "buying division" makes airplanes; the "selling division" makes navigational systems.

Note that the problem with the use of a market price as the transfer price occurred when the selling division operated below capacity. This is likely to be a temporary phenomenon reflecting short-term conditions.

In short, when there are competitive markets for products transferred between divisions and the selling division operates at capacity, transfer prices based on market prices are ideal. Division managers who make decisions in response to such transfer prices to maximize division profits also maximize company-wide profits.

Situations in which there are competitive markets for a product being transferred between divisions are rare, however. The fact that two responsibility centers are part of one company indicates that there may be some advantages from being part of one company and not being two separate companies dealing with each other in the market. For example, there may be more certainty about the internal supplier's product quality or delivery reliability. Or the selling division may make a specialized product for which there are no substitutes in the market. Hence, it may not be possible to use market prices.

In the following section, we show that the use of market prices when selling divisions operate at capacity is part of a general rule for transfer prices that induces division managers to make decisions that are in the company's best interests.

Differential Cost Plus Opportunity Cost: A General Rule

The general rule for setting transfer prices such that the buying division makes the economic decisions that are optimal from the viewpoint of the total company is to transfer at:[5]

$$\begin{array}{c} \text{Differential Cost} \\ \text{to the Selling} \\ \text{Division} \end{array} + \begin{array}{c} \text{Implicit Opportunity} \\ \text{Cost to Company If} \\ \text{Goods Are Transferred} \\ \text{Internally.} \end{array}$$

In the Magna-Products example, the differential cost to the selling division (that is, the Systems Division) was $1 million per unit. What was the implicit opportunity cost to the company if the Systems Division made the systems and transferred them to the buyer (that is, the Aircraft Division)? Recall that both the Systems and Aircraft divisions were operating below capacity. *If there are no alternative uses for the idle capacity, the implicit opportunity cost to the company is zero.* Thus, the transfer price should have been $1 million, and the Aircraft Division's costs would have been the total differential costs of producing an airplane—$17 million.

If the Systems Division had been operating at capacity, there would have been an implicit opportunity cost of internal transfers. The Systems Division would have forgone a sale of a system in the intermediate market to make the internal transfer. The implicit opportunity cost to the company is the lost contribution margin (for example, $2.5 million − $1.0 million = $1.5 million) from not selling the system in the intermediate market.

Thus, if the selling division had sufficient sales in the intermediate market such that it would have had to forgo those sales to transfer internally, the transfer price should have been:

---

[5]Other terms that are sometimes used instead of differential cost are "marginal cost," "outlay cost," or "variable cost." We use differential cost to be consistent with our terminology throughout the book.

Economists will sometimes refer to the general rule as "transfer at marginal opportunity cost." We find it useful to distinguish between the differential cost, which can usually be derived from the accounting records, and implicit opportunity cost, which requires an "off-the-books" calculation.

$$
\begin{array}{ccc}
\begin{array}{c}\text{Differential Cost}\\\text{to the Selling}\\\text{Division}\end{array} & + & \begin{array}{c}\text{Implicit Opportunity}\\\text{Cost to Company If}\\\text{Goods Are Transferred}\\\text{Internally}\end{array}
\end{array}
$$

$$= \$1,000,000 \quad + \$1,500,000$$

$$= \$2,500,000.$$

(Note that this rule is the same as the market price-based transfer price *when the selling division operates at capacity*.)

The buying division would have appropriately treated the $2.5 million as part of *its* differential cost of making and selling airplanes. Now compare the effects of this rule on each division and the company, both when the selling division is below capacity and when it operates at capacity, as shown in Exhibit 14.3. Note that when the selling division operates at capacity and the transfer price is $2.5 million, the buying division manager decides not to sell the airplane. The selling division therefore sells the system in the external market for $2.5 million, and the company makes a profit of $1.5 million.

Exhibit 14.3
Applying the General Transfer Price Rule to Magna-Products, Incorporated

	Company (000,000)	Buying (Aircraft) Division (000,000)	Selling (Systems) Division (000,000)
Facts			
Price per Airplane	$18.0	$18	—
Differential Cost of the System	$(1.0)	—	$(1)
Differential Cost of the Remainder of the Airplane. .	$(16.0)	$(16)	—
Case 1: Selling (Systems) Division Operates Below Capacity			
Transfer Price	—	$(1)	$1
Profit (Loss) If:			
Airplane Sold and System Purchased Internally. .	$1.0	$1	$0
Airplane Sold and System Purchased Externally for $2,500,000	$(.5)	$(.5)	$0
Airplane Not Sold	$0	$0	$0
Optimal Decision: Sell Airplane and Purchase System Internally.			
Case 2: Selling (Systems) Division Operates at Capacity			
Transfer Price	—	$(2.5)	$2.5
Profit (Loss) If:			
Airplane Sold and System Purchased Internally. .	$1.0	$(.5)	$1.5
Airplane Sold and System Purchased Externally .	$1.0	$(.5)	$1.5
Airplane Not Sold	$1.5	$0	$1.5
Optimal Decision: Do Not Sell Airplane, Continue Selling Systems in Outside Market.			

Is opportunity cost always based on the intermediate market for the product?
No. The rule that the transfer price should include the opportunity cost of the
transfer applies to any forgone alternative use of resources because the transfer is
made. For example, suppose that the Systems Division is operating below capacity,
but the idle capacity could be rented to an outsider. The opportunity cost of an
internal transfer would be the forgone rent from the outsider. In short, the general
transfer pricing rule applies to any type of opportunity cost.

Use of Full Costs and Standard Costs

Measurement Problems When market prices are the appropriate transfer prices,
and information about them is readily available, implementing a transfer price
policy is not very costly. But measurement problems, and costs of implementing
a transfer pricing policy, can be substantial when market prices are not known.
Differential costs are often difficult to measure, and implicit opportunity costs may
be next to impossible to measure. Consequently, many companies transfer at full
cost, or full cost plus a markup.

Use of Standard Costs Whether transferring at differential cost or full cost, standard
costs, where available, are often used as the basis for the transfer. This encourages
efficiency in the selling division because inefficiencies are not passed on to the
buyer. With standard costs, variances in the selling division are not transferred to
the buying division. Otherwise, the selling division can transfer cost inefficiencies
to the buying division. Use of standard costs reduces risk to the buyer. The buyer
knows that standard costs will be transferred and avoids being charged with the
supplier's cost overruns.

Motivational Problems When the Selling
Division Receives No ''Profits''

The transfer pricing ''rule'' may not give the selling division a profit on the transaction when transfers are made at actual differential cost. For example, when the
selling division operates below capacity and there is no opportunity for the use of
idle facilities, the selling division receives only a price that equals differential cost.
(Note Case 1 in Exhibit 14.3.) Under these circumstances, a criticism of the transfer
price rule is that it does not provide incentives to the selling division to transfer
internally, because the selling division can seldom, if ever, expect to profit from
internal transfers. There are several ways to deal with this situation.

Cost Centers If nearly all of the selling division's transfers are internal, the seller's
responsibility center is probably a cost center. As such, the division (if it could be
called a division under these circumstances) would normally be responsible for
costs, but not for revenues.

Hybrid Centers: Cost and Profit Suppose that the selling division does business
with both internal and external customers. It could be set up as a profit center for
the external business, where the manager has some responsibility for setting prices,

and as a cost center for the internal business, where the manager does not. Performance for external business could be measured as if the center were a profit center, whereas performance for internal business could be measured as if the center were a cost center.

Dual Transfer Prices There is no reason why the price paid to the selling division *has* to equal the price paid by the buying division on an internal transaction. The buying division could be charged differential costs while the selling division is credited with differential costs plus a markup. Referring to the Magna-Products example, suppose that top management decides to charge the Aircraft (buying) Division with differential cost (which was $1 million), but credit the selling division with the intermediate market price of $2.5 million, *when the selling division operated below capacity.* This retains the transfer pricing rule, so the Aircraft Division manager makes the correct decision to acquire the system internally, and manufacture the airplane. Yet the System Division is provided with profits on the internal transfer.

Incentive Systems We have assumed that selling division managers are rewarded based only on their division's performance. Selling division managers will have incentives to transfer internally, even if their division earns no profits on the transaction, *if* they are rewarded in some other fashion. Thus, many companies will recognize internal transfers and incorporate them into the reward system. Other companies base part of the selling managers' rewards on the buying division's performance. In short, there are numerous ways of creating incentives for managers to trade internally without losing the benefit of the transfer pricing rule.

Negotiated Transfer Prices

Transfer prices based on differential cost represent a lower limit on the price that selling divisions are willing to accept. Transfer prices based on market prices represent an upper limit on the price that buying divisions are willing to absorb. The difference between these two prices is the total margin on the transfer. Many firms permit divisional managers to negotiate among themselves as to how the margin is to be split. If both divisions are free to deal either with each other or in the external market, the negotiated price will likely be close to the external market price. If all of a selling division's output cannot be sold on the external market (that is, a portion must be sold to the buying division), the negotiated price will likely be less than the market price and the total margin will be shared by the divisions. The use of negotiated transfer prices is consistent with the concept of decentralized decision making in divisionalized firms.

One of the principal disadvantages of negotiated transfer prices is that significant time may be required by the divisions to carry out the negotiating process. Also, interdivision hostility may result, which could hurt overall company performance.

As we mentioned previously, no particular transfer pricing scheme is best in all circumstances. The choice revolves around such factors as the extent of intermediate markets, the extent top management chooses to intervene in divisional decisions, the amount of trading among divisions, and other factors.

Current Practices

Some results of a survey of transfer pricing practices appear in Exhibit 14.4.[6] As shown, nearly half of the companies reported use a cost basis for setting transfer prices. Thirty-one percent use market prices, and the remainder use negotiated prices.

Exhibit 14.4
Transfer Pricing Practices

	Respondents Specifying Method Used	
	Number of Companies	**Percent**
Market Price:		
Competitor's Price	28	
Market Price—List	41	
Market Price—Bid	5	
Total Market Price Based.	74	31.0
Cost:		
Variable Cost: Actual	4	
Variable Cost: Standard	7	
Full Cost: Actual.	31	
Full Cost: Standard.	30	
Total Cost Based	72	30.1
Cost Plus	40	16.7
Negotiation	53	22.2
Total	239	100.0

Source: Richard F. Vancil, *Decentralization* (Homewood, Ill.: Dow Jones-Irwin, 1978), p. 180.

Note: Questionnaires were mailed to 1,010 companies, 404 were returned, of which 357 were usable. Of these 357 companies, 249 reported that they transfer goods between profit centers; 239 of these reported their transfer pricing policy.

Measuring Divisional Operating Costs

The key issue in measuring divisional operating costs is to ascertain how the following costs are treated: (1) controllable, direct operating costs; (2) noncontrollable, direct operating costs; (3) controllable, indirect operating costs; and (4) noncontrollable, indirect operating costs. Direct versus indirect refers to whether the cost is attributable directly to the division; controllable versus noncontrollable refers to whether the division manager has control over the cost. Exhibit 14.5 shows examples of each.

Direct Costs

A division's direct operating costs, whether controllable by the division manager or not, are virtually always deducted from divisional revenues in measuring divisional operating profits. From top management's perspective, any cost attributable

---

[6]Richard F. Vancil, *Decentralization* (Homewood, Ill.: Dow Jones-Irwin, 1978).

Exhibit 14.5

Examples of Direct (Indirect) and Controllable (Noncontrollable) Costs

Direct	Indirect
Controllable	
Labor Used in the Division's Production	Costs of Providing Centralized Services, Such as Data Processing and Employee Training, That Are at Least Partially Affected by the Division's Use of Those Services
Noncontrollable	
Salary of the Division Manager (controlled by top management)	Company President's Salary

directly to a division is necessary for that division to operate, even if the cost is not controllable by the division manager. If top management believes that division managers should not be held responsible for things outside their control, then top management can separate the measure of costs assigned to a *division* from the costs assigned to a division *manager*—the latter measure could exclude direct costs of the division that are not controllable by the division manager (for example, the division manager's salary).

Indirect, Controllable Operating Costs[7]

Indirect, controllable costs are at least partially controllable by divisions. These services are usually centralized because there are economies of scale in doing so. In some companies, costs would exceed benefits if each division had its own legal staff, research department, data processing department, employee training department, and so forth.

For example, many companies have centralized employee training departments. Should divisions be charged for sending their people to these centralized departments? As you might expect, the experiences in most companies follow fundamental laws of economics: The use of centralized services and the price charged for those services are inversely related. When companies charge a high price for employee training, attendance by people from the divisions drops, and vice versa. Top management can use this experience to decide the desired usage, and set the price accordingly. Centralized service departments are treated as profit or investment centers in some companies; if so, the transfer pricing issues discussed earlier are relevant.

Indirect, Noncontrollable Operating Costs

Indirect, noncontrollable operating costs are essentially independent of a division, although they may be necessary costs company-wide. The salaries and staff support

[7]The issue raised in this chapter about assigning central headquarters' costs to divisions is part of a more general cost allocation problem. Cost allocation methods are discussed in Chapter 15.

of corporate top management are examples. The most frequently cited arguments against allocation of these costs are based on the divisions' inability to control the amount of costs incurred and to the arbitrary allocation bases that must be used. For example, on what basis should the president's salary be allocated to the divisions—sales, number of employees, square footage of space used? Any allocation base is likely to be meaningless.

One argument advanced for allocation is that, unless these costs are allocated to the divisions, the divisions will underprice their products and cause the company as a whole to operate at a loss. That is, the revenues generated by the divisions would be insufficient to cover both the direct operating costs of the divisions and the indirect operating costs incurred at central headquarters.

This argument is not particularly convincing in the short run. Prices are likely to be determined by competitive market conditions. These prices will be the same whether central corporate operating costs are allocated or not. Over the long run, these central corporate operating costs must be covered by the divisions, and a stronger case can therefore be made for allocation. As a basis for evaluating the month-to-month performance of divisional managers, however, attention should be directed to the divisional contribution to coverage of central corporate operating costs and profit (that is, divisional operating profits before allocation of central corporate operating costs). If divisions seek to optimize this divisional contribution amount, they will also optimize divisional operating profits after allocation of central corporate operating costs, however allocated.

Another argument for allocation is that it keeps division managers aware of the existence of central headquarters costs, to keep them aware of the need for the company as a whole to cover those costs, and to encourage them to monitor those costs and put pressure on top management if those costs become too great. A top manager of a retail company told us that central headquarters costs were allocated to the stores to keep them aware of these costs. "We want our store managers to recognize that it's not enough for stores to make a profit for the company to be profitable." The corporate manager went on to say that part of a store manager's bonus was based on the store's profit after central headquarters costs had been allocated to stores. "This makes them very aware of central headquarters costs, and it makes us [top management] sensitive to their criticisms about administrative costs" (that is, central headquarters' costs).

Financing Costs and Income Taxes

Some companies do not allocate nonoperating costs, such as interest on debt and income axes, to divisions. Corporate headquarters nearly always makes decisions about the terms and type of financing—issuing short-term versus long-term bonds, issuing common versus preferred shares, and so forth. Consequently, many companies do not charge divisions with financing costs. Those that do often charge an implicit interest cost to cover both the opportunity cost of equity capital and interest on debt. This implicit interest indicates the minimum desired rate of return that the division should generate.

In the vast majority of cases, income taxes are assessed on the taxable income of the company as a whole rather than on each division. Should these income taxes be allocated to individual divisions?

The principal argument favoring allocating income taxes to divisions is that managers should be encouraged to make decisions keeping in mind the income tax consequences. For example, consideration should be given to the investment tax credit, the tax savings from depreciation deductions, and the tax consequences of selling versus trading-in old equipment in capital budgeting decisions. To the extent that division managers have authority to make these types of decisions, they should be held accountable for the income tax consequences.

The arguments against allocation are similar to those against allocating central corporate expenses. The amount of income taxes assessed is often beyond the control of divisional managers. In addition, the amount of income taxes that would be paid on divisional income if it were a separate taxable entity may be different from the amount actually assessed when it is aggregated with income of other divisions. Thus, the income taxes of one division are not independent of income generated by other divisions.

Measuring the Investment in Divisions

Most companies use some measure of capital employed, or invested, in each division in calculating ROI. Our concerns in this section are (1) what assets are to be included in the investment base; and (2) what valuation basis is to be used.

Assets Included in the Investment Base

Two guidelines can be suggested in selecting assets to be included in the investment base. First, to the extent that top management wants to hold division managers accountable for what they control, the assets included should be those for which divisions have significant control. For assets physically located in a division and used only in the division's operations, there is little question that they should be included. More difficult problems arise with respect to assets shared with other divisions (for example, a manufacturing plant) and assets acquired by centralized services departments (for example, equipment used in personnel training). For example, the cost of a shared manufacturing plant might be allocated between divisions based on square footage used. Where only highly arbitrary allocation bases are possible, it may be best not to attribute common investment facilities to the divisions.

The second general guideline for selecting assets to be included in the investment base is *consistency*. Whatever base a company selects, if that base is followed consistently across time and across divisions, the effects of any biases in the investment base and managers' reactions to them will be stabilized.

Valuation of Assets in the Investment Base

Once the assets to be included in the investment base are chosen, a monetary amount must be assigned to them. Most firms use acquisition cost as the valuation basis. The necessary amounts can be obtained directly from the company's records

Exhibit 14.6
Comparison of Alternative Methods of Valuing the Investment Base in ROI Computations

Facts
Operating profits before depreciation is subtracted (all in cash flows at end of year):
  Year 1, $100; Year 2, $120; and Year 3, $144.
Annual rate of price changes, 20 percent. This applies both to asset replacement costs and annual cash flows.
Asset cost at *beginning* of Year 1, $500. The only asset is depreciable with 10-year life and no salvage value.
  Straight-line depreciation is used; straight-line rate is 10% per year for managerial purposes. The denominator in the ROI computation is based on *end*-of-year asset value.
The numerator in the ROI computation equals operating profits (equals cash flow minus depreciation for the year).

Year	Historical Cost		Current Replacement Cost	
	Net Book Value (1)	Gross Book Value (2)	Net Book Value (3)	Gross Book Value (4)
1	$\text{ROI} = \dfrac{\$100^a - (.1 \times \$500)^b}{\$500^c - (.1^f \times \$500)^d}$ $= \dfrac{\$50}{\$450} = \underline{11.1\%}$	$\text{ROI} = \dfrac{\$50}{\$500}$ $= \underline{10\%}$	$\text{ROI} = \dfrac{\$100 - (.1 \times 1.2^e \times \$500)}{(1.2^e \times \$500) - (.1 \times 1.2^e \times \$500)}$ $= \dfrac{\$100 - \$60}{\$600 - \$60} = \dfrac{\$40}{\$540} = \underline{7.4\%}$	$\text{ROI} = \dfrac{\$100 - \$60}{(1.2 \times \$500)}$ $= \dfrac{\$40}{\$600} = \underline{6.7\%}$
2	$\text{ROI} = \dfrac{\$120 - (.1 \times \$500)}{\$500 - (.2^f \times \$500)}$ $= \dfrac{\$70}{\$400} = \underline{17.5\%}$	$\text{ROI} = \dfrac{\$70}{\$500}$ $= \underline{14\%}$	$\text{ROI} = \dfrac{\$120 - (.1 \times 1.2 \times \$600)}{(1.2 \times \$600) - (.2^f \times 1.2 \times \$600)}$ $= \dfrac{\$120 - \$72}{\$720 - \$144} = \dfrac{\$48}{\$576} = \underline{8.3\%}$	$\text{ROI} = \dfrac{\$120 - \$72}{(1.2 \times \$600)}$ $= \dfrac{\$48}{\$720} = \underline{6.7\%}$
3	$\text{ROI} = \dfrac{\$144 - (.1 \times \$500)}{\$500 - (.3^f \times \$500)}$ $= \dfrac{\$94}{\$350} = \underline{26.9\%}$	$\text{ROI} = \dfrac{\$94}{\$500}$ $= \underline{18.8\%}$	$\text{ROI} = \dfrac{\$144 - (.1 \times 1.2 \times \$720)}{(1.2 \times \$720) - (.3^f \times 1.2 \times \$720)}$ $= \dfrac{\$144 - \$86.4}{\$864 - \$259.2} = \dfrac{\$57.6}{\$604.8} = \underline{9.5\%}$	$\text{ROI} = \dfrac{\$144 - \$86.4}{(1.2 \times \$720)}$ $= \dfrac{\$57.6}{\$864} = \underline{6.7\%}$

[a] The first term in the numerator is the annual operating profit before depreciation.
[b] The second term in the numerator is depreciation for the year.
[c] The first term in the denominator is the beginning of the first year value of the assets used in the investment base.
[d] The second term in the denominator reduces the beginning-of-first-year value of the asset by the amount of depreciation.
[e] This term (1.2) adjusts the beginning-of-year asset value to the end-of-year value (current value).
[f] This term reduces the net book value of the asset. The net book value is reduced by 10 percent for depreciation at the end of Year 1, by 20 percent at the end of Year 2, and by 30 percent at the end of Year 3.

and accounts. Also, this valuation basis is consistent with the measurement of cost of goods sold and depreciation expense in the numerator of ROI.

The use of book values of assets, particularly fixed assets, in the denominator of ROI can have undesirable results. The manager of a division with old, low-cost, and almost fully depreciated assets may be reluctant to replace the assets with newer, more efficient, but more costly assets. Replacing old assets with new, more costly ones decreases the numerator—operating profits—of the ROI calculation because of increased depreciation charges. It also increases the denominator—cost of total assets—of the ROI calculation. These two effects combine to reduce calculated ROI.

If use of book values in the investment base does have this effect on divisional investment behavior, there are at least two possible ways to deal with the problem. One is to state all assets at gross book value, rather than at net book value (that is, net of accumulated depreciation). Assets will therefore be stated at their full acquisition cost regardless of age. Another approach is to state assets at their current replacement cost. Exhibit 14.6 presents a comprehensive example of ROI computations, using different valuation bases. Note that the older the assets (compare Year 3 to Year 1, for example) the higher the ROI under net book value compared to gross book value. Also, note that ROI is relatively higher under historical cost compared to current replacement cost as the assets get older.

According to a survey of companies in the "Fortune 1000" listing, most companies (about 84 percent of those surveyed) use historical cost, net book value in the investment base.[8]

The best approach is to select the measurement methods that management believes most accurately reflect performance and effectively communicate the reasons for using these measurement methods to divisional personnel, and then to apply them consistently over time.

Divisional Performance Measurement Practices

Exhibit 14.7 summarizes current divisional performance measurement practices based on a survey of the "Fortune 1000" industrial companies.[9] As shown at the top of Exhibit 14.7, 59 percent of the companies use measures of divisional operating profits that are different from the measures of net income they use in external financial reports to their shareholders. These variations between external and internal reporting practices can be almost entirely related to things over which division managers have little control—central corporate administration costs, income taxes, and interest. In a similar fashion, only a minority of companies allocate common assets to divisions, as shown in the bottom of Exhibit 14.7.

Hence, we conclude that a slight majority of companies do not allocate common costs and assets to divisions. In companies that use the same measure of profits and assets for both divisional reporting and external financial reporting, top management may nevertheless take into account things outside the divisions' and their managers' control in evaluating performance.

---

[8]James S. Reece and William R. Cool, "Measuring Investment Center Performance," *Harvard Business Review* (May–June 1978).

[9]Reece and Cool, "Measuring Investment Center Performance," *Harvard Business Review* (May–June, 1978).

Exhibit 14.7
Divisional Performance Measurement Practices: Allocation of
Common Costs and Assets to Divisions

Measuring Divisional Profit

Consistent with the Way Net Income Is Calculated for External Financial Reports to Shareholders?	Number	Percent of 594 Companies[a]
Yes	239	40
No	351	59
No Answer	4	1
	594	100

If No (from above) (multiple responses allowed):	Number	Percent of 351 Companies[b]
No Taxes Assessed to Divisions.	249	71
No Corporate Administrative Costs Allocated to Divisions	173	49
No Interest Charges on Corporate Debt Allocated to Divisions	225	64
All Other Variations	100	28

Measuring Divisional Investment Base

Selected Items Included in the Division's Investment Base (multiple responses allowed):	Number	Percent of 459 Companies Having Investment Centers
Land and Buildings Used Solely by the Division	430	94
Prorated Share of Land and Buildings Used by Two or More Divisions.	207	45
Equipment Used Solely by the Division	380	83
Prorated Share of Equipment Used by Two or More Divisions	188	41

[a]*Source:* James S. Reece and William R. Cool, "Measuring Investment Center Performance," *Harvard Business Review* (May–June 1978). Questionnaires were sent to 1,000 companies; 620 companies responded; 594 of these had profit centers (135 companies) or investment centers (459 companies).

[b]Companies could respond to more than one reason for the measures of profit for internal reporting and measures of net income for external reporting.

Interpreting Divisional ROI

In previous sections, we have discussed some of the factors to be considered in calculating ROI. In this section, we discuss several additional considerations in using and interpreting ROI as a basis for evaluating divisional performance.

We have suggested that a firm should settle on the way it is going to calculate ROI and then use it consistently. There is a tendency, however, to overemphasize this single statistic. Exhibit 14.8 presents a divisional performance report in a format that facilitates a variety of uses. For example, by separating controllable from noncontrollable items, the report could be used to evaluate the division and its manager's performance based only on controllable items. Further, the report provides data about the division's performance after all central administrative costs have been allocated. Some corporate managers like to see the "bottom line" after all costs have been taken into account, even if some of those are indirect, noncontrollable costs that have been allocated to divisions.

Exhibit 14.8
Suggested Format for a Divisional Performance Report[a]

		Dollars	ROI
Revenues:			
Sales to Outside Customers		$XXX	
Sales to Other Divisions		XXX	
Total Revenues		$XXX	
Less Controllable Operating Costs:			
Variable Direct	$XXX		
Variable Indirect	XXX	XXX	
Contribution Margin		$XXX	
Fixed Direct	$XXX		
Fixed Indirect	XXX	XXX	
Controllable Operating Profit Margin		$XXX	XX.X%[b]
Less Noncontrollable Direct Operating Costs		XXX	
Operating Profit Before Allocated Share of Central Headquarters' Costs, Interest, and Income Taxes . . .		$XXX	
Less Allocated Share of Central Headquarters' Costs . .		XXX	
Operating Profit Before Interest and Income Taxes . . .		$XXX	
Less Interest[c]		XXX	
Less Income Taxes[d]		XXX	XX.X%[e]
Profit After Income Taxes and Interest		$XXX	XX.X%[e]

[a]The actual performance report should include columns for both budgeted and actual amounts.
[b]The investment base in this ROI calculation would *exclude* the allocation of shared central facilities to each division.
[c]This is usually implicit interest charged to divisions.
[d]This is usually a flat rate charged to divisions.
[e]The investment base in this calculation would include an allocation of shared central facilities.

Sales and Divisional Expenses

Note that the statement distinguishes between sales to outsiders and those to other divisions. The purpose of this distinction is to show the extent to which the division is dependent on orders from other divisions for its business. The statement also indicates the variable and fixed cost structure under the control of the division. This information might be used for breakeven and other cost-volume-profit analyses.

Profit Margins

The controllable profit margin and the corresponding ROI are measures of the return generated from decisions made within the division. The controllable profit margin and its corresponding ROI are often used for evaluating the performance of the division manager. When noncontrollable direct expenses, such as the division manager's salary, are deducted from the controllable profit margin, we obtain the division's operating profit before allocated shares of central headquarters costs and its corresponding ROI. These are often used by top management to evaluate a division (as contrasted to the division manager) in relation to other divisions, and to similar divisions or companies in the same line of business.

Central Headquarters' Costs, Interest, and Income Taxes

We suggested earlier that it may not be desirable to allocate central headquarters' costs to divisions if the purpose is to obtain a measure for evaluating divisional performance. Divisions do not have control over these costs and, therefore, should not be held accountable for them. However, divisional personnel must be conscious of the need to provide a positive contribution margin to the coverage of central corporate expenses and to profits. One means of communicating this to divisional personnel is to show on the performance report the relationship between the division's contribution and the amount that top management feels is the division's share of central headquarters' costs.

Many divisional performance reports end with "Income Before Income Taxes." In some companies, it is argued that income taxes are part of controllable costs, if they are derived from controllable revenues and controllable costs. In our example, placement of income taxes at the bottom of the report is a compromise between the two positions. This placement recognizes that allocation of income taxes to divisions may be as difficult as the allocation of central headquarters' costs. However, it emphasizes to division managers the importance of income taxes in decisions and the need that they be covered before profits are generated for the company's owners.

Disaggregating Return on Investments

The rate of return on investment can be disaggregated into profit margin and asset turnover components.

Return on Investment = Profit Margin Percentage × Investment Turnover Ratio

$$\frac{\text{Controllable Profit Margin (or other divisional income measure)}}{\text{Divisional Investment}} = \frac{\text{Controllable Profit Margin (or other divisional income measure)}}{\text{Divisional Revenues}} \times \frac{\text{Divisional Revenues}}{\text{Divisional Investment}}.$$

To illustrate the usefulness of disaggregating the ROI, assume the following information about Division A:

Year	Sales	Profit	Investment
1983	$1,000,000	$100,000	$ 500,000
1984	2,000,000	160,000	1,000,000
1985	4,000,000	400,000	2,500,000

The ROI for each of the 3 years and the associated profit margin percentages and investment turnover ratios are shown on the following page.

Year	ROI	=	Profit Margin Percentage	×	Investment Turnover Ratio
1983	20%	=	10%	×	2.0
1984	16%	=	8%	×	2.0
1985	16%	=	10%	×	1.6

The profit margin percentage provides information for assessing divisional management's ability to combine inputs to generate outputs. That is, various cost inputs (materials, labor, depreciation) are combined to generate revenue outputs (sales of goods and services). The profit margin percentage indicates the portion of each dollar of revenue that is in excess of the costs incurred. It is often used as a measure for assessing efficiency in producing and selling goods and services. The profit margin percentage for Division A in the example above decreased from 10 percent to 8 percent between 1983 and 1984. Because the investment turnover ratio remained the same between the 2 years, it appears that the decrease in ROI is caused by an inability to control costs or an inability to raise selling prices as costs have increased, or both.

We indicated earlier that divisional profits are divided by investment as a means of scaling divisions of different size so that their performance measures are more comparable. When ROI is disaggregated, however, potentially useful information can be obtained on how effectively the capital invested in the division has been used. The investment turnover ratio indicates the dollars of revenue that the division was able to generate for each dollar of invested capital. Returning to the example above, Division A was unable to increase its ROI between 1984 and 1985, despite an increase in its profit margin percentage, because its investment turnover ratio decreased. The division was unable to generate $2 of revenue for each dollar invested in 1985, as it had done in previous years.

More useful information is likely to be provided by studying profit margin percentages and investment turnover ratios for a given division over several periods than by looking at these ratios for all divisions in a particular period. This is because some divisions, because of the nature of their activities, require more capital than others. For example, a division involved in manufacturing and selling heavy equipment is likely to require more capital than one selling management consulting or advertising and promotion services. The investment turnover ratios of these two divisions are inherently likely to differ and should not cause concern for top management. A significant change in the ratio of either division between two periods, however, may signal the need for corrective action. For example, a significant decrease in investment turnover for the manufacturing division may indicate excess capacity and suggest disposal of some facilities.

Setting Minimum Desired ROIs

If the ROI is to serve as an effective measure for controlling divisional performance, a standard, or desired, rate may be set each period. A minimum desired ROI for each division, given their particular operating characteristics, is usually specified. Some divisions are in more risky businesses than others, hence their expected return may be higher. Some divisions have a very low investment base (for example, professional services, consulting), thus ROI is sometimes quite high. In short, it makes sense to recognize the particular characteristics of a division in setting minimum ROIs.

Some companies carry this a step further to compute a minimum rate of return for various classes of divisional assets and then aggregate to obtain a required ROI.[10] For example, assume that fixed assets are required to generate a return of 22 percent, inventories 14 percent, and accounts receivable 7 percent. If a division had $500,000, $400,000, and $100,000 invested on average in these three types of assets, respectively, its minimum required ROI would be 17.3 percent [= (.22 × $500,000) + (.14 × $400,000) + (.07 × $100,000)] ÷ ($500,000 + $400,000 + $100,000).

Residual Income

A criticism of the use of return on investment (ROI) is that if managers are encouraged to have a high ROI, they may turn down investment opportunities that are above the minimum acceptable rate, but below the ROI that is currently being earned by the manager. For example, suppose that the division currently earns:

$$\text{ROI} = \frac{\$1,000,000}{\$4,000,000} = 25\%.$$

Suppose that there is an opportunity to make an additional investment. This investment would return $400,000 per year for 5 years for a $2 million investment. At the end of 5 years, the $2 million investment would be returned. Assume that there is no inflation. The ROI each year is

$$\text{ROI} = \frac{\$400,000}{\$2,000,000} = 20\%.$$

The company requires a minimum return of 15 percent for this type of investment. This investment clearly qualifies, but it would lower the investment center ROI to 23.3 percent:

$$\text{ROI} = \frac{\$1,000,000 + \$\ 400,000}{\$4,000,000 + \$2,000,000} = 23.3\%.$$

[10]For example, Donald Hughes reports the use of this method at Burlington Industries in "The Behavioral Aspects of Accounting Data for Performance Evaluation at Burlington Industries, Inc.," in Thomas Burns, ed., *The Behavioral Aspects of Accounting Data for Performance Evaluation* (Columbus, Ohio: Ohio State University College of Administrative Science, 1970).

A comparison of the old (25 percent) and new (23.3 percent) returns would imply performance has worsened, consequently a manager might decide not to make such an investment.

An alternative to ROI is *residual income* (RI).[11] Residual income is defined as

$$\begin{array}{c} \text{Residual} \\ \text{Income} \end{array} = \begin{array}{c} \text{Division} \\ \text{Operating} \\ \text{Profits} \end{array} - \left(\begin{array}{c} \text{Percent} \\ \text{Capital} \\ \text{Charge} \end{array} \times \begin{array}{c} \text{Division} \\ \text{Investment} \end{array} \right),$$

where the percent capital charge is the minimum acceptable rate of return. The terms "division operating profits" and "division investment" are defined as for ROI. Residual income is similar in concept to economists' definition of profits. If managers are encouraged to maximize RI, they will accept all projects above the minimum acceptable rate of return.

Using data from the example just discussed to see the impact of the investment on residual income, we find:

Before the investment, the residual income is $400,000:

$$\text{RI} = \$1,000,000 - (.15 \times \$4,000,000)$$

$$= \$1,000,000 - \$600,000$$

$$= \$400,000.$$

The residual income from the additional investment is $100,000:

$$\text{RI} = \$400,000 - (.15 \times \$2,000,000)$$

$$= \$400,000 - \$300,000$$

$$= \$100,000.$$

Hence, *after the additional investment*, the residual income of the division increases to $500,000:

$$\text{RI} = (\$1,000,000 + \$400,000) - [.15 \times (\$4,000,000 + \$2,000,000)]$$

$$= \$1,400,000 - (.15 \times \$6,000,000)$$

$$= \$1,400,000 - \$900,000$$

$$= \$500,000.$$

The additional investment *increases* residual income, appropriately improving the measure of performance, whereas the use of ROI worsened the measure of performance.

Managers generally recognize this "problem" with ROI, and they may take it into account when ROI is lowered by a new investment. This may explain why residual income does not dominate ROI in practice as a performance measure. Most

---

[11]For a discussion of the use of residual income in companies, see David Solomons, *Divisional Performance Measurement and Control* (Homewood, Ill.: Richard D. Irwin, 1968).

of the companies studied by Reece and Cool use ROI. Only 2 percent used residual income only, and 28 percent used both ROI and residual income.[12] Further, a "benefit" of ROI is that it is expressed as a percentage that can be intuitively compared with related percentages—like the cost of capital, the prime interest rate, and the Treasury Bill rate.

Summary

A major objective of this chapter has been to convey the message that companies use a variety of divisional performance measurement methods. Most methods are imperfect; most methods have some merit. One of top management's most challenging jobs is to design and implement divisional performance measurement methods that induce division managers to act in the best interests of the company as a whole. At a minimum, performance measurement methods should not create conflicts such that when division managers take actions that are in the company's best interests, they look bad.

The key issues in divisional performance measurement deal with measuring division revenues, division costs, and investment in the division. For profit centers, the most important measure is

$$\text{Division Operating Profits} = \text{Division Revenues} - \text{Division Costs};$$

for investment centers it is

$$\text{ROI} = \frac{\text{Division Revenues} - \text{Division Costs}}{\text{Division Investment}}.$$

(We assume that divisions are investment centers unless otherwise stated.)

When one division's output can be sold to another division, a *transfer price* is set that becomes a revenue to the selling division and a cost to the buying division. Selecting the transfer price can have a significant effect on decision making. Ideally, the transfer price will be set so that when divisions internally optimize their buy and sell decisions, they also optimize from a company-wide viewpoint.

There are numerous solutions to the transfer pricing "problem," including direct intervention by top management in buy and sell decisions, top management-established transfer pricing policy, and transfer prices negotiated among division managers. Direct intervention by top management could be expected to induce managers to make the "right" decision for the company for a particular transaction. Direct intervention reduces some of the advantages of decentralization, however, because it overrides delegation of responsibility.

When a transfer pricing policy is set, the general rule is to transfer *a differential*

---

[12]Reece and Cool, "Measuring Investment Center Performance," *Harvard Business Review* (May–June, 1978).

cost to the selling division plus the implicit opportunity cost to the company if the goods are transferred internally. When there are competitive external markets for the product being exchanged between divisions, and the selling division operates at capacity, the product's external market price satisfies the general rule. The optimal rule can be costly to implement because of the difficulty in measuring differential costs and opportunity costs. Consequently, many companies transfer at some measure of cost found in the accounting records—for example, standard full cost or standard variable cost—plus a markup.

Many companies carry decentralization to the limit by allowing division managers to set their own prices—so-called negotiated prices. The key transfer pricing problem facing top management is the trade-off between intervening to ensure that a transaction is optimal from a company-wide viewpoint and delegating decisions to division managers. Delegation requires top management to tolerate occasional decisions that are suboptimal from a company-wide perspective.

The key issue in measuring divisional operating costs is to ascertain which costs should be allocated to divisions. Should central headquarters costs—say top management's salaries—be allocated to divisions, for example? The arguments against allocation to divisions are usually based on the divisions' inability to control these costs and the arbitrary allocation bases that must be used. The arguments favoring allocation point out the need to make divisions aware of central headquarters' costs. The costs and benefits of allocation are different in different situations, which makes it impossible to generalize about the optimal amount of cost allocation to divisions. From an accounting viewpoint, top management can "have it both ways." As shown in Exhibit 14.8, division profits can be calculated after deducting only controllable costs, and after deducting noncontrollable allocated costs.

The issues in measuring the investment of capital in divisions are (1) what assets to include in the investment base, and (2) what valuation basis is to be used. For assets physically located in a division, there is little question that they be included in the investment bases. Assets that are shared by divisions, or with central headquarters, are usually assigned to divisions if reasonable allocation bases can be used. A general guideline for including assets in the investment base is to develop a reasonable policy and to follow it consistently. The use of historical cost and net book value has been criticized on the grounds that managers of divisions with old, low-cost, and almost fully depreciated assets may be reluctant to replace these with newer, more costly assets that reduce calculated ROI. The vast majority of companies in the Reece and Cool study use historical cost, net book value, however.

A criticism of ROI is that if managers are encouraged to have a high ROI, they may turn down investment opportunities that are above the minimum acceptable rate but below the ROI currently being earned. An alternative measure that is not worsened by projects earning less than the current ROI but greater than the minimum acceptable rate of return is residual income (RI), where

$$\begin{matrix} \text{Residual} \\ \text{Income} \end{matrix} = \begin{matrix} \text{Division} \\ \text{Operating} \\ \text{Profits} \end{matrix} - \left(\begin{matrix} \text{Percent} \\ \text{Capital} \\ \text{Charge} \end{matrix} \times \begin{matrix} \text{Division} \\ \text{Investment} \end{matrix} \right).$$

Any project accepted with a return above the minimum acceptable rate (that is, the percent capital charge) will increase residual income. Hence, projects that are profitable for the company also improve the division manager's performance measure.

Problem 1 for Self-Study

The Venus Division of Hyperspace Company has assets of $2.4 billion, operating profits of $.60 billion, and a cost of capital of 20 percent.

Compute return on investment and residual income.

Suggested Solution

$$ROI = \frac{\$.60 \text{ Billion}}{2.4 \text{ Billion}} = 25\%.$$

$$\text{Residual Income} = \$.60 \text{ Billion} - (.20 \times \$2.4 \text{ Billion})$$

$$= \$.60 \text{ Billion} - \$.48 \text{ Billion}$$

$$= \$.12 \text{ Billion (that is, residual income of } \$120 \text{ million).}$$

Problem 2 for Self-Study

The T Division of A.T. Enterprises has depreciable assets costing $2 million. The cash flows from these assets for 3 years were as follows:

Year	Cash Flow
1	$600,000
2	$700,000
3	$810,000

The replacement costs of these assets were expected to increase 25 percent per year. Depreciation of these assets for managerial purposes was 10 percent per year; the assets have no salvage value. The denominator in the ROI calculation is based on *end* of year asset values.

Compute the ROI for each year under each of the following methods:

a. Historical cost, net book value.

b. Historical cost, gross book value.

c. Replacement cost, net book value.

d. Replacement cost, gross book value.

Suggested Solution

a, b. Historical cost:

Year	Net Book Value	Gross Book Value
1	$ROI = \dfrac{\$600,000 - (.10 \times \$2,000,000)^a}{\$2,000,000 - (.10 \times \$2,000,000)}$	$ROI = \dfrac{\$400,000}{\$2,000,000}$
	$= \dfrac{\$400,000}{1,800,000} = \underline{\underline{22.22\%}}$	$= \underline{\underline{20\%}}$
2	$ROI = \dfrac{\$700,000 - (.10 \times \$2,000,000)}{1,800,000 - (.10 \times \$2,000,000)}$	$ROI = \dfrac{\$500,000}{\$2,000,000}$
	$= \dfrac{\$500,000}{\$1,600,000} = \underline{\underline{31.25\%}}$	$= \underline{\underline{25\%}}$
3	$ROI = \dfrac{\$810,000 - (.10 \times \$2,000,000)}{1,600,000 - (.10 \times \$2,000,000)}$	$ROI = \dfrac{\$610,000}{\$2,000,000}$
	$= \dfrac{\$610,000}{\$1,400,000} = \underline{\underline{43.57\%}}$	$= \underline{\underline{30.5\%}}$

[a]The first term in the numerator is annual cash flow; the second term in the numerator is annual depreciation; the first term in the denominator is the beginning of year net book value of the asset; the second term in the denominator reduces the beginning of the year value by the amount of the current year's depreciation.

c, d. Replacement Cost:

Year	Net Book Value	Gross Book Value
1	$ROI = \dfrac{\$600,000 - (.10 \times 1.25^a \times \$2,000,000)}{(1.25 \times \$2,000,000) - (.10^b \times 1.25 \times \$2,000,000)}$	$ROI = \dfrac{\$350,000}{\$2,500,000}$
	$= \dfrac{\$600,000 - \$250,000}{\$2,500,000 - \$250,000} = \underline{\underline{15.6\%}}$	$= \underline{\underline{14\%}}$
2	$ROI = \dfrac{\$700,000 - (.10 \times 1.25 \times \$2,500,000)}{(1.25 \times \$2,500,000) - (.20^b \times 1.25 \times \$2,500,000)}$	$ROI = \dfrac{\$387,500}{\$3,125,000}$
	$= \dfrac{\$700,000 - \$312,500}{\$3,125,000 - \$625,000} = \underline{\underline{15.5\%}}$	$= \underline{\underline{12.4\%}}$
3	$ROI = \dfrac{\$810,000 - (.10 \times 1.25 \times \$3,125,000)}{(1.25 \times \$3,125,000) - (.30^b \times 1.25 \times \$3,125,000)}$	$ROI = \dfrac{\$419,375}{\$3,906,250}$
	$= \dfrac{\$810,000 - \$390,625}{\$3,906,250 - \$1,171,875}$	$= \underline{\underline{10.7\%}}$
	$= \dfrac{\$419,375}{\$2,734,375} = \underline{\underline{15.3\%}}$	

[a]This term increases asset value to replacement cost.
[b]This term reduces the net book value of the asset by 10 percent after 1 year, by 20 percent after 2 years, and by 30 percent after 3 years.

Problem 3 for Self-Study

The Lee Lewis Company has two divisions: Production and Marketing. Production manufactures designer pants, which it sells to both the Marketing Division and to other retailers (the latter under a different brand name). Marketing operates numerous pants stores. Marketing sells both Lee Lewis pants and other brands.

Sales price to retailers if sold by Production: $38 per pair.

Variable cost to produce: $19 per pair.

Fixed costs: $200,000 per month.

Production is operating far below its capacity.

Sales price to customers if sold by Marketing: $50 per pair.

Variable marketing costs: 5 percent of sales price.

Marketing has decided to reduce the sales price of Lee Lewis pants. The company's variable manufacturing and marketing costs are differential to this decision, while *fixed* manufacturing and marketing costs are not.

a. What is the *minimum* price that can be charged for the pants and still cover differential manufacturing and marketing costs?

b. What is the appropriate transfer price for this decision?

c. What if the transfer price were set at $38? What effect would this have on the minimum price set by the marketing manager?

Suggested Solution

a. From the company's perspective, the minimum price would be the variable cost of producing and marketing the goods. They would solve for this minimum price, P_C (the subscript C means that this is the minimum price that is in the *company's* best interest), as follows:

$$P_C = \$19 + .05 \, P_C$$

$$P_C - .05 P_C = \$19$$

$$.95 P_C = \$19$$

$$P_C = \underline{\$20}.$$

The *minimum* price the company should accept is $20. If the company were centralized, we would expect that this information would be conveyed to the manager of Marketing, who would be instructed not to set a price below $20.

b. The transfer price that correctly informs the marketing manager about the differential costs of manufacturing is $19. Production is operating below capacity, so there is no opportunity cost of transferring internally.

c. If the production manager set the price at $38, the marketing manager would solve for the minimum price (which we call P_M for *Marketing's* solution):

$$P_M = \$38 + .05P_M$$

$$P_M - .05P_M = \$38$$

$$.95P_M = \$38$$

$$P_M = \underline{\underline{\$40}}.$$

So the marketing manager sets the price in excess of $40 per pair when, in fact, prices greater than $20 would have generated a positive contribution margin from the production and sale of pants.

Problem 4 for Self-Study

How would your answer to Problem 3 for Self-Study change if the Production Division had been operating at full capacity?

Suggested Solution

If the Production Division had been operating at capacity, there would have been an implicit opportunity cost of internal transfers. Production would have forgone a sale in the wholesale market to make the internal transfer. The implicit opportunity cost to the company is the lost contribution margin ($38 − $19 = $19) from not selling in the wholesale market.

Thus, if Production had sufficient sales in the wholesale market such that it would have had to forgo those sales to transfer internally, the transfer price should have been

$$\begin{matrix} \text{Differential Cost} \\ \text{to Production} \end{matrix} + \begin{matrix} \text{Implicit Opportunity Cost} \\ \text{to Company If Goods Are} \\ \text{Transferred Internally} \end{matrix} = \$19 + \$19$$

$$= \$38.$$

Marketing would have appropriately treated the $38 as part of *its* differential cost of buying and selling the pants. When Production was operating below full capacity (hence, the implicit opportunity cost of transferring to marketing was zero), the minimum price for the pants was derived as follows:

$$P_M = \$19 + .05\, P_M$$

$$.95P_M = \$19$$

$$P_M = \$20.$$

However, if Production is operating at full capacity, the minimum price is

$$P_M = \$38 + .05P_M$$

$$.95P_M = \$38$$

$$P_M = \$40.$$

Questions

1. Review the meaning of the following concepts or terms discussed in this chapter.

<table>
<tr><td>**a.**</td><td>Divisions.</td><td>**i.**</td><td>Common costs.</td></tr>
<tr><td>**b.**</td><td>Decentralized decision making.</td><td>**j.**</td><td>Centralized service department costs.</td></tr>
<tr><td>**c.**</td><td>Profit center.</td><td></td><td></td></tr>
<tr><td>**d.**</td><td>Return on investment.</td><td>**k.**</td><td>Central administration costs.</td></tr>
<tr><td>**e.**</td><td>Transfer pricing problem.</td><td>**l.**</td><td>Profit margin percentage.</td></tr>
<tr><td>**f.**</td><td>Cost-based transfer price.</td><td>**m.**</td><td>Investment turnover ratio.</td></tr>
<tr><td>**g.**</td><td>Market-based transfer price.</td><td>**n.**</td><td>Residual income.</td></tr>
<tr><td>**h.**</td><td>Negotiated transfer price.</td><td></td><td></td></tr>
</table>

2. "It may be desirable to use a different ROI measure for evaluating the performance of a division and the performance of the division's manager." Explain.

3. "An action that is optimal for a division may not be optimal for the company as a whole." Explain.

4. Why are transfer prices necessary?

5. In what sense is the term "transfer price" a misnomer?

6. "The case for allocating central service department costs is stronger than the case for allocating central administration costs to divisions." Explain.

7. "The return on investment measure may be biased in favor of divisions with older plant and equipment." Explain.

8. What are the advantages of using ROI measure rather than the value of division profits as a performance evaluation technique?

9. Under what conditions would the use of ROI measures inhibit goal-congruent decision making by a division manager?

10. What are the advantages of using residual income instead of ROI?

11. Why might gross book value and/or replacement cost be used instead of net book value and/or historical cost to measure the denominator (investment) in the ROI computation?

12. Describe the bases for establishing transfer prices.

13. Why might transfer prices exist even in highly centralized organizations?

14. Why are market-based transfer prices considered optimal under many circumstances?

15. What are the limitations to market-based transfer prices?

16. What are the advantages of a centrally administered transfer price (that is, direct intervention)? What are the disadvantages of such a transfer price?

17. Why do companies often use prices other than market prices for interdivisional transfers?

18. Division A has no external markets. It produces a product that is used by Division B. Division B cannot purchase this product from any other source. What transfer pricing system would you recommend for the interdivisional sale of the product? Why?

19. What are the disadvantages of a negotiated transfer price system?

20. Describe the economic basis for transfer pricing systems.

Exercises

21. *Transfer Pricing Computations.* Whitmyer Chemical Company began business in January 19X0. It produces various chemical products that pass through two divisions. Division A refines the basic chemicals. These refined chemicals are then immediately transferred to Division B, which combines them into several chemical products. During 19X0, Division A refined 12,000 pounds of chemicals at a cost of $180,000. Its administration and other expenses amounted to $40,000. Division B incurred $120,000 of additional manufacturing costs in completing 10,000 pounds. No work was done on the remaining 2,000 pounds received from Division A. Division B sold the 10,000 pounds of completed units for $500,000. Its selling and administration expenses for 19X0 were $80,000.

  a. Prepare divisional income statements for each of these two divisions for 19X0 assuming that the transfer price is equal to Division A's total cost.

  b. Repeat part **a**, assuming that the transfer price is based on the external market price of $20 per pound.

  c. Repeat part **a**, assuming that the transfer price is based on a negotiated price of $19 per pound.

  d. Respond to the following statement: "It is immaterial to the company as a whole which transfer price is used."

22. *Return on Investment Computations.* The following information relates to the operating performance of three divisions of Langston Products Corporation for 19X0.

	Division A	Division B	Division C
Divisional Contribution to Central			
Corporate Expenses	$ 500,000	$ 500,000	$ 500,000
Divisional Investment	$ 4,000,000	$ 5,000,000	$ 6,000,000
Divisional Sales	$24,000,000	$20,000,000	$16,000,000
Divisional Employees	22,500	12,000	10,500

Langston evaluates divisional performance using rate of return on investment (ROI) after allocating a portion of the central corporate expenses to each division. Central corporate expenses for 19X0 were $900,000.

  a. Determine the ROI of each division before allocation of central corporate expenses.

b.   Determine the ROI of each division assuming central corporate expenses are allocated based on divisional investments (that is, allocate 4/15 to Division A, 5/15 to Division B, and 6/15 to Division C).

c.   Repeat part **b**, assuming that central corporate expenses are allocated based on divisional sales.

d.   Repeat part **b**, assuming that central corporate expenses are allocated based on the number of employees.

23. *ROI Computations with a Capital Charge.* The following information relates to the operating performance of three divisions of Dees Manufacturing Company for 19X0.

	Division A	Division B	Division C
Operating Profit	$ 640,000	$ 3,000,000	$ 6,000,000
Investment.	8,000,000	15,000,000	37,500,000

a.   Determine the rate of return on investment (ROI) of each division for 19X0.

b.   Assume that a charge is levied on each division for the use of capital. The charge is 10 percent on investment and is deducted in determining divisional net income. Recalculate ROI using divisional net income after deduction of the use of capital charge in the numerator.

c.   Which of these two measures do you feel gives the better indication of operating performance? Explain your reasoning.

24. *ROI Computations with Replacement Costs.* The following information relates to the operating performance of two divisions of Pratt Electronics Corporation for 19X0.

	Division A	Division B
Operating Profit.	$ 400,000	$ 600,000
Total Assets (based on acquisition cost)	4,000,000	7,500,000
Total Assets (based on current replacement costs)	6,000,000	8,000,000

a.   Determine the return on investment (ROI) of each division, using total assets stated at acquisition cost as the investment base.

b.   Determine the ROI of each division, using total assets based on current replacement cost as the investment base.

c.   Which of the two measures do you feel gives the better indication of operating performance? Explain your reasoning.

25. *ROI Computations Comparing Net and Gross Book Value.* The following information relates to the operating performance of two divisions of the Hargrave Company for 19X0.

	Division A	Division B
Operating Profit	$ 500,000	$ 800,000
Total Assets (at gross acquisition cost)	6,250,000	20,000,000
Total Assets (net of accumulated depreciation)	5,000,000	5,000,000

a. Determine the return on investment (ROI) of each division, using total assets at gross book value as the investment base.

b. Determine the ROI of each division, using total assets net of accumulated depreciation (net book value) as the investment base.

c. Which of the two measures do you feel gives the better indication of operating performance? Explain your reasoning.

26. *Comparing Profit Margin and ROI as Performance Measures.* The operating performance of the three divisions of Bobel Corporation for 19X0 is as follows:

	Division A	Division B	Division C
Sales	$3,800,000	$17,000,000	$20,000,000
Operating Profit	200,000	500,000	1,000,000
Investment.	2,000,000	6,250,000	8,000,000

a. Using the operating profit margin percentage as the criterion, which is the most profitable division?

b. Using the rate of return on investment as the criterion, which is the most profitable division?

c. Which of the two measures do you feel gives the better indication of overall operating performance? Explain your reasoning.

27. *Profit Margin and Investment Turnover Ratio Computations.* The Assembly Division of the Whitley Manufacturing Company had a rate of return on investment (ROI) of 10 percent (= $200,000 ÷ $2,000,000) during 19X0, based on sales of $4,000,000. In an effort to improve its performance during 19X1, the division instituted several cost-saving programs, including the substitution of automatic equipment for work previously done by workers and the purchase of raw materials in large quantities to obtain quantity discounts. Despite these cost-saving programs, the division's ROI for 19X1 was 8 percent (= $220,000 ÷ $2,750,000), based on sales of $4,000,000.

a. Disaggregate the ROI for 19X0 and 19X1 into profit margin and investment turnover ratios.

b. Explain the reason for the decrease in ROI between the 2 years, using results from part **a**.

28. *ROI Computations with Net and Gross Book Values.* The Raiders Division of Shark Company has just started operations. It purchased depreciable assets costing $1,000,000 that have an expected life of 4 years, after which the assets can be salvaged for $200,000. In addition, the division has $1,000,000 in assets that are not depreciable. After 4 years, the division will have $1,000,000 available from these assets. In short, the division has invested $2,000,000 in assets that will last 4 years, after which it will salvage $1,200,000. Assume that annual cash operating profits are $400,000. In computing ROI, this division uses *end*-of-year asset values in the denominator.

    a. Compute ROI using net book value.

    b. Compute ROI using gross book value.

29. *ROI Computations Using Historical Cost and Replacement Costs.* Assume the same facts as in Exercise **28**, except that all cash flows increase 10 percent at the end of the year. This has the following effect on the assets' replacement cost and annual cash flows:

End of Year	Replacement Cost	Annual Cash Flow
1	$2,000,000 × 1.1 = $2,200,000	$400,000 × 1.1 = $440,000
2	$2,200,000 × 1.1 = $2,420,000	$440,000 × 1.1 = $484,000
⋮	Etc.	Etc.

    a. Compute ROI using historical cost gross book value.

    b. Compute ROI using historical cost net book value.

    c. Compute ROI using replacement cost gross book value.

    d. Compute ROI using replacement cost net book value.

30. *ROI and Residual Income Computations.* A division is considering acquisition of a new asset. The asset will cost $160,000 and have a cash flow of $70,000 per year (excluding depreciation) for each of the 5 years of the asset life. The asset will have no salvage value after 5 years.

    a. What is the ROI for each year of the asset life if the division is using beginning-of-year asset balances for the computation?

    b. What is the residual income each year if the cost of capital is 25 percent?

31. *Transfer Pricing (CPA adapted).* Mar Company has two decentralized divisions, X and Y. Division X has always purchased certain units from Division Y at $75 per unit. Because Division Y plans to raise the price to $100 per unit, Division X desires to purchase these units from outside suppliers for $75 per unit. Division Y's costs follow:

Y's variable costs per unit: $70.

Y's annual fixed costs: $15,000.

Y's annual production of these units for X: 1,000 units.

If Division X buys from an outside supplier, the facilities Division Y uses to manufacture these units would remain idle. What would be the result if Mar enforces a transfer price of $100 per unit between Divisions X and Y?

32. *Transfer Pricing.* Selling Division offers its product to outside markets at a price of $200. Selling incurs variable costs of $70 per unit and fixed costs of $50,000 per month based on monthly production of 1,000 units.

Buying Division can acquire the product from an alternate supplier at a cost of $210 per unit. Buying Division can also acquire the product from Selling Division for $200, but must pay $15 per unit in transportation costs in addition to the transfer price charged by Selling Division.

    a. What are the costs and benefits of the alternatives available to Selling and Buying Divisions with respect to the transfer of Selling Division's product? Assume that Selling Division can market all that it can produce.

    b. How would your answer change if Selling Division had idle capacity sufficient to cover all of Buying Division's needs?

Problems and Cases

33. *Transfer Pricing.* Robinson Manufacturing Company produces heavy-duty equipment used in construction work. The company is organized into several divisions that operate essentially as autonomous companies. Division managers are permitted to make capital investment and production-level decisions. They can also decide whether to sell to other divisions or to outside customers.

Division A produces a critical component in the construction of cranes manufactured by Division B. It has been selling this component to Division B for $1,500 per unit. Division A recently purchased new equipment for producing the component. To offset its higher depreciation charges, Division A increased its price to $1,600 per unit. The manager of Division A has asked the president to instruct Division B to purchase the component for the $1,600 price rather than permit Division B to purchase externally for $1,500 per unit. The following information is obtained from the company's records:

Division B's Annual Purchases of the Component	100 Units
Division A's Variable Costs per Unit	$1,200
Division A's Fixed Costs per Unit	$ 300

    a. Assume that there are no alternative uses for Division A's idle capacity. Will the company as a whole benefit if Division B purchases the component externally for $1,500? Explain.

    b. Assume that the idle capacity of Division A can be used for other purposes, resulting in cash operating savings of $20,000. Will the company as a whole benefit if Division B purchases the component externally for $1,500? Explain.

    c. Assume the same facts as in part **b** except that the outside market price drops to $1,350 per unit. Will the company as a whole benefit if Division B purchases the component externally for $1,350? Explain.

    d. As president, how would you respond to the manager of Division A?

34. *Biases in ROI Computations.* The Champion Manufacturing Company uses rate of return on investment (ROI) as a basis for determining the annual bonus of divisional managers. Before calculating ROI at year-end, all manufacturing cost variances are assigned to units produced, whether sold or in ending inventory, so that standard costs are converted into actual costs. Central corporate expenses are allocated to the divisions based on total sales. The calculation of ROI for 19X0 for two independent manufacturing divisions is as follows:

	Division A	Division B
Division Contribution to Central Corporate Expenses and Operating Profit	$100,000	$ 500,000
Share of Central Corporate Expenses	(10,000)	(25,000)
Divisional Operating Profit.	$ 90,000	$ 475,000
Divisional Investment (assets)	$600,000	$4,750,000
ROI	15 Percent	10 Percent

Indicate several factors that, if present, would bias the ROI measure as calculated by Champion and lead to possible inequities in determining the annual bonus.

35. *Issues in Designing ROI Measures.* The Domestic Corporation manufactures and sells a patented electronic device for detecting burglaries. Return on investment is used as a measure for the control of operations for each of its 16 U.S. divisions.

A new division has been recently organized in Brazil. Domestic contributed the necessary capital for the construction of manufacturing and sales facilities in Brazil, whereas debt financing was obtained locally for working capital requirements. The new division will remit the following amounts annually to the U.S. central corporate office: **(1)** a royalty of $10 for each burglary device sold in Brazil, **(2)** a fee of $40 per hour plus traveling expenses for central corporate engineering services used by the division, and **(3)** a dividend equal to 10 percent of the capital committed by Domestic. Remaining funds generated by operations will be retained by the division for its own use. The division will receive the right to produce and market in Brazil any future electronic devices developed by the central corporate research and development staff.

List some of the questions that must be addressed in designing a ROI measure for this division.

36. *Issues in Designing ROI Measures.* Durham Industries is one of the largest and most diversified textile companies in the world. Its products are manufactured and sold through 25 individual divisions, which operate much like autonomous companies. Each division has its own manufacturing plants for making the division's products, a sales staff to market them, and an administrative staff to provide financial assistance and control. Broad policy and financial guidance are received from corporate management, and technical assistance can be obtained from the corporate staff. The latter includes treasurer, legal, personnel, advertising, engineering, and purchasing groups.

Although several measures of divisional performance are used, the most significant yardstick is return on investment. The numerator of ROI is calculated as follows:

Divisional Revenues (sales to outsiders plus sales to other divisions based on negotiated transfer price)

Less Direct Divisional Costs (excluding income taxes)

Less Charge for Central Corporate Costs (the costs of central administration and service departments are allocated to the divisions according to each division's investment as a percentage of the total of all of the divisions' investments)

Equals Divisional Operating Profit.

The investment measure in the denominator of ROI is based on the book value of the following assets: **(1)** accounts receivable net of accounts payable, **(2)** inventories, including supplies, raw materials, work in process, and finished goods, and **(3)** long-term depreciable assets (net of accumulated depreciation). Accounting methods are set by the central corporate controller's staff and used uniformly by all divisions.

The actual ROI is calculated monthly for each division. In evaluating ROI, corporate management uses two bases. First, management pays great attention to trends rather than absolute goals or standards. Maximum interest centers on divisions that are either improving or getting worse. Second, management sets a minimum satisfactory ROI for each division. This represents a lower limit below which the division manager's job is in jeopardy. The minimum is set rather loosely and is easily attainable in almost all cases. The minimum ROI is determined by applying different weights to the three investment components: 20 percent for depreciable assets, 12 percent for inventories, and 6 percent for accounts receivable net of accounts payable.

Discuss the strengths and weaknesses of the return on investment measure as used by Durham as a basis for controlling divisional performance.

37. *Analyzing Performance Reports (CMA adapted)*. Bio-grade Products is a multiproduct company manufacturing animal feeds and feed supplements. The need for a widely based manufacturing and distribution system has led to a highly decentralized management structure. Each divisional manager is responsible for production and distribution of corporate products in one of eight geographic areas of the country.

Residual income is used to evaluate divisional managers. The residual income for each division equals each division's contribution to corporate profits before taxes less a 20 percent investment charge on a division's investment base. The investment base for each division is the sum of its year-end balances of accounts receivable, inventories, and net plant fixed assets (cost less accumulated depreciation). Corporate policies dictate that divisions minimize their investments in receivables and inventories. Investments in plant fixed assets are a joint division/corporate decision based on proposals made by divisional plant managers, available corporate funds, and general corporate policy.

Alex Williams, divisional manager for the Southeastern Sector, prepared the 1985 and preliminary 1986 budgets in late 1984 for his division. Final approval of the 1986 budget took place in late 1985, after adjustments for trends and other information developed during 1985. Preliminary work on the 1987 budget also took

Exhibit 14.9
BIO-GRADE PRODUCTS
Southeastern Sector
(in thousands)

	1986			1985	
	Annual Budget	Nine-Month Budget[a]	Nine-Month Actual	Annual Budget	Actual Results
Sales	$2,800	$2,100	$2,200	$2,500	$2,430
Divisional Costs and Expenses:					
Direct Materials and Labor	$1,064	$ 798	$ 995	$ 900	$ 890
Supplies	44	33	35	35	43
Maintenance and Repairs	200	150	60	175	160
Plant Depreciation	120	90	90	110	110
Administration	120	90	90	90	100
Total Divisional Costs and Expenses	$1,548	$1,161	$1,270	$1,310	$1,303
Divisional Margin	1,252	939	930	1,190	1,127
Allocated Corporate Fixed Costs	360	270	240	340	320
Divisional Profits	$ 892	$ 669	$ 690	$ 850	$ 807
Cost of Capital of Divisional Investment (20 percent)	420	321[b]	300[b]	370	365
Divisional Residual Income	$ 472	$ 348	$ 390	$ 480	$ 442

	Budgeted Balance 12/31/86	Budgeted Balance 9/30/86	Actual Balance 9/30/86	Budgeted Balance 12/31/85	Actual Balance 12/31/85
Division Investment:					
Accounts Receivable	$ 280	$ 290	$ 250	$ 250	$ 250
Inventories	500	500	650	450	475
Plant Fixed Assets (net)	1,320	1,350	1,100	1,150	1,100
Total	$2,100	$2,140	$2,000	$1,850	$1,825
Cost of Capital (20 percent)	$ 420	$ 321[b]	$ 300[b]	$ 370	$ 365

[a]Bio-grade's sales occur uniformly throughout the year.
[b]Imputed interest is calculated at only 15 percent to reflect that only 9 months or three-fourths of the fiscal year has passed.

place at that time. In early October of 1986, Williams asked the divisional controller to prepare a report that presents performance for the first 9 months of 1986. The report is reproduced in Exhibit 14.9.

　a. Evaluate the performance of Alex Williams for the 9 months ending September 1986. Support your evaluation with pertinent facts from the problem.

　b. Identify the features of Bio-grade Products divisional performance measurement reporting and evaluating system that need to be revised if it is to reflect effectively the responsibilities of the divisional managers.

38. *ROI and Management Behavior (CMA adapted).* The Notewon Corporation is a highly diversified company that grants its divisional executives a significant amount of authority in operating the divisions. Each division is responsible for its own sales, pricing, production, costs of operations, and management of accounts receivable, inventories, accounts payable, and use of existing facilities. Cash is managed by corporate headquarters; all cash in excess of normal operating needs of the divisions is transferred periodically to corporate headquarters for redistribution or investment.

The divisional executives are responsible for presenting requests to corporate management for investment projects. The proposals are analyzed and documented at corporate headquarters. The final decision to commit funds to acquire equipment, to expand existing facilities, or for other investment purposes rests with corporate management. This procedure for investment projects is necessitated by Notewon's capital allocation policy.

The corporation evaluates the performance of division executives by the ROI measure. The asset base is composed of fixed assets employed plus working capital exclusive of cash.

The ROI performance of a divisional executive is the most important appraisal factor for salary changes. In addition, the annual performance bonus is based on the ROI results, with increases in ROI having a significant impact on the amount of the bonus.

The Notewon Corporation adopted the ROI performance measure and related compensation procedures about 10 years ago. The corporation did so to increase the awareness of divisional management of the importance of the profit/asset relationship and to provide additional incentive to the divisional executives to seek investment opportunities.

The corporation seems to have benefited from the program. The ROI for the corporation as a whole increased during the first years of the program. Although the ROI has continued to grow in each division, the corporate ROI has declined in recent years. The corporation has accumulated a sizable amount of cash and short-term marketable securities in the past 3 years.

The corporation management is concerned about the increase in short-term marketable securities. A recent article in a financial publication suggested that the use of ROI was overemphasized by some companies, with results similar to those experienced by Notewon.

    a. Describe the specific actions division managers might have taken to cause the ROI to grow in each division but decline for the corporation. Illustrate your explanation with appropriate examples.

    b. Explain, using the concepts of goal congruence and motivation of divisional executives, how Notewon Corporation's overemphasis on the use of the ROI measure might result in the recent decline in the corporation's return on investment and the increase in cash and short-term marketable securities.

    c. What changes could be made in Notewon Corporation's compensation policy to avoid this problem? Explain your answer.

39. *Evaluating Profit Impact of Alternative Transfer Decisions (CMA adapted).* A. R. Oma, Inc., manufactures a line of men's colognes and aftershave lotions. The manufacturing process is basically a series of mixing operations with the addition of certain aromatic and coloring ingredients; the finished product is packaged in a company-produced glass bottle and packed in cases containing 6 bottles.

A. R. Oma feels that the sale of its product is heavily influenced by the appearance and appeal of the bottle and has, therefore, devoted considerable managerial effort to the bottle production process. This has resulted in the development of certain unique bottle production processes in which management takes considerable pride.

The two areas (that is, perfume production and bottle manufacture) have evolved over the years in an almost independent manner; in fact, a rivalry has developed between management personnel as to "which division is the more important" to A. R. Oma. This attitude is probably intensified because the bottle manufacturing plant was purchased intact 10 years ago, and no real interchange of management personnel or ideas (except at the top corporate level) has taken place.

Since the acquisition, all bottle production has been absorbed by the perfume manufacturing plant. Each area is considered a separate profit center and evaluated as such. As the new corporate controller, you are responsible for the definition of a proper transfer value to use in crediting the bottle production profit center and in debiting the packaging profit center.

At your request, the bottle division general manager has asked certain other bottle manufacturers to quote a price for the quantity and sizes demanded by the perfume division. These competitive prices are as follows:

Volume	Total Price	Price per Case
2,000,000 Eq. Cases[a]	$ 4,000,000	$2.00
4,000,000 Eq. Cases	7,000,000	1.75
6,000,000 Eq. Cases	10,000,000	1.67

[a]An "equivalent case" represents 6 bottles each.

A cost analysis of the internal bottle plant indicates that they can produce bottles at these costs:

Volume	Total Price	Cost per Case
2,000,000 Eq. Cases	$3,200,000	$1.60
4,000,000 Eq. Cases	5,200,000	1.30
6,000,000 Eq. Cases	7,200,000	1.20

(Your cost analysts point out that these costs represent fixed costs of $1,200,000 and variable costs of $1 per equivalent case.)

These figures have given rise to considerable corporate discussion as to the proper value to use in the transfer of bottles to the perfume division. This interest is heightened because a significant portion of a division manager's income is an incentive bonus based on profit center results.

The perfume production division has the following costs in addition to the bottle costs:

Volume	Total Cost	Cost per Case
2,000,000 Cases	$16,400,000	$8.20
4,000,000 Cases	32,400,000	8.10
6,000,000 Cases	48,400,000	8.07

After considerable analysis, the marketing research department has furnished you with the following price-demand relationship for the finished product:

Sales Volume	Total Sales Revenue	Sales Price per Case
2,000,000 Cases	$25,000,000	$12.50
4,000,000 Cases	45,600,000	11.40
6,000,000 Cases	63,900,000	10.65

    a. The A. R. Oma Company has used market price transfer prices in the past. Using the current market prices and costs, and assuming a volume of 6,000,000 cases, calculate the income for
      (1) The bottle division.
      (2) The perfume division.
      (3) The corporation.
    b. Is this production and sales level the most profitable volume for:
      (1) The bottle division?
      (2) The perfume division?
      (3) The corporation?

Explain your answer.

40. *Analyzing Transfer Pricing Policy (CMA adapted).* PortCo Products is a divisionalized furniture manufacturer. The divisions are autonomous segments, with each division being responsible for its own sales, costs of operations, working capital management, and equipment acquisitions. Each division serves a different market in the furniture industry. Because the markets and products of the divisions are so different, there have never been any transfers between divisions.

The Commercial Division manufactures equipment and furniture that is purchased by the restaurant industry. The division plans to introduce a new line of counter and chair units that feature a cushioned seat for the counter chairs. John Kline, the division manager, has discussed the manufacturing of the cushioned seat with Russ Fiegel of the Office Division. They both believe that a cushioned seat currently made by the Office Division for use on its deluxe office stool could be modified for use on the new counter chair. Consequently, Kline has asked Russ Fiegel for a price for 100-unit lots of the cushioned seat. The following conversation took place about the price to be charged for the cushioned seats.

    Fiegel: John, we can make the necessary modifications to the cushioned seat easily. The direct materials used in your seat are slightly different and should cost about 10 percent more than those used in our deluxe office stool. However, the labor time should be the same because the seat fabrication operation basically is the same. I would price the seat at our regular rate—full cost plus 30 percent markup.

Kline: That's higher than I expected, Russ. I was thinking that a good price would be your variable manufacturing costs. After all, your capacity costs will be incurred regardless of this job.

Fiegel: John, I'm at capacity. By making the cushion seats for you, I'll have to cut my production of deluxe office stools. Of course, I can increase my production of economy office stools. The labor time freed by not having to fabricate the frame or assemble the deluxe stool can be shifted to the frame fabrication and assembly of the economy office stool. Fortunately, I can switch my labor force between these two models of stools without any loss of efficiency. As you know, overtime is not a feasible alternative in our community. I'd like to, sell it to you at variable cost, but I have excess demand for both products. I don't mind changing my product mix to the economy model if I get a good return on the seats I make for you. Here are my standard costs for the two stools and a schedule of my manufacturing overhead. (See Exhibit 14.10 for standard costs, and see Exhibit 14.11 for the overhead schedule.)

Kline: I guess I see your point, Russ, but I don't want to price myself out of the market. Maybe we should talk to corporate to see if they can give us any guidance.

a. John Kline and Russ Fiegel did ask PortCo corporate management for guidance on an appropriate transfer price. Corporate management suggested

Exhibit 14.10
Office Division Standard Costs and Prices

	Deluxe Office Stool		Economy Office Stool
Direct Materials:			
Framing	$ 8.15		$ 9.76
Cushioned Seat:			
Padding	2.40		—
Vinyl	4.00		—
Molded Seat (purchased)	—		6.00
Direct Labor:			
Frame Fabrication (.5 × $7.50 per direct labor hour)	3.75	(.5 × $7.50 per direct labor hour)	3.75
Cushion Fabrication (.5 × $7.50 per direct labor hour)	3.75		—
Assembly[a] (.5 × $7.50 per direct labor hour)	3.75	(.3 × $7.50 per direct labor hour)	2.25
Manufacturing:			
Overhead (1.5 direct labor hours × $12.80 per direct labor hour).	19.20	(.8 direct labor hour × $12.80 per direct labor hour)	10.24
Total Standard Cost	$45.00		$32.00
Selling Price (30 percent markup) . .	$58.50		$41.60

[a]Attaching seats to frames and attaching rubber feet.

Exhibit 14.11
Office Division
Manufacturing
Overhead Budget

Overhead Item	Nature	Amount
Supplies	Variable—at Current Market Prices	$ 420,000
Indirect Labor	Variable	375,000
Supervision	Nonvariable	250,000
Power	Use Varies with Activity; Rates Are Fixed	180,000
Heat and Light	Nonvariable—Light Is Fixed Regardless of Production; Heat/Air Conditioning Varies with Fuel Charges	140,000
Property Taxes and Insurance	Nonvariable—Any Change in Amounts/Rates Is Independent of Production	200,000
Depreciation.	Fixed-Dollar Total	1,700,000
Employee Benefits . .	20 Percent of Supervision, Direct and Indirect Labor	575,000
	Total Overhead	$3,840,000
	Capacity in Direct Labor Hour	300,000
	Overhead Rate per Direct Labor Hour	$12.80

they consider using a transfer price based on variable manufacturing cost plus opportunity cost. Calculate a transfer price for the cushioned seat based on variable manufacturing cost plus opportunity cost.

b. Which alternative transfer price system—full cost, variable manufacturing cost, or variable manufacturing cost plus opportunity cost—would be better as the underlying concept for an intracompany transfer price policy? Explain your answer.

41. *Transfer Pricing and Differential Analysis (CMA adapted).* National Industries is a diversified corporation with separate and distinct operating divisions. Each division's performance is evaluated on the basis of total dollar profits and return on division investment.

The WindAir Division manufactures and sells air conditioner units. The coming year's budgeted income statement, based on a sales volume of 15,000 units, appears in Exhibit 14.12.

WindAir's division manager believes that sales can be increased if the unit selling price of the air conditioners is reduced. A market research study conducted by an independent firm at the request of the manager indicates that a 5 percent reduction in the selling price ($20) would increase sales volume by 16 percent, or 2,400 units. WindAir has sufficient production capacity to manage this increased volume with no increase in fixed costs.

At the present time, WindAir uses a compressor in its units that it purchases from an outside supplier at a cost of $70 per compressor. The division manager of WindAir has approached the manager of the Compressor Division regarding the sale of a compressor unit to WindAir. The Compressor Division currently manufactures and sells exclusively to outside firms a unit that is similar to the unit used

Exhibit 14.12
WindAir Division
Budgeted Income Statement
for the Fiscal Year

	Per Unit	Total (in thousands)
Sales Revenue	$400	$6,000
Manufacturing Costs:		
Compressor	70	1,050
Other Direct Materials	37	555
Direct Labor	30	450
Variable Overhead	45	675
Fixed Overhead	32	480
Total Manufacturing Costs	$214	$3,210
Gross Margin	$186	$2,790
Operating Costs:		
Variable Marketing	$ 18	270
Fixed Marketing	19	285
Fixed Administrative	38	570
Total Operating Costs	$ 75	$1,125
Operating Profit Before Taxes	$111	$1,665

by WindAir. The specifications of the WindAir compressor are slightly different, which would reduce the Compressor Division's direct material cost by $1.50 per unit. In addition, the Compressor Division would not incur any variable selling costs in the units sold to WindAir. The manager of WindAir wants all of the compressors it uses to come from one supplier, and has offered to pay $50 for each compressor unit.

The Compressor Division has the capacity to produce 75,000 units. The coming year's budgeted income statement for the Compressor Division is shown in Exhibit 14.13 and is based on a sales volume of 64,000 units without considering WindAir's proposal.

   a. Should WindAir Division institute the 5 percent price reduction on its air conditioner units even if it cannot acquire the compressors internally for $50 each? Support your conclusion with appropriate calculations.

   b. Without prejudice to your answer to part **a**, assume that WindAir needs 17,400 units. Should the Compressor Division be willing to supply the compressor units for $50 each? Support your conclusions with appropriate calculations.

   c. Without prejudice to your answer to part **a**, assume that WindAir needs 17,400 units. Would it be in the best interest of National Industries for the Compressor Division to supply the compressor units at $50 each to the WindAir Division? Support your conclusions with appropriate calculations.

42. *Transfer Pricing and Organizational Structure.*[13] "If I were to price these boxes any lower than $480 a thousand," said Mr. Brunner, manager of Birch Paper

[13]Copyright (1957) by the President and Fellows of Harvard College. This case was prepared by William Rotch under the direction of Neil E. Harlan as a basis for class discussion rather than to illustrate effective or ineffective handling of an administrative situation. Reprinted by permission of the Harvard Business School.

Exhibit 14.13
Compressor Division
Budgeted Income Statement
for the Fiscal Year

	Per Unit	Total (in thousands)
Sales Revenues.	$100	$6,400
Manufacturing Costs:		
Direct Materials	12	768
Direct Labor	8	512
Variable Overhead	10	640
Fixed Overhead	11	704
Total Manufacturing Costs	$ 41	$2,624
Gross Margin.	$ 59	$3,776
Operating Costs:		
Variable Marketing	$ 6	$ 384
Fixed Marketing	4	256
Fixed Administrative	7	448
Total Operating Costs	17	$1,088
Operating Profit Before Taxes.	$ 42	$2,688

Company's Thompson division, "I'd be countermanding my order of last month for our salesmen to stop shaving their bids and to bid full cost quotations. I've been trying for weeks to improve the quality of our business, and if I turn around now and accept this job at $430 or $450 or something less than $480, I'll be tearing down this program I've been working so hard to build up. The division can't very well show a profit by putting in bids which don't even cover a fair share of overhead costs, let alone give us a profit."

Birch Paper Company was a medium-sized, partly integrated paper company, producing white and kraft papers and paperboard. A portion of its paperboard output was converted into corrugated boxes by the Thompson division, which also printed and colored the outside surface of the boxes. Including Thompson, the company had four producing divisions and a timberland division, which supplied part of the company's pulp requirements.

For several years each division had been judged independently on the basis of its profit and return on investment. Top management had been working to gain effective results from a policy of decentralizing responsibility and authority for all decisions except those relating to overall company policy. The company's top officials felt that in the past few years the concept of decentralization had been applied successfully and that the company's profits and competitive position had definitely improved.

Early in 19X0 the Northern division designed a special display box for one of its papers in conjunction with the Thompson division, which was equipped to make the box. Thompson's package design and development staff spent several months perfecting the design, production methods, and materials that were to be used; because of the unusual color and shape, these were far from standard. According to an agreement between the two divisions, the Thompson division was reimbursed by the Northern division for the cost of its design and development work.

When the specifications were all prepared, the Northern division asked for bids on the box from the Thompson division and from two outside companies, West Paper Company and Erie Papers, Ltd. Each division manager normally was free to buy from whichever supplier he wished, and even on sales within the company, divisions were expected to meet the going market price if they wanted the business.

Early in 19X0 the profit margins of converters such as the Thompson division were being squeezed. Thompson, as did many other similar converters, bought its board, liner, or paper; and its function was to print, cut, and shape it into boxes. Though it bought most of its materials from other Birch divisions, most of Thompson's sales were to outside customers. If Thompson got the order from Northern, it probably would buy its liner, board, and corrugating medium from the Southern division of Birch. The walls of a corrugated box consist of outside and inside sheets of linerboard sandwiching the corrugating medium.

About 70 percent of Thompson's out-of-pocket cost of $400 a thousand for the order represented the cost of linerboard and corrugating medium. Though Southern division had been running below capacity and had excess inventory, it quoted the market price, which had not noticeably weakened as a result of the oversupply. Its out-of-pocket costs on both liner and corrugating medium were about 60 percent of the selling price.

The Northern division received bids on the boxes of $480 a thousand from the Thompson division, $430 a thousand from West Paper Company, and $432 a thousand from Erie Papers, Ltd. Erie Papers offered to buy from Birch the outside linerboard with the special printing already on it, but would supply its own liner and corrugating medium. The outsider liner would be supplied by the Southern division at a price equivalent to $90 a thousand boxes, and would be printed for $30 a thousand by the Thompson division. Of the $30, about $25 would be out-of-pocket costs.

Since this situation appeared to be a little unusual, Mr. Kenton, manager of the Northern division, discussed the wide discrepancy of bids with Birch's commercial vice-president. He told the commercial vice-president, "We sell in a very competitive market, where higher costs cannot be passed on. How can we be expected to show a decent profit and return on investment if we have to buy our supplies at more than 10 percent over the going market?"

Knowing that Mr. Brunner had on occasion in the past few months been unable to operate the Thompson division at capacity, the commercial vice-president thought it odd that Mr. Brunner would add the full 20 percent overhead and profit charge to his out-of-pocket costs. When he asked Mr. Brunner about this over the telephone, his answer was the statement that appears at the beginning of the case. Mr. Brunner went on to say that having done the developmental work on the box, and having received no profit on that, he felt entitled to a good markup on the production of the box itself.

The vice-president explored further the cost structures of the various divisions. He remembered a comment the controller had made at a meeting the week before to the effect that costs that for one division were variable could be largely fixed for the company as a whole. He knew that in the absence of specific orders from top management, Mr. Kenton would accept the lowest bid, namely, that of the West Paper Company for $430. However, it would be possible for top management to order the acceptance of another bid if the situation warranted such action. And though the volume represented by the transactions in question was less than 5 percent of the volume of any of the divisions involved, other transactions could conceivably raise similar problems later.

> **a.** Does the system motivate Mr. Brunner in such a way that actions he takes in the best interest of the Thompson division are also in the best interest of the Birch Paper Company? If your answer is "no," give some specific instances related as closely as possible to the type of situation described in the case. Would the managers of *other* divisions be correctly motivated?
>
> **b.** What should the vice-president do?

43. *Impact of Division Performance Measures on Management Incentives.* The home office staff of The Nomram Group evaluates managers of the Nomram divisions by keeping track of the rate of return earned by each division on the average level of assets invested at the division. The home office staff considers 20 percent, which is the aftertax cost of capital of The Nomram Group, to be the minimum acceptable annual rate of return on average investment. When a division's rate of return drops below 20 percent, division management can expect an unpleasant investigation by the home office and, perhaps, some firings. When the rate of return exceeds 20 percent and grows through time, the home office staff is invariably pleased and rewards division management. When the rate of return exceeds 20 percent but declines over time, the home office staff sends out unpleasant memorandums and cuts the profit-sharing bonuses of the division managers.

In Division A, average assets employed during the year amount to $60,000. Division A has been earning 40 percent per year on its average investment for several years. Management of Division A is proud of its extraordinary record— earning a steady 40 percent per year.

In Division B, average assets employed during the year also amount to $60,000. Division B has been earning 25 percent per year on its average investment. In the preceding 3 years, the rate of return on investment was 20 percent, 22 percent, and 23 percent, respectively. Management of Division B is proud of its record of steadily boosting earnings.

New investment opportunities have arisen at both Division A and Division B. In both cases, the new investment opportunity will require a cash outlay today of $30,000 and will provide a rate of return on investment of 30 percent for each of the next 8 years. The average amount of assets invested in the project will be $30,000 for each of the next 8 years. Both new investment opportunities have positive net present values when the discount rate is 20 percent per year (the after tax cost of capital of The Nomram Group).

When word of the new opportunities reached the home office staff, it was pleased at the prospects of the two new investments, because both of them would yield a better return than the average for The Nomram Group.

Management of Division A computed its rate of return on investment both with and without the new investment project and decided not to undertake the project. Management of Division B computed its rate of return on investment both with and without the new investment project and decided to undertake it.

When word of the actions taken by the two divisions reached the home office staff, it was perplexed. Why did Division A's management turn down such a good opportunity? What was it about the behavior of the home office staff that induced Division A's management to reject the new project? Is management of Division B doing a better job than management of Division A? What might the home office do to give Division A an incentive to act in a way more consistent with the well-being of The Nomram Group?

44. *Capital Investment Analysis and Decentralized Performance Measurement—A Comprehensive Case.*[14]
The following exchange occurred just after a capital investment proposal was rejected at Diversified Electronics.

Ralph Browning (Product Development): I just don't understand why you have rejected my proposal. This new investment is going to be a sure money maker for the Residential Products division. No matter how we price this new product, we can expect to make $230,000 on it before tax.

Sue Gold (Finance): I am sorry that you are upset with our decision, but this product proposal just does not meet our short-term ROI target of 15 percent after tax.

Ralph Browning: I'm not so sure about the ROI target, but it goes a long way toward meeting our earnings-per-share growth target, by contributing more than 5 cents per share to corporate earnings after tax.

Phil Carlson (Executive Vice-President): Ralph, you are right, of course, about the importance of earnings per share. However, we view our three divisions as investment centers. Proposals like yours must meet our ROI targets. It is not enough that you show an earnings-per-share increase.

Sue Gold: We feel that a company like Diversified Electronics should have a return on investment of 12 percent after tax, especially given the interest rates we have had to pay recently. This is why we have targeted 12 percent as the appropriate minimum ROI for each division to earn next year.

Phil Carlson: If it were not for the high interest rates and poor current economic outlook, Ralph, we would not be taking such a conservative position in evaluating new projects. This past year has been particularly rough for our industry. Our two major competitors had ROIs of 10.8 and 12.3 percent. Though our ROI of 10.9 percent after tax was reasonable (see Exhibit 14.16), performance varied from division to division. Professional Services did very well with 15 percent ROI, while the Residential Products division managed just 11 percent. The performance of the Aerospace Products division was especially dismal, with an ROI of only 7 percent. We expect divisions in the future to carry their share of the load.

Chris McGregor (Aerospace Products): My division would be showing much higher ROI if we had a lot of old equipment like the Residential Products or relied heavily on human labor like Professional Services.

Phil Carlson: I don't really see the point you are trying to make, Chris.

Diversified Electronics, a growing company in the electronics industry, had grown to its present size of more than $74 billion in sales. (See Exhibits 14.14, 14.15, and 14.16 for financial data for 1982 and 1983.) Diversified Electronics has

[14]J. M. Lim, M. W. Maher, and J. S. Reece, copyright © 1983. This case requires knowledge of discounted cash flow methods (see Chapter 9).

Exhibit 14.14
DIVERSIFIED ELECTRONICS
Income Statement
for 1982 and 1983
(000s, except earnings-per-share figures)

	Year Ended December 31	
	1982	**1983**
Sales	$141,462	$148,220
Cost of Goods Sold	108,118	113,115
Gross Margin	$ 33,344	$ 35,105
Selling and General	13,014	13,692
Profit Before Taxes and Interest	$ 20,330	$ 21,413
Interest Expense	1,190	1,952
Profit Before Taxes	$ 19,140	$ 19,461
Income Tax Expense	7,886	7,454
Net Income	$ 11,254	$ 12,007
Earnings per Share (2,000 shares outstanding in 1982 and 1983)	$5.63	$6.00

Exhibit 14.15
DIVERSIFIED ELECTRONICS
Balance Sheets
for 1982 and 1983
(000s)

	December 31	
	1982	**1983**
Assets		
Cash and Temporary Investments	$ 1,404	$ 1,469
Accounts Receivable	13,688	15,607
Inventories	42,162	45,467
Total Current Assets	$ 57,254	$ 62,543
Plant and Equipment:		
Original Cost	107,326	115,736
Accumulated Depreciation	42,691	45,979
Net	$ 64,635	$ 69,757
Investments and Other Assets	3,143	3,119
Total Assets	$125,032	$135,419
Liabilities and Owner's Equity		
Accounts Payable	$ 10,720	$ 12,286
Taxes Payable	1,210	1,045
Current Portion of Long-Term Debt	—	1,634
Total Current Liabilities	$ 11,930	$ 14,965
Deferred Income Taxes	559	985
Long-Term Debt	12,622	15,448
Total Liabilities	$ 25,111	$ 31,398
Common Stock	47,368	47,368
Retained Earnings	52,553	56,653
Total Owner's Equity	$ 99,921	$104,021
Total Liabilities and Owners' Equity	$125,032	$135,419

Exhibit 14.16
DIVERSIFIED ELECTRONICS
Ratio Analysis
for 1982 and 1983

	1982	1983
Net Income ÷ Total Assets	$\dfrac{\$\ 11,254}{\$125,032} = 9.0\%$	$\dfrac{\$\ 12,007}{\$135,419} = 8.9\%$
Return on Investment.	$\text{Average Tax Rate} = \dfrac{\$\ 7,886}{\$19,140}$	$\text{Average Tax Rate} = \dfrac{\$\ 7,454}{\$19,461}$
	$= .412$	$= .383$
	$\text{ROI} = \dfrac{\$20,330\ (1 - 0.412)}{\$12,622 + \$99,921}$	$\text{ROI} = \dfrac{\$21,413\ (1 - 0.383)}{\$1,634 + \$15,448 + \$104,021}$
	$= \dfrac{\$\ 11,954}{\$112,543}$	$= \dfrac{\$\ 13,212}{\$121,103}$
	$= 10.6\ \text{Percent}$	$= 10.9\ \text{Percent}$

three divisions, Residential Products, Aerospace Products, and Professional Services, each of which accounts for about one-third of Diversified Electronics' sales. Residential Products, the oldest division, produces furnace thermostats and similar products. The Aerospace Products division is a large ''job shop'' that builds electronic devices to customer specifications. A typical job or batch takes several months to complete. About one-half of Aerospace Products' sales are to the U.S. Defense Department. The newest of the three divisions, Professional Services, provides consulting engineering services. This division has shown tremendous growth since its acquisition by Diversified Electronics 4 years ago.

Each division operates independently of the others and is treated essentially as a separate entity. Many of the operating decisions are made at the division level. Corporate management coordinates the activities of the various divisions, which includes review of all investment proposals over $400,000.

Diversified Electronic's measure of return on investment is defined to be the division's ''adjusted'' net income profit before taxes and interest times (one minus the income tax rate) divided by interest bearing debt plus owners' equity. Each division's expenses includes an allocated portion of corporate administrative expenses. (See Exhibit 14.16.)

Since each of Diversified Electronics' divisions is located in a separate facility, it is easy to attribute most assets, including receivables, to specific divisions. The corporate office assets, including the centrally controlled cash account, are allocated to the divisions on the basis of divisional revenues.

The details of Ralph Browning's rejected product proposal are shown in Exhibit 14.17.

a. Why did corporate headquarters reject Ralph Browning's product proposal? Was their decision the right one? What would the results of their evaluation have been if they had used the discounted cash flow (DCF) method

Exhibit 14.17
DIVERSIFIED ELECTRONICS
Financial Data for New Product Proposal

1. Projected Asset Investment:[a]
   Cash $200,000
   Plant and Equipment[b] $800,000
      Total $1,000,000
2. Cost Data, Before Taxes (first year):
   Variable Cost per Unit $3.00
   Differential Fixed Costs[c] $170,000
3. Price/Market Estimate (first year):
   Unit Price $7.00
   Sales . . . . 100,000 Units
4. Taxes: The company assumes a 46 percent tax rate for investment analyses. Depreciation of plant and equipment according to tax law is as follows: Year 1, 15 percent; Year 2, 22 percent; Year 3, 21 percent; Year 4, 21 percent; Year 5, 21 percent. The plant and equipment qualify for the 10 percent investment tax credit. According to tax law, the asset base must be reduced by 5 percent for depreciation purposes because the investment tax credit is taken. Taxes are paid for taxable income in Year 1 at the end of Year 1, taxes for Year 2 at the end of Year 2, etc.
5. Inflation is assumed to be 10 percent per year and applies to revenues and all costs except depreciation. A 10 percent increase in cash investment is needed at the end of each year.

[a]Assumes sales of 100,000 units.

[b]Annual capacity of 120,000 units.

[c]Includes straight-line depreciation on new plant and equipment. Plant and equipment are expected to last 8 years and to have no net salvage value at the end of 8 years.

instead? The company uses a 15 percent cost of capital (i.e., hurdle rate) in evaluating projects such as these.

b. Evaluate the manner in which Diversified Electronics has implemented the investment center concept. What pitfalls did they apparently not anticipate? What, if anything, should be done with regard to the investment center approach and the use of ROI as a measure of performance?

c. What conflicting incentives for managers can occur between the use of a yearly ROI performance measure and DCF for capital budgeting?

Suggested Solutions to Even-Numbered Exercises

22. *Return on Investment Computations.*

   a. Division A: $\dfrac{\$500,000}{\$4,000,000} = 12.5\%$;

      Division B: $\dfrac{\$500,000}{\$5,000,000} = 10\%$;

      Division C: $\dfrac{\$500,000}{\$6,000,000} = 8.33\%$.

b. Division A: $$\frac{\$500,000 - (\$4,000,000 \div \$15,000,000)(\$900,000)}{\$4,000,000}$$

= 6.5%;

Division B: $$\frac{\$500,000 - (\$5,000,000 \div \$15,000,000)(\$900,000)}{\$5,000,000}$$

= 4.0%;

Division C: $$\frac{\$500,000 - (\$6,000,000 \div \$15,000,000)(\$900,000)}{\$6,000,000}$$

= 2.33%;

c. Division A: $$\frac{\$500,000 - (\$24,000,000 \div \$60,000,000)(\$900,000)}{\$4,000,000}$$

= 3.5%;

Division B: $$\frac{\$500,000 - (\$20,000,000 \div \$60,000,000)(\$900,000)}{\$5,000,000}$$

= 4.0%;

Division C: $$\frac{\$500,000 - (\$16,000,000 \div \$60,000,000)(\$900,000)}{\$6,000,000}$$

= 4.33%.

d. Division A: $$\frac{\$500,000 - (22,500 \div 45,000)(\$900,000)}{\$4,000,000}$$

= 1.25%;

Division B: $$\frac{\$500,000 - (12,000 \div 45,000)(\$900,000)}{\$5,000,000}$$

= 5.2%;

Division C: $$\frac{\$500,000 - (10,500 \div 45,000)(\$900,000)}{\$6,000,000}$$

= 4.83%.

24. *ROI Computations with Replacement Costs.*

a. Division A: $\dfrac{\$400,000}{\$4,000,000} = 10\%$;   Division B: $\dfrac{\$600,000}{\$7,500,000} = 8\%$.

b. Division A: $\dfrac{\$400,000}{\$6,000,000} = 6.67\%$;   Division B: $\dfrac{\$600,000}{\$8,000,000} = 7.5\%$.

c. There are two principal arguments for using acquisition cost in the denominator as in part **a**. First, it is easily obtained from the firm's records and does not require estimates of current replacement costs. Second, it is consistent with the measurement of net income in the numerator (that is, depreciation expense is based on acquisition cost and unrealized holding gains are excluded). There are also two principal arguments for using current replacement cost in the denominator as in part **b**. First, it eliminates the effects of price changes and permits the division that can use the depreciable assets most efficiently to show a better ROI. Second, as discussed in the chapter, it may lead division managers to make better equipment-replacement decisions. If acquisition cost is used as the valuation basis in calculating ROI, divisions with older, more fully depreciated assets may be reluctant to replace them and thereby introduce higher, current amounts in the denominator. If current replacement cost is used in the denominator, the asset base will be the same regardless of whether or not the assets are replaced. Thus, the replacement decision can be made properly (that is, based on net present value), independent of any effects on ROI.

26. *Comparing Profit Margin and ROI as Performance Measures.* The return on investment (ROI), profit margin percentage, and asset turnover ratio of the three divisions are as follows.

	$\dfrac{\text{Return on}}{\text{Investment}}$	$=$	$\dfrac{\text{Profit Margin}}{\text{Percentage}}$	$\times$	$\dfrac{\text{Asset Turnover}}{\text{Ratio}}$
Division A:	$\dfrac{\$200,000}{\$2,000,000}$	$=$	$\dfrac{\$200,000}{\$3,800,000}$	$\times$	$\dfrac{\$3,800,000}{\$2,000,000}$
	10%	$=$	5.26%	$\times$	1.9
Division B:	$\dfrac{\$500,000}{\$6,250,000}$	$=$	$\dfrac{\$500,000}{\$17,000,000}$	$\times$	$\dfrac{\$17,000,000}{\$6,250,000}$
	8%	$=$	2.94%	$\times$	2.72
Division C:	$\dfrac{\$1,000,000}{\$8,000,000}$	$=$	$\dfrac{\$1,000,000}{\$20,000,000}$	$\times$	$\dfrac{\$20,000,000}{\$8,000,000}$
	12.5%	$=$	5%	$\times$	2.5

a. Using the profit margin percentage, the ranking of the divisions is Division A, Division C, and Division B.
b. Using ROI, the ranking of divisions is Division C, Division A, and Division B.
c. The ROI is a better measure of overall performance because it relates profits to the investment, or capital, required to generate those profits. Division A had the largest profit margin percentage. It required more capital to generate a dollar of sales than did Division C. Thus its overall profitability is less. Note that Division B had the largest asset turnover ratio. However, it generated the smallest amount of net income per dollar of sales, resulting in the lowest ROI of the three divisions.

28. *ROI Computations with Net and Gross Book Values.*

	a. Net Book Value	b. Gross Book Value
Year 1	$\dfrac{(\$400{,}000 - \$200{,}000)}{(\$2{,}000{,}000 - \$200{,}000)}$	$\dfrac{(\$400{,}000 - \$200{,}000)}{\$2{,}000{,}000}$
	$= \dfrac{\$200{,}000}{\$1{,}800{,}000} = 11.1$ Percent	$= \dfrac{\$200{,}000}{\$2{,}000{,}000} = 10$ Percent
Year 2	$\dfrac{(\$400{,}000 - \$200{,}000)}{[\$2{,}000{,}000 - (2 \times \$200{,}000)]}$	$\dfrac{(\$400{,}000 - \$200{,}000)}{\$2{,}000{,}000}$
	$= \dfrac{\$200{,}000}{\$1{,}600{,}000} = 12.5$ Percent	$= \dfrac{\$200{,}000}{\$2{,}000{,}000} = 10$ Percent
Year 3	$\dfrac{(\$400{,}000 - \$200{,}000)}{[\$2{,}000{,}000 - (3 \times \$200{,}000)]}$	$\dfrac{(\$4{,}000{,}000 - \$200{,}000)}{\$2{,}000{,}000}$
	$= \dfrac{\$200{,}000}{\$1{,}400{,}000} = 14.3$ Percent	$= \dfrac{\$200{,}000}{\$2{,}000{,}000} = 10$ Percent
Year 4	$\dfrac{(\$400{,}000 - \$200{,}000)}{[\$2{,}000{,}000 - (4 \times \$200{,}000)]}$	$\dfrac{(\$400{,}000 - \$200{,}000)}{\$2{,}000{,}000}$
	$= \dfrac{\$200{,}000}{\$1{,}200{,}000} = 16.7$ Percent	$= \dfrac{\$200{,}000}{\$2{,}000{,}000} = 10$ Percent

30. *ROI and Residual Income Computations.*

$$\text{Annual Income} = \$70{,}000 - \frac{\$160{,}000}{5} = \$38{,}000.$$

Year	Investment Base	a. ROI $38,000 ÷ Base	b. Residual Income $38,000 − 25 Percent × Base
1	$160,000	23.8 Percent	$(2,000)
2	128,000[a]	29.7 Percent	6,000
3	96,000	39.6 Percent	14,000
4	64,000	59.4 Percent	22,000
5	32,000	118.8 Percent	30,000

[a]Base decreases by annual depreciation of $32,000.

32. *Transfer Pricing.*

a.

	Buying Division	Selling Division		Company	
Transfer Internally	Pays $215	Receives	$200	Pays	$ 70
		Pays	70	Pays	15
				Pays	$ 85
Transfer Externally	Pays $210	Receives	$200	Pays	$ 70
		Pays	70	Pays	210
				Receives	200
				Pays	$ 80

Hence, it is advantageous to transfer externally.

b.

	Buying Division	Selling Division		Company	
Transfer Internally	Pays $215	Receives	$200	Pays	$ 70
		Pays	70	Pays	15
				Pays	$ 85
Transfer Externally	Pays $210	Receives and		Pays	$210
		Pays	0		

Hence, it is optimal to transfer internally.

Part Five **Special Topics**

This part contains four chapters that deal with special topics. Chapters 15 and 16 integrate managerial accounting material from previous chapters. Chapter 15 discusses cost allocation to products, departments, and divisions, including the rationale for cost allocation, cost allocation methods, and pitfalls of misusing cost allocation in decision making. Chapter 16 synthesizes managerial accounting topics from previous chapters. It also shows possible conflicts between managerial decisions and the way managerial actions are reflected in accounting reports.

Chapters 17 and 18 provide an overview of financial accounting topics. Chapter 17 provides an overview of financial reporting, and Chapter 18 discusses methods of analyzing financial statements, including ratio analysis.

Chapter 15   Cost Allocation

This chapter discusses concepts and methods of assigning costs to departments, products, and other cost objects. This cost assignment is known as *cost allocation*. Critics of accounting have suggested that cost allocations made in preparing accounting reports cause more misleading and incorrect interpretations than any other single factor. Why are cost allocations made? How can they cause misleading or incorrect interpretations? Are there some cost allocation methods that are better than others? This chapter attempts to answer these questions.

The Nature of Common Costs

Accounting distinguishes between a *direct cost* and a *common cost*. (Common costs are also known as *indirect costs*.) A direct cost is one that can be identified specifically with, or traced directly to, a particular product, department, or process. For example, direct materials and direct labor costs are direct costs with respect to products manufactured. A department manager's salary is a *direct* cost of the department, but *common* to the units produced by the department. A *common cost*, in contrast, results from the joint use of a facility (for example, plant or machines) or a service (for example, fire insurance) by several products, departments, or processes. There is no way to disaggregate this common, or shared, cost and to attribute its parts directly to particular products, departments, or processes. For some reporting purposes, however, common costs must be disaggregated. It is necessary in these cases to develop some reasonably systematic basis for allocating common costs.

Common costs pervade accounting to a much greater extent than one might initially suppose. In financial accounting, most questions of allocating costs to accounting periods involve common costs. That is, many costs are common, or joint, to more than one reporting period. For example, the cost of a depreciable asset must be allocated through depreciation to the years of the asset's useful life.

In addition, there are many costs that are common to products manufactured. In order to develop product cost information, these common costs must be allocated. Examples include the following:

1. Fixed manufacturing overhead costs in a factory or department are all allocated to each of the products produced to obtain a value for inventory and to calculate cost of goods sold in external financial statements.

2. The costs of operating service departments (for example, employee cafeteria, maintenance department) are allocated to individual manufacturing departments for several purposes, discussed later in the chapter. This is called *service department cost allocation*.

3. The costs incurred in a manufacturing process that jointly produces several different products simultaneously (for example, beef and hides obtained from cattle) are allocated to each of the products for inventory valuation. This is called *joint cost allocation*.

Other examples of common costs include central corporate expenses common to each of the corporate divisions and costs incurred in paying property taxes (for example, on land, building, and inventory) that must be allocated to the individual assets under certain circumstances.

The purpose of listing these examples is to emphasize the extent to which common cost allocations pervade accounting reports, both internal and external. In order to understand accounting reports and make appropriate interpretations, one must be familiar with the alternative allocation methods used and their effects on the resulting reports.

Purpose of Common Cost Allocations

Common cost allocations are made to allocate costs to units of product for external financial reporting and tax purposes. Also, many contracts require cost allocations.

Allocations in Contract Disputes

Example Two companies entered into a joint venture and agreed to "split the costs 50-50." Each partner was to be reimbursed for the partner's own "costs" and was to receive an equal share of the profits. The first partner submitted an itemized list of costs chargeable to the joint venture, which included an allocation of $500,000 of corporate headquarters' costs. The second partner argued that these were not chargeable to the partnership. The first partner replied by asserting that without corporate headquarters the company would not exist and, hence, the costs of the headquarters were necessary for the operation of the partnership.

Should the partnership be charged with a share of one partner's headquarters' costs? If so, what method should be used to allocate those costs? Settling disputes like these is seldom simple or straightforward. Indeed, the settlement process may involve costly litigation.

Cost Accounting Standards Board Contracts between companies in the defense industry and the U.S. government are frequently made on a "cost-plus-a-profit" basis. These contracts require the companies to allocate costs between government and commercial work. Further allocations are often needed among several contracts within a particular company. There are enough such disputes that the *Cost Accounting Standards Board* (CASB) was formed in 1971 to establish standards for cost allocation to government contracts. Although the CASB operated only from 1971 until mid-1980, its standards are still in effect.

Misleading Cost Allocations

The dilemma with cost allocations is that they are often needed for a particular purpose, such as product costing for external financial reporting and to satisfy contract requirements. They can be misleading, however, and lead to incorrect decisions, inaccurate plans, and misinterpretations of performance, as demonstrated by the following examples.

Example 1 Technotronics Corporation manufactures a wide line of electronic equipment. One product, a signal detection device, has a unit production cost (direct material, labor, and manufacturing overhead) of $40, of which $10 is fixed manufacturing overhead allocated to each unit. Technotronics has been asked to accept a special order for 500 signal detection devices for $35 each. The devices can be produced with capacity that is currently not being used. Fixed manufacturing costs, and marketing and administrative costs, would be unaffected by this order. Accepting the order would not affect the regular market for this product.

The decision to accept or to reject the order should be based on an assessment of the differential costs of accepting the order. As long as the differential costs to produce the product (that is, the variable costs) are less than $35, the order should be accepted. Using the $40 unit cost, which includes an allocation of fixed manufacturing overhead cost, could lead to an incorrect decision. All other things being equal, the appropriate information to use in the decision is the $30 unit variable cost before allocation of fixed costs to the product.

Example 2 Wharton Products Corporation allocates the cost of operating service departments (for example, the maintenance department) to each of the manufacturing departments for purposes of product costing. These costs are included in manufacturing overhead. Division A of Wharton Products Corporation is attempting to estimate its overhead cost for the coming year. To develop estimates of fixed and variable overhead costs, it has analyzed past overhead cost behavior using statistical regression and developed the following budget equation: total costs = $100,000 + $5 per unit produced. It used these estimates in planning for the coming year.

In the past, maintenance department costs have been allocated to manufacturing divisions using square footage occupied by each division. This year, corporate management decided to use maintenance hours worked in each division as the basis for allocating maintenance costs in the future. Because the costs allocated under the new rule will differ significantly from those using the old allocation base, using past cost data to construct a budget for total costs can lead to inaccurate plans for the coming year.

Example 3 Diversified Industries, Inc., is organized into 40 autonomous operating divisions. Corporate management uses the divisional rate of return on investment for evaluating the performance of the division managers. In calculating divisional net income, an allocated share of central corporate expenses is deducted. The expenses are allocated to divisions based on divisional sales. Division B increased its sales by 25 percent during the current year. Because of an increase in total central corporate expenses and an increase in the relative share of these expenses allocated to Division B, the 25 percent increase in sales resulted in only a 5 percent increase in Division B's operating profits.

Including a share of central corporate expenses in Division B's performance report can give a misleading picture of its operations. If Division B has no control over these costs, then it is questionable for the division to be held accountable for them. More important, allocation of these costs based on sales could lead division managers to reduce sales efforts, to the detriment of the company as a whole.

The message of this section should be fairly clear. Accounting data that include common cost allocations must be interpreted carefully. As a rule, decisions should be made using unallocated costs.

Use of Cost Allocation for Managerial Purposes

Although we have emphasized the need to be wary of using allocated costs, there are times when cost allocation is useful for managerial purposes. Full product costs are sometimes used as inputs to pricing and planning decisions. Such questions as "Will the price received for product A cover all of its costs in the long run?" require knowledge of full product costs, including common or joint costs allocated to the product. Other managerial reasons for allocating costs are discussed below.

Charging the Cost of Service Departments to Users Virtually every organization has departments whose main job is to service other departments. These include the laundry in a hospital, the computer center in a university, maintenance in a factory, security in a retail store, and so forth. Because the output of these departments is not sold to customers outside the organization, their costs must be covered by the contribution margins of revenue-generating departments. Thus, organizations often allocate the costs of departments that do not generate revenue (which we call "service departments") to revenue-generating departments as an "attention-getting device."[1] The allocation makes managers of user departments aware that it is not enough to cover just the direct department costs in order for the organization as a whole to break even or make a profit; indirect costs must be covered as well.

Example The Allen Company did not allocate the costs of its computer department to user departments. In 1982, top management noted that computer department costs had increased 400 percent over the level of costs in 1979. Although an increasing need for computer services was acknowledged by top management, an increase of this magnitude far exceeded expectations. Top management learned, upon investigation, that user departments were not charged for using the computer or computer department staff, so they treated the computer and computer staff as if they were free.

To deal with this problem, Allen Company started allocating computer department costs to user departments using a rate per unit of the computer's time and

---

[1] A study of corporate cost allocation found that 84 percent of companies participating in the survey reported allocating some indirect costs. The study indicated that cost allocation for managerial purposes was primarily an attention-getting device to *remind* responsibility center managers that common costs exist and must be recovered by responsibility center profits. See J. M. Fremgen and S. S. Liao, *The Allocation of Corporate Indirect Costs* (New York: National Association of Accountants, 1981).

space, and a rate per unit of computer personnel time. As a result, user departments reduced their demand for the computer and related services to only those uses for which the benefits to the user department were believed to exceed the cost charged or allocated to the user. When computer personnel assisted a user department, the user department's manager monitored the computer personnel's work habits to avoid being charged for time inefficiently spent by computer personnel.

Preventing Users from Treating Services as Free The previous example demonstrates how cost allocation gives users incentives to control the costs of services. In theory, the user should use a service as long as the marginal benefit of a unit of service exceeds its marginal cost. Thus, the marginal cost of supplying a unit of service should be charged to the user to get the user to make the correct (economic) decision about how much of the service to use. Marginal costs are difficult to measure, however, so variable costs or other surrogates for marginal costs are often used. Cost allocation also encourages "interdepartment monitoring." If the costs of a service department are allocated to user departments, managers of user departments have incentives to monitor the service department's costs. Presumably, the more efficient the service department, the lower the costs that will be passed on to the user departments.

Problems with Allocating Fixed Service Department Costs

The allocation of fixed costs can have unintended effects, as demonstrated by the following example.

Example[2] The top administrators of Southwest University observed that faculty and staff were using the University's WATS (Wide Area Telephone Service) so much that the lines were seldom free during the day. WATS allowed the university unlimited toll-free service within the United States. The fixed cost of WATS was $10,000 per month; variable cost per call was zero.

The top administrators learned that there was an average usage of 50,000 minutes per month on the WATS line, so they initially allocated the $10,000 monthly charge to callers (that is, departments) at a rate of $.20 per minute (= $10,000 ÷ 50,000 minutes). Now that they were being charged for the use of WATS, faculty and staff reduced their usage of WATS. Hence, the number of minutes used on WATS dropped to 25,000 per month, which increased the rate charged to $.40 per minute (= $10,000 ÷ 25,000 minutes). This continued until the internal cost allocation per minute exceeded the normal long-distance rates, and the use of WATS dropped almost to zero. Southwest University's total telephone bill increased dramatically.[3]

---

[2]This example is based on one given by Jerold L. Zimmerman, "The Costs and Benefits of Cost Allocations," *The Accounting Review* (July 1979), pp. 510–511.

[3]According to Zimmerman (ibid.), the correct price to charge users is ". . . the cost imposed by forcing others who want to use the WATS line to either wait or place a regular toll call . . . this cost varies between zero (if no one is delayed) to, at most, the cost of a regular toll call if a user cannot use the WATS line" (p. 510). The necessary procedure to implement such a pricing system would be difficult and costly. Zimmerman suggests that fixed allocations could be a simplified way of approximating the results of the more complicated, though theoretically correct, pricing system.

The top administrators subsequently compromised by charging a nominal fee of $.10 per minute. According to the university's chief financial officer, ''The $.10 per minute charge made us aware that there was a cost to the WATS service, albeit a fixed cost. The charge was sufficiently low, however, so as not to discourage bona fide use of WATS.''

Cost Allocation: A Note of Caution

In short, cost allocations are common in organizations. Although they often have a purpose, they can easily be misleading because users of accounting information often do not appreciate how arbitrarily most costs are allocated. We caution the reader to use allocated costs carefully.

Cost allocation is so prevalent that it is often taken for granted. It is wise to continually challenge the need for cost allocation in companies—to ask ''Why allocate?'' The absence of a sound reason for the cost allocation is a signal that it is not needed. If there is a reason for cost allocation, be sure that costs allocated for the particular purpose are not misused for another purpose.

Given this word of caution, we now discuss *methods* of allocating costs.

General Principles of Cost Allocation

The cost allocation process involves three principal steps:

1. Accumulating the costs that relate to the product, department, or division (for example, manufacturing overhead, service department costs, central corporate expenses).
2. Identifying the recipient of the allocated costs (this may be a product, department, or division).
3. Selecting a method or basis for relating the costs in step 1 with the recipient in step 2.

This third step is the most difficult, because common costs cannot be associated directly with a single product, department, or division. The aim is to find an indirect relation that can serve as a meaningful allocation base. Some of the guidelines to be applied in selecting an allocation base are as follows:

1. Does an analysis of past cost behavior suggest a relationship between the incurrence of the cost and an allocation base (for example, manufacturing overhead cost and the number of units produced)?
2. Does knowledge of operations suggest a logical relationship between the incurrence of cost and an allocation base (for example, the relationship between manufacturing overhead and either the number of labor hours worked or the dollar investment in depreciable assets)?
3. If an allocation base cannot be selected on empirical or logical grounds, is there general acceptance among the parties affected that the allocations must be arbitrary? If not, then perhaps the common costs should not be allocated at all, or if allocated, a consensus of those affected should be reached on the most acceptable base.

Illustrations of Cost Allocation Procedures

In the sections that follow, we illustrate allocation procedures for manufacturing overhead, joint product costs, and selling and administrative expenses.

Manufacturing Overhead and Service Department Costs

The illustration that follows indicates the types of problems involved in allocating manufacturing overhead costs. The manufacturing division of Berdan Products Company is composed of five departments. Departments A, B, and C are production departments. Departments M and S are service departments (that is, they exist to provide support to the production departments). Records are kept of the direct material and direct labor costs incurred in each of the three production departments. All other manufacturing costs are considered to be overhead and are initially accumulated at the level of the manufacturing division, not by department. Exhibit 15.1 summarizes these relations.

The accumulation of overhead costs at the divisional level is done for control purposes. For product costing purposes, these overhead costs must be allocated to

Exhibit 15.1
BERDAN PRODUCTS COMPANY
Organization Chart

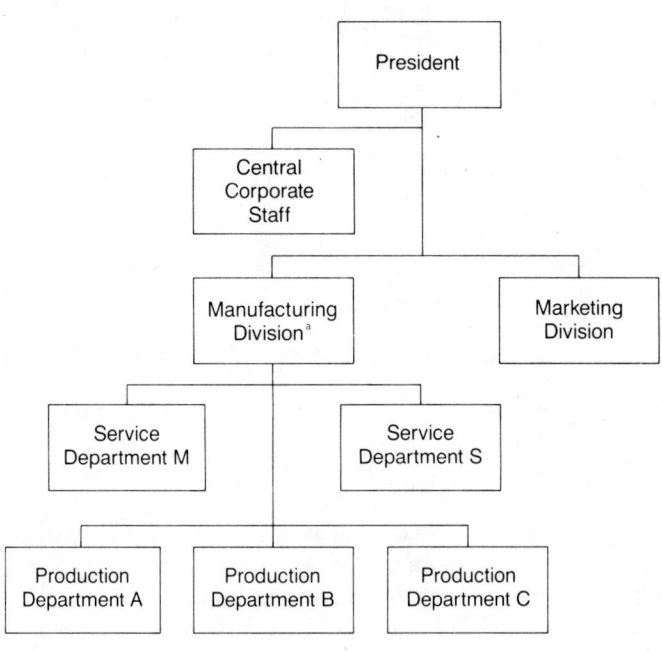

[a]All manufacturing costs other than direct material and direct labor used in the production departments are initially accumulated at the divisional level.

the production departments and then to individual products. The allocation procedure is outlined below.

1. Any overhead costs that can be attributed directly to a service or production department are allocated first (for example, salary of a foreman in one of the production departments).

2. Next, the remaining manufacturing overhead costs are allocated to the service and production departments, using a base selected because of an empirical or logical relationship between the cost and the department.

3. Next, the costs allocated to the service departments in steps 1 and 2 are reallocated to all the three production departments.

4. The direct material, direct labor, and share of manufacturing overhead allocated to each production department are then allocated to the units produced during the period.

Column (1) of Exhibit 15.2 shows a listing of the manufacturing overhead costs incurred during the month of March for Berdan Products Company. The first step

Exhibit 15.2
BERDAN PRODUCTS COMPANY
Manufacturing Overhead Costs
for the Month of March

	Total (1)	Dept. A (2)	Dept. B (3)	Dept. C (4)	Dept. M (5)	Dept. S (6)	Indirect Costs (7)
*Foreman's Salary—Dept. A	$ 2,100	$2,100					
*Foreman's Salary—Dept. B	1,950		$1,950				
*Foreman's Salary—Dept. C	1,500			$1,500			
*Foreman's Salary—Dept. M (Maintenance)	2,100				$2,100		
*Maintenance Labor—Dept. M	6,000				6,000		
*Storeroom Labor—Dept. S	2,400					$2,400	
Security Guard's Salary	500						$ 500
*Supplies Used—Dept. A	600	600					
*Supplies Used—Dept. B	900		900				
*Supplies Used—Dept. C	300			300			
*Supplies Used—Dept. S	800					800	
*Supplies Used—Dept. M	450				450		
Property Taxes	1,200						1,200
Fire Insurance.	300						300
Workmen's Compensation Insurance .	800						800
Payroll Taxes	5,000						5,000
*Depreciation of Equipment—Dept. A. .	1,200	1,200					
*Depreciation of Equipment—Dept. B. .	900		900				
*Depreciation of Equipment—Dept. C. .	330			330			
*Depreciation of Equipment—Dept. S. .	180					180	
*Depreciation of Equipment—Dept. M. .	120				120		
Rent—Factory Building	720						720
Electricity, Gas, and Water	600						600
Miscellaneous Factory Costs	750						750
Total	$31,700	$3,900	$3,750	$2,130	$8,670	$3,380	$9,870

*Each item marked with an asterisk can be assigned directly to a department.

is to allocate overhead costs that can be attributed directly to one of the five departments. Costs in this category include salaries and labor, supplies used, and depreciation. These costs are shown in the appropriate departmental columns of Exhibit 15.2. Technically, these costs are direct rather than common costs with respect to the departments.

The next step is to allocate manufacturing overhead costs that are not attributable directly to one of the departments. These costs appear in column (7) of Exhibit 15.2 and include the security guard's salary, property taxes, fire insurance, workmen's compensation insurance, payroll taxes, rent, electricity, gas, and water, and miscellaneous factory costs. At this stage it is necessary to select an allocation base. Exhibit 15.3 shows the allocation of each of these costs to the five departments. Note the types of additional information that must be available in order to make these distributions.

(1) The security guard's salary, $500, is distributed in proportion to the number of visits made to each department during a typical night. Section (1) of Exhibit 15.3 shows the distributions of the security guard's salary.

(2) Property taxes and fire insurance are distributed in proportion to the book value of the equipment and inventories in each department. See (2) in Exhibit 15.3.

(3) Workmen's compensation insurance and payroll taxes are distributed in proportion to departmental labor costs. In the schedule the amounts shown for direct labor indicate the amount of compensation earned by production-line workers in

Exhibit 15.3
BERDAN PRODUCTS COMPANY
Distribution of Various Overhead Costs for March

(1) Security Guard's Salary

Dept.	No. Visits	Percent	Distribution
A	8	20	$100
B	8	20	100
C	8	20	100
S	16	40	200
M	0	—	—
Totals	40	100	$500

(2) Property Taxes and Fire Insurance

Dept.	Book Value of Assets	Percent	Distribution of Property Taxes	Fire Insurance
A	$100,000	50	$ 600	$150
B	60,000	30	360	90
C	10,000	5	60	15
S	26,000	13	156	39
M	4,000	2	24	6
Totals	$200,000	100	$1,200	$300

Exhibit 15.3 (*continued*)
BERDAN PRODUCTS COMPANY
Distribution of Various Overhead Costs for March

(3) Workmen's Compensation Insurance and Payroll Taxes

Dept.	Direct Labor	Indirect Labor	Total Labor	Percent
A	$17,100	$ 2,200	$ 19,300	19.3
B	37,950	2,050	40,000	40.0
C	28,400	1,600	30,000	30.0
S	—	2,600[a]	2,600	2.6
M	—	8,100[b]	8,100	8.1
Totals	$83,450	$16,550	$100,000	100.0

		Distribution of	
Dept.	Percent	Work. Comp. Ins.	Payroll Taxes
A	19.3	$154	$ 965
B	40.0	320	2,000
C	30.0	240	1,500
S	2.6	21	130
M	8.1	65	405
Totals	100.0	$800	$5,000

(4) Rent—Factory Building

Dept.	Square Feet of Floor Space	Percent	Distribution
A	15,000	37.50	$270
B	15,000	37.50	270
C	8,500	21.25	153
S	1,000	2.50	18
M	500	1.25	9
Totals.	40,000	100.00	$720

(5) Electricity, Gas, and Water

Dept.	Utility Services (percent)	Distribution
A	50	$300
B	30	180
C	15	90
S	3	18
M	2	12
Totals	100	$600

[a]$2,600 = $2,400 (storeroom labor from Exhibit 15.2) + $200 [security guard's salary allocated in step (**1**)].

[b]$8,100 = $2,100 (foreman's salary—Department M from Exhibit 15.2) + $6,000 (maintenance labor—Department M from Exhibit 15.2).

each production department. The indirect labor in the production departments is the foreman's salary plus the guard's allocated salary in step (1). In the service departments, the indirect labor total is made up of department labor plus the foreman's salary for Department M plus the allocated security guard's salary for Department S. See (3) in Exhibit 15.3.

(4) The rent of the factory building is distributed in proportion to the floor space occupied by each department. See (4) in Exhibit 15.3.

(5) Electricity, gas, and water are distributed according to the capacity of equipment and needs of each department. The distribution results from a study of the departmental requirements. See (5) in Exhibit 15.3.

(6) Miscellaneous factory costs are distributed equally over the five production and service departments because there is no other logical basis for an allocation. Exhibit 15.4 shows the results of these allocations of overhead costs.

Exhibit 15.4
BERDAN PRODUCTS COMPANY
Allocation of Overhead by Step Allocation Procedure
Overhead Allocation Schedule
Month Ending March 31

	Total	Dept. A	Dept. B	Dept. C	Dept. S Storeroom	Dept. M Maintenance	Reference[a]
Foremen's Salaries	$ 7,650	$ 2,100	$ 1,950	$ 1,500	$ —	$ 2,100	*
Maintenance Labor	6,000	—	—	—	—	6,000	*
Storeroom Labor	2,400	—	—	—	2,400	—	*
Security Guard's Salary	500	100	100	100	200	—	(1)
Supplies Used	3,050	600	900	300	800	450	*
Property Taxes	1,200	600	360	60	156	24	(2)
Fire Insurance.	300	150	90	15	39	6	(2)
Workmen's Compensation Insurance	800	154	320	240	21	65	(3)
Payroll Taxes	5,000	965	2,000	1,500	130	405	(3)
Depreciation of Equipment	2,730	1,200	900	330	180	120	*
Rent—Factory Building	720	270	270	153	18	9	(4)
Electricity, Gas, and Water	600	300	180	90	18	12	(5)
Miscellaneous Factory Costs . . .	750	150	150	150	150	150	(6)
Totals	$31,700	$ 6,589	$7,220	$ 4,438	$4,112	$ 9,341	
Redistribution—Dept. M	—	3,736	1,868	2,989	748	(9,341)	
	$31,700	$10,325	$ 9,088	$ 7,427	$4,860		
Redistribution—Dept. S	—	1,620	1,620	1,620	(4,860)		
Total Production Department Costs	$31,700	$11,945	$10,708	$ 9,047			

[a]Each item marked with an asterisk is allocated directly to a department. The number in parentheses refers to a section of Exhibit 15.3 and to a discussion reference in the text.

When the initial distribution of the overhead accounts to the various departments has been completed, it is then necessary to redistribute the totals of the service departments to the production departments. One logical method, where two or more service departments serve each other as well as the production departments, requires an algebraic solution. This method, which is discussed in the appendix, requires the use of matrix algebra to allocate costs simultaneously from each service department to the other service departments and to production departments.

A less exact, but simpler solution, is as follows: (1) distribute the total costs of the service department that receives the smallest dollar amount of service from the other service departments over the other service and production departments; (2) then, in the same manner, distribute the total costs of the service department receiving the next smallest amount of service from other service departments; and so on until all service department costs have been allocated to the production departments. Once a given service department's costs have been allocated to other departments, no further costs are allocated to that given service department. This is sometimes called a *step allocation* method.

In the illustration it is assumed that Department M is the Maintenance Department. It receives little or no service from Department S, the Storeroom Department. The redistribution therefore begins by allocating the total costs of Department M in proportion to the time spent doing work specifically for certain departments.

Allocation of Department M Costs

Department	Chargeable Hours	Percent	Distribution
A	400	40	$3,736
B	200	20	1,868
C	320	32	2,989
S	80	8	748
Totals	1,000	100	$9,341

This allocation appears in the lower part of Exhibit 15.4.

It is difficult to find a logical, and at the same time practical, basis for spreading of storeroom costs. They should bear some relationship to the quantity of supplies and materials that have been issued, and in part they may be interpreted as a cost of the materials and supplies on hand. The number of requisitions made by each of the departments might be used, but the benefits from "improved" cost allocation by counting numbers of requisitions are probably not worth the effort. If the inventories at the end of the period are small compared to the quantities used during the period, storeroom costs might be allocated on the basis of a physical measure or dollar value of materials issued. If, in the example, materials and supplies are requisitioned in about equal quantities by Departments A, B, and C, the costs of Department S might be apportioned about equally among those departments, as is done in Exhibit 15.4.

Summary of Cost Allocation Steps There are three allocation steps: (1) allocation of costs associated directly with departments, (2) allocation of costs not associated directly with departments, and (3) allocation of service department costs to the production departments. Thus, the total manufacturing overhead of $31,700 is allocated $11,945 to Department A, $10,708 to Department B, and $9,047 to Department C. The next step is to allocate these amounts to the products manufactured in the three production departments. This allocation is usually based on the number of units produced, direct labor hours, direct labor cost, or some other activity base.

Joint Products and By-Products

A cost allocation problem arises when more than one product emerges from a single production process. The numerous products of meat-packing plants, the variety of metals often found and extracted together in mining operations, the inevitable production of various grades of finished lumber in the operation of a lumber mill, and the several products made from the original material in the dairy and petroleum industries are common examples of jointly produced goods.

The problems of joint production are not limited to manufacturing and mining. For instance, in real estate a similar problem exists in the development of a subdivision. The total cost of developing the tract represents a joint cost for all of the lots that are to be sold. Some reasonable method of allocating this total figure among the lots must be found if a cost and profit are to be calculated for each lot sold and a cost assigned to the unsold lots.

To understand the problems of joint cost allocations requires familiarity with some special terminology. Exhibit 15.5 presents the following information graphically. Direct materials are initially introduced into processing. After the incurrence of some direct labor and manufacturing overhead costs, two identifiable products, product A and product B, emerge from the production process. Product A is processed further. Product B is sold immediately. The point at which the identifiable products emerge is called the *splitoff point*. Costs incurred up to the splitoff point are the *joint costs*. Costs incurred after the splitoff point are called *additional processing costs*.

Exhibit 15.5
Joint Production Process

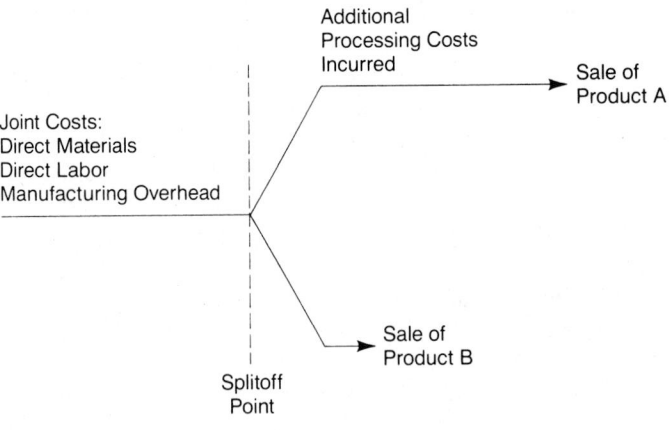

Allocation of Joint Production Costs Strictly speaking, it is impossible to compute the cost of each product produced under a joint process. Total cost can usually be computed with a satisfactory degree of accuracy, but there is no theoretically correct or objective method of spreading the total cost over the various joint products. The methods used can best be described as feasible, reasonable, or expedient. In spite of this apparently insurmountable barrier, attempts are nevertheless made to allocate joint costs, primarily in order to provide figures that can be used for cost of goods sold and inventory purposes.

Joint costs are usually allocated by either of two methods: the relative sales value method or the physical units method. Both are described in the following illustration based on a real estate development. Sorter Homes Development Company purchases a 2-acre tract of land adjoining a lake for $38,000 and spends $2,000 in legal fees to have the land subdivided into five lots. Houses are built on each of the lots. Exhibit 15.6 shows the various costs and price data.

Exhibit 15.6
SORTER HOMES DEVELOPMENT COMPANY
Data for Joint Cost Allocations

Lot Number (1)	Size (in acres) (2)	Resale Price After Subdivision (3)	Selling Price for House and Lot (4)	Cost to Build House (5)	Approximate Sales Value of Land at Splitoff (6)
1	½	$16,000	$ 75,000	$ 50,000	$ 25,000
2	½	25,000	80,000	50,000	30,000
3	½	25,000	80,000	50,000	30,000
4	¼	4,000	35,000	30,000	5,000
5	¼	10,000	40,000	30,000	10,000
	2	$80,000	$310,000	$210,000	$100,000

(3) Market prices given.
(6) = (4) − (5).

The differing prices for the half-acre and quarter-acre lots result from differing proximity to the lake. The joint cost problem in this context is to allocate the $40,000 cost of the land to each of the five lots.

Relative Sales Value Method First, suppose that once the land is legally subdivided, there is a ready market for the lots without houses and that the market prices for the five lots are as shown in column (3) of Exhibit 15.6. If such information is available, then the method of allocating the $40,000 of joint cost is to allocate that cost to the lots in proportion to their relative current market values. Because the cost is 50 percent of the sum of the current market values ($40,000 ÷ $80,000), each lot would be assigned a cost of 50 percent of its current market value. The cost allocated to lot 1 would be $8,000. The cost allocated to the other lots would be as follows: lots 2 and 3, $12,500 each; lot 4, $2,000; lot 5, $5,000. Under this method, then, each lot is assigned a portion of the joint cost such that it yields a profit equal to 50 percent of selling price.

Approximate Relative Sales Value Method To alter the illustration, suppose that the legal agreement allowing subdivision prohibits Sorter Homes from reselling the lots without houses or that for some other reason the information shown in column **(3)** is not available.

The only information directly available is that shown in columns **(4)** and **(5)**, from which column **(6)** is calculated. It would not be logical to make the assignment of the land's cost on the basis of the information in column **(4)**, because those prices include the house as well as the land. For example, the selling price of lot-house combination 4 is $35,000, which is about 11 percent of the total selling prices of $310,000. We can see from the information in column **(3)** that lot 4 represents only 5 percent of (= $4,000 ÷ $80,000) of the value of the total land package. Using final selling prices of lot-house combinations from column **(4)** to allocate land costs would intermingle land and house prices and would assign 11 percent of the land costs to lot 4, whereas 5 percent of the cost is more appropriate. The *approximate relative sales value method* is designed to achieve an allocation much like the one obtained from column **(3)** when the information about the sales value at the splitoff point is unavailable.

The diagram in Exhibit 15.7 may help in understanding the nature of the problem. Such a diagram will usually be helpful in analyzing joint cost allocation problems. The splitoff point comes just before the costs of the individual houses are incurred. To use the approximate relative sales value method, relative sales values at the splitoff must be derived, as shown in column **(6)** of Exhibit 15.6.

Exhibit 15.7
Splitoff Point in Allocating Joint Costs

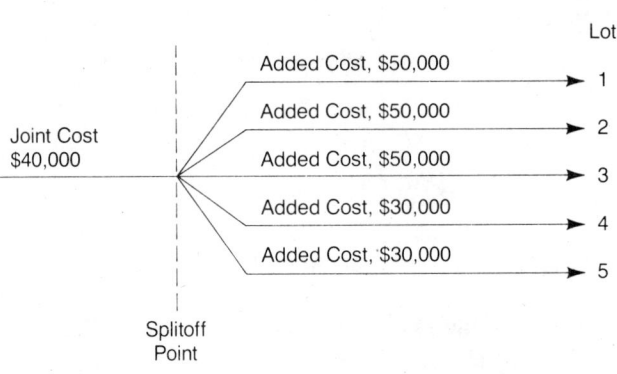

The approximate sales value of a lot (joint product) is defined to be the selling price of the lot-house combination (final product) less the cost to complete the lot-house combination. Here, the cost to complete is the cost of building the house. The approximate sales value of lot 1 is $25,000, or the price of the house-lot combination, $75,000, less the cost of the house, $50,000. The sum of the approximate sales values of the lots at the splitoff point is $100,000. Because the cost of the land ($40,000) is 40 percent of the sum of the approximate sales values, each lot would be assigned a cost of 40 percent (= $40,000 ÷ $100,000) of its approximate sales value. Lot 1, for example, would be allocated $10,000 (= .4 × $25,000). Allocations for the other lots are shown in column **(2)** of Exhibit 15.8.

Physical Units Method The physical units method is not based on dollar costs but on some obvious physical measure. Here, the obvious measure is area in acres. In other contexts the obvious physical measure might be weight or volume. Because lots 1, 2, and 3 each contain ½ acre out of 2 acres, each would be allocated (½) ÷ 2 × $40,000 or $10,000. Each ¼-acre lot would be allocated (¼) ÷ 2 × $40,000 or $5,000.

The physical units method is usually easy to apply, but its results may not make good sense. For example, if the physical units method using pounds of salable product is used to allocate the cost of beef cattle to cuts of meat, tenderloin will carry the same cost per pound as liver. Then the sales of tenderloin will appear extraordinarily profitable, whereas liver will seem to be sold at a loss. The relative sales value method will allocate more of the joint costs of beef cattle to a pound of tenderloin than to a pound of liver.

Accounting for By-Products In accounting for jointly produced products, it is customary to distinguish between by-products and joint products. A by-product is produced as the inevitable result of the production of a main product and is of a

Exhibit 15.8
SORTER HOMES DEVELOPMENT COMPANY
Joint Cost Allocation Under Various Methods
With and Without By-Products

Lot Number	Joint Product Cost = $40,000			By-Product Cost = $2,000 Joint Product Cost = $38,000		
	Basis of Allocation			Basis of Allocation		
	Relative Sales Values (1)[a]	Approximate Relative Sales Values (2)[b]	Physical Units (3)[c]	Relative Sales Values (4)[d]	Approximate Relative Sales Values (5)[e]	Physical Units (6)[f]
1	$ 8,000	$10,000	$10,000	$ 7,600	$ 9,500	$ 9,500
2	12,500	12,000	10,000	11,875	11,400	9,500
3	12,500	12,000	10,000	11,875	11,400	9,500
4	2,000	2,000	5,000	1,900	1,900	4,750
5	5,000	4,000	5,000	4,750	3,800	4,750
Total	$40,000	$40,000	$40,000	$38,000	$38,000	$38,000

[a](1) = column (3) of Exhibit 15.6 × 40/80.
[b](2) = column (6) of Exhibit 15.6 × 40/100.
[c](3) = $40,000 × [column (2) of Exhibit 15.6 ÷ 2].
[d](4) = (1) × 38/40 = column (3) of Exhibit 15.6 × 38/80.
[e](5) = (2) × 38/40 = column (3) of Exhibit 15.6 × 38/100.
[f](6) = (3) × 38/40.

relatively small value. For example, steel shavings in a machine shop, scraps of lumber in a furniture factory, and buttermilk in a dairy are typical instances of by-products. A joint product is one that is treated as equally significant with other products that emerge from a process. The different grades of lumber in a lumber mill, milk and butter in dairy operations, and subdivision lots are examples of joint products. The difference between by-products and joint products, then, is one of degree; the dividing line is not distinct. A power plant, for instance, that produces both electricity and steam may consider one or the other as a by-product or may treat them both as joint products.

In accounting for by-products, just as for joint products, no processing cost is assigned to the by-product until it is separated from the joint process. The distinctive feature of by-product accounting is that when the by-product is separated from the joint process, the by-product is then assigned a cost equal to its net realizable (or sales) value. The *net realizable sales value* of the by-product is its estimated selling price less any costs yet to be incurred for further processing, handling, and disposal. The cost assigned to by-products is then deducted from the total accumulated joint costs and the remaining joint costs become the cost of the main product or products. By-products are assigned a cost so that the expected gain or loss on their sale is zero. The cost assigned to the by-products reduces the cost of the main product or products and thereby increases the profits of the main product or products.

To illustrate the accounting for by-products, reconsider the Sorter Homes example. Suppose that at the time Sorter Homes arranged for legal subdivision of the land purchase, it also sold to the city the rights for the public to use the lake for $2,000. The rights to the lake probably should be viewed as a by-product in this case, so they would be treated as a reduction in the cost of the land. The joint costs of the land to be allocated to the five lots would be only $38,000. The right-hand panel of Exhibit 15.8 summarizes the allocation of the joint costs.

An alternative is to treat the income from the by-product as other income, and assign all by-product costs to the main product.

Marketing and Administrative Expenses

Techniques similar to those employed in manufacturing cost analysis are often applied in allocating marketing and administrative costs. A department store, for example, may wish to have its operating costs and cost of goods sold allocated, as far as possible, by departments; a wholesaler may wish to have information as to the profitability of different territories and types of customers; or a manufacturer may be interested in the cost of handling and selling various products.

Department Store Cost Analysis   The calculation of departmental operating costs in a department store is much the same as the allocation of departmental overhead in a manufacturing plant. Some items, such as salaries and commissions of salespeople, are assignable directly to departments. Others, such as rent, insurance, and supervision, have to be allocated after a preliminary accumulation in an overhead control account. Appropriate bases for the allocation of such costs are adopted, as is done for manufacturing overhead costs. For example, floor space may be used as the basis for the spreading of building service costs, but usually on a weighted basis. The different weights applied to the area occupied by different departments makes allowance for the greater value of certain sections of the store. For example, first-floor space of a given size would be weighted more heavily than the same amount of space on an upper floor.

In a manufacturing plant, all manufacturing costs must be completely allocated so that they can be assigned to units produced and unit costs for inventories can be derived for external financial reporting. By contrast, the operating costs of a department store are not included in cost of goods sold or inventory valuations. In the department store, the results of allocations of operating costs are used only for managerial purposes. Such purposes will be served better if the allocations are limited to those that can be assigned on some reasonably logical basis. Attempts to allocate the more general costs such as office salaries, executives' salaries, general store advertising, and warehouse costs will usually be arbitrary.

We list below some of the bases of allocation that have been suggested for marketing and administrative costs. One striking aspect of the problem of such cost analysis is that extensive data must be accumulated in addition to the regular accounting information. Some of the data can be accumulated regularly; other items, because of the cost of obtaining the information, will be made the subject of occasional studies in order to establish or to correct normal or standard costs of the operation.

For Allocation of	Basis
1. Insurance	Average Value of Finished Goods
2. Storage and Building Costs	Floor Space
3. Cost of Sending Monthly Statements, Credit Investigations, etc.	Number of Customers
4. Various Joint Costs Such as Advertising and Supervision of Selling Activities	Sales, Classified by Dealers, Territories, or Products
5. Credit Investigation, Postage, Stationery, and Other Such Expenses	Number of Orders Received
6. Handling Costs	Tonnage Handled
7. Salespersons' Expenses	Number of Salespersons' Calls
8. Order Writing and Filling	Number of Items on an Order
9. Stenographic Expense	Number of Letters Written
10. Automobile Operation, Delivery Expense, etc.	Number of Miles Operated

Fixed Costs and Interim Earnings Reports

The illustrations of common cost allocations considered thus far have been concerned with allocations to products, departments, or processes. An equally perplexing problem arises in allocating costs that are fixed for a year, such as insurance and property taxes, to interim periods within the year. Most firms prepare monthly or quarterly reports for evaluating the performance of departments or divisions. Performance is often judged on the department's or division's net income for the month or quarter. In order to calculate net income for an interim period within a year, a portion of the annual fixed selling and administrative expenses (and perhaps fixed manufacturing expenses, if direct costing is used for internal performance evaluation) must be deducted.

The principal problems involved in preparing and interpreting interim reports arise for departments and divisions that have substantial seasonal variations in revenues. Professional sport teams, vacation resorts, and most department stores, for example, sell their goods and services at a nonuniform rate throughout the year. Many operating costs, however, are incurred at a relatively uniform rate throughout the year. Examples include rent, property taxes, insurance, and most salaries. The principal accounting question is how these operating costs are to be assigned to each of the months or quarters during the year.

Example A summer resort generates 80 percent of its revenues during the third quarter of the year. Should the interim report for the first quarter of the year, January through March, which shows little or no revenue, show one-fourth of the year's property taxes, insurance, and other similar costs and thereby report a loss? Alternatively, should the interim report for the third quarter, which shows 80 percent of the year's revenues, show 80 percent of the year's costs as expenses and thereby report 80 percent of the anticipated net income for the year?

Illustration of Fixed Cost Allocation to Periods The illustration that follows demonstrates the issues involved in allocating fixed costs to interim periods.

Example Division C of Montsinger Corporation grows citrus fruits. Exhibit 15.9, column (1), shows the estimated revenues of Division C during each quarter of the coming year. Seasonal sales are expected to occur in the percentages of .10, .60, .20, and .10. That is, 10 percent of the year's sales is expected to occur in the first quarter of the year. Column (2) shows the expected production costs of the citrus fruit sold. Production costs are expected to be 60 percent of selling price.

Exhibit 15.9
MONTSINGER CORPORATION—DIVISION C
Estimated Revenues, Expenses, and Net Income for the Next Four Quarters
and Year Based on Two Different Allocations of Common Costs

				Method 1		Method 2	
Quarter	Estimated Revenues (1)	Production Costs (2)	Gross Profit (3)	Equal Allocation of Other Expenses (4)	Net Income (5)	Seasonal Allocation of Other Expenses (6)	Net Income (7)
1	$ 100,000	$ 60,000	$ 40,000	$ 50,000	$ (10,000)	$ 20,000	$ 20,000
2	600,000	360,000	240,000	50,000	190,000	120,000	120,000
3	200,000	120,000	80,000	50,000	30,000	40,000	40,000
4	100,000	60,000	40,000	50,000	(10,000)	20,000	20,000
Total . .	$1,000,000	$600,000	$400,000	$200,000	$200,000	$200,000	$200,000

(3) = (1) − (2).
(5) = (3) − (4).
(7) = (3) − (6).

Column (3) shows the expected gross profit. Selling and administrative expenses, which are largely fixed for the year, are expected to be $200,000.

Assume that sales and production costs during the first quarter of the year occur as expected. What is Division C's net income for the first quarter? Two alternative procedures for allocating selling and administrative expenses to the quarters during the year are illustrated in Exhibit 15.9. Column (4) shows an equal allocation to each of the four quarters. Division C therefore shows a net loss of $10,000 for the first quarter. Column (6) shows a seasonal allocation of costs to the four quarters. That is, selling and administrative expenses are allocated according to the proportion of the year's sales expected in each quarter. For example, 10 percent of the year's selling and administrative expenses are allocated to the first quarter.

Before selecting an allocation method, management must decide how it intends to use the interim earnings report. If the report is to be used to evaluate Division C's actual performance during the first quarter and management wishes to view the first quarter as a discrete accounting period, then an equal allocation is reasonable. If management intends to use the interim earnings report to help predict the division's net income for the year, then a seasonal allocation of costs makes more sense. The expected divisional net income for the year is $200,000. Using a seasonal assignment of selling and administrative expenses, the first quarter's net income is $20,000. This amount is 10 percent of the expected net income for the year, in direct proportion to the seasonal sales percentage.

The manner in which fixed costs are allocated to interim periods can have a significant effect on reported interim net income. Interpretations of interim earnings reports must therefore be made cautiously, only after knowing the methods used to assign annual fixed costs to the interim periods.[4]

Summary

Common cost allocations permeate accounting reports, both financial and managerial. Accounting reports should be read and interpreted carefully, taking into account the effects of common cost allocations that have been made. For most decision making, planning, and control purposes, accounting reports should be based on a minimum of cost allocations.

Costs are accumulated due to transactions with outsiders. The accumulated costs are then allocated to various cost objects. The cost allocation process involves (1) accumulating costs to be allocated, (2) identifying cost objects, and (3) selecting a basis for relating costs to cost objects.

A common reason for cost allocation is to satisfy external reporting requirements (for example, to value inventory on external financial reports). Cost-plus contracts and cost-based rate regulations require allocations of common costs. Service department costs are also allocated for managerial purposes (1) to charge users for the cost of services and (2) to encourage interdepartment cost monitoring.

---

[4]For an expanded discussion of interim period accounting problems, see David Green, Jr., "Towards a Theory of Interim Reports," *Journal of Accounting Research* 2, 1 (Spring 1964), pp. 35–49.

A common method of cost allocation is the *step* method, in which costs are allocated in steps, usually beginning with an allocation from the service department that provides the greatest portion of its services to other service departments, and continuing until all costs are allocated to manufacturing and marketing departments. Once an allocation is made *from* a service department, no more costs can be allocated *to* it under the step method.

Joint cost allocations are sometimes made when two or more products are output from a common input. Two common methods are the *relative sales value* method, which allocates costs in proportion to their relative sales value, and the *physical units* method, which allocates in proportion to a physical measure.

By-products are like joint products except that they are relatively minor outputs from a joint production process.

Appendix: Matrix Allocation of Service Department Costs

As mentioned in the text of the chapter, a logical method for allocating service departments' costs to production departments requires algebra. The presentation and derivation of this method are easiest with the algebra of matrices. Readers who are not prepared to deal with matrix algebra may skip this appendix without fear of losing continuity with the rest of the book.[5]

The problem is to allocate logically to production departments the costs of service departments that serve each other as well as the production departments. The data necessary to perform the logical allocation are shown for Berdan Products Company in Exhibit 15.10. The maintenance and storeroom service departments both provide service to each other as well as to production Departments A, B, and C.

The costs of the service departments to be allocated are $9,341 in maintenance and $4,112 in the storeroom. In the simplified procedure explained in the text in Exhibit 15.3, it was assumed that the storeroom's costs were allocable equally to the three production departments. A more realistic treatment assumes that the costs should be allocated in proportion to the cost of factory supplies issued by the storeroom for use by each of the departments. The total of factory supplies used is $3,050. Note that maintenance consumed $450 or 14.8 percent of that total. Consequently, in the schedule that shows the fractions of storeroom services consumed by the five departments, the storeroom column contains the figure .148 to indicate the maintenance department's consumption. The other entries in the storeroom column (including the self-service in the storeroom $800 ÷ $3,050 = .262) are derived by dividing the factory supplies used in that department by the total factory supplies used, $3,050. The basis for distributing Maintenance Department costs is the same as that used in the step procedure explained in the text.

Notice that each column in the schedule adds exactly to one. One hundred percent

---

[5]Readers who are comfortable with matrix algebra and who wish to pursue this problem further should refer to Robert S. Kaplan, "Variable and Self-Service Costs in Reciprocal Allocation Models," *The Accounting Review,* 48 (October 1973), pp. 738–748.

Exhibit 15.10
BERDAN PRODUCTS COMPANY
Fractions of Service Departments' Outputs Used by
Service and Production Departments for March

	Services Performed Here	
	Maintenance (M)	Storeroom (R)
Services Used Here		
Service Departments		
Maintenance	0	.148
Storeroom	.08	.262 } Matrix S
Production Departments		
A	.40	.197
B	.20	.295 } Matrix P
C	.32	.098
	1.00	1.000
Costs to Be Allocated.	$9,341	$4,112

of a service department's output is used somewhere. The top portion of the schedule shows the service department use of service department outputs. That section of the schedule is denoted by matrix S, where s_{ij} represents the fraction of service department j's output used by service department i. For example, $s_{MR} = .148$, or 14.8 percent of the storeroom's (R) output is used by the maintenance department (M). (The abbreviation for the storeroom is R so that it will not be confused with "S," which stands for the entire service department matrix.) The bottom portion of the schedule shows the production department usage. That section of the schedule is denoted by matrix P, where p_{ij} represents the fraction of service department j's output used by production department i. To allocate the service department costs to production departments, we need an allocation matrix such as the one shown in Exhibit 15.11. In matrix A, a_{ij} represents the fraction of service department j's cost that is allocable to production department i after taking account of mutual use of service department output by service departments.

Exhibit 15.11
BERDAN PRODUCTS COMPANY
Allocation Matrix for March

	Services Performed Here	
	Maintenance (M)	Storeroom (R)
Service Costs Allocated Here		
Production Departments		
A	.428	.353
B	.236	.447 } Matrix A
C	.336	.200
	1.000	1.000

The matrix A is calculated by the matrix equation $A = P(I - S)^{-1}$, where I is the identity matrix and $(I - S)^{-1}$ means the inverse of the matrix $(I - S)$. The derivation of the equation for A is not difficult. For example, a_{CM} represents the fraction of the maintenance department's (M) output allocable to product Department C. That fraction is

$$a_{CM} = p_{CM} + a_{CM}s_{MM} + a_{CR}s_{RM}$$

$$= .32 + a_{CM} \times 0 + a_{CR} \times .08$$

or the direct use of maintenance by Department C (p_{CM}) plus the fraction of maintenance costs used by maintenance that is allocable to Department C ($a_{CM}s_{MM}$) plus the fraction of maintenance costs used by the storeroom, that is, allocable to Department C ($a_{CR}s_{RM}$). Notice that a_{CM} is defined in terms of itself and other a_{ij} so that a system of simultaneous equations for the a_{ij} results.

Consider another example, a_{BR}:

$$a_{BR} = p_{BR} + a_{BM}s_{MR} + a_{BR}s_{RR}$$

$$= .295 + a_{BM} \times .148 + a_{BR} \times .262.$$

The fraction of storeroom costs allocable to Department B is the sum of the direct use of the storeroom by Department B (p_{BR}) plus the fraction of storeroom costs used by maintenance that is allocable to Department B ($a_{BM}s_{MR}$) plus the fraction of storeroom costs used by the storeroom that is allocable to Department B ($a_{BR}s_{RR}$).

Writing out a similar equation for each a_{ij}, where i represents production Department A, B, or C, and j represents service Department M or R, the entire system can be represented by the matrix equation

$$a_{ij} = p_{ij} + \sum_{k=M,R} a_{ik}s_{kj}$$

or

$$A = P + AS.$$

Rearranging terms yields:

$$A - AS = P$$

or

$$A(I - S) = P.$$

Postmultiply both sides by $(I - S)^{-1}$ to get[6]

$$A = P(I - S)^{-1}.$$

---

[6]If the inverse of $(I - S)$ does not exist, then a subset of the service departments completely uses the entire output of themselves without providing any service to the other service departments or to production departments. If the subset of service departments that mutually consume the output of each other is eliminated from the problem, then the procedure can be carried out.

Exhibit 15.12
BERDAN PRODUCTS COMPANY
Allocation of Service Department Costs to Production Departments, March

Production Department	Service Departments			
	Matrix Method			Step Approximation Method
	Maintenance	Storeroom	Total	
A	$3,998	$1,452	$ 5,450	$ 5,356
B	2,204	1,838	4,042	3,488
C	3,139	822	3,961	4,609
	$9,341	$4,112	$13,453	$13,453

Once the matrix A is calculated, the allocation of service department costs to production departments is straightforward. The allocation is shown in Exhibit 15.12 along with the allocation provided by the easier, but approximate, step procedure demonstrated earlier.

Observe that the matrix method gives different answers from the approximation. The matrix method is cumbersome to carry out by hand. The solution to the set of simultaneous equations (or the matrix inversion) is tedious and, except for small problems, should be done on a computer. Only when all entries in the S matrix are zero, that is, when all service department outputs are used directly by production departments, will the matrix procedure and the approximate step procedure give the same answer.

Problem 1 for Self-Study

See the partially completed overhead distribution schedule shown in Exhibit 15.13. The costs are to be distributed on the following bases.

(1) Janitor's wages and rent of building: on basis of floor space.

(2) Fire insurance and property taxes: on basis of value of assets in each department.

(3) Workman's compensation insurance and payroll taxes: on basis of proportions of total labor costs, including allocated portion of janitor's wages.

(4) Electricity, gas, and water, and miscellaneous factory costs: on basis of percentages given.

(5) Maintenance costs: on basis of chargeable maintenance hours.

(6) Storeroom costs: on basis of proportions of number of requisitions drawn.

Prepare a schedule of allocated costs and use the step method to distribute service department costs. Round all percentages to one decimal place and all dollars to the nearest dollar.

Exhibit 15.13
MERRIAM COMPANY
Overhead Distribution Schedule
Month of February

	Total	Dept. A	Dept. B	Dept. C	Dept. S Storeroom	Dept. M Maintenance
Foremen's Salaries	$ 2,550.00	$ 600.00	$ 675.00	$ 637.50		$ 637.50
Maintenance Wages . . .	1,870.00					1,870.00
Storeroom Wages	530.00				$ 530.00	
(1) Janitor's Wages	350.00					
Supplies Used	1,350.00	200.00	300.00	100.00	600.00	150.00
(2) Fire Insurance.	150.00					
(3) Workmen's Compensation Insurance	260.00					
(3) Payroll Taxes	1,320.00					
(2) Property Taxes	300.00					
(1) Rent—Factory Building . .	550.00					
Depreciation of Machinery and Equipment	450.00	202.50	144.00	45.00	36.00	22.50
(4) Electricity, Gas, and Water	200.00					
(4) Miscellaneous Factory Costs	1,270.00					
Total	$ 11,150.00					

	Total	Dept. A	Dept. B	Dept. C	Storeroom	Maintenance
Direct Labor Costs	$ 44,700.00	$14,000.00	$15,800.00	$14,900.00	—	—
Value of Assets	$100,000.00	$45,000.00	$32,000.00	$10,000.00	$8,000.00	$5,000.00
Floor Space (square feet) .	50,000	16,000	12,000	20,000	1,600	400
Chargeable Maintenance Hours	500	160	200	120	20	—
Requisitions Drawn	200	140	50	10	—	—
Other Distribution Data:						
Electricity, Gas, and Water	100%	40%	30%	20%	6%	4%
Miscellaneous Factory Costs	100%	30%	25%	25%	10%	10%

Suggested Solution

MERRIAM COMPANY
Overhead Distribution Schedule
Month of February

	Total	Dept. A	Dept. B	Dept. C	Dept. S Storeroom	Dept. M Maintenance
Foremen's Salaries	$ 2,550.00	$ 600.00	$ 675.00	$ 637.50	$ —	$ 637.50
Maintenance Wages	1,870.00	—	—	—	—	1,870.00
Storeroom Wages	530.00	—	—	—	530.00	—
Janitor's Wages	350.00	112.00	84.00	140.00	11.20	2.80
Supplies Used	1,350.00	200.00	300.00	100.00	600.00	150.00
Fire Insurance	150.00	67.50	48.00	15.00	12.00	7.50

MERRIAM COMPANY
Overhead Distribution Schedule
Month of February (*continued*)

	Total	Dept. A	Dept. B	Dept. C	Dept. S Storeroom	Dept. M Maintenance
Workmen's Compensation Insurance	260.00	76.44	86.06	81.64	2.86	13.00
Payroll Taxes	1,320.00	388.08	436.92	414.48	14.52	66.00
Property Taxes	300.00	135.00	96.00	30.00	24.00	15.00
Rent—Factory Building	550.00	176.00	132.00	220.00	17.60	4.40
Depreciation of Machinery and Equipment	450.00	202.50	144.00	45.00	36.00	22.50
Electricity, Gas, and Water	200.00	80.00	60.00	40.00	12.00	8.00
Miscellaneous Factory Costs	1,270.00	381.00	317.50	317.50	127.00	127.00
Totals	$11,150.00	$2,418.52	$2,379.48	$2,041.12	$1,387.18	$2,923.70
Redistribution—Dept. M	—	935.58	1,169.48	701.69	116.95	(2,923.70)
	$11,150.00	$3,354.10	$3,548.96	$2,742.81	$1,504.13	
Redistribution—Dept. S	—	1,052.89	376.03	75.21	(1,504.13)	
Total Productive Department Overhead Costs	$11,150.00	$4,406.99	$3,924.99	$2,818.02		

Total Labor Costs

	Direct Labor	Janitor's Wages	Other Labor	Total
Dept. A	$14,000.00	$112.00	$ 600.00	$14,712.00
Dept. B	15,800.00	84.00	675.00	16,559.00
Dept. C	14,900.00	140.00	637.50	15,677.50
Dept. S	—	11.20	530.00	541.20
Dept. M	—	2.80	2,507.50	2,510.30
Total	$44,700.00	$350.00	$4,950.00	$50,000.00

Allocation Percentages

	Floor Space	Value of Assets	Labor Costs	Maintenance	Requisitions
Dept. A	32.0%	45%	29.4%	32%	70%
Dept. B	24.0%	32%	33.1%	40%	25%
Dept. C	40.0%	10%	31.4%	24%	5%
Dept. S	3.2%	8%	1.1%	4%	—
Dept. M	0.8%	5%	5.0%	—	—
Total	100.0%	100%	100.0%	100%	100%

Problem 2 for Self-Study

Up to the point of separation of joint products X, Y, and Z, total production costs amount to $51,500. The following quantities are produced:

Product X: 3,000 units with an estimated sales value of $3 per unit.

Product Y: 4,500 units with an estimated sales value of $4 per unit.

Product Z: 9,700 units with an estimated sales value of $5 per unit.

a. Prepare a schedule showing the allocation of production costs to the three joint products and the unit cost of each product, using the relative sales value method.

b. Repeat part **a** assuming that product X is treated as a by-product.

Suggested Solution

a.

	Units	Unit Price	Total Sales Value	Percent of Value	Cost Allocation	Unit Cost
Product X . . .	3,000	$3	$ 9,000	11.92	$ 6,139	$2.046
Product Y . . .	4,500	4	18,000	23.84	12,278	2.728
Product Z . . .	9,700	5	48,500	64.24	33,083	3.411
Total			$75,500	100.00	$51,500	

b.

Total Cost	$51,500
Value of Product X	9,000
Costs to Be Allocated to Y and Z	$42,500

$$\text{Product Y} = \frac{\$18,000}{\$66,500} \times \$42,500$$

$$= .2707 \times \$42,500 = \$11,505.$$

Unit cost = $2.56.

$$\text{Product Z} = \frac{\$48,500}{\$66,500} \times \$42,500$$

$$= .7293 \times \$42,500 = \$30,995.$$

Unit cost = $3.20.

Problem 3 for Self-Study

At the conclusion of process 4, the total cost of processing 25,000 gallons of chemical product K is $362,000. At this point, 5,000 gallons of by-product Y emerge and the remaining 20,000 gallons of K are transferred to process 5 for further work. The Y material will require further processing at an estimated cost of $1 per gallon and then it can be sold for $3 per gallon. Determine the cost per gallon of chemical product K transferred to process 5.

Suggested Solution

The by-product has a net realizable value of $10,000 [= 5,000 × ($3 − $1)]. This amount is subtracted from the joint cost of $362,000. The remaining $352,000 is allocated to Product K. The cost per gallon, therefore, is $352,000 ÷ 20,000 gallons = $17.60 per gallon.

Problem 4 for Self-Study (Appendix)

The following data describe services produced and consumed by the four departments of the Oak Bank during October. Using these data, write the system of simultaneous equations describing the proper allocation of service department costs to the production departments. Solve for the final allocation of costs with simultaneous equations or the matrix method explained in the appendix to Chapter 15.

OAK BANKS
Fractions of Service Departments' Output Used by Service and Production Department for October

	Services Performed Here	
	Personnel (P)	Administration (A)
Services Used Here		
Service Departments		
Personnel (P)	—	.30
Administration (A)	.10	—
Production Departments		
Services (S)	.60	.20
Loans (L)	.30	.50
Costs to Be Allocated	$40,000	$60,000

Suggested Solution

Using Simultaneous Equations.

1. Set up equations to reflect service department usage and costs for each department.

Production Departments:

    (1) S (Services) = $.6P$ (Personnel) + $.2A$ (Administration)

    (2) L (Loans) = $.3P + .5A$.

Service Departments:

    (3) $P = .3A + \$40,000$

    (4) $A = .1P + \$60,000$.

2. Solve for P in terms of A by substituting equation (4) into equation (3).

$$(3)\ P = .3A + \$40,000$$
$$= .3(.1P + \$60,000) + \$40,000$$
$$= .03P + \$18,000 + \$40,000$$
$$P - .03P = \$58,000$$
$$.97P = \$58,000$$
$$P = \frac{\$58,000}{.97} = \underline{\underline{\$59,794}}.$$

3. Now substitute $P = \$59{,}794$ into equation (4).

$$(4)\ A = .1P + \$60{,}000$$
$$= .1(\$59{,}794) + \$60{,}000$$
$$= \underline{\$65{,}979}.$$

4. Finally, substitute values for A and P into the production department equations and solve to derive the service department cost allocations.

$$S\ (\text{Services}) = .6P + .2A$$
$$= .6(\$59{,}794) + .2(\$65{,}979)$$
$$= \underline{\$49{,}072}.$$

$$L\ (\text{Loans}) = .3P + .5A$$
$$= .3(\$59{,}794) + .5(\$65{,}979)$$
$$= \underline{\$50{,}928}.$$

Using Matrix Algebra.

Let a_{ij} represent the percent of service department j's cost allocable to production department i, after accounting for service department usage of service department output.

Let p_{ij} represent the direct use of department j by department i.

Let s_{ij} represent the use of department j by department i, when i and j are both service departments.

$$a_{sp} = p_{sp} + a_{sa}s_{ap} + a_{sp}s_{pp} = .63918$$
$$a_{sa} = p_{sa} + a_{sa}s_{aa} + a_{sp}s_{pa} = .39175$$
$$a_{lp} = p_{lp} + a_{la}s_{ap} + a_{lp}s_{pp} = .36082$$
$$a_{la} = p_{la} + a_{lp}s_{pa} + a_{la}s_{aa} = .60825.$$

Using the same notation as in the appendix, we find that

$$S = \begin{bmatrix} 0 & .3 \\ .10 & 0 \end{bmatrix} \qquad P = \begin{bmatrix} .60 & .20 \\ .30 & .50 \end{bmatrix}.$$

Now,

$$(I - S) = \begin{bmatrix} 1 & -.3 \\ -.1 & 1 \end{bmatrix},$$

where I is an identity matrix. The inverse matrix of $(I - S)$, $(I - S)^{-1}$, is

$$\begin{bmatrix} 1.03093 & 0.30928 \\ 0.10309 & 1.03093 \end{bmatrix}.$$

Thus,

$$A = P(I - S)^{-1} = \begin{bmatrix} .63918 & .39175 \\ .36082 & .60825 \end{bmatrix}.$$

The allocation of service department to production departments is as follows:

	From	
To	**Personnel**	**Administrative**
Services	.63918 × $40,000 = $25,567	.39175 × $60,000 = $23,505
Loans	.36082 × $40,000 = $14,433	.60825 × $60,000 = $36,495

Total allocation:

Services: $25,567 + $23,505 = $49,072.

Loans: $14,433 + $36,495 = $50,928.

Questions

1. Review the meaning of the following concepts or terms discussed in this chapter.

a. Common cost.
b. Direct cost.
c. Allocation base.
d. Service department.
e. Step allocation method.
f. Joint product.
g. By-product.
h. Splitoff point.
i. Relative sales value method.
j. Approximate relative sales value method.
k. Physical units method.
l. Net realizable sales value.
m. Joint cost allocation.
n. Additional processing costs.
o. Interdepartment monitoring.
p. Matrix allocation method (appendix).

2. When service department costs are allocated to production departments, why are these costs first accumulated at the service department level rather than assigned directly to production departments?

3. Distinguish between a production department and a service department.

4. What is the reasoning behind the opinion that, in merchandising (as opposed to manufacturing) enterprises, only those costs that can be assigned on some obviously logical basis should be allocated?

5. Comment on this statement: "The purpose of cost accounting is to compute the cost of producing a unit of product, so that this production cost can be used to determine a sales price that yields the desired gross profit margin."

6. Why are service department costs allocated to production departments?

7. Distinguish between a joint product and a by-product.

8. Comment on the following statement: "The relative sales value method is the best method to use in decisions concerning whether a joint product should be sold at splitoff or processed further."

9. What are some of the costs and benefits of cost allocation?

10. A critic of cost allocation noted: "You can avoid arbitrary cost allocations by not allocating any costs." Comment.

11. What are the steps in the cost allocation process?

12. For each of the types of common cost in the first column, select the most appropriate allocation base from the second column:

Common Cost	Allocation Base
Building Utilities	Value of Equipment and Inventories
Payroll Accounting	Number of Units Produced
Property Taxes on Personal Property	Number of Employees
Equipment Repair	Space Occupied
Quality Control Inspection	Number of Service Calls

Exercises

13. *Allocating Overhead to Departments and Jobs.* The following estimates for a year were made by the accountants of the Roberts Specialty Company:

	Cutting Department	Assembling Department	Painting Department
Estimated Overhead	$36,000	$50,000	$56,000
Estimated Direct Labor Cost	$60,000	$50,000	$70,000
Estimated Direct Labor Time	12,000 Hours	12,500 Hours	14,000 Hours

a. Compute the departmental overhead allocation rates using **(1)** direct labor cost and **(2)** direct labor hours as a basis.

b. Apply the results obtained in part **a** to the data given below for job no. 407. Show the total cost of the job for each basis of overhead allocation.

	Cutting Department	Assembling Department	Painting Department
Direct Material	$ 600	—	$ 80
Direct Labor Cost	$1,500	$2,000	$200
Direct Labor Time	250 Hours	400 Hours	38 Hours

14. *Allocating Overhead.* The Hamilton Company has two producing departments and a maintenance department. In addition, the upkeep costs for the entire plant are kept in a separate account. The estimated cost data for 19X0 are as follows:

Cost	Producing Dept. 1	Producing Dept. 2	Maintenance	General Plant
Direct Labor	$50,000	$30,000	—	—
Indirect Labor	28,000	14,000	$22,500	$20,000
Indirect Materials. . . .	9,000	7,000	900	8,000
Miscellaneous.	3,000	5,000	1,600	5,000
	$90,000	$56,000	$25,000	$33,000
Maintenance	7,000 Hours	13,000 Hours	—	—

The "general plant" services the other three departments in the following proportions: 50 percent (Department 1); 30 percent (Department 2); 20 percent (Maintenance). Allocate maintenance costs based on maintenance hours.

Compute the overhead allocation rates for Departments 1 and 2, including the allocations of the service department and the general plant.

15. *Allocating Overhead to Jobs.* The Burns Company uses a job order system of cost accounting. The data presented below relate to operations in its plant during January.

There are two production departments and one service department. The factory overhead costs accumulated during the month are $4,000. At the end of the period the overhead costs are allocated as follows: Department A, $2,100; Department B, $1,600; Department C, $300. The service department (Department C) overhead is redistributed as follows: two-thirds to Department A, one-third to Department B.

Factory overhead is applied to job orders at the following predetermined rates: 60 percent of direct labor costs in Department A, and 80 percent in Department B. The jobs are delivered upon completion. Job orders completed in January are nos. 789, 790, and 791. Job 788 is still in process on January 31.

Complete job order production record below by filling in appropriate amounts. Be sure to show supporting calculations.

Job Order Production Record

Job Order No.	Jobs In Process Jan. 1	Direct Labor Dept. A	Direct Labor Dept. B	Direct Matl. Dept. A	Direct Matl. Dept. B	Overhead Dept. A	Overhead Dept. B	Total Costs	Jobs in Process Jan. 31	Com-pleted Jobs
788.	$1,200	$ 300	$ 150	$ 250	$ 150	$	$	$	$	$
789.	850	600	300	450	300					
790.		800	450	550	350					
791.		1,000	600	600	450					
792.		1,200	650	900	400					
Totals	$2,050	$3,900	$2,150	$2,750	$1,650	$	$	$	$	$

16. *Allocating Service Department Costs Using the Step Method.* Meridian Box Company has two service departments (maintenance and general factory administration) and two operating departments (cutting and assembly). Management has decided to allocate maintenance costs on the basis of the area in each department and general factory administration costs on the basis of labor hours worked by the employees in each of their respective departments.

The following data appear in the company records for the current period:

	General Factory Administration	Maintenance	Cutting	Assembly
Area Occupied (square feet). .	1,000	—	1,000	3,000
Labor Hours	—	100	100	400
Direct Labor Costs (operating departments only)			$1,500	$4,000
Service Cost Center Direct Costs	$1,200	$2,400		

Use the step method to allocate these service department costs to the operating departments, starting with maintenance.

17. *Allocating Service Department Costs Directly to Operating Departments.* Using the data in Exercise **16,** allocate service department costs directly to the operating departments without allocating any to other service departments.

18. *Allocating Service Department Costs Directly to Operating Departments.* Greene's Good Burgers has a commissary with two operating departments: P1 (food inventory control) and P2 (paper goods inventory control). There are two service departments: S1 (computer services) and S2 (administration, maintenance, and all other). Each department's direct costs are as follows:

```
P1  . . .  $90,000
P2  . . .   60,000
S1  . . .   20,000
S2  . . .   30,000
```

S1's services are used as follows:

```
P1  . . .  10 Percent
P2  . . .  10 Percent
S2  . . .  80 Percent
```

S2's services are used as follows:

```
P1  . . .  50 Percent
P2  . . .  30 Percent
S1  . . .  20 Percent
```

Compute the allocation of service center costs to operating departments. Allocate directly to operating departments. Do not allocate costs from one service center to another.

19. *Allocating Service Department Costs Using the Step Method.* Using the data for Exercise **18,** allocate service department costs using the step allocation method, in which service center costs are allocated to other service centers as well as to operating departments.

20. *Joint Cost Allocations—Relative Sales Value Method.* A company processes Chemical XX-12 to produce two outputs: D and T. The monthly costs of processing XX-12 amount to $45,000 for materials and $160,000 for conversion costs. This processing results in outputs that sell for a total of $455,000. The sales revenue from D amounts to $273,000 of the total.

Compute the costs to be assigned to D and T in a typical month using the relative sales value method.

21. *Joint Cost Allocations—Approximate Relative Sales Value Method.* A batch of ore yields three refined products: lead, copper, and manganese. The costs of processing the ore up to the splitoff point, including ore costs, are $55,000 per batch. Selling prices and additional processing costs after splitoff are as follows (per batch):

Product	Additional Processing Cost	Sales Price
Lead	$8,000	$20,000
Copper	1,000	40,000
Manganese	6,000	30,000

Use the approximate relative sales value method to allocate joint costs to the three refined products.

22. *Joint Cost Allocations Using the Physical Quantities Method—By-Products.* The following diagram presents the facts for a group of products:

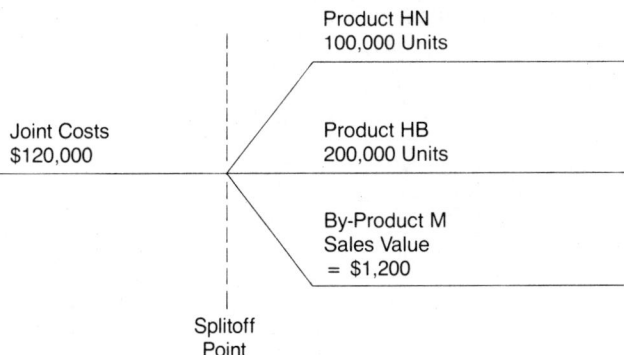

By-product sales value is used to reduce joint product costs before allocation. The $120,000 is before reduction for by-product sales value. Allocate joint costs.

23. *Joint Costing—Solving for Unknowns (CPA adapted).* O'Connor Company manufactures Product J and Product K from a joint process. For product J, 4,000 units were produced having a sales value at the splitoff point of $15,000. If Product J were processed further, the additional costs would be $3,000 and the sales value would be $20,000. For Product K, 2,000 units were produced having a sales value at splitoff of $10,000. If Product K were processed further, the additional costs would be $1,000 and the sales value would be $12,000. Using the relative sales value at splitoff approach, the portion of the total joint product costs allocated to Product J was $9,000.

Compute the total joint product costs.

24. *Joint Costing—Finding Missing Values (CPA adapted).* A company manufactures products A, B, and C from a joint process. Additional data are as follows:

	Product			
	A	**B**	**C**	**Total**
Units Produced	8,000	4,000	2,000	14,000
Joint Costs	$ 72,000	a	b	$120,000
Sales Value at Splitoff	c	d	$30,000	200,000
Additional Costs to Process Further . . .	14,000	$10,000	6,000	30,000
Sales Value if Processed Further	140,000	60,000	40,000	240,000

Derive the values for the lettered spaces.

Problems and Cases

25. *Allocating Overhead.* The APCO Company applies manufacturing overhead to all departments by means of allocation ratios. The two departments are Melting and Molding.

From the data shown below, prepare an overhead distribution schedule showing in detail the manufacturing overhead chargeable to each department. Round all decimals to three places and all dollars to whole dollars.

APCO COMPANY
Manufacturing Overhead Costs During the Month

Indirect Labor:	
Melting	$ 6,600
Molding	3,600
Supplies Used:	
Melting	1,500
Molding	900
Taxes (machinery and equipment, $72; building, $144)	216
Compensation Insurance	906
Power	300
Heat and Light	480
Depreciation: Building	384
Machinery and Equipment	360
Total	$15,246

APCO COMPANY
Other Operating Data

	Floor Space (square feet)	Cost of Machinery and Equipment	Direct Labor per Month	Horsepower Rating
Department:				
Melting	2,000	$35,000	$ 2,000	120
Molding	6,000	25,000	10,000	180
Total	8,000	$60,000	$12,000	300

26. *Allocating Unassigned Costs to Retail Store Departments.* The Kellermeyer Specialty Shop has two departments: Clothing and Accessories. The operating expenses for the year ending December 31 are shown below.

    a. Prepare a three-column statement of operating expenses with columns headed as follows: Clothing; Accessories; Total. Begin with direct departmental expenses and show a subtotal. Then continue with the allocated expenses, assigning each item to the various departments. Round all values to the nearest dollar and all percentages to one decimal place.

    b. Prepare a condensed income statement with the following columnar headings: Clothing; Accessories; Total. Show the total of operating expenses calculated in part **a** as a single deduction from gross margin.

KELLERMEYER SPECIALTY SHOP

	Clothing	Accessories	Unassigned	Total
Salaries:				
Clerks	$78,240	$69,360	—	$147,600
Others			$48,000	48,000
Supplies Used	3,800	3,200	1,400	8,400
Depreciation of Equipment . . .	1,600	4,800	—	6,400
Advertising	3,726	8,586	3,888	16,200
Building Rent			19,000	19,000
Payroll Taxes			12,300	12,300
Workman's Compensation Insurance			2,080	2,080
Fire Insurance			1,000	1,000
Delivery Expense			1,800	1,800
Miscellaneous Expenses . . .	1,000	800	600	2,400

KELLERMEYER SPECIALTY SHOP

	Clothing	Accessories	Total
Sales	$600,000	$400,000	$1,000,000
Cost of Goods Sold	$440,000	$240,000	$ 680,000
Equipment	$ 10,080	$ 24,960	$ 35,040
Inventory (average)	$100,800	$139,200	$ 240,000
Floor Space (square feet)	2,400	3,600	6,000
Number of Employees	10	15	25

KELLERMEYER SPECIALTY SHOP

Expense	Basis of Allocation
Salaries—Other	Gross Margin
Supplies Used (unassigned)	Sales
Advertising (unassigned).	Sales
Building Rent.	Floor Space
Payroll Taxes.	Salaries (including both direct and other allocated salaries)
Workmen's Compensation Insurance	Salaries (including both direct and other allocated salaries)
Fire Insurance	Cost of Equipment and Inventory
Delivery Expense	Sales
Miscellaneous Expenses (unassigned)	Number of Employees

27. *Allocating Service Department Costs.* The Schneider Spaghetti Company has two production departments: Tubing and Packing. There are also two service departments: Quality Control and Maintenance. In June, the Quality Control Department provided 2,000 hours of service: 995 hours to Tubing, 255 hours to Maintenance, and 750 hours to Packing. In the same month, Maintenance provided 2,700 hours to Tubing, 1,800 hours to Packing, and 500 hours to Quality Control. Costs incurred for Quality Control were $50,000 and costs incurred for Maintenance were $105,000.

Use the step method to allocate service department costs sequentially. Start with Maintenance and then allocate Quality Control. Check your solution by making certain that $155,000 is finally allocated to the production departments.

28. *Allocating Service Department Costs.* The Horton Hose Factory is engaged in the manufacture and sale of garden hoses. The firm's two production departments are Slicing and Nozzles. These departments are served by the Personnel and Administration Departments. In January, the Slicing Department consumed the following services: 750 hours from Personnel and 300 hours from Administration. Nozzles consumed 450 hours from Personnel and 300 hours from Administration. In addition, Personnel supplied Administration with 150 hours and consumed 200 hours from Administration. Costs for the Personnel Department were $60,000 and for Administration, $50,000.

Allocate all service costs using the step procedure. Treat service departments in the following order: Personnel and then Administration. Round answers to the nearest dollar and decimals to three places.

29. *Joint Cost Allocations.* The Roving Eye Cosmetics Company buys bulk flowers and processes them into perfumes. Their highest-grade perfume, Seduction, and a residue that is processed into a medium-grade perfume called Romance come from a certain mix of petals. In July, the company used 25,000 pounds of petals. Costs involved in Process A, reducing the petals to Seduction and the residue, were

$200,000 direct materials,

$110,000 direct labor,

$90,000 overhead and other costs.

The additional costs of producing Romance in Process B were

$22,000 direct materials,

$50,000 direct labor,

$40,000 overhead and other costs.

At the end of the month, total completed production was 5,000 ounces of Seduction and 28,000 ounces of Romance. In addition, 5,000 ounces of Seduction and 25,000 ounces of Romance were still in Process A (a continuous process). These units were on the average one-half complete. There was no beginning inventory on July 1, and all materials, labor, and overhead are applied evenly throughout Process A. There are no uncompleted units in Process B.

Packaging costs incurred for each product as completed were Seduction, $40,000, and Romance, $161,000. The sales price of Seduction is $90 an ounce and of Romance, $31.50 per ounce.

 a. Allocate joint costs using the approximate relative sales value method.

 b. Allocate the joint costs using the physical units method. Round all percentages to one decimal place.

 c. Is there any inconsistency in using the physical units method in this case?

 d. Assume that Roving Eye can sell the squeezed petals from Process A to greenhouses for use as fertilizer. In July, there were 12,000 pounds of squeezed petals left over that sold for $.75 per pound. The squeezed petals are a by-product of Process A. With this new information, answer parts **a** and **b**.

30. *Cost Allocation over Time Periods.* Gaffney Tax Services, Inc., provides income tax preparation services to its customers. Fee revenues are highly seasonal during the four quarters of the calendar year and occur in the following proportions: .60, .20, .10, .10. That is, 60 percent of the firm's revenues are usually generated during the months of January through March. The following operating costs were anticipated and actually incurred evenly throughout the year ended December 31, 19X5.

Salaries	$250,000
Rent	125,000
Insurance	25,000
Total	$400,000

During the first quarter of 19X5, fee revenues totaled $360,000.

 a. Compute operating profit for the first quarter, assuming that operating costs are assigned equally to each of the four quarters during the year.

 b. Compute operating profit for the first quarter, assuming that operating costs are assigned to each quarter in proportion to the percentage of the anticipated year's revenues recognized during each quarter.

 c. If the pattern of fee revenues during 19X5 occurs as anticipated (that is, .60, .20, .10, .10), what is the anticipated net income for the year?

 d. Which of the interim earnings measures determined in parts **a** and **b** will lead to the more accurate prediction of the annual operating profit calculated in part **c**?

31. *Cost Allocation over Time Periods.* St. Nicholas Tailors rents out a single Santa Claus costume for the months of November and December each year. Its transactions are as follows:

(1) The company commences business on January 1, 19X1.
(2) October 1, 19X1. One Santa Claus costume is purchased for $100. The costume will last for 10 annual rental periods and is depreciated on a straight-line basis. The costume has a zero estimated salvage value. The company takes a full year of depreciation in the first year.
(3) The costume is rented for the months of November and December 19X1, for $70, total.
(4) January 2, 19X2. Cleaning costs of $5 are incurred for the costume, which has been returned to St. Nicholas Tailors.
(5) The costume is stored for the months of January through October 19X2, at a cost of $2 per month.
(6) The costume is rented for the months of November and December 19X2, for $70, total.
(7) The books are closed annually on December 31. Income taxes are to be paid at the rate of 20 percent of the first $5 of taxable income and 40 percent of the rest.

Income statements for the years 19X1 and 19X2 are shown below.

ST. NICHOLAS TAILORS
Income Statements for the Years 19X1 and 19X2

	19X1	19X2
Revenues	$70	$70
Costs:		
Storage Costs	$–0–	$20
Depreciation	10	10
Cleaning Costs	–0–	5
Income Taxes	23	13
Total	$33	$48
Operating Profit	$37	$22

Prepare interim quarterly reports for March 31, June 30, September 30, and December 31, 19X1 and 19X2. If interim reports would be inadequate or inappropriate, discuss why.

32. *Joint Cost Allocations.* The Tru-Life Mannequin Company manufactures female, male, and infant mannequins. The process consists of melting, molding, shaping, sanding, assembling, painting, and producing wigs and painted hair.

In October, the following types of costs were incurred and assigned to the classes of products as follows:

Unassigned process costs (other than related to wigs and painted hair): 250,000 pounds of plaster, costing $.10 per pound; labor costs, $90,000; other costs, $35,000.

Assigned processing costs (other than related to wigs and painted hair): female, $8 each; male, $9 each; infant, $2 each.

Wigs for female mannequins: material, $1 each; labor, $10,000; overhead, $7,500.

Painted hair for male and infant mannequins: material, males, $.15 each; material, infants, $.05 each; labor, $18,000; other, $12,000.

Production for October (with no beginning or ending work-in-process inventories): 50,000 female mannequins, 60,000 male mannequins, and 30,000 infant mannequins. Female mannequins sell for $15 each; male mannequins, for $11 each; and infant mannequins, for $8 each.

    a.   Allocate joint costs using the approximate relative sales value method.

    b.   Allocate the joint costs using the physical units method.

33. *Sell or Process Further.* A joint production process results in the splitoff of three products: product A, product B, and product C. Joint costs incurred total $100,000. At splitoff, 10,000 units of product A, 10,000 units of product B, and 20,000 units of product C emerge.

    a.   The units can be sold at splitoff at the following prices: product A, $3 each; product B, $6 each; product C, $4.50 each. Using the relative sales value method, determine the net income of each product if they are sold at splitoff.

    b.   By incurring additional processing costs of $1 per unit, product A can be sold for $5 a unit. By incurring additional processing costs of $3 a unit, product C can be sold for $8 a unit. Using the approximate relative sales value at splitoff method, determine the net income of each product if additional processing takes place.

    c.   Which products should be sold at splitoff and which products should be processed further? Explain.

34. *Joint Cost Allocations (CPA adapted).* Harrison Corporation produces three products: Alpha, Beta, and Gamma. Alpha and Gamma are main products, whereas Beta is a by-product of Alpha. Information on the past month's production processes is given as follows:

(1) In Department I, 110,000 units of raw material Rho are processed at a total cost of $120,000. After processing in Department I, 60 percent of the units are transferred to Department II and 40 percent of the units (now unprocessed Gamma) are transferred to Department III.

(2) In Department II, the materials received from Department I are processed at a total additional cost of $38,000. Seventy percent of the units become Alpha and are transferred to Department IV. The remaining 30 percent emerge as Beta and are sold at $2.10 per unit. The selling costs for the Beta amount to $8,100.

(3) In Department III, the Gamma is processed at an additional cost of $165,000. A normal loss of units of Gamma occurs in this department. The loss is equal to 10 percent of the units of good output. The remaining good output is then sold for $12 per unit.

(4) In Department IV, Alpha is processed at an additional cost of $23,660. After this processing, the Alpha can be sold for $5 per unit.

Prepare a schedule showing the allocation of the $120,000 joint cost between Alpha and Gamma using the relative sales value approach. Revenue from sales of by-products should be credited to the manufacturing costs of the related main product.

35. *Allocation for Economic Decisions and Motivation (CMA adapted).* Bonn Company recently reorganized its computer and data processing activities. The small installations located within the accounting departments at its plants and subsidiaries have been replaced with a single data processing department at corporate headquarters responsible for the operations of a newly acquired large-scale computer system. The new department has been in operation for 2 years and has been regularly producing reliable and timely data for the past 12 months.

Because the department has focused its activities on converting applications to the new system and producing reports for the plant and subsidiary managements, little attention has been devoted to the costs of the department. Now that the department's activities are operating relatively smoothly, company management has requested that the departmental manager recommend a cost accumulation system to facilitate cost control and the development of suitable rates to charge users for service.

For the past 2 years, the departmental costs have been recorded in one account. The costs have then been allocated to user departments on the basis of computer time used. The schedule below reports the costs and charging rate for 1984.

Data Processing Department
Costs for the Year Ended December 31, 1984

(1)	Salaries and Benefits	$ 622,600
(2)	Supplies	40,000
(3)	Equipment Maintenance Contract	15,000
(4)	Insurance	25,000
(5)	Heat and Air Conditioning	36,000
(6)	Electricity	50,000
(7)	Equipment and Furniture Depreciation	285,400
(8)	Building Improvements Depreciation	10,000
(9)	Building Occupancy and Security	39,300
(10)	Corporate Administrative Charges	52,700
	Total Costs	$1,176,000
	Computer Hours for User Processing[a]	2,750
	Hourly Rate ($1,176,000 ÷ 2,750)	$428

[a]Use of available computer hours:

Testing and Debugging Programs	250
Setup of Jobs	500
Processing Jobs	2,750
Downtime for Maintenance	750
Idle Time	742
	4,992

The department manager recommends that the department costs be accumulated by five activity centers within the department: systems analysis, programming, data preparation, computer operations (processing), and administration. He then suggests that the costs of the administration activity should be allocated to the other four activity centers before a separate rate for charging users is developed for each of the first four activities.

The manager made the following observations regarding the charges to the several subsidiary accounts within the department after reviewing the details of the accounts:

(1) Salaries and benefits—records the salary and benefit costs of all employees in the department.

(2) Supplies—records punch-card costs, paper costs for printers, and a small amount for miscellaneous other costs.

(3) Equipment maintenance contracts—records charges for maintenance contracts; all equipment is covered by maintenance contracts.

(4) Insurance—records cost of insurance covering the equipment and the furniture.

(5) Heat and air conditioning—records a charge from the corporate heating and air conditioning department estimated to be the incremental costs to meet the special needs of the computer department.

(6) Electricity—records the charge for electricity based on a separate meter within the department.

(7) Equipment and furniture depreciation—records the depreciation charges for all owned equipment and furniture within the department.

(8) Building improvements—records the amortization charges for the building changes required to provide proper environmental control and electrical service for the computer equipment.

(9) Building occupancy and security—records the computer department's share of the depreciation, maintenance, heat, and security costs of the building; these costs are allocated to the department on the basis of square feet occupied.

(10) Corporate administrative charges—records the computer department's share of the corporate administrative costs. They are allocated to the department on the basis of number of employees in the department.

a. For each of the 10 cost items, state whether or not it should be distributed to the five activity centers; and for each cost item that should be distributed, recommend the basis on which it should be distributed. Justify your conclusion in each case.

b. Assume that the costs of the computer operations (processing) activity will be charged to the user departments on the basis of computer hours. Using the analysis of computer utilization shown as a footnote to the department cost schedule presented in the problem, determine the total number of hours that should be employed to determine the charging rate for computer operations (processing). Justify your answer.

36. *Cost Allocation and Decision Making (CMA adapted).* The Promotion Department of the Doxolby Company is responsible for the design and development of all promotional materials for the corporation. This includes all promotional campaigns and related literature, pamphlets, and brochures. Top management is reviewing the effectiveness of the promotion department to determine if the department's activities could be managed better and more economically by an outside promotion agency. As a part of this review, top management has asked for a summary of the promotion department's costs for the most recent year. The following cost summary was supplied:

Promotion Department
Costs for the Year

Direct Department Costs	$257,500
Charges from Other Departments	44,700
Allocated Share of General Administrative Overhead	22,250
Total Costs	$324,450

The direct department costs consist of those costs that can be traced directly to the activities of the promotion department such as staff and clerical salaries including related employee benefits, supplies, and so on. The charges from other departments represent the costs of services that are provided by other departments of Doxolby at the request of the promotion department. The company has developed a charging system for such interdepartmental uses of services. For instance, the "in-house" printing department charges the promotion department for the promotional literature printed. All such services provided to the promotion department by other departments of Doxolby are included in the "Changes from Other Departments." General administrative overhead comprises such costs as top management salaries and benefits, depreciation, heat, insurance, property taxes, and so on. These costs are allocated to all departments in proportion to the number of employees in each department.

Discuss the usefulness of the cost figures as presented for the promotion department of Doxolby, Inc., as a basis for a comparison with a bid from an outside agency to provide the same type of activities as Doxolby's own promotion department.

37. *Allocating Service Department Costs (CPA adapted).* The Parker Manufacturing Company has three service departments (general factory administration, factory maintenance, and factory cafeteria), and two production departments (fabrication and assembly). A summary of costs and other data for each department prior to allocation of service department costs for the year ended June 30, 1984, are as follows:

	General Factory Administration	Factory Maintenance	Factory Cafeteria	Fabrication	Assembly
Direct Material Costs	–0–	$65,000	$91,000	$3,130,000	$ 950,000
Direct Labor Costs	$90,000	82,100	87,000	1,950,000	2,050,000
Manufacturing Overhead Costs . . .	70,000	56,100	62,000	1,650,000	1,850,000
Direct Labor Hours	31,000	27,000	42,000	562,500	437,500
Number of Employees	12	8	20	280	200
Square Footage Occupied	1,750	2,000	4,800	88,000	72,000

The costs of the general factory administration department, factory maintenance department, and factory cafeteria are allocated on the basis of direct labor hours, square footage occupied, and number of employees, respectively. Round all final calculations to the nearest dollar.

    a.   Assuming that Parker elects to distribute service department costs directly to production departments without interservice department cost allocation, what would be the amount of factory maintenance department costs allocated to the fabrication department?

    b.   Assuming the same method of allocation as in part **a**, what would be the amount of general factory administration department costs allocated to the assembly department?

    c.   Assuming that Parker elects to distribute service department costs to other service departments (starting with the service department with the greatest total costs) as well as the production departments, what would be the amounts of factory cafeteria department costs allocated to the factory maintenance department? (Note: Once a service department's costs have been allocated, no subsequent service department costs are allocated back to it.)

    d.   Assuming the same method of allocation as in part **c**, what would be the amount of factory maintenance department costs allocated to the factory cafeteria?

38. *Allocating Service Department Costs Using Simultaneous Solution of Equations (CMA adapted).* (Note: Matrix algebra is not required for this problem. An algebraic equation can be set up for the costs of each of the two service departments and solved by substitution.)

    Barrylou Corporation is developing departmental overhead rates based on direct labor hours for its two production departments—molding and assembly. The molding department employs 20 people, and the assembly department employs 80 people. Each person in these two departments works 2,000 hours per year. The production related overhead costs for the molding department are budgeted at $200,000, and the assembly department costs are budgeted at $320,000. Two service departments—repair and power—directly support the two production departments and have budgeted costs of $48,000 and $250,000, respectively. The production department's overhead rates cannot be determined until the service department's costs are properly allocated. The following schedule reflects the use of the repair department's and power department's output by the various departments.

	Department			
	Repair	**Power**	**Molding**	**Assembly**
Repair Hours	–0–	1,000	1,000	8,000
Kilowatt-Hours	240,000	–0–	840,000	120,000

    a.   Calculate the overhead rates per direct labor hour for the molding department and the assembly department, allocating service department costs directly to production departments, without interservice department cost allocation.

    b.   Calculate the overhead rates per direct labor hour for the molding department and the assembly department, using the simultaneous solution method to charge service department costs to each other and to the production department.

39. *Analyzing Performance Based on Allocated Costs (CMA adapted).* The Herbert Manufacturing Co. is a manufacturer of custom-designed restaurant and kitchen furniture. Herbert Manufacturing uses a job-order cost accounting system. Actual overhead costs incurred during the month are applied to the products on the basis of actual direct labor hours required to produce the products. The overhead consists primarily of supervision, employee benefits, maintenance costs, property taxes, and depreciation.

Herbert Manufacturing recently won a contract to manufacture the furniture for a new fast-food chain that is expanding rapidly in the area. In general, this furniture is durable but of a lower quality than Herbert Manufacturing normally manufactures. To produce this new line, Herbert Manufacturing must purchase more molded plastic parts for the furniture than for its current line. Through innovative industrial engineering, an efficient manufacturing process for this new furniture has been developed that requires only a minimum capital investment. Management is very optimistic about the profit improvement the new product line will bring.

At the end of October, the startup month for the new line, the controller has prepared a separate income statement for the new product line. On a consolidated basis, the gross profit percentage was normal; however, the profitability for the new line was less than expected.

The president of the corporation is concerned that shareholders will criticize the decision to add this lower-quality product line at a time when profitability appeared to be increasing with the standard product line.

The results as published for the first 9 months, for October, and for November are presented below.

HERBERT MANUFACTURING COMPANY
(000 omitted)

	Fast-Food Furniture	Custom Furniture	Consolidated
Nine Months Year-to-Date			
Gross Sales	—	$8,100	$8,100
Direct Material	—	$2,025	$2,025
Direct Labor			
Forming	—	758	758
Finishing	—	1,314	1,314
Assembly	—	558	558
Overhead	—	1,779	1,779
Cost of Sales	—	$6,434	$6,434
Gross Profit	—	$1,666	$1,666
Gross Profit Percentage	—	20.6%	20.6%
October			
Gross Sales	$400	$ 900	$1,300
Direct Material	$200	$ 225	$ 425
Direct Labor			
Forming	17	82	99
Finishing	40	142	182
Assembly	33	60	93
Overhead	60	180	240
Cost of Sales	$350	$ 689	$1,039
Gross Profit	$ 50	$ 211	$ 261
Gross Profit Percentage	12.5%	23.4%	20.1%

	Fast-Food Furniture	Custom Furniture	Consolidated
November			
Gross Sales	$800	$ 800	$1,600
Direct Material	$400	$ 200	$ 600
Direct Labor			
Forming	31	72	103
Finishing	70	125	195
Assembly	58	53	111
Overhead	98	147	245
Cost of Sales	$657	$ 597	$1,254
Gross Profit	$143	$ 203	$ 346
Gross Profit Percentage	17.9%	25.4%	21.6%

Ms. Jameson, the cost accounting manager, has stated that the overhead allocation based only on direct labor hours is no longer appropriate. On the basis of a recently completed study of overhead accounts, Jameson feels that only the supervision and employee benefits should be allocated on the basis of direct labor hours and the balance of the overhead should be allocated on a machine hour basis. In Jameson's judgment, the increase in the profitability of the custom design furniture is due to a misallocation of overhead in the present system.

The actual direct labor hours and machine hours for the past 2 months are shown below.

	Fast-Food Furniture	Custom Furniture
Machine Hours		
October		
Forming	660	10,700
Finishing	660	7,780
Assembly	—	—
	1,320	18,480
November		
Forming	1,280	9,640
Finishing	1,280	7,400
Assembly	—	—
	2,560	17,040
Direct Labor Hours		
October		
Forming	1,900	9,300
Finishing	3,350	12,000
Assembly	4,750	8,700
	10,000	30,000
November		
Forming	3,400	8,250
Finishing	5,800	10,400
Assembly	8,300	7,600
	17,500	26,250

The actual overhead costs for the past 2 months were as follows:

	October	November
Supervision	$ 13,000	$ 13,000
Employee Benefits.	95,000	109,500
Maintenance	50,000	48,000
Depreciation	42,000	42,000
Property Taxes	8,000	8,000
All other	32,000	24,500
Total	$240,000	$245,000

a. Reallocate the overhead for October and November, using direct labor hours as the allocation base for supervision and employee benefits. Use machine hours as the base for the remaining overhead costs.

b. Support or criticize the conclusion that the increase in custom design profitability is due to a misallocation of overhead. Use the data developed in part **a** to support your analysis.

40. *Relating Allocation Methods to Organizational Characteristics for a Retailer (CMA adapted).* Columbia Company is a regional office supply chain with 26 independent stores. Each store has been responsible for its own credit and collections. The assistant manager in each store is assigned the responsibility for credit activities including the collection of delinquent accounts because the stores do not need a full-time employee assigned to credit activities. The company has experienced a sharp rise in uncollectibles the last 2 years. Corporate management has decided to establish a collections department in the home office to be responsible for the collection function company-wide. The home office of Columbia Company will hire the necessary full-time personnel. The size of this department will be based on the historical credit activity of all the stores.

The new centralized collections department was discussed at a recent management meeting. A method to assign the costs of the new department to the stores has been difficult because this type of home office service is unusual. Alternative methods are being reviewed by top management.

The controller favored using a predetermined rate for charging the costs to the stores. The predetermined rate would be based on budgeted costs. The vice president for sales had a strong preference for an actual cost charging system.

In addition, the basis for the collection charges to the stores was also discussed. The controller identified the following four measures of services (allocation bases) that could be used:

(1) Total dollar sales.
(2) Average number of past-due accounts.
(3) Number of uncollectible accounts written off.
(4) One twenty-sixth of the cost to each of the stores.

The executive vice-president stated that he would like the accounting department to prepare a detailed analysis of the two charging methods and the four service measures (allocation bases).

a. Evaluate the two methods identified—predetermined rate versus actual cost—that could be used to charge the individual stores the costs of Columbia Company's new collections department in terms of:

(1) Practicality of application and ease of use; and

(2) Cost control.

Also indicate whether a centralized or decentralized type of organization structure would be more conducive for each charging method.

b. For each of the four measures of services (allocation bases) identified by the Controller of Columbia Company:

(1) Discuss whether the service measure (allocation base) is appropriate to use in this situation; and

(2) Identify the behavioral problems, if any, that could arise as a consequence of adopting the service measure (allocation base).

41. *Allocation of Fixed Manufacturing Overhead and Decision Making (CMA adapted).* Jenco, Inc., manufactures a combination fertilizer/weed killer under the name Fertikil. This is the only product Jenco produces at the present time. Fertikil is sold nationwide through normal marketing channels to retail nurseries and garden stores.

Taylor Nursery plans to sell a similar fertilizer/weed killer compound through its regional nursery chain under its own private label. Taylor has asked Jenco to submit a bid for a 25,000-pound order of the private-brand compound. Although the chemical composition of the Taylor compound differs from that of Fertikil, the manufacturing process is very similar.

The Taylor compound would be produced in 1,000-pound lots. Each lot would require 60 direct labor hours and the following chemicals:

Chemicals	Quantity in Pounds
CW-3	400
JX-6	300
MZ-8	200
BE-7	100

The first three chemicals (CW-3, JX-6, MZ-8) are all used in the production of Fertikil. BE-7 was used in a compound that Jenco has discontinued. This chemical was not sold or discarded because it does not deteriorate and there have been adequate storage facilities. Jenco could sell BE-7 at the prevailing market price less $.10 per pound selling/handling expenses.

Jenco also has on hand a chemical called CN-5, which was manufactured for use in another product that is no longer produced. CN-5, which cannot be used in Fertikil, can be substituted for CW-3 on a one-for-one basis without affecting the quality of the Taylor compound. The quantity of CN-5 in inventory has a salvage value of $500.

Inventory and cost data for the chemicals that can be used to produce the Taylor compound are as shown below.

Raw Material	Pounds in Inventory	Actual Price per Pound When Purchased	Current Market Price per Pound
CW-3	22,000	$ .80	$ .90
JX-6	5,000	$ .55	$ .60
MZ-8	8,000	$1.40	$1.60
BE-7	4,000	$ .60	$ .65
CN-5	5,500	$ .75	(salvage)

The current direct labor rate is $7.00 per hour. The manufacturing overhead rate is established at the beginning of the year and is applied consistently throughout the year, using direct labor hours (DLH) as the base. The predetermined overhead rate for the current year, based on a two-shift capacity of 400,000 total DLH with no overtime, is as follows:

Variable Manufacturing Overhead . . . . $2.25 per DLH
Fixed Manufacturing Overhead . . . . 3.75 per DLH
Combined Rate . . . . $6.00 per DLH

Jenco's production manager reports that the present equipment and facilities are adequate to manufacture the Taylor compound. However, Jenco is within 800 hours of its two-shift capacity this month before it must schedule overtime. If need be, the Taylor compound could be produced on regular time by shifting a portion of Fertikil production to overtime. Jenco's rate for overtime hours is one-and-one-half times the regular pay rate or $10.50 per hour. There is no allowance for any overtime premium in the manufacturing overhead rate.

Jenco's standard markup policy for new products is 25 percent of full manufacturing cost.

a. Assume that Jenco, Inc., has decided to submit a bid for a 25,000-pound order of Taylor's new compound. The order must be delivered by the end of the current month. Taylor has indicated that this is a one-time order that will not be repeated.

Calculate the lowest price that Jenco should bid for the order and not reduce its operating profit.

b. Without prejudice to your answer to part **a**, assume that Taylor Nursery plans to place regular orders for 25,000-pound lots of the new compound during the coming year. Jenco expects the demand for Fertikil to remain strong again in the coming year. Therefore, the recurring orders from Taylor will put Jenco over its two-shift capacity. However, production can be scheduled so that 60 percent of each Taylor order can be completed during regular hours, or Fertikil production could be shifted temporarily to overtime so the Taylor orders could be produced on regular time. Jenco's production manager has estimated that the prices of all chemicals will stabilize at the current market rates for the coming year and that all other manufacturing costs are expected to be maintained at the same rates or amounts.

Calculate the price that Jenco, Inc., should quote Taylor Nursery for each 25,000-pound lot of the new compound assuming that there will be recurring orders during the coming year.

42. *Using Matrix Algebra for Cost Allocations (Appendix).* Refer to the problem data for Schneider Spaghetti Company, Problem **27.**

    a. Following the method outlined in the appendix to Chapter 15, set up the full matrices of services output, S, and usage, P, based on the above data.

    b. Express algebraically the fraction of the Maintenance department's output allocable to Tubing. Use the notation described in the appendix to Chapter 15 for the Berdan Products example.

    c. Express algebraically the fraction of the Quality Control department's output allocable to Packing. Use the notation described in the appendix for the Berdan Products example.

    d. Use matrices S and P to solve for matrix A, the allocation matrix.

    e. Use the results of matrix A to allocate the service department costs.

43. *Using Matrix Algebra for Cost Allocation (Appendix).* Refer to the problem data for Horton Hose Factory, Problem **28.**

    a. Set up matrices S and P as described in the appendix to the chapter. Round entries to two decimal places but make sure that all columns sum to 1 by allocating any rounding error.

    b. Using the notation explained in the appendix to the chapter for the Berdan Products example, express algebraically the following fractions:

        (1) Fraction of Administrative output allocable to Slicing.

        (2) Fraction of Personnel output allocable to Nozzles; to Slicing.

    Use matrices S and P to solve for matrix A, the allocation matrix.

    c. Use the results of matrix A to allocate the service department costs.

44. *Cost Allocations with Matrices Given (Appendix).* The allocation matrices (A) for the Twin City Manufacturing Company for April, May, and June were derived and are shown below.

TWIN CITY MANUFACTURING COMPANY
Allocation Matrices

	Services Performed Here	
	Repairs (R)	Administration (A)
Services Used Here		
April		
Production Departments		
Cleaning (C)	.435	.343
Mixing (M).	.215	.358
Pouring (P)	.350	.299
	1.000	1.000
Cost to Be Allocated	$50,000	$60,000

	Services Performed Here	
	Repairs (R)	**Administration (A)**
Services Used Here		
May		
Production Departments		
Cleaning (C)	.40	.30
Mixing (M).	.40	.20
Pouring (P)	.20	.50
	1.00	1.00
Costs to Be allocated	$52,000	$58,000

	Services Performed Here	
	Repairs (R)	**Administration (A)**
Services Used Here		
June		
Production Departments		
Cleaning (C)	.45	.35
Mixing (M).	.25	.40
Pouring (P)	.30	.25
	1.00	1.00
Costs to Be allocated	$55,000	$64,000

Use the allocation matrices to determine how much each production department should be charged for service costs for the month of

    a. April.

    b. May.

    c. June.

45. *Issues in Cost Allocations: What Price Progress?*[7] In discussing the costs incident to various types of operations, the analogy was drawn of the restaurant that adds a rack of peanuts to the counter, intending to pick up a little additional profit in the usual course of business. This analogy was attacked as an oversimplification. However, the accuracy of the analogy is evident when one considers the actual problem faced by the restaurateur (Joe) as revealed by his accountant-efficiency expert.

    Expert: Joe, you said you put in these peanuts because some people ask for them, but do you realize what this rack of peanuts is *costing* you?

    Joe: It's not going to cost! It's going to be a profit. Sure, I had to pay $25 for a fancy rack to hold the bags, but the peanuts cost 6¢ a bag and I sell 'em for 10¢. Suppose I sell 50 bags a week to start. It'll take 12½ weeks to cover

---

[7]This piece appeared in a publication by Coopers and Lybrand as a reprint. The author is unknown to us.

the cost of the rack. After that I have a clear profit of 4¢ a bag. The more I sell, the more I make.

Expert: That is an antiquated and completely unrealistic approach, Joe. Fortunately, modern accounting procedures permit a more accurate picture which reveals the complexities involved.

Joe: Huh?

Expert: To be precise, those peanuts must be integrated into your entire operation and be allocated their appropriate share of business overhead. They must share a proportionate part of your expenditures for rent, heat, light, equipment depreciation, decorating, salaries for your waitresses, cook, . . .

Joe: The *cook?* What's he got to do with the peanuts? He doesn't even know I have them.

Expert: Look, Joe, the cook is in the kitchen, the kitchen prepares the food, the food is what brings people in here, and the people ask to buy peanuts. *That's* why you must charge a portion of the cook's wages, as well as a part of your own salary to peanut sales. This sheet contains a carefully calculated cost analysis which indicates the peanut operation should pay exactly $1,278 per year toward these general overhead costs.

Joe: The peanuts? $1,278 a year for overhead? Nuts?

Expert: It's really a little more than that. You also spend money each week to have the windows washed, to have the place swept out in the mornings, keep soap in the washroom and provide free cokes to the police. That raises the total to $1,313 per year.

Joe: (Thoughtfully) But the peanut salesman said I'd make money—put 'em on the end of the counter, he said—and get 4¢ a bag profit—

Expert: (With a sniff) He's not an accountant. Do you actually know what the portion of the counter occupied by the peanut rack is worth to you?

Joe: Nothing. No stool there—just a dead spot at the end.

Expert: The modern cost picture permits no dead spots. Your counter contains 60 square feet and your counter business grosses $15,000 a year. Consequently, the square foot of space occupied by the peanut rack is worth $250 per year. Since you have taken that area away from general counter use, you must charge the value of the space to the occupant.

Joe: You mean I have to add *$250 a year more to the peanuts?*

Expert: Right. That raises their share of the general operating costs to a grand total of $1,563 per year. Now then, if you sell 50 bags of peanuts per week, these allocated costs will amount to 60¢ per bag.

Joe: WHAT?

Expert: Obviously, to that must be added your purchase price of 6¢ per bag, which brings the total to 66¢. So you see, by selling peanuts at 10¢ per bag you are losing 56¢ on every sale.

Joe: Something's crazy!

Expert: Not at all! Here are the *figures.* They *prove* your peanut operation cannot stand on its own feet.

Joe: (Brightening) Suppose I sell *lots* of peanuts—thousand bags a week instead of fifty?

Expert: (Tolerantly) Joe, you don't understand the problem. If the volume of peanut sales increases, your operating costs will go up—you'll have to handle more bags, with more time, more depreciation, more everything. The basic principle of accounting is firm on that subject: "*The bigger the operation, the more general overhead costs that must be allocated.*" No, increasing the volume of sales won't help.

Joe: Okay. You're so smart, *you* tell *me* what I have to do!

Expert: (Condescendingly) Well—you could first reduce operating expenses.

Joe: How?

Expert: Move to a building with cheaper rent. Cut salaries. Wash the windows bi-weekly. Have the floor swept only on Thursday. Remove the soap from the washrooms. Decrease the square-foot value of your counter. For example, if you can cut your expenses 50 percent, that will reduce the amount allocated to peanuts from $1,563 down to $781.50 per year, reducing the cost to 36¢ per bag.

Joe: (Slowly) That's better?

Expert: Much, much better. However, even then you would lose 26¢ per bag if you charge only 10¢. Therefore, you must also raise your selling price. If you want a net profit of 4¢ per bag you would have to charge 40¢.

Joe: (Flabbergasted) You mean even after I cut operating costs 50 percent I still have to charge 40¢ for a 10¢ bag of peanuts? Nobody's that nuts about nuts! Who'd buy them?

Expert: That's a secondary consideration. The point is, at 40¢ you'd be selling at a price based on a true and proper evaluation of your then reduced costs.

Joe: (Eagerly) Look! I have a better idea. Why don't I just throw the nuts out—put them in a trash can?

Expert: Can you afford it?

Joe: Sure. All I have is about 50 bags of peanuts—cost about three bucks—so I lose $25 on the rack, but I'm out of this nutsy business and no more grief.

Expert: (Shaking head) Joe it isn't quite that simple. You are *in* the peanut business! The minute you throw those peanuts out you are adding $1,563 of annual overhead to the *rest* of your operation. Joe—be realistic—*can you afford to do that?*

Joe: (Completely crushed) It's unbelievable! Last week I was making money. Now I'm in trouble—just because I think peanuts on a counter are going to bring me some extra profit—just because I believe 50 bags of peanuts a week is easy.

Expert: (With raised eyebrow) That is the object of modern cost studies, Joe—to dispel those false illusions.

What should Joe do?

46. *Cost-Based Reimbursement for Hospitals.*[8] The annual costs of hospital care under the medicare program amount to $20 billion per year. In the medicare leg-

---

islation, Congress mandated that reimbursement to hospitals would be limited to the costs of treating medicare patients. Ideally, neither the patients nor the hospitals would bear the costs of the medicare patients nor would the government bear costs of nonmedicare patients. Given the large sums involved, it is not surprising that cost reimbursement specialists, computer programs, publications, and other products and services have arisen to provide hospital administrators with the assistance needed to obtain an appropriate reimbursement for medicare patient services.

Hospital departments may be divided into two categories: (1) revenue-producing departments and (2) nonrevenue-producing departments. This classification seems mundane; but it is useful, for the traditional accounting concepts associated with "service department cost allocation," while appropriate to this context, lead to a great deal of confusion in terminology since all of the hospital's departments are considered to be rendering services.

Costs of revenue-producing departments are charged to medicare and nonmedicare patients on the basis of actual usage of the departments. These costs are relatively simple to apportion. The costs of nonrevenue-producing departments are somewhat more difficult to apportion. The approach to finding the appropriate distribution of these costs begins with the establishment of a reasonable basis for allocating nonrevenue-producing department costs to revenue-producing departments. Statistical measures of the relationships between departments must be ascertained. The cost allocation bases listed in Exhibit 15.14 have been established by medicare regulations as acceptable for cost reimbursement purposes. The regulated order of allocation must be used for medicare reimbursement even though the general rule may call for another order.

Exhibit 15.14
Bases for Allocating Nonrevenue Department Costs
to Revenue-Producing Departments

Nonrevenue Cost Center	Basis for Allocation
Depreciation—Buildings	Square Feet in Each Department
Depreciation—Movable Equipment	Dollar Value of Equipment in Each Department
Employee Health and Welfare	Gross Salaries in Each Department
Administrative and General	Accumulated Costs by Department
Maintenance and Repairs	Square Feet in Each Department
Operation of Plant	Square Feet in Each Department
Laundry and Linen Service	Pounds Used in Each Department
Housekeeping	Hours of Service to Each Department
Dietary	Meals Served in Each Department
Maintenance of Personnel	Number of Departmental Employees Housed
Nursing Administration	Hours of Supervision in Each Department
Central Supply	Costs of Requisitions Processed
Pharmacy	Costs of Drug Orders Processed
Medical Records	Hours Worked for Each Department
Social Service	Hours Worked for Each Department
Nursing School	Assigned Time by Department
Intern/Resident Service	Assigned Time by Department

A hospital may then use either a simultaneous solution method to the cost allocation problem or they may use the step method. If the step method is used, the order of departments for allocation is the same order as that by which the departments are listed in Exhibit 15.14. Thus, depreciation of buildings is allocated before depreciation of movable equipment. Cost centers must be established for each of these nonrevenue-producing costs that are relevant to a particular hospital's operations.

In the past year, the hospital reported the following departmental costs:

Nonrevenue-Producing:
Laundry and Linen. . . . . $ 250,000
Depreciation—Buildings   830,000
Employee Health and Welfare.   375,000
Maintenance of Personnel   210,000
Central Supply   745,000
Revenue-Producing:
Operating Room $1,450,000
Radiology   160,000
Laboratory   125,000
Patient Rooms 2,800,000

Percentage usage of services by one department from another department were as follows:

From	Laundry and Linen	Depreciation— Buildings	Employee Health and Welfare	Maintenance of Personnel	Central Supply
Laundry and Linen . .		.05	.10	–0–	–0–
Depreciation— Buildings.	.10		–0–	.10	–0–
Employee Health and Welfare	.15	–0–		.05	.03
Maintenance of Personnel	–0–	–0–	–0–		.12
Central Supply . . .	.10	–0–	–0–	.08	

	Operating Rooms	Radiology	Laboratory	Patient Rooms
Laundry and Linen.	.30	.10	.05	.40
Depreciation—Buildings	.05	.02	.02	.71
Employee Health and Welfare. . .	.25	.05	.04	.43
Maintenance of Personnel	.36	.10	.08	.34
Central Supply	.09	.04	.03	.66

The proportional usage of revenue-producing department services by medicare and other patients was as follows:

	Medicare	Other
Operating Rooms	25%	75%
Radiology	20	80
Laboratory	28	72
Patient Rooms	36	64

Determine the amount of the reimbursement claim for medicare services using the step method of allocation.

Suggested Solutions to Even-Numbered Exercises

14. *Allocating Overhead.*

	Department			
	No. 1	**No. 2**	**Maintenance**	**General Plant**
Charged Directly to Department:				
Indirect Labor	$28,000	$14,000	$22,500	$20,000
Indirect Material	9,000	7,000	900	8,000
Miscellaneous	3,000	5,000	1,600	5,000
	$40,000	$26,000	$25,000	$33,000
Allocations:				
General Plant	16,500	9,900	6,600	(33,000)
Maintenance[a]	11,060	20,540	(31,600)	
Total Overhead[b]	$67,560	$56,440	–0–	–0–
Direct Labor Cost	$50,000	$30,000		
Overhead Allocation Rate . .	135.12%	188.13%		

[a]Total costs to be allocated: $25,000 + $6,600 = $31,600. Allocate on the basis of maintenance hours.
[b]$67,560 + $56,440 = $40,000 + $26,000 + $25,000 + $33,000.

16. *Allocating Service Department Costs Using the Step Method.*

	General Factory Administration	Maintenance	Cutting	Assembly
Service Department Costs	$1,200	$2,400	NA	NA
Maintenance Allocation[a]	480 (⅕)	(2,400)	$480(⅕)	$1,440(⅗)
General Factory Administration Allocation	(1,680)		336(⅕)	1,344(⅘)
Total Costs Allocated . .			$816	$2,784

[a]Allocated first because we assume that maintenance renders more service to general factory administration than vice versa.

18. *Allocating Service Department Costs Directly to Operating Departments.*

	To	
From	**P1**	**P2**
S1	$10,000[a]	$10,000[a]
S2	18,750[b]	11,250[b]
	$28,750	$21,250

[a]$10,000 = .10 \times \dfrac{\$20,000}{.10 + .10}$ (80 percent of S1's costs used by S2 are ignored).

[b]$18,750 = .50 \times \dfrac{\$30,000}{.50 + .30}$.

$$$11,250 = .30 \times \dfrac{\$30,000}{.50 + .30}$.

20. *Joint Cost Allocations—Relative Sales Value Method.* Total joint costs are $205,000 (based on the $45,000 materials plus $160,000 conversion). These costs are allocated as follows:

$$\text{To Output D:} \quad \frac{\$273,000}{\$455,000} \times \$205,000 = \underline{\$123,000}.$$

$$\text{To Output T:} \quad \frac{\$455,000 - \$273,000}{\$455,000} \times \$205,000 = \underline{\$82,000}.$$

22. *Joint Cost Allocations Using the Physical Quantities Method—By-Products.* The net realizable value of M ($1,200) is deducted from the total processing costs ($120,000) to obtain the net processing costs to be allocated ($118,800). The allocation computations are

$$\text{To HN:} \quad \frac{100,000 \text{ Units}}{100,000 \text{ Units} + 200,000 \text{ Units}} \times \$118,800 = \underline{\$39,600}.$$

$$\text{To HB:} \quad \frac{200,000 \text{ Units}}{100,000 \text{ Units} + 200,000 \text{ Units}} \times \$118,800 = \underline{\$79,200}.$$

24. *Joint Costing—Finding Missing Values.* Since joint costs are allocated on the basis of relative sales value, we know that the fraction

$$\frac{\text{Joint Cost}}{\text{Sales Value at Splitoff}}$$

will be the same for all three products and for the total.
    For total costs, the ratio is

$$\frac{\$120,000}{\$200,000} = .6.$$

For product A, since the allocated costs are known, we can express the relationship between allocated costs and sales value at splitoff as

$$.6X = \$72,000$$

$$X = \frac{\$72,000}{.6}$$

$$= \underline{\$120,000} \quad \text{(Answer \textbf{c}).}$$

For product C, allocated joint costs are unknown. Since the costs equal .6 of the relative sales value at splitoff, the costs allocated to C are

$$X = \$30,000 \times .6$$

$$= \underline{\$18,000} \quad \text{(Answer \textbf{b}).}$$

Having found the costs and relative sales values for A and C, we subtract them from the total to find the missing values for Product B.

Total Relative Sales Value	$200,000
Less:	
Value of A	(120,000)
Value of C	(30,000)
Value of B	$ 50,000

    (Answer **d**).

Since allocated joint costs are .6 of relative sales value.

$$\$50,000 \times .6 = \underline{\$30,000} \quad \text{(Answer \textbf{a})}$$

Proof:

$$\text{Total Allocated Costs} = \$120,000$$

$$\$72,000 + \$30,000 + \$18,000 = \$120,000.$$

Chapter 16

Synthesis: Managerial Accounting and External Reporting

This book has focused on three principal uses of accounting information: (1) decision making; (2) planning, control, and internal performance evaluation; and (3) external financial reporting. Data appropriate for one of these purposes may be inappropriate for another. Many managers view external reporting as unproductive—a needless cost imposed by the securities market regulators. In other cases, in an effort to get more output per dollar of accounting input, managers will sometimes try to use data designed for external reporting to do double duty and serve in decision-making or planning and control functions. This chapter reviews the data needed for each of these purposes and provides examples of how errors can result when data designed for one purpose are used for a different purpose.

The material in this chapter is presented in a different format from that in previous chapters. This chapter synthesizes concepts discussed in previous chapters. We use case studies, both in the chapter and in the end-of-chapter materials, to bring out the key issues. Our intent is to raise these issues here so that you will be aware of them and prepared to deal with them in your career.

Illustration

This section contains an illustration based on discussions between a firm's president (John Presley), its controller (Jill Contreras), and the manager of a division (Tom Divito). The initial setting takes place during January, Year 2, at a meeting of the three.

Presley (President): Tom, I have just received a report on the first year of operations for your division (Exhibit 16.1), and the results look bad. You show a loss of $2,000 for the year. Our shareholders want to see increasing net income and earnings per share each year. We can't afford to have one division pulling down the rest of the company.

Divito (Division Manager): But Mr. Presley, we operated exactly according to plan during Year 1. We anticipated producing 12,000 units, and we were right on the mark. At this production level, we projected a unit production cost of $4.50, and that's right where we came out.

Presley: I'm still not happy. I've received an offer from a competitor to purchase your inventory and plant assets for $17,000, and I'm inclined to accept.

Contreras (Controller): I think such a decision would be unwise until we do more analysis. Basing such a decision on the divisional profit report for Year 1 could lead to a bad decision. For one thing, Exhibit 16.1 reports the results

Exhibit 16.1
Divisional Performance Report for Year 1

Sales (10,000 × $5)		$50,000
Cost of Goods Sold:		
Beginning Inventory	$ –0–	
Direct Materials (12,000 × $2.00)	24,000	
Direct Labor (12,000 × $1.50).	18,000	
Overhead:		
Variable (12,000 units × $.75 per unit).	9,000	
Fixed (12,000 units × $.25[a] per unit)	3,000	
Total	$54,000	
Less Ending Inventory (2,000 × $4.50)	(9,000)	
Cost of Goods Sold		(45,000)
Gross Margin		$ 5,000
Selling Expenses (.04 × $50,000)		(2,000)
Share of Corporate Administrative Costs (.10 × $50,000). . . .		(5,000)
Divisional Net Loss		$ (2,000)

[a] $\dfrac{\text{Budgeted and Actual Fixed Overhead Costs}}{\text{Budgeted and Actual Production in Units}} = \dfrac{\$3,000}{12,000} = \$.25$ per unit.

for last year. That's history now; there's nothing we can do about the loss incurred. What's important for decision making is what we expect to happen in the future.

Presley: Okay, Jill. You've just finished the budget for Year 2. What do you show for Tom's division this year?

Contreras: Exhibit 16.2 presents the expected results for Year 2. Sales are expected to increase to 12,000 units, which should improve things a bit. Tom expects to produce 12,000 units again at a unit cost of $4.50. The higher sales

Exhibit 16.2
Divisional Budget for Year 2

Sales (12,000 × $5)		$60,000
Cost of Goods Sold:		
Beginning Inventory (2,000 × $4.50)	$ 9,000	
Direct Materials (12,000 × $2.00)	24,000	
Direct Labor (12,000 × $1.50).	18,000	
Overhead:		
Variable (12,000 units × $.75 per unit).	9,000	
Fixed (12,000 units × $.25[a] per unit)	3,000	
Total	$63,000	
Less Ending Inventory (2,000 × $4.50)	(9,000)	
Cost of Goods Sold		(54,000)
Gross Margin		$ 6,000
Selling Expenses (.04 × $60,000)		(2,400)
Share of Corporate Administrative Costs (.10 × $60,000). . . .		(6,000)
Divisional Net Loss		$ (2,400)

[a] $\dfrac{\text{Budgeted Fixed Overhead Costs}}{\text{Budgeted Production}} = \dfrac{\$3,000}{12,000} = \$.25$ per unit.

level, however, will mean that Tom's division must absorb a higher portion of central corporate costs. Thus a loss of $2,400 is projected for next year.

Presley: You mean with an increase in sales of $10,000, we expect an even *bigger* loss next year? That about does it for me. How much loss will I report to shareholders if I sell the division for $17,000?

Contreras: The inventory on hand at the beginning of Year 2 costs us $9,000 (= 2,000 × $4.50) to produce. The plant assets were acquired at the beginning of Year 1 for $10,000. Based on straight-line depreciation and a 10-year life, they now have a book value of $9,000. Thus, the loss on the sale would be $1,000 (= $17,000 − $9,000 − $9,000) before taxes.

Presley: I am inclined to cut my losses and get rid of the division. I'll report a loss of $1,000 instead of $2,400 for Year 2, and I won't have to worry about the division dragging down my profits in future years.

Contreras: That may be the correct decision, but I think we should think this thing through more clearly. Exhibit 16.2 does show the expected divisional profit for Year 2 instead of actual for Year 1, but it would be inappropriate to base a decision on this analysis alone.

First, Exhibit 16.2 was prepared using generally accepted accounting principles (GAAP). While we must follow GAAP for external reporting, we're not constrained to do so for internal managerial purposes. We should be looking at the future cash flows under each of our alternatives, not accounting profits.

Presley: Because most of our sales are for cash or on short-term credit and most of our expenses are paid soon after purchase, can't we assume that the revenues and expenses in Exhibit 16.2 are essentially the same as cash receipts and disbursements?

Contreras: That's okay for most items, but not for all. For example, fixed manufacturing overhead includes a $1,000 depreciation charge, which is not a cash flow. Furthermore, we should be focusing primarily on those future cash flows that differ between alternatives.

Presley: Jill, why don't you show me what Exhibit 16.2 would look like if it focused just on those cash flows for Year 2 that would differ between alternatives?

Contreras: I thought you might want such analysis. Exhibit 16.3 shows what I came up with. As you can see, cash outflows for fixed manufacturing overhead will be $2,000 if we operate the division; depreciation of $1,000 does not require a cash outflow. The $2,000 includes property taxes and insurance on the division's inventory and plant assets. Also, I have left out the $6,000 share of central corporate expenses.

Presley: Wait a minute! Your salary and my salary will require cash next year. I don't intend to work for nothing. The division's fair share of central corporate expenses is $6,000. Thus, the net cash inflow from operating the division of $4,600 in your analysis must be changed to a net cash outflow of $1,400.

Contreras: Mr. Presley, I don't intend to work for nothing, any more than you do. I left the $6,000 out of the analysis because that cost will be incurred whether we continue to operate the division or whether we sell it off. Future

Exhibit 16.3
Cash Flows Comparison:
Keep Division Versus Sell Division

	Keep Division (1)	Sell Division (2)	Keep-Sell Differential Cash Flows = (1) − (2) (3)
Sales Revenue (12,000 × $5.00)	$ 60,000	$ —	$ 60,000
Direct Materials (12,000 × $2.00)	(24,000)	—	(24,000)
Direct Labor (12,000 × $1.50).	(18,000)	—	(18,000)
Variable Overhead (12,000 × $.75).	(9,000)	—	(9,000)
Fixed Overhead ($3,000 − $1,000)	(2,000)	—	(2,000)
Selling Expense ($60,000 × .04).	(2,400)	—	(2,400)
Selling Price of Division	—	17,000	(17,000)
Net Cash Flows	$ 4,600	$17,000	$(12,400)

cash flows that will not differ between alternatives can be safely ignored because they won't be a factor in *differentiating* between the alternatives.

Presley: I'm not totally convinced yet, but let's see where we stand. If I sell the division outright, I will get $17,000 in cash. If I operate the division next year, I will receive $4,600. I am inclined to stick by my earlier inclination to sell the division for the $12,400 differential cash flow. Jill, is this right, or am I missing some other point?

Contreras: Possibly. You have compared the two alternatives over different time periods. The plant assets in the division have a remaining useful life of 9 years, not just 1 year. We have to look at the cash flows that would be generated over the next 9 years to see the benefit of keeping the division.

Presley: Assuming that the division will be able to generate a net cash inflow of $4,600 each year during the next 9 years, we will generate $41,400 of cash flow. But I know that the $41,400 is not comparable to the $17,000 cash we would get from selling the division, because the $41,400 inflows are spread out more. To make the two sets of cash flows comparable, I must discount the annual $4,600 cash flows back for 9 years at our cost of capital of 12 percent. That results in a net present value of $24,510.[1] The present value of selling the division is, of course, $17,000. Maybe we shouldn't sell the division.

Divito: That's what I like to hear. I was beginning to wonder where I would be working next year.

Presley: Jill, as I understand it, we've calculated the present value of the future cash flows that will differ between the alternatives. I think I understand now why this is the correct basis for making managerial decisions. Before bringing important nonquantitative factors into the decision, have we left out anything?

Contreras: Unfortunately, yes. We have given no consideration to income

---

[1] $24,510 = $4,600 × 5.32825; see Table 4, 9-period row, 12 percent column.

Exhibit 16.4
Aftertax Cash Flow Comparison:
Keep Division Versus Sell Division

	Present Value at 12 Percent	End of Period								
		2	3	4	5	6	7	8	9	10
Keep Division										
Cash Receipts from Sales	$319,695[a]	$ 60,000	$ 60,000	$ 60,000	$ 60,000	$ 60,000	$ 60,000	$ 60,000	$ 60,000	$ 60,000
Cash Expenditures for Variable Manufacturing Costs	(271,741)[a]	(51,000)	(51,000)	(51,000)	(51,000)	(51,000)	(51,000)	(51,000)	(51,000)	(51,000)
Cash Expenditures for Fixed Manufacturing Costs	(10,657)[a]	(2,000)	(2,000)	(2,000)	(2,000)	(2,000)	(2,000)	(2,000)	(2,000)	(2,000)
Cash Expenditures for Selling Expenses	(12,788)[a]	(2,400)	(2,400)	(2,400)	(2,400)	(2,400)	(2,400)	(2,400)	(2,400)	(2,400)
Depreciation for Tax Purposes		(2,200)	(2,100)	(2,100)	(2,100)	—	—	—	—	—
Taxable Income		$ 2,400	$ 2,500	$ 2,500	$ 2,500	$ 4,600	$ 4,600	$ 4,600	$ 4,600	$ 4,600
Cash Expenditures for Income Taxes at 40 Percent	(7,217)	(960)	(1,000)	(1,000)	(1,000)	(1,840)	(1,840)	(1,840)	(1,840)	(1,840)
Net Present Value	$ 17,292									
Sell Division										
Selling Price	$ 17,000									
Tax Effect of Loss on Sale	200[b]									
Net Present Value	$ 17,200									

[a]See Table 4 (page 880), 9-period row, 12-percent column; factor is 5.32825.
[b]Cash inflow is 40 percent of loss at $500 = $17,000 − $9,000 − $8,500; .40 × $500 loss is $200.

taxes. Because 12 percent is the *aftertax* cost of capital, we must compute the income tax ramifications of this decision.

Presley: But Jill, you know that we have centralized our income tax planning and strategy function in central corporate headquarters. We don't hold the divisions responsible for the impact of income taxes on their decisions. We report divisional profit performance on a before-tax basis.

Contreras: Our treatment of income taxes may or may not be appropriate for internal performance reporting. But for decision making, income taxes affect cash flows and must be considered. At our tax rate of 40 percent, income taxes can have a major effect on the decision.

Presley: Well, Jill let's see the analysis.

Contreras: Exhibit 16.4 gives the figures. The top panel shows the present value of the cash inflows and outflows along with the related tax effects, assuming that we continue to operate the division. While depreciation is itself not a cash flow, depreciation can be subtracted in calculating taxable income. Thus, it indirectly affects cash flows. The amounts reported as depreciation for tax purposes are based on the accelerated cost recovery system. Depreciation for tax purposes is as follows:

Year 1: $1,500.

Year 2: $2,200.

Year 3: $2,100.

Year 4: $2,100.

Year 5: $2,100.

The net present value if the division continues to operate is $17,292.

If we sell the division, there'll be a loss on the disposal of the inventory and equipment. As I indicated earlier, the inventory has a book value of $9,000 for both tax and financial reporting. The plant assets, however, were depreciated during Year 1 at $1,000 for financial reporting and $1,500 for tax reporting. In calculating the tax consequences of the sale, the *tax* basis of the plant assets of $8,500 (= $10,000 − $1,500) is relevant. The loss on the sale for tax purposes is $500 (= $17,000 − $9,000 − $8,500) and the tax savings are $200 (= .40 × $500).

Presley: As I see it, the net present value of the aftertax cash flows favors keeping the division, but it's so close that I think selling is more prudent—"a bird in the hand," you know.

Divito: Before you make up your mind, Mr. Presley, I would like to put in my two cents about delaying such a sale for a while. The market for our products is expanding. With aggressive promotion, I feel that we can increase our market share. Given this potential for growth, I feel that we can cover not only our own costs but provide for coverage of central corporate costs as well. We also anticipate that through more efficient purchasing of raw materials and better training of our workers, we can reduce our direct manufacturing costs.

Presley: OK, Tom, I'll let you have a go at it for another year. Perhaps one year of operations is not enough to form a judgment on the profit-generating ability of your division. Good luck.

One Year Later

John Presley, Jill Contreras, and Tom Divito meet to review the performance of Tom's division for Year 2.

Presley: Well, Tom, now is the time of reckoning. I've kept a copy of the budget for your division for Year 2 (Exhibit 16.2) in my desk for the last year. I have asked Jill to show your actual results for Year 2 side by side with your budget so that I can see clearly how you've done. Jill, have you prepared the analysis?

Contreras: Yes; Exhibit 16.5 presents the results.

Exhibit 16.5
Comparison of Budgeted and Actual Performance for Year 2

	Budget	Actual	Variance
Sales	$ 60,000	$ 61,200	$ 1,200
Cost of Goods Sold:			
Beginning Inventory	$ 9,000	$ 9,000	—
Direct Materials.	24,000	28,500	$(4,500)
Direct Labor	18,000	21,750	(3,750)
Overhead:			
Variable	9,000	10,500	(1,500)
Fixed	3,000	3,750	(750)
Total.	$ 63,000	$ 73,500	$(10,500)
Less Ending Inventory	(9,000)	(21,500)	12,500
Cost of Goods Sold	$ 54,000	$ 52,000	$ 2,000
Gross Margin	$ 6,000	$ 9,200	$ 3,200
Fixed Overhead Variance	—	750	750
Selling Expenses	(2,400)	(2,520)	(120)
Share of Corporate Administrative Costs	(6,000)	(6,030)	(30)
Division Net Profit (Loss)	$(2,400)	$ 1,400	$ 3,800

Presley: Well, I like your actual bottom line for Year 2—a profit of $1,400 instead of a loss of $2,400. I'm not happy, though, with the large production cost variances. In contrast to the promises made a year ago, your production costs have been much larger than expected. It looks to me like you have been grossly inefficient. There are two things I don't understand about this performance report. What do the $12,500 variance relating to ending inventory and the $750 fixed overhead variance mean?

Contreras: In Exhibit 16.5, the budget amounts are based on a production level of 12,000 units. But actual production was 15,000 units. The unfavorable manufacturing cost variances and the ending inventory variance are due in part to the fact that manufactured costs expected to be incurred in producing

12,000 units are being compared with the actual costs of producing 15,000 units.

Presley: I read the other day about something called a ''flexible budget.'' It seemed to apply when you produced or sold a different number of units than you expected.

Contreras: That's right. We know what the manufacturing costs should have been to produce 12,000 units. We can now see what they should have been to produce the 15,000 units actually produced. Exhibit 16.6 presents the analysis. As you can see, the actual manufacturing costs for direct material, direct labor, and variable manufacturing overhead were less than they should have been for 15,000 units. Thus, the efficiencies that Tom promised you have been realized.

Exhibit 16.6
Comparison of Flexible Budget and Actual Performance for Year 2

	Flexible Budget	Actual	Variance
Sales	$ 60,000	$ 61,200	$ 1,200
Cost of Goods Sold:			
Beginning Inventory	$ 9,000	$ 9,000	$ —
Direct Materials	30,000	28,500	1,500
Direct Labor	22,500	21,750	750
Overhead:			
Variable	11,250	10,500	750
Fixed	3,000	3,750	(750)
Total	$ 75,750	$ 73,500	$ 2,250
Less Ending Inventory	(21,500)	(21,500)	—
Cost of Goods Sold	$ 54,250	$ 52,000	$ 2,250
Gross Margin	$ 5,750	$ 9,200	$ 3,450
Fixed Overhead Variance	—	750	750
Selling Expenses	(2,400)	(2,520)	(120)
Share of Corporate Administrative Costs.	(6,000)	(6,030)	(30)
Division Net Profit.	$(2,650)	$ 1,400	$ 4,050

Divito: I'm glad to see that they show up in my performance report. I increased production this year because I anticipate that we will be able to capture a larger market share in Year 3. I was concerned, though, as to how the increase in costs required for these additional units would show up in my performance report, because the budgeted costs based on 12,000 units were so much less. I like this flexible budget report.

Presley: You have answered my question about the large variable manufacturing cost variances and about the ending inventory variance. I can see now that they relate to the larger production volume achieved. But what about the $750 fixed overhead variance? What's that?

Contreras: That variance is also due to producing more units than anticipated. Fixed overhead costs for Year 2 were budgeted to be $3,000. With anticipated production of 12,000 units, the fixed overhead rate was set at $.25 per unit. By producing 15,000 units, $3,750 (= 15,000 × $.25) has been applied to units produced. The difference of $750 is not really a variance at all. The division manager should not receive any credit for such a variance.

Divito: Now wait a minute. I was able to use my plant assets more efficiently this year, producing 15,000 units instead of 12,000 units. The $750 fixed overhead variance is a measure of the benefit of this more efficient utilization, and I should get credit for it.

Contreras: The variance is caused by the practice under absorption costing of treating fixed costs like a variable cost. Exhibit 16.6 was prepared in accordance with absorption costing as required under GAAP for financial reporting. Fixed manufacturing costs for the year are divided by the expected level of production to obtain a rate per unit, $.25 in this case. Each unit produced is allocated a share of the fixed cost using this rate. Because you produced 3,000 more units than anticipated, you applied $750 (= 3,000 × $.25) more fixed overhead to production than you would have *had you anticipated that you would produce 15,000 units during Year 2*. Note that the unfavorable variance of $750 for fixed overhead in the upper portion of Exhibit 16.6 is offset by the $750 favorable variance in the lower portion. Absorption costing can do some crazy things to your performance report when expected and actual production differ.

Presley: What you say makes sense, but we've little choice. We must use absorption costing in our external financial statements.

Contreras: Yes, but we're not constrained by GAAP in our internal reports. With some modifications, our accounting system can be adapted to generate data both on an absorption costing basis for external reporting and on another basis for internal performance evaluation.

Presley: What are you suggesting be done?

Contreras: We should classify our costs according to their behavior, either variable or fixed. Raw materials and direct labor are variable. Except for a few easily identifiable overhead items (depreciation, insurance, property taxes), our overhead costs are essentially variable as well. Selling costs are also variable. The performance report would then distinguish costs by their behavior rather than by their nature (that is, production, selling). Exhibit 16.7 shows what I mean. Product costs include only variable material, labor, and overhead costs. Fixed costs are treated as an expense of the period. This report was prepared on a variable costing, instead of absorption costing, basis. There is no overapplied fixed overhead, nor is there a favorable overhead variance, as a result of producing more than expected. This format has the added advantage of classifying data in a form useful for decisions. For many decisions, incremental costs will be the variable costs. If the time horizon is short enough, fixed costs often do not change. Of course, in the long run even the fixed costs can be altered by decisions.

Presley: The only thing that bothers me with the performance report you have prepared in Exhibit 16.7 is that you have deleted the division's share of central costs. I can buy the fact that these costs are not affected by our decision to continue running the division or to sell it and, therefore, are irrelevant

Exhibit 16.7
Comparison of Flexible Budget and Actual Performance
for Year 2 Using Variable Costing

	Flexible Budget		Actual		
	Per Unit	Total	Per Unit	Total	Variance
Sales	$5.00	$ 60,000	$5.10	$ 61,200	$ 1,200
Variable Costs:					
Manufacturing:					
Beginning Inventory . . .		$ 8,500		$ 8,500	
Direct Materials	$2.00	30,000	$1.90	28,500	$ 1,500
Direct Labor	1.50	22,500	1.45	21,750	750
Variable Overhead . . .	.75	11,250	.70	10,500	750
Total	$4.25	$ 72,250	$4.05	$ 69,250	$ 3,000
Less Ending Inventory . .		(21,250)		(20,250)	(1,000)
Goods Sold		$ 51,000		$ 49,000	$ 2,000
Selling	.20	2,400	.21	2,520	(120)
Total Variable Costs . . .	$4.45	$ 53,400	$4.25	$ 51,520	$ 1,880
Contribution Margin	$ .55	$ 6,600	$ .84	$ 9,680	$ 3,080
Fixed Costs:					
Manufacturing.	—	(3,000)	—	(3,000)	—
Contribution to Corporate Administrative Costs and Corporate Profits.		$ 3,600		$ 6,680	

to that decision. However, these costs must be covered by someone if the company is to survive in the long run.

Divito: This is a good place for me to sound off. It really bothers me that my division can operate at a positive divisional profit before allocation of central corporate costs, but my bottom line really gets hit by costs over which I have no control. Not only can't I control these costs, but I get penalized when my sales go up. Central corporate headquarters provides us with little or no marketing support. So why should they get a bigger piece of the action when my division increases its sales?

Contreras: You have both made legitimate points. Mr. Presley, you are correct that these costs must be covered by revenues from the operating divisions if the firm is to survive. Tom, you have grounds for complaining that these costs are not under your control. The primary benefits of the decentralized, divisional corporate structure is that each operating unit feels that it is running its own separate company. If the allocation of central corporate costs to the division has the effect of motivating you to hold back on sales increases, then something must be done about the allocation. We either have to stop allocating or else find a more appropriate allocation method. Placing your share of central corporate costs at the bottom of your divisional performance report should make you aware that you are part of the larger company and must do your share to cover costs of running the company. Yet your performance will be judged primarily on your division's contribution to central corporate expenses and net income.

Divito: This seems reasonable to me.

Presley: Good, then we have developed a new basis for internal performance evaluation. We will break out costs by responsibility center according to their behavior (variable or fixed). The performance report will be designed in a variable costing format. Jill, at the end of each year, you can make the necessary adjustments to convert to an absorption costing basis for external reporting.

Contreras: Now we see the three different uses of accounting data and the appropriate model for each one. In managerial decision making, we are concerned with the differential future cash flows between alternatives. The three key words are (1) future, (2) cash flows, and (3) differential. In many cases, variable costs will be differential and fixed costs will not. However, some fixed costs may also be differential if they can be eliminated or altered even in the short run. In the long run, all costs can be changed and thus potentially become differential. If the decision horizon extends beyond 1 year, then the differential cash flows should be discounted to their present value when comparing alternatives.

In planning, control, and internal performance evaluation, the focus is on individual responsibility centers. We want to attribute revenues and costs to those units within a firm that have control over the amounts. Because unitizing fixed manufacturing overhead under absorption costing can lead to confusing results, the performance report should be prepared on a variable costing basis. Variable costs should be subtracted from revenue to obtain the contribution margin. Fixed costs of the responsibility center should then be subtracted to obtain the center's contribution to coverage of central corporate expenses and to corporate profits.

For external reporting, we are required to follow generally accepted accounting principles. The main point to keep in mind is that we do not and, in general, should not use these same reports for managerial decision making, planning, and control. These latter purposes are concerned primarily with the economic effects of decisions on a firm. While GAAP theoretically should also be concerned primarily with economic effects, accounting standards for financial reporting are often set based on objectivity, practicability, or political pressure.

Different Data for Different Purposes

Accounting data have several different uses: decision making, managerial planning, control, internal performance evaluation, external financial reporting, income tax reporting, and reporting to various regulatory agencies. Data appropriate for one of these purposes is sometimes inappropriate for another.

Exhibit 16.8 summarizes some of the uses of accounting information and contrasts the data necessary for different uses. If you read across the exhibit from left to right, you will see how accounting requirements change as you move from decision making to planning to performance evaluation. The remainder of this

Exhibit 16.8
Different Data for Different Purposes

	Purpose			
	Internal			
	Decision Making	**Planning (budgeting)**	**Control and Performance Evaluation**	**External Financial Reporting**
Activity	Differential Analysis; Selecting from Alternatives for Action	Expressing Expectations for Alternatives Selected	Comparing Actual Results with Expectations	Reporting Actual Results to Owners and Other External Entities
Accounting Reports . . .	Differential Cash Flows	Static Budgets; Profit Plans and Capital Budgets	Flexible Budgets; Performance Reports; Variances	Financial Statements
Time Orientation.	Future	Future	Past and Current (input to future)	Past and Current
Focus of Accounting . . .	Decision Specifics	Responsibility Centers	Responsibility Centers	Companywide plus Segments
Model	Short Run: Differential Cash Flows; Long Run: Net Present Value	Short Run: Profit; Long Run: Capital Budgets	ROI	Earnings, ROI, EPS
Variables in the Model . .	Differential Future Cash Flows	Revenues, Variable Costs, Fixed Costs	Revenues, Variable Costs, Fixed Costs, Investment in Division	Revenues Matched with Expenses in Compliance with GAAP

Consistent with Variable Costing   Full-Absorption Costing

section elaborates on particular cases where different data are required for different purposes.

The Projected Future Versus the Actual Past

For decision making, the concern of the decision makers is: What will happen? There is no more difficult task in business than trying to forecast the future. Chapter 6 discusses the techniques for cost estimation and forecasts of market demands. Good management requires skillful guesses about the future and how to adapt to it. Accounting provides a structure for gathering and analyzing data on managers' expectations that is useful for decisions.

Once a decision is made, a plan or budget to implement the decision is constructed. As Chapters 12 and 13 point out, budgets can be either static or flexible. A static budget assumes a particular level of output and projects costs based on that level. A flexible budget, based on fixed and variable cost components, can show expected costs for various levels of output.

Once plans are being carried out, management wants to know if processes are in control. For these purposes, one needs both projections originally made and actual outcomes. Comparison of projections and outcomes helps pinpoint the causes of deviations from expectations. This comparison serves both as a basis for evaluating past performance and for testing actions that will help assure that future performance will coincide with expectations.

Current Costs Versus Historical Costs

In evaluating a lower-level manager or a division, one compares profits generated with the investment necessary in that division (for example, plant, inventory, and working capital) to generate those profits. Typically (and misleadingly), the historical cost of the assets (adjusted downward for amortization, if plant assets) is used as the denominator in a rate-of-return calculation or in deriving the capital charge in a residual income analysis. Some firms recognize that a more appropriate asset basis for these purposes is the current exit value (opportunity cost) of the assets. If, for example, a plant can be sold for $10 million, then the cost of using the asset is $10 million even if its depreciated historical cost is only $4 million and its replacement cost is $13 million.

Throughout accounting, the benefits of the added relevance obtained from using current cost data may be offset by reduced objectivity and verifiability. Nowhere, however, is the benefit/cost ratio more favorable than for internally evaluating management. Although it is tempting to use historical cost data, as required for external financial reporting, in making internal evaluations, resulting comparisons can mislead. The objection to current cost data—reduced precision—is less severe when the data are used internally and not subject to official scrutiny through securities regulation or tax reporting.

Interest on Funds: Explicit, Implicit, or Ignored

Other things being equal, cash received sooner is more valuable than cash received later; cash paid later is less costly than cash paid sooner. Effective decision making requires that the time value of money be taken explicitly into account. Chapter 9 explains and illustrates the techniques. In planning and control, the time horizon—usually a single accounting period—is so short that ignoring the time value of money is cost-effective. In internal evaluations, typically there is no net present value analysis, but the cost of capital tied up while operations are carried out is recognized. In a rate-of-return computation (such as return on investment, ROI), the charge for capital occurs when the profit is divided by the average amount of assets employed during the period: The larger the amount of assets employed, the larger is the denominator and the smaller is the computed rate of return. The resulting rate is compared to some norm. That norm is at least in part a function of the cost of funds.

Chapter 14 points out the problems caused by using the rate of return for internal evaluation. Projects are compared to an average, rather than a marginal, cost of funds; managers will have incentives to dispose of assets (or not undertake new projects) whenever the return on them is less than the average earned by the division, even though the assets can earn a rate larger than the cost of capital. Chapter 14 suggests that an alternative method for making internal evaluations is to measure residual income: Rather than divide earnings by average assets to get an average rate of return, subtract an explicit charge from income for capital used.

Economics and Accounting Define Costs and Profits Differently

To economists, the cost of capital is a cost of doing business. In economics, there are no profits until funds employed in a business have been paid a market wage, just as there is no profit until labor has been paid its market wage. Whereas the economist will subtract from revenues both interest on borrowed funds and the opportunity cost of owners' funds invested, accounting net income results from subtracting only the cost of borrowed funds from revenues. Thus, whereas economic analysis (for decision making and internal evaluation) explicitly takes into account the cost of all funds used, externally reported net income does not.

Similarly, external financial reporting and internal accounting sometimes ignore the time value of money. In external financial reporting and income tax reporting, there is positive income so long as revenues (measured by amounts of cash eventually collected) exceed expenses (measured over long enough time periods in amounts equal to cash expenditures). Economic analysis will report losses for the same transactions if the cash collections are delayed so long that assets do not earn the opportunity cost of the funds invested in them.

Allocations and Unit Costs

External financial reporting and income tax accounting require the allocation of fixed costs to individual units of inventory produced. A major theme of this book is that using unit costs that include an allocation of fixed costs is likely to lead managers to incorrect internal decisions. Chapter 15 points out, however, that allocating the costs of service departments to producing departments may have beneficial effects on incentives and, hence, total costs. When managers of producing departments are charged an allocated portion of service department costs, those managers will have an incentive to press the service departments to operate more efficiently. Such pressure may help in reducing costs in the service departments.

Illustrations of Contrasting Uses

Static Versus Flexible Budgeting In budgeting, the plan usually forecasts an expected level of activity, such as sales, and projects total costs based on that level of activity. In assessing whether operations are in control, deviations from plan can be understood only if they are separated into deviations from the forecast of activity and deviations from meeting the cost targets per unit of activity.

Variable Costs Versus Fully Absorbed Costs For decision making and control, variable costs per unit are treated separately from fixed costs per period. In external financial and income tax reporting, the fully absorbed costs are computed for ending inventories and cost of goods sold.

Controllable Costs Versus Absorption Costs When managers are evaluated, they are generally held responsible for costs they can control but not for costs beyond their control. Controllable costs are often variable costs, but need not be. For example, the cost per pound of copper is generally not controllable by a manufacturing department, although the amount of copper used in production is. The *total* cost of copper used in manufacturing varies with the number of units produced but is not controllable by the manufacturing department. The cost of a quality control inspector is fixed because its cost does not vary with output, but the decision whether to hire one is made by the manufacturing supervisor. Thus the cost is controllable, but does not vary with output, at least within wide ranges of output. For external and income tax reporting, all manufacturing costs—whether controllable or not, whether variable or not—are allocated to ending inventory and cost of goods sold.

ROI or Residual Income Versus Earnings per Share Effective internal evaluation measures performance against the cost of generating that performance. Thus, for internal purposes, managers look at ROI, or better yet, at residual income. Externally, security analysts focus on earnings per share, which generally is net income divided by average shares outstanding during the period. If managers focus on earnings per share, they must inevitably focus on earnings, computed from generally accepted accounting principles. Conflicts between effective decisions and reported earnings arise here as well.

Revenues Versus Receipts In external financial reporting, income is measured as revenues less expenses. Revenue is the present value of cash to be collected from rendering services. A firm can recognize revenue, such as from credit sales, in a period before it receives the cash. For external reporting, the revenues will be recognized in the period of sale. For income taxes, the income from the sale need not be reported until the later period when the cash is collected. Because it is generally wise to delay tax payments as long as possible (assuming that tax rates do not change over time), the manager will want to focus on receipts in tax reporting while reporting revenues in external financial statements.

Accounting for Inventories: Variable Versus Absorption Costing

Could a business report increasing profits year after year and still be approaching bankruptcy? Yes: If production exceeds sales period after period, a manufacturing business can report increasing profits while it is becoming insolvent. Effective management requires a good understanding of how the methods of accounting for inventories might cause such a misleading picture of operating performance.

Chapters 3 and 4 discuss two approaches to measuring manufacturing costs to be included in product cost: absorption costing and variable costing. Under *absorption costing,* all manufacturing costs, whether direct or indirect and whether fixed or variable, are included in a product's cost. Absorption costing is required for external financial reporting and for income tax reporting. Many businesses use it for managerial purposes as well. Herein lies a potential problem: Decisions based on absorption costing can be in error, because absorption costing does not reflect differential cost behavior. That is, absorption costing treats fixed manufacturing costs as if they were unit costs and, therefore, variable. Under *variable costing,* only the variable manufacturing costs are considered to be unit product costs. All costs of being a going concern, the ongoing costs of remaining in business, or fixed costs, are treated as expenses of the period when the costs are incurred.

Absorption Versus Variable Costing: Reporting Effects Consider a simplified situation where one, two, or three units of a product may be produced each period. Variable costs of production are $30 per *unit* produced, and fixed costs are $120 per *period*. Thus, the total cost per unit under absorption costing will be $150, $90, or $70 per unit, depending on whether one, two, or three units are produced during the period. Each unit sells for $100. Exhibit 16.9 shows the income and the balance sheet amounts for ending inventory under both absorption and direct costing for each of five cases. In each case, production and sales over the two periods total four units. Only the timing of production and sales changes. Total income over the two periods is $40 for each case. This equality over the two periods stems from both beginning and ending inventory being zero. Under these conditions, total expenses must equal cash expenditures.

   All else being equal, the larger are long-run revenues, the larger must be the costs of producing those revenues. Thus, assuming that costs are under control and are as expected, accurate reporting to management will show increased operating profit and cost in periods when there is increased revenue. Notice in cases IV and V that under absorption costing, reported income varies more strongly with production than with sales; whereas under variable costing, reported income varies with sales. Even in case II, the relation between income and sales, though positive for both absorption and variable costing, is stronger under variable costing than under absorption costing.

Justification for Variable Costing Fixed manufacturing costs provide the capacity to produce this period and are not avoided if for some reason, such as a shut-down of the production line, no product is manufactured. Consider the rent on a factory. A company is obligated to pay that rent even when its factory lies idle, producing nothing. Factory rent is a cost of being a going concern. Under absorption costing, factory rent is part of inventory produced. If rent for the month is $500 and 100 parts are produced, then each part will carry $5 (= $500 ÷ 100 units) of costs for rent; but if 200 units are produced, then each part will probably carry $2.50 (= $500 ÷ 200 units) of costs for rent. Under absorption costing, the cost of each unit produced varies inversely with the total number of units produced. Management that wants to know short-run costs of units produced needs to know the incremental costs of production—direct labor, direct materials, and variable overhead. In variable costing, only the variable costs of production are included as product costs. All fixed costs are treated as period expenses.

   All costs are variable if the time horizon is long enough. Leases need not be renewed, salaried workers need not be replaced as they retire, equipment need not

Exhibit 16.9
Absorption Versus Variable Costing
(variable costs are $30 per unit; fixed costs are $120 per period; units sell for $100 each)

	Case I		Case II		Case III		Case IV		Case V	
	Period 1	Period 2	Period 1	Period 2	Period 1	Period 2	Period 1	Period 2	Period 1	Period 2
Production in Units	2	2	2	2	3	1	3	1	3	1
Sales in Units (at $100)	2	2	1	3	3	1	2	2	1	3
Absorption Costing										
Average Unit Cost of Production[a]	$ 90	$ 90	$ 90	$ 90	$ 70	$150	$ 70	$150	$ 70	$150
Sales	$200	$200	$100	$300	$300	$100	$200	$200	$100	$300
Cost of Goods Sold	(180)	(180)	(90)	(270)	(210)	(150)	(140)	(220)	(70)	(290)
Income (Loss)	$ 20	$ 20	$ 10	$ 30	$ 90	$ (50)	$ 60	$ (20)	$ 30	$ 10
Ending Inventory	$ -0-	$ -0-	$ 90	$ -0-	$ -0-	$ -0-	$ 70	$ -0-	$140	$ -0-
Variable Costing										
Sales	$200	$200	$100	$300	$300	$100	$200	$200	$100	$300
Variable Cost of Goods Sold	(60)	(60)	(30)	(90)	(90)	(30)	(60)	(60)	(30)	(90)
Fixed Expenses	(120)	(120)	(120)	(120)	(120)	(120)	(120)	(120)	(120)	(120)
Income (Loss)	$ 20	$ 20	$ (50)	$ 90	$ 90	$ (50)	$ 20	$ 20	$ (50)	$ 90
Ending Inventory	$ -0-	$ -0-	$ 30	$ -0-	$ -0-	$ -0-	$ 30	$ -0-	$ 60	$ -0-

[a]Equal to $30 + $120/n, where n is the number of units produced that period.

be replaced, and so on. But management is concerned with assessing performance over shorter time horizons. Variable costing often provides information that is more useful to management in the short run. The basic question asked of each cost incurred in variable costing is: "Does incurring this cost today avoid having to incur that cost in the future?" If the answer is *yes*, then the cost in question is an incremental cost and is included in product cost. If the answer is *no*, variable costing treats the cost as an expense of the period. Because raw materials used today in producing a particular unit eliminates the need to use raw materials tomorrow for that unit, raw materials are incremental product costs under variable costing. But factory rent must be paid whether any product is made or not, so variable costing treats factory rent as a period expense rather than as a production cost. Many factory overhead costs—salaries of factory supervisors and guards, depreciation, and property taxes, for example—will not be less next period for having been incurred this period. These costs are, therefore, period expenses in variable costing.

Selling Profits to Inventory Earlier, we pointed out that a firm could report increasing profits year after year, all the while approaching bankruptcy. We can now see how this might occur. As long as production exceeds sales, absorption costing will transfer fixed costs into ending inventory, increasing reported profits. Even if sales decline, income under absorption costing can continue to increase as long as production exceeds sales. Eventually, there can be a large amount of inventory, and a firm will become insolvent or bankrupt in spite of its increasing reported income. Absorption costing "sells profits" to inventory. A firm would not, of course, normally continue to increase production in the face of stable or declining sales.

Inventory valuation, cost of goods sold, and income are affected by the decision as to how much fixed costs are allocated to inventory and how much to expenses for the period.

Summary

This chapter illustrates the importance of using appropriate data for the particular task at hand. It also indicates areas where sound management decisions and financial reporting may conflict. There is a common thread running through these examples and others that could be offered. Managerial decisions must rely on estimates of current and future cash flows. Financial reporting focuses on past cash flows and the allocation of those cash flows to periods in accordance with generally accepted accounting principles. These "principles" are more often guided by considerations of conservatism and objectivity than by the present value of future cash flows.

There are some important implications for accounting system design. In designing a home, ideally we start with the major uses and activities, then design the structure. Similarly, in accounting we start with uses of data and work back to the appropriate system. All of this is done keeping both the costs and benefits in mind.

Questions

Note: Because of the unique nature of this chapter, we have not included self-study problems or exercises. The questions and the problems and cases are intended to synthesize concepts discussed in prior chapters or to illustrate potential conflicts between managerial decision making and accounting reporting.

1. Review the meaning of the following concepts or terms discussed in this chapter:

    a. Cash flows versus income flows.

    b. Receipts versus revenues.

    c. Unitizing fixed costs.

    d. Static versus flexible budgeting.

2. Each of the following terms contains the word *cost*. These terms are used in various ways in accounting, business, and economics. The terms are explained in the Glossary at the back of the book under the heading *cost terminology*. Review the meaning and usage of each of these terms.

    a. Avoidable cost.

    b. Book cost.

    c. Common cost.

    d. Current cost.

    e. Direct cost.

    f. Escapable cost.

    g. Fixed cost.

    h. Historical cost.

    i. Incremental cost.

    j. Indirect cost.

    k. Inescapable cost.

    l. Marginal cost.

    m. Out-of-pocket cost.

    n. Standard cost.

    o. Sunk cost.

    p. Traceable cost.

    q. Unavoidable cost.

    r. Variable cost.

3. Assume 2 years of constant production quantities, decreasing sales, and, hence, rising end-of-year inventory quantities. In Year 2, fixed costs are substantially higher than in Year 1. Compare the differences in reported income resulting from using absorption costing on the one hand and variable costing on the other in Years 1 and 2.

4. Under what circumstances would the shift from absorption costing to variable costing have little effect on the balance sheet and income statement?

5. Inventory valuations appear only on the balance sheet. How is it, then, that inventory valuations affect net income for the period?

6. How does the economist's view of profit differ from the accountant's?

7. Meals in restaurants are not inventoriable (usually). That is, once prepared, a meal cannot be saved until the next accounting period. Yet the cost of meals is computed using absorption and variable costing methods, methods generally used only for inventoriable items.

    Explain how the full absorption costing versus variable costing accounting methods could be relevant for analysis of such noninventoriable items.

8. Over long enough time periods, income is cash-in less cash-out. Eventually the entire book value of an owned asset will be written off through depreciation or on disposal of the asset, regardless of the depreciation method used by accountants.

What difference could it possibly make whether or not accountants use straight-line or accelerated depreciation methods for external financial reporting?

9. "Because the FASB does not allow a firm generally to capitalize its research and development (R&D) costs, internal financial statements will not be consistent with external financial reports unless R&D costs are expensed internally. Therefore, R&D costs should be expensed for internal evaluation of managerial performance."
Comment.

10. Explain how interest costs that enter into managerial decision making are often ignored in financial reporting.

Problems and Cases

11. *Inventory Costing.*[2] The All Fixed Costs Company is so named because it has no variable costs—all of its costs are fixed and vary with time rather than output. The All Fixed Costs Company is located on the back of a river and has its own hydroelectric plant to supply power, light, and heat. The company manufactures a synthetic material from air and river water, and sells its product on a long-term, fixed-price contract. It has a small staff of employees, all hired on an annual salary basis. The output of the plant can be increased or decreased by adjusting a few dials on the control panel. Exhibit 16.10 presents data on production, sales, and cost information for the first 2 months of operations.

Exhibit 16.10
ALL FIXED COSTS COMPANY

	Month 1	Month 2
Production	20,000 Tons	0 Tons
Sales	10,000 Tons	10,000 Tons
Selling Price per Ton.	$ 30	$ 30
Costs (all fixed):		
Production	$280,000	$280,000
General and Administrative	$ 40,000	$ 40,000

a. Prepare income statements for each of the 2 months, using absorption costing.
b. Prepare income statements for each of the 2 months, using variable costing.
c. Which costing method is management likely to prefer? Why?

12. *Inventory Costing.* The Semi-Fixed Cost Company is just like the All Fixed Cost Company (see the preceding problem) except that its production costs are

[2]This problem and the next are adapted from an article by Raymond P. Marple in *The Accounting Review* (July 1956). They are presented in Chapter 3 and repeated here.

$210,000 per month and $7 per ton. The production, sales, and general and administrative cost data for months 1 and 2 for the All Fixed Cost Company apply to the Semi-Fixed Cost Company as well.

   a. Prepare income statements for each of the 2 months, using absorption costing.

   b. Prepare income statements for each of the 2 months, using direct costing.

   c. Which costing method is management likely to prefer? Why?

13. *Divisional Performance Reports.* A manufacturing company segments its operations into two divisions for purposes of internal performance evaluation. Division A assembles the firm's product, whereas Division B conducts the finishing, packing, and selling activities. Quarterly sales during the first year of operations are expected to be seasonal in the following percentages: 20 percent, 30 percent, 30 percent, 20 percent.

Division A plans to produce units at a reasonably uniform rate throughout the year. Units completed by Division A are immediately transferred to Division B on the basis of cost of manufacturing plus a 25 percent markup on cost. A representative market price for the product at this stage is $22. Divisional fixed selling and administrative expenses are allocated equally to each quarter during the year. Central corporate expenses are allocated to divisions on the basis of total sales.

A performance report for the first quarter appears in Exhibit 16.11.

Exhibit 16.11
Performance Report for Critique

	Division A	Division B
Annual Budgeted Production (units)	48,000	40,000
Budgeted Production—First Quarter (units)	12,000	8,000
Units Produced	10,000	8,000
Units Sold	10,000	5,000
Sales	$250,000	$500,000
Cost of Goods Sold:		
Variable Expenses	(150,000)	(375,000)
Fixed Expenses[a]	(50,000)	(50,000)
Gross Profit	$ 50,000	$ 75,000
Divisional Fixed Selling and Administrative Expenses	(12,000)	(50,000)
Central Corporate Expenses	(25,000)	(50,000)
Divisional Income (Loss)	$ 13,000	($ 25,000)

[a]Exclusive of any adjustment for under- or overapplied expenses.

   a. What strengths and weaknesses do you see in this divisional performance report?

   b. Making whatever changes you feel are appropriate, prepare a divisional performance report for these two divisions for the first quarter. Describe briefly the justification for your treatment of the transfer price, fixed manufacturing expenses, fixed selling and administrative expenses, and central corporate expenses.

14. *Financial Accounting and Decision Making.* The Manfin Company uses a cost of capital rate of 12 percent in making investment decisions. It currently is considering two projects that are mutually exclusive, each requiring an initial investment of $10 million. The first project has a net present value of $21 million and an internal rate of return of 20 percent. This project will be completed within 1 year and will raise accounting income and earnings per share almost immediately thereafter. The second project has a net present value of $51 million and an internal rate of return of 30 percent. The second project requires incurring large, noncapitalizable expenses over the next few years before net cash inflows from sales revenue result. Thus, accounting income and earnings per share for the next few years will not only be lower than if the first project is accepted, but also lower than earnings currently reported.

    a. Should the short-run effects on accounting income and earnings per share influence the decision as to the choice of projects? Explain.

    b. Should either of the projects be accepted? If so, which one? Why?

15. *Accounting for Advertising.* Equilibrium Company spends $30,000 on advertising the company's brand names and trademarks. As a result of the advertising expenditures, gross margin on sales after taxes has been $33,000 larger each year than it would have been without the advertising expenditures. For the purposes of this problem, assume that all advertising expenditures are made on the first day of each year and that the $33,000 extra aftertax gross margin on sales occurs on the first day of the next year. Excluding any advertising assets, or profits, Equilibrium Company has $100,000 of other assets that have been producing an aftertax income of $10,000 per year. Equilibrium Company has followed a policy of declaring dividends each year equal to net income, and has a cost of capital of 10 percent per year.

    a. Is the advertising policy a sensible one? Explain.

    b. How should the expenditures for advertising be reflected in Equilibrium Company's financial statements in order to reflect accurately the managerial decision of advertising at the rate of $30,000 per year? That is, how can the advertising expenditures be accounted for in such a way that the accounting rate of return for the advertising project and the rate of return on assets for the firm reflect the 10 percent return from advertising?

16. *Management Incentives and Financial Accounting for Research and Development.* Many companies evaluate managerial effectiveness by examining the accounting rate of return of a given manager's division or product lines. If managers think that they are going to be evaluated by an accounting rate of return criterion, they may make decisions in order to increase, or not to decrease, the accounting rate of return. *Statement of Financial Accounting Standards No. 2* requires the immediate expensing of R&D expenditures, whereas capitalization of those expenditures is a reasonable theoretical alternative. Assume that a manager is contemplating making R&D expenditures that have a positive net present value when cash flows are discounted at the firm's cost of capital.

Indicate how generally accepted accounting principles for R&D expenditures are likely to affect the decision making of the manager who is evaluated by the accounting rate of return.

17. *Management Incentives and Accounting for Research and Development.* The Consumer Division is a 100 percent owned subsidiary of Herzlinger Company and has $300,000 of total assets. The Consumer Division has been earning $45,000 per year and generating $45,000 per year of cash flow from assets. The cost of capital of the Herzlinger Company is 15 percent per year. Each year the Consumer Division distributes its earnings and pays cash of $45,000 to the parent company. Management of the Consumer Division has discovered a project involving research and development costs now that will lead to new products. The anticipated cash flows of the project are as follows:

Beginning of Year	Cash (Outflow) Inflow
1	($24,000)
2, 3, and 4	10,000 Each Year

Assume that the project is undertaken, that cash flows are as planned, and that the Consumer Division makes payments to the parent of $45,000 at the end of the first year and $47,000 at the end of each of the next 3 years.

    a. Compute the rate of return on assets of the Consumer Division for each year of the project, assuming that R&D expenditures are expensed as they occur. Use the year-end balance of total assets in the denominator.

    b. Compute the rate of return on assets of the Consumer Division for each year of the project, assuming that R&D costs are capitalized and then amortized on a straight-line basis over the last 3 years of the project. Use the year-end balance of total assets in the denominator.

    c. Compute the accounting rate of return for the new project, independent of the other assets and of the income of the Consumer Division, assuming that R&D costs are capitalized and then amortized on a straight-line basis over the entire 4 years of the project.

    d. How well has the management of the Consumer Division carried out its responsibility to its owners? On what basis do you make this judgment?

18. *Management Incentives and Financial Accounting.* This chapter points out how economically sound managerial decisions can often be reported as poor ones and vice versa, at least in the short run. This case provides an opportunity to explore certain areas where financial accounting rules may impede effective managerial decisions. The financial accounting issues involved in the situations below have not all been discussed in the book. The instructor can provide the student with suitable background, or students may be asked to do their own research in identifying the issues.

    For each of the FASB *Statements* described below, describe the required accounting treatment and reasonable alternatives to it. Then describe how the required treatment might alter the behavior of a manager who is to be evaluated by the accounting statements. Assume that the manager wishes to make decisions that are in the long-run best interests of the firm by maximizing the present value of future cash flows, but that the manager is being evaluated currently by reported net income.

a. FASB *Statement No. 2,* "Accounting for Research and Development Costs." This statement requires the immediate expensing of research and development costs.

b. FASB *Statement No. 5,* "Accounting for Contingencies." In the past, firms often did not carry casualty insurance on some of their assets, but instead spoke of themselves as being "self-insured." They used the following accounting. Each year the firm would charge to income an amount for insurance expense while setting up an estimated liability for losses. Under that practice, firms would later charge catastrophic losses against the estimated liability, rather than against income in the period when the loss occurs. Income under this method would be smoother than when the losses are charged to income in the period of the loss. *Statement No. 5* forbids this practice; it requires that such expense or loss be recognized only in the period when an actual loss occurs.

c. FASB *Statement No. 7,* "Accounting and Reporting by Development Stage Enterprises." This statement, in effect, requires expensing of (rather than capitalization of, followed by amortization of) preoperating costs incurred by new businesses. Preoperating costs are those costs incurred before a business has begun its intended operations.

19. *Puzzling Accounting Reports Including Inventory Costing.* Lucius Green runs a distillery under the corporate name Green's Distillery. Each year Green distills 10,000 barrels of whiskey, puts the product in barrels, and stores the barrels for 4 years. Each year Green sells 10,000 barrels of 4-year-old whiskey to a retail chain, which bottles the whiskey and puts its own label on the product. The retailer has a long-term, fixed-price contract with Green. The retailer is so pleased with Green's product that it is willing to buy the whiskey at any age. The contract specifies that the retailer will buy a barrel of newly distilled whiskey for $100, a barrel of 1-year-old whiskey for $118, a barrel of 2-year-old whiskey for $140, a barrel of 3-year-old whiskey for $168, and a barrel of 4-year-old whiskey for $200. In the past, Green has always sold only 4-year-old whiskey. Prices and costs have been stable for several years and are expected to remain so. An income statement for Green's Distillery for a typical year, when 10,000 barrels are distilled and 10,000 barrels of 4-year-old whiskey are sold, appears in Exhibit 16.12.

Exhibit 16.12
GREEN'S DISTILLERY
Income Statement for Typical Year When 10,000 Barrels Are Produced and 10,000 Barrels Are Sold

Sales (10,000 barrels at $200)		$2,000,000
Cost of Goods Sold:		
Variable Costs ($50 per barrel, 10,000 barrels)	$500,000	
Depreciation of Distilling Equipment	100,000	
Storage Costs of Aging Whiskey ($20 per barrel per year, 40,000 barrels)	800,000	(1,400,000)
General and Administrative Expenses		(200,000)
Income Before Taxes		$ 400,000

During Year 0, the retailer suggested to Lucius Green that the distillery be doubled in capacity and that the contract be rewritten so that the retailer would promise to buy as much as Green wanted to produce.

Assume that Green doubled capacity and, starting in Year 1, distilled 20,000 barrels of whiskey each year to be aged. All costs shown on the income statement for 10,000 barrels doubled (that is, *unit costs* including depreciation remained constant) except for general and administrative expenses, which increased $100,000 a year to $300,000 a year. By Year 5, the first batch of extra product was fully aged, and, starting in Year 5, Green sold 20,000 barrels of 4-year-old whiskey to the retail chain. During Year 1 through Year 4, 10,000 barrels were sold.

a.   Prepare income statements for each of the Years 1 through 5 using absorption costing.

b.   Prepare income statements for each of the Years 1 through 5 using variable costing.

c.   Which of the costing methods appears to give a better picture of the results of Green's Distillery for Years 2 through 4?

d.   You will probably judge in part **c** that absorption costing better reflects the situation. Why is it that variable costing appears to fail in this case, and what should be concluded from this?

20. *Incremental Analysis and Decisions Involving Patents.* Southeast Industries is a conglomerate firm. In the past several years, two matters involving its patents have required analysis. This case illustrates one use of incremental analysis and cost allocations in decision making.

Plywood Division In its plywood division, Southeast Industries manufactures striated (decorative) plywood that sells in the marketplace for a premium over ordinary plywood. Southeast Industries owns the patent, called the Deskey patent, on the striation process, and currently is the only producer of striated plywood. The machinery required (in addition to the machinery usually required to make plywood) for the striation process costs $15,000 and lasts 5 years. Southeast Industries is currently operating its plywood manufacturing operation at 80 percent of normal capacity. The specialized machinery currently used for striation is also operating at only 80 percent of normal capacity. The variable (direct) cost of producing 1,000 board feet of striated plywood is $100. The total fixed cost for producing 1,000 board feet of striated plywood at present levels of output is $10. The selling price of 1,000 board feet of striated plywood is $160.

The market demand for striated plywood appears to be increasing. Industry forecasts are that the demand for striated plywood will increase by about 25 percent next year and remain at that level for the next 5 years. Southeast Industries can acquire additional striating machinery, if necessary, and produce more striated plywood in a plant in South Carolina that currently is able to produce only ordinary plywood. The costs in the South Carolina plant will be comparable to current costs.

A competitor in the ordinary plywood business, Alabama Atlantic Company, has approached Southeast and asked to purchase nonexclusive rights to use the Deskey patent. Alabama Atlantic Company has calculated that, aside from the cost of the patent license to use the Deskey patent, it can make a net incremental profit (after taxes) of $50 per 1,000 board feet of striated plywood produced. Alabama Atlantic has sufficient capacity to match Southeast's production of striated plywood.

    a. What is the maximum price that Alabama Atlantic should be willing to pay, per 1,000 board feet, as a royalty for the right to use the Deskey patent?

    b. What is the minimum price that Southeast Industries should be willing to accept from Alabama Atlantic as a royalty to use the Deskey patent?

    c. Explain why the two companies are, or are not, likely to reach a mutually agreeable price. In your opinion, what is that price likely to be?

Chemical Division In its chemical division, Southeast Industries manufactures several kinds of flux used in welding. In particular, it owns the patent for flux no. 660; the patent on flux no. 660 expires in 4 years. At the end of that time, anyone else can manufacture the no. 660 flux without paying a royalty to Southeast Industries.

    The Jefferson Electric Company requires a flux in its manufacturing of electric motors. Currently, Jefferson Electric Company owns the right to use both the no. 620 and the no. 650 fluxes, but does not own the right to use the no. 660 flux. Engineers at Jefferson Electric Company state that neither the no. 620 nor the no. 650 flux is suitable for the line of electric motors that Jefferson wishes to build over the next decade. The no. 660 flux is suitable. The engineers are also certain that the series 700 fluxes, just developed at Jefferson Electric Company, will be ideal for these motors. Unfortunately, the series 700 fluxes are not scheduled to come off the production line in large quantities until 2 years from now. All estimates are that the series 700 fluxes will be substantially cheaper to manufacture than any of the series 600 fluxes (nos. 620, 650, and 660).

    If Jefferson Electric Company were to purchase all of its fluxes from Southeast Industries, at Southeast's normal selling prices, then Southeast would make a net incremental aftertax profit of $300,000 per year.

    The two companies are attempting to negotiate an agreement whereby Jefferson Electric Company pays Southeast Industries for the right to manufacture the no. 660 flux. Assume that the companies consider each year separately in the negotiations.

    d. Explain why the two companies are, or are not, likely to reach a mutually agreeable royalty for each of the next 10 years. In your opinion, what payment is likely to be agreed to for each of the years? Why? What other factors, if any, would you want to consider?

21. *Management Analysis of Standard Cost Variances; Absorption and Variable Costing.*[3] As a member of the board of directors of Advanced Resource Technology, you have been attempting to track down rumors of cost overruns at the Bio-Tech Division, which produces a single product (a liquid protein supplement). You have just returned from a brief inspection of the production facilities. While there, you picked up various pieces of possibly relevant information. The first is the published version of the division's income statement from the preceding year based

---

[3]By James M. Patell.

on *standard absorption* costing, and the second is an internal reconstruction of the same statement based on variable costing. Both appear in Exhibit 16.13; on both statements all production variances have been carried to the cost of goods sold. Actual output for the year exceeded originally forecast output by 10,000 units. Information about unit costs appears in Exhibit 16.14.

Exhibit 16.13
ADVANCED RESOURCE TECHNOLOGY

Income Statement—Published Version
Standard Absorption Costing

Sales		$2,240,000
Cost of Goods Sold		
Beginning Inventory	$ –0–	
+ Goods Produced	2,200,000	
– Ending Inventory	440,000	
= Standard Cost of Goods Sold	$1,760,000	
+ Correction for *All* Variances	44,500	
= Cost of Goods Sold		$1,804,500
Gross Margin		$ 435,500
Selling and Administrative Expenses		150,000
Net Income		$ 285,500

Income Statement—For Internal Use Only
Variable Costing

Sales		$2,240,000
Cost of Goods Sold		
Beginning Inventory	$ –0–	
+ Goods Produced	1,900,500	
– Ending Inventory	380,100	
= Cost of Goods Sold	$1,520,400	
– Correction for Overapplied Overhead[a]	21,000	
= Cost of Goods Sold		$1,499,400
Selling Expenses		80,000
Contribution Margin		$ 660,600
Factory Overhead		365,000
Selling and Administrative Expenses		70,000
Operating Profit		$ 225,600

[a]Overhead was applied based on actual hours × overhead application rate.

Exhibit 16.14
ADVANCED RESOURCE TECHNOLOGY
Cost per Unit of Protein Supplement

	Standard		Actual	
	Quantity	**Cost**	**Quantity**	**Cost**
Materials	2 Quarts	$2.00 per Quart	1.9 Quarts	$2.10 per Quart
Labor	2 Hours	$6.00 per Hour	2.1 Hours	$6.15 per Hour
Total Overhead	2 Hours	$3.00 per Hour		

Construct a complete variance analysis, including price, efficiency, volume, flexible budget, and production volume variances, for all input categories (including variable and fixed overhead). (There were no raw materials inventories.) Another member of the board of directors is impressed that the external report shows higher net income than the internal report. This person wonders, "Why do we control costs better on one report than the other?" How would you respond?

22. *Pricing Decisions and Accounting Data.*[4] In July 1977, John Marmon, founder of Marmon Metals Corporation, said to his son Frank, "We have held the price line for 3 years, and since we have driven one major competitor almost out of the grinding and plating business, I think our strategy paid off in getting productivity and product quality up while maintaining constant prices to keep competition out."

"I agree, Dad," said Frank Marmon. "It's been a great year, but there are a couple of things that bother me. With steel prices going up some 7 percent next month, it could be the time to change our pricing strategy."

"I'll listen," said John, "but we are doing pretty well. I'd hate to see us either price ourselves out of the market or hold a profit umbrella over the heads of our competitors—and potential competitors as well. We didn't get 40 percent of the market by raising prices."

History In 1951, John Marmon founded Marmon Metals to clean steel castings used in large generators. In 1954, Marmon bought two multiple-spindle drill presses, which looked like a real bargain. Later, General Telephone approached Marmon Metals and suggested that it tool up to make mounting bars for direct dialing systems. At that time Marmon was the only company in the country with any surplus drilling equipment suitable for the job. Marmon accepted.

Gradually, John Marmon embarked on a planned program of buying grinding machines on the used machine market and from war surplus. He financed his purchases largely by selling time on his machines to other companies and partly from expanding grinding and plating operations. By 1977, in the Chicago plant alone, Marmon Metals employed seven people manufacturing tooling full time. In addition, it was carrying between $250,000 and $300,000 worth of consumable supplies.

In 1966, it became apparent that Marmon Metals had neither the plant nor the people in Chicago to handle all the business available. The company expanded to a small town in central Indiana, which put up $25,000 as a down payment on the new plant and helped Marmon Metals borrow the rest through local banks.

Early in 1970, Frank Marmon got out of the army and decided to expand Marmon Metals into an emerging California market. In May, Frank Marmon went to California to find a site. He found it; ground was broken in July; and the first piece of bar was ground and plated in November 1970. From May 1971, the California plant, under Frank's management, made a profit and, within 1 year, a second bay had to be built, which doubled the size of the plant.

With the start of the California venture, Marmon moved, in all its locations,

---

[4]Adapted from Olson Metals case prepared by Professor Neil C. Churchill and Research Associate Ashis Gupta.

toward selling the "total product" to its customers rather than just providing a grinding and plating service. This permitted Marmon Metals, in John Marmon's words, "to go along without price increases and to maintain profit margins by selling steel. Increasingly, we have been buying, grinding and plating, and selling as a package instead of processing other people's steel." By 1977, John estimated that Marmon Metals held between 40 and 50 percent of the piston rod market other than the substantial "captive" market of original equipment manufacturers such as Caterpillar and International Harvester. The size of the "noncaptive" market was approximately $20 million per year.

Financial and Accounting Procedures By 1977, Frank Marmon had become concerned that Marmon Metals had not been "managing its margins" in the face of inflation. Exhibit 16.15 shows gross margin on a product-line basis. Frank calculated that whereas the margin on material sales had remained at 11 percent from 1976 to 1977, the margin on grinding had decreased from 23.5 percent to 13.4 percent on a historical cost basis. Thus, although profits had increased substantially, the increase had come from operating leverage—increased sales without proportional increases in administrative expenses. Frank had come to recognize the basically conservative nature of Marmon's accounting system. It had been on a

Exhibit 16.15
MARMON METALS
Income Statements

	Year Ended June 30, 1976		Year Ended June 30, 1977	
	Historical Cost (1)	Replacement Cost (2)	Historical Cost (3)	Replacement Cost (4)
Material Sales	$3,055,217	$3,055,217	$5,928,705	$5,928,705
Total Cost of Material . . .	2,716,652	2,716,652	5,260,211	5,260,211
Margin on Material Sales . . . . . . (1)	$ 338,565	$ 338,565	$ 668,494	$ 668,494
Grinding and Plating Sales . .	$3,832,850	$3,832,850	$5,066,196	$5,066,196
Inventory Reduction . . .	—	—	39,523	39,523
Total Factory Compensation.	1,187,032	1,187,032	2,047,039	2,047,039
Depreciation on Machinery	90,300	367,100[a]	118,300	373,400[a]
Depreciation on Buildings .	100,500	225,000[b]	100,500	236,800[b]
Other Operating Expenses	1,447,040	1,447,040	1,982,606	1,982,606
Margin on Grinding and Plating . . . . . (2)	$1,007,978	$ 606,678	$ 778,228	$ 386,828
Total Margin = (1) + (2) . .	$1,346,543	$ 945,243	$1,446,722	$1,055,322
Administrative Expenses . .	822,322	822,322	529,614	529,614
Income Before Taxes. . . .	$ 524,221	$ 122,921	$ 917,108	$ 525,708
Provision for Taxes	251,626	59,002	440,212	252,340
Net Income from Operations.	$ 272,595	$ 63,919	$ 476,896	$ 273,368

[a]See Exhibit 16.18.
[b]See Exhibit 16.19.

Exhibit 16.16
MARMON METALS
Balance Sheets

	June 30, 1976		June 30, 1977	
	Historical Cost (1)	Replacement Cost (2)	Historical Cost (3)	Replacement Cost (4)
Assets				
Current Assets				
Cash	$ 88,472	$ 88,472	$ 183,634	$ 183,634
Accounts Receivable. . .	1,184,109	1,184,109	1,164,987	1,164,987
Inventory	887,910	1,051,800[a]	1,527,071	1,764,500[a]
Total Current Assets. . . .	$2,160,491	$ 2,324,381	$2,875,692	$ 3,113,121
Plant Assets				
Land	$ 92,894	$ 92,894	$ 92,894	$ 92,894
Buildings (net)	457,241	4,195,000	391,041	4,286,000
Machinery (net)	648,630	5,506,000[b]	590,568	5,601,000[b]
Cars and Trucks (net) . .	55,092	55,092	78,008	78,008
Total Plant Assets	$1,253,857	$ 9,848,986	$1,152,511	$10,057,902
Other Assets	80,714	80,714	138,893	138,893
Total Assets	$3,495,062	$12,254,081	$4,167,096	$13,309,916
Liabilities and Equities				
Current Liabilities				
Accounts Payable. . . .	$ 445,500	$ 445,500	$ 167,642	$ 167,642
Wages and Payroll Taxes Payable	4,907	4,907	36,916	36,916
Corporate Income Taxes	63,766	18,850	372,992	239,474
Other	27,582	27,582	31,315	31,315
Total Current Liabilities. . .	$ 541,755	$ 496,839	$ 608,865	$ 475,347
Long-Term Liabilities. . .	1,238,315	1,238,325	1,384,776	1,384,776
Owners' Equity				
Capital Stock	56,048	56,048	56,048	56,046
Retained Earnings (historical cost)	1,658,944	1,658,944	2,117,407[c]	2,117,407
Additional Owners' Equity from Revaluation to Current Cost	—	8,803,925	—	9,276,340
Total Equities	$3,495,062	$12,254,081	$4,167,096	$13,309,916

[a]See Exhibit 16.17.
[b]See Exhibit 16.18.
[c]Dividends for the year ended June 30, 1977, were $18,433.

cash basis until 1973, and its underlying philosophy was that "an expenditure is an expense." The company had consistently "expensed" the costs of refurbishing and improving old grinding machines and producing new plating tools. This practice had increased expenses in recent years, when many of the old grinding machines had been refurbished as the business expanded and new plating fixtures were purchased and expensed. Where machinery had been capitalized and then depreciated, the depreciable life was 10 years. Frank estimated that the company had written off some $1,060,500 of machinery over the 7 years from 1971 to 1977.

From a public reporting point of view, this machinery would have been capitalized. For public reporting, all machinery would have been depreciated over 15 years.

Replacement Cost Analysis Frank knew that since 1976, the Securities and Exchange Commission had required large corporations to show the effects of inflation on their assets and profits by calculating the replacement cost of inventories, assets, cost of goods sold, and depreciation. Frank thought that this approach might be helpful for his father and him in their pricing decision, so he compiled additional data.

Inventories To adjust inventories, Frank constructed an index of steel prices and applied them to the LIFO layers of inventory beginning in 1970, the year Marmon Metals went on LIFO (see Exhibit 16.17). Because LIFO costs closely approximated replacement costs on the income statement,[5] Frank made no adjustment to the cost of purchased materials sold.

Machinery and Equipment For the machinery, Frank prepared a list of all items still in use, mostly used machines that had been extensively reengineered and refurbished. John Marmon estimated the cost to Marmon Machines of acquiring these machines in their present condition as of June 30, 1977. The results of the calculations appear in Exhibit 16.18. Because the values were estimated as those at June 30, 1977, no accumulated depreciation was shown on the balance sheet, although 1/15 of the reported cost was taken as depreciation on the 1976 and 1977 income statements.

Exhibit 16.17
MARMON METALS
Replacement Cost of Inventory
(convert LIFO cost to replacement cost)

Year	LIFO Layer	Index[a]	Replacement Cost on June 30, 1977 (rounded to nearest $100)
1970	$ 44,400	1.70	$ 75,500
1971	99,500	1.56	155,200
1972	174,700	1.42	248,100
1973	6,800	1.28	8,700
1974	—	1.21	—
1975	514,600	1.14	586,600
1976	47,900	1.07	51,300
1977	639,100	1.00	639,100
	$1,527,000		$1,764,500

Replacement Cost on June 30, 1976 = ($1,764,500 − $639,100) ÷ 1.07 = $1,051,800.

[a]Index developed from Marmon Metals purchasing records.

[5]Inventory turned over more than four times a year.

Exhibit 16.18
MARMON METALS
Schedule of Machinery

Purchase Year	Cost	Book Value Using 10-Year Life on June 30		Estimated Market Value (used) as of June 30, 1977
		1976	1977	
1960	$ 7,965	—	—	$ 261,000
1961	2,445	—	—	7,000
1962	45,086	—	—	182,000
1963	70,871	—	—	473,000
1964	41,835	—	—	371,000
1965	12,150	—	—	183,000
1966	9,113	—	—	173,000
1967	12,957	—	—	11,000
1968	73,919	$ 10,885	—	293,000
1969	37,109	7,398	$ 4,388	183,000
1970	54,749	14,548	9,072	309,000
1971	159,255	67,774	51,848	1,100,000
1972	106,789	53,155	42,475	419,000
1973	48,256	31,460	26,060	81,000
1974	398,678	278,906	236,412	1,009,000
1975	59,415	49,860	42,823	184,000
1976	164,002	134,644	131,778	267,000
		$648,630		$5,506,000
1977	52,140		45,711	95,000
Total			$590,567	$5,601,000

	1976	1977
Replacement Cost of Used Machinery at Year End.	$5,506,000[a]	$5,601,000
Annual Depreciation over 15 Years	$ 367,100	$ 373,400
Less Depreciation over 10 Years Included in Historical Cost Income Statement.	(90,300)	(118,300)
Additional Depreciation Expense for Income Statement . . .	$ 276,800	$ 255,100

[a]Note probable misstatement in June 30, 1976, balance sheet of using used asset values from June 30, 1977; actual amount might be somewhat larger or smaller.

Buildings For the buildings in California and Indiana, John and Frank estimated the cost of constructing the same facilities today. For Chicago, John estimated their present market value. See Exhibit 16.19.

Income Taxes Frank was puzzled when it came to calculation of the income tax on replacement cost-based income. On the one hand, the company owed $440,212 for 1977, and that is what they would pay even if they kept their books on a replacement cost basis. On the other hand, a new company coming into the industry would find its actual costs equal to Marmon's replacement costs. Taxes at 48 percent would be paid on lower actual profits. Thus Frank chose this second alternative. Frank estimated the aftertax cost of capital for such a new entrant to be about 10 percent.

Exhibit 16.19
MARMON METALS
Schedule of Buildings
(depreciable life of 25 years)

Site of Buildings	Approximate Construction Year of Buildings	Estimated Value as of June 30, 1977	Accumulated Depreciation	
			6/30/76	6/30/77
Chicago	1951	$ 800,000	$ —a	$ —b
Indiana	1967	1,670,000	601,000	668,000
California.	1970	3,450,000	828,000	966,000
		$5,920,000	$1,429,000	$1,634,000
			1976	1977
Replacement Cost of Buildings			$5,624,000b	$5,920,000
Annual Depreciation over 25 Years			$ 225,000	$ 236,800
Less Depreciation Accounted for in Historical Cost Figures.			(100,500)	(100,500)
Additional Depreciation Expense for Income Statement			$ 124,500	$ 136,300

aZero because current market value is being used.
b1976 value estimated at 95 percent of 1977 values.

The Pricing Decision Frank and John Marmon met in early August 1977 to discuss the results of the replacement cost analysis. They had confirmed the news that steel prices would go up 7 percent later in the month and that, if Marmon was to change its prices, this would be the appropriate time.

John Marmon believed that a 6 percent price rise by Marmon Metals would be followed by their competition. Lincoln Steel, a $300 million steel company, was their major competitor—although in John's opinion, they did plating and grinding primarily to sell more steel. John also believed that they probably sold the service side of the product at or below cost, because they didn't have the equipment edge that Marmon had. The other competitor, Geiger Machinery, had dropped from a 40 percent to a 10 percent market share under Marmon Metals pricing policies and was not, in John's eyes, a factor in the market any more. John was hesitant, however, to raise prices more than 6 percent. "We have a fascinating business here," he told Frank, "I don't know if we've priced our products properly or not, according to your new theories, but we're making profits, increasing our market share, and getting rid of some of our competition. And that I like. I also think that keeping prices low has expanded the market—people won't do it themselves if they can get it done cheaply enough."

"I know it, Dad," Frank replied, "but look at the numbers. Our aftertax return on assets was 7.8 percent in 1976 and 11.4 percent in 1977—if you believe our accounting figures. Now, a competitor who comes in with the same equipment and facilities as we have would have to invest $13 million, and the aftertax rate of return on the assets would be 2.1 percent. I still think the figures show that we can raise our prices by at least 9 percent, get our margins under control and our return on investment up to where it should be, and still not be too fat a target for others to shoot at."

''Well, I don't know, Frank,'' said John. ''It sounds logical, and your figures show what I always said, 'we need a dollar of investment to produce a dollar of sales.' But you've put in a lot of assumptions. I would sure hate to raise prices and lose our competitive edge. We have kept our prices down and still made profits, and not only kept competition away but driven one of our competitors out. So what if we have a little inflation—our business is fundamentally sound. I'm inclined toward 6 percent and no more, but I can be convinced otherwise.''

    a.   Reproduce Frank's analysis to derive the rates of return in the next-to-last paragraph.

    b.   What income tax data should be used in the analysis? Why?

    c.   What would you do about prices and why?

23. *Measuring Managerial Performance: New Challenges.*[6] Many commentators about North American business have argued that the relative deterioration in manufacturing productivity compared to Japanese manufacturers results from a preoccupation with short-term financial performance measures. Many bonus plans for senior executives are based on annual accounting income. This provides incentives to take actions that enhance short-term earnings performance that might not be in the best long-term interests of the firm. By contrast, Japanese executives have incentives to endure the long-run viability of their companies. Consequently, they are more concerned than their North American counterparts with long-run productivity, quality control, and managing the company's physical assets.

Not everyone agrees with the observation that North American business executives are preoccupied with short-term financial performance to such an extent that they would take actions contrary to the best long-run economic interests of the organization just to make themselves look good on the performance measures. But suppose that an executive faces a choice between an action that has a positive short-run effect on performance measures and one that has better long-run consequences for the organization but does not have a positive effect on short-run performance measures. It is hard to fault a rational executive for taking the action that looks good in the short run. As the saying goes, ''you have to look good in the short run to be around in the long run.''

How would you design a control system that gives incentives to top-level managers to be concerned about long-run productivity, quality of products, and long-run economic well being of the company? Assume that these managers have previously focused on maximizing quarterly and annual earnings numbers to the detriment of these other factors.

24. *Accounting for Partial Obsolescence—Conflict Between Historical Costs and Opportunity Costs.* The chief financial executive of a firm made the following statement:

Production methods change. Robotics, nuclear power, and computers are only eye-catching examples of technological changes that take place. Financial ac-

---

[6]This case was influenced by an article by Robert S. Kaplan, ''Measuring Manufacturing Performance: A New Challenge for Managerial Accounting Research,'' *The Accounting Review* (October 1983). Also, see Robert H. Hayes and William H. Abernathy, ''Managing Our Way to Economic Decline,'' *Harvard Business Review* (July–August 1981).

counting has done little to adapt to and report specifically on the effects of technological obsolescence, which can render already-owned assets significantly less valuable than before.

As new equipment and processes become available, capable management discovers and evaluates them. If the analysis calls for the disposition of old equipment, and the disposal is made, then financial accounting, using generally accepted accounting principles (GAAP), writes off the old equipment and, in doing so, recognizes the complete obsolescence of the old equipment.

In other cases, the net present value analysis may indicate that the operating cost savings of the new equipment are not enough to justify its substitution for the old, even though the economic value of the old equipment has been reduced. So long as the firm holds the older, partially obsolete equipment, financial accounting, using GAAP, does not report the loss in economic value from partial obsolescence.

A machine now owned by the firm has a book value of $200,000. (This means that the original cost of the machine less the depreciation recognized to date, as shown in the accounting records, is $200,000.) The machine has no current resale value because the costs of removal equal the salvage proceeds. The machine will be able to produce 1,000 units of product during each of the next 5 years if $50,000 cash is spent each year for materials and labor. A new machine has been developed that costs $200,000, that will also last for 5 years, and that will also produce 1,000 units of product each year. The yearly costs of materials and labor to use the modern machine are, however, only $20,000.

What should be done?

25. *Management Decisions and External Financial Reports.* "Squeezing oranges in your idle time is not a by-product," said the Big Eight partner in charge of the audit of Regent Company, disapprovingly.

"But," replied the president of Regent, "squeezing oranges is not our usual business, and your accounting plan will make us show a substantial decline in income. We all know that our decision this year to squeeze oranges was a good one that is paying off handsomely."

The argument concerned the accounting for income during the year 1983 by Regent Company.

Background In 1976, the Alcoholic Control Board (ACB) of Georgia, a state not known for its production of grapes and wines, wanted to encourage the production of wine within the state. The Regent Company was formed in response to the encouragement of the ACB. The production process for wine involves aging the product. The company commenced production in 1977, but the first batch of wine was not sold until 1979. Regent made a cash investment at the start of 1977 of $4,400,000 in grape-pressing equipment and a facility to house that equipment. The ACB has promised to buy the output of the Regent Company for 10 years, starting with the first batch in 1979. Regent Company decided to account for its operations by including in the cost of the wine all depreciation on the grape-pressing equipment and on the facility to house it. The economic life of the equipment was judged to be 10 years, the life of the contract with the ACB. Regent Company reported general and administrative expenses in external financial reports, for both 1977 and 1978, of $100,000 per year.

Regent Company's contract with the ACB promised payments of $1.8 million per year. The direct costs of labor and materials for each year's batch of wine are $130,000 each year. Depreciation is charged on a straight-line basis over a 10-year life. The income taxes were 40 percent of pretax income.

The wine sales commenced in 1979 and operations were carried out as planned. The income statements for the years 1979 through 1982 appeared as shown in Exhibit 16.20.

By 1982, operations were running so smoothly that the time required to press the grapes and to put the young wine into barrels for storage took only two and one-half months of the year.

In late 1979, management of Regent Company was approached by a large manufacturer of frozen orange juice concentrate with headquarters in Florida. The juice manufacturer wanted Regent to squeeze oranges for input to its processes. The manufacturer pointed out to Regent Company that the pressing equipment was now standing idle 80 percent of the year and that for no additional capital costs, the equipment could be put to use squeezing oranges during the otherwise idle months. The manufacturer was willing to pay directly all out-of-pocket costs of squeezing oranges plus $100,000 per year to Regent.

Exhibit 16.20
REGENT COMPANY
Income Statements
(in thousands)

| | 1979 to 1982 Each Year, Actual | For 1983 | |
		Management's View	Auditor's View
Revenues:			
From Wine Put into Production 2 Years Previously	$1,800	$1,800	$1,800
From Orange Juice Squeezed in Current Year	—	100[a]	100[a]
Total Revenues.	$1,800	$1,900	$1,900
Cost of Goods Sold:			
Direct Costs of Wine Put into Production 2 Years Previously	$ 300	$ 300	$ 300
Depreciation of Buildings and Equipment:			
From 2 Years Prior, Carried in Inventory until Wine Is Sold	440	440	440
From Current Year, Allocated to Orange Juice	—	100	352
Selling, General, and Administrative Expenses	130	130[a]	130[a]
Income Taxes at 40 Percent	372	372	271
Total Expenses	$1,242	$1,342	$1,493
Net Income	$ 558	$ 558	$ 407

[a]Manufacturer of orange juice pays out-of-pocket costs directly. These items are not shown here.

Management of Regent Company was delighted with the offer to put its idle capacity to work. It contracted with the manufacturer to perform the services. At the end of 1983, it compiled the income statement shown in Exhibit 16.20 as "Management's View."

The Accounting Issue   Management of Regent Company suggested that the revenues from squeezing oranges are an incremental by-product of owning the wine-making machinery. The wine-making process was undertaken on its own merits and has paid off according to schedule. The revenues from squeezing oranges are a by-product of the main purpose of the business. Ordinarily, the accounting for by-products assigns to them costs equal to their net realizable value. That is, costs are assigned in exactly the amount that will make the sale of the by-products show neither gain nor loss. In this case, because the incremental revenue of squeezing oranges is $100,000, Regent Company assigns $100,000 of the overhead to this process, reducing from $440,000 to $340,000 the overhead assigned to the main product. This will make the main product appear more profitable when it is sold.

Management of Regent Company was aware that its income for 1983 would appear no different from that of the preceding year. Management knew that the benefits from squeezing oranges began to occur in 1983, but was willing for the benefits to appear on the financial statements later.

The Big Eight auditor who saw management's proposed income statement disapproved. The partner in charge of the audit spoke as quoted at the beginning of this case.

The auditor's position was that the squeezing of oranges in these circumstances is not a by-product and that by-product accounting is inappropriate. The overhead costs must be allocated between the two processes of grape pressing and orange squeezing according to some reasonable basis. The most reasonable basis, the auditor thought, was the time devoted to each of the processes. Because grape pressing used about 20 percent of the year, whereas orange squeezing used 80 percent of the year, the auditor assigned $352,000, or 80 percent, of the overhead costs to orange squeezing and $88,000, or 20 percent, to the wine production. Exhibit 16.20 shows the auditor's income statement.

The president of Regent Company was upset. Reported net income in 1983 is down almost 30 percent from 1982; yet things have improved. The president fears the reaction of the board of directors and of shareholders. The president wonders what has happened and what to do.

    a.   Assuming that the Regent Company faces an aftertax cost of capital of 10 percent, did the company in fact make a good decision in 1976 to enter into an agreement with the state to produce wine? Explain.

    b.   Did the company in fact make a good decision in 1982 to enter into the agreement with the manufacturer of frozen orange juice?

    c.   Using management's view of the proper accounting, construct financial statements for the years 1984, 1985, and 1986, assuming that events occur as planned and in the same way as in 1983. Generalize these statements to later years.

    d.   Are management's statements correct given its interpretation of by-product accounting? If not, construct an income statement for 1983 that is consistent with by-product accounting.

e. Is management correct in its interpretation that the orange juice is a by-product?

f. Using the auditor's view of the situation and assuming the same facts as in part **c**, construct income statements for the years 1984, 1985, and 1986. Generalize these statements to later years.

g. Assuming that the auditor is right, what might management of Regent Company do to solve its problem?

26. *Managing Earnings.* Champion Clothiers, Inc., owns and operates 80 retailing establishments throughout New England, specializing in quality men's and women's clothing. The company was established in 1908 by James Champion and has been run by a member of the Champion family since that time. Currently, Ronald Champion, grandson of the founder, is president and chief executive officer. The company's shares are held by members of the Champion family.

The setting for this case is March 1983. The following conversation takes place between Ronald Champion and the company's accountant, Tom Morrissey.

Champion (President): Tom, you said on the telephone that the financial statements for 1982 were now complete. How much did we earn last year?

Morrissey (Accountant): net income was $800,000, with earnings per share at $1.60. With the $1.20 per share earned in 1980 and $1.38 earned in 1981, we have maintained our 15 percent growth rate in profits.

Champion: That sounds great! Tom, at our board meeting next week I am going to announce that the Champion family has decided to take the company public. We will be issuing shares equal to a 30 percent stake in the company early in 1984. It is important that our earnings for 1983 continue to reflect the growth rate we have been experiencing. By my calculations, we need an earnings per share for 1983 in the neighborhood of $1.84. Does this seem likely?

Morrissey: I'm afraid not. Our current projections indicate an earnings per share around $1.65 for this year. Major unexpected style changes earlier this year have left us with obsolete inventory that will have to be written off. In addition, increased competition in several of our major markets is putting a squeeze on margins. Even the acquisition of Green Trucking Company in June of this year will not help earnings that much.

Champion: I know that you accountants have all kinds of games you can play to doctor up the numbers. There must be something we can do to increase earnings to the desired level. What about our use of LIFO for inventories?

Morrissey: We have been using LIFO in the past because it reduces income and saves taxes during a period of rising prices. The more recent, higher acquisition costs of inventory items are used in computing cost of goods sold in the income statement. The older, lower acquisition prices are used in the valuation of inventory on the balance sheet. We could switch to FIFO for 1983. That would add about $.21 to earnings per share. However, we would probably have to use FIFO for tax purposes as well, increasing our taxes for the year by about $50,000.

Champion: I don't like paying more taxes, but FIFO certainly more closely approximates the physical flow of our goods. If we decide to stay on LIFO, is there anything we can do in applying the LIFO method that would prop up earnings?

Morrissey: We now classify our inventory very broadly into two LIFO groups, or pools: one for men's clothing and one for women's clothing. We do this to minimize the possibility of dipping into an old LIFO layer. As you will recall, if we sell more than we purchase during a given period, we dip into an old LIFO layer. These LIFO layers are valued using acquisition costs of the year the layer was added. Some of these layers reflect costs of the mid-1950s. When we dip into one of these layers, we have to use these old, lower costs in figuring cost of goods sold and net income. By defining our LIFO pools broadly to include our dollar investment in men's clothing and our dollar investment in women's clothing, we minimize the probability of liquidating an old LIFO layer. We could define our LIFO pools more narrowly to increase the possibility of dipping. We could then let the inventory of particular items run down at the end of the year, dip into the LIFO layer to increase earnings, and then rebuild the inventory early in the next year. I suspect that we could add about $.02 a share to 1983 earnings if we went with narrower pools.

Champion: We own all of our store buildings and display counters. Is there anything we can do with depreciation expense?

Morrissey: We now depreciate these items using the shortest lives allowed and the fastest write-off permitted by tax law. However, unlike LIFO, we do not have to calculate depreciation for financial reporting the same as we do for tax reporting. We could depreciate these items over the expected economic life of each asset, which would be longer than the tax life. That should add about $.04 to earnings per share for 1983. We could also use the straight-line depreciation method for financial reporting. Although our depreciable assets probably decrease in value faster than the straight-line method would indicate, we would be using the depreciation method that most of our competitors use for financial reporting. The use of straight-line depreciation would add another $.08.

Champion: Now you're talking. What else can we do?

Morrissey: There are some possibilities with respect to the acquisition of Green Trucking later this year. We currently plan to account for this acquisition using the purchase method. Under the purchase method, we will record the assets (and liabilities) of Green Trucking on our books at their market value on the date of acquisition. Since we expect to pay a price higher than the market value of Green's identifiable assets, there will also be some goodwill recorded.

Champion: How does the acquisition impact earnings for 1983?

Morrissey: On the plus side, we will include the earnings of Green Trucking from the date of acquisition in June until the end of the year. However, cost of goods sold and depreciation expense must be based on the higher current market values recorded on our books for Champion's assets rather than the lower recorded amounts on Green's books. In addition, we will have to amortize the goodwill. I expect to pick up $.08 per share in earnings for 1983 from the Green acquisition, but this is already reflected in my $1.65 estimate for the year.

Champion: Can we account for the acquisition any differently?

Morrissey: If we can qualify, we may be able to use the pooling-of-interests method. Under the pooling method, we would record Green's assets (and liabilities) on our books at the amounts at which they are stated on Green's books. That is, the older, lower book values would be carried over. This means that cost of goods sold and depreciation expense will be lower this year and in the future than if we used the purchase method. In addition, no goodwill would be recognized, and therefore no goodwill amortization would have to be recorded. Also, we would reflect in our earnings for 1983 the earnings of Green Trucking for all of 1983, not just that portion after June. Using the pooling method, earnings per share should increase $.10 more than the purchase method.

Champion: That sounds great, but what do we have to do to qualify?

Morrisey: To justify carrying over the old book values of Green Trucking, we have to show that we are merely combining the predecessor companies *and their shareholders*. The shareholders of Green Trucking must receive common stock of Champion Clothiers in exchange for their shares in Green Trucking. The shareholders in each of the predecessor companies then become shareholders in the new combined company (which will carry the Champion name). The Green shareholders would own 10 percent of Champion after the acquisition. Accountants view such a transaction as a change in form rather than in substance and permit the carryover of the old book values of Green.

Champion: My family may not be too happy about this arrangement, but let's move on.

Morrissey: Well, there is one thing we can do very easily with our pension plan to improve earnings. When we adopted the pension plan 2 years ago, we gave all employees credit for their service prior to adoption. This created an immediate obligation for past service. We are amortizing this obligation as a charge against earnings over a 15-year period, which is the average remaining work life of our employees. Generally accepted accounting principles permit us to use 30 years instead of 15 years as the amortization period; that switch would increase earnings per share by $.05 for 1983.

Champion: All of the things you have suggested deal with the selection or application of accounting methods. Can we do anything with the timing of expenditures to help 1983's earnings?

Morrissey: Well, painting and other maintenance of our stores scheduled for the last quarter of this year could be postponed until the first quarter of next year. That would add $.02 to earnings per share. In addition, we anticipate running a major advertising campaign just after Christmas. Although the advertising expenditure will be made in 1983 and will reduce earnings per share by $.03, all of the benefits of the campaign will be realized in greater sales early in 1984. Finally, capital expenditures scheduled for the first quarter of 1984 could be moved back to the fourth quarter of this year. We realize a tax saving from the investment tax credit on these expenditures. By realizing these credits this year, we could increase earnings per share by $.04.

Champion: I hadn't realized how much flexibility we had in managing our earnings. Before we decide which choices to make, can you think of any other avenues open to us?

Morrissey: We could always sell off assets on which we have potential gain. For example, we hold some marketable securities that we purchased last year. Selling those securities would net us an additional $.02 in earnings per share. In addition, we own two parcels of land that we hope to use some day for new stores. These parcels could be sold at a gain of $.04 per share.

Champion: It strikes me that these alternatives could increase earnings per share for 1983 to the $2.00-plus range. This level is a lot more appealing than the $1.65 per share anticipated for the year. Will we have to do anything to earnings per share for prior years, if we adopt any of these alternatives?

Morrissey: I have set out in Exhibit 16.21 the impact of each of the choices on earnings per share for 1983 as well as any retroactive adjustment required for prior years. This summary should be helpful as we decide our strategy.

How much do you think Champion Clothiers should report as earnings per share for 1983?

Exhibit 16.21
Alternative Strategies for Managing Earnings per Share

Alternative	Impact on Earnings per Share			
	1980	1981	1982	1983
Actual or Anticipated	$1.20	$1.38	$1.60	$1.65
Adoption of FIFO	+.15	+.17	+.20	+.21
Use of Narrower LIFO Pools	+.02	+.03	+.02	+.02
Use of Longer Depreciable Lives	—	—	—	+.04
Adoption of Straight-line Depreciation	+.05	+.06	+.07	+.08
Adoption of Pooling of Interests	+.02	+.04	+.06	+.10
Amortization of Pension Obligation over 30 Years	—	—	—	+.05
Deferral of Maintenance	—	—	—	+.02
Deferral of Advertising	—	—	—	+.03
Acceleration of Capital Expenditures	—	—	—	+.04
Sale of Marketable Securities	—	—	—	+.02
Sale of Land	—	—	—	+.04

Chapter 17 Overview of Financial Statements

Accounting is a system for *measuring* the effects, or results, of business activities and *communicating* those measurements to interested users. Previous chapters have explored the types of measurements made to assist managers in making decisions, planning operations, and evaluating performance. Consideration has also been given to the appropriate formats of various managerial accounting reports (for example, income statement in contribution format, performance report in flexible budgeting format). In designing accounting systems for internal, or managerial, uses, considerable flexibility exists in the manner in which business activities are measured and reported.

The results of a firm's business activities must also be reported to individuals and entities outside the firm: owners, creditors, governmental agencies, labor unions, and others. Given this wide variety of users and the various uses made of financial accounting reports, the need exists for some degree of standardization in both measurement methods and reporting formats. This chapter and the next explore the content of the principal financial statements prepared for external users and the techniques used for analyzing and interpreting them. An understanding of the external reporting process will help the manager see how the results of various financing, investment, and operating decisions are communicated to owners, creditors, and others. It should also provide insights as to how the external reporting process itself might be "managed."

This chapter examines the purpose and content of the principal financial statements included in annual reports to owners and other external users. Chapter 18 explores techniques for analyzing these financial statements.

Overview of Business Activities

The financial statements prepared for external users attempt to capture in a meaningful way the results of a firm's business activities. An understanding of these financial statements requires an understanding of the business activities they attempt to portray.

Example Bill Marsh and Janet Nelson, while working on a degree in engineering, developed a computerized mechanism for monitoring automobile engine performance. They received a patent on the device and, having recently graduated, want to set up their own firm to manufacture and sell it. The firm will be called Marnel Corporation.

The firm will need either to construct or to purchase a manufacturing facility. Once the facility is ready for production, the firm will need to purchase raw materials and hire factory workers. It will also need to pursue advertising and other marketing efforts.

Before these purchasing, hiring, and other activities can occur, Marnel Corporation will need funds, or capital. There are two primary sources of capital for a firm: creditors and owners. Creditors provide funds but require that the funds be repaid, usually with interest, at some date in the future. Owners also provide funds. In return, they receive some evidence of their ownership in the firm. When the firm is organized as a corporation, ownership is evidenced by shares of capital stock. Unlike capital provided by creditors, there is generally no requirement that funds provided by owners be repaid at a particular date in the future. The amount of capital to be obtained from creditors versus that to be obtained from owners is a decision faced by all firms. We explore some of the more important factors in such *financing decisions* in Chapter 18.

Once the firm has obtained capital, it must invest it. Some of the capital will be invested in land, buildings, and equipment. Chapters 9 and 10 discussed techniques for making these capital budgeting, or capacity *investment decisions*. Some of the capital will also be invested in raw materials, employee training, and other goods and services required to carry out *operating activities*. A firm's business activities might thus be depicted as comprising three components:

1. Financing activities.
2. Investing activities.
3. Operating activities.

As described for Marnel Corporation, financing activities are concerned with obtaining capital, investing activities are concerned with acquiring particular types of resources with the capital, and operating activities are concerned with using the resources to carry out the firm's principal business activities. Exhibit 17.1 depicts these three dimensions of business activity.

Exhibit 17.1
Overview of Business Activities

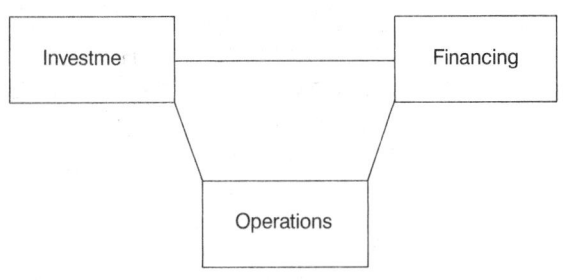

Overview of Principal Financial Statements

Three principal financial statements are included in periodic reports to external users:

1. Statement of financial position, or balance sheet.
2. Income statement.
3. Statement of changes in financial position.

The purpose and content of each of these three financial statements are considered next.

The Balance Sheet—Measuring Financial Position

The statement of financial position, or balance sheet, presents a ''snapshot'' of the resources of a firm (assets) and claims on those resources (liabilities and owners' equity) as of a specific time. Exhibit 17.2 presents a balance sheet for Marnel Corporation as of December 31, Year 1, and December 31, Year 2. The assets portion of the balance sheet reports as of a specific time the effects of all of a firm's past investment decisions. In this case, Marnel Corporation has invested in accounts receivable, merchandise, inventory, land, buildings, and equipment. The equities portion of the balance sheet reports as of a specific time the effects of all of a firm's past financing decisions. Capital has been obtained from both short- and long-term creditors and from owners.

The balance sheet derives its name from the fact that it shows the following balance, or equality:

$$\text{Assets} = \text{Liabilities} + \text{Owners' Equity}.$$

That is, a firm's assets or resources are in balance with, or equal to, the claims on those assets by creditors and owners. The balance sheet views resources from two angles: a listing of the specific forms in which they are held (for example, cash, inventory, equipment), and a listing of the persons or interests that provided the funds to obtain the assets and therefore have claims on them (for example, suppliers, employees, governments, shareholders). Thus, the balance sheet portrays the equality of investing (assets) and financing (equities) activities.

Several important questions must be addressed before the balance sheet can be fully understood:

1. Which resources of a firm are recognized as assets?
2. What valuations are placed on these assets?
3. How are assets classified, or grouped, within the balance sheet?
4. Which claims against a firm's assets are recognized as liabilities?
5. What valuations are placed on these liabilities?
6. How are liabilities classified within the balance sheet?
7. What valuation is placed on the owner's equity in a firm, and how is the owner's equity disclosed?

Exhibit 17.2
MARNEL CORPORTION
Comparative Balance Sheets
for December 31, Year 1 and Year 2

	December 31, Year 1	December 31, Year 2
Assets		
Current Assets		
Cash.	$ 30,000	$ 3,000
Accounts Receivable	20,000	55,000
Merchandise Inventory	40,000	50,000
Total Current Assets	$ 90,000	$108,000
Noncurrent Assets		
Buildings and Equipment (cost)	$100,000	$225,000
Accumulated Depreciation	(30,000)	(40,000)
Total Noncurrent Assets	$ 70,000	$185,000
Total Assets	$160,000	$293,000
Equities		
Current Liabilities		
Accounts Payable—Merchandise		
Suppliers	$ 30,000	$ 50,000
Accounts Payable—Other Suppliers. . .	10,000	12,000
Salaries Payable	5,000	6,000
Total Current Liabilities	$ 45,000	$ 68,000
Noncurrent Liabilities		
Bonds Payable	–0–	100,000
Total Liabilities	$ 45,000	$168,000
Owners' Equity		
Capital Stock ($10 par value)	$100,000	$100,000
Retained Earnings	15,000	25,000
Total Owners' Equity	$115,000	$125,000
Total Equities	$160,000	$293,000

In seeking answers to these questions, we must explore briefly several accounting concepts and conventions that underlie the balance sheet. This discussion not only provides a background for understanding the statement as it is currently prepared, it also permits an assessment of alternative methods of measuring financial position.

Asset Recognition

Assets are resources that have the potential for providing a firm with future economic benefits. That benefit is the ability to generate future cash inflows or to reduce future cash outflows. The resources that are recognized as assets are those (1) for which the firm has acquired rights to their future use as a result of a past transaction or exchange and (2) for which the value of the future benefits can be measured, or quantified, with a reasonable degree of precision.[1]

Example 1 Marnel Corporation sold merchandise and received a note from the customer who agreed to pay $2,000 within 4 months. This note receivable is an asset of Marnel Corporation, because a right has been established to receive a definite amount of cash in the future as a result of the previous sale of merchandise.

Example 2 Marnel Corporation acquired manufacturing equipment costing $40,000 and agreed to pay the seller over 3 years. After the final payment, legal title to the equipment will be transferred to Marnel Corporation. Even though Marnel Corporation does not possess legal title, the equipment is Marnel's asset because it has obtained the rights and responsibilities of ownership and can sustain those rights as long as the payments are made on schedule.

Example 3 Marnel Corporation plans to acquire a fleet of new trucks next year to replace those wearing out. These new trucks are not now assets, because no exchange has taken place between Marnel Corporation and a supplier and, therefore, no right to the future use of the trucks has been established.

Example 4 Marnel Corporation has developed a good reputation with its employees, customers, and citizens of the community. This good reputation is expected to provide benefits to the firm in its future business activities. A good reputation, however, is generally *not* recognized as an asset. Although Marnel Corporation has made various expenditures in the past to develop the reputation, the future benefits are considered to be too difficult to quantify with a sufficient degree of precision to warrant recognition as an asset.

Most of the difficulties in deciding which items to recognize as assets are related to unexecuted or partially executed contracts. In Example 3, suppose that Marnel Corporation entered into a contract with a local truck dealer to acquire the trucks next year at a cash price of $60,000. Marnel Corporation has acquired rights to future benefits, but the contract has not been executed. Unexecuted contracts of this nature are generally not recognized as assets in accounting. Marnel Corportion will recognize an asset for the trucks when they are received next year.

To take the illustration one step further, assume that Marnel Corporation advances the truck dealer $15,000 of the purchase price upon signing the contract. Marnel Corporation has acquired rights to future benefits and has exchanged cash. Current accounting practice treats the $15,000 as an advance on the purchase of equipment and reports it as an asset under a title such as Advances to Suppliers. The trucks would not be shown as assets at this time, however, because Marnel Corporation is not yet deemed to have received sufficient future rights to justify their inclusion in the balance sheet. Similar asset recognition questions arise when a firm leases buildings and equipment for its own use under long-term leases or manufactures custom-design products for particular customers.

---

[1]Financial Accounting Standards Board, *Statement of Financial Accounting Concepts No. 3,* "Elements of Financial Statements of Business Enterprises," 1980, par. 19. See the Glossary for the Board's specific definition at "asset."

Asset Valuation Bases

An amount must be assigned to each asset in the balance sheet. Several methods of computing this amount might be used.

Acquisition or Historical Cost The acquisition, or historical, cost of an asset is the amount of cash payment (or cash equivalent value of other forms of payment) made in acquiring the asset. This amount can generally be found by referring to contracts, invoices, and canceled checks. Because a firm is not compelled to acquire a given asset, it must expect the future benefits from that asset to be at least as large as its acquisition cost. Historical cost, then, is a lower limit on the amount that a firm considered the future benefits of the asset to be worth at the time of acquisition.

Current Replacement Cost Each asset might be shown on the balance sheet at the current cost of replacing it. Current replacement cost is often referred to as an *entry value,* because it represents the amount required currently to acquire, or "enter" into, the rights to receive future benefits from the asset.

For assets purchased frequently, such as merchandise inventory, current replacement cost can often be calculated by consulting suppliers' catalogs or price lists. The replacement cost of assets purchased less frequently, such as land, buildings, and equipment, is more difficult to ascertain. A major obstacle to implementing current replacement cost is the absence of well-organized secondhand markets for many used assets. Ascertaining current replacement cost in these cases requires finding the cost of a similar new asset and then adjusting that amount downward somehow for the services of the asset already used. There may be difficulties, however, in finding a similar asset. With technological improvements and other quality changes, equipment purchased currently will likely be quite different from that acquired 10 years previously but that is still being used. Thus, there may be no similar equipment on the market for which replacement cost can be found. Alternatively, the current replacement cost of an asset capable of rendering equivalent services might be substituted when the replacement cost of the specific asset is not readily available. This approach, however, is also subject to a high degree of subjectivity in the identification of assets with equivalent service potential.

Current Net Realizable Value Net realizable value is the net amount of cash (selling price less selling costs) that the firm would receive currently if it sold each asset separately. This amount is often referred to as an *exit value,* because it reflects the amount obtainable if the firm currently disposed of the asset, or "exited" ownership. In measuring net realizable value, one generally assumes that the asset is sold in an orderly fashion, rather than through a forced sale at some "distress" price.

Measuring net realizable value entails difficulties similar to those in measuring current replacement cost. There may be no well-organized secondhand market for used equipment, particularly when the equipment was specially designed for a single firm's needs. In this case, the current selling price of the asset (value in exchange) may be substantially less than the value of the future benefits to the firm from using the asset (value in use).

Present Value of Future Net Cash Flows Another possible valuation basis is the present value of future net cash flows. An asset is a resource that provides a future benefit. This future benefit is the ability of an asset either to generate future net cash receipts or to reduce future cash expenditures. For example, accounts receivable from customers will lead directly to future cash receipts. Merchandise inventory can be sold for cash or promises to pay cash. Equipment can be used to manufacture products that can then be sold for cash. A building that is owned reduces future cash outflows for rental payments. Because these cash flows represent the future services, or benefits, of assets, they might be used in the valuation of assets. Because cash can be invested to yield interest revenue over time, today's value of a stream of future cash flows, called the *present value,* is worth less than the sum of the cash amounts to be received or saved over time. The balance sheet is to be prepared as of a current date. If future cash flows are to be used to measure an asset's value, the future net cash flows must be ''discounted'' to find their present value as of the date of the balance sheet.

Using discounted cash flows in the valuation of individual assets requires solving several problems. One is the difficulty caused by the uncertainty of the amounts of future cash flows. The amounts to be received can depend on whether or not competitors introduce new products, the rate of inflation, and many other factors. A second problem is allocating the cash receipts from selling a single item of merchandise inventory to all of the assets involved in its production and distribution (for example, equipment, buildings, sales staff's automobiles). A third problem is selecting the appropriate rate to be used in discounting the future cash flows back to the present. Is the interest rate at which the firm could borrow the appropriate one? Or is the rate at which the firm could invest excess cash the one that should be used? Or is the appropriate rate the firm's cost of capital?

Generally Accepted Accounting Asset Valuation Bases The financial statements currently prepared by publicly held firms for external users are based on one of two valuation bases: one for monetary assets and one for nonmonetary assets.

Monetary assets, such as cash and accounts receivable, are generally shown on the balance sheet at their net present value—their current cash, or cash equivalent, value. Cash is stated at the amount of cash on hand or in the bank. Accounts receivable from customers are stated at the amount of cash expected to be collected in the future. If the period of time until a receivable is to be collected spans more than 1 year, then the expected future cash receipt is discounted to a present value. Most accounts receivable, however, are collected within 1 to 3 months. The amount of future cash flows is approximately equal to the present value of these flows, and the discounting process is ignored.

Nonmonetary assets, such as merchandise inventory, land, buildings, and equipment, are stated at acquisition cost, in some cases adjusted downward for depreciation reflecting the services of the assets that have been consumed.

The acquisition cost of an asset may include more than its invoice price. Cost includes all expenditures made or obligations incurred in order to put the asset into usable condition. Transportation cost, costs of installation, handling charges, and any other necessary and reasonable costs incurred in connection with the asset up to the time it is put into service should be considered as part of the total cost assigned to the asset. For example, the cost of an item of equipment might be calculated as follows:

Invoice Price of Equipment.	$12,000
Less: 2 Percent Discount for Prompt Cash Payment.	240
Net Invoice Price	$11,760
Transportation Cost	326
Installation Costs	735
Total Cost of Equipment	$12,821

The acquisition cost of this equipment to be recorded in the accounting records is $12,821.

Instead of disbursing cash or incurring a liability, other forms of consideration (for example, common stock, merchandise inventory, land) may be given in acquiring an asset. In these cases, acquisition cost is measured by the market value of the consideration given or the market value of the asset received, depending on which market value is more reliably measured.

Accounting's use of acquisition cost valuations for nonmonetary assets rests on three important concepts or conventions. First, a firm is assumed to be a *going concern*. That is, it is assumed that the firm will remain in operation long enough for all of its current plans to be carried out. Any increases in the market value of assets held will be realized in the normal course of business when the firm receives higher prices for its products. Current values of the individual assets are therefore assumed to be largely unimportant. Second, acquisition cost valuations are considered to be more objective than those obtained from using the other valuation methods. *Objectivity* in accounting refers to the ability of several independent measurers to come to the same conclusion about the valuation of an asset. It is relatively easy to obtain consensus on what constitutes the acquisition cost of an asset. Differences among measurers can arise in ascertaining an asset's current replacement cost, current net realizable value, or present value of future cash flows. A reasonable degree of consensus is necessary if financial statements are to be subject to audits by independent accountants. Third, acquisition cost generally provides more conservative valuations of assets (and measures of earnings) relative to the other valuation methods. Many accountants feel that the possibility of misleading financial statement users will be minimized when assets are stated at lower rather than higher amounts. Thus, *conservatism* has evolved as a convention to justify acquisition cost valuations.

The preceding description of generally accepted valuation bases does not justify them. Which basis—the acquisition cost, current replacement cost, current net realizable value, or present value of future cash flows of a firm's assets—is most relevant to investors' decisions is an empirical question for which a definitive answer has not yet been provided. Most publicly held firms are required to provide supplementary information on the current cost of their inventories, property, plant, and equipment. The required disclosure of such information is, to some extent, a response to the recognized deficiencies of historical cost valuations during periods of inflation.

Asset Classification

The classification of assets within the balance sheet varies widely in published annual reports. The principle asset categories are described below.

Current Assets The term *current assets* designates "cash and other assets or resources commonly identified as those which are reasonably expected to be realized in cash or sold or consumed during the normal operating cycle of the business."[2] The operating cycle refers to the period of time that elapses for a given firm during which cash is converted into salable goods and services, goods and services are sold to customers, and customers pay for their purchases with cash. Included in current assets are cash, marketable securities held for the short term, accounts and notes receivable net of allowance for uncollectible accounts, inventories of merchandise, raw materials, supplies, work in process, and finished goods and prepaid operating costs (for example, prepaid insurance, and prepaid rent). Prepaid costs, or prepayments, are current assets to the extent that if they were not paid in advance, current assets would be required within the next operating cycle to acquire those services.

Investments A second section of the balance sheet, labeled "Investments," includes long-term investments in securities of other firms. For example, a firm might purchase shares of common stock of a supplier to help assure continued availability of raw materials. Or shares of common stock of a firm in another area of business activity might be acquired to permit the acquiring firm to diversify its operations. When one corporation (the parent) owns more than 50 percent of the voting stock in another corporation (the subsidiary), a single set of "consolidated" financial statements is usually prepared. That is, the specific assets, liabilities, revenues, and expenses of the subsidiary are merged, or consolidated, with those of the parent corporation. The securities shown in the Investments section of the balance sheet are therefore investments in firms whose assets and liabilities have *not* been consolidated with the parent or investor firm.

Property, Plant, and Equipment Property, plant, and equipment (sometimes called *plant assets* or *fixed assets*) designates the tangible, long-lived assets used in a firm's operations over a period of years and generally not acquired for resale. This category includes land, buildings, machinery, automobiles, furniture, fixtures, computers, and other equipment. The amount shown on the balance sheet for each of these items (except land) is acquisition cost less accumulated depreciation since the asset was acquired. Frequently, only the net balance, or book value, is disclosed on the balance sheet. Land is presented at acquisition cost.

Intangible Assets Intangible assets include such items as patents, trademarks, franchises, and goodwill. The expenditures made by the firm in developing intan-

---

[2]Committee on Accounting Research, *Accounting Research Bulletin No. 43*, 1953, chap. 3.A.

gible assets are usually not recognized as assets, because of the difficulty of ascertaining the existence and amount of future benefits. Only when intangible assets
are acquired from other entities are they reorganized as assets.[3]

Liability Recognition

A liability represents a firm's obligation to make payment of cash, goods, or
services in a reasonably definite amount at a reasonably definite future time for
benefits or services received currently or in the past.[4]

Example 1 Marnel Corporation purchased merchandise inventory and agreed to
pay the supplier $8,000 within 30 days. This obligation is a liability, because
Marnel Corporation has received the goods and must pay a definite amount at a
reasonably definite future time.

Example 2 Marnel Corporation borrowed $4 million by issuing long-term bonds.
Annual interest payments of 10 percent must be made on December 31 of each
year, and the $4 million principal must be repaid in 20 years. This obligation is a
liability, because Marnel Corporation has received the cash and must repay the
debt in a definite amount at a definite future time.

Example 3 Marnel Corporation provides a 3-year warranty on its products. The
obligation to maintain the products under warranty plans creates a liability. The
selling price for its products implicitly includes a charge for future warranty services.
As customers pay the selling price, Marnel Corporation receives a benefit (that is,
the cash received). Past experience provides a basis for estimating the proportion
of customers who will seek services under the warranty agreement and the expected
cost of providing warranty services. Thus, the amount of obligation can be estimated with a reasonable degree of accuracy, and it is shown as a liability.

Example 4 Marnel Corporation has signed an agreement with its employees' labor
union, promising to increase wages 6 percent and to provide for medical and life
insurance. This agreement does not immediately create a liability, because services
have not yet been received from employees that would require any payments for
wages and insurance. As labor services are received, a liability will arise.

The most troublesome questions of liability recognition relate to unexecuted
contracts. The labor union agreement in Example 4 is an unexecuted contract.
Other examples include leases, pension agreements, and purchase order commitments. Whether or not unexecuted contracts should be recognized as liabilities has
been and continues to be controversial.

---

[3]Financial Accounting Standards Board, *Statement of Financial Accounting Standards
No. 2*, ''Accounting for Research and Development Costs,'' 1974.

[4]Financial Accounting Standards Board, *Statement of Financial Accounting Concepts
No. 3*, par. 28. See the Glossary for the Board's specific definition at ''liability.''

Liability Valuation

Most liabilities are monetary, requiring payments of specific amounts of cash. Those due within 1 year or less are stated at the amount of cash expected to be paid to discharge the obligation. If the payment dates extend more than 1 year into the future (for example, as in the case of the bonds in Example 2), the liability is stated at the present value of the future cash outflows.

A liability that requires delivering goods or rendering services, rather than paying cash, is nonmonetary. For example, magazine publishers typically collect cash for subscriptions, promising delivery of magazines over many months. Cash is received currently, whereas the obligation under the subscription is discharged by delivering magazines in the future. Theaters and football teams receive cash for season tickets and in return incur an obligation to admit the ticket holder to future performances. Landlords receive cash in advance and are obligated to let the tenant use the property. Such nonmonetary obligations are included among liabilities. They are stated, however, at the amount of cash received rather than at the expected cost of publishing the magazines or of providing the theatrical or sporting entertainment. The title frequently used for liabilities of this type is Advances from Customers.

Liability Classification

Liabilities in the balance sheet are typically classified in one of the following categories.

Current Liabilities The term *current liabilities* ''is used principally to designate obligations whose liquidation is reasonably expected to require the use of existing resources properly classified as current assets, or the creation of other current liabilities.''[5] Included in this category are liabilities to merchandise suppliers, employees, and governmental units. Notes and bonds payable are also included to the extent that they require the use of current assets within a relatively short period of time, typically during the next 12 months.

Long-Term Debt Obligations having due dates, or maturities, more than 1 year after the balance sheet date are generally classified as long-term debt. Included are bonds, mortgages, and similar debts, as well as some obligations under long-term leases.

Other Long-Term Liabilities Obligations not properly considered as current liabilities or long-term debt are classified as *other long-term liabilities* or *indeterminate-term liabilities*. Included are such items as deferred income taxes and some deferred compensation obligations.

---

[5]Committee on Accounting Procedure, *Accounting Research Bulletin No. 43*, chap. 3.A.

Owners' Equity Valuation and Disclosure

The owners' equity in a firm is a residual interest.[6] That is, the owners have a claim on all assets not required to meet the claims of creditors.[7] The valuation of the assets and liabilities included in the balance sheet therefore determines the valuation of total owners' equity.

The remaining question concerns the manner of disclosing this total owners' equity. Accounting draws a distinction between contributed capital and earnings retained by a firm. The balance sheet for a corporation generally separates the amounts contributed directly by shareholders for an interest in the firm (that is, capital stock) from the subsequent earnings realized by the firm in excess of dividends declared (that is, retained earnings).

In addition, the amount received from shareholders is usually further disaggregated into the *par* or *stated value* of the shares and *amounts contributed in excess of par value or stated value*. The par or stated value of a share of stock is a somewhat arbitrary amount assigned to comply with the corporation laws of each state, and will rarely equal the market price of the shares at the time they are issued. As a result, the distinction between par or stated value and amounts contributed in excess of par or stated value is of questionable informational value, but is typically shown nonetheless.

Example 1 Stephens Corporation was formed on January 1, Year 1. It issued 15,000 shares of $10 par value common stock for $10 cash per share. During Year 1, Stephens Corporation had net income of $30,000 and paid dividends of $10,000 to shareholders. The shareholders' equity section of the balance sheet of Stephens Corporation on December 31, Year 1, is as follows:

Common Stock (par value of $10 per share, 15,000 shares issued and outstanding)	$150,000
Retained Earnings	20,000
Total Shareholders' Equity	$170,000

Example 2 Instead of issuing $10 par value common stock as in Example 1, assume that Stephens Corporation issued 15,000 shares of $1 par value common stock for $10 cash per share. (The market price of a share of common stock depends on the economic value of the firm and not on the par value of the shares.) The shareholders' equity section of the balance sheet of Stephens Corporation on December 31, Year 1, is as follows:

Common Stock (par value of $1 per share, 15,000 shares issued and outstanding)	$ 15,000
Capital Contributed in Excess of Par Value	135,000
Retained Earnings	20,000
Total Shareholders' Equity	$170,000

---

[6]Although owners' equity is equal to assets minus liabilities, accounting provides an independent method for computing the amount. This method is discussed in financial accounting texts.

[7]Financial Accounting Standards Board, *Statement of Financial Accounting Concepts No. 3,* par. 43. See the Glossary for the Board's specific definition at "owners' equity."

Balance Sheet Account Titles

The following list shows balance sheet account titles that are commonly used. The descriptions should help in your understanding the nature of various assets, liabilities, and owners' equities. Alternative account titles can be easily devised. The list does not show all the account titles used in this book or appearing in the financial statements of publicly held firms.

Assets

Cash on Hand. Coins and currency, and such items as bank checks and money orders. The latter items are merely claims against individuals or institutions, but by custom are called "cash."

Cash in Bank. Strictly speaking, merely a claim against the bank for the amount deposited. Cash in bank consists of demand deposits, against which checks can be drawn, and time deposits, usually savings accounts and certificates of deposit. In published statements, the two items of Cash on Hand and Cash in Bank usually are combined under the title *Cash.*

Marketable Securities. Government bonds, or stocks and bonds of corporations, which the firm plans to hold for a relatively short period of time. The word *marketable* implies that they can be bought and sold readily through a security exchange such as the New York Stock Exchange.

Accounts Receivable. Amounts due from customers of a business from the sale of goods or services. The collection of cash occurs some time after the sale. These accounts are also known as "charge accounts" or "open accounts." The general term Accounts Receivable is used in financial statements to describe the figure representing the total amount receivable from all customers but, of course, the firm keeps a separate record for each customer.

Notes Receivable. Amounts due from customers or from others to whom loans have been made or credit extended, when the claim has been put into writing in the form of a promissory note.

Interest Receivable. Interest on assets such as promissory notes or bonds that has accrued, or come into existence, through the passing of time but that has not been collected as of the date of the balance sheet.

Merchandise Inventory. Goods on hand that have been purchased for resale, such as canned goods on the shelves of a grocery store or suits on the racks of a clothing store.

Finished Goods Inventory. Completed but unsold manufactured products.

Work-in-Process Inventory. Partially completed manufactured products.

Direct Materials Inventory. Unused materials from which manufactured products are to be made. Also called *Raw Materials Inventory.*

Supplies Inventory. Lubricants, cleaning rags, abrasives, and other incidental materials used in manufacturing operations; stationery, computer disks, pens, and other office supplies; bags, twine, boxes, and other store supplies; gasoline, oil, spare parts, and other delivery supplies. Alternative titles, such as *Factory Supplies, Office Supplies, Store Supplies,* and *Delivery Supplies,* could be used.

Prepaid Insurance. Insurance premiums paid for future coverage.

Prepaid Rent. Rent paid in advance for futher use of land, buildings, or equipment.

Advances to Suppliers. The general name used to indicate payments made in advance for goods to be received at a later date. If no cash is paid by a firm when it places an order, no asset is recognized.

Investment in Securities. The cost of shares of stock in other companies, where the firm's purpose is to hold the shares for relatively long periods of time.

Land. Land occupied by buildings or used in operations.

Buildings. Factory buildings, store buildings, garages, warehouses, and so forth.

Equipment. Lathes, ovens, tools, boilers, computers, motors, bins, cranes, conveyors, automobiles, and so forth.

Furniture and Fixtures. Desks, tables, chairs, counters, showcases, scales, and other such store and office equipment.

Accumulated Depreciation. This account shows the cumulative amount of the cost of long-term assets (such as buildings and equipment) that has been allocated to prior periods in measuring net income or to the costs of production. The amount in this account is subtracted from the acquisition cost of the long-term asset to which it relates in ascertaining the *net book value* of the asset to be shown in the balance sheet.

Leasehold. The right to use property owned by someone else.

Organization Costs. Amounts paid for legal and incorporation fees, for printing the certificates for shares of stock, and for accounting and any other costs incurred in organizing the business so it can begin to function. This asset is seen most commonly on the balance sheets of corporations.

Patents. A right granted for up to 17 years by the federal government to exclude others from manufacturing, using, or selling a certain process or device. Under current generally accepted accounting principles, research and development costs must be treated as an expense in the year incurred rather than being recognized as an asset with future benefits.[8] (This treatment seems to us to be at odds with good accounting theory.) As a result, a firm that develops a patent will not normally show it as an asset. On the other hand, a firm that purchases a patent from another firm or from an individual will recognize the patent as an asset.

Goodwill. An amount paid by one firm in acquiring another business enterprise that is greater than the sum of the values assignable to individual, identifiable

---

[8]Financial Accounting Standards Board, *Statement of Financial Accounting Standards No. 2.*

assets. A good reputation and other desirable attributes are generally not recognized as assets by the firm that creates or develops them. However, when one firm acquires another firm, these desirable attributes are indirectly recognized as assets, because they are a factor in the measurement of goodwill.

Liabilities

Accounts Payable. Amounts owed for goods or services acquired under an informal credit agreement. These accounts are usually payable within 1 or 2 months. The same items appear as Accounts Receivable on the creditor's books.

Notes Payable. The face amount of promissory notes given in connection with loans from the bank or the purchase of goods or services. The same items appear as Notes Receivable on the creditor's books.

Payroll Taxes Payable. Amounts withheld from wages and salaries of employees for federal and state payroll taxes that have not yet been remitted to tax authorities as well as the employer's share of such taxes.

Withheld Income Taxes. Amounts withheld from wages and salaries of employees for income taxes that have not yet been remitted to the taxing authority. This is a tentative income tax on the earnings of employees, and the employer acts merely as a tax-collecting agent for the federal and state governments. A few cities also levy income taxes, which the employer must withhold from wages.

Interest Payable. Interest on obligations that has accrued or accumulated with the passage of time but that has not been paid as of the date of the balance sheet. The liability for interest is customarily shown separately from the face amount of the obligation.

Income Taxes Payable. The estimated liability for income taxes, accumulated and unpaid, based on the taxable income of the business from the beginning of the taxable year to the date of the balance sheet.

Advances from Customers. The general name used to indicate payments received in advance for goods to be delivered or services to be furnished to customers in the future; a nonmonetary liability. If no cash is received when a customer places an order, no liability is shown.

Rent Received in Advance. Another example of a nonmonetary liability. The business owns a building that it rents to a tenant. The tenant has prepaid the rental charge for several months in advance. The amount applicable to future months cannot be considered a component of income until the rent is earned as service is rendered with the passage of time. Meanwhile, the advance payment results in a liability payable in services (that is, in the use of the building). On the records of the tenant, the same amount would appear as an asset, Prepaid Rent.

Mortgage Payable. Long-term promissory notes that have been given greater protection by the pledge of specific pieces of property as a security for their payment. If the loan or interest is not paid according to the agreement, the property can be sold for the benefit of the creditor.

Bonds Payable. Amounts borrowed by the business for a relatively long period of time under a formal written contract or indenture. The loan is usually obtained from a number of lenders, each of whom receives one or more bond certificates as written evidence of his or her share of the loan.

Debenture Bonds. The most common type of bond, except in the railroad and public utility industries. This type of bond carries no specific security or collateral; instead it is issued on the basis of the general credit of the business. If other bonds have a prior claim on the assets of the business, then the debenture is called *subordinated*.

Convertible Bonds. A bond that the holder can *convert* into or ''trade in'' for shares of common stock. The number of shares to be received when the bond is converted into stock, the dates when conversion can occur, and other details are specified in the bond indenture.

Capitalized Lease Obligations. The present value of future commitments for cash payments to be made in return for the right to use property owned by someone else.

Deferred Income Taxes. Certain income tax payments are delayed beyond the current accounting period.

Owners' Equity

Common Stock. Amounts received for the par value of a firm's principal class of voting stock.

Preferred Stock. Amounts received for the par value of a class of a firm's stock that has some preference relative to the common stock. This preference is usually with respect to dividends and to assets in the event the corporation is liquidated. Sometimes preferred stock is convertible into common stock.

Capital Contributed in Excess of Par or Stated Value. Amounts received from the issuance of common or preferred stock in excess of such shares' par value or stated value. This account is also referred to as *Additional Paid-in Capital* or sometimes as *Premium on Preferred* (or *Common*) *Stock*.

Retained Earnings. An account reflecting the increase in net assets since the business was organized as a result of generating earnings in excess of dividend declarations. When dividends are declared, net assets are decreased, and retained earnings are reduced by an equal amount.

Treasury Shares. This account shows the cost of shares of stock originally issued but subsequently reacquired by the corporation. Treasury shares are not entitled to dividends and are not considered to be ''outstanding'' shares. The cost of treasury shares is almost always shown on the balance sheet as a deduction from the total of the other shareholders' equity accounts.

Summary of Balance Sheet Concepts

The balance sheet, or statement of financial position, comprises three major classes of items—assets, liabilities, and owners' equity.

Resources are recognized as assets when a firm has acquired rights to their future use as a result of a past transaction or exchange and when the value of the future benefits can be measured with a reasonable degree of precision. Monetary assets are, in general, stated at their current cash, or cash equivalent, values. Nonmonetary assets are stated at acquisition cost, in some cases adjusted downward for the cost of services that have been consumed.

Liabilities represent obligations of a firm to make payments of a reasonably definite amount at a reasonably definite future time for benefits already received. Owners' equity is the difference between total assets and total liabilities and, for corporations, is typically segregated into contributed capital and retained earnings.

The Income Statement—Measuring Operating Performance

The total assets of a firm may change over time because of financing and investment activities. For example, common stock may be issued for cash, a building may be acquired and a mortgage assumed for part or all of the purchase price, or holders of convertible bonds may exchange them for shares of common stock. These financing and investment activities affect the amount and structure of a firm's assets and equities.

The total assets of a firm may also change over time because of operating activities. Goods or services are sold to customers for an amount that is hoped to be larger than the cost to the firm of acquiring or producing the goods and services. Capital is provided to a firm by creditors and owners with the expectation that the capital will be used by the firm to generate a profit and provide an adequate return to the suppliers of the capital. The second principal financial statement, the income statement, provides information about the operating performance of a firm for some particular period of time.

Exhibit 17.3 presents an income statement for Marnel Corporation for Year 2. Net income is equal to revenues minus expenses. Revenues measure the inflows of net assets (assets less liabilities) from selling goods and providing services. Expenses measure the outflows of net assets that are used up, or consumed, in the process of generating revenues. As a measure of operating performance, revenues reflect the services rendered by the firm, and expenses indicate the efforts required or expended.

The Accounting Basis for Measuring Performance

Some operating activities are both started and completed within a given accounting period. For example, merchandise might be purchased from a supplier, sold to a customer on account, and the account collected in cash, all within a particular accounting period. Few difficulties are encountered in measuring performance in these cases. The difference between the cash received from customers and the cash disbursed to acquire, sell, and deliver the merchandise represents net income from this series of transactions.

Exhibit 17.3
MARNEL CORPORTION
Income Statement
for Year 2

Sales Revenue	$125,000
Less Expenses:	
Cost of Goods Sold	$ 60,000
Salaries	19,667
Depreciation	10,000
Interest	2,000
Income Taxes	13,333
Total Expenses.	$105,000
Net Income	$ 20,000

Many operating activities, however, are started in one accounting period and completed in another. Buildings and equipment are acquired in one period but used over a period of several years. Merchandise is sometimes purchased in one accounting period, sold during the next period, with cash collected from customers during a third period. A significant problem in measuring performance for a specific accounting period is measuring the amount of revenues and expenses from operating activities that are in process as of the beginning of the period or are incomplete as of the end of the period. Two approaches to measuring operating performance are (1) the cash basis of accounting and (2) the accrual basis of accounting.

Cash Basis of Accounting Under the *cash basis of accounting,* revenues from selling goods and providing services are recognized in the period when cash is received from customers. Expenses are typically reported in the period in which expenditures are made for merchandise, salaries, insurance, taxes, and similar items. To illustrate the measurement of performance under the cash basis of accounting, consider the following example.

Donald and Joanne Allens open a hardware store on January 1, Year 1. They contribute $20,000 in cash and borrow $12,000 from a local bank. The loan is repayable on June 30, Year 1, with interest charged at the rate of 12 percent per year. A store building is rented on January 1, and 2 months' rent of $4,000 is paid in advance. The premium of $2,400 for property and liability insurance coverage for the year ending December 31, Year 1, is paid on January 1. During January, merchandise costing $40,000 is acquired, of which $26,000 is purchased for cash and $14,000 is purchased on account. Sales to customers during January total $50,000, of which $34,000 is sold for cash and $16,000 is sold on account. The acquisition cost of the merchandise sold during January is $32,000, and various employees are paid $5,000 in salaries.

Exhibit 17.4 presents a performance report for Allen's Hardware Store for the month of January Year 1, using the cash basis. Cash receipts from sales of merchandise of $34,000 represent the portion of the total sales of $50,000 made during January that was collected in cash. Whereas merchandise costing $40,000 was acquired during January, only $26,000 cash was disbursed to suppliers, and only this amount is subtracted in measuring performance under the cash basis. Cash

Exhibit 17.4
ALLENS' HARDWARE STORE
Performance Measurement on a Cash Basis
for the Month of January Year 1

Cash Receipts from Sales of Merchandise		$34,000
Less Cash Expenditures for Merchandise and Services:		
Merchandise	$26,000	
Salaries.	5,000	
Rental	4,000	
Insurance	2,400	
Total Cash Expenditures		37,400
Excess of Cash Expenditures over Cash Receipts		($ 3,400)

expenditures during January for salaries, rent, and insurance are also subtracted in measuring performance, without regard to whether or not the services acquired were fully consumed by the end of the month. Cash expenditures made for merchandise and services exceeded receipts from customers during January by $3,400.[9]

As a basis for measuring performance for a particular accounting period (for example, January Year 1 for Allens' Hardware Store), the cash basis of accounting is subject to two related criticisms. First, the cost of the efforts required in generating revenues is not adequately matched with those revenues. Performance of one period therefore gets mingled with the performance of preceding and succeeding periods. The store rental payment of $4,000 provides rental services for both January and February, but under the cash basis, the full amount is subtracted in measuring performance during January. Likewise, the annual insurance premium provides coverage for the full year, whereas under the cash basis of accounting, none of this insurance cost will be subtracted in measuring performance during the months of February through December.

The longer the period over which future benefits are received, the more serious is this criticism of the cash basis of accounting. Consider, for example, the investments of a capital-intensive firm in buildings and equipment that might be used for 10, 20, or more years. The length of time between the purchase of these assets and the collection of cash for goods produced and sold can span many years.

A second, and probably less serious, criticism of the cash basis of accounting is that it postpones unnecessarily the time when revenue is recognized. In most cases, the sale (delivery) of goods or rendering of services is the critical event in generating revenue. Collecting cash is relatively routine, or at least highly predictable. In these cases, recognizing revenue at the time of cash collection may result in reporting the effects of operating activities one or more periods after the critical revenue-generating activity has occurred. For example, sales to customers during January by Allens' Hardware Store totaled $50,000. Under the cash basis

---

[9]Note that, under the cash method, cash receipts and disbursements from financing and investment activities are not included in the performance report. Only those cash receipts and disbursements from the firm's operating activities are included.

Exhibit 17.5
ALLENS' HARDWARE STORE
Income Statement
for the Month of January Year 1
(accrual basis of accounting)

Sales Revenue		$50,000
Less Expenses:		
Cost of Goods Sold	$32,000	
Salaries Expense	5,000	
Rent Expense	2,000	
Insurance Expense	200	
Interest Expense	120	
Total Expenses		39,320
Net Income		$10,680

of accounting, $16,000 of this amount will not be recognized until February or later, when the cash is collected. If the credit standings of customers have been checked prior to making sales on account, it is highly probable that cash will be collected, and there is little reason to postpone recognition of the revenue.

The cash basis of accounting is used principally by lawyers, accountants, and other professional people. These professionals have relatively small investments in multiperiod assets, such as buildings and equipment, and usually collect cash from their clients soon after services are rendered. Most such firms actually use a *modified cash basis of accounting*, under which the costs of buildings, equipment, and similar items are treated as assets when purchased. A portion of the acquisition cost is then recognized as an expense when services of these assets are consumed. Except for the treatment of these long-lived assets, revenues are recognized at the time cash is received and expenses are reported when cash disbursements are made.

Most individuals use the cash basis of accounting for the purpose of computing personal income and personal income taxes. Where inventories are an important factor in generating revenues, such as for a merchandising or manufacturing firm, the Internal Revenue Code prohibits a firm from using the cash basis of accounting in its income tax returns.

Accrual Basis of Accounting Under the *accrual basis of accounting*, revenue is recognized when some critical event or transaction occurs that is related to the earnings process. In most cases, this critical event is the sale (delivery) of goods or the rendering of services. Under the accrual basis of accounting, costs incurred are reported as expenses in the period when the revenues which they helped produce are recognized. Thus, an attempt is made to *match* expenses with associated revenues. When particular types of costs incurred cannot be closely identified with specific revenue streams, they are treated as expenses of the period in which services of an asset are consumed or future benefits of an asset disappear.

Exhibit 17.5 presents an income statement for Allens' Hardware Store for January Year 1, using the accrual basis of accounting. The entire $50,000 of sales during January is recognized as revenue, even though cash in that amount has not yet been received. Because of the high probability that outstanding accounts receivable will be collected, the critical revenue-generating event is the sale of the goods rather than the collection of cash from customers. The acquisition cost of the merchandise sold during January is $32,000. Recognizing this amount as cost-of-goods-sold expense leads to an appropriate matching of sales revenue and merchandise expense in the income statement. Of the advance rental payment of $4,000, only $2,000 applies to the cost of services consumed during January. The remaining rental of $2,000 applies to the month of February. Likewise, only $200 of the $2,400 insurance premium represents coverage used up during January. The remaining $2,200 of the insurance premium provides coverage for February through December and will be recognized as an expense during those months. The interest expense of $120 represents 1 month's interest on the $12,000 bank loan at an annual rate of 12 percent $(= \$12,000 \times .12 \times \frac{1}{12})$. Although the interest will not be paid until the loan becomes due on June 30, Year 1, the firm benefited from having the funds available for its use during January; an appropriate portion of the total interest cost on the loans should therefore be recognized as a January expense. The salaries, rental, insurance, and interest expenses, unlike the cost of merchandise sold, cannot be associated directly with revenues recognized during the period. These costs are therefore reported as expenses of January to the extent that services were consumed during the month.

The accrual basis of accounting provides a better measure of earnings performance for Allens' Hardware Store for the month of January than does the cash basis for two reasons:

1. Revenues are measured in a more meaningful way.
2. Expenses are associated more closely with reported revenues.

Likewise, the accrual basis will provide a superior measure of performance for future periods, because activities of those periods will be charged with their share of the costs of rental, insurance, and other services to be consumed. Thus, the accrual basis focuses on the *use* of assets in operations rather than on their financing (that is, the receipt and expenditure of cash).

Most business firms, particularly those involved in merchandising and manufacturing activities, use the accrual basis of accounting. The next section examines in greater depth the measurement principles of accrual accounting.

Measurement Principles of Accrual Accounting

In recognizing revenues and expenses under the accrual basis of accounting, we are concerned with when revenues and expenses are recognized (timing questions) and how much is recognized or reported (measurement questions).

Timing of Revenue Recognition The earnings process for the acquisition and sale of merchandise might be depicted as shown in Exhibit 17.6. Revenue could conceivably be recognized at the time of purchase, sale, or cash collection, at some point(s) between these events, or even continuously. To answer the timing question, we must have a set of criteria for revenue recognition.

Exhibit 17.6
Earnings Process for the Acquisition and Sale of Merchandise

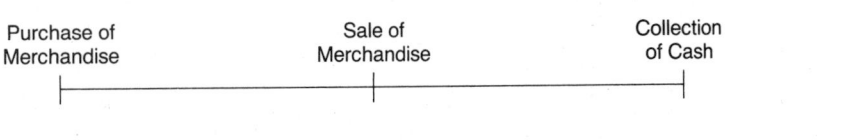

Criteria for Revenue Recognition The criteria currently required to be met before revenue is recognized under the accrual basis of accounting are as follows:

1. All, or a substantial portion, of the services to be provided have been performed.
2. Cash, a receivable, or some other asset susceptible to reasonably precise measurement has been received.

For the vast majority of firms involved in selling goods and services, revenue is recognized at the time of sale (delivery). This method of recognizing revenues is called the *completed sale,* or in some contexts the *completed contract,* method of revenue recognition. The goods have been transferred to the buyer or the services have been performed. Future services, such as for warranties, are likely to be insignificant, or if significant, can be estimated with reasonable precision. An exchange between an independent buyer and seller has occurred that provides an objective measure of the amount of revenue. If the sale is made on account, past experience and an assessment of customers' credit standings provide a basis for predicting the amount of cash that will be collected. The sale of the goods or services is therefore the critical revenue-generating event. Under the accrual basis of accounting, revenue is typically recognized at the time of sale.

Measurement of Revenue The amount of revenue recognized is generally measured by the cash or cash equivalent value of other assets received from customers. As a starting point, this amount is the agreed-upon price between buyer and seller at the time of sale. Some adjustments to this amount may be necessary, however, if revenue is recognized in a period prior to the collection of cash.

Uncollectible Accounts If some portion of the sales for a period is not expected to be collected, the amount of revenue recognized for that period must be adjusted for estimated uncollectible accounts arising from those sales. Logic suggests that this adjustment of revenue should occur in the period when revenue is recognized and not in a later period when specific customers' accounts are found to be uncollectible. If the adjustment is postponed, reported income of subsequent periods will be affected by earlier decisions to extend credit to customers. Thus, the performance of the firm for both the period of sale and the period when the account is judged uncollectible would be measured inaccurately.

Sales Discounts and Allowances Customers may take advantage of discounts for prompt payment, or allowances may be granted for unsatisfactory merchandise. In these cases, the amount of cash eventually to be received can be expected to be less than the stated selling price. Appropriate reductions should therefore be made at the time of sale in measuring the amount of revenue to be recognized.

Delayed Payments If the period between the sale of the goods or services and the time of cash collection extends over several years and there is no provision for explicit interest payments, it is likely that the selling price includes an interest charge for the right to delay payment. Under the accrual basis of accounting, this interest element should be recognized as interest revenue during the periods between sale and collection when the loan is outstanding. To recognize all potential revenue entirely in the period of sale would be to recognize too soon the return for services rendered over time in lending money. Thus, when cash collection is to be delayed, the measure of revenue for the current period should be the selling price reduced to account for interest during future periods. Only the *present value* at the time of sale of the amount to be received should be recognized as revenue during the period of sale. For most accounts receivable, the period between sale and collection spans only 2 to 3 months. The interest element is likely to be relatively insignificant in these cases. As a result, in accounting practice no reduction for interest on delayed payments is made for receivables to be collected within 1 year or less. This procedure is a practical expedient rather than a strict following of the underlying accounting theory.

Timing of Expense Recognition Assets provide future benefits to the firm. *Expenses* are a measurement of the assets consumed in generating revenue. Assets are *unexpired costs* and expenses are *expired costs* or "gone assets." Our attention focuses on *when* the asset expiration takes place. The critical question is "When have asset benefits expired—leaving the balance sheet—and become expenses—entering the income statement as reductions in owners' equity?" Thus:

Balance Sheet	**Income Statement**
Assets or Unexpired Costs ⟶	Expenses or Expired Costs.

Expense Recognition Criteria The criteria used in accrual accounting are these:

1. Asset expirations directly associated with particular types of revenue are expenses in the period in which the revenues are recognized. This treatment is called the *matching convention,* because cost expirations are matched with revenues.
2. Asset expirations not associated with revenues are expenses of the period in which services are consumed in operations.

Product Costs The cost of goods or merchandise sold is perhaps the easiest expense to associate with revenue. At the time of sale, the asset physically changes hands. Revenue is recognized, and the cost of the merchandise transferred is treated as an expense.

A *merchandising firm* purchases inventory and later sells it without changing its physical form. The inventory is shown as an asset stated at acquisition cost on the balance sheet. Later, when the inventory is sold, the same amount of acquisition cost is shown as an expense (cost of goods sold) on the income statement.

A *manufacturing firm,* on the other hand, incurs various costs in changing the physical form of the goods it produces. These costs are typically of three types: (1) direct material, (2) direct labor, and (3) manufacturing overhead (sometimes called indirect manufacturing costs). Direct material and direct labor costs can be associated directly with particular products manufactured. Manufacturing overhead includes a mixture of costs that provide a firm with a capacity to produce. Examples of manufacturing overhead costs are expenditures for utilities, property taxes, and insurance on the factory, as well as depreciation on manufacturing plant and equipment. The services of each of these items are used up, or consumed, during the period while the firm is creating new assets—the inventory of goods being worked on or held for sale. Benefits from direct material, direct labor, and manufacturing overhead are, in a sense, transferred to, or become embodied in, the asset represented by units of inventory. Because the inventory items are assets until sales are made to customers, the various direct material, direct labor, and manufacturing overhead costs incurred in producing the goods are included in the manufacturing inventory under the titles Work-in-Process Inventory and Finished Goods Inventory. Such costs, which are assets transformed from one form to another, are called *product costs.* Product costs are assets; they become expenses only when the goods in which they are embodied are sold.

Selling Costs In most cases, the costs incurred in selling, or marketing, a firm's products relate to the units sold during the period. For example, salaries and commissions of the sales staff, sales literature used, and most advertising costs are incurred in generating revenue currently. Because these selling costs are associated with the revenues of the period, they are reported as expenses in the period when the services provided by these costs are used. It can be argued that some selling costs, such as advertising and other sales promotion, provide future period benefits for a firm and should continue to be treated as assets. However, distinguishing what portion of the cost relates to the current period to be recognized as an expense and what portion relates to future periods to be treated as an asset can be extremely difficult. Therefore, accountants typically treat selling and other marketing activity costs as expenses of the period when the services are used. These selling costs are treated as *period expenses* rather than as assets, even though they may enhance the future marketability of a firm's products.

Administrative Costs The costs incurred in administering, or directing, the activities of a firm cannot be closely associated with units produced and sold and are, therefore, like selling costs, treated as period expenses. Examples include the president's salary, accounting and data processing costs, and the costs of conducting various supportive activities, such as legal services and corporate planning.

Measurement of Expenses Expenses represent assets consumed during the period. The amount of an expense is therefore the cost of the expired asset. Thus, the basis for expense measurement is the same as for asset valuation. Because assets are primarily stated at acquisition cost on the balance sheet, expenses are measured by the acquisition cost of the assets that were either sold or used during the period.

Format and Classification Within the Income Statement

The income statement might contain some or all of the following sections or categories, depending on the nature of the firm's income for the period:

1. Income from continuing operations.
2. Income, gains, and losses from discontinued operations.
3. Adjustments for changes in accounting principles.
4. Extraordinary gains and losses.
5. Earnings per share.

The great majority of income statements include only the first section. The other sections are added if necessary.

Income from Continuing Operations Revenues, gains, expenses, and losses from the continuing areas of business activity of a firm are presented in the first section of the income statement.

Income, Gains, and Losses from Discontinued Operations If a firm sells a major division or segment of its business during the year or contemplates its sale within a short time after the end of the accounting period, Accounting Principles Board *Opinion No. 30* requires that any income, gains, and losses related to that segment be disclosed separately from ordinary, continuing operations in a section of the income statement entitled "Income, Gains, and Losses from Discontinued Operations."[10] This section follows the section presenting Income from Continuing Operations.

Adjustments for Changes in Accounting Principles A firm that changes its principles, or methods, of accounting during the period is required in some cases to disclose the effects of the change on current and prior years' net income.[11] This information is presented in a separate section, after Income, Gains, and Losses from Discontinued Operations.

Extraordinary Gains and Losses Extraordinary gains and losses are presented in a separate section of the income statement. For an item to be extraordinary, it must generally meet both of the following criteria:

1. Unusual in nature.
2. Infrequent in occurrence.[12]

An example of an item likely to be extraordinary for most firms would be a loss from expropriation or confiscation of assets by a foreign government. Such items are likely to be rare. Since 1973, when Accounting Principles Board *Opinion No. 30* was issued, extraordinary items have seldom been seen in published annual reports (except for gains or losses on bond retirements).[13]

---

[10]Accounting Principles Board, *Opinion No. 30*, "Reporting the Results of Operations," 1973.
[11]Accounting Principles Board, *Opinion No. 20*, "Accounting Changes," 1971.
[12]Accounting Principles Board, *Opinion No. 30*.
[13]Financial Accounting Standards Board, *Statement of Financial Accounting Standards No. 4*, "Reporting Gains and Losses from Extinguishment of Debt," 1975.

Earnings per Share Earnings-per-share data must be shown in the body of the income statement.[14] Earnings per common share is conventionally calculated by dividing net income minus preferred stock dividends by the average number of outstanding common shares during the accounting period. For example, assume that a firm had net income of $500,000 during the year. Dividends declared and paid on outstanding preferred stock were $100,000. The average number of shares of outstanding common stock during the year was 1 million shares. Earnings per common share would be $.40 [= ($500,000 − $100,000) ÷ 1,000,000].

If a firm has securities outstanding that can be converted into common stock (for example, convertible bonds) or exchanged for common stock (for example, stock options), it may be required to present two sets of earnings-per-share amounts: primary earnings per share and fully diluted earnings per share.[15] The calculation of primary and fully diluted earnings per share is discussed in financial accounting texts.

Summary of Income Statement Concepts

Net income is equal to the excess of revenues over expenses for a particular period of time. Most firms use the accrual basis for measuring net income and financial position. A few firms use the cash basis or modified cash basis.

Under the cash basis, revenue is recognized when cash is received, and expenses are recognized when cash expenditures are made for merchandise, salary, and similar operating items. The cash basis suffers from two weaknesses: (1) It unnecessarily delays the recognition of revenue, and (2) it recognizes expenses in periods that may differ from those when economic benefits are received as revenues.

The accrual basis is not subject to these important weaknesses of the cash basis. Revenue is typically recognized at the time of sale and stated at the amount of cash expected to be collected from customers. Costs that can be associated directly with particular revenues become expenses in the period when revenues are recognized. The cost of acquiring or manufacturing inventory items is treated in this manner. Costs that cannot be associated closely with particular revenue streams become expenses of the period when goods or services are consumed in operations. Most selling and administrative costs are treated in this manner.

The Statement of Changes in Financial Position

The third principal financial statement is the statement of changes in financial position. This statement reports the inflows, or sources, and outflows, or uses, of cash during a period of time. Exhibit 17.7 presents a statement of changes in financial position for Marnel Corporation for Year 2.

Rationale for the Statement of Changes in Financial Position

W. T. Grant Company filed for bankruptcy in 1975. For virtually all years prior to 1975, Grant had operated profitably. It had a positive balance in retained earnings

---

[14]Accounting Principles Board, *Opinion No. 15*, ''Earnings per Share,'' 1969.
[15]Accounting Principles Board, *Opinion No. 15*.

Exhibit 17.7
MARNEL CORPORATION
Statement of Changes in Financial Position
for Year 2

Sources of Cash		
Operations:		
Net Income	$20,000	
Plus Expenses Not Using Cash:		
Depreciation	10,000	
Plus Increases in Current Liabilities:		
Accounts Payable—Merchandise Suppliers	20,000	
Accounts Payable—Other Suppliers	2,000	
Salaries Payable	1,000	
Less Increases in Current Assets Other Than Cash:		
Accounts Receivable	(35,000)	
Merchandise Inventory	(10,000)	
Cash Provided by Operations.		$ 8,000
Receipts from Issuing Long-Term Bonds.		100,000
Total Sources of Cash		$108,000
Uses of Cash		
Disbursements for Dividends		$ 10,000
Disbursements for Equipment		125,000
Total Uses of Cash		$135,000
Net Decrease in Cash		$ 27,000

at the time of bankruptcy. Despite generating net income each year, Grant continually found itself strapped for cash and unable to pay suppliers, employees, and other creditors.

The experience of Grant is not unusual. Many firms, particularly those experiencing rapid growth, discover that their cash position is deteriorating despite an excellent earnings record. This occurs for two principal reasons.

1. The timing of cash receipts from customers does not necessarily coincide with the recognition of revenue, and the timing of cash expenditures to suppliers, employees, and other creditors does not necessarily coincide with the recognition of expenses under the accrual basis of accounting. In the usual case, cash expenditures precede the recognition of expenses, whereas cash receipts occur after the recognition of revenue. Thus, net income might be positive, but more cash is used in operations than is provided by operations.

2. The firm may be obligated to retire outstanding debt or need to acquire new plant or equipment at a time when there is insufficient cash available.

In many cases, a profitable firm that finds itself short of cash will be able to obtain the funds required from either short- or long-term creditors or from owners. Amounts borrowed from creditors, however, must be repaid with interest. Owners may require that periodic dividends be paid in cash. Eventually, cash must be generated internally by operations if the firm is to survive. *Cash flows are the connecting link among financing, investment, and operating activities. They permit each of these three principal business activities to continue functioning smoothly and effectively.*

Objective of the Statement of Changes in Financial Position

The statement of changes in financial position presents information on the sources (increases) and uses (decreases) of cash during a period. Exhibit 17.8 shows the major sources and uses. These are described below.

1. *Sources—Operations.* The excess of revenues increasing cash over expenses using cash is the most important source of funds. When assessed over several years, cash from operations indicates the extent to which the operating or earnings activities have generated more cash than is used. The excess from operations can then be used for dividends, acquisition of buildings and equipment, or repayment of long-term debt if necessary. As Exhibit 17.7 shows, the statement of changes in financial position usually begins with net income for the period. Adjustments are then made to net income to derive the net amount of cash derived from operations.

2. *Sources—Issuance of Long-Term Debt or Capital Stock.* In contrast to the short-term nature of cash from operations, increases in long-term debt or capital stock represent longer-term sources of financing for a firm.

3. *Sources—Sale of Noncurrent Assets.* The sale of buildings, equipment, and other noncurrent assets results in an increase in cash. These sales generally cannot be viewed as a major source of financing for a firm, because the amounts received from the sales are not likely to be sufficient to replace the assets sold.

Exhibit 17.8
Sources and Uses of Cash

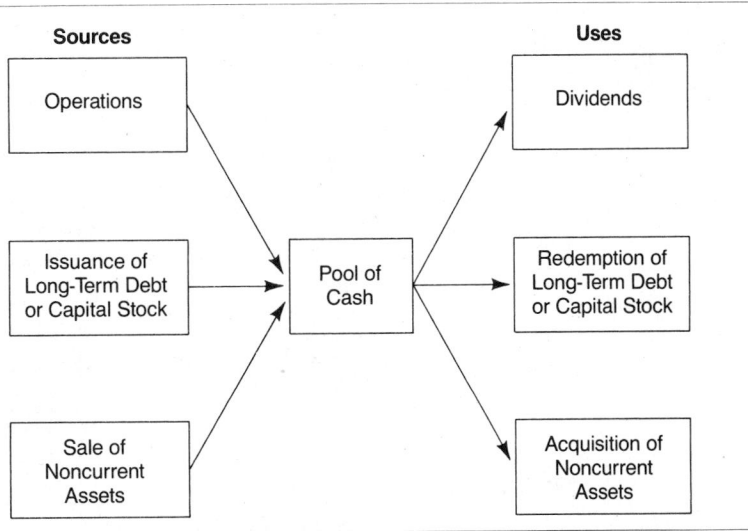

4. *Uses—Dividends.* Dividends are generally a recurring use of cash, because most publicly held firms are reluctant to reduce or omit the payment of dividends, even during a year of poor earnings performance.

5. *Uses—Redemption of Long-Term Debt or Capital Stock.* In most instances, publicly held firms redeem or pay long-term debt at maturity with the proceeds of another bond issue. Thus, these redemptions often have little effect on the *net* change in cash. Some firms also occasionally reacquire or redeem their own capital stock for various reasons.

6. *Uses—Acquisition of Noncurrent Assets.* The acquisition of noncurrent assets such as building and equipment usually represents an important use of cash. These assets must be replaced as they wear out, and additional noncurrent assets must be acquired if a firm is to grow.

Firms sometimes issue long-term debt or capital stock directly to the vendor, or seller, in acquiring buildings, equipment, or other noncurrent assets. These transactions technically do not affect their cash balance. However, the transaction is reported in the statement of changes in financial position as though two transactions took place: the issuance of long-term debt or capital stock for cash and the immediate use of the cash in the acquisition of noncurrent assets. This is called the *dual transactions assumption.* Such a transaction would normally be disclosed in the statement of changes in financial position as both a source and use of cash of equal amounts.

Uses of Information in the Statement of Changes in Financial Position

The statement of changes in financial position provides information that may be used in:

1. Assessing changes in a firm's liquidity; and
2. Assessing changes in the structure of a firm's assets and equities.

Liquidity Perhaps the most important factor not reported on the balance sheet and income statement alone is how the operations of a period affect the liquidity of a firm. It is easy to assume that increased earnings mean increased cash or other liquid assets. However, a new plant may have been acquired and other similar events could have occurred. On the other hand, increased liquidity can accompany reduced earnings, if cash is allowed to accumulate rather than being used to replace plant and equipment.

Structure of Assets and Equities In addition to providing information about changes in a firm's liquidity during a period, the statement of changes in financial position also indicates the major transactions causing changes in the structure of a firm's assets and equities. For example, acquisitions and sales of specific types of noncurrent assets (buildings, equipment, patents) are reported. Likewise, issues and redemptions of long-term debt and capital stock are disclosed. These transactions are difficult to observe by looking at either the income statement or balance sheet alone. For example, the change in the account, "Buildings and Equipment— Net of Accumulated Depreciation," could be attributable to depreciation charges, to acquisition of new buildings and equipment, to disposition of old buildings and equipment, or to a combination of these. The income statement and comparative balance sheets do not provide sufficient information about these three items individually for the reader to disaggregate the net change in the account during the period. A statement of changes in financial position is required to report this information.

Other Items in External Financial Reports

Supporting Schedules and Notes

Published financial statements are supplemented with various supporting schedules and notes to assist users in analysis and interpretation. Among the supporting schedules are a reconciliation of the beginning and ending amounts of contributed capital and retained earnings, and data on sales, earnings, assets, and capital expenditures for the various operating segments of the firm. The notes to the financial statements include additional narrative and quantitative information, such as details of income tax expense (for example, federal, foreign, state, and local taxes); amounts, interest rates, and maturities of long-term debt outstanding; and data on the performance of the firm's pension fund.

Summary of Significant Accounting Policies

A summary of significant accounting policies is required as an integral part of the financial statement presentation.[16] The disclosure of accounting policies identifies the accounting principles adopted by the reporting enterprise and the methods of applying those principles that substantially affect the measurement of income, financial position, and changes in financial position. The summary statement may be given either in a separate "Summary of Significant Accounting Policies" preceding the notes to the financial statements, or in the first note to the statements.

The following list indicates the areas of accounting principles and methods of application frequently presented in a summary statement of accounting policies:

Basis for consolidation

Basis for foreign currency translation

Method of recognizing income on long-term construction contracts

Method of recognizing revenue from franchising and leasing operations

Basis for valuation of inventory

---

[16]Accounting Principles Board, *Opinion No. 22*, "Disclosure of Accounting Policies," 1972.

Methods of accounting for:

Investments

Property, plant, and equipment

Intangibles, such as patents and goodwill

Retirement and pension plans

Leases and rentals

Income taxes and investment tax credits

Earnings per share

Auditor's Opinion

An important section of the external financial report is the opinion of the independent certified public accountant on the financial statements, supporting schedules, and notes. Exhibit 17.9 illustrates an auditor's opinion.

The opinion usually follows a standard format and contains two paragraphs—a *scope* paragraph and an *opinion* paragraph. The scope paragraph indicates the financial presentations covered by the opinion and affirms that auditing standards and practices generally accepted by the accounting profession have been adhered to unless otherwise noted and described. Exceptions to the statement that the auditor's "examination was made in accordance with generally accepted auditing standards" are seldom, if ever, seen in published annual reports. There are occasional references to the auditor's having relied on financial statements examined by other auditors, particularly for subsidiaries or for data from prior periods.

Exhibit 17.9
Example of Auditor's Opinion

Report of Independent Accountants
To the Board of Directors and
Shareholders of
Marnel Corporation

We have examined the statement of financial position of Marnel Corporation and consolidated subsidiaries as of December 31, Year 1 and Year 2, and the related statements of current and retained earnings and changes in financial position for the years then ended. Our examination was made in accordance with generally accepted auditing standards, and accordingly included such tests of the accounting records and such other auditing procedures as we considered necessary in the circumstances.

In our opinion, the aforementioned financial statements present fairly the financial position of Marnel Corporation and consolidated subsidiaries at December 31, Year 1 and Year 2, and the results of their operations and the changes in their financial position for the years then ended, in conformity with generally accepted accounting principles applied on a consistent basis.

Stuckney, Wells + Co.

5836 South Greenwood Avenue
Chicago, Illinois 60637

February 11, Year 3

The opinion expressed by the auditor in the second paragraph is the heart of the independent auditor's report. The opinion may be *unqualified* or *qualified*. The great majority of opinions are unqualified; that is, there are no exceptions or qualifications to the auditor's opinion that the statements "present fairly the financial position . . . and the results of operations and the changes in financial position . . . in conformity with generally accepted accounting principles applied on a consistent basis."

Qualifications to the opinion result primarily from the material uncertainties regarding valuation or realization of assets, outstanding litigation or tax liabilities, or accounting inconsistencies between periods caused by changes in the application of accounting principles. An opinion qualified as to fair presentation is usually noted by the phrase *subject to;* an opinion qualified as to consistency in application of accounting principles is usually noted by *except for,* with an indication of the auditor's approval of the change.

A qualification so material that the auditor feels an opinion cannot be expressed as to the fairness of the financial statements as a whole must result in either a *disclaimer of opinion* or an *adverse opinion*. Adverse opinions and disclaimers of opinion are extremely rare in published reports.

Management's Discussion and Analysis of Operations and Financial Position

The annual report to shareholders must include a discussion by management of the reasons for important changes in a firm's profitability, liquidity, and capital structure. Management must also comment on the impact of inflation on the firm.[17]

Summary

This chapter has provided an overview of the manner in which the results of a firm's activities are measured and disclosed in published accounting reports. The relationships among the three principal financial statements might be depicted as follows:

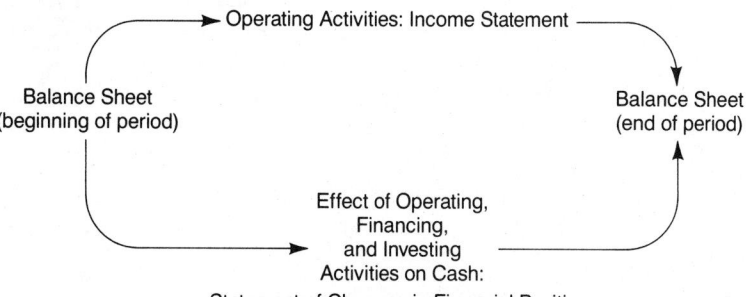

Perhaps the most effective overview of external financial reporting is obtained by reading and studying the annual reports of several publicly held corporations.

---

[17]Securities and Exchange Commission, *Accounting Series Release No. 279*, 1980.

Problem for Self-Study

The accounting records of Digital Electronics Corporation reveal the following:

	Dec. 31, Year 1	Dec. 31, Year 2
Balance Sheet Items		
Accounts Payable to Suppliers	$250,000	$ 295,000
Accounts Receivable from Customers	240,000	320,000
Bonds Payable	100,000	120,000
Buildings (net of accumulated depreciation)	150,000	140,000
Cash	30,000	50,000
Common Stock	100,000	100,000
Equipment (net of accumulated depreciation)	140,000	220,000
Income Taxes Payable	40,000	70,000
Land.	60,000	70,000
Merchandise Inventory	380,000	400,000
Retained Earnings	500,000	600,000
Salaries Payable	10,000	15,000
Income Statement Items for Year 2		
Cost of Merchandise Sold		$ 620,000
Depreciation Expense		40,000
Income Tax Expense		100,000
Insurance Expense		3,000
Interest Expense		10,000
Property Tax Expense		2,000
Rental Revenue (rental of part of building)		30,000
Salary Expense		135,000
Sales Revenue		1,000,000
Dividend Information for Year 2		
Dividends Declared and Paid		$ 20,000

a. Prepare a comparative balance sheet for Digital Electronics Corporation as of December 31, Year 1 and Year 2. Classify the balance sheet items into the following categories: current assets, noncurrent assets, current liabilities, noncurrent liabilities, or shareholders' equity.

b. Prepare an income statement for Digital Electronics Corporation for Year 2. Separate income statement items into revenues and expenses.

c. Prepare a schedule explaining or accounting for the changes in retained earnings between the beginning and end of Year 2.

Suggested Solution

Exhibit 17.10 presents a comparative balance sheet, Exhibit 17.11 presents an income statement, and Exhibit 17.12 analyzes the change in retained earnings for Digital Electronics Corporation for Year 2.

Exhibit 17.10
DIGITAL ELECTRONICS CORPORATION
Comparative Balance Sheet December 31, Year 1 and Year 2

	December 31	
	Year 1	Year 2
Assets		
Current Assets		
Cash	$ 30,000	$ 50,000
Accounts Receivable from Customers	240,000	320,000
Merchandise Inventory.	380,000	400,000
Total Current Assets.	$ 650,000	$ 770,000
Noncurrent Assets		
Land	$ 60,000	$ 70,000
Equipment (net of accumulated depreciation).	140,000	220,000
Buildings (net of accumulated depreciation)	150,000	140,000
Total Noncurrent Assets	$ 350,000	$ 430,000
Total Assets	$1,000,000	$1,200,000
Liabilities and Shareholders' Equity		
Current Liabilities		
Accounts Payable to Suppliers	$ 250,000	$ 295,000
Salaries Payable.	10,000	15,000
Income Taxes Payable	40,000	70,000
Total Current Liabilities.	$ 300,000	$ 380,000
Noncurrent Liabilities		
Bonds Payable	100,000	120,000
Total Liabilities.	$ 400,000	$ 500,000
Shareholders' Equity		
Common Stock	$ 100,000	$ 100,000
Retained Earnings	500,000	600,000
Total Shareholders' Equity	$ 600,000	$ 700,000
Total Liabilities and Shareholders' Equity	$1,000,000	$1,200,000

Exhibit 17.11
DIGITAL ELECTRONICS CORPORATION
Income Statement for Year 2

Revenues		
Sales Revenue	$1,000,000	
Rental Revenue	30,000	
Total Revenues		$1,030,000
Expenses		
Cost of Merchandise Sold	$ 620,000	
Salary Expense	135,000	
Property Tax Expense.	2,000	
Insurance Expense	3,000	
Depreciation Expense	40,000	
Interest Expense.	10,000	
Income Tax Expense	100,000	
Total Expenses		910,000
Net Income		$ 120,000

Exhibit 17.12
DIGITAL ELECTRONICS CORPORATION
Analysis of Change in
Retained Earnings
for Year 2

Retained Earnings, January 1, Year 2	$500,000
Plus Net Income.	120,000
Less Dividends Declared and Paid	(20,000)
Retained Earnings, December 31, Year 2.	$600,000

Questions

1. Review the meaning of the following concepts or terms discussed in this chapter.

a. Balance sheet.
b. Asset.
c. Liability.
d. Owners' equity.
e. Monetary assets and liabilities.
f. Nonmonetary assets and liabilities.
g. Current asset.
h. Current liability.
i. Net income.
j. Revenue.
k. Expense.
l. Product cost.
m. Period expense.

n. Cash basis of accounting.
o. Accrual basis of accounting.
p. Income from continuing operations.
q. Income, gains, and losses from discontinued operations.
r. Extraordinary items.
s. Earnings per share.
t. Cash flow.
u. Summary of significant accounting policies.
v. Auditor's opinion.
w. Unqualified opinion.

2. The *book* value of owners' equity is equal to assets minus liabilities, or owners' equity. The *market* value of owners' equity is equal to the market price per share times the number of shares outstanding. The market value can be divided by the book value to obtain an index of market to book. When the index exceeds 1.0, market value exceeds book value. When the index is less than 1.0, market value is less than book value.

The indexes of market to book for several firms at the end of a recent year are shown below. Indicate the likely reasons for a difference between market value and book value in each case.

Company	Index
a. Eli Lilly (drug company)	2.78
b. Standard Oil of Ohio	1.92
c. Boeing	1.84
d. Union Pacific Railroad	1.34
e. Citicorp (bank holding company)	.76

3. A group of investors owns an office building, which is rented unfurnished to tenants. The building was purchased 5 years previously from a construction company and, at that time, was expected to have a useful life of 40 years. Indicate the procedures you might follow in determining the amount at which the building would be stated under each of the following valuation methods.

    a. Acquisition cost.
    b. Current replacement cost.
    c. Current net realizable value.
    d. Present value of future cash flows.

4. Suggest procedures that you would follow in ascertaining the amounts at which each of the following resources would be stated on a balance sheet if they were recognized as assets:

    a. Well-known trademark or other product symbol.
    b. Well-trained employee labor force.

5. ''Accrual accounting focuses on the use, rather than the financing, of assets.'' Explain.

6. Under the accrual basis of accounting, cash receipts and disbursements may precede, coincide with, or follow the period in which revenues and expenses are recognized. Give an example of each of the following:

    a. A cash receipt that precedes the period in which revenue is recognized.
    b. A cash receipt that coincides with the period in which revenue is recognized.
    c. A cash receipt that follows the period in which revenue is recognized.
    d. A cash disbursement that precedes the period in which expense is recognized.
    e. A cash disbursement that coincides with the period in which expense is recognized.
    f. A cash disbursement that follows the period in which expense is recognized.

7. If the total net income from a particular business activity is equal to the difference between cash inflows and cash outflows, why isn't the cash basis of accounting generally used rather than the accrual basis?

8. ''The use of the accrual basis of accounting for measuring operating performance gives rise to the need for a statement of changes in financial position.'' Explain.

9. ''Over long enough time periods, cumulative net income equals cumulative cash provided by operations.'' Do you agree? Why or why not?

10. Refer to Exhibit 17.8 in the text, which shows the various sources and uses of cash. For a healthy, growing firm, what should be the relationship among the three sources? Among the three uses?

Exercises

11. *Preparation of Personal Balance Sheet*. Prepare a balance sheet of your personal assets, liabilities, and owner's equity. How does the presentation of owner's equity on your balance sheet differ from that in Exhibit 17.2?

12. *Concept of an Accounting Asset*. Indicate whether or not each of the following items would be recognized as an asset by a firm according to generally accepted accounting principles.
    a.   A patent on a new invention purchased from its creator.
    b.   A firm's chief scientist, who has twice won the Nobel prize.
    c.   The right to use a building during the coming year. The rent for the period has already been paid.
    d.   An automobile acquired with the issue of a note payable. Because the note has not been paid, legal title to the automobile has not yet passed to the firm.
    e.   A degree in engineering from a reputable university, awarded to the firm's chief executive.
    f.   A contract signed by a customer to purchase $1,000 worth of goods next year.
    g.   A favorable reputation.

13. *Concept of an Accounting Asset*. Indicate whether or not each of the following immediately gives rise to an asset under generally accepted accounting principles. If an asset is recognized, state the account title and amount.
    a.   A check for $300 has been sent to an insurance company for property insurance. The period of coverage begins next month (consider from the standpoint of the firm making the cash expenditure).
    b.   A check for $3,000 is issued as a deposit on specially designed equipment. The equipment is to have a total purchase price of $20,000 and will be completed and delivered next year (consider from the standpoint of the firm making the cash expenditure).
    c.   Shares of common stock of General Electric Company are acquired with temporarily excess cash for $12,000.
    d.   Merchandise inventory with a list price of $800 is acquired, with payment made in time to secure a 3 percent discount for prompt payment. Cash discounts are treated as a reduction in the acquisition cost of the inventory.
    e.   A well-known scientist has been hired to manage the firm's research and development activity. Employment begins next month. One-twelfth of the annual salary of $90,000 is payable at the end of each month worked.
    f.   Bonds with a face value of $200,000 are purchased for $206,000. The bonds mature in 20 years. Interest is payable by the issuer at the rate of 10 percent annually.
    g.   An order for $700 worth of merchandise is received from a customer.
    h.   Notice has been received from a manufacturer that raw materials billed at $2,000, with payment due in 30 days, have been shipped by freight. The buyer obtains title to the goods as soon as they are shipped by the seller.

14. *Concept of an Accounting Liability.* Indicate whether or not each of the following items is recognized as a liability according to generally accepted accounting principles.

a. An obligation to provide magazines next year to subscribers who have paid 1 year's subscription fees in advance (consider from the standpoint of the magazine publisher).

b. The reputation for poor quality control on products manufactured.

c. An obligation to provide warranty services for 3 years after customers purchase the firm's products.

d. The outstanding common stock of a corporation.

e. Unpaid property taxes for the preceding year.

f. The amount payable by a firm for a television advertisement that has appeared but for which payment is not due for 30 days.

g. A tenant's obligation to maintain a rented warehouse in good repair.

h. The firm's president has an incompetent son who is employed in the business.

15. *Concept of an Accounting Liability.* Indicate whether or not each of the following events immediately gives rise to the recognition of a liability under generally accepted accounting principles. If a liability is recognized, state the account title and amount.

a. A company hires its president under a 5-year contract beginning next month. The contract calls for $300,000 compensation per year.

b. An insurance company receives $2,000 for 6 months' insurance coverage in advance (consider from the standpoint of the insurance company).

c. A manufacturer agrees to produce a specially designed piece of equipment for $3 million. A down payment of $300,000 is received upon signing the contract, and the remainder is due when the equipment is completed. Consider from the standpoint of the manufacturer.

d. Additional common stock with a par value of $75,000 is issued for $80,000.

e. Employees earned wages totaling $6,000 during the last pay period for which they have not been paid. The employer is also liable for payroll taxes of 8 percent of the wages earned.

f. A firm signs a contract agreeing to sell $6,000 of merchandise to a particular customer.

16. *Expense Measurement Under the Accrual Basis.* Assume that the accrual basis of accounting is used and that revenue is recognized at the time goods are sold or services are rendered. Indicate the amount of expense recognized during March, if any, from each of the following transactions or events.

a. An insurance premium of $1,800 is paid on March 1 for 1 year's coverage beginning on that date.

b. On April 3, a utilities bill totaling $460 for services during March is received.

c. $700 worth of supplies were purchased on account during March. $500 of these purchases on account were paid in March, and the remainder was paid in April. On March 1, supplies were on hand that cost $300. At March 31, supplies that cost $350 were still on hand.

d.   Data of **c**, except that $200 of supplies were on hand at March 1.

e.   Property taxes of $4,800 on an office building for the year were paid in January.

f.   An advance of $250 on the April salary is paid to an employee on March 29.

Problems and Cases

17. *Cash Versus Accrual Basis.* J. Thompson opened a hardware store on January 1, Year 1. Thompson invested $10,000 and borrowed $8,000 from the local bank. The loan is repayable on June 30, Year 1, with interest at the rate of 9 percent per year.

Thompson rented a building on January 1, and paid 2 months' rent in advance in the amount of $2,000. Property and liability insurance coverage for the year ending December 31, Year 1, was paid on January 1 in the amount of $1,200.

Thompson purchased $28,000 of merchandise inventory on account on January 2 and paid $10,000 of this amount on January 25. The cost of merchandise on hand on January 31 was $15,000.

During January, cash sales to customers totaled $20,000 and sales on account totaled $9,000. Of the sales on account, $2,000 had been collected as of January 31.

Other costs incurred and paid in cash during January were as follows: utilities, $400; salaries, $650; taxes, $350.

a.   Prepare an income statement for January, assuming that Thompson uses the accrual basis of accounting with revenue recognized at the time goods are sold (delivered).

b.   Prepare an income statement for January, assuming that Thompson uses the cash basis of accounting.

c.   Which basis of accounting do you feel provides a better indication of the operating performance of the hardware store during January? Why?

18. *Cash Versus Accrual Basis.* Management Consultants, Inc., opened a consulting business on July 1, Year 1. Roy Bean and Sarah Bower each contributed $7,000 cash for shares of the firm's common stock. The corporation borrowed $8,000 from a local bank on August 1, Year 1. The loan is repayable on July 31, Year 2, with interest at the rate of 9 percent per year.

Office space was rented on August 1, with 2 months' rent paid in advance. The remaining monthly rental fees of $900 per month were made on the first of each month, beginning October 1. Office equipment with a 4-year life was purchased for cash on August 1 for $4,800.

Consulting services rendered for clients between August 1 and December 31, Year 1, were billed at $15,000. Of this amount, $9,000 was collected by year-end.

Other costs incurred and paid in cash by the end of the year were as follows: utilities, $450; salary of secretary, $7,500; supplies, $450. Unpaid bills at year-end are as follows: utilities, $80; salary of secretary, $900; supplies, $70. All supplies acquired were used.

a. Prepare an income statement for the 5 months ended December 31, Year 1, assuming that the corporation uses the accrual basis of accounting, with revenue recognized at the time services are rendered.

b. Prepare an income statement for the 5 months ended December 31, Year 1, assuming that the corporation uses the cash basis of accounting.

c. Which basis of accounting do you feel provides a better indication of operating performance of the consulting firm for the period? Why?

19. *Preparation of Income Statement and Balance Sheet.* B. Stephens, L. Harris, and G. Winkle, recent business school graduates, set up a management consulting practice on December 31, Year 1, by issuing common stock for $950,000. The accounting records of the S, H, & W Corporation as of December 31, Year 2, reveal the following:

Balance Sheet Items:

Cash	$ 240,000
Accounts Receivable from Clients	230,000
Supplies Inventory	20,000
Office Equipment (net of depreciation)	260,000
Office Building (net of depreciation)	360,000
Accounts Payable to Suppliers	8,000
Payroll Taxes Payable	40,000
Income Taxes Payable	30,000
Common Stock	950,000

Income Statement Items:

Revenue from Consulting Services	$1,100,000
Rental Revenue (from renting part of building)	150,000
Salaries Expense	890,000
Property Taxes and Insurance Expense	80,000
Supplies Expense	10,000
Depreciation Expense	30,000
Income Tax Expense	80,000

Dividend Information:

Dividends Declared and Paid	$ 78,000

a. Prepare an income statement for S, H, & W Corporation for the year ending December 31, Year 2. Refer to Exhibit 17.3 for help in designing the format of the statement.

b. Prepare a comparative balance sheet for S, H, & W Corporation on December 31, Year 1, and December 31, Year 2. Refer to Exhibit 17.2 for help in designing the format of the statement.

20. *Preparation of Income Statement and Balance Sheet.* The accounting records of Laser Sales Corporation reveal the following:

	December 31	
	Year 1	Year 2
Balance Sheet Items:		
Accounts Payable	$1,247,000	$1,513,000
Accounts Receivable	740,000	820,000
Bank Loan Payable (due April 10, Year 3).	—	15,000
Bonds Payable (due Year 16)	80,000	100,000
Building (net of accumulated depreciation).	460,000	440,000
Cash	270,000	315,000
Common Stock	1,190,000	1,240,000
Equipment (net of accumulated depreciation).	825,000	1,023,000
Income Taxes Payable	25,000	30,000
Land	40,000	50,000
Merchandise Inventory.	550,000	610,000
Note Receivable (due June 15, Year 3).	—	20,000
Note Receivable (due December 31, Year 10)	100,000	100,000
Retained Earnings	430,000	470,000
Salaries Payable.	28,000	32,000
Supplies Inventory	15,000	22,000
Income Statement Items for Year 2:		
Cost of Merchandise Sold		$2,611,000
Depreciation Expense		45,000
Income Tax Expense		55,000
Insurance Expense		8,000
Interest Expense.		16,000
Interest Revenue.		15,000
Payroll Tax Expense		80,000
Salary Expense		640,000
Sales Revenue		3,500,000
Dividend Information:		
Dividends Declared and Paid during Year 2		$ 20,000

    a. Prepare a comparative balance sheet for Laser Sales Corporation as of December 31, Year 1 and Year 2. Classify the balance sheet items into one of the following categories: current assets, noncurrent assets, current liabilities, noncurrent liabilities, or shareholders' equity.

    b. Prepare an income statement for Laser Sales Corporation for Year 2. Separate income items into revenues and expenses.

    21. *Relations Among Principal Financial Statements.* The purpose of this problem is to illustrate the relations among the three principal financial statements. Exhibit 17.13 presents a comparative balance sheet for Articulation Corporation as of December 31, Year 1 and Year 2. Exhibit 17.14 presents an income statement, and Exhibit 17.15 presents a statement of changes in financial position (funds defined as cash) for Articulation Corporation for Year 2.

Exhibit 17.13
ARTICULATION CORPORATION
Comparative Balance Sheets
December 31, Year 1 and Year 2

	December 31	
	Year 1	**Year 2**
Assets		
Current Assets		
Cash.	$ 80	$180
Accounts Receivable from Customers	300	340
Merchandise Inventory	150	160
Total Current Assets	$530	$680
Noncurrent Assets		
Land.	$ 40	$ 55
Buildings and Equipment (net of accumulated depreciation)	130	165
Total Noncurrent Assets	$170	$220
Total Assets	$700	$900
Liabilities and Shareholders' Equity		
Current Liabilities		
Accounts Payable	$310	$350
Income Taxes Payable	40	60
Total Current Liabilities	$350	$410
Noncurrent Liabilities		
Bonds Payable	20	25
Total Liabilities	$370	$435
Shareholders' Equity		
Common Stock	$200	$245
Retained Earnings	130	220
Total Shareholders' Equity	$330	$465
Total Liabilities and Shareholders' Equity	$700	$900

Exhibit 17.14
ARTICULATION CORPORATION
Income Statement
for Year 2

Sales Revenue	$1,000
Expenses	
Cost of Merchandise Sold $600	
Salary Expense 100	
Depreciation Expense. 50	
Interest Expense 20	
Income Tax Expense 120	
Total Expenses	890
Net Income	$ 110

Exhibit 17.15
ARTICULATION CORPORATION
Statement of Changes in
Financial Position
for Year 2

Sources of Cash

Operations:

Revenues Increasing Cash	$960
Expenses Decreasing Cash	790
Total from Operations	$170
Issue of Bonds	5
Issue of Common Stock	45
Total Sources	$220

Uses of Cash

Dividends Declared and Paid	$ 20
Land Acquired	15
Buildings and Equipment Acquired	85
Total Uses	120

Net Change in Cash	$100

Using amounts from these three financial statements, demonstrate that the following relationships are correct:

a. Retained earnings at the beginning of Year 2 plus net income for Year 2 minus dividends declared and paid for Year 2 equal retained earnings at the end of Year 2.

b. Change in total assets equals change in total liabilities plus change in contributed capital plus net income minus dividends.

c. Accounts receivable at the beginning of Year 2 plus sales (all on account) to customers less cash collections from customers (see statement of changes in financial position) equal accounts receivable at the end of Year 2.

d. Buildings and equipment at the beginning of Year 2 plus acquisitions of buildings and equipment minus dispositions of buildings and equipment minus depreciation for Year 2 equal buildings and equipment at the end of Year 2.

e. Bonds payable at the beginning of Year 2 plus new bonds issued during Year 2 minus outstanding bonds redeemed during year 2 equal bonds payable at the end of Year 2.

f. Common stock at the beginning of Year 2 plus common stock issued during Year 2 minus outstanding common stock redeemed during Year 2 equal common stock at the end of Year 2.

22. *Relation Between Income and Cash Flows.* The ABC Company started the year in fine shape. The firm made widgets—just what the customer wanted. It made them for $.75 each and sold them for $1.00. The ABC Company kept an inventory equal to shipments of the past 30 days, paid its bills promptly, and collected cash from customers within 30 days after the sale. The sales manager predicted a steady increase of 500 widgets each month beginning in February. It looked like a great year, and it began that way:

January 1. Cash, $875; receivables, $1,000; inventory, $750.

January. In January, 1,000 widgets costing $750 were sold on account for $1,000. Receivables outstanding at the beginning of the month were collected. Production totaled 1,000 units at a total cost of $750. Net income for the month was $250.

February 1. Cash, $1,125; receivables, $1,000; inventory $750.

February. This month's sales jumped, as predicted, to 1,500 units. With a corresponding step-up in production to maintain the 30-day inventory, ABC Company made 2,000 units at a cost of $1,500. All receivables from January sales were collected. Net income so far, $625.

March 1. Cash, $625; receivables, $1,500; inventory, $1,125.

March. March sales were even better: 2,000 units. Collections: On time. Production, to adhere to the inventory policy: 2,500 units. Operating results for the month, net income of $500. Net income to date: $1,125.

April 1. Cash, $250; receivables, $2,000; inventory, $1,500.

April. In April, sales jumped another 500 units to 2,500, and the manager of ABC Company patted the sales manager on the back. Customers were paying right on time. Production was pushed to 3,000 units, and the month's business netted $625 for a net income to date of $1,750. The manager of ABC Company took off for Miami before the accountant's report was issued. Suddenly a phone call came from the treasurer: "Come home! We need money!"

May 1. Cash, $000; receivables, $2,500; inventory, $1,875.

    a. Prepare an analysis that explains what happened to ABC Company. (*Hint:* Compute the amount of cash receipts and cash disbursements for each month during the period January 1 to May 1.)

    b. How can a firm show increasing net income but a decreasing amount of cash?

    c. What insights are provided by the problem about the need for all three financial statements: balance sheet, income statement, and statement of changes in financial position?

23. *Relation Between Income and Cash Flows. (Adapted from a problem by Professor Leonard Morrissey.)* RV Suppliers, Incorporated, founded in July Year 1, manufactures "Kaps." A "Kap" is a relatively low-cost camping unit attached to a pickup truck. Most units consist of an extruded aluminum frame and a fiberglass skin.

After a loss in its initial (Year 1–2) year, the company was barely profitable in fiscal Year 3 and Year 4. More substantial profits were realized in fiscal Year 5 and Year 6, as indicated in the financial statements shown in Exhibits 17.16 and 17.17.

However, in fiscal Year 7, ended just last month, the company suffered a loss of $13,400. Sales dropped from $424,000 in fiscal Year 6 to $247,400 in fiscal Year 7. The outlook for fiscal Year 8 is not encouraging. Potential buyers continue to shun pickup trucks in preference to more energy-efficient small foreign and domestic automobiles.

How did the company finance its rapid growth during the year ended June 30, Year 6? What were the sources and uses of cash during the year? Similarly, how did the company manage its financial affairs during the abrupt contraction in business during the year just ended last month?

Exhibit 17.16
RV SUPPLIERS, INCORPORATED
Income Statements (amounts in 000's)

	Fiscal Years Ended June 30		
	Year 5	Year 6	Year 7
Net Sales	$266.4	$424.0	$247.4
Cost of Goods Sold	191.4	314.6	210.6
Gross Margin	$ 75.0	$109.4	$ 36.8
Operating Expenses[a]	35.5	58.4	55.2
Income (Loss) Before Income Taxes	$ 39.5	$ 51.0	$ (18.4)
Income Taxes	12.3	16.4	(5.0)
Net Income (Loss)	$ 27.2	$ 34.6	$ (13.4)

[a]Includes depreciation expense of $1.7 in Year 5, $4.8 in Year 6, and $7.6 in Year 7.

Exhibit 17.17
RV SUPPLIERS, INCORPORATED
Balance Sheet (amounts in 000's)

	June 30, Year 5	June 30, Year 6	June 30, Year 7
Assets			
Current Assets			
Cash	$ 14.0	$ 12.0	$ 5.2
Accounts Receivable	28.8	55.6	24.2
Inventories	54.0	85.6	81.0
Tax Refund Receivable	–0–	–0–	5.0
Prepayments	4.8	7.4	5.6
Total Current Assets	$101.6	$160.6	$121.0
Property, Plant, Equipment—Net[a]	30.2	73.4	72.2
Total Assets	$131.8	$234.0	$193.2
Liabilities and Shareholders' Equity			
Current Liabilities			
Bank Notes Payable	$ 10.0	$ 52.0	$ 70.0
Accounts Payable	31.6	53.4	17.4
Income Taxes Payable	5.8	7.0	–0–
Other Current Liabilities	4.2	6.8	4.4
Total Current Liabilities	$ 51.6	$119.2	$ 91.8
Shareholders' Equity			
Capital Stock	$ 44.6	$ 44.6	$ 44.6
Retained Earnings	35.6	70.2	56.8
Total Shareholders' Equity	$ 80.2	$114.8	$101.4
Total Liabilities and Shareholders' Equity	$131.8	$234.0	$193.2

	Year 5	Year 6	Year 7
[a]Acquisitions	$ 13.4	$ 48.4	$ 11.8
Depreciation Expense	(1.7)	(4.8)	(7.6)
Book Value and Sales Proceeds from Retirements . .	(.4)	(.4)	(5.4)
Net Change in Property, Plant, and Equipment . . .	$ 11.3	$ 43.2	$ (1.2)

Suggested Solutions to Even-Numbered Exercises

12. *Concept of an Accounting Asset.*
    a. Yes. The patent will provide future benefits. Its acquisition resulted from a past exchange.
    b. No. The employment of the scientist might lead to future benefits, but those benefits are considered too difficult to quantify to justify recognition as an asset.
    c. Yes. The right to use the building has been established in the signing of the rental contract and payment of the rental amount.
    d. Yes. The right to use the automobile has been fixed and will be sustained as long as payments on the note are made on time.
    e. No, for reasons similar to those in part **b**.
    f. No, because there has been no mutual performance.
    g. No, for reasons similar to those in part **b**.

14. *Concept of an Accounting Liability.*
    a. Yes. Cash has been received, and future goods or services must be provided.
    b. No. It is difficult to measure the amount and timing of future cash flows, if any, from such a reputation.
    c. Yes. In contrast to part **b**, there is a specific warranty agreement that specifies the conditions when warranty services will be provided and over what period. Past experience under the warranty plan should provide an adequate basis for estimating the amount and timing of future cash flows.
    d. No, common stock has no maturity date or amount under the assumption that the firm is a going concern.
    e. Yes, benefits have been received (governmental services) for which a known amount is due.
    f. Yes, benefits have been received that create a legal obligation to make payment. The due date merely indicates the latest time before the obligation is considered past due.
    g. Probably not, unless specific damage has occurred that must be repaired.
    h. No, because it is questionable whether benefits have been received in the past or if future cash payments will be required.

16. *Expense Measurement Under the Accrual Basis.*
    a. $150.
    b. $460.
    c. $650 (= $300 + $700 − $350).
    d. $550 (= $200 + $700 − $350).
    e. $400 (= $4,800 ÷ 12).
    f. Zero (an expense of April).

Chapter 18   Analysis of Financial Statements

The financial statements prepared for external users are analyzed by investors, bankers, and others in making their investment, credit, and similar decisions. Financial statements, either for a firm as a whole or for segments thereof, are also analyzed by management in evaluating the performance of the firm and its various operating units. This chapter describes some of the techniques commonly used by investors and other external users in analyzing financial statements. Many of the same techniques can be used by management, however, in evaluating performance internally.

Objectives of Financial Statement Analysis

The first question likely to be raised in analyzing a set of financial statements is "What do I look for?" The response to this question requires an understanding of investment decisions.

To illustrate, assume that you recently inherited $25,000 and must decide what to do with the bequest. You have narrowed the investment decision to purchasing either a certificate of deposit at a local bank or shares of common stock of Horrigan Corporation, currently selling for $40 per share. Your decision will be based on the *return* anticipated from each investment and the *risk* associated with that return.

The bank is currently paying interest at the rate of 12 percent annually on certificates of deposit. Because it is unlikely that the bank will go out of business, you are virtually certain of earning 12 percent each year.

The return from investing in the shares of common stock of Horrigan Corporation has two components. First, the firm paid a cash dividend in their most recent year of $.625 per share, and it is anticipated that this dividend will continue in the future. Second, the market price of the stock is likely to change between the date the shares are purchased and the date in the future when they are sold. The difference between the eventual selling price per share and the $40 purchase price, often called a *capital gain,* is a second component of the return from buying the stock.

Compared to the interest on the certificate of deposit, the return from the common stock investment is more risky. Future dividends and market price changes are likely to be associated, at least partially, with the profitability of the firm. Future income might be less than is currently anticipated if competitors introduce new products that erode Horrigan Corporation's share of its sales market. Future income might be greater than currently anticipated if Horrigan Corporation makes important discoveries or introduces successful new products.

The market price of Horrigan Corporation's shares will probably also be affected by economy-wide factors such as inflation and unemployment. Also, specific industry factors, such as raw materials shortages or government antitrust actions, may influence the market price of the shares. Because most individuals prefer less risk to more risk, you will probably demand a higher expected return from the purchase of Horrigan Corporation's shares than if you invest the inheritance in a certificate of deposit.

Theoretical and empirical research has shown that the expected return from investing in a firm is, in part, related to the expected profitability of the firm.[1] A firm's past earnings performance can be analyzed as a basis for predicting its future profitability.

Investment decisions also require that the risk associated with the expected return be assessed.[2] A firm may find itself, for example, with a shortage of cash and near-cash assets and be unable to repay a short-term bank loan coming due. Or the amount of long-term debt in the capital structure may be so large that the firm has difficulty meeting the required fixed interest payments. The financial statements provide information for assessing how these and other elements of risk affect expected return.

Usefulness of Ratios

The various items in financial statements may be difficult to interpret in the form in which they are presented. For example, the profitability of a firm may be difficult to assess by looking at the amount of net income alone. It is helpful to compare earnings with the assets or capital required to generate those earnings. This relationship, and other important ones between various items in the financial statements, can be expressed in the form of ratios. Some ratios compare items within the income statement; some use only balance sheet data, others relate items from more than one statement. Ratios are useful tools of financial statement analysis because they conveniently summarize data in a form that is more easily understood, interpreted, and compared.

Ratios are, by themselves, difficult to interpret. For example, does a rate of return on common stock of 8.6 percent reflect a good performance? Once calculated, the ratios must be compared with some standard. Several possible standards might be used:

1. The planned ratio for the period being analyzed.
2. The corresponding ratio during the preceding period for the same firm.
3. The corresponding ratio for a similar firm in the same industry.
4. The average ratio for other firms in the same industry.

---

[1] Ray Ball and Philip Brown, "An Empirical Evaluation of Accounting Income Numbers," *Journal of Accounting Research* (Autumn 1968), pp. 159–178.

[2] Modern portfolio theory makes a distinction between systematic (market) risk and nonsystematic (firm-specific) risk. The discussion in this chapter does not differentiate between these two dimensions of risk.

Exhibit 18.1
HORRIGAN CORPORATION
Comparative Balance Sheets
(amounts in millions)

	December 31			
	Year 1	Year 2	Year 3	Year 4
Assets				
Cash	$ 10	$ 10	$ 8	$ 10
Accounts Receivable (net)	26	40	46	78
Inventories	14	30	46	83
Total Current Assets	$ 50	$ 80	$100	$171
Land.	$ 20	$ 30	$ 60	$ 60
Building	150	150	150	190
Equipment	70	192	276	313
Less Accumulated Depreciation	(40)	(52)	(66)	(84)
Total Noncurrent Assets	$200	$320	$420	$479
Total Assets	$250	$400	$520	$650
Liabilities and Shareholders' Equity				
Accounts Payable	$ 25	$ 30	$ 35	$ 50
Salaries Payable	10	13	15	20
Income Taxes Payable	5	7	10	20
Total Current Liabilities	$ 40	$ 50	$ 60	$ 90
Bonds Payable	50	50	100	150
Total Liabilities	$ 90	$100	$160	$240
Common Stock ($10 par value)	$100	$150	$160	$160
Additional Paid-in Capital	20	100	120	120
Retained Earnings.	40	50	80	130
Total Shareholders' Equity	$160	$300	$360	$410
Total Liabilities and Shareholders' Equity . .	$250	$400	$520	$650

Difficulties encountered in using each of these bases for comparison are discussed later.

In the sections that follow, we describe several ratios that are useful for assessing profitability and various dimensions of risk. To demonstrate the calculation of various ratios, we use data for Horrigan Corporation for the years 2 through 4 as shown in Exhibit 18.1 (comparative balance sheets), Exhibit 18.2 (comparative income statements), and Exhibit 18.3 (comparative statements of changes in financial position). Our analysis for Horrigan Corporation is based on a study of the changes in its various ratios over the 3-year period. Such an analysis is referred to as *time-series analysis*.

Measures of Profitability

Usually the most important question asked about a business is "How profitable is it?" Most financial statement analysis is directed at various aspects of this question. Some measures of profitability relate earnings to resources or capital employed; other computations relate earnings and various expenses to sales; a third group

Exhibit 18.2
HORRIGAN CORPORATION
Comparative Income Statements
(amounts in millions)

	Years Ended December 31		
	Year 2	Year 3	Year 4
Sales	$210	$310	$475
Less Expenses:			
Cost of Goods Sold	$119	$179	$280
Selling	36	38	46
Administrative	12	13	15
Depreciation	12	14	18
Interest	5	10	16
Total	$184	$254	$375
Net Income Before Taxes	$ 26	$ 56	$100
Income Tax Expense	10	22	40
Net Income	$ 16	$ 34	$ 60

Exhibit 18.3
HORRIGAN CORPORATION
Comparative Statements of Changes in Financial Position
(amounts in millions)

	Years Ended December 31		
	Year 2	Year 3	Year 4
Sources of Cash			
Operations:			
Net Income	$ 16	$ 34	$ 60
Add Back Expenses Not Using Cash:			
Depreciation	12	14	18
Add Increases in Current Operating Liability Accounts:			
Accounts Payable	5	5	15
Salaries Payable	3	2	5
Income Taxes Payable	2	3	10
Subtract Increases in Current Operating Asset Accounts Other Than Cash:			
Accounts Receivable	(14)	(6)	(32)
Inventories	(16)	(16)	(37)
Cash Flow Provided by Operations	$ 8	$ 36	$ 39
Other Sources:			
Issuance of Bonds	—	50	50
Issuance of Common Stock	130	30	—
Total Sources	$138	$116	$ 89
Uses of Cash			
Dividends	$ 6	$ 4	$ 10
Purchase of Land	10	30	—
Purchase of Building	—	—	40
Purchase of Equipment	122	84	37
Total Uses	$138	$118	$ 87
Net Increase (Decrease) in Cash	$–0–	($ 2)	$ 2

seeks to explain profitability by measuring the efficiency with which inventories, receivables, or other assets have been managed.

Rate of Return on Assets

The rate of return on assets is a measure for assessing a firm's performance in using assets to generate earnings independent of the financing of those assets. The rate of return on assets is calculated as follows:

$$\frac{\text{Net Income Plus Interest Expense}}{\text{Net of Income Tax Savings}} \Big/ \text{Average Total Assets}.$$

Because the rate of return on assets measures a firm's performance in using assets independent of the financing of those assets, the earnings figure used in calculating the rate of return on assets is income before deducting any payments or distributions to the providers of capital. Because interest is a payment to a furnisher of capital, interest expense should not be deducted in measuring the return on total assets. To derive income before interest charges, it is usually easier to start with net income and add to that figure. The amount added to net income is not, however, the interest expense shown on the income statement. Because interest expense is deductible in calculating taxable income, interest expense does not reduce *aftertax* net income by the full amount of interest expense. The amount added back to net income is interest expense reduced by income tax savings.

For example, interest expense for Horrigan Corporation for Year 4, as shown in Exhibit 18.2, is $16 million. The income tax rate is assumed to be 40 percent of pretax income. The income taxes saved, because interest is deductible in computing taxable income, is $6.4 million ($= .40 \times$ $16 million). The amount of interest expense net of income tax savings that is added back to net income is therefore $9.6 million ($= $16 million $-$ $6.4 million). There is no need to add back dividends paid to shareholders, because they are not deducted as an expense in calculating net income.

Because the earnings rate *during the year* is being computed, the measure of investment should reflect the average amount of assets in use during the year. A crude, but usually satisfactory, figure for average total assets is one-half the sum of total assets at the beginning and at the end of the year.[3]

The calculation of rate of return on assets for Horrigan Corporation for Year 4 follows:[4]

---

[3]The rate of return on assets (ROA) is similar in concept to divisional return on investment, or ROI, discussed in Chapter 14, but its measurement is somewhat different. ROA is calculated using amounts from the external financial statements and focuses on net income, interest expense, and assets for the firm as a whole. ROI is calculated using amounts from internal records for divisions and is based on controllable operating profit and investment for each division.

[4]Throughout the remainder of this chapter, we omit reference to the fact that the amounts for Horrigan Corporation are in millions of dollars.

$$\frac{\begin{array}{c}\text{Net Income Plus}\\\text{Interest Expense}\\\text{Net of Income Tax}\\\text{Savings}\end{array}}{\text{Average Total Assets}} = \frac{\$60 + (\$16 - \$6.4)}{\frac{1}{2}(\$520 + \$650)} = 11.9 \text{ percent.}$$

Thus, for each dollar of assets used, the management of Horrigan Corporation was able to earn $.119 during Year 4 before payments to the suppliers of capital. The rate of return on assets was 5.8 percent in Year 2 and 8.7 percent in Year 3. Thus, the rate of return has increased steadily during this 3-year period.

One might question the rationale for a measure of return that is independent of the means of financing. After all, the assets must be financed, and the cost of that financing must be covered by revenues if the firm is to be profitable. A firm's creditors may find that rate of return on assets provides useful information. Creditors have a senior claim on earnings and assets relative to common and preferred shareholders. Creditors receive their return in the form of interest. This return typically comes from the earnings generated from assets before any other suppliers of capital receive a return (for example, dividends). In extending credit or providing debt capital to a firm, creditors would want to be sure that the return generated by the firm on that capital (assets) exceeded its cost.

The rate of return on assets is also useful to common shareholders in assessing financial leverage, a topic discussed later in this chapter.

Disaggregating the Rate of Return on Assets

One means of studying changes in the rate of return on assets is to disaggregate the ratio into two other ratios as follows:

$$\begin{array}{c}\text{Rate of}\\\text{Return}\\\text{on Assets}\end{array} = \begin{array}{c}\text{Profit Margin Ratio}\\\text{(before interest expense}\\\text{and related income tax effects)}\end{array} \times \begin{array}{c}\text{Total Assets}\\\text{Turnover}\\\text{Ratio,}\end{array}$$

or

$$\frac{\begin{array}{c}\text{Net Income Plus}\\\text{Interest Expense}\\\text{Net of Income}\\\text{Tax Savings}\end{array}}{\begin{array}{c}\text{Average Total}\\\text{Assets}\end{array}} = \frac{\begin{array}{c}\text{Net Income Plus}\\\text{Interest Expense}\\\text{Net of Income}\\\text{Tax Savings}\end{array}}{\text{Revenues}} \times \frac{\text{Revenues}}{\begin{array}{c}\text{Average Total}\\\text{Assets}\end{array}}.$$

The profit margin ratio is a measure of a firm's ability to control the level of costs, or expenses, relative to revenues generated. By holding down costs, a firm will be able to increase the profits from a given amount of revenue and thereby improve its profit margin ratio. The total assets turnover ratio is a measure of a firm's ability to generate revenues from a particular level of investment in assets or, to put it another way, the total assets turnover measures the firm's ability to control the level of investment in assets for a particular level of revenues.

Exhibit 18.4 shows the disaggregation of the rate of return on assets for Horrigan Corporation for Year 2, Year 3, and Year 4 into profit margin and total assets

Exhibit 18.4
Disaggregation of Rate of Return on Assets for Horrigan
Corporation for Year 2, Year 3, and Year 4

	Net Income Plus Interest Expense Net of Income Tax Savings / Average Total Assets	=	Net Income Plus Interest Expense Net of Income Tax Savings / Revenues	×	Revenues / Average Total Assets
Year 2:	$\dfrac{\$16 + (\$5 - \$2)}{\frac{1}{2}(\$250 + \$400)}$	=	$\dfrac{\$16 + (\$5 - \$2)}{\$210}$	×	$\dfrac{\$210}{\frac{1}{2}(\$250 + \$400)}$
	5.8 Percent	=	9.05 Percent	×	.646
Year 3:	$\dfrac{\$34 + (\$10 - \$4)}{\frac{1}{2}(\$400 + \$520)}$	=	$\dfrac{\$34 + (\$10 - \$4)}{\$310}$	×	$\dfrac{\$310}{\frac{1}{2}(\$400 + \$520)}$
	8.7 Percent	=	12.90 Percent	×	.674
Year 4:	$\dfrac{\$60 + (\$16 - \$6.4)}{\frac{1}{2}(\$520 + \$650)}$	=	$\dfrac{\$60 + (\$16 - \$6.4)}{\$475}$	×	$\dfrac{\$475}{\frac{1}{2}(\$520 + \$650)}$
	11.9 Percent	=	14.65 Percent	×	.812

turnover ratios. Much of the improvement in the rate of return on assets between Year 2 and Year 3 can be attributed to an increase in the profit margin ratio from 9.05 percent to 12.90 percent. The total assets turnover ratio remained relatively stable between these 2 years. On the other hand, most of the improvement in the rate of return on assets between Year 3 and Year 4 can be attributed to the increased total assets turnover. The firm was able to generate $.812 of sales from each dollar invested in assets during Year 4 as compared to $.674 of sales per dollar of assets in Year 3. The increased total assets turnover, coupled with an improvement in the profit margin ratio, permitted Horrigan Corporation to increase its rate of return on assets during Year 4. We must analyze the changes in the profit margin ratio and total assets turnover ratio in greater depth to pinpoint the causes of the changes in Horrigan Corporation's profitability over this 3-year period. We return to this analysis shortly.

Improving the rate of return on assets can be accomplished by increasing the profit margin ratio, the rate of asset turnover, or both. Some firms, however, may have little flexibility in altering one of these components. For example, a firm committed under a 3-year labor union contract may have little control over wage rates paid. Or a firm operating under market- or government-imposed price controls may not be able to increase the prices of its products. In these cases, the opportunities for improving the profit margin ratio may be limited. In order to increase the rate of return on assets, the level of investment in assets such as inventory, plant, and equipment must be reduced or, to put it another way, revenues per dollar of assets must be increased.

Analyzing Changes in the Profit Margin Ratio

Profit, or net income, is measured by subtracting various expenses from revenues. To identify the reasons for a change in the profit margin ratio, changes in a firm's expenses relative to revenues must be examined. One approach is to express individual expenses and net income as a percentage of revenues. Such an analysis is presented in Exhibit 18.5 for Horrigan Corporation. Note that we have altered somewhat the conventional income statement format in this analysis by subtracting interest expense (net of its related income tax effects) as the last expense item. The percentages on the line, Income Before Interest and Related Income Tax Effect, correspond (except for rounding) to the profit margin ratios (before interest and related tax effects) shown in Exhibit 18.4.

The analysis in Exhibit 18.5 indicates that the improvement in the profit margin ratio over the 3 years for Horrigan Corporation can be attributed primarily to decreases in selling, administrative, and depreciation expenses as a percentage of sales. The reasons for these decreasing percentages should be explored further with management. Does the decrease in selling expenses as a percentage of sales reflect a reduction in the rate of advertising expenditures that could hurt future sales? Does the decrease in depreciation expense as a percentage of sales reflect a failure to expand plant and equipment as sales have increased? On the other hand, do these decreasing percentages merely reflect the realization of economies of scale as fixed selling, administrative, and depreciation expenses are being spread over a larger number of units?[5] The amount or trend in a particular ratio cannot, by itself, be the basis for investing or not investing in a firm. Ratios merely indicate areas where

Exhibit 18.5

Net Income and Expenses as a Percentage of Sales for Horrigan Corporation for Year 2, Year 3, and Year 4

	Years Ended December 31		
	Year 2	Year 3	Year 4
Sales	100.0%	100.0%	100.0%
Less Operating Expenses:			
Cost of Goods Sold	56.7%	57.7%	58.9%
Selling	17.1	12.3	9.7
Administrative	5.7	4.2	3.2
Depreciation	5.7	4.5	3.8
Total	85.2%	78.7%	75.6%
Income Before Income Taxes and Interest	14.8%	21.3%	24.4%
Income Taxes at 40 percent	5.9	8.5	9.8
Income Before Interest and Related Income Tax Effect	8.9%	12.8%	14.6%
Interest Expense Net of Income Tax Effect.	1.4	1.9	2.0
Net Income	7.5%	10.9%	12.6%

[5]This phenomenon is called *operating leverage* and is discussed more fully in managerial economics textbooks.

additional analysis is required. For example, the increasing percentage of cost of goods sold to sales should be explored further. It may reflect a successful, planned pricing policy of reducing gross margin (selling price less cost of goods sold) in order to increase the volume of sales. On the other hand, the replacement costs of inventory items may be increasing without corresponding increases being made in selling prices. Or the firm may be accumulating excess inventories that are physically deteriorating or becoming obsolete.

Analyzing Changes in the Total Assets Turnover Ratio

The total assets turnover ratio depends on the turnover ratios for its individual asset components. Three turnover ratios are commonly calculated: accounts receivable turnover, inventory turnover, and fixed asset turnover.

Accounts Receivable Turnover The rate at which accounts receivable turn over gives an indication of their nearness to being converted into cash. The accounts receivable turnover is calculated by dividing net sales on account by average accounts receivable. For Horrigan Corporation, the accounts receivable turnover for Year 4, assuming that all sales are on account (that is, none are for immediate cash), is calculated as follows:

$$\frac{\text{Net Sales on Account}}{\text{Average Accounts Receivable}} = \frac{\$475}{\frac{1}{2}(\$46 + \$78)} = 7.66 \text{ times per year.}$$

The concept of accounts receivable turnover is often expressed in terms of the average number of days that receivables are outstanding before cash is collected. The calculation is to divide the accounts receivable turnover ratio into 365 days. The average number of days that accounts receivable are outstanding for Horrigan Corporation for Year 4 is 47.6 days (= 365 days ÷ 7.66 times per year). Thus, on average, accounts receivable are collected approximately $1\frac{1}{2}$ months after the date of sale. The interpretation of this average collection period depends on the terms of sale. If the terms of sale are "net 30 days," the accounts receivable turnover indicates that collections are not being made in accordance with the stated terms. Such a ratio would warrant a review of the credit and collection activity for an explanation and for possible corrective action. If the firm offers terms of "net 45 days," then the results indicate that accounts receivable are being handled better.

Inventory Turnover The inventory turnover ratio is considered to be a significant indicator of the efficiency of operations for many businesses. It is calculated by dividing cost of goods sold by the average inventory during the period. The inventory turnover for Horrigan Corporation for Year 4 is calculated as follows:

$$\frac{\text{Cost of Goods Sold}}{\text{Average Inventory}} = \frac{\$280}{\frac{1}{2}(\$46 + \$83)} = 4.34 \text{ times per year.}$$

Thus, inventory is typically on hand an average of 84.1 days (= 365 days ÷ 4.34 times per year) before it is sold.

The interpretation of the inventory turnover figure involves two opposing considerations. Management would like to sell as many goods as possible with a minimum of capital tied up in inventories. An increase in the rate of inventory turnover between periods would seem to indicate more profitable use of the investment in inventory. On the other hand, management does not want to have so little inventory on hand that shortages result and customers are turned away. An increase in the rate of inventory turnover in this case may mean a loss of customers and thereby offset any advantage gained by decreased investment in inventory. Some trade-offs are therefore required in deciding the optimum level of inventory for each firm, and thus the desirable rate of inventory turnover. (Chapter 8 describes techniques for making optimal inventory investment decisions.)

The inventory turnover ratio is sometimes calculated by dividing sales, rather than cost of goods sold, by the average inventory. As long as there is a relatively constant relationship between selling prices and cost of goods sold, changes in the *trend* of the inventory turnover can usually be identified with either measure. It is inappropriate to use sales in the numerator if the inventory turnover ratio is to be used to calculate the average number of days inventory is on hand until sale.

Plant Asset Turnover The plant asset turnover ratio is a measure of the relationship between sales and the investment in plant assets such as property, plant, and equipment. It is calculated by dividing sales by average plant assets during the year. The plant assets turnover ratio for Horrigan Corporation for Year 4 is

$$\frac{\text{Sales}}{\text{Average Plant Assets}} = \frac{\$475}{\frac{1}{2}(\$420 + \$479)} = 1.06 \text{ times per year.}$$

Thus, for each dollar invested in plant assets during Year 4, $1.06 was generated in sales.

Changes in the plant asset turnover ratio must be interpreted carefully. Investments in plant assets (for example, production facilities) are often made several periods before the time when sales are generated from products manufactured in the plant. Thus, a low or decreasing rate of plant asset turnover may be indicative of an expanding firm preparing for future growth. On the other hand, a firm may cut back its capital expenditures if the near-term outlook for its products is poor. Such action could lead to an increase in the plant asset turnover ratio.

We noted earlier that the total assets turnover for Horrigan Corporation was relatively steady between Year 2 and Year 3 but increased dramatically in Year 4. Exhibit 18.6 presents the four turnover ratios we have discussed for Horrigan Corporation over this 3-year period. The accounts receivable turnover ratio increased steadily over the 3 years, indicating either more careful screening of credit applications or more effective collection efforts. The inventory turnover ratio decreased during the 3 years. Coupling this result with the increasing percentage of cost of goods sold to sales shown in Exhibit 18.5 indicates that there may be excessive investments in inventories that are physically deteriorating or becoming obsolete.

Most of the increase in the total assets turnover between Year 3 and Year 4 can be attributed to an increase in the plant assets turnover. We note in the statement

Exhibit 18.6
Asset Turnover Ratios for Horrigan Corporation
for Year 2, Year 3, and Year 4

	Year 2	Year 3	Year 4
Total Assets Turnover	.646	.674	.812
Accounts Receivable Turnover	6.36	7.21	7.66
Inventory Turnover	5.41	4.71	4.34
Plant Asset Turnover	.81	.84	1.06

of changes in financial position for Horrigan Corporation in Exhibit 18.3 that total capital expenditures on land, building, and equipment decreased over the 3-year period, possibly accounting for the increase in the plant asset turnover. The reasons for this decrease in capital expenditures should be investigated.

Summary of the Analysis of the Rate of Return on Assets This section began by stating that the rate of return on assets is a useful measure for assessing a firm's performance in using assets to generate earnings. The rate of return on assets was then disaggregated into profit margin and total assets turnover components. The profit margin ratio was, in turn, disaggregated by relating various expenses and net income to sales. The total assets turnover was further analyzed by calculating turnover ratios for accounts receivable, inventory, and plant assets.

The analysis revealed the following:

1. The rate of return on assets increased steadily over the 3-year period from Year 2 to Year 4.

2. The improved rate of return on assets can be attributed to an increasing profit margin over all 3 years and an improved total asset turnover during Year 4.

3. The improved profit margin is in large measure attributable to a decrease in the percentage of selling expenses to sales. The reason for this decrease should be explored further to ascertain whether advertising and selling efforts are being curtailed currently that might adversely affect future sales.

4. The changes in the total assets turnover reflect the effects of increasing accounts receivable and plant asset turnovers and a decreasing inventory turnover. The increasing plant asset turnover might be attributable to a reduction in the level of investment in new property, plant, and equipment that could hurt future productive capacity and should be explored further. The decreasing rate of inventory turnover coupled with the increasing percentage of cost of goods sold to sales may be indicative of inventory control problems (build-up of obsolete inventory) and should likewise be explored further.

Rate of Return on Common Stock Equity

The investor in a firm's common stock is probably more interested in the *rate of return on common stock equity* than the rate of return on assets. The rate of return on common stock equity is calculated as follows:

$$\frac{\text{Net} \quad \text{Dividends on}}{\text{Income} - \text{Preferred Stock}}$$
$$\text{Average Common}$$
$$\text{Shareholders' Equity}$$

To calculate the amount of earnings assignable to common stock equity, the earnings allocable to any preferred stock equity—usually the dividends on preferred stock declared during the period—must be deducted from net income. The capital provided during the period by common shareholders can be calculated by averaging the aggregate par value of common stock, capital contributed in excess of par value on common stock, and retained earnings (or by deducting the equity of preferred shareholders from total shareholders' equity) at the beginning and end of the period.

The rate of return on common stock equity by Horrigan Corporation for Year 4 is calculated as

$$\frac{\text{Net Income} - \text{Dividends on Preferred Stock}}{\text{Average Common Shareholders' Equity}} = \frac{\$60 - \$0}{\frac{1}{2}(\$360 + \$410)} = 15.6 \text{ percent.}$$

The rate of return on common stock equity by Horrigan Corporation, 15.6 percent, is larger than the rate of return on assets (11.9 percent). The return to the common stock equity is larger than the rate of return on assets because the payments to the other suppliers of capital (for example, creditors and bondholders) are less than the overall 11.9 percent rate of return generated from capital that they provided. Observe that current liabilities carry no explicit interest payment and bonds carry an average interest rate of less than 11 percent (= \$16 ÷ \$150).

The common stock equity earned a higher rate of return only because the shareholders undertook more risk in their investment. They were placed in a riskier position because the firm incurred debt obligations with fixed payment dates. In each of the years 2 through 4, the rate of return on assets exceeded the average cost of debt, so that the rate of return on common stock equity exceeded the rate of return on assets. The phenomenon of common shareholders trading extra risk for a potentially higher return is called *financial leverage* and is described next.

Financial Leverage: Trading on the Equity

Financing with debt and preferred stock to increase the potential return to the residual common shareholders' equity is referred to as *financial leverage* or *trading on the equity*. So long as a higher rate of return can be earned on assets than is paid for the capital used to acquire those assets, then the rate of return to common shareholders can be increased. Exhibit 18.7 explores this phenomenon. Leveraged Company and No-Debt Company both have \$100,000 of assets. Leveraged Company borrows \$40,000 at a 10 percent annual rate. No-Debt Company raises all its capital from common shareholders. Both companies pay income taxes at the rate of 40 percent.

Consider first a "good" earnings year. Both companies earn \$10,000 before interest charges (but after taxes except for tax effects of interest charges).[6] This

---

[6]That is, income before taxes and before interest charges is \$16,667; \$10,000 = (1 − .40) × \$16,667.

Exhibit 18.7
Effects of Financial Leverage on Rate of Return of Common Shareholders' Equity
(income tax rate is 40 percent of pretax income)

	Long-Term Equities		Income After Taxes but Before Interest Charges[a]	Aftertax Interest Charges[b]	Net Income	Rate of Return on Total Assets[c] (percent)	Rate of Return on Common Shareholders' Equity (percent)
	Long-Term Borrowing at 10 Percent per Year	Shareholders' Equity					
Good Earnings Year							
Leveraged Company.	$40,000	$ 60,000	$10,000	$2,400	$ 7,600	10.0	12.7
No-Debt Company.	—	100,000	10,000	—	10,000	10.0	10.0
Neutral Earnings Year							
Leveraged Company.	40,000	60,000	6,000	2,400	3,600	6.0	6.0
No-Debt Company.	—	100,000	6,000	—	6,000	6.0	6.0
Bad Earnings Year							
Leveraged Company.	40,000	60,000	4,000	2,400	1,600	4.0	2.7
No-Debt Company.	—	100,000	4,000	—	4,000	4.0	4.0

[a]But not including any income tax savings caused by interest charges. Income before taxes and interest for *good* year is $16,667; for *neutral* year is $10,000; for *bad* year is $6,667.
[b]$40,000 (borrowed) × .10 (interest rate) × [1 − .40 (income tax rate)]. The numbers shown in the preceding column for aftertax income do not include the effects of interest charges on taxes.
[c]In each year, the rate of return on assets is the same for both companies as the rate of return on common shareholders' equity for No-Debt Company: 10 percent, 6 percent, and 4 percent, respectively.

represents a rate of return on assets for both companies of 10 percent (= $10,000 ÷ $100,000). Leveraged Company's net income is $7,600 [= $10,000 − (1 − .40 tax rate) × (.10 interest rate × $40,000 borrowed)], representing a rate of return on common shareholders' equity of 12.7 percent (= $7,600 ÷ $60,000). Net income of No-Debt Company is $10,000, representing a rate of return on shareholders' equity of 10 percent. Leverage increased the rate of return to shareholders of Leveraged Company, because the capital contributed by the long-term debtors earned 10 percent but required an aftertax interest payment of only 6 percent [= (1 − .40 tax rate) × (.10 interest rate)]. This additional 4 percent return on each dollar of assets increases the return to the common shareholders.

Although leverage increased the return to the common stock equity during the "good" earnings year, the increase would be larger if a larger proportion of the assets were financed with long-term borrowing and the firm were made more risky. For example, assume that the assets of $100,000 were financed with $50,000 of long-term borrowing and $50,000 of shareholders' equity. Net income of Leveraged Company in this case would be $7,000 [= $10,000 − (1 − .40 tax rate) × (.10 × $50,000 borrowed)]. The rate of return on common stock equity would be 14 percent (= $7,000 ÷ $50,000). This rate compares with a rate of return on common stock equity of 12.7 percent when long-term debt was only 40 percent of the total capital provided.

Financial leverage increases the rate of return on common stock equity when the rate of return on assets is higher than the aftertax cost of debt. The greater the proportion of debt in the capital structure, however, the greater the risk borne by the common shareholders. Debt cannot, of course, be increased without limit. As more debt is added to the capital structure, the risk of default or insolvency becomes greater. Lenders, including investors in a firm's bonds, will require a higher and higher return (interest rate) to compensate for this additional risk. A point will be reached when the aftertax cost of debt will exceed the rate of return that can be earned on assets. At this point, leverage can no longer increase the potential rate of return to common stock equity. For most large manufacturing firms, liabilities represent between 30 percent and 60 percent of total capital.

Exhibit 18.7 also demonstrates the effect of leverage in a "neutral" earnings year and in a "bad" earnings year. In the "neutral" earnings year, the rate of return to common shareholders is neither increased nor decreased by leverage, because the return on assets is 6 percent and the aftertax cost of long-term debt is 6 percent. In the "bad" earnings year, the return on assets of 4 percent is less than the aftertax cost of debt of 6 percent. The return on common stock equity therefore drops—to only 2.7 percent—below the rate of return on assets. Clearly, financial leverage can work in two ways. It can enhance owners' rate of return in good years, but owners run the risk that bad earnings years will be even worse than they would be without the borrowing.

Earnings per Share of Common Stock

Earnings per share of common stock is calculated by dividing net income applicable to common shareholders by the average number of common shares outstanding during the period.

Earnings per share for Horrigan Corporation for Year 4 is calculated as follows:

$$\frac{\text{Net Income} - \text{Preferred Stock Dividend}}{\text{Weighted Average Number of Common Shares Outstanding During the Period}} = \frac{\$60 - \$0}{16 \text{ Shares}^7} = \$3.75 \text{ per share}.$$

Earnings per share were \$1.28 (= \$16 ÷ 12.5) for Year 2 and \$2.19 (= \$34/15.5) for Year 3.

If a firm has securities outstanding that can be converted into or exchanged for common stock, it may be required to present two earnings-per-share amounts: *primary earnings per share* and *fully diluted earnings per share*. For example, some firms issue convertible bonds or convertible preferred stock that can be exchanged directly for shares of common stock. Also, many firms have employee stock option plans under which shares of the company's common stock may be acquired by employees under special arrangements. If these convertible securities were converted or stock options were exercised and additional shares of common stock were issued, the amount conventionally shown as earnings per share would probably decrease, or become *diluted*. When a firm has outstanding securities that, if exchanged for shares of common stock, would decrease earnings per share by 3 percent or more, a dual presentation of primary and fully diluted earnings per share is required.[8]

Interpreting Earnings per Share Earnings per share has been criticized as a measure of profitability because it does not consider the amount of assets or capital required to generate that level of earnings. Two firms with the same earnings and earnings per share will not be equally profitable if one of the firms requires twice the amount of assets or capital to generate that earnings than does the other firm.

Earnings-per-share amounts are also difficult to interpret when comparing firms. For example, assume that two firms have identical earnings, common shareholders' equity, and rates of return on common shareholders' equity. One firm may have a lower earnings per share simply because it has a larger number of shares outstanding (due perhaps to the use of a lower par value for its shares or to different earnings retention policies; see Exercise 15 at the end of this chapter).

Price-Earnings Ratio

Earnings-per-share amounts are often compared with the market price of the stock. This is usually expressed as a *price-earnings ratio* (= market price per share ÷

---

[7]Exhibit 18.1 indicates that the par value of a common share is \$10 and that the common stock account has a balance of \$160 million throughout Year 4. The shares outstanding were therefore 16 million.

[8]Accounting Principles Board, *Opinion No. 15*, ''Earnings per Share,'' 1969.

earnings per share). For example, the common stock of Horrigan Corporation is selling for $40 per share at the end of Year 4. The price-earnings ratio, often called the P/E ratio, is 10.67 to 1 (= $40 ÷ $3.75). This ratio is often presented in tables of stock market prices and in financial periodicals. The relationship is sometimes expressed by saying that "the stock is selling at 10.7 times earnings."

The relation between earnings and market price per share might be expressed as a rate (= earnings per share ÷ market price per share). This calculation, 9.4 percent (= $3.75 ÷ $40) for Horrigan Corporation, is seen less often than the price-earnings ratio.

Measures of Risk

Two dimensions of risk are discussed in the sections that follow: (1) short-term liquidity risk, and (2) long-run solvency, or capital structure, risk.

Measures of Short-Term Liquidity Risk

Investors or creditors whose claims will become payable in the near future are interested in the short-term liquidity or "nearness to cash" of a firm's assets. One tool for predicting whether or not cash will be available when the claims become due is a budget of cash receipts and disbursements for several months or quarters in the future. Such budgets are often prepared for management and used internally for planning cash requirements. Budgets of cash receipts and disbursements are not generally available for use by persons outside a firm. Investors must, therefore, use other tools in assessing short-term liquidity.

The statement of changes in financial position is one published source of information for assessing liquidity. The amount of cash provided by operations indicates the extent to which the operating activities have generated sufficient cash for the payment of dividends and the acquisition of fixed assets. The statement also discloses the extent to which additional financing has been used for those purposes. Exhibit 18.3 indicated that cash provided by operations for Horrigan Corporation increased each year between Year 2 and Year 4. Although a substantial portion of cash generated by operations each year was reinvested in receivables and inventories, operations nonetheless produced increasing amounts of cash flows over the 3-year period.

Several ratios are also useful in assessing the short-term liquidity risk of a firm. The most popular ones are the current ratio, the quick ratio, and the accounts receivable turnover ratio.

Current Ratio The *current ratio* is calculated by dividing current assets by current liabilities. It is commonly expressed as a ratio such as "2 to 1" or "2:1," meaning that current assets are twice as large as current liabilities. The current ratio of Horrigan Corporation on December 31, Year 1, Year 2, Year 3, and Year 4, is

$$\frac{\text{Current}}{\text{Ratio}} = \frac{\text{Current Assets}}{\text{Current Liabilities}}$$

December 31, Year 1: $\dfrac{\$\ 50}{\$\ 40} = $ 1.25 to 1.0

December 31, Year 2: $\dfrac{\$\ 80}{\$\ 50} = $ 1.60 to 1.0

December 31, Year 3: $\dfrac{\$100}{\$\ 60} = $ 1.67 to 1.0

December 31, Year 4: $\dfrac{\$171}{\$\ 90} = $ 1.90 to 1.0

This ratio is presumed to indicate the ability of the concern to meet its current obligations, and is therefore of particular significance to short-term creditors. Although an excess of current assets over current liabilities is generally considered desirable from the creditor's viewpoint, changes in the trend of the ratio may be difficult to interpret. For example, when the current ratio is larger than 1 to 1, an increase of equal amount in both current assets and current liabilities results in a decline in the ratio, whereas equal decreases result in an increased current ratio.

If a corporation has a particularly profitable year, the large current liability for income taxes may cause a decline in the current ratio. In a recession period, business is contracting, current liabilities are paid, and even though the current assets may be at a low point, the ratio may go to high levels. In a boom period, just the reverse effect might occur. In other words, a very high current ratio may accompany unsatisfactory business conditions, whereas a falling ratio may accompany profitable operations.

Furthermore, the current ratio is susceptible to "window dressing"; that is, management can take deliberate steps to produce a financial statement that presents a better current ratio at the balance sheet date than the average or normal current ratio. For example, toward the close of a fiscal year normal purchases on account may be delayed. Or loans to officers, classified as noncurrent assets, may be collected and the proceeds used to reduce current liabilities. These actions may be taken so that the current ratio will appear as favorable as possible in the annual financial statements at the balance sheet date.

Although the current ratio is probably the most common ratio presented in statement analysis, there are limitations in its use as discussed above. Its trends are difficult to interpret and, if overemphasized, it can easily lead to undesirable business practices as well as misinterpretation of financial condition.

Quick Ratio A variation of the current ratio, usually known as the *quick ratio* or *acid test ratio,* is computed by including in the numerator of the fraction only those current assets that could be converted quickly into cash. The numerator customarily includes cash, marketable securities, and receivables, but it would be better to make a study of the facts in each case before deciding whether or not to include receivables and to exclude inventories. In some businesses, the inventory of merchandise might be converted into cash more quickly than the receivables of other businesses.

Assuming that the accounts receivable of Horrigan Corporation are included but that inventory is excluded, the quick ratio on December 31, Year 1, Year 2, Year 3, and Year 4, is

$$\text{Quick Ratio} = \frac{\text{Cash, Marketable Securities, Accounts Receivable}}{\text{Current Liabilities}}$$

December 31, Year 1: $\dfrac{\$36}{\$40} =$ .90 to 1.0

December 31, Year 2: $\dfrac{\$50}{\$50} =$ 1.0 to 1.0

December 31, Year 3: $\dfrac{\$54}{\$60} =$ .90 to 1.0

December 31, Year 4: $\dfrac{\$88}{\$90} =$ .98 to 1.0

Whereas the current ratio increased steadily over the period, the quick ratio remained relatively constant. The increase in the current ratio results primarily from a build-up of inventories.

Accounts Receivable Turnover Ratio The accounts receivable turnover ratio, discussed earlier in the section on profitability ratios, also provides useful information about a firm's liquidity. The ratio is calculated by dividing net sales on account by the average amount of accounts receivable during the period. In assessing short-term liquidity, it is helpful to reexpress the ratio in terms of the average number of days accounts receivable are outstanding. Using the accounts receivable turnover amounts from Exhibit 18.6, the average number of days Horrigan Corporation's receivables were outstanding during Year 2, Year 3, and Year 4 were

$$\text{Average Number of Days Accounts Receivable Are Outstanding} = \frac{365}{\text{Accounts Receivable Turnover Ratio}}$$

Year 2: $\dfrac{365}{6.36} =$ 57.4 days

Year 3: $\dfrac{365}{7.21} =$ 50.6 days

Year 4: $\dfrac{365}{7.66} =$ 47.6 days

Over the 3-year period, the accounts receivable of Horrigan Corporation have become more liquid.

Other Short-Term Liquidity Ratios Several other ratios are sometimes used to assess short-term liquidity. One ratio relates cash *inflow* from operations to the average amount of current liabilities during a period. This ratio is intended to provide information similar to the current ratio but is not as susceptible to year-end window dressing. Another ratio sometimes encountered is the *defensive interval*.[9] It is calculated by dividing the average daily cash expenditures for operating expenses into a firm's most liquid assets, generally cash, marketable securities, and accounts receivable. The defensive interval is the number of days the firm could theoretically remain in business without additional sales or new financing. This ratio has been found to be a good predictor of bond default and bankruptcy.

Summarizing the analysis of Horrigan Corporation's short-term liquidity, we have noted the following:

1. Cash flow provided by operations has been positive and growing at a reasonably stable rate with sales and net income. Operations are now the primary source of liquid assets for the firm.
2. The current ratio has been improving over the last 3 years, but most of the improvement is explained by a build-up of inventories.
3. The average collection period for accounts receivable has been decreasing during the past 3 years, indicating that they are becoming more liquid, or that collection policy has been more stringent, or both.

Measures of Long-Term Solvency Risk

Measures of long-term solvency, or capital structure, risk are used in assessing the firm's ability to meet interest and principal payments on long-term debt and similar obligations as they become due. If the payments cannot be made on time, the firm becomes *insolvent* and may have to be reorganized or liquidated.

Perhaps the best indicator of long-term solvency is a firm's ability to generate profits over a period of years. If a firm is profitable, it will either generate sufficient capital from operations or be able to obtain needed capital from creditors and owners. The measures of profitability discussed previously are therefore applicable for this purpose as well. Two other commonly used measures of long-term solvency risk are debt ratios and the number of times that interest charges are earned.

Debt Ratios There are several variations of the debt ratio, but the one most commonly encountered in financial analysis is the *long-term debt ratio*. It reports the portion of the firm's long-term capital that is furnished by debt holders. To calculate this ratio, divide total noncurrent liabilities by the sum of total noncurrent liabilities and total shareholders' equity.

Another form of the debt ratio is the *debt-equity ratio*. To calculate the debt-equity ratio, divide total liabilities (current and noncurrent) by total equities (liabilities plus shareholders' equity = total assets).

The two forms of the debt ratio for Horrigan Corporation on December 31, Year 1, Year 2, Year 3, and Year 4, are shown in Exhibit 18.8. In general, the higher

---

[9]George H. Sorter and George Benston, "Appraising the Defensive Position of a Firm: The Interval Measure," *The Accounting Review* (October 1960), pp. 633–640.

Exhibit 18.8
Debt Ratios
for Horrigan Corporation

	Long-Term Debt Ratio $=$ $\dfrac{\text{Total Noncurrent Liabilities}}{\substack{\text{Total Noncurrent Liabilities}\\\text{Plus Shareholders'}\\\text{Equity}}}$		Debt-Equity Ratio $=$ $\dfrac{\text{Total Liabilities}}{\substack{\text{Total Liabilities Plus}\\\text{Shareholders'}\\\text{Equity}}}$
Dec. 31, Year 1:	$\dfrac{\$\ 50}{\$210} = 24$ Percent	Dec. 31, Year 1:	$\dfrac{\$\ 90}{\$250} = 36$ Percent
Dec. 31, Year 2:	$\dfrac{\$\ 50}{\$350} = 14$ Percent	Dec. 31, Year 2:	$\dfrac{\$100}{\$400} = 25$ Percent
Dec. 31, Year 3:	$\dfrac{\$100}{\$460} = 22$ Percent	Dec. 31, Year 3:	$\dfrac{\$160}{\$520} = 31$ Percent
Dec. 31, Year 4:	$\dfrac{\$150}{\$560} = 27$ Percent	Dec. 31, Year 4:	$\dfrac{\$240}{\$650} = 37$ Percent

these ratios, the higher the likelihood that the firm may be unable to meet fixed interest and principal payments in the future. The decision for most firms is how much financial leverage with its attendant risk they can afford to assume. Funds obtained from issuing bonds or borrowing from a bank have a relatively low interest cost but require fixed, periodic payments that increase the likelihood of bankruptcy.

In assessing the debt ratios, analysts customarily vary the standard in direct relation to the stability of the firm's earnings. The more stable the earnings, the higher the debt ratio that is considered acceptable or safe. The debt ratios of public utilities are customarily high, frequently on the order of 60 to 70 percent. The stability of public utility earnings makes these ratios acceptable to many investors who would be dissatisfied with such large leverage for firms with less stable earnings.

Because several variations of the debt ratio appear in corporate annual reports, care in making comparisons of debt ratios among firms is necessary.

Interest Coverage: Times Interest Charges Earned Another measure of long-term solvency is the *number of times that interest charges are earned,* or covered. This ratio is calculated by dividing net income before interest and income tax expenses by interest expense. For Horrigan Corporation, the times interest earned ratios for Year 2, Year 3, and Year 4 are

$$\frac{\text{Times Interest}}{\text{Charges Earned}} = \frac{\text{Net Income Before Interest and Income Taxes}}{\text{Interest Expense}}$$

$$\text{Year 2:} \quad \frac{\$16 + \$5 + \$10}{\$5} = 6.2 \text{ times}$$

$$\text{Year 3:} \quad \frac{\$34 + \$10 + \$22}{\$10} = 6.6 \text{ times}$$

$$\text{Year 4:} \quad \frac{\$60 + \$16 + \$40}{\$16} = 7.3 \text{ times}$$

Thus, whereas the bonded indebtedness increased sharply during the 3-year period, the growth in net income before interest and income taxes was sufficient to provide increasing coverage of the fixed interest charges.

The purpose of this ratio is to indicate the relative protection of bondholders and to assess the probability that the firm will be forced into bankruptcy by a failure to meet required interest payments. If periodic repayments of principal on long-term liabilities are also required, the repayments might also be included in the denominator of the ratio. The ratio would then be described as the *number of times that fixed charges were earned,* or covered.

The times interest or fixed charges earned ratios can be criticized as measures for assessing long-term solvency because the ratios use earnings rather than cash flows in the numerator. Interest and other fixed payment obligations are paid with cash, and not with earnings. When the value of the ratio is relatively low (for example, two to three times), some measure of cash flows, such as cash flows from operations, may be preferable in the numerator.

Limitations of Ratio Analysis

For convenient reference, Exhibit 18.9 summarizes the calculation of the ratios discussed in this chapter.

The analytical computations discussed in this chapter have a number of limitations that should be kept in mind by anyone preparing or using them. Several of the more important limitations are the following:

1. The ratios are based on financial statement data and are therefore subject to the same criticisms as the financial statements (for example, use of acquisition cost rather than current replacement cost or net realizable value; the latitude permitted firms in selecting from among various generally accepted accounting principles).

2. Changes in many ratios are highly associated with each other. For example, the changes in the current ratio and quick ratio between two different times are often in the same direction and approximately proportional. It is therefore not necessary to compute all the ratios to assess a particular factor.

3. When comparing the size of a ratio between periods for the same firm, one must recognize conditions that have changed between the periods being compared (for example, different product lines or geographic markets served, changes in economic conditions, changes in prices).

4. When comparing ratios of a particular firm with those of similar firms, one must recognize differences between the firms (for example, use of different methods of accounting, differences in the method of operations, type of financing, and so on).

Results of financial statement analyses cannot be used by themselves as direct indications of good or poor management. Such analyses merely indicate areas that might be investigated further. For example, a decrease in the turnover of raw materials inventory, ordinarily considered to be an undesirable trend, may reflect the accumulation of scarce materials that will keep the plant operating at full

Exhibit 18.9
Summary of Financial
Statement Ratios

Ratio	Numerator	Denominator
Rate of Return on Assets	Net Income + Interest Expense (net of tax effects)[a]	Average Total Assets During the Period
Profit Margin Ratio (before interest effects)	Net Income + Interest Expense (net of tax effects)[a]	Revenues
Various Expenses Ratios	Various Expenses	Revenues
Total Assets Turnover Ratio	Revenues	Average Total Assets During the Period
Accounts Receivable Turnover Ratio	Net Sales on Accounts	Average Accounts Receivable During the Period
Inventory Turnover Ratio	Cost of Goods Sold	Average Inventory During the Period
Plant Asset Turnover Ratio	Sales	Average Plant Assets During the Period
Rate of Return on Common Stock Equity	Net Income − Preferred Stock Dividends	Average Common Shareholders' Equity During the Period
Earnings per Share of Stock[b]	Net Income − Preferred Stock Dividends	Weighted Average Number of Common Shares Outstanding During the Period
Current Ratio	Current Assets	Current Liabilities
Quick or Acid Test Ratio	Highly Liquid Assets (ordinarily, cash, marketable securities, and receivables)[c]	Current Liabilities
Long-Term Debt Ratio	Total Noncurrent Liabilities	Total Noncurrent Liabilities Plus Shareholders' Equity
Debt-Equity Ratio	Total Liabilities	Total Equities (liabilities plus shareholders' equity)
Times Interest Charges Earned	Net Income Before Interest and Income Taxes	Interest Expense

[a]If a consolidated subsidiary is not owned entirely by the parent corporation, the minority interest share of earnings must also be added back to net income.

[b]This calculation can be more complicated when there are convertible securities, options, or warrants outstanding.

[c]Receivables could conceivably be excluded for some firms and inventories included for others. Such refinements are seldom employed in practice.

capacity during shortages when competitors have been forced to restrict operations or to close down. Ratios derived from financial statements must be combined with an investigation of other facts before valid conclusions can be drawn.

Summary

Earlier in this chapter we raised the question: "Should you invest your inheritance in a certificate of deposit or in the shares of common stock of Horrigan Corporation?" Our analysis of Horrigan Corporation's financial statements indicates that it has been a growing, profitable company with few indications of either short-term liquidity or long-term solvency problems. At least three additional inputs are necessary before making the investment decisions. First, you must consider other sources of information besides the financial statements to assess whether additional information for projecting rates of return or for assessing risk needs to be considered. Second, you must decide your attitude toward, or willingness to assume, risk. Third, you must decide if you think the stock market price of the shares makes them an attractive purchase.[10] It is at this stage in the investment decision that the analysis becomes particularly subjective.

---

[10]Other important factors cannot be discussed here, but are in finance texts. Perhaps the most important question of all is how a particular investment fits in with the investor's entire portfolio. Modern research suggests that the suitability of a potential investment depends more on the attributes of the other components of an investment portfolio and the risk attitude of the investor than it does on the attributes of the potential investment itself.

Exhibit 18.10
COX CORPORATION
Comparative Balance Sheet
December 31, Year 1 and Year 2

	December 31	
	Year 1	Year 2
Assets		
Current Assets		
Cash.	$ 600	$ 750
Accounts Receivable	3,600	4,300
Merchandise Inventories.	5,600	7,900
Prepayments.	300	380
Total Current Assets	$10,100	$13,330
Property, Plant, and Equipment		
Land.	$ 500	$ 600
Buildings and Equipment (net).	9,400	10,070
Total Property, Plant, and Equipment	$ 9,900	$10,670
Total Assets	$20,000	$24,000
Liabilities and Shareholders' Equity		
Current Liabilities		
Notes Payable	$ 2,000	$ 4,000
Accounts Payable	3,500	3,300
Other Current Liabilities	1,500	1,900
Total Current Liabilities	$ 7,000	$ 9,200
Noncurrent Liabilities		
Bonds Payable	4,000	2,800
Total Liabilities	$11,000	$12,000
Shareholders' Equity		
Preferred Stock	$ 1,000	$ 1,000
Common Stock	2,000	2,500
Additional Paid-in Capital	1,500	1,800
Retained Earnings	4,500	6,700
Total Shareholders' Equity	$ 9,000	$12,000
Total Liabilities and Shareholders' Equity	$20,000	$24,000

Problem for Self-Study

Exhibit 18.10 on the opposite page presents a comparative balance sheet for Cox Corporation as of December 31, Year 1 and Year 2, and Exhibit 18.11 presents an income statement for Year 2. Using information from these financial statements, compute the following ratios. The income tax rate is 40 percent.

a. Rate of return on assets.
b. Profit margin ratio (before interest and related tax effects).
c. Cost of goods sold to sales percentage.
d. Selling expense to sales percentage.
e. Total assets turnover.
f. Accounts receivable turnover.

g. Inventory turnover
h. Plant asset turnover.
i. Rate of return on common stock equity.
j. Current ratio (both dates).
k. Quick ratio (both dates).
l. Long-term debt ratio (both dates).
m. Debt-equity ratio (both dates).
n. Times interest charges earned.

Exhibit 18.11
COX CORPORATION
Income and Retained Earnings Statement
for the Year Ended December 31, Year 2

Sales Revenue		$30,000
Less Expenses:		
Cost of Goods Sold	$18,000	
Selling	4,500	
Administrative	1,800	
Interest	700	
Income Taxes	2,000	
Total Expenses		27,000
Net Income		$ 3,000
Less Dividends:		
Preferred	$ 100	
Common	700	800
Increase in Retained Earnings for Year 2		$ 2,200
Retained Earnings, December 31, Year 1		4,500
Retained Earnings, December 31, Year 2		$ 6,700

Suggested Solution

a. Rate of Return on Assets $= \dfrac{\$3,000 + (1 - .40)(\$700)}{.5(\$20,000 + \$24,000)} = 15.5$ percent.

b. Profit Margin Ratio $= \dfrac{\$3,000 + (1 - .40)(\$700)}{\$30,000} = 11.4$ percent.

c. Cost of Goods Sold to Sales Percentage $= \dfrac{\$18,000}{\$30,000} = 60.0$ percent.

d. Selling Expense to Sales Percentage $= \dfrac{\$4,500}{\$30,000} = 15.0$ percent.

e. Total Assets Turnover $= \dfrac{\$30,000}{.5(\$20,000 + \$24,000)} = 1.4$ times per year.

f. Accounts Receivable Turnover $= \dfrac{\$30,000}{.5(\$3,600 + \$4,300)} = 7.6$ times per year.

g. Inventory Turnover $= \dfrac{\$18,000}{.5(\$5,600 + \$7,900)} = 2.7$ times per year.

h. Plant Asset Turnover $= \dfrac{\$30,000}{.5(\$9,900 + \$10,670)} = 2.9$ times per year.

i. Rate of Return on Common Stock Equity $= \dfrac{\$3,000 - \$100}{.5(\$8,000 + \$11,000)} = 30.5$ percent.

j. Current Ratio:

December 31, Year 1: $\dfrac{\$10,100}{\$7,000} = 1.4:1.$

December 31, Year 2: $\dfrac{\$13,330}{\$9,200} = 1.4:1.$

k. Quick Ratio:

December 31, Year 1: $\dfrac{\$4,200}{\$7,000} = .6:1.$

December 31, Year 2: $\dfrac{\$5,050}{\$9,200} = .5:1.$

l. Long-Term Debt Ratio:

December 31, Year 1: $\dfrac{\$4,000}{\$13,000} = 30.8$ percent.

December 31, Year 2: $\dfrac{\$2,800}{\$14,800} = 18.9$ percent.

m. Debt-Equity Ratio:

December 31, Year 1: $\dfrac{\$11,000}{\$20,000} = 55.0$ percent.

December 31, Year 2: $\dfrac{\$12,000}{\$24,000} = 50.0$ percent.

n. Times Interest Charges Earned $= \dfrac{\$3,000 + \$2,000 + \$700}{\$700} = 8.1$ times.

Questions

1. Review the meaning of the following concepts or terms discussed in this chapter.

a. Expected return and risk.	**i.** Financial leverage.
b. Rate of return on assets.	**j.** Earnings per common share.
c. Profit margin ratio (before interest and related tax effects).	**k.** Price-earnings ratio.
	l. Short-term liquidity risk.
	m. Long-term solvency risk.
d. Total assets turnover.	**n.** Current ratio.
e. Accounts receivable turnover.	**o.** Quick ratio.
f. Inventory turnover.	**p.** Long-term debt ratio.
g. Plant asset turnover.	**q.** Debt-equity ratio.
h. Rate of return on common stock equity.	**r.** Times interest charges earned.
	s. Time-series analysis.

2. Describe several factors that might limit the comparability of a firm's current ratio over several periods.

3. Describe several factors that might limit the comparability of one firm's current ratio with that of another firm in the same industry.

4. Under what circumstances will the rate of return on the common stock equity be more than the rate of return on assets? Under what circumstances will it be less?

5. A company president recently stated: "The operations of our company are such that we can use effectively only a small amount of financial leverage." Explain.

Exercises

6. *Disaggregation of Rate of Return on Assets.* The following data are taken from the Year 2 annual reports of Alabama Company and Carolina Company.

	Alabama Co.	Carolina Co.
Sales	$2,000,000	$2,400,000
Expenses Other Than Interest and Income Taxes.	1,700,000	2,150,000
Interest Expense	100,000	50,000
Income Tax Expense at 40 Percent.	80,000	80,000
Net Income	120,000	120,000
Average Total Assets During the Year.	1,500,000	1,000,000

a. Calculate the rate of return on assets for each company.
b. Disaggregate the rate of return in part **a** into profit margin and total assets turnover components.
c. Comment on the relative performance of the two companies.

7. *Accounting Versus Market Measures of Return.* Net income attributable to common shareholders' equity of Florida Corporation during Year 2 was $250,000. Earnings per share was $.50 during the period. The average common shareholders' equity during Year 2 was $2,500,000. The market price at year-end was $6.00 per share.

    a. Calculate the rate of return on common shareholders' equity for Year 2.

    b. Calculate the rate of return currently being earned on the market price of the stock (the ratio of earnings per common share to market price per common share).

    c. Why is there a difference between the rates of return calculated in parts **a** and **b**?

8. *Working Backwards from Ratios to Financial Statements.* The revenues of Lev Company were $1,000 for the year. A financial analyst computed the following ratios for Lev Company, using the year-end balances for balance sheet amounts.

Debt-Equity Ratio (all liabilities/all equities)	$73\frac{1}{3}\%$
Income Tax Expense as a Percentage of Pretax Income	40%
Net Income as a Percentage of Revenue	12%
Rate of Return on Shareholders' Equity	10%
Rate of Return on Assets	6%

From this information, compute each of the following items.

    a. Interest expense.

    b. Income tax expense.

    c. Total expenses.

    d. Net income.

    e. Total assets.

    f. Total liabilities.

9. *Relation of Profitability to Risk.* Refer to the data below for the Adelsman Company.

	Year 1	Year 2	Year 3
Rate of Return on Common Shareholders' Equity	8%	10%	11%
Earnings per Share	$3.00	$4.00	$4.40
Net Income/Total Interest Expense[a]	10	5	4
Debt-Equity Ratio (liabilities/all equities).	20%	50%	60%

[a]Note that this computation does not represent "times interest earned" as defined in the chapter.

The income tax rate was 40 percent in each year and 100,000 common shares were outstanding throughout the period.

    a. Did the company's profitability increase over the 3-year period? How can you tell? (*Hint:* Compute the rate of return on assets.)

    b. Did risk increase? How can you tell?

    c. Are shareholders better off in Year 3 than in Year 1?

10. *Profitability Analysis of Two Industries.* The following information is taken from the annual reports of two companies, one of which is a retailer of quality men's clothes and the other of which is a discount household goods store. Neither company had any interest-bearing debt during the year. Identify which of these companies is likely to be the clothing retailer and which is likely to be the discount store. Explain.

	Company A	Company B
Sales	$3,000,000	$3,000,000
Net Income	60,000	300,000
Average Total Assets	600,000	3,000,000

11. *Profitability Analysis of Three Industries.* Exhibit 18.12 shows five items from the financial statements for three companies for a recent year:

Exhibit 18.12
Comparison of Operations and Investment
(Problem 11)

	Company A	Company B	Company C
For Year			
Operating Revenues	$28,947,200	$13,639,900	$9,716,900
Income Before Interest and Dividends[a] . .	4,295,800	824,600	156,400
Net Income to Common Shareholders[b] . .	2,915,800	522,600	148,600
Average During Year			
Total Assets	77,107,200	10,885,000	1,532,400
Common Shareholders' Equity	29,769,200	5,118,800	743,830

[a]Net income + interest charges × (1 − tax rate).
[b]Net income − preferred stock dividends.

   a. Compute the income to sales (or income to operating revenues) ratio for each company. Which company seems to be the most successful according to this ratio?

   b. How many dollars of sales on average does each of the companies make for each dollar's worth of average assets held during the year?

   c. Compute the rate of return on assets for each company. Which company seems to be the most successful according to this ratio?

   d. Compute the rate of return on common shareholders' equity for each company. Which company seems to be the most successful according to this ratio?

   e. The three companies are American Telephone & Telegraph, Safeway Stores, and Sears, Roebuck and Company. (Dollar amounts shown are actually in thousands.) Which of the companies corresponds to A, B, and C? What clues did you use in reaching your conclusion?

12. *Relation of Profitability to Financial Leverage.* The Borrowing Company has total assets of $100,000 during the year. It has borrowed $20,000 at a 10 percent annual rate and pays income taxes at a rate of 40 percent of pretax income. Shareholders' equity is $80,000.

    a. What must net income be for the rate of return on shareholders' equity to equal the rate of return on assets (the all capital earnings rate)?

    b. What is the rate of return on shareholders' equity for the net income determined above in part **a**?

    c. What must income before interest and income taxes be to achieve this net income?

    d. Repeat parts **a**, **b**, and **c** assuming borrowing of $80,000 and shareholders' equity of $20,000.

    e. Compare the results from the two different debt-equity relations. What generalizations can be made?

13. *Relation of Profitability to Financial Leverage*

    a. Compute the ratio of return on common shareholders' equity in each of the independent cases below.

Case	Total Assets	Interest-Bearing Debt	Common Shareholders' Equity	Rate of Return on Assets	Aftertax Cost of Interest-Bearing Debt
A	$200	$100	$100	6%	6%
B	$200	$100	$100	8%	6%
C	$200	$120	$ 80	8%	6%
D	$200	$100	$100	4%	6%
E	$200	$ 50	$100	6%	6%
F	$200	$ 50	$100	5%	6%

    b. In which cases is leverage working to the advantage of the common shareholders?

14. *Earnings per Share Versus Rates of Return (CMA adapted).* The Virgil Company is planning to invest $10 million in an expansion program that is expected to increase income before interest and taxes by $2.5 million. Currently, Virgil Company has total equities of $40 million, 25 percent of which is debt and 75 percent of which is shareholders' equity, represented by 1 million shares. The expansion can be financed with the issuance of 200,000 new shares at $50 each or by issuing long-term debt at an annual interest rate of 10 percent. The following is an excerpt from the most recent income statement.

Earnings Before Interest and Taxes	$10,500,000
Less: Interest Charges	500,000
Earnings Before Income Taxes	$10,000,000
Income Taxes (at 40 percent)	4,000,000
Net Income	$ 6,000,000

Assume that Virgil Company maintains its current earnings on its present assets, achieves the planned earnings from the new program, and that the tax rate remains at 40 percent.

    a. What will be earnings per share if the expansion is financed with debt?

    b. What will be earnings per share if the expansion is financed by issuing new shares?

    c. At what level of earnings before interest and taxes will earnings per share be the same, whichever of the two financing programs is used?

    d. At what level of earnings before interest and taxes will the rate of return on shareholders' equity be the same, whichever of the two financing plans is used?

15. *Earnings per Share Versus Rates of Return.* Company A and Company B both start Year 2 with $1 million of shareholders' equity and 100,000 shares of common stock outstanding. During Year 2, both companies earn net income of $100,000, a rate of return of 10 percent on shareholders' equity. Company A declares and pays $100,000 of dividends to common shareholders at the end of Year 2, whereas Company B retains all its earnings, declaring no dividends. During Year 3, both companies earn net income equal to 10 percent of shareholders' equity at the beginning of Year 3.

    a. Compute earnings per share for Company A and for Company B for Year 2 and for Year 3.

    b. Compute the rate of growth in earnings per share for Company A and Company B, comparing earnings per share in Year 3 with earnings per share in Year 2.

    c. Using the rate of growth in earnings per share as the criterion, which company's management appears to be doing a better job for its shareholders? Comment on this result.

16. *Calculation and Interpretation of Current Ratio.* Following is a schedule of the current assets and current liabilities of the Lewis Company:

	December 31	
	Year 2	**Year 1**
Current Assets		
Cash	$ 355,890	$ 212,790
Accounts Receivable	389,210	646,010
Inventories	799,100	1,118,200
Prepayments.	21,600	30,000
Total Current Assets	$1,565,800	$2,007,000
Current Liabilities		
Accounts Payable	$ 152,760	$ 217,240
Accrued Payroll, Taxes, etc.	126,340	318,760
Notes Payable	69,500	330,000
Total Current Liabilities	$ 348,600	$ 866,000

The Lewis Company operated at a loss during Year 2.

    a. Calculate the current ratio for each date.

    b. Explain how the improved current ratio is possible under the Year 2 operating conditions.

17. *Calculation and Interpretation of Accounts Receivable Turnover*. The following information relates to the activities of Tennessee Corporation and Kentucky Corporation for Year 2.

	Tennessee Corp.	Kentucky Corp.
Sales on Account, Year 2	$4,050,000	$2,560,000
Accounts Receivable, December 31, Year 1	960,000	500,000
Accounts Receivable, December 31, Year 2	840,000	780,000

    a. Compute the accounts receivable turnover of each company.

    b. Compute the average number of days that accounts receivable are outstanding for each company.

    c. Which company is managing its accounts receivable more efficiently?

Problems and Cases

18. *Interpretation of Financial Statement Ratios (CMA adapted)*. Thorpe Company is a wholesale distributor of professional equipment and supplies. The company's sales have averaged about $900,000 annually for the 3-year period Year 6–Year 8. The firm's total assets at the end of Year 8 amounted to $850,000.

The president of Thorpe Company has asked the controller to prepare a report that summarizes the financial aspects of the company's operations for the past 3 years. This report will be presented to the board of directors at their next meeting.

In addition to comparative financial statements, the controller has decided to present a number of relevant financial ratios that can assist in the identification and interpretation of trends. At the request of the controller, the accounting staff has calculated the following ratios for the 3-year period Year 6–Year 8.

	Year 6	Year 7	Year 8
Current Ratio	2.00	2.13	2.18
Acid Test (Quick) Ratio	1.20	1.10	0.97
Accounts Receivable Turnover	9.72	8.57	7.13
Inventory Turnover	5.25	4.80	3.80
Sales to Fixed Assets (Fixed Asset Turnover)	1.75	1.88	1.99
Sales as a Percent of Year 5 Sales	1.00	1.03	1.06
Gross Margin Percentage	40.0	38.6	38.5
Net Income to Sales	7.8%	7.8%	8.0%
Return on Total Assets	8.5%	8.6%	8.7%
Return on Shareholders' Equity	15.1%	14.6%	14.1%
Percent of Total Debt to Total Assets	44.0%	41.0%	38.0%
Percent of Long-Term Debt to Total Assets	25.0%	22.0%	19.0%

In the preparation of the report, the controller has decided first to examine the financial ratios independently of any other data to determine if the ratios themselves reveal any significant trends over the 3-year period.

a. The current ratio is increasing while the acid test (quick) ratio is decreasing. Using the ratios provided, identify and explain the contributing factor(s) for this apparently divergent trend.

b. In terms of the ratios provided, what conclusion(s) can be drawn regarding the company's use of financial leverage during the period Year 6–Year 8?

c. Using the ratios provided, what conclusion(s) can be drawn regarding the company's net investment in plant and equipment?

19. *Calculation and Interpretation of Financial Statement Ratios.* The income statements and balance sheets of Illinois Corporation and Ohio Corporation are presented in Exhibits 18.13 and 18.14. Assume that the balances in asset and equity

Exhibit 18.13
Income Statements
for Year 3
(Problem 19)

	Illinois Corp.	Ohio Corp.
Sales	$4,300,000	$3,000,000
Less Expenses:		
Cost of Goods Sold	$2,800,000	$1,400,000
Selling and Administrative Expenses	330,000	580,000
Interest Expense	100,000	200,000
Income Tax Expense	428,000	328,000
Total Expenses	$3,658,000	$2,508,000
Net Income	$ 642,000	$ 492,000

Exhibit 18.14
Balance Sheets
December 31, Year 3
(Problem 19)

	Illinois Corp.	Ohio Corp.
Assets		
Cash	$ 100,000	$ 50,000
Accounts Receivable (net).	700,000	400,000
Merchandise Inventory	1,200,000	750,000
Plant and Equipment (net).	4,000,000	4,800,000
Total Assets	$6,000,000	$6,000,000
Equities		
Accounts Payable.	$ 572,000	$ 172,000
Income Taxes Payable	428,000	328,000
Long-Term Bonds Payable (10 percent)	1,000,000	2,000,000
Capital Stock	2,000,000	2,000,000
Retained Earnings	2,000,000	1,500,000
Total Equities	$6,000,000	$6,000,000

accounts at year-end approximate the average balances during the period. The income tax rate is 40 percent. On the basis of this information, which company is

   a. More profitable?
   b. More liquid?
   c. More secure in terms of long-term solvency?

Use financial ratios, as appropriate, in doing your analysis.

20. *Calculation and Interpretation of Financial Statement Ratios.* The comparative balance sheets and the income statement of Solinger Electric Corporation for Year 2 are shown in Exhibits 18.15 and 18.16, respectively. Income taxes are 40 percent of pretax income.

   a. Calculate the ratios for Solinger Electric Corporation for Year 2 listed on the next page.

Exhibit 18.15
SOLINGER ELECTRIC CORPORATION
Comparative Balance Sheets
for December 31, Year 1 and Year 2
(Problem 20)

	December 31 Year 1	December 31 Year 2
Assets		
Current Assets		
Cash	$ 30,000	$ 3,000
Accounts Receivable	20,000	55,000
Merchandise Inventory	40,000	50,000
Total Current Assets	$ 90,000	$108,000
Noncurrent Assets		
Buildings and Equipment (cost)	$100,000	$225,000
Accumulated Depreciation	(30,000)	(40,000)
Total Noncurrent Assets	$ 70,000	$185,000
Total Assets	$160,000	$293,000
Equities		
Current Liabilities		
Accounts Payable—Merchandise Suppliers	$ 30,000	$ 50,000
Accounts Payable—Other Suppliers	10,000	12,000
Salaries Payable	5,000	6,000
Total Current Liabilities	$ 45,000	$ 68,000
Noncurrent Liabilities		
Bonds Payable	–0–	100,000
Total Liabilities	$ 45,000	$168,000
Owners' Equity		
Capital Stock ($10 par value)	$100,000	$100,000
Retained Earnings	15,000	25,000
Total Owners' Equity	$115,000	$125,000
Total Equities	$160,000	$293,000

Exhibit 18.16
SOLINGER ELECTRIC CORPORATION
Income Statement
for Year 2
(Problem 20)

Sales Revenue	$125,000
Less Expenses:	
Cost of Goods Sold.	$ 60,000
Salaries	19,667
Depreciation	10,000
Interest	2,000
Income Taxes.	13,333
Total Expenses	$105,000
Net Income.	$ 20,000

    (1) Rate of return on assets.
    (2) Rate of return on common shareholders' equity.
    (3) Earnings per share.
    (4) Accounts receivable turnover (assuming that all sales are made on account).
    (5) Inventory turnover.
    (6) Plant asset turnover.
    (7) Current ratio on December 31, Year 1, and December 31, Year 2.
    (8) Quick ratio on December 31, Year 1, and December 31, Year 2 (assuming that merchandise inventories are excluded from quick assets).
    (9) Debt-equity ratio on December 31, Year 1, and December 31, Year 2.
    (10) Times interest charges earned ratio.
  b. Was Solinger Electric Corporation successfully leveraged during Year 2?
  c. Assume that the bonds were issued on November 1, Year 2. At what annual interest rate were the bonds apparently issued?
  d. If Solinger Electric Corporation earns the same rate of return on assets in Year 3 as it realized in Year 2, and issues no more debt, will the firm be successfully leveraged in Year 3?

21. *Calculation and Interpretation of Financial Statement Ratios.* Comparative balance sheets and the income statement of Nykerk Electronics Corporation for Year 2 are presented in Exhibits 18.17 and 18.18, respectively.
  a. Calculate the following ratios for Nykerk Electronics Corporation for Year 2.
    (1) Rate of return on assets.
    (2) Rate of return on common shareholders' equity.
    (3) Earnings per share.
    (4) Accounts receivable turnover (assuming that all sales are made on account).
    (5) Inventory turnover.
    (6) Plant asset turnover.
    (7) Current ratio on December 31, Year 1, and December 31, Year 2.

Exhibit 18.17
NYKERK ELECTRONICS CORPORATION
Comparative Balance Sheets
(Problem 21)

	(in 000's of dollars)	
	December 31	
	Year 2	**Year 1**
Assets		
Current Assets		
Cash.	$ 1,300	$ 1,100
Marketable Securities	300	300
Accounts Receivable (net)	2,600	2,500
Inventories.	7,300	6,900
Total Current Assets	$11,500	$10,800
Noncurrent Assets		
Plant and Equipment	$ 5,200	$ 4,500
Less Accumulated Depreciation	1,300	1,000
Net Plant and Equipment	$ 3,900	$ 3,500
Land.	1,200	1,200
Total Noncurrent Assets	$ 5,100	$ 4,700
Total Assets	$16,600	$15,500
Liabilities and Shareholders' Equity		
Current Liabilities		
Accounts Payable	$ 1,600	$ 1,700
Accrued Payables	800	900
Income Taxes Payable	300	200
Notes Payable	1,900	1,200
Total Current Liabilities	$ 4,600	$ 4,000
Long-Term Liabilities		
Bonds Payable (8 percent)	$ 2,000	$ 2,100
Mortgage Payable	200	200
Total Long-Term Liabilities	$ 2,200	$ 2,300
Total Liabilities	$ 6,800	$ 6,300
Shareholders' Equity		
Preferred Stock (6 percent, $100 par)	$ 2,000	$ 2,000
Common Stock ($1 par)	500	500
Additional Paid-in Capital	2,500	2,500
Total Contributed Capital	$ 5,000	$ 5,000
Retained Earnings	4,800	4,200
Total Shareholders' Equity	$ 9,800	$ 9,200
Total Liabilities and Shareholders' Equity	$16,600	$15,500

    (8) Quick ratio on December 31, Year 1, and December 31, Year 2.

    (9) Debt-equity ratio on December 31, Year 1, and December 31, Year 2.

    (10) Times interest charges earned ratio.

    b. Was Nykerk Electronics Corporation successfully leveraged during Year 2?

Exhibit 18.18
NYKERK ELECTRONICS CORPORATION
Statement of Income and Retained Earnings
Year 2
(Problem 21)

	(in 000's of dollars)
Revenues	
Sales	$26,500
Less Sales Allowances, Returns, and Discounts	600
Net Sales	$25,900
Interest and Other Revenues	200
Total Revenues	$26,100
Expenses	
Cost of Goods Sold	$20,500
Selling and Administrative Expenses:	
Selling Expenses $2,120	
Administrative Expenses 1,000	
Depreciation 300	
Total Selling and Administrative Expenses	3,420
Interest Expense	180
Income Tax Expense	800
Total Expenses	$24,900
Net Income to Shareholders	$ 1,200

22. *Industry Differences in Financial Statement Ratios.* In this problem, you become a financial analyst/detective. The condensed financial statements in Exhibit 18.19 are constructed on a percentage basis. In all cases, total sales revenues are shown as 100.00 percent. All other numbers were divided by sales revenue for the year. The 13 companies (all corporations except for the accounting firm) shown here represent the following industries:

(1) Advertising and public opinion survey firm.
(2) Beer brewery.
(3) Department store chain (which carries its own receivables).
(4) Distiller of hard liquor.
(5) Drug manufacturer.
(6) Finance company (lends money to consumers).
(7) Grocery store chain.
(8) Insurance company.
(9) Manufacturer of tobacco products, mainly cigarettes.
(10) Public accounting (CPA) partnership.
(11) Soft drink bottler.
(12) Steel manufacturer.
(13) Utility company.

Use whatever clues you can to match the companies in Exhibit 18.19 with the industries listed above. You may find it useful to refer to average industry ratios compiled by Dun & Bradstreet, Prentice-Hall, Robert Morris Associates, and the Federal Trade Commission. Copies of these documents can be found in most libraries.

Exhibit 18.19
Data for Ratio Detective Exercise
(Problem 22)

	Company Numbers						
	(1)	(2)	(3)	(4)	(5)	(6)	(7)
Balance Sheet at End of Year							
Current Receivables	0.31%	29.11%	6.81%	25.25%	3.45%	38.78%	17.64%
Inventories	7.80	0.00	3.14	0.00	6.45	14.94	20.57
Net Plant and Equipment*	8.50	9.63	11.13	19.88	49.87	15.59	37.60
All Other Assets	2.16	7.02	25.59	32.93	24.05	15.54	30.07
Total Assets	18.78%	45.76%	46.67%	78.06%	83.83%	84.85%	105.88%
*Cost of Plant and Equipment (gross) . . .	14.64%	14.80%	19.57%	29.03%	79.03%	24.80%	59.73%
Current Liabilities	6.08%	9.82%	6.41%	17.49%	14.83%	35.28%	27.68%
Long-Term Liabilities . . . . . . : .	2.12	7.96	0.00	0.00	0.00	8.33	1.33
Owners' Equity	10.58	27.98	40.25	60.57	69.00	41.24	76.86
Total Equities	18.78%	45.76%	46.67%	78.06%	83.83%	84.85%	105.88%
Income Statement for Year							
Revenues	100.00%	100.00%	100.00%	100.00%	100.00%	100.00%	100.00%
Cost of Goods Sold (excluding depreciation) or Operating Expenses[a] . .	78.97	53.77	48.21	59.07	68.62	60.88	33.29
Depreciation	1.04	1.39	1.72	2.07	4.07	1.09	3.02
Interest Expense	0.16	.52	0.00	0.08	0.02	1.35	0.73
Advertising Expense	3.72	0.00	11.43	0.06	4.39	2.93	2.28
Research and Development Expense	0.00	1.00	0.00	0.00	0.15	0.00	9.06
Income Taxes	1.28	.53	9.59	6.52	7.87	3.78	8.55
All Other Items (net)	13.34	18.88	18.58	24.52	6.40	24.39	27.66
Total Expenses	98.50%	76.08%	89.53%	92.32%	91.51%	94.41%	84.59%
Net Income	1.50%	23.92%	10.47%	7.68%	8.49%	5.59%	15.41%

[a]Represents operating expenses for the following companies: advertising/public opinion survey firm, insurance company, finance company, and the public accounting partnership.

Suggested Solutions to Even-Numbered Exercises

6. *Disaggregation of Rate of Return on Assets.*

    a. Alabama Co.:
$$\frac{\$120,000 + (1 - .40)(\$100,000)}{\$1,500,000} = 12 \text{ percent.}$$

           Carolina Co.:
$$\frac{\$120,000 + (1 - .40)(\$50,000)}{\$1,000,000} = 15 \text{ percent.}$$

    b.   Rate of Return on Assets =   Profit Margin Ratio   ×   Total Assets Turnover Ratio

Alabama Co.:
$$\frac{\$120,000 + (1 - .40)(\$100,000)}{\$1,500,000} = \frac{\$120,000 + (1 - .40)(\$100,000)}{\$2,000,000} \times \frac{\$2,000,000}{\$1,500,000}$$

$$12 \text{ percent} = \quad 9 \text{ percent} \quad \times \quad 1.33$$

	Company Numbers					
	(8)	(9)	(10)	(11)	(12)	(13)
Balance Sheet at End of Year						
Current Receivables	12.94%	9.16%	25.18%	27.07%	13.10%	653.94%
Inventories	15.47	56.89	79.53	0.00	1.62	0.00
Net Plant and Equipment*	70.29	28.36	19.22	2.64	251.62	2.88
All Other Assets	18.37	26.42	24.72	223.91	23.68	200.37
Total Assets	117.08%	120.82%	148.65%	253.63%	290.01%	857.18%
*Cost of Plant and Equipment (gross)	167.16%	42.40%	35.08%	4.45%	320.90%	3.81%
Current Liabilities	19.37%	33.01%	20.42%	161.37%	28.01%	377.56%
Long-Term Liabilities	20.62	34.07	36.09	10.62	115.50	280.79
Owners' Equity	77.09	53.74	92.13	81.63	146.51	198.83
Total Equities	117.08%	120.82%	148.65%	253.63%	290.01%	857.18%
Income Statement for Year						
Revenues	100.00%	100.00%	100.00%	100.00%	100.00%	100.00%
Cost of Goods Sold (excluding depreciation) or						
Operating Expenses[a]	81.92	57.35	42.92	82.61	45.23	47.69
Depreciation	5.81	1.90	1.97	0.05	14.55	0.00
Interest Expense	1.23	2.69	3.11	1.07	7.15	24.33
Advertising Expense	0.00	6.93	13.04	0.00	0.00	0.00
Research and Development Expense	0.76	0.00	0.00	0.00	0.71	0.00
Income Taxes	2.15	7.47	10.63	3.92	8.73	12.89
All Other Items (net)	3.81	14.82	17.99	2.97	11.51	−5.57
Total Expenses	95.68%	91.16%	89.66%	90.62%	87.89%	79.35%
Net Income	4.32%	8.84%	10.34%	9.38%	12.11%	20.65%

Carolina Co.:

$$\frac{\$120,000 + (1 - .40)(\$\,50,000)}{\$1,000,000} = \frac{\$120,000 + (1 - .40)(\$\,50,000)}{\$2,400,000} \times \frac{\$2,400,000}{\$1,000,000}$$

$$15 \text{ percent} = 6.25 \text{ percent} \times 2.40$$

c. Although the profit margin percentage of Carolina Company is smaller than that for Alabama Company, Carolina Company generated more sales per dollar of investment in assets as indicated by the larger asset turnover. The return on assets of Carolina Company is, therefore, higher than for Alabama Company.

8. *Working Backwards from Ratios to Financial Statements.*
   a. $250.
   b. $80.
   c. $880.
   d. $120.
   e. $4,500.
   f. $3,300.
   The computation of the amounts is shown below.

LEV COMPANY
Income Statement

Revenues		$1,000 **(1)**
Other Expenses	$550 **(10)**	
Interest	250 **(9)**	
Income Taxes	80 **(4)**	
Total Expenses		880 **(3)**
Net Income		$ 120 **(2)**

LEV COMPANY
Balance Sheet

Assets . . . . $4,500 **(8)**	Liabilities	$3,300	**(6)**
	Owners' Equity	1,200	**(5)**
		$4,500	**(7)**

(1) Revenues = $1,000.

(2) Net Income = $0.12 \times \$1,000 = \$120$.

(3) Total Expenses = $\$1,000 - \$120 = \$880$.

(4) Income Tax Expense = $0.40 \times \dfrac{\$120}{1 - 0.40} = \$80$.

(5) Owners' Equity = $\dfrac{\$120}{0.10} = \$1,200$.

(6) Liabilities = $\dfrac{\$73\frac{1}{3}\% \times \$1,200}{26\frac{2}{3}\%} = \$3,300$.

(7) Total Equities = $\$1,200 + \$3,300 = \$4,500$.

(8) Assets = $\$4,500$

(9) $\dfrac{\$120 + (1 - 0.40) \text{ Interest Expense}}{\$4,500} = 0.06$

$$\text{Interest Expense} = \$250.$$

(10) Other Expenses = $\$880 - \$80 - \$250 = \$550$.

10. *Profitability Analysis of Two Industries.* Company A is likely to be the discount store because it has a smaller profit margin and larger total assets turnover than Company B, the clothing retailer. The analysis is presented below.

$$\begin{array}{ccc} \text{Rate of} & & \text{Total} \\ \text{Rate of} & \text{Profit} & \text{Assets} \\ \text{Return} & = & \text{Margin} & \times & \text{Turnover} \\ \text{On Assets} & & \text{Ratio} & & \text{Ratio} \end{array}$$

Company A:
$$\frac{\$\ 60,000}{\$\ 600,000} = \frac{\$\ 60,000}{\$3,000,000} \times \frac{\$3,000,000}{\$\ 600,000}$$

$$10\ \text{Percent} = 2\ \text{Percent} \times 5.0.$$

Company B:
$$\frac{\$\ 300,000}{\$3,000,000} = \frac{\$\ 300,000}{\$3,000,000} \times \frac{\$3,000,000}{\$3,000,000}$$

$$10\ \text{Percent} = 10\ \text{Percent} \times 1.0.$$

12. *Relationship of Profitability to Financial Leverage.*
  a. Let Y represent net income. Then

$$\frac{Y + .60(.10 \times \$20,000)}{\$100,000} = \frac{Y}{\$80,000}$$

$$\$100,000Y = \$80,000(Y + \$1,200)$$

$$20Y = \$96,000$$

$$Y = \$4,800\ \text{net income.}$$

  b. $\$4,800 \div \$80,000 = 6$ percent rate of return on shareholders' equity.
  c. Let X represent pretax income. Then $.6X = \$4,800$; $X = \$8,000$; and income before interest and taxes must be $\$8,000 + \$2,000 = \$10,000$.
  d.
$$\frac{Y + .60(.10 \times \$80,000)}{\$100,000} = \frac{Y}{\$20,000}$$

$$\$100,000Y = \$20,000(Y + \$4,800)$$

$$80Y = \$96,000$$

$$Y = \$1,200$$

$$\frac{\$\ 1,200}{\$20,000} = 6\ \text{percent.}$$

$.6X = \$1,200$; $X = \$2,000$; income before interest and taxes must be $\$2,000 + \$8,000 = \$10,000$.
  e. The breakeven rates of return are identical, 6 percent, although the net incomes are quite different. The required incomes before interest and taxes are the same. Breakeven occurs when the rate of return on owners' equity equals the aftertax interest rate for borrowing: $(1 - .40) \times 10$ percent equals 6 percent, in this example.

14. *Earnings per Share Versus Rates of Return.*

	(Amounts in Thousands)	
	a. (Debt)	b. (Equity)
Earnings Before Interest and Taxes:		
Present Assets	$10,500	$10,500
Expansion	2,500	2,500
Total	$13,000	$13,000
Interest:		
Present	$ 500	$ 500
Additional	1,000	—
Total Interest	$ 1,500	$ 500
Pretax Income	$11,500	$12,500
Income Taxes (40 percent)	4,600	5,000
Net Income	$ 6,900	$ 7,500
Common Shares Outstanding	1,000,000	1,200,000
Earnings per Share	$6.90	$6.25

c. Let X represent required earnings before interest and taxes. Then

$$\frac{(X - \text{Interest})(1 - \text{Tax Rate})}{\text{Number of Shares}} = \text{Earnings per Share}$$

$$\frac{(X - \$1,500,000)(1 - .40)}{\$1,000,000} = \frac{(X - \$500,000)(1 - .40)}{\$1,200,000}$$

$$1.2 \times .60(X - \$1,500,000) = 1.0 \times .60(X - \$500,000)$$

$$.12X = \$1,080,000 - \$300,000$$

$$X = \$6,500,000.$$

d. Let Y represent required earnings before interest and taxes. Then

$$\frac{(Y - \text{Interest})(1 - \text{Tax Rate})}{\text{Shareholders' Equity}} = \text{Rate of Return on Shareholders' Equity}$$

$$\frac{(Y - \$1,500,000)(1 - .40)}{\$30,000,000} = \frac{(Y - \$500,000)(1 - .40)}{\$40,000,000}$$

$$4 \times .6(Y - \$1,500,000) = 3 \times .6(Y - \$500,000)$$

$$.6Y = \$2,700,000.$$

$$Y = \$4,500,000.$$

16. *Calculation and Interpretation of Current Ratio.*

a. December 31, Year 1:   December 31, Year 2:

$$\frac{\$2,007,000}{\$866,000} = 2.32:1. \qquad \frac{\$1,565,800}{\$348,600} = 4.49:1.$$

b. The reduction in both current assets and current liabilities appears to be largely the result of a retrenchment program. The proceeds from reductions in inventories and collections of receivables have chiefly been applied to reducing current indebtedness. The working capital has increased slightly, probably through the sale of noncurrent assets. The working capital from operations would not be reduced by the full amount of the operating loss, but rather by the operating loss less expenses not requiring the use of funds, such as depreciation.

| Appendix | **Compound Interest Concepts and Applications** |

Money is a scarce resource, which its owner can use to command other resources. Like owners of other scarce resources, owners of money can permit others (borrowers) to rent the use of their money for a period of time. Payment for the use of money differs little from other rental payments, such as those made to a landlord for the use of property or to a car rental agency for the use of a car. Payment for the use of money is called *interest*. Accounting is concerned with interest because it must record transactions in which the use of money is bought and sold.

Managerial accountants and managers are concerned with interest calculations for another, equally important, reason. Expenditures for an asset most often do not occur at the same time as the receipts for services produced by that asset. Money received sooner is more valuable than money received later. The difference in timing can affect whether or not acquiring an asset is profitable. Amounts of money received at different times are different commodities. Managers use interest calculations to make amounts of money to be paid or received at different times comparable.

A series of money payments over time, such as from an investment project or from a bond, are evaluated by finding the *present value* of the stream of payments. The present value of a stream of payments is a single amount of money at the present time that is the economic equivalent of the entire stream.

Compound Interest Concepts

The quotation of interest "cost" is typically specified as a percentage of the amount borrowed per unit of time. Examples are 10 percent per year and 1 percent per month.

The amount borrowed or loaned is called the *principal*. To *compound* interest means that the amount of interest earned during a period is added to the principal and the principal for the next interest period is correspondingly larger.

For example, if you deposit $1,000 in a savings account that pays compound interest at the rate of 10 percent per year, you will earn $100 by the end of 1 year. If you do not withdraw the $100, then $1,100 will be earning interest during the second year. During the second year your principal of $1,100 will earn $110 interest, $100 on the initial deposit of $1,000 and $10 on the $100 earned during the first year. By the end of the second year, you will have $1,210.

Problems involving compound interest generally fall into two groups with respect to time: First, there are the problems for which we want to know the future value of money invested or loaned today; second, there are the problems for which we want to know the present value, or today's value, of money to be received or paid at later dates. In addition, the accountant must compute the rate of interest implied by certain payment streams.

Future Value

When $1.00 is invested today at 10 percent compounded annually, it will grow to $1.10000 at the end of 1 year, $1.21000 at the end of 2 years, $1.33100 at the end of 3 years, and so on according to the formula

$$F_n = P(1 + r)^n,$$

where

F_n represents the accumulation or future value,

P represents the one-time investment today,

r is the interest rate per period, and

n is the number of periods from today.

The amount F_n is the future value of the present payment. P, compounded at r percent per period for n periods. Table 1, at the end of this appendix, shows the future values of $P = \$1$ for various numbers of periods and for various interest rates. Excerpts from that table are shown here in Table A.1.

Example Problem in Determining Future Value

Example 1 How much will $1,000 deposited today at 8 percent compounded annually be worth 10 years from now?

One dollar deposited today at 8 percent will grow to $2.15892; therefore $1,000 will grow to $1,000(1.08)^{10} = \$1,000 \times 2.15892 = \$2,158.92$.

Table A.1
(Excerpts from Table 1)
Future Value of $1 at 8 Percent
and 12 Percent per Period
$F_n = P(1 + r)^n$

Number of Periods = n	Rate = r	
	8 Percent	12 Percent
1	1.08000	1.12000
2	1.16640	1.25440
3	1.25971	1.40493
10	2.15892	3.10585
20	4.66096	9.64629

Present Value

The preceding section developed the tools for computing the future value, F_n, of a sum of money, P, deposited or invested today. P is known; F_n is calculated. This section deals with the problems of calculating how much principal, P, has to be invested today in order to have a specified amount, F_n, at the end of n periods. The future amount, F_n, the interest rate, r, and the number of periods, n, are known; P is to be found. In order to have $1 one year from today when interest is earned at 8 percent, P of .92593 must be invested today. That is, $F_1 = P(1.08)^1$ or $1 = \$.92593 \times 1.08$. Because $F_n = P(1 + r)^n$, dividing both sides of the equation by $(1 + r)^n$ yields

$$\frac{F_n}{(1 + r)^n} = P,$$

or

$$P = \frac{F_n}{(1 + r)^n} = F_n(1 + r)^{-n}.$$

Present Value Terminology

The number $(1 + r)^{-n}$ is the present value of $1 to be received after n periods when interest is earned at r percent per period. The term *discount* is used in this context as follows: The *discounted* present value of $1 to be received n periods in the future is $(1 + r)^{-n}$ when the *discount* rate is r percent per period for n periods. The number r is the discount *rate* and the number $(1 + r)^{-n}$ is the discount *factor* for n periods. A discount factor $(1 + r)^{-n}$ is merely the reciprocal, or inverse, of a number, $(1 + r)^n$, in Table A.1. Therefore, tables of discount factors are not necessary for present value calculations if tables of future values are at hand. But present value calculations are so frequently needed, and division is so onerous, that tables of discount factors are as widely available as tables of future values. Table 2 at the end of this appendix shows discount factors or, equivalently, present values of $1 for various interest (or discount) rates for various numbers of periods. Table A.2 shows excerpts from that table.

Table A.2
(Excerpts from Table 2)
Present Value of $1 at 8 Percent
and 12 Percent per Period
$P = F_n(1 + r)^{-n}$

Number of Periods = n	Rate = r	
	8 Percent	12 Percent
1	.92593	.89286
2	.85734	.79719
3	.79383	.71178
10	.46319	.32197
20	.21455	.10367

Example Problems in Determining Present Value

Example 2 What is the present value of $1 due 10 years from now if the interest rate (or equivalently, the discount rate) r is 12 percent per year?

From Table A.2, 12 percent column, 10 percent row, the present value of $1 to be received 10 periods hence at 12 percent is $.32197.

Example 3 An investment is projected to generate cash of $13,500 three years from today. What is the net present value of this cash receipt today if the discount rate is 8 percent per year?

One dollar received 3 years hence discounted at 8 percent has a present value of $.79383. Thus, the promise is worth $13,500 × .79383 = $10,717. Exhibit A.1 shows how $10,717 grows to $13,500 in 3 years.

Exhibit A.1
Verification of Net Present Value of $10,717
Single Cash Flow of $13,500 at the End of Year 3
Discounted at 8 Percent per Year

Year	Beginning Amount	+	Interest at 8 Percent	=	Ending Amount
1	$10,717		$ 857		$11,574
2	11,574		926		12,500
3	12,500		1,000		13,500

Changing the Compounding Period: Nominal and Effective Rates

"Twelve percent, compounded annually" is the price for a loan; this means that interest is added to or *converted* into principal once a year at the rate of 12 percent. Often, however, the price for a loan states that compounding is to take place more than once a year. A savings bank may advertise that it pays 6 percent, compounded quarterly. This means that at the end of each quarter the bank credits savings accounts with interest calculated at the rate of 1.5 percent (= 6 percent ÷ 4). The interest payment can be withdrawn or left on deposit to earn more interest.

If $10,000 is invested today at 12 percent compounded annually, its future value 1 year later is $11,200. If the rate of interest is stated as 12 percent compounded semiannually, then 6 percent interest is added to the principal every 6 months. At the end of the first 6 months, $10,000 will have grown to $10,600, so that the accumulation will be $10,600 × 1.06 = $11,236 by the end of the year. Notice that 12 percent compounded *semiannually* is equivalent to 12.36 percent compounded *annually*.

Suppose that the price is quoted as 12 percent, compounded quarterly. Then an additional 3 percent of the principal will be added to, or converted into, principal every 3 months. By the end of the year, $10,000 will grow to $10,000 × $(1.03)^4$ = $10,000 × 1.12551 = $11,255. Twelve percent compounded quarterly is equivalent to 12.55 percent compounded annually. If 12 percent is compounded monthly, then $1 will grow to $1 $\times$ $(1.01)^{12}$ = $1.12683 and $10,000 will grow to $11,268. Thus, 12 percent compounded monthly is equivalent to 12.68 percent compounded annually.

For a given *nominal* rate, such as the 12 percent in the examples above, the more often interest is compounded or converted into principal, the higher the *effective* rate of interest paid. If a nominal rate, r, is compounded m times per year, then the effective rate is $[1 + (r \div m)]^m - 1$.

In practice, to solve problems that require computation of interest quoted at a nominal rate of r percent per period compounded m times per period for n periods, merely use the tables for rate $r \div m$ and $m \times n$ periods. For example, 12 percent compounded quarterly for 7 years is equivalent to the rate found in the interest tables for r = 12 $\div$ 4 = 3 percent for $m \times n$ = 4 $\times$ 7 = 28 periods.

Some savings banks advertise that they compound interest daily or even continuously. The mathematics of calculus provides a mechanism for finding the effective rate when interest is compounded continuously. We shall not go into details but merely state that if interest is compounded continuously at nominal rate r per year, then the effective annual rate is $e^r - 1$, where e is the base of the natural logarithms. Tables of values of e^r are widely available.[1] Six percent per year compounded continuously is equivalent to 6.18 percent compounded annually; 12 percent per year compounded continuously is equivalent to 12.75 percent compounded annually. Do not confuse the compounding period with the payment period. Some banks, for example, compound interest daily but pay interest quarterly. You can be sure that such banks do not employ clerks or even computers to calculate interest every day. They merely use tables to derive an equivalent effective rate to apply at the end of each quarter.

Example Problems in Changing the Compounding Period

Example 4 What is the future value 5 years hence of $600 invested at 8 percent compounded quarterly?

Eight percent compounded four times per year for 5 years is equivalent to 2 percent per period compounded for 20 periods. Table 1 shows the value of F_{20} = $(1.02)^{20}$ to be 1.48595. Six hundred dollars, then, would grow to $600 $\times$ 1.48595 = $891.57.

Example 5 How much money must be invested today at 12 percent compounded semiannually in order to have $1,000 four years from today?

Twelve percent compounded two times a year for 4 years is equivalent to 6 percent per period compounded for 8 periods. The *present* value, Table 2, of $1 received 8 periods hence at 6 percent per period is $.62741. That is, $.62741 invested today for 8 periods at an interest rate of 6 percent per period will grow to $1. To have $1,000 in 8 periods (4 years), $627.41 (= $1,000 $\times$ .62741) must be invested today.

---

[1]See, for example, Sidney Davidson and Roman L. Weil (eds.), *Handbook of Modern Accounting*, 3rd ed. (New York: McGraw-Hill Book Company, 1983), Chap. 9, Exhibit 1.

Example 6 A local department store offers its customers credit and advertises its interest rate at 18 percent per year, compounded monthly at the rate of 1½ percent per month. What is the effective annual interest rate?

One and one-half percent per month for 12 months is equivalent to $(1.015)^{12} - 1 = 19.562$ percent per year. See Table 1, 12 period row, 1½ percent column, where the factor is 1.19562.

Example 7 If prices increased at the rate of 6 percent during each of two consecutive 6-month periods, how much did prices increase during the entire year?

If a price index is 100.00 at the start of the year, it will be $100.00 \times (1.06)^2 = 112.36$ at the end of the year. The price change for the entire year is $(112.36 \div 100.00) - 1 = 12.36$ percent.

Annuities

An *annuity* is a series of equal payments made at the beginning or end of equal periods of time. Examples of annuities include monthly rental payments, semiannual corporate bond coupon (or interest) payments, and annual payments to a lessor under a lease contract. Armed with an understanding of the tables for future and present values, you can solve any annuity problem. Annuities arise so often, however, and their solution is so tedious without special tables, that annuity problems warrant special study and the use of special tables.

Terminology

The terminology used for annuities can be confusing because not all writers use the same terms. Definitions of the terms used in this text follow.

An annuity whose payments occur at the *end* of each period is called an *ordinary annuity* or an *annuity in arrears*. Semiannual corporate bond coupon payments are usually paid in arrears or, equivalently, the first payment does not occur until after the bond has been outstanding for 6 months.

An annuity whose payments occur at the *beginning* of each period is called an *annuity due* or an *annuity in advance*. Rent is usually paid in advance, so that a series of rental payments is an annuity due.

A *deferred* annuity is one whose first payment is at some time later than the end of the first period.

Annuities can be paid forever. Such annuities are called *perpetuities*. Bonds that promise payments forever are called *consols*. The British and Canadian governments have, from time to time, issued consols. A perpetuity can be in arrears or in advance. The only difference between the two is the timing of the first payment.

Annuities can be confusing. Their study is made easier with a *time line* such as the one shown below.

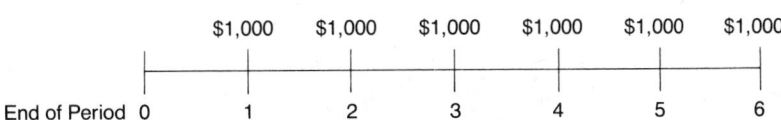

A time line marks the end of each period, numbers the period, shows the payments to be received or paid, and shows the time at which the annuity is valued. The time line just pictured represents an ordinary annuity (in arrears) for six periods of $1,000 to be valued at the end of period 6. The end of period 0 is "now." The first payment is to be received one period from now. Note that the general term "period" is used instead of "years." The period may be 1 month, 3 months, 6 months, 12 months, or some other length of time.

Ordinary Annuities (Annuities in Arrears)

Table 3 at the end of this appendix shows the future values of ordinary annuities. Table A.3 reproduces excerpts from that table.

Table A.3
(Excerpts from Table 3)
Future Value of an Ordinary Annuity of $1 per Period at 8 Percent and 12 Percent

$$F_A = \frac{[(1 + r)^n - 1]}{r}$$

Number of Periods = n	Rate = r	
	8 Percent	12 Percent
1	1.00000	1.00000
2	2.08000	2.12000
3	3.24640	3.37440
5	5.86660	6.35285
10	14.48656	17.54874
20	45.76196	72.05244

Consider an ordinary annuity for three periods at 12 percent. The time line for the future value of such an annuity is

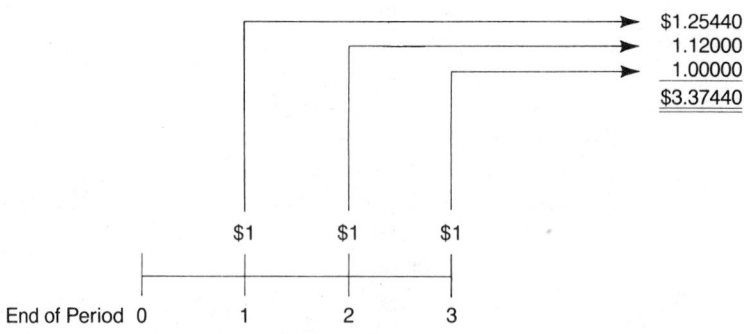

The $1 received at the end of the first period earns interest for two periods, so it is worth $1.25440 at the end of period 3. (See Table A.1.) The $1 received at the

end of the second period grows to $1.12000 by the end of period 3, and the $1 received at the end of period 3 is, of course, worth $1.00000 at the end of period 3. The entire annuity is worth $3.37440 at the end of period 3. This is the amount shown in Table A.3 for the future value of an ordinary annuity for three periods at 12 percent. Factors for the future value of an annuity for a particular number of periods are merely the sum of the factors for the future value of $1 for each of the periods. The future value of an ordinary annuity is calculated as follows:

$$\text{Future Value of Ordinary Annuity} = \text{Periodic Payment} \times \text{Factor for the Future Value of an Ordinary Annuity.}$$

Thus,

$$\$3.37440 = \$1 \times 3.37440.$$

Table 4 at the end of this appendix shows the present value of ordinary annuities. Table A.4 reproduces excerpts from Table A.4.

Table A.4
(Excerpts from Table 4)
Present Value of an Ordinary Annuity of $1 per Period at 8 Percent and 12 Percent

$$P_A = \frac{[1 - (1 + r)^{-n}]}{r}$$

Number of Periods = n	Rate = r	
	8 Percent	12 Percent
1	.92593	.89286
2	1.78326	1.69005
3	2.57710	2.40183
5	3.99271	3.60478
10	6.71008	5.65022
20	9.81815	7.46944

The time line for the present value of an ordinary annuity of $1 per period for three periods, discounted at 12 percent, is

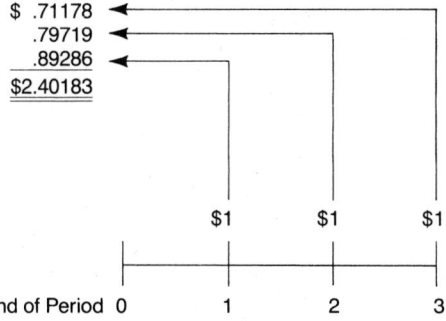

The $1 to be received at the end of period 1 has a present value of $.89286, the $1 to be received at the end of period 2 has a present value of $.79719, and the dollar to be received at the end of the third period has a present value of $.71178. Each of these numbers comes from Table A.2. The present value of the annuity is the sum of these individual present values, $2.40183, shown in Table A.4.

The present value of an ordinary annuity for n periods is the sum of the present value of $1 received one period from now plus the present value of $1 received two periods from now, and so on until we add on the present value of $1 received n periods from now. The present value of an ordinary annuity is calculated as follows:

$$\begin{matrix} \text{Present Value} \\ \text{of an} \\ \text{Ordinary Annuity} \end{matrix} = \begin{matrix} \text{Periodic} \\ \text{Payment} \end{matrix} \times \begin{matrix} \text{Factor for the} \\ \text{Present} \\ \text{Value of an Ordinary} \\ \text{Annuity.} \end{matrix}$$

Thus,

$$\$2.40183 \quad = \quad \$1 \quad \times \quad 2.40183.$$

Example Problems Involving Ordinary Annuities

Example 8 An investment is projected to generate $1,000 at the end of each of the next 20 years. If the interest rate is 8 percent compounded annually, what will be the future value of these flows at the end of 20 years?

The time line for this problem is

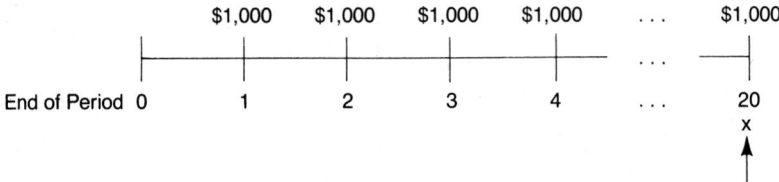

The symbol x denotes the amount to be calculated. Table 3 indicates that the factor for the future value of an annuity at 8 percent for 20 periods is 45.76196. Thus,

$$\begin{matrix} \text{Future Value} \\ \text{of an} \\ \text{Ordinary Annuity} \end{matrix} = \begin{matrix} \text{Periodic} \\ \text{Payment} \end{matrix} \times \begin{matrix} \text{Factor for} \\ \text{the Future} \\ \text{Value of an} \\ \text{Ordinary Annuity} \end{matrix}$$

$$x \quad = \$ \ 1,000 \ \times \quad 45.76196$$

$$x \quad = \$45,762.$$

The cash flows have future value of $45,762.

Example 9 Parents are accumulating a fund to send their child to college. The parents will invest a fixed amount at the end of each calendar quarter for the next

10 years. The funds will accumulate in a savings certificate that promises to pay 8 percent interest compounded quarterly. What amount must be invested to accumulate a fund of $25,000?

The time line for this problem is

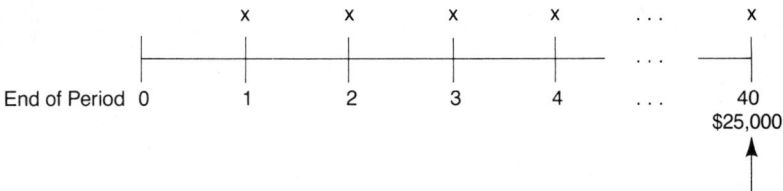

This problem is similar to Example 8 because both involve periodic investments of cash that accumulate interest over time until a specific time in the future. In Example 8, the periodic investment is given and the future value is computed. In Example 9, the future value is given and the periodic investment is computed. Table 3 indicates that the future value of an annuity at 2 percent ($= 8$ percent per year $\div$ 4 quarters per year) per period for 40 ($= 4$ quarters per year $\times$ 10 years) periods is 60.40198. Thus,

$$\begin{array}{ccc}
\begin{array}{c}\text{Future Value}\\\text{of an}\\\text{Ordinary Annuity}\end{array} & = & \begin{array}{c}\text{Periodic}\\\text{Payment}\end{array} \times \begin{array}{c}\text{Factor for}\\\text{the Future}\\\text{Value of an}\\\text{Ordinary Annuity}\end{array}
\end{array}$$

$$\$25,000 = x \times 60.40198$$

$$x = \frac{\$25,000}{60.40198}$$

$$x = \$414.$$

Because the periodic payment is being calculated, the future value amount of $25,000 is divided by the future value factor.

Example 10 A company borrows $30,000 from an insurance company. The interest rate on the loan is 8 percent compounded semiannually. The company agrees to repay the loan in equal semiannual installments over the next 5 years. The first payment is to be made 6 months from now. What is the amount of the required semiannual payment?

The time line is

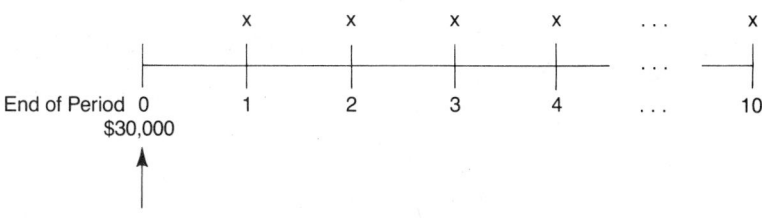

The present value is given and the periodic payment is computed. Table 4 indicates that the present value of annuity at 4 percent ($= 8$ percent per year $\div$ 2 semiannual periods per year) for 10 periods ($=$ 2 periods per year $\times$ 5 years) is 8.11090. Thus,

$$\begin{array}{ccc}
\begin{array}{c}\text{Present Value} \\ \text{of an} \\ \text{Ordinary Annuity}\end{array} & = & \begin{array}{c}\text{Periodic} \\ \text{Payment}\end{array} \times \begin{array}{c}\text{Factor for} \\ \text{the Present} \\ \text{Value of an} \\ \text{Ordinary Annuity}\end{array}
\end{array}$$

$$\$30{,}000 = x \times 8.11090$$

$$x = \frac{\$30{,}000}{8.11090}$$

$$x = \$3{,}699.$$

Because the periodic payment is being calculated, the present value amount of $30,000 must be divided by the present value factor. Exhibit A.2 shows how periodic payments of $3,700 "amortize" the loan. Such a schedule is often called an "amortization schedule." If the periodic payments were $3,699, not $3,700, the "error" in the final payment would be even smaller.

Exhibit A.2
Amortization Schedule for $30,000 Mortgage, Repaid in
10 Semiannual Installments of $3,700, Interest Rate of 8 Percent,
Compounded Semiannually

6-Month Period (1)	Mortgage Principal Start of Period (2)	Interest Expense for Period (3)	Payment (4)	Portion of Payment Reducing Principal (5)	Mortgage Principal End of Period (6)
0					$30,000
1	$30,000	$1,200	$3,700	$2,500	27,500
2	27,500	1,100	3,700	2,600	24,900
3	24,900	996	3,700	2,704	22,196
4	22,196	888	3,700	2,812	19,384
5	19,384	775	3,700	2,925	16,459
6	16,459	658	3,700	3,042	13,417
7	13,417	537	3,700	3,163	10,254
8	10,254	410	3,700	3,290	6,964
9	6,964	279	3,700	3,421	3,543
10	3,543	142	3,685	3,543	–0–

Column (2) = column (6) from previous period.
Column (3) = .04 $\times$ column (2).
Column (4) is given, except row 10, where it is the amount such that column (4) = column (2) + column (3).
Column (5) = column (4) − column (3).
Column (6) = column (2) − column (5).

Example 11 A company signs a lease acquiring the right to use property for 3 years. Lease payments of $19,709 are to be made annually at the end of this and the next 2 years. The discount, or interest, rate is 15 percent per year. What is the present value of the lease payments, which is the equivalent cash purchase price for this property?

The time line is

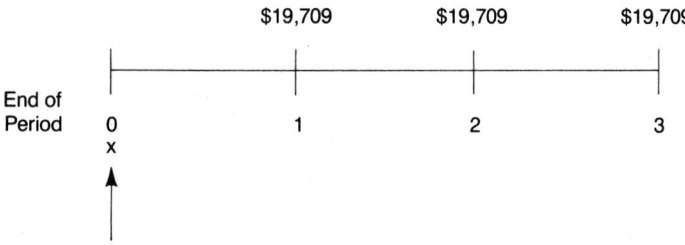

The factor from Table 4 for the present value of an annuity at 15 percent for 3 periods is 2.28323. Thus,

$$
\begin{array}{c}
\text{Present Value} \\
\text{of an} \\
\text{Ordinary Annuity}
\end{array}
=
\begin{array}{c}
\text{Periodic} \\
\text{Payment}
\end{array}
\times
\begin{array}{c}
\text{Factor for} \\
\text{the Present} \\
\text{Value of an} \\
\text{Ordinary Annuity}
\end{array}
$$

$$ x = \$19{,}709 \times 2.28323 $$

$$ x = \$45{,}000. $$

Exhibit A.3 is an amortization schedule for the lease.

Exhibit A.3
Amortization Schedule for $45,000 Lease Liability,
Repaid in Three Annual Installments of $19,709 Each,
Interest Rate 15 Percent, Compounded Annually

Year (1)	Lease Liability Start of Year (2)	Interest Expense for Year (3)	Payment (4)	Portion of Payment Reducing Lease Liability (5)	Lease Liability End of Year (6)
0					$45,000
1	$45,000	$6,750	$19,709	$12,959	32,041
2	32,041	4,806	19,709	14,903	17,138
3	17,138	2,571	19,709	17,138	–0–

Column (2) = Column (6), previous period.
Column (3) = .15 × column (2).
Column (4)   Given.
Column (5) = Column (4) − column (3).
Column (6) = Column (2) − column (5).

Example 12 Mr. Mason is 62 years old. He wishes to invest equal amounts on his sixty-third, sixty-fourth, and sixty-fifth birthdays so that starting on his sixty-

sixth birthday he can withdraw $50,000 on each birthday for 10 years. His in-
vestments will earn 8 percent per year. How much should be invested on the sixty-
third through sixty-fifth birthdays?

The time line for this problem is

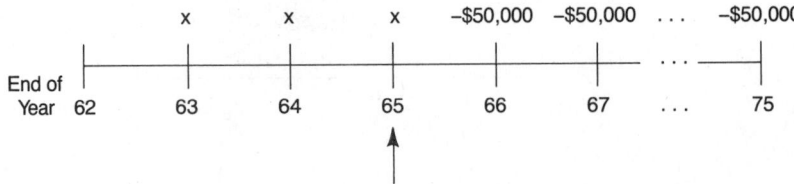

On his sixty-fifth birthday, Mr. Mason needs to have accumulated a fund equal to
the present value of an annuity of $50,000 per period for 10 periods, discounted
at 8 percent per period. The factor from Table 4 for 8 percent and 10 periods is
6.71008. Thus,

$$
\begin{array}{ccc}
\begin{array}{c}\text{Present Value} \\ \text{of an} \\ \text{Ordinary Annuity}\end{array} & = & \begin{array}{c}\text{Period} \\ \text{Payment}\end{array} \times \begin{array}{c}\text{Factor for} \\ \text{the Present} \\ \text{Value of an} \\ \text{Ordinary Annuity}\end{array}
\end{array}
$$

$$x = \$50{,}000 \times 6.71008$$

$$x = \$335{,}504.$$

The time line now appears as follows:

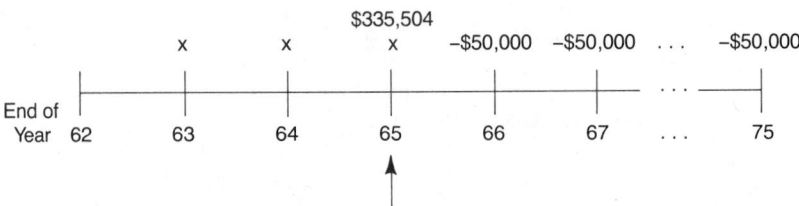

The question now becomes: How much must be invested on Mr. Mason's sixty-
third, sixty-fourth, and sixty-fifth birthdays to accumulate to a fund of $335,504
on his sixty-fifth birthday? The factor for the future value of an annuity for three
periods at 8 percent is 3.24640. Thus,

$$
\begin{array}{ccc}
\begin{array}{c}\text{Future Value} \\ \text{of an} \\ \text{Ordinary Annuity}\end{array} & = & \begin{array}{c}\text{Periodic} \\ \text{Payment}\end{array} \times \begin{array}{c}\text{Factor for} \\ \text{the Future} \\ \text{Value of an} \\ \text{Ordinary Annuity}\end{array}
\end{array}
$$

$$\$335{,}504 = x \times 3.24640$$

$$x = \frac{\$335{,}504}{3.24640}$$

$$x = \$103{,}346.$$

Annuities in Advance (Annuities Due)

The time line for the future value of a three-period annuity in advance is

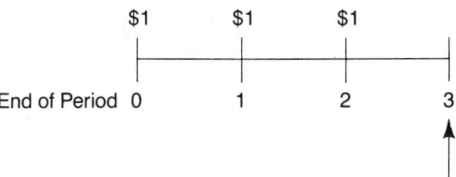

Notice that the future value is defined for the *end* of the period at the start of which the last payment is made. When tables of ordinary annuities are available, tables for annuities due are unnecessary.

Compare the time line for the future value of an annuity in advance for three periods *with the time axis relabeled to show start of period* and the time line for the future value of an ordinary annuity (in arrears) for four periods.

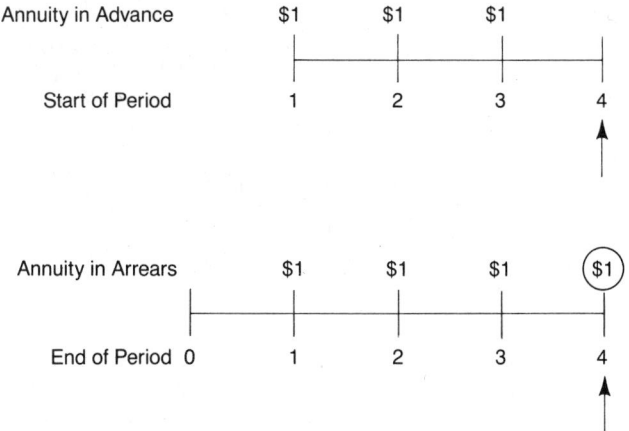

A $1 annuity in advance for *n* periods has a future value equal to the future value of a $1 annuity in arrears for *n* + 1 periods *minus* $1. The $1 circled in the time line for the annuity in arrears is the $1 that must be subtracted to calculate the future value of an annuity in advance, because no annuity payment is made at the end of period 3. The "note" at the foot of Table 3 states: "To convert from this table to values of an annuity in advance, determine the annuity in arrears above for one more period and subtract 1.00000."

Example Problem Involving Future Value of Annuity Due

Example 13 A student plans to invest $1,000 a year at the beginning of each of the next 10 years in a savings certificate paying interest of 12 percent per year. The first payment is to be made today. What will be the amount in the savings account at the end of the tenth year?

The time line is

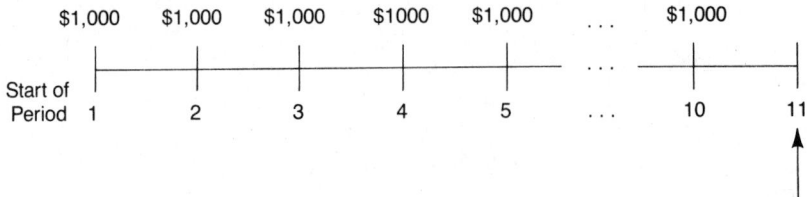

The factor for the future value of an annuity for 11 (= 10 + 1) periods is 20.65458. Because a $1,000 investment is not made at the end of the tenth year, 1.00000 is subtracted from 20.65458 to obtain the factor for the annuity in advance of 19.65458. The future value of the annuity in advance is

$$
\begin{array}{ccc}
\text{Future Value} & & \text{Factor for} \\
\text{of an} & = \text{Periodic} \times & \text{the Future Value} \\
\text{Annuity} & \text{Payment} & \text{of an} \\
\text{in Advance} & & \text{Annuity} \\
& & \text{in Advance}
\end{array}
$$

$$ x = \$1,000 \times 19.65458 $$

$$ x = \$19,655. $$

Example Problem Involving Present Value of Annuity Due

The time line for the present value of an annuity in advance for three periods is

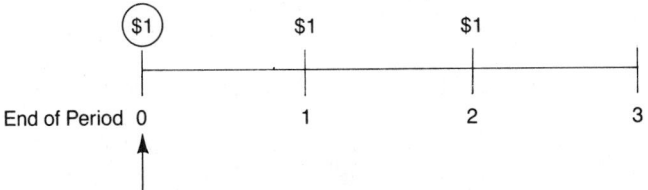

Notice that except for the first, circled payment, it looks just like the present value of an ordinary annuity for two periods. A $1 annuity in advance for n periods has a present value equal to the present value of a $1 annuity in arrears for $n - 1$ periods *plus* $1. The "note" at the foot of Table 4 states: "To convert from this table to values of an annuity in advance, determine the annuity in arrears above for one less period and add 1.00000."

Example 14 What is the present value of rents of $350 to be paid monthly, in advance, for 1 year when the discount rate is 1 percent per month?
   The time line is

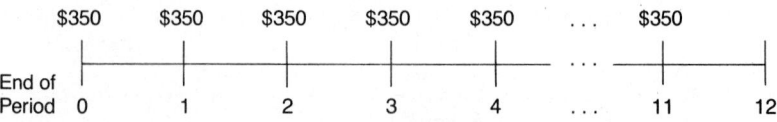

The present value of $1 per period *in arrears* for 11 periods at 1 percent per period is $10.36763; the present value of $1 per period in advance for 12 periods is $10.36763 + $1.00 = $11.36763, and the present value of this year's rent is $350 × 11.36763 = $3,979.

Deferred Annuities

When the first payment of an annuity occurs some time after the end of the first period, the annuity is *deferred*. The time line for an ordinary annuity of $1 per period for four periods deferred for two periods is

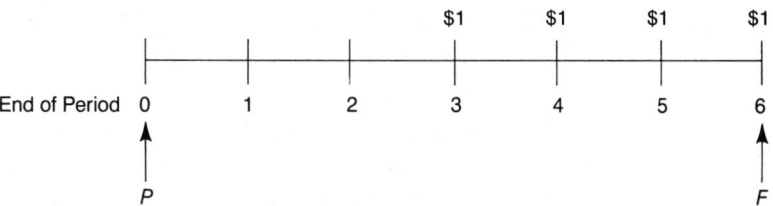

The arrow marked *P* shows the time for which the present value is calculated; the arrow marked *F* shows when the future value is calculated. The *future* value is not affected by the deferral and equals the future value of an ordinary annuity for four periods.

Notice that the time line for the present value looks like one for an ordinary annuity for six periods *minus* an ordinary annuity for two periods:

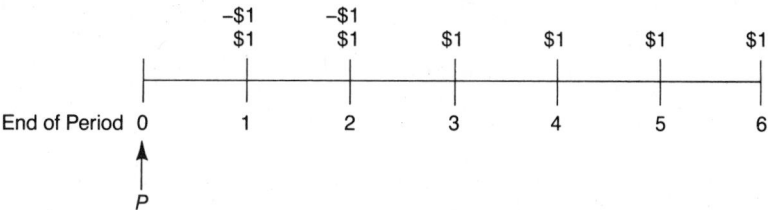

Calculate the present value of an annuity of *n* payments deferred for *d* periods by subtracting the present value of an annuity for *d* periods from the present value of an annuity for *n* + *d* periods.

Example Problem Involving Deferred Annuities

Example 15 Refer to the data in Example 12. Recall that Mr. Mason wants to withdraw $50,000 per year on his sixty-sixth through his seventy-fifth birthdays. He wishes to invest a sufficient amount on his sixty-third, sixty-fourth, and sixty-fifth birthdays to provide a fund for the later withdrawals.

The time line is

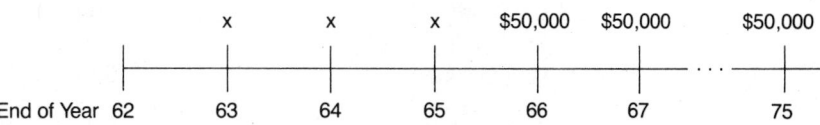

As of his sixty-second birthday, the $50,000 series of payments on Mr. Mason's sixty-sixth through seventy-fifth birthdays is a deferred annuity. The interest rate is 8 percent per year.

The present value amount can be calculated using the factor for the present value of an annuity for 13 periods (10 payments deferred for three periods) of 7.90378 and subtracting the factor for the present value of an annuity for three periods of 2.57710. The net amount is 5.32668 (= 7.90378 − 2.57710). Multiplying by the $50,000 payment amount, we find the present value of the deferred annuity on Mr. Mason's sixty-second birthday ($266,334 = $50,000 × 5.32668).

Perpetuities

A periodic payment to be received forever is called a *perpetuity*. Future values of perpetuities are undefined. If $1 is to be received at the end of every period and the discount rate is r percent, then the present value of the perpetuity is $1 ÷ r. This expression can be derived with algebra or by observing what happens in the expression for the present value of an ordinary annuity of $A per payment as n, the number of payments, approaches infinity:

$$P_A = \frac{A[1 - (1 + r)^{-n}]}{r}.$$

As n approaches infinity, $(1 + r)^{-n}$ approaches zero, so P_A approaches $A(1 ÷ r)$. If the first payment of the perpetuity occurs now, the present value is $A[1 + (1 ÷ r)]$.

Example of Perpetuities

Example 16 The Canadian government offers to pay $30 every 6 months forever in the form of a perpetual bond. What is that bond worth if the discount rate is 14 percent compounded semiannually?

Fourteen percent compounded semiannually is equivalent to 7 percent per 6-month period. If the first payment occurs 6 months from now, the present value is $30 ÷ .07 = $429. If the first payment occurs today, the present value is $30 + $429 = $459.

Implicit Interest Rates: Finding Internal Rates of Return

In the preceding examples, we knew the interest rate and computed a future value or a present value given stated cash payments. Or we computed the required payments given their known future value or their known present value. In some calculations, we know the present or future value and the periodic payments; we must find the implicit interest rate. Assume, for example, a case in which we know that a cash investment of $10,500 will grow to $13,500 in 3 years. What is the implicit interest rate, or material rate of return, on this investment? The time line for this problem is

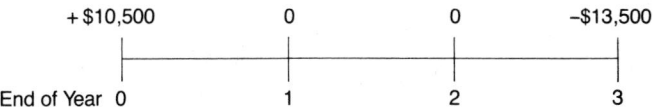

The implicit interest rate is r, such that

$$(I) \qquad \$10,500 = \frac{\$13,500}{(1 + r)^3}.$$

$$(II) \qquad 0 = \$10,500 - \frac{\$13,500}{(1 + r)^3}.$$

That is, the present value of $13,500 discounted three periods at r percent per period is $10,500. The present value of all current and future cash flows nets to zero when future flows are discounted at r per period. In general, the only way to find such an r is a trial-and-error procedure.[2] The procedure is called "finding the internal rate of return" of a series of cash flows. The *internal rate of return* of a series of cash flows is the discount rate that equates the net present value of that series of cash flows to zero. The steps in finding the internal rate of return are as follows:

1. Make an educated guess, called the "trial rate," at the internal rate of return. If you have no idea what to guess, try zero.
2. Calculate the present value of all the cash flows (including the one at the end of year 0).
3. If the present value of the cash flows is zero, stop. The current trial rate is the internal rate of return.
4. If the amount found in step 2 is less than zero, try a larger interest rate as the trial rate and go back to step 2.
5. If the amount found in step 2 is greater than zero, try a smaller interest rate as the new trial rate and go back to step 2.

The iterations below illustrate the process for the example in equation (II).

Iteration Number	Trial Rate $= r$	Net Present Values: Right-Hand Side of (II)
1	0.00%	− $3,500
2	10.00	+ 357
3	5.00	− 1,162
4	7.50	− 367
5	8.75	+ 3

[2]In cases where r appears in only one term, as here, r can be found analytically. Here, $r = (\$13,500 \div \$10,500)^{1/3} - 1 = .087380$.

With a trial rate of 8.75 percent, the right-hand side is close enough to zero so that 8.75 percent can be used as the implicit interest rate. Continued iterations would find trial rates even closer to the true rate, which is about 8.7380 percent.

Finding the internal rate of return for a series of cash flows can be tedious and should not be attempted unless one has at least a desk calculator. An exponential feature, the feature that allows the computation of $(1 + r)$ raised to various powers, helps.[3]

Example Problems Involving Finding Implicit Interest Rates

Example 17 The Alexis Company acquires a machine with a cash price of $10,500. It pays for the machine by giving a note promising to make payments equal to 7 percent of the face value, $840, at the end of each of the next 3 years and a single payment of $12,000 in 3 years. What is the implicit interest rate in the loan?

The time line for this problem is

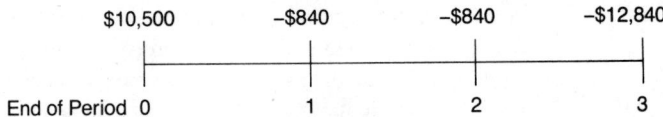

The implicit interest rate is r, such that[4]

$$(III) \quad \$10,500 = \frac{\$840}{(1 + r)} + \frac{\$840}{(1 + r)^2} + \frac{\$12,840}{(1 + r)^3}.$$

The internal rate of return is found to the nearest tenth of 1 percent to be 12.2 percent:

Iteration Number		Trial Rate	Right-Hand Side of (III)
1	. . . .	7.0%	$12,000
2	. . . .	15.0	9,808
3	. . . .	11.0	10,827
4	. . . .	13.0	10,300
5	. . . .	12.0	10,559
6	. . . .	12.5	10,428
7	. . . .	12.3	10,480
8	. . . .	12.2	10,506
9	. . . .	12.1	10,533

[3]There are ways to guess the trial rate that will approximate the true rate in fewer iterations than the method described here. If you want to find internal rates of return efficiently with successive trial rates, refer to a mathematical reference book to learn about the "Newton search" method, sometimes called the "method of false position."

[4]Compare this formulation to that in equation (II), above. Note that the left-hand side is zero in one case but not in the other. The left-hand side can be either a nonzero number or zero, depending on what seems convenient for the particular context.

Example 18 In some contexts, such as mortgages or leases, one knows the amount of a series of future periodic payments, which are identical in all periods, and the present value of those future payments. For example, a firm may borrow $100,000 and agree to repay the loan in 20 payments of $11,746 each at the end of each of the next 20 years. In order to calculate interest expense each period, the interest rate implicit in the loan must be found.

The given information might be summarized as follows:

$$\begin{matrix} \text{Present Value} \\ \text{of an} \\ \text{Ordinary Annuity} \end{matrix} = \begin{matrix} \text{Periodic} \\ \text{Payment} \end{matrix} \times \begin{matrix} \text{Factor for} \\ \text{the Present} \\ \text{Value of an} \\ \text{Ordinary Annuity} \end{matrix}$$

$$\$100,000 = \$11,746 \times x$$

$$x = \frac{\$100,000}{\$11,746}$$

$$x = 8.51354.$$

The factor that will discount 20 payments of $11,746 to a present value of $100,000 is 8.51354. To find the interest rate implicit in the discounting, scan the 20-payment row of Table 4 to find the *factor* 8.51354. The interest rate at the head of the column is the implicit interest rate, approximately 10 percent in the example.

Example 19 An investment costing $11,400 today provides the following aftertax cash inflows at the ends of each of the next five periods: $5,000, $4,000, $3,000, $2,000, $1,000. What is the internal rate of return on these flows? That is, find r such that

$$\text{(IV)} \qquad 0 = -\$11,400 + \frac{\$5,000}{(1 + r)} + \frac{\$4,000}{(1 + r)^2} + \frac{\$3,000}{(1 + r)^3} + \frac{\$2,000}{(1 + r)^4} + \frac{\$1,000}{(1 + r)^5}.$$

Trial rates r produced the following sequence of estimates of the internal rate of return:

Iteration Number	Trial Rate	Right-Hand Side of (IV)
1	0.00%	+$3,600
2	10.00	+ 692
3	15.00	− 414
4	12.50	+ 115
5	13.50	− 102
6	13.00	+ 6
7	13.10	− 16
8	13.01	+ 4
9	13.02	+ 2
10	13.03	− 1

The estimating process is carried several steps further than is necessary. To the nearest whole percentage point, the internal rate of return is 13 percent.

To the nearest one-hundredth of a percent, the internal rate of return is 13.03 percent. Further trials find an even more accurate answer, $r = 13.027$ percent. Physical scientists learn early in their training not to use more significant digits in calculations than are warranted by the accuracy of the measuring devices. Accountants, too, should not carry calculations beyond the point of accuracy. Given the likely uncertainty in the estimates of cash flows, an estimate of the internal rate of return accurate to the nearest whole percentage point likely will serve its intended purpose.

Summary

To compare or to compute with payments made at different times requires that the payments be made comparable. The methods of compound interest are used. Given a set of payments and an interest rate, either a future value or a present value can be computed. Given future value or present value and an interest rate, the required payments can be computed. Given payments and either the present value or the future value, the interest rate can be computed, generally by a trial-and-error process. That interest rate is often called the "implicit interest rate" or the "internal rate of return."

Problem for Self-Study

A group of investors has decided to purchase a large herd of beef cattle, to sell cattle as calves are born, and to sell the entire herd after 6 years. They have also agreed that no investment of the syndicate should return less than 10 percent per year. They purchase the cattle on January 1, Year 1, for a price of $1,200,000, and they expect to sell the herd remaining on December 31, Year 6, for the same price. The projected net cash flows from sale of beef during the 6 years is $200,000 per year.

On December 31, Year 1, the syndicate finds that its cash flow from the herd is $210,000. But during December the herd was stricken with a disease and 20 percent of the cattle died. The syndicate wants to restock the herd, and they decide to sell only enough beef to cover expenses until the herd grows to its original size. They anticipate that this process will result in zero cash flow for Year 2, and $200,000 for each of the remaining 4 years.

Ignore tax considerations in your calculations.

a. Calculate the present value of the herd to the syndicate at time of purchase.

b. If there had been no disease, what would have been the value of the herd on January 1, Year 2? Use only future cash flows for this and subsequent computations.

c. What was the value of the herd on January 1, Year 2, after the disease and the decision to restock?

d. What was the cost to the syndicate of the disease?

e. On January 1, Year 2, an investor who has a 25 percent interest in the herd decides to sell out. What is the least amount that the investor should be willing to accept for the 25 percent share? Assume that the investor is looking at alternative investments that would yield 10 percent per year.

Suggested Solution

a. $200,000 for 6 years plus present value of sale of herd in 6 years:

$$
\begin{array}{rl}
\$\ 200,\!000 \times 4.35526 = & \$\ 871,\!052 \\
1,\!200,\!000 \times\ \ .56447 = & 677,\!364 \\
\hline
& \$1,\!548,\!416
\end{array}
$$

b. $200,000 for 5 years and present value of sale of herd in 5 years:

$$
\begin{array}{rl}
\$\ 200,\!000 \times 3.79079 = & \$\ 758,\!158 \\
1,\!200,\!000 \times\ \ .62092 = & 745,\!104 \\
\hline
& \$1,\!503,\!262
\end{array}
$$

c. Value as computed in part **b** less 1 year's revenue:

$$
\begin{array}{rl}
& \$1,\!503,\!262 \\
(\$200,\!000) \times .90909 = & (181,\!818) \\
\hline
& \$1,\!321,\!444
\end{array}
$$

d.
$$
\begin{array}{lcl}
\$1,\!503,\!262 & & \$200,\!000 \\
\underline{(1,\!321,\!444)} & \text{or} & \underline{\times .90909} \\
\$\ \ \ 181,\!818 & & \$181,\!818
\end{array}
$$

e. $.25 \times$ **c** $= .25 \times \$1,\!321,\!444 = \$330,\!361.$

Questions

1. Review the following concepts or terms discussed in this appendix.

a. Compound interest.	**i.** Ordinary annuity (annuity in
b. Principal.	arrears).
c. Simple interest.	**j.** Annuity in advance (annuity
d. Future value.	due).
e. Present value.	**k.** Perpetuity.
f. Discounted value.	**l.** Deferred annuity.
g. Discount factor.	**m.** Implicit interest rate (internal
h. Discount rate.	rate of return).

2. What is interest?

3. Distinguish between simple and compound interest.

4. Distinguish between the discounted present value of a stream of future payments and their net present value. If there is no distinction, then so state.

5. Distinguish between an annuity due and an ordinary annuity.

6. Decribe the "implicit interest rate" for a series of cash flows and a procedure for finding it.

7. Does the present value of a given amount to be paid in 10 years increase or decrease if the interest rate increases? Suppose that the amount were due in 5 years? 20 years? Does the present value of an annuity to be paid for 10 years increase or decrease if the discount rate decreases? Suppose that the annuity were for 5 years? 20 years?

8. Rather than pay you $100 a month for the next 20 years, the person who injured you in an automobile accident is willing to pay a single amount now to settle your claim for injuries. Would you rather an interest rate of 6 percent or 12 percent be used in computing the present value of the lump-sum settlement? Comment or explain.

Exercises

9. *Number of periods and interest rate.* State the rate per period and the number of periods, in each of the following:
   a.   12 percent per annum, for 5 years, compounded annually.
   b.   12 percent per annum, for 5 years, compounded semiannually.
   c.   12 percent per annum, for 5 years, compounded quarterly.
   d.   12 percent per annum, for 5 years, compounded monthly.

Exercises **10** *through* **21** *and* **23** *through* **27** *involve calculations of present and future value for single payments and for annuities, both ordinary and in arrears. To make the exercises more realistic, specific guidance is not given with each individual exercise.*

10. Compute the future value of:
   a. $100 invested for 5 periods at 4 percent compounded once per period.
   b. $500 invested for 15 periods at 2 percent compounded once per period.
   c. $2,500 invested for 14 years at 8 percent compounded quarterly.
   d. $1,000 invested for 2 years at 12 percent compounded monthly.

11. *See note at Exercise* **10.** Compute the present value of:
   a. $100 due in 33 periods compounded at 4 percent per period.
   b. $50 due in 27 periods at 6 percent compounded twice per period.
   c. $250 due in 8 years at 8 percent compounded quarterly.
   d. $1,000 due in 2 years at 12 percent compounded monthly.

12. *See note at Exercise* **10.** Compute the amount (future value) of an ordinary annuity (an annuity in arrears) of:
   a.   13 rents of $100 at 1½ percent per period.
   b.   8 rents of $850 at 6 percent per period.
   c.   27 rents of $375 at 4 percent per period.
   d.   35 rents of $1,400 at 3 percent per period.

13. *See note at Exercise* **10.** What is the amount (future value) of an annuity due (in advance) of:
    a.   13 rents of $200 each at 6 percent per period?
    b.   9 rents of $75 each at 4 percent per period?
    c.   24 rents of $100 each at 2 percent per period?

14. *See note at Exercise* **10.** Compute the present value of an ordinary annuity (an annuity in arrears) of:
    a. $1,000 for 29 periods at 4 percent per period.
    b. $1,500 for 31 periods at 6 percent per period.
    c. $400 for 41 years at 8 percent per year.
    d. $750 for 75 years at 10 percent per year.

15. *See note at Exercise* **10.** What is the present value of an annuity due (in advance) of:
    a.   28 rents of $50 at 12 percent per period?
    b.   32 rents of $45 at 10 percent per period?

16. *See note at Exercise* **10.** Mr. Adams has $500 to invest. He wishes to know how much it will amount to if he invests it at:
    a.   6 percent per year for 21 years.
    b.   8 percent per year for 33 years.

17. *See note at Exercise* **10.** Ms. Black wishes to have $15,000 at the end of 8 years. How much must she invest today to accomplish this purpose if the interest rate is
    a.   6 percent per year?
    b.   8 percent per year?

18. *See note at Exercise* **10.** Mr. Case plans to set aside $4,000 each year, the first payment to be made on January 1, Year 1, and the last on January 1, Year 10. How much will he have accumulated by January 1, Year 10, if the interest rate is
    a.   6 percent per year?
    b.   8 percent per year?

19. *See note at Exercise* **10.** Ms. David is 57 and wants to have $450,000 on her sixty-fifth birthday. She asks you to tell her how much she must deposit on each birthday from her fifty-eighth to sixty-fifth, inclusive, in order to receive this amount. Assume an interest rate of:
    a.   8 percent per year.
    b.   10 percent per year.

20. *See note at Exercise* **10.** Mr. Edwards invests $900 on June 1 of each year from Year 1 to Year 11, inclusive, 11 payments total. How much will he have accumulated on June 1, Year 12 (note that 1 year elapses after last payment), if the interest rate is
    a.   12 percent per year?
    b.   10 percent per year?

21. *See note at Exercise* **10.** Ms. Frank has $145,000, which she deposits with an insurance company on February 1, Year 1, to purchase an annuity. The annuity consists of six annual payments, the first to be made on February 1, Year 2. How much will she receive in each payment? Assume an interest rate of:

    a.   8 percent per year.

    b.   12 percent per year.

22. *Symbolic notation for compound interest tables.* In the preceding Exercises **9** through **21,** you have been asked to compute a number. First you must decide what factor from the tables is appropriate and then you use that factor in the appropriate calculation. Notice that the last step could be omitted. You could write an arithmetic expression showing the factor you want to use without actually copying down the number and doing the arithmetic. For example, define the following notation: T(i, p, r) means Table i (1, 2, 3, or 4), row p (periods 1 to 20, 22, 24, . . . , 40, 45, 50, 100), and column r (interest rates from ½ percent up to 20 percent). Thus, T(3, 16, 12) would be the factor in Table 3 for 16 periods and an interest rate of 12 percent per period, which is 42.75328. Using this notation, you can write an expression for any compound interest problem.

You can check that you understand this notation by observing that the following are true statements:

$$\text{T}(1,\ 20,\ 8) = \quad 4.66096.$$

$$\text{T}(2,\ 12,\ 5) = \quad .55684.$$

$$\text{T}(3,\ 16,\ 12) = 42.75328.$$

$$\text{T}(4,\ 10,\ 20) = \quad 4.19247.$$

In the following questions, write an expression for the correct answer using the notation introduced here, but do not attempt to evaluate the expression.

    a.   Work the **a** parts of Exercises **16** and **17.**

    b.   Work the **b** parts of Exercises **18** through **21.**

    c.   How might the use of this notation make it easier for your instructor to write examination questions on compound interest?

23. *See note at Exercise* **10.** How much must Mr. Grady invest on July 1 of each of Years 1 through 7, inclusive, to have $300,000 on July 1, Year 8? Assume an interest rate of:

    a.   8 percent per year.

    b.   10 percent per year.

24. *See note at Exercise* **10.** Ms. Howe wishes to provide her two sons with an income of $7,500 each for 5 years. How much must she invest on January 1, Year 1, to provide for five such payments, the first to be made on January 1, Year 3? Assume interest rates of:

    a.   15 percent per year.

    b.   10 percent per year.

25. *See note at Exercise* **10.** Mr. Irons borrowed money from a friend, and he agreed to repay $8,000 on March 1 of this year. On that date he was unable to pay his friend, so he made the following arrangement with the Regional Loan Company: The loan company paid the friend the $8,000 on March 1, and Mr. Irons agreed to repay the loan in a series of five equal annual payments. Assume an interest rate of 20 percent per year. How much must Mr. Irons pay each year if he makes the first payment on March 1 of:

    a. This year?
    b. Next year?
    c. Two years from now?

26. *See note at Exercise* **10.** Ms. Jones bought a car for $14,500, and agreed to pay for it in 12 equal monthly installments with interest at 12 percent per year, the first payment to be made immediately. What is the monthly payment?

27. *See note at Exercise* **10.** Mr. Karls agrees to lease a certain property for 10 years at the following annual rentals, payable in advance:

Years 1 and 2—$1,000 per year.

Years 3 to 6—$2,000 per year.

Years 7 to 10—$2,500 per year.

What single immediate sum will pay all of these rents if they are discounted at:

    a. 8 percent per year?
    b. 10 percent per year?

28. *Perpetuity.* In order to establish a fund that will provide a scholarship of $3,000 a year indefinitely, with the first award to occur now, how much must be deposited if the fund earns:

    a. 10 percent per period?
    b. 8 percent per period?

29. *Delayed Perpetuity.* Consider the scholarship fund in the preceding problem. Suppose that the first scholarship is not to be awarded until 1 year from now. How much should be deposited if the fund earns:

    a. 10 percent per period?
    b. 8 percent per period?

Suppose that the first scholarship is not to be awarded until 5 years from now. How much should be deposited if the fund earns:

    c. 10 percent per year?
    d. 8 percent per year?

30. *Internal Rate of Return.* Find the internal rate of return for the following investments, each of which requires $10,000 now and generates cash inflows as shown:

    a. $5,530.67 at the end of Years 1 and 2.
    b. $1,627.45 at the end of Years 1 through 10.
    c. $1,556.66 at the end of Years 1 through 13.
    d. $2,053.39 at the end of Years 1 through 20.

31. *Internal Rate of Return.* Find the internal rate of return for the following investments, each of which requires $10,000 now and generates cash inflows as shown:

    a. $2,921.46 at the end of Years 3 through 7.

    b. $2,101.77 at the end of Years 2 through 10.

    c. $24,883.20 at the end of Year 5 only.

32. *Internal Rate of Return.* Compute the implicit interest rates for each of the following single-payment notes:

    a. $10,000 is borrowed: a payment of $15,208.75 is due in 3 years.

    b. $10,000 is borrowed: a payment of $15,036.30 is due in 3½ years. (Find a semiannual rate.)

    c. $10,000 is borrowed: a payment of $21,068.50 is due in 4¾ years. (Find a quarterly rate.)

Problems and Cases

33. *Relations Between Present Value Tables.* Describe each of the arithmetic relations between numbers in compound interest tables described below.

    a. A number in Table 1 (future value of a single payment) and the corresponding number (same row and same column) in Table 2 (present value of a single payment).

    b. A number in Table 4 (present value of an ordinary annuity) and the numbers in Table 2 (present value of a single payment) for the same column as the number in Table 4.

    c. A number in Table 3 (future value of an ordinary annuity) and the corresponding number (same row and same column) in Table 4 (present value of an ordinary annuity).

    d. Note that no similarly simple statement can relate numbers in Table 3 to Table 1.

34. *Interest Rate Implied by Sales Discount.* The terms of sale "2/10, net/30" mean that a discount of 2 percent from gross invoice price can be taken if the invoice is paid within 10 days and that otherwise the full amount is due within 30 days.

    a. Write an expression for the implied annual rate of interest being offered, if the entire discount is viewed as being interest for funds received sooner rather than later. (Note that 98 percent of the gross invoice price is being borrowed for 20 days.)

    b. The tables at the back of the book do not permit the exact evaluation of the expression derived in part **a**. The rate of interest implied is 44.59 percent per year. Use the tables to convince yourself that this astounding (to some) answer must be close to correct.

35. *Changing Compounding Period for an Annuity.* The state helps a rural county maintain a bridge and has agreed to pay $6,000 now and every 2 years thereafter forever toward the expenses. The state wishes to discharge its obligation by paying a single sum to the county now in lieu of the payment due and all future payments.

How much should the state pay the county if the discount rate is 10 percent per year?

36. *Changing Compounding Period for a Perpetuity.* Mr. and Mrs. Clark want to establish a fund that will pay a $25,000 prize to an outstanding academic accountant. The first prize is to be awarded 4 years from now, and the prize is to be awarded every 10 years thereafter. How much should be deposited if the fund earns:

a. 8 percent per year?

b. 10 percent per year?

37. *Single Sum and Perpetuity.* An oil-drilling company figures that $300 must be spent for an initial supply of drill bits and that $100 must be spent every month to replace the worn-out bits. What is the present value of the cost of the bits if the company plans to be in business indefinitely and discounts payments at 2 percent per month?

38. *Working Backwards.* If you promise to leave $25,000 on deposit at the Quarter Savings Bank for 4 years, the bank will give you a new car now and your $25,000 back at the end of 4 years. How much are you, in effect, paying today for the car if the bank pays 8 percent interest compounded quarterly (2 percent paid four times per year)?

39. *Breakeven Analysis Involving Annuity.* When the General Electric Company first introduced the Lucalox ceramic, screw-in light bulb, the bulb cost 3½ times as much as an ordinary bulb but lasted 5 times as long. An ordinary bulb cost $.50 and lasted about 8 months. If a firm has a discount rate of 12 percent compounded three times a year, how much would it save in present value dollars by using one Lucalox bulb?

40. *Breakeven Analysis Involving an Annuity.* The Roberts Dairy Company switched from delivery trucks with regular gasoline engines to ones with diesel engines. The diesel trucks cost $2,000 more than the ordinary gasoline trucks, but $600 per year less to operate. Assume that the operating costs are saved at the end of each month. If Roberts Dairy uses a discount rate of 1 percent per month, approximately how many months, at a minimum, must the diesel trucks remain in service for the switch to be worthwhile?

41. *Converting Lease Payments for Decision Analysis.* In the mid-1950s, International Business Machines Corporation (IBM) entered into a consent judgment with the U.S. Justice Department by agreeing to offer its business machines for sale. Prior to that time IBM would only rent its machines.

a. Assume that the type 402 accounting machine had been renting for $5,220 per year, paid in advance, and the selling price of $27,950 was set so that it was equal to the present value of seven rental payments. What annual discount rate did IBM use in determining the selling price?

b. If a type 82 card sorter had been rented for $55 a month, paid in advance, and the purchase price had been set at $3,400, what number of rental payments would be equivalent to the purchase price? Assume that the rental payments were discounted at ½ percent per month.

    c. If a type 24 keypunch machine had been rented for $40 per month, paid in advance, and if IBM wanted to set a purchase price so that the price would be equal to the discounted present value of 48 months' rent discounted at ½ percent per month, what should the purchase price be?

42. *Net Present Value Graph.* The Danos Company invests $10,000 at the end of year 0 so that it may receive the following stream of payments (initial investment also shown):

End of Year	Cash Payment
0	− $10,000
1	4,000
2	3,400
3	3,100
4	2,800

What is the present value at the end of Year 0 of that stream of payments if the discount rate is

    a. 0 percent per year?
    b. 2 percent per year?
    c. 6 percent per year?
    d. 10 percent per year?
    e. 14 percent per year? (Use these discount factors: 1,000, .877, .769, .675, and .592.)
    f. Construct a graph that shows the discount rate on the horizontal axis and the net present value on the vertical axis. Plot the points derived in **a–e**.
    g. Is the line connecting the plotted points a straight line?
    h. What is the implicit interest rate for these flows?

43. *Deferred Annuity.* Two parents are accumulating a fund to send their child to college. The parents are investing a fixed amount in a savings certificate at the end of each calendar quarter starting on March 30, 1981. The savings certificate earns 12 percent compounded quarterly. Starting March 30, 1987, the parents will withdraw $1,000 at the end of each calendar quarter for 4 years to pay bills.

    The parents expect to make payments through the end of 1990 (for a total of 10 years and 40 payments). How much must be paid into the fund quarterly for 10 years so that $1,000 can be withdrawn quarterly for the last 4 years?

44. *Effective Interest Rate.* September 1 of Year 1, the partnership of Charles, Leslie, and Eli received $5,000 cash from Davis for a single-payment note promising a single payment of principal and interest to Davis of $5,450 due August 31 of Year 2. The interest rate stated in the note was 9 percent per year. On January 1 of Year 2, the holder of the note, Davis, needed cash and offered to return the note to the partnership for a single payment of $4,500.

    What was the implicit annual interest rate in Davis' offer to sell the note back to the partnership for a single payment of $4,500?

45. *Amortization Schedules.* Avner Company issues a $100,000 face value note that promises to pay $15,000 at the end of Year 1, $15,000 at the end of Year 2, and $115,000 at the end of Year 3. Assume a market interest rate of 10 percent per year.

    a. Discounting cash flows at 10 percent, compute the net present value of these promises. Avner Company receives this amount in return for its note.

    b. Construct an amortization schedule showing the balance of the note payable at the start of each period, the interest for each period, the periodic payment, the amount of each payment increasing or decreasing the principal amount, and the loan balance at the end of each period.

46. *Decision Case.* On January 1, Year 1, Outergarments, Inc., opened a new textile plant for the production of synthetic fabrics. The plant is on leased land; 20 years remain on the nonrenewable lease.

    The cost of the plant was $2 million. Net cash flow to be derived from the project is estimated to be $300,000 per year. The company does not normally invest in such projects unless the anticipated yield is at least 12 percent.

    On December 31, the company finds cash flows from the plant to be $280,000 for the year. On the same day, farm experts predict cotton production to be unusually low for the next 2 years. Outergarments estimates the resulting increase in demand for synthetic fabrics to boost cash flows to $350,000 for each of the next 2 years. Subsequent years' estimates remain unchanged. Ignore tax considerations.

    a. Calculate the present value of the future expected cash flows from the plant when it was opened.

    b. What is the present value of the plant 1 year later, immediately after the reestimation of future cash flows?

    c. On the day following the cotton production news release, Overalls Company announces plans to build a synthetic fabrics plant to be opened in 3 years. Outergarments, Inc., makes no further changes in estimates for Years 2 through 4, but reduces the estimated annual cash flows for subsequent years to $200,000. What is the value of the Outergarments' present plant on January 1, Year 2, after the new projections?

    d. On January 2, Year 2, an investor contacts Outergarments about purchasing a 20 percent share of the plant. If the investor expects to earn at least a 12 percent annual return on the investment, what is the maximum amount that the investor should pay? Assume that the investor and Outergarments, Inc. use the same estimates of annual cash flows as found in part **c**.

Suggested Solutions to Even-Numbered Exercises

10. a. $100 \times 1.21665 = \$121.67$.
    b. $500 \times 1.34587 = \$672.94$.
    c. $2,500 \times (1.74102 \times 1.74102) = \$7,577.88$. $(1.02)^{56} = (1.02)^{28}(1.02)^{28}$.
    d. $1,000 \times 1.26973 = \$1,269.73$.

12. a. $100 × 14.23683 = $1,423.68.
  b. $850 × 9.89747 = $8,412.85.
  c. ($375 × 44.31174 × 1.04) + $375 = $17,656.58.
  d. ($1,400 × 57.73018 × 1.03) + $1,400 = $84,646.92.

14. a. $1,000(17.29203 − .30832) = $16,983.71.
  b. $1,500(14.08404 − .15496) = $20,893.62.
  c. $400(11.92461 + .31524 × .13520) = $4,786.89.
  d. $750(9.86281 × .05731 + 9.42691) = $7,494.11.

16. a. $500(3.20714 × 1.06) = $1,699.78.
  b. $500(11.73708 × 1.08) = $6,338.02.

18. a. $4,000 × 13.18079 = $52,723.16.
  b. $4.000 × 14.48656 = $57,946.24.

20. a. $900 × (24.13313 − 1.0) = $20,819.82.
  b. $900 × (21.38428 − 1.0) = $18,345.85.

22. *Symbolic notation for compound interest tables.*
  a. (16) $500 × T(1, 20, 6) × T(1, 1, 6) = $500 × T(1, 20, 6) × 1.06
      = $500 × T(1, 21, 6)—but this is not in the tables.
      (17) $15,000 × T(2, 8, 6).
  b. (18) $4,000 × T(3, 10, 8).
      (19) $450,000/T(3, 8, 10).
      (20) $900 × [T(3, 12, 10) − 1.0] = $900 × T(3, 11, 10) ×
      T(1, 1, 10).
      (21) $145,000/T(4, 6, 12).
  c. Asking questions about compound interest calculations on examinations presents a difficult logistical problem to teachers. They may want the students to use compound interest tables, but not wish to incur the costs of reproducing them in sufficient numbers for each student to have a copy. They may not wish to give an open book test. This device is useful for posing test questions about compound interest, because the notation shows that the student understands what factors should be used without testing students' ability to do arithmetic. Teachers want to be sure that students know how to use the tables and calculating devices efficiently such that humans do the thinking and calculators do the multiplications and divisions.

24. a. $15,000 × (3.78448 − .86957) = $43,723.65.
  b. $15,000 × (4.35526 − .90909) = $51,692.55.

26. $14,500 ÷ (10.36763 + 1.0) = $1,275.55.

28. *Perpetuity*
  a. $3,000 + ($3,000 ÷ .10) = $33,000.
  b. $3,000 + ($3,000 ÷ .08) = $40,500.

30. *Internal Rate of Return*
   a.   7 percent.
   b.   10 percent.
   c.   12 percent.
   d.   20 percent.

32. *Internal Rate of Return*
   a.   15 percent: $(1.520875)^{1/3} - 1 = .15$. Or, scan Table 1, 3-period row.
   b.   6 percent per 6 months: $(1.503630)^{1/7} - 1 = .06$. Or, scan Table 1, 7-period row.
   c.   4 percent per quarter: $(2.10685)^{1/19} - 1 = .04$. Or, scan Table 1, 19-period row.

Compound Interest and Annuity Tables

Table 1
Future Value of $1

$$F_n = P(1 + r)^n$$

r = Interest rate; n = number of periods until valuation; P = $1

Periods = n	1/2%	1%	1½%	2%	3%	4%	5%	6%	7%	8%	10%	12%	15%	20%	25%
1	1.00500	1.01000	1.01500	1.02000	1.03000	1.04000	1.05000	1.06000	1.07000	1.08000	1.10000	1.12000	1.15000	1.20000	1.25000
2	1.01003	1.02010	1.03022	1.04040	1.06090	1.08160	1.10250	1.12360	1.14490	1.16640	1.21000	1.25440	1.32250	1.44000	1.56250
3	1.01508	1.03030	1.04568	1.06121	1.09273	1.12486	1.15763	1.19102	1.22504	1.25971	1.33100	1.40493	1.52088	1.72800	1.95313
4	1.02015	1.04060	1.06136	1.08243	1.12551	1.16986	1.21551	1.26248	1.31080	1.36049	1.46410	1.57352	1.74901	2.07360	2.44141
5	1.02525	1.05101	1.07728	1.10408	1.15927	1.21665	1.27628	1.33823	1.40255	1.46933	1.61051	1.76234	2.01136	2.48832	3.05176
6	1.03038	1.06152	1.09344	1.12616	1.19405	1.26532	1.34010	1.41852	1.50073	1.58687	1.77156	1.97382	2.31306	2.98598	3.81470
7	1.03553	1.07214	1.10984	1.14869	1.22987	1.31593	1.40710	1.50363	1.60578	1.71382	1.94872	2.21068	2.66002	3.58318	4.76837
8	1.04071	1.08286	1.12649	1.17166	1.26677	1.36857	1.47746	1.59385	1.71819	1.85093	2.14359	2.47596	3.05902	4.29982	5.96046
9	1.04591	1.09369	1.14339	1.19509	1.30477	1.42331	1.55133	1.68948	1.83846	1.99900	2.35795	2.77308	3.51788	5.15978	7.45058
10	1.05114	1.10462	1.16054	1.21899	1.34392	1.48024	1.62889	1.79085	1.96715	2.15892	2.59374	3.10585	4.04556	6.19174	9.31323
11	1.05640	1.11567	1.17795	1.24337	1.38423	1.53945	1.71034	1.89830	2.10485	2.33164	2.85312	3.47855	4.65239	7.43008	11.64153
12	1.06168	1.12683	1.19562	1.26824	1.42576	1.60103	1.79586	2.01220	2.25219	2.51817	3.13843	3.89598	5.35025	8.91610	14.55192
13	1.06699	1.13809	1.21355	1.29361	1.46853	1.66507	1.88565	2.13293	2.40985	2.71962	3.45227	4.36349	6.15279	10.69932	18.18989
14	1.07232	1.14947	1.23176	1.31948	1.51259	1.73168	1.97993	2.26090	2.57853	2.93719	3.79750	4.88711	7.07571	12.83918	22.73737
15	1.07768	1.16097	1.25023	1.34587	1.55797	1.80094	2.07893	2.39656	2.75903	3.17217	4.17725	5.47357	8.13706	15.40702	28.42171
16	1.08307	1.17258	1.26899	1.37279	1.60471	1.87298	2.18287	2.54035	2.95216	3.42594	4.59497	6.13039	9.35762	18.48843	35.52714
17	1.08849	1.18430	1.28802	1.40024	1.65285	1.94790	2.29202	2.69277	3.15882	3.70002	5.05447	6.86604	10.76126	22.18611	44.40892
18	1.09393	1.19615	1.30734	1.42825	1.70243	2.02582	2.40662	2.85434	3.37993	3.99602	5.55992	7.68997	12.37545	26.62333	55.51115
19	1.09940	1.20811	1.32695	1.45681	1.75351	2.10685	2.52695	3.02560	3.61653	4.31570	6.11591	8.61276	14.23177	31.94800	69.38894
20	1.10490	1.22019	1.34686	1.48595	1.80611	2.19112	2.65330	3.20714	3.86968	4.66096	6.72750	9.64629	16.36654	38.33760	86.73617
22	1.11597	1.24472	1.38756	1.54598	1.91610	2.36992	2.92526	3.60354	4.43040	5.43654	8.14027	12.10031	21.64475	55.20614	135.5253
24	1.12716	1.26973	1.42950	1.60844	2.03279	2.56330	3.22510	4.04893	5.07237	6.34118	9.84973	15.17863	28.62518	79.49685	211.7582
26	1.13846	1.29526	1.47271	1.67342	2.15659	2.77247	3.55567	4.54938	5.80735	7.39635	11.91818	19.04007	37.85680	114.4755	330.8722
28	1.14987	1.32129	1.51722	1.74102	2.28793	2.99870	3.92013	5.11169	6.64884	8.62711	14.42099	23.88387	50.06561	164.8447	516.9879
30	1.16140	1.34785	1.56308	1.81136	2.42726	3.24340	4.32194	5.74349	7.61226	10.06266	17.44940	29.95992	66.21177	237.3763	807.7936
32	1.17304	1.37494	1.61032	1.88454	2.57508	3.50806	4.76494	6.45339	8.71527	11.73708	21.11378	37.58173	87.56507	341.8219	1262.177
34	1.18480	1.40258	1.65900	1.96068	2.73191	3.79432	5.25335	7.25103	9.97811	13.69013	25.54767	47.14252	115.80480	492.2235	1972.152
36	1.19668	1.43077	1.70914	2.03989	2.89828	4.10393	5.79182	8.14725	11.42394	15.96817	30.91268	59.13557	153.15185	708.8019	3081.488
38	1.20868	1.45953	1.76080	2.12230	3.07478	4.43881	6.38548	9.15425	13.07927	18.62528	37.40434	74.17966	202.54332	1020.675	4814.825
40	1.22079	1.48886	1.81402	2.20804	3.26204	4.80102	7.03999	10.28572	14.97446	21.72452	45.25926	93.05097	267.86355	1469.772	7523.164
45	1.25162	1.56481	1.95421	2.43785	3.78160	5.84118	8.98501	13.76461	21.00245	31.92045	72.89048	163.9876	538.76927	3657.262	22958.87
50	1.28323	1.64463	2.10524	2.69159	4.38391	7.10668	11.46740	18.42015	29.45703	46.90161	117.3909	269.0022	1083.65744	9100.438	70064.92
100	1.64667	2.70481	4.43205	7.24465	19.21863	50.50495	131.5013	339.3021	867.7163	2199.761	13780.61	83522.27	117×10^4	828×10^5	491×10^7

Table 2
Present Value of $1

$$P = F_n(1 + r)^{-n}$$

r = discount rate; n = number of periods until payment; F_n = \$1

Periods = n	½%	1%	1½%	2%	3%	4%	5%	6%	7%	8%	10%	12%	15%	20%	25%
1	.99502	.99010	.98522	.98039	.97087	.96154	.95238	.94340	.93458	.92593	.90909	.89286	.86957	.83333	.80000
2	.99007	.98030	.97066	.96117	.94260	.92456	.90703	.89000	.87344	.85734	.82645	.79719	.75614	.69444	.64000
3	.98515	.97059	.95632	.94232	.91514	.88900	.86384	.83962	.81630	.79383	.75131	.71178	.65752	.57870	.51200
4	.98025	.96098	.94218	.92385	.88849	.85480	.82270	.79209	.76290	.73503	.68301	.63552	.57175	.48225	.40960
5	.97537	.95147	.92826	.90573	.86261	.82193	.78353	.74726	.71299	.68058	.62092	.56743	.49718	.40188	.32768
6	.97052	.94205	.91454	.88797	.83748	.79031	.74622	.70496	.66634	.63017	.56447	.50663	.43233	.33490	.26214
7	.96569	.93272	.90103	.87056	.81309	.75992	.71068	.66506	.62275	.58349	.51316	.45235	.37594	.27908	.20972
8	.96089	.92348	.88771	.85349	.78941	.73069	.67684	.62741	.58201	.54027	.46651	.40388	.32690	.23257	.16777
9	.95610	.91434	.87459	.83676	.76642	.70259	.64461	.59190	.54393	.50025	.42410	.36061	.28426	.19381	.13422
10	.95135	.90529	.86167	.82035	.74409	.67556	.61391	.55839	.50835	.46319	.38554	.32197	.24718	.16151	.10737
11	.94661	.89632	.84893	.80426	.72242	.64958	.58468	.52679	.47509	.42888	.35049	.28748	.21494	.13459	.08590
12	.94191	.88745	.83639	.78849	.70138	.62460	.55684	.49697	.44401	.39711	.31863	.25668	.18691	.11216	.06872
13	.93722	.87866	.82403	.77303	.68095	.60057	.53032	.46884	.41496	.36770	.28966	.22917	.16253	.09346	.05498
14	.93256	.86996	.81185	.75788	.66112	.57748	.50507	.44230	.38782	.34046	.26333	.20462	.14133	.07789	.04398
15	.92792	.86135	.79985	.74301	.64186	.55526	.48102	.41727	.36245	.31524	.23939	.18270	.12289	.06491	.03518
16	.92330	.85282	.78803	.72845	.62317	.53391	.45811	.39365	.33873	.29189	.21763	.16312	.10686	.05409	.02815
17	.91871	.84438	.77639	.71416	.60502	.51337	.43630	.37136	.31657	.27027	.19784	.14564	.09293	.04507	.02252
18	.91414	.83602	.76491	.70016	.58739	.49363	.41552	.35034	.29586	.25025	.17986	.13004	.08081	.03756	.01801
19	.90959	.82774	.75361	.68643	.57029	.47464	.39573	.33051	.27651	.23171	.16351	.11611	.07027	.03130	.01441
20	.90506	.81954	.74247	.67297	.55368	.45639	.37689	.31180	.25842	.21455	.14864	.10367	.06110	.02608	.01153
22	.89608	.80340	.72069	.64684	.52189	.42196	.34185	.27751	.22571	.18394	.12285	.08264	.04620	.01811	.00738
24	.88719	.78757	.69954	.62172	.49193	.39012	.31007	.24698	.19715	.15770	.10153	.06588	.03493	.01258	.00472
26	.87838	.77205	.67902	.59758	.46369	.36069	.28124	.21981	.17220	.13520	.08391	.05252	.02642	.00874	.00302
28	.86966	.75684	.65910	.57437	.43708	.33348	.25509	.19563	.15040	.11591	.06934	.04187	.01997	.00607	.00193
30	.86103	.74192	.63976	.55207	.41199	.30832	.23138	.17411	.13137	.09938	.05731	.03338	.01510	.00421	.00124
32	.85248	.72730	.62099	.53063	.38834	.28506	.20987	.15496	.11474	.08520	.04736	.02661	.01142	.00293	.00079
34	.84402	.71297	.60277	.51003	.36604	.26355	.19035	.13791	.10022	.07305	.03914	.02121	.00864	.00203	.00051
36	.83564	.69892	.58509	.49022	.34503	.24367	.17266	.12274	.08754	.06262	.03235	.01691	.00653	.00141	.00032
38	.82735	.68515	.56792	.47119	.32523	.22529	.15661	.10924	.07646	.05369	.02673	.01348	.00494	.00098	.00021
40	.81914	.67165	.55126	.45289	.30656	.20829	.14205	.09722	.06678	.04603	.02209	.01075	.00373	.00068	.00013
45	.79896	.63905	.51171	.41020	.26444	.17120	.11130	.07265	.04761	.03133	.01372	.00610	.00186	.00027	.00004
50	.77929	.60804	.47500	.37153	.22811	.14071	.08720	.05429	.03395	.02132	.00852	.00346	.00092	.00011	.00001
100	.60729	.36971	.22563	.13803	.05203	.01980	.00760	.00295	.00115	.00045	.00007	.00001	.00000	.00000	.00000

Table 3
Future Value of an Annuity of $1 in Arrears

$$F_A = \frac{(1 + r)^n - 1}{r}$$

r = Interest rate; n = number of payments

No. of Payments = n	1/2%	1%	1½%	2%	3%	4%	5%	6%	7%	8%	10%	12%	15%	20%	25%
1	1.00000	1.00000	1.00000	1.00000	1.00000	1.00000	1.00000	1.00000	1.00000	1.00000	1.00000	1.00000	1.00000	1.00000	1.00000
2	2.00500	2.01000	2.01500	2.02000	2.03000	2.04000	2.05000	2.06000	2.07000	2.08000	2.10000	2.12000	2.15000	2.20000	2.25000
3	3.01503	3.03010	3.04522	3.06040	3.09090	3.12160	3.15250	3.18360	3.21490	3.24640	3.31000	3.37440	3.47250	3.64000	3.81250
4	4.03010	4.06040	4.09090	4.12161	4.18363	4.24646	4.31013	4.37462	4.43994	4.50611	4.64100	4.77933	4.99338	5.36800	5.76563
5	5.05025	5.10101	5.15227	5.20404	5.30914	5.41632	5.52563	5.63709	5.75074	5.86660	6.10510	6.35285	6.74238	7.44160	8.20703
6	6.07550	6.15202	6.22955	6.30812	6.46841	6.63298	6.80191	6.97532	7.15329	7.33593	7.71561	8.11519	8.75374	9.92992	11.25879
7	7.10588	7.21354	7.32299	7.43428	7.66246	7.89829	8.14201	8.39384	8.65402	8.92280	9.48717	10.08901	11.06680	12.91590	15.07349
8	8.14141	8.28567	8.43284	8.58297	8.89234	9.21423	9.54911	9.89747	10.25980	10.63663	11.43589	12.29969	13.72682	16.49908	19.84186
9	9.18212	9.36853	9.55933	9.75463	10.15911	10.58280	11.02658	11.49132	11.97799	12.48756	13.57948	14.77566	16.78584	20.79890	25.80232
10	10.22803	10.46221	10.70272	10.94972	11.46388	12.00611	12.57789	13.18079	13.81645	14.48656	15.93742	17.54874	20.30372	25.95868	33.25290
11	11.27917	11.56683	11.86326	12.16872	12.80780	13.48635	14.20679	14.97164	15.78360	16.64549	18.53117	20.65458	24.34928	32.15042	42.56613
12	12.33556	12.68250	13.04121	13.41209	14.19203	15.02581	15.91713	16.86994	17.88845	18.97713	21.38428	24.13313	29.00167	39.58050	54.20766
13	13.39724	13.80933	14.23683	14.68033	15.61779	16.62684	17.71298	18.88214	20.14064	21.49530	24.52271	28.02911	34.35192	48.49660	68.75958
14	14.46423	14.94742	15.45038	15.97394	17.08632	18.29191	19.59863	21.01507	22.55049	24.21492	27.97496	32.39260	40.50471	59.19592	86.94947
15	15.53655	16.09690	16.68214	17.29342	18.59891	20.02359	21.57856	23.27597	25.12902	27.15211	31.77248	37.27971	47.58041	72.03511	109.6868
16	16.61423	17.25786	17.93237	18.63929	20.15688	21.82453	23.65749	25.67253	27.88805	30.32428	35.94973	42.75328	55.71747	87.44213	138.1085
17	17.69730	18.43044	19.20136	20.01207	21.76159	23.69751	25.84037	28.21288	30.84022	33.75023	40.54470	48.88367	65.07509	105.9306	173.6357
18	18.78579	19.61475	20.48938	21.41231	23.41444	25.64541	28.13238	30.90565	33.99903	37.45024	45.59917	55.74971	75.83636	128.1167	218.0446
19	19.87972	20.81090	21.79672	22.84058	25.11687	27.67123	30.53900	33.75999	37.37896	41.44626	51.15909	63.43968	88.21181	154.7400	273.5558
20	20.97912	22.01900	23.12367	24.29737	26.87037	29.77808	33.06595	36.78559	40.99549	45.76196	57.27500	72.05244	102.4435	186.6880	342.9447
22	23.19443	24.47159	25.83758	27.29898	30.53678	34.24797	38.50521	43.39229	49.00574	55.45676	71.40275	92.50258	137.63164	271.0307	538.1011
24	25.43196	26.97346	28.63352	30.42186	34.42647	39.08260	44.50200	50.81558	58.17667	66.76476	88.49733	118.1552	184.16784	392.4842	843.0329
26	27.69191	29.52563	31.51397	33.67091	38.55304	44.31174	51.11345	59.15638	68.67647	79.95442	109.1818	150.3339	245.71197	567.3773	1319.489
28	29.97452	32.12910	34.48148	37.05121	42.93092	49.96758	58.40258	68.52811	80.69769	95.33883	134.2099	190.6989	327.10408	819.2233	2063.952
30	32.28002	34.78489	37.53868	40.56808	47.57542	56.08494	66.43885	79.05819	94.46079	113.2832	164.4940	241.3327	434.74515	1181.881	3227.174
32	34.60862	37.49407	40.68829	44.22703	52.50276	62.70147	75.29883	90.88978	110.2181	134.2135	201.1378	304.8477	577.10046	1704.109	5044.710
34	36.96058	40.25770	43.93309	48.03380	57.73018	69.85791	85.06696	101.1838	128.2588	158.6267	245.4767	384.5210	765.36535	2456.118	7884.609
36	39.33610	43.07688	47.27597	51.99437	63.27594	77.59831	95.83632	119.1209	148.9135	187.1022	299.1268	484.4631	1014.34568	3539.009	12321.95
38	41.73545	45.95272	50.71989	56.11494	69.15945	85.97034	107.7095	135.9042	172.5610	220.3159	364.0434	609.8305	1343.62216	5096.373	19255.30
40	44.15885	48.88637	54.26789	60.40198	75.40126	95.02552	120.7998	154.7620	199.6351	259.0565	442.5926	767.0914	1779.09031	7343.858	30088.66
45	50.32416	56.48107	63.61420	71.89271	92.71986	121.0294	159.7002	212.7435	285.7493	386.5056	718.9048	1358.230	3585.12846	18281.31	91831.50
50	56.64516	64.46318	73.68283	84.57940	112.7969	152.6671	209.3480	290.3359	406.5289	573.7702	1163.909	2400.018	7217.71628	45497.19	280255.7
100	129.33370	170.4814	228.8030	312.2323	607.2877	1237.624	2610.025	5638.368	12381.66	27484.52	137796.1	696010.5	783×10^4	414×10^6	196×10^8

Note: To convert from this table to values of an annuity in advance, determine the annuity in arrears above for one more period and subtract 1.00000.

Table 4
Present Value of an Annuity of $1 in Arrears

$$P_A = \frac{1 - (1 + r)^{-n}}{r}$$

r = discount rate; n = number of payments

No. of Payments = n	1/2%	1%	1½%	2%	3%	4%	5%	6%	7%	8%	10%	12%	15%	20%	25%
1	0.99502	.99010	.98522	.98039	.97087	.96154	.95238	.94340	.93458	.92593	.90909	.89286	0.86957	.83333	.80000
2	1.98510	1.97040	1.95588	1.94156	1.91347	1.88609	1.85941	1.83339	1.80802	1.78326	1.73554	1.69005	1.62571	1.52778	1.44000
3	2.97025	2.94099	2.91220	2.88388	2.82861	2.77509	2.72325	2.67301	2.62432	2.57710	2.48685	2.40183	2.28323	2.10648	1.95200
4	3.95050	3.90197	3.85438	3.80773	3.71710	3.62990	3.54595	3.46511	3.38721	3.31213	3.16987	3.03735	2.85498	2.58873	2.36160
5	4.92587	4.85343	4.78264	4.71346	4.57971	4.45182	4.32948	4.21236	4.10020	3.99271	3.79079	3.60478	3.35216	2.99061	2.68928
6	5.89638	5.79548	5.69719	5.60143	5.41719	5.24212	5.07569	4.91732	4.76654	4.62288	4.35526	4.11141	3.78448	3.32551	2.95142
7	6.86207	6.72819	6.59821	6.47199	6.23028	6.00205	5.78637	5.58238	5.38929	5.20637	4.86842	4.56376	4.16042	3.60459	3.16114
8	7.82296	7.65168	7.48593	7.32548	7.01969	6.73274	6.46321	6.20979	5.97130	5.74664	5.33493	4.96764	4.48732	3.83716	3.32891
9	8.77906	8.56602	8.36052	8.16224	7.78611	7.43533	7.10782	6.80169	6.51523	6.24689	5.75902	5.32825	4.77158	4.03097	3.46313
10	9.73041	9.47130	9.22218	8.98259	8.53020	8.11090	7.72173	7.36009	7.02358	6.71008	6.14457	5.65022	5.01877	4.19247	3.57050
11	10.67703	10.36763	10.07112	9.78685	9.25262	8.76048	8.30641	7.88687	7.49867	7.13896	6.49506	5.93770	5.23371	4.32076	3.65640
12	11.61893	11.25508	10.90751	10.57534	9.95400	9.38507	8.86323	8.38384	7.94269	7.53608	6.81369	6.19437	5.42062	4.43922	3.72512
13	12.55615	12.13374	11.73153	11.34837	10.63496	9.98565	9.39357	8.85268	8.35765	7.90378	7.10336	6.42355	5.58315	4.53268	3.78010
14	13.48871	13.00370	12.54338	12.10625	11.29607	10.56312	9.89864	9.29498	8.74547	8.24424	7.36669	6.62817	5.72448	4.61057	3.82408
15	14.41662	13.86505	13.34323	12.84926	11.93794	11.11839	10.37966	9.71225	9.10791	8.55948	7.60608	6.81086	5.84737	4.67547	3.85926
16	15.33993	14.71787	14.13126	13.57771	12.56110	11.65230	10.83777	10.10590	9.44665	8.85137	7.82371	6.97399	5.95423	4.72956	3.88741
17	16.25863	15.56225	14.90765	14.29187	13.16612	12.16567	11.27407	10.47726	9.76322	9.12164	8.02155	7.11963	6.04716	4.77463	3.90993
18	17.17277	16.39827	15.67256	14.99203	13.75351	12.65930	11.68959	10.82760	10.05909	9.37189	8.20141	7.24967	6.12797	4.81219	3.92794
19	18.08236	17.22601	16.42617	15.67846	14.32380	13.13394	12.08532	11.15812	10.33560	9.60360	8.36492	7.36578	6.19823	4.84350	3.94235
20	18.98742	18.04555	17.16864	16.35143	14.87747	13.59033	12.46221	11.46992	10.59401	9.81815	8.51356	7.46944	6.25933	4.86958	3.95388
22	20.78408	19.66038	18.62082	17.65805	15.93692	14.45112	13.16300	12.04158	11.06124	10.20074	8.77154	7.64465	6.35866	4.90943	3.97049
24	22.56287	21.24339	20.03041	18.91393	16.93554	15.24696	13.79864	12.55036	11.46933	10.52876	8.98474	7.78432	6.43377	4.93710	3.98111
26	24.32402	22.79520	21.39863	20.12104	17.87684	15.98277	14.37519	13.00317	11.82578	10.80998	9.16095	7.89566	6.49056	4.95632	3.98791
28	26.06769	24.31644	22.72672	21.28127	18.76411	16.66306	14.89813	13.40616	12.13711	11.05108	9.30657	7.98442	6.53351	4.96967	3.99226
30	27.79405	25.80771	24.01584	22.39648	19.60044	17.29203	15.37245	13.76483	12.40904	11.25778	9.42691	8.05518	6.56596	4.97894	3.99505
32	29.50328	27.26959	25.26714	23.46833	20.38877	17.87355	15.80268	14.08404	12.64656	11.43500	9.52638	8.11159	6.59053	4.98537	3.99683
34	31.19555	28.70267	26.48173	24.49859	21.13184	18.41120	16.19290	14.36814	12.85401	11.58693	9.60857	8.15656	6.60910	4.98984	3.99797
36	32.87102	30.10751	27.66068	25.48884	21.63225	18.90826	16.54685	14.62099	13.03521	11.71719	9.67651	8.19241	6.62314	4.99295	3.99870
38	34.52985	31.48466	28.80505	26.44064	22.49246	19.36786	16.86786	14.84602	13.19347	11.82887	9.73265	8.22099	6.63375	4.99510	3.99917
40	36.17223	32.83469	29.91585	27.35548	23.11477	19.79277	17.15909	15.04630	13.33171	11.92461	9.77905	8.24378	6.64178	4.99660	3.99947
45	40.20710	36.09451	32.55234	29.49016	24.51871	20.72004	17.77407	15.45583	13.60552	12.10840	9.86281	8.28252	6.65429	4.99863	3.99983
50	44.14279	39.19612	34.99969	31.42361	25.72976	21.48218	18.25593	15.76186	13.80075	12.23348	9.91481	8.30450	6.66051	4.99945	3.99994
100	78.54264	63.02888	51.62470	43.09635	31.59891	24.50500	19.84791	16.61755	14.26925	12.49432	9.99927	8.33323	6.66666	5.00000	4.00000

Note: To convert from this table to values of an annuity in advance, determine the annuity in arrears above for one less period and add 1.00000.

Glossary[1]

A

AAA. *American Accounting Association.*

Abacus. A scholarly journal containing articles on theoretical aspects of accounting. Published twice a year by the Sydney University Press, Sydney, Australia.

abatement. A complete or partial cancellation of a levy imposed by a government unit.

abnormal spoilage. Actual spoilage exceeding that expected to occur if operations are normally efficient. Usual practice treats this cost as an *expense* of the period rather than as a *product cost*. Contrast with *normal spoilage*.

aboriginal cost. In public utility accounting, the *acquisition cost* of an *asset* incurred by the first *entity* devoting that asset to public use. Most public utility regulation is based on aboriginal cost. If it were not, then public utilities could exchange assets among themselves at ever-increasing prices in order to raise the rate base and, then, prices based thereon.

absorbed overhead. *Overhead* costs allocated to individual products at some *overhead rate*.

absorption costing. The generally accepted method of *costing* that assigns all types of *manufacturing costs* (direct material and labor as well as fixed and variable overhead) to units produced. Sometimes called "full costing." Contrast with *direct costing*.

Accelerated Cost Recovery System. ACRS. A form of *accelerated depreciation* enacted by the Congress in 1981. The system provides percentages of the asset's cost to be depreciated each year for tax purposes. *Salvage value* is ignored. For income tax purposes, almost all *depreciable assets* are grouped into one of four classes: those to be depreciated for tax purposes over 3 years (such as automobiles), those to be depreciated for tax purposes over 5 years (such as most machinery and equipment), those to be depreciated over 10 years (such as railroad

[1]Many words and phrases in the Glossary are defined in terms of other words and phrases. Terms in a given definition that are themselves explained elsewhere under their own listings are *italicized*.

tankcars), and those to be depreciated over 15 years (such as most plant assets owned by public utilities). For financial reporting, the depreciable life is chosen as the best estimate of its useful life. Income tax *timing differences* for depreciation are created when a shorter life is used for tax reporting than for financial reporting.

accelerated depreciation. Any method of calculating *depreciation* charges where the charges become progressively smaller each period. Examples are *double-declining-balance* and *sum-of-the-years'-digits* methods.

acceptance. A written promise to pay that is equivalent to a *promissory note*.

account. Any device for accumulating additions and subtractions relating to a single *asset*, *liability*, or *owners' equity* item, including *revenues* and *expenses*.

account form. The form of *balance sheet* where *assets* are shown on the left and *equities* are shown on the right. Contrast with *report form*. See also *T-account*.

account payable. A *liability* representing an amount owed to a *creditor*, usually arising from purchase of *merchandise* or materials and supplies; not necessarily due or past due. Normally, a *current* liability.

account receivable. A claim against a *debtor* usually arising from sales or services rendered; not necessarily due or past due. Normally, a *current* asset.

accountability center. *Responsibility center.*

accountancy. The British word for *accounting*. In the United States, it means the theory and practice of accounting.

Accountants' Index. A publication of the *AICPA* that indexes, in detail, the accounting literature of the period.

accountant's opinion. *Auditor's report.*

accountant's report. *Auditor's report.*

accounting. An *information system* conveying information about a specific *entity*. The information is in financial terms and is restricted to information that can be made reasonably precise. The *AICPA* defines accounting as a service activity whose "function is to provide quantitative information, primarily financial in nature, about economic entities that is intended to be useful in making economic decisions."

accounting changes. As defined by *APB Opinion* No. 20, a change in (1) an *accounting principle* (such as a switch from *FIFO* to *LIFO* or from *sum-of-the-years'-digits* to *straight-line depreciation*), (2) an accounting estimate (such as estimated useful lives or salvage value of depreciable assets and estimates of *warranty* costs or *uncollectible accounts*), and (3) the reporting *entity*. Changes of type (1) should be disclosed. The cumulative effect of the change on *retained earnings* at the start of the period during which the change was made should be included in reported earnings for the period of change. Changes of type (2) should be treated as affecting only the period of change and, if necessary, future periods. The reasons for changes of type (3) should be disclosed and, in statements reporting on operations of the period of the change, the effect of the change on all other periods reported on for comparative purposes should also be shown. In some cases (such as a change from *LIFO* to another inventory *flow assumption* or in the method of accounting for long-term construction contracts), changes of type (1) are treated like changes of type (3). That is, for these changes all statements shown for prior periods must be restated to show the effect of adopting the change for those periods as well. See *all-inclusive concept* and *accounting errors*.

accounting conventions. Methods or procedures used in accounting. This term tends to be used when the method or procedure has not been given official authoritative sanction by a pronouncement of a group such as the *APB*, *FASB*, or *SEC*. Contrast with *accounting principles*.

accounting cycle. The sequence of accounting procedures starting with *journal entries* for various transactions and events and ending with the *financial statements* or, perhaps, the *post-closing trial balance*.

accounting entity. See *entity*.

accounting equation. *Assets* = Equities.
Assets = Liabilities + Owners' Equity.

accounting errors. Arithmetic errors and misapplications of *accounting principles* in previously published financial statements that are corrected in the current period with direct *debits* or *credits* to *retained earnings*. In this regard, they are treated like *prior-period adjustments*, but, technically, they are not classified by *APB Opinion* No. 9 as prior-period adjustments. See *accounting changes* and contrast with changes in accounting estimates as described there.

accounting event. Any occurrence that is recorded in the accounting records.

accounting methods. *Accounting principles*. Procedures for carrying out accounting principles.

accounting period. The time period for which *financial statements* that measure *flows*, such as the *income statement* and the *statement of changes in financial position*, are prepared. Should be clearly identified on the financial statements. See *interim statements*.

accounting policies. *Accounting principles* adopted by a specific *entity*.

accounting principles. The methods or procedures used in accounting for events reported in the *financial statements*. This term tends to be used when the method or procedure has been given official authoritative sanction by a pronouncement of a group such as the *APB*, *FASB*, or *SEC*. Contrast with *accounting conventions* and *conceptual framework*.

Accounting Principles Board. See *APB*.

accounting procedures. See *accounting principles*, but usually this term refers to the methods for implementing accounting principles.

accounting rate of return. Income for a period divided by average investment during the period. Based on income, rather than discounted cash flows and, hence, a poor decision-making aid or tool. See *ratio*.

Accounting Research Bulletin. *ARB*. The name of the official pronouncements of the former *Committee on Accounting Procedure* of the *AICPA*. Fifty-one bulletins were issued between 1939 and 1959. *ARB No. 43* summarizes the first 42 bulletins.

Accounting Research Study. *ARS*. One of a series of studies published by the Director of Accounting Research of the *AICPA* "designed to provide professional accountants and others interested in the development of accounting with a discussion and documentation of accounting problems." Fifteen such studies were published between 1961 and 1974.

The Accounting Review. Scholarly publication of the *American Accounting Association*.

Accounting Series Release. *ASR*. See *SEC*.

accounting standards. *Accounting principles*.

Accounting Standards Executive Committee. AcSEC. The senior technical committee of the *AICPA*, authorized to speak for the AICPA in the areas of *financial accounting* and reporting as well as *cost accounting*.

accounting system. The procedures for collecting and summarizing financial data in a firm.

Accounting Terminology Bulletin. *ATB*. One of four releases of the Committee on Terminology of the *AICPA* issued in the period 1953-1957.

Accounting Trends and Techniques. An annual publication of the *AICPA* that surveys the reporting practices of 600 large corporations. It presents tabulations of specific practices, terminology, and disclosures along with illustrations taken from individual annual reports.

accounts receivable turnover. *Net sales* on account for a period divided by the average balance of net accounts receivable. See *ratio*.

accretion. Increase in economic worth through physical change, usually said of a natural resource such as an orchard, caused by natural growth. Contrast with *appreciation*.

accrual. Recognition of an *expense (or revenue)* and the related *liability (or asset)* that is caused by an *accounting event*, frequently by the passage of time, and that is not signaled by an explicit cash transaction. For example, the recognition of interest expense or revenue (or wages, salaries, or rent) at the end of a period even though no explicit cash transaction is made at that time. Cash flow occurs after accounting recognition; contrast with *deferral*.

accrual basis of accounting. The method of recognizing *revenues* as *goods* are sold (or delivered) and as *services* are rendered, independent of the time when cash is received. *Expenses* are recognized in the period when the related revenue is recognized, independent of the time when cash is paid out. *SFAC No. 1* says that "accrual accounting attempts to record the financial effects on an enterprise of transactions and other events and circumstances that have cash consequences for the enterprise in the periods in which those transactions, events, and circumstances occur rather than only in the periods in which cash is received or paid by the enterprise." Contrast with the *cash basis of accounting*. See *accrual* and *deferral*. The basis would more correctly be called "accrual/deferral" accounting.

accrued. Said of a *revenue (expense)* that has been earned (recognized) even though the related *receivable (payable)* is not yet due. This adjective should not be used as part of an account title. Thus, we prefer to use Interest Receivable (Payable) as the account title, rather than Accrued Interest Receivable (Payable). See *matching convention*. See *accrual*.

accrued depreciation. An incorrect term for *accumulated depreciation*. Acquiring an asset with cash, capitalizing it, and then amortizing its cost over periods of use is a process of *deferral* and allocation, not of *accrual*.

accrued payable. A *payable* usually resulting from the passage of time. For example, *salaries* and *interest* accrue as time passes. See *accrued*.

accrued receivable. A *receivable* usually resulting from the passage of time. See *accrued*.

accumulated depreciation. A preferred title for the *contra-asset* account that shows the sum of *depreciation* charges on an asset since it was acquired. Other titles used are *allowance* for *depreciation* (acceptable term) and *reserve* for *depreciation* (unacceptable term).

accurate presentation. The qualitative accounting objective suggesting that information reported in financial statements should correspond as precisely as possible with the economic effects underlying transactions and events. See *fair presentation* and *full disclosure*.

acid test ratio. *Quick ratio.*

acquisition cost. Of an *asset*, the net *invoice* price plus all *expenditures* to place and ready the asset for its intended use. The other expenditures might include legal fees, transportation charges, and installation costs.

ACRS. *Accelerated Cost Recovery System.*

AcSEC. *Accounting Standards Executive Committee* of the *AICPA*.

activity accounting. *Responsibility accounting.*

activity-based depreciation. *Production method of depreciation.*

actual cost (basis). *Acquisition* or *historical cost*. Contrast with *standard* cost.

actual costing. Method of allocating costs to products using actual *direct materials*, actual *direct labor*, and actual *factory overhead*. Contrast with *normal costing* and *standard cost system*.

actuarial. Usually said of computations or analyses that involve both *compound interest* and probabilities, such as the computation of the *present value* of a life-contingent *annuity*. Sometimes the term is used if only one of the two is involved.

actuarial accrued liability. A 1981 *report* of the Joint Committee on Pension Terminology (of various actuarial societies) stated that the terms "supplemental actuarial value," "past service cost," and "prior service cost" are no longer recommended and that this term be used instead. It will take a few years for this term to become standard in accounting. The Joint Committee defines this term as "the portion . . . of the actuarial present value of pension plan benefits . . . not provided for by future normal costs." *Present value* at a given time of a *pension plan's* unrecognized benefits assigned to employees for their service before that given time. Called "prior service cost" in *APB Opinion* No. 8 and supplemental actuarial value in *SFAS No. 35*; includes *past service cost*. Such obligations are not recognized as liabilities in the accounting records but must be disclosed in the notes to the financial statements; contrast with *normal cost*.

additional paid-in capital. An acceptable alternative title for the *capital contributed in excess of par (or stated) value account*.

adequate disclosure. *Fair presentation* of *financial statements* requires *disclosure* of *material* items. This *auditing standard* does not, however, require publicizing all information detrimental to a company. For example, the company may be threatened with a lawsuit and disclosure might seem to require a *debit* to a *loss* account and a *credit* to an *estimated liability* account. But the mere making of this entry might adversely affect the actual outcome of the suit. Such entries need not be made, although impending suits should be disclosed.

adjunct account. An *account* that accumulates additions to another account. For example, Premium on Bonds Payable is adjunct to the liability Bonds Payable; the effective liability is the sum of the two account balances at a given date. Contrast with *contra account*.

adjusted acquisition (historical) cost. Cost adjusted to a *constant dollar amount* to reflect *general price level changes*. See also *book value*.

adjusted bank balance of cash. The *balance* shown on the statement from the bank plus or minus amounts, such as for unrecorded deposits or outstanding checks, to reconcile the bank's balance with the correct cash balance. See *adjusted book balance of cash*.

adjusted basis. The *basis* used to compute gain or loss for tax purposes upon disposition of an *asset*. See also *book value*.

adjusted book balance of cash. The *balance* shown in the firm's account for cash in the bank plus or minus amounts, such as for *notes* collected by the bank or bank service charges, to reconcile the account balance with the correct cash balance. See *adjusted book balance of cash*.

adjusted trial balance. *Trial balance* taken after *adjusting entries* but before *closing entries*. Contrast with *pre-* and *post-closing trial balances*. See *unadjusted trial balance* and *post-closing trial balance*. See also *work sheet*.

adjusting entry. An entry made at the end of an *accounting period* to record a *transaction* or other *accounting event*, which for some reason has not been recorded or has been improperly recorded during the accounting period. An entry to update the accounts. See *work sheet*.

adjustment. A change in an *account* produced by an *adjusting* entry. Sometimes the term is used to refer to the process of restating *financial statement* amounts to *constant dollars*.

administrative expense. An *expense* related to the enterprise as a whole, as contrasted to expenses related to more specific functions such as manufacturing or selling.

admission of partner. Legally, when a new partner joins a *partnership*, the old partnership is dissolved and a new one comes into being. In practice, however, the old accounting records may be kept in use and the accounting entries reflect the manner in which the new partner joined the firm. If the new partner merely purchases the interest of another partner, the only accounting is to change the name for one capital account. If the new partner contributes *assets* and *liabilities* to the partnership, then the new assets must be recognized with debits and the liabilities and other sources of capital with credits. See *bonus method*.

ADR. See *asset depreciation range*.

advances from (by) customers. A preferred title for the *liability* account representing *receipts* of *cash* in advance of delivering the *goods* or rendering the *service* (that will cause *revenue* to be recognized). Sometimes called "deferred revenue" or "deferred income."

advances to affiliates. *Loans* by a parent company to a *subsidiary*. Frequently combined with "investment in subsidiary" as "investments and advances to subsidiary" and shown as a *noncurrent asset* on the parent's *balance sheet*. These advances are eliminated in *consolidated financial statements*.

advances to suppliers. A preferred term for *disbursements* of cash in advance of receiving *assets* or *services*.

adverse opinion. An *auditor's report* stating that the financial statements are not fair or are not in accord with *GAAP*.

affiliated company. Said of a company controlling or controlled by another company.

after closing. *Post-closing trial balance*; said of a *trial balance* at the end of the period.

aftercost. Said of *expenditures* to be made subsequent to *revenue* recognition. For example, *expenditures* for *repairs* under warranty are aftercosts. Proper recognition of aftercosts involves a debit to expense at the time of the sale and a credit to an *estimated liability*. When the liability is discharged, the debit is to the estimated liability and the credit is to the assets consumed.

agency fund. An account for *assets* received by governmental units in the capacity of trustee or agent.

agency theory. A branch of economics relating the behavior of principals (such as owner nonmanagers or bosses) and their *agents* (such as nonowner managers or subordinates). The principal assigns responsibility and authority to the agent, but the agent has his or her own risks and preferences different from those of the principal. The principal is unable to observe all activities of the agent. Thus the principal must be careful about the kinds of observations of or reports sought from the agent, perhaps through an independent *auditor,* and the sorts of incentive contracts that the principal makes with the agent.

agent. One authorized to transact business, including executing contracts, for another.

aging accounts receivable. The process of classifying *accounts receivable* by the time elapsed since the claim came into existence for the purpose of estimating the amount of uncollectible accounts receivable as of a given date. See *sales contra, estimated uncollectibles*, and *allowance for uncollectibles*.

aging schedule. A listing of *accounts receivable*, classified by age, used in *aging accounts receivable*.

AICPA. American Institute of Certified Public Accountants. The national organization that represents *CPA*s. See *AcSEC*. It oversees the writing and grading of the Uniform CPA Examination. Each state, however, sets its own requirements for becoming a CPA in that state. See *certified public accountant*.

all financial resources. All *assets* less all *liabilities*. Sometimes the *statement of changes in financial position* explains the changes in all financial resources rather than only the changes in *working capital*.

all-capital earnings rate. *Rate of return on assets*.

all-inclusive (income) concept. Under this concept, no distinction is drawn between *operating* and *nonoperating revenues* and *expenses*; thus, the only entries to retained earnings are for *net income* and *dividends*. Under this concept all *income, gains*, and *losses* are reported in the *income statement*; thus, events usually reported as *prior-period adjustments* and as *corrections of errors* are included in net income. This concept in its pure form is not the basis of *GAAP*, but *APB Opinions* No. 9 and 30 move very far in this direction. They do permit retained earnings entries for prior-period adjustments and correction of errors.

allocate. To spread a *cost* from one *account* to several accounts, to several products or activities, or to several periods.

allocation of income taxes. See *deferred income tax*.

allowance. A balance sheet *contra account* generally used for *receivables* and depreciable assets. See *sales (or purchase) allowance* for another use of this term.

allowance for funds used during construction. One principle of public utility regulation and rate setting is that customers should pay the full costs of producing the services (e.g., electricity) that they use—nothing more and nothing less. Thus an electric utility is even more careful than other businesses to capitalize in an *asset account* the full costs, but no more, of producing a new electric power generating plant. One of the costs of building a new plant is the *interest* cost on money tied up during construction. If *funds* are explicitly borrowed by an ordinary business, the journal entry for interest of $1,000 is typically:

Interest Expense	1,000	
Interest Payable		1,000

Interest expense for the period.

If the firm is constructing a new plant, then another entry would be made capitalizing interest into the plant-under-construction account:

Construction Work in Progress	750	
Interest Expense		750

Capitalize relevant portion of interest relating to construction work in progress into the asset account.

The cost of the *plant asset* is increased; when the plant is used, *depreciation* is charged; the interest will become an expense through the depreciation process in the later periods of use, not currently as the interest is paid. Thus the full cost of the electricity generated during a given period is reported as expense in that period.

But suppose, as is common, that the electric utility does not explicitly borrow the funds, but uses some of its own funds, including funds raised from equity shares as well as from debt. Even though there is not explicit interest expense, there is the *opportunity cost* of the funds. Put another way, the cost of the plant under construction is not less in an economic sense just because the firm used its own cash rather than borrowing. The public utility using its own funds, on which $750 of interest would be payable if the funds had been explicitly borrowed, will make the following entry:

Construction Work in Progress	750	
Allowance for Funds Used During Construction		750

Recognition of interest, an opportunity cost, on own funds used.

The allowance account is a form of *revenue*, to appear on the income statement, and will be closed to Retained Earnings, increasing it. On the *funds statement*, it is an income or revenue item not producing funds and so must be subtracted from net income in deriving *funds provided by operations*. *SFAS No. 34* specifically prohibits nonutility companies from capitalizing the opportunity cost (interest) on own funds used into plant under construction.

allowance for uncollectibles (accounts receivable). A *contra* to Accounts Receivable that shows the estimated amount of *accounts receivable* that will not be collected. When such an allowance is used, the actual *write-off* of specific accounts receivable (*debit* allowance, *credit* specific account) does not affect *revenue* or *expense* at the time of the write-off. The revenue reduction is recognized when the allowance is credited; the amount of the credit to the allowance may be based on a percentage of sales on account for a period of time or computed from *aging accounts receivable*. This contra account enables an estimate to be shown of the amount of receivables that will be collected without identifying specific uncollectible accounts. See *allowance method*.

allowance method. A method of attempting to *match* all *expenses* of a transaction with its associated *revenues*. Usually involves a debit to expense and a credit to an *estimated liability*, such as for estimated warranty expenditures, or a debit to a revenue (*contra*) account and a credit to an asset (*contra*) account, such as for uncollectible accounts. See *allowance for uncollectibles* for further explanation. When the allowance method is used for *sales discounts*, sales are recorded at *gross invoice* prices (not reduced by the amounts of discounts made available). An estimate of the amount of discounts to be taken is debited to a *revenue contra account* and *credited* to an allowance account, shown contra to *accounts receivable*.

American Accounting Association. AAA. An organization primarily for academic accountants, but open to all interested in accounting. It publishes *The Accounting Review*.

American Institute of Certified Public Accountants. See *AICPA*.

American Stock Exchange. AMEX. ASE. A public market where various corporate *securities* are traded.

AMEX. *American Stock Exchange*.

amortization. Strictly speaking, the process of liquidating or extinguishing (''bringing to death'') a *debt* with a series of payments to the *creditor* (or to a *sinking fund*). From that usage has evolved a related use involving the accounting for the payments themselves: an ''amortization schedule'' for a mortgage, which is a table showing the allocation between *interest* and *principal*. The term has come to mean writing off (''liquidating'') the cost of an asset. In this context it means the general process of *allocating acquisition cost* of an asset to either the periods of benefit as *expenses* or to *inventory* accounts as *product costs*. Called *depreciation* for *plant assets, depletion* for *wasting assets* (natural resources), and ''amortization'' for *intangibles*. *SFAC No. 3* refers to amortization as ''the accounting process of reducing an amount by periodic payments or write-downs.'' The expressions ''unamortized debt discount or premium'' and ''to amortize debt discount or premium'' relate to *accruals*, not to *deferrals*. The expressions ''amortization of long-term assets'' and ''to amortize long-term assets'' refer to deferrals, not accruals.

analysis of changes in working capital accounts. The *statement of changes in financial position* explains the causes of the changes in *working capital* during a period. This part of the statement, which may appear in footnotes, shows the net changes in the specific working capital accounts that have been explained in the main section of the statement.

analysis of variances. See *variance analysis*.

annual report. A report for shareholders and other interested parties prepared once a year; includes a *balance sheet*, an *income statement*, a *statement of changes in financial position*, a reconciliation of changes in *owners' equity* accounts, a *summary of significant accounting principles*, other explanatory *notes*, the *auditor's report*, and comments from management about the year's events. See *10-K* and *financial statements*.

annuitant. One who receives an *annuity*.

annuity. A series of payments, usually made at equally spaced time intervals.

annuity certain. An *annuity* payable for a definite number of periods. Contrast with *contingent annuity*.

annuity due. An *annuity* whose first payment is made at the start of period 1 (or at the end of period 0). Contrast with *annuity in arrears*.

annuity in advance. An *annuity due*.

annuity in arrears. An *ordinary annuity* whose first payment occurs at the end of the first period.

annuity method of depreciation. See *compound interest depreciation*.

antidilutive. Said of a *potentially dilutive security* that will increase *earnings per share* if it is *exercised* or *converted* into common stock. In computing *primary* and *fully diluted earnings per share*, antidilutive securities may not be assumed to be exercised or converted and hence do not affect reported earnings per share in a given period.

APB. Accounting Principles Board of the *AICPA*. It set *accounting principles* from 1959 through 1973, issuing 31 *APB Opinions*. It was superseded by the *FASB*.

APB Opinion. The name given to pronouncements of the *APB* that make up much of *generally accepted accounting principles*; there are 31 *APB Opinions*, issued from 1962 through 1973.

APB Statement. The *APB* issued four *Statements* between 1962 and 1970. The *Statements* were approved by at least two-thirds of the board, but they are recommendations, not requirements. For example, *Statement* No. 3 (1969) suggested the publication of *constant dollar financial statements* but did not require them.

APBs. An abbreviation used for *APB Opinions*.

application of funds. Any transaction that reduces *funds* (however "funds" is defined). A *use of funds*.

applied cost. A *cost* that has been *allocated* to a department, product, or activity; need not be based on actual costs incurred.

applied overhead. *Overhead costs* charged to departments, products, or activities.

appraisal. The process of obtaining a valuation for an *asset* or *liability* that involves expert opinion rather than evaluation of explicit market transactions.

appraisal method of depreciation. The periodic *depreciation* charge is the difference between the beginning- and end-of-period appraised values of the *asset* if that difference is positive. If negative, there is no charge. Not generally accepted.

appreciation. An increase in economic worth caused by rising market prices for an *asset*. Contrast with *accretion*.

appropriated retained earnings. See *retained earnings, appropriated*.

appropriation. In governmental accounting, an *expenditure* authorized for a specified amount, purpose, and time.

appropriation account. In governmental accounting, an account set up to record specific authorizations to spend; it is credited with appropriation amounts. *Expenditures* during the period and *encumbrances* outstanding at the end of the period are closed (debited) to this account at the end of the period.

ARB. Accounting Research Bulletin.

arbitrage. Strictly speaking, the simultaneous purchase in one market and sale in another of a *security* or commodity in hope of making a *profit* on price differences in the different markets. Often this term is used loosely when the item sold is somewhat different from the item purchased; for example, the sale of shares of *common stock* and the simultaneous purchase of a *convertible bond* that is convertible into identical common shares.

arm's length. Said of a transaction negotiated by unrelated parties, each acting in his or her own self-interest; the basis for a *fair market value* determination.

arrears. Said of *cumulative preferred stock dividends* that have not been declared up to the current date. See *annuity in arrears* for another context.

ARS. Accounting Research Study.

articles of incorporation. Document filed with state authorities by persons forming a corporation. When the document is returned with a certificate of incorporation, it becomes the corporation's *charter*.

articulate. Said of the relationship between any operating statement (for example, *income statement* or *statement of changes in financial position*) and *comparative balance sheets*, where the operating statement explains (or reconciles) the change in some major balance sheet category (for example, *retained earnings* or *working capital*).

ASE. American Stock Exchange.

ASR. Accounting Series Release. See *SEC*.

assess. To value property for the purpose of property taxation; the assessment is computed by the taxing authority. To levy a charge on the owner of property for improvements thereto, such as for sewers or sidewalks.

assessed valuation. A dollar amount for real estate or other property used by a government as a basis for levying taxes. The amount may or may not bear some relation to *market value*.

asset. *SFAC No. 3* defines assets as "probable future economic benefits obtained or controlled by a particular entity as a result of past transactions. An asset has three essential characteristics: (a) it embodies a probable future benefit that involves a capacity, singly or in combination with other assets, to contribute directly or indirectly to future net cash inflows, (b) a particular enterprise can obtain the benefit and control others' access to it, and (c) the transaction or other event giving rise to the enterprise's right to or control of the benefit has already occurred." A footnote points out that "probable" means that which can be reasonably expected or believed but is neither certain nor proved. May be *tangible* or *intangible*, *short-term* (current) or *long-term* (noncurrent).

asset depreciation range. ADR. The range of *depreciable lives* allowed by the *Internal Revenue Service* before the adoption of *ACRS* for a specific depreciable *asset*.

asset turnover. Net sales divided by average assets. See *ratio*.

assignment of accounts receivable. Transfer of the legal ownership of an *account receivable* through its sale. Contrast with *pledging* accounts receivable, where the receivables serve as *collateral* for a *loan*.

ATB. Accounting Terminology Bulletin.

at par. Said of a *bond* or *preferred stock* issued or selling at its *face amount*.

attachment. The laying claim to the *assets* of a borrower or debtor by a lender or creditor when the borrower has failed to pay debts on time.

attest. Rendering of an *opinion* by an auditor that the *financial statements* are fair. This procedure is called the "attest function" of the CPA. See *fair presentation*.

attribute measured. When making physical measurements, such as of a person, one needs to decide the units with which to measure, such as inches or centimeters or pounds or grams. One chooses the attribute—height or weight—independently of the measuring unit—English or metric. In conventional accounting the attribute measured is *historical cost* and the measuring unit is *nominal dollars*. Some theorists argue that accounting is more useful when the attribute measured is *current cost*. Others argue that accounting is more useful when the measuring unit is *constant dollars*. Some, including us, think both changes from conventional accounting should be made. The attribute historical cost can be measured in nominal dollars or in constant dollars. The attribute current cost can also be measured in nominal dollars or constant dollars. Choosing between two attributes and two measuring units implies four different accounting systems. Each of these four has its uses.

audit. Systematic inspection of accounting records involving analyses, tests, and *confirmations*. See *internal audit*.

audit committee. A committee of the board of directors of a *corporation*, usually consisting of outside directors who nominate the independent auditors and discuss the auditors' work with them. If the auditors believe that certain matters should be brought to the attention of shareholders, the auditors first bring these matters to the attention of the audit committee.

Audit Guides. See *Industry Audit Guides*.

audit program. The procedures followed by the *auditor* in carrying out the *audit*.

audit trail. A reference accompanying an *entry*, or *posting*, to an underlying source record or document. A good audit trail is essential for efficiently checking the accuracy of accounting entries. See *cross-reference*.

Auditing Research Monograph. Publication series of the *AICPA*.

auditing standards. A set of 10 standards promulgated by the *AICPA*, including three general standards, three standards of field work, and four standards of reporting. According to the *AICPA*, these standards "deal with the measures of the quality of the performance and the objectives to be attained," rather than with specific auditing procedures.

Auditing Standards Advisory Council. An *AICPA* committee.

Auditing Standards Board. Operating committee of the *AICPA* promulgating auditing rules.

auditor. One who checks the accuracy, fairness, and general acceptability of accounting records and statements, and then *attests* to them.

auditor's opinion. *Auditor's report*.

auditor's report. The auditor's statement of the work done and an opinion of the *financial statements*. Opinions are usually unqualified ("clean"), but may be *qualified*, or the auditor may disclaim an opinion in the report. Often called the "accountant's report." See *adverse opinion*.

AudSEC. The former Auditing Standards Executive Committee of the *AICPA*, now functioning as the *Auditing Standards Board*.

authorized capital stock. The number of *shares* of stock that can be issued by a corporation; specified by the *articles of incorporation*.

average. The arithmetic mean of a set of numbers; obtained by summing the items and dividing by the number of items.

average collection period of receivables. See *ratio*.

average tax rate. The rate found by dividing *income tax expense* by *net income* before taxes. Contrast with *marginal tax rate, statutory tax rate*.

average-cost flow assumption. An *inventory flow assumption* where the cost of units is the *weighted average* cost of the *beginning inventory* and purchases. See *inventory equation*.

avoidable cost. A *cost* that will cease if an activity is discontinued. An *incremental* or *variable cost*. See *programmed cost*.

B

backlog. Orders for which insufficient *inventory* is on hand for current delivery and which will be filled in a later period.

backlog depreciation. In *current cost accounting*, a problem arising for the *accumulated depreciation* on *plant assets*. Consider an *asset* costing $10,000 with a 10-year life depreciated with the *straight-line method*. Assume that a similar asset has a current cost of $10,000 at the end of the first year but $12,000 at the end of the second year. Assume that the depreciation charge is based on the average current cost during the year, $10,000 for the first year and $11,000 for the second. The depreciation charge for the first year is $1,000 and for the second is $1,100 ($=.10 \times \$11,000$), so the *accumulated depreciation account* is $2,100 after 2 years. Note that at the end of the second year, 20 percent of the asset's future benefits have been used, so the accounting records based on current costs must show a *net book value* of $9,600 ($=.80 \times \$12,000$), which would result if accumulated depreciation of $2,400 were subtracted from a current cost of $12,000. But the sum of the depreciation charges has been only $2,100. The *journal entry* to increase the accumulated depreciation account requires a *credit* to that account of $300. The question arises, what account is to be debited? That is the problem of backlog depreciation. Some theorists would *debit* an *income* account and others would *debit* a *balance sheet owners' equity* account without reducing current-period earnings. The answer to the question of what to do with the debit is closely tied to the problem of how *holding gains* are recorded. When the asset account is debited for $2,000 to increase the recorded amount from $10,000 to $12,000, a holding gain or $2,000 must be recorded with a credit. Many theorists believe that whatever account is credited for the holding gains is the same account that should be debited for backlog depreciation. Sometimes called "catch-up depreciation."

bad debt. An *uncollectible account receivable*; see *sales contra, estimated uncollectibles*.

bad debt expense. See *sales contra, estimated uncollectibles*.

bad debt recovery. Collection, perhaps partial, of a specific account receivable previously written off as uncollectible. If the *allowance method* is used, the *credit* is usually to the *allowance* account. If the direct write-off method is used, the credit is to a *revenue account*.

bailout period. In a *capital budgeting* context, the total time that must elapse before net accumulated cash inflows from a project, including potential *salvage value* of assets at various times, equal or exceed the accumulated cash outflows. Contrast with *payback period*, which assumes completion of the project and uses terminal salvage value. Bailout is superior to payback because bailout takes into account, at least to some degree, the *present value* of the cash flows after the termination date being considered. The potential salvage value at any time includes some estimate of the flows that can occur after that time.

balance. The sum of *debit* entries minus the sum of *credit* entries in an *account*. If positive, the difference is called a debit balance; if negative, a credit balance.

balance sheet. Statement of financial position that shows *Total Assets* = Total Liabilities + Owners' Equity.

balance sheet account. An account that can appear on a balance sheet. A *permanent account*; contrast with *temporary account*.

bank balance. The amount of the balance in a checking account shown on a *bank statement*. Compare with *adjusted bank balance* and see *bank reconciliation schedule*.

bank prime rate. See *prime rate*.

bank reconciliation schedule. A schedule that shows how the difference between the book balance of the cash in a bank account and the bank's statement can be explained. Takes into account the amount of such items as checks issued that have not cleared or deposits that have not been recorded by the bank, as well as errors made by the bank or the firm.

bank statement. A statement sent by the bank to a checking account customer showing deposits, checks cleared, and service charges for a period, usually 1 month.

bankrupt. Said of a company whose *liabilities* exceed its *assets* where a legal petition has been filed and accepted under the bankruptcy law. A bankrupt firm is usually, but need not be, *insolvent*.

base stock method. A method of inventory valuation that assumes that there is a minimum normal or base stock of goods that must be kept on hand at all times for effective continuity of operations. This base quantity is valued at *acquisition cost* of the inventory on hand in the earliest period when inventory was on hand. The method is not allowable for income tax purposes and is no longer used, but is generally considered to be the forerunner of the *LIFO* method.

basic accounting equation. *Accounting equation*.

basis. *Acquisition cost*, or some substitute therefor, of an asset used in computing gain or loss upon disposition or retirement. *Attribute measured*.

basket purchase. Purchase of a group of assets for a single price; *costs* must be assigned to each of the assets so that the individual items can be recorded in the *accounts*.

bear. One who believes that security prices will fall. A "bear market" refers to a time when stock prices are generally declining. Contrast with *bull*.

bearer bond. See *registered bond* for contrast and definition.

beginning inventory. Valuation of *inventory* on hand at the beginning of the accounting period.

betterment. An *improvement*, usually *capitalized*.

bid. An offer to purchase, or the amount of the offer.

big bath. A *write off* of a substantial amount of costs previously treated as *assets*. Usually caused when a corporation drops a line of business that required a large investment but that proved to be unprofitable. Sometimes used to describe a situation where a corporation takes a large write off in one period in order to free later periods of gradual write offs of those amounts. In this sense, it frequently occurs when there is a change in top management.

Big Eight. Eight large *public accounting (CPA)* partnerships; in alphabetical order: Arthur Andersen & Co.; Coopers & Lybrand; Deloitte Haskins & Sells; Ernst & Whinney; Peat, Marwick, Mitchell & Co.; Price Waterhouse & Co.; Touche Ross & Co.; and Arthur Young & Company. Klynveld Main Goerdeler (KMG) is actually larger than many of these when worldwide operations are measured. An international firm, KMG's U.S. affiliate is Main Hurdman.

Big Nine. See *Big Eight*.

bill. An *invoice* of charges and *terms of sale* for *goods and services*. Also, a piece of currency.

bill of materials. A specification of the quantities of *direct materials* expected to be used to produce a given job or quantity of output.

board of directors. The governing body of a corporation elected by the shareholders.

bond. A certificate to show evidence of debt. The *par value* is the *principal* or face amount of the bond payable at maturity. The *coupon rate* is the amount of interest payable in 1 year divided by the principal amount. Coupon bonds have attached to them coupons that can be redeemed at stated dates for interest payments. Normally, bonds carry semiannual coupons.

bond conversion. The act of exchanging *convertible bonds* for *preferred* or *common stock*.

bond discount. From the standpoint of the issuer of a *bond* at the issue date, the excess of the *par value* of a bond over its initial sales price; at later dates the excess of par over the sum of initial issue price plus the portion of discount already amortized. From the standpoint of a bondholder, the difference between par value and selling price when the bond sells below par.

bond indenture. The contract between an issuer of *bonds* and the bondholders.

bond premium. Exactly parallel to *bond discount* except that the issue price (or current selling price) is higher than *par value*.

bond ratings. Ratings of corporate and *municipal bond* issues by Moody's Investors Service and by Standard & Poor's Corporation, based on the issuer's existing *debt* level, its previous record of payment, the *coupon rate* on the bonds, and the safety of the *assets* or *revenues* that are committed to paying off *principal* and *interest*. Moody's top rating is Aaa; Standard & Poor's is AAA.

bond redemption. Retirement of *bonds*. A *corporation* acquires its *bonds* from the *bondholders*. Bonds can be retired at *maturity* or before, either by paying *cash*, exchanging *shares* of *stock* (if the bond is *convertible*), by serial retirement (for *serial bonds*), by setting up a *sinking fund*, or by replacing one bond issue with another (*bond refunding*).

bond refunding. To incur *debt*, usually through the issue of new *bonds*, intending to use the proceeds to retire an *outstanding* bond issue.

bond sinking fund. See *sinking fund*.

bond table. A table showing the current price of a *bond* as a function of the *coupon rate*, years to *maturity*, and effective *yield to maturity* (or *effective rate*).

bonus. Premium over normal *wage* or *salary*, paid usually for meritorious performance.

bonus method. When a new partner is admitted to a *partnership* and the new partner is to be credited with *capital* in excess proportion to the amount of *tangible* assets he or she contributes, two methods may be used to recognize this excess, say, $10,000. First, $10,000 may be transferred from the old partners to the new one. This is the bonus method. Second, goodwill in the amount of $10,000 may be recognized as an asset, with the credit to the new partner's capital account. This is the *goodwill method*. (Notice that the new partner's percentage of total ownership is not the same under the two methods.) If the new partner is to be credited with capital in smaller proportion than the amount of contribution, then there will be bonus or goodwill for the old partners.

book. As a verb, to record a transaction. As a noun, usually plural, the *journals* and *ledgers*. As an adjective, see *book value*.

book inventory. An *inventory* amount that results, not from physical count, but from the amount of beginning inventory plus *invoice* amounts of net purchases less invoice amounts of *requisitions* or withdrawals; implies a *perpetual* method.

book of original entry. A *journal*.

book value. The amount shown in the books or in the *accounts* for an *asset, liability*, or *owners' equity* item. Generally used to refer to the net amount of an *asset* or group of assets shown in the account that records the asset and reductions, such as for *amortization*, in its cost. Of a firm, the excess of total assets over total liabilities. *Net assets*.

book value per share of common stock. Common *shareholders' equity* divided by the number of shares of *common stock outstanding*. See *ratio*.

bookkeeping. The process of analyzing and recording transactions in the accounting records.

boot. The additional money paid or received along with a used item in a trade-in or exchange transaction for another item. See *trade-in transaction*.

borrower. See *loan*.

branch. A sales office or other unit of an enterprise physically separated from the home office of the enterprise but not organized as a legally separate *subsidiary*. The term is rarely used to refer to manufacturing units.

branch accounting. An accounting procedure that enables the financial position and operations of each *branch* to be reported separately but later combined for published statements.

breakeven analysis. See *breakeven chart.*

breakeven chart. Two kinds of breakeven charts are shown here. The charts are based on the information for a month shown below. Revenue is $30 per unit.

Cost Classification	Variable Cost, per Unit	Fixed Cost, per Month
Manufacturing costs:		
Direct material	$ 4	—
Direct labor	9	—
Overhead	4	$3,060
Total manufacturing costs	$17	$3,060
Selling, general, and administrative costs.	5	1,740
Total cost	$22	$4,800

The cost-volume-profit graph presents the relationship of changes in volume to the amount of *profit*, or *income*. On such a graph, total *revenue* and total *costs* for each volume level are indicated and profit or loss at any volume can be read directly from the chart. The profit-volume graph does not show revenues and costs but more readily indicates profit (or loss) at various output levels.

Two caveats should be kept in mind about these graphs. Although the curve depicting *variable cost* and total cost is shown as being a straight line for its entire length, it is likely that at very low or very high levels of output, variable cost would probably be different from $22 per unit. The variable cost figure was probably established by studies of operations at some broad central area of production, called the *relevant range*. For very low (or very high) levels of activity, the chart may not be applicable. For this reason, the total cost and profit-loss curves are sometimes shown as dotted lines at lower (or higher) volume levels. Second, this chart is simplified because it assumes a single-product firm. For a multiproduct firm, the horizontal axis would have to be stated in dollars rather than in physical units of output. Breakeven charts for multiproduct firms necessarily assume that constant proportions of the several products are sold, and changes in this mixture as well as in costs or selling prices would invalidate such a chart.

breakeven point. The volume of sales required so that total *revenues* and total *costs* are equal. May be expressed in units (*fixed costs/contribution per unit*) or in sales dollars [selling price per unit × (fixed costs/contribution per unit)].

A. Cost-Volume-Profit Graph

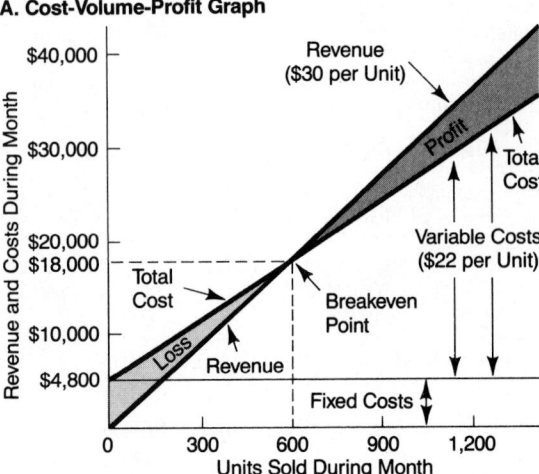

B. Profit-Volume Graph

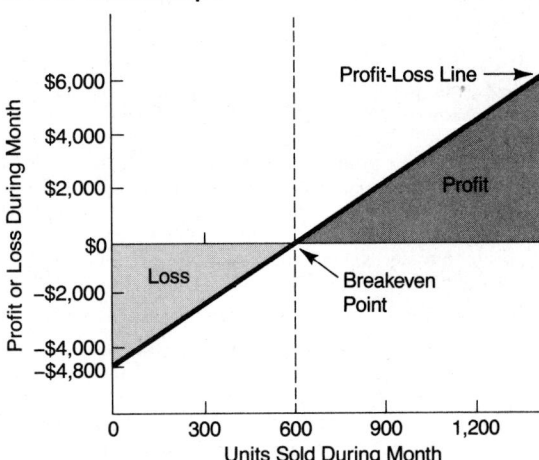

budget. A financial plan used to estimate the results of future operations. Frequently used to help control future operations. In governmental operations, budgets often become the law.

budgetary accounts. In governmental accounting, the accounts that reflect estimated operations and financial condition, as affected by estimated *revenues, appropriations,* and *encumbrances*. Contrast to *proprietary accounts*, which record the transactions.

budgetary control. Management of a governmental (nongovernmental) unit in accordance with an official (approved) *budget* in order to keep total expenditures within authorized (planned) limits.

budgeted cost. See *standard cost* for definition and contrast.

budgeted statements. *Pro forma* statements prepared before the event or period occurs.

bull. One who believes that security prices will rise. A "bull market" refers to a time when stock prices are generally rising. Contrast with *bear*.

burden. See *overhead costs*.

business combination. As defined in *APB Opinion* No. 16, the bringing together into a single accounting *entity* of two or more incorporated or unincorporated businesses. The *merger* will be accounted for either with the *purchase method* or the *pooling-of-interests method*. See *conglomerate*.

business entity. *Entity. Accounting entity.*

bylaws. The rules adopted by the shareholders of a corporation that specify the general methods for carrying out the functions of the corporation.

by-product. A *joint product* whose sales value is so small relative to the sales value of the other joint product(s) that it does not receive normal accounting treatment. The costs assigned to by-products reduce the costs of the main product(s). By-products are allocated a share of joint costs such that the expected gain or loss upon their sale is zero. Thus, by-products are shown in the *accounts* at *net realizable value*.

C

CA. *Chartered accountant.*

call. An option to buy *shares* of a publicly-traded corporation at a fixed price during a fixed time span. Contrast with *put*.

call premium. See *callable bond*.

call price. See *callable bond*.

callable bond. A *bond* for which the issuer reserves the right to pay a specific amount, the call price, to retire the obligation before *maturity* date. If the issuer agrees to pay more than the *face amount* of the bond when called, the excess of the payment over the face amount is the "call premium."

Canadian Institute of Chartered Accountants. The national organization that represents *chartered accountants* in Canada.

cancelable lease. See *lease*.

capacity. Stated in units of product, the amount that can be produced per unit of time. Stated in units of input, such as *direct labor* hours, the amount of input that can be used in production per unit of time. This measure of output or input is used in allocating *fixed costs* if the amounts producible are normal, rather than maximum, amounts.

capacity costs. A *fixed cost* incurred to provide a firm with the capacity to produce or to sell. Consists of *standby costs* and *enabling costs*. Contrast with *programmed costs*.

capacity variance. Standard fixed *overhead* rate per unit of normal *capacity* (or base activity) times (units of base activity budgeted or planned for a period minus actual units of base activity worked or assigned to product during the period). Often called a "volume variance."

capital. *Owners' equity* in a business. Often used, equally correctly, to mean the total assets of a business. Sometimes used to mean *capital assets*. Sometimes used to mean *cash* or *funds*.

capital asset. Properly used, a designation for income tax purposes that describes property held by a taxpayer, except *cash*, inventoriable *assets*, goods held primarily for sale, most depreciable property, *real estate, receivables*, certain *intangibles*, and a few other items. Sometimes this term is used imprecisely to describe *plant* and *equipment*, which are clearly not capital assets under the income tax definition. Often the term is used to refer to an *investment* in *securities*.

capital budget. Plan of proposed outlays for acquiring long-term *assets* and the means of *financing* the acquisition.

capital budgeting. The process of choosing *investment* projects for an enterprise by considering the *present value* of cash flows and deciding how to raise the funds required by the investment.

capital consumption allowance. The term used for *depreciation expense* in national income accounting and the reporting of funds in the economy.

capital contributed in excess of par (or stated) value. A preferred title for the account that shows the amount received by the issuer for *capital stock* in excess of *par (or stated) value*.

capital expenditure (outlay). An *expenditure* to acquire long-term *assets*.

capital gain. The excess of proceeds over *cost*, or other *basis*, from the sale of a *capital asset* as defined by the Internal Revenue Code. If the capital asset has been held for a sufficiently long time before sale, then the tax on the gain is computed at a rate lower than is used for other gains and ordinary income.

capital lease. A *lease* treated by the *lessee* as both the borrowing of funds and the acquisition of an *asset* to be *amortized*. Both the *liability* and the asset are recognized on the balance sheet. Expenses consist of *interest* on the *debt* and *amortization* of the asset. The *lessor* treats the lease as the sale of the asset in return for a series of future cash receipts. Contrast with *operating lease*.

capital loss. A negative capital gain; see *capital gain*.

capital rationing. In a *capital budgeting* context, the imposing of constraints on the amounts of total capital expenditures in each period.

capital stock. The ownership shares of a corporation. Consists of all classes of *common* and *preferred stock*.

capital structure. The composition of a corporation's equities; the relative proportions of *short-term debt, long-term debt*, and *owners' equity*.

capital surplus. An inferior term for *capital contributed in excess of par (or stated) value*.

capitalization of a corporation. A term used by investment analysts to indicate *shareholders' equity* plus *bonds outstanding*.

capitalization of earnings. The process of estimating the economic worth of a firm by computing the *net present value* of the predicted *net income* (not *cash flows*) of the firm for the future.

capitalization rate. An *interest rate* used to convert a series of payments or receipts or earnings into a single *present value*.

capitalize. To record an *expenditure* that may benefit a future period as an *asset* rather than to treat the expenditure as an *expense* of the period of its occurrence. Whether or not expenditures for advertising or for research and development should be capitalized is controversial, but *SFAS No. 2* requires expensing of *R&D* costs. We believe that expenditures should be capitalized if they lead to future benefits and thus meet the criterion to be an asset.

carryback, carryforward, carryover. The use of losses or tax credits in one period to reduce income taxes payable in other periods. There are three common kinds of carrybacks: for net operating losses, for *capital losses*, and for the *investment credit*. The first two are applied against taxable income and the third against the actual tax. In general, carrybacks are for 3 years, with the earliest year first. Operating losses and the investment credit can be carried forward for 15 years. Corporate capital loss carryforwards are for 5 years. The capital loss for individuals can be carried forward indefinitely.

carrying cost. Costs (such as property taxes and insurance) of holding, or storing, *inventory* from the time of purchase until the time of sale or use.

carrying value (amount). *Book value*.

CASB. Cost Accounting Standards Board. A board of five members authorized by the U.S. Congress to ''promulgate cost-accounting standards designed to achieve uniformity and consistency in the cost-accounting principles followed by defense contractors and subcontractors under federal contracts.'' The *principles* promulgated by the CASB are likely to have considerable weight in practice where the *FASB* has not established a standard. The CASB started work in 1970; although it ceased operations in 1980, its standards have the same force as before.

cash. Currency and coins, negotiable checks, and balances in bank accounts.

cash basis of accounting. In contrast to the *accrual basis of accounting*, a system of accounting in which *revenues* are recognized when *cash* is received and *expenses* are recognized as *disbursements* are made. No attempt is made to *match revenues* and *expenses* in determining *income*. See *modified cash basis*.

cash budget. A schedule of expected cash *receipts* and *disbursements*.

cash collection basis. The *installment method* for recognizing *revenue*. Not to be confused with the *cash basis of accounting*.

cash cycle. The period of time that elapses during which *cash* is converted into *inventories*, inventories are converted into *accounts receivable*, and receivables are converted back into cash. *Earnings cycle*.

cash disbursements journal. A specialized *journal* used to record *expenditures* by *cash* and by *check*. If a *check register* is also used, a cash disbursements journal records only expenditures of currency and coins.

cash discount. A reduction in sales or purchase price allowed for prompt payment.

cash dividend. See *dividend*.

cash equivalent value. A term used to describe the amount for which an *asset* could be sold. *Market value*. *Fair market price (value)*.

cash flow. Cash *receipts* minus *disbursements* from a given *asset*, or group of assets, for a given period. A term used imprecisely by financial analysts to mean *net income* plus *depreciation changes* as an approximation to *funds* from *operations*.

cash flow statement. A statement similar to the typical *statement of changes in financial position* where the flows of cash, rather than of *working capital*, are explained.

cash receipts journal. A specialized *journal* used to record all *receipts* of *cash*.

cash (surrender) value of life insurance. An amount equal, not to the face value of the policy to be paid in event of death, but to the amount that could be realized if the policy were immediately canceled and traded with the insurance company for cash. If a firm owns a life insurance policy, the policy is reported as an asset at an amount equal to this value.

cash yield. See *yield*.

cashier's check. A bank's own *check* drawn on itself and signed by the cashier or other authorized official. It is a direct obligation of the bank. Compare with *certified check*.

catch-up depreciation. *Backlog depreciation*.

CCA. *Current cost accounting; current value accounting*.

central corporate expenses. General *overhead expenses* incurred in running the corporate headquarters and related supporting activities of a corporation. These expenses are treated as *period expenses*. Contrast with *manufacturing overhead*. A major problem in *line-of-business reporting* is the treatment of these expenses.

certificate. The document that is the physical embodiment of a *bond* or a *share of stock*. A term sometimes used for the *auditor's report*.

Certificate in Management Accounting. *CMA*.

certificate of deposit. Federal law constrains the *rate of interest* that banks can pay. Under current law, banks are allowed to pay a rate higher than the one allowed on a *time deposit* if the depositor promises to leave funds on deposit for several months or more. When the bank receives such funds, it issues a certificate of deposit. The depositor can withdraw the funds before maturity if a penalty is paid.

certified check. The *check* of a depositor drawn on a bank on the face of which the bank has inserted the words "accepted" or "certified" with the date and signature of a bank official. The check then becomes an obligation of the bank. Compare with *cashier's check*.

certified financial statement. A financial statement attested to by an independent *auditor* who is a *CPA*.

certified internal auditor. See *CIA*.

certified public accountant. CPA. An accountant who has satisfied the statutory and administrative requirements of his or her jurisdiction to be registered or licensed as a public accountant. In addition to passing the Uniform CPA Examination administered by the *AICPA*, the CPA must meet certain educational, experience, and moral requirements that differ from jurisdiction to jurisdiction. The jurisdictions are the 50 states, the District of Columbia, Guam, Puerto Rico, and the Virgin Islands.

chain discount. A series of *discount* percentages; for example, if a chain discount of 10 and 5 percent is quoted, then the actual, or *invoice*, price is the nominal, or list, price times .90 times .95, or 85.5 percent of invoice price.

change fund. Coins and currency issued to cashiers, delivery drivers, and so on.

changes, accounting. See *accounting changes*.

changes in financial position. See *statement of changes in financial position*.

charge. As a noun, a *debit* to an account; as a verb, to debit.

charge off. To treat as a *loss* or *expense* an amount originally recorded as an *asset*; use of this term implies that the charge is not in accord with original expectations.

chart of accounts. A list of names and numbers of *accounts* organized systematically.

charter. Document issued by a state government authorizing the creation of a corporation.

chartered accountant. CA. The title used in Australia, Canada, and the United Kingdom for an accountant who has satisfied the requirements of the institute of his or her jurisdiction to be qualified to serve as a *public accountant*. In Canada, each provincial institute or order has the right to administer the examination and set the standards of performance and ethics for Chartered Accountants in its province. For a number of years, however, the provincial organizations have pooled their rights to qualify new members through the Inter-provincial Education Committee and the result is that there are nationally set and graded examinations given in English and French. The pass/fail grade awarded by the Board of Examiners (a subcommittee of the Inter-provincial Education Committee) is rarely deviated from.

check. The Federal Reserve Board defines a check as "a *draft* or order upon a bank or banking house purporting to be drawn upon a deposit of funds for the payment at all events of a certain sum of money to a certain person therein named or to him or his order or to bearer and payable instantly on demand." It must contain the phrase "pay to the order of." The amount shown on the check's face must be clearly readable, and it must have the signature of the drawer. Checks need not be dated, although they usually are. The *balance* in the *cash account* is usually reduced when a check is issued, not later when it clears the bank and reduces cash in bank.

check register. A *journal* to record *checks* issued.

CIA. Certified Internal Auditor. One who has satisfied certain requirements of the *Institute of Internal Auditors* including experience, ethics, education, and passing examinations.

CICA. *Canadian Institute of Chartered Accountants*.

CIF. Cost, insurance, and freight; a term used in contracts along with the name of a given port to indicate that the quoted price includes insurance, handling, and freight charges up to delivery by the seller at the given port.

circulating capital. *Working capital*.

clean opinion. See *auditor's report*.

clean surplus concept. The notion that the only entries to the *retained earnings* account are to record *net income* and *dividends*. See *comprehensive income*. Contrast with *current operating performance concept*. This concept, with minor exceptions, is now controlling in *GAAP*. (See *APB Opinions* Nos. 9 and 30.)

clearing account. An account containing amounts to be transferred to another account(s) before the end of the *accounting period*. Examples are the *income summary* account (whose balance is transferred to *retained earnings*) and the purchases account (whose balance is transferred to *inventory* or to *cost of goods sold*).

close. As a verb, to transfer the *balance* of a *temporary* or *contra* or *adjunct* account to the main account to which it relates; for example, to transfer *revenue* and *expense* accounts directly, or through the *income summary* account, to an *owners' equity* account, or to transfer *purchase discounts* to purchases.

closed account. An account with equal debits and credits, usually as a result of a closing entry. See *ruling an account*.

closing entries. The entries that accomplish the transfer of balances in temporary accounts to the related balance sheet accounts. See *work sheet*.

closing inventory. *Ending inventory*.

CMA. Certificate in Management Accounting. Awarded by the Institute of Management Accounting of the *National Association of Accountants* to those who pass a set of examinations and meet certain experience and continuing education requirements.

CoCoA. *Continuously Contemporary Accounting*.

coding of accounts. The numbering of *accounts*, as for a *chart of accounts*, which is particularly necessary for computerized accounting.

coinsurance. Insurance policies that protect against hazards such as fire or water damage often specify that the owner of the property may not collect the full amount of insurance for a loss unless the insurance policy covers at least some specified "coinsurance" percentage, usually about 80 percent, of the *replacement cost* of the property. Coinsurance clauses induce the owner to carry full, or nearly full, coverage.

COLA. Cost-of-living adjustment. See *indexation*.

collateral. Assets pledged by a *borrower* that will be given up if the *loan* is not paid.

collectible. Capable of being converted into cash; now, if due; later, otherwise.

combination. See *business combination*.

commercial paper. *Short-term notes* issued by corporate borrowers.

commission. Remuneration, usually expressed as a percentage, to employees based on an activity rate, such as sales.

committed costs. *Capacity costs*.

Committee on Accounting Procedure. CAP. Predecessor of the *APB*. The *AICPA's* principles-promulgating body from 1939 through 1959. Its 51 pronouncements are called *Accounting Research Bulletins*.

common cost. *Cost* resulting from use of *raw materials*, a facility (for example, plant or machines), or a service (for example, fire insurance) that benefits several products or departments and must be allocated to those products or departments. Common costs result when multiple products are produced together although they could be produced separately; joint costs occur when multiple products are of necessity produced together. Many writers use common costs and *joint costs* synonymously. See *joint costs, indirect costs*, and *overhead*. See *sterilized allocation*.

common dollar accounting. *Constant dollar accounting*.

common monetary measuring unit. For U.S. corporations, the dollar. See also *stable monetary unit assumption* and *constant dollar accounting*.

common shares. *Shares* representing the class of owners who have residual claims on the assets and earnings of a corporation after all debt and preferred shareholders' claims have been met.

common stock equivalent. A *security* whose primary value arises from its ability to be exchanged for *common shares*; includes *stock options, warrants*, and also *convertible bonds* or *convertible preferred stock* whose cash *yield* for any year within 5 years of issue is less than two-thirds the *prime rate* at the time of issue.

common-size statement. A *percentage statement* usually based on total *assets* or *net sales* or *revenues*.

company-wide control. See *control system*.

comparative (financial) statements. Financial statements showing information for the same company for different times, usually two successive years. Nearly all published financial statements are in this form. Contrast with *historical summary*.

compensating balance. When a bank lends funds to a customer, it often requires that the customer keep on deposit in his or her checking account an amount equal to some percentage—say, 20 percent—of the loan. The amount required to be left on deposit is the compensating balance. Such amounts effectively increase the *interest rate*. The amounts of such balances must be disclosed in *notes* to the *financial statements*.

completed contract method. Recognizing *revenues* and *expenses* for a job or order only when it is finished, except that when a loss on the contract is expected, revenues and expenses are recognized in the period when the loss is first forecast. This term is generally used only for long-term contracts. It is otherwise equivalent to the *sales basis* of *revenue recognition*.

completed sales basis. See *sales basis of revenue recognition*.

compliance audit. Objectively obtaining and evaluating evidence regarding assertions, actions, and events to ascertain the degree of correspondence between them and established performance criteria.

composite depreciation. *Group depreciation* of dissimilar items.

composite life method. *Group depreciation*, which see, for items of unlike kind. The term may be used when a single item, such as a crane, which consists of separate units with differing service lives, such as the chassis, the motor, the lifting mechanism, and so on, is depreciated as a whole rather than treating each of the components separately.

compound entry. A *journal entry* with more than one *debit* or more than one *credit*, or both. See *trade-in transaction* for an example.

compound interest. *Interest* calculated on *principal* plus previously undistributed interest.

compound interest depreciation. A method designed to hold the *rate of return* on an asset constant. First find the *internal rate of return* on the cash inflows and outflows of the asset. The periodic depreciation charge is the cash flow for the period less the internal rate of return multiplied by the asset's book value at the beginning of the period. When the cash flows from the asset are constant over time, the method is sometimes called the "annuity method" of depreciation.

compounding period. The time period for which *interest* is calculated. At the end of the period, the interest may be paid to the lender or added (that is, converted) to principal for the next interest-earning period, which is usually a year or some portion of a year.

comprehensive budget. *Master budget*.

comprehensive income. Defined in *SFAS No. 3* as "the change in equity (net assets) of an entity during a period from transactions and other events and circumstances from nonowner sources. It includes all changes in equity during a period except those resulting from investments by owners and distributions to owners." In this definition, "equity" means *owners' equity*.

comptroller. Same meaning and pronunciation as *controller*.

conceptual framework. A coherent system of interrelated objectives and fundamentals, promulgated by the *FASB* primarily through its *SFAC* publications, expected to lead to consistent standards for *financial accounting* and reporting.

confirmation. A formal memorandum delivered by the customers or suppliers of a company to its independent *auditor* verifying the amounts shown as receivable or payable. The confirmation document is originally sent by the auditor to the customer. If the auditor asks that the document be returned whether the *balance* is correct or incorrect, then it is called a "positive confirmation." If the auditor asks that the document be returned only if there is an error, it is called a "negative confirmation."

conglomerate. *Holding company*. This term is used when the owned companies are in dissimilar lines of business.

conservatism. A *reporting objective* that calls for anticipation of all *losses* and *expenses* but defers recognition of *gains* or *profits* until they are *realized* in *arm's-length* transactions. In the absence of certainty, events are to be reported in a way that tends to minimize cumulative income.

consignee. See *on consignment*.

consignment. See *on consignment*.

consignor. See *on consignment*.

consistency. Treatment of like *transactions* in the same way in consecutive periods so that financial statements will be more comparable than otherwise. The reporting policy implying that procedures, once adopted, should be followed from period to period by a reporting *entity*. See *accounting changes* for the treatment of inconsistencies.

consol. A *bond* that never matures; a *perpetuity* in the form of a bond. Originally issued by Great Britain after the Napoleonic wars to consolidate debt issues of that period. The term arose as an abbreviation for "consolidated annuities."

consolidated financial statements. Statements issued by legally separate companies that show financial position and income as they would appear if the companies were one economic *entity*.

constant dollar. A hypothetical unit of *general purchasing power*, denoted "C$" by the *FASB*.

constant dollar accounting. Accounting where items are measured in *constant dollars*. See *historical cost/constant* *dollar accounting* and *current cost/nominal dollar accounting*.

constant dollar date. The time at which the *general purchasing power* of one *constant dollar* is exactly equal to the *general purchasing power* of one *nominal dollar*; that is, the date when C$1 = $1. When the constant dollar date is mid-period, then the nominal amounts of *revenues* and *expenses* spread evenly throughout the period are equal to their constant dollar amounts, but end-of-period *balance sheet* amounts measured in constant mid-period dollars differ from their nominal dollar amounts. When the constant dollar date is at the end of the period, then the constant dollar and nominal dollar amounts on a balance sheet for that date are identical.

constructive receipt. An item is included in taxable income when the taxpayer can control funds whether or not cash has been received. For example, *interest* added to *principal* in a savings account is deemed by the *IRS* to be constructively received.

Consumer Price Index. CPI. A *price index* computed and issued monthly by the Bureau of Labor Statistics of the U.S. Department of Labor. The index attempts to track the price level of a group of goods and services purchased by the average consumer. The *FASB* requires use of the CPI in *constant dollar accounting*. Contrast with *GNP Implicit Price Deflator*.

contingency. A potential *liability*; if a specified event were to occur, such as losing a lawsuit, a liability would be recognized. The contingency is merely disclosed in notes, rather than shown in the balance sheet. *SFAS No. 5* requires treatment as a contingency until the outcome is "probable" and the amount of payment can be reasonably estimated, perhaps within a range. When the outcome becomes probable (the future event is "likely" to occur) and the amount can be reasonably estimated (using the lower end of a range if only a range can be estimated), then the liability is recognized in the accounts, rather than being disclosed in the notes. A *material* contingency may lead to a qualified, "*subject to,*" auditor's opinion. *Gain* contingencies are not recorded in the accounts, but are merely disclosed in notes.

contingent annuity. An *annuity* whose number of payments depends on the outcome of an event whose timing is uncertain at the time the annuity is set up; for example, an annuity payable for the life of the *annuitant*. Contrast with *annuity certain*.

contingent issue (securities). Securities issuable to specific individuals upon the occurrence of some event, such as the firm's attaining a specified level of earnings.

contingent liability. *Contingency*. This term is to be avoided because it refers to something that is not a *liability* on the *balance sheet*.

continuing appropriation. A governmental *appropriation* automatically renewed without further legislative action until it is altered or revoked or expended.

continuing operations. See *income from continuing operations*.

continuity of operations. The assumption in accounting that the business *entity* will continue to operate long enough for current plans to be carried out. The *going-concern assumption*.

continuous budget. A *budget* that perpetually adds a month in the future as the month just ended is dropped.

continuous compounding. *Compound interest* where the *compounding period* is every instant of time. See *e* for the computation of the equivalent annual or periodic rate.

continuous inventory method. The *perpetual inventory* method.

Continuously Contemporary Accounting. CoCoA. A name coined by the Australian theorist, Raymond J. Chambers, to indicate a combination of *current value accounting* where amounts are measured in *constant dollars* and based on exit values.

contra account. An *account*, such as *accumulated depreciation*, that accumulates subtractions from another account, such as machinery. Contrast with *adjunct account*.

contributed capital. The sum of the balances in *capital stock* accounts plus *capital contributed in excess of par (or stated) value* accounts. Contrast with *donated capital*.

contributed surplus. An inferior term for *capital contributed in excess of par value*.

contribution approach. Method of preparing *income statements* that separates *variable costs* from *fixed costs* in order to emphasize the importance of cost behavior patterns for purposes of planning and control.

contribution margin. *Revenue* from *sales* less all variable *expenses*. See *gross margin*.

contribution per unit. Selling price less *variable costs* per unit.

contributory. Said of a *pension plan* where employees, as well as employers, make payments to a pension *fund*. Note that the provisions for *vesting* are applicable only to the employer's payments. Whatever the degree of vesting of the employer's payments, the employee typically gets back all of his or her payments, with interest, in case of death, or other cessation of employment, before retirement.

control (controlling) account. A summary *account* with totals equal to those of entries and balances that appear in individual accounts in a *subsidiary ledger*. Accounts Receivable is a control account backed up with an account for each customer. The balance in a control account should not be changed unless a corresponding change is made in the subsidiary accounts.

control system. A device for ensuring that actions are carried out according to plan or for safeguarding *assets*. A system for ensuring that actions are carried out according to plan can be designed for a single function within the firm, called "operational control"; for autonomous segments within the firm that generally have responsibility for both revenues and costs, called "divisional control"; or for activities of the firm as a whole, called "company-wide control." Systems designed for safeguarding *assets* are called "internal control" systems.

controllable cost. A *cost* whose amount can be influenced by the way in which operations are carried out, such as advertising costs. These costs can be *fixed* or *variable*. See *programmed costs* and *managed costs*.

controlled company. A company, a majority of whose voting stock is held by an individual or corporation. Effective control can sometimes be exercised when less than 50 percent of the stock is owned.

controller. The title often used for the chief accountant of an organization. Often spelled *comptroller*.

conversion. The act of exchanging a convertible security for another security.

conversion cost. *Direct labor* costs plus factory *overhead* costs incurred in producing a product. That is, the cost to convert raw materials to finished products. *Manufacturing cost*.

conversion period. *Compounding period*. Period during which a *convertible bond* or *convertible preferred stock* can be converted into *common stock*.

convertible bond. A *bond* that may be converted into a specified number of shares of *capital stock* during the *conversion period*.

convertible preferred stock. *Preferred shares* that may be converted into a specified number of shares of *common stock*.

co-product. A product sharing production facilities with another product. For example, if an apparel manufacturer produces shirts and jeans on the same line, these are co-products. Co-products are distinguished from *joint products* and *by-products*, which by their very nature must be produced together, such as the various grades of wood produced in a lumber factory.

copyright. Exclusive right granted by the government to an individual author, composer, playwright, and the like for the life of the individual plus 50 years. If the copyright is granted to a firm, then the right extends 75 years after the original publication. The *economic life* of a copyright may be considerably less than the legal life as, for example, the copyright of this book.

corporation. A legal entity authorized by a state to operate under the rules of the entity's *charter*.

correcting entry. An *adjusting entry* where an improperly recorded *transaction* is properly recorded. Not to be confused with entries that correct *accounting errors*.

correction of errors. See *accounting errors*.

cost. The sacrifice, measured by the *price* paid or required to be paid, to acquire *goods* or *services*. See *acquisition cost* and *replacement cost*. The term "cost" is often used when referring to the valuation of a good or service acquired. When "cost" is used in this sense, a cost is an *asset*. When the benefits of the acquisition (the goods or services acquired) expire, the cost becomes an *expense* or *loss*. Some writers, however, use cost and expense as synonyms. Contrast with *expense*.

cost accounting. Classifying, summarizing, recording, reporting, and allocating current or predicted *costs*. A subset of *managerial accounting*.

Cost Accounting Standards Board. See *CASB*.

cost accumulation. Bringing together, usually in a single *account*, all *costs* of a specified activity. Contrast with *cost allocation*.

cost allocation. Assigning *costs* to individual products or time periods. Contrast with *cost accumulation*.

cost behavior. The functional relation between changes in activity and changes in *cost*. For example, *fixed* versus *variable costs*; *linear* versus *curvilinear cost*.

cost center. A unit of activity for which *expenditures* and *expenses* are accumulated.

cost effective. Among alternatives, the one whose benefit, or payoff, per unit of cost is highest. Sometimes said of an action whose expected benefits exceed expected costs whether or not there are other alternatives with larger benefit/cost ratios.

cost estimation. The process of measuring the functional relation between changes in activity levels and changes in cost.

cost flow assumption. See *flow assumption*.

cost flows. Costs passing through various classifications within an entity. See *flow of costs* for a diagram.

cost method (for investments). Accounting for an investment in the *capital stock* or *bonds* of another company where the investment is shown at *acquisition cost*, and only *dividends* declared or *interest receivable* is treated as *revenue*.

cost method (for treasury stock). The method of showing *treasury stock* as a *contra* to all other items of *shareholders' equity* in an amount equal to that paid to reacquire the stock.

cost objective. Any activity for which a separate measurement of costs is desired. Examples include departments, products, and territories.

cost of capital. *Opportunity cost* of funds invested in a business. The rate of return required to be earned on an asset before the rational owner will devote that asset to a particular purpose. Sometimes measured as the average rate per year a company must pay for its *equities*. In efficient capital markets, the *discount rate* that equates the expected *present value* of all future cash flows to common shareholders with the market value of common stock at a given time.

cost of goods manufactured. The sum of all costs allocated to products completed during a period; includes materials, labor, and *overhead*.

cost of goods purchased. Net purchase price of goods acquired plus costs of storage and delivery to the place where the items can be productively used.

cost of goods sold. Inventoriable *costs* that are expensed because the units are sold; equals beginning inventory plus *cost of goods purchased* or *manufactured* minus *ending inventory*.

cost of sales. Generally refers to *cost of goods sold*; occasionally, to *selling expenses*.

cost or market, whichever is lower. See *lower of cost or market*.

cost percentage. One less *markup percentage*. *Cost* of *goods available for sale* divided by selling prices of goods available for sale (when *FIFO* is used). With *LIFO*, cost of *purchases* divided by selling price of purchases. See *markup* for further detail on inclusions in calculation of cost percentage.

cost pool. *Indirect cost pool*.

cost principle. The *principle* that requires reporting *assets* at *historical* or *acquisition cost*, less accumulated *amortization*. This principle is based on the assumption that cost is equal to *fair market value* at the date of acquisition and that subsequent changes are not likely to be significant.

cost sheet. Statement that shows all the elements comprising the total cost of an item.

cost terminology. The word "cost" appears in many accounting terms. The accompanying exhibit classifies some of these by the distinctions the terms are used to make. Joel Dean was, to our knowledge, the first to attempt such distinctions; we have used some of his ideas here. Some terms have more detailed discussion under their own listings.

cost-recovery-first method. A method of *revenue* recognition that *credits inventory* as collections are received until all costs are recovered. Only after costs are completely recovered is *income* recognized. To be used in financial reporting only when the total amount of collections is highly uncertain. Can never be used in income tax reporting. Contrast with the *installment method*, where *constant proportions* of each collection are credited both to cost and to income.

cost-to-cost. The *percentage-of-completion method*, where the estimate of completion is the ratio of costs incurred to date divided by total costs expected to be incurred for the entire project.

cost-volume-profit graph (chart). A graph that shows the relation between *fixed costs, contribution per unit, breakeven point*, and *sales*. See *breakeven chart*.

costing. The process of calculating the cost of activities, products, or services. The British word for *cost accounting*.

coupon. That portion of a *bond* document redeemable at a specified date for *interest* payments. Its physical form is much like a ticket; each coupon is dated and is deposited at a bank, just like a check, for collection or is mailed to the issuer's agent for collection.

coupon rate. Of a *bond*, the amount of annual coupons divided by par value. Contrast with *effective rate*.

covenant. A promise with legal validity.

CPA. See *certified public accountant*. The *AICPA* suggests that no periods be shown in the abbreviation.

CPI. *Consumer Price Index*.

CPP. Current purchasing power; usually used as an adjective modifying the word "accounting" to mean the accounting that produces *constant dollar financial statements*.

Cr. Abbreviation for *credit*.

credit. As a noun, an entry on the right-hand side of an *account*. As a verb, to make an entry on the right-hand side of an account. Records increases in *liabilities, owners' equity, revenues*, and *gains*; records decreases in *assets* and *expenses*. See *debit and credit conventions*. Also the ability or right to buy or borrow in return for a promise to pay later.

credit loss. The amount of *accounts receivable* that is, or is expected to become, *uncollectible*.

credit memorandum. A document used by a seller to inform a buyer that the buyer's *account receivable* is being credited (reduced) because of *errors, returns*, or *allowances*. Also, the document provided by a bank to a depositor to indicate that the depositor's balance is being increased because of some event other than a deposit, such as the collection by the bank of the depositor's *note receivable*.

Cost Terminology: Distinctions Among Terms Containing the Word ''Cost''

Terms (Synonyms Given in Parentheses)			Distinctions and Comments
			1. The following pairs of terms distinguish the "attribute" or "basis" measured in accounting.
Historical Cost (Acquisition Cost)	vs.	Current Cost	A distinction used in financial accounting. Current cost can be used more specifically to mean replacement cost, net realizable value, or present value of cash flows. "Current cost" is often used narrowly to mean replacement cost.
Historical Cost (Actual Cost)	vs.	Standard Cost	The distinction between historical and standard costs arises in product costing for inventory valuation. Some systems record actual costs while others record the standard costs.
			2. The following pairs of terms denote various distinctions among historical costs. For each pair of terms, the sum of the two kinds of costs equals total historical cost used in financial reporting.
Variable Cost	vs.	Fixed Cost (Constant Cost)	Distinction used in breakeven analysis and in designing cost accounting systems, particularly for product costing. See (4), below, for a further subdivision of fixed costs and (5), below, for an economic distinction closely paralleling this one.
Traceable Cost	vs.	Common Cost (Joint Cost)	Distinction arises in allocating manufacturing costs to product. Common costs are allocated to product, but the allocations are more-or-less arbitrary. The distinction also arises in segment reporting and in separating manufacturing from nonmanufacturing costs.
Direct Cost	vs.	Indirect Cost	Distinction arises in designing cost accounting systems and in product costing. The distinction generally applies only to manufacturing costs.
Out-of-Pocket Cost (Outlay Cost; Cash Cost)	vs.	Book Cost	Virtually all costs recorded in financial statements require a cash outlay at one time or another. The distinction here separates expenditures to occur in the future from those already made and is used in making decisions. Book costs, such as for depreciation, reduce income without requiring a future outlay of cash. The cash has already been spent. See future vs. past costs in (5), below.
Incremental Cost (Marginal Cost) (Differential Cost)	vs.	Sunk Cost	Distinction used in making decisions. Incremental costs will be incurred (or saved) if a decision is made to go ahead (or to stop) some activity, but not otherwise. Sunk costs will be reported in financial statements whether the decision is made to go ahead or not, because cash has already been spent or committed. Not all sunk costs are book costs, as, for example, a salary promised but not yet earned, that will be paid even if a no-go decision is made.
			The economist restricts the term marginal cost to the cost of producing one more unit. Thus the next unit has a marginal cost; the next week's output has an incremental cost. If a firm produces and sells a new product the related new costs would properly be called incremental, not marginal. If a factory is closed, the costs saved are incremental, not marginal.
Escapable Cost	vs.	Inescapable Cost (Unavoidable Cost)	Same distinction as incremental vs. sunk costs, but this pair is used only when the decision maker is considering stopping something—ceasing to produce a product, closing a factory, or the like. See next pair.
Avoidable Cost	vs.	Unavoidable Cost	A distinction sometimes used in discussing the merits of variable and absorption costing. Avoidable costs are treated as product cost and unavoidable costs are treated as period expenses under variable costing.
Controllable Cost	vs.	Uncontrollable Cost	The distinction here is used in allocating responsibility and in setting bonus or incentive plans. All costs can be affected by someone in the entity; those who design incentive schemes attempt to hold a person responsible for a cost only if that person can influence the amount of the cost.

Terms (Synonyms Given in Parentheses)			Distinctions and Comments
			3. In each of the following pairs, used in historical cost accounting, the word "cost" appears in one of the terms where "expense" is meant.
Expired Cost	vs.	Unexpired Cost	The distinction is between *expense* and *asset*.
Product Cost	vs.	Period Cost	The terms distinguish product cost from period expense. When a given asset is used, is its cost converted into work in process and then finished goods on the balance sheet until the goods are sold or is it an expense shown on this period's income statement? Product costs appear on the income statement as part of cost of goods sold in the period when the goods are sold. Period expenses appear on the income statement with an appropriate caption for the item in the period when the cost is incurred or recognized.
			4. The following subdivisions of fixed (historical) costs are used in analyzing operations. The relation between the components of fixed costs is:

$$\text{Fixed Costs} = \text{Capacity Costs} + \text{Programmed Costs}$$

$$\underbrace{\text{Semifixed} + \text{"Pure" Fixed Costs} + \text{Fixed Portions of Semivariable Costs}} \quad \underbrace{\text{Standby Costs} + \text{Enabling Costs}}$$

Capacity Cost (Committed Cost)	vs.	Programmed Cost (Managed Cost; Discretionary Cost)	Capacity costs give a firm the capability to produce or to sell. Programmed costs, such as for advertising or research and development, may not be essential, but once a decision to incur them is made, they become fixed costs.
Standby Cost	vs.	Enabling Cost	Standby costs will be incurred whether capacity, once acquired, is used or not, such as property taxes and depreciation on a factory. Enabling costs, such as for security force, can be avoided if the capacity is unused.
Semifixed Cost	vs.	Semivariable Cost	A cost fixed over a wide range but that can change at various levels is a semifixed cost or "step cost." An example is the cost of rail lines from the factory to the main rail line where fixed cost depends on whether there are one or two parallel lines, but are independent of the number of trains run per day. Semivariable costs combine a strictly fixed component cost plus a variable component. Telephone charges usually have a fixed monthly component plus a charge related to usage.
			5. The following pairs of terms distinguish among economic uses or decision making uses or regulatory uses of cost terms.
Fully Absorbed Cost (Full Cost)	vs.	Variable Cost (Direct Cost)	Fully absorbed costs refer to costs where fixed costs have been allocated to units or departments as required by generally accepted accounting principles. Variable costs, in contrast, may be more relevant for making decisions, such as in setting prices.
Opportunity Cost	vs.	Outlay Cost (Out-of-Pocket Cost)	Opportunity cost refers to the economic benefit foregone by using a resource for one purpose instead of for another. The outlay cost of the resource will be recorded in financial records. The distinction arises because a resource is already in the possession of the entity with a recorded historical cost. Its economic value to the firm, opportunity cost, generally differs from the historical cost; it can be either larger or smaller.
Future Cost	vs.	Past Cost	Effective decision making analyzes only present and future outlay costs, or out-of-pocket costs. Opportunity costs are relevant for profit maximizing; past costs are used in financial reporting.

Terms (Synonyms Given in Parentheses)			Distinctions and Comments
Short-Run Cost	vs.	Long-Run Cost	Short-run costs vary as output is varied for a given configuration of plant and equipment. Long-run costs can be incurred to change that configuration. This pair of terms is the economic analog of the accounting pair, see (2) above, variable and fixed costs. The analogy is not perfect because some short-run costs are fixed, such as property taxes on the factory, from the point of view of breakeven analysis.
Imputed Cost	vs.	Book Cost	In a regulatory setting some costs, for example the cost of owners' equity capital, are calculated and used for various purposes. Imputed costs are not recorded in the historical cost accounting records for financial reporting. Book costs are recorded.
Average Cost	vs.	Marginal Cost	The economic distinction equivalent to fully absorbed cost of product and direct cost of product. Average cost is total cost divided by number of units. Marginal cost is the cost to produce the next unit (or the last unit).

creditor. One who lends.

cross-reference (index). A number placed by each *account* in a *journal entry* indicating the *ledger* account to which the entry is posted and placing in the ledger the page number of the journal where the entry was made. Used to link the *debit* and *credit* parts of an entry in the ledger accounts back to the original entry in the journal. See *audit trail*.

cross-section analysis. Analysis of *financial statements* of various firms for a single period of time, as opposed to time-series analysis, where statements of a given firm are analyzed over several periods of time.

cumulative dividend. Preferred stock *dividends* that, if not paid, accrue as a commitment that must be paid before dividends to common shareholders can be declared.

cumulative preferred shares. *Preferred* shares with *cumulative dividend* rights.

current asset. *Cash* and other *assets* that are expected to be turned into cash, sold, or exchanged within the normal operating cycle of the firm, usually 1 year. Current assets include *cash, marketable securities, receivables, inventory*, and *current prepayments*.

current cost. *Cost* stated in terms of current values (of *productive capacity*) rather than in terms of *acquisition cost*. See *net realizable value, current selling price*.

current cost accounting. The *FASB's* term for *financial statements* where the *attribute measured* is *current cost*.

current cost/nominal dollar accounting. Accounting based on *current cost* valuations measured in *nominal dollars*. Components of *income* include an *operating margin* and *holding gains and losses*.

current exit value. *Exit value*.

current fund. In governmental accounting, a synonym for general fund.

current funds. *Cash* and other assets readily convertible into cash. In governmental accounting, funds spent for operating purposes during the current period. Includes *general, special revenue, debt service*, and *enterprise funds*.

current liability. A debt or other obligation that must be discharged within a short time, usually the *earnings cycle* or 1 year, normally by expending *current assets*.

current (gross) margin. See *operating margin (based on current costs)*.

current operating performance concept. The notion that reported *income* for a period ought to reflect only ordinary, normal, and recurring operations of that period. A consequence is that *extraordinary* and nonrecurring items are entered directly in the Retained Earnings account. Contrast with *clean surplus concept*. This concept is no longer acceptable. (See *APB Opinions* Nos. 9 and 30.)

current ratio. Sum of *current assets* divided by sum of *current liabilities*. See *ratio*.

current realizable value. *Realizable value*.

current replacement cost. Of an *asset*, the amount currently required to acquire an identical asset (in the same condition and with the same service potential) or an asset capable of rendering the same service at a current *fair market price*. If these two amounts differ, the lower is usually used. Contrast with *reproduction cost*.

current selling price. The amount for which an *asset* could be sold as of a given time in an *arm's-length* transaction, rather than in a forced sale.

current value accounting. The form of accounting where all assets are shown at *current replacement cost (entry value)* or *current selling price* or *net realizable value (exit value)* and all *liabilities* are shown at *present value*. Entry and exit values may be quite different from each other, so there is no general agreement on the precise meaning of current value accounting.

current yield. Of a *bond*, the annual amount of *interest coupons* divided by the current market price of the bond. Contrast with *yield to maturity*.

currently attainable standard cost. *Normal standard cost.*

curvilinear (variable) cost. A continuous, but not necessarily linear (straight-line), functional relation between activity levels and *costs*.

customers' ledger. The *ledger* that shows accounts receivable of individual customers. It is the *subsidiary ledger* for the *controlling account*, Accounts Receivable.

D

days of average inventory on hand. See *ratio*.

DCF. *Discounted cash flow.*

DDB. *Double-declining-balance depreciation.*

debenture bond. A *bond* not secured with *collateral*.

debit. As a noun, an entry on the left-hand side of an *account*. As a verb, to make an entry on the left-hand side of an account. Records increases in *assets* and *expenses*; records decreases in *liabilities, owners' equity*, and *revenues*. See *debit and credit conventions*.

debit and credit conventions. The equality of the two sides of the *accounting equation* is maintained by recording equal amounts of *debits* and *credits* for each *transaction*. The conventional use of the *T-account* form and the rules for debit and credit in *balance sheet accounts* are summarized as follows.

Any Asset Account

Opening Balance Increase + Dr. Ending Balance	Decrease − Cr.

Any Liability Account

Decrease − Dr.	Opening Balance Increase + Cr. Ending Balance

Any Owners' Equity Account

Decrease − Dr.	Opening Balance Increase + Cr. Ending Balance

Revenue and expense accounts belong to the owner's equity group. The relationship and the rules for debit and credit in these accounts can be expressed as follows.

Owners' Equity

Decrease − Dr. Expenses		Increase + Cr. Revenues	
Dr. + *	Cr. −	Dr. −	Cr. + *

*Normal balance prior to closing.

debit memorandum. A document used by a seller to inform a buyer that the seller is debiting (increasing) the amount of the buyer's *account receivable*. Also, the document provided by a bank to a depositor to indicate that the depositor's *balance* is being decreased because of some event other than payment for a *check*, such as monthly service charges or the printing of checks.

debt. An amount owed. The general name for *notes, bonds, mortgages*, and the like that are evidence of amounts owed and have definite payment dates.

debt capital. *Noncurrent liabilities*. See *debt financing* and contrast with *equity financing*.

debt financing. Raising *funds* by issuing *bonds, mortgages*, or *notes*. Contrast with *equity financing*. *Leverage*.

debt guarantee. See *guarantee*.

debt ratio. *Debt-equity ratio*.

debt service fund. In governmental accounting, a *fund* established to account for payment of *interest* and *princi-*

pal on all general-obligation *debt* other than that payable from special *assessments*.

debt service requirement. The amount of cash required for payments of *interest*, current maturities of *principal* on outstanding *debt*, and payments to *sinking funds* (corporations) or to the *debt service fund* (governmental).

debt-equity ratio. Total *liabilities* divided by total equities. See *ratio*. Sometimes the denominator is merely total shareholders' equity. Sometimes the numerator is restricted to *noncurrent debt*.

debtor. One who borrows.

declaration date. Time when a *dividend* is declared by the *board of directors*.

declining-balance depreciation. The method of calculating the periodic *depreciation* charge by multiplying the *book value* at the start of the period by a constant percentage. In pure declining-balance depreciation the constant percentage is $1 - \sqrt[n]{s/c}$, where n is the *depreciable life*, s is *salvage value*, and c is *acquisition cost*. See *double-declining-balance depreciation*.

deep discount bonds. Said of *bonds* selling much below (exactly how much is not clear) *par value*.

defalcation. Embezzlement.

default. Failure to pay *interest* or *principal* on a *debt* when due.

defensive interval. A financial *ratio* equal to the number of days of normal cash *expenditures* covered by *quick assets*. It is defined as

$$\frac{\text{Quick Assets}}{(\text{All Expenses Except Amortization and Others Not Using Funds}/365)}$$

The denominator of the ratio is the cash expenditure per day. This ratio has been found useful in predicting *bankruptcy*.

deferral. The accounting process concerned with past *cash receipts* and *payments*; in contrast to *accrual*. Recognizing a liability resulting from a current cash receipt (as for magazines to be delivered) or recognizing an asset from a current cash payment (or for prepaid insurance or a long-term depreciable asset).

deferral method. See *flow-through method* (of accounting for the *investment credit*) for definition and contrast.

deferred annuity. An *annuity* whose first payment is made sometime after the end of the first period.

deferred asset. *Deferred charge*.

deferred charge. *Expenditure* not recognized as an *expense* of the period when made but carried forward as an *asset* to be *written off* in future periods, such as for advance rent payments or insurance premiums. See *deferral*.

deferred cost. *Deferred charge*.

deferred credit. Sometimes used to indicate *advances from customers*. Also sometimes used to describe the *deferred income tax liability*.

deferred debit. *Deferred charge*.

deferred expense. *Deferred charge*.

deferred gross margin. *Unrealized gross margin*.

deferred income. *Advances from customers*.

deferred income tax (liability). Generally a *credit* balance on the *balance sheet* that arises when the pretax income shown on the tax return is less than what it would have been had the same *accounting principles* been used in tax returns as used for financial reporting. *APB Opinion* No. 11 requires that the firm debit income tax *expense* and credit deferred income tax with the amount of the taxes delayed by using different accounting principles in tax returns from those used in financial reports. See *timing difference* and *permanent difference*. See *installment sales*. Although the item is often reported as a *liability* on the balance sheet, there is no obligation to pay. If, as a result of timing differences, cumulative taxable income exceeds cumulative reported income before taxes, the deferred income tax account will have a *debit* balance and will be reported as a *deferred charge*.

deferred performance liability. *Estimated liability* that arises under product *warranty*. Sometimes used to mean *advances from customers*.

deferred revenue. Sometimes used to indicate *advances from customers*.

deferred tax. See *deferred income tax*.

deficit. A *debit balance* in the Retained Earnings account; presented on the balance sheet as a *contra* to shareholders' equity. Sometimes used to mean negative *net income* for a period.

defined-benefit plan. A *pension plan* where the employer promises specific dollar amounts to each eligible employee; the amounts usually depend on a formula that takes into account such things as the employee's earnings, years of employment, and age. The employer's cash contributions and pension expense are adjusted in relation to *actuarial* experience in the eligible employee group and investment performance of the pension *fund*. Sometimes called a "fixed-benefit" pension plan. Contrast with *money purchase plan*.

defined-contribution plan. A *money purchase (pension) plan* or other arrangement, based on formula or discretion, where the employer makes cash contributions to eligible individual employee *accounts* under the terms of a written plan document.

deflation. A period of declining *general price changes*.

demand deposit. *Funds* in a *checking account* at a bank.

demand loan. See *term loan* for definition and contrast.

denominator volume. Capacity measured in expected number of units to be produced this period; divided into *budgeted fixed costs* to obtain fixed costs applied per unit of product.

depletion. Exhaustion or *amortization* of a *wasting asset* or natural resource. See also *percentage depletion*.

depletion allowance. See *percentage depletion*.

deposit method (of revenue recognition). This method of *revenue* recognition is not distinct from the *completed sale* or *completed contract method*. In some contexts such as retail land sales, the customer must make substantial payments while still having the right to back out of the deal and receive a refund. When there is uncertainty about whether the deal will be completed but a cash collection is made by the seller, the seller must *credit* deposits, a *liability account*, rather than *revenue*. (In this regard, the accounting differs from the completed contract method, where the account credited is offset against the *work-in-process inventory* account.) When the *sale* becomes complete, a revenue account is credited and the deposit account is *debited*.

deposit, sinking fund. Payments made to a *sinking fund*.

deposits (by customers). A *liability* arising upon receipt of *cash* (as in a bank, or in a grocery store when the customer pays cash for sodapop bottles to be repaid when the bottles are returned).

deposits in transit. Deposits made by a firm but not yet reflected on the *bank statement*.

depreciable cost. That part of the *cost* of an asset, usually *acquisition cost* less *salvage value*, that is to be charged off over the life of the asset through the process of *depreciation*.

depreciable life. For an *asset*, the time period or units of activity (such as miles driven for a truck) over which *depreciable cost* is to be allocated. For tax returns, depreciable life may be shorter than estimated *service life*.

depreciation. *Amortization of plant assets*; the process of allocating the cost of an asset to the periods of benefit— the *depreciable life*. Classified as a *production cost* or a *period expense*, depending on the asset and whether *absorption* or *direct costing* is used. Depreciation terms described in this glossary include the *annuity method*, *appraisal method*, *backlog depreciation*, *composite de-*

preciation, compound interest depreciation, declining-balance depreciation, double-declining-balance depreciation, production method, replacement cost method, retirement method, sinking fund method, straight-line depreciation, and *sum-of-the-years'-digits depreciation*.

depreciation reserve. An inferior term for *accumulated depreciation*. See *reserve*. Do not confuse with a replacement *fund*.

Descartes' rule of signs. In a *capital budgeting* context, the rule says that a series of cash flows will have a nonnegative number of *internal rates of return*. The number is equal to the number of variations in the sign of the cash flow series or is less than that number by an even integer. Consider the following series of cash flows, the first occurring now and the others at subsequent yearly intervals: $-100, -100, +50, +175, -50, +100$. The internal rates of return are the numbers for r that satisfy the equation

$$-100 - \frac{100}{(1 + r)} + \frac{50}{(1 + r)^2} + \frac{175}{(1 + r)^3} - \frac{50}{(1 + r)^4} + \frac{100}{(1 + r)^5} = 0.$$

The series of cash flows has three variations in sign: a change from minus to plus, a change from plus to minus, and a change from minus to plus. The rule says that this series must have either one or three internal rates of return; in fact, it has only one, about 12 percent. But see also *reinvestment rate*.

determination. See *determine*.

determine. The verb ''determine'' and the noun ''determination'' are often used (in our opinion, overused) by accountants and those who describe the accounting process. A leading dictionary associates the following meanings with the verb ''determine'': settle, decide, conclude, ascertain, cause, affect, control, impel, terminate, and decide upon. In addition, accounting writers can mean any one of the following: measure, allocate, report, calculate, compute, observe, choose, and legislate. In accounting, there are two distinct sets of meanings—those encompassed by the synonym ''cause or legislate'' and those encompassed by the synonym ''measure.'' The first set of uses conveys the active notion of causing something to happen and the second set of uses conveys the more passive notion of observing something that someone else has caused to happen. An accountant who writes of cost or income ''determination'' generally means measurement or observation, not causation; management and economic conditions cause costs or income to be what they are. One who writes of accounting principles ''determination'' can mean choosing or applying (as in ''determining depreciation charges'' from an allowable set) or causing to be acceptable (as in the FASB ''determining'' the accounting for *leases*). In the long run, income is cash in less cash out, so management and economic conditions ''determine'' (cause) income to be what it is. In the short run, reported income is a function of accounting principles chosen and applied, so the accountant ''determines'' (measures) income. A question such as "Who determines income?" has, therefore, no unambiguous answer. The meaning of "an accountant determining acceptable accounting principles" is also vague. Does the clause mean merely choosing one from the set of generally acceptable principles, or does it mean using professional judgment to decide that some of the generally accepted principles are not correct under the current circumstances? We try never to use "determine" unless we mean "cause." Otherwise we use "measure," "report," "calculate," "compute," or whatever specific verb seems appropriate. We suggest that careful writers will always "determine" to use the most specific verb to convey meaning. "Determine" is seldom the best choice to convey specifity in describing a process where those who make decisions often differ from those who apply technique.

development-stage enterprise. As defined in *SFAS No. 7*, a firm whose planned principal *operations* have not commenced or, having commenced, have not generated significant *revenue*. Such enterprises should be so identified, but no special *accounting principles* apply to them.

differential analysis. Analysis of *incremental costs*.

differential cost. *Incremental cost*.

dilution. A potential reduction in *earnings per share* or *book value* per share by the potential *conversion* of securities or by the potential exercise of *warrants* or *options*.

dilutive. Said of a *security* that would reduce *earnings per share* if it were exchanged for *common stock*.

dipping into LIFO layers. See *LIFO inventory layer*.

direct cost. Cost of *direct material* and *direct labor* incurred in producing a product. See *prime cost*. In some accounting literature, this term is used to mean the same thing as *variable cost*.

direct costing. This method of allocating costs assigns only *variable manufacturing costs* to product and treats *fixed manufacturing costs* as *period* expenses. A better term for this concept is "variable costing." Contrast with *absorption costing*.

direct labor (material) cost. Cost of labor (material) applied and assigned directly to a product; contrast with *indirect labor (material)*.

direct posting. A method of bookkeeping where *entries* are made directly in *ledger accounts*, without the use of a *journal*.

direct write-off method. See *write-off method*.

disbursement. Payment by *cash* or by *check*. See *expenditure*.

DISC. Domestic International Sales Corporation. A U.S. *corporation*, usually a *subsidiary*, whose *income* is attributable primarily to exports. *Income tax* on 50 percent of a DISC's income is usually deferred for a long period. Generally, this results in a lower overall corporate tax for the *parent* than would otherwise be incurred.

disclaimer of opinion. An *auditor's report* stating that an opinion cannot be given on the *financial statements*. Usually results from *material* restrictions on the scope of the audit or from material uncertainties about the accounts that cannot be resolved at the time of the audit.

disclosure. The showing of facts in *financial statements*, *notes* thereto, or the *auditor's report*.

discontinued operations. See *income from discontinued operations*.

discount. In the context of *compound interest*, *bonds*, and *notes*, the difference between *face* or *future value* and *present value* of a payment. In the context of *sales* and *purchases*, a reduction in price granted for prompt payment. See also *chain discount*, *quantity discount*, and *trade discount*.

discount factor. The reciprocal of 1 plus the *discount rate*. If the discount rate is 10 percent per period, the discount factor for three periods is $(1.10)^{-3} = 0.75131$.

discount rate. *Interest rate* used to convert future payments to *present values*.

discounted bailout period. In a *capital budgeting* context, the total time that must elapse before discounted value of net accumulated cash flows from a project, including potential *salvage value* at various times of assets, equals or exceeds the *present value* of net accumulated cash outflows. Contrast with *discounted payback period*.

discounted cash flow. DCF. Using either the *net present value* or the *internal rate of return* in an analysis to measure the value of future expected cash *expenditures* and *receipts* at a common date.

discounted payback period. Amount of time over which the discounted present value of cash inflows from a project, excluding potential *salvage value* at various times of assets, equals the discounted *present value* of the cash outflows.

discounting a note. See *note receivable discounted* and *factoring*.

discounts lapsed (lost). The sum of *discounts* offered for prompt payment that were not taken (or allowed) because of expiration of the discount period. See *terms of sale*.

discovery value accounting. See *reserve recognition accounting*.

Discussion Memorandum. A neutral discussion of all the issues concerning an accounting problem of current concern to the *FASB*. The publication of such a document usually implies that the FASB is considering issuing an *SFAS* or *SFAC* on this particular problem. The Discussion Memorandum brings together material about the particular problem to facilitate interaction and comment by those interested in the matter. It may lead to an *Exposure Draft*.

dishonored note. A *promissory note* whose maker does not repay the loan at *maturity* for a *term loan*, or on demand, for a *demand loan*.

disintermediation. Federal law regulates the maximum *interest rate* that both banks and savings and loan associations can pay for *time deposits*. When free-market interest rates exceed the regulated interest ceiling for such time deposits, some depositors withdraw their funds and invest them elsewhere at a higher interest rate. This process is known as "disintermediation."

distributable income. The portion of conventional accounting net income that can be distributed to owners (usually in the form of *dividends*) without impairing the physical capacity of the firm to continue operations at current levels. Pretax distributable income is conventional pretax income less the excess of *current cost* of goods sold and *depreciation* charges based on the replacement cost of *productive capacity* over cost of goods sold and depreciation on an *acquisition cost basis*. Contrast with *sustainable income*. See *inventory profit*.

distribution expense. *Expense* of selling, advertising, and delivery activities.

dividend. A distribution of assets generated from *earnings* to owners of a corporation; it may be paid in cash (cash dividend), with stock (stock dividend), with property, or with other securities (dividend in kind). Dividends, except stock dividends, become a legal liability of the corporation when they are declared. Hence, the owner of stock ordinarily recognizes *revenue* when a dividend, other than a stock dividend, is declared. See also *liquidating dividend* and *stock dividend*.

dividend yield. *Dividends* declared for the year divided by market price of the stock as of a given time of the year.

dividends in arrears. Dividends on *cumulative preferred stock* that have not been declared in accordance with the preferred stock contract. Such arrearages must usually be cleared before dividends on *common stock* can be declared.

dividends in kind. See *dividend*.

divisional control. See *control system*.

divisional reporting. *Line-of-business reporting*.

dollar sign rules. In presenting accounting statements or schedules, place a dollar sign beside the first figure in each column and beside any figure below a horizontal line drawn under the preceding figure.

dollar-value LIFO method. A form of *LIFO* inventory accounting with inventory quantities *(layers)* measured in dollar, rather than physical, terms. Adjustments to account for changing prices are made by use of specific price indexes appropriate for the kinds of items in the inventory.

Domestic International Sales Corporation. See *DISC*.

donated capital. A *shareholders' equity* account credited when contributions, such as land or buildings, are freely given to the company. Do not confuse with *contributed capital*.

double entry. The system of recording transactions that maintains the equality of the accounting equation; each entry results in recording equal amounts of *debits* and *credits*.

double T-account. *T-account* with an extra horizontal line showing a change in the account balance to be explained by the subsequent entries into the account, such as:

Plant

42,000	

This account shows an increase in the asset account, plant, of $42,000 to be explained. Such accounts are useful in preparing the *statement of changes in financial position*; they are not a part of the formal record-keeping process.

double taxation. Corporate income is subject to the corporate income tax, and the aftertax income, when distributed to owners, is subject to the personal income tax.

double-declining-balance depreciation. DDB. *Declining-balance depreciation*, which see, where the constant percentage used to multiply by book value in determining the depreciation charge for the year is $2/n$ and n is the *depreciable life* in periods. Maximum declining-balance rate permitted in the *income tax* laws. *Salvage value* is omitted from the depreciable amount. Thus if the asset cost $100 and has a depreciable life of 5 years, the depreciation in the first year would be $40 = 2/5 \times \$100$, in the second would be $24 = 2/5 \times (\$100 - \$40)$, and in the third year would be $14.40 = 2/5 \times (\$100 - \$40 - \$24)$. By the fourth year, the remaining undepreciated cost could be depreciated under the straight-line method at $10.80 = 1/2 \times (\$100 - \$40 - \$24 - \$14.40)$ per year for tax purposes.

doubtful accounts. *Accounts receivable* estimated to be *uncollectible*.

Dr. The abbreviation for *debit*.

draft. A written order by the first party, called the drawer, instructing a second party, called the drawee (such as a bank) to pay a third party, called the payee. See also *check, cashier's check, certified check, NOW account, sight draft,* and *trade acceptance.*

drawee. See *draft.*

drawer. See *draft.*

drawing account. A *temporary account* used in *sole proprietorships* and *partnerships* to record payments to owners or partners during a period. At the end of the period, the drawing account is closed by crediting it and debiting the owner's or partner's share of income or, perhaps, his or her capital account.

drawings. Payments made to a *sole proprietor* or to a *partner* during a period. See *drawing account.*

dry-hole accounting. See *reserve recognition accounting* for definition and contrast.

dual transactions assumption (fiction). In presenting the *statement of changes in financial position,* some transactions not involving *working capital* accounts are reported as though working capital was generated and then used. For example, the issue of *capital stock* in return for the *asset,* land, is reported in the statement of changes in financial position as though stock were issued for *cash* and cash were used to acquire land. Other examples of transactions that require the dual transaction fiction are the issue of the *mortgage* in return for a noncurrent asset and the issue of stock to bondholders upon *conversion* of their *convertible bonds.*

duality. The axiom of *double-entry* record keeping that every *transaction* is broken down into equal *debit* and *credit* amounts.

E

e. The base of natural logarithms; 2.71828182846. . . . If *interest* is compounded continuously during a period at a stated rate of *r* per period, then the effective *interest rate* is equivalent to interest compounded once per period at rate *i,* where $i = e^r - 1$. Tables of e^r are widely available. If 12 percent annual interest is compounded continuously, the effective rate is $e^{.12} - 1 = 12.75$ percent.

earned surplus. A term once used, but no longer considered proper, for *retained earnings.*

earnings. *Income,* or sometimes *profit.*

earnings cycle. The period of time that elapses for a given firm, or the series of transactions, during which *cash* is converted into *goods* and *services,* goods and services are sold to customers, and customers pay for their purchases with cash. *Cash cycle.*

earnings per share (of common stock). *Net income* to common shareholders (net income minus *preferred dividends*) divided by the weighted average number of *common shares* outstanding; see also *primary earnings per share* and *fully diluted earnings per share.* See *ratio.*

earnings per share (of preferred stock). *Net income* divided by the weighted average number of *preferred shares* outstanding during the period. This ratio indicates how well the preferred dividends are covered or protected; it does not indicate a legal share of *earnings.* See *ratio.*

earnings, retained. See *retained earnings.*

earnings statement. *Income statement.*

earn-out. An agreement between two merging firms under which the amount of payment by the acquiring firm to the acquired firm's shareholders depends on the future earnings of the *consolidated entity.*

easement. The acquired right or privilege of one person to use, or have access to, certain property of another. For example, a public utility's right to lay pipes or lines under property of another and to service those facilities.

economic depreciation. Decline in *current cost* of an *asset* during a period.

economic entity. See *entity.*

economic life. The time span over which the benefits of an *asset* are expected to be received. The economic life of a *patent, copyright,* or *franchise* may be less than the legal life. *Service life.*

economic order quantity. In mathematical *inventory* analysis, the optimal amount of stock to order when inventory is reduced to a level called the "reorder point." If *A* represents the *incremental cost* of placing a single order, *D* represents the total demand for a period of time in units, and *H* represents the incremental holding cost during the period per unit of inventory, then the economic order quantity $Q = \sqrt{2AD/H}$. *Q* is sometimes called the "optimal lot size."

ED. *Exposure Draft.*

effective interest method. A systematic method for computing *interest expense* (or *revenue*) that makes the interest expense for each period divided by the amount of the net *liability (asset)* at the beginning of the period equal to the *yield rate* on the bond at the time of issue (acquisition). Interest for a period is the yield rate (at time of issue) multiplied by the net liability (asset) at the start of the period. The *amortization* of discount or premium is the *plug* to give equal *debits* and *credits.* (Interest expense is a debit and the amount of coupon payments is a credit.)

effective (interest) rate. Of a bond, the *internal rate of return* or *yield to maturity* at the time of issue. Contrast with *coupon rate*. If the bond is issued for a price below *par*, the effective rate is higher than the coupon rate; if it is issued for a price greater than par, then the effective rate is lower than the coupon rate. In the context of *compound interest*, when the *compounding period* on a *loan* is different from 1 year, such as a nominal interest rate of 12 percent compounded monthly, then the single rate that could be applied at the end of a year to the beginning balance is economically equivalent to the series of compound interest calculations. If 12 percent per year is compounded monthly, the effective interest rate is 12.683 percent. In general, if the nominal rate is r percent per year and is compounded m times per year, then the effective rate is $(1 + r/m)^m - 1$.

efficiency variance. A term used for the *quantity variance* for labor or *variable overhead* in a *standard cost system*.

efficient market hypothesis. The supposition in finance that securities' prices reflect all available information and react nearly instantaneously and in an unbiased fashion to new information.

eliminations. *Work sheet* entries to prepare *consolidated statements* that are made to avoid duplicating the amounts of *assets, liabilities, owners' equity, revenues*, and *expenses* of the consolidated *entity* when the accounts of the *parent* and *subsidiaries* are summed.

Employee Retirement Income Security Act. See *ERISA*.

employee stock option. See *stock option*.

Employee Stock Ownership Trust (or Plan). See *ESOT*.

employer, employee payroll taxes. See *payroll*.

enabling costs. A type of *capacity cost* that will stop being incurred if operations are shut down completely but must be incurred in full if operations are carried out at any level. Costs of a security force or of a quality control inspector for an assembly line might be examples. Contrast with *standby costs*.

encumbrance. In governmental accounting, an anticipated *expenditure*, or *funds* restricted for an anticipated expenditure, such as for outstanding purchase orders. *Appropriations* less expenditures less outstanding encumbrances yields unencumbered balance.

ending inventory. The *cost of inventory* on hand at the end of the *accounting period*, often called "closing inventory." The dollar amount of inventory to be carried to the subsequent period.

endorsee. See *endorser*.

endorsement. See *draft*. The *payee* signs the draft and transfers it to a fourth party, such as the payee's bank.

endorser. The *payee* of a *note* or *draft* signs it, after writing "Pay to the order of X," transfers the note to person X, and presumably receives some benefit, such as cash, in return. The payee who signs over the note is called the endorser and person X is called the endorsee. The endorsee then has the rights of the payee and may in turn become an endorser by endorsing the note to another endorsee.

enterprise. Any business organization, usually defining the accounting *entity*.

enterprise fund. A *fund* established by a governmental unit to account for acquisition, operation, and maintenance of governmental services that are supposed to be self-supporting from user charges, such as for water or airports.

entity. A person, *partnership, corporation*, or other organization. The *accounting entity* for which accounting statements are prepared may not be the same as the entity defined by law. For example, a *sole proprietorship* is an accounting entity, but the individual's combined business and personal assets are the legal entity in most jurisdictions. Several affiliated corporations may be separate legal entities although *consolidated financial statements* are prepared for the group of companies operating as a single economic entity.

entity theory. The view of the corporation that emphasizes the form of the *accounting equation* that says *assets = equities*. Contrast with *proprietorship theory*. The entity theory is less concerned with a distinct line between *liabilities* and *shareholders' equity* than is the proprietorship theory. Rather, all equities are provided to the corporation by outsiders who merely have claims of differing legal standings. The entity theory implies using a *multiple-step* income statement.

entry value. The *current cost* of acquiring an asset or service at a *fair market price*. *Replacement cost*.

EOQ. *Economic order quantity*.

EPS. *Earnings per share*.

EPVI. *Excess present value index*.

equalization reserve. An inferior title for the allowance account when the *allowance method* is used for such things as maintenance expenses. Periodically, maintenance *expense* is debited and the allowance is credited. As maintenance *expenditures* are actually incurred, the allowance is debited and cash or the other asset expended is credited.

equities. *Liabilities* plus *owners' equity*. See, however, *equity*.

equity. A claim to *assets*; a source of assets. *SFAS No. 3* defines equity as "the residual interest in the assets of an entity that remains after deducting its liabilities.'' Usage may be changing so that ''equity'' will exclude liabilities. We prefer to keep the broader definition, including liabilities, because there is no other single word that serves this useful purpose.

equity financing. Raising *funds* by issuance of *capital stock*. Contrast with *debt financing*.

equity method. A method of accounting for an *investment* in the stock of another company in which the proportionate share of the earnings of the other company is debited to the investment account and credited to a *revenue* account as earned. When *dividends* are received, *cash* is debited and the investment account is credited. Used in reporting when the investor owns sufficient shares of stock of an unconsolidated company to exercise significant control over the actions of that company. One of the few instances where revenue is recognized without a change in *working capital*.

equity ratio. *Shareholders' equity* divided by total *assets*. See *ratio*.

equivalent production. *Equivalent units*.

equivalent units (of work). The number of units of completed output that would require the same costs as were actually incurred for production of completed and partially completed units during a period. Used primarily in *process costing* calculations to measure in uniform terms the output of a continuous process.

ERISA. Employee Retirement Income Security Act of 1974. The federal law that sets *pension plan* requirements.

error accounting. See *accounting errors*.

ESOP. Employee Stock Ownership Plan. See *ESOT*.

ESOT. Employee stock ownership trust. A trust *fund* created by a corporate employer that can provide certain tax benefits to the corporation while providing for employee stock ownership. The corporate employer can contribute up to 25 percent of its payroll per year to the trust. The contributions are *deductions* from otherwise taxable income for federal *income tax* purposes. The assets of the trust must be used for the benefit of employees—for example, to fund death or retirement benefits. The assets of the trust are usually the *common stock*, sometimes nonvoting, of the corporate employer. As an example of the potential *tax shelter*, consider the case of a corporation with $1 million of *debt* outstanding, which it wishes to retire, and an annual payroll of $2 million. The corporation sells $1 million of common stock to the ESOT. The ESOT borrows $1 million with the loan guaranteed by, and therefore a *contingency* of, the corporation. The corporation uses the $1 million proceeds of the stock issue to retire its outstanding debt. (The debt of the corporation has been replaced with the debt of the ESOT.) The corporation can contribute $500,000 (= .25 × $2 million payroll) to the ESOT each year and treat the contribution as a deduction

for tax purposes. After a little more than 2 years, the ESOT has received sufficient funds to retire its loan. The corporation has effectively repaid its original $1 million debt with pretax dollars. Assuming an income tax rate of 40 percent, it has saved $400,000 (= .40 × $1 million) of aftertax dollars *if* the $500,000 expense for the contribution to the ESOT for the pension benefits of employees would have been made, in one form or another, anyway. Observe that the corporation could use the proceeds ($1 million in the example) of the stock issue to the ESOT for any of several different purposes: financing expansion, replacing plant assets, or acquiring another company.

Basically this same form of pretax dollar financing through pensions is "almost" available with any corporate pension plan, but with one important exception. The trustees of an ordinary pension trust must invest the assets "prudently"; if they do not, they are personally liable to employees. Current judgment about "prudent" investment requires diversification—pension trust assets should be invested in a wide variety of investment opportunities. (Not more than 10 percent of a pension trust's assets can ordinarily be invested in the parent's common stock.) Thus the ordinary pension trust cannot, in practice, invest all, or even most, of its assets in the parent corporation's stock. This constraint does not apply to the investments of an ESOT. All ESOT assets may be invested in the parent company's stock.

The ESOT also provides a means for closely held corporations to achieve wider ownership of shares without *going public*. The laws enabling ESOTs provide for independent professional appraisal of shares not traded in public markets and for transactions between the corporation and the ESOT or between the ESOT and the employees to be based on the appraised values of the shares.

estimated expenses. See *aftercost*.

estimated liability. The preferred terminology for estimated costs to be incurred for such uncertain things as repairs under *warranty*. An estimated liability is shown in the *balance sheet*. Contrast with *contingency*.

estimated revenue. A term used in governmental accounting to designate revenue expected to accrue during a period whether or not it will be collected during the period. A *budgetary account* is usually established at the beginning of the budget period.

estimated salvage value. Synonymous with *salvage value* of an *asset* before its retirement.

estimates, changes in. See *accounting changes*.

except for. Qualification in an *auditor's report*, usually caused by a change, approved by the auditor, from one acceptable accounting principle or procedure to another.

excess present value. In a *capital budgeting* context, *present value* of anticipated net cash inflows minus cash outflows, including initial cash outflow for a project.

excess present value index. *Present value* of future *cash* inflows divided by initial cash outlay.

exchange. The generic term for a transaction (or, more technically, a reciprocal transfer) between one entity and another. In another context, the name for a market, such as the New York Stock Exchange.

exchange gain or loss. The phrase used by the *FASB* for *foreign exchange gain or loss*.

exchange rate. The *price* of one country's currency in terms of another country's currency. For example, the British pound might be worth $1.50 at a given time. The exchange rate would be stated as "one pound is worth one dollar fifty cents" or "one dollar is worth .67 (= £ 1/$1.50) pounds."

excise tax. Tax on the manufacture, sale, or consumption of a commodity.

ex-dividend. Said of a stock at the time when the declared *dividend* becomes the property of the person who owned the stock on the *record date*. The payment date follows the ex-dividend date.

executory contract. An agreement providing for payment by a payor to a payee upon the performance of an act or service by the payee, such as a labor contract. Obligations under such contracts generally are not recognized as *liabilities*. Some contracts are partially executory; these give rise to an *asset* or *liability* to the extent of partial performance. An example is the downpayment on a purchase.

exemption. A term used for various amounts subtracted from gross income in computing taxable income. Not all such subtractions are called "exemptions." See *tax deduction*.

exercise. When the owner of an *option* or *warrant* purchases the security that the option entitles him or her to purchase, he or she has exercised the option or warrant.

exercise price. See *option*.

exit value. The proceeds that would be received if assets were disposed of in an *arm's-length transaction. Current selling price. Net realizable value.*

expected value. The mean or arithmetic *average* of a statistical distribution or series of numbers.

expendable fund. In governmental accounting, a *fund* whose resources, *principal*, and earnings may be distributed.

expenditure. Payment of *cash* for goods or services received. Payment may be made either at the time the goods or services are received or at a later time. Virtually synonymous with *disbursement* except that disbursement is a broader term and includes all payments for goods or services. Contrast with *expense*.

expense. As a noun, a decrease in *owners' equity* caused by the using up of *assets* in producing *revenue* or carrying out other activities that are part of the entity's *operations*. A "gone" asset; an expired cost. The amount is the *cost* of the assets used up. Do not confuse with *expenditure* or *disbursement*, which may occur before, when, or after the related expense is recognized. Use the word "cost" to refer to an item that still has service potential and is an asset. Use the word "expense" after the asset's service potential has been used. As a verb, to designate a past or current expenditure as a current expense.

expense account. An *account* to accumulate *expenses*; such accounts are closed at the end of the accounting period. A *temporary owners' equity* account. Also used to describe a listing of expenses by an employee submitted to the employer for reimbursement.

expense center. *Cost center.*

experience rating. A term used in insurance, particularly unemployment insurance, to denote changes from ordinary rates to reflect extraordinarily large or small amounts of claims over time by the insured.

expired cost. An *expense* or a *loss*.

Exposure Draft. ED. A preliminary statement of the *FASB* (or *APB* between 1962 and 1973) that shows the contents of a pronouncement the board is considering making effective.

external reporting. Reporting to shareholders and the public, as opposed to internal reporting for management's benefit. See *financial accounting* and contrast with *managerial accounting*.

extraordinary item. A *material expense* or *revenue* item characterized both by its unusual nature and infrequency of occurrence that is shown along with its income tax effects separately from ordinary income and *income from discontinued operations* on the *income statement*. A *loss* from an earthquake would probably be classified as an extraordinary item. Gain (or loss) upon retirement of *bonds* is treated as an extraordinary item under the terms of *SFAS No. 4*.

F

face amount (value). The nominal amount due at *maturity* from a *bond* or *note* not including contractual interest that may also be due on the same date. The corresponding amount of a stock certificate is best called the *par* or *stated value*, whichever is applicable.

factoring. The process of buying *notes* or *accounts receivable* at a *discount* from the holder to whom the debt is owed; from the holder's point of view, the selling of such notes or accounts. When a single note is involved, the process is called "discounting a note."

factory. Used synonymously with *manufacturing* as an adjective.

factory burden. *Manufacturing overhead.*

factory cost. *Manufacturing cost.*

factory expense. *Manufacturing overhead. Expense* is a poor term in this context because the item is a *product cost.*

factory overhead. Usually an item of *manufacturing cost* other than *direct labor* or *direct materials.*

fair market price (value). Price (value) negotiated at *arm's length* between a willing buyer and a willing seller, each acting rationally in his or her own self-interest. May be estimated in the absence of a monetary transaction.

fair presentation (fairness). When the *auditor's report* says that the *financial statements* "present fairly. . . ," the auditor means that the accounting alternatives used by the entity are all in accordance with *GAAP*. In recent years, however, courts are finding that conformity with *generally accepted accounting principles* may be insufficient grounds for an opinion that the statements are fair. *SAS No. 5* requires that the auditor judge the accounting principles used "appropriate in the circumstances" before attesting to fair presentation.

FASB. Financial Accounting Standards Board. An independent board responsible, since 1973, for establishing *generally accepted accounting principles*. Its official pronouncements are called *Statements of Financial Accounting Concepts (SFAC), Statements of Financial Accounting Standards (SFAS)*, and *Interpretations of Financial Accounting Standards*. See also *Discussion Memorandum* and *Technical Bulletin*.

FASB Interpretation. An official statement of the *FASB* interpreting the meaning of *Accounting Research Bulletins, APB Opinions*, and *Statements of Financial Accounting Standards*.

FASB Technical Bulletin. See *Technical Bulletin*.

favorable variance. An excess of actual *revenues* over expected revenues. An excess of *standard cost* over actual cost.

federal income tax. *Income tax* levied by the U.S. government on individuals and corporations.

Federal Insurance Contribution Act. *FICA.*

Federal Unemployment Tax Act. See *FUTA.*

feedback. The process of informing employees about how their actual performance compares with the expected or desired level of performance in the hope that the information will reinforce desired behavior and reduce unproductive behavior.

FEI. *Financial Executives Institute.*

FICA. Federal Insurance Contributions Act. The law that sets *Social Security taxes* and benefits.

fiduciary. Someone responsible for the custody or administration of property belonging to another, such as an executor (of an estate), agent, receiver (in *bankruptcy*), or trustee (of a trust).

FIFO. First in, first out; the *inventory flow assumption* by which *ending inventory* cost is computed from most recent purchases and *cost of goods sold* is computed from oldest purchases including beginning inventory. See *LISH*. Contrast with *LIFO.*

finance. As a verb, to supply with *funds* through the *issue* of stocks, bonds, notes, or mortgages, or through the retention of earnings.

financial accounting. The accounting for *assets, equities, revenues*, and *expenses* of a business. Concerned primarily with the historical reporting of the *financial position* and operations of an *entity* to external users on a regular, periodic basis. Contrast with *managerial accounting.*

Financial Accounting Foundation. The independent foundation (board of trustees) that raises funds to support the *FASB*, appoints its members, approves its operating policies and procedures, and appoints members of the *Financial Accounting Standards Advisory Council*.

Financial Accounting Standards Advisory Council. A committee giving advice to the *FASB* on matters of strategy and emerging issues.

Financial Accounting Standards Board. *FASB.*

Financial Executives Institute. An organization of financial executives, such as chief accountants, *controllers*, and treasurers, of large businesses.

financial expense. An *expense* incurred in raising or managing *funds*.

financial position (condition). Statement of the *assets* and *equities* of a firm displayed as a *balance sheet*.

financial ratio. See *ratio*.

financial reporting objectives. FASB *Statement of Financial Accounting Concepts No. 1* sets out the broad objectives of financial reporting that are intended to guide the development of specific *accounting standards*.

Financial Reporting Release. New series of releases, issued by the SEC, since 1982. Replaces the *Accounting Series Releases*. See *SEC*.

financial statements. The *balance sheet, income statement, statement of retained earnings, statement of changes in financial position*, statement of changes in *owners' equity accounts*, and *notes* thereto.

Flow of Costs (and Sales Revenue)

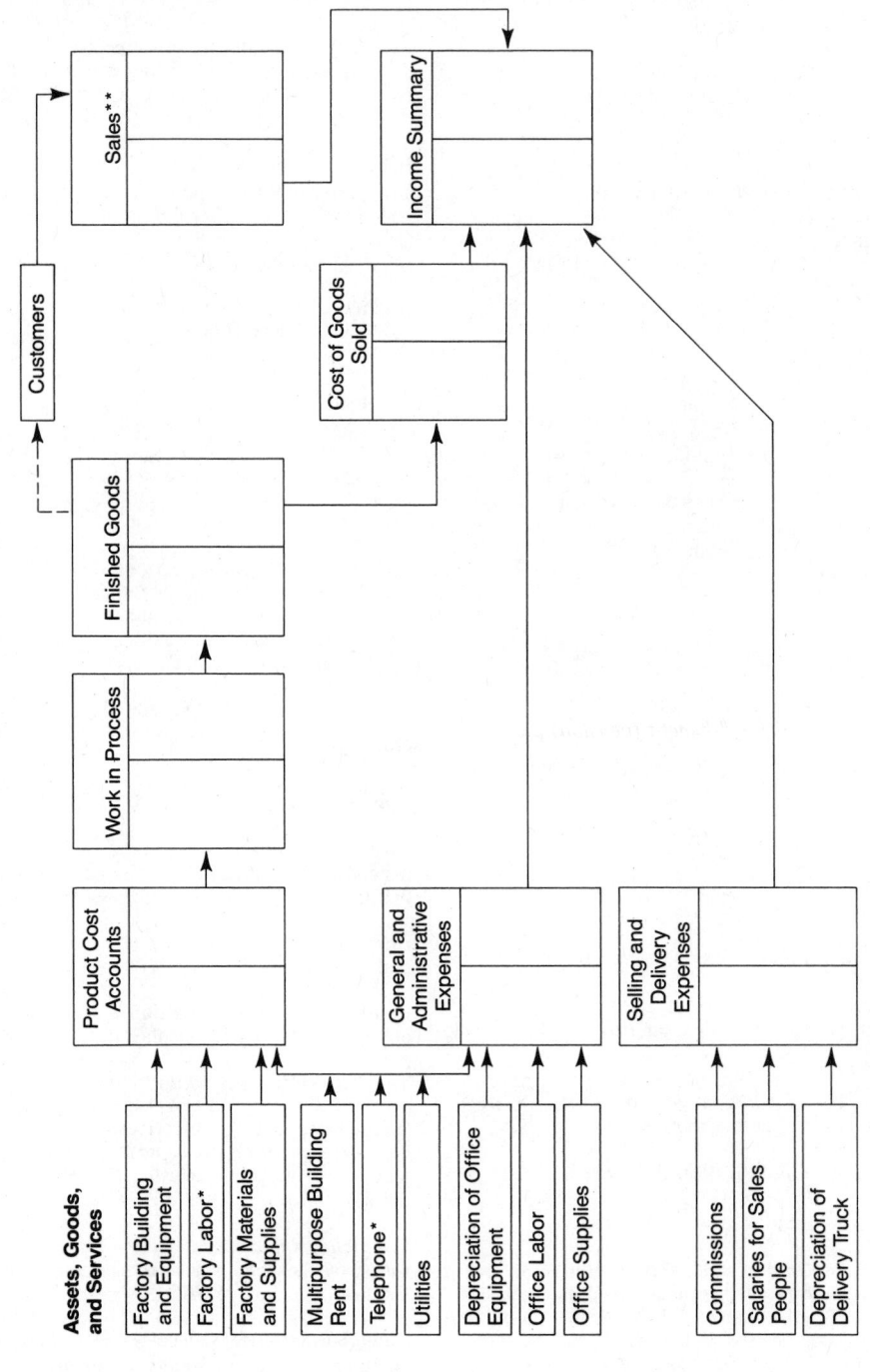

*The credit in the entry to record these items is usually to a payable; for all others, the credit is usually to an asset, or to an asset contra account.
**When sales to customers are recorded, the Sales account is credited. The debit is usually to Cash or Accounts Receivable.

financial structure. *Capital structure.*

financial year. The term for *fiscal year* in Australia and Britain.

financing lease. *Capital lease.*

finished goods. Manufactured product ready for sale; a *current asset (inventory) account.*

firm. Informally, any business entity. (Strictly speaking, a firm is a *partnership*.)

first in, first out. See *FIFO.*

fiscal year. A period of 12 consecutive months chosen by a business as the *accounting period* for annual reports. May or may not be a *natural business year* or a calendar year. Called *financial year* in Australia and Britain.

FISH. An acronym, conceived by George H. Sorter, for *first in, still here.* FISH is the same cost flow assumption as *LIFO.* Many readers of accounting statements find it easier to think about inventory questions in terms of items still on hand. Think of LIFO in connection with *cost of goods sold* but of FISH in connection with *ending inventory.* See *LISH.*

fixed assets. *Plant assets.*

fixed assets turnover. *Sales* divided by average total *fixed assets.*

fixed benefit plan. A *defined-benefit (pension) plan.*

fixed budget. A plan that provides for specified amounts of *expenditures* and *receipts* that do not vary with activity levels. Sometimes called a "static budget." Contrast with *flexible budget.*

fixed charges earned (coverage) ratio. *Income* before *interest expense* and *income tax expense* divided by interest expense.

fixed cost (expense). An *expenditure* or *expense* that does not vary with volume of activity, at least in the short run. See *capacity costs*, which include *enabling costs* and *standby costs*, and *programmed costs* for various subdivisions of fixed costs. See *cost terminology.*

fixed liability. *Long-term* liability.

fixed manufacturing overhead applied. The portion of *fixed manufacturing overhead cost* allocated to units produced during a period.

flexible budget. *Budget* that projects receipts and expenditures as a function of activity levels. Contrast with *fixed budget.*

flexible budget allowance. With respect to manufacturing overhead, the total cost that should have been incurred at the level of activity actually experienced during the period.

float. *Checks* whose amounts have been *added* to the depositor's bank account, but not yet subtracted from the *drawer's* bank account.

flow. The change in the amount of an item over time. Contrast with *stock.*

flow assumption. When a *withdrawal* is made from *inventory*, the cost of the withdrawal must be computed by a flow assumption if *specific identification* of units is not used. The usual flow assumptions are *FIFO, LIFO,* and *weighted-average.*

flow of costs. *Costs* passing through various classifications within an *entity.* See the diagram on page 914 for a summary of *product* and *period cost* flows.

flow-through method. Accounting for the *investment credit* to show all income statement benefits of the credit in the year of acquisition, rather than spreading them over the life of the asset acquired, called the "deferral method." The *APB* preferred the deferral method in *Opinion* No. 2 (1962) but accepted the flow-through method in *Opinion* No. 4 (1964). The term is also used in connection with *depreciation* accounting, where the *straight-line method* is used for financial reporting and an *accelerated* method for tax reporting. Followers of the flow-through method would not recognize a *deferred tax liability. APB Opinion* No. 11 prohibits the use of the flow-through approach in financial reporting, although it has been used by some regulatory commissions.

FOB. Free on board some location (for example, FOB shipping point; FOB destination); the *invoice* price includes delivery at seller's expense to that location. Title to goods usually passes from seller to buyer at the FOB location.

footing. Adding a column of figures.

footnotes. More detailed information than that provided in the *income statement, balance sheet, statement of retained earnings*, and *statement of changes in financial position*; these are considered an integral part of the statements and are covered by the *auditor's report.* Sometimes called "notes."

forecast. An estimate or projection of costs or revenues or both.

foreclosure. The borrower fails to make a required payment on a *mortgage*; the lender takes possession of the property for his or her own use or sale. Assume that the lender sells the property but the proceeds of sale are insufficient to cover the outstanding balance on the loan at the time of foreclosure. Under the terms of most mortgages, the lender becomes an unsecured creditor of the borrower for the still-unrecovered balance of the loan.

foreign currency. For *financial statements* prepared in a given currency, any other currency.

foreign exchange gain or loss. Gain or loss from holding *net* foreign *monetary items* during a period when the *exchange rate* changes.

Form 10-K. See *10-K*.

forward exchange contract. An agreement to exchange at a specified future date currencies of different countries at a specified rate called the "forward rate."

franchise. A privilege granted or sold, such as to use a name or to sell products or services.

free on board. *FOB*.

freight-in. The *cost* of freight or shipping incurred in acquiring *inventory*, preferably treated as a part of the cost of *inventory*. Often shown temporarily in an *adjunct account* that is closed at the end of the period with other purchase accounts to the inventory account by the acquirer.

freight-out. The *cost* of freight or shipping incurred in selling *inventory*, treated by the seller as a selling *expense* in the period of sale.

full (aborption) costing. *Absorption costing*; the "full" is not necessary, but is often used for emphasis. See *reserve recognition accounting* for another definition in the context of accounting for natural resources.

full disclosure. The reporting policy requiring that all significant or *material* information is to be presented in the financial statements. See *fair presentation*.

fully diluted earnings per share. Smallest *earnings per share* figure on *common stock* that can be obtained by computing earnings per share for all possible combinations of assumed *exercise* or *conversion* of *potentially dilutive securities*. Must be reported on the *income statement* if it is 97 percent or less of earnings available to common shareholders divided by the average number of common shares outstanding during the period.

fully vested. Said of a *pension plan* when an employee (or his or her estate) has rights to all the benefits purchased with the employer's contributions to the plan even if the employee is not employed by this employer at the time of death or retirement.

function. In governmental accounting, said of a group of related activities for accomplishing a service or regulatory program for which the governmental unit is responsible. In mathematics, a rule for associating a number, called the dependent variable, with another number or numbers, called independent variable(s).

functional classification. *Income statement* reporting form in which *expenses* are reported by functions, that is,

cost of goods sold, administrative expenses, financing expenses, selling expenses; contrast with *natural classification*.

fund. An *asset* or group of assets set aside for a specific purpose. See also *fund accounting*.

fund accounting. The accounting for resources, obligations, and *capital* balances, usually of a not-for-profit or governmental *entity*, which have been segregated into *accounts* representing logical groupings based on legal, donor, or administrative restrictions or requirements. The groupings are described as "funds." The accounts of each fund are *self-balancing* and from them a *balance sheet* and an operating statement for each fund can be prepared. See *fund* and *fund balance*.

fund balance. In governmental accounting, the excess of assets of a *fund* over its liabilities and reserves; the not-for-profit equivalent of *owners' equity*.

funded. Said of a *pension plan* or other obligation when *funds* have been set aside to meet the obligation when it becomes due. The federal law for pension plans requires that all *normal costs* be funded as recognized. In addition, *actuarial accrued liability* of pension plans must be funded over 30 or over 40 years, depending on the circumstances.

funding. Replacing *short-term* liabilities with *long-term* debt.

funds. Generally *working capital*; current assets less current liabilities. Sometimes used to refer to *cash* or to cash and *marketable securities*.

funds provided by operations. An important subtotal in the *statement of changes in financial position*. This amount is the total of revenues producing *funds* less *expenses* requiring funds. Often, the amount is shown as *net income* plus expenses not requiring funds (such as depreciation charges) minus revenues not producing funds (such as revenues recognized under the *equity method* of accounting for a long-term investment). The statement of changes in financial position maintains the same distinctions between *continuing operations, discontinued operations*, and *income* or *loss* from *extraordinary items* as does the *income statement*.

funds statement. An informal name often used for the *statement of changes in financial position*.

funny money. Said of securities such as *convertible preferred stock, convertible bonds, options*, and *warrants* that have aspects of *common stock* equity but that did not reduce reported *earnings per share* prior to the issuance of *APB Opinions* No. 9, in 1967, and No. 15, in 1969.

FUTA. Federal Unemployment Tax Act, which provides for taxes to be collected at the federal level to help subsidize the individual states' administration of their unemployment compensation programs.

future value. Value at a specified future date of a sum increased at a specified *interest rate*.

G

GAAP. *Generally accepted accounting principles.* A plural noun.

gain. Increase in *owners' equity* caused by a transaction not part of a firm's typical, day-to-day operations and not part of owners' *investment* or *withdrawals*. The term "gain" (or "*loss*") is distinguished in two separate ways from related terms. First, gains (and losses) are generally used for nonoperating, incidental, peripheral, or nonroutine transactions: gain on sale of land in contrast to *gross margin* on *sale* of *inventory*. Second, gains and losses are *net* concepts, not gross concepts: gain or loss results from subtracting some measure of *cost* from the measure of inflow. *Revenues* and *expenses*, on the other hand, are gross concepts; their difference is a net concept. Gain is nonroutine and net, *profit* or *margin* is routine and net; revenue is routine and gross. Loss is net but can be either routine ("loss on sale of inventory") or not ("loss on disposal of segment of business").

gain contingency. See *contingency*.

gearing. British term for *financial leverage*.

gearing adjustment. Consider a firm, part of whose assets are *noncurrent liabilities* and who has experience *holding gains* on its *assets* during a period. All of the increase in wealth caused by the holding gains belongs to the owners; none typically belongs to the lenders. Some British accounting authorities believe that published *income statements* should show the part of the holding gain as financed with debt in *income* for the period. That part is called the "gearing adjustment."

general debt. Debt of a governmental unit legally payable from general revenues and backed by the full faith and credit of the governmental unit.

general expenses. *Operating expenses* other than those specifically assigned to cost of goods sold, selling, and administration.

general fixed asset (group of accounts). Accounts showing those long-term assets of a governmental unit not accounted for in *enterprise, trust,* or intragovernmental service funds.

general fund. Assets and liabilities of a nonprofit entity not specifically earmarked for other purposes; the primary operating fund of a governmental unit.

general journal. The formal record where transactions, or summaries of similar transactions, are recorded in *journal entry* form as they occur. Use of the adjective "general" usually implies only two columns for cash amounts

or that there are also various *special journals*, such as a *check register* or *sales journal*, in use.

general ledger. The name for the formal *ledger* containing all of the financial statement accounts. It has equal debits and credits as evidenced by the *trial balance*. Some of the accounts in the general ledger may be *controlling accounts*, supported by details contained in *subsidiary ledgers*.

general partner. Member of *partnership* personally liable for all debts of the partnership; contrast with *limited partner*.

general price index. A measure of the aggregate prices of a wide range of goods and services in the economy at one time relative to the prices during a base period. See *Consumer Price Index* and *GNP Implicit Price Deflator*. Contrast with *specific price index*.

general price level changes. Changes in the aggregate prices of a wide range of goods and services in the economy. These price changes are measured using a *general price index*. Contrast with *specific price changes*.

general price level-adjusted statements. See *constant dollar accounting*.

general purchasing power. The command of the dollar over a wide range of goods and services in the economy. The general purchasing power of the dollar is inversely related to changes in a general price index. See *general price index*.

general purchasing power accounting. See *constant dollar accounting*.

generally accepted accounting principles. GAAP. As previously defined by the *APB* and now by the *FASB*, the conventions, rules, and procedures necessary to define accepted accounting practice at a particular time; includes both broad guidelines and relatively detailed practices and procedures.

generally accepted auditing standards. The standards, as opposed to particular procedures, promulgated by the *AICPA* (in *Statements on Auditing Standards*) that concern "the auditor's professional quantities" and "the judgment exercised by him in the performance of his examination and in his report." Currently, there are 10 such standards: three general ones (concerned with proficiency, independence, and degree of care to be exercised), three standards of field work, and four standards of reporting. The first standard of reporting requires that the *auditor's report* state whether or not the *financial statements* are prepared in accordance with *generally accepted accounting principles*. Thus, the typical auditor's report says that the examination was conducted in accordance with generally accepted auditing standards and that the statements are prepared in accordance with generally accepted accounting principles. See *auditor's report*.

GNP Implicit Price Deflator (Index). A *price index* issued quarterly by the Office of Business Economics of the U.S. Department of Commerce. This index attempts to trace the price level of all *goods and services* comprising the *gross national product*. Contrast with *Consumer Price Index*.

going public. Said of a business when its *shares* become widely traded, rather than being closely held by relatively few shareholders. Issuing shares to the general investing public.

going-concern assumption. For accounting purposes a business is assumed to remain in operation long enough for all its current plans to be carried out. This assumption is part of the justification for the *acquisition cost* basis, rather than a *liquidation* or *exit value* basis, of accounting.

goods. Items of merchandise, supplies, raw materials, or finished goods. Sometimes the meaning of ''goods'' is extended to include all *tangible* items, as in the phrase ''goods and services.''

goods available for sale. The sum of *beginning inventory* plus all acquisitions of merchandise or finished goods during an *accounting period*.

goods in process. *Work in process.*

goodwill. The excess of cost of an acquired firm (or operating unit) over the current of *fair market value* of the separately identifiable *net assets* of the acquired unit. Before goodwill is recognized, all identifiable assets, whether or not on the books of the acquired unit, must be given a *fair market value*. For example, a firm has developed a *patent* that is not recognized on its books because of *SFAS No. 2*. If another company acquires the firm, the acquirer will recognize the patent at an amount equal to its estimated fair market value. Informally, the term is used to indicate the value of good customer relations, high employee morale, a well-respected business name, and so on, that are expected to result in greater than normal earning power.

goodwill method. A method of accounting for the *admission* of a new partner to a *partnership* when the new partner is to be credited with a portion of capital different from the value of the *tangible* assets contributed as a fraction of tangible assets on the partnership. See *bonus method* for a description and contrast.

GPL. General price level; usually used as an adjective modifying the word ''accounting'' to mean *constant dollar accounting*.

GPLA. General price level-adjusted accounting; *constant dollar accounting*.

GPP. General purchasing power; usually used as an adjective modifying the word ''accounting'' to mean *constant dollar accounting*.

graded vesting. Said of a *pension plan* where not all employee benefits are currently *vested*. By law, the benefits must become vested according to one of several formulas as time passes.

grandfather clause. An exemption in new accounting *pronouncements* exempting transactions that occurred before a given date from the new accounting treatment. For example, *APB Opinion* No. 17, adopted in 1970, exempted *goodwill* acquired before 1970 from required *amortization*. The term ''grandfather'' appears in the title to *SFAS No. 10*.

gross. Not adjusted or reduced by deductions or subtractions. Contrast with *net*.

gross margin. *Net sales* minus *cost of goods sold*.

gross margin percent. $100 \times (1 - cost\ of\ goods\ sold/ net\ sales) = 100 \times (gross\ margin/net\ sales)$.

gross national product. GNP. The market value within a nation for a year of all goods and services produced as measured by final sales of goods and services to individuals, corporations, and governments plus the excess of exports over imports.

gross price method (of recording purchase or sales discounts). The *purchase* (or *sale*) is recorded at its *invoice price*, not deducting the amounts of *discounts* available. Discounts taken are recorded in a *contra* account to purchases (or sales). Information on discounts lapsed is not made available, and for this reason, most firms prefer the *net price method* of recording purchase discounts.

gross profit. *Gross margin.*

gross profit method. A method of estimating *ending inventory* amounts. *Cost of goods sold* is measured as some fraction of sales; the *inventory equation* is then used to value *ending inventory*.

gross profit ratio. *Gross margin* divided by *net sales*.

gross sales. All *sales* at *invoice* prices, not reduced by *discounts, allowances, returns*, or other adjustments.

group depreciation. A method of calculating *depreciation* charges where similar assets are combined rather than depreciated separately. No gain or loss is recognized upon retirement of items from the group until the last item in the group is sold or retired. See *composite life method*.

guarantee. A promise to answer for payment of debt or performance of some obligation if the person liable for the debt or obligation fails to perform. A guarantee is a *contingency* of the *entity* making the promise. Often, the words ''guarantee'' and ''warranty'' are used to mean the same thing. In precise usage, however, ''guarantee'' means a promise to fulfill the promise of some person to perform a contractual obligation such as to pay a sum of money, whereas ''warranty'' is most often used to refer to promises about pieces of machinery or other products. See *warranty*.

H

half-year convention. An assumption used in *tax accounting* under *ACRS*, and sometimes in *financial accounting*, that *depreciable assets* were acquired at midyear of the year of acquisition. When this convention is used, the *depreciation charge* for the year is computed as one-half the charge that would be used if the assets had been acquired at the beginning of the year.

hidden reserve. The term refers to an amount by which *owners' equity* has been understated, perhaps deliberately. The understatement arises from an undervaluation of *assets* or overvaluation of *liabilities*. By undervaluing assets on this period's *balance sheet*, *net income* in some future period can be made to look artificially high by disposing of the asset: Actual *revenues* less artificially low cost of assets sold yields artificially high net income. There is no *account* that has this title.

historical cost. *Acquisition cost; original cost;* a *sunk cost.*

historical cost/constant dollar accounting. Accounting based on *historical cost* valuations measured in *constant dollars*. *Nonmonetary items* are restated to reflect changes in the *general purchasing power* of the dollar since the time the specific *assets* were acquired or *liabilities* were incurred. A *gain* or *loss* is recognized on *monetary items* as they are held over time periods when the general purchasing power of the dollar changes.

historical summary. A part of the *annual report* to shareholders that shows important items, such as *net income, revenues, expenses, asset* and *equity* totals, *earnings per share*, and the like, for 5 or 10 periods including the current one. Usually not as much detail is shown in the historical summary as in *comparative statements*, which typically report as much detail for the two preceding years as for the current year. Annual reports may contain both comparative statements and a historical summary.

holding company. A company that confines its activities to owning *stock* in, and supervising management of, other companies. A holding company usually owns a controlling interest in, that is, more than 50 percent of the voting stock of, the companies whose stock it holds. Contrast with *mutual fund*. See *conglomerate*. In British usage, the term refers to any company with controlling interest in another company.

holding gain or loss. Difference between end-of-period price and beginning-of-period price of an asset held during the period. Realized holding gains and losses are not ordinarily separately reported in financial statements. Unrealized gains are not usually reflected in income at all. Some unrealized losses, such as on inventory or marketable securities, are reflected in income or *owners' equity* as the losses occur; see *lower of cost or market*. See *inventory profit* for further refinement, including *gains* on *assets* sold during the period. See also *backlog depreciation*.

holding gain or loss net of inflation. Increase or decrease in the *current cost* of an asset while it is held measured in units of *constant dollars*.

holding period. The time between acquisition and disposition of an *asset*. The length of the holding period can affect the tax rate applied to the *gain* or *loss* upon sale.

horizontal analysis. *Time-series analysis.*

human resource accounting. A term used to describe a variety of proposals that seek to report and emphasize the importance of human resources—knowledgeable, trained, and loyal employees—in a company's earning process and total assets.

hurdle rate. Required rate of return in a *discounted cash flow* analysis.

hybrid security. *Security*, such as a *convertible bond*, containing elements of both *debt* and *owners' equity*.

hypothecation. The *pledging* of property, without transfer of title or possession, to secure a loan.

I

I. *Identity matrix.*

IAA. *Interamerican Accounting Association.*

ideal standard costs. *Standard costs* set equal to those that would be incurred under the best possible conditions.

identity matrix. A square *matrix* with ones on the main diagonal and zeros elsewhere; a matrix **I** such that for any other matrix **A**, **IA** = **AI** = **A**. The matrix equivalent to the number one.

IIA. *Institute of Internal Auditors.*

IMA. Institute of Management Accounting. See *CMA* and *National Association of Accountants*.

implicit interest. *Interest* not paid or received. See *interest, imputed*. All transactions involving the deferred payment or receipt of cash involve interest, whether explicitly mentioned or not. The implicit interest on a single-payment *note* is the difference between the amount collected at maturity less the amount lent at the start of the loan. The implicit *interest rate* per year can be computed from

$$\frac{\text{Cash Received at Maturity}}{\text{Cash Lent}^{(1/t)}} - 1$$

where t is the term of the loan in years; t need not be an integer.

imprest fund. *Petty cash fund.*

improvement. An *expenditure* to extend the useful life of an *asset* or to improve its performance (rate of output, cost) over that of the original asset. Such expenditures are *capitalized* as part of the asset's cost. Sometimes called "betterment." Contrast with *maintenance* and *repair.*

imputed cost. A cost that does not appear in accounting records, such as the *interest* that could be earned on cash spent to acquire inventories rather than, say, government bonds. Or, consider a firm that owns the buildings it occupies. This firm has an imputed cost for rent in an amount equal to what it would have to pay to use similar buildings owned by another.

imputed interest. See *interest, imputed.*

in the black (red). Operating at a profit (loss).

income. *Excess of revenues* and *gains* over *expenses* and *losses* for a period; *net income.* Sometimes used with an appropriate modifier to refer to the various intermediate amounts shown in a *multiple-step income statement.* Sometimes used to refer to revenues, as in "rental income." See *comprehensive income.*

income accounts. *Revenue* and *expense accounts.*

income before taxes. On the *income statement,* the difference between all *revenues* and *expenses* except *income tax* expense. Contrast with *net income* and *taxable income.*

income (revenue) bond. See *special revenue debt.*

income determination. See *determine.*

income distribution account. *Temporary account* sometimes debited when *dividends* are declared; closed to *retained earnings.*

income from continuing operations. As defined by *APB Opinion* No. 30, all *revenues* less all *expenses* except for the following: results of operations (including income tax effects) that have been or will be discontinued; *gains* or *losses,* including income tax effects, on disposal of segments of the business; gains or losses, including income tax effects, from *extraordinary items*; and the cumulative effect of *accounting changes.*

income from discontinued operations. *Income,* net of tax effects, from parts of the business that have been discontinued during the period or are to be discontinued in the near future. Such items are reported on a separate line of the *income statement* after *income from continuing operations* but before *extraordinary items.*

income smoothing. A method of timing business *transactions* or choosing *accounting principles* so that variations in reported *income* from year to year are reduced from what they would otherwise be. Although income smooth-

ing is an objective of some managements, it is not an official *accounting principle* or *reporting objective.*

income statement. The statement of *revenues, expenses, gains,* and *losses* for the period, ending with *net income* for the period. The *earnings-per-share* amount is usually shown on the income statement; the *reconciliation* of beginning and ending balances of *retained earnings* may also be shown in a combined statement of income and retained earnings. See *income from continuing operations, income from discontinued operations, extraordinary items, multiple-step, single-step.*

income summary. An *account* used in problem solving that serves as a surrogate for the *income statement.* All *revenues* are closed to the income summary account as *credits,* and all *expenses* as *debits.* The *balance* in the account, after all other *closing entries* are made, is then closed to the retained earnings or other *owners' equity* account and represents *net income* for the period.

income tax. An annual tax levied by the federal and other governments on the income of an entity.

income tax allocation. See *deferred tax liability* and *tax allocation: intrastatement.*

incremental. An adjective used to describe the change in *cost, expense, investment, cash flow, revenue, profit,* and the like if one or more units are produced or sold or if an activity is undertaken.

indenture. See *bond indenture.*

independence. The mental attitude required of the *CPA* in performing the *attest* function. It implies impartiality and that the members of the auditing CPA firm own no stock in the corporation being audited.

independent accountant. The *CPA* who performs the *attest* function for a firm.

indeterminate-term liability. An obligation not due at a definite time. This term is our own coinage to encompass the *deferred income tax credit* and *minority interest.*

indexation. An attempt by lawmakers or parties to a contract to cope with the effects of *inflation.* Amounts fixed in law or contracts are "indexed" when these amounts change as a given measure of price changes. For example, a so-called escalator clause (*COLA*) in a labor contract might provide that hourly wages will be increased as the *Consumer Price Index* increases. Many economists have suggested the indexation of numbers fixed in the *income tax* laws. If, for example, the personal *exemption* is $1,000 at the start of the period, prices rise by 10 percent during the period, and the personal exemption is indexed, then the personal exemption would automatically rise to $1,100 (= $1,000 + .10 × 1,000) at the end of the period.

indirect cost pool. Any grouping of individual costs that are not identified with a *cost objective.*

indirect costs. Costs of production not easily associated with the production of specific goods and services; *overhead costs*. May be *allocated* on some arbitrary basis to specific products or departments.

indirect labor (material) cost. An *indirect cost* for labor (material), such as for supervisors (supplies).

individual proprietorship. *Sole proprietorship.*

Industry Audit Guide. A series of publications by the *AICPA* providing specific *accounting* and *auditing principles* for specialized situations. Audit guides have been issued covering government contractors, state and local government units, investment companies, finance companies, brokers and dealers in securities, and many others.

inflation. A time of generally rising prices.

inflation accounting. Strictly speaking, *constant dollar accounting*. Some writers use the term, incorrectly, to mean *current cost accounting*.

information system. A system, sometimes formal and sometimes informal, for collecting, processing, and communicating data that are useful for the managerial functions of decision making, planning, and control, and for financial reporting under the *attest* requirement.

insolvent. Unable to pay debts when due. Said of a company even though *assets* exceed *liabilities*.

installment. Partial payment of a debt or collection of a receivable, usually according to a contract.

installment contracts receivable. The name used for *accounts receivable* when the *installment method* of recognizing revenue is used. Its *contra, unrealized gross margin*, is shown on the balance sheet as a subtraction from the amount receivable.

installment (sales) method. Recognizing *revenue* and *expense* (or *gross margin*) from a sales transaction in proportion to the fraction of the selling price collected during a period. Allowed by the *IRS* for income tax reporting, but acceptable in *GAAP (APB Opinion* No. 10) only when cash collections are reasonably uncertain. See *realized* (and *unrealized*) *gross margin.*

installment sales. Sales on account where the buyer promises to pay in several separate payments, called *installments*. Sometimes are, but need not be, accounted for on the *installment method*. If installment sales are accounted for with the sales *basis of revenue recognition* for financial reporting, but with the installment method for income tax returns, then a *deferred income tax liability* arises.

Institute of Internal Auditors. IIA. The national association of accountants who are engaged in internal auditing and are employed by business firms. Administers a comprehensive professional examination; those who pass qualify to be designated CIA, certified internal auditor.

Institute of Management Accounting. See *CMA.*

insurance. A contract for reimbursement of specific losses; purchased with insurance premiums. Self-insurance is not insurance but merely the willingness to assume risk of incurring losses while saving the premium.

intangible asset. A nonphysical, *noncurrent* right that gives a firm an exclusive or preferred position in the marketplace. Examples are a *copyright, patent, trademark, goodwill, organization costs, capitalized* advertising cost, computer programs, licenses for any of the preceding, government licenses (e.g., broadcasting or the right to sell liquor), *leases*, franchises, mailing lists, exploration permits, import and export permits, construction permits, and marketing quotas.

Interamerican Accounting Association. An organization, headquartered in Mexico City, devoted to facilitating interaction among accounting practitioners in Central America, North America, and South America.

intercompany elimination. See *eliminations.*

intercompany profit. If one *affiliated company* sells to another, and the goods remain in the second company's *inventory* at the end of the period, then the first company's *profit* has not been realized by a sale to an outsider. That profit is called "intercompany profit" and is eliminated from net *income* in *consolidated income statements* or when the *equity method* is used.

intercompany transaction. *Transaction* between *parent company* and *subsidiary* or between subsidiaries in a *consolidated entity* whose effects are eliminated in preparing *consolidated financial statements*. See *intercompany profit.*

intercorporate investment. A given *corporation* owns *shares* or *debt* issued by another.

interest. The charge or cost for using money; the earnings from lending money; expressed as a rate per period, usually 1 year, called the interest rate. See *effective interest rate* and *nominal interest rate.*

interest, imputed. If a borrower merely promises to pay a single amount, sometime later than the present, then the present value (computed at a *fair market* interest rate, called the "imputed interest rate") of the promise is less than the *face amount* to be paid at *maturity*. The difference between the face amount and the present value of a promise is called imputed interest. See also *imputed cost.*

interest factor. One plus the *interest* rate.

interest method. See *effective interest method.*

interest rate. See *interest*.

interfund accounts. In governmental accounting, the accounts that show transactions between funds, especially interfund receivables and payables.

interim statements. Statements issued for periods less than the regular, annual *accounting period*. Most corporations are required to issue interim statements on a quarterly basis. The basic issue in preparing interim reports is whether their purpose is to report on the interim period (1) as a self-contained accounting period, or (2) as an integral part of the year of which they are a part so that forecasts of annual performance can be made. *APB Opinion* No. 28 and the *SEC* require that interim reports be constructed largely to satisfy the second purpose.

internal audit. An *audit* conducted by employees to ascertain whether or not *internal control* procedures are working, as opposed to an external audit conducted by a *CPA*.

internal control. See *control system*.

internal rate of return. The discount rate that equates the net *present value* of a stream of cash outflows and inflows to zero.

internal reporting. Reporting for management's use in planning and control; contrast with *external reporting* for financial statement users.

Internal Revenue Service. IRS. Agency of the U.S. Treasury Department responsible for administering the Internal Revenue Code and collecting income, and certain other, taxes.

International Accounting Standards Committee. An organization that promotes the establishment of international accounting standards.

interperiod tax allocation. *Income tax expense* is assigned to the period when *income* is earned for *financial reporting* purposes rather than to the period when an obligation to pay *income taxes* is generated. This process is sometimes called "normalization" of income tax expense. See *deferred income tax liability*.

interpolation. The estimation of an unknown number intermediate between two (or more) known numbers.

Interpretations of Statements of Financial Accounting Standards. See *FASB Interpretations*.

intrastatement tax allocation. See *tax allocation: intrastatement*.

inventoriable costs. *Costs* incurred that are added to the cost of manufactured products. *Product costs (assets)* as opposed to *period expenses*.

inventory. As a noun, the *balance* in an asset *account* such as raw materials, supplies, work in process, and finished goods. As a verb, to calculate the *cost* of goods on hand at a given time or physically to count items on hand.

inventory equation. *Beginning inventory* + net additions − withdrawals = ending inventory. Ordinarily, additions are net purchases and withdrawals are *cost of goods sold*. Notice that ending inventory, to be shown on the balance sheet, and cost of goods sold, to be shown on the income statement, are not independent of each other. The larger is one, the smaller must be the other. In valuing inventories, beginning inventory and net purchases are usually known. In some inventory methods (for example, some applications of the *retail inventory method*), costs of goods sold is measured and the equation is used to find the cost of ending inventory. In most methods, cost of ending inventory is measured and the equation is used to find the cost of goods sold (withdrawals). In *current cost* (in contrast to *historical cost*) accounting, *additions* (in the equation) include holding gains, whether realized or not. Thus the current cost inventory equation is: Beginning Inventory (at Current Cost) + Purchases (Where Current Cost Is Historical Cost) + Holding Gains (Whether Realized or Not) − Ending Inventory (at Current Cost) = Cost of Goods Sold (Current Cost).

inventory flow assumption. *Flow assumption* for measuring *inventory* and *cost of goods sold*.

inventory holding gains. See *inventory profit*.

inventory layer. See *LIFO inventory layer*.

inventory profit. This term has several possible meanings. Consider the data in the accompanying illustration. The *historical cost* data are derived in the conventional manner; the firm uses a *FIFO cost flow assumption*. The *current cost* data are assumed, but are of the kind that the *FASB* requires in *SFAS No. 33*.

The term *income from continuing operations* refers to revenues less expenses based on current, rather than historical, costs. To that subtotal add realized holding gains to arrive at realized (conventional) income. To that, add unrealized holding gains to arrive at *economic income*.

The term "inventory profit" often refers (for example, in some *SEC* releases) to the realized holding gain, $110 in the illustration. The amount of inventory profit will usually be material when FIFO is used and prices are rising.

Others, including ourselves, prefer to use the term "inventory profit" to refer to the total *holding gain*, $300 (=$110 + $190, both realized and unrealized), but this appears to be a lost cause.

In periods of rising prices and increasing inventories, the realized holding gains under a FIFO cost flow assumption will be substantially larger than under LIFO. In the illustration, for example, assume under LIFO that the historical cost of goods sold is $4,800, that historical LIFO cost of beginning inventory is $600, and that historical LIFO cost of ending inventory is $800. Then income from

Inventory Profit Illustration

	(Historical) Acquisition Cost Assuming FIFO	Current Cost
Assumed Data		
Inventory, 1/1/82	$ 900	$1,100
Inventory, 12/31/82	1,160	1,550
Cost of Goods Sold for 1982 . .	4,740	4,850
Sales for 1982	$5,200	$5,200
INCOME STATEMENT FOR 1982		
Sales	$5,200	$5,200
Cost of Goods Sold.	4,740	4,850
(1) Income from Continuing Operations		$ 350
Realized Holding Gains		110[a]
(2) Realized Income = Conventional Net Income (under FIFO)	$ 460	$ 460
Unrealized Holding Gain		190[b]
(3) Economic income		$ 650

[a]Realized holding gain during a period is current cost of goods sold less historical cost of goods sold; for 1982 the realized holding gain under FIFO is $110 = $4,850 − $4,740. Some refer to this as "inventory profit."

[b]The total unrealized holding gain at any time is current cost of inventory on hand at that time less historical cost of that inventory. The unrealized holding gain during a period is unrealized holding gain at the end of the period less the unrealized holding gain at the beginning of the period. Unrealized holding gain prior to 1982 is $200 = $1,100 − $900. Unrealized holding gain during 1982 = ($1,550 − $1,160) − ($1,100 − $900) = $390 − $200 = $190.

continuing operations, based on current costs, remains $350 (=$5,200 − $4,850), realized holding gains are $50 (=$4,850 − $4,800), realized income is $400 (=$350 + $50), the unrealized holding gain for the year is $250 [=($1,550 − $800) − ($1,100 − $600)], and economic income is $650 (=$350 + $50 + $250). Because the only real effect of the cost flow assumption is to split the total holding gain into realized and unrealized portions, economic income is the same, independent of the cost flow assumption. The total of holding gains is $300 in the illustration. The choice of cost flow assumption merely determines the portion reported as realized.

inventory turnover. Number of times the average *inventory* has been sold during a period; *cost of goods sold* for a period divided by average inventory for the period. See *ratio*.

invested capital. *Contributed capital.*

investee. A company whose *stock* is owned by another.

investment. An *expenditure* to acquire property or other assets in order to produce *revenue;* the *asset* so acquired; hence a *current* expenditure made in anticipation of future income. Said of *securities* of other companies held for the long term and shown in a separate section of the *balance sheet;* in this context, contrast with *marketable securities.*

investment credit. A reduction in income tax liability granted by the federal government to firms that buy new equipment. This item is a credit, in that it is deducted from the tax bill, not from pretax income. The tax credit has been a given percentage of the purchase price of certain assets purchased. The actual rules and rates have changed over the years. See *flow-through method* and *carryforward.*

investment tax credit. *Investment credit.*

invoice. A document showing the details of a sale or purchase transaction.

IRR. *Internal rate of return.*

IRS. *Internal Revenue Service.*

issue. When a corporation exchanges its stock (or bonds) for cash or other assets, the corporation is said to issue, not sell, that stock (or bonds). Also used in the context of withdrawing supplies or materials from inventory for use in operations and drawing of a *check.*

issued shares. Those shares of *authorized capital stock* of a *corporation* that have been distributed to the shareholders. See *issue.* Shares of *treasury stock* are legally issued but are not considered to be *outstanding* for the purpose of voting, *dividend declarations,* and *earnings-per-share* calculations.

J

job cost sheet. A schedule showing actual or budgeted inputs for a special order.

job development credit. The name used for the *investment credit* in the 1971 tax law on this subject.

job-order costing. Accumulation of *costs* for a particular identifiable batch of product, known as a job, as it moves through production.

joint cost. Cost of simultaneously producing or otherwise acquiring two or more products, called joint products, that must, by the nature of the process, be produced or acquired together, such as the cost of beef and hides of cattle. Generally, the joint costs of production are allocated to the individual products in proportion to their respective sales value at the *splitoff point.* Other examples include central *corporate expenses, overhead* of a department when several products are manufactured, and *basket purchases.* See *common cost.* See *sterilized allocation.*

joint product. One of two or more outputs with significant value produced by a process that must be produced or acquired simultaneously. See *by-product* and *joint cost*.

journal. The place where transactions are recorded as they occur. The book of original entry.

journal entry. A recording in a *journal*, of equal *debits* and *credits*, with an explanation of the *transaction*, if necessary.

Journal of Accountancy. A monthly publication of the *AICPA*.

Journal of Accounting Research. Scholarly journal containing articles on theoretical and empirical aspects of accounting. Published three times a year by the Graduate School of Business of the University of Chicago.

journal voucher. A *voucher* documenting (and sometimes authorizing) a transaction, leading to an entry in the *journal*.

journalize. To make an entry in a *journal*.

K

kiting. This term means slightly different things in banking and auditing contexts. In both, however, it refers to the wrongful practice of taking advantage of the *float*, the time that elapses between the deposit of a *check* in one bank and its collection at another. In the banking context, an individual deposits in Bank A a check written on Bank B. He (or she) then writes checks against the deposit created in Bank A. Several days later, he deposits in Bank B a check written on Bank A, to cover the original check written on Bank B. Still later, he deposits in Bank A a check written on Bank B. The process of covering the deposit in Bank A with a check written on Bank B and vice versa is continued until an actual deposit of cash can be arranged. In the auditing context, kiting refers to a form of *window dressing* where the amount of the account Cash in Bank is made to appear larger than it actually is by depositing in Bank A a check written on Bank B without recording the check written on Bank B in the *check register* until after the close of the *accounting period*.

know-how. Technical or business information of the type defined under *trade secret*, but that is not maintained as a secret. The rules of accounting for this asset are the same as for other *intangibles*.

L

labor variances. The *price* (or *rate*) and *quantity* (or *usage*) *variances* for *direct labor* inputs in a *standard cost system*.

land. An *asset shown at acquisition cost* plus the *cost* of any nondepreciable *improvements*. In accounting, implies use as a plant or office site, rather than as a *natural resource*, such as timber land or farm land.

lapping (accounts receivable). The theft, by an employee, of cash sent in by a customer to discharge the latter's *payable*. The theft from the first customer is concealed by using cash received from a second customer. The theft from the second customer is concealed by using the cash received from a third customer, and so on. The process is continued until the thief returns the funds or can make the theft permanent by creating a fictitious *expense* or receivable write-off, or until the fraud is discovered.

lapse. To expire; said of, for example, an insurance policy or discounts made available for prompt payment that are not taken.

last in, first out. See *LIFO*.

layer. See *LIFO inventory layer*.

lead time. The time that elapses between placing an order and receipt of the *goods* or *services* ordered.

learning curve. A mathematical expression of the phenomenon that incremental unit costs to produce decrease as managers and labor gain experience from practice.

lease. A contract calling for the lessee (user) to pay the lessor (owner) for the use of an asset. A cancelable lease is one the lessee can cancel at any time. A noncancelable lease requires payments from the lessee for the life of the lease and usually has many of the economic characteristics of *debt financing*. Most long-term noncancelable leases meet the usual criteria to be classified as a *liability*, but some leases entered into before 1977 need not be shown as a liability. *SFAS No. 13* and the *SEC* require disclosure in notes to the financial statements of the commitments for long-term noncancelable leases. See *capital lease* and *operating lease*.

leasehold. The *asset* representing the right of the *lessee* to use leased property. See *lease* and *leasehold improvement*.

leasehold improvement. An *improvement* to leased property. Should be *amortized* over *service life* or the life of the lease, whichever is shorter.

least and latest rule. Pay the least amount of taxes as late as possible within the law to minimize the *present value* of tax payments for a given set of operations.

ledger. A book of accounts. See *general ledger* and *subsidiary ledger*; contrast with *journal*. Book of final entry.

legal capital. The amount of *contributed capital* that, according to state law, must remain permanently in the firm as protection for creditors.

legal entity. See *entity*.

lender. See *loan*.

lessee. See *lease*.

lessor. See *lease*.

letter stock. Privately placed *common shares*; so called because the *SEC* requires the purchaser to sign a letter of intent not to resell the shares.

leverage. "Operating leverage" refers to the tendency of *net income* to rise at a faster rate than sales when there are *fixed costs*. A doubling of sales, for example, usually implies a more than doubling of net income. "Financial leverage" (or "capital leverage") refers to the increased rate of return on *owners' equity* (see *ratio*) when an investment earns a return larger than the *interest rate* paid for *debt* financing. Because the interest charges on debt are usually fixed, any *incremental* income benefits owners and none explicitly benefits debtors. When "leverage" is used without a qualifying adjective, it usually refers to financial leverage and means the use of *long-term* debt in securing *funds* for the *entity*.

leveraged lease. A special form of *lease* involving three parties—a *lender*, a *lessor*, and a *lessee*. The lender, such as a bank or insurance company, lends a portion, say, 80 percent, of the cash required to acquire the *asset*. The lessor puts up the remainder, 20 percent, of the cash required. The lessor acquires the asset with the cash, using the asset as security for the loan, and leases it to the lessee on a *noncancelable* basis. The lessee makes periodic lease payments to the lessor, who in turn makes payments on the loan to the lender. Typically, the lessor has no obligation for the debt to the lender other than transferring a portion of the receipts from the lessee. If the lessee should default on required lease payments, then the lender can repossess the leased asset. The lessor is usually entitled to deductions for tax purposes for depreciation on the asset, for interest expense on the loan from the lender, and for any investment credit. The lease is leveraged in the sense that the lessor, who enjoys most of the risks and rewards of ownership, usually borrows most of the funds needed to acquire the asset. See *leverage*.

liability. A probable future sacrifice of economic benefits arising from present obligations of a particular *entity* to *transfer assets* or to provide services to other entities in the future as a result of past *transactions* or events. *SFAC No. 3* says that "probable" refers to that which can reasonably be expected or believed but is neither certain nor proved. A liability has three essential characteristics: (1) transfer of assets or services at a specified or determinable date; (2) the entity has little or no discretion to avoid the transfer; and (3) the event causing the obligation has already happened.

lien. The right of person A to satisfy a claim against person B by holding B's property as security or by seizing B's property.

life annuity. A *contingent annuity* in which payments cease at death of a specified person(s), usually the *annuitant(s)*.

LIFO. *Last in, first out*. An *inventory* flow assumption where the *cost of goods sold* is the cost of the most recently acquired units and the *ending inventory cost* is computed from costs of the oldest units; contrast with *FIFO*. In periods of rising prices and increasing inventories, LIFO leads to higher reported expenses and therefore lower reported income and lower balance sheet inventories than does FIFO. See also *FISH* and *inventory profit*.

LIFO conformity rule. The *IRS* requires that companies which use a *LIFO cost flow assumption* for *income taxes* also use LIFO in computing *income* reported in *financial statements* and forbids disclosure of *pro forma* results from using any other cost flow assumption. During 1981, this rule was challenged by a federal court decision in the Insilco case.

LIFO, dollar-value method. See *dollar-value LIFO method*.

LIFO inventory layer. The *ending inventory* for a period is likely to be larger than the *beginning inventory*. Under a *LIFO cost flow assumption*, this increase in physical quantities is given a value computed by the prices of the earliest purchases during the year. The LIFO inventory then consists of layers, sometimes called "slices," which typically consist of relatively small amounts of physical quantities from each of the past several years. Each layer carries the prices from near the beginning of the period when it was acquired. The earliest layers will typically (in periods of rising prices) have prices very much less than current prices. If inventory quantities should decline in a subsequent period, the latest layers enter cost of goods sold first.

LIFO reserve. *Unrealized holding gain* in *ending inventory*: current or *FIFO historical* cost of ending inventory less LIFO *historical cost*. See *reserve*.

limited liability. Shareholders of corporations are not personally liable for debts of the company.

limited partner. Member of a *partnership* not personally liable for debts of the partnership; every partnership must have at least one *general partner* who is fully liable.

line of credit. An agreement with a bank or set of banks for short-term borrowings on demand.

line-of-business reporting. See *segment reporting*.

liquid. Said of a business with a substantial amount (the amount is unspecified) of *working capital*, especially *quick assets*.

liquid assets. *Cash, current marketable securities*, and, sometimes, *current receivables*.

liquidating dividend. *Dividend* declared in the winding up of a business to distribute the assets of the company to the shareholders. Usually treated by recipient as a return of *investment*, not as *revenue*.

liquidation. Payment of a debt. Sale of assets in closing down a business or a segment thereof.

liquidation value per share. The amount each *share* of stock will receive if the corporation is dissolved. For *preferred stock* with a *liquidation preference*, a stated amount per share.

liquidity. Refers to the availability of *cash*, or near cash resources, for meeting a firm's obligations.

LISH. An acronym, conceived by George H. Sorter, for *last in, still here.* LISH is the same cost flow assumption as *FIFO*. Many readers of accounting statements find it easier to think about inventory questions in terms of items still on hand. Think of FIFO in connection with *cost of goods sold* but of LISH in connection with *ending inventory.* See *FISH.*

list price. The published or nominally quoted price for goods.

list price method. See *trade-in transaction.*

loan. An arrangement where the owner of property, called the lender, allows someone else, called the borrower, the use of the property for a period of time that is usually specified in the agreement setting up the loan. The borrower promises to return the property to the lender and, often, to make a payment for use of the property. Generally used when the property is *cash* and the payment for its use is *interest.*

long-lived (term) asset. An asset whose benefits are expected to be received over several years. A *noncurrent* asset; usually includes *investments, plant assets*, and *intangibles.*

long-term (construction) contract accounting. The *percentage-of-completion method* of *revenue* recognition. Sometimes used to mean the *completed contract method.*

long-term liability (debt). *Noncurrent liability.*

loss. Excess of *cost* over net proceeds for a single transaction; negative *income* for a period. A cost expiration that produced no *revenue.* See *gain* for a discussion of related and contrasting terms.

loss contingency. See *contingency.*

lower of cost or market. A basis for valuation of *inventory* or *marketable equity securities*. The inventory value is set at the lower of *acquisition cost* or *current replacement cost* (market), subject to the following constraints: First, the market value of an item used in the computation cannot exceed its *net realizable value*—an amount equal to selling price less reasonable costs to complete production and to sell the item. Second, the market value of an item used in the computation cannot be less than the net realizable value minus the normal *profit* ordinarily realized on disposition of completed items of this type. The lower-of-cost-or-market valuation is chosen as the lower of acquisition *cost* or replacement cost *(market)* subject to the upper and lower bounds on replacement cost established in the first two steps. Thus,

Market Value = Midvalue of (Replacement Cost, Net Realizable Value, Net Realizable Value Less Normal Profit Margin)

Lower-of-Cost- = Minimum of (Acquisition Cost, or-Market   Market Value) Valuation

The accompanying exhibit illustrates the calculation of the lower-of-cost-or-market valuation for four inventory items. Notice that each of the four possible outcomes occurs once in determining lower of cost or market. Item 1 uses acquisition cost; item 2 uses net realizable value; item 3 uses replacement cost; and item 4 uses net realizable value less normal profit.

	Item			
	1	2	3	4
Calculation of Market Value				
(a) Replacement Cost	$92	$96	$92	$96
(b) Net Realizable Value	95	95	95	95
(c) Net Realizable Value Less Normal Profit Margin [= (b) − $9]	86	86	86	86
(d) Market = Midvalue [(a), (b), (c)]	92	95	92	86
Calculation of Lower of Cost or Market				
(e) Acquisition Cost...........	90	97	96	90
(f) Market [= (d)]	92	95	92	86
(g) Lower of Cost or Market = Minimum [(e), (f)]	90	95	92	86

Lower of cost or market cannot be used for inventory on tax returns in combination with a *LIFO* flow assumption.

In the context of inventory, once the asset is written down, a new "original cost" basis is established and subsequent increases in market value are ignored in the accounts.

In the context of *marketable equity securities*, the method is applied separately to short-term and long-term portfolios of securities. Losses in market value on the short-term portfolio (and any subsequent recoveries in value up to original cost) are reported as part of *income from continuing operations* for the period. For the long-term portfolio, the losses (and subsequent recoveries, if any) are *debited* (or *credited*) directly to an *owners' equity contra account*.

Note that hyphens are not used when the term is used as a noun but hyphens are used when the term is used as an adjectival phrase.

lump-sum acquisition. *Basket purchase.*

M

maintenance. *Expenditures* undertaken to preserve an *asset's* service potential for its originally intended life; these expenditures are treated as *period expenses* or *product costs*; contrast with *improvement*. See *repair*.

make-or-buy decision. A managerial decision about whether the firm should produce a product internally or purchase it from others. Proper make-or-buy decisions in the short run result when *opportunity costs* are the only costs considered in decision making.

maker (of note) (of check). One who signs a *note* to borrow. One who signs a *check*; in this context synonymous with drawer; see *draft*.

management. Executive authority that operates a business.

Management Accounting. Monthly publication of the *NAA.*

management (managerial) accounting. Reporting designed to enhance the ability of management to do its job of decision making, planning, and control; contrast with *financial accounting*.

management audit. An audit conducted to ascertain whether the objectives, policies, and procedures for a firm or one of its operating units are properly carried out. Generally applies only to activities for which qualitative standards can be specified. See *audit* and *internal audit*.

management by exception. A principle of management where attention is focused only on performance that is significantly different from that expected.

managerial accounting. See *management accounting*.

manufacturing cost. Cost of producing goods, usually in a factory.

manufacturing expense. An imprecise, and generally incorrect, alternative title for *manufacturing overhead*.

manufacturing overhead. General manufacturing *costs* incurred in providing a capacity to carry on productive activities but that are not directly associated with identifiable units of product. *Fixed* manufacturing overhead costs are treated as a *product cost* under *absorption costing* but as an *expense* of the period under *direct costing*.

margin. *Revenue* less specified expenses. See *contribution margin*, *gross margin*, and *current margin*.

margin of safety. Excess of actual, or budgeted, sales over *breakeven* sales. Usually expressed in dollars; may be expressed in units of product.

marginal cost. The *incremental cost* or *differential cost* of the last unit added to production or the first unit subtracted from production. See *cost terminology*.

marginal costing. *Direct costing.*

marginal revenue. The increment in *revenue* from sale of one additional unit of product.

marginal tax rate. The tax imposed on the next dollar of taxable income generated; contrast with *average tax rate*.

markdown. See *markup* for definition and contrast.

markdown cancellation. See *markup* for definition and contrast.

market price. See *fair market price*.

market rate. The rate of *interest* a company must pay to borrow *funds* currently. See *effective rate*.

marketable equity securities. *Marketable securities* representing *owners' equity* interest in other companies, rather than *loans* to them.

marketable securities. *Stocks* and *bonds* of other companies held that can be readily sold on stock exchanges or over-the-counter markets and that the company plans to sell as cash is needed. Classified as *current assets* and as part of *working capital*. The same securities held for *long-term* purposes would be classified as *noncurrent assets*. *SFAS No. 12* requires the *lower-of-cost-or-market* valuation basis for all marketable equity securities but different accounting treatments (with differing effect on income) depending on whether the security is a *current* or a *noncurrent asset*.

markon. See *markup* for definition and contrast.

markup. When a retailer acquires items for *inventory*, the items are given a selling price. The difference between the original selling price and cost is most precisely called "markon," although many business people use the term "markup," and because of confusion of this use of "markup" with its precise definition (see below), "original markup'' is sometimes used. If the originally established retail price is increased, the precise term for the amount of price increase is ''markup,'' although ''additional markup'' is sometimes used. If a selling price is lowered, the terms ''markdown'' and ''markup cancellation'' are used. ''Markup cancellation'' refers to reduction in price following ''additional markups'' and can, by definition, be no more than the amount of the additional markup; ''cancellation of additional markup,'' although not used, is descriptive. ''Markdown'' refers to price reductions from the original retail price. A price increase after a markdown is a ''markdown cancellation.'' If original cost is $12 and original selling price is $20, then markon (original markup) is $8; if the price is later increased to $24, the $4 increase is markup (additional markup); if the price is later lowered to $21, the $3 reduction is markup cancellation; if price is lowered further to $17, the $4 reduction is $1 markup cancellation and $3 markdown; if price is later increased to $22, the $5 increase is $3 of markdown cancellation and $2 of markup (additional markup). Markup cancellations and markdowns are counted separately because the former are deducted (whereas the latter are not) in computing the selling prices of goods available for sale for the denominator of the *cost percentage* used in the conventional *retail inventory method*.

markup cancellation. See *markup* for definition and contrast.

markup percentage. *Markup* divided by (acquisition cost plus *markup*).

master budget. A *budget* projecting all *financial statements* and their components.

matching convention. The concept of recognizing cost expirations *(expenses)* in the same accounting period when the related *revenues* are recognized. Combining or simultaneously recognizing the revenues and expenses that jointly result from the same *transactions* or other events.

material. As an adjective, it means relatively important. See *materiality*. Currently, no operational definition exists. As a noun, *raw material*.

material variances. *Price* and *quantity variances* for *direct materials* in *standard cost systems*. Sometimes used to mean variances that are significant; see *materiality*.

materiality. The concept that accounting should disclose separately only those events that are relatively important (no operable definition yet exists) for the business or for understanding its statements. *SFAC No. 2* suggests that accounting information is material if ''the judgment of a reasonable person relying on the information would have been changed or influenced by the omission or misstatement.''

matrix. A rectangular array of numbers or mathematical symbols.

matrix inverse. For a given square *matrix* $\mathbf{A}$, the square matrix inverse is the matrix, $\mathbf{A}^{-1}$, such that $\mathbf{A}\mathbf{A}^{-1} = \mathbf{A}^{-1}\mathbf{A} = \mathbf{I}$, the *identity matrix*. Not all square matrices have inverses. Those that do not are called singular; those that do are nonsingular.

maturity. The date at which an obligation, such as the *principal* of a *bond* or a *note*, becomes due.

maturity value. The amount expected to be collected when a loan reaches *maturity*. Depending on the context, the amount may be *principal* or principal and *interest*.

measuring unit. See *attribute measured* for definition and contrast.

merchandise. *Finished goods* bought by a retailer or wholesaler for resale; contrast with finished goods of a manufacturing business.

merchandise turnover. *Inventory turnover* for merchandise; see *ratio*.

merchandising business. As opposed to a manufacturing or service business, one that purchases (rather than manufactures) *finished goods* for resale.

merger. The joining of two or more businesses into a single *economic entity*. See *holding company*.

minority interest. A *balance sheet account* on *consolidated statements* showing the *equity* in a less-than-100-percent-owned *subsidiary* company allocable to those who are not part of the controlling (majority) interest. May be classified either as shareholders' equity or as a liability of *indeterminate term* on the consolidated balance sheet. On the *income statement*, the minority's interest in the current period's income of the less-than-100-percent-owned subsidiary must be subtracted to arrive at consolidated *net income* for the period.

minority investment. A holding of 50 percent or less of the *voting stock* in another corporation. Accounted for with the *equity method* when sufficient shares are owned so that the investor can exercise ''significant influence,'' and with the *lower-of-cost-or-market* method otherwise. See *mutual fund*.

minutes book. A record of all actions authorized at corporate *board of directors'* or shareholders' meetings.

mixed cost. A *semifixed* or a *semivariable* cost.

modified cash basis. The *cash basis of accounting* with long-term assets accounted for with the *accrual basis of accounting*. Most uses of the term ''cash basis of accounting'' actually mean ''modified cash basis.''

monetary assets, liabilities. See *monetary items*.

monetary gain or loss. The *gain* or loss *in general purchasing power* as a result of holding *monetary assets* or liabilities during a period when the *general purchasing power of the dollar* changes. During periods of *inflation*, holders of net monetary assets lose, and holders of net monetary liabilities gain, general purchasing power. During periods of *deflation*, holders of net monetary assets gain, and holders of net monetary liabilities lose, general purchasing power. Explicitly reported in *constant dollar accounting*.

monetary items. Amounts fixed in terms of dollars by statute or contract. *Cash, accounts receivable, accounts payable*, and *debt*. The distinction between monetary and nonmonetary items is important for *constant dollar accounting* and for *foreign exchange gain* or *loss* computations. In the foreign exchange context, account amounts denominated in dollars are not monetary items, whereas amounts denominated in any other currency are monetary.

money. A word seldom used with precision in accounting, at least in part because economists have not yet agreed on its definition. Economists use the term to refer to both a medium of exchange and a unit of value. See *cash* and *monetary items*.

money purchase plan. A *pension plan* where the employer contributes a specified amount of cash each year to each employee's pension fund. Benefits ultimately received by the employee are not specifically defined but depend on the rate of return on the cash invested. Sometimes called a "defined-contribution" pension plan; contrast with *defined-benefit plan*. As of the mid-1980s, most corporate pension plans were defined-benefit plans because both the law and *generally accepted accounting principles* for pensions made defined-benefit plans more attractive than money purchase plans. *ERISA* makes money purchase plans relatively more attractive than they had been. We expect the relative number of money purchase plans to increase.

mortality table. Data of life expectancies or probabilities of death for persons of specified ages and sex.

mortgage. A claim given by the borrower (mortgagor) to the lender (mortgagee) against the borrower's property in return for a loan.

moving average. An *average* computed on observations over time. As a new observation becomes available, the oldest one is dropped so that the average is always computed for the same number of observations and only the most recent ones. Sometimes, however, this term is used synonymously with *weighted average*.

moving average method. *Weighted-average inventory method.*

multiple-step. Said of an *income statement* where various classes of *expenses* and *losses* are subtracted from *revenues* to show intermediate items such as *operating income*, income of the enterprise (operating income plus *interest* income), income to investors (income of the enterprise less *income taxes*), net income to shareholders (in- come to investors less interest charges), and income retained (income to shareholders less dividends). See *entity theory*.

municipal bond. A *bond* issued by a village, town, or city. *Interest* on such bonds is generally exempt from federal *income taxes* and from some state income taxes. Because bonds issued by state and county governments often have these characteristics, such bonds are often called "municipals" as well. Sometimes referred to as "tax exempts."

mutual fund. An investment company that issues its own stock to the public and uses the proceeds to invest in securities of other companies. A mutual fund usually owns less than 5 or 10 percent of the stock of any one company and accounts for its investments using current *market values*; contrast with *holding company*.

mutually exclusive projects. Competing investment projects, where accepting one project eliminates the possibility of undertaking the remaining projects.

N

NAARS. *National Automated Accounting Research System.*

National Association of Accountants. NAA. A national society generally open to all engaged in activities closely associated with *managerial accounting*. Oversees the administration of the *CMA* Examinations through the Institute of Management Accounting.

National Automated Accounting Research System. NAARS. A computer-based information retrieval system containing, among other things, the complete text of most public corporate annual reports and *Forms 10-K*. The system is available to users through the *AICPA*.

natural business year. A 12-month period chosen as the reporting period so that the end of the period coincides with a low point in activity or inventories. See *ratio* for a discussion of analyses of financial statements of companies using a natural business year.

natural classification. *Income statement* reporting form in which *expenses* are classified by nature of items as acquired, that is, materials, wages, salaries, insurance, and taxes, as well as depreciation; contrast with *functional classification*.

natural resources. Timber land, oil and gas wells, ore deposits, and other products of nature that have economic value. The cost of natural resources is subject to *depletion*. Natural resources are "nonrenewable" (for example, oil, coal, gas, ore deposits) or "renewable" (timber land, sod fields); the former are often called "wasting assets." See also *reserve recognition accounting* and *percentage depletion*.

negative confirmation. See *confirmation*.

negative goodwill. Refer to *goodwill*. When the purchase price of the company acquired is less than the sum of the *fair market value* of the *net assets* acquired, *APB Opinion* No. 16 requires that the valuation of noncurrent assets (except long-term *investments* in *marketable securities*) acquired be reduced proportionately until the purchase price equals the adjusted valuation of the fair market value of net assets acquired. If, after the adjusted valuation of noncurrent assets is reduced to zero, the purchase price is still less than the net assets acquired, then the difference is shown as a credit balance in the balance sheet as negative goodwill and is amortized to income over a period not to exceed 40 years. For negative goodwill to exist, someone must be willing to sell a company for less than the fair market value of net current assets and marketable securities. Because such a bargain purchase is rare, negative goodwill is rarely found in the financial statements; when it does appear, it generally signals unrecorded obligations, such as for *pensions*.

negotiable. Legally capable of being transferred by endorsement. Usually said of *checks* and *notes* and sometimes of *stocks* and *bearer bonds*.

net. Reduced by all relevant deductions.

net assets. *Owners' equity*; total *assets* minus total *liabilities*.

net bank position. From a firm's point of view, *cash* in a specific bank less *loans* payable to that bank.

net book value. *Book value*.

net current asset value (per share). *Working capital* divided by the number of common shares outstanding. Many security analysts think that when a common share trades in the market for an amount less than net current asset value, then the share is undervalued and should be purchased. We find this view naive because it ignores the efficiency of capital markets generally and, specifically, unrecorded obligations such as for *pension plans*, not currently reported as liabilities in the *balance sheet* under *GAAP*.

net current assets. *Working capital* = current assets − current liabilities.

net income. The excess of all *revenues* and *gains* for a period over all *expenses* and *losses* of the period. See *comprehensive income*.

net loss. The excess of all *expenses* and *losses* for a period over all *revenues* and *gains* of the period. Negative *net income*.

net markup. In the context of *retail inventory methods*, *markups* less markup cancellations; a figure that usually ignores *markdowns* and markdown cancellations.

net of tax method. A nonsanctioned method for dealing with the problem of income tax allocation; described in *APB Opinion* No 11. Deferred tax credit items are subtracted from specific asset amounts rather than being shown as a deferred credit or liability.

net of tax reporting. Reporting, such as for *income from discontinued operations, extraordinary items*, and *prior-period adjustments*, where the amounts presented in *financial statements* have been adjusted for all income tax effects. For example, if an extraordinary loss amounted to $10,000 and the marginal tax rate were 40 percent, then the extraordinary item would be reported "net of taxes" as a $6,000 loss. Hence, all income taxes may not be reported on one line of the income statement. The taxes will be allocated to *income from continuing operations, income from discontinued operations, extraordinary items*, cumulative effects of *accounting changes*, and *prior-period adjustments*.

net operating profit. Income from *continuing operations*.

net present value. Discounted or *present value* of all cash inflows and outflows of a project or from an *investment* at a given *discount rate*.

net price method (of recording purchase or sales discounts). The *purchase* (or *sale*) is recorded at its *invoice* price less all *discounts* made available under the assumption that nearly all discounts will be taken. Discounts lapsed through failure to pay promptly are recorded in an *adjunct account* to purchases (or sales) or, in the purchasing context, to an *expense* account. For purchases, management usually prefers to know about the amount of discounts lost because of inefficient operations, not the amounts taken, so that most managers prefer the net price method to the *gross price method*.

net realizable value. Selling price of an item less reasonable further costs to make the item ready for sale and to sell it. See *lower of cost or market*.

net sales. Sales (at gross invoice amount) less *returns, allowances*, freight paid for customers, and *discounts* taken.

net working capital. *Working capital;* the "net" is redundant in accounting. Financial analysts sometimes mean *current assets* when they speak of working capital, so for them the "net" is not redundant.

net worth. A misleading term, to be avoided, that means the same as *owners' equity*.

New York Stock Exchange. NYSE. A public market where various corporate *securities* are traded.

next in, first out. See *NIFO*.

NIFO. Next *in, first out*. In making decisions, many managers consider *replacement costs* (rather than *historical costs*) and refer to them as NIFO costs.

no par. Said of *stock* without a *par value*.

nominal accounts. *Temporary accounts* as opposed to *balance sheet accounts*. All nominal accounts are *closed* at the end of each *accounting period*.

nominal amount (value). An amount stated in dollars, in contrast to an amount stated in *constant dollars*. Contrast with *real amount (value)*.

nominal dollars. The measuring unit giving no consideration to differences in the *general purchasing power of the dollar* over time. The face amount of currency or coin, a *bond*, an *invoice*, a *receivable* is a nominal dollar amount. When that amount is adjusted for changes in *general purchasing power*, it is converted into a *constant dollar* amount.

nominal interest rate. A rate specified on a *debt* instrument, which usually differs from the market or *effective rate*. Also, a rate of *interest* quoted for a year. If the interest is compounded more often than annually, then the *effective interest rate* is higher than the nominal rate.

noncancelable. See *lease*.

nonconsolidated subsidiary. An *intercorporate investment* where more than 50 percent of the shares of the *subsidiary* are owned but the investment is accounted for with the *equity method* or, in some rare circumstances, the *cost method*.

noncontributory. Said of a *pension plan* where only the employer makes payments to a pension *fund*; contrast with *contributory*.

noncurrent. Due more than 1 year (or more than one *operating cycle*) hence.

nonexpendable fund. A governmental fund, whose *principal*, and sometimes earnings, may not be spent.

non-interest-bearing note. A *note* that bears no explicit interest. The *present value* of such a note at any time before *maturity* is less than the *face value* so long as *interest rates* are positive. *APB Opinion* No. 21 requires that the present value, not face value, of long-term non-interest-bearing notes be reported as the *asset* or *liability* amount in financial statements. See *interest, imputed*.

nonmanufacturing costs. All *costs* incurred other than those to produce goods.

nonmonetary items. All items that are not monetary; see *monetary items*.

nonoperating. In the *income statement* context, said of revenues and expenses arising from transactions incidental to the company's main line(s) of business. In the *statement of changes in financial position* context, said of all sources or uses of *working capital* other than working capital provided by operations. See *operations*.

nonprofit corporation. An incorporated *entity*, such as a hospital, with owners who do not share in the earnings. It usually emphasizes providing services rather than maximizing income.

nonrecurring. Said of an event that is not expected to happen often for a given firm. Under *APB Opinion* No 30, the effects of such events should be disclosed separately, but as part of *ordinary* items unless the event is also unusual. See *extraordinary* item.

normal cost. *Pension plan expenses* incurred during an *accounting period* for employment services performed during that period; contrast with *actuarial accrued liability* and see *funded*.

normal costing. Method of charging costs to products using actual *direct materials*, actual *direct labor*, and predetermined *factory overheard* rates.

normal spoilage. Costs incurred because of ordinary amounts of spoilage; such costs should be prorated to units produced as *product costs*; contrast with *abnormal spoilage*.

normal standard cost. The *cost* expected to be incurred under reasonably efficient operating conditions with adequate provision for an average amount of rework, spoilage, and the like.

normal volume. The level of production over a time span, usually 1 year, that will satisfy demand by purchasers.

normalization. See *interperiod tax allocation*.

note. An unconditional written promise by the maker (borrower) to pay a certain amount on demand or at a certain future time. See *footnotes* for another context.

note receivable discounted. A *note* assigned by the holder to another. If the note is assigned with recourse, it is the *contingent liability* of the assignor until the debt is paid. See *factoring*.

NOW account. Negotiable order of withdrawal. A *savings account* on which orders to pay, much like *checks* but technically not checks, can be drawn and given to others who can redeem the orders at the savings institution.

number of days sales in inventory (or receivables). Days of average inventory on hand (or average collection period for receivables). See *ratio*.

NYSE. *New York Stock Exchange*.

O

OASD(H)I. *Old Age, Survivors, Disability, and (Hospital) Insurance*.

objective. See *reporting objectives* and *objectivity*.

objectivity. The reporting policy implying that formal recognition will not be given to an event in financial statements until the magnitude of the events can be measured with reasonable accuracy and is subject to independent verification.

obsolescence. A decline in *market value* of an *asset* caused by improved alternatives becoming available that will be more *cost effective*; the decline in market value is unrelated to physical changes in the asset itself. See *partial obsolescence*.

Occupational Safety and Health Act. *OSHA*.

off-balance-sheet financing. A description often used for a *long-term, noncancelable lease* accounted for as an *operating lease* and other means of borrowing that do not qualify as *liabilities*.

Old Age, Survivors, Disability, and (Hospital) Insurance. The technical name for Social Security under the Federal Insurance Contribution Act (FICA).

on (open) account. Said of a *purchase* or *sale* when payment is expected sometime after delivery and no *note* evidencing the *debt* is given or received. The purchaser has generally signed an agreement sometime in the past promising to pay for such purchases according to an agreed time schedule. When a sale (purchase) is made on open account, *Accounts Receivable (Payable)* is *debited (credited)*.

on consignment. Said of goods delivered by the owner (the consignor) to another (the consignee) to be sold by the consignee; the owner is entitled to the return of the property or payment of an amount agreed upon in advance. The goods are assets of the consignor.

one-line consolidation. Said of an *intercorporate investment* accounted for with the *equity method*. The effects of this method on reported *income* and *balance sheet* total *assets* and *equities* are identical to those that would appear if the investee firm were consolidated, even though the income from the investment appears on a single line of the income statement and the net investment appears on a single line in the assets section of the balance sheet.

open account. Any *account* with a nonzero *debit* or *credit balance*. See *on (open) account*.

operating. An adjective used to refer to *revenue* and *expense* items relating to the company's main line(s) of business. See *operations*.

operating accounts. *Revenue, expense,* and *production cost accounts*; contrast with *balance sheet accounts*.

operating cycle. *Earnings cycle*.

operating expenses. *Expenses* incurred in the course of *ordinary* activities of an *entity*. Frequently, a classification including only *selling, general,* and *administrative* *expenses*, thereby excluding *cost of goods sold, interest,* and *income tax* expenses. See *operations*.

operating income. *Income from continuing operations*.

operating lease. A *lease* accounted for by the *lessee* without showing an *asset* for the lease rights *(leasehold)* or a *liability* for the lease payment obligations. Rental payments of the lessee are merely shown as *expenses* of the period. The asset remains on the lessor's *books*, where rental collections appear as *revenues*; contrast with *capital lease*.

operating leverage. Usually said of a firm with a large proportion of *fixed costs* in its *total costs*. Consider a book publisher or a railroad; the *incremental costs* of producing another book or transporting another freight car are much less than *average cost*, so the *gross margin* upon sale of the unit is relatively large. Contrast, for example, a grocery store, where the *cost of goods sold* is usually more than 95 percent of the selling price. For firms with equal profitability, however defined, the one with the larger percentage increase in income from a given percentage increase in unit sales is said to have the larger operating leverage. See *leverage* for contrast of this term with "financial leverage." See *cost terminology* for definition of terms involving the word "cost."

operating margin (based on current costs). *Revenues* from *sales* minus *current cost* of goods sold. A measure of operating efficiency that is independent of the *cost flow assumption* for *inventory*. Sometimes called "current (gross) margin." See *inventory profit* for illustrative computations.

operating ratio. See *ratio*.

operational control. See *control system*.

operations. A word not precisely defined in *accounting*. Generally, operating activities (producing and selling *goods* or *services*) are distinguished from financing activities (raising funds). Acquiring goods on account and then paying for them in one month, though generally classified as an operating activity, has the characteristics of a financing activity. Or consider the transaction of selling plant assets for a price in excess of book value. On the *income statement*, the gain is part of income from operations (continuing operations or discontinued operations, depending on the circumstances), but on the *statement of changes in financial position*, all of the funds received on disposition are reported below the "funds from operations" section, as a nonoperating source of funds, disposition of noncurrent assets. In income tax accounting an "operating loss" results whenever deductions are greater than taxable revenues.

opinion. The *auditor's report* containing an attestation or lack thereof. Also, *APB Opinion*.

opinion paragraph. Section of *auditor's report*, generally following the *scope paragraph*, giving the auditor's conclusion that the *financial statements* are (rarely, are not) in accordance with *GAAP* and present fairly the *financial position*, changes in financial position, and the results of *operations*.

opportunity cost. The *present value* of the *income* (or *costs*) that could be earned (or saved) from using an *asset* in its best alternative use to the one being considered.

option. The legal right to buy something during a specified period at a specified price, called the *exercise* price. Employee stock options should not be confused with put and call options traded in various public markets.

ordinary annuity. An *annuity in arrears*.

ordinary income. For income tax purposes, reportable *income* not qualifying as *capital gains*.

organization costs. The *costs* incurred in planning and establishing an *entity*; example of an *intangible* asset. Often, since the amounts are not *material*, the costs are treated as *expenses* in the period incurred even though the *expenditures* clearly provide future benefits and should be treated as *assets*.

original cost. *Acquisition cost*. In public utility accounting, the acquisition cost of the *entity* first devoting the asset to public use.

original entry. Entry in a *journal*.

OSHA. Occupational Safety and Health Act. The federal law that governs working conditions in commerce and industry.

outlay. The amount of an *expenditure*.

out-of-pocket. Said of an *expenditure* usually paid for with cash. An *incremental* cost.

out-of-stock cost. The estimated decrease in future *profit* as a result of losing customers because insufficient quantities of *inventory* are currently on hand to meet customers' demands.

output. Physical quantity or monetary measurement of *goods* and *services* produced.

outside director. A member of a corporate board of directors who is not a company officer and does not participate in the corporation's day-to-day management.

outstanding. Unpaid or uncollected. When said of *stock*, the shares issued less *treasury stock*. When said of checks, it means a check issued that did not clear the *drawer's* bank prior to the *bank statement* date.

over-and-short. Title for an *expense account* used to account for small differences between book balances of cash and actual cash and vouchers or receipts in *petty cash* or *change funds*.

overapplied (overabsorbed) overhead. An excess of costs applied, or *charged*, to product for a period over actual *overhead* costs during the period. A *credit balance* in an overhead account after overhead is assigned to product.

overdraft. A check written on a checking account that contains funds less than the amount of the check.

overhead costs. Any *cost* not associated directly with the production or sale of identifiable goods and services. Sometimes called "burden" or "indirect costs" and, in Britain, "oncosts." Frequently limited to manufacturing overhead. See *central corporate expenses* and *manufacturing overhead*.

overhead rate. Standard, or other predetermined rate at which *overhead costs* are applied to products or to services.

over-the-counter. Said of a *security* traded in a negotiated transaction, rather than in an auctioned one on an organized stock exchange, such as the *New York Stock Exchange*.

owners' equity. *Proprietorship; assets* minus *liabilities; paid-in capital* plus *retained earnings* of a corporation; partners' capital accounts in a *partnership*; owner's capital account in a *sole proprietorship*.

P

P&L. Profit and loss statement; *income statement*.

paid-in capital. Sum of balances in *capital stock* and *capital contributed in excess of par (or stated) value* accounts. Same as *contributed capital* (minus *donated capital*). Some use the term to mean only *capital contributed in excess of par (or stated) value*.

paid-in surplus. See *surplus*.

paper profit. A *gain* not yet realized through a *transaction*. An *unrealized holding gain*.

par. See *at par* and *face amount*.

par value. *Face amount* of a *security*.

par value method. The method of accounting for *treasury stock* that *debits* a common stock account with the *par value* of the shares required and allocates the remaining debits between the *additional paid-in capital* and *retained earnings* accounts; contrast with *cost method*.

parent company. Company owning more than 50 percent of the voting shares of another company, called the *subsidiary*.

partial obsolescence. As technology improves, the economic value of existing *assets* declines. In many cases, however, it will not pay a firm to replace the existing asset with a new one even though the new type, rather than the old, would be acquired if the acquisition were to be made currently. In these cases, the accountant should theoretically recognize a loss from partial obsolescence from the firm's owning an old, out-of-date asset, but *GAAP* does not permit recognition of partial obsolescence. The old asset will be carried at *cost* less *accumulated depreciation* until it is retired from service. See *obsolescence*.

partially funded. Said of a *pension plan* where not all earned benefits have been funded. See *funded* for funding requirements.

partially vested. Said of a *pension plan* where not all employee benefits are *vested*. See *graded vesting*.

participating dividend. *Dividend* paid to preferred shareholders in addition to the minimum preferred dividends when the *preferred stock* contract allows such sharing in earnings. Usually applied after dividends on *common stock* have reached a certain level.

participating preferred stock. *Preferred stock* with rights to *participating dividends*.

partner's drawing. A payment to a partner to be charged against his or her share of income or capital. The name of a *temporary account* to record such payments.

partnership. Contractual arrangement between individuals to share resources and operations in a jointly run business. See *general* and *limited partner* and *Uniform Partnership Act*.

past service cost. *Present value* at a given time of a *pension plan's* unrecognized, and usually unfunded, benefits assigned to employees for their service before the inception of the plan. A part of *actuarial accrued liability*. See *funded*; contrast with *normal cost*.

patent. A right granted for up to 17 years by the federal government to exclude others from manufacturing, using, or selling a claimed design, product, or plant (e.g., a new breed of rose) or from using a claimed process or method of manufacture. An asset if acquired by purchase. If developed internally, the development costs are *expensed* when incurred under current *GAAP*.

pay as you go. Said of an *income tax* scheme where periodic payments of income taxes are made during the period when the income to be taxed is being earned; in contrast to a scheme where no payments are due until the end of, or after, the period whose income is being taxed. (Called PAYE—pay as you earn—in Britain.) Sometimes used to describe an *unfunded pension plan*, where payments to pension plan beneficiaries are made from general corporate funds, not from cash previously contributed to a pension fund. Not acceptable as a method of accounting for pension plans.

payable. Unpaid but not necessarily due or past due.

payback period. Amount of time that must elapse before the cash inflows from a project equal the cash outflows.

payback reciprocal. One divided by the *payback period*. This number approximates the *internal rate of return* on a project when the project life is more than twice the payback period and the cash inflows are identical in every period after the initial period.

PAYE. See *pay as you go*.

payee. The person or entity to whom a cash payment is made or who will receive the stated amount of money on a check. See *draft*.

payout ratio. *Common stock dividends* declared for a year divided by net *income* to common stock for the year. A term used by financial analysts; contrast with *dividend yield*.

payroll taxes. Taxes levied because salaries or wages are paid; for example, *FICA* and unemployment compensation insurance taxes. Typically, the employer pays a portion and withholds part of the employee's wage fund.

P/E ratio. *Price-earnings ratio*.

Pension Benefit Guarantee Corporation. PBGC. A federal corporation established under *ERISA* to administer terminated pension plans and impose *liens* on corporate assets for certain unfunded pension liabilities.

pension fund. *Fund*, the assets of which are to be paid to retired ex-employees, usually as a *life annuity*. Usually held by an independent trustee and thus not an *asset* of the employer.

pension plan. Details or provisions of employer's contract with employees for paying retirement *annuities* or other benefits. See *funded*, *vested*, *normal cost*, *past service cost*, *prior service cost*, *actuarial accrued liability*, *money purchase plan*, and *defined-benefit plan*.

per books. An expression used to refer to the *book value* of an item at a specific time.

percent. Any number, expressed as a decimal, multiplied by 100.

percentage depletion (allowance). Deductible *expense* allowed in some cases by the federal *income tax* regulations; computed as a percentage of gross income from a *natural resource* independent of the unamortized cost of the asset. Because the amount of the total deductions for tax purposes is usually greater than the cost of the asset being *depleted*, many people think the deduction is an unfair tax advantage or "loophole."

percentage statement. A statement containing, in addition to (or instead of) dollar amounts, ratios of dollar amounts to some base. In a percentage *income statement*, the base is usually either *net sales* or total *revenues*; in a percentage *balance sheet*, the base is usually total *assets*.

percentage-of-completion method. Recognizing *revenues* and *expenses* on a job, order, or contract (1) in proportion to the *costs* incurred for the period divided by total costs expected to be incurred for the job or order ("cost-to-cost"), or (2) in proportion to engineers' or architects' estimates of the incremental degree of completion of the job, order, or contract during the period. Contrast with *completed contract method.*

period. *Accounting period.*

period cost. An inferior term for *period expense.*

period expense (charge). *Expenditure*, usually based on the passage of time, charged to operations of the accounting period rather than *capitalized* as an asset; contrast with *product cost.*

periodic inventory. A method of recording *inventory* that uses data on beginning inventory, additions to inventories, and ending inventory to find the cost of withdrawals from inventory.

periodic procedures. The process of making *adjusting entries*, *closing entries*, and preparing the *financial statements*, usually by use of *trial balances* and *work sheets.*

permanent account. An account that appears on the *balance sheet*; contrast with *temporary account.*

permanent capital. *Noncurrent liabilities* and *owners' equity.*

permanent difference. Difference between reported income and taxable income that will never be reversed and, hence, requires no entry in the *deferred income tax (liability)* account. An example is the difference between taxable and reportable income from interest earned on state and municipal bonds; contrast with *timing difference* and see *deferred income tax liability.*

perpetual annuity. *Perpetuity.*

perpetual inventory. Records on quantities and amounts of *inventory* that are changed or made current with each physical addition to or withdrawal from the stock of goods; an inventory so recorded. The records will show the physical quantities so and, frequently, the dollar valuations that should be on hand at any time. Because *cost of goods sold* is computed explicitly, the *inventory equation* can be used to compute *ending inventory.* The computed amount of ending inventory can be compared to the actual amount of ending inventory as a *control* device. Contrast with *periodic inventory.*

perpetuity. An *annuity* whose payments continue forever. The *present value* of a perpetuity in *arrears* is p/r where p is the periodic payment and r is the *interest rate* per period. If $100 is promised each year, in arrears, forever and the interest rate is 20 percent per year, then the value of the perpetuity is $500 = $100/.20.

personal account. *Drawing account.*

petty cash fund. Currency and coins maintained for expenditures that are made with cash on hand.

physical verification. *Verification*, by an *auditor*, performed by actually inspecting items in *inventory, plant assets*, and the like; may be based on statistical sampling procedures; in contrast to mere checking of written records.

plant. *Plant assets.*

plant asset turnover. Number of dollars of *sales* generated per dollar of *plant assets.* Equal to sales divided by average *plant assets.*

plant assets. Buildings, machinery, equipment, land, and natural resources. The phrase "property, plant, and equipment" is, therefore, a redundancy. In this context, "plant" means buildings.

pledging. The borrower assigns *assets* as security or *collateral* for repayment of a loan.

pledging of receivables. The process of using expected collections on accounts receivable as *collateral* for a loan. The borrower remains responsible for collecting the receivable but promises to use the proceeds to repay the debt.

plow back. To retain assets generated by earnings for continued investment in the business.

plug. For any *account*, beginning balance + additions − deductions = ending balance; if any three of the four items are known, the fourth can be found by plugging. In making a *journal entry*, often all *debits* are known, as are all but one of the *credits* (or vice versa). Because *double-entry* bookkeeping requires equal debits and credits, the unknown quantity can be computed by subtracting the sum of the known credits from the sum of all the debits (or vice versa). This process is also known as plugging. The unknown found is called the plug. For example, if a *discount* on *bonds payable* is being *amortized* with the *straight-line method*, then *interest expense* is a plug: interest expense = interest payable + discount amortization. See *trade-in transaction* for an example.

pooling-of-interests method. Accounting for a *business combination* by merely adding together the *book value* of the *assets* and *equities* of the combined firms. Contrast with *purchase method.* Generally leads to a higher reported *net income* for the combined firms than would be reported had the business combination been accounted for as a purchase, because the *market values* of the merged assets are generally larger than their book values. See *APB Opinion* No. 16 for the conditions that must be met before the pooling-of-interests treatment is acceptable.

positive confirmation. See *confirmation.*

post. To record entries in an *account* in a *ledger*; usually the entries are transferred from a *journal*.

post-closing trial balance. *Trial balance* taken after all *temporary accounts* have been closed.

post-statement events. Events with *material* impact that occur between the end of the *accounting period* and the formal publication of the *financial statements*. Such events must be disclosed in notes for the auditor to give a *clean opinion*, even though the events are subsequent to the period being reported on.

potentially dilutive. A *security* that may be converted into, or exchanged for, common stock and thereby reduce reported *earnings per share: options, warrants, convertible bonds*, and *convertible preferred stock*.

PPB. *Program budgeting;* the second "P" means "plan."

practical capacity. Maximum level at which the plant or department can operate efficiently.

preclosing trial balance. *Trial balance* taken at the end of the period before *closing entries*. In this sense an *adjusted trial balance*. Sometimes taken before *adjusting entries* and then synonymous with *unadjusted trial balance*.

predetermined (factory) overhead rate. Rate used in applying *overhead* to products or departments developed at the start of a period by dividing estimated overhead cost by the estimated number of units of the overhead allocation base (or *denominator volume*) activity.

preemptive right. The privilege of a shareholder to maintain a proportionate share of ownership by purchasing a proportionate share of any new stock issues.

preference as to assets. The rights of *preferred shareholders* to receive certain payments in case of dissolution before common shareholders receive payments.

preferred shares. *Capital stock* with a claim to *income* or *assets* after *bondholders* but before *common shares*. *Dividends* on preferred shares are *income distributions*, not *expenses*. See *cumulative preferred stock*.

premium. The excess of issue (or market) price over *par value*. For a different context, see *insurance*.

premium on capital stock. Alternative but inferior title for *capital contributed in excess of (par) or stated value*.

prepaid expense. An *expenditure* that leads to a *deferred charge* or *prepayment*; strictly speaking, a contradiction in terms, for an *expense* is a gone asset and this title refers to past *expenditures*, such as for rent or insurance premiums, that still have future benefits and thus are *assets*.

prepaid income. An inferior alternative title for *advances from customers*. An item should not be called *revenue* or *income* until earned, when goods are delivered or services are rendered.

prepayments. *Deferred charges. Assets* representing *expenditures* for future benefits. Rent and insurance premiums paid in advance are usually classified as *current* prepayments.

present value. Value today of an amount or amounts to be paid or received later, discounted at some *interest* or *discount rate*.

price. The quantity of one *good* or *service*, usually *cash*, asked in return for a unit of another good or service. See *fair market price*.

price index. A series of numbers, one for each period, that purports to represent some *average* of prices for a series of periods, relative to a base period.

price level. The number from a *price index* series for a given period or date.

price level-adjusted statements. *Financial statements* expressed in terms of dollars of uniform purchasing power. *Nonmonetary* items are restated to reflect changes in general *price levels* since the time specific *assets* were acquired and *liabilities* were incurred. A *gain* or *loss* is recognized on *monetary items* as they are held over time periods when the general *price level changes*. Conventional financial statements show *historical costs* and ignore differences in purchasing power in different periods.

price variance. In accounting for *standard costs* (actual cost per unit − standard cost per unit) times quantity purchased.

price-earnings ratio. At a given time, the market value of a company's *common stock*, per share, divided by the *earnings per common share* for the past year. See *ratio*.

primary earnings per share. Net *income* to *common shareholders* plus *interest (net of tax* effects*)* or *dividends* paid on *common stock equivalents* divided by (weighted average of common shares outstanding plus net increase in the number of common shares that would become *outstanding* if all common stock equivalents were exchanged for common shares, with cash proceeds, if any, used to retire common shares).

prime cost. Sum of *direct materials* plus *direct labor* costs assigned to product.

prime rate. The rate for loans charged by commercial banks to their most preferred risks. For the purpose of deciding whether a security is or is not a *common stock equivalent* in calculating *earnings per share*, the corporation should use the rate in effect at the bank at which it does business or an average of such rates if the corporation does business with more than one bank. The *Federal Reserve Bulletin* is considered the authoritative source of information about historical prime rates.

principal. An amount on which *interest* is charged or earned.

principle. See *generally accepted accounting principles*.

prior service cost. *Actuarial accrued liability*.

prior-period adjustment. A *debit* or *credit* made directly to *retained earnings* (which does not affect *income* for the period) to adjust earnings as calculated for prior periods. Such adjustments are now extremely rare. Theory might suggest that corrections of errors in accounting estimates (such as the *depreciable life* or *salvage value* of an asset) should be treated as adjustments to retained earnings. But *GAAP* require that corrections of such estimates flow through current, and perhaps future, *income statements*. See *accounting changes* and *accounting errors*.

pro forma statements. Hypothetical statements. Financial statements as they would appear if some event, such as a *merger* or increased production and sales had occurred or were to occur. Pro forma is often spelled as one word.

proceeds. The *funds* received from disposition of assets or from the issue of securities.

process costing. A method of *cost accounting* based on average costs (total cost divided by the *equivalent units* of work done in a period). Typically used for assembly lines or for products that are produced in a series of steps that are more continuous than discrete.

product. *Goods* or *services* produced.

product cost. Any *manufacturing cost* that can be inventoried. See *flow of costs* for example and contrast with *period expenses*.

production cost. *Manufacturing cost*.

production cost account. A *temporary account* for collecting *manufacturing costs* during a period.

production department. A department producing salable *goods* or *services*; contrast with *service department*.

production method (depreciation). The depreciable asset is given a *depreciable life* measured, not in elapsed time, but in units of output or perhaps in units of time of expected use. Then the *depreciation* charge for a period is a portion of depreciable cost equal to a fraction computed by dividing the actual output produced during the period by the expected total output to be produced over the life of the asset. Sometimes called the "units-of-production (or output) method."

production method (revenue recognition). *Percentage-of-completion method* for recognizing *revenue*.

productive capacity. In computing *current cost* of *long-term assets*, we are interested in the cost of reproducing the productive capacity (for example, the ability to manufacture 1 million units a year), not the cost of reproducing the actual physical assets currently used (see *reproduction cost*). Replacement cost of productive capacity will be the same as reproduction cost of assets only in the unusual case when there has been no technological improvement in production processes and the relative prices of goods and services used in production have remained approximately the same as when the currently used ones were acquired.

profit. Excess of *revenues* over *expenses* for a *transaction*; sometimes used synonymously with *net income* for the period.

profit and loss sharing ratio. The fraction of *net income* or loss allocable to a partner in a *partnership*. Need not be the same fraction as the partner's share of capital.

profit and loss statement. *Income statement*.

profit center. A unit of activity for which both *revenue* and *expenses* are accumulated; contrast with *cost center*.

profit margin. *Sales* minus all *expenses* as a single amount. Frequently used to mean ratio of sales minus all *operating* expenses divided by sales.

profit maximization. The doctrine that a given set of operations should be accounted for so as to make reported *net income* as large as possible; contrast with *conservatism*. This concept in accounting is slightly different from the profit-maximizing concept in economics, where the doctrine states that operations should be managed to maximize the present value of the firm's wealth, generally by equating *marginal costs* and *marginal revenues*.

profitability accounting. *Responsibility accounting*.

profit-volume graph. See *breakeven chart*.

profit-volume ratio. *Net income* divided by net sales in dollars.

program budgeting. Specification and analysis of inputs, outputs, costs, and alternatives that link plans to *budgets*.

programmed costs. A *fixed cost* not essential for carrying out operations. Research and development and advertising designed to generate new business are controllable, but once a commitment is made to incur them, they become fixed costs. Sometimes called *managed costs* or *discretionary costs*; contrast with *capacity costs*.

progressive tax. Tax for which the rate increases as the taxed base, such as income, increases; contrast with *regressive tax*.

project financing arrangement. As defined by *SFAS No. 47*, the financing of an investment project in which the lender looks principally to the *cash flows* and *earnings* of the project as the source of funds for repayment and to the *assets* of the project as *collateral* for the loan. The general *credit* of the project entity is usually not a significant factor, either because the entity is a *corporation* without other assets or because the financing is without direct *recourse* to the entity's owners.

projected financial statement. *Pro forma* financial statement.

promissory note. An unconditional written promise to pay a specified sum of money on demand or at a specified date.

proof of journal. The process of checking arithmetic accuracy of *journal entries* by testing for the equality of all *debits* with all *credits* since the last previous proof.

property dividend. A *dividend in kind*.

proprietary accounts. See *budgetary accounts* for contrast in context of governmental accounting.

proprietorship. *Assets* minus *liabilities* of an *entity*; equals *contributed capital* plus *retained earnings*.

proprietorship theory. The view of the corporation that emphasizes the form of the *accounting equation* that says *assets* − liabilities = owners' equity; contrast with *entity theory*. The major implication of a choice between these theories deals with the treatment of *subsidiaries*. For example, the view that *minority interest* is an *indeterminate-term liability* is based on the proprietorship theory. The proprietorship theory implies using a *single-step income statement*.

prorate. To *allocate* in proportion to some base; for example, allocate *service department* costs in proportion to hours of service used by the benefited department.

prospectus. Formal written document describing *securities* to be issued. See *proxy*.

protest fee. Fee charged by banks or other financial agencies when items (such as checks) presented for collection cannot be collected.

provision. Often the exact amount of an *expense* is uncertain, but must be recognized currently anyway. The entry for the estimated expense, such as for *income taxes* or expected costs under *warranty*, is

Expense (Estimated).	X
Liability (Estimated)	X

In American usage, the term "provision" is often used in the expense account title of the above entry. Thus, Provision for Income Taxes is used to mean the estimate of income tax expense. (In British usage, the term "provision" is used in the title for the estimated liability of the above entry, so that Provision for Income Taxes is a balance sheet account.)

proxy. Written authorization given by one person to another so that the second person can act for the first, such as to vote shares of stock. Of particular significance to accountants because the *SEC* presumes that financial information is distributed by management along with its proxy solicitations.

public accountant. Generally, this term is synonymous with *certified public accountant*. In some jurisdictions, individuals have been licensed as public accountants without being CPAs.

public accounting. That portion of accounting primarily involving the *attest* function, culminating in the *auditor's report*.

PuPU. An acronym for *pu*rchasing *p*ower *u*nit conceived by John C. Burton, former Chief Accountant of the *SEC*. Those who think *constant dollar accounting* is not particularly useful poke fun at it by calling it "PuPU accounting."

purchase allowance. A reduction in sales *invoice price* usually granted because the *goods* received by the purchaser were not exactly as ordered. The goods are not returned to the seller, but are purchased at a price lower than originally agreed upon.

purchase discount. A reduction in purchase *invoice price* granted for prompt payment. See *sales discount* and *terms of sale*.

purchase method. Accounting for a *business combination* by adding the acquired company's assets at the price paid for them to the acquiring company's assets. Contrast with *pooling-of-interests method*. The acquired assets are put on the books at current values, rather than original costs, the *amortization expenses* are usually larger (and reported income, smaller) than for the same business combination accounted for as a pooling of interests. The purchase method is required unless all criteria to be a pooling are met.

purchase order. Document authorizing a seller to deliver goods, with payment to be made later.

purchasing power gain or loss. *Monetary gain or loss*.

push-down accounting. Assume that Company A purchases substantially all of the *common shares* of Company B but that Company B must still issue its own *financial statements*. The question arises, shall the *basis* for Company B's *assets* and *equities* be changed on its own books to the same updated amounts at which they are shown on Company A's *consolidated* statements. When Company B shows the new asset and equity bases reflecting Company A's purchase, Company B is using "push-down accounting," because the new bases are "pushed down" from Company A (where they are required in *GAAP* to Company B (where the new bases would not appear in *historical cost accounting*). Since 1983, the *SEC* has required push-down accounting under some circumstances.

put. An option to sell *shares* of a publicly-traded corporation at a fixed price during a fixed time span. Contrast with *call*.

Q

qualified report (opinion). *Auditor's report* containing a statement that the auditor was unable to complete a satisfactory examination of all things considered relevant or that the auditor has doubts about the financial impact of some material item reported in the financial statements. See *except for* and *subject to*.

quantity discount. A reduction in purchase price as quantity purchased increases; amount of the discount is constrained by law (Robinson-Patman Act). Not to be confused with *purchase discount*.

quantity variance. In *standard cost* systems, the standard price per unit times (actual quantity used minus standard quantity that should be used).

quasi-reorganization. A *reorganization* where no new company is formed or no court has intervened, as would happen in *bankruptcy*. The primary purpose is to absorb a *deficit* and get a "fresh start."

quick assets. *Assets* readily convertible into *cash*; includes cash, *current marketable securities,* and *current receivables*.

quick ratio. Sum of (*cash, current marketable securities,* and *receivables*) divided by *current liabilities*. Some nonliquid receivables may be excluded from the numerator. Often called the "acid test ratio." See *ratio*.

R

R&D. See *research* and *development*.

Railroad Accounting Principles Board. RAPB. A board brought into existence by the Staggers Rail Act of 1980 to advise the Interstate Commerce Commission on matters of accounting affecting railroads. The RAPB had not started work by the time this book went to press.

RAPB. *Railroad Accounting Principles Board.*

rate of return (on total capital). See *ratio* and *rate of return on assets*.

rate of return on assets. *Net income* plus aftertax *interest charges* plus *minority interest* in income divided by average total *assets*. Perhaps the single most useful ratio for assessing management's overall operating performance. See *ratio*.

rate of return on common stock equity. See *ratio*.

rate of return on shareholders' (owners') equity. See *ratio*.

rate variance. *Price variance,* usually for *direct labor costs*.

ratio. The number resulting when one number is divided by another. Ratios are generally used to assess aspects of profitability, solvency, and liquidity. The commonly used financial ratios are of three kinds:

1. Those that summarize some aspect of *operations* for a period, usually a year.
2. Those that summarize some aspect of *financial position* at a given moment—the moment for which a balance sheet has been prepared.
3. Those that relate some aspect of operations to some aspect of financial position.

Exhibit 18.9 lists the most common financial ratios and shows separately both the numerator and denominator used to calculate the ratio.

For all ratios that require an average balance during the period, the average is most often derived as one-half the sum of the beginning and ending balances. Sophisticated analysts recognize, however, that when companies use a fiscal year different from the calendar year, this averaging of beginning and ending balances may be misleading. Consider, for example, the *rate of return on assets* of a retailing firm, such as J.C. Penney, which chooses a fiscal year to end in late January. It chooses a late January closing date at least in part because inventories are at a low level and are therefore easy to count—the Christmas merchandise has been sold and the Easter merchandise has not yet all been received. Furthermore, by January 31, most Christmas sales have been collected or returned, so receivable amounts are not unusually large. Thus at January 31, the amount of total assets is lower than at many other times during the year. Consequently, the denominator of the rate of return on assets, total assets, for the retailing firm is more likely to represent a smaller amount of total assets on hand during the year than the average amount. The rate of return on assets for companies that choose a fiscal year-end to coincide with low points in the inventory cycle is likely to be larger than if a more accurate estimate of the average amounts of total assets were used.

raw material. Goods purchased for use in manufacturing a product.

reacquired stock. *Treasury stock.*

real accounts. *Balance sheet accounts;* as opposed to *nominal accounts.* See *permanent accounts.*

real amount (value). An amount stated in *constant dollars.* For example, if an investment costing $100 is sold for $130 after a period of 10 percent general *inflation*, the *nominal amount* of *gain* is $30 (= $130 − $100) but the real amount of gain is C$ 20 (= $130 − 1.10 × $100), where "C$" denotes constant dollars of purchasing power on the date of sale.

real estate. *Land* and its *improvements*, such as landscaping and roads, but not buildings.

realizable value. *Market value* or, sometimes, *net realizable value.*

realization convention. The accounting practice of delaying the recognition of *gains* and *losses* from changes in the market price of *assets* until the assets are sold. However, unrealized losses on *inventory* and *marketable securities* classified as *current assets* are recognized prior to sale when the *lower-of-cost-or-market* valuation basis is used.

realize. To convert into *funds*. When applied to a *gain* or *loss*, implies that an *arm's-length transaction* has taken place. Contrast with *recognize*; a loss (as for example on *marketable equity securities*) may be recognized in the financial statements even though it has not yet been realized in a transaction.

realized gain (or loss) on marketable equity securities. An income statement account title for the difference between the proceeds of disposition and the *original cost* of *marketable equity securities.*

realized holding gain. See *inventory profit* for definition and an example.

rearrangement costs. Costs of reinstalling assets, perhaps in a different location. May be *capitalized* as part of the assets cost, just as is original installation cost.

recapitalization. *Reorganization.*

recapture. Various provisions of the *income tax* rules require refund by the taxpayer (recapture by the government) of various tax advantages under certain conditions. For example, the tax savings provided by the *investment credit* or by *accelerated depreciation* must be repaid if the item providing the tax savings is retired prematurely.

receipt. Acquisition of *cash.*

receivable. Any *collectible*, whether or not it is currently due.

receivable turnover. See *ratio.*

reciprocal holdings. Company A owns stock of Company B and Company B owns stock of Company A.

recognize. To enter a transaction in the accounts. Not synonymous with *realize.*

reconciliation. A calculation that shows how one balance or figure is derived systematically from another, such as a *reconciliation of retained earnings* or a *bank reconciliation schedule.* See *articulate.*

record date. *Dividends* are paid on payment date to those who own the stock on the record date.

recourse. See *note receivable discounted.*

recovery of unrealized loss on marketable securities. An *income statement account title* for the *gain* during the current period on the current asset portfolio of *marketable equity securities*. This gain will be *recognized* only to the extent that net losses have been recognized in preceding periods in amounts no smaller than the current gain. (The Allowance for Declines in Marketable Equity Securities account can never have a *debit balance.*)

redemption. Retirement by the issuer, usually by a purchase or *call*, of *stocks* or *bonds.*

redemption premium. *Call premium.*

redemption value. The price to be paid by a corporation to retire *bonds* or *preferred stock* if called before *maturity.*

refunding bond issue. Said of a *bond* issue whose proceeds are used to retire bonds already *outstanding.*

register. Collection of consecutive entries, or other information, in chronological order, such as a check register or an insurance register, which lists all insurance policies owned. If entries are recorded, it may serve as a *journal.*

registered bond. *Principal* of such a *bond* and *interest*, if registered as to interest, is paid to the owner listed on the books of the issuer. As opposed to a bearer bond, where the possessor of the bond is entitled to interest and principal.

registrar. An *agent*, usually a bank or trust company, appointed by a corporation to keep track of the names of shareholders and distributions of earnings.

registration statement. Statement required by the Securities Act of 1933 of most companies wishing to have their securities traded in public markets. The statement discloses financial data and other items of interest to potential investors.

regression analysis. A method of *cost estimates* based on statistical techniques for fitting a line (or its equivalent in higher mathematical dimensions) to an observed series of data points, usually by minimizing the sum of squared deviations of the observed data from the fitted line.

regressive tax. Tax for which the rate decreases as the taxed base, such as income, increases. Contrast with *progressive tax*.

Regulation S-X. The *SEC*'s regulation specifying the form and content of financial reports to the SEC.

rehabilitation. The improving of a used *asset* via an extensive repair. Ordinary *repairs* and *maintenance* restore or maintain expected *service potential* of an asset and are treated as *expenses*. A rehabilitation improves the asset beyond its current service potential, restoring the service potential to a significantly higher level than before the rehabilitation. Once rehabilitated, the asset may be better, but need not be, than it was when new. *Expenditures* for rehabilitation, like those for *betterments* and *improvements*, are *capitalized*.

reinvestment rate. In a *capital budgeting* context, the rate at which cash inflows from a project occurring before the project's completion are invested. Once such a rate is assumed, there will never be multiple *internal rates of return*. See *Descartes' rule of signs*.

relative sales value method. A method for *allocating joint costs* in proportion to *realizable values* of the joint products. For example, joint products A and B together cost $100; A sells for $60, whereas B sells for $90. Then A would be allocated ($60/$150) × $100 = .40 × $100 = $40 of cost, whereas B would be allocated ($90/$150) × $100 = $60 of cost.

relevant cost. *Incremental cost. Opportunity cost.*

relevant range. Activity levels over which costs are linear or for which *flexible budget* estimates and *breakeven charts* will remain valid.

remittance advice. Information on a *check* stub, or on a document attached to a check by the *drawer*, which tells the *payee* why a payment is being made.

rent. A charge for use of land, buildings, or other assets.

reorganization. A major change in the *capital structure* of a corporation that leads to changes in the rights, interests, and implied ownership of the various security owners. Usually results from a *merger* or agreement by senior security holders to take action to forestall *bankruptcy*.

repair. An *expenditure* to restore an *asset's* service potential after damage or after prolonged use. In the second sense, after prolonged use, the difference between repairs and maintenance is one of degree and not of kind. Treated as an *expense* of the period when incurred. Because repairs and maintenance are treated similarly in this regard, the distinction is not important. A repair helps to maintain capacity intact at levels planned when the *asset* was acquired; contrast with *improvement*.

replacement cost. For an asset, the current fair market price to purchase another, similar asset (with the same future benefit or service potential). *Current cost.* See *reproduction cost* and *productive capacity*. See also *distributable income* and *inventory profit*.

replacement cost method of depreciation. The original-cost *depreciation* charge is augmented by an amount based on a portion of the difference between the *current replacement cost* of the asset and its *original cost*.

replacement system of depreciation. See *retirement method of depreciation* for definition and contrast.

replacement value accounting. The Dutch term for *current cost accounting*.

report. *Financial statement; auditor's report.*

report form. This form of *balance sheet* typically shows *assets* minus *liabilities* as one total. Then, below that it shows the components of *owners' equity* summing to the same total. Often, the top section shows *current* assets less current liabilities before *noncurrent assets* less noncurrent liabilities. Contrast with *account form*.

reporting objectives (policies). The general purposes for which financial statements are prepared. The FASB has discussed these in *SFAC* No. 1.

reproduction cost. The *cost* necessary to acquire an *asset* similar in all physical respects to another asset for which a *current value* is wanted. See *replacement cost* and *productive capacity* for further contrast.

required rate of return. The opportunity *cost of capital*.

requisition. A formal written order or request, such as for withdrawal of supplies from the storeroom.

resale value. *Exit value. Net realizable value.*

research and development. Research is activity aimed at discovering new knowledge in hopes that such activity will be useful in creating a new product, process, or service or improving a present product, process, or service. Development is the translation of research findings or other knowledge into a new or improved product, process, or service. *SFAS No. 2* requires that costs of such activities be *expensed* as incurred, on the grounds that the future benefits are too uncertain to warrant *capitalization* as an asset. This treatment seems questionable to us, because we wonder why firms would continue to undertake R&D if there were no expectation of future benefit; if future benefits exist, then the *costs* should be assets.

reserve. When properly used in accounting, the term refers to an account that appropriates *retained earnings* and restricts dividend declarations. Appropriating retained earnings is itself a poor and vanishing practice, so the word should seldom be used in accounting. In addition, used in the past to indicate an *asset contra* (for example, "reserve for depreciation") or an *estimated liability* (for example, "*reserve for warranty costs*"). In any case, reserve accounts have *credit* balances and are not pools of *funds*, as the unwary reader might infer. If a company has set aside a pool of *cash* or *marketable securities*, then that cash will be called a *fund*. No other word in accounting is so misunderstood and misused, even by "experts" who should know better. A leading unabridged dictionary defines *reserve* as "Cash, or assets readily convertible into cash, held aside, as by a corporation, bank, state or national government, etc., to meet expected or unexpected demands." This definition is absolutely wrong in accounting. Reserves are not funds. For example, a contingency fund of $10,000 is created by depositing cash in a fund, and this entry is made:

Dr. Contingency Fund	10,000	
Cr. Cash		10,000

The following entry may accompany this entry if retained earnings are to be appropriated:

Dr. Retained Earnings.	10,000	
Cr. Reserve for Contingencies . .		10,000

The transaction leading to the first entry is an event of economic significance. The second entry has little economic impact for most firms. The problem with the word "reserve" arises because the second entry can be made without the first—a company can create a reserve, that is, appropriate retained earnings, without creating a fund. The problem is caused at least in part by the fact that, in common usage, "reserve" means a pool of assets, as in the phrase "oil reserves." The *Internal Revenue Service* does not help in dispelling confusion about the term *reserves*. The federal *income tax* return for corporations uses the title "Reserve for Bad Debts" to mean the "Allowance for Uncollectible Accounts" and speaks of the "Reserve Method" in referring to the *allowance method* for estimating *revenue* or *income* reductions from estimated *uncollectibles*. *Accounting Terminology Bulletin No. 1*, issued in 1953, suggested that the word should seldom be used.

reserve recognition accounting. In exploration for natural resources, there is the problem of what to do with the expenditures for exploration. Suppose that $10 million is spent to drill 10 holes ($1 million each) and that nine of them are dry, whereas one is a gusher containing oil with a *net realizable value* of $40 million. Dry hole, or *successful efforts*, accounting would *expense* $9 million and *capitalize* $1 million to be *depleted* as the oil was lifted from the ground. *SFAS No. 19*, now suspended, requires successful efforts accounting. Full costing would expense nothing but capitalize the $10 million of drilling costs to be depleted as the oil is lifted from the single productive well. Reserve recognition accounting would capitalize $40 million to be depleted as the oil is lifted, with a $30 million *credit* to *income* or *contributed capital*. The *balance sheet* shows the *net realizable value* of proven oil

and gas reserves. The *income statement* has three sorts of items: (1) current income resulting from production or "lifting profit," which is the *revenue* from sales of oil and gas less the expense based on the current valuation amount at which these items had been carried on the balance sheet; (2) profit or loss from exploration efforts, where the current value of new discoveries is revenue and all the exploration cost is expense; and (3) gain or loss on changes in current value during the year, which is in other contexts called a *holding gain or loss*.

residual income. In an external reporting context, this term refers to *net income* available for *common shares* (= net income less *preferred stock dividends*). In *managerial accounting*, this term refers to the excess of income for a division or *segment* of a company over the product of the *cost of capital* for the company multiplied by the average amount of capital invested in the division during the period over which the income was earned.

residual security. A *potentially dilutive security*. *Options, warrants, convertible bonds*, and *convertible preferred stock*.

residual value. At any time, the estimated or actual, *net realizable value* (that is, proceeds less removal costs) of an *asset*, usually a depreciable *plant asset*. In the context of depreciation accounting, this term is equivalent to *salvage value* and is preferable to *scrap value*, because the asset need not be scrapped. Sometimes used to mean net *book value*. In the context of a *noncancelable* lease, the estimated value of the leased asset at the end of the lease period. See *lease*.

responsibility accounting. Accounting for a business by considering various units as separate entities, or *profit centers*, giving management of each unit responsibility for the unit's *revenues* and *expenses*. Sometimes called "activity accounting." See *transfer price*.

responsibility center. Part or *segment* of an organization that is accountable for a specified set of activities. Also called *"accountability center."*

restricted assets. Governmental resources restricted by legal or contractual requirements for specific purposes.

restricted retained earnings. That part of *retained earnings* not legally available for *dividends*. See *retained earnings, appropriated*. Bond indentures and other loan contracts can curtail the legal ability of the corporation to declare dividends without formally requiring a retained earnings appropriation, but disclosure is required.

retail inventory method. Ascertaining cost amounts of *ending inventory* as follows (assuming *FIFO*): cost of ending inventory = (selling price of *goods available for sale − sales*) × *cost percentage*. *Cost of goods sold* is then computed from the *inventory equation*; costs of *beginning inventory, purchases*, and ending inventory are all known. (When *LIFO* is used, the method is similar to the *dollar-value LIFO method*). See *markup*.

retail terminology. See *markup*.

retained earnings. Net *income* over the life of a corporation less all *dividends* (including capitalization through *stock dividends*); *owners' equity* less *contributed capital*.

retained earnings, appropriated. An *account* set up by crediting it and debiting *retained earnings*. Used to indicate that a portion of retained earnings is not available for dividends. The practice of appropriating retained earnings is misleading unless all capital is earmarked with its use, which is not practicable. Use of formal retained earnings appropriations is declining.

retained earnings statement. *Generally accepted accounting principles* require that whenever *comparative balance sheets* and an *income statement* are presented, there must also be presented a *reconciliation* of the beginning and ending balances in the *retained earnings account*. This reconciliation can appear in a separate statement, in a combined statement of income and retained earnings, or in the balance sheet.

retirement method of depreciation. No entry is recorded for *depreciation expense* until an *asset* is retired from service. Then, an entry is made *debiting* depreciation expense and *crediting* the asset account for the cost of the asset retired. If the retired asset has a *salvage value*, the amount of the debit to depreciation expense is reduced by the amount of salvage value with a corresponding debit to cash, receivables, or salvaged materials. The "replacement system of depreciation" is similar, except that the debit to depreciation expense equals the cost of the new asset less the salvage value, if any, of the old asset. These methods were used by some public utilities. For example, if 10 telephone poles are acquired in Year 1 for $60 each and are replaced in Year 10 for $100 each, when the salvage value of the old poles is $5 each, then the accounting would be as follows:

Retirement Method.

Plant Assets.	600	
Cash		600

To acquire assets in Year 1.

Depreciation Expense	550	
Salvage Receivable	50	
Plant Assets.		600

To record retirement and depreciation in Year 10.

Plant Assets.	1,000	
Cash		1,000

To record acquisition of new assets in Year 10.

Replacement Method.

Plant Assets.	600	
Cash		600

To acquire assets in Year 1.

Depreciation Expense	950	
Salvage Receivable	50	
Cash		1,000

To record depreciation on old asset in amount quantified by net cost of replacement asset in Year 10.

The retirement method is like *FIFO* in that the cost of the first asset is recorded as depreciation and the cost of the second asset is put on the balance sheet. The replacement method is like *LIFO* in that the cost of the second asset determines the depreciation expense and the cost of the first asset remains on the balance sheet.

retirement plan. *Pension plan.*

return. A schedule of information required by governmental bodies, such as the tax return required by the *Internal Revenue Service*. Also the physical return of merchandise. See also *return on investment*.

return on investment. return on capital. *Income* (before distributions to suppliers of capital) for a period. As a rate, this amount divided by average total assets. *Interest*, net of tax effects, should be added back to *net income* for the numerator. See *ratio*.

revenue. The increase in *owners' equity* caused by a service rendered or the sale of goods. The monetary measure of a service rendered. *Sales* of products, merchandise, and services, and earnings from *interest, dividends*, rents, and the like. The amount of revenue is the expected *net present value* of the *net assets* received. Do not confuse with *receipt of funds*, which may occur before, when, or after revenue is recognized. Contrast with *gain* and *income*. See also *holding gain*. Some writers use the term *gross income* synonymously with *revenue*; such usage is to be avoided.

revenue center. A *responsibility center* within a firm that has control only over revenues generated; contrast with *cost center*. See *profit center*.

revenue expenditure. A phrase sometimes used to mean an *expense*, in contrast to a capital *expenditure* to acquire an *asset* or to discharge a *liability*. Avoid using this phrase; use *period expense* instead.

revenue received in advance. An inferior term for *advances from customers*.

reversal (reversing) entry. An *entry* in which all *debits* and *credits* are the credits and debits, respectively, of another entry, and in the same amounts. It is usually made on the first day of an *accounting period* to reverse a previous *adjusting entry*, usually an *accrual*. The purpose of such entries is to make the bookkeeper's tasks easier. Suppose that salaries are paid every other Friday, with paychecks compensating employees for the 2 weeks just ended. Total salaries accrue at the rate of $5,000 per 5-day work week. The bookkeeper is accustomed to making the following entry every other Friday:

(1) Salary Expense	10,000	
Cash		10,000
To record salary expense and salary payments.		

If paychecks are delivered to employees on Friday, June 25, then the *adjusting entry* made on June 30 (or, perhaps, later) to record accrued salaries for June 28, 29, and 30 would be

(2) Salary Expense	3,000	
Salaries Payable		3,000
To charge second-quarter operations with all salaries earned in second quarter.		

The Salary Expense account would be closed as part of the June 30 *closing entries*. On the next payday, July 9, the salary entry would have to be

(3) Salary Expense	7,000	
Salaries Payable	3,000	
Cash		10,000
To record salary payments split between expense for the third quarter (7 days) and liability carried over from the second quarter.		

To make entry (3), the bookkeeper must look back into the records to see how much of the debit is to Salaries Payable accrued from the previous quarter so that total debits are properly split between third-quarter expense and the liability carried over from the second quarter. Notice that this entry forces the bookkeeper both (a) to refer to balances in old accounts and (b) to make an entry different from the one customarily made, entry (1).

The reversing entry, made just after the books have been closed for the second quarter, makes the salary entry for July 9, the same as that made on all other Friday paydays. The reversing entry merely *reverses* the adjusting entry (2):

(4) Salaries Payable	3,000	
Salary Expense		3,000
To reverse the adjusting entry.		

This entry results in a zero balance in the Salaries Payable account and a *credit* balance in the Salary Expense account. If entry (4) is made just after the books are closed for the second quarter, then the entry on July 9 will be the customary entry (1). Entries (4) and (1) together have exactly the same effect as entry (3).

The procedure for using reversal entries is as follows: The required adjustment to record an accrual (*payable* or *receivable*) is made at the end of an *accounting period*; the closing entry is made as usual; as of the first day of the following period, an entry is made reversing the adjusting entry; when a payment is made (or received), the entry is recorded as though no adjusting entry had been recorded. Whether or not reversal entries are used affects the record-keeping procedures, but not the financial statements.

Also used to describe the entry reversing an incorrect entry before recording the correct entry.

reverse stock split. A stock split in which the number of shares *outstanding* is decreased. See *stock split*.

revolving fund. A *fund* whose amounts are continually expended and then replenished; for example, a *petty cash fund*.

revolving loan. A *loan* that is expected to be renewed at *maturity*.

right. The privilege to subscribe to new *stock* issues or to purchase stock. Usually, rights are contained in securities called *warrants*, and the warrants may be sold to others. See also *preemptive right*.

risk. A measure of the variability of the *return on investment*. For a given expected amount of return, most people prefer less risk to more risk. Therefore, in rational markets, investments with more risk usually promise, or are expected to yield, a higher rate of return than investments with lower risk. Most people use "risk" and "uncertainty" as synonyms. In technical language, however, these terms have different meanings. "Risk" is used when the probabilities attached to the various outcomes are known, such as the probabilities of heads or tails in the flip of a fair coin. "Uncertainty" refers to an event where the probabilities of the outcomes, such as winning or losing a lawsuit, can only be estimated.

An Open Account, Ruled and Balanced
(Steps indicated in parentheses correspond to steps described in "ruling an account.")

	Date 1985	Explanation	Ref.	Debit (1)		Date 1985	Explanation	Ref.	Credit (2)		
	Jan. 1	Balance	✔	100	00						
	Jan. 13		VR	121	37	Sept. 15		J		42	
	Mar. 20		VR	56	42	Nov. 12		J	413	15	
	June 5		J	1,138	09	Dec. 31	Balance	✔	1,050	59	(3)
	Aug. 18		J	1	21						
	Nov. 20		VR	38	43						
	Dec. 7		VR	8	64						
(4)	1986			1,464	16	1986			1,464	16	(4)
(5)	Jan. 1	Balance	✔	1,050	59						

risk premium. Extra compensation paid to an employee or extra interest paid to a lender, over amounts usually considered normal, in return for their undertaking to engage in activities more risky than normal.

risk-adjusted discount rate. In a *capital budgeting* context, a decision maker compares projects by comparing their *net present values* for a given *interest* rate, usually the *cost of capital*. If a given project's outcome is considered to be much more or much less risky than the normal undertakings of the company, then the interest rate will be increased (if the project is more risky) or decreased (if less risky) and the rate used is said to be risk-adjusted.

ROI. *Return on investment*, but usually used to refer to a single project and expressed as a ratio: *income* divided by average *cost* of *assets* devoted to the project.

royalty. Compensation for the use of property, usually a patent, copyrighted material, or natural resources. The amount is often expressed as a percentage of receipts from using the property or as an amount per unit produced.

RRA. See *Reserve recognition accounting*.

RRR. Required rate of return.

rule of 69. An amount of money invested at r percent per period will double in $69/r + .35$ periods. This approximation is accurate to one-tenth of a period for interest rates between $r\frac{1}{4}$ and 100 percent per period. For example, at 10 percent per period, the rule says that a given sum will double in $69/10 + .35 = 7.25$ periods. At 10 percent per period, a given sum actually doubles in 7.27+ periods.

rule of 72. An amount of money invested at r percent per period will double in $72/r$ periods. A reasonable approxi-

mation but not nearly as accurate as the *rule of 69*. For example, at 10 percent per period, the rule says that a given sum will double in $72/10 = 7.2$ periods.

rule of 78. The rule followed by many finance companies for allocating earnings on *loans* among the months of a year on the sum-of-the-months'-digits basis when equal monthly payments from the borrower are to be received. The sum of the digits from 1 through 12 is 78, so 12/78 of the year's earnings are allocated to the first month, 11/78 to the second month, and so on. See *sum-of-the-years' digits depreciation*.

ruling (and balancing) an account. The process of summarizing a series of entries in an *account* by computing a new *balance* and drawing double lines to indicate that the information above the double lines has been summarized in the new balance. The process is illustrated below. The steps are as follows. (1) Compute the sum of all *debit* entries including opening debit balance, if any—$1,464.16. (2) Compute the sum of all credit entries including opening credit balance, if any—$413.57. (3) If the amount in (1) is larger than the amount in (2), write the excess as a credit with a check mark—$1,464.16 − $413.57 = $1,050.59. (4) Add both debit and credit columns, which should both now sum to the same amount, and show that identical total at the foot of both columns. (5) Draw double lines under those numbers and write the excess of debits over credits as the new debit balance with a check mark. (6) If the amount in (2) is larger than the amount in (1), write the excess as a debit with a check mark. (7) Do steps (4) and (5) except that the excess becomes the new credit balance. (8) If the amount in (1) is equal to the amount in (2), the balance is zero and only the totals with the double lines beneath them need be shown. This process is illustrated in the figure above.

S

SAB. *Staff Accounting Bulletin* of the *SEC*.

safe-harbor lease. See *tax-transfer lease*.

salary. Compensation earned by managers, administrators, and professionals, not based on an hourly rate. Contrast with *wage*.

sale. A *revenue* transaction where *goods* or *services* are delivered to a customer in return for cash or a contractual obligation to pay.

sale and leaseback. Phrase used to describe a *financing* transaction where improved property is sold but is taken back for use on a long-term *lease*. Such transactions often have advantageous income tax effects, but usually have no effect on *financial statement income*.

sales allowance. A reduction in sales *invoice* price usually given because the goods received by the buyer are not exactly what was ordered. The amounts of such adjustments are often accumulated by the seller in a temporary *revenue contra account* having this, or a similar, title. See *sales discount*.

sales basis of revenue recognition. *Revenue* is recognized, not as goods are produced nor as orders are received, but only when the sale (delivery) has been consummated and cash or a legal receivable obtained. Most revenue is recognized on this basis. Compare with the *percentage-of-completion method* and the *installment method*. Identical with the *completed contract method*, but this latter term is ordinarily used only for *long-term* construction projects.

sales contra, estimated uncollectibles. A title for the *contra-revenue account* to recognize estimated reductions in income caused by accounts receivable that will not be collected. See *allowance for uncollectibles* and *allowance method*.

sales discount. Reduction in sales *invoice* price usually offered for prompt payment. See *terms of sale* and *2/10, n/30*.

sales return. The physical return of merchandise; the amounts of such returns are often accumulated by the seller in a temporary *revenue contra account*.

sales value method. *Relative sales value method*.

salvage value. Actual or estimated selling price, net of removal or disposal costs, of a used *plant asset* to be sold or otherwise retired. See *residual value*.

SAS. *Statement on Auditing Standards* of the *AICPA*.

SAV. *Supplemental actuarial value*.

schedule. Supporting set of calculations that show how figures in a statement or tax return are derived.

scientific method. *Effective interest method* of amortizing *bond discount* or *premium*.

scope paragraph. Section of *auditor's report* containing a description of the work done by the auditor.

scrap value. *Salvage value* assuming that item is to be junked. A *net realizable value*. *Residual value*.

SEC. Securities and Exchange Commission, an agency authorized by the U.S. Congress to regulate, among other things, the financial reporting practices of most public corporations. The SEC has indicated that it will usually allow the *FASB* to set accounting principles but it reserves the right to require more disclosure than required by the FASB. The SEC's accounting requirements are stated in its *Financial Reporting Releases* (formerly called *Accounting Series Releases, ASRs*) and *Regulation S-X*. See also *registration statement* and *10-K*.

secret reserve. *Hidden reserve*.

Securities and Exchange Commission. *SEC*.

security. Document that indicates ownership or indebtedness or potential ownership, such as an *option* or *warrant*.

segment (of a business). As defined by *APB Opinion No. 30*, "a component of an *entity* whose activities represent a separate major line of business or class of customer. . . . [It may be] a *subsidiary*, a division, or a department, . . . provided that its *assets*, results of *operations*, and activities can be clearly distinguished, physically and operationally for financial reporting purposes, from the other assets, results of operations, and activities of the entity." In *SFAS No. 14* a segment is defined as "A component of an enterprise engaged in promoting a product or service or a group of related products and services primarily to unaffiliated customers . . . for a profit."

segment reporting. Reporting of *sales*, *income*, and *assets* by *segments of a business*, usually classified by nature of products sold but sometimes by geographic area where goods are produced or sold, or by type of customers. Sometimes called "line-of-business reporting." *Central corporate expenses* are not allocated to the segments.

self-balancing. A set of records with equal *debits* and *credits*, such as the *ledger* (but not individual accounts), the *balance sheet*, and a *fund* in nonprofit accounting.

self-insurance. See *insurance*.

selling and administrative expenses. *Expenses* not specifically identifiable with, nor assigned to, production.

semifixed costs. *Costs* that increase with activity as a step function.

semivariable costs. *Costs* that increase strictly linearly with activity but that are positive at zero activity level. Royalty fees of 2 percent of sales are variable; royalty fees of $1,000 per year plus 2 percent of sales are semivariable.

senior securities. *Bonds* as opposed to *preferred stock; preferred stock* as opposed to *common stock.* The senior security has a claim against *earnings* or *assets* that must be met before the claim of less senior securities.

serial bonds. An *issue* of *bonds* that mature in part at one date, another part on another date, and so on; the various maturity dates usually are equally spaced; contrast them with *term bonds.*

service basis of depreciation. *Production method.*

service department. A department, such as the personnel or computer department, that provides services to other departments, rather than direct work on a salable product; contrast with *production department.* Costs of service departments whose services benefit manufacturing operations must be *allocated* to *product costs* under *absorption costing.*

service life. Period of expected usefulness of an asset; may not coincide with *depreciable life* for income tax purposes.

service potential. The future benefits embodied in an item that cause the item to be classified as an *asset.* Without service potential, there are no future benefits and the item should not be classified as an asset. *SFAS No. 3* suggests that the primary characteristic of service potential is the ability to generate future net cash inflows.

services. Useful work done by a person, a machine, or an organization. See *goods and services.*

setup. The time or costs required to prepare production equipment for doing a job.

SFAC. *Statement of Financial Accounting Concepts* from the *FASB.*

SFAS. *Statement of Financial Accounting Standards* from the *FASB.*

share. A unit of *stock* representing ownership in a corporation.

shareholders' equity. *Proprietorship* or *owners' equity* of a corporation. Because *stock* means inventory in Australian, British, and Canadian usage, the term "shareholders' equity" is usually used by Australian, British, and Canadian writers.

short-term. Current; ordinarily, due within 1 year.

shrinkage. An excess of *inventory* shown on the *books* over actual physical quantities on hand. Can result from theft or shoplifting as well as from evaporation or general wear and tear.

sight draft. A demand for payment drawn by a person to whom money is owed. The *draft* is presented to the borrower's (the debtor's) bank in expectation that the borrower will authorize its bank to disburse the funds. Such drafts are often used when a seller sells goods to a new customer in a different city. The seller is not sure whether the buyer will pay the bill. The seller sends the *bill* of lading, or other evidence of ownership of the goods, along with a sight draft to the buyer's bank. Before the goods can be released to the buyer, the buyer must instruct its bank to honor the sight draft by withdrawing funds from the buyer's account. Once the sight draft is honored, the bill of lading or other document evidencing ownership is handed over to the buyer and the goods become the property of the buyer.

simple interest. *Interest* calculated on *principal* where interest earned during periods before maturity of the loan is neither added to the principal nor paid to the lender. *Interest* = principal × interest rate × time. Seldom used in economic calculations except for periods less than 1 year; contrast with *compound interest.*

single proprietorship. *Sole proprietorship.*

single-entry accounting. Accounting that is neither *self-balancing* nor *articulated*; that is, it does not rely on equal *debits* and *credits.* No *journal entries* are made. *Plugging* is required to derive *owners' equity* for the *balance sheet.*

single-step. Said of an *income statement* where *ordinary revenue* and *gain* items are shown first and totaled. Then all ordinary *expenses* and *losses* are totaled. Their difference, plus the effect of *income from discontinued operations* and *extraordinary items*, is shown as *net income*; contrast with *multiple-step* and see *proprietorship theory.*

sinking fund. *Assets* and their earnings earmarked for the retirement of bonds or other long-term obligations. Earnings of sinking fund investments are taxable income of the company.

sinking fund method of depreciation. The periodic charge is an amount such that when the charges are considered to be an *annuity*, the value of the annuity at the end of its depreciable life is equal to the *acquisition cost* of the asset. In theory, the charge for a period ought to include interest on the accumulated depreciation at the start of the period as well. A *fund* of cash is not necessarily, or even usually, accumulated. This method is rarely used.

skeleton account. *T-account.*

slide. The name of the error made by a bookkeeper in recording the digits of a number correctly with the decimal point misplaced, for example, recording $123.40 as $1,234.00 or as $12.34.

soak-up method. The *equity method.*

Social Security taxes. Taxes levied by the federal government on both employers and employees to provide *funds* to pay retired persons (or their survivors) who are entitled to receive such payments, either because they paid Social Security taxes themselves or because the Congress has declared them eligible. See *Old Age, Survivors, Disability*, and *(Hospital) Insurance*.

sole proprietorship. All *owners' equity* belongs to one person.

solvent. Able to meet debts when due.

SOP. *Statement of Position* (of *AcSEC* of the *AICPA*).

sound value. A phrase used mainly in appraisals of *fixed assets* to mean *fair market value* or *replacement cost* in present condition.

source of funds. Any *transaction* that increases *working capital*.

sources and uses statement. *Statement of changes in financial position*.

SOYD. *Sum-of-the-years'-digits depreciation*.

special assessment. A compulsory levy made by a governmental unit on property to pay the costs of a specific improvement, or service, presumed not to benefit the general public but only the owners of the property so assessed. Accounted for in a special assessment fund.

special journal. A *journal*, such as a sales journal or cash disbursements journal, to record *transactions* of a similar nature that occur frequently.

special revenue debt. Debt of a governmental unit backed only by revenues from specific sources such as tolls from a bridge.

specific identification method. Method for valuing *ending inventory* and *cost of goods sold* by identifying actual units sold and in inventory and summing the actual costs of those individual units. Usually used for items with large unit value, such as jewelry, automobiles, and fur coats.

specific price changes. Changes in the market prices of specific *goods and services*; contrast with *general price level changes*.

specific price index. A measure of the price of a specific good or service, or a small group of similar goods or services, at one time relative to the price during a base period; contrast with *general price index*. See *dollar-value LIFO method*.

spending variance. In *standard cost systems*, the difference between *budgeted overhead* (for a given production plan) and actual *overhead costs* incurred.

split. *Stock split*. Sometimes called "splitup."

splitoff point. The point where all costs are no longer *joint costs* but can be identified with individual products or perhaps with a smaller number of *joint products*.

spoilage. See *abnormal spoilage* and *normal spoilage*.

spread sheet. A *work sheet* organized like a *matrix* that provides a two-way classification of accounting data. The rows and columns are both labeled with *account* titles. An entry in a row represents a *debit*, whereas an entry in a column represents a *credit*. Thus, the number "100" in the "cash" row and the "accounts receivable" column records an entry debiting cash and crediting accounts receivable for $100. A given row total indicates all debit entries to the account represented by that row, and a given column total indicates the sum of all credit entries to the account represented by the column.

squeeze. A term sometimes used for *plug*.

SSARS. See *Statement on Standards for Accounting and Review Services*.

stabilized accounting. *Constant dollar accounting*.

stable monetary unit assumption. In spite of *inflation* that appears to be a way of life, the assumption that underlies *historical cost/nominal dollar accounting*—namely, that current dollars and dollars of previous years can be meaningfully added together. No specific recognition is given to changing values of the dollar in the usual *financial statements*. See *constant dollar accounting*.

Staff Accounting Bulletin. An interpretation issued by the Staff of the Chief Accountant of the *SEC* "suggesting" how the various *Accounting Series Releases* should be applied in practice.

standard cost. Anticipated *cost* of producing a unit of output; a predetermined cost to be assigned to products produced. Standard cost implies a norm: what costs should be. Budgeted cost implies a forecast: something likely, but not necessarily a "should," as implied by a norm. Standard costs are used as the benchmark for gauging good and bad performance. While a budget may be used similarly, it need not be. A budget may be simply a planning document, subject to changes whenever plans change, whereas standard costs are usually not changed until technology changes or costs of labor and materials change.

standard cost system. *Product costing* using *standard costs* rather than actual costs. May be based on either *absorption* or *direct costing* principles.

standard manufacturing overhead. *Overhead costs* expected to be incurred per unit of time and per unit produced.

standard price (rate). Unit price established for materials or labor used in *standard cost systems*.

standard quantity allowed. The quantity of direct material or direct labor (inputs) that should have been used if the units of output had been produced in accordance with preset *standards*.

standby costs. A type of *capacity cost*, such as property taxes, incurred even if operations are shut down completely. Contrast with *enabling costs*.

stated capital. Amount of capital contributed by shareholders. Sometimes used to mean *legal capital*.

stated value. A term sometimes used for the *face amount of capital stock*, when no *par value* is indicated. Where there is a stated value per share, it may be set by the directors (in which case, capital *contributed in excess of stated value* may come into being).

statement of affairs. A *balance sheet* showing immediate *liquidation* amounts, rather than *historical costs*, usually prepared when *insolvency* or *bankruptcy* is imminent. The *going-concern assumption* is not used.

statement of changes in financial position. As defined by *APB Opinion No. 19,* a statement that explains the changes in *working capital* (or cash) balances during a period and shows the changes in the working capital (or cash) accounts themselves. Sometimes called the "funds statement." See *dual transactions assumption* and *all financial resources*.

Statement of Financial Accounting Concepts. SFAC. One of a series of *FASB* publications in its *conceptual framework* for *financial accounting* and reporting. Such statements set forth objectives and fundamentals to be the basis for specific financial accounting and reporting standards.

Statement of Financial Accounting Standards. SFAS. See *FASB*.

statement of financial position. *Balance sheet.*

Statement of Position. SOP. A recommendation on an emerging accounting problem issued by the *AcSEC* of the *AICPA*. The AICPA's Code of Professional Ethics specifically states that *CPAs* need not treat *SOPs* as they do rules from the FASB, but a CPA would be wary of departing from the recommendations of a *SOP*.

statement of retained earnings (income). A statement that reconciles the beginning-of-period and end-of-period balances in the *retained earnings* account. It shows the effects of *earnings, dividend declarations*, and *prior-period adjustments*.

Statement on Auditing Standards. SAS. *No. 1* of this series (1973) codifies all statements on auditing standards previously promulgated by the AICPA. Later numbers deal with specific auditing standards and procedures.

Statement on Standards for Accounting and Review Services. SSARS. Pronouncements issued by the *AICPA* on *unaudited financial statements* and unaudited financial information of nonpublic entities.

static budget. *Fixed budget.*

statutory tax rate. The tax rate specified in the *income tax* law for each type of income (for example, *ordinary income, capital gain or loss*).

step cost. *Semifixed cost.*

step-down method. The method for *allocating service department* costs that starts by allocating one service department's costs to *production departments* and to all other service departments. Then a second service department's costs, including costs allocated from the first, are allocated to production departments and to all other service departments except the first one. In this fashion, the costs of all service departments, including previous allocations, are allocated to production departments and to those service departments whose costs have not yet been allocated.

sterilized allocation. Optimal decisions result from considering *incremental costs*, only. *Allocations* of *joint* or *common costs* are never required for optimal decisions. An allocation of these costs that causes the optimal decision choice not to differ from the one that occurs when joint or common costs are unallocated is "sterilized" with respect to that decision. The term was first used in this context by Arthur L. Thomas. Because *absorption costing* requires that all manufacturing costs be allocated to product, and because some allocations can lead to bad decisions, Thomas (and we) advocate that the allocation scheme chosen lead to sterilized allocations that do not alter the otherwise optimal decision. There is, however, no single allocation scheme that is always sterilized with respect to all decisions. Thus, Thomas (and we) advocate that decisions be made on the basis of incremental costs before any allocations.

stock. *Inventory. Capital stock.* A measure of the amount of something on hand at a specific time; in this sense, contrast with *flow*.

stock appreciation rights. The employer promises to pay to the employee an amount of *cash* on a certain future date. The amount of cash is the difference between the *market value* of a certain number of *shares* of *stock* in the employer's company on a given future date and some base price set on the date the rights are granted. This is a form of compensation used because both changes in tax laws in recent years and stock market performance have made *stock options* relatively less attractive. *GAAP* computes compensation based on the difference between market value of the shares and the base price set at the time of the grant. *Expense* is recognized as the holder of the rights performs the services required for the rights to be exercised.

stock dividend. A so-called *dividend* where additional *shares* of *capital stock* are distributed, without cash payments, to existing shareholders. It results in a *debit* to *retained earnings* in the amount of the market value of the shares issued and a *credit to capital stock* accounts. It is ordinarily used to indicate that earnings retained have been permanently reinvested in the business; contrast with a *stock split*, which requires no entry in the capital stock accounts other than a notation that the *par* or *stated value* per share has been changed.

stock option. The right to purchase a specified number of shares of *stock* for a specified price at specified times, usually granted to employees; contrast with *warrant*.

stock right. See *right*.

stock split. Increase in the number of common shares outstanding resulting from the issuance of additional shares to existing shareholders without additional capital contributions by them. Does not increase the total *par* (or *stated*) *value of common stock* outstanding because par (or stated) value per share is reduced in inverse proportion. A three-for-one stock split reduces par (or stated) value per share to one-third of its former amount. Stock splits are usually limited to distributions that increase the number of shares outstanding by 20 percent or more; compare with *stock dividend*.

stock subscriptions. See *subscription* and *subscribed stock*.

stock warrant. See *warrant*.

stockholders' equity. See *shareholders' equity*.

stores. *Raw materials*, parts, and supplies.

straight-debt value. An estimate of what the *market value* of a *convertible bond* would be if the bond did not contain a conversion privilege.

straight-line depreciation. If the *depreciable life* is *n* periods, then the periodic *depreciation* charge is $1/n$ of the *depreciable cost*. Results in equal periodic charges and is sometimes called "straight-time depreciation."

Subchapter S Corporation. A firm legally organized as a *corporation* but taxed as if it were a *partnership*.

subject to. Qualifications in an *auditor's report* usually caused by a *material* uncertainty in the valuation of an item, such as future promised payments from a foreign government or outcome of pending litigation.

subordinated. Said of *debt* whose claim on income or assets is junior to, or comes after, claims of other debt.

subscribed stock. A *shareholders' equity* account showing the capital that will be contributed as soon as the subscription price is collected. A subscription is a legal contract, so an entry is made debiting an owners' equity contra account and crediting subscribed stock as soon as the stock is subscribed.

subscription. Agreement to buy a *security*, or to purchase periodicals such as magazines.

subsequent events. *Post-statement events*.

subsidiary. Said of a company more than 50 percent of whose voting stock is owned by another.

subsidiary (ledger) accounts. The *accounts* in a *subsidiary ledger*.

subsidiary ledger. The *ledger* that contains the detailed accounts whose total is shown in a *controlling account* of the *general ledger*.

successful efforts accounting. In petroleum accounting, the *capitalization* of the drilling costs of only those wells that contain oil. See *reserve recognition accounting* for an example.

summary of significant accounting principles. *APB Opinion* No. 22 requires that every *annual report* summarize the significant *accounting principles* used in compiling the annual report. This summary may be a separate exhibit or the first *note* to the financial statements.

sum-of-the-years'-digits depreciation. SYD. SOYD. An *accelerated depreciation* method for an asset with *depreciable life* of *n* years, where the charge in period *i* $(i = 1, \ldots, n)$ is the fraction $(n + 1 - i)/[n(n + 1)/2]$ of the *depreciable cost*. If an asset has a depreciable cost of $15,000 and a 5-year depreciable life, for example, the depreciation charges would be $5,000 $(= 5/15 \times \$15,000)$ in the first year, $4,000 in the second, $3,000 in the third, $2,000 in the fourth, and $1,000 in the fifth.

sunk costs. *Costs* incurred in the past that are not affected by, and hence irrelevant for, current decisions, aside from *income tax* effects; contrast with *incremental costs* and *imputed costs*. For example, the *acquisition cost* of machinery is irrelevant to a decision of whether or not to scrap the machinery. The current *exit value* of the machine is the imputed cost of continuing to own it, and the cost of, say, electricity to run the machine is an incremental cost of its operation. Sunk costs become relevant for decision making when *income taxes* (*gain* or *loss* on disposal of asset) are taken into account because the cash payment for income taxes depends on the tax basis of the asset.

supplemental actuarial value. Actuarial accrued liability.

supplementary statements (schedules). Statements (schedules) in addition to the four basic *financial statements* (including the retained earnings reconciliation as a basic statement).

surplus. A word once used but now considered poor terminology; prefaced by "earned" to mean *retained earnings* and prefaced by "capital" to mean *capital contributed in excess of par* (or *stated*) *value*.

surplus reserves. Of all the words in accounting, *reserve* is the most objectionable and *surplus* is the second most objectionable. This phrase, then, has nothing to recommend it. It means, simply, *appropriated retained earnings*.

suspense account. A *temporary account* used to record part of a transaction prior to final analysis of that transaction. For example, if a business regularly classifies all sales into a dozen or more different categories but wants to deposit the proceeds of cash sales every day, it may credit a sales suspense account pending detailed classification of all sales into sales, type 1; sales, type 2; and so on.

sustainable income. The part of *distributable income* (computed from *current cost* data) that the firm can be expected to earn in the next accounting period if operations are continued at the same levels as during the current period. *Income from discontinued operations*, for example, may be distributable but not sustainable.

S-X. See *Regulation S-X*.

SYD. *Sum-of-the-years'-digits depreciation. SOYD.*

syndicate. A group of *underwriters*, who have joined together to market a particular *issue* of *securities*.

T

T-account. Account form shaped like the letter T with the title above the horizontal line. *Debits* are shown to the left of the vertical line, *credits* to the right.

take-home pay. The amount of a paycheck; earned wages or *salary* reduced by deductions for *income taxes, Social Security taxes*, contributions to fringe benefit plans, union dues, and so on. Take-home pay might be as little as 60 percent of earned compensation.

take-or-pay contract. As defined by *SFAS No. 47*, an agreement between a purchaser and a seller that provides for the purchaser to pay specified amounts periodically in return for products or services. The purchaser must make specified minimum payments even if it does not take delivery of the contracted products or services.

taking a bath. To incur a large loss. See *big bath*.

tangible. Having physical form. Accounting has never satisfactorily defined the distinction between tangible and *intangible assets*. Typically, intangibles are defined by giving an exhaustive list and everything not on the list is defined as tangible.

target cost. *Standard cost*.

tax. A nonpenal, but compulsory, charge levied by a government on income, consumption, wealth, or other basis for the benefit of all those governed. The term does not include fines or specific charges for benefits accruing only to those paying the charges, such as licenses, permits, special assessments, admissions fees, and tolls.

tax accounting. tax reporting. Process of measuring *taxable income* according to regulations of the *IRS*. Contrast with *financial accounting* and *managerial accounting*.

tax allocation: interperiod. See *deferred income tax liability*.

tax allocation: intrastatement. The showing of income tax effects on *extraordinary items, income from discontinued operations*, and *prior-period adjustments* along with these items, separately from income taxes on other income. See *net-of-tax reporting*.

tax avoidance. See *tax shelter*.

tax credit. A subtraction from taxes otherwise payable; contrast with *tax deduction*.

tax deduction. A subtraction from *revenues* and *gains* to arrive at taxable income. Tax deductions are technically different from tax *exemptions*, but the effect of both is to reduce gross income in computing taxable income. Both are different from *tax credits*, which are subtracted from the computed tax itself in determining taxes payable. If the tax rate is the fraction t of pretax income, then a *tax credit* of \$1 is worth \$1/t of *tax deductions*.

tax evasion. The fraudulent understatement of taxable revenues or overstatement of deductions and expenses or both; contrast with *tax shelter*.

tax exempts. See *municipal bonds*.

tax shelter. The legal avoidance of, or reduction in, *income taxes* resulting from a careful reading of the complex income tax regulations and the subsequent rearrangement of financial affairs to take advantage of the regulations. Often the term is used pejoratively, but the courts have long held that an individual or corporation has no obligation to pay taxes any larger than the legal minimum. If the public concludes that a given tax shelter is "unfair," then the laws and regulations can be changed. Sometimes used to refer to the investment that permits tax avoidance.

tax shield. The amount of an *expense* that reduces taxable income but does not require *working capital*, such as *depreciation*. Sometimes this term is expanded to include expenses that reduce taxable income and use working capital. A depreciation deduction (or *R&D expense* in the expanded sense) of \$10,000 provides a tax shield of \$4,600 when the marginal tax rate is 46 percent.

taxable income. *Income* computed according to *IRS* regulations and subject to *income taxes*. Contrast with *income, net income, income before taxes* (in the *income statement*), and *comprehensive income* (a *financial reporting* concept).

tax-transfer lease. The Congress has provided business with an incentive to invest in qualifying *plant and equipment* by granting an *investment credit*, which though it occurs as a reduction in *income taxes* otherwise payable, is effectively a reduction in the purchase price of the assets. Similarly, the Congress has granted an incentive to acquire such assets by allowing *Accelerated Cost Recovery* (*ACRS*, a form of unusually *accelerated depreciation*). Accelerating depreciation for tax purposes allows a reduction of taxes paid in early years of an asset's life, which provides the firm with an increased *net present value* of *cash flows*. Both of these incentives are administered by the *IRS* through the income tax laws, rather than being granted as an outright cash payment by some other government agency. A business with no taxable income in many cases had difficulty reaping the benefits of the investment credit or of accelerated depreciation because the Congress had not provided for tax refunds to those who acquire qualifying assets but who have no taxable income. In principle, a company without taxable income could lease from another firm with taxable income an asset that would otherwise have been purchased by the first company. The second firm acquires the asset, gets the tax reduction benefits from the acquisition, and becomes a lessor, leasing the asset (presumably at a lower price reflecting its own costs lowered by the tax reductions) to the unprofitable company. Such leases were discouraged by the tax laws prior to 1981. That is, although firms could enter into such leases, the tax benefits could not be legally transferred. Under certain conditions, the tax law allows a profitable firm to earn tax credits and take deductions while leasing to the firm without tax liability in such leases. These leases have sometimes been called "safe-harbor leases."

Technical Bulletin. The *FASB* has authorized its staff to issue bulletins to provide guidance on financial accounting and reporting problems. Although the FASB does not formally approve the contents of the bulletins, their contents are presumed to be part of *GAAP*.

technology. The sum of a firm's technical *trade secrets* and *know-how*, as distinct from its *patents*.

temporary account. *Account* that does not appear on the *balance sheet. Revenue* and *expense* accounts, their *adjuncts* and *contras, production cost accounts, dividend distribution accounts*, and purchases-related accounts (which are closed to the various inventories). Sometimes called a "nominal account."

temporary difference. See *timing difference.*

temporary investments. Investments in *marketable securities* that the owner intends to sell within a short time, usually 1 year, and hence classified as *current assets*.

10-K. The name of the annual report required by the *SEC* of nearly all publicly held corporations.

term bonds. A *bond issue* whose component bonds all mature at the same time; contrast with *serial bonds*.

term loan. A loan with a *maturity* date, as opposed to a demand loan, which is due whenever the lender requests payment. In practice, bankers and auditors use this phrase only for loans for a year or more.

terms of sale. The conditions governing payment for a sale. For example, the terms *2/10, n(et)/30* mean that if payment is made within 10 days of the invoice date, a *discount* of 2 percent from *invoice* price can be taken; the invoice amount must be paid, in any event, within 30 days or it becomes overdue.

throughput contract. As defined by *SFAS No. 47*, an agreement between a shipper (processor) and the owner of a transportation facility (such as an oil or natural gas pipeline or a ship) or a manufacturing facility that provides for the shipper (processor) to pay specified amounts periodically in return for the transportation (processing) of a product. The shipper (processor) is obligated to make cash payments even if it does not ship (process) the contracted quantities.

tickler file. A collection of vouchers or other memoranda arranged chronologically to remind the person in charge of certain duties to make payments (or to do other tasks) as scheduled.

time cost. *Period cost.*

time deposit. Cash in bank earning interest; contrast with *demand deposit.*

time-adjusted rate of return. *Internal rate of return.*

time-series analysis. See *cross-section analysis* for definition and contrast.

times-interest earned. Ratio of pretax *income* plus *interest* charges to interest charges. See *ratio.*

timing difference. A difference between taxable income and pretax income reported to shareholders that will be reversed in a subsequent period and requires an entry in the *deferred income tax* account. For example, the use of *accelerated depreciation* for tax returns and *straight-line depreciation* for financial reporting. Contrast with *permanent difference.*

total assets turnover. *Sales* divided by average total *assets*. Contrast with *permanent difference.*

total overhead variance. Difference between total *overhead* costs and *absorbed overhead*.

trade acceptance. A *draft* drawn by a seller that is presented for signature (acceptance) to the buyer at the time goods are purchased and that then becomes the equivalent of a *note receivable* of the seller and the *note payable* of the buyer.

trade credit. One business allows another to buy from it in return for a promise to pay later. As contrasted with consumer credit, where a business extends the privilege of paying later to a retail customer.

trade discount. A *discount* from *list price* offered to all customers of a given type; contrast with a *discount* offered for prompt payment and *quantity discount*.

trade payables (receivables). *Payables (receivables)* arising in the ordinary course of business transactions. Most accounts payable (receivable) are of this kind.

trade secret. Technical or business information such as formulas, recipes, computer programs, and marketing data not generally known by competitors and maintained by the firm as a secret. A famous example is the secret formula for *Coca-Cola* (a registered *trademark* of the company). Compare with *know-how*. Theoretically capable of having an infinite life, this intangible asset is capitalized only if purchased and then amortized over a period not to exceed 40 years. If it is developed internally, then no asset will be shown.

trade-in. Acquiring a new *asset* in exchange for a used one and perhaps additional cash. See *boot* and *trade-in transaction*.

trade-in transaction. The accounting for a trade-in depends on whether or not the asset received is "similar" to the asset traded in and whether the accounting is for *financial statements* or for *income tax* returns. Assume that an old asset cost $5,000, has $3,000 of *accumulated depreciation* (after recording depreciation to the date of the trade in), and hence has a *book value* of $2,000. The old asset appears to have a market value of $1,500, according to price quotations in used-asset markets. The old asset is traded in on a new asset with a list price of $10,000. The old asset and $5,500 cash *(boot)* are given for the new asset. The generic entry for the trade-in transaction is

New Asset.	A		
Accumulated Depreciation			
(Old Asset)	3,000		
Adjustment on Exchange of Asset .	B	or	B
Old Asset			5,000
Cash			5,500

1. The *list price* method of accounting for trade-ins rests on the assumption that the list price of the new asset closely approximates its market value. The new asset is recorded at its list price (A = $10,000 in the example); B is a *plug* (= $2,500 credit in the example). If B requires a *debit* plug, the Adjustment on Exchange of Asset is a *loss*; if a *credit* plug is required (as in the example), the adjustment is a *gain*.

2. Another theoretically sound method of accounting for trade-ins rests on the assumption that the price quota-

tion from used-asset markets gives a more reliable measure of the market value of the old asset than is the list price a reliable measure of the market value of the new asset. This method uses the *fair market value* of the old asset, $1,500 in the example, to determine B (= $2,000 book value − $1,500 assumed proceeds on disposition = $500 debit or loss). The exchange results in a loss if the book value of the old asset exceeds its market value and in a gain if the market value exceeds the book value. The new asset is recorded on the books by plugging for A (= $7,000 in the example).

3. For income tax reporting, no gain or loss may be recognized on the trade-in. Thus the new asset is recorded on the books by assuming that B is zero and plugging for A (= $7,500 in the example). In practice, firms that wish to recognize the loss currently will sell the old asset directly, rather than trading it in, and acquire the new asset entirely for cash.

4. *Generally accepted accounting principles (APB Opinion No. 29)* require a variant of these methods. The basic method is (1) or (2), depending on whether the list price of the new asset (1) or the quotation of the old asset's market value (2) is the more reliable indication of market value. If, when applying the basic method, a debit entry, or loss, is required for the Adjustment on Exchange of Asset, then the trade-in is recorded as described in (1) or (2) and the full amount of the loss is recognized currently. If, however, a credit entry, or gain, is required for the Adjustment on Exchange of Asset, then the amount of gain recognized currently depends on whether or not the old asset and the new asset are "similar." If the assets are not similar, then the entire gain is recognized currently. If the assets are similar and cash is not received by the party trading in, then no gain is recognized and the treatment is like that in (3): that is, B = 0, plug for A. If the assets are similar and cash is received by the party trading in—a rare case—then a portion of the gain is recognized currently. The portion of the gain recognized currently is the fraction *cash received/fair market value of total consideration received*. [When the list price method (1) is used, the market value of the old asset is assumed to be the list price of the new asset plus the amount of cash received by the party trading in.]

The results of applying *GAAP* to the example can be summarized as follows:

More Reliable Information as to Fair Market Value	Old Asset Compared with New Asset	
	Similar	Not Similar
New Asset List. . .	A = $7,500	A = $10,000
Price	B = 0	B = 2,500 gain
Old Asset Market. .	A = $7,000	A = $ 7,000
Price	B = 500 loss	B = 500 loss

trademark. A distinctive word or symbol affixed to a product, its package, or dispenser, which uniquely identifies the firm's products and services. See *trademark right*.

trademark right. The right to exclude competitors in sales or advertising from using words or symbols that may be confusingly similar to the firm's *trademarks*. Trademark rights last as long as the firm continues to use the trademarks in question. In the United States, trademark rights arise from use and not from government registration. They therefore have a legal life independent of the life of a registration. Registrations last 20 years and are renewable as long as the trademark is being used. Thus, as an asset, purchased trademark rights might, like land, not be subject to amortization if management believes that the life of the trademark is indefinite. In practice, accountants amortize a trademark right over some estimate of its life, not to exceed 40 years. Under *SFAS No. 2*, internally developed trademark rights must be *expensed*.

trading on the equity. Said of a firm engaging in *debt financing*; frequently said of a firm doing so to a degree considered abnormal for a firm of its kind. *Leverage*.

transaction. A *transfer* between the accounting *entity* and another party, or parties.

transfer. *SFAC No. 3* distinguishes "reciprocal" and "nonreciprocal" transfers. In a reciprocal transfer, or "exchange," the entity both receives and sacrifices. In a nonreciprocal transfer, the entity sacrifices but does not receive (examples include gifts, distributions to owners) or receives but does not sacrifice (investment by owner in entity). *SFAC No. 3* suggests that the term "internal transfer" is self-contradictory and that the term "internal event" be used instead.

transfer agent. Usually a bank or trust company designated by a corporation to make legal transfers of *stock (bonds)* and, perhaps, to pay *dividends (coupons)*.

transfer price. A substitute for a *market*, or *arm's-length, price* used in *profit center*, or *responsibility, accounting* when one segment of the business "sells" to another segment. Incentives of profit center managers will not coincide with the best interests of the entire business unless transfer prices are properly set.

translation gain (or loss). *Foreign exchange gain (or loss)*.

transportation-in. *Freight-in*.

transposition error. An error in record keeping resulting from reversing the order of digits in a number, such as recording "32" for "23." If an error of this sort has been made in a number added in a total, then the incorrect total will differ from the correct total by a number divisible by nine. Thus if *trial balance* sums differ by a number divisible by nine, one might search for a transposition error.

treasury bond. A bond issued by a corporation and then reacquired; such bonds are treated as retired when reacquired and an *extraordinary gain or loss* on reacquisition is recognized. Also, a *bond* issued by the U.S. Treasury Department.

treasury shares. *Capital stock* issued and then reacquired by the corporation. Such reacquisitions result in a reduction of *shareholders' equity*, and are usually shown on the balance sheet as *contra* to shareholders' equity. Neither *gain* nor *loss* is recognized on transactions involving treasury stock. Any difference between the amounts paid and received for treasury stock transactions is debited (if positive) or credited (if negative) to *additional paid-in capital*. See *cost method* and *par value method*.

treasury stock. *Treasury shares*.

trial balance. A listing of *account balances*; all accounts with *debit* balances are totaled separately from accounts with *credit* balances. The two totals should be equal. Trial balances are taken as a partial check of the arithmetic accuracy of the entries previously made. See *adjusted, preclosing, post-closing, unadjusted, trial balance*.

troubled debt restructuring. As defined in *SFAS No. 15*, a concession (changing of the terms of a *debt*) granted by a *creditor* for economic or legal reasons related to the *debtor's* financial difficulty that the creditor would not otherwise consider.

turnover. The number of times that *assets*, such as *inventory* or *accounts receivable*, are replaced on average during the period. Accounts receivable turnover, for example, is total sales on account for a period divided by average accounts receivable balance for the period. See *ratio*.

turnover of plant and equipment. See *ratio*.

two-T-account method. A method for computing either (1) *foreign exchange gains and losses* or (2) monetary gains or *losses* for *constant dollar accounting statements*. The left-hand *T-account* shows actual net balances of *monetary items* and the right-hand T-account shows implied *(common) dollar* amounts.

2/10, *n*(et)/30. See *terms of sale*.

U

unadjusted trial balance. *Trial balance* before *adjusting* and *closing entries* are made at the end of the period.

unappropriated retained earnings. *Retained earnings* not appropriated and therefore against which *dividends* can be charged in the absence of retained earnings restrictions. See *restricted retained earnings*.

uncertainty. See *risk* for definition and contrast.

uncollectible account. An *account receivable* that will not be paid by the *debtor*. If the preferable *allowance method* is used, the entry upon judging a specific account to be uncollectible is to *debit* the allowance for uncollectible accounts and to *credit* the specific account receivable. See *sales contra, estimated uncollectibles*.

unconsolidated subsidiary. A *subsidiary* not consolidated and, hence, accounted for on the *equity method*.

uncontrollable cost. The opposite of *controllable cost*.

underapplied (underabsorbed) overhead. An excess of actual *overhead costs* for a period over costs applied, or charged, to products produced during the period. A *debit balance* remaining in an overhead account after overhead is assigned to product.

underlying document. The record, memorandum, *voucher*, or other signal that is the authority for making an *entry* into a *journal*.

underwriter. One who agrees to purchase an entire *security issue* for a specified price, usually for resale to others.

undistributed earnings. *Retained earnings*; typically, this term refers to that amount retained for a given year.

unearned income (revenue). *Advances from customers;* strictly speaking, a contradiction in terms.

unemployment tax. See *FUTA*.

unencumbered appropriation. In governmental accounting, portion of an *appropriation* not yet spent or *encumbered*.

unexpired cost. An *asset*.

unfavorable variance. In *standard cost* accounting, an excess of actual cost over standard cost assigned to product.

unfunded. Not *funded*. An obligation or *liability*, usually for *pension costs*, exists but no *funds* have been set aside to discharge the obligation or liability.

Uniform Partnership Act. A model law, enacted by many states, to govern the relations between partners where the *partnership* agreement fails to specify the agreed-upon treatment.

unissued capital stock. *Stock* authorized but not yet issued.

unitary taxation. Many states believe that *corporations* unfairly avoid paying *income taxes* in their state by using artificially concocted *transfer prices* to show high income in locations with low income tax rates and low income in locations with high income tax rates. Unitary taxation is a method used by some states to *allocate* worldwide corporate income so that income taxes can be levied. The allo-

cation formulas take into account *revenues*, *plant assets*, and employment in various locations.

units-of-production method. The *production method of depreciation*.

unlimited liability. The liability of *general partners* or the sole proprietor for all debts of the *partnership* or *sole proprietorship*.

unqualified opinion. See *auditor's report*.

unrealized appreciation. An *unrealized holding gain;* frequently used in the context of *marketable securities*.

unrealized gross margin (profit). A *contra* account to *installment accounts receivable* used with the *installment method* of revenue recognition. Shows the amount of profit that will eventually be realized when the receivable is collected. Some accountants show this account as a *liability*.

unrealized holding gain. See *inventory profit* for definition and an example.

unrealized loss on marketable securities. An *income statement account* title for the amount of *loss* during the current period on the portfolio of *marketable securities* below the beginning-of-period *book value* of that portfolio. *SFAS No. 12* requires that losses caused by declines in price below market be *recognized* in the income statement, even though they have not been *realized*.

unrecovered cost. *Book value* of an *asset*.

usage variance. *Quantity variance*.

use of funds. Any transaction that reduces funds (however funds is defined).

useful life. *Service life*.

V

valuation account. A *contra account* or *adjunct account*. When *marketable securities* are reported at *lower of cost or market*, any declines in market value below cost will be credited to a valuation account. In this way, the acquisition cost and the amount of price declines below cost can both be shown. *SFAS No. 3* says that a valuation account is "a separate item that reduces and increases the carrying amount" of an asset (or liability). The accounts are part of the related assets (or liabilities) and are neither assets (nor liabilities) in their own right.

value. Monetary worth; the term is usually so subjective that it ought not to be used without a modifying adjective unless most people would agree on the amount; not to be confused with *cost*. See *fair market value, entry value, exit value*.

value added. *Cost* of a product or *work in process*, minus the cost of the material purchased for the product or work in process.

value variance. *Price variance.*

variable annuity. An *annuity* whose periodic payments depend on some uncertain outcome, such as stock market prices.

variable budget. *Flexible budget.*

variable costing. *Direct costing.* Contrast with *absorption costing.*

variable costs. *Costs* that change as activity levels change. Strictly speaking, variable costs are zero when the activity level is zero. See *semivariable costs.* In accounting, this term most often means the sum of *direct costs* and variable *overhead.*

variance. Difference between actual and *standard costs* or between *budgeted* and actual *expenditures* or, sometimes, *expenses.* The word has completely different meanings in accounting and statistics, where it is a measure of dispersion of a distribution.

variance analysis. The investigation of the causes of *variances* in a *standard cost system.* This term has a different meaning in statistics.

variation analysis. Analysis of the causes of changes in items of interest in financial statements such as net *income* or *gross margin.*

vendor. A seller. Sometimes spelled ''vender.''

verifiable. A qualitative *objective* of financial reporting specifying that items in *financial statements* can be checked by tracing back to *underlying documents*—supporting *invoices,* canceled *checks,* and other physical pieces of evidence.

verification. The auditor's act of reviewing or checking items in *financial statements* by tracing back to *underlying documents*—supporting *invoices,* canceled *checks,* and other business documents—or sending out *confirmations* to be returned. Compare with *physical verification.*

vertical analysis. Analysis of the financial statements of a single firm or across several firms for a particular time, as opposed to *horizontal* or time-series analysis, where items are compared over time for a single firm or across firms.

vested. Said of an employee's *pension plan* benefits that are not contingent on the employee continuing to work for the employer.

volume variance. *Capacity variance.*

voucher. A document that signals recognition of a *liability* and authorizes the disbursement of cash. Sometimes used to refer to the written evidence documenting an *accounting entry,* as in the term *journal voucher.*

voucher system. A method for controlling *cash,* that requires each *check* to be authorized with an approved *voucher.* No cash *disbursements* are made except from *petty cash funds.*

W

wage. Compensation of employees based on time worked or output of product for manual labor. But see *take-home pay.*

warrant. A certificate entitling the owner to buy a specified number of shares at a specified time(s) for a specified price. Differs from a *stock option* only in that options are granted to employees and warrants are issued to the public. See *right.*

warranty. A promise by a seller to correct deficiencies in products sold. When warranties are given, proper accounting practice recognizes an estimate of warranty *expense* and an *estimated liability* at the time of sale. See *guarantee* for contrast in proper usage.

wash sale. The sale and purchase of the same or similar *asset* within a short time period. For *income tax* purposes, *losses* on a sale of stock may not be recognized if equivalent stock is purchased within 30 days before or 30 days after the date of sale.

waste. Residue of material from manufacturing operations with no sale value. Frequently, it has negative value because additional costs must be incurred for disposal.

wasting asset. A *natural resource* having a limited *useful life* and, hence, subject to *amortization,* called *depletion.* Examples are timber land, oil and gas wells, and ore deposits.

watered stock. *Shares* issued for *assets* with *fair market value* less than *par* or *stated value.* The assets are put onto the books at the overstated values. In the law, for shares to be considered watered, the *board of directors* must have acted in bad faith or fraudulently in issuing the shares under these circumstances. The term originated from a former practice of cattlemen who fed cattle (''stock'') large quantities of salt to make them thirsty. The cattle then drank a lot of water before being taken to market. This was done to make the cattle appear heavier and more valuable than otherwise.

weighted average. An average computed by counting each occurrence of each value, not merely a single occurrence of each value. For example, if one unit is purchased for $1 and two units are purchased for $2 each, then the simple average of the purchase prices is $1.50 but the weighted average price per unit is $5/3 = $1.67. Contrast with *moving average.*

weighted-average inventory method. Valuing either *withdrawals* or *ending inventory* at the *weighted-average* purchase price of all units on hand at the time of withdrawal or of computing ending inventory. The *inventory equation* is used to calculate the other quantity. If the *perpetual inventory* method is in use, often called the "moving average method."

where-got, where-gone statement. A term used by W. M. Cole for a statement much like the *statement of changes in financial position*.

window dressing. The attempt to make financial statements show *operating* results, or *financial position*, more favorable than would otherwise be shown.

with recourse. See *note receivable discounted*.

withdrawals. *Assets* distributed to an owner. *Partner's drawings*. See *inventory equation* for another context.

withheld income taxes. See *withholding*.

withholding. Deductions from *salaries* or *wages*, usually for *income taxes*, to be remitted by the employer, in the employee's name, to the taxing authority.

without recourse. See *note receivable discounted*.

work in process. Partially completed product; an *asset* that is classified as *inventory*.

work sheet. A tabular schedule for convenient summary of *adjusting* and *closing entries*. The work sheet usually begins with an *unadjusted trial balance*. Adjusting entries are shown in the next two columns, one for *debits* and one for *credits*. The horizontal sum of each line is then carried to the right into either the *income statement* or *balance sheet* column, as appropriate. The *plug* to equate the income statement column totals is the income, if a debit plug is required, or loss, if a credit plug is required, for the period. That income will be closed to retained earnings on the balance sheet. The income statement credit columns are the revenues for the period and the debit columns are the expenses (and revenue *contras*) to be shown on the income statement.

Work sheet is also used to refer to *schedules* for computing other items appearing on the *financial statements* that require adjustment or compilation.

working capital. *Current assets* minus *current liabilities*. The *statement of changes in financial position* usually explains the changes in working capital for a period.

working capital equation. The *balance sheet* states that *assets* = equities. The information in comparative balance sheets from the start and end of a period can be restated as:

$$\text{Change in Assets} = \text{Change in Equities}$$

This equation can be further broken down to say that

$$\begin{array}{l}\text{Change in Current} \\ \text{Assets Plus Change} = \\ \text{in Noncurrent Assets}\end{array} \begin{array}{l}\text{Change in Current} \\ \text{Liabilities Plus Change} \\ \text{in Noncurrent Equities}\end{array}$$

which is equivalent to

$$\begin{array}{l}\text{Change in Current} \\ \text{Assets Less Change} = \\ \text{in Current Liabilities}\end{array} \begin{array}{l}\text{Change in Noncurrent} \\ \text{Equities Less Change} \\ \text{in Noncurrent Assets}\end{array}$$

The left-hand side of this equation is the change in *working capital* for the period. The items on the right-hand side cause the change in working capital during the period. The *statement of changes in financial position* typically shows the causes of the changes (right-hand side of the equation) at the top of the statement and the way working capital has changed (left-hand side of the equation) at the bottom of the statement.

working capital provided by operations. See *funds provided by operations*.

working papers. The schedules and analyses prepared by the *auditor* in carrying out investigations prior to issuing an *opinion* on *financial statements*.

worth. *Value*. See *net worth*.

worth-debt ratio. Reciprocal of the *debt-equity ratio*. See *ratio*.

write down. *Write off*, except that not all the assets' cost is charged to expense or *loss*. Generally used for nonrecurring items.

write off. *Charge* an *asset* to *expense* or *loss*; that is, *debit* expense (or loss) and *credit* asset.

write up. To increase the recorded *cost* of an *asset* with no corresponding *disbursement* of *funds*; that is, *debit* asset and *credit revenue*, or perhaps, *owners' equity*. Seldom done because currently accepted accounting principles are based on actual transactions. When a portfolio of *marketable equity securities* increases in market value subsequent to a previously recognized decrease, the *book value* of the portfolio is written up—the debit is to the *contra account*.

write-off method. A method for treating *uncollectible accounts* that charges *bad debt expense* and credits accounts receivable of specific customers as uncollectible amounts are identified. May not be used when uncollectible amounts are significant and can be estimated. See *sales contra, estimated uncollectibles*, and the *allowance method* for contrast.

Y

yield. *Internal rate of return* of a stream of cash flows. Cash yield is cash flow divided by book value. See also *dividend yield*.

yield to maturity. At a given time, the *internal rate of return* of a series of cash flows, usually said of a *bond*. Sometimes called the "effective rate."

Z

zero salvage value. If the *salvage value* of a *depreciable asset* is estimated to be less than 10 percent of its *cost*, the tax regulations permit an assumption of zero salvage value in computing *depreciation* for federal *income tax* purposes. This convention is often used in financial reporting as well, but seldom in textbooks.

zero-base(d) budgeting. ZBB. In preparing an ordinary *budget* for the next period, a manager starts with the budget for the current period and makes adjustments as seem necessary, because of changed conditions for the next period. Because most managers like to increase the scope of the activities managed and because most prices increase most of the time, amounts in budgets prepared in the ordinary, incremental way seem to increase period after period. The authority approving the budget assumes that operations will be carried out in the same way as in the past and that next period's expenditures will have to be at least as large as the current period's. Thus, this authority tends to study only the increments to the current period's budget. In ZBB, the authority questions the process for carrying out a program and the entire budget for the next period. Every dollar in the budget is studied, not just the dollars incremental to the previous period's amounts. The advocates of ZBB claim that in this way: (1) programs or divisions of marginal benefit to the business or governmental unit will more likely be deleted from the program, rather than being continued with costs at least as large as the present ones; and (2) alternative, more cost-effective, ways of carrying out programs are more likely to be discovered and implemented. ZBB implies questioning the existence of programs, and the fundamental nature of the way they are carried out, not merely the amounts used to fund them. Experts appear to be evenly divided as to whether the middle word should be "base" or "based."

Index